# Coins and Samian Ware

A study of the dating of coin-loss and the deposition of samian ware (terra sigillata), with a discussion of the decline of samian ware manufacture in the NW provinces of the Roman Empire, late 2nd to mid 3rd centuries AD

Anthony C. King

BAR International Series 2573
2013

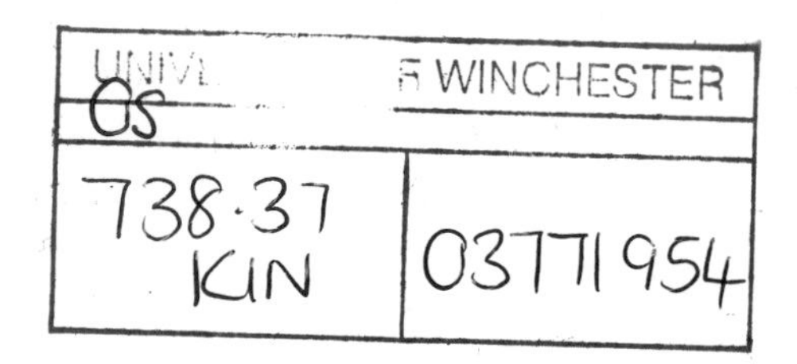


Published by

Archaeopress
Publishers of British Archaeological Reports
Gordon House
276 Banbury Road
Oxford OX2 7ED
England
bar@archaeopress.com
www.archaeopress.com

BAR S2573

*Coins and Samian Ware: A study of the dating of coin-loss and the deposition of samian ware (terra sigillata), with a discussion of the decline of samian ware manufacture in the NW provinces of the Roman Empire, late 2nd to mid 3rd centuries AD*



ISBN 978 1 4073 1194 4

Cover image: mould for Drag. form 37, with signature of Dubitatus. Trier group IIIa, 2nd quarter of the 3rd century AD. From Trier, Pacelliufer; Rheinisches Landesmuseum Trier inv. no. 1935, 260. Photo: A. C. King.

Printed in England by CMP (UK) Ltd

All BAR titles are available from:

Hadrian Books Ltd
122 Banbury Road
Oxford
OX2 7BP
England
www.hadrianbooks.co.uk

The current BAR catalogue with details of all titles in print, prices and means of payment is available free from Hadrian Books or may be downloaded from www.archaeopress.com

# Contents

# List of Tables

# List of Figures

# SUMMARY

The first part of this book is concerned with a review of the chronology for samian ware of the late second and early/mid third centuries AD (*c*. AD 150-275). The currently accepted dating scheme is shown to have an uncertain basis, mainly due to the use of historically dated sites without clear regard to the nature of the historical dating as applied to archaeological sites and deposits (chapters 1 and 2). In place of this scheme another is proposed, based upon the stratigraphic association of samian ware with coins in specific deposits, and using the statistical strength of association between potters or styles with each other and with dated deposits (chapters 4 and 5). The use of coins in this way has necessitated an extensive numismatic analysis that establishes a scheme for estimating approximate time-lapses between minting and loss for coins of the period under consideration (chapter 3).

The results of the new chronology are mainly an extension of the period of manufacture of Central Gaulish samian ware later than hitherto supposed, together with revisions in the existing relative sequence of potters. The relationships between kiln-centres in Central Gaul, Eastern Gaul and elsewhere, in terms of their concurrence of deposition, is analysed and discussed. Some of the consequences of these results are brought out, e.g. the average period of use of samian vessels would appear to be quite long in many instances, and therefore, reliance on samian sherds for accurate dating is called into question (chapter 5).

The discussion that follows proposes a revision of ideas about the decline of samian ware manufacture, revolving around economic and cultural models, rather than historical interpretations (chapters 6 and 7). Mechanisms for the trade in samian ware are discussed, and emphasis is placed on the collapse of an adequate monetary base and the breakdown of long-distance communications as key factors in the decline. Changes in consumer preferences are also considered to be an important element, and are discussed in the light of the general social climate of the period, and in terms of present-day observations of stylistic change.

The book includes an appendix, listing samian ware kiln sites and finds of moulds in north-west Europe dating to the mid-second to mid-third centuries, together with bibliography for each site. A gazetteer of deposits and assemblages used for the analysis in chapters 4 and 5, and an extensive bibliography, complete the volume.

Anthony King is Professor of Roman Archaeology at the University of Winchester and researches in Romano-Celtic religion, ancient diet and Romano-British rural settlement, as well as the subject matter of this volume. He has excavated on many Roman sites in Britain, Italy and Gaul, notably Hayling Island temple, Meonstoke and Dinnington villas, and the early Christian church and villa at Monte Gelato. He is author of The Archaeology of the Roman Empire (1982), Roman Gaul and Germany (1990), British and Irish Archaeology: a bibliographical guide (1994), Excavations at the Mola di Monte Gelato. A Roman and Medieval settlement in South Etruria (1997, with T W Potter), and A Sacred Island. Iron Age, Roman and Saxon temples and ritual on Hayling Island (2013, with G Soffe). He has co-edited The Roman West in the Third Century (1981, with M Henig), Military and Civilian in Roman Britain (1984, with T F C Blagg), Pagan Gods and Shrines of the Roman Empire (1986, with M Henig) and Continuity and Innovation in Religion in the Roman West (2007/8, with R Haeussler).

# Preface

This volume arises out of a PhD thesis, completed a good many years ago.[1] The question that probably leaps to readers' minds above all is, 'Why publish it now – isn't it out of date?' To which my answer is No, from two different points-of-view.

Many revisions and updated sections have been inserted for the present volume. The data for the coins and coin-hoards analysis have been augmented by the considerable number of new finds since the mid 1980s, whilst the data analysis for the samian ware associated deposits has also been reworked. New samian ware deposits associated with coins have been examined, particularly from France, and their evidence for dating samian ware incorporated into the discussion.[2] However, the gazetteer of deposits used for the primary analysis in chapter 5 has not been augmented, as the sample was considered to be good enough for the analysis conducted for the thesis.

The second reason for saying 'No, it isn't out-of-date', is that nearly all the background issues that originally led to the research project being set up, are still in place. There has certainly been a good deal of research on kiln-centre chronologies and sequences (discussed in chapter 1 and the Appendix to chapter 7),[3] but an attempt to reconcile the different chronologies has not happened to any great extent, nor has there been extensive discussion of the economic and social factors affecting change in samian production and consumption in the third century.

An important aspect that arose from reactions to the conclusions of the original thesis, is a level of uncertainty concerning dating of production as against dating of disposal.[4] Samian specialists are naturally interested in when the pottery was made, and in establishing chronological parameters for particular potters or styles. But how is this done? The simple answer is by examining the context of samian of a particular type within archaeological sites, and assigning a date to it. The date can be derived from internal means, e.g. coins found with the samian ware, or by externally assigned dates, such as a historical event thought to be associated with the archaeological context (discussed further in chapters 1 and 2). Whatever method is used for deriving a date, it remains the case that the samian ware being dated is actually pottery that has had usage, however brief or lengthy, and then been disposed of, either in a structured deposit such as a burial, or more usually in a less deliberative deposit such as a dump or fill. In other words, all our data for dating leads to chronologies that define disposal of the pottery, not its manufacture.[5] Therein lies the confusion, as a significant proportion of the samian literature talks of dates of production, and for Britain in particular, of importation. The truth of the matter is that we literally do not know this information, except by intelligent estimation about the likely 'life' of a samian vessel (discussed in chapter 5). The hard data we have is the original archaeological context of the pottery and any absolute dates assigned to it, and that is what forms the primary focus of this volume (chapters 4 and 5).

Coins, too, are objects that have been lost or disposed of when found in archaeological contexts, even if they are found in a hoard. Therefore, as archaeological artefacts they are subject to the same methodological strictures as samian ware. We may have a much better idea of when a particular coin type was produced than for samian or any other type of pottery, but the time-lapse between production and loss is a matter of considerable speculation and research (as discussed in chapter 3). It is tempting for archaeologists to use the device of the *terminus post quem* to provide a dating framework derived from coins, based on their production dates, but this has the effect of systematically pushing the dates of archaeological contexts back to their *termini post quem*, and thus shortening overall chronologies. As discussed in chapter 3, this poses a significant problem for the early third century, when coin circulation was problematic in outlying provinces such as Britain, and old bronze coinage remained in circulation in this period for longer than would be expected for much of the first or second centuries. Chapter 3 is an attempt to model likely dates of deposition of coins in this period, and therefore by extension establish a chronology of disposal for samian ware, in chapters 4 and 5. From this scheme as a basis, we can then make an estimate of pottery usage and work back towards likely production dates.

Despite the apparent controversy over Central Gaulish production running into the third century, continuing excavation and study in France has demonstrated that this was exactly the case. In particular, excavations at Lezoux revealed a third-century samian ware kiln,[6] and the clear continuation of activity there into the third and fourth centuries.[7] Elsewhere, coin-dated deposits showed that

[1] King 1985.

[2] They are summarised in the Gazetteer, section D.

[3] E.g. Heiligmann 1990; Rogers 1999; Delage 1998; 1999a; Mees 2002.

[4] Responses to a later chronology for late Central Gaulish products, as proposed in the thesis, and in King 1981 and 1984, have tended to focus on the difficulties of extending the working lives of individual potters, such as Cinnamus (cf. Simpson 1992; Ward 1993, 17; Hartley & Dickinson 2008a, 5). Bird, in a considered and helpful response (1986, 146), also highlights the issue of the Cinnamus workshop's lifespan, in connection with the now much-discussed assemblage at St Magnus House, London (cf. Wallace 2006, 259-60; see also below, chapter 5, and gazetteer entry A 90). See also Willis 2005, section 5.8.5, for a general reflection on the debate about third-century Central Gaulish ware in Britain.

[5] Ward (1993, 17-18) gives instances of Central Gaulish decorated vessels remaining in use for a considerable time at Piercebridge.

[6] Bet & Gangloff 1987.

[7] Bet & Wittmann 1995. Cf. Rogers 1999, 22.

the model of contraction in the market for late Central Gaulish products (see chapter 7) was a valid one, rather than the curtailment of production due to historical events. In Britain, this was picked up in 2006 by Wallace, in an article entitled 'Long-lived samian?',[8] which effectively revived the debate about the nature and chronology of samian ware in the third century, especially for Britain. Wallace referred to the arguments laid out in the thesis of 1985 on which this volume is based, in effect laying down a friendly challenge to publish the thesis and bring it up to date.[9] This is what I have attempted to do, as part of the current renaissance of British and European samian ware studies that is apparent from recent publications and conferences.[10]

In preparing this volume, the essential argument and methodology in the thesis of 1985 has been preserved, but the opportunity has been taken to bring the interpretation and discussion up to date. Critiques of the thesis, recent discussions of chronology and samian economics, together with published assemblages, have all been consulted, and incorporated where appropriate.[11] In effect, this is a second, revised edition.

Sway, Hampshire
July 2013

## Preface 1985

The history of this thesis is soon told. Its origins lie in the Roman pottery course for undergraduate students given at the Institute of Archaeology. In 1974 the course was taught by Michael Fulford, whose remarks on the lack of knowledge of third-century Roman pottery provided the impetus for the study. At first, while the author was working for the Royal Commission on Historical Monuments (England) in 1975-6, the thesis was begun part-time, and its scope was very wide: the development of the pottery industry in the north-west provinces during the third century. Rapidly, this nebulous scheme of research was modified and narrowed. An initial decision was taken to restrict the study to samian ware, since it is the most important type of pottery for our understanding of both chronology and manufacture. There also appeared to be inconsistencies and problems in existing chronologies, which have eventually needed, for the products of some kiln-centres, considerable modification.

Chronological problems, therefore, were the major target of research during the period of full-time study, 1976-9. It was decided to concentrate on the dating of decorative styles, since these were felt to vary sufficiently rapidly to give the possibility of a relatively close chronology. This possibility has not been fully realised, for a variety of reasons discussed in the main text, since the new chronology is, if anything, less precise than previous ones. However, since plain samian forms are much less variable than decorative styles, and since the chronology of potter's stamps (the other fairly sensitive indicator of date) is being studied elsewhere, the decision to concentrate on the decorated forms still appears to be one of the most productive lines of enquiry for this particular area of research.

The method adopted to investigate late samian chronology was one that relied on detailed associations between finds of the pottery and other, independently dated, materials. In this way, some of the problems that had occurred in previous chronologies could be avoided. Accordingly, the main activity throughout this period was the gathering of data, by making searches through the literature, and by visiting museums and excavation units. Two long visits were made in 1977-8, to the Rhineland and eastern Gaul, and to northern Britain.

Bibliographic information was, surprisingly, much more valuable than that from museums, since most museum collections were found to be unstratified finds or not capable of association with their original contexts. The information made available by excavation units was, generally speaking, more useful than museum-derived data, although there was a tendency for associations between finds of samian and other artefacts (especially coins) to be difficult to ascertain if post-excavation work was in its early stages, whilst if such associations were readily available, the excavation details were on the point of being published anyway. As a result, it became apparent that detailed associations were best obtained from published reports and recently compiled excavation archives, and it also became very clear that despite the massive quantity of samian ware available for study, only a tiny percentage of it was stratified, particularly for the period under consideration. It is paradoxical that there should eventually be unexpectedly little material upon which to base a study of this kind, when it had been decided at an earlier stage to narrow the scope of the study to samian ware alone because the original subject area was deemed too large. Such unanticipated problems probably beset many schemes of research, but they can of course lead to beneficial results in the end.

In this particular case the result was the decision to expand what was originally conceived as a minor section on matters other than chronological to a significant proportion of the whole work. The basis for this expansion was laid with the writing of a paper for the 1980 conference on *The Roman West in the Third Century*, which can be

[8] Wallace 2006.

[9] *Ibid.*, 268.

[10] See, for instance, Bird (D) 2012; Bird (J) 1998; 2003; Delage 1998; 1999a; 1999b; 2001a; Fulford & Durham 2013 (especially Fulford 2013); Hartley & Dickinson 2008a-2012; Mees 1995; 2002; 2011; Mees & Polak 2013; Riedl 2011; Willis 1998; 2005; 2011.

[11] The gist of the thesis was given in presentations at the Roman Pottery Study Group conference at Lincoln, 1992, and a Roman research seminar at Oxford, Institute of Archaeology, 2011. Grateful thanks are due to participants in the discussions at both these events, and to correspondence over the years with both samian specialists and others. The author is very grateful to the University of Winchester for providing the facilities and time that enabled this revision to be completed.

regarded as an interim report on the thesis.[12] Research was undertaken into the interpretation of the decline of samian ware manufacture, and the wider issue of the theory of fashion change, the latter being felt to be a crucial factor in understanding this episode in ceramic history. Most of this work was done in 1979-82, on a part-time basis since full-time grant aid had expired. The bulk of the thesis was written in 1982-5.

Research of this kind almost inevitably involves discussion with other people. The author is happy to acknowledge the valuable criticisms and contributions made on the thesis as it developed over many years, by his supervisor, Richard Reece, who in addition was sufficiently impatient and goading to ensure that other work was laid aside so that the thesis could be finished. Work on the initial stages of research was stimulated by discussions with the late John Morris, whose breadth of vision made the final goal seem worth attaining. Others who freely gave of their time to discuss the problems that came to the fore during research were Joanna Bird, T F C Blagg, Brian Hartley, Martin Henig, Catherine Johns, Bernard Lovell, Geoff Marsh, Martin Millett, Michael Pitts, Tim Potter and Michael Vanderhoeven. The examiners of the thesis, Professors Michael Fulford and John Wilkes, gave very helpful advice, both at the examination itself and subsequently. The author is also very grateful to all the curators of museums and directors of excavation units, too numerous to mention individually, who were so generous with their time, and did many unexpected kindnesses to make the task of data collection easier. Full-time work on the thesis was funded by a Major State Studentship awarded by the Department of Education and Science, which also provided for the considerable travelling costs. Acknowledgement is also made here to a University of London Postgraduate Studentship which was awarded at the same time as the DES studentship, and therefore not taken up. The thesis was originally typed by Lyn Greenwood who admirably coped with the many intractable lists and tables.

Clapham Common, London
September 1985

[12] King 1981. A paper given at the Rei Cretariae Fautores conference at Munich in 1982 (King 1984a) is also an interim statement on the thesis methodology. Chronological considerations, particularly relating to northern Britain, are discussed in King 1991.

# Chapter 1

# Introduction: a 'historical' problem

*La contribution de la céramique sigillée à la datation des contextes archéologiques n'est pas sans poser des problèmes.*[1]

Before outlining the current *status quaestionis* it is first necessary to define the *quaestio* itself. It can be most simply put in the form of two related questions, the answers to which will form the backbone of this volume:- What is the basis for dating late-second- and early-third-century samian ware?[2] Why did manufacture of samian ware fall into decline in the northern provinces during this period? A brief examination of previous work on these subjects will give an indication of what is currently known, and why it is worthwhile asking these questions. As will be seen, it is the decorated rather than the plain ware which is more important in providing answers, and consequently the arguments presented here will be concerned almost exclusively with the former.

The basis for the study of late Central Gaulish samian ware has for many years been Stanfield and Simpson's *Central Gaulish Potters,* which gives definitions and examples of the style of each of those decorated ware potters sufficiently known at that time to be included.[3] Work has continued since on attributions of styles by Bémont, Delage, Hartley, Rogers, Simpson and others,[4] and there is much further work to be done to refine some of the more problematic styles.[5] The process of identifying the styles of individual potters or workshops forms the essential under-pinning of all other work on the subject, without which the student cannot proceed further, in much the same way as work on the identification of coin types forms the basis of numismatics. Stylistic studies of the products of the other kiln-centres include Ricken and Fischer on Rheinzabern, Huld-Zetsche on Trier and Lutz on various of the Moselle potters.[6] The working method in all these studies is more or less the same – decorated bowls or their moulds signed by potters or mould-makers are 'dissected' for their constituent decorative elements, and the overall designs formed by the elements are noted. The corpus of elements unique to that potter or style are then regarded as an identifying 'trademark' while those elements which are shared with other potters are used to establish stylistic links and sequences.[7] Not all potters signed their work, though, and much of the recent stylistic study has centred on defining these anonymous potters (and the related matter of the anonymous sub-styles sheltering under the signature of some of the major potters who did not produce all their own work). The process of attributing styles is in part mechanical, in the identification of the decorative elements, and in part intuitive, in the separation of what can often be virtually identical vessels on the basis of the indefinable imprint of a particular potter's individual style. This has led to changes and variations in existing schemes of attribution as notions change in what constitutes a potter's individual style.[8] Computerised methods of analysis have been brought to bear on this subject, as an aid in clarifying styles.[9]

Stylistic analysis of samian ware is a very valuable study in its own right, and a vital part of the subject. However, most samian specialists are equally concerned with dating, since the pottery is widely regarded as a sensitive chronological indicator by Roman archaeologists. There are some grounds for doubting the confident and precise dates that are often given to pieces of samian ware,[10] but generally the chronological aspect is the main justification of samian ware studies to the archaeological world at large.[11] The dating scheme in Stanfield and Simpson[12] is based largely on the historical dates then attributed to the mainly military sites in northern Britain. Similarly, Rheinzabern and other East Gaulish products have been dated by reference to the developments along the German and Raetian *limes*.[13] This reliance on sites dated by reference to historical events poses problems, as will be discussed in chapter 2, and can lead to peculiar and sometimes erroneous datings. The best

[1] Delage 2003, 183.

[2] The term 'samian' is used instead of *terra sigillata* throughout this volume, as it is the general, if perhaps colloquial English terminology. For the possibility that *samia vasa* was an ancient usage, see King 1980.

[3] 1st edition issued in 1958; revised edition in French, *Les Potiers de la Gaule Centrale*, 1990.

[4] Cf. bibliography in the entry Lezoux in the Appendix 7.1.

[5] See, for instance, the analysis of Cracina (Delage & Séguier 2009).

[6] Ricken & Fischer 1963; Huld-Zetsche 1972; Lutz 1960; 1970a; 1977a.

[7] Cf. Vertet 1976a for discussion.

[8] For instance, Pugnus in Stanfield and Simpson 1958 is now divided into Pugnus and Secundus.

[9] Bémont *et al.* 1980; Bernhard 1981a; Kortüm & Mees 1998; Mees 2002.

[10] See the discussion at end of chapter 4; for earlier consideration of this topic, see the critiques by Miller 1921; MacDonald 1935; Simpson 1966.

[11] In recent years, however, the economic and social interpretation of this class of pottery has come much more to the fore, and now represents a third major area of samian ware studies. See discussion in chapters 6 and 7; many of the papers in Fulford & Durham 2013; Bird, D. 2012; also Aubert 1994, chap. 4; Biddulph 2012; Bird, J. 2012; 2013; Dannell 2002; Dark 2001; Delage 1998; 2001a; 2004; Fülle 1997; Liesen 2011; Marsh 1981; Mees 1994a; 2002; 2007; Middleton 1979; 1980; 1983; Monteil 2004; Peacock 1982; Polak 1998; 2000; Pucci 1983; Raepsaet 1987; Raepsaet-Charlier & Raepsaet-Charlier 1988; Rhodes 1989; Strobel 1992; 2000; Vertet 1998; Weber 2012; Webster 2001; Willis 1997; 1998; 2005; 2011. For more theoretical/philosophical discussions of the study of samian ware, see Roth 2003; Van Oyen 2012; Biddulph 2013.

[12] 1958; 1990.

[13] Cf. Nuber 1969; Bernhard 1981a; Fischer 1981.

example to demonstrate this is the well-known 'AD 197' destruction debris level at Corbridge.

This deposit has been excavated at various times from the beginning of the twentieth century onward, and various dates proposed for the burning levels and associated pottery. In the 1950s and 1960s the consensus of opinion was that the burning represented destruction caused by a hypothetical barbarian incursion in the wake of Clodius Albinus' presumed withdrawal of frontier troops in AD 196-7 to support his civil war campaign.[14] Consequently this dating was applied to the large quantity of samian ware from the destruction level, notably to pieces by Cinnamus and his contemporaries. The destruction was taken to be one of the latest in Britain that contained a large assemblage of samian ware, and therefore its dating provided a guide to the end of Central Gaulish samian production as a whole. However, problems in the chronology soon arose, as Maxfield relates, with the consequence that thinking in the 1980s inclined more to *c.* 180 and the destruction attested in literary sources prior to the governorship of Ulpius Marcellus.[15] The dating of the samian ware had already been questioned before the moving of the historical date, and Hartley adopted an intermediate position by proposing that much of the samian was earlier material redeposited in 197.[16] The stratigraphy of the deposit in question is difficult, but insofar as it can now be interpreted, there is a lower burning level which appears to contain much of the samian ware together with coins up to the reign of Marcus Aurelius, and therefore consonant with the 180 destruction.[17] The lower level may also contain a coin of AD 198,[18] which would nominally place the whole deposit after the presumed 197 destruction, but the coin's uncertain stratigraphic circumstances mean that it is best set aside as good-quality evidence for a *terminus post quem* for the stratum. A result of the move in the historical dating of this deposit has been a general earlier shift in many dates by a couple of decades, which has unfortunately continued to cause chronological problems, e.g. in the dating of earthen town defences.

The German equivalent to Corbridge in terms of late samian ware[19] dating is Niederbieber, although the problem posed by this site is slightly different. It is a so-called 'dated site' in the sense that there are fairly well-defined chronological limits for its beginning and its end.[20] The large quantity of samian and other pottery has been carefully studied and has provided the basis for a 'Niederbieber-Horizont' on many other sites.[21] The problem here is not caused by misapplication of a historically attested date, but by having parameters of *c.* 70 years to date a single, essentially unstratified group of pottery. At the time Oelmann studied the material this was the best approach, since excavation methods were not sufficiently developed to disentangle the exact sequence of layers on the site. However, it inevitably raises the question as to whether the pottery assemblage is representative of the entire date range for the site, or concentrated in one or more periods of activity, or even entirely from the rubbish left behind when the site was abandoned. This group of pottery has, like Corbridge, been used to date the end of samian ware production, the date veering between *c.* 260, the *terminus ante quem* of Niederbieber itself, and as early as *c.* 233, the date of an Alemannic incursion in the southern Rhineland, thought by some to mark the destruction of the Rheinzabern kiln-centre.[22] Current views favour a later rather than an earlier date.[23]

The general problem with historically dated deposits and 'dated sites' as exemplified above is that there are various inherent difficulties in marrying archaeological and historical data in this way (as discussed in chapter 2), and there are too few of them, with the consequence that much emphasis is put on those that do exist. Nevertheless the existing chronology is to a great extent based on such sites, and on stylistic analysis, which helps to link the dated deposits in a sequence. Details of this chronology are given in Table 1.I, which also serves to introduce the sub-groups of the major kiln-centres used in the detailed analysis in chapter 5.[24] The minor kilns are not given here but are discussed in chapter 4 and listed in Appendix 10. If the reader wishes to compare the existing chronology with that proposed in this thesis, reference should be made to Table 5.XIV. The revision in the chronology carried out in

[14] Stanfield & Simpson 1958, xl; Frere 1978, 217, n. 3; Hartley 1972a, App. II.

[15] Maxfield 1982, 79; Dio 72.8; Breeze and Dobson 1976, 118; Bruce 1978, 90ff.

[16] Hartley 1972a, 46. In Hartley & Dickinson (2008a, 5) it is clear that Hartley considers this group unreliable for dating purposes.

[17] See detailed discussion in the Gazetteer under deposits A54-5; also Simpson 1974a, 329-39; Brassington 1975; Simpson and Brassington 1980.

[18] Craster 1911. However, the stratigraphic information presented by the excavators and the coin specialist are inconsistent, as discussed in detail by Gillam (nd), in a typescript response to Hartley 1972a, 45-8. See Dore 1988, 220-1, for a pessimistic assessment of the value of the recording of this deposit. Cf. also King 1991, 44-5.

[19] Throughout this volume, 'late samian ware' refers to products of the mid/late 2nd to mid 3rd century, not the rather different late 3rd and 4th century products manufactured at centres such as Lezoux and the Argonne.

[20] Oswald & Pryce 1920, chap. III; beginning date: tile-stamps in the bath-house dated 185-192; Schönberger 1969, 173; Schallmayer 1987, 487; end date: two coin hoards of the late 250s; Ritterling 1901; 1936.

[21] Oelmann 1914. Schallmayer 1996 provides full discussion of this site in the context of the end of the *limes*. Cf. also Jost 2009, 9-10; Friedrich 2012.

[22] Cf. discussion in Nuber 1969; Müller 1968; Schallmayer 1987, 487-8.

[23] Bernhard 1981a.

[24] The original system of sub-groups was applied to Rheinzabern (e.g. Bernard 1981a), but has been extended in this volume to include Central Gaul and Trier as well, since for many purposes of analysis groupings are more useful than individual potters. Since the original study for this volume in the 1980s, a sub-group scheme was developed for Central Gaul (Heiligmann 1990, 156) which is virtually identical to that given in Table 1.I. Central Gaulish chronology in the Table is based on Stanfield and Simpson 1958, pl 170; Hartley 1972a, Tables IV-V; Rogers 1974; 1990; Heiligmann 1990, 156; Hartley & Dickinson 2008a-2012; Delage 1999a; 1999b; 2000; 2012; Delage & Séguier 2009. Rheinzabern chronology is based on Ricken & Fischer 1963; Ricken & Thomas 2005; Simon 1968, 22; Bernhard 1981a; cf. also Bittner 1986; 1996; Gimber 1993; 1999; Mees 1993; 1994a; 2002; Kortüm & Mees 1998) The Bernhard 1981a scheme has been used for the analysis in chapters 4 and 5, and is given here in the Table. See Appendix 5 for further discussion of Rheinzabern chronological schemes. Trier chronology is based on Huld-Zetsche 1971a; 1993; Pferdehirt 1976, 37.

*Table 1.1 Chronology for Central Gaul, Rheinzabern and Trier, divided into the sub-groups used in chapters 4 and 5. The dates given here are the conventional date-ranges.*

Not all known potters are listed. Central Gaul can be taken to mean mainly the Lezoux kiln-centre in periods II-IV and mainly Les Martres-de-Veyre kiln-centre in period I, but there is some overlap, and many other lesser, but significant, kiln-sites were in operation during the period as well (see Appendix 10 for list of production sites and maps).

**Central Gaul**

I *c.* AD 100-120

Drusus I (X-3), Igocatus (X-4), Sacirius (X-13), Libertus, potter of the rosette, X-I, X-2, X-8/10, X-11/12

II *c.* AD 120-145

Avitus-Vegetus, Quintilianus group, Geminus, Sacer-Attianus, Drusus II, Birrantus II, Secundinus I, Butrio, Acaunissa, Austrus, Docilis, Arcanus, Acurio, Tittius, Sissus I-II, Tetturo, Ianuaris II-Paternus I, Pugnus-Mapillio, X-5, X-6 (Catul ... ), large S potter, Me ...

III *c.* AD 145-75

Criciro, Cettus, Cinnamus-Cerialis, Cinnamus early style, Cinnamus main styles, Secundus, Pugnus, Paullus, Laxtucissa, Albucius, Q I Balbinus, Servus I, Carantinus II, Illixo, Divixtus, Lastuca, Martialis, Moxius, Cantomallus, P-18, P-19, P-22, P-23

IV *c.* AD 160-200

Casurius, Paternus II, Censorinus, Mercator II, Advocisus, Iustus, Iullinus, Doeccus I, Banvus (probably continuing after 200), Cracina, Servus II-VI, Severus, Caletus (probably continuing after 200), Priscus, Antistii, Caratillus, Fgientinus, Atilianus, Ollognatus, Marcus (probably continuing after 200), Lucinus (perhaps after 200), P-33

**Rheinzabern**

Ia *c.* AD 140-70

Janu[arius] I, Reginus I, Cobnertus I-III, Firmus I

Ib *c.* AD 170-early 3rd century

Cerialis I-V, Arvernicus-Lutaevus, Comitialis I-III, Belsus I, Lucanus, Reginus II-Virilis, Cerialis group wares A & B

IIa dated as Ib, probably starting later

Comitialis IV-VI, B F Attoni (= Atto I), Belsus II-III, Cerialis VI, Castus, Respectus, Florentinus, Mammilianus, Firmus II, Iustinus, Iuvenis I, Pupus-Iuvenis II, Pupus, Atto II, Reginus II, Attillus, Augustinus I, E25/26

IIb dated as IIa, probably starting later

Augustinus II-III, Julius I, Lupus, Victorinus I, E8

IIc probably early third century

Verecundus I-II, Regulinus, Peregrinus, Helenius, Marcellus I-II, Augustalis, Primitivus I-IV, wares A & B with 0 382/383

IIIa *c.* AD 230-260

Julius II-Julianus I, Victorinus II-III, Janu[arius] II, Respectinus I-II, Marcellinus, E 48/49

IIIb *c.* AD 230 or later - 275

Victor I, Victor II-Januco, Victor III, Perpetuus, Julianus II, Statutus I-II, Severianus, Severianus-Gemellus, Pervincus I, E30/34, Pervincus II (= E31), E35

**Trier**

I *c.* AD 130-65

Werkstatt I, Werkstatt II

IIa *c.* AD 160-90+

Comitialis, Dexter, Censor, Maiiaavus

IIb *c.* AD 190-210

Criciro, Censor/Dexter successors, Marcellinus, Victor, Tordilo, Amator, Catu ...

IIc *c.* AD 205-225

Atillus-Pussosus, Afer, Afer-Marinus

IIIa *c.* AD 225 or later - 250

Dubitatus-Dubitus, Paternianus, Primanus, Dignus, Perpetuus, Gard 1937, Taf 27, nos 1-21

IIIb *c.* AD 245-275

Succio, Equitius, TPCFR, späte Waren, Spätausformungen

chapters 4 and 5 has effectively ignored all but one or two of the existing historically dated chronological pegs, and used other methods, notably the association of coins and samian ware together in individual deposits. For reasons outlined in chapter 2, this is felt to be more satisfactory.

Explanations of the decline in manufacture of samian ware have not been discussed by samian ware specialists to any great extent.[25] Probably the most explicit is one that is

[25] This was true for the 1970s-80s, but is less so now. Cf. fn 29.

firmly based in historical events. Eric Birley and Grace Simpson[26] used as a basis the proposition that Clodius Albinus removed troops from the northern frontier of Britain to form part of his army that eventually fought and lost the battle of Lyon in AD 197.[27] In the aftermath of this battle, the victorious Septimius Severus in some manner caused the destruction of the Central Gaulish samian industry. The reasons they put forward for inferring this were that the 'AD 197' deposit at Corbridge (as it was dated at the time) contained late samian ware, but that overlying levels did not, to any great extent. Therefore samian ware was not being supplied after this date, and the kilns must have come to a sudden end. The most convenient historical event to account for this was the battle of Lyon, which was therefore taken as a firm date after which no Central Gaulish ware was produced. This self-contained explanation is, of course, plausible, but is uncorroborated in any way (e.g. with independent evidence from the kiln-sites) and depends heavily on the Corbridge evidence. Since, as shown above, the latter has a distinctly weak historical date, which has now been moved earlier, the explanation is no longer tenable. In addition, the argument that lack of samian ware in overlying levels at Corbridge is evidence of lack of supply generally is not a strong one – it is likely that this part of the site was little used after the deposit was laid out, and also it is clearly the case that samian ware is present in deposits elsewhere of later date.

An additional facet of the explanation given in Stanfield and Simpson was that Niederbieber had no Central Gaulish ware, and since it had been dated almost entirely to the period after the presumed end of Central Gaulish manufacture, this was explicable in chronological terms. In fact, Niederbieber was outside the market area for late Central Gaulish samian ware (see chapter 7) and the lack of this pottery on the site is a result of differences in distribution, not chronology.

## THE DECLINE OF SAMIAN WARE MANUFACTURE: TWO HYPOTHESES

The existing conceptual framework for the decline of samian ware manufacture, as we have seen, is based upon historical rather than archaeological paradigms. Dating is founded upon historically-dated sites and deposits; and explanations, where offered, seek to link the end of manufacture with events known or inferred from the written sources. As a result, the end of Central Gaulish manufacture has been placed at *c.* 197, while that of the East Gaulish kilns has a date of *c.* 260 (but with the possibility that other historically important dates, e.g. 233 or 275, may also be relevant). There is a presumption in the conceptual framework that external catastrophe caused the end of manufacture, and that production, especially as far as Central Gaulish samian is concerned, continued at an optimal level until the catastrophic event. Little mention is made of possible problems in the system of distribution or internal changes to the organisation and level of production (except in terms of crudeness of manufacture and the implication that late products were artistically decadent).[28] In other words, the end of samian ware production has not been conceived in economic or cultural terms to any great extent.[29] This is an omission that this volume seeks to rectify, at the same time removing the explanatory framework from its historical basis and placing it more in the realm of archaeologically recognisable processes and sequences. In this way, it is hoped that the dating and explanation proposed here for the decline of manufacture will be more in keeping with the nature of the evidence itself, namely a ceramic product (unattested historically for the period under consideration) only known from the archaeological record.

To this end, two working hypotheses have been created to act as a focus for the study as a whole. They are based on the questions asked at the beginning of this chapter, and are:-

1. That the main agents of decline in manufacture were economic and cultural changes, for whatever reason, throughout the NW provinces.

2. Given that 1 is an admissible hypothesis; that manufacture started to decline in the major kiln-centres in Central and East Gaul at approximately the same time.

These hypotheses have been phrased so that, to a certain extent, they are deliberately contrary to current datings and explanations, the reason for this being that the evidence presented in subsequent chapters can be tested against these hypotheses. If the hypotheses are disproved, it would then be in order to return to the earlier explanatory framework (or, of course, create new working hypotheses); but if maintained, they can continue to be put forward as valid propositions. Analysis will concentrate on the subject matter of the second hypothesis, namely chronology, first (chapters 2-5) and go on to reasons for the decline in chapters 6-7.

[26] In Stanfield & Simpson 1958, xl-xli; for a recent statement of this historical context for Central Gaulish decline, see Ward 2008, 171, and also King 1990, 172-3.

[27] Herodian 3.7.7; Cassius Dio 75.5-7. Cf Ferdière 2011, 17. Symonds (1992, 46) discusses Wightman's (1970, 52) view that the Treveran region and East Gaul may have benefitted from the disruption to Central Gaul at this time.

[28] Cf. Dragendorff 1895, 132, or more recently Simpson 1974b, 114, no. 9.

[29] This was certainly the case when the original PhD thesis was written in the 1980s, but less so in more recent times, when researchers such as Delage (1999a; 2001a) have interpreted the end of samian ware production in largely economic terms.

# CHAPTER 2

# THE METHODOLOGY AND THEORY OF SAMIAN WARE CHRONOLOGY

Despite the general acceptance of samian ware as one of the basic tools available to the archaeologist for site chronology, there has been remarkably little discussion of the methods used to date the pottery itself.[1] In part this is due to the complexity of the pottery styles and their inter-relationships, which has apparently discouraged the non-specialist from investigating the theoretical basis of the chronology, and in part there has been an empirical tradition of scholarship amongst samian specialists. This chapter is devoted to a discussion of the methodology of dating samian ware and its theoretical basis, in an attempt to evaluate the suitability of existing and possible methods.

## CHRONOLOGY BY MEANS OF HISTORICALLY-DATED SITES

As outlined in chapter 1, the existing framework for dating late samian ware is a series of dated sites whose pottery assemblages are linked together by stylistic and other characteristics. The framework can be criticised in its details, but there are also more serious problems of methodology which are best brought out by means of an example.

This type of chronological method is, in fact, in general use for samian ware of all periods. Any site with a restricted period of occupation is amenable to being used as a fixed point in the chronology of both samian ware and other artefacts, provided that the site itself can be accurately and independently dated. One such is the famous legionary base at Haltern, in all likelihood occupied on historical and numismatic grounds between *c.* 8-7 BC and AD 9 during the Roman advance into Germany.[2] From it came a vast collection of artefacts, including a notable series of early samian wares from Italy and South Gaul.[3] In order to make use of this pottery for chronological purposes, the assumption is generally made that the potters (whose names are found on stamped vessels, and consequently are held to be the basic unit for most purposes of analysis; see below) were active during the period of occupation of the site, or at a period that had a fixed relationship with the period of occupation and can therefore be discounted. When sherds of these potters are found on other sites, it is usually taken that the site from which they came had a clear chronological relationship with Haltern. If there are only a few samian sherds on the site to be dated, all of which have analogues at Haltern, contemporaneity is assumed. This relationship is expressed diagrammatically in Fig 2.1. However, it is often the case with a large assemblage such as that from Oberaden, not far from Haltern, that there are samian sherds and potters represented that were not found at the original dated site.[4] Oberaden has consequently been given an earlier date in order to account for the differences in the assemblages (and, it must be said, for historical and numismatic reasons also). Similar differences have been used to give later dates in other cases (Fig. 2.2).

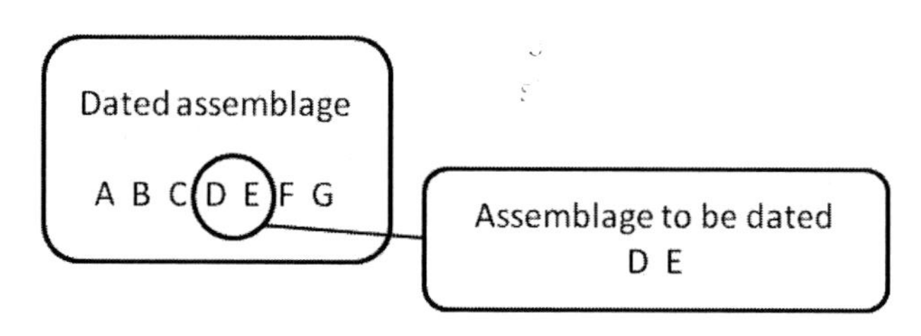


*Fig. 2.1 Diagram showing use of a dated assemblage to establish the contemporaneity of another site. Each letter represents an artefact in the assemblage.*

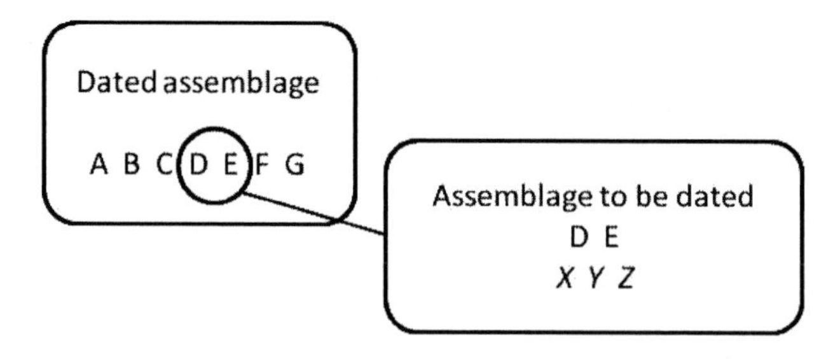


*Fig 2.2 Diagram showing use of a dated assemblage to establish earlier or later occupation of another site. Artefacts X, Y, Z represent items not present in the dated assemblage, which could be earlier or later in date.*

The simple example given here serves to introduce the application in practice of this particular dating method. It also helps to expose the logic of its application, which can be seen to be that of a closed set of occurrences or presences of the pottery, which if repeated in another assemblage, means that they are contemporary, but if not repeated, means that they are not of the same date. These relationships can be described very simply in terms of mathematical set theory.[5] Each assemblage is a finite set - A, B, C, etc. The sherds that make up each assemblage are elements of that set, i.e. in set notation, sherds $x_1 ... x_n \in A$, $y_1 ... y_n \in B$, etc. If the sherds in one assemblage are similar to another (i.e. $x_1 ... x_n = y_1 ... y_n$) then the assemblages are also similar (i.e. A = B). It can be seen that assemblages

[1] However, work on ceramic chronologies in general has encompassed considerable discussion of the underlying issues, e.g. Orton & Orton 1975; Millett 1979; 1987a; 1987b; Going 1992; Isserlin 2012.

[2] Wells 1972, 169; von Schnurbein 1981, 39-44.

[3] Loeschcke 1909; Gechter 1979, 3ff.

[4] Wells 1972, 261.

[5] See, for instance, Green 1965.

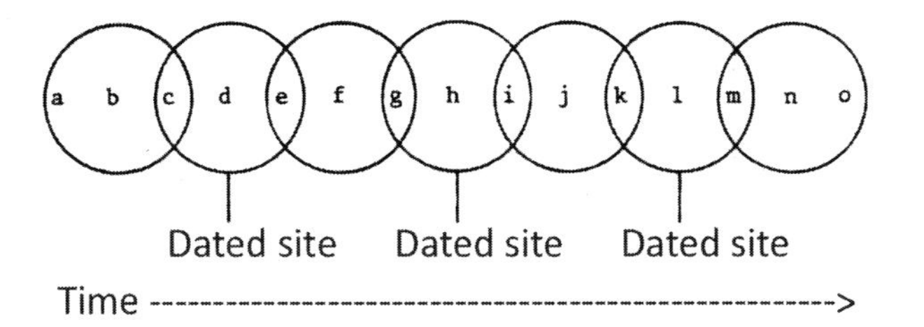


*Fig. 2.3 An idealised chain linking dated assemblages. Each letter could represent a sherd, or a potter's stamp, or a decorative style.*

A. Convergence around fixed points

B. Convergence between fixed points

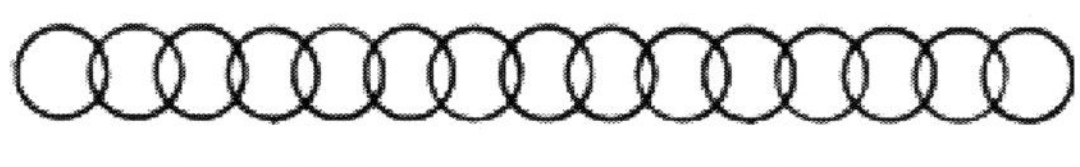


C. An even sequence

*Fig. 2.4 possible variations in a dated chain of assemblages, in which the fixed links are infrequent*

can only be deemed similar if their constituent elements are identical. The process of seeking links between assemblages is known in set theory as the mapping of the elements of one set onto another. If the elements are not identical and cannot be mapped precisely, the unmapped elements become the focus of interest. In most cases of dating by this method the unmapped sherds are accounted for diachronically, resulting in earlier or later dates being suggested for the site. In other words, *in extremis*, a comparison between two assemblages that reveals one sherd of a particular potter present on one site but not on another, all the other sherds being identical, would result in the conclusion that the two sites were not exactly contemporary: that there was considerable overlap in the periods of occupation of the two sites, but that the 'spare' sherd indicates that one of the sites was started earlier or ran later than the other.

In its developed form, this dating scheme is usually applied roughly on the lines given above. The assemblages from dated sites are defined and used as the key sets onto which sherds from assemblages to be dated are mapped. If there are enough sites, both those with previously defined dates and those to be dated, a chain can be established formed of interlinked assemblages. Within the terms of this methodology the chain is a relative chronology, anchored into an absolute dating framework at those links in the chain which are formed of the dated sites (Fig 2.3). If a reasonable proportion of the sites are independently datable, it is usually taken that fairly firm absolute dates can be applied to the other sites. Less confidence can be assumed, however, if there are long gaps between independently dated sites, for the other sites and assemblages may be bunched together at one particular point in the chronology (Fig 2.4).

Such long gaps, and such bunching are indeed two of the problems of this type of chronological method when applied to late samian ware.[6] It is often thought, for instance, that a large number of sites was destroyed in Raetia in AD 233 at the time of the first great Alamannic incursion.[7] Therefore, many sites with traces compatible with destruction, such as burning levels, are assumed to end at this time, thus giving a date to the associated samian ware. Further to this, similar pottery on other sites in the region has been used to establish the same end-date for those sites too, even if there were no traces compatible with destruction or the site had been inadequately recorded. Therefore, the dating of the pottery in similar styles has tended to converge on this historical date. This process can also be seen in other circumstances, such as the '197' destruction of parts of Hadrian's Wall, and the abandonment of the *agri decumates* in *c.* AD 260. It conforms with the generalised model given in Fig 2.4 A, its variants (2.4 B and C) being much less usual, and in the case of 2.4 B (convergence around an unattested 'historical' event) being difficult to propose and sustain.

A major difficulty in using the dated sites method as presently constituted is the definition of the absolute dates for the fixed points in the chronology. Virtually all the dates are provided by historical events which are thought to relate to the sites and assemblages in question. In rare cases it is possible to accept the dates proposed with confidence, the most obvious example being the ash layer covering Pompeii, which is described by Pliny and can be dated precisely.[8] The example of Pompeii,

[6] And indeed in earlier periods, cf. Hogg & Stevens 1936, 71-2.
[7] Kellner 1971a, 138-42.

[8] 24th August, 79; Pliny, *Ep* 6.16; 6.20. Cf. Hartley & Dickinson 2008a, 4-8, and Rogers 1999, 11-16, for discussion of historically dated sites and samian ware. Pavlinec (1992) uses a combination of historical and archaeological parameters to establish a sequence of Swiss dated sites. Cf. also Schaub 1994, Tab. 2, for sequencing of sites linked to the Marcomannic Wars. Cf. fn. 11.

*Table 2.1 Variables affecting the composition of an archaeological pottery assemblage*

| | *Variable mainly dependent upon:-* | | | |
|---|---|---|---|---|
| | **Potter** | **User** | **Excavator** | **Ceramicist** |
| | *who treats the pottery as:-* **a product** | *who treats the pottery as:-* **a consumable** | *who treats the pottery as:-* **in a context** | *who treats the pottery as:-* **an artefact** |
| 1 Availability of vessels of different styles and functions | X | | | |
| 2 Desirability of vessels of different styles and functions (plus continued desirability after acquisition) | X | X | | |
| 3 Use of vessels in different processes | X | X | | |
| 4 Fragility during use | X | X | | |
| 5 Reusability after breakage | X | X | | |
| 6 'Events' affecting vessel users (flight, death, etc.) | | X | | |
| 7 Rubbish disposal methods | | X | | |
| 8 Post-depositional disturbance | | | X | |
| 9 Post-recovery selection | | | X | X |

in fact, highlights the guiding principles which must be followed when attempting to link a historical event with an archaeologically attested episode. Firstly, the event should be accurately delineated in the historical sources, with a reference to the precise scene of action, the material effect of the action and exactly when it occurred. The event should preferably be either construction *ab novo* or destruction and abandonment, since such activities are easiest to detect archaeologically. Secondly, the archaeological episode should be distinctive, in the same way as the Pompeii ash layer is; compatible with the events described, and, most importantly, the relationship of the finds to be dated with the remnants of the episode should be well understood. If these principles can be satisfied, it can be taken that, generally speaking, a construction episode provides a *terminus post quem* for the use of the pottery on that site, and conversely, a destruction episode provides a *terminus ante quem*. There are remarkably few such episodes in the late second and early third centuries, but they are principally the building of the Antonine Wall by *c.* 143,[9] the advance to the outer German *limes* by 161,[10] the destruction associated with the Marcomannic Wars, and the subsequent founding of Regensburg fortress, 179-80,[11] the founding of Carpow fortress by 212,[12] and possibly also to be admitted as a historically attested event, the abandonment of the outer German *limes* and *agri decumates* in *c.* 259-60.[13] Nearly all of these, it should be noted, are dated by inscriptions rather than specific literary references, which are extremely rare.

At this stage, it is useful to recall the case of Niederbieber, mentioned in chapter 1. Its dating parameters of *c.* 190-260, provided by inscribed tiles and a historical event give a probable *terminus post quem* for the deposition of finds within the fort and a *terminus ante quem* for the cessation of deposition. It should be noted that neither date can be referred directly to the finds; only the period within which their loss took place can be defined. In addition, definition of the period of finds-deposition is a maximum. At its minimum, all the finds *may* have found their way into archaeological contexts at the same time, at any point between the two *termini.* A point to be stressed is that the dates provided by historical events and similar parameters only apply to the *activities* that took place at the sites concerned. They do not date the finds themselves. For instance, the presumed abandonment of a site at a specific date can shed no light on whether samian ware of similar styles to that found on the site was in use, and lost, after that date on sites not affected by the historical events that led to its abandonment. Similarly, a foundation date does not necessarily mean that the pottery from a site cannot be found on earlier sites elsewhere. Thus, strictly speaking, all that a set of, dates applied to a site can do is date that site alone. Associated material may have different dates on other sites.

Such strictures lead to grave difficulties in the application of this dating method, and appear to run counter to the way in which the method is normally applied, to the extent that it is no longer possible to accept in its present form. In fact, the basic definition of assemblages as sets is still perfectly valid. The problems centre around the assumptions made

[9] Hist. Aug., *Antoninus* 5; *RIB* 2191-2.
[10] *CIL* XIII, 6561.
[11] *CIL* III, 11965. Fischer (T) 1981; 1994; 2009. Cf. also Scherrer 1994; Stuppner 1994; Jilek 1994 and Gabler 1994 for the Marcomannic Wars in the Danube region, and samian ware finds.
[12] Wright 1965, 223; Herodian 3.14.5; Dio 77.13.1.
[13] Cf. Schönberger 1969, 176; Schallmayer 1996.

when the elements of one set are mapped onto another. It does not seem in reality to be at all likely that the variation between assemblages is monocausal, in other words solely as a result of the chronology of the pottery.[14]

Even a brief reflection on the processes that go towards the placing of a samian sherd in an archaeological context forces a realisation that a wide variety of human behaviour and natural processes has contributed to the selection of sherds found by the archaeologist.[15] Only a few of these are necessarily related to the availability and supply of pottery of different styles (Table 2.I, no. 1), which is the only variable directly related to the chronology of pottery production, In other words, factors such as the type of site from which the assemblage came may have had an important bearing on the presence or absence of vessels in particular styles. A military establishment, for instance, may have favoured certain decorative styles, or even have had a contract for exclusive supply from one source. The other factors given in Table 2.I, nearly all related to disposal and taphonomy of sherds, may cause considerable variation between different sites and different types of site. Thus, it may easily be that two sites or assemblages usually considered to be of different dates, could be contemporary on the basis of the samian ware, with all the variation being accounted for by the non-chronological factors.[16]

## Stylistic typology and chronology

At this point it is apposite to discuss another method of creating a dating sequence, stylistic typology. This seeks to make an order out of pottery styles by internal means, using criteria such as decorative traits present on the sherds themselves. The chronology so produced is implicitly one of production rather than of disposal, which makes it inherently different from dating from dated sites and a matter worthy of further consideration.

The process of creating an ordered sequence through typological means involves the establishment of a set in which the constituent elements (i.e. styles) have a sequence according to the order in which they were produced. Each potter or group of potters may be considered a sub-set of the whole, with an individual suite of elements or styles. The whole production set should strictly be defined as the entire samian pottery production, both discovered, yet-to-be discovered, and even destroyed pieces. This theoretically could be ordered sequentially (by sub-set and within sub-set) by date of production, although of course our knowledge is incomplete since the surviving assemblage is a part only of the whole. It is, in fact, a 'fuzzy' set, as it is not possible exactly to circumscribe the number of elements within the set.[17]

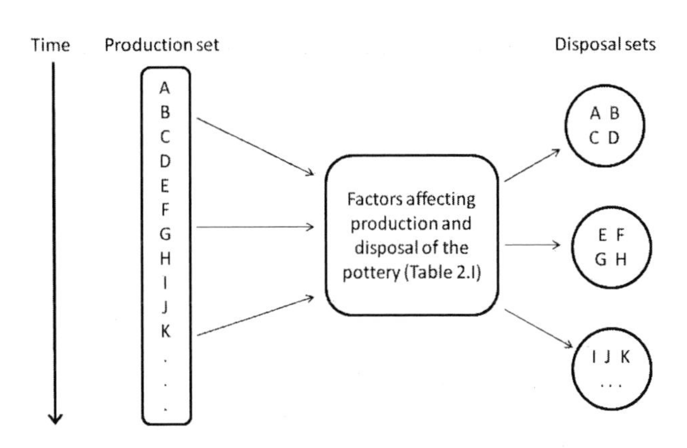


*Fig. 2.5 Mapping of a production set (i.e. a typology) to a series of disposal sets (i.e. dated assemblages), and vice versa. Each letter could represent a sherd, or the presence of a particular decorative style.*

The reason for putting stylistic typology in terms of set theory is that most chronological systems for pottery are in fact a combination of a typological sequence and an absolute chronology from dated assemblages. This involves the combination of production sets (typology) and disposal sets (dated assemblages), and that process effectively requires the mapping of the elements in each type of set to the other, since the elements (i.e. individual sherds) are repeated in both sets. The mapping is not easy since there are many variables that affect the mapping 'pathways' (Fig 2.5), mainly those given in Table 2.I. In practice, the chronological sequence of the production set. tends to be an estimate, especially at the detailed level of individual potters' styles, and it can be revised as a consequence of a strong input of new data from the corpus of disposal sets, for instance when a new group of pottery is excavated. Also, the opposite can occur for when new typological deductions are made which alter the production sequence, the sequence of disposal sets may change, especially those with insecure dating evidence. In other words there is a continual interaction between the work of stylistic analysis for typology and the analysis of dated assemblages. Each supports the other, and each is 'tested' against the other when comparisons (i.e. mappings) are made.

So far, the term typology has been used without elaborating exactly how it reflects a production sequence. A classic typology usually does this by application of one or more guiding principles that are assumed to replicate the original sequence. A good and common example of this is the use of normative aesthetic criteria as the dynamic elements of the typology. One style or group of styles is regarded as the ideal or near the ideal that manufacturers of the pottery were striving to achieve.[18] Supposedly earlier groups are regarded as developmental or experimental, the ideal is called the classic or mature phase, and subsequent groups are deemed decadent. Thus a value is placed on the ideal

[14] See Millett 1979; 1983 for further discussion.

[15] Peña 2007, esp. chapters 1 and 11, provides an extended discussion and modeling of Roman pottery use, discard and incorporation into archaeological deposits.

[16] See the discussion accompanying Table 5.X in chapter 5.

[17] Cf. Zadeh *et al.* 1975; Wang & Chang 1980. Additional 'fuzziness' is created by the problem of defining exactly what is, and what is not, samian ware (cf. Rigoir *et al.* 1973).

[18] Cf. Klejn 1982, 49ff, 190ff.

and the others are implicitly or explicitly measured against it. As far as samian ware is concerned, the generalisation is sometimes made in early works that Arretine ware is regarded as the ideal, and all subsequent samian wares are decadent, with the underlying assumption that the latest products are more decadent than the others. In this way, many badly styled and manufactured sherds are automatically accorded a late date.

An alternative to this set of assumptions is one that presupposes technical or economic changes to be most important. An example may be the assumption that there was a trend through time to simplify production processes and reduce costs, and which therefore regards more elaborate vessels as early and simpler ones as later. This, too, has been applied to samian ware.

The application of such assumptions to samian ware typology is not done without reference to other factors, however, such as the known absolute dating framework. There is also a mitigating feature inherent in the decoration of the pottery that helps a great deal to create a stable stylistic sequence. The individual decorative elements are derived from punches that appear to have been passed between potters, handed from one generation to another, and in the process broken or copied.[19] Broken or worn punches can be traced in styles and the potters who used them positioned later in the sequence than those who used the punches in more pristine condition. Similarly, copies tend to be reproduced on bowls at a slightly smaller scale than the originals due to shrinkage of the clay when the copy punch is fired. Therefore, copyists can be traced and placed later in the sequence. This characteristic of the pottery gives it a distinct advantage over other types when it comes to establishing the minutiae of a sequence.

An interesting offshoot from this characteristic is that it is possible to estimate the intensity of interaction between potters by counting the number of borrowings and copyings. Potters working contemporaneously in a kiln-centre appear to follow the precepts of the social interaction theory proposed by various American archaeologists,[20] in which proximity of the potters in time and space to one another determines their intensity of interchanges and links. At least, this theory is implicit in most discussions of samian potter's styles - those with closely similar styles usually being taken as working at the same time and perhaps in cooperation.

## Dating by means of coin-associated deposits

Given the difficulties in some aspects of the dated-sites method, but also the need for a system of absolute dating that can provide a good chronology for the stylistic typology, it may reasonably be asked what may be available to supplant the dated sites and their assemblages. To answer in brief, it appears that the association of coins and samian ware together in individual deposits currently offers the best hope of establishing a more broadly-based chronology. This is not a new approach, since Paul Karnitsch based a chronology of Rheinzabern ware upon a version of coin-associated deposits, and Nuber has examined the end of Rheinzabern production in this way.[21]

Coin-associated deposits are conceptually exactly the same as assemblages from dated sites, in being disposal sets with all the potential hazards in interpretation outlined in Table 2.1. However, generally speaking, the assemblages are smaller and more controlled, so that some of the non-chronological variation can be eliminated. Also, since the circumstances of deposition are known, it is easier to estimate how and how fast the assemblages came to be formed, rather than guessing when within the time-span of a dated site (such as Niederbieber) the assemblage was deposited. A further advantage is that the three features of every deposit – the coins, the samian ware, and the depositional matrix itself – are all in physical proximity to one another, and therefore avoid the problems associated with the linking of vague historical references with possibly relevant archaeological strata.

There have been objections to the use of artefacts in association as a means of dating, chiefly by Barker:-[22]

> 'Pottery cannot be dated by "association" with a coin. It is only too easy for a stray Roman coin to get into a Medieval rubbish pit. No one would redate a group of glazed jugs to the Roman period on that evidence alone. But how many times have we seen objects and pottery dated by association with coins when the dates look more plausible?'
>
> '...objects retrieved from a layer or feature are "associated" only in the sense that they have a common context in the excavation. Their "association" implies nothing about their relative or absolute dates, or ultimate provenance.'

Logically, Barker's strictures are true, but he effectively denies the dating value of most artefactual material, Associative datings are in fact made on the basis of the *probability* of their association being contemporary. That probability is established by examining a statistically viable number of associations, on the basis of which the presence of coins of particular dates with particular samian styles can be correlated and the strength of association noted. In other words the method mainly uses statistical techniques rather than strictly logical ones (e.g. *terminus*

[19] Cf. Vertet 1976a.

[20] Cf. Plog 1980, 115-7; Hill 1985, 363-4; also Lathrap 1983. Rheinzabern provides the best example of close interaction for the period under study for this volume, and La Graufesenque for the 1st century; cf. Mees 2002.

[21] Karnitsch 1960; Nuber 1969. Karnitsch's coin-associations have been criticised (cf. Bird 1986, 146), and there is unease about using coins for dating samian ware amongst some specialists (e.g. Hartley & Dickinson 2008a, 5-6; Rogers 1999, 11). As Rogers says, 'Malheureusement l'expérience démontre que les monnaies sont presque toujours plus anciennes que les sigillées'; he makes, in effect, a probabilistic statement of association between coins and samian ware, which this volume seeks to test and validate in chapters 3-5.

[22] Barker 1977, 196, 195. See also Hartley & Dickinson 2008a, 5-6.

*post* and *ante quem*). Barker himself implies this when he asks how many times associated dates have been given when the material in association looks 'plausible'. The word plausible presumably means that similar associations have been met with previously, and therefore the associated dating has some backing from other associations. An approach which examines the probability of associated material coming together is explicitly concerned with assessing how 'plausible' that association is.

The three variables in coin-associated deposits, mentioned above, cannot, however, simply be placed in conjunction with one another to yield an absolute date for the deposit. The coins in the deposit, the ultimate source of any absolute date, give a *terminus post quem* from the date of the latest coin. The *terminus post quem*, though, is not what is of interest here, rather it is the estimated date at which the deposit is *most likely* to have come together. This depends on the number of coins in the deposit, their denominations and dates. It also depends on their estimated life in circulation, which has to be obtained by examining coin hoards (discussed in detail in chapter 3). The depositional matrix also has an effect on the actual date of deposition and the strength of association. The main factors of concern here are the rate of accumulation of the deposit (fast or slow) and the source of the matrix (i.e. how much redeposited material it contains). This is discussed in chapter 4, together with the third variable, the samian ware itself, which of course is the subject under investigation, whose variation when the other two are accounted for will give us date ranges for the most likely period of deposition of particular potters' styles.

Coin-associated deposits have the advantage of being a data-source that can continuously produce new material to refine the existing chronology, as newly excavated groups are processed and published. Also, they can come from all periods and types of site, and potentially from anywhere within the distribution area of the pottery, thus avoiding the 'bunching' of dates alluded to earlier, and opening the way for detailed regional or socially-stratified chronologies of distribution and marketing. This contrasts with the source material available from the dated sites approach, which tends to be restricted for the most part to military and frontier sites, as a result of the pre-eminence of these types of site in the literary and epigraphic record. Towns are only occasionally mentioned in the historical sources, and villas or rural settlements scarcely ever. Consequently it is a military pattern of use and disposal that dominates the current chronology. The only viable means of assessing civilian patterns is through the use of coin-dated associations.

# Chapter 3

# Coin-Life and Coin-Loss in the Late Second and Early Third Centuries

This chapter explores the dates provided by coins for archaeological deposits of the late second and early third centuries in the north-west provinces. 'Date' in this exercise means, of course, the likely date of loss of a coin, not its date of issue, since it is well known that a single coin in an archaeological deposit has a strong possibility of being lost some considerable time after it was minted. The questions addressed here are whether we can assess the probability of loss by specified elapsed times after the date of issue, and whether it is possible to quantify the probabilities meaningfully so as to be able to give a likely date-of-loss to a coin in an archaeological context.[1] The answer to these questions would almost certainly be no if coins were always found singly, but luckily they are quite frequently found in groups, either as associated site-finds or hoards. By analysing the composition of these groups it may be possible to answer the questions posed above. Associated site-finds will be examined first, as hoards represent a distinctive and specialised type of coin-loss, to be discussed below.

## Coins found in association

Two or more coins found together will be able to yield valuable data on circulation pattern, provided it is assumed that the coins came to the deposit at the same time, or at least close enough together in archaeological time to have had no effect. For the purpose of this exercise it has been taken that all the coins in the deposits came together within *c.* 10 years as this is comfortably inside the scale of accuracy that can best be achieved. The latest coin in an associated group can, on this assumption, be taken to provide a *terminus post quem* for all the earlier coins. This means that the difference between the date of the latest coin and each of the earlier coins is the minimum period of circulation for each of those coins.

## Zugmantel: a case study

In order to examine this approach to investigating periods of circulation, the finds from the fort and *vicus* at Zugmantel have been used. A large number of cellars and wells were excavated at this site,[2] most with homogeneous

*Table 3.I Period divisions for coin groups*

*Note:* The periods are based on Reece 1973, but differ in some of the details, notably the division of IX into 3 instead of 2, and the start of XI at 282 instead of 275.

| *Period* | *Emperor* | *Date* | *Length of period in years* |
|---|---|---|---|
| Ia | Republic-Augustus | up to 14 | - |
| Ib | Tiberius-Caligula | 14-41 | 27 |
| IIa | Claudius | 41-54 | 13 |
| IIb | Nero-Vitellius | 54-69 | 15 |
| III | Vespasian-Domitian | 69-96 | 27 |
| IV | Nerva-Trajan | 96-117 | 21 |
| V | Hadrian | 117-38 | 21 |
| VI | Antoninus | 138-61 | 22 |
| VIIa | Aurelius | 161-80 | 18 |
| VIIb | Commodus | 180-92 | 13 |
| VIIIa | Pertinax-Severus | 193-211 | 18 |
| VIIIb | Caracalla-Elagabalus | 211-22 | 11 |
| IXa | Alexander-Maximinus | 222-38 | 16 |
| IXb | Gordian-Philip II | 238-49 | 11 |
| IXc | Decius-Valerian | 249-59/60 | 10 |
| Xa | Gallienus-Quintillus Postumus-Victorinus | 260-70 | 10 |
| Xb | Aurelian-Probus Tetricus | 270-82 | 12 |
| XI | Carus-Diocletian Carausius-Allectus | 282-94 | 12 |
| XII | Diocletian reform coinage and later | from 294 | - |

stratigraphy and many having two or more coins in the fill (Appendix 3, Table B). The quantity of coins from this single site is fortunate, since if several sites had had to be used the vagaries of regional circulation patterns may have had an effect on the data.[3] As it is, the periods of circulation that can be extracted from this body of data presumably reflect a single circulation pattern, that of the Rhineland area.

Appendix 3 gives the coins in each context by type and period, using the scheme given in Reece 1973 and elsewhere: the reigns and dates of these periods are given in Table 3.I. Silver denotes mainly *denarii*, since few radiates (*antoniniani*) were found: there is also one *aureus*

[1] The problems associated with using coins for dating archaeological contexts have most recently been discussed by Lockyear 2012, especially pp. 203-7 for some of the issues touched on in this chapter.

[2] The main reference to Zugmantel is now Sommer 1988, in which there is a major reconsideration of the site. The original excavation data are in Jacobi 1930, 36f. and earlier references therein. See also Kortüm 1998, 47, Abb. 70-2, for discussion of the coin finds from the site, and its end-date. He also shows that Severan coins are relatively more common in the fort than the *vicus*, the latter being from which the data analysed here is drawn.

[3] Reece 1973; Hodder & Reece 1980.

*Table 3.II Zugmantel: coins in associated groups in relation to the latest coin in each group*

| **SILVER** | *Number of periods earlier than latest coin (silver or bronze) in group* | | | | | | | | | | | |
|---|---|---|---|---|---|---|---|---|---|---|---|---|
| *Period of issue* | *0* | *1* | *2* | *3* | *4* | *5* | *6* | *7* | *8* | *9* | *10* | *11* |
| Ia | - | - | - | - | - | - | - | - | - | 2 | - | 1 |
| Ib | - | - | - | - | - | - | - | - | - | - | - | - |
| IIa | - | - | - | - | - | - | - | - | - | - | - | - |
| IIb | - | - | - | - | - | - | - | - | - | 1 | - | |
| III | - | - | - | - | 4 | 5 | 3 | 1 | 3 | 2 | | |
| IV | - | - | - | 1 | 3 | - | - | 4 | 4 | | | |
| V | 1 | - | 1 | - | 1 | 1 | - | 2 | | | | |
| VI | - | 2 | 1 | 1 | - | 4 | 2 | | | | | |
| VIIa | 1 | 1 | 3 | - | 3 | 3 | | | | | | |
| VIIb | 2 | 2 | 2 | 1 | 1 | | | | | | | |
| VIIIa | 16 | 4 | 19 | 6 | | | | | | | | |
| VIIIb | 10 | 8 | 7 | | | | | | | | | |
| IXa | 27 | 3 | | | | | | | | | | |
| IXb | 10 | | | | | | | | | | | |

| **BRONZE** | *Number of periods earlier than latest coin (silver or bronze) in group* | | | | | | | | | | | | |
|---|---|---|---|---|---|---|---|---|---|---|---|---|---|
| *Period of issue* | *0* | *1* | *2* | *3* | *4* | *5* | *6* | *7* | *8* | *9* | *10* | *11* | *12* |
| Ia | - | - | - | - | - | - | - | - | 2 | 1 | - | - | 1 |
| Ib | - | - | - | - | - | - | - | - | - | - | - | 2 | - |
| IIa | - | - | - | - | - | - | 1 | - | - | - | - | - | |
| IIb | - | - | - | - | - | - | - | 2 | - | - | - | | |
| III | - | - | 1 | 1 | 3 | 3 | 5 | 2 | 14 | 7 | | | |
| IV | - | - | 2 | 3 | 9 | 4 | 5 | 10 | 2 | | | | |
| V | 7 | 2 | 2 | 17 | 16 | 11 | 9 | 8 | | | | | |
| VI | 4 | 6 | 13 | 8 | 8 | 19 | 10 | | | | | | |
| VIIa | 19 | 19 | 17 | 7 | 21 | 8 | | | | | | | |
| VIIb | 10 | 3 | 4 | 3 | 4 | | | | | | | | |
| VIIIa | - | - | - | - | | | | | | | | | |
| VIIIb | 1 | - | - | | | | | | | | | | |
| IXa | - | - | | | | | | | | | | | |
| IXb | - | | | | | | | | | | | | |

in the total. Bronze includes *sestertii*, *dupondii* and *asses*, since little distinction could be observed in the pattern for these bronze denominations, and consequently it was not thought worthwhile keeping them separate.

When the data are arranged to show the timespan of each coin relative to the latest in each respective context (Table 3.II), an interesting pattern emerges. It is immediately apparent that the majority of silver coins is lost within three periods of the latest in the group, whereas bronze coins are frequently much older at the time of loss.[4] It is also clear that little, if any, bronze reached Zugmantel after period VIIb (Commodus), which was almost certainly a contributory factor to the longevity of much of the bronze in the deposits, in that bronze coins were retained in circulation longer and thus presumably conserved more carefully.

Another observation to be made from Table 3.II is that all the early coins, both silver and bronze, were very old by the time they were incorporated in their respective deposits. This is because all the contexts studied from Zugmantel must date from the second half of the second century or first half of the third. This much is clear from the latest coin in each context. In other words, the coins from, for instance, period III (Flavian) were in circulation for 50-180 years before loss, although that is not to say that period III coins were not also lost closer to their period of issue – simply that within the period of circulation under study, old coins are surprisingly common.

A second method of examining the data is to plot the number of coins in each deposit against the period of the latest coin (Table 3.III). This shows that there is a relationship between these two variables, since deposits with few coins tend to be grouped in the earlier part of the range of periods (VIIa-VIIIa), whereas larger numbers of coins (6+) are more often in the later periods (VIIIb-IXb). A linear correlation coefficient of -0.462 lends some support to this relationship. The inference from this

[4] Scrutiny of individual contexts in Appendix 3, Table B, confirms that silver coins are usually younger than the bronze ones in their group.

*Table 3.III Zugmantel: number of coins (including unidentified coins) in each deposit plotted against the period of the latest coin in the deposit (Cellar 168 not included)*

| Period of latest coin | Number of coins in deposit 2 | 3 | 4 | 5 | 6 | 7 | 8 | 9 | 10 | 11 | 12 | 13 | 14 | 15 | 16 | 17 | 18 | 19 | 20 | 21 | 22 | 23 | 24 | 25 |
|---|---|---|---|---|---|---|---|---|---|---|---|---|---|---|---|---|---|---|---|---|---|---|---|---|
| V | - | - | - | 1 | 1 | - | - | - | - | - | - | - | - | - | - | - | - | - | - | - | - | - | - | - |
| VI | 1 | 1 | 1 | - | - | - | - | - | - | - | - | - | - | - | - | - | - | - | - | - | - | - | - | - |
| VIIa | 4 | 3 | 4 | - | 1 | 1 | - | - | - | - | - | - | - | - | - | - | - | - | - | - | - | - | - | - |
| VIIb | - | 3 | 1 | - | - | 1 | - | - | 1 | 1 | - | - | - | - | - | - | - | - | - | - | - | - | - | - |
| VIIIa | 2 | 4 | 3 | 1 | - | 2 | 2 | - | 1 | 1 | - | - | - | - | - | - | - | - | - | - | - | - | - | - |
| VIIIb | 1 | 1 | 2 | - | - | 4 | - | 1 | - | 1 | - | - | - | - | - | - | - | - | - | - | - | - | - | - |
| IXa | 1 | 2 | 2 | - | 2 | 5 | 1 | - | 1 | 1 | 1 | 1 | - | - | - | - | 1 | - | - | - | - | - | - | 1 |
| IXb | - | - | - | 1 | - | 3 | - | - | - | - | - | 1 | - | - | - | - | - | - | - | 1 | - | 1 | - | - |

is not the obvious one that earlier deposits have fewer coins in them and *vice versa*, but given what we know of circulation life of the coins, it is more likely that Table 3.III reflects the relationship of the number of coins in the deposit to the actual date of deposition. This means that the greater the number of coins in the deposit, the greater is the chance that the latest represents the period when the deposit was formed. Such an inference is unsurprising when viewed in the light of the probability that all coins of the same denomination have an equal chance of being lost, for deposits that have had greater 'exposure' to coins being lost will incorporate a greater range of periods in their coin sample, and thus are more likely to have coins more or less contemporary with the *terminus ad quem* of the deposit.

This relationship is a valuable tool in assessing likely dates of loss of coins, and will be returned to later in this chapter. However, Table 3.III yields one further point that is pertinent to this matter. The regression line used to calculate the correlation coefficient intercepts the $x$ axis at 10.77 coins. In other words, the best-fit regression line predicts that a group of eleven coins will be deposited at the period of its latest coin. This information, too, will be useful in assessing likely dates of loss.

## Coin hoards

In a general sense, coin hoards can be taken to be fossilised reflections of the pattern of circulation at the time of their deposition, although individual cases may show idiosyncracies of collection. The effect of such cases can be minimised if numbers of contemporary hoards can be grouped together. The main type of hoard that would not reflect the circulation pattern at the time of burial is the 'life-savings' hoard, built up over a period of time, but since it is impossible to estimate their proportion to the total, it will have to be accepted that they exist in the hoard population, and due allowance made for their lengthening effect on the date-ranges derived for any particular coin. It would seem, however, that the numbers of such hoards and hence their effect on date-range estimation is fairly limited, for Reece has shown that the composition of *denarius* hoards of Severus in Britain tend to conform to a particular pattern which may be graphically characterised as a bell-shaped histogram skewed towards the later periods.[5] This is best accounted for by suggesting that it reflects the circulation pattern at the time of deposition which, in theory at least, should consist mainly of coins that came into use in the few years preceding the date of deposition, coins of earlier periods being present but rare, and coins of the period current at the time of deposition being uncommon due to the delay between issue and use, a phenomenon prevalent in the Roman Empire, particularly before regional mints were established.[6] In the case of the Severan data, if many 'life-savings' hoards had been present the shape of the histogram would have been more even, with less prominence in the peak preceding the final period, if indeed it would have been present at all. As we shall see, the Severus histogram is not peculiar to that

[5] Reece 1981; 1974. For hoard types and hoarding behaviour: Abdy 2002, 9-10; Bourne 2001, 32-9; Bland 1996. Duncan-Jones (1994, 67-85) puts a determinedly official and military complexion on hoard composition, arguing (p. 83); 'Most surviving hoards seem to owe their composition to army paymasters, who may occasionally have paid out in older worn coins for preference'. This interpretation has not found favour amongst numismatists (cf. Howgego, *JRS* 86, 1996, 208-9; Cheesman, *NC* 156, 1996, 358), and in more recent studies mainly run along lines iterated in this chapter (see above). Hobley (1998, 105-8) demonstrates that coin-types in 2nd-century *sestertii* hoards tend to be selected specifically for the hoards, unlike the coin-types from site finds. This phenomenon seems to affect the percentage of coin-types, but not the overall circulation pattern, nor the regional variation in the hoards. For a 3rd-century deposit resembling a hoard, of sacrificial origin but apparently with the same characteristics as other hoards, in Barbaricum at Illerup, Denmark, see Bursche 2011.

[6] The pattern observable in modern coinage is similar, although the fall-off in the proportion of the most recent coins is less marked due to more efficient distribution of new coin. Collis 1974 presents the theory of the mechanics of coin distribution but his imaginary examples using modern pennies do not conform to the fall-off pattern observable in tests of 5p/ls and 10p/2s coins carried out by the author which have higher proportions of recent coinage.

period, and it may be taken to be a normal shape for late second and early third century silver coinage.

A particular problem that faces the student wishing to use coin hoards as indicators of the pattern of coin loss is that hoards are deliberate artefacts, whereas losses are non-systematic and random, to all intents and purposes. This has been touched on above in that different ways of making up the hoard will be reflected in the overall sample. In an ideal situation all hoards would be 'spot' hoards, accumulated immediately prior to deposition.[7] The indications are that these hoards do in fact predominate over 'life-savings' hoards, to a great extent. There are four other ways in which a hoard may not be a reflection of the circulation pattern:-

1. If the method of saving is altered during compilation of the hoard
2. If saving is not continuous
3. If a selected part of the hoard is returned to circulation (e.g. if a denomination is in danger of demonetisation)
4. If Gresham's law is operating in favour of hoard compilation. This would be the case if under-valued issues are hoarded either with the intention of melting them down, or if there is the hope that values might be restored.

As far as 1 and 2 are concerned, if the sample of hoards is sufficient, these may be regarded as idiosyncracies that will not affect the overall picture. Number 3 is one of the factors that is of interest in predicting coin loss, for if a coin is demonetised or effectively useless due to inflation, it will go out of circulation quite quickly, and unless there is an incentive to recover them, nearly all possible losses will have been made by the time this occurs. A case in point is that the *denarius* was effectively demonetised by the Gallienic and Postuman issues of radiates and the contemporary inflation. Very few *denarii* remained in circulation after the 260s.

Another factor was also probably in operation in this period, namely that under-valued currency was being driven out of circulation by over-valued denominations (Gresham's law). This happened when debased issues were made and the government attempted to melt down and replace all the earlier under-valued coin. Private withdrawals of under-valued coin for melting down may also have been made, although illegal. This was almost certainly the case for *denarii* from the 240s onward, after the probably still over-valued radiate had been introduced in strength. Debasements of the *denarius* itself seem to have been less effective in driving earlier issues out of circulation, if the hoard evidence is valid in this respect.[8] The relevant hoards all have numbers of coins spanning the periods of debasement that occurred throughout the late second and early third centuries, and unless they were all being collected under the influence of factor 4 above, namely with the intention of keeping under-valued coins for melting down, or for a future restoration of value, which is doubtful, then not much notice seems to have been taken of old coins as intrinsically under-valued items.[9] Certainly central treasuries must have withdrawn many old coins from circulation,[10] but not enough to eradicate the surprisingly large numbers of old *denarii* surviving in hoards to the early third century. Perhaps a general shortage of coin in the first part of the third century led to their remaining in circulation, a problem which was otherwise solved by casting and counterfeiting,[11] or overstriking.[12] Thus the presence of old and new coin together in hoards, along with circumstantial evidence for a general shortage of currency, would militate against the existence in the hoard population of numbers of hoards accumulated with a view to withdrawing under-valued coins from circulation.

The conclusion of this brief survey of hoarding is that the majority was built up during a short period of time and, as such, may be taken to reflect the circulation pattern at the time of deposition. There may also be a minority of hoards which was the product of saving over a period, or which for other particular reasons would not bear a strong relationship to the circulation pattern. The effect of these anomalies, and the probable presence in nearly every hoard of an admixture of old coin, is to make the apparent life of individual issues longer than in fact would have been the case. This overestimate of coin life is not one that can be easily quantified, but a reasonable assumption to make, until further research proves otherwise, is to reduce the upper limit of a coin's established date-range by 10-20%.

### Calculating coin life from coin hoards

The method adopted here to assess a coin's date-range is to calculate the percentage of a particular coin type in hoards of different periods. In this way ranges and means of percentages can be built up for the total of individual scores. This method was proposed in theoretical terms by Collis and used in two examples by Reece, but the

[7] The Beau Street hoard, Bath, with its packets or bags of coins of different denominations (Ghey 2013), opens up the discussion concerning the nature of hoarding behaviour. Part of the hoard may have been old coin saved up, while other packets probably represent 'spot' hoarding just prior to deposition. The discovery of the different packets was due to careful, forensic excavation of the hoard, and it remains unknown how far its taphonomic formation process would apply to other hoards, too.

[8] Walker 1978, 139-40; Bland 1996, 76-80; Abdy 2002, 28-9. Duncan-Jones (2001, 81-2) has established that the later *denarii* of Severus were being removed from circulation in preference to the lighter early *denarii* of his reign, due presumably to melting down for their silver content.

[9] *Contra* Bolin 1958, chap. 9 and Bruun 1978, who assumes, on the basis of the proportion of different denominations in hoards, that Gresham's law did in fact operate in favour of hoards. However, the proportion of denominations in hoards is never the same as site proportions, even in stable currency conditions.

[10] As they seem to have done under Trajan; Bolin 1958, 208ff; Reece 1974, 83.

[11] Boon 1974, 110ff.; King (C) 1996.

[12] From 249 onwards; Walker 1978, 140.

potential pointed out by these contributions for assessing coin loss systematically has not hitherto been exploited.[13]

The most convenient unit to use for the period of each stage of coin loss is the reign of particular emperors, as this enables a fairly large sample to be drawn on for assessing each stage, and also tends to coincide with variations in the coin issue rate of each ruler or group of rulers (Table 3.I).[14]

The data from the coin hoards examined are presented in Appendices 1 and 2, where the percentage of coins of each period for each hoard is given, together with its position chronologically in relation to the latest coin in the hoard. Thus, for the first entry, Itteringham, the number 3 indicates that coins of Antoninus accounted for 3% of the total in the hoard (all the rest being earlier in date), and the column heading *VI* indicates the Antonine period. This is also the period of the latest coin for this particular hoard, and thus there are no further entries along the row. The data in the Appendices are re-arranged in the graphs (Figs 3.1-3.8; 3.10-3.16), in order to show the percentages of coins in each period together. As the diagrams indicate, the cumulative effect of grouping the percentages together is to allow averages to be calculated that can potentially be used in a predictive way (see below). These averages are presented as a line graph, with the data for each period as box-and-whisker plots.[15]

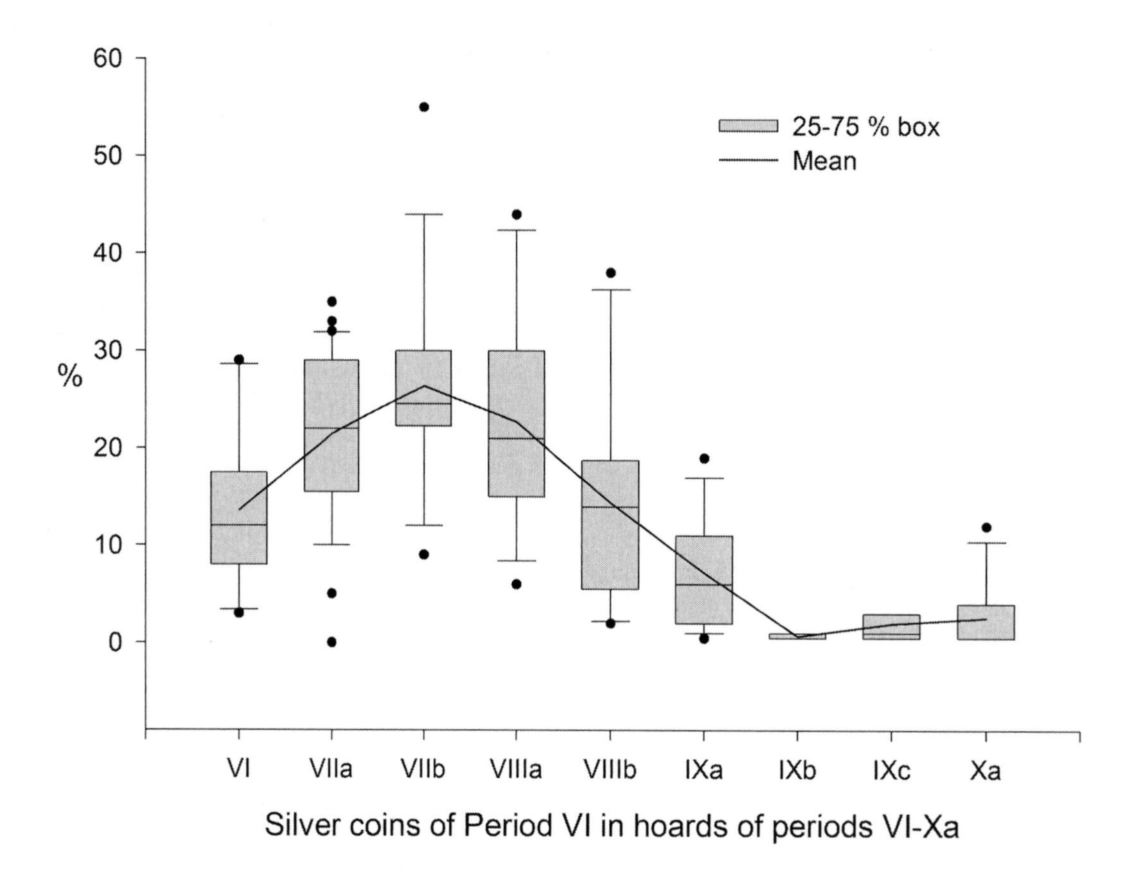


*Fig. 3.1 Graph showing the mean percentage of silver coins of Period VI (Antoninus Pius, 138-161) in hoards from the NW provinces of periods VI-Xa (data from Appendix 1). The mean for hoards of each period is linked by the line plot across the graph, and the box-and-whisker plots give an indication of the dispersion of percentages in the hoards of each period.*

[13] Collis 1974, 178ff; Reece 1974, 83.

[14] It should be noted that coins of Pertinax, Didius Julianus, Gordian I and II, Balbinus, and Pupienus are not included in the hoard statistics. All were rulers for short periods only, which makes the calculation of coin loss per year inaccurate in their cases, and the two periods into which they fall are both ones of uncertainty in monetary terms, Pertinax being involved in a sharp revaluation of the *denarius*, and Balbinus and Pupienus being the last emperors to issue *denarii* to any great extent. See Carson (1983) for the utility of hoards in establishing dating sequences for coin issues within an emperor's reign. This level of detail is not, however, the concern of the methodology put forward in this chapter. Cf. Peter (1996) for an assessment of the circulation of Antonine and Aurelian bronze by issue year, in the NW provinces.

[15] The method for calculating the mean line in Figs 3.1-8 is to take the mean for each group as representing the number of scores for that group. In other words, in Fig 3.1 group 1 has 11 scores (after conversion of the mean, 11.3, to an integer value), group 2 has 20, group 3 has 27 etc.

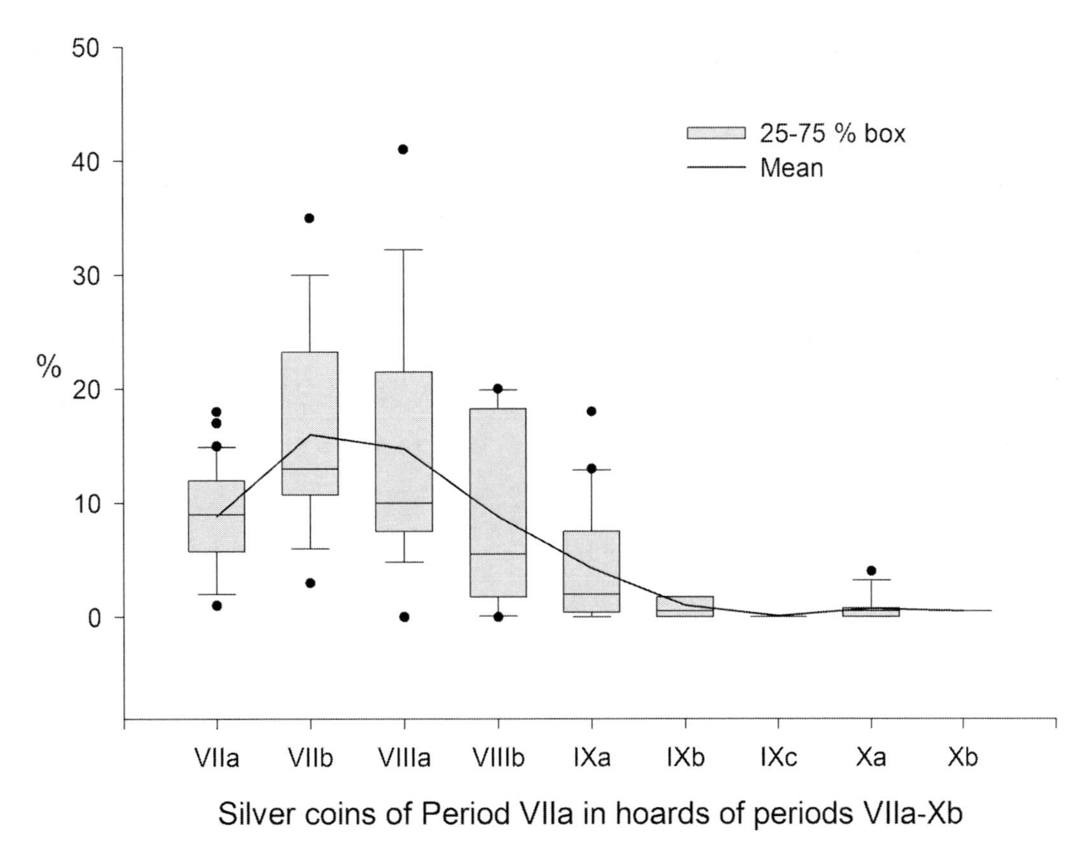


*Fig. 3.2 Graph showing the mean percentage of silver coins of Period VIIa (Marcus Aurelius and Lucius Verus, 161-180) in hoards from the NW provinces of periods VIIa-Xb (data from Appendix 1).*

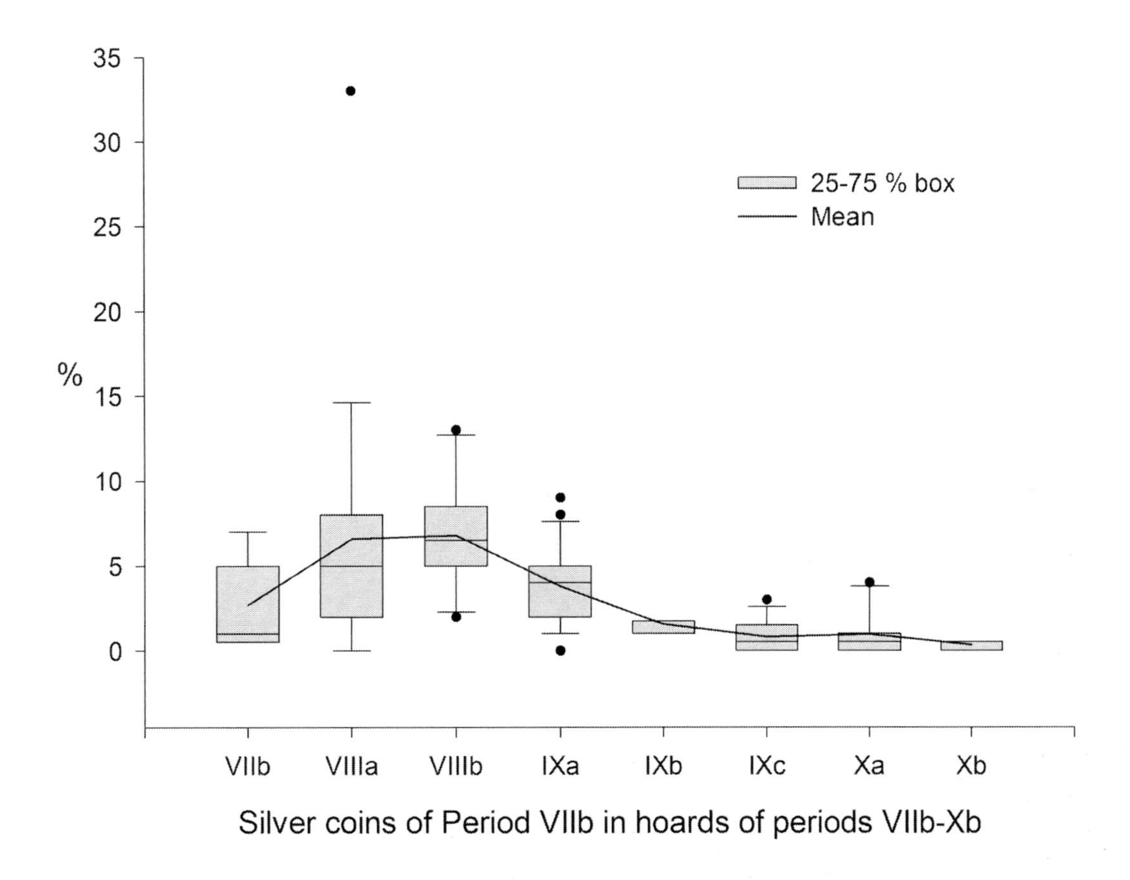


*Fig. 3.3 Graph showing the mean percentage of silver coins of Period VIIb (Commodus, 180-192) in hoards from the NW provinces of periods VIIb-Xb (data from Appendix 1).*

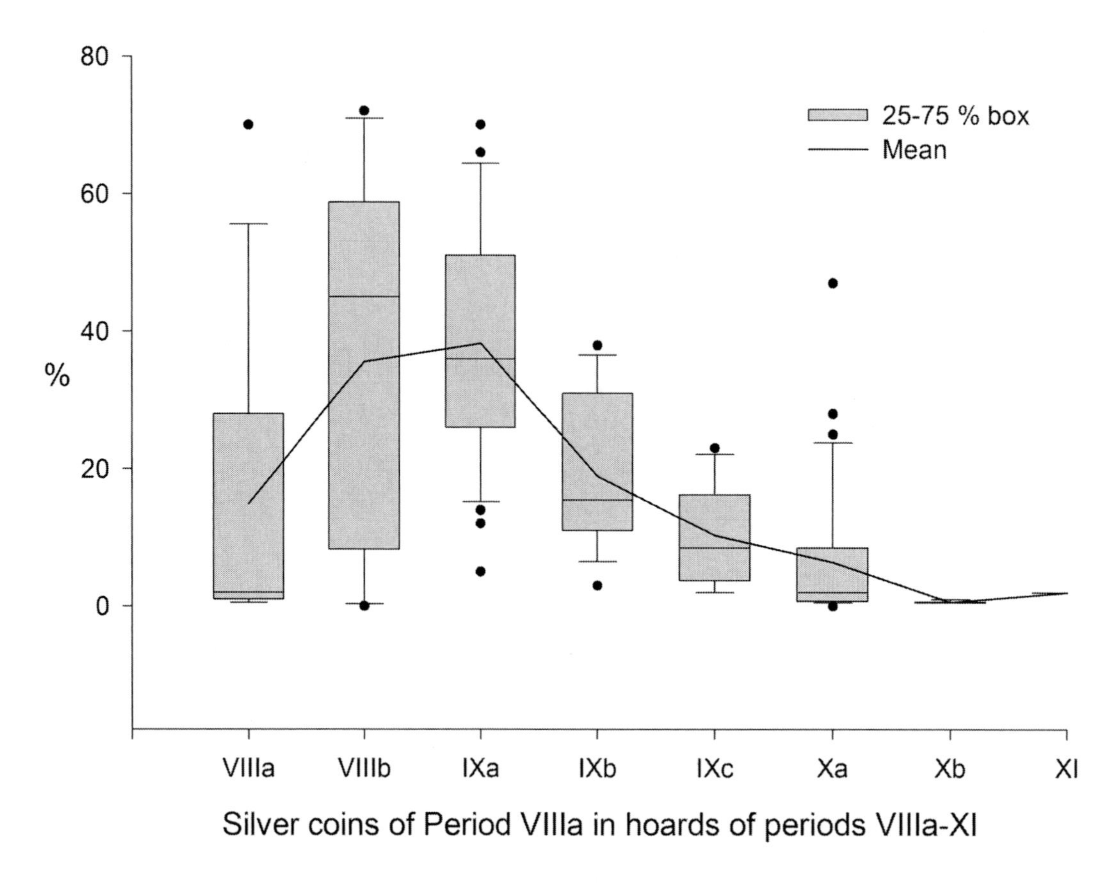


*Fig. 3.4 Graph showing the mean percentage of silver coins of Period VIIIa (Septimius Severus, 193-211) in hoards from the NW provinces of periods VIIIa-XI (data from Appendix 1).*

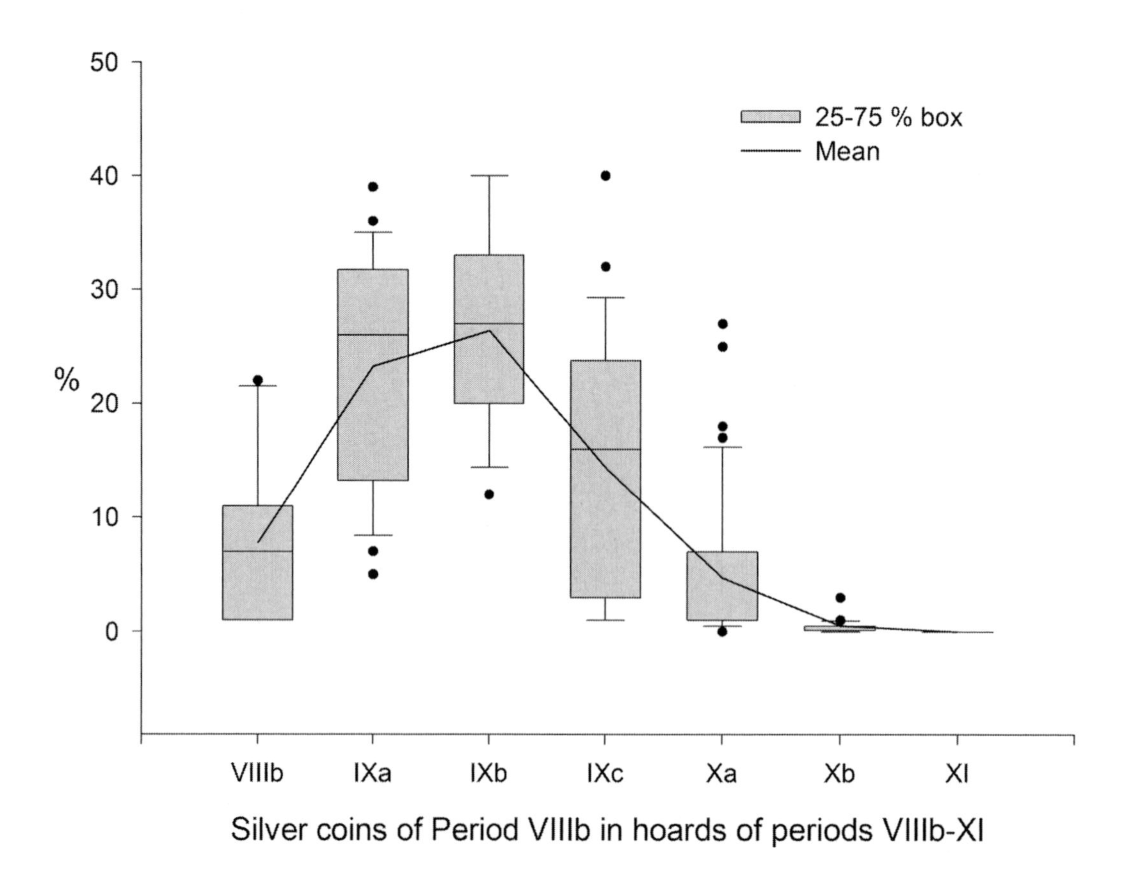


*Fig. 3.5 Graph showing the mean percentage of silver coins of Period VIIIb (Caracalla to Elagabalus, 211-222) in hoards from the NW provinces of periods VIIIb-XI (data from Appendix 1).*

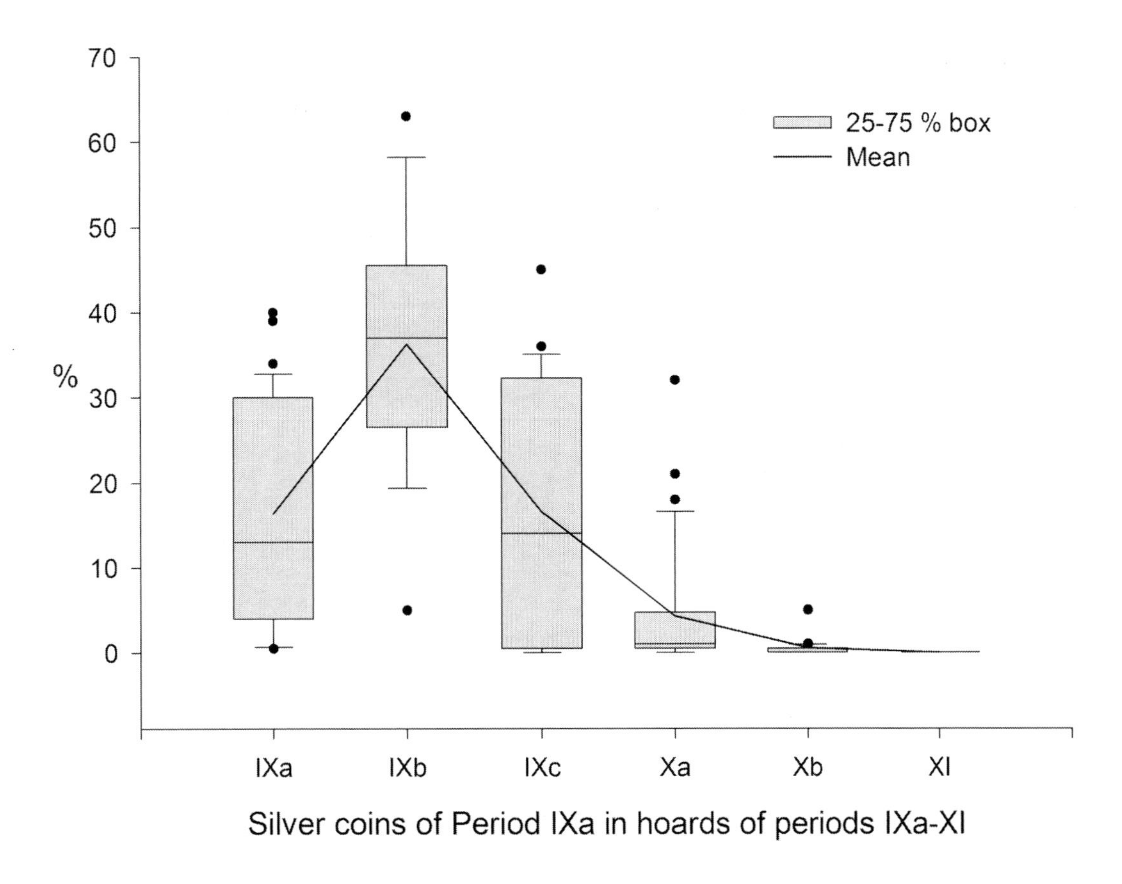


*Fig. 3.6 Graph showing the mean percentage of silver coins of Period IXa (Severus Alexander to Maximinus Thrax, 222-238) in hoards from the NW provinces of periods IXa-XI (data from Appendix 1).*

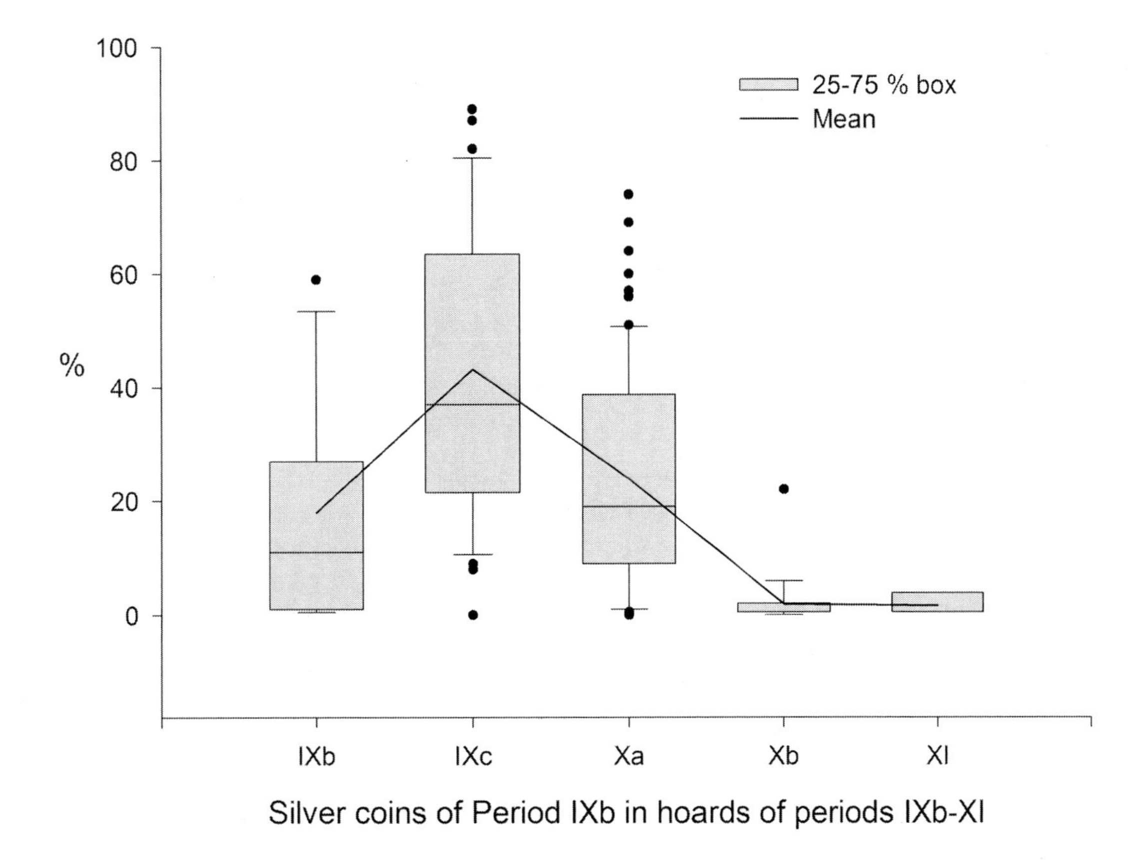


*Fig. 3.7 Graph showing the mean percentage of silver coins of Period IXb (Gordian III to Philip I/II, 238-249) in hoards from the NW provinces of periods IXb-XI (data from Appendix 1).*

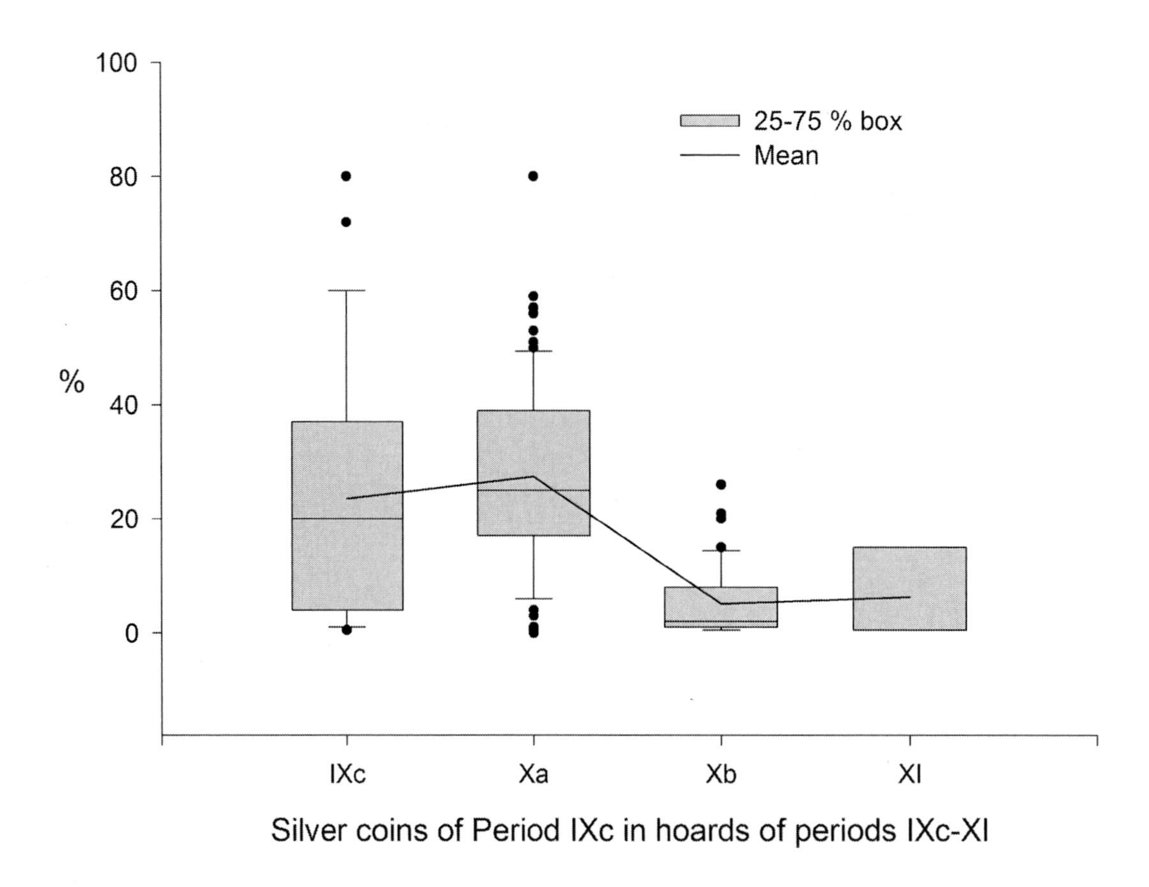


*Fig. 3.8 Graph showing the mean percentage of silver coins of Period IXc (Decius to Valerian, 249-259/60) in hoards from the NW provinces of periods IXc-XI (data from Appendix 1).*

SILVER COINS IN HOARDS

The initial point to note is that all the silver hoards conform to a roughly similar pattern, which is of the type presaged by the work of Reece and Collis,[16] whereas the bronze averages show a markedly different and less consistent pattern, that seems to follow neither the theoretical notions of coin circulation and loss, nor the empirical evidence available for other denominations and other periods. In fact the nature of the pattern of the averages makes the derivation of parameters for coin loss much easier for silver than for bronze, and so it is to the former that attention will be turned first.

Fig. 3.9 shows the averages for each period in each reign recalculated as percentages and displayed as a stacked percentage bar for each period.[17] In this way it can be seen how long after the moment of issue it takes for a certain percentage of the coins in hoards to be hoarded. The percentage that is of interest here is 80-90%, for that is the value arbitrarily chosen to represent the upper limit of the date-range of a particular issue (see above). Coincidentally, the 80% value is at roughly the point where the rate of hoarding of most of the silver issues in the period under consideration falls off quite significantly, and so it can be taken to mark a change in the hoarding characteristic of the particular issue. In this way, we are in a position to say that, for instance, 80% of hoarded *denarii* of Antoninus have entered their respective hoards by the reign of Severus (i.e. 50-60 years after minting), and, by extension, that nearly all site losses will probably have been made by this time. Put in another way, a single *denarius* of Antoninus has a 0.8 or greater probability of being lost or otherwise withdrawn from circulation by the early 200s. Conversely, if the other end of each bar is inspected, it may be seen that only *c.* 10% of the coins have entered hoards of Antoninus himself, which makes it unlikely (i.e. *c.* 0.1 probability) that site losses will have been made in the first 10-20 years after minting. In fact, if the information presented on Fig. 3.9 is coupled with that on Fig. 3.1 the suggestion can be made that a single coin of Antoninus found in an excavation or elsewhere is *most* likely to have been lost in the reigns of Commodus or Severus, and that it is *more* likely to have been lost in the period Antoninus-Caracalla than at a later date.

The example of the *denarii* of Antoninus illustrates the method used to extrapolate site losses from hoard percentages. When the same method is applied to the other periods under consideration, Table 3.IV can be constructed which incorporates the significant points from Figs 3.1-3.9 together with an estimate in years of circulation expectancy. The estimates are very rough, because of the difficulties of

[16] Standard deviations were given on these graphs in King 1985, figs 3.18-3.19, but box-and whisker plots have been preferred here for clarity..

[17] The strictures of Kerrick & Clarke 1967 on cumulative percentage graphs in archaeology are not relevant here.

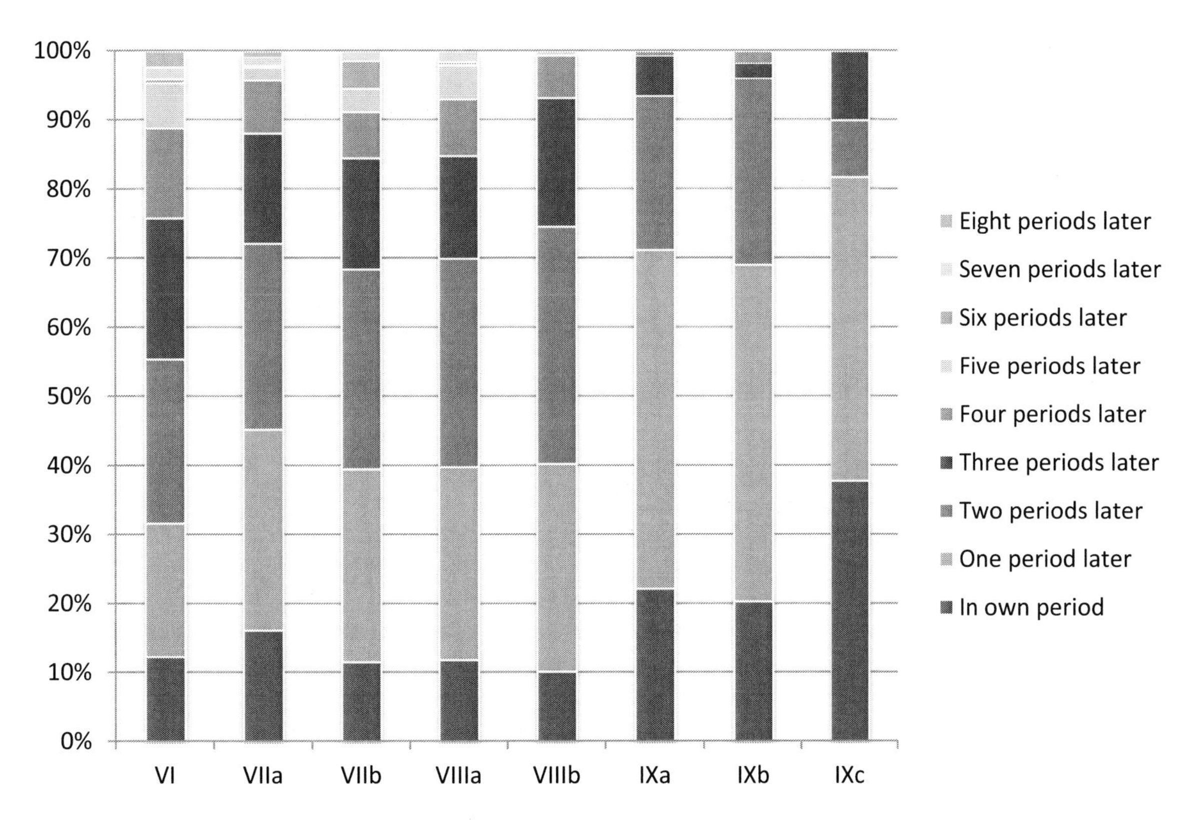


*Fig. 3.9 Stacked percentage bars showing silver coin percentages in hoards of periods VI-IXc. The lowest band shows the percentage hoarded within the coin period itself, the next band up shows the percentage hoarded one period later, and so on.*

*Table 3.IV Probabilities of coin-loss dates: silver, 138-260*

| *Period of issue* | *Most likely period of loss (Fig. 3.1-8)* | *80% hoarded by (Fig. 3.9)* | *Likely date-range for site finds* | *Estimated circulation expectancy in years* |
|---|---|---|---|---|
| VI, 138-61 | VIIb-VIIIa | 193-211 | 138-222 | 40 ± 30 |
| VIIa, 161-80 | VIIb-VIIIa | 193-211 | 161-222 | 30 ± 25 |
| VIIb, 180-92 | VIIIa-VIIIb | 211-22 | 180-238 | 25 ± 20 |
| VIIIa, 193-211 | VIIIb-IXa | 238-49 | 193-259 | 25 ± 20 |
| VIIIb, 211-22 | IXa-IXb | 238-49 | 211-59 | 20 ± 15 |
| IXa, 222-38 | IXb | 238-49 | 222-59 | 15 ± 10* |
| IXb, 238-49 | IXc | 249-59 | 238-70 | 10 ± 8 |
| IXc, 249-59 | IXc | 260-70 | 249-70 | 8 ± 6* |

* The later issues in this period are likely to have shorter circulation expectancies due to currency changes early in the following period.

expressing coin issue periods of at least ten years in yearly terms. However, the first figure can be taken to be the numerical equivalent of the most likely period of loss, and the plus-or-minus figure the equivalent of the likely range of date of loss. Another difficulty found when transferring coin periods into years is that, for certain periods such as Alexander-Maximinus and Decius-Valerian, coins issued at the beginning of the period may have a longer life than those at the end of the period because of the effect of monetary changes in the succeeding periods that tended to drive earlier issues out of circulation.

As far as the results are concerned, the most obvious numismatic point to emerge is a confirmation of Reece's observation that the silver coinage has a tendency to get into circulation, and thus be hoarded or lost, at a faster and faster rate through the late second and early third centuries,[18] culminating in the pattern of the period Decius-Valerian, which is one of almost 50% hoarded and presumably a slighter lower percentage lost within the period itself. A preliminary assessment of the later third century suggests that this pattern is the dominant one after the 250s, and that the earlier patterns with much longer

[18] Reece 1973; see also Bourne 2001, 38-40; Abdy 2002, 33-6; Lockyear 2012, 197-8. Bland (1996, 77-80) gives the relative representation of *denarii* and radiates in hoards of this period - it is clear that *denarii*, although progressively disappearing from circulation after the 240s, were not rapidly driven out, and remained in appreciable numbers up to the 260/70s.

time scales of circulation and loss are not re-established. The explanation of this trend is not relevant here: what is of interest is the implications of this overall pattern for the technique of associative dating. For instance, it can be seen that *denarii* of both Antoninus and Aurelius are most likely to have been lost in the reigns of Commodus and Severus, and that there is a good chance of a coin of Antoninus being lost at the same time as, or even later than, one of Aurelius. The natural tendency of archaeologists to date finds, layers and phases of excavations to the date provided by the *terminus post quem* of the coin has resulted in a tendency to date the finds and phases systematically too early. This has resulted in erroneous interpretations, particularly of military monuments with a certain body of known literary history.[19] In fact, for the later second century and also for earlier periods, back to the conquest of AD 43 as far as Britain is concerned, the use of the *terminus post quem* derived from coins is misleading and should be replaced by the 'most likely *terminus ad quem*'. The difference between the most likely date and the date of the coin is not so great for the early third century or later, but the same misleading tendency occurs if the *terminus post quem* principle is closely applied.

### Bronze coins in hoards

For bronze coinage in the period 138-260/70, the dangers of applying the coin date rigidly to archaeological deposits are even more acute (Figs 3.10-3.17). As Figs 3.10-3.12 show, bronze of Antoninus-Commodus has a tendency to remain at a relatively high percentage of the total bronze in each hoard right through the period up to the 270s. Carson has summarised the situation thus:[20]

> 'In the majority of hoards in categories 4 and 5 (mainly bronze and only bronze) where the coins extend up to the end of the second century or into the third, a consistent pattern can be observed. The graph of the coin population of each reign rises steadily from the Flavians through Trajan and Hadrian to a peak under Antoninus Pius and Marcus Aurelius; it shows a marked drop under Commodus, though the quantities here are still quite substantial, but thereafter it falls precipitously, showing the barest representation of early third century emperors and then only of some few.'

After the 270s, although it is not shown in the data in Appendix 2 and the figures, bronze virtually disappears from all site and hoard finds, and the relative percentages of different periods becomes unreliable due to the small sample. This is also the case to a large extent with the representation of early bronze in hoards of the period Aurelian-Probus which is shown on the figures. For instance the large rise in the final period for Aurelius bronze is due to the presence of only three hoards, which consisted of 38, 38 and 31% coins of Aurelius respectively.

[19] See chapter 1.

[20] Carson 1971a, 182.

In this way, the apparent continuance of high percentages after the period under consideration can be explained.

In terms of the implications for coin loss, the lack of an obvious peak in the rate of hoarding for most of the bronze coinage would appear to indicate that a coin of, for instance, Antoninus has an equal chance of being lost at any time between his own reign and that of Postumus, when the majority of the residue of early coins was finally hoarded, lost or otherwise withdrawn from circulation. In numismatic terms, this phenomenon can be explained as a disruption of circulation of new bronze coinage in the northern provinces after the reign of Commodus, and consequent continued use of older coins.[21] As Abdy says, in respect of Britain:[22] 'in broad terms, the latest *sestertii* to arrive and circulate ... were those of the Adoptive and Antonine emperors, which remained long in circulation and became increasingly worn'. This disruption may have been partly due to a change in pay scales and payment method in the army under Severus and his successors, for the army appears to have been the principal agent of distribution of new coin in the outlying provinces.[23] Disruption of supply reached its nadir in the period Decius-Valerian, to judge from the hoard evidence (which is almost entirely zero for Period IXc, and therefore has not been presented in a graph). In this period, virtually no bronze coinage at all reached the northern provinces, although it continued to circulate to a significant degree in Italy and the Mediterranean.[24] The demonstration of regional variations in supply, and hence loss, opens up the possibilities of such variation occurring within the northern provinces, which will be considered further below. Suffice it to say here that a coin of Antoninus found on a Mediterranean site has a much greater chance of being lost before the end of the second century than a similar coin found on a site further north.

A major problem encountered with the bronze hoards of the early third century is the actual date of deposition. This can be illustrated by the hoard from Froidmont, which has as its latest coin a *sestertius* of Macrinus, dated AD 217-8.[25] This was taken to be the date of deposition until reconsidered by Buttrey, who noted that a *sestertius* of Trajan had an overstrike consisting of lozenges stamped over the emperor's hair.[26] This is a well-known overstrike of Postumus, who was attempting to double the value of the coin by adding a radiate crown.[27] Thus the hoard was laid down in the 260s. In the words of Buttrey:[28]

[21] See principally Bastien 1967; Thirion 1967; Callu 1967; Carson 1971a; Buttrey 1972; Reece 1973; Bourne 2001, 32-4.

[22] Abdy 2003, 142.

[23] Watson 1969, 91; Hobley 1998, 128. The effect must have been similar to the 1970s shortfalls in the supply of small denominations in Italy, where a minor system of bartering sprang up as a method of repaying small debts (cf. also Humphrey 1985).

[24] See Appendix 2, g and h, where this is dramatically shown for Italy and North Africa. Cf. also Cesano 1919 and Callu 1967, 117ff.

[25] RIC 201; Thirion 1967, no.120.

[26] Buttrey 1972, 46-7.

[27] Bastien 1967, 91-2. See Hollard 1992b; Groot *et al.* 2012, 36-42 for recent discussions of Postuman hoards.

[28] Buttrey 1972, 47.

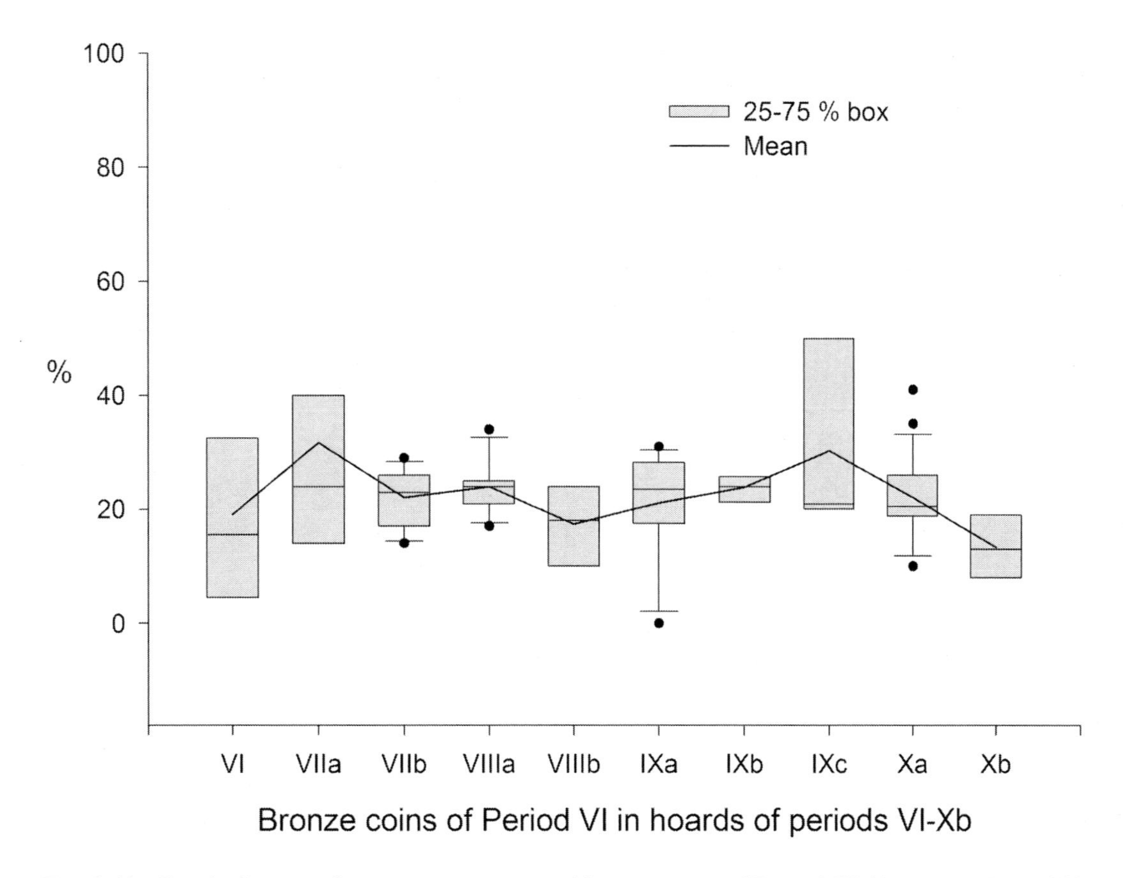


*Fig. 3.10 Graph showing the mean percentage of bronze coins of Period VI (Antoninus Pius, 138-161) in hoards from the NW provinces of periods VI-Xb (data from Appendix 2). The mean for hoards of each period is linked by the line plot across the graph, and the box-and-whisker plots give an indication of the dispersion of percentages in the hoards of each period.*

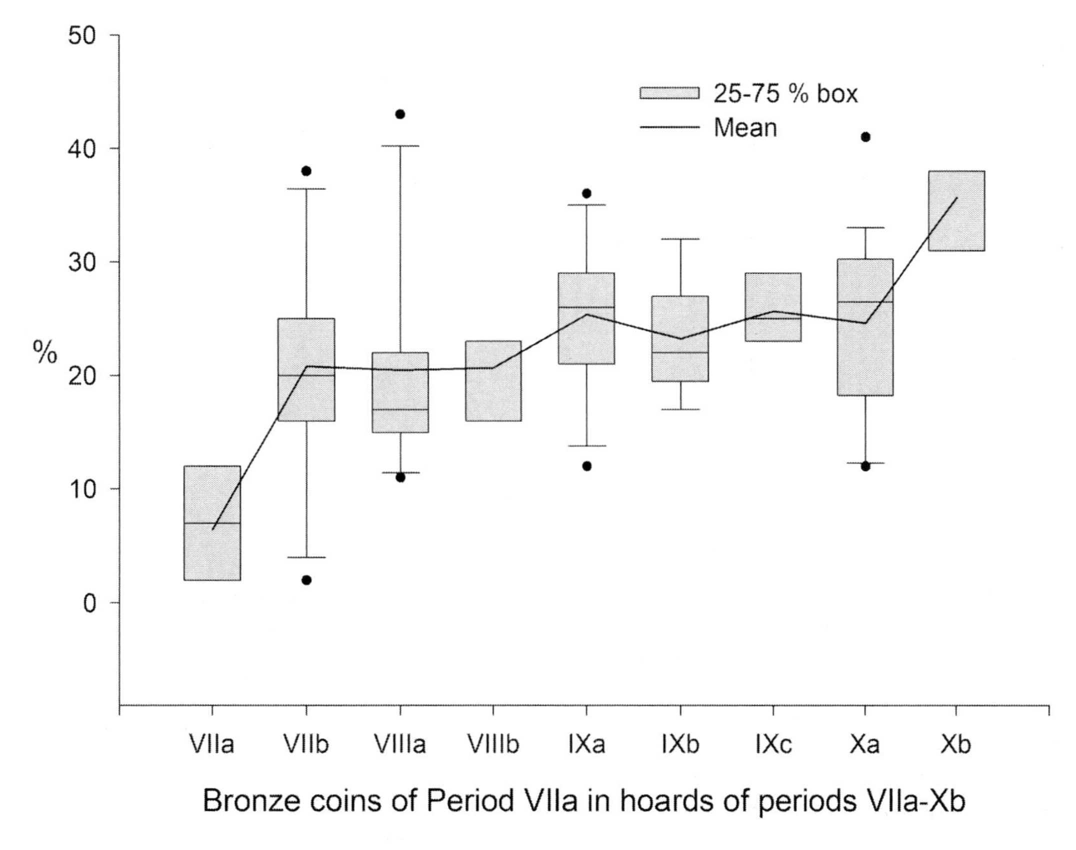


*Fig. 3.11 Graph showing the mean percentage of bronze coins of Period VIIa (Marcus Aurelius and Lucius Verus, 161-180) in hoards from the NW provinces of periods VIIa-Xb (data from Appendix 2).*

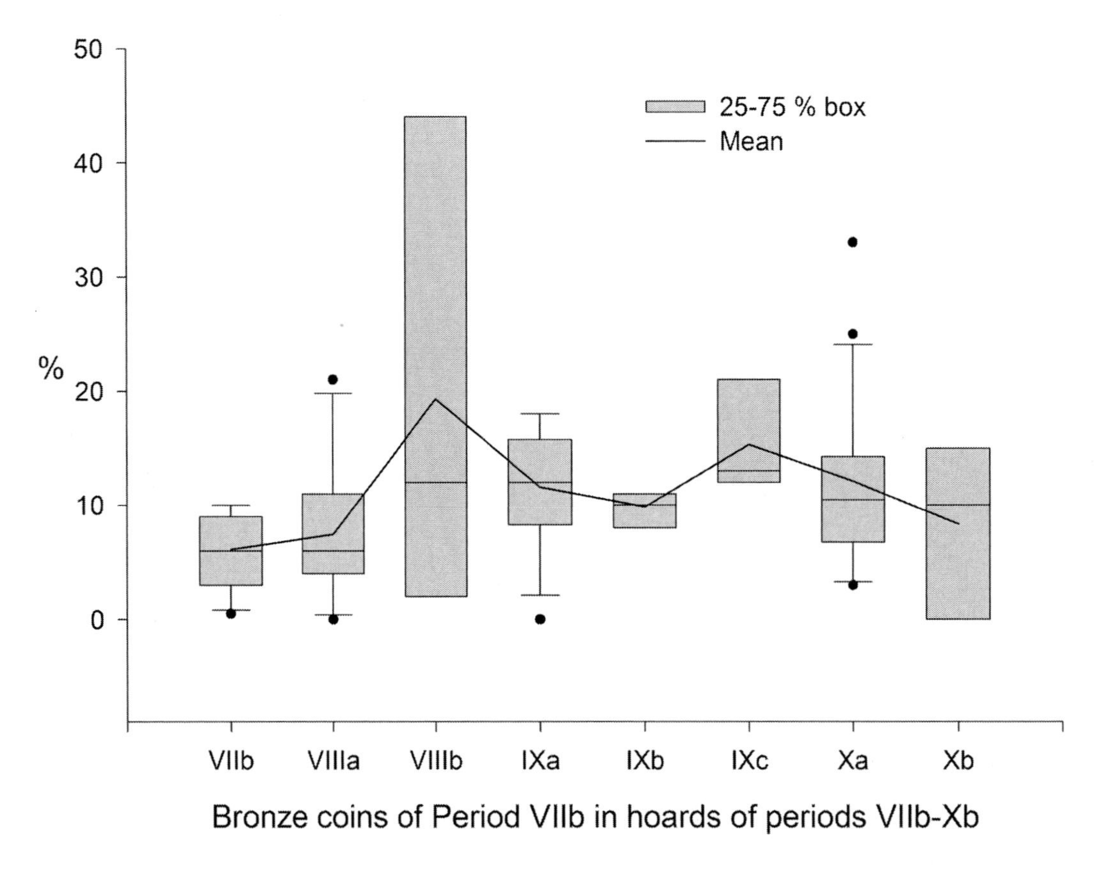


*Fig. 3.12 Graph showing the mean percentage of bronze coins of Period VIIb (Commodus, 180-192) in hoards from the NW provinces of periods VIIb-Xb (data from Appendix 2).*

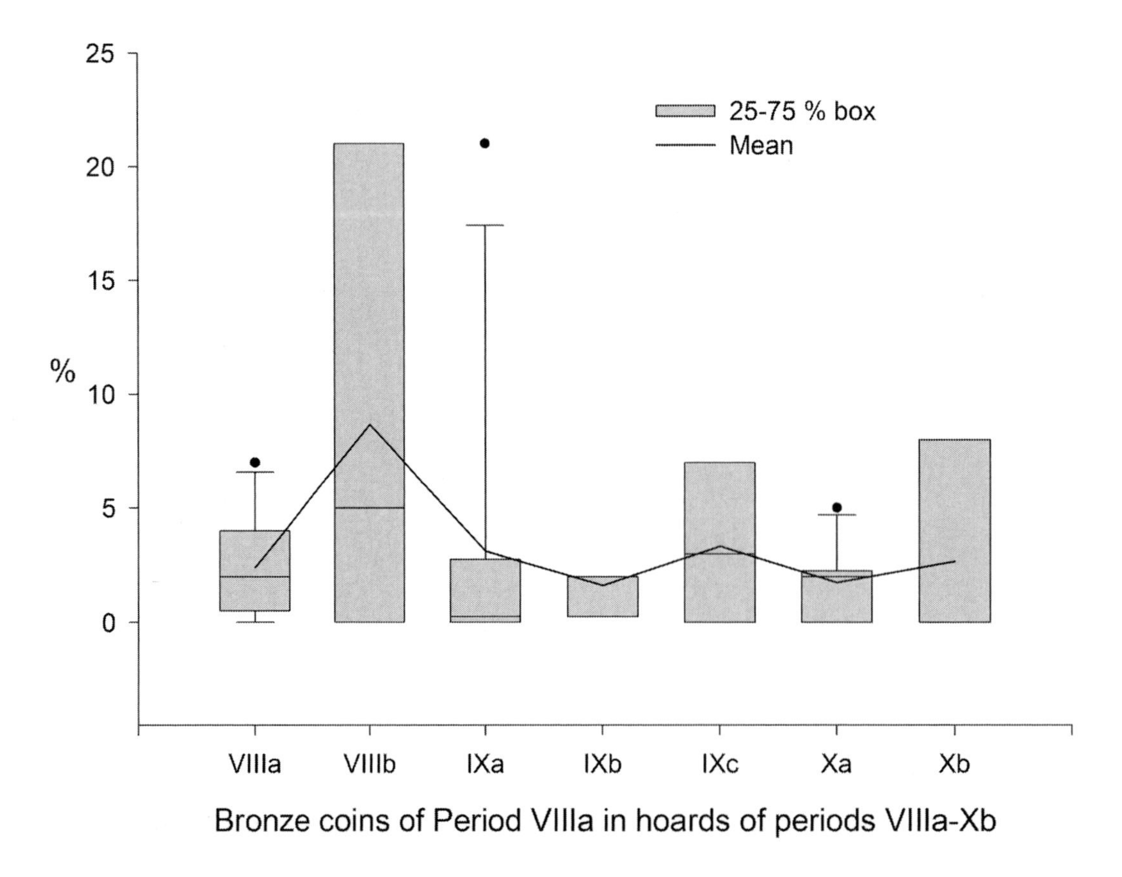


*Fig. 3.13 Graph showing the mean percentage of bronze coins of Period VIIIa (Septimius Severus, 193-211) in hoards from the NW provinces of periods VIIIa-Xb (data from Appendix 2).*

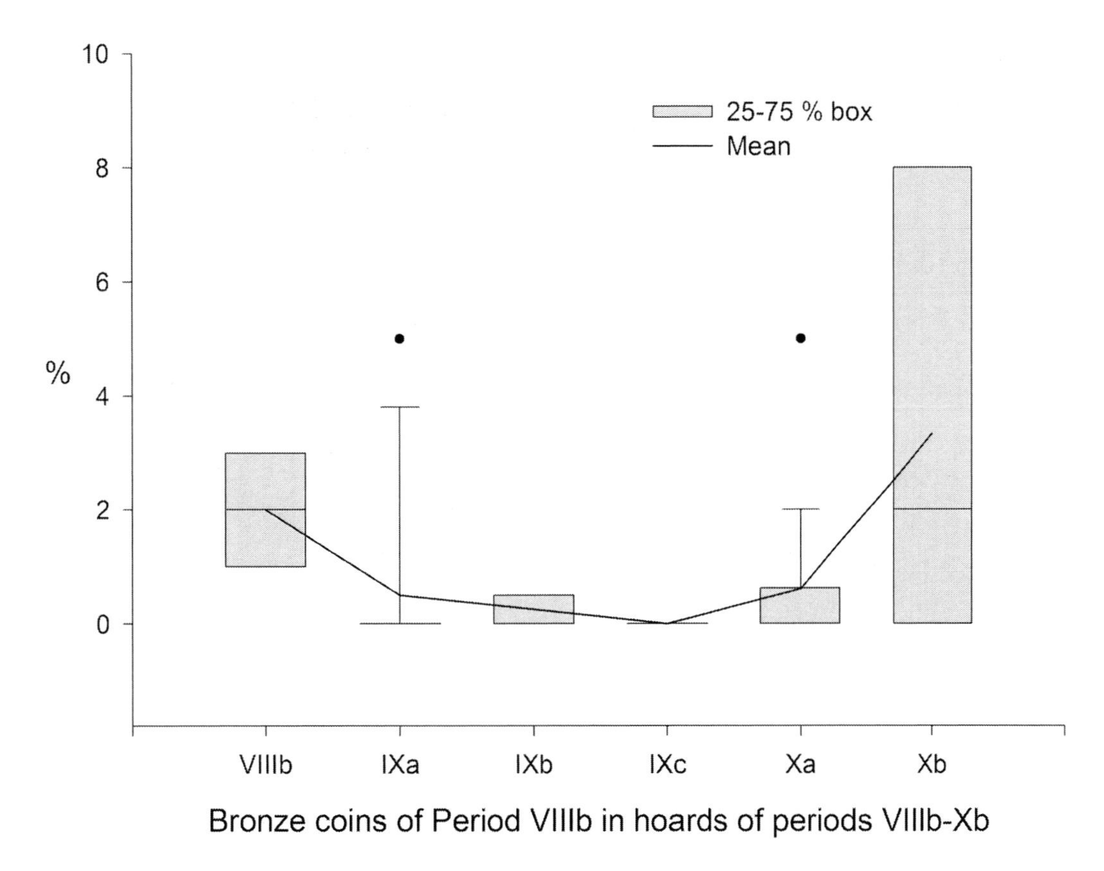


*Fig. 3.14 Graph showing the mean percentage of bronze coins of Period VIIIb (Caracalla to Elagabalus, 211-222) in hoards from the NW provinces of periods VIIIb-Xb (data from Appendix 2).*

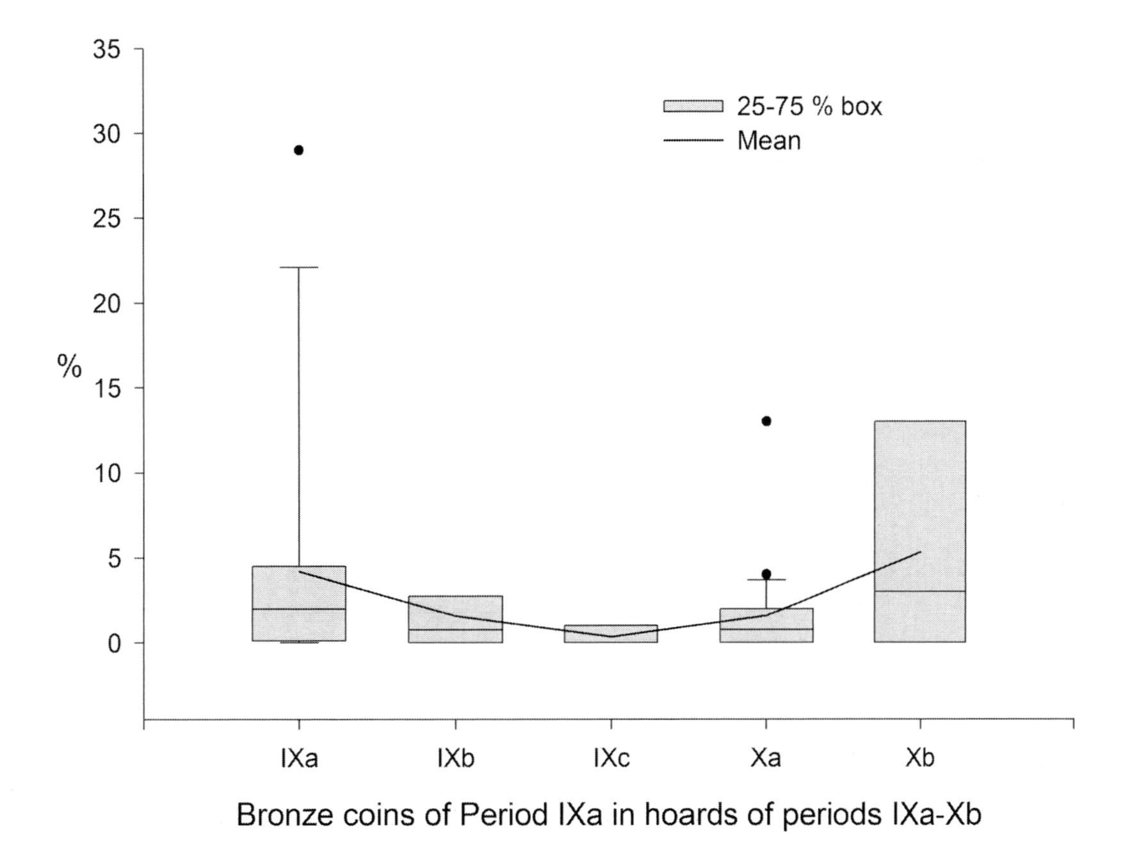


*Fig. 3.15 Graph showing the mean percentage of bronze coins of Period IXa (Severus Alexander to Maximinus Thrax, 222-238) in hoards from the NW provinces of periods IXa-Xb (data from Appendix 2).*

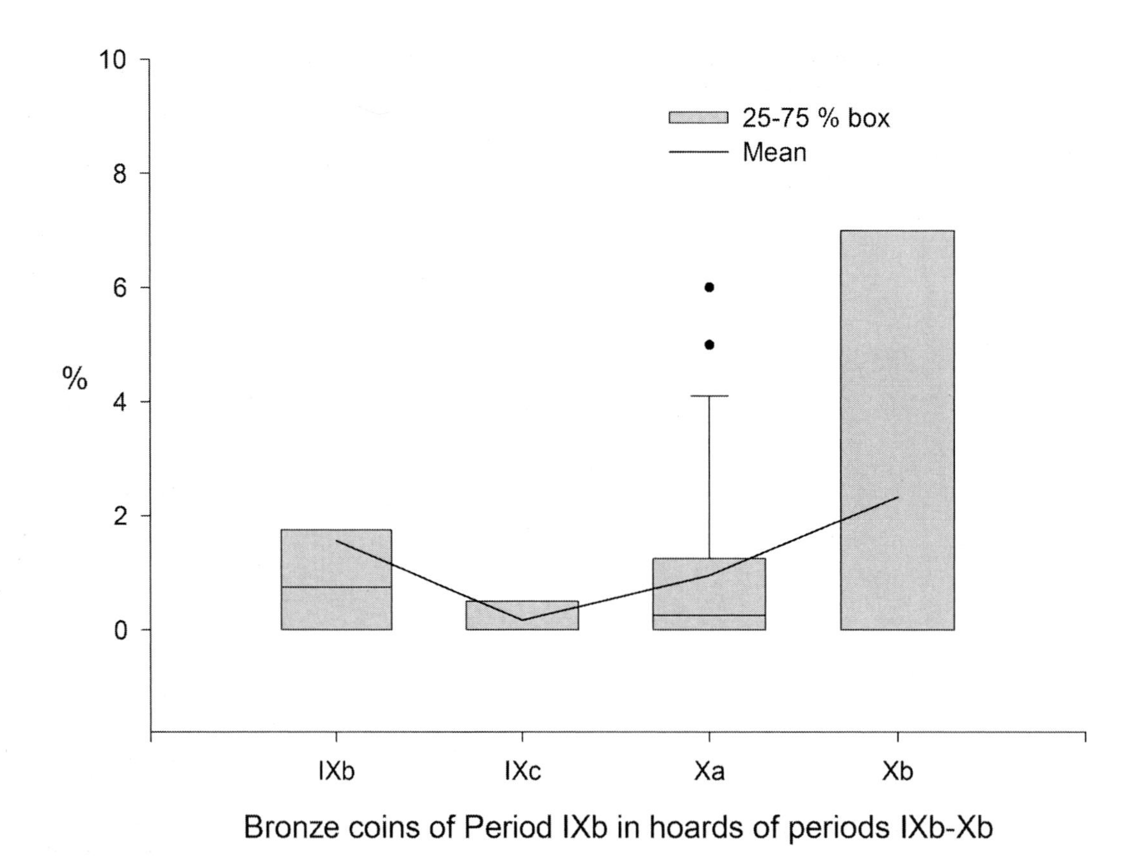


*Fig. 3.16 Graph showing the mean percentage of bronze coins of Period IXb (Gordian III to Philip I/ II, 238-249) in hoards from the NW provinces of periods IXb-Xb (data from Appendix 2).*

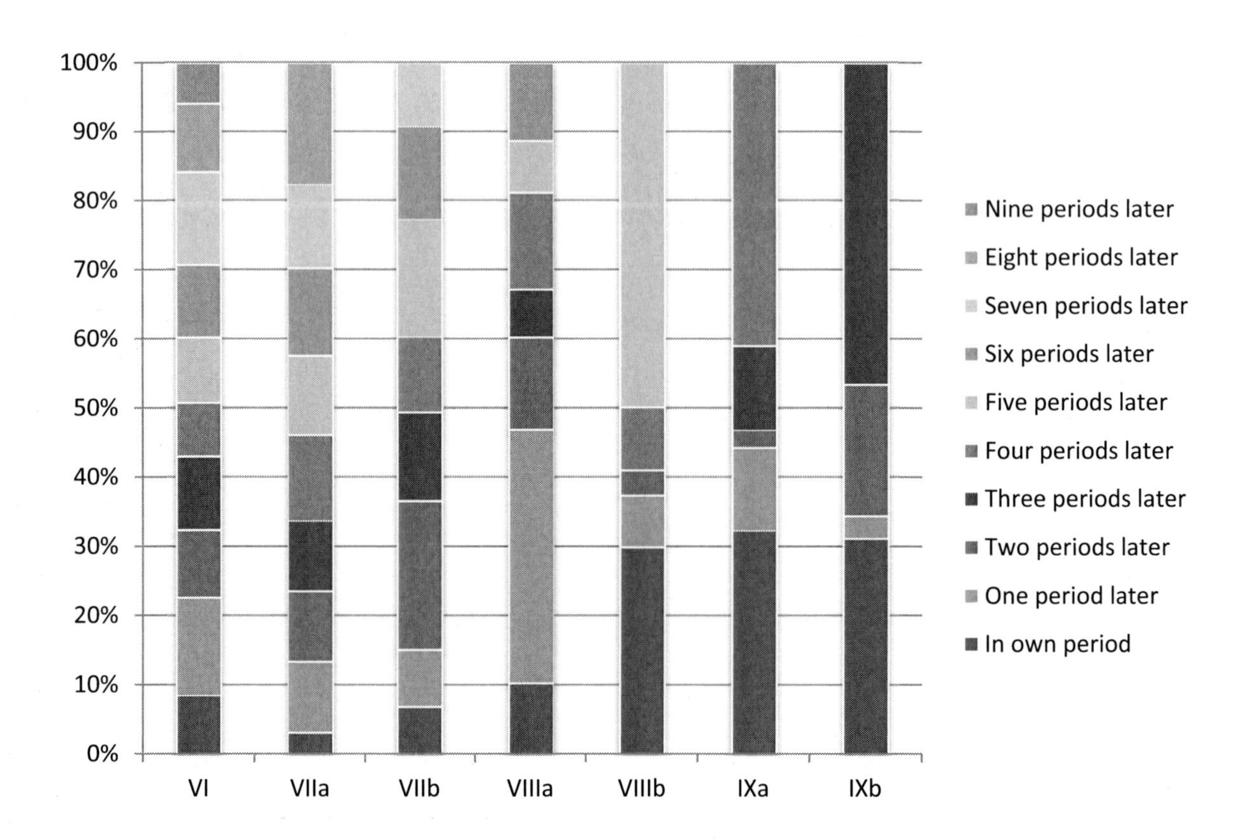


*Fig. 3.17 Stacked percentage bars showing bronze coin percentages in hoards of periods VI-IXb. The lowest band shows the percentage hoarded within the coin period itself, the next band up shows the percentage hoarded one period later, and so on.*

> 'If a hoard buried under Postumus need contain no coin of the immediately preceding emperors, or indeed of Postumus himself, the dating of the hoard by means of the latest coin it contains is impossible. No Gallic bronze hoard whose latest coin was struck by Commodus or any of his successors to the 260s can be securely dated.'

This judgement is a bit severe, for the *terminus post quem* of each hoard provides some sort of indication, but it remains the case that many, if not all, of such hoards could have been deposited well after their apparent end-dates. This is corroborated by the existence of several mixed hoards with *denarii* or radiates of later date than any bronze coins present.[29] Some of these have silver coins that are up to thirty years later than the latest bronze ones, which elegantly confirm the suggestion prompted by the graphs that the rate of silver circulation and loss is much faster than that for bronze. For such mixed hoards, it is reasonable to assume that the date of burial is not much later than the latest (silver) coin and is almost certainly within the same period. However, there remain a number of hoards which have no silver coins and no overstrikes from which a more accurate date can be obtained. If all these 'uncertainly-dated' hoards ending with Commodus or later emperors are taken to end in the period Gallienus-Quintillus, it is interesting to note that the average percentage of Antonine coins in Gallienic-Quintillan hoards is hardly altered at all by the addition of the new group, being 21.3% as opposed to 21.4%.[30] For other periods the same occurs: Aurelius 23.5% (old 24.3%), Commodus 11.3% (12.3%), Severus 2.4% (1.4%), Caracalla-Elagabalus 0.6% (0.8%), Alexander-Maximinus 2.1% (1.8%), Gordian-Philip 0.4% (0.9%), Decius-Valerian 0% (0%), and Gallienus-Quintillus 2.4% (5.8%). In other words, the average percentage 'profile' of Gallienic (Postuman) hoards is not significantly altered by more than doubling the sample, and it may be quite seriously considered that many of the 'uncertainly-dated' bronze hoards were in fact deposited in the 260s, as Buttrey implied.

These suggestions, however, do nothing but hinder the search for probabilities of coin loss and date-ranges for bronze coins. It is likely that any bronze coins in circulation after the reign of Commodus have an equal chance of being

*Table 3.V Probabilities of coin-loss dates: bronze, 138-260*

| *Period of issue* | *80% hoarded by (Fig. 3.17)* | *Likely date-range for site finds* |
|---|---|---|
| VI, 138-61 | 249-59 | 161-270 |
| VIIa, 161-80 | 260-70 | 180-270 |
| VIIb, 180-92 | 249-59 | 193-270 |
| VIIIa, 193-211 | 249-59 | 211-70 |
| VIIIb, 211-22 | 270-82 | 211-70 |
| IXa, 222-38 | 270-82 | 222-70 |
| IXb, 238-49 | 260-70 | 238-70 |
| IXc, 249-59 | 270-82 | 249-70 |

lost at any time in the period Severus-Gallienus. There are no peaks of loss of coins according to the hoard evidence, and this has to be taken into account for assessing individual site losses. For bronze in circulation up to Commodus, it is very likely that quite opposite considerations apply, since evidence from the mid second century indicates that bronze coins were being lost *faster* than silver. The total of bronze and silver from the Antonine Wall shows this quite clearly,[31] and emphasizes the strong contrast with the pattern of loss in the early third century. The indications from this are that bronze coins are as useful for dating as silver up to the late second century, perhaps even more useful at periods when they were coming into and going out of circulation more rapidly than silver. The great problem, of course, is that it is almost impossible to ascertain which coins have crossed the 'Commodus threshold' and entered the pool of aged bronze, with its quite different pattern of circulation and loss. The only clue to this, as far as site finds are concerned, is the state of wear of individual coins; unworn second century bronze being unlikely to have continued beyond the 'Commodus threshold', while conversely, very worn coins, especially the quite commonly found completely illegible specimens, being much more likely to have circulated well into the third century.

Table 3.V takes most of these problems into consideration, by being simpler and less precise than its equivalent for silver. Since there are no peaks in the hoard graphs, the most likely period of loss cannot be predicted, and so only the likely range of date of loss is given, together with the 80% hoarded figure taken from the cumulative percentage graphs. For all periods the terminal date for circulation lies in the mid third century, and in all likelihood the pattern would also be the same for earlier second century coins.

### Regional variations in the hoarding pattern

So far, interpretation of the hoard evidence has been gathered from the sample as a whole, ignoring regional hoarding and circulation patterns. It is well known, though, and has been alluded to above, that within the area under consideration there were variations in these patterns. Therefore, an

[29] Appendix 2; Heidelberg, Malonne, Petigny, Solre-St-Géry, Werken, Paris 1927, Strijp, Aardenburg, Roksem, Celle-Conde, Bourne End, Gare, Owston Ferry and Adderstone. Cf. also Bastien 1967, 95ff. The find at Merbes-le-Château, Belgium, is an interesting variant on this pattern, in that a group of 4 very worn or worn *sestertii* up to AD 168/9 was found with 119 *antoniniani* of Caracalla to Gallienus (to AD 260). The silver coins were all together, probably originally in a purse, while the bronze coins and a votive plaque were adjacent, in a *tubulus*. The excavators interpret this as two separate groups, both deposited *c.* AD 260; Heesch 2010.

[30] The hoards added are Bernbeuren, Mainz, Faha, Scheidgen, Beveren, Bornem, Destelbergen, Hautrage I and II, Manage, Mélin, Meux, Humbeek, Geilenkirchen, Paris 1968, Merelbeke III, Château-Renaud, Upchurch, Knapwell and Maidstone; the new total being 36 as opposed to 16. The data presented here are based on the hoard sample taken up to 1985, and more recent hoards have not been included. See King 1985, Fig. 3.22. For discussion of Postuman bronze hoards, see Hollard 1992b; 1996, 213-6; Groot *et al.* 2012.

[31] Robertson 1983

assessment of how significant these variations are for the prediction of coin losses is attempted here.

When the average hoard percentages given in Figs 3.1-8 and 3.10-16 are subdivided into area averages (Figs 3.18-19), a number of differences emerge, particularly for silver hoards. The areas used are Britain, France and the Low Countries, the Rhine and Danube region: it was difficult to use smaller subdivisions because the sample sizes would have been too small. Even so there are too few relevant hoards for the France/Low Countries area for several periods of silver hoards, and similarly for British bronze hoards.

The British silver hoard percentages for period VI-VIIIa coins all have characteristics of an earlier peak than their Rhine/Danube counterparts (Fig. 3.18). This implies that British silver was entering and leaving circulation more rapidly, and thus for the purposes of dating, provides a slightly narrower date range when dates of loss are being assessed. However, these British hoards also have lower peak percentages than those from the Rhine/Danube area, except for period VIIIa, which may imply that relatively low quantities of period VI-VIIb coinage were being brought into circulation in the province. Certainly, it would appear that period VIIb percentages are low because Commodus produced fewer coins than his predecessors. Following this period, it is not surprising to see relatively high peak percentages for period VIIIa coins, as they were rapidly brought into circulation to make up the shortfall. The impression, then, for British silver is that it may well have been in shorter supply than in the Rhine/Danube area, and consequently new issues were hoarded, circulated and lost fairly rapidly, while in the latter area circulation was smoother and quantities probably more plentiful.[32]

In periods VIIIb-IXc, all regions (France and the Low Countries also being included for these later periods) are more or less the same, since the hoarding peaks are all very soon after the period of issue. The peak percentages are also similar in the three regions, and it is probably fair to say that supply and circulation were equivalent as well. Only in period IXc is there a marked disparity, occurring in the initial (i.e. contemporary with period of issue) hoard percentages. The samples of relevant hoards in each region for this period are quite respectable (see Appendix 1), and so it is probably regional differences in supply that account for the fluctuations in the percentages. However, this is of no great consequence for the issue of coin loss dates, since it is clear in all regions that period IXc coins are going out of circulation very soon after issue.

Regional differences in bronze hoards are less easy to perceive, mainly because the data are more unbalanced, with only France/Low Countries region being consistently well represented. It is possible that most of the differences may be accounted for by the vagaries of small sample sizes, but equally there are some consistent differences that may have explanations in numismatic terms. Rhine/Danube bronze in periods VI-VIIb appears to fall away from an initial peak, for the first 3-4 periods after the period of issue. This may reflect a circulation pattern in a region where coinage was probably fairly plentiful due to the presence of the army, and therefore old coin did not continue in circulation for long periods. By contrast, France and the Low Countries may have had problems with the supply of bronze, since old coins are clearly conserved there for long periods.[33] In this area, it is notable that peak percentages occur in periods VIIb and VIIIa, somewhat similar to the silver peaks, implying that bronze in that area was in reasonable supply and circulation for a while in the early third century. After the peaks in these periods, there are long 'tails' in the percentages, showing that the shortage of bronze in the middle of the century was leading to conservation of old issues; the familiar pattern. Some British bronze hoards have been included for periods VI-VIIb, mainly to show that they are effectively the same as elsewhere, rather than to indicate any distinctive regional characteristic.[34]

## The estimation of dates-of-loss for site finds of coins

Examination of site finds and hoards in the sections above has given a variety of patterns in circulation of coinage and has provided pointers to the estimation of dates-of-loss. It remains to draw this information together in the form of a scheme that can be used in a practical way to yield dates for coin-associated excavation contexts. The accuracy of the dates being sought is not, of course, to the nearest year or even five years, but at a minimum to a 10/12 year date range (Tables 3.IV-V) and often considerably longer.[35]

One of the most important factors to affect the estimation of coin-loss is the number of coins in the deposit. It is well known that a single coin is not of great value for dating purposes, and for deposits of this type there is little that can be done other than to apply the full likely date-range given in Tables 3.IV-V. Information on the wear of the coin may be available, in which case a refinement of the date-range is possible: little worn coins coming in the earliest

[32] This impression is given some backing by the relative quantities of silver and bronze from coin-associated samian ware deposits, since silver is relatively rarer in Britain than in the Rhine or Danube areas (see Table 4.1). Duncan-Jones (1996) has established regional variations for Period VI *denarius* circulation, from hoard evidence, and interprets this as the result of regional coin supply and circulation areas. For discussion of Severan silver hoards in northern Britain, and the hoards from Birnie, see Holmes 2006; also Bland & Abdy 2002.

[33] This is also the conclusion of Hollard (1996, 211-3), who contrasts the northern provinces with Spain, the western Mediterranean and Italy, where bronze maintained a prominent role, with new issues coming into circulation. See also Hobley 1998, 105-8; Bourne 2001, 32-4.

[34] For a survey of 2nd- and 3rd-century British bronze hoards, see King (C) 1997a.

[35] The comments by Hobley (1998, 132) about the dangers of using 1 or 2 coins for dating purposes should be noted, but apply specifically if single-year *termini post quem* derived from the year of issue are relied upon. The argument of this chapter runs counter to reliance on the *terminus post quem* alone (see chapters 1-2 above).

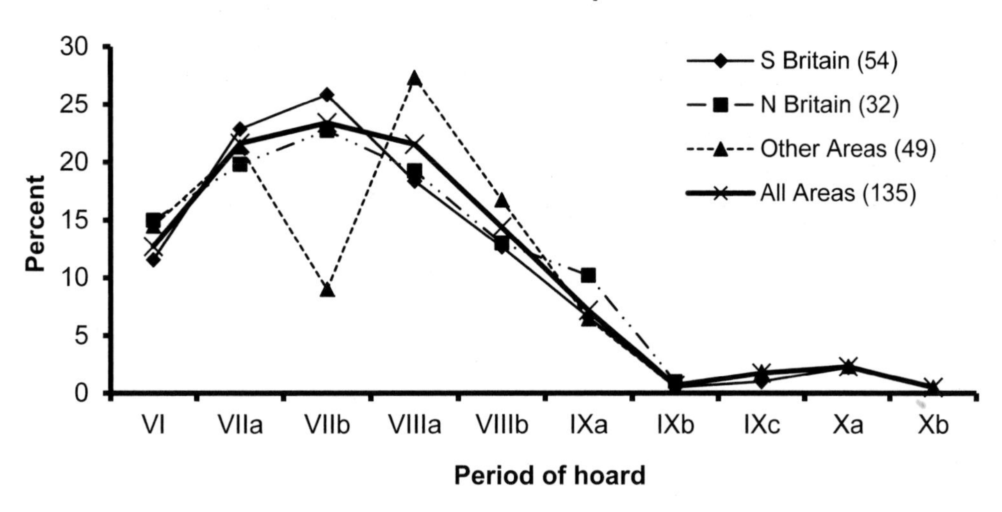
Silver coins 138-61 in hoards of periods VI-Xb
Percent
30
25
20
15
10
5
0
S Britain (54)
N Britain (32)
Other Areas (49)
All Areas (135)
VI
VIIa
VIIb
VIIIa
VIIIb
IXa
IXb
IXc
Xa
Xb
Period of hoard

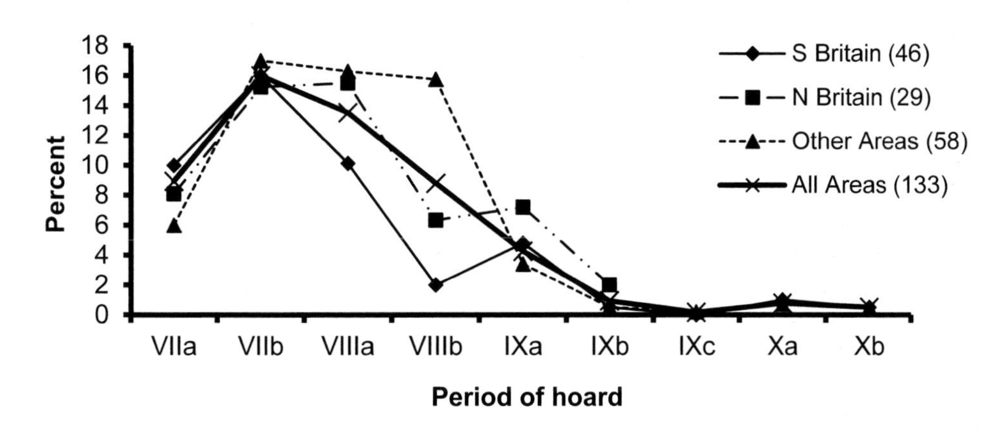
Silver coins 161-80 in hoards of periods VIIa-Xb
Percent
18
16
14
12
10
8
6
4
2
0
S Britain (46)
N Britain (29)
Other Areas (58)
All Areas (133)
VIIa
VIIb
VIIIa
VIIIb
IXa
IXb
IXc
Xa
Xb
Period of hoard

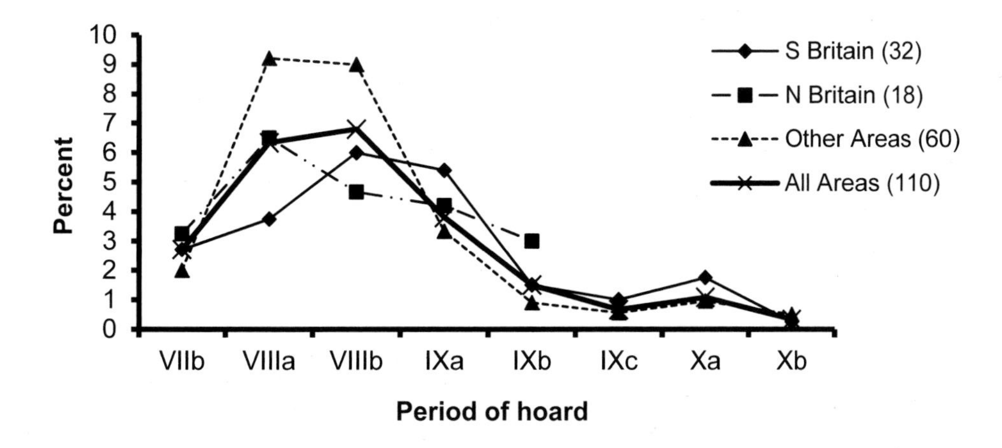
Silver coins 180-92 in hoards of periods VIIb-Xb
Percent
10
9
8
7
6
5
4
3
2
1
0
S Britain (32)
N Britain (18)
Other Areas (60)
All Areas (110)
VIIb
VIIIa
VIIIb
IXa
IXb
IXc
Xa
Xb
Period of hoard

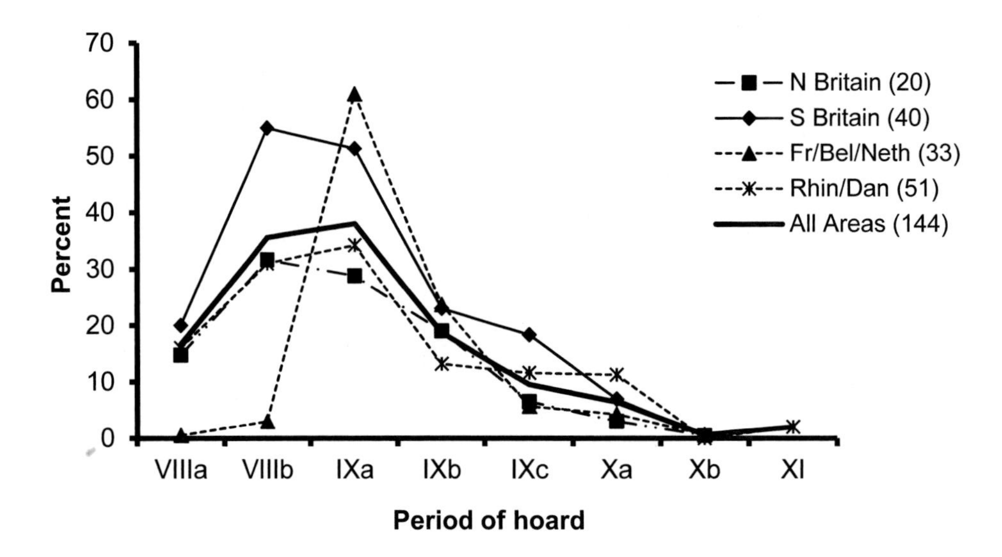
Silver coins 193-211 in hoards of periods VIIIa-XI
Percent
Period of hoard
VIIIa VIIIb IXa IXb IXc Xa Xb XI
0 10 20 30 40 50 60 70
N Britain (20)
S Britain (40)
Fr/Bel/Neth (33)
Rhin/Dan (51)
All Areas (144)

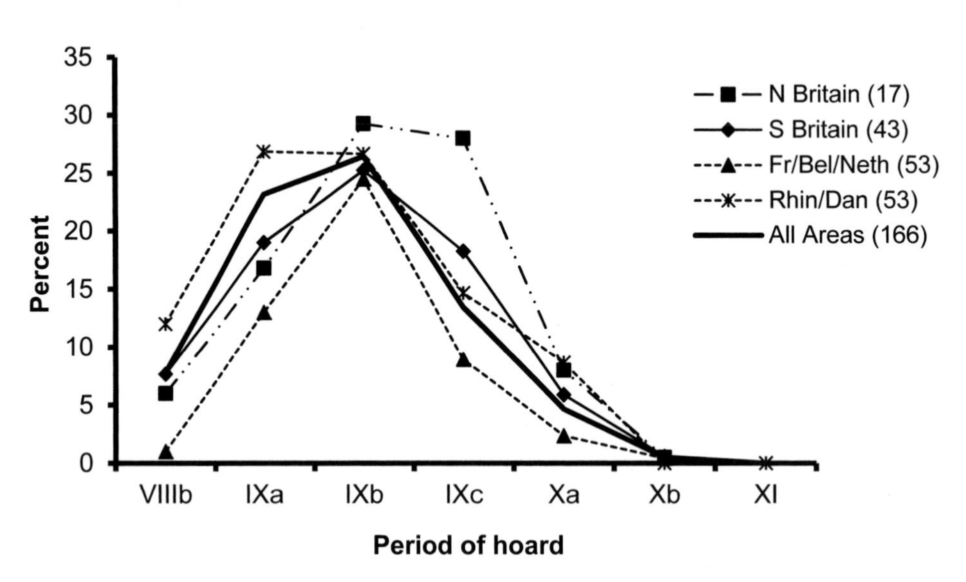
Silver coins 211-22 in hoards of periods VIIIb-XI
Percent
Period of hoard
VIIIb IXa IXb IXc Xa Xb XI
0 5 10 15 20 25 30 35
N Britain (17)
S Britain (43)
Fr/Bel/Neth (53)
Rhin/Dan (53)
All Areas (166)

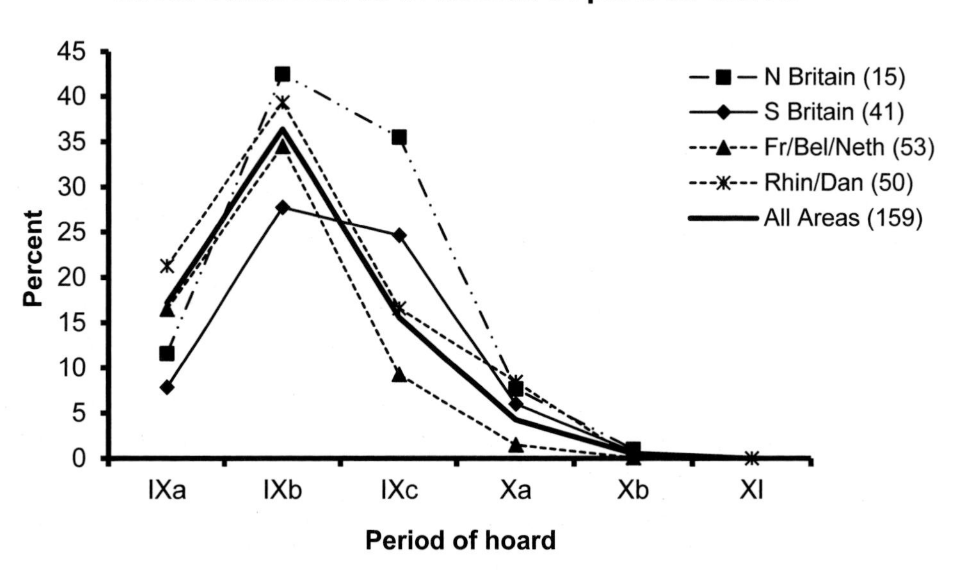
Silver coins 222-38 in hoards of periods IXa-XI
Percent
Period of hoard
IXa IXb IXc Xa Xb XI
0 5 10 15 20 25 30 35 40 45
N Britain (15)
S Britain (41)
Fr/Bel/Neth (53)
Rhin/Dan (50)
All Areas (159)

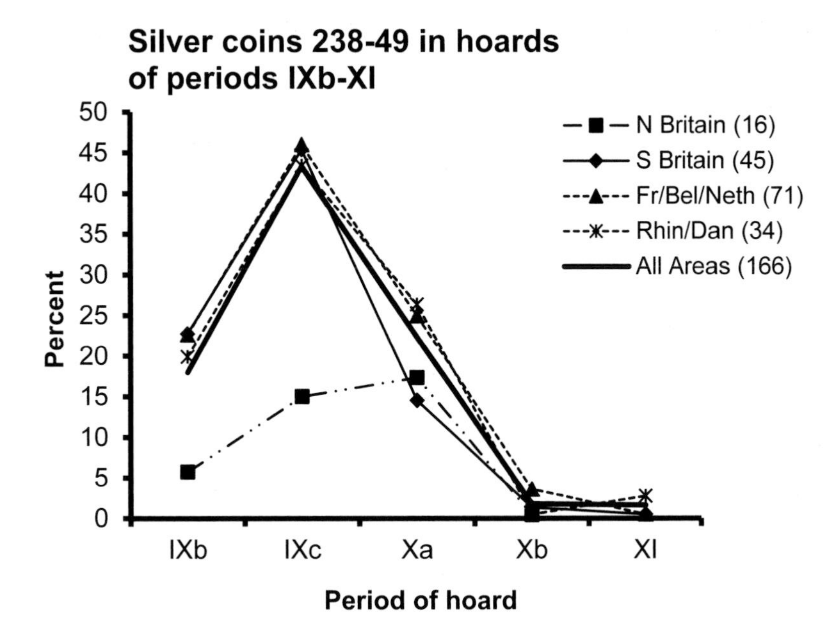


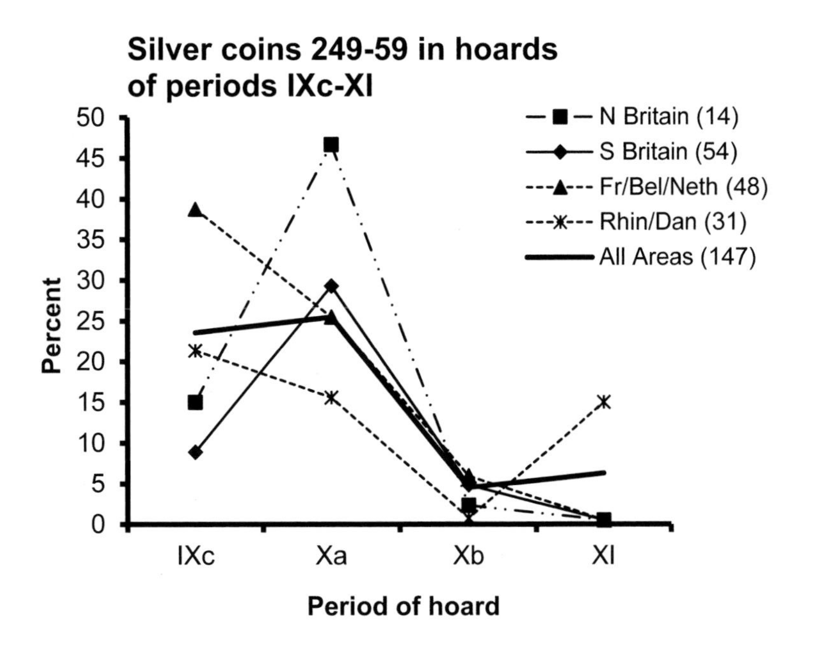


*Fig. 3.18 Regional variation in hoarding patterns for silver coins of periods VI-IXc, showing the means for different regions of the NW provinces.*

part of the date-range, and the converse being likely in the case of more heavily worn coins.[36]

For deposits with a large number of coins, it is also quite easy to apply a date, in this case simply the period of the latest coin in the group. This is based on the assumption that as the number of coins in a group increases, so does the likelihood that the latest coin is contemporary with or close to the date of deposition, i.e. that the proximity of the *terminus ad quem* to the *terminus post quem* of the latest coin is a function of the number of coins in the deposit. The Zugmantel data discussed above give support to this assumption. However, for this assumption to hold true, another has to be made, that the deposit was accumulated over a short period of time, and contains no redeposited material. This is a major issue, but for the moment, it will be taken that coin-loss estimates are being applied to groups of coins from single deposition events.[37]

[36] For discussion of wear, cf. Doyen 2011, 34-7. He discusses data from Reims indicating that bronze coins of Trajan and Hadrian have bimodal states of wear, i.e. coins with little wear, presumably lost soon after issue, and a peak of very worn coins, which could have been in circulation for a century or so.

[37] It is instructive, in this respect, to look at the coins found at Pompeii in the AD 79 destruction levels, as they indicate a range through the 1st

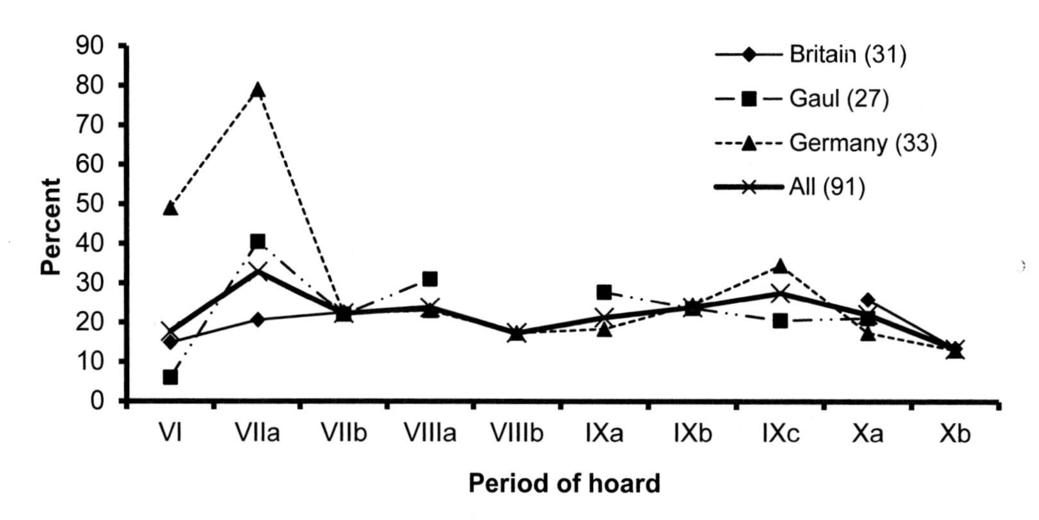
Bronze coins 138-61 in hoards of periods VI-Xb
Britain (31)
Gaul (27)
Germany (33)
All (91)
Percent
90
80
70
60
50
40
30
20
10
0
VI
VIIa
VIIb
VIIIa
VIIIb
IXa
IXb
IXc
Xa
Xb
Period of hoard

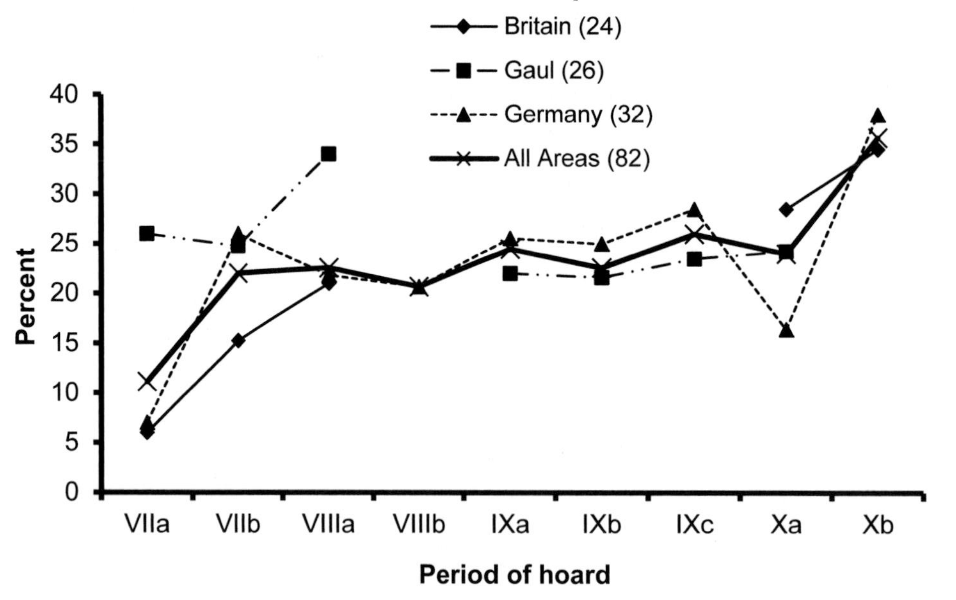
Bronze coins 161-80 in hoards of periods VIIa-Xb
Britain (24)
Gaul (26)
Germany (32)
All Areas (82)
Percent
40
35
30
25
20
15
10
5
0
VIIa
VIIb
VIIIa
VIIIb
IXa
IXb
IXc
Xa
Xb
Period of hoard

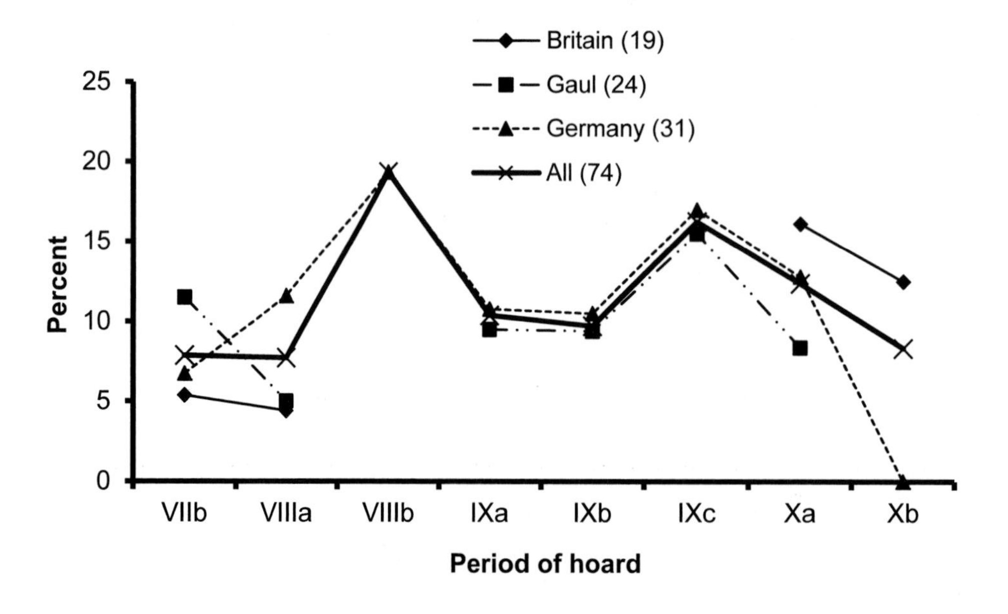
Bronze coins 180-92 in hoards of periods VIIb-Xb
Britain (19)
Gaul (24)
Germany (31)
All (74)
Percent
25
20
15
10
5
0
VIIb
VIIIa
VIIIb
IXa
IXb
IXc
Xa
Xb
Period of hoard

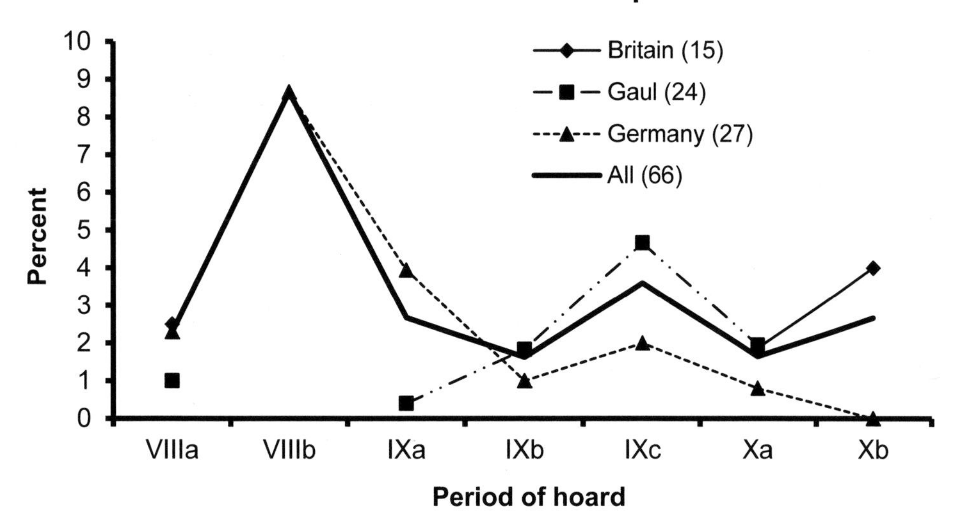
Bronze coins 193-211 in hoards of periods VIIIa-Xb
10
9
8
7
6
5
4
3
2
1
0
Percent
Britain (15)
Gaul (24)
Germany (27)
All (66)
VIIIa
VIIIb
IXa
IXb
IXc
Xa
Xb
Period of hoard

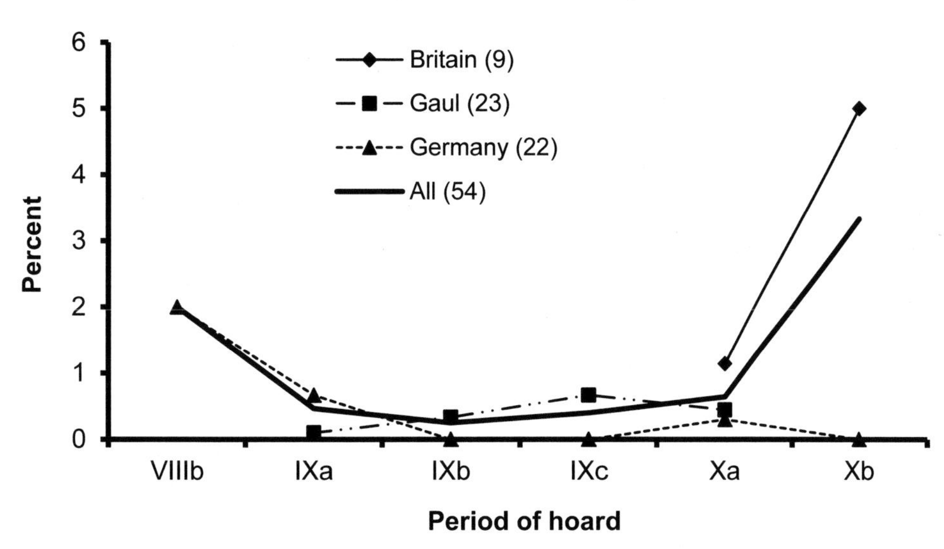
Bronze coins 211-222 in hoards of periods VIIIb-Xb
6
5
4
3
2
1
0
Percent
Britain (9)
Gaul (23)
Germany (22)
All (54)
VIIIb
IXa
IXb
IXc
Xa
Xb
Period of hoard

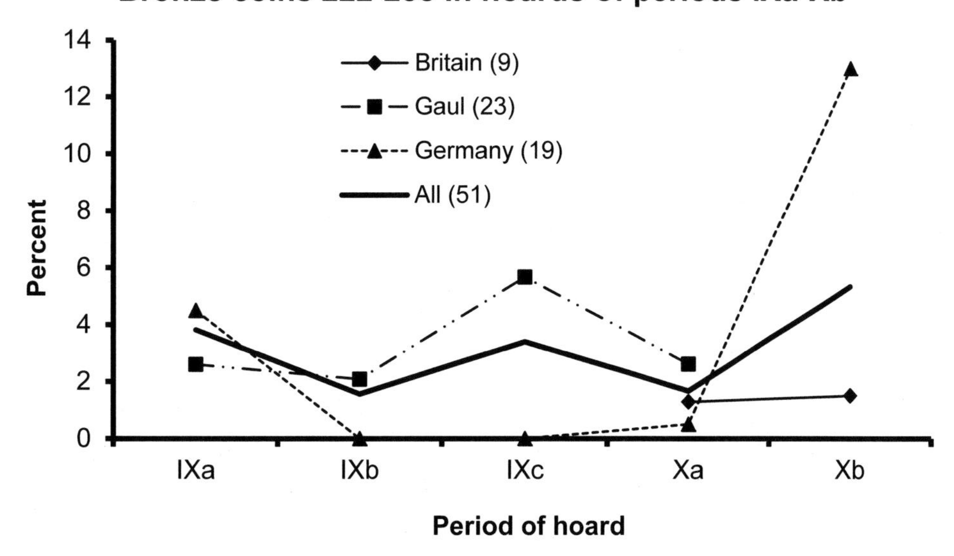
Bronze coins 222-238 in hoards of periods IXa-Xb
14
12
10
8
6
4
2
0
Percent
Britain (9)
Gaul (23)
Germany (19)
All (51)
IXa
IXb
IXc
Xa
Xb
Period of hoard

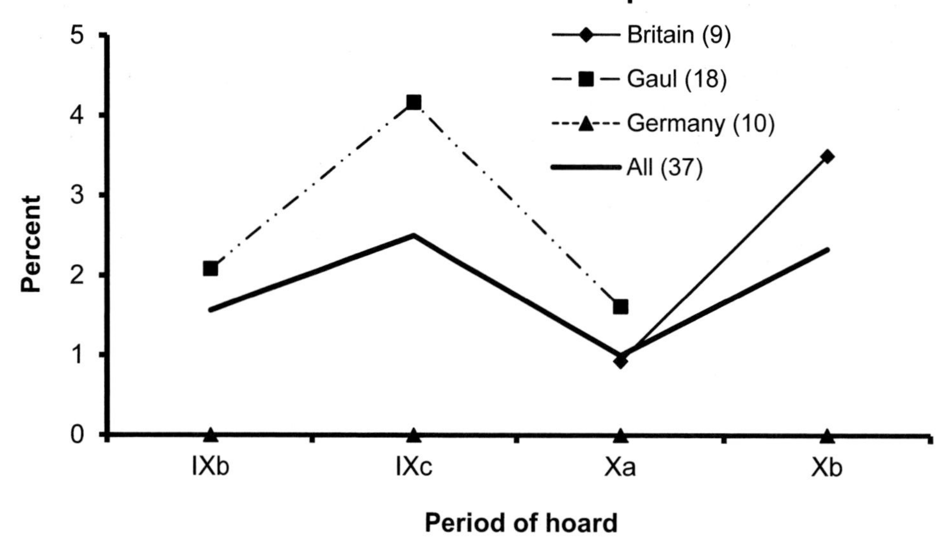


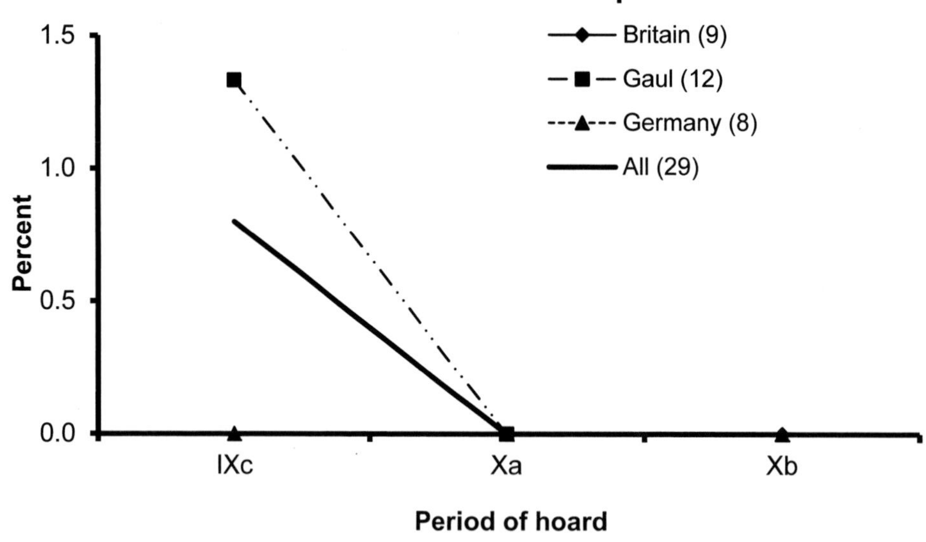


*Fig. 3.19 Regional variation in hoarding patterns for bronze coins of periods VI-IXc, showing the means for different regions of the NW provinces.*

Two methods arise from the case of deposits with large numbers of coins. Firstly, how large is 'large' in this context, and secondly, how should dates-of-loss be estimated when the coin group falls below the 'large' criterion? To a certain extent, the first question has to be answered in an arbitrary fashion, for there is no way of checking whether a large deposit really is contemporary with the period of its latest coin. The Zugmantel data give a pointer to the number of coins above which a deposit could be regarded as large, since the calculations associated with Table 3.III yielded a figure of eleven coins as the size of deposit that could be predicted to be contemporary with the latest coin. In the absence of any conflicting indications, it would seem reasonable to take this figure as the lower limit of the 'large' size group.

century AD; Morelli del Franco & Vitale 1989; Dapoto 1987.

For groups with between two and ten coins, estimation is more complicated. Since silver coins are generally more precise indicators of dates-of-loss, in groups where silver coins are present, these should be taken by preference. An estimation of the likely date-range can then be made by taking the date-range of the latest silver coin and subtracting $(n-1)/10$ parts of the range from the later end, where $n$ is the total number of coins in the group. This is a rough reflection of the observation that the size of the group is an influence upon the length of the date-range. The earlier limit of the date-range is, of course, provided by the *terminus post quem* of the latest coin, whether silver or bronze. Such a method works for most cases, the main exception being where there are bronze coins much later than silver ones, since the *terminus post quem* of the latest coin may then be later than the estimated limit of the date-range from the silver coin. It is probably best in this case to use the date-range of the latest coin instead as the basis for estimating the date-of-loss. In groups where there are only bronze coins, any estimate of date-of-loss is likely to have a fairly wide range, since the circulation patterns of bronze during much of the period under consideration are unusual. However, it seems reasonable to apply the same method as for groups with silver coins, i.e. lowering the later limit of the date-range of the latest coin by $(n\text{-}1)/10$ parts of the range. Considerations of wear in groups of bronze coins may be important as a guide to narrowing the date-range.

In conclusion, therefore, information from hoards and site-finds of coins can be brought to bear on the matter of estimating dates-of-loss. Estimates can be made only after taking account of the denomination of the coins, the total number in the group, the state of wear, and the extent to which redeposition has taken place. All these factors have been provided for in the scheme for estimation presented above, with the exception of the last, which would need to be considered on a case-by-case basis for each deposit being dated.

# Chapter 4

# Associated Groups of Samian Ware: compiling a database

Having considered dating methodology and a framework for using coins for dating in previous chapters, the chronology of late samian ware is now in a position to be reassessed. The main source of information is the large number of groups of samian ware from the north-west provinces dating approximately to the period under study. These are given in detail in the Gazetteer at the end of the volume, to which the reader is referred for specific comments on individual deposits.

## The compilation and arrangement of the gazetteer

There are four major divisions within the gazetteer, of which the first two are used extensively in the analysis that follows in this and the next chapter. Part A is concerned with groups of decorated samian that are associated with coins, together with any plain wares noted for those groups. Occasionally other independent dating indicators have been used, such as tile stamps or dendrochronological dates. Part B consists of groups of decorated samian ware without independent dating evidence. These have been collected together to enlarge the corpus of associated groups, for, as will be seen below, a vital component of the chronology is the information to be gained from analysis of the way in which samian vessels are associated together. Included in this section of the gazetteer are a number of groups from sites with restricted date-ranges or with clear historical *termini*, even though some of the groups are not stratified deposits in the strict sense, but from the site as a whole. Part C is a smaller section, in which coin-dated groups made up only of plain samian ware are presented, with a view to investigating whether plain wares continued to be made after decorated ware manufacture was abandoned, as some have maintained. Part D is a selection, mainly from Gaul and Germany, of coin-dated and other groups of decorated samian, compiled from data available after c. 1985; it has not been used for the analysis in chapters 4 and 5, but has informed the discussion of the results. Parts A and D present a very similar picture of coin-dated deposits, and in effect, Part D is a check upon the results obtained from the pre-1985 data.

## Geographical area

The geographical area from which the groups come is mainly the NW provinces, with an important extension eastwards to include the middle Danube area (see index of sites at the end of the Gazetteer). Britain provides the bulk of the entries, due to the number of well-documented excavation reports and records. Southern Britain in particular has many stratified deposits of samian ware that have not previously been taken into account, given the emphasis on military sites in earlier chronologies. Sites in the Low Countries and Germany are also relatively plentiful, especially along the Rhine and Danube *limes*. These yield the most useful information about East Gaulish wares, but often have the disadvantage of being imperfectly recorded due to the difficulties of defining stratigraphic groups using the 'planum' method of excavation. Danube and Alpine sites are few in number, but of great importance in the case of Enns-Lorch (A 206) and *Aquincum* (B 162). France, unfortunately, provides relatively few good groups, apparently due to the lack of interest in the past in making stratigraphic records about finds from excavations. Generally speaking, it is the exceptional groups that tend to be published from this area. However, this situation is changing, so that more detail about groups in the vital areas around the Central Gaulish kiln centres themselves will eventually be available.

## Date-range of the entries

In terms of the general date-range of the deposits selected for the gazetteer, limits of roughly the mid-second century and the late third century have been chosen. It is probable, though, that some deposits of mid-second century date that might justifiably have been included here have in fact been omitted. This is because their associated coins are somewhat earlier than this date, but when adjusted coin-loss dates are applied as defined in the previous chapter, they appear to have been deposited in the mid-second century or later. It was not thought worthwhile to examine all this type of deposit in order to seek out those that could fall within the date limits, especially as the main focus of attention in matters of chronology is the late-second century and later. The younger date-limit chosen is fairly arbitrary, since many deposits of late third century date are manifestly redeposited, a factor which applies even more strongly in fourth century deposits, which have not been considered, with one or two exceptions. However, a late third century limit is useful in that it includes some sites which have almost certain survival use of samian ware, e.g. Portchester (A 99), and also contains the initial period when 'post-samian' fine pottery was coming into widespread use.

## Sources of information

Most of the groups in the gazetteer were gathered from published sources. It may seem surprising at first that this was so, given the wide variation in standards of publication, but it is sad to report that in several of the cases where potentially useful but inadequately published groups were investigated further, the original records were either lost or inaccessible, or the pieces of samian ware disassociated from their original groups. For most published reports, the standard of presentation of the stratigraphic details accurately reflected the standard of original recording, and therefore inadequate reports were usually not worth pursuing further. However, this was not the case with more recent reports from Britain, where the effects of changes in publishing policy have been felt in the form of the division between printed summaries and archive reports. For these, the printed summary only gave a rough indication of the value of individual contexts, and consequently in many cases the archive was consulted. It proved much easier to consult the archive when it was in some type of microform publication than in its original state, mainly due to ease of accessibility. The experience of attempting to consult archive reports has convinced the writer that these archives must be carefully organised and widely available, either in microform publication or in centralised information centres. The expense of consulting archives in regional centres, with no guarantee of emerging with information on useful groups of associated samian ware, was with rare exceptions, not justified.

Much of the same comment about value for research time and money could be said about many museum collections. Several expeditions to museums were made to record material. Generally, it can be said that the pottery itself was often carefully preserved and easily accessible, but that associated documentation was not. In many cases, original stratigraphic connections had been lost, particularly between coins and samian ware, since these two classes of object were often kept separate from the other material from excavations. Museum collections, therefore, proved most useful in checking pieces of samian against published reports and drawings, rather than in yielding previously unrecorded associated groups. In contrast to this, unpublished groups being actively worked on by excavation units were a most useful addition to the gazetteer. These had the advantage of having staff familiar with the groups and their stratification on hand to assist in explaining the samian or the archive reports, and in this respect particular acknowledgement is due to the Department of Urban Archaeology, London, the Central Excavation Unit, Portsmouth, and the Circonscription des Antiquités Historiques, Lyon. However, it was usually advantageous to examine unpublished groups in this way when they were at a particular stage of analysis, i.e. when the material had been analysed sufficiently for the excavators to know precisely what the samian and coins actually were, and before relevant staff had gone on to other jobs.

Having outlined some of the vicissitudes of records of samian ware groups other than in published sources, the variety and the standard of the published reports needs to be examined, in order to give a picture of the reliability of the main source of information. The reports used in the gazetteer were mainly contained in excavation reports in learned journals or monographs, with a small number coming from articles specifically about samian ware or some aspect of the pottery industry. As the bibliography demonstrates, the number of different journals that needed to be searched for this information was vast, and indeed the time taken to locate samian ware reports in this way was a not inconsiderable proportion of the total research time for the thesis. This source of information was naturally dependent on the comprehensiveness of the libraries used,[1] and eventually, virtually all potential sources could be traced, so that it is reasonable to claim that the cull of useful reports from Britain in particular was effectively complete, although, as in all such searches, some reports may have slipped past. Coverage of the Low Countries, the Rhineland and northern France was almost as good, with the main problem being that some monographs with samian ware reports were impossible to find. For areas further afield, e.g. the Danube or SW France, searches for reports were less comprehensive, since some sources were difficult to obtain and useful reports were few and far between.

As far as the standard and reliability of the published information are concerned, samian ware, particularly decorated ware, has the distinct advantage over many other classes of material in being amenable to standardised, accurate recording.[2] A consensus has arisen amongst specialists that decorated pieces should be reported on in a fair degree of detail, with both drawings of the decoration, and the routine use of the standard reference works for identification of the decorative types. It is in fact quite possible to publish decorated samian by means of these standard references alone, but drawings are highly desirable, both as a means of checking the identifications and for information about the style and spacing of the decorative elements, which at present can only be reported on by means of visual representations. In Germany and the Low Countries, drawings are often dispensed with in favour of the equally useful means of photographs of flattened latex or plaster casts.

To a great extent, a report on decorated samian ware can be judged by the standard of its illustrations. The authors of good reports have invariably taken pains over the preparation of the illustrations by ensuring that the diagnostic features are properly delineated (or lit, in the case of photographs) and not, for instance, leaving them obscured, as has been the case in several recent reports, by over-zealous use of shading lines. A particular criterion for assessing the accuracy of many samian drawings is the way in which repetitive features such as ovolos are depicted. Often it can be seen that the draughtsman has failed to appreciate the minor, but crucial, details that differentiate the ovolos, etc, of different potters and their styles. On the whole, though, nearly all published drawings have proved to be sufficiently detailed for the purposes of this thesis - namely, the checking of original attributions,

[1] Acknowledgement is gladly given to the libraries at the Institute of Archaeology, London, the Institute of Classical Studies, London, Senate House Library, London, the British Library, the Society of Antiquaries, London, the Warburg Institute, London, the Ashmolean Museum and the Heberden Coin Room, Oxford, the Sackler Library, Oxford, Durham University, the Rijksdienst voor Opgravingen, Amersfoort, the Rheinisches Landesmuseum, Trier, and the Bibliothèque Nationale, Paris.

[2] Cf. Hartley 1969; Bulmer 1979; Webster 2005.

the re-allocation and updating of identifications in the light of current knowledge, and in some cases, the making of initial identifications where reports have contained drawings but no detailed text. From this point of view alone, it can easily be appreciated that the effort and the cost of publishing samian illustrations is well justified. The field of study where drawings or photographs are inadequate, however, is that of quantified analysis of the size of decorative elements or the spacing between them, since different methods of representation introduce a variety of irreconcilable distortions in order to reduce the curvature of the common bowl types to a two-dimensional plane. This is a pity, since quantified work of this sort is likely to be one of the main future developments in stylistic analysis of decoration, and the corpus of existing illustrative material seems unsuitable for the purpose.

There are two aspects of samian ware reports that contrast with this relatively standardised approach in being very variable. Firstly, it is evident that many reports are on material that has been selected to a greater or lesser extent. Sometimes this is made explicit by a statement to the effect that only the more interesting pieces have been published, but it is equally the case that the selection is often unstated and only apparent after detailed perusal of the report. Usually, the form that selection takes is the omission of small pieces or the omission of pieces that the samian specialist considers too early in their context to be other than redeposited. All the entries in the gazetteer have been considered from the point of view of selection having taken place, and some have not been used in compilation of certain of the tables given later in this chapter. A number of potentially useful groups of samian ware have unfortunately had to be left out of consideration, and the gazetteer, because of this problem.

Selection of material has been detected in both early and more recent reports, but generally those produced in the last few years have less selection, mainly due to a more widespread appreciation of quantification and the writing of reports that are consonant with current ideas about the publication of ancient pottery in general. Quantification has also had an effect on the other, often somewhat variable, aspect of samian ware reports, namely the presentation of the plain pieces. In many reports, it is clear that these have been ignored or selected for the larger and more interesting sherds only, or reported on in the form of presence/absence of the forms identified. Counts of pieces, vessels or estimated vessel equivalents[3] are not very common except in the more recent reports – and there are two difficulties with many reports that do quantify: the failure to specify whether pieces or vessels are being counted, and the giving of accurate figures for small quantities but generalised figures for larger counts or the use of words like 'several'. In this last case, it has sometimes proved possible to make an estimate of what 'several' might actually mean in terms of figures, and to substitute a figure. A good criterion of a well-quantified report has proved to be whether the number of unattributable or unidentifiable pieces was given. Plain ware, despite these problems, has been given in most of the gazetteer entries, both as an aid to understanding the deposit as a whole, and to provide a basis for some comments on plain ware chronology. Stamps on plain ware have also been listed, but little comment is made on them in the text due to the on-going and recently completed reassessment of their chronology.[4]

### Level of identification

The gazetteer entries for each piece of decorated ware have as their basic unit of identification the potter or anonymous style to which the piece can best be attributed. On most occasions this is obvious, especially if the piece has a name-stamp, and for some potters with distinctive styles, even small areas of surviving decoration can be attributed with confidence. Generally, it can be said that the certainty of an attribution increases with the number of decorative elements present, and that it is by a process of reduction of possibilities that a single choice of potter is eventually arrived at. This is best illustrated by a classic example given by J A Stanfield (Fig. 4.1):[5]

> 'This fragment provides the excuse for as good an exercise in attribution by elimination as could be desired. To begin with, the Cupid bearing torches, D 265, was used by Albucius, Banvus, Lastuca, Laxtucissa, Libertus, Paternus, Austrus, Birrantus, Putriu, Q I Balbinus, and Advocisus. Next, the Victory, D 484, was used by Albucius, Aventinus, Banvus, Decimanus, Attianus, and occurs on fragments in the style of Docilis and Q I Balbinus. The Dolphin, D 1052 reversed, the tail of which is seen on the right, was used by very many potters, among whom (of the potters mentioned above) was Paternus. It was also used by Servus. The little feline, D 805, was used by Albucius, Cinnamus, and others. The 'fasces' (usually of three joints but here only two) were used by Albucius, Paternus, Laxtucissa, Cinnamus, Q I Balbinus, Servus, Butrio, and occurs on fragments in the style of Justus. The small baluster ornament was used by Butrio, Januaris, and Servus.
>
> 'It will be seen that the figure types by themselves are much too common to assist in the identification of the potter. The next step, therefore, is, on grounds of style, to reject most of the above-mentioned potters, leaving for consideration Albucius, Laxtucissa, Paternus, Q I Balbinus, Servus, Cinnamus, and Butrio. The decisive factors are the panel borders which are composed of small conjoined astragali, and the small baluster ornament free in the field behind the Victory. Here again Butrio, Laxtucissa, and Paternus may be ruled out, as they did not use this type of border (Paternus occasionally used a border of larger astragali).

[3] *Sensu* Orton 1980, 164f.

[4] Initiated by Brian Hartley and Brenda Dickinson of Leeds University, now published in 9 volumes as Hartley & Dickinson 2008a-2012.

[5] Stanfield 1940, 202; D = Déchelette 1904.

*Fig. 4.1 Decorated piece by Q I Balbinus, used to illustrate aspects of identification of potters' styles. Drawing by J A Stanfield* (1940, fig. 5, no. 39) *(reproduced here not-to-scale).*

> 'This reduces the choice to Albucius, Q I Balbinus, Servus, and Cinnamus, who all used the border. Of these again Albucius and Cinnamus may be eliminated, as the baluster does not occur in their work so far as I know it. We are therefore left with Servus and Q I Balbinus, and although the former (in his work of this date) used the baluster, astragali, and fasces, I have not met with the figure-stamps in his work.
>
> 'Q I Balbinus alone remains, and the Wroxeter fragment may be attributed to him. The evidence of final proof rests in the Guildhall Museum in which there is a piece of form 37, on which occurs the 'fasces', the free baluster, the astragalus bead-rows, the Cupid with torches, and the advanced foot and part of the dress of the Victory, all together. It bears the stamp Q I B.'

Although the details of potters' names, decorative types and references used would be different today,[6] the thrust of his exposition gives exactly the processes that those identifying samian ware have to go through. For small pieces the choice may not be narrowed down to one potter alone, and as can be seen in the gazetteer, these have to be left as uncertain identifications. In the example that Stanfield gives, had the sherd been half the size that survived, for instance, the level of identification may have remained at between three and four potters. There is also a tendency for small pieces to be attributed to dominant potters within their style group. Thus, the bottom half of Fig 4.1 would appear most likely to have been by Albucius, as the style is very similar to his work, and he is much more commonly met with then Q I Balbinus or Servus I, whose pieces can frequently be in equivalent style. In the Gazetteer, where pieces can be attributed to a number of potters, the most likely on grounds of quantity of production is usually put first, and where the choice of potters is limited to two, the most likely has been used in certain aspects of the analysis given later in the chapter.

The level of identification is to a great extent limited by the amount of work that has been done in analysing styles and attributing them to potters. In this respect, Rheinzabern products have been best served, for with publication of Ricken's, and Ricken and Fischer's catalogues,[7] most adequately sized pieces can be confidently identified. For Central Gaulish (chiefly Lezoux and Les Martres-de-Veyre) potters, great strides have been made by Stanfield and Simpson, Rogers, and in other publications,[8] allowing most pieces to be allocated to potter or anonymous style. There remain some areas of uncertainty, however, principally (as far as the date limits of this thesis are concerned) in the mid-second century potters and those working at the very end of Central Gaulish production. The former group is composed of a number of combines and very closely associated potters (e.g. Sacer and Attianus) whose work cannot be easily distinguished, together with some anonymous potters who appear to be derivatives of the main styles of this period. The very late potters are difficult for a different reason, for many were borrowing and reusing earlier potters' decorative elements, and thus definition of their styles is not easy. In addition, many of them (e.g. Marcus or Lucinus) are only rarely met with and there is an insufficient corpus of data for clear attributions. In general, Central Gaulish ware is identified according to the names and groups given by Rogers.[9]

Other kiln-centres have varying degrees of precision in their levels of identification. Trier is well-served for the early period of production,[10] less so for later periods. The Argonne potters, meanwhile, largely remain to be properly sorted out, despite several publications about their products.[11] Many of the minor kilns with few potters, especially those in Germany and Britain, have good definitions of individual styles.[12] All such variations between kilns contribute to the different levels of precision possible in the establishment of chronologies. It should be stated at this point that no new stylistic definitions are attempted in the thesis, the database being drawn up with a view to examining chronologies and distribution, and therefore not properly constituted for detailed stylistic work.)

The decorative elements of each piece have been given in detail in the gazetteer for the British entries. This enables attributions to be checked by those who wish to do so, and also gives precise or updated identifications to many pieces

[6] See Gazetteer A 130 for the same piece described afresh. See Delage 1999b, 322, for discussion of Q I Balbinus and the possibility that he was a proprietor linked to several other potters, such as Cinnamus, Albucius and Marcus, ranging over the late 2nd-early 3rd century. In the same article, Delage articulates a more developed methodology of attribution to styles, with less reliance on attribution to potters' names. He also defines sub-styles for a number of potters' style-groups, including Iullinus, Paternus and Banvus.

[7] Ricken 1948; Ricken & Fischer 1963.

[8] Stanfield & Simpson 1958, revised ed. 1990; Rogers 1974; 1999. See also references in Appendix 10, sv. Lezoux.

[9] Rogers 1974, 20-4.

[10] Huld-Zetsche 1972.

[11] Ricken 1934; Oswald 1945; Chenet & Gaudron 1955; Hofmann 1968. A correspondence table of Argonne potters and ovolos is given as Appendix 4.

[12] See bibliography in the list of kiln-centres, Appendix 10, for details.

for the first time. A number of original identifications have been changed, particularly for Rheinzabern pieces published before Ricken and Fischer's catalogue and Central Gaulish pieces before Rogers' catalogues were available. There were also several reports where the text was imprecise but the drawings good enough to allow identifications to be made which had not previously been attempted. Drawings of the pieces have not been given, since in almost every case these have been published elsewhere, and repetition here is superfluous.

Non-British entries have not been accorded so much detail, although the process of identification was carried out in exactly the same way. This is principally due to reasons of space, since it was felt that the British entries demonstrated the level at which identification was carried out sufficiently well. In addition, the majority of the foreign entries were composed of Rheinzabern products, for which uncertainties of attribution were few and fairly well-defined, thus requiring less by way of corroborative detail in the gazetteer. One exception to this is *Aquincum* (B 162), where an important group of Central Gaulish ware, hitherto only available in a Hungarian report with German summary,[13] is given in full. Plain wares for non-British entries are given in parts A and B, but no attempt has been made to compile non-British type C entries (plain ware only, plus coin associations), which accordingly are confined to British entries, with a few from France and Belgium illustrative of specific points.

[13] Juhász 1936.

### Arrangement of entries

Information in each gazetteer entry has been arranged in a numbered sequence, so as to allow for easy consultation. The name of the site, the type of the site and the excavator's reference for the deposit are given first. Then follow two coded sections, giving the type of deposit and the standard of recording and recovery - details of the codes are in the key prefacing the gazetteer itself. The most important part of each entry is in the fourth section, in which the samian ware pieces are described. Decorated pieces are listed first, then plain ware stamps and lastly plain pieces. Other pottery of interest is noted in the following section. Any coins associated with the deposit are then listed in section six, and the last two sections are concerned with comments about the deposit, particularly from a stratigraphical point of view, and with bibliographic and other references, respectively. Not all sections have been completed for each entry, since sections 5, 6, or 7 in particular are superfluous for some deposits. Two deposits, Zugmantel (A 202) and Enns-Lorch (A 206) are arranged slightly differently from the sequence given above, since they had many subdivisions within the main deposit group, and therefore are given with sections 4 and 6 combined in a column format.

*Table 4.1 Totals of coins found in type A deposits*

Ar = silver, Ae = bronze
See index at the end of the Gazetteer for the areas used.

| *Period* | *Coin Type* | *S Brit* | *Wales* | *N Brit* | *France* | *Low C* | *Rhine* | *Danube* |
|---|---|---|---|---|---|---|---|---|
| I-III | Ar | 4 | 1 | 10 | 0 | 0 | 12 | 2 |
| | Ae | 15 | 4 | 3 | 3 | 6 | 17 | 1 |
| IV | Ar | 1 | 3 | 0 | 1 | 0 | 9 | 0 |
| | Ae | 18 | 10 | 5 | 1 | 3 | 12 | 1 |
| V | Ar | 5 | 1 | 0 | 0 | 0 | 5 | 3 |
| | Ae | 17 | 6 | 2 | 4 | 5 | 33 | 5 |
| VI | Ar | 2 | 2 | 3 | 0 | 0 | 6 | 2 |
| | Ae | 36 | 9 | 7 | 4 | 2 | 37 | 10 |
| VIIa | Ar | 4 | 1 | 1 | 1 | 0 | 5 | 1 |
| | Ae | 21 | 4 | 2 | 6 | 3 | 57 | 14 |
| VIIb | Ar | 2 | 1 | 0 | 0 | 0 | 2 | 4 |
| | Ae | 5 | 1 | 3 | 4 | 1 | 10 | 5 |
| VIIIa | Ar | 12 | 6 | 9 | 0 | 1 | 36 | 28 |
| | Ae | 1 | 0 | 0 | 0 | 0 | 1 | 9 |
| VIIIb | Ar | 8 | 3 | 4 | 0 | 2 | 18 | 14 |
| | Ae | 0 | 0 | 1 | 0 | 0 | 0 | 2 |
| IXa | Ar | 3 | 2 | 1 | 1 | 2 | 23 | 14 |
| | Ae | 2 | 1 | 0 | 0 | 1 | 2 | 4 |
| IXb | Ar | 2 | 0 | 0 | 0 | 0 | 13 | 3 |
| | Ae | 0 | 0 | 0 | 0 | 0 | 0 | 2 |
| IXc | Ar | 0 | 0 | 0 | 0 | 0 | 5 | 0 |
| Xa-b | | 142 | 19 | 8 | 4 | 5 | 68 | 29 |
| I-IX illeg | Ar | 0 | 1 | 0 | 0 | 1 | 0 | 0 |
| | Ae | 5 | 0 | 1 | 1 | 3 | 5 | 0 |

## Variability in the database

### Assessing bias in the sample as a whole

The easiest way of establishing whether the sample is biased, chronologically or geographically, is not by looking at the samian at all, but by examining the characteristics of the coin sample in type A deposits. The reason for this is that suitable comparanda are available for coins but not for samian ware. Table 4.I gives the totals of coins arranged according to the regions used in the area analysis given later in the text. Three of these areas are used for comparison with various regional listings of coins (Tables 4.II-IV).

The bronze coins in the associated groups (Table 4.II) compare very well with site collections from their respective areas in the cases of South Britain and the Rhineland. The correlation coefficients are high, and a brief inspection of the figures confirms that, by-and-large, the pairs of percentages move in step. A minor exception to this is in the last two periods, where both South British and Rhenish groups are high by comparison with the samian-associated coins. In the South British case this may in fact be due to an anomaly in the site collections given by Reece,[14] rather than a bias against this later end of the date-range in the samian ware groups, since the high site collection percentage is almost entirely accounted for by one collection, in Cirencester Museum. With the possible exception of this, therefore, it is fair to say that the coin-associated groups appear to form a representative sample when compared in this way.

The Danube area, however, poses more of a problem, for when the samian-associated coins are compared with those listed in the relevant volumes of the *Fundmünzen der Römischen Zeit in Deutschland*, the correlation is relatively low, mainly, it appears, because of high

[14] Reece 1972.

*Table 4.II Percentages of bronze coins from type A deposits, compared with site collections, periods V-IXc*

FMRD = *Fundmünzen der Römischen Zeit in Deutschland*

Rhineland area FMRD volumes: Chantraine 1965; Christ 1963; 1964a; 1964b; Franke 1960; Kellner *et al.* 1975; Kienast 1962; Weiller 1972; and those sites in Christ & Franke 1964 allocated to Germania Superior.

Danube area FMRD volumes: Alföldi *et al.* 1962; Kellner 1960a; 1963a; 1970; Kellner & Overbeck 1978; and those sites in Christ & Franke 1964 allocated to Raetia.

| *Period* | *S Brit* | *Reece 1972* | *Rhine* | *FMRD* | *Danube* | *FMRD* | *Hahn 1976* |
|---|---|---|---|---|---|---|---|
| V | 20.7 | 27.7 | 23.6 | 24.3 | 9.8 | 31.4 | 15.1 |
| VI | 43.9 | 35.9 | 26.4 | 30.7 | 19.6 | 30.9 | 23.4 |
| VIIa | 25.6 | 21.7 | 40.7 | 29.0 | 27.5 | 22.3 | 29.8 |
| VIIb | 6.1 | 7.3 | 7.1 | 8.5 | 9.8 | 6.2 | 6.3 |
| VIIIa | 1.2 | 1.1 | 0.7 | 1.4 | 17.6 | 3.3 | 4.0 |
| VIIIb | 0.0 | | 0.0 | 1.0 | 3.9 | 1.4 | 3.6 |
| IXa | 2.4 | 2.8 | 1.4 | 2.7 | 7.8 | 2.1 | 12.7 |
| IXb | 0.0 | 3.5 | 0.0 | 2.3 | 3.9 | 1.8 | 4.4 |
| IXc | 0.0 | | 0.0 | 0.1 | 0.0 | 0.5 | 0.7 |
| *N of coins* | 82 | 1101 | 140 | 1525 | 51 | 840 | 1375 |
| *Corr coeff* | | 0.96 | | 0.96 | | 0.61 | 0.82 |

*Table 4.III Percentages of silver coins from type A deposits, compared with site collections, periods V-IXc*

FMRD = *Fundmünzen der Römischen Zeit in Deutschland*

Rhineland area FMRD volumes: Chantraine 1965; Christ 1963; 1964a; 1964b; Franke 1960; Kellner *et al.* 1975; Kienast 1962; Weiller 1972; and those sites in Christ & Franke 1964 allocated to Germania Superior.

Danube area FMRD volumes: Alföldi *et al.* 1962; Kellner 1960a; 1963a; 1970; Kellner & Overbeck 1978; and those sites in Christ & Franke 1964 allocated to Raetia.

| *Period* | *S Brit* | *Reece 1972* | *Rhine* | *FMRD* | *Danube* | *FMRD* | *Hahn 1976* |
|---|---|---|---|---|---|---|---|
| V | 13.2 | 6.6 | 4.4 | 5.2 | 4.3 | 6.7 | 4.2 |
| VI | 5.3 | 8.4 | 5.4 | 7.0 | 2.9 | 8.8 | 4.1 |
| VIIa | 10.5 | 4.2 | 4.4 | 4.0 | 1.4 | 5.0 | 3.4 |
| VIIb | 5.3 | 0.9 | 1.8 | 2.1 | 5.8 | 1.9 | 1.9 |
| VIIIa | 31.6 | 41.3 | 31.9 | 19.7 | 40.6 | 28.3 | 25.5 |
| VIIIb | 21.1 | | 15.9 | 17.9 | 20.3 | 16.8 | 16.5 |
| IXa | 7.9 | 15.5 | 20.4 | 20.0 | 20.3 | 21.6 | 19.1 |
| IXb | 5.3 | 23.0 | 11.5 | 12.9 | 4.3 | 7.5 | 12.7 |
| IXc | 0.0 | | 4.4 | 11.3 | 0.0 | 3.4 | 9.7 |
| *N of coins* | 38 | 760 | 113 | 1316 | 69 | 477 | 1719 |
| *Corr coeff* | | 0.81 | | 0.88 | | 0.95 | 0.88 |

percentages of samian-associated coins in periods VIIIa-b, and low percentages in periods V-VI. It is possible that this is due to the relatively low numbers of coins in the Danubian sample, resulting in a simple case of sampling error, but an examination of the groups involved suggests another solution. Enns-Lorch (*Lauriacum*) provides the great majority of associated groups (cf A 206) in this region, and therefore the bias of data in the levels from this site could well account for the difference. It is also, in fact, rather to the east of most of the other sites, both those with samian-associated coins and those in *FMRD*. Therefore, it is possible that there is an area bias in operation here, a hypothesis given some support by the correlation with the last column in the Table, which is from *Carnuntum*, further down the Danube valley. Possibly there is a distinction to be made between the Upper Danube and the Middle Danube in terms of coin circulation (and perhaps samian distribution) patterns at this time. Unfortunately, the sample of groups from this area is too small to subdivide without losing confidence in the resulting statistics.

In the case of the silver coins from the Danube area (Table 4.III), there are, by contrast, surprisingly high correlations with both the *FMRD* sites and *Carnuntum*, the former, in fact, being more highly correlated. In all probability the silver coins, being more numerous than bronze in both the samian-associated groups and *Carnuntum* (Table 4.IV), give a more representative view of the potential bias in the samian ware groups, and allow the suggestion that there is less bias than had been feared when the bronze coins were examined in isolation. Nevertheless, of the three regions being compared, the Danube is the one where bias in the sample is most likely to exist.

Silver coins in South Britain and the Rhineland are generally fairly well correlated between samian-associated and site collection coin lists, but the correlations are lower than for bronze. This may be accounted for by the lower numbers of silver coins in these areas, especially in the case of South Britain. In the latter area also, what might be termed the 'Cirencester anomaly' has probably elevated the site collection percentage for the last two periods and accordingly lowered the correlation coefficient.

*Table 4.IV Ratio of silver to bronze coins, periods V-IXc*

CASG = coins in coin-associated samian ware groups

| | Silver | Bronze | Ratio |
|---|---|---|---|
| S Britain CASG | 38 | 82 | 1:2.2 |
| Reece 1972 | 760 | 1101 | 1:1.4 |
| Rhineland CASG | 113 | 140 | 1:1.2 |
| FMRD | 1316 | 1525 | 1:1.2 |
| Danube CASG | 69 | 51 | 1:0.7 |
| FMRD | 477 | 840 | 1:1.8 |
| Hahn 1976 | 1719 | 1375 | 1:0.8 |
| Wales CASG | 16 | 21 | 1:1.3 |
| N Britain CASG | 18 | 15 | 1:0.8 |
| France CASG | 2 | 18 | 1:9.0 |
| Low Countries CASG | 5 | 12 | 1:2.4 |

In sum, then, the coins from the coin-associated samian groups appear to reflect the general coin finds, and hence circulation patterns, of their respective areas, with some minor exceptions that have been discussed above. Therefore, there appear to be representative coin samples in the type A samian groups, and consequently it has been assumed that the composition of the samian ware itself in these groups is also more or less a representative sample, In the absence of an accessible database of identifications from site collections with which direct comparison of the samian ware sample can be made, this conclusion is probably as far as the question of the assessment of bias in the sample can be taken.

For the areas given in Table 4.I, but not used for comparison with site collections, namely North Britain, Wales and the Marches, France, and the Low Countries, it is difficult to assess whether bias exists or not. The small size of the coin samples, and in fact the relatively small size of the samian ware samples, as will be seen below, would logically lead to the supposition that bias due to sampling error could well have occurred. Subjectively, the least representative sample is probably that from France, followed by the Low Countries (fairly dependent on one group from Zwammerdam, A 158), Wales and the Marches (fairly dependent on groups from Caerleon, A 20-28, Chester, A 41-5, and Wroxeter, A 130-2), and North Britain. The number of groups relative to the overall area of each region is also probably a contributory factor in the inherent representativeness of the groups.[15] France fares by far the least well in this respect, although the Danube and Wales, superficially at least, also appear to be thin on the ground.

### Variability in the type of deposit: the question of residuality and survival

A different cause of variability and bias to that discussed above concerns the way in which individual deposits came together, and whether the type of feature or stratum affects what might be termed the taphonomy of the samian ware.

Each deposit in the gazetteer has been classified into a scheme that divides the deposits into different types, as follows: A, burial; B, occupation layer, 'build-up' or road-surface; C, pit or well; D, ditch; E, destruction debris, burnt levels or dumps; F, general associations, often between several types of deposit within one phase; G, other (which in the event, consisted mainly of riverine silt deposits). Of these, only type A consists inherently of artefacts that are deliberately buried and which therefore can be assumed to made up of vessels in 'use' at the time of burial. All the other classes have at least the risk of residual material being present. Since residuality is clearly an important factor in the method of chronological assessment being

[15] See list of sites prefacing the Gazetteer.

used in the thesis, it requires some discussion of the nature of residuality and analysis of its effect.

Residual material can be defined fairly simply as material from a context other than its position of first disposal, in other words having the same meaning as 'redeposited' or 'derived' artefacts. This follows the definition in Crummy and Terry,[16] and is perhaps narrower than the definition of residuality frequently used in archaeological texts, that all material out of its chronological context is residual. However, the narrower definition is essential for the analysis of samian ware, since it distinguishes post-depositional residuality from survival in use. Survival in use is one of the aspects implicitly under investigation in any assessment of samian ware chronology that uses disposal sets as the main data-base. However, there are several problems in seeking to distinguish residual from survival pieces, since there is no easy way of deciding which pieces fall into which category.

The best previous discussion of this matter is in Crummy and Terry.[17] They show that late Roman levels in Portchester and post-Roman levels in Colchester contain high proportions of residual coins and pottery respectively. The method used for Portchester was to plot the coin histogram for one of the late Roman periods and compare the date-range with that expected for that period from coin-hoard evidence. This gave a figure of 30% of the coins probably being residual (and by extension, probably a similar percentage of pottery also). Such an approach is theoretically possible for the late second and early third century deposits under consideration here, but in practice the long circulation period of most coins at this time precludes effective analysis. The Colchester analysis showed that some of the medieval pits contained up to 90% residual Roman pottery, whereas the ditches had a lower percentage, being relatively uncontaminated. Their conclusion was that some deposit types were very prone to having a residual element, e.g. pits, whereas some were variable, depending on the individual circumstances of deposition, e.g. ditches, and some were usually free of much contamination, e.g. burials, occupation layers on floors, destruction debris, primary silts and 'pure' tip-lines. The main source of residual material was soil scraped or dug up in order to fill features deliberately, and from this it follows that the residual element is likely to be greatest at the end of an occupation sequence, rather than at the time of initial use of the site.

An aspect not discussed by Crummy and Terry, but important for the dating of associated material, is the question of slow and rapid rates of deposition. Rapid deposition involves the inclusion of coins, samian ware and other finds that should be in roughly contemporaneous use (as well, of course, as residual pieces incorporated in the fill). A long period of deposition, on the other hand (e.g. the natural silting of a ditch) can result in an accumulation of artefacts that were in use at different times, so that it is possible to have coins much earlier than the associated samian, or *vice versa*, none of which is residual in the narrow sense but simply the outcome of a long-term process. Indeed, many cases of slow deposition do not involve the deliberate redeposition of earth from one feature to another, and therefore have few residual pieces. As far as dating of these deposits is concerned, a single coin-date is not of great use, since it marks merely one episode of deposition amongst the many that may be both earlier, contemporary and later. In other words, the *terminus post quem* that a coin can supply is not of great significance, and the conventional wisdom about dating deposits, as represented by the quote below, is wrong.[18]

> 'A datable object such as a coin, or other datable find, such as a radio-carbon sample from a layer or feature, only gives the date *on or after which the feature was deposited*, that is, the so-called *terminus post quem.*'

In fact, where there are a number of coins in a slowly-accumulating deposit, they may give a rough indication of the overall date-range of accumulation, if they came to the deposit individually at intervals. This also is counter to the generally received notion that it is the latest coin that provides the *terminus post* or *ad quem* for a deposit – it may even be the earliest coins that give the best guide as to when the deposit started accumulating.[19] Slowly-accumulating deposits, therefore, have to be regarded in a different light from that which most archaeologists regard as typical, i.e. fairly rapidly accumulating strata. The dating evidence they provide has to be regarded loosely, and the associations of artefacts within them as general only.

A final point to be made about deposition and redeposition is that the redeposited material may, in itself, be useful for dating. If there is a clear distinction between the contemporary and the residual artefacts, e.g. second century pottery in a late fourth century context, and there is good reason to suppose that the residual material derives from a single context,[20] then the possibility exists of using the residual coin-associations to provide a *terminus ad quem* for the residual samian. This has to be done cautiously, of course, because the original circumstances of deposition for the residual material are effectively unknown.

In sum, there are two major factors affecting residuality and survival; the extent of redeposition from other archaeological strata, and the rate of accumulation. When these are applied to the categories of deposit used in the gazetteer (Table 4.V) it can be seen that, in terms of usefulness for dating purposes, burials are hypothetically

[16] Crummy & Terry 1979. See also Lockyear 2012, 195; Guidobaldi *et al.* 1998. The debate about samian ware and residuality has focused on late-2nd- and 3rd-century deposits; cf. Ward 1996, 76-7 and Evans 1996, for the site of Alcester in this respect.

[17] *Op. cit.*

[18] Barker 1977, 193.

[19] Cf King 1983 for an example of this argument applied to a fourth century context.

[20] As in gazetteer entry A 69, Enfield.

*Table 4.V Factors affecting residuality in deposit types*

| | *Presence of redeposited strata* | *Rate of accumulation* |
|---|---|---|
| A: Burial | Rare | Fast |
| B: Occupation layer, etc | Rare | Variable, often slow |
| C: Pit, etc | Common | Variable, often fast |
| D: Ditch | Variable | Fast or slow |
| E: Destruction debris, etc | Variable | Fast |

best (although there are other factors, e.g. the burial rite, that may alter the deposition pattern), followed by categories B, E, D, C in that order, but with much variation in reliability in the last three.

The application of these notions to the deposits in the Gazetteer is best conceived in terms of a grading scheme, as in Appendix 6. This gives a choice of three grades to the extent of residuality, the rate of accumulation and the overall reliability/usefulness of the context. Clearly, it is not possible to be wholly objective in grading deposits in this way, since pertinent information may not have been provided by the excavator. Therefore, it is assumed, for instance, that burning deposits and burials are generally accumulated at a fast rate unless specified otherwise. In some cases, assessment of residuality has depended on the internal consistency of the artefacts in the assemblage, which unavoidably raises the problem of circularity of argument, but this has been kept to a minimum. Grading of the overall usefulness of the deposit has not been carried out simply by reference to the other two factors, but takes account of other aspects of the deposit as well, such as the quality and circumstances of the excavation, and the way in which the samian ware and the coins were referred back to the stratigraphy of the deposit.

The results of applying the scheme outlined above are summarised in Table 4.VI. It can be seen that the deposit type with the greatest variation in the extent of known redeposition is E (destruction debris, burnt levels and dumps), while C (pits) also has a number of cases of known redeposition. The latter conforms with Crummy and Terry's observations at Colchester, but their suggestion that destruction debris should be relatively free of contamination does not appear to be borne out, the same also applying to B, occupation levels. Perhaps the explanation of this difference is that excavators have not always made clear how disturbed their destruction and occupation levels might have been, and if only the relatively clear-cut cases are taken (and dumps are excluded altogether from category E), then the results should conform more closely with Crummy & Terry's hypotheses.

The most reliable of the deposit types is A, burials, both in terms of having little evidence of redeposition, and being accumulated into archaeological strata at a fast rate. This would, on the face of it, make this category the best for constructing a chronology, but there are two other factors that reduce this apparent advantage. Firstly, most burial groups are small, and decorated samian ware is in fact an unusual grave-offering, particularly in Britain.[21] This means that associations of coins and decorated samian ware in burials are quite rare, and consequently there are not

[21] Bird 2013, 334.

*Table 4.VI Summary of deposit types (see Appendix 6)*

*Extent of redeposition*

| | **Deposit type** | | | | | | |
|---|---|---|---|---|---|---|---|
| | **A** | **B** | **C** | **D** | **E** | **F** | **G** |
| * | 24 | 56 | 85 | 30 | 99 | 32 | 8 |
| ** | - | 10 | 20 | 10 | 39 | 7 | 1 |
| *** | - | 1 | - | - | 7 | 1 | - |
| Total | 24 | 67 | 105 | 40 | 145 | 40 | 9 |

*Rate of accumulation*

| | **Deposit type** | | | | | |
|---|---|---|---|---|---|---|
| | **A** | **B** | **C** | **D** | **E** | **G** |
| * | - | 7 | 9 | 3 | 9 | 5 |
| ** | - | 32 | 31 | 15 | 49 | 1 |
| *** | 24 | 3 | 13 | 6 | 56 | - |

enough data to construct a chronology from burials alone. Secondly, burials are the only 'deliberate' deposit type, in that vessels were presumably chosen to go into the grave, and have therefore undergone a process of selection which is unlikely to have affected the other categories. Samian ware from burials may, therefore, be a biased set of data when compared with that from settlement debris deposits.

Category E deposits follow burials in having a large percentage accumulated at a fast rate, which is helpful for the purposes of creating a chronology, but mitigated by the large proportion showing evidence of redeposition. However, this category is probably the most useful for samian ware chronology, since they are common deposits and often with large quantities of pottery. Categories B, C and D appear to be similar to one another when considered in this way, while G, mainly riverine silts, is markedly different, being mainly deposits of slow accumulation, but with little residual material.

In sum, deposit types vary in ways that are to a certain extent predictable, but when compared with Crummy and Terry's observations and those put forward in Table 4.VI, the actual results show several differences in detail, mainly to do with the greater variation noted in practice, than might have been predicted in theory. Each deposit, therefore, has to be taken on its own merits and carefully appraised for reliability. With that in mind, it is now possible to examine the chronology of the samian ware itself, and put forward sequences of deposits.

# Chapter 5

# Coin-associated groups of samian ware

## Unadjusted Coin Dates

The initial approach to establishing a chronology from coin-associated deposits should clearly be to take the raw, unadjusted coin dates from section A of the gazetteer and tabulate them against potters/styles (Appendix 7). We know that the coin-dates will need eventual adjustment (as was established in chapter 3), so the dates themselves are merely a guide to *termini post quem* rather than realistic date-ranges. However, the unadjusted dates are useful in that they give the simplest appraisal of the overall range of dates and quantities of samian ware for each potter (see also Appendix 8). They also provide the starting point for adjusting for bias in the sample.

The presentation of the data in Appendix 7 is in the form of the number of sherds of each potter in each coin-period (cf. Table 3.I for details of the coin-periods), and the number of deposits containing sherds of each potter in each coin-period. The former figure is more of a quantitative statistic than the latter, which is more of a presence-absence type of count. There are advantages in both methods of counting. The number of sherds can be taken as equivalent to the number of vessels, since joining pieces of single vessels were noted in the gazetteer but counted as one only when compiling the statistics. As a result this can provide a basis for estimating comparative levels of production at different periods. However, the number of sherds count can be distorted by large assemblages (e.g. Gauting, A 165, with 67 sherds of Cinnamus from one deposit), and so the number of deposits is useful in showing the presence of particular potters in association with coins of each period.

As can be seen from a perusal of Appendix 7, the majority of potters are represented by fewer than 10 sherds. This makes for some anomalous datings, due simply to small

*Table 5.I Summary of number of sherds in coin-dated associations for deposits c. 150-280+. All deposits in Gazetteer section A.*

Key to kiln-centre abbreviations: **CG**, Central Gaul; **Rh**, Rheinzabern; **Tr**, Trier; **West**, Westerndorf; **Pfaff**, Pfaffenhofen; **Arg**, Argonne; **La Mad**, La Madeleine; **Chém/Mitt**, Chémery and Mittelbronn; **Sinz**, Sinzig; **Heil**, Heiligenberg; **Itten**, Ittenwiller; **Kräh**, Kräherwald; **Waib**, Waiblingen; **EG**, East Gaulish unlocated; **Brit**, British samian
*, large quantity (unspecified)

| | *Coin-periods* | | | | | | | | | | | | |
|---|---|---|---|---|---|---|---|---|---|---|---|---|---|
| **Kiln-centre** | *I-III* | *IV* | *V* | *VI* | *VIIa* | *VIIb* | *VIIIa* | *VIIIb* | *IXa* | *IXb* | *IXc* | *Xa-b* | *XI+* |
| **CG I** | - | 1 | 1 | 9 | 7 | 2 | 1 | 1 | 1 | - | - | 6 | - |
| **CG II** | - | 2 | 5 | 18 | 20 | 11 | 7 | 3 | 21 | - | - | 5 | 3 |
| **CG III** | 7 | 1 | 11 | 92 | 50 | 16 | 60 | 19 | 105 | 2 | - | 18 | 11 |
| **CG IV** | - | - | 3 | 56 | 20 | 10 | 27 | 35 | 19 | 4 | - | 16 | 15 |
| **Rh Ia** | 1 | - | 8 | 2 | 7 | 3 | 10 | 5 | 12 | 1 | 1 | 3 | - |
| **Rh Ib** | 1 | 1 | 1 | 5 | 2 | 4 | 16 | 15 | 5 | 3 | 1 | 4 | - |
| **Rh IIa** | - | 1 | 11 | 10 | 11 | 7 | 24 | 23 | 18 | 8 | 3 | 3 | 1 |
| **Rh IIb-c** | - | 2 | - | - | 3 | 2 | 17 | 15 | 16 | 4 | 2 | 7 | - |
| **Rh III** | 1 | - | 1 | 3 | 3 | 2 | 6 | 10 | 22 | 7 | 2 | 10 | 2 |
| **Tr** | - | - | 3 | 3 | 9 | 2 | 95 | 15 | 8 | - | 76 | 6 | 1 |
| **West** | - | - | - | 2 | 2 | 12 | 2 | 1 | 94 | 12 | - | 27 | 3 |
| **Pfaff** | - | - | 1 | 1 | - | 27 | - | - | 2 | - | - | 17 | 1 |
| **Arg** | - | - | 5 | 2 | 4 | 4 | 9 | 2 | - | 1 | - | 9 | 1 |
| **La Mad** | - | - | 1 | 6 | 6 | - | 14 | 2 | - | - | - | 2 | - |
| **Chém/Mitt** | - | - | 1 | - | 1 | 1 | 5 | 1 | 1 | - | - | - | - |
| **Sinz** | - | - | - | - | 11 | - | - | - | - | - | - | - | - |
| **Heil** | 1 | - | - | 7 | 1 | 1 | - | - | 4 | - | - | 1 | 1 |
| **Blick** | - | - | 1 | 4 | 4 | - | 9 | - | - | 1 | - | - | - |
| **Itten** | - | - | - | - | - | - | - | - | - | 1 | - | - | - |
| **Kräh** | - | - | 1 | 2 | - | - | - | - | - | - | - | - | - |
| **Waib** | - | - | - | - | 2 | - | - | - | - | - | - | - | - |
| **EG** | - | - | 1 | - | - | - | - | - | 1 | - | - | 2 | - |
| **Brit** | - | - | - | - | * | - | - | - | - | - | - | 1 | 1 |
| **Total** | 11 | 8 | 55 | 222 | 163 | 104 | 302 | 147 | 329 | 44 | 85 | 137 | 40 |

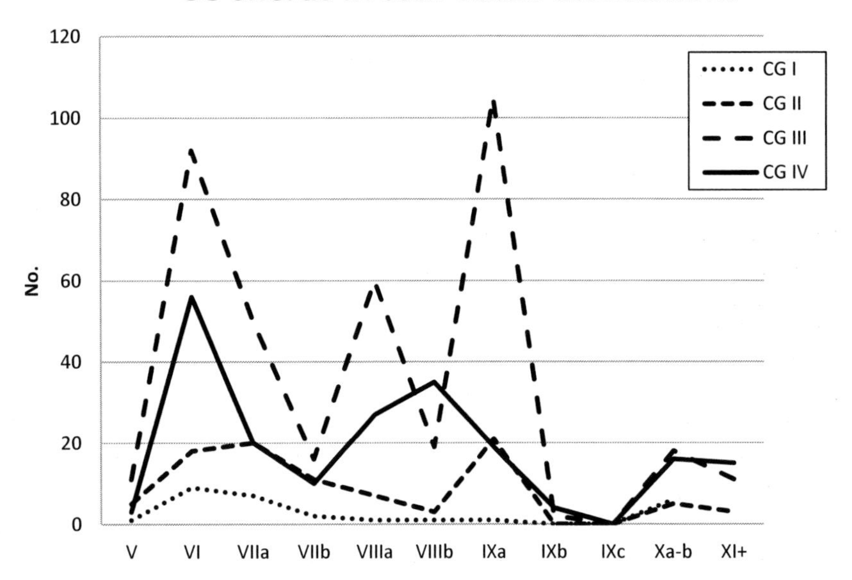


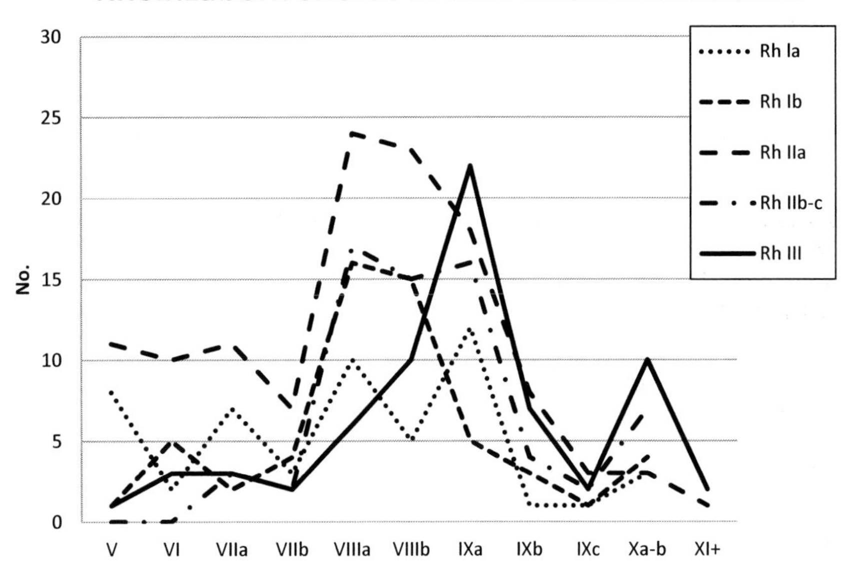


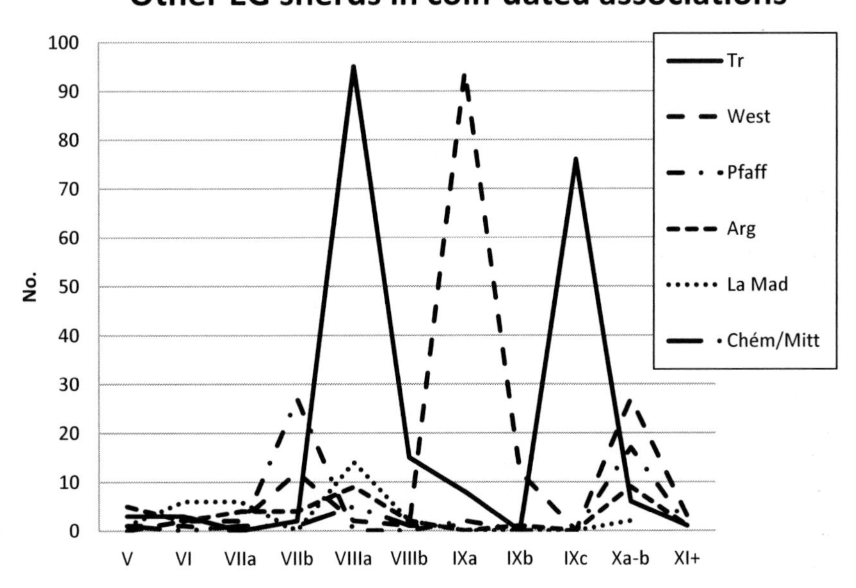


*Fig. 5.1 Central Gaul, Rheinzabern and other East Gaulish sherds in coin-dated associations. Unadjusted coin dates. All deposits. Data from Table 5.I.*

sample size, such as X-2 (an early 2nd century CG potter) being represented only by one sherd associated with a coin of the mid third century. More sense in the figures comes with potters being grouped together, which has been done in Table 5.I and Fig. 5.1 using the subdivisions defined in chapter 1, and Table 5.II and Fig. 5.2 where percentages of sherds found with pre-Severan and Severan or later coins are given. It can be seen that the divisions within the two largest kiln-centres do fall along roughly chronological lines, even using these raw, unadjusted dates. CG III and IV are similar to one another, but definitely later than CG I and II. Rh Ia-b and IIa are also earlier than Rh IIb-c and III, but with a slight anomaly in the case of Rh Ib (Cerialis, Comitialis I-III, etc). Of the minor kilns, all those generally thought to be earlier are earlier, but Heiligenberg appears to have an over-preponderance of early deposits. The later kilns are somewhat anomalous, especially Pfaffenhofen which should be mainly third century but is heavily biased

*Table 5.II Numbers of sherds associated with pre Severan and Severan or later coins. Unadjusted coin dates, all deposits.*

Key: as Table 5.I

| | Pre-Severan I-VIIb | Severan and later VIIIa-IX+ | Pre-Severan as % of Severan and later |
|---|---|---|---|
| **CG I** | 20 | 9 | 222 |
| **CG II** | 56 | 39 | 144 |
| **CG III** | 177 | 215 | 82 |
| **CG IV** | 89 | 116 | 77 |
| | | | |
| **Rh Ia** | 21 | 32 | 66 |
| **Rh Ib** | 14 | 44 | 32 |
| **Rh IIa** | 50 | 11 | 17 |
| **Rh IIb-c** | 7 | 61 | 11 |
| **Rh III** | 10 | 59 | 17 |
| | | | |
| **Tr** | 17 | 201 | 8 |
| **West** | 16 | 139 | 12 |
| **Pfaff** | 29 | 20 | 145 |
| **Arg** | 15 | 22 | 68 |
| **La Mad** | 13 | 18 | 72 |
| **Heil** | 10 | 6 | 167 |
| **Blick** | 9 | 10 | 90 |

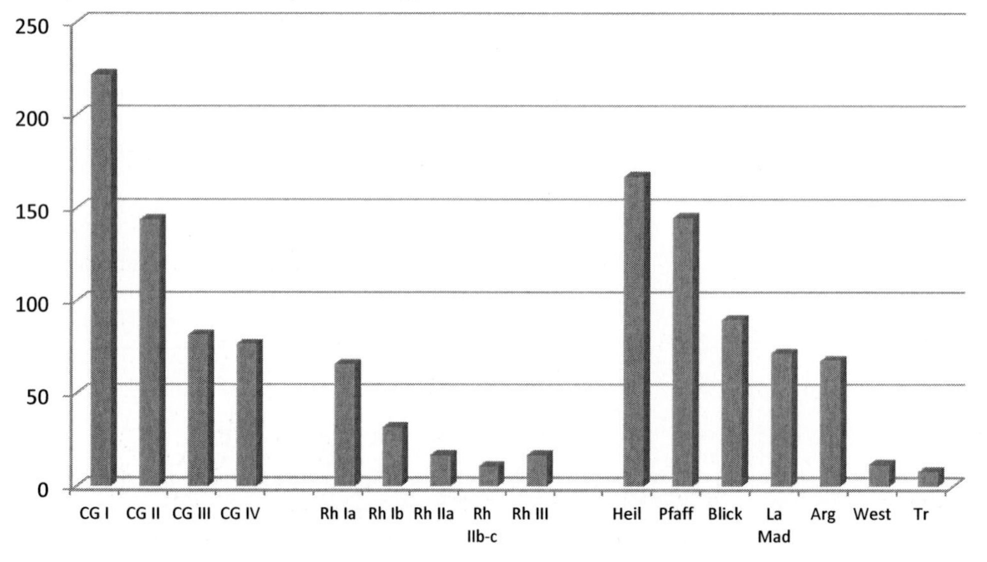


*Fig. 5.2 Numbers of sherds associated with pre-Severan and Severan or later coins. Unadjusted coin dates. All deposits. Data from Table 5.II.*

by a large kiln-site deposit. Also, Trier is abnormally deficient in pre-Severan deposits, and its percentage is biased by the inclusion of A 187, Niederbieber.

Taken as a whole, the raw coin-dates certainly seem to suggest later dates for many of the potters than are usually given, but nevertheless appear to support the existing relative chronology and go against the hypothesis presented in chapter 1. CG products, even those of late potters, are generally earlier than those of Rheinzabern and Trier. However, it must be stressed that the coin-dates are unadjusted, and that there is the additional factor of distributional differences. Most of the CG ware in the gazetteer comes from Britain, which, as Tables 4.II and 4.III show, has fewer early third century coins than the Rhineland, from which the bulk of the Rheinzabern and Trier ware comes. There is also the question of individual deposits that may bias the results.

### ADJUSTING FOR BIAS IN THE SAMPLE

A basic adjustment to be made is the removal of deposits badly affected by residual material (see Appendix 6). These are A 1, A 22, A 27, A 33, A 53, A 72, A 73, A 82, A 129, A 154 and A 165. Of these only A 165, Gauting, has a large quantity of samian ware. Further to this, there are some F type deposits which have not got sufficiently restricted time-spans to be particularly useful. Chief of these is A 187, Niederbieber, which has been discussed already in chapter 1. Others are A 163, Degerfeld unsealed deposits, and A 100, Rapsley. In addition there is a B type deposit from Caerleon, A 25, which seems anomalous in having a wide range of samian ware and coins up to Severus Alexander. It may be disturbed or built up over a period, like Gauting. A 25 has in fact been included in the counts of sherds and deposits, but its somewhat doubtful status should be borne in mind. Some of the series B gazetteer entries have in fact got usable dates, and have been included; these are B 52, B 67, B 97, B 107, B 108, B 118, B 143, B 148, B 160.

### ADJUSTED COIN DATES

Conversion of the coin dates from dates of minting to estimated dates of loss has been done by applying the scheme given at the end of chapter 3. The results for each deposit have been listed in Appendix 6 and the date-ranges

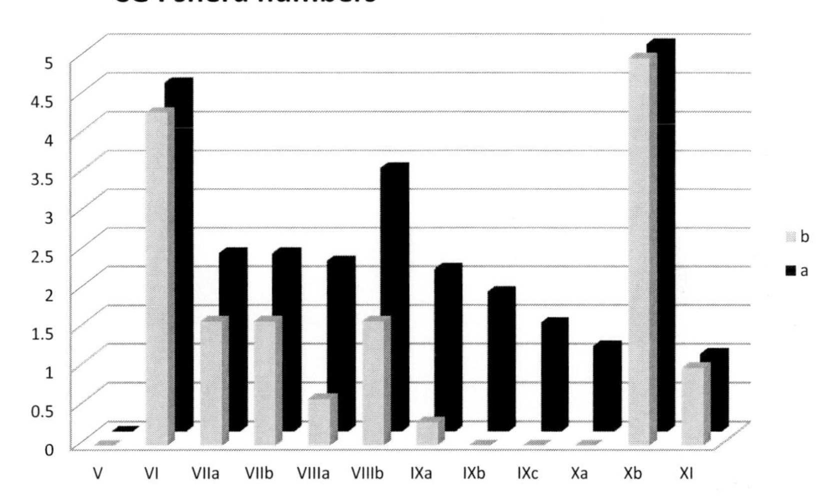


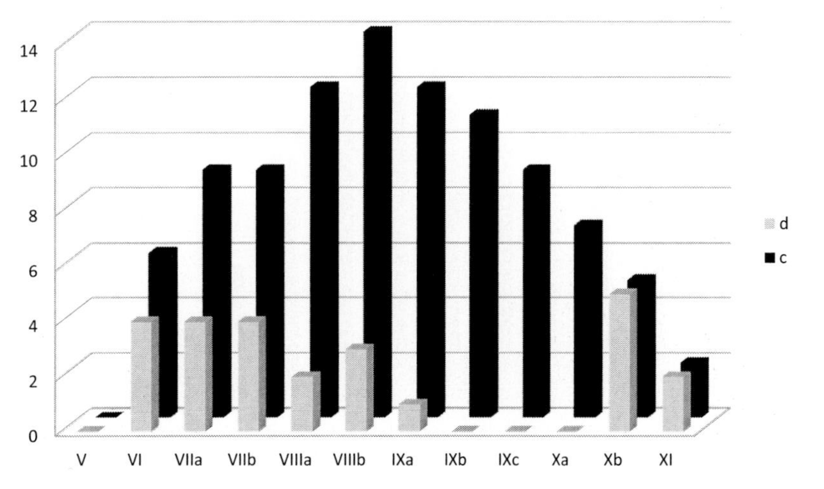


*Fig. 5.3 Central Gaulish group I, in adjusted coin-dated deposits.* ***a*** *number of sherds per coin-period;* ***b*** *as a but well-dated deposits only;* ***c*** *number of deposit-equivalents per coin-period;* ***d*** *as c but well-dated deposits only.*

for each kiln-centre and the better-represented potters are given in Appendix 8 and Figs 5.3-5.17. It has not been thought worthwhile giving those potters represented by only a few sherds, or indeed those kiln-centres where the evidence is thin (i.e. Sinzig, Ittenwiller, Kräherwald, Waiblingen and the British kilns). However, what is known of their chronology will be discussed where relevant.

Four different categories of data are given in Appendix 8 and the Figures. The number of sherds per coin-period is the basic listing (cf. Fig. 5.3**a**), calculated by taking each deposit and distributing the number of constituent sherds over the date-range of coin-periods. Thus, if a potter is represented by, for instance, 4 sherds in a deposit that dates to periods VIIb-VIIIb (i.e. 3 coin-periods), then 1.3 sherds are allocated to each of those 3 periods. The numbers for each potter or style are totalled for each kiln-centre, or where appropriate, the relevant kiln-centre sub group. A refinement of the number of sherds listing has been done by taking only the better-dated deposits (cf. Fig. 5.3**b**), which have been deemed all those having date-ranges of four coin-periods or less. In several of the Figures this gives a clearer picture of dating than the more spread out and therefore vaguer, general count of sherd numbers. A third method of display of the data has been to count what may be termed the deposit-equivalents (cf. Fig. 5.3**c**). These are calculated by totalling for each potter the number of deposits present in each coin-period, regardless of whether individual deposits are spread over a number of periods. Therefore, in the example given above, there would be three deposit-equivalents recorded, one for each of the coin-periods. This calculation has the effect of emphasising deposits spread over a number of periods, and of playing down deposits with a large number of constituent sherds. In this way, the sherd number count is effectively smoothed, and the Figures show more gradual rises and falls for the deposit-equivalent counts. Finally, this calculation has been refined to form the fourth category, by taking only the better dated deposits as for sherd numbers (cf. Fig. 5.3**d**). This last method of representing the data (despite being a considerable adjustment of the raw coin/deposit listings) probably gives the clearest picture of the chronology of the coin-dated deposits.

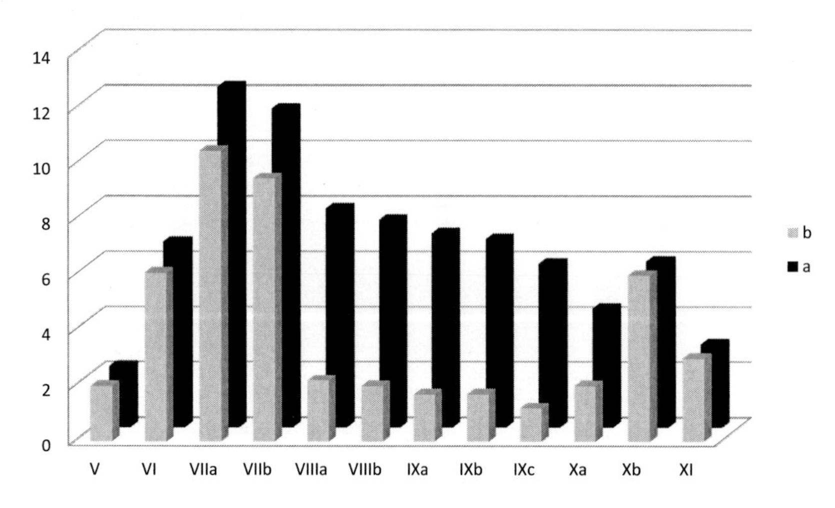


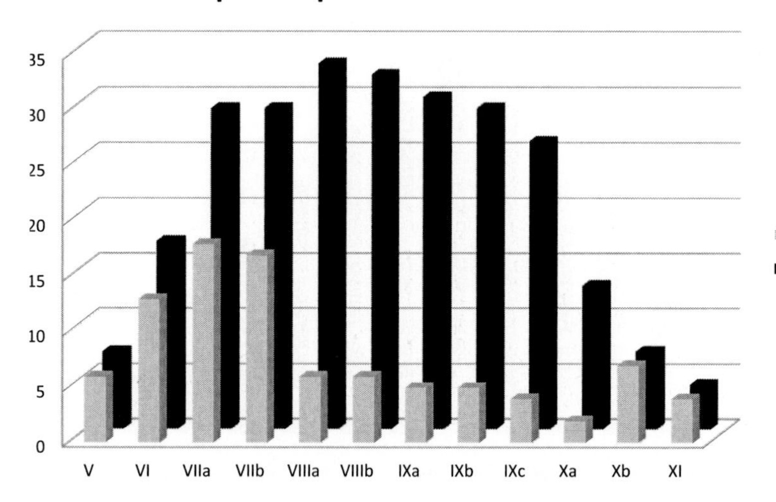


*Fig. 5.4 Central Gaulish group II, in adjusted coin-dated deposits. Key as Fig 5.3.*

In detail, the evidence can be used to chart the varying fortunes of the different kiln-centres as they neared the end of their production, although it should always be remembered that the Tables and Figures are giving the evidence for when the pottery was disposed of, not when it was made.

### CENTRAL GAUL

Central Gaulish group I potters are conventionally dated to the Trajanic period (i.e. coin period IV), but it is clear from Fig. 5.3 that sherds of these potters, although not plentiful, are met with up to the end of the second century, with a number of presumably residual pieces in mid-third century and later contexts. Period V is distinctly under-represented for CG I (and probably for CG II and III) because few deposits with early second century *termini post quem* were examined (for reasons given earlier in this chapter). CG II (Fig. 5.4) has a strong grouping in the later second century, peaking at the time of Marcus Aurelius (VIIa). This is followed by a tail of sherds in early third century deposits, with numbers rising again in periods Xb-XI. When deposit equivalents are considered, the apparent CG II peak is later, in the Severan period (VIIIa). This is due to the large number of less well-dated deposits that have spread the dates into the third. The part of the graph showing only the better-dated deposits peaks in the Aurelian period and shows the same characteristics as the sherd-number graph.

CG III is given both with its largest constituent potter, Cinnamus, and without (Figs 5.5-5.6). This is because the numbers for Cinnamus are so high compared with the rest of the group that there is the danger of distortion of the statistics of the group as a whole, a danger borne out to a certain extent by the graphs for Cinnamus alone (Fig. 5.8), where by comparison with the CG III (without Cinnamus) graph on Fig. 5.6, the potter appears to be somewhat later. CG III has two main peaks, in periods VI and IXa, plus the upswing in numbers in the mid/late third century. The first peak is, to a certain extent, distorted by a few deposits each having a considerable number of CG III sherds, e.g. A 131, Wroxeter, as the smoother deposit-equivalent graph makes clear. However, the bulk of CG III pottery is in deposits of late second century date, but with considerable numbers still being found in deposits up to the 220s/230s.

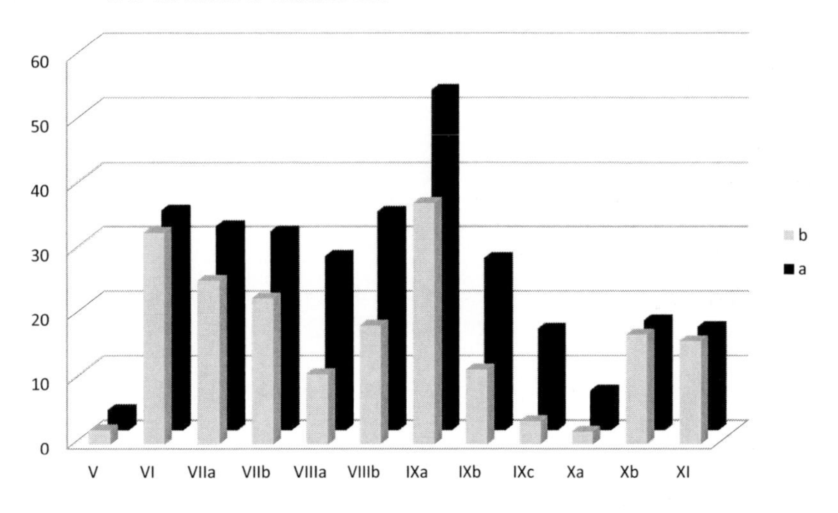


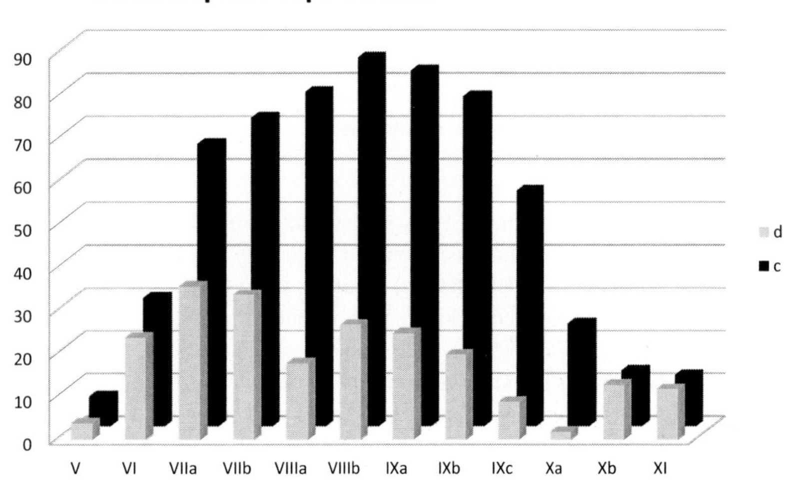


*Fig. 5.5 Central Gaulish group III, including Cinnamus, in adjusted coin-dated deposits. Key as Fig 5.3.*

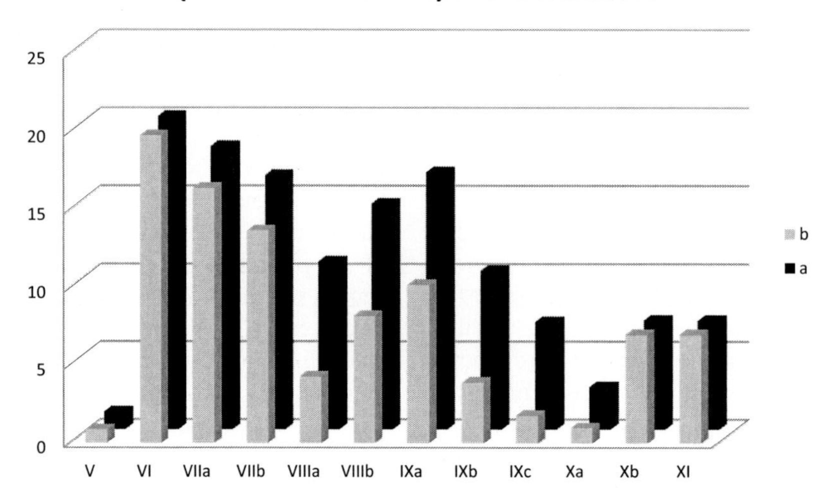


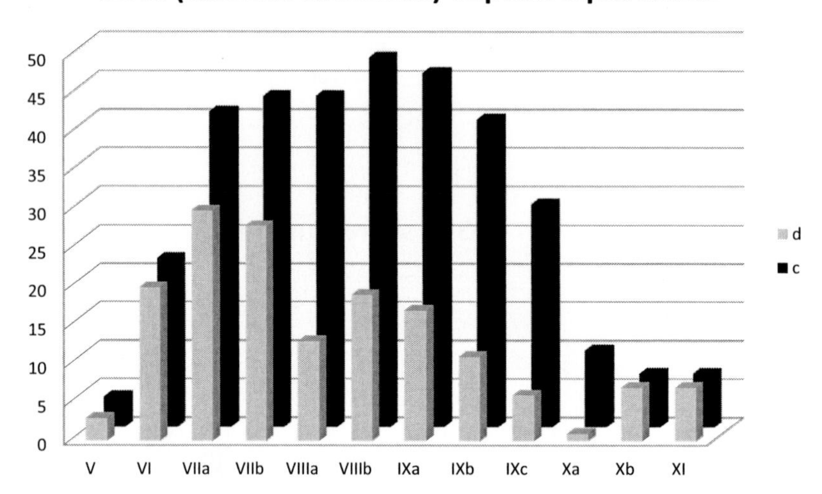


*Fig. 5.6 Central Gaulish group III, without Cinnamus, in adjusted coin-dated deposits. Key as Fig 5.3.*

The phenomenon of the two peaks may be an artificial effect due to the relative lack of Commodan (VIIb) coins (displaced by a period to VIIIa because of the calculation of dates of loss), although it has to be admitted that the precise reason is difficult to discern. It seems unlikely that there were two peaks in production of the pottery, since CG IV is affected in the same way, but the possibility exists of there being two peaks in the disposal deposits used for the gazetteer.

When Cinnamus (i.e. his main styles, to be distinguished from his early style, which has been counted separately and included in the general CG III listing) is added to CG III the 'later' peak is accentuated in Fig. 5.5**a** & **b**, but remains virtually unaltered in Fig. 5.5**c** & **d**. It seems possible that the bulk of this potter's output is late in terms of overall CG III production, and that Cinnamus's main styles occupy a border-line position between CG III and CG IV.

CG IV (Fig. 5.7) is in many ways similar to CG III - there are two peaks in periods VI and VIIIb and a general date-range of Aurelius-230s/240s. There are also distortions, which add greatly to the sherd numbers in periods VI (A 131, Wroxeter) and VIIIb (A 90, London). These are smoothed out in the deposit-equivalent count, and Fig. 4.3 in fact shows that there are some significant differences between CG III and CG IV, in that the latter is more heavily represented in well-dated deposits of periods VIIb-IXb than the former, which is conversely better represented in periods VI-VIIb. Thus, if deposit-equivalent counts really do give a clearer picture of the chronology, the bulk of CG III pottery is being deposited in the late second century, while that of CG IV is mainly early third century, up to the 240s. There is also a considerable representation of CG IV in periods Xb-XI, probably more than can be accounted for by residuality alone, and the survival of vessels into those periods is an active possibility. If this is so, the trough in period Xa is accounted for by the lack of IXc coins (displaced due to the dates of loss calculation).

When we turn to those individual CG potters sufficiently well represented to merit separate tabulation (Fig. 5.8), it seems, not unnaturally, that in general they are representative of their groups. Criciro has an earlier profile than the other CG III potters, particularly Cinnamus, who stands out from the other CG III potters by virtue of a strong late representation, as pointed out earlier. Sacer-Attianus, the only CG II potter group given here, has, on the face of it, a later profile than Criciro, although still well within the CG II overall grouping. However, Sacer-Attianus is often found in late deposits and occurs surprisingly frequently in association with potters such as Cinnamus (see below). It may be that this potter group, particularly Attianus, who is thought to be the later of the two, was in fact working later than usually considered, perhaps being on the border line between CG II and CG III. Advocisus seems to have an earlier profile than the other CG IV potters, and may be early in the group. The others all conform to the main CG IV pattern, especially when the deposit-equivalent graphs are compared. Of note is the anomalous period VI representation for Paternus II sherds, due to A 131, Wroxeter, and the unusual profile for Iullinus who is only represented in well-dated deposits.

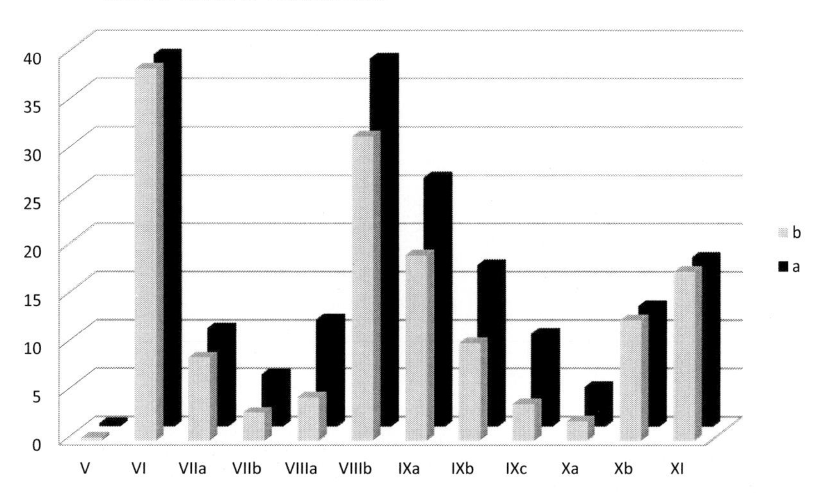


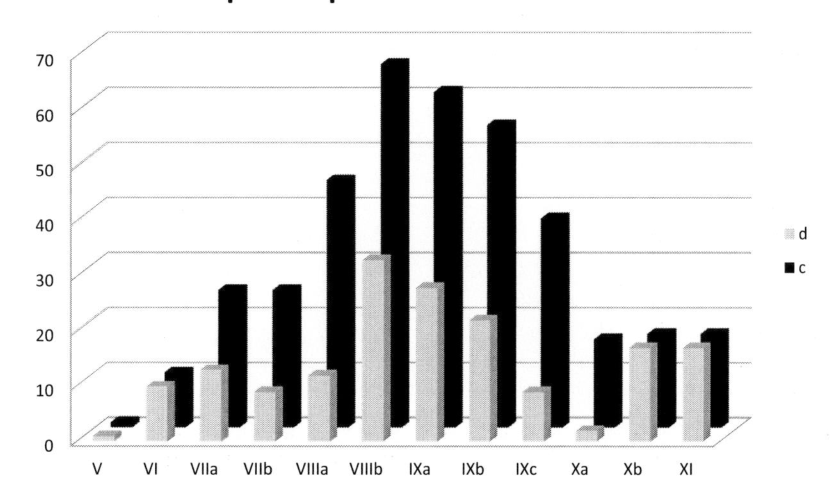


*Fig. 5.7 Central Gaulish group IV, in adjusted coin-dated deposits. Key as Fig 5.3.*

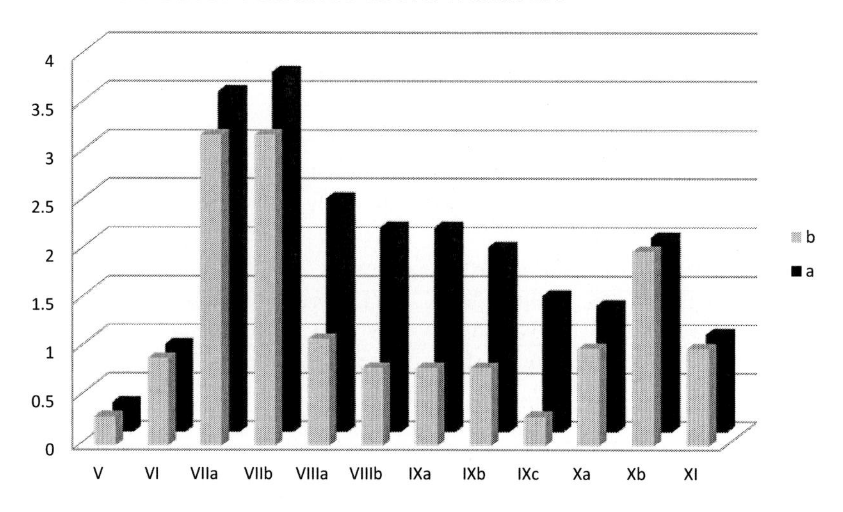
CG Sacer-Attianus sherd numbers
4
3.5
3
2.5
2
1.5
1
0.5
0
V
VI
VIIa
VIIb
VIIIa
VIIIb
IXa
IXb
IXc
Xa
Xb
XI
b
a

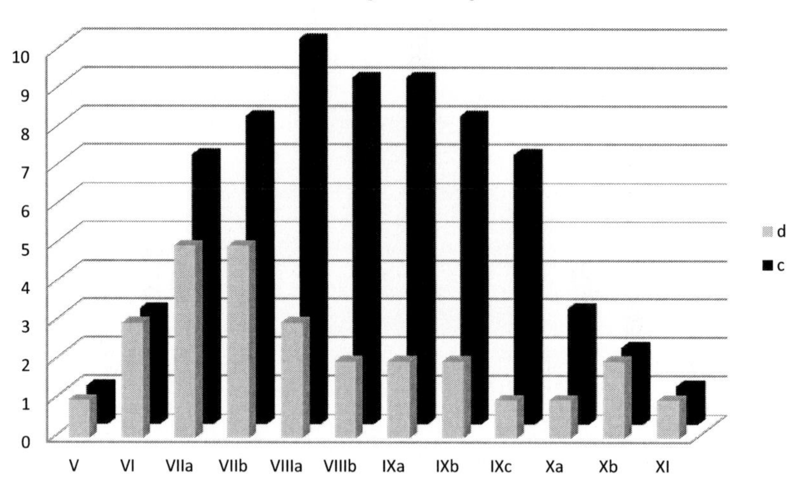
CG Sacer-Attianus deposit equivalents
10
9
8
7
6
5
4
3
2
1
0
V
VI
VIIa
VIIb
VIIIa
VIIIb
IXa
IXb
IXc
Xa
Xb
XI
d
c

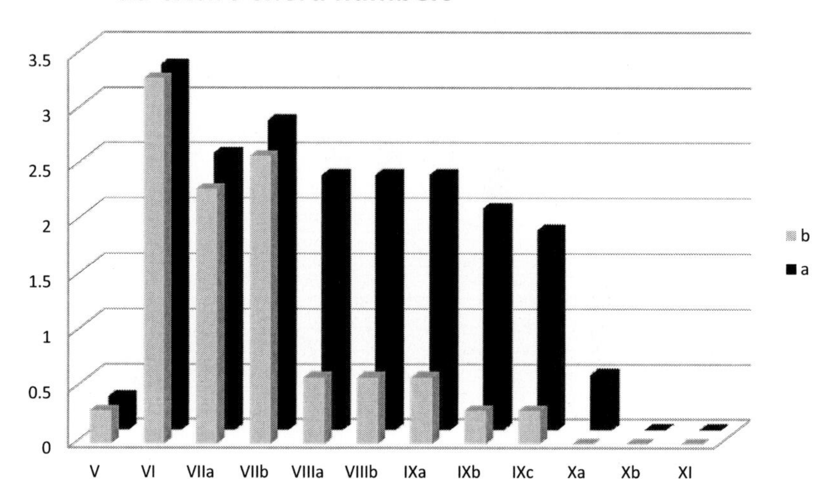
CG Criciro sherd numbers
3.5
3
2.5
2
1.5
1
0.5
0
V
VI
VIIa
VIIb
VIIIa
VIIIb
IXa
IXb
IXc
Xa
Xb
XI
b
a

*Fig. 5.8*

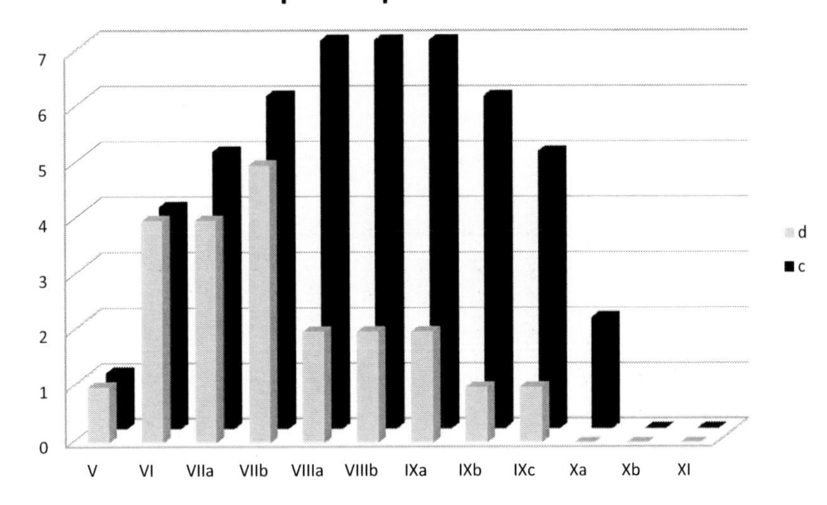
CG Criciro deposit equivalents
7
6
5
4
3
2
1
0
V
VI
VIIa
VIIb
VIIIa
VIIIb
IXa
IXb
IXc
Xa
Xb
XI
d
c

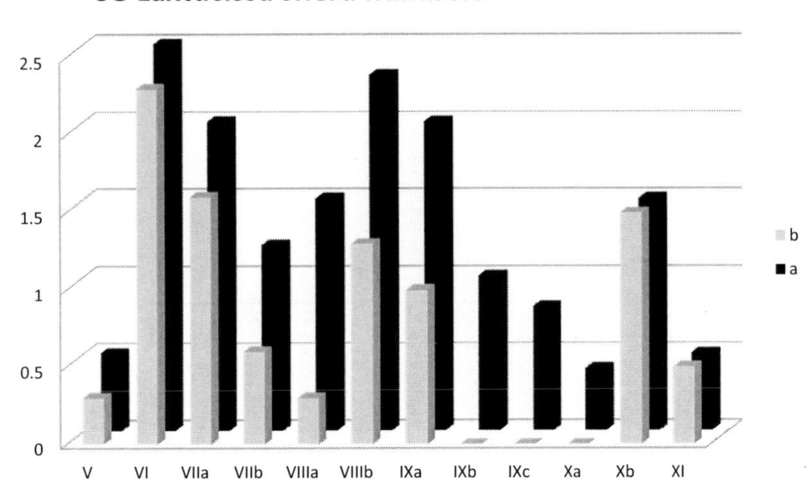
CG Laxtucissa sherd numbers
2.5
2
1.5
1
0.5
0
V
VI
VIIa
VIIb
VIIIa
VIIIb
IXa
IXb
IXc
Xa
Xb
XI
b
a

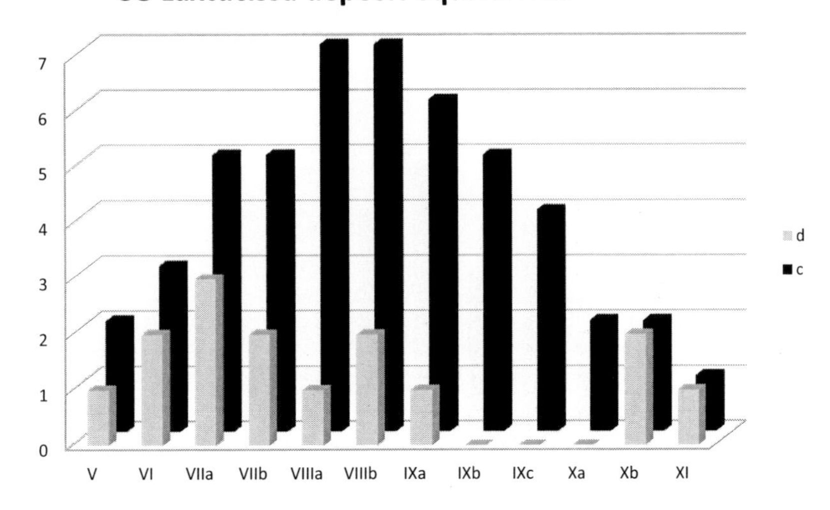
CG Laxtucissa deposit equivalents
7
6
5
4
3
2
1
0
V
VI
VIIa
VIIb
VIIIa
VIIIb
IXa
IXb
IXc
Xa
Xb
XI
d
c

*Fig. 5.8 Cont.*

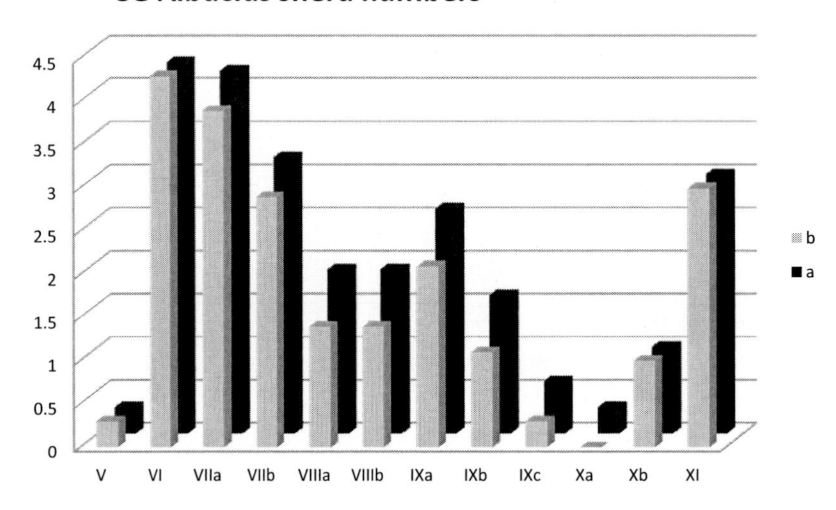
CG Albucius sherd numbers
4.5
4
3.5
3
2.5
2
1.5
1
0.5
0
V
VI
VIIa
VIIb
VIIIa
VIIIb
IXa
IXb
IXc
Xa
Xb
XI
b
a

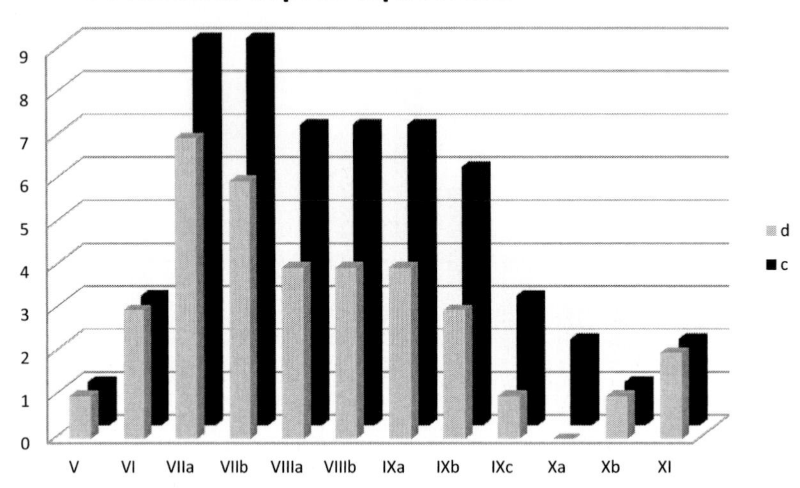
CG Albucius deposit equivalents
9
8
7
6
5
4
3
2
1
0
V
VI
VIIa
VIIb
VIIIa
VIIIb
IXa
IXb
IXc
Xa
Xb
XI
d
c

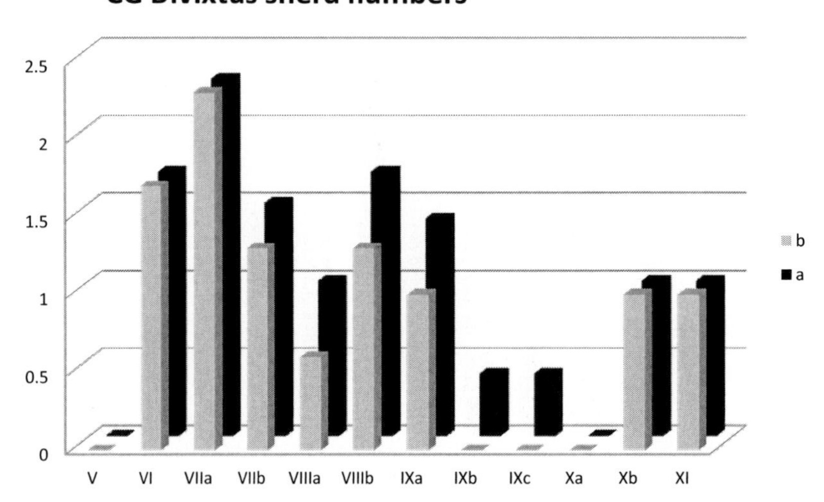
CG Divixtus sherd numbers
2.5
2
1.5
1
0.5
0
V
VI
VIIa
VIIb
VIIIa
VIIIb
IXa
IXb
IXc
Xa
Xb
XI
b
a

*Fig. 5.8 Cont.*

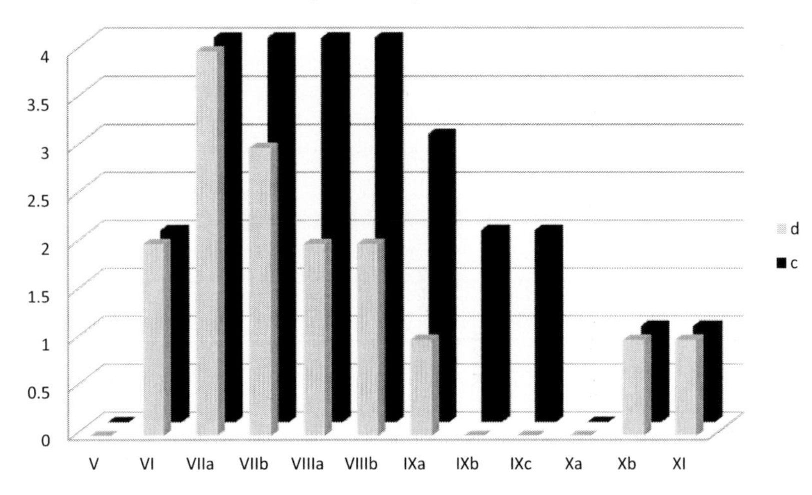
CG Divixtus deposit equivalents
4
3.5
3
2.5
2
1.5
1
0.5
0
V VI VIIa VIIb VIIIa VIIIb IXa IXb IXc Xa Xb XI
d
c

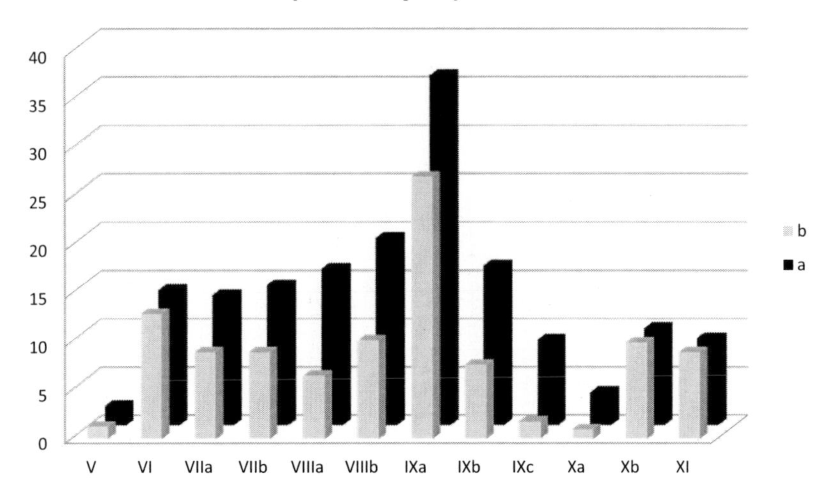
CG Cinnamus (main styles) sherd numbers
40
35
30
25
20
15
10
5
0
V VI VIIa VIIb VIIIa VIIIb IXa IXb IXc Xa Xb XI
b
a

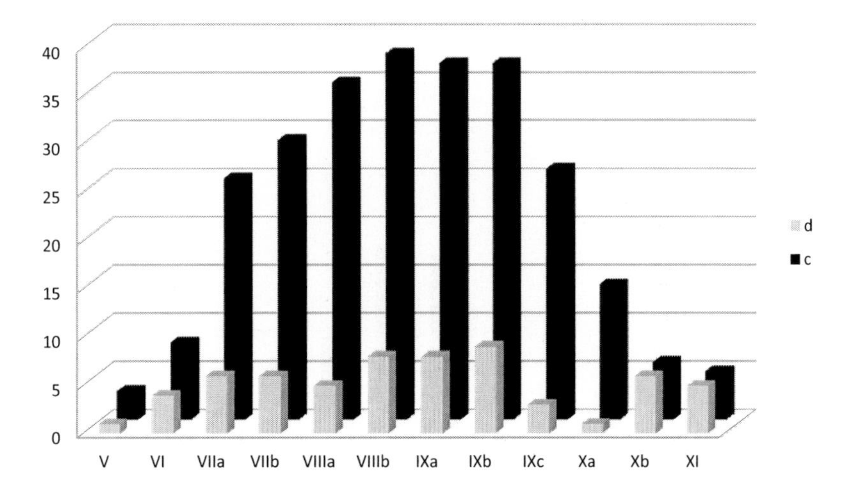
CG Cinnamus (main styles) deposit equivalents
40
35
30
25
20
15
10
5
0
V VI VIIa VIIb VIIIa VIIIb IXa IXb IXc Xa Xb XI
d
c

*Fig. 5.8 Cont.*

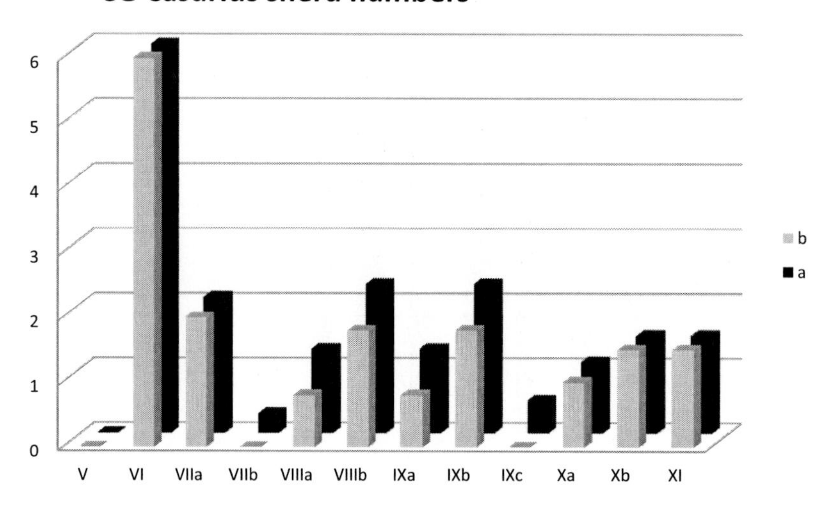
CG Casurius sherd numbers
6
5
4
3
2
1
0
V
VI
VIIa
VIIb
VIIIa
VIIIb
IXa
IXb
IXc
Xa
Xb
XI
b
a

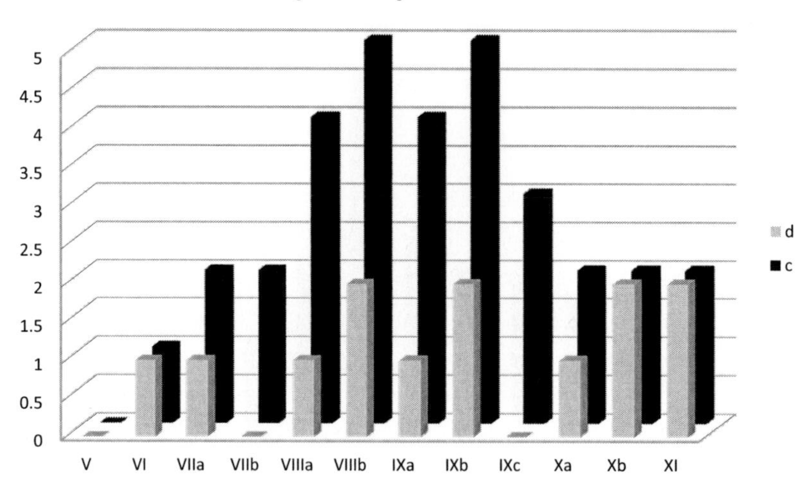
CG Casurius deposit equivalents
5
4.5
4
3.5
3
2.5
2
1.5
1
0.5
0
V
VI
VIIa
VIIb
VIIIa
VIIIb
IXa
IXb
IXc
Xa
Xb
XI
d
c

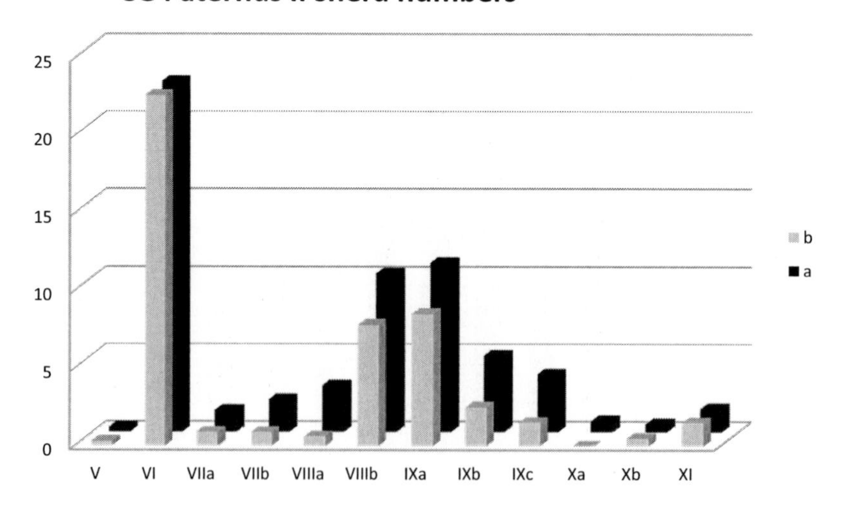
CG Paternus II sherd numbers
25
20
15
10
5
0
V
VI
VIIa
VIIb
VIIIa
VIIIb
IXa
IXb
IXc
Xa
Xb
XI
b
a

*Fig. 5.8 Cont.*

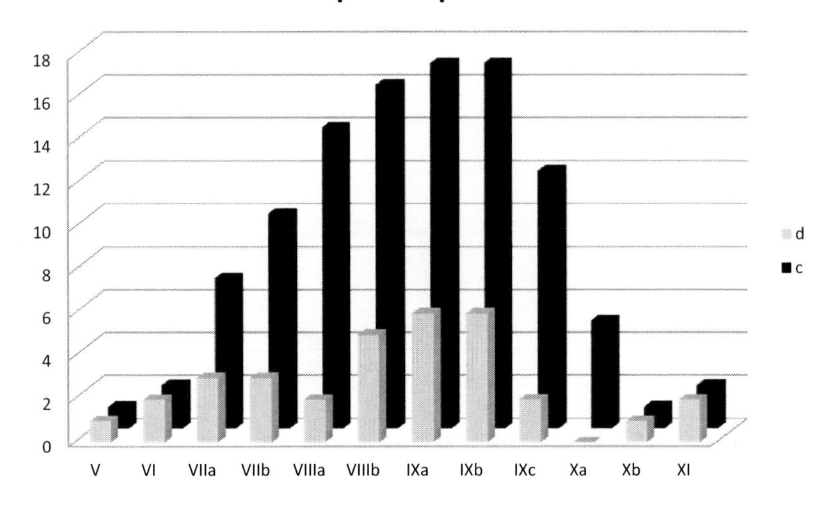
CG Paternus II deposit equivalents
18
16
14
12
10
8
6
4
2
0
d
c
V VI VIIa VIIb VIIIa VIIIb IXa IXb IXc Xa Xb XI

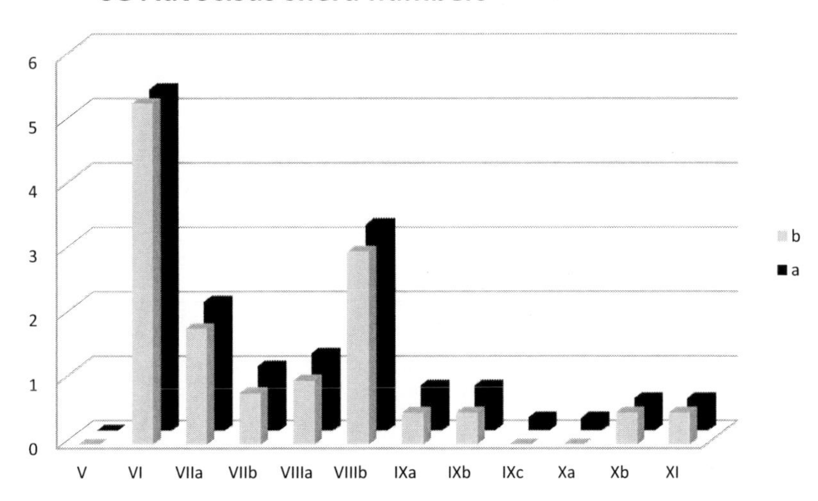
CG Advocisus sherd numbers
6
5
4
3
2
1
0
b
a
V VI VIIa VIIb VIIIa VIIIb IXa IXb IXc Xa Xb XI

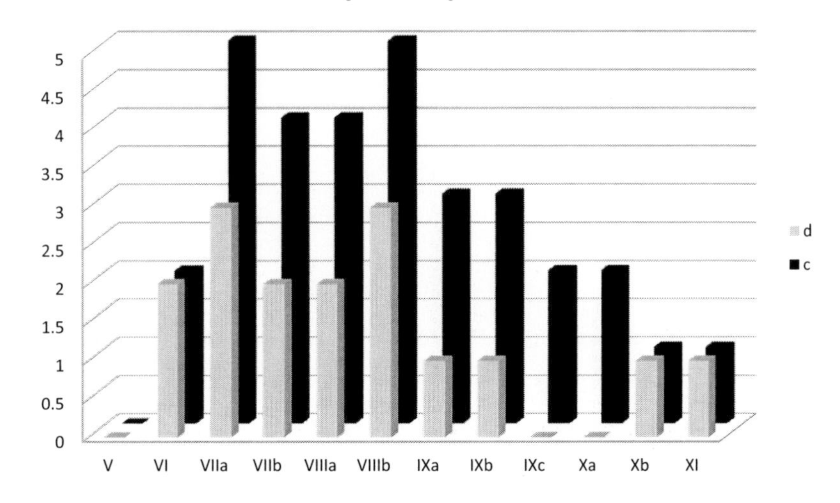
CG Advocisus deposit equivalents
5
4.5
4
3.5
3
2.5
2
1.5
1
0.5
0
d
c
V VI VIIa VIIb VIIIa VIIIb IXa IXb IXc Xa Xb XI

*Fig. 5.8 Cont.*

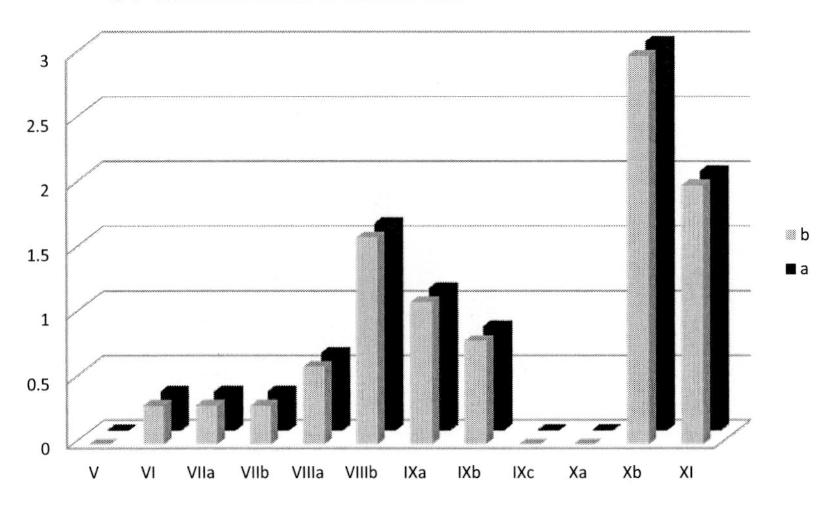
CG Iullinus sherd numbers
3
2.5
2
1.5
1
0.5
0
V
VI
VIIa
VIIb
VIIIa
VIIIb
IXa
IXb
IXc
Xa
Xb
XI
b
a

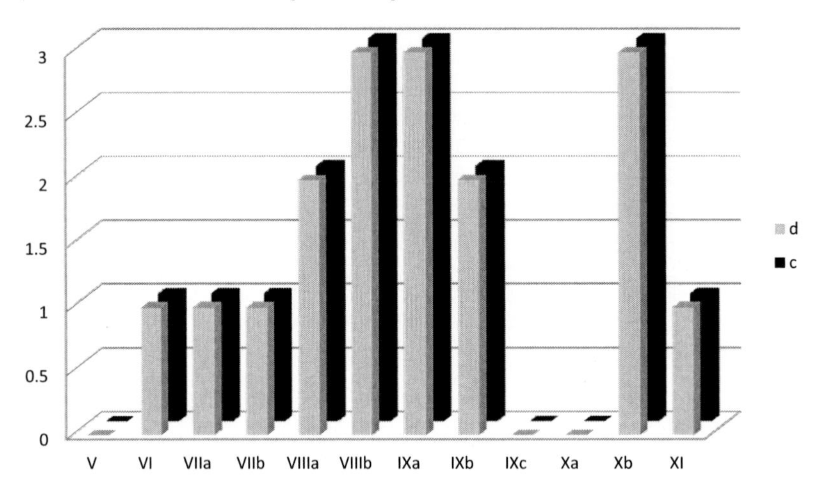
CG Iullinus deposit equivalents
3
2.5
2
1.5
1
0.5
0
V
VI
VIIa
VIIb
VIIIa
VIIIb
IXa
IXb
IXc
Xa
Xb
XI
d
c

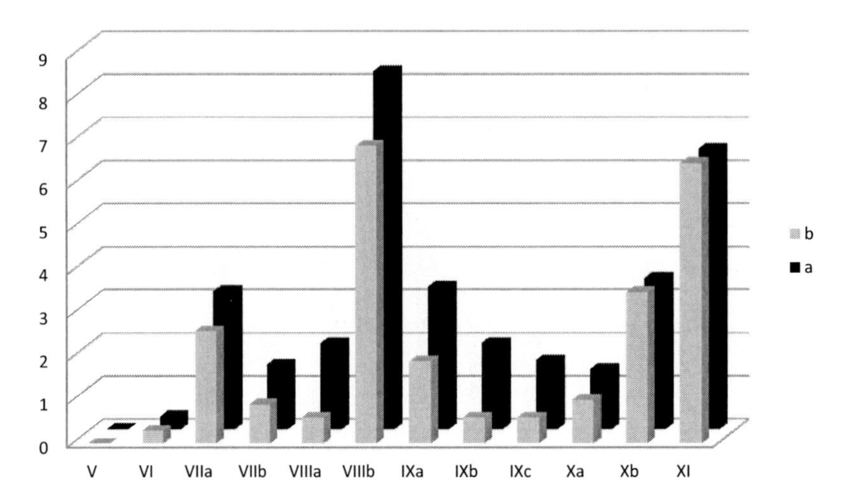
CG Doeccus sherd numbers
9
8
7
6
5
4
3
2
1
0
V
VI
VIIa
VIIb
VIIIa
VIIIb
IXa
IXb
IXc
Xa
Xb
XI
b
a

*Fig. 5.8 Cont.*

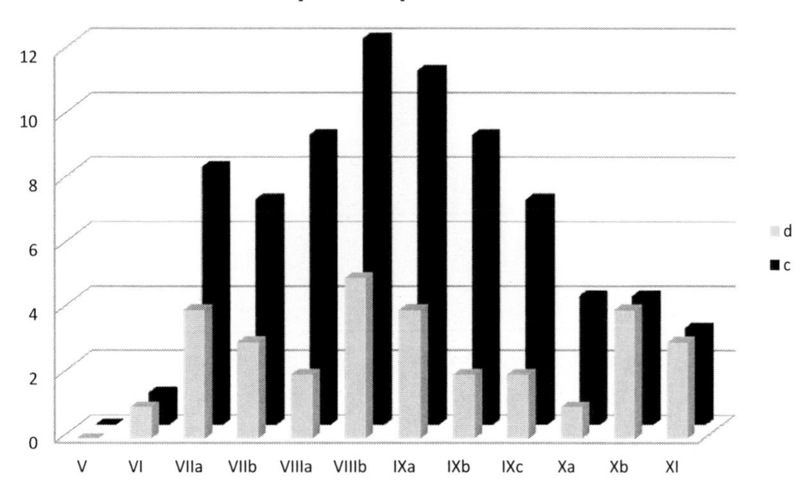


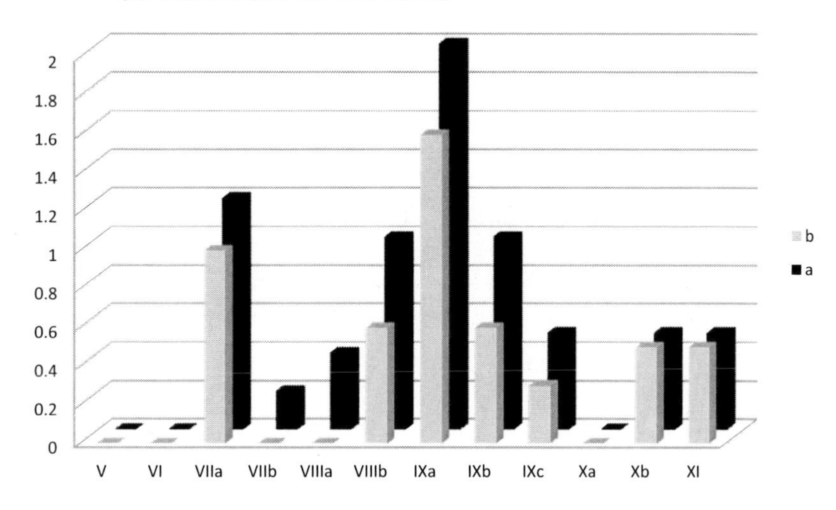


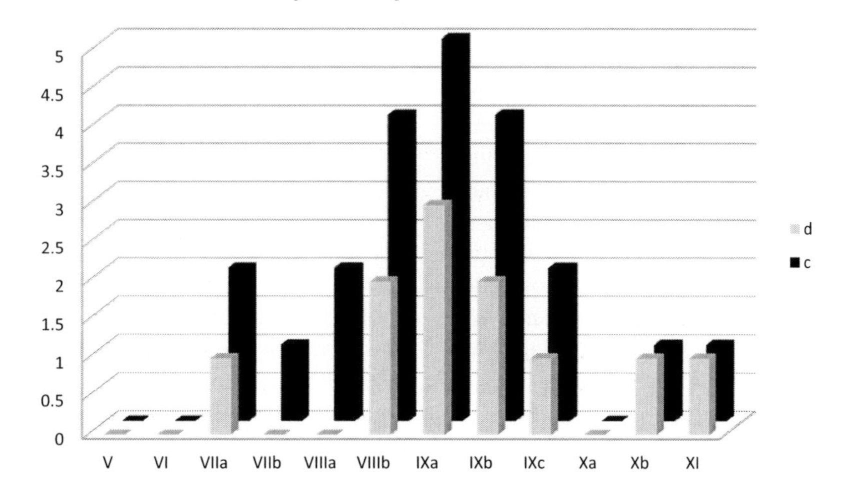


*Fig. 5.8 Central Gaulish profiles for individual potters. Key as Fig. 5.3.*

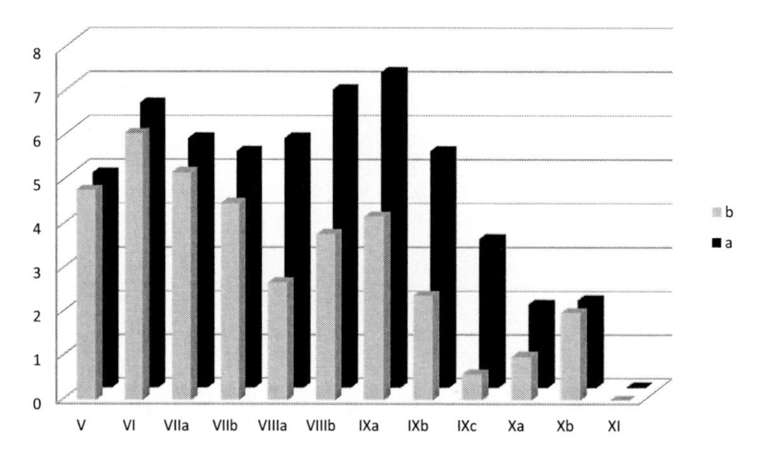


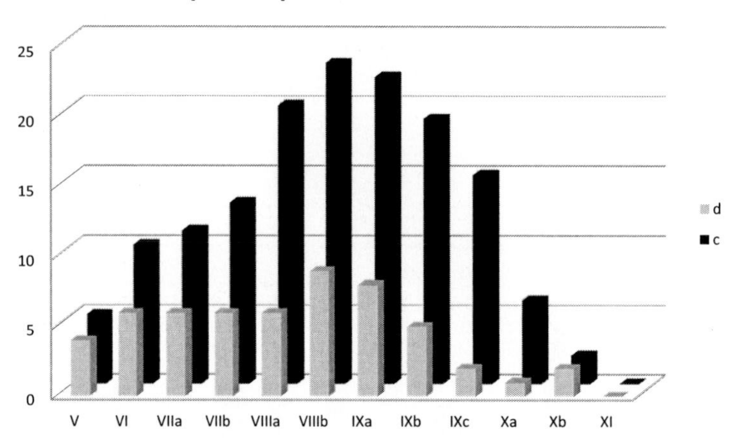


*Fig. 5.9 Rheinzabern group Ia, in adjusted coin-dated deposits. **a** number of sherds per coin-period; **b** as a but well-dated deposits only; **c** number of deposit-equivalents per coin-period; **d** as c but well-dated deposits only.*

RHEINZABERN

Rheinzabern is strikingly different from CG (Figs 5.9-5.13). Only Rh la has relative numbers in the early periods that approach CG and this group is clearly differentiated from the later ones. In part this is due to strong representation of Rh la in a number of British deposits of this period, and also to the clear chronological division of Rh into those potters operating before the foundation of Regensburg legionary fortress in the 170s (i.e. Rh la) and those after (i.e. Rh Ib-III; cf. B 146-8). Rh Ib-III are all similar to one another, and have definite peaks (especially Rh IIa, which closely resembles the statistician's normal curve). Rh Ib peaks in period VIIIb, while the others peak in period IXa. Of interest is the observation that the picture painted by the unadjusted coin dates (Table 5.III) in which Rh Ib seemed to be later than IIa, is apparently changed about in the adjusted figures. The sherd number and deposit equivalent graphs are similar to each other in all cases, except Rh la where the high early representation has been smoothed away to a certain extent in Fig. 5.9**c** & **d**. It would seem that Rh Ib-III pottery is primarily of early third century date, and that the conventional divisions may represent stylistic groupings rather than chronological divisions, with the exception of Rh la. Of course, an alternative interpretation is that the chronological system used here is not sufficiently precise to separate out the chronological divisions between the groupings, if it is assumed that they succeeded each other fairly rapidly.

The general period of fall-off is period IXc, with in some cases a revival in period Xb. There is little evidence, unlike CG, for survival/residuality into period XI and later, but there are few deposits of this period in the areas where Rheinzabern is best represented. Rh III maintains a reasonable representation until period Xb, and does not have an intervening trough. This may indicate a distinct chronological difference, with Rheinzabern late products being generally in use until this period. Because of the compactness of the graphs, Rheinzabern products can probably be more accurately dated than those of CG.

Individual Rheinzabern potters, like those of CG, conform to their groups (Fig. 5.14). Janu I and particularly Reginus I (Rh la) have significant early representation, while the

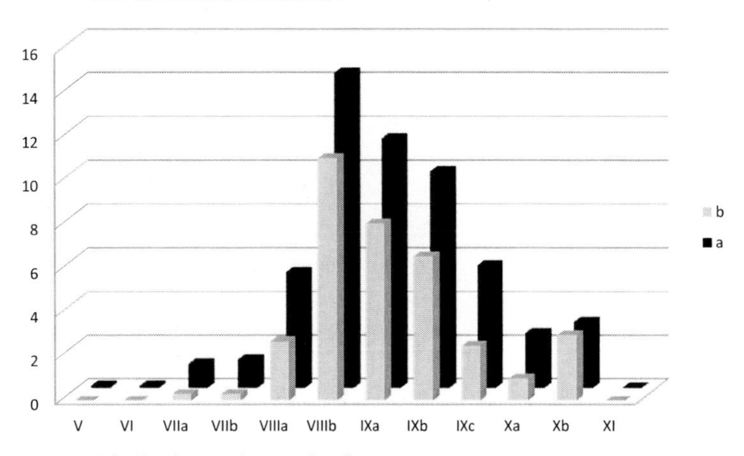


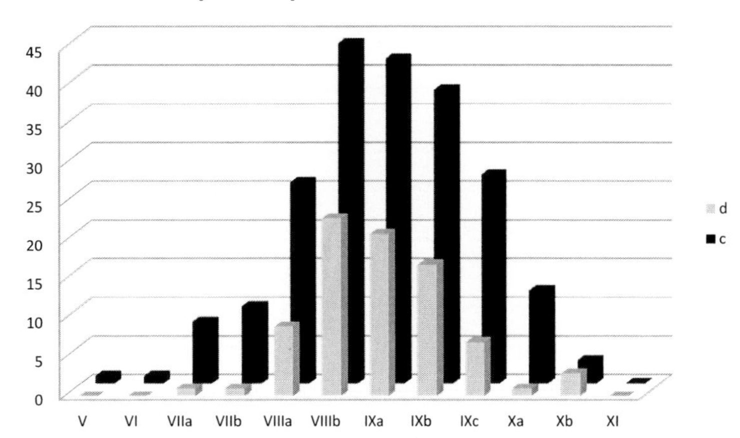


*Fig. 5.10 Rheinzabern group Ib, in adjusted coin-dated deposits. Key as Fig 5.9.*

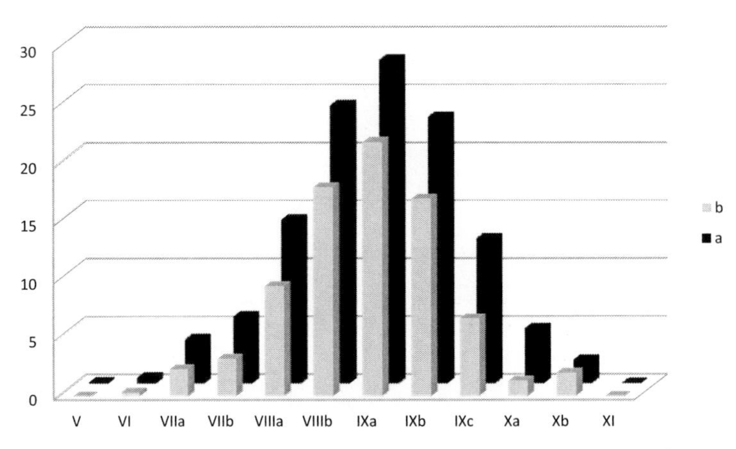


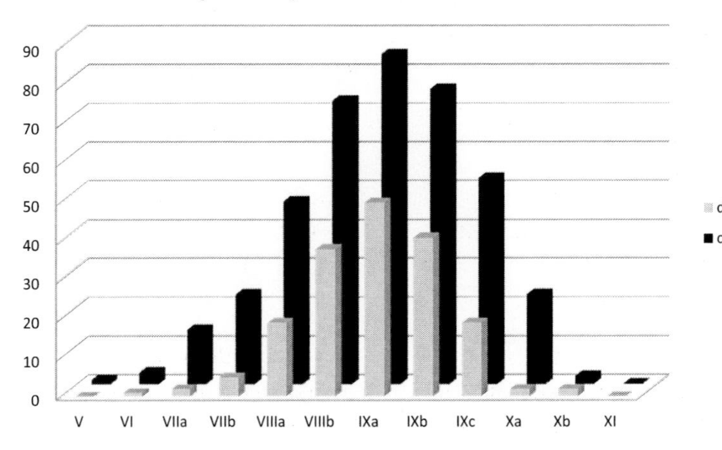


*Fig. 5.11 Rheinzabern group IIa, in adjusted coin-dated deposits. Key as Fig 5.9.*

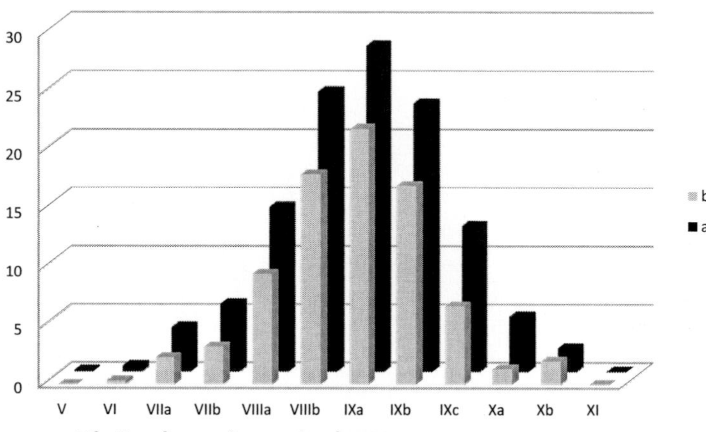


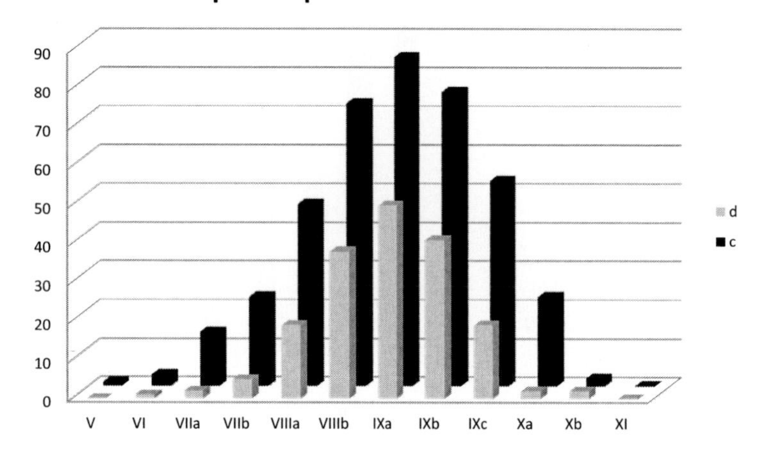


*Fig. 5.12 Rheinzabern group IIb-c, in adjusted coin-dated deposits. Key as Fig 5.9.*

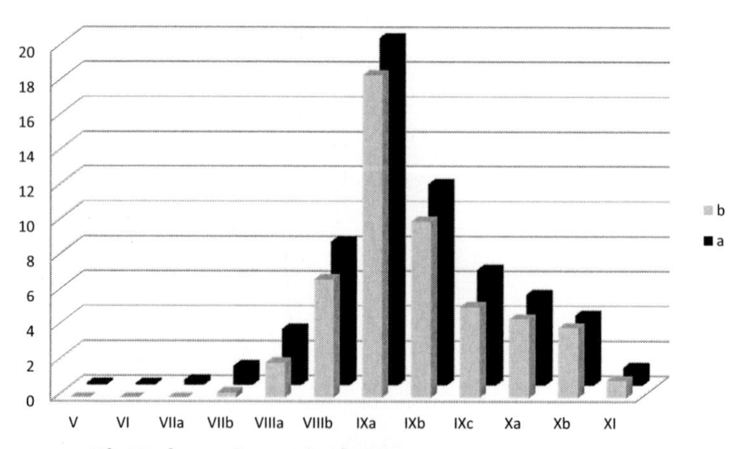


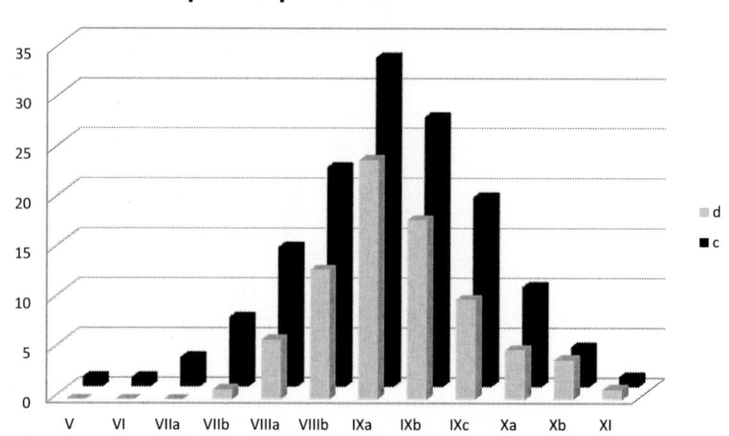


*Fig. 5.13 Rheinzabern group III, in adjusted coin-dated deposits. Key as Fig 5.9.*

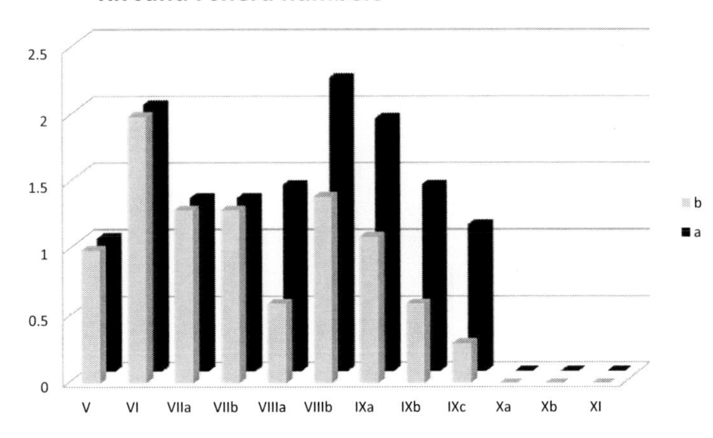


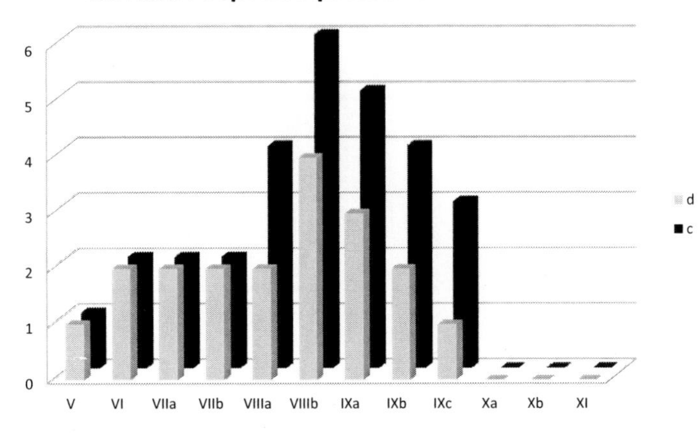


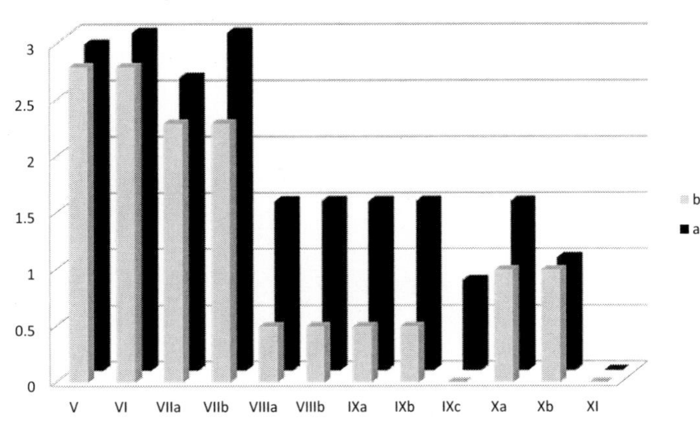


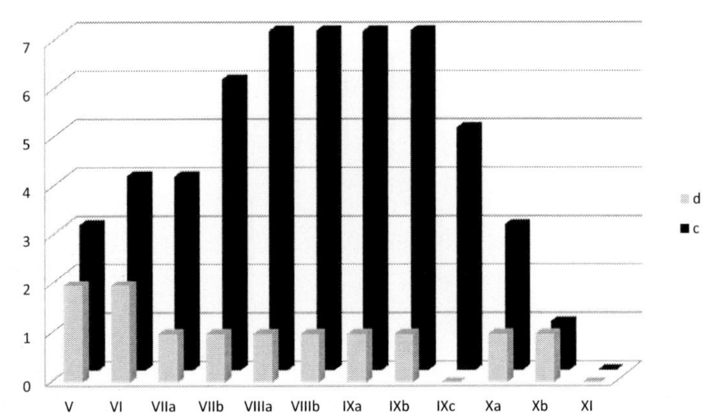


*Fig. 5.14 (continued on next page)*

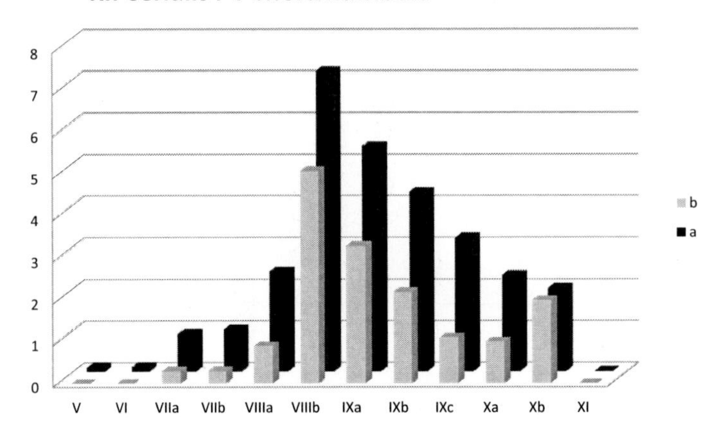
Rh Cerialis I-V sherd numbers
8
7
6
5
4
3
2
1
0
V VI VIIa VIIb VIIIa VIIIb IXa IXb IXc Xa Xb XI
b
a

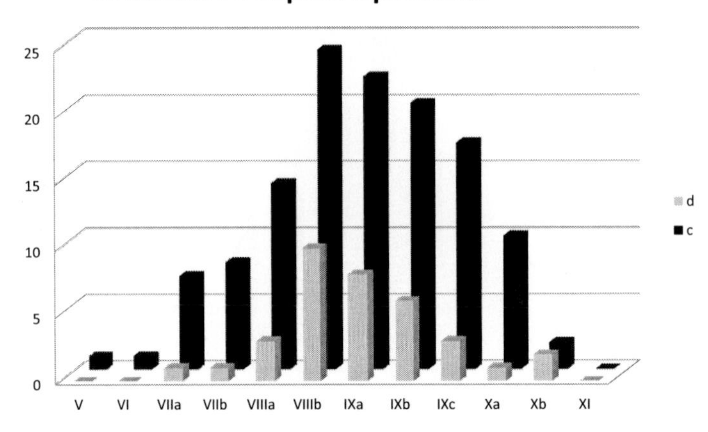
Rh Cerialis I-V deposit equivalents
25
20
15
10
5
0
V VI VIIa VIIb VIIIa VIIIb IXa IXb IXc Xa Xb XI
d
c

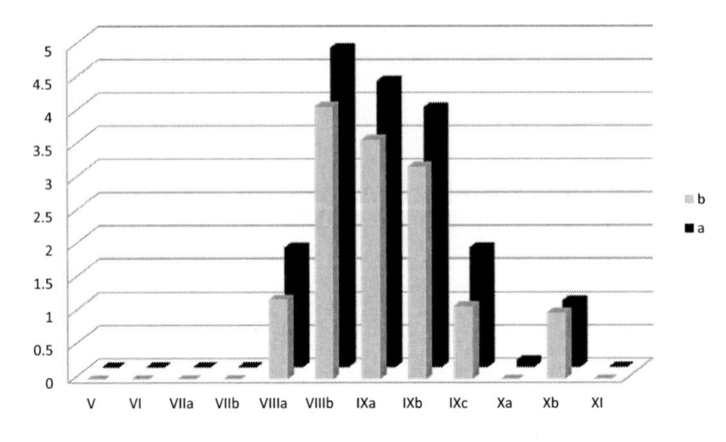
Rh Comitialis II-III sherd numbers
5
4.5
4
3.5
3
2.5
2
1.5
1
0.5
0
V VI VIIa VIIb VIIIa VIIIb IXa IXb IXc Xa Xb XI
b
a

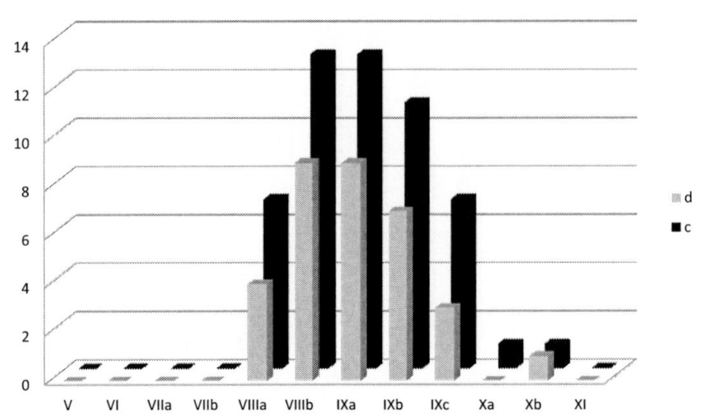
Rh Comitialis II-III deposit equivalents
14
12
10
8
6
4
2
0
V VI VIIa VIIb VIIIa VIIIb IXa IXb IXc Xa Xb XI
d
c

*Fig. 5.14 (cont,)*

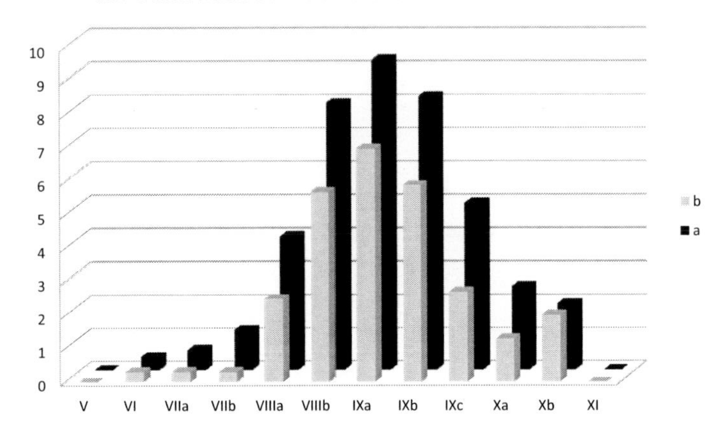
Rh Comitialis IV-VI sherd numbers
10
9
8
7
6
5
4
3
2
1
0
V
VI
VIIa
VIIb
VIIIa
VIIIb
IXa
IXb
IXc
Xa
Xb
XI
b
a

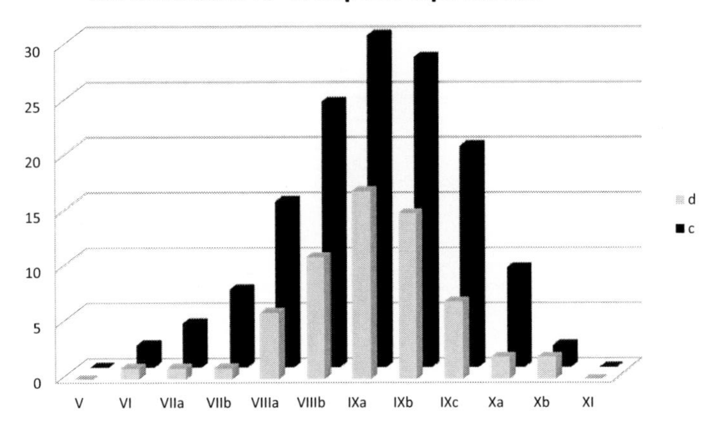
Rh Comitialis IV-VI deposit equivalents
30
25
20
15
10
5
0
V
VI
VIIa
VIIb
VIIIa
VIIIb
IXa
IXb
IXc
Xa
Xb
XI
d
c

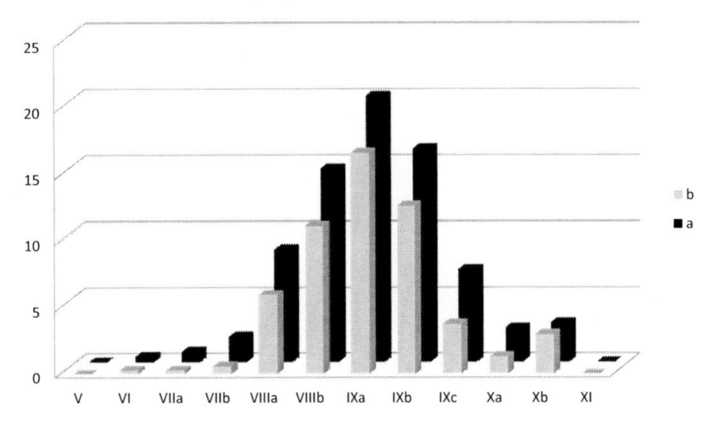
Rh Comitialis (all) sherd numbers
25
20
15
10
5
0
V
VI
VIIa
VIIb
VIIIa
VIIIb
IXa
IXb
IXc
Xa
Xb
XI
b
a

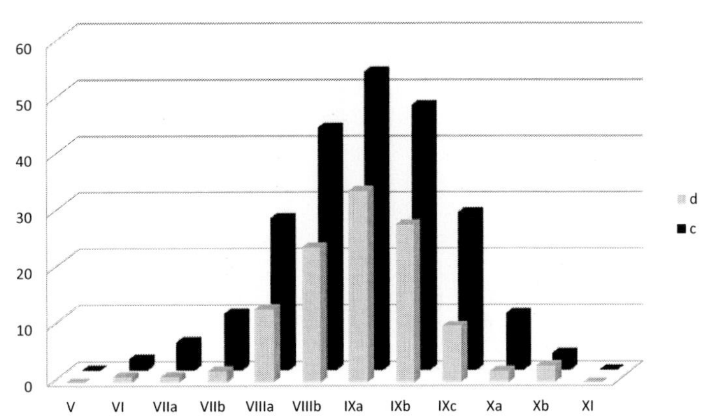
Rh Comitialis (all) deposit equivalents
60
50
40
30
20
10
0
V
VI
VIIa
VIIb
VIIIa
VIIIb
IXa
IXb
IXc
Xa
Xb
XI
d
c

*Fig. 5.14 (cont,)*

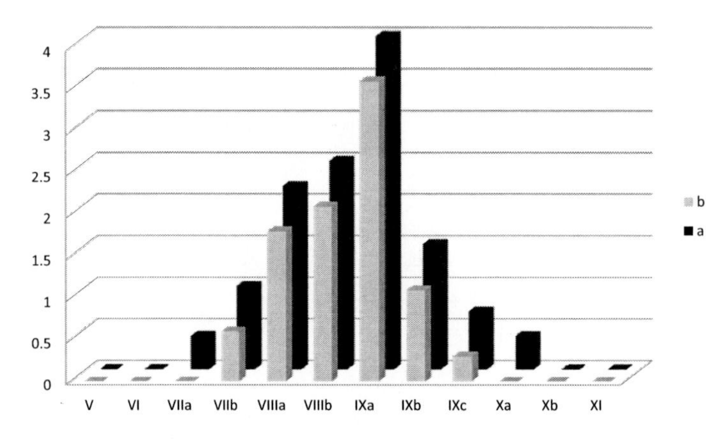
Rh B F Attoni sherd numbers
4
3.5
3
2.5
2
1.5
1
0.5
0
V VI VIIa VIIb VIIIa VIIIb IXa IXb IXc Xa Xb XI
b
a

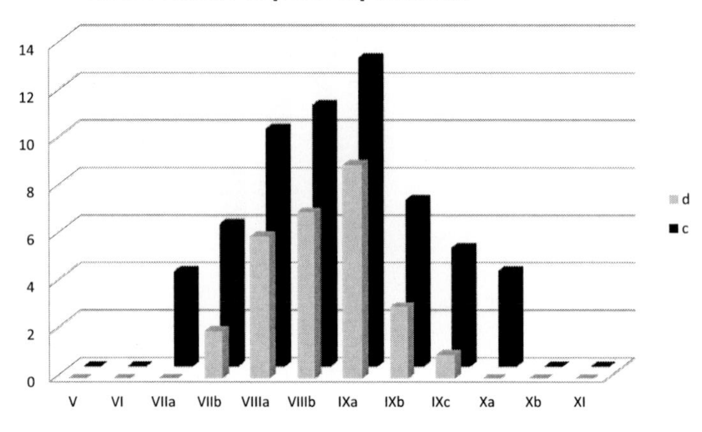
Rh B F Attoni deposit equivalents
14
12
10
8
6
4
2
0
V VI VIIa VIIb VIIIa VIIIb IXa IXb IXc Xa Xb XI
d
c

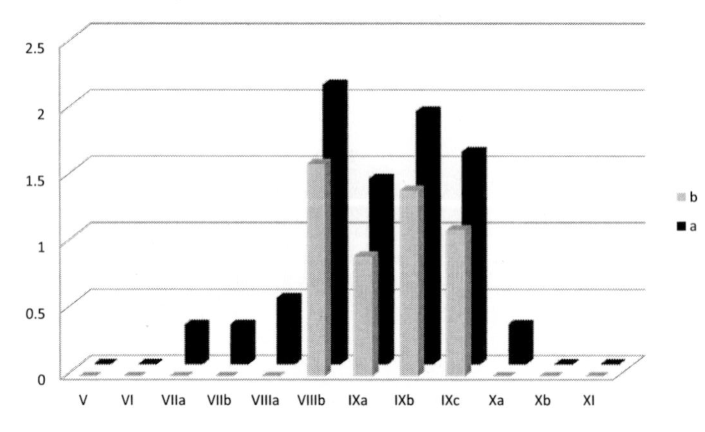
Rh E25/26 sherd numbers
2.5
2
1.5
1
0.5
0
V VI VIIa VIIb VIIIa VIIIb IXa IXb IXc Xa Xb XI
b
a

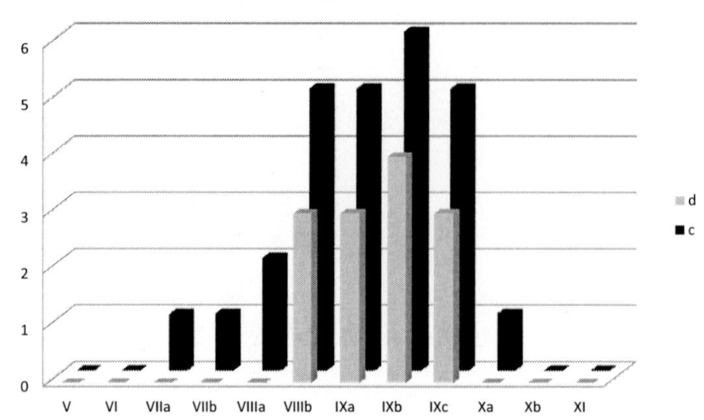
Rh E25/26 deposit equivalents
6
5
4
3
2
1
0
V VI VIIa VIIb VIIIa VIIIb IXa IXb IXc Xa Xb XI
d
c

*Fig. 5.14 (cont,)*

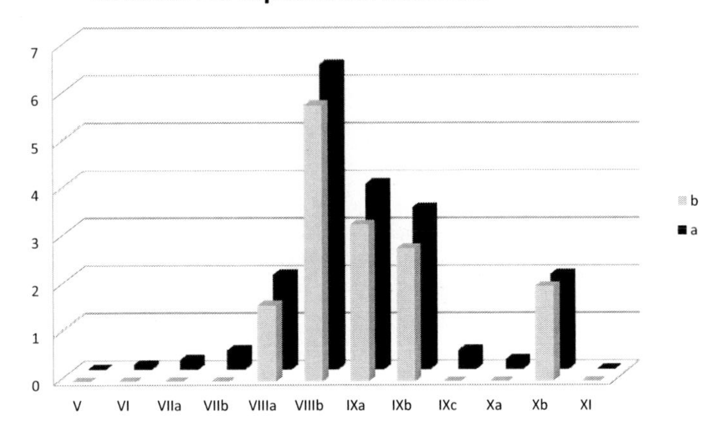
Rh Julius I & Lupus sherd numbers
7
6
5
4
3
2
1
0
V VI VIIa VIIb VIIIa VIIIb IXa IXb IXc Xa Xb XI
b
a

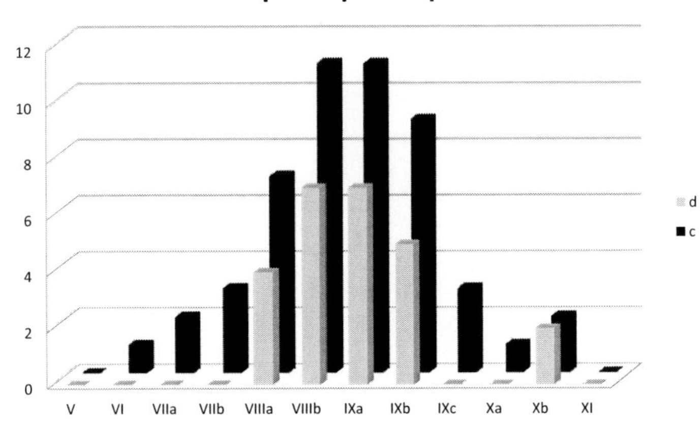
Rh Julius I & Lupus deposit equivalents
12
10
8
6
4
2
0
V VI VIIa VIIb VIIIa VIIIb IXa IXb IXc Xa Xb XI
d
c

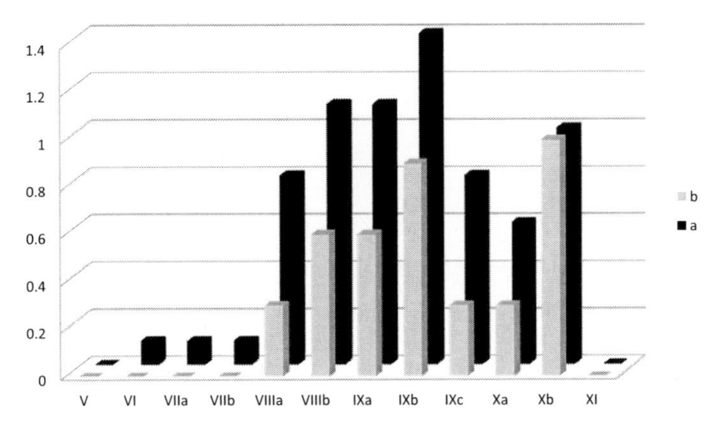
Rh Helenius sherd numbers
1.4
1.2
1
0.8
0.6
0.4
0.2
0
V VI VIIa VIIb VIIIa VIIIb IXa IXb IXc Xa Xb XI
b
a

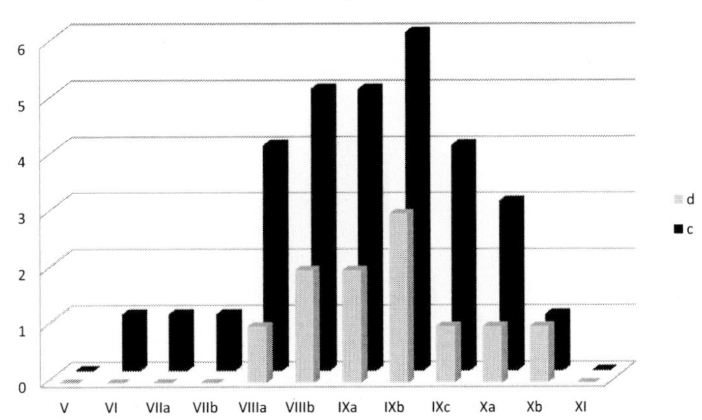
Rh Helenius deposit equivalents
6
5
4
3
2
1
0
V VI VIIa VIIb VIIIa VIIIb IXa IXb IXc Xa Xb XI
d
c

*Fig. 5.14 (cont,)*

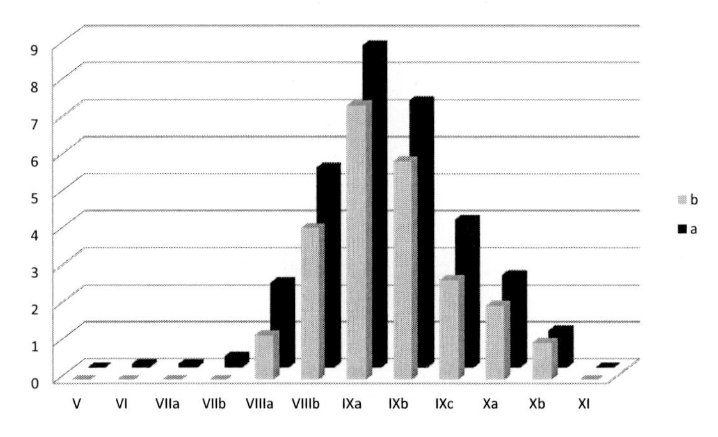
Rh Primitivus I-IV sherd numbers
9
8
7
6
5
4
3
2
1
0
V VI VIIa VIIb VIIIa VIIIb IXa IXb IXc Xa Xb XI
b
a

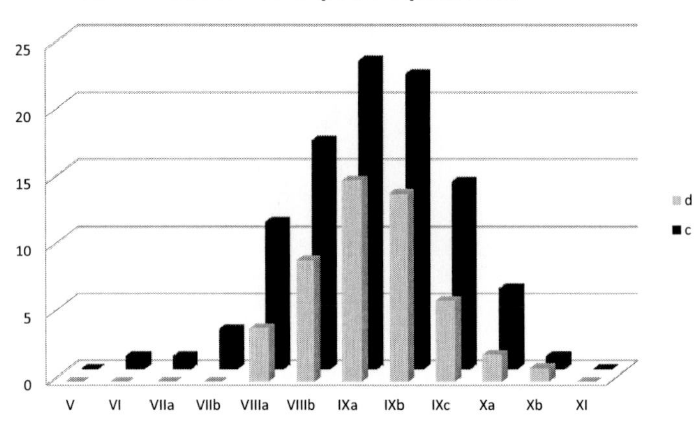
Rh Primitivus I-IV deposit equivalents
25
20
15
10
5
0
V VI VIIa VIIb VIIIa VIIIb IXa IXb IXc Xa Xb XI
d
c

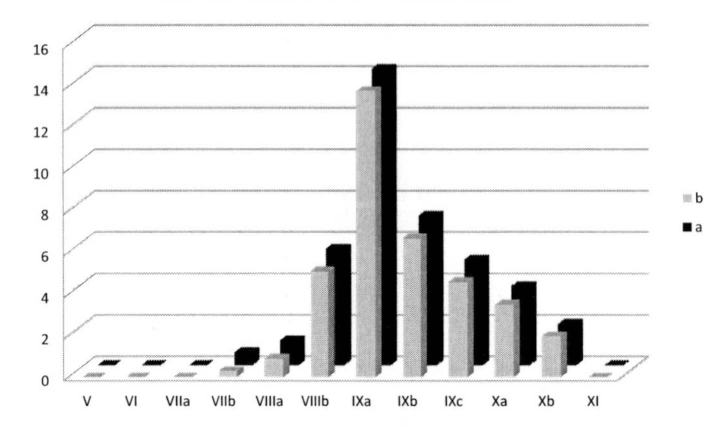
Rh Julius II-Julianus I sherd numbers
16
14
12
10
8
6
4
2
0
V VI VIIa VIIb VIIIa VIIIb IXa IXb IXc Xa Xb XI
b
a

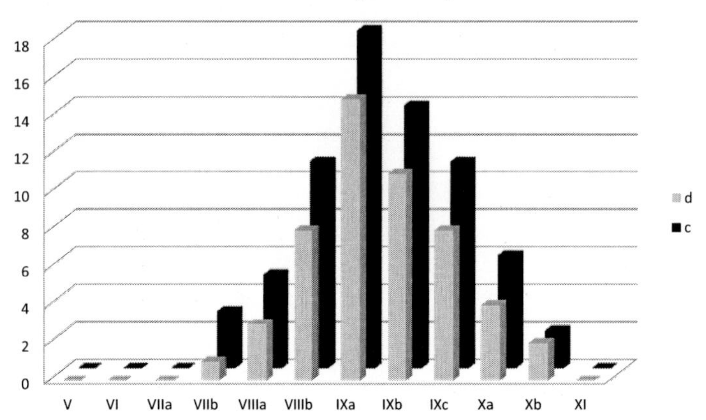
Rh Julius II-Julianus I deposit equivalents
18
16
14
12
10
8
6
4
2
0
V VI VIIa VIIb VIIIa VIIIb IXa IXb IXc Xa Xb XI
d
c

*Fig. 5.14 (cont,)*

Rh Janu II sherd numbers

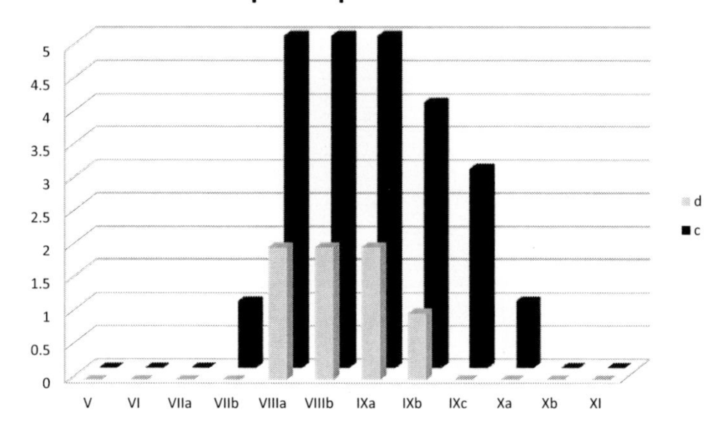


*Fig. 5.14 Rheinzabern profiles for individual potters. Key as Fig. 5.9.*

others peak in the early third century. Cerialis I-V and Comitialis II-III belong to Rh Ib, and it may be significant that both these potter groups peak in period VIIIb, earlier than those in Rh II-III. This shows that the division between Comitialis II-III and Comitialis IV-VI does seem to have some chronological significance, and that the placing of the latter in Rh Ila is justified. Comitialis was one of the most prolific Rheinzabern potters and falls mainly in the early third century. The Julius I and Lupus group is interesting, in that it has a profile that peaks in period VIIIb, like Cerialis. This potter group is the main constituent of Rh llb, and it may be that this is evidence for Rh IIb being a stylistic grouping (as mooted above) which may in fact be contemporary with or earlier than Rh IIa. The profile for Rh Ib is in fact the one that is most similar to the Julius I and Lupus group, and may give some indication of its relative chronological position. Primitivus I-IV (Rh IIc) and Julius II-Julianus I (Rh IIIa) are the main, apparently late potter groups, and present no anomalies in their profiles. Most of the later potters have virtually no representation in deposits dated to before VIIIa, and are clearly early to mid third century in their chronologies. A profile for Janu II has been included because this potter was moved by Bernhard from an early date stylistically to one in Rh IIIa.[1] The coin associations justify this change, since the profile is of late not early type. However, sherds of Janu II are frequently found with those of early potters such as Janu I and Reginus I (see below), which complicates this particular issue.

### OTHER EAST GAULISH KILN-CENTRES

Trier (Fig. 5.15), although appearing to be straightforward in its adjusted chronology, is not in fact easy to interpret, since it is known that there is a fairly wide chronological spread for Trier products, and the date ranges given here are dominated by a large group, A 158, from Zwammerdam

[1] Bernhard 1981a. This change is supported by Gimber (1999), and by Mees (1994, Fig. 3), in which Janu II is in his Jaccard-group 2 with Julius II-Julianus I, whilst Janu(arius) I is in Jaccard-group 1 with other earlier potters. Kortüm and Mees (1998, Abb. 1 & 4) also place Janu II in a position that is chronologically about a third across their seriation sequence, but not as late as Julius II-Julianus I or other Rh IIIa potters. Bittner (1986, Beil. B & C; 1996) places Janu II early, but with many stylistic links to a range of later potters. Schaub (1996) prefers an earlier date, on the basis of the Sulz cellar (D 95; Table 5.X, Group A), but acknowledges that Janu II is found in deposits ranging up to the mid 3rd century. See the discussion by Huld-Zetsche in Bittner 1986, 259; Zanier 1994, 66-7; and this volume, Appendix 5.

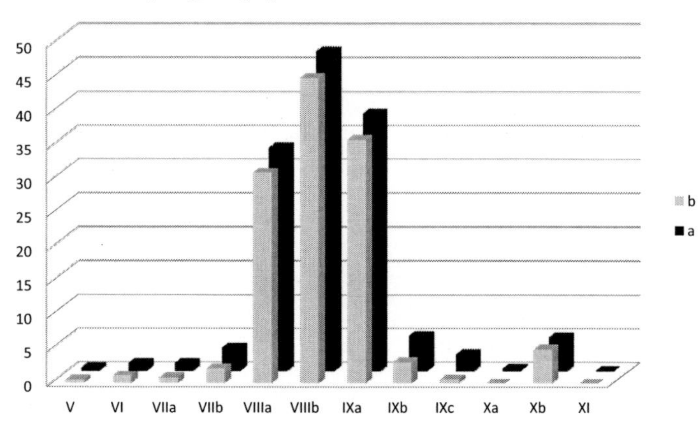


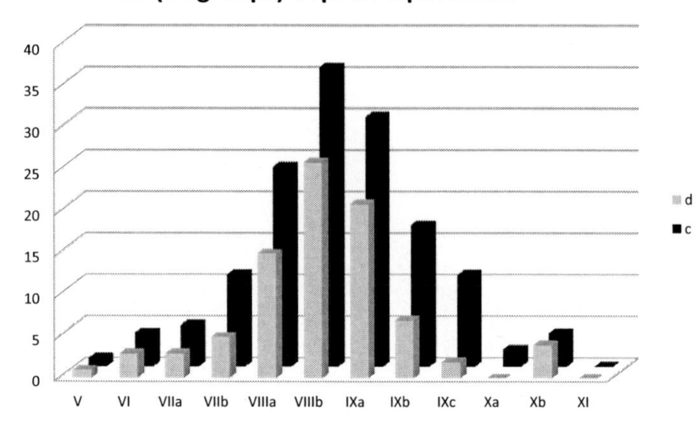


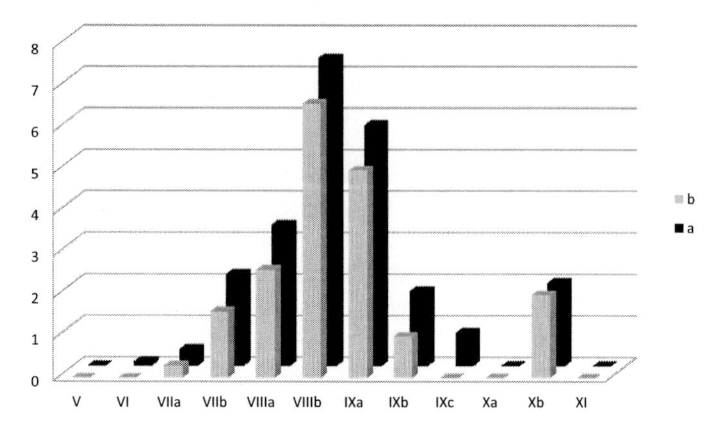


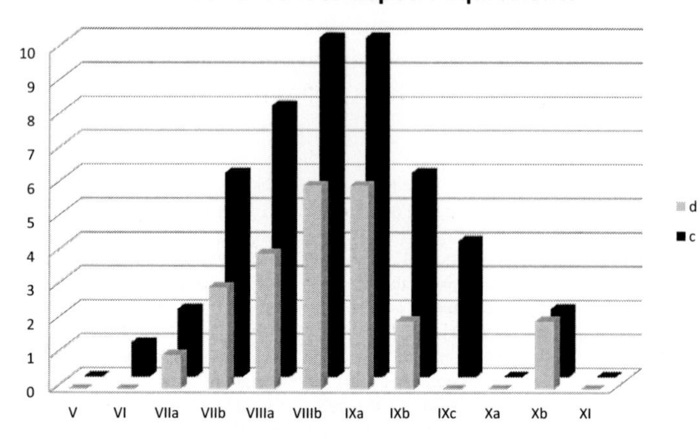


*Fig. 5.15 Trier (all groups), and profile for Dexter and Censor, in adjusted coin-dated deposits. Key as Fig 5.9.*

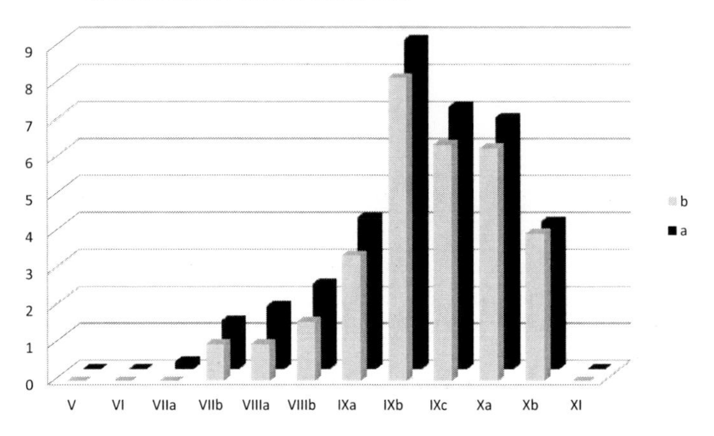


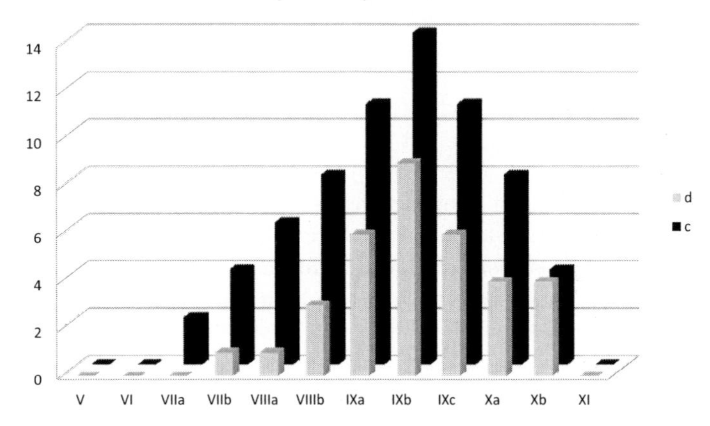


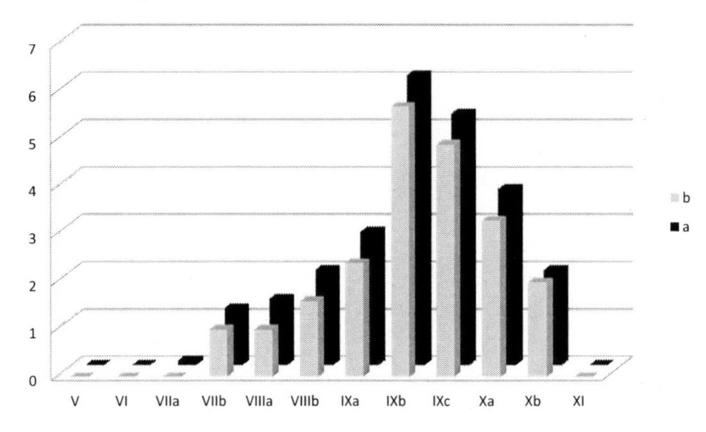


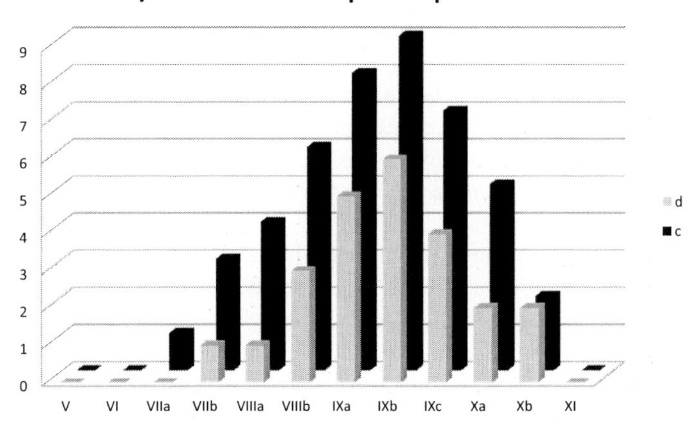


*Fig. 5.16 Westerndorf, Pfaffenhofen, and profile for Helenius, in adjusted coin-dated deposits. Key as Fig. 5.9.*

(periods VIIIa-IXc, sherd numbers 30.7 per period, deposit equivalents 11 per period). If these are removed the profile is much flatter, with a peak in period VIIIb. Exactly the same applies to the Dexter and Censor group (i.e. Trier IIa), the only individual potters well enough represented to be separated out.[2] It seems that Trier pottery is mostly found in early third century deposits, but also has a reasonable representation in the late second century. At the other end of the chronology, there is a fall-off in period IXb, and then a number of deposits in period-Xb. The profile is similar to Rh Ib, rather than to the later Rheinzabern groups, and therefore there seems no justification in suggesting large-scale late production. One of the main planks used in conventionally taking Trier down to the mid third century is B 155, Trier, which is in fact without independent dating evidence. However, it is clear that Trier products are in use in period Xb, as witnessed by the well-dated groups A 146, Titelberg, and A 164, Froitzheim.

Westerndorf and Pfaffenhofen products are definitely late in date (Fig. 5.16), in fact the latest of any considered here. Pfaffenhofen is very poorly represented, but Westerndorf has a good profile, peaking in period IXb and clearly going to period Xb before falling away. The potter Helenius, from both Westerndorf and Pfaffenhofen, shows the same characteristics. No light can be shed on the suggestion made by Kellner[3] that Westerndorf came to an end in the 230s, but Pfaffenhofen continued to the mid third century, although the profile for Westerndorf would appear to support a later dating than that. The figures for sherds and moulds from the Pfaffenhofen kiln site, not given in Fig. 5.16, but entered as row *e* on the relevant parts of Appendix 8, show that much kiln debris was being deposited in periods VIIb-IXa and IXb (but the latter could be redeposited).

Of the smaller kiln centres (Fig. 5.17), La Madeleine, Blickweiler and to a certain extent Chémery and Mittelbronn present early characteristics, while the Argonne has a surprisingly late profile, especially when considered against the figures presented for the unadjusted coin dates in Tables 5.I-5.II and Appendix 7. All the Argonne potters and styles are found in third century deposits, Gesatus being the main potter attested for the late second century as well. It seems very likely that the main period of Argonne pottery production is later than usually thought. The strong representation of Argonne products in mid third century deposits is also of interest, since it is known that the roller-stamped late Argonne products were coming into use at this time or not long afterwards (see chapter 7): continuity between early and late Argonne wares therefore seems a strong possibility.

The suggestion that Argonne may be later than usually thought can also be made for La Madeleine, Blickweiler, Mittelbronn and Heiligenberg, although the last kiln centre has poor coin dated evidence.[4] (Chémery has been included with Mittelbronn because of the association of Saturninus/Satto with both kiln centres; see Table 5.V for differentiation of the products and Appendix 10 for chronology and bibliography of the problem.) All of these are thought to have been in operation mainly in the mid-late second century and to have stopped production some time before the end of the century. However, there is no independent dating evidence for this, and the profiles in Fig. 5.17 do not have the heavy early representation of, e.g. CG II-III or Rh la. On the other hand they are not as late in profile as Rh Ib-III. Somewhat later production, up to the end of the century and a little beyond may be the best explanation of this. Certainly the products of these kilns were still circulating and being disposed of well into the third century.

The minor kilns not given in Table 5.V or the Figures are not easy to date from the coin associations, due to the paucity of the evidence. Kräherwald and Waiblingen can be considered together.[5] The best dated deposit is of period VI-VIII date, with others coming in the early third century. The pottery is stylistically related to Rh la, and thus the late second century date would be consonant with this. Ittenwiller is only represented by one sherd in a mid third century deposit, definitely later than what little is known of production at this kiln site.

Three of the EG unlocated wares have adjusted coin dates, all in mid third century. These are ovolo X, possibly produced in Mainz,[6] dated to periods IXa-IXc, a ware local to A 164, Froitzheim, dated to Xb, and a piece from A 206, Enns-Lorch,[7] dated to the same period.[8]

Finally there are Sinzig and the British kilns, which can be examined together because the only dated group of Sinzig ware found in fact comes from the Colchester samian kiln site. Colchester potters A and B, and Sinzig potter group 1, Werkstatt 2, were found in a deposit over the samian kiln, with an adjusted date of VIIIa-IXb, i.e. early third century. This clearly must be after the kiln ceased production, both stratigraphically and chronologically. Unfortunately, therefore, little can be said about the dating of these products. The same goes for Pulborough, with one sherd found in a deposit dated to period Xa, clearly later than the stylistic date of the pottery, which is equivalent to CG II-III.

[2] A 158 sherd numbers 2.0 per period, deposit equivalents 2 per period.

[3] Kellner in Christlein *et al* 1976.

[4] The stylistic links between Heiligenberg and Rheinzabern Ia are significant, in view of the probable movement of potters from the former to the latter; see discussion at the end of this chapter. Blickweiler (and Eschweiler-Hof) now have good evidence for reuse of moulds as late as the mid 3rd century; Gazetteer D 51; Petit 1989; 2001.

[5] Cf. Riedl 2011, especially Abb. 66 and pp. 225ff.

[6] Schleiermacher 1958.

[7] Karnitsch 1955, Taf 92 nos 2-3.

[8] The potter Clamosus is also unlocated, but on the basis of many finds at Bliesbruck (Moselle), may possibly be linked to Blickweiler or Eschweiler-Hof. Dating of Clamosus is early to mid 3rd century (Schaub 1989; Petit 2001, 73-4, phases D-E).

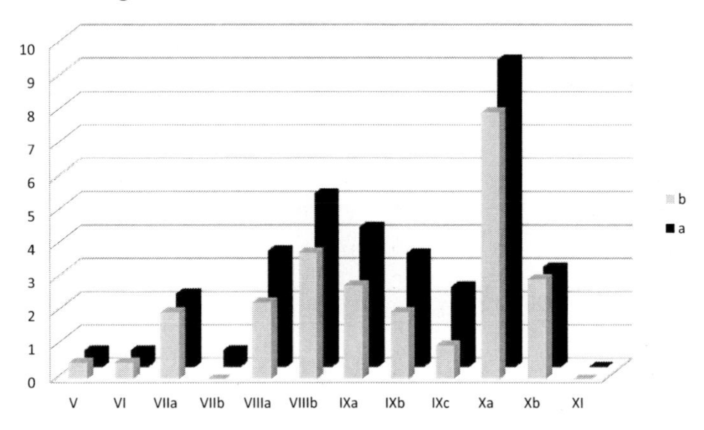

Argonne sherd numbers
10
9
8
7
6
5
4
3
2
1
0
b
a
V
VI
VIIa
VIIb
VIIIa
VIIIb
IXa
IXb
IXc
Xa
Xb
XI


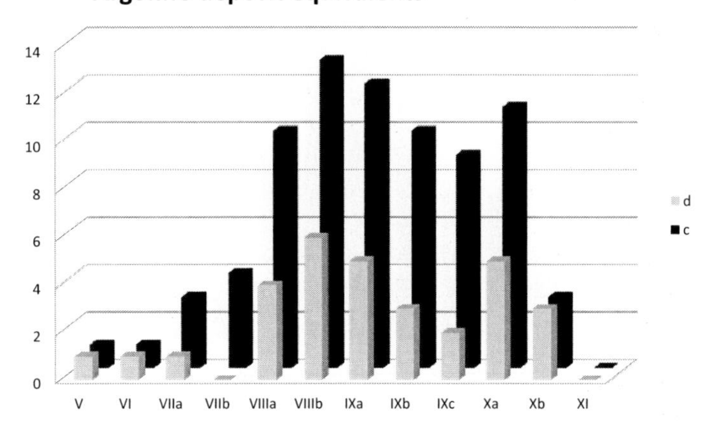

Argonne deposit equivalents
14
12
10
8
6
4
2
0
d
c
V
VI
VIIa
VIIb
VIIIa
VIIIb
IXa
IXb
IXc
Xa
Xb
XI


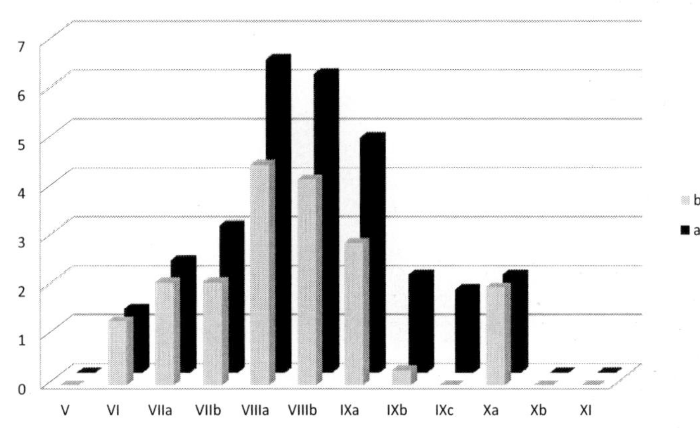

La Madeleine sherd numbers
7
6
5
4
3
2
1
0
b
a
V
VI
VIIa
VIIb
VIIIa
VIIIb
IXa
IXb
IXc
Xa
Xb
XI


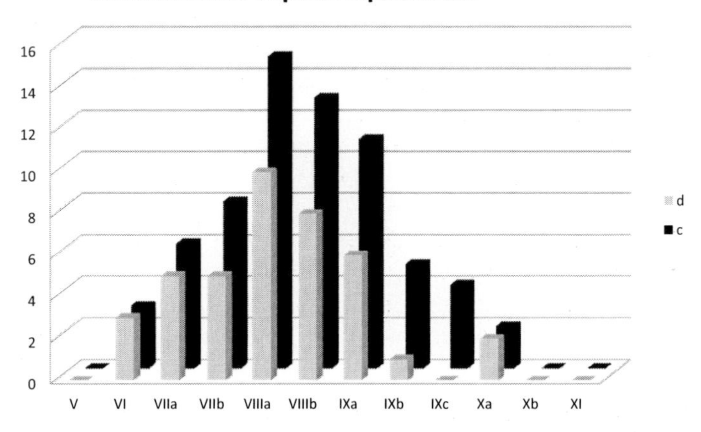

La Madeleine deposit equivalents
16
14
12
10
8
6
4
2
0
d
c
V
VI
VIIa
VIIb
VIIIa
VIIIb
IXa
IXb
IXc
Xa
Xb
XI


*Fig. 5.17.*

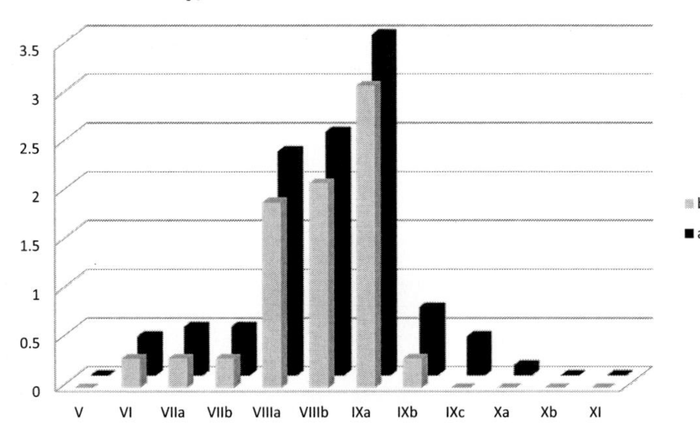


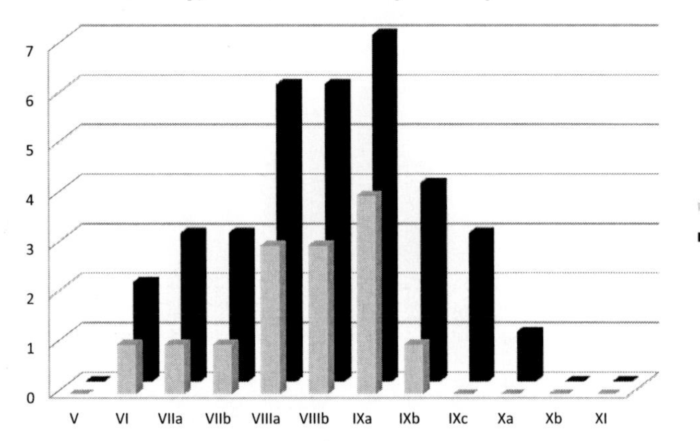


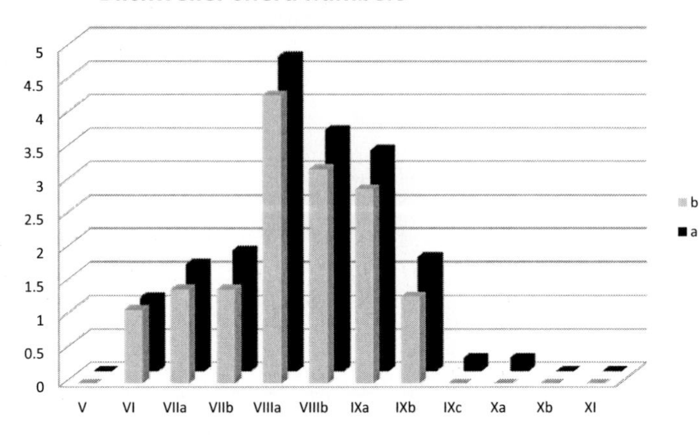


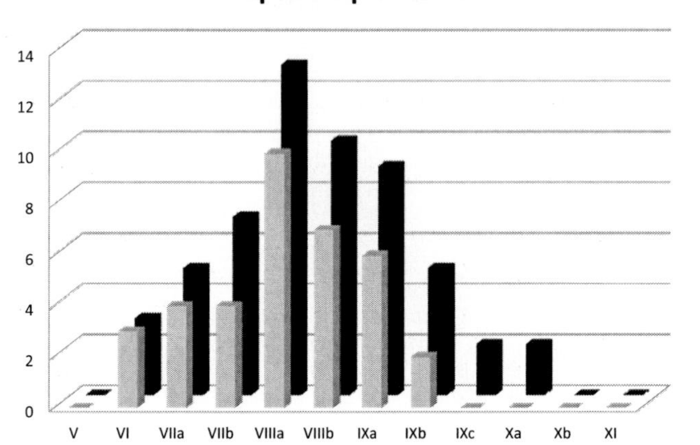


*Fig. 5.17 Argonne, La Madeleine, Chémery/ Mittelbronn and Blickweiler, in adjusted coin-dated deposits. Key as Fig. 5.9.*

*Table 5.III Matrix of internal associations of kiln-centres and their sub-groups within deposits.*

Key to kiln-centre abbreviations: CG, Central Gaul; Rh, Rheinzabern; Tr, Trier; West, Westerndorf; Pfaff, Pfaffenhofen; Arg, Argonne; La Mad, La Madeleine; Chém/Mitt, Chémery and Mittelbronn Sinz, Sinzig; Heil, Heiligenberg; Itten, Ittenviller; Kräh, Kräherwald; Waib, Waiblingen; EG, East Gaulish unlocated; Colch, Colchester; Pulb, Pulborough

| CG I | CG II | CG III | CG Cinn | CG IV | Rh Ia | Rh Ib | Rh IIa | Rh IIb | Rh IIc | Rh IIIa | Rh IIIb | Tr Ia | Tr IIa | Tr IIb | Tr IIc | Tr IIIa | Tr IIIb | West | Pfaff | Arg | La Mad | Ch/Mitt | Blick | Esch | Heil | Itten | Kräh | Waib | EG | Colch | Pulb | | Tot Assocs |
|---|---|---|---|---|---|---|---|---|---|---|---|---|---|---|---|---|---|---|---|---|---|---|---|---|---|---|---|---|---|---|---|---|---|
| 8 | 17 | 16 | 17 | 11 | 9 | 2 | 1 | 1 | 3 | 2 | 0 | 2 | 0 | 0 | 0 | 0 | 0 | 2 | 1 | 3 | 2 | 1 | 0 | 0 | 1 | 0 | 0 | 0 | 1 | 0 | 0 | CG I | 100 |
| | 37 | 43 | 50 | 30 | 13 | 2 | 5 | 1 | 3 | 2 | 0 | 3 | 1 | 0 | 0 | 0 | 0 | 4 | 1 | 8 | 6 | 3 | 3 | 0 | 4 | 0 | 0 | 0 | 1 | 1 | 1 | CG II | 239 |
| | | 43 | 51 | 44 | 10 | 5 | 8 | 2 | 2 | 3 | 0 | 5 | 2 | 1 | 1 | 1 | 0 | 3 | 0 | 9 | 8 | 3 | 3 | 0 | 5 | 0 | 0 | 0 | 1 | 1 | 0 | CGIII | 270 |
| | | | 49 | 44 | 16 | 10 | 16 | 3 | 5 | 4 | 2 | 5 | 1 | 1 | 1 | 1 | 0 | 7 | 1 | 10 | 7 | 5 | 1 | 0 | 8 | 1 | 0 | 0 | 0 | 2 | 2 | CG Cinn | 320 |
| | | | | 62 | 15 | 6 | 12 | 4 | 5 | 5 | 0 | 3 | 3 | 1 | 1 | 1 | 0 | 5 | 0 | 13 | 7 | 3 | 2 | 0 | 6 | 1 | 0 | 0 | 0 | 1 | 0 | CG IV | 285 |
| | | | | | 12 | 11 | 16 | 6 | 8 | 8 | 5 | 4 | 5 | 1 | 1 | 1 | 1 | 4 | 3 | 8 | 3 | 5 | 3 | 0 | 3 | 1 | 0 | 2 | 1 | 0 | 0 | Rh Ia | 175 |
| | | | | | | 12 | 31 | 16 | 22 | 14 | 7 | 8 | 10 | 6 | 5 | 4 | 1 | 5 | 1 | 7 | 3 | 5 | 8 | 0 | 3 | 0 | 0 | 0 | 2 | 0 | 0 | Rh Ib | 206 |
| | | | | | | | 47 | 19 | 27 | 24 | 13 | 6 | 12 | 7 | 5 | 4 | 1 | 11 | 4 | 7 | 4 | 6 | 6 | 1 | 4 | 1 | 0 | 1 | 2 | 0 | 0 | Rh IIa | 301 |
| | | | | | | | | 8 | 12 | 18 | 8 | 8 | 9 | 5 | 4 | 4 | 2 | 4 | 0 | 8 | 2 | 2 | 3 | 0 | 1 | 1 | 0 | 0 | 1 | 0 | 0 | Rh IIb | 152 |
| | | | | | | | | | 11 | 17 | 8 | 6 | 6 | 2 | 2 | 2 | 0 | 5 | 0 | 3 | 1 | 0 | 3 | 0 | 2 | 0 | 0 | 0 | 1 | 0 | 0 | Rh IIc | 156 |
| | | | | | | | | | | 15 | 11 | 8 | 9 | 4 | 7 | 7 | 1 | 7 | 2 | 6 | 2 | 2 | 2 | 0 | 2 | 1 | 0 | 0 | 1 | 0 | 0 | Rh IIIa | 184 |
| | | | | | | | | | | | 3 | 2 | 3 | 1 | 3 | 2 | 2 | 1 | 1 | 2 | 0 | 1 | 1 | 0 | 0 | 0 | 0 | 0 | 1 | 0 | 0 | Rh IIIb | 76 |
| | | | | | | | | | | | | 7 | 9 | 6 | 5 | 5 | 1 | 1 | 0 | 6 | 5 | 2 | 3 | 0 | 1 | 0 | 0 | 0 | 0 | 0 | 0 | Tr Ia | 111 |
| | | | | | | | | | | | | | 9 | 6 | 7 | 5 | 2 | 1 | 0 | 8 | 6 | 2 | 3 | 0 | 1 | 0 | 0 | 0 | 2 | 0 | 0 | Tr IIa | 122 |
| | | | | | | | | | | | | | | 5 | 4 | 4 | 1 | 0 | 0 | 3 | 3 | 1 | 1 | 0 | 0 | 0 | 0 | 0 | 0 | 0 | 0 | Tr IIb | 63 |
| | | | | | | | | | | | | | | | 5 | 6 | 1 | 1 | 0 | 3 | 2 | 1 | 1 | 0 | 1 | 0 | 0 | 0 | 1 | 0 | 0 | Tr IIc | 68 |
| | | | | | | | | | | | | | | | | 4 | 1 | 1 | 0 | 2 | 1 | 1 | 0 | 0 | 1 | 0 | 0 | 0 | 0 | 0 | 0 | Tr IIIa | 58 |
| | | | | | | | | | | | | | | | | | 2 | 0 | 0 | 2 | 0 | 0 | 0 | 0 | 0 | 0 | 0 | 0 | 1 | 0 | 0 | Tr IIIb | 19 |
| | | | | | | | | | | | | | | | | | | 11 | 8 | 3 | 0 | 1 | 0 | 0 | 4 | 1 | 0 | 0 | 0 | 0 | 0 | West | 90 |
| | | | | | | | | | | | | | | | | | | | 5 | 0 | 0 | 0 | 0 | 0 | 1 | 0 | 0 | 0 | 0 | 0 | 0 | Pfaff | 28 |
| | | | | | | | | | | | | | | | | | | | | 10 | 6 | 4 | 5 | 0 | 3 | 0 | 0 | 0 | 2 | 0 | 0 | Arg | 141 |
| | | | | | | | | | | | | | | | | | | | | | 5 | 3 | 5 | 0 | 0 | 0 | 0 | 0 | 1 | 1 | 0 | La Mad | 83 |
| | | | | | | | | | | | | | | | | | | | | | | 2 | 5 | 0 | 1 | 0 | 0 | 0 | 1 | 0 | 0 | Ch/Mitt | 60 |
| | | | | | | | | | | | | | | | | | | | | | | | 5 | 0 | 0 | 0 | 0 | 0 | 2 | 0 | 0 | Blick | 65 |
| | | | | | | | | | | | | | | | | | | | | | | | | 1 | 1 | 0 | 0 | 0 | 1 | 0 | 0 | Esch | 4 |
| | | | | | | | | | | | | | | | | | | | | | | | | | 2 | 0 | 0 | 0 | 1 | 0 | 0 | Heil | 56 |
| | | | | | | | | | | | | | | | | | | | | | | | | | | 0 | 0 | 0 | 0 | 0 | 0 | Itten | 7 |
| | | | | | | | | | | | | | | | | | | | | | | | | | | | 1 | 0 | 0 | 0 | 0 | Kräh | 1 |
| | | | | | | | | | | | | | | | | | | | | | | | | | | | | 1 | 0 | 0 | 0 | Waib | 4 |
| | | | | | | | | | | | | | | | | | | | | | | | | | | | | | 0 | 0 | 0 | EG | 24 |
| | | | | | | | | | | | | | | | | | | | | | | | | | | | | | | 1 | 0 | Colch | 6 |
| | | | | | | | | | | | | | | | | | | | | | | | | | | | | | | | 0 | Pulb | 3 |

## INTERNAL ASSOCIATIONS OF POTTERS WITHIN DEPOSITS

Another approach to the information contained in the Gazetteer, besides that of the coin-associations, is to examine which potters, etc., are found in association with each other within deposits.

Table 5.III is a matrix of associations within deposits, using both sections A and B of the gazetteer. It has been compiled by counting up the presences of products of one kiln-centre or kiln-centre sub group with the others in each deposit. As an example, if a deposit has two CG II and one Argonne sherds, the presence of the former with the latter (and the latter with the former) is recorded in the matrix. Also, because there are two CG II sherds, this is counted as a self-association and included as well. In this way the level of association of products both within their own groups and with others can be measured. However, the matrix is not a complete numerical record of all associations, since it has been decided to count all large assemblages from one kiln centre or sub-group as 2 only, in order to reduce the distortion that would be caused by large deposits. Table 5.III should be looked at in conjunction with Table 5.IV, which gives the same data in the form of percentages totalled for each kiln-centre or sub group across each row, which therefore should be read across, not up and down.

### ASSOCIATIONS BETWEEN KILN-CENTRES AND THEIR SUB-PHASES

The two major kiln-centres, CG and Rheinzabern, have a tendency to be associated most strongly with other sub groups of their own kiln-centre. This is probably the outcome of a distribution system that favoured quasi-monopolistic dominance by CG and Rheinzabern of their respective market areas.[9] CG IV is the best case of this since 22% of its associations are with other sherds of CG IV, and a total of 67% of associations are with CG as a whole. The only other groups well associated with CG IV are Rh Ia, Rh IIa and Argonne, and even these are at the low level of 4-5%. Rh Ia is something of an exception, with its best associations being with CG Cinnamus and CG IV (as well as Rh IIa). This may be because early Rheinzabern products had no well defined market and therefore were more widely distributed. It is noticeable in fact that a

[9] Discussed further in chapter 7.

*Table 5.IV Percentages derived from Table 5.III, for the better-represented kiln-centres. The percentages total 100% row-wise for each kiln-centre.*

| CG I | CG II | CG III | CG Cinn | CG IV | Rh Ia | Rh Ib | Rh IIa | Rh IIb | Rh IIc | Rh IIIa | Rh IIIb | Tr Ia | Tr IIa | Tr IIb | Tr IIc | Tr IIIa | Tr IIIb | West | Pfaff | Arg | La Mad | Ch/Mitt | Blick | Esch | Heil | Itten | Kräh | Waib | EG | Colch | Pulb | |
|---|---|---|---|---|---|---|---|---|---|---|---|---|---|---|---|---|---|---|---|---|---|---|---|---|---|---|---|---|---|---|---|---|
| 8 | 17 | 16 | 17 | 11 | 9 | 2 | 1 | 1 | 3 | 2 | 0 | 2 | 0 | 0 | 0 | 0 | 0 | 2 | 1 | 3 | 2 | 1 | 0 | 0 | 1 | 0 | 0 | 0 | 1 | 0 | 0 | CG I |
| 7 | 15 | 18 | 21 | 13 | 5 | 1 | 2 | 1 | 1 | 1 | 0 | 1 | 1 | 0 | 0 | 0 | 0 | 2 | 1 | 3 | 3 | 1 | 1 | 0 | 2 | 0 | 0 | 0 | 1 | 1 | 1 | CG II |
| 6 | 16 | 16 | 19 | 16 | 4 | 2 | 3 | 1 | 1 | 1 | 0 | 2 | 1 | 1 | 1 | 1 | 0 | 1 | 1 | 3 | 3 | 1 | 1 | 0 | 2 | 0 | 0 | 0 | 1 | 1 | 0 | CGIII |
| 5 | 6 | 16 | 15 | 14 | 5 | 3 | 5 | 1 | 2 | 1 | 1 | 2 | 1 | 1 | 1 | 1 | 0 | 2 | 0 | 3 | 2 | 2 | 1 | 0 | 3 | 1 | 0 | 0 | 0 | 1 | 1 | CG Cinn |
| 4 | 11 | 15 | 15 | 22 | 5 | 2 | 4 | 1 | 2 | 2 | 0 | 1 |  | 1 | 1 | 1 | 0 | 2 | 1 | 5 | 2 | 1 | 1 | 0 | 2 | 1 | 0 | 0 | 0 | 1 | 0 | CG IV |
| 5 | 7 | 6 | 9 | 9 | 7 | 6 | 9 | 3 | 5 | 5 | 3 | 2 | 3 | 1 | 1 | 1 | 1 | 2 | 0 | 5 | 2 | 3 | 2 | 0 | 2 | 1 | 0 | 1 | 1 | 0 | 0 | Rh Ia |
| 1 | 1 | 2 | 5 | 3 | 5 | 6 | 15 | 8 | 11 | 7 | 3 | 4 | 5 | 3 | 2 | 2 | 1 | 2 | 2 | 3 | 1 | 2 | 4 | 0 | 1 | 0 | 0 | 0 | 1 | 0 | 0 | Rh Ib |
| 1 | 2 | 3 | 5 | 4 | 5 | 10 | 16 | 6 | 9 | 8 | 4 | 2 | 4 | 2 | 2 | 1 | 1 | 4 | 1 | 2 | 1 | 2 | 2 | 1 | 1 | 1 | 0 | 1 | 1 | 0 | 0 | Rh IIa |
| 1 | 1 | 1 | 2 | 3 | 4 | 11 | 13 | 5 | 8 | 12 | 5 | 5 | 6 | 3 | 3 | 3 | 1 | 3 | 1 | 5 | 1 | 1 | 2 | 0 | 1 | 1 | 0 | 0 | 1 | 0 | 0 | Rh IIb |
| 2 | 2 | 1 | 3 | 3 | 5 | 14 | 17 | 8 | 7 | 11 | 5 | 4 | 4 | 1 | 1 | 1 | 0 | 3 | 0 | 2 | 1 | 0 | 2 | 0 | 1 | 0 | 0 | 0 | 1 | 0 | 0 | Rh IIc |
| 1 | 1 | 2 | 2 | 3 | 4 | 8 | 13 | 10 | 9 | 8 | 6 | 4 | 5 | 2 | 4 | 4 | 1 | 4 | 0 | 3 | 1 | 1 | 1 | 0 | 1 | 1 | 0 | 0 | 1 | 0 | 0 | Rh IIIa |
| 0 | 0 | 0 | 3 | 0 | 7 | 9 | 17 | 11 | 11 | 14 | 4 | 3 | 4 | 1 | 4 | 3 | 3 | 1 | 1 | 3 | 0 | 1 | 1 | 0 | 0 | 0 | 0 | 0 | 1 | 0 | 0 | Rh IIIb |
| 2 | 3 | 5 | 5 | 3 | 4 | 7 | 5 | 7 | 5 | 7 | 2 | 6 | 8 | 5 | 5 | 5 | 1 | 1 | 1 | 5 | 5 | 2 | 3 | 0 | 1 | 0 | 0 | 0 | 0 | 0 | 0 | Tr Ia |
| 0 | 1 | 2 | 1 | 2 | 4 | 8 | 10 | 7 | 5 | 7 | 2 | 7 | 7 | 5 | 6 | 4 | 2 | 1 | 0 | 7 | 5 | 2 | 2 | 0 | 1 | 0 | 0 | 0 | 2 | 0 | 0 | Tr IIa |
| 0 | 0 | 2 | 2 | 2 | 2 | 10 | 11 | 8 | 3 | 6 | 2 | 10 | 10 | 8 | 6 | 6 | 2 | 0 | 0 | 5 | 5 | 2 | 2 | 0 | 0 | 0 | 0 | 0 | 0 | 0 | 0 | Tr IIb |
| 0 | 0 | 1 | 1 | 1 | 1 | 7 | 7 | 6 | 3 | 10 | 4 | 7 | 10 | 6 | 7 | 9 | 1 | 1 | 0 | 4 | 3 | 1 | 1 | 0 | 1 | 0 | 0 | 0 | 1 | 0 | 0 | Tr IIc |
| 0 | 0 | 2 | 2 | 2 | 2 | 9 | 9 | 7 | 3 | 12 | 3 | 9 | 9 | 7 | 10 | 7 | 2 | 2 | 0 | 3 | 2 | 2 | 0 | 0 | 2 | 0 | 0 | 0 | 0 | 0 | 0 | Tr IIIa |
| 0 | 0 | 0 | 0 | 0 | 5 | 5 | 5 | 11 | 0 | 5 | 11 | 5 | 11 | 5 | 5 | 5 | 11 | 0 | 0 | 11 | 0 | 0 | 0 | 0 | 0 | 0 | 0 | 0 | 5 | 0 | 0 | Tr IIIb |
| 2 | 4 | 3 | 8 | 6 | 4 | 6 | 12 | 4 | 6 | 8 | 1 | 1 | 1 | 0 | 1 | 1 | 0 | 12 | 9 | 3 | 0 | 1 | 0 | 0 | 4 | 1 | 0 | 0 | 0 | 0 | 0 | West |
| 4 | 4 | 0 | 4 | 0 | 11 | 4 | 14 | 0 | 0 | 7 | 4 | 0 | 0 | 0 | 0 | 0 | 0 | 29 | 18 | 0 | 0 | 0 | 0 | 0 | 4 | 0 | 0 | 0 | 0 | 0 | 0 | Pfaff |
| 2 | 6 | 6 | 7 | 9 | 6 | 5 | 5 | 6 | 2 | 4 | 1 | 4 | 6 | 2 | 2 | 1 | 1 | 2 | 0 | 7 | 4 | 3 | 4 | 0 | 2 | 0 | 0 | 0 | 1 | 0 | 0 | Arg |
| 2 | 7 | 10 | 8 | 8 | 4 | 4 | 5 | 2 | 1 | 2 | 0 | 6 | 7 | 4 | 2 | 1 | 0 | 0 | 0 | 7 | 6 | 4 | 6 | 0 | 0 | 0 | 0 | 0 | 1 | 1 | 0 | La Mad |
| 2 | 5 | 5 | 8 | 5 | 8 | 8 | 10 | 3 | 0 | 3 | 2 | 3 | 3 | 2 | 2 | 2 | 0 | 2 | 0 | 7 | 5 | 3 | 8 | 0 | 2 | 0 | 0 | 0 | 2 | 0 | 0 | Ch/Mitt |
| 0 | 5 | 5 | 2 | 3 | 5 | 12 | 9 | 5 | 5 | 3 | 2 | 5 | 5 | 2 | 2 | 0 | 0 | 0 | 0 | 8 | 8 | 8 | 8 | 0 | 0 | 0 | 0 | 0 | 3 | 0 | 0 | Blick |
| 2 | 7 | 9 | 14 | 11 | 3 | 5 | 7 | 2 | 4 | 4 | 0 | 2 | 2 | 0 | 2 | 2 | 0 | 7 | 2 | 5 | 0 | 2 | 0 | 2 | 4 | 0 | 0 | 0 | 2 | 0 | 0 | Heil |

significant amount of Rh Ia pottery reaches Britain, which accounts for the relatively high level of association with CG. Trier has strong associations with Rheinzabern as well as internally, the former also being a feature of the smaller kiln-centres within the ambit of the Rheinzabern distribution network (Westerndorf, Pfaffenhofen, Argonne, La Madeleine, etc.). Few of these smaller centres have strong internal associations, mainly because their products tend to be found singly in most deposits, and in association with sherds from the major kilns. Westerndorf and Pfaffenhofen are the exceptions to this, due to the presence in the gazetteer of a number of kiln-site deposits from Pfaffenhofen. It is also the case that these two kiln-centres managed to build up a strong presence in their own, Danubian, distribution area. Argonne, La Madeleine, Chémery/Mittelbronn, Blickweiler and Heiligenberg are of interest in that they have equally strong associations with both CG (mainly III-IV) and Rheinzabern (mainly Ia-IIa). Their distribution areas overlapped with those of the two main producers and therefore should be of some help in assessing the relative chronology of CG and Rheinzabern.

A more detailed association of potters from these minor kiln-centres with CG and Rheinzabern is given in Table 5.V. The use of individual potters or styles should give a clearer picture of the contemporaneity of CG and Rheinzabern sub groups, and at the same time clarify the chronology of the minor kiln-centres. From this it appears that Tribunus is later than Gesatus of Argonne, the former inclining to CG IV and CG Cinnamus and also having fairly high representation in the later Rheinzabern groups IIb and IIIa. Albillus of La Madeleine is best associated with CG II and III, and is only weakly linked with Rheinzabern (which may be due to distributional factors). Ovolo C of La Madeleine appears to be later than Albillus. All the potters on the Table for Heiligenberg seem to be contemporary and, taken together, are associated mainly with CG III, IV and Cinnamus, and Rh Ia-IIa. The Blickweiler potters are clearly linked more with Rheinzabern and CG and fit with Rh Ib-IIc best. However, Chémery/Mittelbronn probably yields the best evidence. When Saturninus/Satto products are differentiated, as far as is possible given the way in which the gazetteer was compiled, Chémery clearly is associated with CG II-III and to a lesser extent CG Cinnamus, while Mittelbronn is later, linked with CG Cinnamus and Rh Ia-IIa. Cibisus of Mittelbronn comes probably after Saturninus/Satto and is linked weakly with CG IV but mainly with Rh IIa. In sum, these links point to the contemporaneity of CG III and Cinnamus (and to a lesser extent CG IV) with Rh la, while CG IV (and to a lesser extent CG Cinnamus) link with Rh Ib-IIa and perhaps later Rheinzabern groups. CG IV potters almost

*Table 5.V Associations between selected potters of the minor kilns and CG and Rheinzabern.*

| | | CG II | CG III | CG Cinn | CG IV | Rh Ia | Rh Ib | Rh IIa | Rh IIb | Rh IIc | Rh IIIa |
|---|---|---|---|---|---|---|---|---|---|---|---|
| **Arg** | Gesatus | 4 | 3 | 3 | 3 | 4 | 1 | 3 | 1 | 1 | 2 |
| | Tribunus | 5 | 5 | 7 | 6 | 4 | 3 | 2 | 3 | 0 | 3 |
| **La Mad** | Albillus | 3 | 3 | 1 | 2 | 1 | 1 | 1 | 1 | 0 | 0 |
| | Ov B | 1 | 1 | 1 | 1 | 0 | 1 | 1 | 1 | 0 | 0 |
| | Ov C | 2 | 3 | 3 | 4 | 1 | 0 | 0 | 0 | 0 | 0 |
| **Heil** | Janu | 0 | 2 | 3 | 2 | 1 | 2 | 1 | 1 | 1 | 1 |
| | Ciriuna | 2 | 2 | 3 | 2 | 2 | 1 | 3 | 0 | 0 | 1 |
| | F-master | 1 | 1 | 2 | 1 | 1 | 1 | 1 | 0 | 0 | 1 |
| **Blick** | Avitus | 0 | 0 | 0 | 0 | 1 | 2 | 3 | 1 | 2 | 0 |
| | Ov 32 | 1 | 1 | 1 | 0 | 0 | 2 | 2 | 1 | 1 | 0 |
| **Chém** | Satto/ Saturn. | 3 | 3 | 2 | 1 | 1 | 0 | 0 | 0 | 0 | 0 |
| **Mitt** | Satto/ Saturn. | 0 | 0 | 2 | 1 | 2 | 3 | 2 | 1 | 0 | 0 |
| | Cibisus | 0 | 0 | 0 | 1 | 1 | 1 | 3 | 1 | 0 | 1 |

certainly started before Rh Ia ends, but they continued into the main production period of Rheinzabern. These indications are confirmed by the direct links between CG and Rheinzabern given in Tables 5.III-5.IV, where Rh Ia has good associations with all CG groups but principally with CG Cinnamus and IV, while Rh Ib-IIa links mainly with CG Cinnamus and IV, and Rh IIb-IIIa with CG IV.

### ASSOCIATIONS WITHIN KILN-CENTRES

The internal associations of CG and Rheinzabern also give useful chronological information and serve to strengthen the suggestion that Rheinzabern groups succeed each other rapidly, and that there is a more orderly progression in the CG groups.

If we pass over CG I on Tables 5.III-5.IV since it consists mainly of survival and/or residual pieces, it can be seen that the other CG groups have percentages that rise to a peak and then fall away, for CG II-III the peak is at CG Cinnamus, for CG Cinnamus at CG II-III, and for CG IV at CG IV. This would suggest that the dominance that Cinnamus has over production in CG III has led to a

*Table 5.VI Matrix of associations between CG potters within deposits, expressed as permillages of total CG associations (n = 6499)*

| CG I | CG I | CG I | CG I | CG II | CG II | CG II | CG II | CG III | CG III | CG II | CG II | CG III | CG III | CG III | CG III | CG III | CG III | CG III | CG III | CG IV | CG IV | CG IV | CG IV | CG IV | CG IV | CG IV | |
|---|---|---|---|---|---|---|---|---|---|---|---|---|---|---|---|---|---|---|---|---|---|---|---|---|---|---|---|
| Igocatus | X-8/10 | X-11/12 | Sacirius | Arcanus | Geminus | Drusus II | X-6 | Cinn-Cer | Cettus | Quitilianus | Sacer-Att | Criciro | Cinnamus | Secundus | Pugnus | Paullus | Laxtucissa | Albucius | Divixtus | Casurius | Paternus II | Censorinus | Advocisus | Doeccus I | Banvus | Iustus | |
| X | 0.2 | 0.3 | - | - | - | 0.6 | - | 0.3 | - | - | 0.6 | 0.5 | 2.5 | 0.3 | 0.2 | 0.3 | 0.3 | 0.5 | 0.2 | 0.9 | 3.4 | 0.5 | 0.8 | - | 0.3 | - | Igocatus |
| | X | - | - | - | - | 0.5 | - | 0.6 | 1.4 | 0.5 | 0.8 | - | 9.4 | 0.3 | - | - | 0.5 | 0.8 | 0.6 | - | 0.2 | - | 0.3 | - | - | - | X-8/10 |
| | | X | 0.3 | 0.5 | 0.3 | 0.3 | - | - | 0.2 | - | 0.6 | 0.9 | 4.3 | 0.3 | 0.3 | 0.6 | 0.6 | 1.1 | 0.5 | 2.0 | 6.8 | 0.9 | 1.5 | - | 0.3 | - | X-11/12 |
| | | | X | 0.3 | 0.3 | 0.5 | 1.1 | 0.3 | 0.5 | 0.9 | 0.9 | 0.8 | 12.9 | 0.3 | 0.2 | - | - | 0.2 | 0.3 | 0.2 | 0.5 | - | - | - | - | - | Sacirius |
| | | | | X | - | 0.2 | 1.1 | - | 0.3 | 0.8 | 0.8 | 0.3 | 11.4 | - | - | - | - | 0.2 | 0.2 | 0.2 | 0.2 | - | - | - | - | - | Arcanus |
| | | | | | X | 0.2 | 3.1 | 0.3 | 0.6 | 3.1 | 1.5 | 1.8 | 5.1 | - | 0.3 | - | 1.2 | 0.2 | 0.6 | - | 0.8 | - | 0.8 | - | - | - | Geminus |
| | | | | | | X | 1.1 | 1.7 | 0.5 | 1.2 | 2.8 | 0.6 | 14.2 | 0.8 | - | - | 0.2 | 0.3 | 0.3 | 0.2 | 0.2 | - | - | - | - | - | Drusus II |
| | | | | | | | X | - | 1.2 | 8.8 | 6.3 | 3.5 | 74.9 | - | 0.2 | - | 1.5 | 0.2 | 1.2 | 1.2 | 1.4 | 0.2 | 0.9 | 0.2 | - | - | X-6 |
| | | | | | | | | X | 2.0 | 2.0 | 1.7 | 2.0 | 12.2 | 1.4 | 0.2 | - | 1.2 | 1.4 | 0.3 | - | 0.6 | - | 0.6 | - | - | - | Cinnamus-Cerialis |
| | | | | | | | | | X | 2.9 | 0.9 | 2.5 | 30.0 | 0.5 | - | 0.8 | 1.1 | 1.7 | 1.4 | 0.2 | 1.4 | - | - | 0.5 | - | - | Cettus |
| | | | | | | | | | | X | 5.5 | 4.8 | 65.2 | 0.6 | 0.6 | 1.2 | 2.2 | 2.5 | 1.8 | 1.1 | 2.0 | 0.2 | 0.8 | 0.3 | 0.2 | 0.2 | Quntilianus |
| | | | | | | | | | | | X | 2.6 | 53.7 | 0.9 | 0.3 | 0.9 | 1.4 | 2.0 | 2.0 | 1.4 | 1.8 | 0.5 | 1.5 | 0.9 | 0.6 | 0.3 | Sacer-Attianus |
| | | | | | | | | | | | | X | 38.0 | 1.4 | 0.5 | 2.3 | 2.2 | 3.8 | 1.8 | 2.3 | 10.0 | 1.1 | 1.7 | 0.5 | 0.3 | - | Criciro |
| | | | | | | | | | | | | | X | 6.5 | 13.2 | 8.3 | 15.1 | 34.2 | 23.7 | 24.5 | 84.8 | 11.4 | 14.0 | 9.5 | 9.4 | 5.1 | Cinnamus |
| | | | | | | | | | | | | | | X | 0.2 | 1.1 | 0.6 | 1.7 | 0.6 | 0.9 | 3.8 | 0.8 | 1.1 | 0.2 | 0.2 | - | Secundus |
| | | | | | | | | | | | | | | | X | 0.3 | 0.8 | 1.1 | 0.8 | 1.1 | 6.2 | 0.9 | 1.2 | 0.8 | 0.6 | 0.5 | Pugnus |
| | | | | | | | | | | | | | | | | X | 0.6 | 3.4 | 1.5 | 1.8 | 6.9 | 0.9 | 1.5 | - | 0.5 | - | Paullus |
| | | | | | | | | | | | | | | | | | X | 2.2 | 1.1 | 2.5 | 9.2 | 1.5 | 2.8 | 1.4 | 0.8 | 0.5 | Laxtucissa |
| | | | | | | | | | | | | | | | | | | X | 2.9 | 3.7 | 17.4 | 2.0 | 3.5 | 2.5 | 0.9 | 0.6 | Albucius |
| | | | | | | | | | | | | | | | | | | | X | 1.8 | 6.5 | 1.1 | 1.8 | 1.8 | 0.5 | 0.3 | Divixtus |
| | | | | | | | | | | | | | | | | | | | | X | 21.8 | 3.4 | 6.5 | 2.3 | 1.8 | 0.6 | Casurius |
| | | | | | | | | | | | | | | | | | | | | | X | 15.1 | 20.2 | 7.5 | 6.0 | 2.6 | Paternus II |
| | | | | | | | | | | | | | | | | | | | | | | X | 3.2 | 2.5 | 1.2 | 0.6 | Censorinus |
| | | | | | | | | | | | | | | | | | | | | | | | X | 1.8 | 1.7 | 0.3 | Advocisus |
| | | | | | | | | | | | | | | | | | | | | | | | | X | 1.7 | 1.2 | Doeccus I |
| | | | | | | | | | | | | | | | | | | | | | | | | | X | 0.6 | Banvus |
| | | | | | | | | | | | | | | | | | | | | | | | | | | X | Iustus |

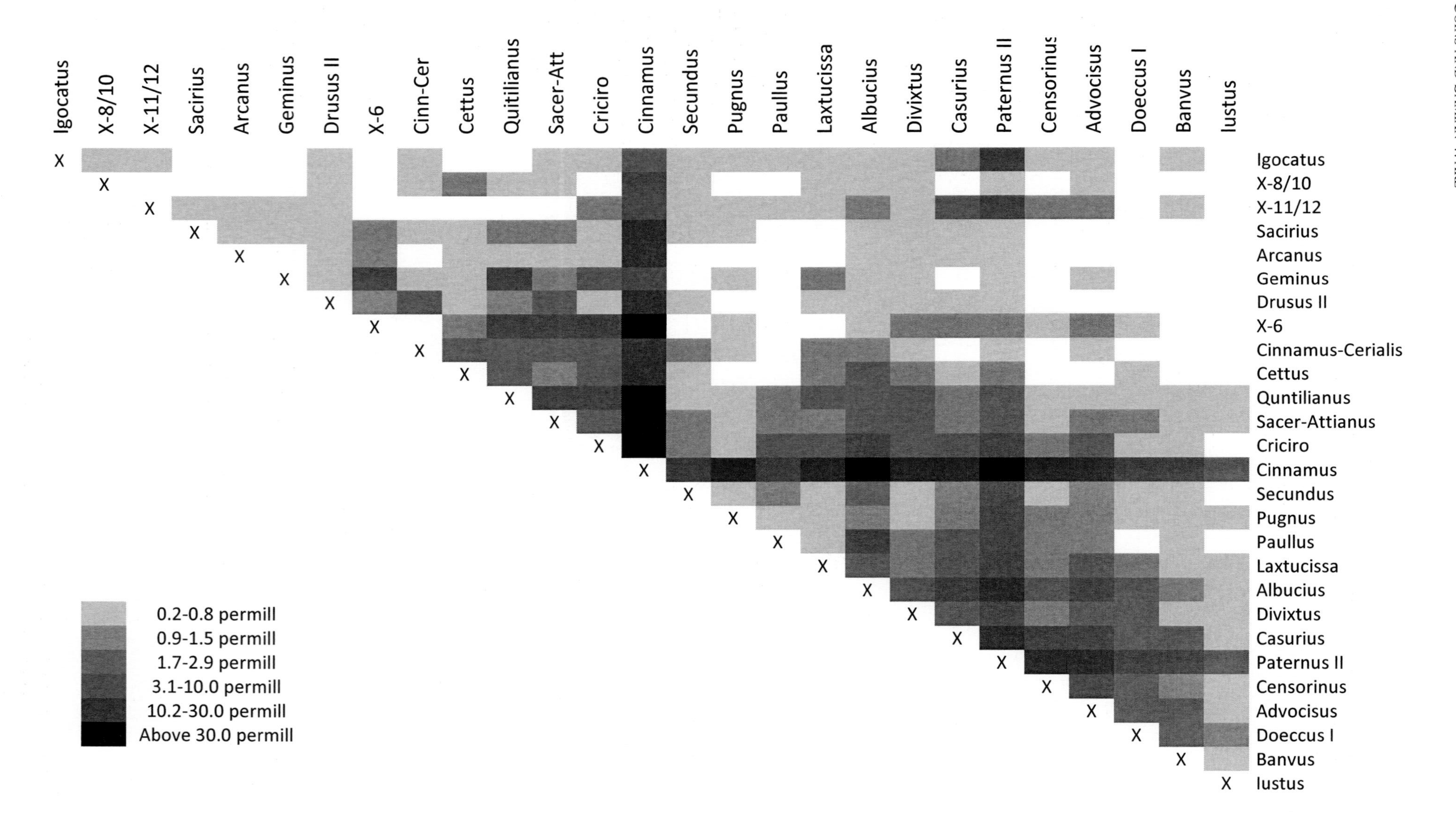


*Fig. 5.18 Matrix of associations between Central Gaulish potters within deposits, data from Table 5.VI.*

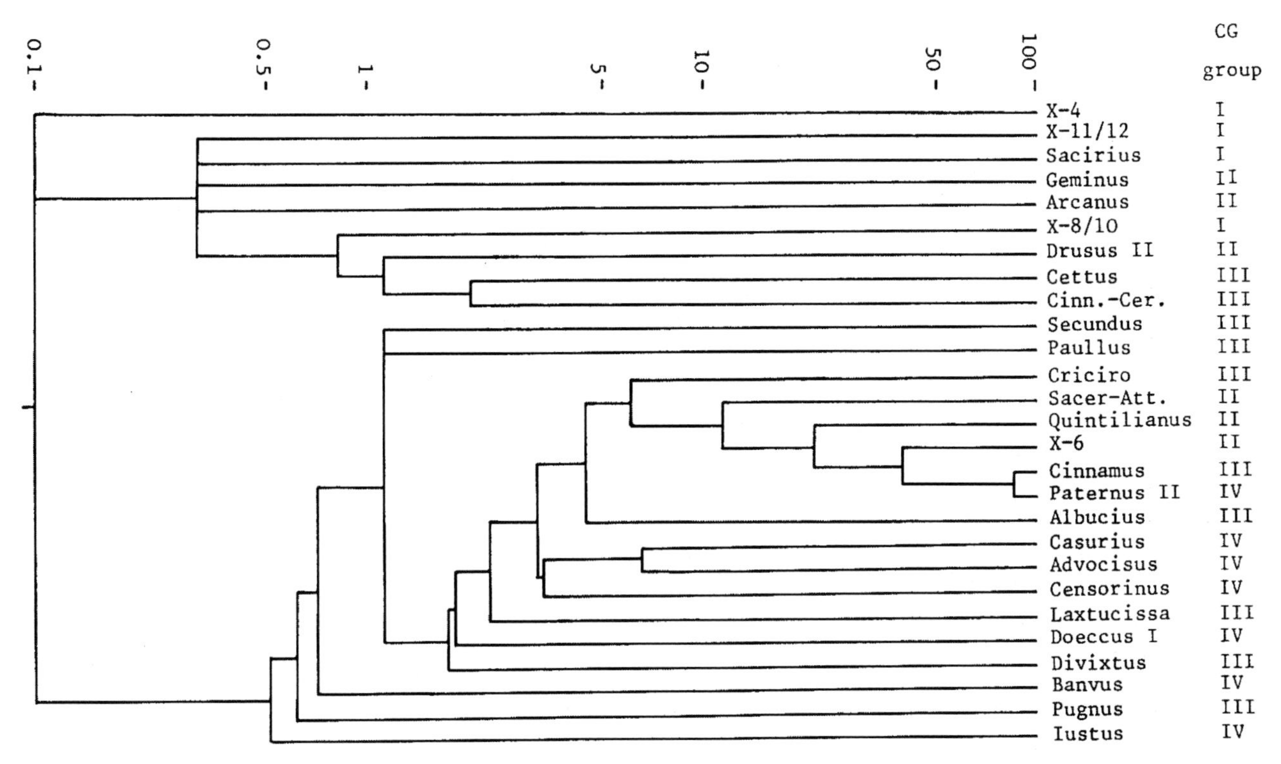


*Fig. 5.19 Average-link dendrogram of the level of association of Central Gaulish potters, data from Table 5.VI.*

swamping of the links in deposits also containing CG II-III pottery. CG IV is more autonomous as a group, since it has a high level of self-associations.

At the more detailed level of individual potters, the better-represented individuals can be plotted against each other on a matrix (Table 5.VI and Fig. 5.18). This is a slightly different type of matrix from Table 5.III in that it shows the permillage of the number of sherd links using the total of links in the whole Table as the base from which the permillage is calculated. All links have been counted, thus accentuating the more prolific potters and the larger deposits (A 202, B 9, B 24, B 51, B 146 and B 149 have been omitted from this and the Rheinzabern matrices). The permillage values are converted to diagrammatic form in Fig. 5.18, and from this the extent to which Cinnamus dominates many deposits can be seen. This potter has got strong links with those in both earlier and later production (in fact 59.33% of all the links recorded) and consequently is to a certain extent difficult to place in a relative chronology. However, his position roughly in the middle of the diagram fits best both with what is known of the chronology and with the visual appearance of the Figure, since it has been arranged so as to group together those potters with similar patterns of links. One result of this has been an alteration to the order of CG groups in the area Cinnamus-Cerialis to Sacer-Attianus to make a better fit. The blocks of similar linkage patterns are Geminus to Cinnamus and Cinnamus to Iustus, with a secondary block linking Cettus-Criciro to Paullus-Advocisus.[10] The CG I potters on the diagram have no strong links with each other, but are often found with Cinnamus and, curiously, Paternus II and Censorinus, presumably in a residual capacity. Some of the CG II potters, too, such as Sacer-Attianus and the Quintilianus group, are often associated with CG III and IV, but in these cases it is possible that some of the links are due to survival of vessels of the earlier potters into the later production periods. Within the main later grouping, it can be seen that the CG IV potters are mainly associated with themselves, and Paullus-Laxtucissa of CG III (plus to a lesser extent Criciro, Secundus and Pugnus). It may be that Paullus-Laxtucissa are part of a later sub-group within CG III. Also, Doeccus, Banvus and Iustus of CG IV have fewer links with any CG III potters than the other representatives of CG IV. These three potters may represent a later sub-group of CG IV.

A different way of presenting the information in Table 5.VI is given in Fig. 5.19. This is an average-link dendrogram of the permillage values in the Table and shows the strength of association between potters and groups of potters.[11] The two potters with the most links with each other, Cinnamus and Paternus II, form by far the closest grouping on the diagram, at 84.8 ‰. If an arbitrary level of 5 ‰ is taken, below which the groups formed on the dendrogram are not significant, then it can be seen that there are only two groups:

(a) Criciro, Sacer-Attianus, Quintilianus, X-6, Cinnamus, Paternus II,
(b) Casurius, Advocisus.

[10] The matrix has a pattern reminiscent of Clarke's ideal model for a sequence of successively dominant attribute states (1968, 172, fig. 34).

[11] See Orton 1980 for methodology of the diagram.

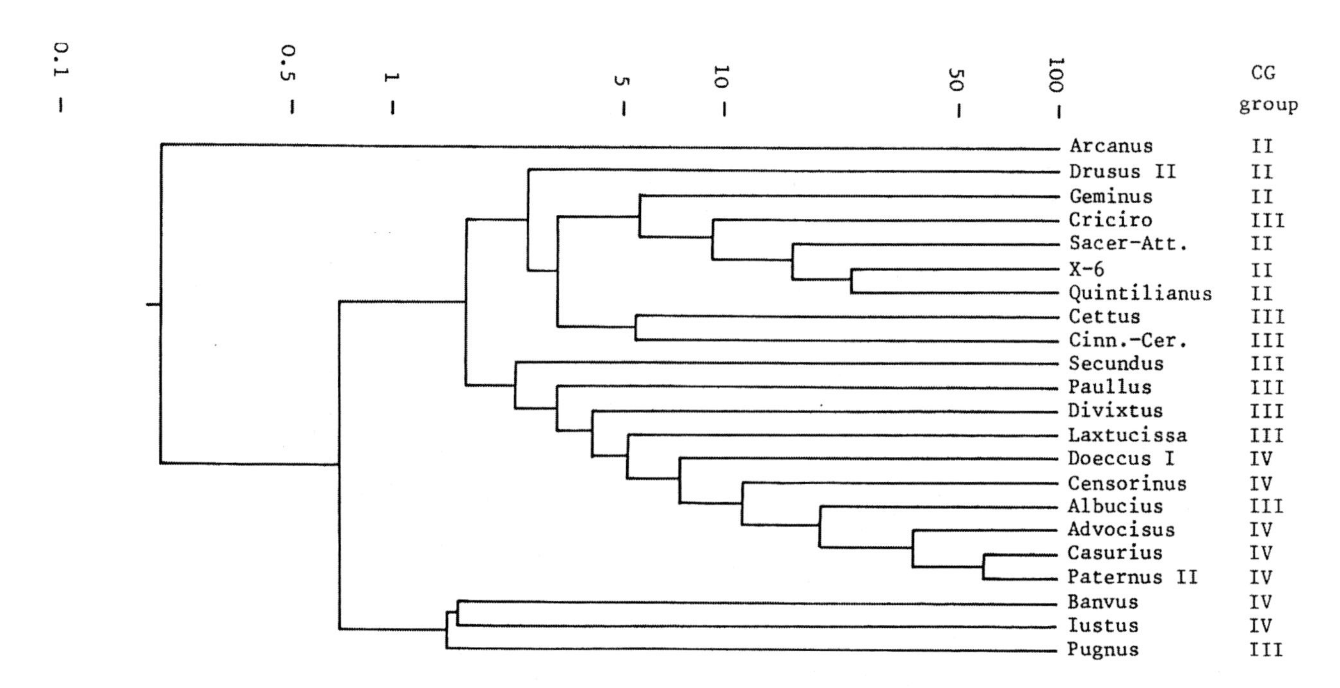


*Fig. 5.20 Average-link dendrogram, as Fig. 5.19, but reworked to remove CG I and Cinnamus.*

The first group is essentially composed of those potters found most frequently with Cinnamus, and corresponds with the dominant position of this potter on Fig. 5.18. The other group consists of two CG IV potters, and is a confirmatory indicator of the high level of internal CG IV links already noted. If Cinnamus is removed (and the CG I potters), the reworked dendrogram (Fig. 5.20) is more balanced and the 5 $^{o}/_{oo}$ level gives us three groups:

(a) Geminus-Quintilianus,
(b) Cettus-Cinnamus/Cerialis,
(c) Laxtucissa-Paternus II.

The first is mainly CG II, the second CG III and the third CG IV, and the diagram generally shows a chronological progression from left (earlier) to right (later). Those potters that do not link with any other above the 5 $^{o}/_{oo}$ level are, for the most part, not well-represented in the gazetteer as a whole, and there is, in fact, a correlation between the rarity of a potter and his low score on the linkage diagrams presented here.

Returning to Tables 5.III-5.IV, the Rheinzabern groups, as suggested above, are not so clearly distinguished as those of CG. Rh Ia is found more frequently with Rh Ia-IIa than later groups, which supports its position as the earliest chronologically. All the groups are dominated by Rh IIa, with a possible distinction to be drawn between Rh Ia-IIa which are weighted towards the earlier groups and Rh IIb-IIIb which are frequently found with Rh IIIa as well, and therefore probably later. Individual potters are shown in Table 5.VII and Figs 5.21-5.22, with similar results. Rh Ia potters form a distinct group at the top left corner of Fig. 5.21, but also include Verecundus I-II, B F Attoni and Respectus. Most of the potters fall into a very loose grouping in the middle of the figure, from Cerialis I to Julius II-Julianus I. There is also a somewhat indistinct and small block of later potters at the bottom of the figure. In its overall pattern Fig. 5.21 is similar to Bernhard's matrix of figure-type correlations,[12] and serves to confirm his suggestion of much borrowing of motifs between potters by indicating that many of the Rh Ib-IIIa potters are found fairly indiscriminately one with another in deposits, and thus may well be contemporary or at least overlapping in their periods of production. The dendrogram (Fig. 5.22) can be used to reach a similar conclusion, since in comparison with the CG dendrograms there are fewer distinctive groups, the links are less strong and are more evenly distributed, and there are many links forming at about the same level, between 1 $^{o}/_{oo}$ and 10 $^{o}/_{oo}$. The groups formed above the 5 $^{o}/_{oo}$ level are:

(a) Janu I, Reginus I, Janu II, Cobnertus III,
(b) Comitialis II, B F Attoni,
(c) Julius I, Helenius,
(d) Cerialis V, Comitialis VI,
(e) Cerialis III, E25/26, Julius I-Lupus, Comitialis V, Primitivus I, Julius II-Julianus I.

Of these, the first is the most interesting since it consists of all the Rh la potters considered for the dendrogram, plus Janu II, who used to be placed early, but has been transferred to Rh IIIa by Bernhard.[13] The transfer received some backing on chronological grounds (see above) but the evidence here seems to be contradictory and requires further investigation (unfortunately beyond the scope of this volume) for a satisfactory explanation. The other groups are all small and mixed, but the last is somewhat larger

[12] Bernhard 1981a; see also Appendix 5.
[13] Bernhard *ibid.* Cf. Schaub 1996 for further discussion, and fn. 1 above.

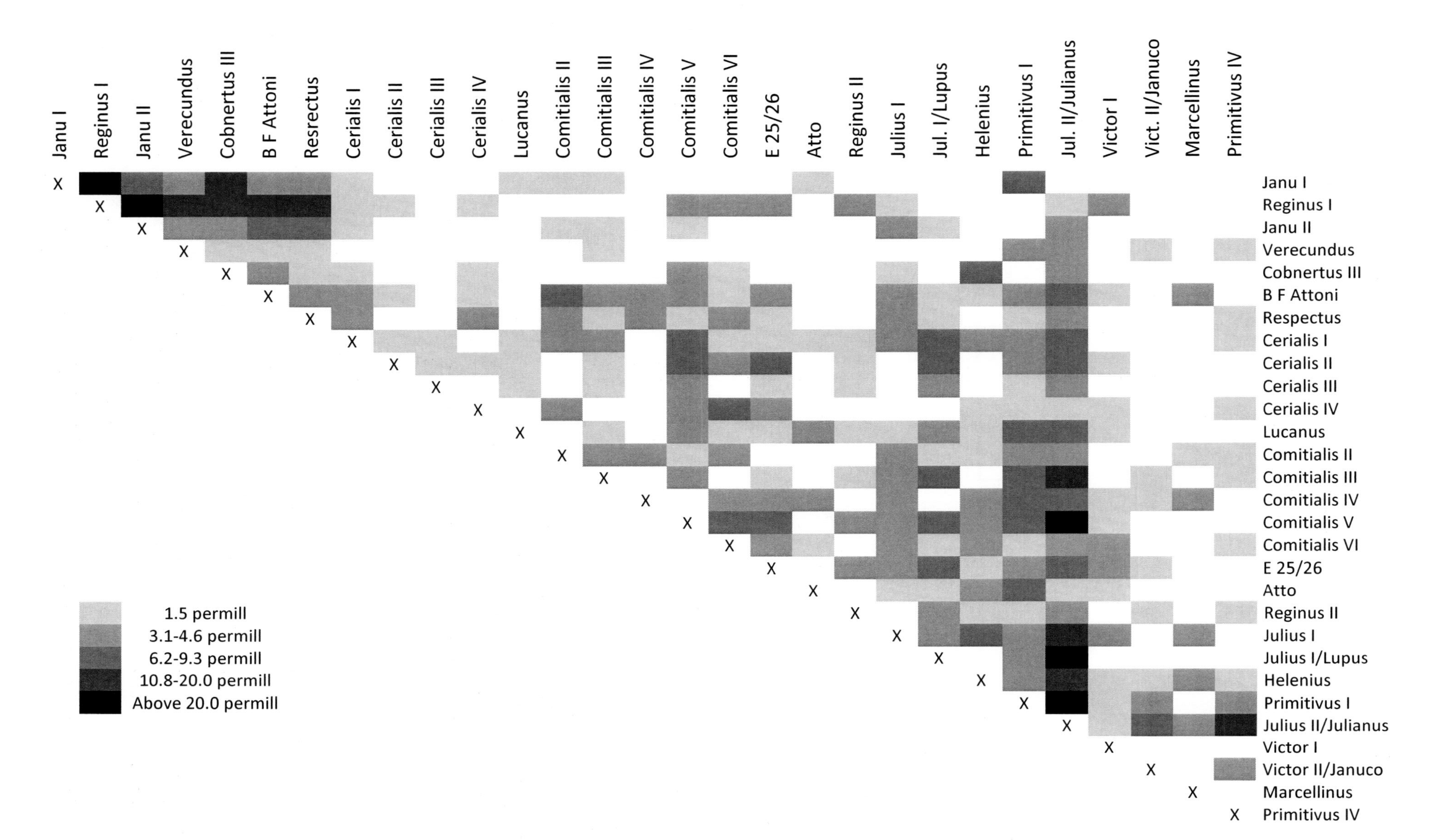


*Fig. 5.21 Matrix of association between Rheinzabern potters within deposits, data from Table 5.VII.*

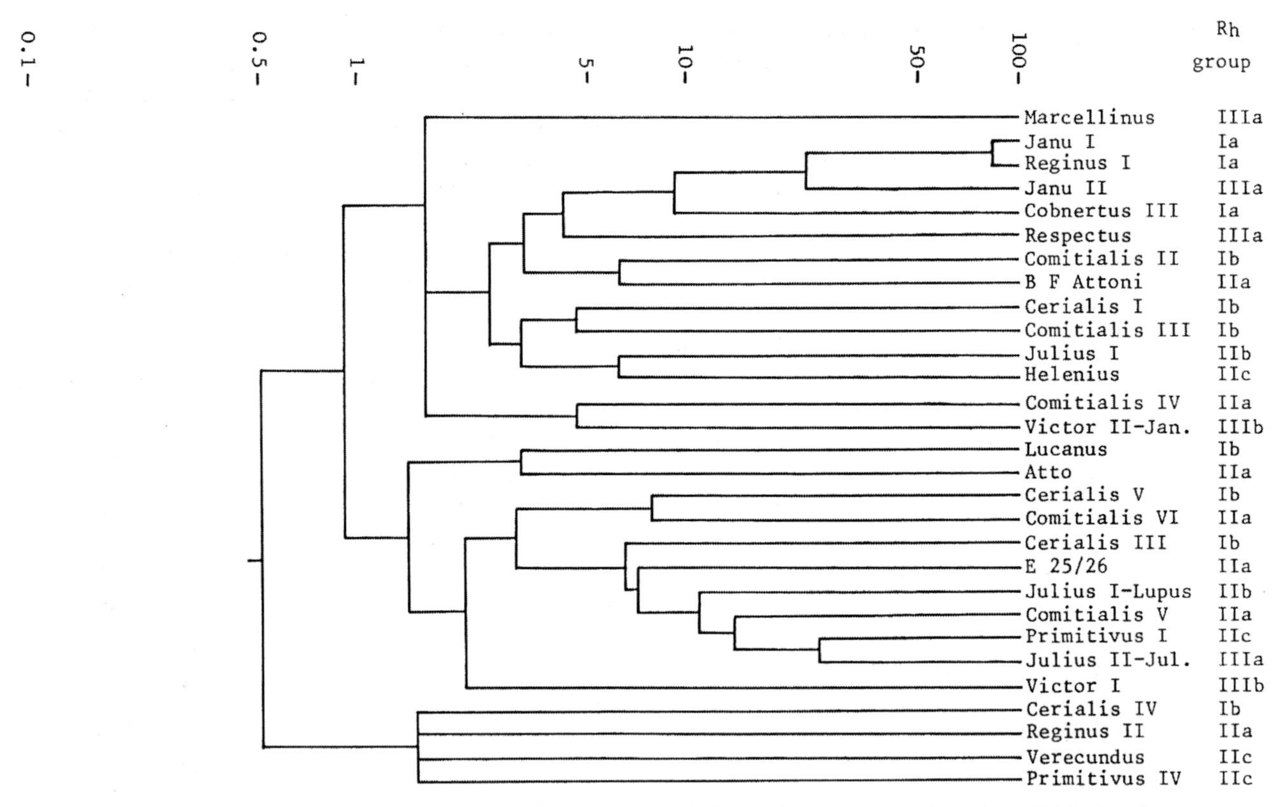


*Fig. 5.22 Average-link dendrogram of the level of association of Rheinzabern potters, data from Table 5.VII.*

*Table 5.VII Matrix of associations between Rheinzabern potters within deposits, expressed as permillages of total Rheinzabern associations (n = 647)*

| Janu I | Reginus I | Janu II | Verec. I-II | Cobnert. III | B F Attoni | Respectus | Cerialis I | Cerialis III | Cerialis IV | Cerialis V | Lucanus | Comit. II | Comit. III | Comit. IV | Comit. V | Comit. VI | E 25/26 | Atto | Reginus II | Julius I | Jul. I-Lupus | Helenius | Primit. I | Jul. II-Jul. I | Victor I | Vict. II-Janu. | Marcellin. | Primit. IV | |
|---|---|---|---|---|---|---|---|---|---|---|---|---|---|---|---|---|---|---|---|---|---|---|---|---|---|---|---|---|---|
| Rh Ia | Rh Ia | Rh IIIa | Rh IIc | Rh Ia | Rh IIa | Rh IIa | Rh Ib | Rh Ib | Rh Ib | Rh Ib | Rh Ib | Rh Ib | Rh Ib | Rh IIa | Rh IIa | Rh IIa | Rh IIa | Rh IIa | Rh IIa | Rh IIb | Rh IIb | Rh IIc | Rh IIc | Rh IIIa | Rh IIIb | Rh IIIb | Rh IIIa | Rh IIc | |
| X | 83.5 | 9.3 | 3.1 | 12.4 | 4.6 | 3.1 | 1.5 | - | - | - | 1.5 | 1.5 | 1.5 | - | - | - | - | 1.5 | - | - | - | - | 6.2 | - | - | - | - | - | Janu I |
| | X | 37.1 | 12.4 | 15.5 | 15.5 | 12.4 | 1.5 | 1.5 | - | 1.5 | - | - | - | - | 3.1 | 3.1 | 3.1 | - | 3.1 | 1.5 | - | - | - | 1.5 | 3.1 | - | - | - | Reginus I |
| | | X | 4.6 | 4.6 | 6.2 | 6.2 | 1.5 | - | - | - | - | 1.5 | 1.5 | - | 1.5 | - | - | - | - | 3.1 | 1.5 | - | - | 3.1 | - | - | - | - | Janu II |
| | | | X | 1.5 | 1.5 | 1.5 | - | - | - | - | - | - | 1.5 | - | - | - | - | - | - | - | - | - | 3.1 | 4.6 | - | 1.5 | - | 1.5 | Verecundus I-II |
| | | | | X | 3.1 | 1.5 | 1.5 | - | - | 1.5 | - | - | - | - | 3.1 | 1.5 | - | - | - | 1.5 | - | 6.2 | - | 4.6 | - | - | - | - | Cobnertus III |
| | | | | | X | 3.1 | 3.1 | 1.5 | - | 1.5 | - | 6.2 | 3.1 | 3.1 | 4.6 | 1.5 | 4.6 | - | - | 4.6 | 1.5 | 1.5 | 3.1 | 6.2 | 1.5 | - | 3.1 | - | B F Attoni |
| | | | | | | X | 3.1 | - | - | 3.1 | - | 3.1 | 1.5 | 3.1 | 1.5 | 3.1 | 1.5 | - | - | 3.1 | 1.5 | - | 1.5 | 3.1 | - | - | - | 1.5 | Respectus |
| | | | | | | | X | 1.5 | 1.5 | - | 1.5 | 3.1 | 4.6 | - | 6.2 | 1.5 | 1.5 | 1.5 | 1.5 | 4.6 | 7.7 | 3.1 | 3.1 | 9.3 | - | - | - | 1.5 | Cerialis I |
| | | | | | | | | X | 1.5 | 1.5 | 1.5 | - | 1.5 | - | 6.2 | 3.1 | 6.2 | - | 1.5 | - | 7.7 | - | 3.1 | 7.7 | 1.5 | - | - | - | Cerialis III |
| | | | | | | | | | X | - | 1.5 | - | 1.5 | - | 3.1 | - | 1.5 | - | 1.5 | - | 4.6 | - | 1.5 | 4.6 | - | - | - | - | Cerialis IV |
| | | | | | | | | | | X | - | 3.1 | - | 1.5 | 3.1 | 7.7 | 4.6 | - | - | - | - | 1.5 | 1.5 | 1.5 | 1.5 | - | - | 1.5 | Cerialis V |
| | | | | | | | | | | | X | - | 1.5 | 1.5 | 3.1 | 1.5 | 1.5 | 3.1 | 1.5 | 1.5 | 4.6 | 1.5 | 7.7 | 6.2 | 1.5 | - | - | - | Lucanus |
| | | | | | | | | | | | | X | 3.1 | 3.1 | 1.5 | 3.1 | - | - | - | 4.6 | 1.5 | 1.5 | 3.1 | 3.1 | - | - | 3.1 | 1.5 | Comitialis II |
| | | | | | | | | | | | | | X | - | 4.6 | - | 1.5 | - | 1.5 | 4.6 | 6.2 | - | 7.7 | 12.4 | - | 1.5 | - | 1.5 | Comitialis III |
| | | | | | | | | | | | | | | X | - | 4.6 | 3.1 | 3.1 | - | 3.1 | - | 4.6 | 6.2 | 7.7 | 1.5 | 4.6 | 3.1 | - | Comitialis IV |
| | | | | | | | | | | | | | | | X | 7.7 | 6.2 | - | 3.1 | 4.6 | 9.3 | 4.6 | 7.7 | 20.1 | 1.5 | - | - | - | Comitialis V |
| | | | | | | | | | | | | | | | | X | 4.6 | 1.5 | - | 3.1 | 1.5 | 4.6 | 1.5 | 6.2 | 3.1 | - | - | 1.5 | Comitialis VI |
| | | | | | | | | | | | | | | | | | X | - | 3.1 | 3.1 | 7.7 | 1.5 | 3.1 | 9.3 | 3.1 | 1.5 | - | - | E 25/26 |
| | | | | | | | | | | | | | | | | | | X | - | 1.5 | 1.5 | 3.1 | 6.2 | 1.5 | 1.5 | - | - | - | Atto |
| | | | | | | | | | | | | | | | | | | | X | - | 4.6 | 1.5 | 1.5 | 4.6 | - | 1.5 | - | 1.5 | Reginus II |
| | | | | | | | | | | | | | | | | | | | | X | 3.1 | 6.2 | 3.1 | 13.9 | 3.1 | - | 3.1 | - | Julius I |
| | | | | | | | | | | | | | | | | | | | | | X | - | 4.6 | 20.1 | - | - | - | - | Julius I-Lupus |
| | | | | | | | | | | | | | | | | | | | | | | X | 3.1 | 10.8 | 1.5 | 1.5 | 3.1 | 1.5 | Helenius |
| | | | | | | | | | | | | | | | | | | | | | | | X | 24.7 | 1.5 | 4.6 | - | 3.1 | Primitivus I |
| | | | | | | | | | | | | | | | | | | | | | | | | X | 1.5 | 9.3 | 3.1 | 12.4 | Julius II-Julianus I |
| | | | | | | | | | | | | | | | | | | | | | | | | | X | - | - | - | Victor I |
| | | | | | | | | | | | | | | | | | | | | | | | | | | X | - | 3.1 | Victor II-Januco |
| | | | | | | | | | | | | | | | | | | | | | | | | | | | X | - | Marcellinus |
| | | | | | | | | | | | | | | | | | | | | | | | | | | | | X | Primitivus IV |

and comprises those later potters most closely associated with Julius II-Julianus I, the chief representative of Rh IIIa (Cerialis III being the early exception in the group).

Having given the main characteristics of the larger kiln-centres and some of the associated smaller kilns, it remains to examine those not considered so far. Trier I has associations with many other groups (Tables 5.III-5.IV), predominantly CG Cinnamus, CG IV, Rh Ib-IIIa, Tr IIa-IIIa, Argonne and La Madeleine. It is difficult to interpret this pattern, except in that it corresponds, in the wide connections made, to the case of Rh la, and may be due to a fairly widespread initial market for Trier ware, before a distinct market area was established in Trier IIa and later. Trier I seems later than Rh la in view of the relatively low level of links between these two groups, and the fact that Rh la is poorly associated the later Trier groups. Trier IIa-b are best associated with Rh IIa, while Trier IIc-IIIa have their highest number of links with Rh IIIa: a chronological sequence is probably the best explanation for this. The later Trier groups have fewer external associations than the early groups, which may be due to the development of a discrete market area, or perhaps chronological factors.[14] The Argonne, for instance, has links with Trier I-IIa, but rather fewer with Trier IIb-IIIb. Trier's internal associations tend to cluster around Trier IIa, the most productive of the Trier groups, but similarly to Rheinzabern, the later Trier groups, especially Trier IIIa, have a tendency to more links with their own later groups, again due, most likely, to the chronological sequence of the groups. However, there was probably much overlapping between the Trier groups, since the internal associations lack the clear-cut trends of CG, and are more similar to Rheinzabern.

Westerndorf is mainly associated externally with CG Cinnamus, CG IV and Rh Ib-IIIa. The Rheinzabern links are most important since they show the rough contemporaneity of Rheinzabern main production period and Westerndorf. The highest level of Westerndorf links is with Rh IIa (as well as internally and with Pfaffenhofen, a feature already explained above by the presence of kiln-site deposits). Pfaffenhofen, to judge from the available data, has a similar linkage pattern to Westerndorf.

Of the remaining small kilns, little can be said except to observe that Waiblingen has links with Rh la, which is in accord with what is known of its chronology, and similarly Colchester and Pulborough have links more with CG Cinnamus than other groups.

The EG unlocated column in Table 5.III consists mainly of Ricken's group 1,[15] which has associations with CG I, II, III, Rh la, Ib, Argonne, La Madeleine, Chémery/Mittelbronn and Blickweiler. It is therefore of an early flavour amongst the kilns considered in the Table. The other unlocated wares are Clamosus, only known from the Bliesbruck area (D 51), dated to the 240/60s;[16] ovolo X, which is linked with Rh IIa and IIc; a ware found at B 124, Holzhausen, linked with Rh Ib, Tr IIa and IIc; a ware found at B 139, Ohringen-West, perhaps from South Germany and linked with Rh IIa, Heiligenberg and Eschweiler-Hof; and finally a ware found at A 164, Froitzheim, with stylistic connections with late Trier ware and linked with Rh IIb, IIIb, Trier IIa and IIIb (definitely late). Little can be said about these unlocated wares apart from the bald record of their associations given here, except for reference back to the adjusted coin dates for ovolo X and Froitzheim above.

## Individual Deposits

So far, discussion of chronology has rested on the deposits in the gazetteer considered as a single group. However, further information can be gained by taking individual deposits and trying to create some sort of sequence with them.

### Central Gaul

Table 5.VIII shows deposits where CG is relatively well-represented, although in no cases are the numbers of sherds very high and thus sampling error variations may have sometimes caused distortions to the figures. Group A consists of three deposits where CG II is the main constituent, B 5 being part of the Vallum filling at Benwell, B 50 a rubbish dump in the *vicus* at Housesteads and B 29 part of the enclosure ditch filling at Ditchley villa. Only B 5 has pieces of Cinnamus or later, and these may be disturbed pieces from the deposit overlying (A 4, see group D).

Group B contains three significant deposits: two burnt assemblages and an apparently unused group in a pit. In terms of sequence, Verulamium (A 122), an amalgam of burning debris layers from Insula XIV, comes first because of its preponderance of CG II. It is similar to group A except for the presence of Cinnamus sherds (all with his largely earlier ovolos 2 and 3). This deposit is dated to 150-60 by Hartley,[17] while the latest coins are of the reign of Antoninus Pius (dated 145-6), with an adjusted coin-date of VIIa-VIIb. Castleford (D 3), one of the most significant mid-second-century groups to be found in the north-west provinces, has a large percentage of CG III, consisting almost exclusively of Cerialis-Cinnamus products. The excavators interpret the burnt deposit as a store or shop, and is dated to 140-50 by Dickinson and Hartley.[18] Much of the samian seems unworn and probably unused, though some of the decorated ware was made from worn moulds, and may have been either seconds, or possibly made from moulds in use for some time. There is some old stock, e.g. by X-9 or X-12, whose moulds originated at Les Martres-de-Veyre, otherwise all of the assemblage comes from

[14] The reuse of moulds at Trier is a well-known phenomenon (Huld-Zetsche 1993, 52-6; 1998). This would increase the associations with later pieces in assemblages, and may account, to a reasonable extent, for the associations in Tables 5.V-VI.

[15] Ricken 1934.

[16] Schaub 1987; Petit 2001.

[17] Hartley 1972c. The deposit also contains pieces from Blickweiler (with Austrus ovolo) and by Satto/Saturninus, probably from Chémery.

[18] Dickinson & Hartley 2000, 33-56; Abramson & Fossick 1999, 132-5; cf. Weber 2012, 64-6; 2013, 192-4.

*Table 5.VIII Sequence of deposits in which CG is well-represented. Key as Table 5.I*

| *Deposit* | | *Coin-date* | CG I | CG II | CG III | CG Cinn | CG IV | Rh Ia | Rh Ib-IIc | Rh III | Tr I | Tr II | Tr III |
|---|---|---|---|---|---|---|---|---|---|---|---|---|---|
| **A** | | | | | | | | | | | | | |
| B50 | Housesteads | - | 1 | 4 | 2 | | | | | | | | |
| B29 | Ditchley | - | 3 | 4 | 1 | | | | | | | | |
| B5 | Benwell | - | | 19 | 3 | 1 | 1 | 1 | | | | | |
| **B** | | | | | | | | | | | | | |
| A122 | *Verulamium* | VIIa-VIIb | 2 | 10 | 3 | 4 | | | | | | | |
| D3 | Castleford | [V-VI/4th cent] | 6 | 97 | 130 | 12 | | | | | | | |
| D1 | Alcester | - | | 4 | 5 | 12 | | | | | | | |
| **C** | | | | | | | | | | | | | |
| A7 | Birrens | VIIa-VIIb | | 2 | 6 | 3 | | | | | | | |
| A94 | Mumrills | VI-VIIIb | | 4 | 14 | 5 | | | | | | | |
| B3 | Bar Hill | - | 3 | 3 | 6 | 17 | | | | | | | |
| B8 | Bothwellhaugh | - | | 1 | 3 | 10 | | | | | | | |
| B63 | Newstead | - | | | 3 | 4 | | | | | | | |
| B71 | Rough Castle | - | | 6 | 13 | 7 | | | | | | | |
| **D** | | | | | | | | | | | | | |
| A4 | Benwell | VIIIa-IXc | 1 | 4 | 8 | 14 | 2 | 5 | | | 2 | | |
| A55 | Corbridge | VIIa-VIIIb | 1 | 2 | 7 | 6+ | 3 | 1 | | | | | |
| B148 | Regensburg-K. | - | | 4 | 3 | 5 | 1 | 13 | | | | | |
| D82 | Regensburg-K. | V-VIIa | | | | | 1 | 2 | 5 | 1 | | | |
| **E** | | | | | | | | | | | | | |
| A25 | Caerleon | IXa | | | 6 | 21 | 10 | | | | | | |
| A48 | Colchester | VIIIa-IXb | | 2 | 2 | 9 | 3 | | | | | | |
| D46 | Ribchester | VIIIa-b | 2 | 6 | | 4 | 3 | | | | | | |
| **F** | | | | | | | | | | | | | |
| A40 | Carrawburgh | VIIIa-IXb | | | | 6 | 6 | 3 | | | | | |
| A45 | Chester | (Xb+) | | 4 | 2 | 8 | 8 | | | | | | |
| **G** | | | | | | | | | | | | | |
| A130 | Wroxeter | VIIIb-IXc | | 1 | 4 | 3 | 6 | | | | | | |
| A133 | York | VIIIa-Xa | | 6 | 5 | 1 | 6 | 2 | 2 | | | | |
| B162 | *Aquincum* | - | | | 6 | 7 | 10 | 1 | | | | | |
| **H** | | | | | | | | | | | | | |
| A131a | Wroxeter | VI | | | 3 | | 10 | | | | | | |
| A131b | Wroxeter | VI | 4 | 2 | 11 | 9 | 30 | 1 | | | | | |
| A38 | Carmarthen | (XII) | | | 3 | | 8 | | | | | | |
| B23 | Chester | - | | 1 | 1 | 2 | 4 | | | | | | |
| D59 | Lezoux | - | | | | 3 | 7 | | | | | | |
| D60 | Lezoux | - | | 1 | 2 | 1 | 3 | | | | | | |
| D68 | St Germain | VI+ | | | 1 | 1 | 4 | | | | | | |
| **I** | | | | | | | | | | | | | |
| B24 | Chester-le-Street | - | 1 | 2 | | 3 | 13 | 2 | 4 | 1 | 1 | | |
| B51 | Ilkley | - | 5 | 2 | 8 | 5 | 38 | 1 | | | | | |
| **J** | | | | | | | | | | | | | |
| A90 | London | VIIIb | | | 3 | 3 | 22 | | 14 | 3 | 1 | 9 | 4 |
| B9 | Brancaster | - | | | 1 | | 15 | | 3 | 1 | | 1 | |
| B87 | Guiry-Gadancourt | - | | 1 | | 1 | 12 | | 1 | | | | |
| D2 | Caister-on-Sea | [4th cent.] | | | | 1 | 14 | | 2 | 1 | 1 | 2 | 1 |
| D64 | Le Mans | Xa | | | | | 11 | | | | | | |

Lezoux. Weber estimates the date of the deposit to be the middle of the second century, to judge from the wear on the associated coins up to Hadrian.[19] There has been some disturbance of the burnt material, however, indicated by the presence of fourth-century coins. The third group, from Alcester (D 1), is also dominated by Cinnamus, nearly all his ovolos 2 and 3. It represents a large and mainly unused group of fairly complete vessels, dumped in a pit, dated to 150-60 by Hartley.[20] The excavator phases the pit to the later second to early third century, while noting that 'there was also a large and clearly *in situ* group of mid-second-century samian and other material',[21] which suggests some mixing of the deposit. It should be noted that the latest material in the pit dates to the late third to fourth century.

The next group (C) is centred on the Antonine Wall area, with deposits from the west ditch of Mumrills fort (A 94), general finds from Bar Hill fort (B 3), general finds from the bath-house of Bothwellhaugh fort (B 8) and general finds from Rough Castle fort (B 71). Also included are the upper burnt layer from Birrens fort (A 7) which has an adjusted coin-date of VIIa-VIIb, and one of the Newstead fort ditch deposits (B 63). A 94 is associated with the abandonment of the Antonine Wall, while the excavator has suggested a date prior to AD 158 for A 7. All these deposits are characterised by having CG III or CG Cinnamus (generally with more ovolo 3 than ovolo 1) as the most common group, and also by having no CG IV. The latter observation is not surprising, since Hartley's definition of CG IV was that it was not present on the Antonine Wall,[22] but it is clear from the reports published subsequently to 1972 (A 7, B 3, B 8, B 71) that this definition still holds good.

Group D does contain CG IV material, but not in great quantity – CG Cinnamus is dominant, and CG III is larger than CG IV. The first deposit concerned is A 4, Benwell, occupation debris over the Vallum filling. This is associated with a coin of Severus (adjusted date VIIIa-IXc) and underlain stratigraphically by a *denarius* of Faustina II. A 55, Corbridge, is part of the so-called 'AD 197' destruction deposit in the vicinity of site XI. It is discussed in detail under the gazetteer entry, where the conclusion is drawn that the bulk of the pottery is from the lower of the burning levels and can be associated with coins up to the reign of Antoninus (dated 155), but with the presence of coins of Faustina II which may be of Aurelianic date (adjusted date VIIa-VIIIb).[23] Unfortunately the assemblage is not quantified or fully recorded, but it is known that Cinnamus was very much the dominant potter present. Also included in this group is B 148, general finds from Regensburg-Kumpfmühl fort, which was apparently abandoned in the 170s (latest coin dated 171-2) when the legionary fortress was built nearby.[24] Of interest to all three deposits is the presence of Rh la and Trier I pottery, but none of later groups.

A 25, Caerleon, Prysg Field barracks, stone phase floor deposits, A 48, Colchester samian ware kiln stoke-hole filling, and D 46, Ribchester phase 5.1, form group E. None of them is a particularly good-quality deposit, since A 25 and D 46 may combine several sub-phases into one, and A 48 has definitely been disturbed by later kiln construction. However, all have CG Cinnamus as the most common of the late CG groups, with CG IV represented more strongly than CG III. Ribchester phase 5.1 is dated by the excavators to the late second to early third century, and has two *denarii* dated 200 and 204; the overlying destruction phase 5.2 is dated third to mid-fourth century.[25]

The following group (F) also has a deposit that is not closely stratified, A 45, Chester fortress, Deanery Field black earth deposit over the barracks. However, this and the Carrawburgh (A 40) *vicus* debris deposit are fairly homogeneous, with CG Cinnamus and CG IV present in equal numbers. Carrawburgh, in fact, has no CG III, and has an adjusted date of VIIIa-IXb.

Group G consists of A 130, Wroxeter baths, third layer above hall of baths, A 133, York, Blossom Street road ditch sealed by road B, and B 162, Aquincum burnt deposit, perhaps from a shop. The York deposit is fairly mixed, but all three have the characteristic of CG IV as the most common group, with in the case of A 130 and A 133, few Cinnamus pieces. A 130 and 133 have adjusted coin-dates in the early third century, but B 162 has been associated with the depredations of the Marcomannic Wars of the 160s (without, however, there being independent dating evidence to confirm this).[26]

In group H there is one of the most interesting deposits in the gazetteer, the Wroxeter 'gutter' shop deposit (A 131a) and associated material in the destruction debris of the forum (A 131b).[27] This has a good coin-date of VI, yet the assemblage is dominated by CG IV, which has a greater representation than all the other CG groups together. As we have seen earlier, this deposit is amongst the earliest known for CG IV, and had a tendency to 'overload' the earlier part of the graph for CG IV in Fig. 5.7. The best explanation for this lies in the fact that the 'gutter' pottery was stacked up as if for sale. A 131 is probably dominated by bowls that were for sale, including numbers of what must have been quite recently produced CG IV products, particularly by Paternus II. This applies not only to the 'gutter' deposit itself but also to the material from elsewhere in the forum, since most of it comes from the

[19] Weber 2012, 64-6; Mattingly & Pirie 1998.

[20] Hartley *et al.* 1994, 106-10; cf. Rhodes 1989, 55.

[21] Langley 1994, 60-3.

[22] Hartley 1972a.

[23] See also the discussion in Chapter 1, and King 1991, 44-5. Gazetteer D 4 contains additional finds linked to this deposit.

[24] See chapter 2, fn. 52, for the historical context, and below, Rheinzabern, Table 5.X, Group A, for further discussion.

[25] Buxton & Howard-Davis 2000, 133.

[26] Juhász 1936. See Friesinger *et al.* 1994, especially Schaub 1994 for discussion of the Marcomannic War and samian ware assemblages.

[27] For recent discussion of this deposit, see Weber 2012, 62-3; 2013, 190-2; also Rhodes 1989, 54-5.

*Table 5.IX St Magnus House (New Fresh Wharf), London (A 90) and Shadwell (D 47): composition of decorated samian ware in the deposits.*

Key as Table 5.I, plus SG, South Gaulish

| | SG | Montans | CG II | CG III | CG Cinn | CG IV | Rh Ia | Rh Ib | Rh IIa | Rh IIb | Rh IIc | Rh IIIa | Rh IIIb | Tr I | Tr IIa | Tr IIb | Tr IIc | Tr IIIa | Tr IIIb | Argonne | La Mad | Colch |
|---|---|---|---|---|---|---|---|---|---|---|---|---|---|---|---|---|---|---|---|---|---|---|
| Early layers [1] | 9 | 2 | 1 | | 2 | | | | | | | | | | | | | | | | | |
| Main deposits [2] | | | | 4 | 2 | 33 | | 10 | 8 | 4 | 1 | 3 | | 1 | 5 | 2 | 3 | 5 | | 1 | 1 | |
| Residual, etc [3] | 2 | | | 1 | | 8 | 1 | 1 | 7 | 3 | 2 | 10 | | 2 | 3 | | 10 | 3 | | | 1 | |
| Shadwell [4] | 5 | 1 | 2 | 1 | 2 | 4 | 1 | 5 | 4 | 8 | 16 | 10 | 3 | 10 | 4 | 3 | 5 | 5 | 3 | 1 | 1 | 1 |

[1] These have been judged to be the layers of Period 1, Phases 1-2, underlying the waterfront structures and the coin of AD 197. They are 286, 350, 357, 527 and 533. Layer 342 also underlies the coin but since it has unused and CG IV vessels, has been left out of consideration. Layer 380 was thought, too, to be uncertain, and thus omitted.

[2] These are all the deposits of Period 1 amongst and in front of the waterfront, and are the pieces listed in the gazetteer. The figures here may differ slightly from the gazetteer, since joins across layers have been separated.

[3] These are layers of Period 2 disturbed in the Saxon period, mainly associated with layers 293, 314, 348, etc.

[4] The figures compiled here are the general finds from the site in Bird 2002; 2011. D 47 is included within these totals.

adjacent part of the portico, East Rooms 1-2, and was probably another part of the shop. The pottery from East Rooms 1-2 is very similar to the 'gutter', with 6 CG III, 5 CG Cinnamus, and 18 CG IV (of which 12 are by Paternus II). There are no pieces of CG I-II, unlike elsewhere in the forum. However, even elsewhere the evidence seems to suggest a scattered shop deposit, since although CG I-II is present, the assemblage is still dominated by CG IV (11 out of 28 total), with a remarkably similar range of CG IV potters to that in the 'gutter' and East Rooms 1-2 (mainly Paternus II, also Advocisus, Casurius, Censorinus). We are clearly in the presence of a highly selective deposit, a batch of new vessels ready to be sold, and as such different in composition from nearly all the other deposits considered, which are usually formed of discards made during the normal course of use of the pottery. If the pottery thought to be for sale is removed, the relatively small remainder has the character of a group C or D deposit. It is instructive to compare A 131 with A 122 of group B; both these deposits are often dated to effectively the same period, late in the reign of Antoninus, and they are both destruction debris, yet their compositions are entirely different, the latter probably representing the general range of bowls actually in use or being thrown away at the time, the former giving a unique insight into the range of vessels that were probably just coming onto the market. The potters represented in the 'gutter' are relatively restricted in number, and unusual in lacking Cinnamus but being dominated by Paternus II. Some common CG IV potters are not present, notably Doeccus, who is probably later (see below).[28]

Two deposits from Lezoux have been included in this group. D 59, from the Serve-d'Ervier kiln F111/112 has no coins, but 2 CG Cinnamus and 7 CG IV, dominated by Paternus II. It has many of the characteristics of Wroxeter and the other assemblages in this group, and is dated by the excavators to the third quarter of the second century.[29] The other Lezoux deposit, D 60, from a waster dump, is more mixed, and earlier than D 59 with more CG III pieces. It includes a mould with the cursive signature of Sanvillus, in a style close to Censorinus and Paternus II.[30]

The other deposits in group H are much less important, but share the characteristic of having an absolute predominance of CG IV. A 38 is a fairly coherent group of material probably redeposited in a well in Carmarthen, and B 23 is from the bottom of a well at Chester, overlain by third century infilling. Group I is similar to H in having more CG IV than the other CG groups combined. Both B 24, Chester-le-Street and B 51, Ilkley, are phase groups rather than individual deposits, but are similar in being forts that have distinctive late second century periods of occupation, the latter in particular being considered to run from AD 169 or a bit earlier. However, both deposits suffer from the common disadvantage of phase groupings, in that it is not known whether the bulk of the samian ware is from early or late in the overall period of the phase, or if there is an even pattern of discard. However, it is clear from the Rheinzabern pieces that B 24, at least, runs into the early decades of the third century.

The last group in Table 5.VIII also contains one of the most important individual deposits, A 90, dump material from the waterfront at St Magnus House (New Fresh Wharf), London. The waterfront timbers have a dendrochronological date of *c.* AD 214, and there is a *terminus post quem* provided by an underlying coin of AD 197. The samian ware includes several unused and virtually complete bowls, apparently dumped deliberately in front of the quayside, perhaps from a store nearby. On conventional dating the CG ware runs to *c.* AD 180, but the Rheinzabern and Trier ware runs to *c.* AD 230. This has led

[28] There is ample scope for re-analysis of A 131, with a view to establishing signs of use, if any, on the bowls, and the chemical composition of their fabrics.

[29] Bet & Delage 2009, 453-64.

[30] *Ibid.*, 464-70.

to the explanation that the CG ware was unused and stored for 20-30 years before being dumped.[31] However, it is clear from the observations made so far in this chapter that CG IV, of which this deposit largely consists, could easily be present as a contemporary ware at the time of the dumping. There are some differences in the internal composition of the deposit (Table 5.IX), as a clear separation can be made between early layers and the main deposit. There are also a number of pieces in residual deposits, and it is interesting to note that in them later pottery (Rh IIIa and Trier IIc) is more common than in the main deposits. This hints at a sequence within the main deposits, in which the upper, later dumps have been truncated by Saxon disturbance. In fact it appears that some of the dumps under the waterfront (e.g. 511) are composed mainly of CG ware, and conversely some in front of the quay (e.g. 269, which is one of the layers truncated by disturbance, and 318) are mainly Trier and Rheinzabern ware. In other words, although there are apparently unused pieces from all parts of the dumps and in all the main wares, the immediate source of the pottery was not the same, and that, whatever the reasons for the dumping, there were probably various episodes all contemporary with or post-dating the VIIIb date for the waterfront.

Table 5.IX also includes the general samian ware finds from Shadwell, East London, mainly as a comparison with St Magnus House, and for the strong presence of Rheinzabern and Trier products, discussed below.[32] These two sites, with Caister-on-Sea (D 2), are the main assemblages with reasonable numbers of late CG, Rheinzabern and Trier examples in association.

The other deposits in group J also have CG IV as the main group with little earlier pottery. In the case of Le Mans (D 64), CG IV is the only group present, and includes pieces of Caletus, Paternus II and Iullinus out of reutilized moulds, together with several pieces by Fgientinus (Cintinus). It has coins to the Gallic Empire, with an adjusted date of period Xa, and clearly represents a third-century assemblage. It is linked to a less well stratified deposit (D 63) with a similar coin-date and pieces by CG IV potters Marcus and Banvus, who are also considered to be late in CG IV.[33] Of relevance to Le Mans and the presence there of Caletus, are D 57-58, Lezoux, Enclos site, kiln F55 and building F83. Both contexts have Caletus as the most common potter, and the excavators consider the large samian ware kiln to be of mid-third century date.[34] D 58 has coins to period IXc. Also relevant is the Poitiers shop deposit (D 67), which has pieces by Caletus and Fgientinus (Cintinus) contemporary with the Lezoux D 57-58 groups. D 67 is a fire destruction deposit dated by the excavators to the second half of the third century, but the basis for this dating is not clear.[35] B 87, the contents of a pit from Guiry-Gadancourt villa, has a similar range of CG IV material, but with a higher preponderance of potters considered to be early CG IV (see Table 5.XIV for proposed division into CG IVa and CG IVb). There is also a deposit from Lyon (B 90) in a drain on the Tolozan site, which consists of 4 pieces of CG IV and a large quantity of TSC (*terre sigillée claire* or *terra sigillata chiara*). It is one of the latest deposits of samian ware from Lyon, but has no independent dating.[36]

B 9 in Group J consists of the general finds from Brancaster fort *vicus*. It is not dated independently, but B 9 is usually considered third century, with an origin in the later second century. All the stratified coins from B 9 excavations of 1974-7 can be dated VI-Xa, implying occupation between the later second and mid/late third centuries.[37] Caister-on-Sea (D 2) is regarded as having been established on unoccupied ground in the early third century, and certainly continued into the fourth century, with hoards of that date placed in the refuse layers of D 2. The composition of D 2 appears to be later in character than B 9, as far as CG IV is concerned.[38]

All group J deposits are notable for lacking Rh la products.

Also of relevance at this point is A 39, general finds from Carpow fortress. There is, unfortunately, only one small decorated sherd published from this closely dated site (*c.* AD 208-11), which is by Casurius, Pugnus or Cettus (CG III-IV). However, it clearly represents a bowl in use on the site at this time. Cramond (D 5) has a Severan phase that is probably contemporary, and a coin-dated deposit of this phase with a single piece in the style of Cettus. At this site, the large quantity of Antonine material, which resulted in redeposition in the Severan phase, makes assessment of late usage difficult, as many of the earlier samian vessels could still have been in use in the later phase. However, there are some definite late CG products in the overall assemblage, brought to the site at the time of the Severan occupation.[39]

Dover (D 6-12) has a stratigraphic sequence with coin-dated samian ware that runs from the later second to the mid third century. All the deposits are small, and there is evidence of redeposition, but CG IV in early-mid third-century contexts is demonstrable.[40] Another site with many coin-dated associations with CG ware is Piercebridge

[31] Bird 1986, 139-47; 1993; cf. Richardson & Tyers 1984, 134. For the stratigraphy and phasing of the site and the chronological evidence from dendrochronology and coins, see Miller *et al.* 1986, 62-72; also Wallace 2006, 259-60; Monteil 1999 (who favours a 'single-group' explanation). Rhodes (1989, 48-9) favours an explanation that the material is primarily breakages 'which accumulated over a long period and were later discarded in the quay fill'.

[32] Gazetteer D 47; Bird 2002; 2011.

[33] Delage & Guillier 1997, 271-6 (D 64), 268-71 (D 63). See also Delage 2003; 1999b; Delage & Séguier 2009 for further discussion of third-century CG IV potters. For other coin-dated late CG IV groups, see D 72, Tavers; D 73, Le Thovey; D 75, Vieux.

[34] Bet & Gangloff 1987, 148-57.

[35] Wittmann & Jouquand 2009.

[36] See also D 61, Lyon, Célestins site, for an early third century deposit, mainly earlier CG IV, that also includes TSC B ware; Bonnet *et al.* 2003.

[37] Dickinson & Bird 1985; Hinchliffe & Sparey Green 1985. Elsewhere on the site, occupation continues into the fourth century. See also Davies 2009, 210-13.

[38] Dickinson & Bird 1993; Darling & Gurney 1993; Davies 2009, 213-6.

[39] Dickinson 2003; Holmes 2003.

[40] Philp 1989; Bird 1989.

(D 14-45). One group (D 14-22) has early third-century material incorporated into ditches and associated features of the mid third century and later. CG IV and Cinnamus are well represented, and were probably part of the legionary presence at the site in the early third century.[41] However, SG samian and other artefacts point to several contexts at the site having redeposited material.

Finally, it is worth singling out A 99, Portchester, where a number of pieces of samian ware including one by Cinnamus were found on an apparently virgin site of AD 286/90+, with little or no evidence of redeposited coarse pottery apart from a small conquest-period group. As Joanna Bird concluded in the report, the best explanation is probably that the samian was brought to the site by the first occupants of the fort.[42]

### Rheinzabern

The individual deposits for Rheinzabern (Table 5.X) are fewer in number than for CG, and less can be said about them. Initially, there is B 148 Regensburg-Kumpfmühl, abandoned in the 170s as pointed out above.[43] It is the only deposit in group A, with only Rh Ia pottery. To this can be added a coin-dated deposit (D 82) from the same site, but with a more mixed Rheinzabern assemblage, including, somewhat surprisingly, a piece in the style of Victor I (Rh IIIb).[44] However, the excavation methods of the early twentieth century used on this deposit, infer caution, and only a general association can be made. Sulz (D 95) also has a majority of Rh Ia pieces, and a coin date of VIIb, i.e. the AD 180s, which would place it slightly later than Regensburg-Kumpfmühl.[45] In this deposit are eight examples of Janu II, conventionally assigned to Rh IIIa, but a potter whose dating and stylistic affiliations have excited a good deal of debate.[46] D 95 has one of the largest dated groups of this potter, and supports Schaub's contention of an early *floruit*, even if the potter continues to be found in third-century assemblages.[47]

The fourth deposit in Group A is Walheim (D 98), a site which has a burning episode of *c.* AD 155/60, with subsequent rebuilding.[48] D 98 probably dates from early in the occupation period that followed.

Group B consists of those deposits where Rh Ib-IIa are the main component when combined. There is A 90, London, New Fresh Wharf, about which no further comment need be made, given what has already been stated earlier. A 158, Zwammerdam fort, A 187, Niederbieber fort and B 146, Regensburg fortress, are all phase groups rather than individual deposits. The first two are very similar in composition, and the date for A 158 is probably more realistic than that for A 187. B 146 dates to the 170s+ on historical ground, but the coin-dating evidence from other sites would put the bulk of the pottery into the third century. A 177 and A 179 are features in Künzing fort, the former apparently slightly earlier than the latter, both in terms of coin-date and composition. A 192 is the upper burnt fill of a cellar in Pocking *vicus*, and besides the pottery listed in the Table, had a number of pieces by Helenius and Comitialis of Westerndorf, for the dating of which it is a key deposit. The pottery from B 105, a pit in Altenstadt fort, and B 108, the ditch of Degerfeld in Butzbach stone fort, are chiefly useful for the links they have between Rh IIa and Trier II. The groups from Walheim are individual deposits in the *vicus*, D 103 being notable for its strong presence of RH IIa pieces, together with an example of the Blickweiler potter L.AT.AT.[49]

Those deposits with Rh IIb-c as the main component form group C. The coin-dated deposits are A 173, a cellar fill from Holzhausen fort (IXa-IXb) and one of the planum levels (am) from A 206, Enns-Lorch fortress (VIIIa-IXb). There is also a similar, but smaller deposit from A 206 (ae) with a coin-date of IXb-IXc. Most significantly of all those in Group C, in view of the large samian ware assemblage, is the Langenhain cellar fill (IXa), which has been dated to AD 233 on historical grounds, and associated with a burning episode.[50] In this deposit, Julius I, Lupus and Julius I/Lupus are dominant, together with Trier II-III potters (Table 5.XI), thus providing a valuable contextual link between the later phases of both kiln-centres.

B 98, Rijswijk settlement general finds, and B 136, Miltenburg-Altstadt fort general finds are two other deposits in Group C. The latter has a date of AD 150s+ by virtue of being on the outer German *limes* (as do A 185 and B 138, Murrhardt, A 199-200, Walldürn, and B 139-141, Ohringen-West), but since this *terminus post quem* covers the entire date-range of Rheinzabern production, it is not useful, and in fact the pottery from B 136 is more likely to be third century. A 200, the later bath-house of Walldürn fort, is relevant in this context, however, since it has Rh IIa (1), Rh IIb (2) and Rh IIIa (1), together with a possible *terminus post quem* provided by a rebuilding inscription dated to AD 232. Lastly, the coin-dated deposit from D 47, Shadwell (Xb) is later than the others in Group C, but is placed in this group because of the dominance of Rh IIb-c. The total samian assemblage from Shadwell (Table 5.IX) is slightly different in composition, inclining to Rh IIc and Rh IIIa, which would place it more in line with Group D than C.

Group D is composed of deposits dominated by Rh IIIa-b. B 149, a pit amongst the Rheinzabern samian kilns is the most interesting of these, because of the large numbers involved. It is important because the assemblage is considered to be probably the dump of a single overfired

[41] Cool & Mason 2008; Ward 2008.
[42] Morris 1975, 277-8.
[43] See chapter 2, fn. 11 for the historical context.
[44] Faber 1994, 349-55.
[45] Schaub 1994, 442; 1996.
[46] Schaub 1996; Gimber 1999, 383-4. See fn. 1 for further details.
[47] Schaub 1996.
[48] Kortüm & Lauber 2004.
[49] Cf. Petit 2001 for discussion of the chronology of this potter. Walheim, D 113 (coin date VI-IXa/c), also has Blickweiler peices in association with Heiligenberg, early Rheinzabern and possibly the Swabian kilns; Kortüm & Lauber 2004, vol. II, 299-304.
[50] Simon & Köhler 1992; Huld-Zetsche & Steidl 1994.

*Table 5.X Sequence of deposits in which Rheinzabern is well-represented. Key as Table 5.I*

| Deposit | | Coin-date | Rh Ia | Rh Ib | Rh IIa | Rh IIb-c | Rh IIIa | Rh IIIb | Tr I | Tr II | Tr III | CG II | CG III | CG Cinn | CG IV |
|---|---|---|---|---|---|---|---|---|---|---|---|---|---|---|---|
| **A** | | | | | | | | | | | | | | | |
| B148 | Regensburg-K. | - | 13 | | | | | | | | | 4 | 3 | 5 | 1 |
| D82 | Regensburg-K. | VI-VIIa | 2 | 3 | 2 | | | 1 | | | | | | | 1 |
| D95 | Sulz | VIIb | 9 | 3 | 1 | | 8 | | | | | | | | |
| D98 | Walheim | VI-IXb | 6 | | 2 | | | | | | | | | | |
| **B** | | | | | | | | | | | | | | | |
| A90 | London | VIIIb | | 5 | 5 | 4 | 3 | | 1 | 9 | 4 | | 3 | 3 | 22 |
| A158 | Zwammerdam | VIIIa-IXa | | 4 | 3 | 3 | 2 | | 31 | 61 | | | | | |
| A187 | Niederbieber | (IXc) | 1 | 1 | 3 | 1 | 1 | 1 | 21 | 63 | 5 | | | | |
| A177 | Künzing | VIIa-Xa | 1 | 2 | 5 | | | 1 | | | | | | 1 | |
| A179 | Künzing | VIIIb-IXc | | 1 | 3 | 2 | 1 | | | | | | | | |
| A192 | Pocking | IXb-IXc | | 1 | 3 | 1 | 1 | | | | | | | 1 | 1 |
| B105 | Altenstadt | - | | 1 | 4 | 2 | 3 | | 1 | 4 | 1 | | | | |
| B108 | Degerfeld in B. | - | | | 4 | | | | | 4 | | | | | |
| B146 | Regensburg | - | 5 | 13 | 25 | 18 | 6 | 1 | | | | | | | |
| D99 | Walheim | VIIb-IXb | 3 | 2 | 7 | 2 | 1 | | | | | | | | |
| D103 | Walheim | VIIb-IXb | | 4 | 11 | 2 | | | | | | | | | |
| D111 | Walheim | (Flav) | 2 | 3 | 4 | 1 | 1 | | | | | | | | |
| **C** | | | | | | | | | | | | | | | |
| A173 | Holzhausen | IXa-IXb | | 1 | | 6 | 3 | 1 | 1 | 1 | | | | | |
| A206 | Enns-Lorch (am) | VIIIa-IXb | | 1 | 3 | 4 | 1 | 1 | | | | | | | |
| B98 | Rijswijk | - | | 1 | 1 | 2 | 1 | | 1 | 6 | 1 | | | | |
| B136 | Miltenburg-A. | - | 1 | 1 | 2 | 3 | 3 | | | 1 | | | | | |
| D47 | Shadwell | Xb | | | 1 | 6 | 1 | 1 | | | | | | | 1 |
| D80 | Langenhain | IXa | | 1 | 3 | 36 | 13 | 1 | 2 | 62 | 68 | | 1 | | |
| **D** | | | | | | | | | | | | | | | |
| A170 | Heddernheim | IXa | | | | 2 | 6 | 1 | | | | | | | |
| B114 | Epfach | - | 1 | 1 | 1 | 2 | 3 | | | | | | | | 1 |
| B129 | Künzing | - | | | 1 | 1 | 1 | 2 | | | | | | | |
| B149 | Rheinzabern | - | 1 | 6 | 13 | 293 | 132 | 181 | | | | | | | |
| A164 | Froitzheim | Xb | | | | 1 | | 1 | | 1 | 1 | | | | |

kiln-load, and therefore represents the activity of a group of contemporary potters, which Bittner dates to AD 235-45.[51] Regulinus (Rh IIc) is the most common in terms of moulds, but the excavator considered the following also to have been working at kilns nearby when the pit was filled:- ovolo E31 = Pervincus II (Rh IIIb), Julius II-Julianus I (Rh IIIa), Primitivus I (Rh IIc), Victorinus I (Rh IIb) and Julianus II (Rh IIIb). All these potters are represented by 45 or more pieces. Two points are clear from this pit, that potters of different Rheinzabern groups were probably at work at the same time, if the excavator's suggestion is correct, and even if it is not, the wide range of Rheinzabern potters present, both in terms of moulds and bowls, demonstrates the extent of mixing that rubbish deposits even at a kiln-site are prone to. The other group D deposits are A 170, a cellar fill at Heddernheim, well dated to period IXa, B 114, a grave at Epfach, B 129, a pit at Künzing, and lastly, the well-dated ditch fills from the short-lived *burgus* of period Xb at Froitzheim. Additionally there is a sherd of Rh IIIb from the fort at Schaan (B 160) which has no occupation earlier than the end of the third century. Presumably this falls into the same survival category as the CG pieces from Portchester mentioned earlier.

### Trier

Trier ware is only well-represented in a few deposits (Table 5.XI), most of which have been referred to in Tables 5.VIII-5.X, and therefore fewer details of date and other products are given here.

The most interesting assemblage in Table 5.XI is B 156, the 'Massenfund' from the kiln-site at Trier. This is similar to the kiln deposit at Rheinzabern in being predominantly of late date (Dubitatus-Dubitus; Trier IIIa) but also having much earlier material. The 'Massenfund' is thought to be a single dump, and Huld-Zetsche uses it as part of her case for

[51] Reutti 1983, 54-6; Bittner 1986, 249-58; 1996; 2011.

*Table 5.XI Deposits in which Trier is well-represented*

| Deposit | | Tr I | Tr IIa | Tr IIb | Tr IIc | Tr IIIa-b |
|---|---|---|---|---|---|---|
| D76 | Echzell | 37 | 96 | 4 | | |
| A158 | Zwammerdam | 31 | 19 | 24 | 18 | |
| A90 | London | 1 | 4 | 2 | 3 | 4 |
| B98 | Rijswijk | 1 | 4 | 1 | 1 | 1 |
| A187 | Niederbieber | 21 | 38 | 23 | 2 | 5 |
| D80 | Langenhain | 2 | 32 | 7 | 23 | 68 |
| B156 | Trier | 9 | 62 | 10 | 50 | 152 |

re-use of earlier moulds by later potters, particularly moulds of Werkstatt I and II (Trier I).[52] This opens up interesting possibilities, particularly at A 187, Niederbieber, where Huld-Zetsche has suggested that 19 out of the 21 pieces of Trier I are in fact from late re-used moulds. If this is the case, this would alter the profile at Niederbieber, and possibly also at Zwammerdam, too, although the excavator there made no mention of re-used moulds.[53] The case for the 'Massenfund' containing moulds that were re-used was based partly on concern by Huld-Zetsche at the mixed nature of the deposit, and her attempt to solve this problem. However, such mixed deposits at kiln-sites are known elsewhere, notably B 149, Rheinzabern, considered above, and A 48, Colchester, and it has also been argued that the Trier 'Massenfund' was built up over a period.[54] In general, mixed rubbish deposits are the rule rather than the exception, and it may be possible to explain the presence of early potters (i.e. those bowls not demonstrably out of re-used moulds) in the 'Massenfund' as mixed material or a fairly slow accumulation. The general case for reuse of moulds remains, of course, and is a significant aspect of samian chronology.[55]

Of the other Trier deposits, D 76, Echzell, is a large dump of material dominated by Werkstatt II (Trier I) and Dexter (Trier IIa), and with a coin-date of VIIa, i.e. AD 180s, thus providing valuable dating to the earlier phases of Trier production. Trier IIa is the most common in A 90, B 98, and A 187, while at A 158 Trier I and IIb are most common.

D 80, Langenhain, provides a link between late Trier and later Rheinzabern products (Table 5.X), and has a valuable coin-date of IXa, i.e. AD 230s, backed up by a possible historical date for the burning episode there of AD 233.[56] The dominant Trier potter in the Langenhain assemblage is Dubitus (Trier IIIa), followed by Dexter (Trier IIa).

Apart from Langenhain, however, Trier III is rare, except at Trier itself, and is probably late and predominantly locally distributed.[57] Relevant in this regard are A 146, a cellar at Titelberg settlement, with two pieces of Trier IIb and a coin-date of Xb, and A 164, Froitzheim *burgus* ditches, with Trier IIa (1), Trier IIIb (1) and a late local Trier-derived ware, plus a coin-date of Xb. Both these sites are fairly close to the kiln-centre.

A general point to emerge from the individual deposits considered here (but somewhat peripheral to the issue of chronology) is that a high proportion of them are from military sites, more than the proportion in the gazetteer generally. There seems to be a greater usage of samian ware on military sites, and therefore a greater concentration of discards in useful deposits. Of course, civilian deposits, particularly from towns, are also important, as Wroxeter and London demonstrate, but it is rare to have deposits from villas, for instance, that are of more than a few pieces. The proportion of samian ware in ceramic assemblages on different types of site is an issue now receiving much-needed further investigation.[58]

### Regional variations in deposits

It is appropriate at this stage to look at regional variations in the representation of potters and kiln products in the deposits considered in the Gazetteer, since distributional factors have some bearing on chronology. Appendix 9 gives the regional distribution by kiln-centre and potter, the sites used for each region being given in the index of deposits at the end of the gazetteer. All deposits have been used, from both sections A and B of the gazetteer, the only exceptions being the kiln-sites, for which the kiln products made at the sites themselves have been excluded because of the heavy bias they give to the figures (the deposits concerned are A 48, B 27, Colchester, A 188-91, B 142-3, Pfaffenhofen, B 149-50, Rheinzabern, B 155-6, Trier). Otherwise the Appendix is a complete listing of all the positive identifications made. Table 5.XII is a summary derived from the longer Appendix.

It should be stressed that the discussion that follows derives mainly from Table 5.XII, but also includes indications, where relevant, from more recent reports and discussion articles. This applies in particular to France, where work on second- and third-century deposits has been very productive, and has resulted in considerable strengthening of the database.[59]

[52] Huld-Zetsche 1972; 1978; 1993, 52-6; 1998.

[53] Moulds may also have been re-used at Rheinzabern and CG, but this has never been investigated in the same detail as at Trier. Cf. Petit 2001 for reuse of moulds at Blickweiler, and Delage 2003 for Lezoux, in this respect. Mees (1993; 2002) does not consider that the evidence from Rheinzabern supports the notion of late reuse of moulds at that kiln-centre. However, Reutti (1983, 54-6) and Bittner (1986, 254-5) consider that reuse of Rheinzabern moulds did take place, based on the kiln-site deposit Rhz. 79/657 (B149). Gimber (1999, 392) considers the practice at Rheinzabern to have varied between workshops. Cf. also Bird (1993, 2; 2002, 33-4) for Shadwell, which has probable Rheinzabern 'Spätausformungen'.

[54] Beckmann 1973.

[55] Delage (2003, 186-8) suggests that CG moulds, once created, could have been used intermittently for long periods, perhaps decades, which would account for the longevity of certain potters' production, e.g. Cinnamus. Cf. Webster 2001, 293, for discussion of this issue. Goubet & Meyer (2006, 549) note that Satto moulds were used at Boucheporn, Chémery, Blickweiler and Mittelbronn over a period of nearly a century, implying both trade in moulds and their use and reuse over long periods.

[56] See fn. 50.

[57] Frey (2000) discusses late Trier decorated wares, in relation to the finds from the Borg villa, a short distance to the south of Trier itself.

[58] Villas and rural sites: Willis 2013; Millett 1980. Samian on civilian and military sites: Ward 2010; Webster 2013; Willis 1998; 2005.

[59] See Gazetteer D; also Delage 1998, and the annual SFECAG volumes

*Table 5.XII Summary and percentages of regional distribution of samian in deposits c. 150-280+, from Gazetteer A-B and Appendix 9. All deposits except for kiln products from kiln-centre deposits. Key as Table 5.I*

| | *S Britain* | | *Wales & W Britain* | | *N Britain* | | *France* | | *Low Countries* | | *Rhineland* | | *Danube* | | *Total* |
|---|---|---|---|---|---|---|---|---|---|---|---|---|---|---|---|
| | n | % | n | % | n | % | n | % | n | % | n | % | n | % | |
| CG I-II | 112 | 21.5 | 28 | 12.5 | 87 | 19.0 | 2 | 2.5 | 2 | 1.0 | 3 | 0.6 | 28 | 5.0 | 262 |
| CG III | 68 | 13.0 | 39 | 17.4 | 90 | 19.6 | 7 | 8.8 | 3 | 1.5 | 1 | 0.2 | 16 | 2.9 | 224 |
| CG Cinn | 89 | 17.0 | 46 | 20 5 | 99 | 21.6 | 3 | 3.8 | 4 | 2.0 | 0 | 0.0 | 95 | 17.1 | 336 |
| CG IV | 117 | 22.4 | 85 | 37.9 | 93 | 20.3 | 40 | 50.0 | 3 | 1.5 | 0 | 0.0 | 16 | 2.9 | 354 |
| CG III/IV | 35 | 6.7 | 14 | 6.3 | 30 | 6.5 | 17 | 21.3 | 3 | 1.5 | 1 | 0.2 | 17 | 3.1 | 117 |
| Rh Ia | 5 | 1.0 | 4 | 1.8 | 20 | 4.4 | 1 | 1.3 | 1 | 0.5 | 20 | 4.0 | 46 | 8.3 | 97 |
| Rh Ib | 12 | 2.3 | 0 | 0.0 | 3 | 0.7 | 0 | 0.0 | 6 | 3.0 | 23 | 4.6 | 55 | 9.9 | 99 |
| Rh IIa | 11 | 2.1 | 2 | 0.9 | 3 | 0.7 | 1 | 1.3 | 5 | 2.5 | 70 | 14.1 | 105 | 18.9 | 197 |
| Rh IIb | 5 | 1.0 | 2 | 0.9 | 2 | 0.4 | 0 | 0.0 | 6 | 3.0 | 46 | 9.3 | 10 | 1.8 | 71 |
| Rh IIc | 8 | 1.5 | 0 | 0.0 | 1 | 0.2 | 0 | 0.0 | 1 | 0.5 | 27 | 5.5 | 41 | 7.4 | 78 |
| Rh II | 2 | 0.4 | 0 | 0.0 | 4 | 0.9 | 0 | 0.0 | 0 | 0.0 | 18 | 3.6 | 4 | 0.7 | 28 |
| Rh IIIa | 6 | 1.2 | 0 | 0.0 | 1 | 0.2 | 0 | 0.0 | 1 | 0.5 | 34 | 6.9 | 29 | 5.2 | 71 |
| Rh IIIb | 1 | 0.2 | 2 | 0.9 | 0 | 0.0 | 0 | 0.0 | 0 | 0.0 | 12 | 2.4 | 7 | 1.3 | 22 |
| Rh III | 0 | 0.0 | 0 | 0.0 | 0 | 0.0 | 1 | 1.3 | 0 | 0.0 | 3 | 0.6 | 0 | 0.0 | 4 |
| Tr I | 3 | 0.6 | 0 | 0.0 | 1 | 0.2 | 0 | 0.0 | 33 | 16.3 | 37 | 7.4 | 0 | 0.0 | 74 |
| Tr IIa | 7 | 1.3 | 0 | 0.0 | 0 | 0.0 | 0 | 0.0 | 24 | 11.9 | 64 | 12.9 | 0 | 0.0 | 95 |
| Tr IIb | 3 | 0.6 | 0 | 0.0 | 0 | 0.0 | 0 | 0.0 | 25 | 12.4 | 29 | 5.9 | 0 | 0.0 | 57 |
| Tr IIc | 3 | 0.6 | 0 | 0.0 | 0 | 0.0 | 0 | 0.0 | 19 | 9.4 | 9 | 1.8 | 0 | 0.0 | 31 |
| Tr IIIa | 3 | 0.6 | 0 | 0.0 | 0 | 0.0 | 0 | 0.0 | 1 | 0.5 | 8 | 1.6 | 0 | 0.0 | 12 |
| Tr IIIb | 0 | 0.0 | 0 | 0.0 | 0 | 0.0 | 0 | 0.0 | 0 | 0.0 | 2 | 0.4 | 0 | 0.0 | 2 |
| Tr | 7 | 1.3 | 0 | 0.0 | 1 | 0.2 | 0 | 0.0 | 9 | 4.5 | 22 | 4.4 | 0 | 0.0 | 39 |
| West | 2 | 0.4 | 0 | 0.0 | 1 | 0.2 | 0 | 0.0 | 2 | 1.0 | 0 | 0.0 | 43 | 7.7 | 48 |
| Pfaff | 0 | 0.0 | 0 | 0.0 | 0 | 0.0 | 0 | 0.0 | 0 | 0.0 | 0 | 0.0 | 21 | 3.8 | 21 |
| Arg | 8 | 1.5 | 0 | 0.0 | 8 | 1.7 | 7 | 8.8 | 30 | 14.9 | 10 | 2.0 | 0 | 0.0 | 63 |
| La Mad | 4 | 0.8 | 0 | 0.0 | 9 | 2.0 | 0 | 0.0 | 11 | 5.4 | 12 | 2.4 | 0 | 0.0 | 36 |
| Heil | 2 | 0.4 | 1 | 0.4 | 1 | 0.2 | 0 | 0.0 | 1 | 0.5 | 1 | 0.2 | 17 | 3.1 | 23 |
| Blick | 2 | 0.4 | 0 | 0.0 | 1 | 0.2 | 0 | 0.0 | 8 | 4.0 | 18 | 3.6 | 0 | 0.0 | 29 |
| Chém | 1 | 0.2 | 0 | 0.0 | 2 | 0.4 | 0 | 0.0 | 0 | 0.0 | 1 | 0.2 | 1 | 0.2 | 5 |
| Mitt | 0 | 0.0 | 0 | 0.0 | 0 | 0.0 | 0 | 0.0 | 4 | 2.0 | 8 | 1.6 | 2 | 0.4 | 14 |
| Itten | 0 | 0.0 | 0 | 0.0 | 0 | 0.0 | 0 | 0.0 | 0 | 0.0 | 0 | 0.0 | 1 | 0.2 | 1 |
| Kräh | 0 | 0.0 | 0 | 0.0 | 0 | 0.0 | 0 | 0.0 | 0 | 0.0 | 3 | 0.6 | 0 | 0.0 | 3 |
| Waib | 0 | 0.0 | 0 | 0.0 | 0 | 0.0 | 0 | 0.0 | 0 | 0.0 | 3 | 0.6 | 0 | 0.0 | 3 |
| Esch | 0 | 0.0 | 0 | 0.0 | 0 | 0.0 | 0 | 0.0 | 0 | 0.0 | 3 | 0.6 | 0 | 0.0 | 3 |
| EG | 3 | 0.6 | 1 | 0.4 | 2 | 0.4 | 1 | 1.3 | 0 | 0.0 | 7 | 1.4 | 1 | 0.2 | 15 |
| Brit | 3 | 0.6 | 0 | 0.0 | 0 | 0.0 | 0 | 0.0 | 0 | 0.0 | 0 | 0.0 | 0 | 0.0 | 3 |
| **Total** | **522** | | **224** | | **459** | | **80** | | **202** | | **495** | | **555** | | |

### BRITAIN

Britain has been divided into three regions, of which southern Britain is the best represented, and appears to suffer from little bias according to the coin evidence considered above (Table 4.I-IV). Northern Britain, too, has a large assemblage and is probably a representative sample. Wales and western Britain, though, has a smaller assemblage and may be biased by the fact that the majority of pieces come from only three sites, Caerleon, Chester, and Wroxeter.

All three areas are dominated by CG products, particularly CG IV and CG Cinnamus, as might be expected. Wales has a very high CG IV percentage due to A 131 from Wroxeter, but when the other two areas are compared with each other, there appears to be a significant difference, in that the ratio CG III and CG Cinnamus to CG IV is 1.34:1 for S Britain but is 2.04:1 for N Britain. There is a greater representation of CG IV in the south, therefore, which may reflect a real difference in the distribution and supply of late CG products. At the level of individual potters, Casurius, Advocisus, Iustus, Mercator II and Servus II are better represented in the north, while Doeccus I, Banvus and Paternus II are relatively more common in the south. It

published during the 1980s-2000s.

is not easy to interpret these differences: some may be due to regional synchronic variations, e.g. Paternus II perhaps having a predominantly civilian market, but some may equally be diachronic in origin, e.g. Doeccus I being a late potter in CG IV and thus found mainly in the south because there are more late deposits there. There are reasons to believe that both are likely inferences, since Paternus II is present in CG IV deposits of all dates, and is known to be early in CG IV (*vide* A 131, Wroxeter), hence should be widely distributed, while Doeccus I is mainly found in the later CG IV deposits (e.g. A 90, London) and is not present in A 131 and other early CG IV deposits. In fact, 13 out of the 19 Doeccus I pieces from northern Britain come from one deposit, B 51, Ilkley, a site that could easily have been occupied into the third century.

There is less to be said about CG III, except that it is not so common in the southern British deposits, for the reasons outlined above. All the potters seem distributed equitably between areas, except Laxtucissa and Pugnus, who have a southern bias.

Rheinzabern ware in Britain reflects the often made observation that the distribution is mainly on the eastern side of the province, since the percentage in Wales and the west is relatively low. However, that observation should mainly be made about the Rh Ib-III since Rh la is relatively equally distributed throughout Britain, with if anything a northern (i.e. Hadrian's Wall) bias. The later Rheinzabern groups have greater representation in the south rather than the N, particularly Rh IIIa-b, and accords with the observations made above about late CG potters.

Trier products are uncommon in Britain except for the south, although the indications from Table 5.XII are that early Trier ware is present in northern Britain, and can be considered in a similar light to the rather stronger representation of Rh la. Shadwell (Table 5.IX), along with A 90, St Magnus House, London, have the largest groups of Trier bowls from Britain. At both, the full range from Trier I to III is represented, and presumably demonstrates continuing if relatively small-scale supply into south-east Britain during the first half of the third century.

The smaller kilns follow the same patterns as Rheinzabern and Trier, being found rarely in the west, and with a greater representation of the earlier products (e.g. La Madeleine) in the north. The presence of Westerndorf products is noteworthy, given the distance to the kiln-centre. British samian is confined to the region in which it was produced, according to the evidence presented here.

#### France

From the CG percentages in Table 5.XII, it is clear that there is a bias towards the later periods in the deposits in Gazetteer A and B, and thus it is difficult to draw conclusions about the internal characteristics of the French CG distribution. Not surprisingly, though, CG provides the great majority of late samian ware in France, *c.* 85%, with the only other kiln-centre showing more than a trace in the percentages being Argonne with *c.* 9%. These overall percentages find confirmation in other studies.[60]

Table 5.XII can be supplemented for CG by the extensive work of Delage in mapping the distribution of CG wares at different phases.[61] His phase 5, AD 140-60, sees CG at its greatest extent, covering most of France, except the south, where late SG wares still held sway with largely local distribution areas. Phase 6, AD 160-90, is the beginning of contraction, with eastern France having a lower representation of CG pottery, as EG kiln-centres start to dominate in that zone. By phase 7, AD 190-240, the lower Loire Valley, Brittany and Normandy form the core area, with a periphery in the lower Seine and lower Garonne basins. The core area itself becomes an area of weak distribution in the final phase 8, AD 240-80.[62] The distribution of individual potters, e.g. Marcus, in phase 7, reflects the north-western France distribution zone, with a few examples also found in south-east Britain.[63]

New work on the Centre-West group, located on the southern margin of the lower Loire Valley, has indicated a distribution area into Brittany and the Sarthe regions, as well as locally.[64] The Centre-West potters appear to have used the same distribution network as CG, but were completely dominated by the latter in terms of volume of production.

The smaller kilns, although often located in France (e.g. La Madeleine, Chémery, Mittelbronn), are unrepresented on Table 5.XII. This is probably due to the phenomenon well known to statisticians whereby those individuals only represented to a very small extent in an assemblage are eliminated completely if the sample size is small,[65] rather than an actual lack of distribution of products of the smaller French kilns in France itself. Sites such as Bliesbruck in eastern France (D 51) have a strong representation of the local kilns at Blickweiler and Eschweiler-Hof, but these samian products are not found to any great extent elsewhere in France, since exportation of their products mainly went east to the Rhineland and upper Danube. The Argonne kilns, too, largely exported to the lower Rhineland, the Moselle area and the Low Countries (see below), with only a marginal distribution west into the heartland of France.[66]

#### Netherlands, Belgium and Luxembourg

It seems clear from Table 5.XII that the Low Countries are outside the main CG distribution area, since CG represents

[60] E.g. Massy 1972; Séguier & Delage 2009.

[61] Delage 1998; 2001a; 2003.

[62] Delage 2001a, Fig. 2; more detailed maps and data in Delage 1998, 286-301.

[63] Delage 2003, 188; Séguier & Delage 2009, 557-8. See also Gazetteer D, sites D 50, Allonnes; D 54, Châteaubleau; D 57-8, Lezoux; D 61, Lyon; D 62-4, Le Mans; D 67, Poitiers; D 72, Tavers; D 73, Le Thovey; D 74-5, Vieux, for presence of late CG potters in dated deposits. See also the Nantes pottery shop deposit of the AD 240s+; Delage *et al.* 2011.

[64] Delage 1997; 2000b; 2010.

[65] Cf. Torrence 1978, 394.

[66] Gazenbeek & Van Der Leeuw 2003; Hanut & Henrotay 2006, 302, fig. 23.

only a modest proportion of the whole, and in fact has a southern and coastal bias in its distribution, being found mainly in Belgium rather than the Netherlands.[67] Rheinzabern, by contrast, has a northerly distribution in the Low Countries, being found mainly on sites along the river Rhine. Rheinzabern ware tends to be early (i.e. Rh Ib-IIb), and is not strongly represented when compared with Trier, which clearly dominated Low Countries distribution in the Rhine river zone from the time that production started at the latter kiln-centre. Again, there are indications that the distribution tended to be northerly within the Low Countries, probably due to the riverine transport system along the Moselle and the Rhine. Later Trier products are rare, but have been found at the mid/late third century site of Oudenburg,[68] and can be linked to supply that went across the Channel to London, Shadwell and elsewhere (see above).

Of the minor kilns, Argonne, La Madeleine, and Blickweiler are relatively common, particularly the first-mentioned. It is probably due to the river Meuse that Argonne achieved its market position in the Low Countries since it dominates such Meuse sites as Namur and Amay,[69] while La Madeleine and Blickweiler were distributed via the Moselle.

### The Rhineland

In the Rhineland, an area that includes the kiln centres of Rheinzabern and Trier (as well as being taken to include the area around Strasbourg in France, and Mosellan sites in Germany and Luxembourg), the distribution pattern is different again. CG is very rare, and tends to be early in date, before Rheinzabern and Trier were producing samian ware in quantity. Rheinzabern is the main constituent, forming *c.* 50% of the total. All Rheinzabern periods are present, Rh IIa-b being most common. Trier appears to be mainly early in the Rhineland (as elsewhere), since the percentages fall away in Trier IIc-IIIb. However, this is partly due to the Trier figures being composed mainly of A 187, Niederbieber, with its concentration of Trier I-IIa products. The kiln-site deposits (B 155-6) have a much higher percentage of late products (which, incidentally, is also true of the Rheinzabern kiln-site deposits). Possibly this is due to difficulties of distribution of late Trier (and Rheinzabern) pottery, since the relative lack of late products on sites distant from the kiln-centre is a real enough phenomenon. Trier has a restricted distribution in the Rhineland due, probably, to competition from Rheinzabern, and it is distinctly rare to find Trier ware south of Mainz.[70] Niederbieber and the Wetterau sites (e.g. Holzhausen) are the effective southern and eastern limits of the distribution network.

The smaller kilns fall into roughly the same pattern as in the Low Countries: Argonne, La Madeleine, Blickweiler and also Mittelbronn are relatively well represented. In this case, though, Argonne, La Madeleine and Blickweiler probably all achieved their distribution via the Moselle, and thereby were ultimately swamped by the growth of Trier, better-placed on the same river. Mittelbronn could well be associated with the Rheinzabern distribution system. Of the other small-scale producers, the local kilns, i.e. Kräherwald, Waiblingen, Eschweiler and some of the EG unlocated wares, all were distributed locally only. Kräherwald and Waiblingen in particular are not found outside their local region of the southern sector of the outer *limes*, and the western sector of the Raetian frontier.[71] Notably absent in the Rhineland are Westerndorf and Pfaffenhofen products, which might be expected in at least one or two deposits, in view of the distribution of Westerndorf products probably through the Rhineland to the Low Countries and Britain.

### Danube Region

The last region on Table 5.XII is the Danube, which mainly means the provinces of Raetia and Noricum. Here, there is a remarkably strong presence of CG products, CG I-II and above all, Cinnamus.[72] Distribution was probably via the Rhône, the Swiss lowland corridor and the river Danube. The strong showing of Cinnamus is particularly notable, but may be artificially enhanced by the large quantity in a single deposit, A 165, Gauting. CG IV is relatively uncommon in the area, and it is very likely that importation of CG products was falling off by the time that CG IV was becoming the main productive group. The reasons for this are probably to be sought in the domination of the Danube market by Rheinzabern, which is present from Rh Ia, rising to a peak in Rh IIa and gradually falling away.[73] Although Rh Ia and CG Cinnamus were probably being distributed in the area at the same time, it is clear that later CG products could not, or did not choose to compete with Rheinzabern.[74] The same can be said, *a fortiori*, about Trier. There is a complete absence of Trier in the Danube, according to the deposits in the gazetteer, which must be due to the same factors that inhibited Trier supply in the Rhineland south of Mainz.

Heiligenberg, often regarded as a predecessor to Rheinzabern in production/stylistic terms, is the main representative of the smaller EG kilns, and indeed must have concentrated its efforts on distribution in the Danube area, since the majority of its products are found there, according to the gazetteer deposits. The route used was

[67] Raepsaet (1987, pl. 2 and Tables I-IV) has a rather stronger representation of CG, but demonstrates well the coastal and Belgian emphasis.

[68] Vanhoutte *et al.* 2009a; 2009b; 2012.

[69] Inf. M. Vanderhoeven; Hanut & Henrotay 2006, fig. 23.

[70] Cf. Oldenstein-Pferdehirt 1983.

[71] Riedl 2011, Abb. 73.

[72] As mapped by Delage (1998, 285, 290, 292; 2001a, fig. 2). There may be a link with the Danubian distribution network of Banassac products; cf. Mees 1994b; Groh 1998; Dannell & Mees 2013, 168. Cf. also Gazetteer D 117, Kaiseraugst.. Kuzmová (1994) lists Cinnamus and other CG III-IV potters in Free Germany north and east of Pannonia.

[73] The decorated samian ware from Ellingen fort on the Raetian *limes* demonstrates this very well; Zanier 1992, 116-31; 1994.

[74] This is exemplified by the Kempten pottery shop deposit, dated to the late 160s or 170s by a coin hoard, where Rheinzabern dominates CG by a ratio of 22:1; Weber 2013, 195; Czysz 1982.

probably the road system leading from Strasbourg to the Upper Danube. The same distribution route probably also applies to Ittenwiller, Chémery and Mittelbronn (and Rheinzabern?). The Swabian kilns of Kräherwald, Waiblingen, etc., also lay on this route, and distributed their products into western Raetia (see above).

Samian ware made locally to the Danube region, represented on Table 5.XII, consists principally of Westerndorf, followed by Pfaffenhofen and with the additional trace of small scale production from an unlocated Danubian kiln (at A 206, Enns-Lorch). Westerndorf and Pfaffenhofen products were distributed downstream along the Inn and the Danube, and achieved a respectable market share in view of the dominant position already held by Rheinzabern. The products of Schwabmünchen and Schwabegg are not present on Table 5.XII, but are known to be distributed locally, with some examples exported to the Middle Danube region.[75]

Rheinzabern, Westerndorf and Pfaffenhofen were all distributed further down the Danube and into Free Germany,[76] but this, and the local samian wares made further east are beyond the scope of this volume.

### Plain wares

So far, all evidence and discussion has been concerned with decorated vessels, because they provide a more coherent basis for understanding chronological matters than plain wares.[77] However, some perusal of the evidence for undecorated samian in late deposits is necessary, in order to check the assumption that decorated ware chronology is representative of samian production as a whole.

Research into late samian manufacture makes clear that plain wares were made later than decorated wares, for instance in the case of the Argonne by Hofmann.[78] Trier also appears to have continued plain ware production up to the early fourth century, although decorated ware appears not to have been produced after 275.[79] Similarly, Rheinzabern seems to have ceased decorated ware production by c. 260, but does have continued manufacture of barbotined, rouletted and incised vessels up to the early fourth century.[80] At Lezoux, plain ware forms are dated at least to the mid third century, and there is evidence for production of pottery there into the fourth century.[81] Later plain ware productions has been suggested particularly for the *mortarium* form 45 with devolved lion's head spout, which Mitard has dated up to the end of the third century.[82] Also, various samian forms in Gose's typology are dated by him to the late third or early fourth century.[83] Clearly pieces are found in contexts up to these dates, as in fact we have seen for decorated wares (e.g. Portchester, Schaan), but some may be survivals rather than late products.[84] The problem is compounded by the difficulty of defining exactly what is and is not samian ware in this period, since bowls and other forms with a samian-type, but usually matt ('non-gresé) slip are being made at various centres, e.g. Oxfordshire and the Argonne.[85] The latter kiln-centre highlights the problem since it produced decorated wares up to the early/mid third century, and then roller-stamped wares thereafter. The quality of the gloss does not alter appreciably between the later moulded and earlier roller-stamped products. Vertet and Rigoir have approached this problem by defining 'derivés de sigillée' (DS), that are composed of such fabrics as Argonne and the early 'paléochrétienne' wares.[86] One of their criteria was a matt rather than a glossy slip. To a certain extent, however, the easiest, but narrow definition of the end of samian production could be when moulded ware manufacture came to an end, although this sidesteps the issue of whether the traditional plain forms made at samian kilns ceased to be made at about the same time.

The deposits listed in section C of the gazetteer show that there are plain wares found in mid-late third century contexts, and sometimes later. Their adjusted coin-dates and assessment of residuality etc., are given in Table Appendix 6. Some of the deposits contain small and abraded pieces (e.g. C 34, Lympne) which are almost certainly residual, while others contain groups or single sherds that just as certainly appear to be survivals (e.g. C 24, Dunstable, C 14, Chew Park). One deposit of eight pieces may be a survival for a special reason, if Boon's suggestion about C 4, Brean Down, is correct.[87] He comments, 'Samian in this sort of quantity is a well-known feature of late Roman sites and does not, of itself, suggest an occupation earlier than the temple. The fact that all the scraps of samian are derived from dishes suggests that they represented the ritual service in the temple.' The site is dated mid to late fourth century, without signs of earlier occupation.

In contrast to the discussion above, it would seem to be the inference from section C of the Gazetteer that plain ware is generally not manufactured later than decorated ware, but there is a caveat, that most of the groups in section C are from Britain, so this may alternatively represent cessation of importation at the same time, whilst plain wares may

[75] Sölch 1999; Sorge 2001.

[76] Gabler 1966; 1978; 1983; Kellner 1962; Radbauer 2013, fig. 11.1. Laser (1998) has catalogued the samian ware in the former East German provinces, largely dominated by Rheinzabern products. See also the articles in Fulford & Durham 2013 that cover this topic.

[77] Apart from plain ware die-stamps, not considered here (cf. Hartley & Dickinson 2008a-2012). See also Weber 2012.

[78] Hofmann 1979, 217-8. See also Roth-Rubi 1990 for discussion of late Roman 'Glanztonkeramik' at Argonne and elsewhere.

[79] Frey 2000, 214.

[80] Bernhard 1985. Cf. Gschwind 2006 for late Rheinzabern products found in Raetia.

[81] Bet *et al.* 1989; Bet & Gangloff 1987; Bet & Wittman 1995.

[82] Mitard 1979, 90; Mitard & Alegoët 1975; Mitard 2005. A full consideration of the issue is forthcoming in Mitard's *Les Mortiers Drag. 45 et leur Ornementation* (Cahiers du Centre Archéologique de Lezoux). For Gueugnon production of form 45 in the 3rd century: Notet & Mitard 1987; Notet 1996, 121.

[83] Gose 1975. See also Bird 1993 for 3rd-century plain ware forms found in Britain.

[84] Cf. Wallace 2006.

[85] Young 1977; Chenet 1941.

[86] Rigoir 1968; Rigoir *et al.* 1973; Rigoir & Rigoir 1985.

[87] Boon 1965b.

*Table 5.XIII Plain wares: basic functional types, from deposits c. 150-280+, from Gazetteer A-C*

| | CG | | EG | |
|---|---|---|---|---|
| | *no* | *%* | *no* | *%* |
| Decorated bowls | 470 | 26.0 | 610 | 33.3 |
| Cups | 341 | 18.8 | 231 | 12.6 |
| Dishes | 831 | 45.9 | 483 | 26.4 |
| Deep bowls | 83 | 4.6 | 140 | 7.6 |
| *Mortaria* | 66 | 3.6 | 320 | 17.5 |
| Jars/Beakers | 20 | 1.1 | 48 | 2.6 |
| Total | 1811 | | 1832 | |

have continued later in terms of local distribution from the kiln-centres.[88] Nearly all the groups recorded are small, and of the sort likely to represent survivals of selected vessels beyond the normal life expectancy of such pottery. The fact that the deposits are small is presumably due to the likelihood that the larger deposits include pieces of decorated ware, and thus are listed in section A rather than section C. Most of the late plain ware deposits include dishes such as form 31, either in CG or EG fabric. This is to be expected since dishes of one form or another were a substantial part of late production, especially by the CG kilns, as Table 5.XIII shows. The table is compiled from the quantified and well-recorded deposits in all three sections of the gazetteer, and is a basic functional breakdown. It shows that there is a considerable difference in emphasis between CG and EG kilns in the late second and early third centuries, which can be summed up as a concentration by CG on cups, dishes and the traditional types of samian tableware, while EG produced more deep bowls (both decorated and plain), and was more adventurous in new forms such as jugs, beakers, etc., that were previously a coarse pottery preserve. A striking difference can be seen in the case of *mortaria* (forms 43, 45 and Niederbieber 21b), which were clearly much more common in EG fabric than CG. Most CG *mortaria* are fairly late, and it may be that CG started to copy vessels that were first produced in Rheinzabern, Trier and other EG kilns. Certainly this is the case at the small CG kiln of Gueugnon, as recorded in C 56, Malain. Since EG *mortaria* are relatively more common, it is probably not surprising that they are often found in late contexts, since they are solid and durable vessels, probably with a longer life expectancy than other samian forms. This may account for their apparent survival in late contexts, rather than Mitard's suggestion of later manufacture.

[88] Cf. Bird 1993 for discussion of plain and decorated EG wares in Britain. Gschwind's (2006) observations on late Rheinzabern ware in Raetia accords with the suggestion of later, local distribution of plain wares. Fulford (1975) shows that New Forest production in its later stages reduced the range of forms, the number per form, and the distribution area, which may provide an analogy for late samian production in the 3rd century. See chapter 7 for further discussion.

Much more could be written about the plain wares in late contexts, and a thorough quantitative study of well-preserved deposits would probably bring great rewards.[89]

## A tentative chronology

All that remains in this chapter is to draw together the threads of what has been presented in detail above, and see how far the chronology differs from that given in chapter 1.

It is important first to clarify and reiterate the type of chronology we are concerned with (see chapter 2). All the evidence comes from disposal sets, even that from deposits at kiln-sites: none of it contains *of itself* evidence for the chronology of production. The patterns revealed in the evidence are, *sensu stricto*, fortuitous in the chronological sense, since they are the result of random and isolated events of rubbish disposal. That there is a pattern at all is due to the behavioural and socially-constrained patterning of Roman disposal practices. If this is granted, then it can be seen that to establish a chronology of production is a move away from the evidence presented in this chapter, and has to involve a number of assumptions (cf. Fig. 2.5 and associated text). Chief of these is that there is a fixed or predictable life-expectancy for samian vessels, which can be applied so as to move back from the disposal chronology to 'the production chronology.

## Life-expectancy of decorated samian ware

Virtually nothing is known of the life expectancy of samian ware itself, unfortunately. The most cogent discussion of this issue is by Orton and Orton, in which they showed that many samian sherds could be several decades old by the time they reached an archaeological context, and they gave an average age of *c.* 10-20 years.[90] However, their work has a flaw, since the samian ware dating they used as a basis was in itself a chronology of disposal not of manufacture, and therefore could not supply reliable life expectancy data.[91] An alternative approach is to look for samian sherds that are independently dated, such as the inscribed South Gaulish bowls dated AD 116-7 that refer to the capture of Decebalus,[92] the mould and bowls of Cerialis IV with a *sestertius* of Antoninus Pius, AD 140-4, impressed at intervals within the decorative zone,[93] or the bowl by Cibisus of Mittelbronn (or Ittenwiller) that has an unworn coin dated AD 169/70 impressed in its decoration,[94] and to

[89] See Wallace 2006 for an appraisal of plain wares in late, mainly funerary contexts.

[90] Orton & Orton 1975.

[91] This is not the Ortons' fault, since all ascribed date-ranges for potters in the standard reference works on samian ware are effectively disposal chronologies, as (it is to be hoped) this volume makes clear. See Millett 1987a, 101; Wallace 2006, 264.

[92] Labrousse 1981.

[93] Mees 2002, 76-8. The impression appears to reflect a worn coin, but this seems to be due to the moulding process rather than the actual state of wear of the coin (*ibid.* 76). The practice of impressing coins into moulds also occurred on Late Italian Sigillata, e.g. the bronze coin of Sabina on an example from Cosa (Marabini Moevs 1980), and on SG and Hispanic pottery (*ibid.*, 322). It seems to have been a 1st and 2nd-century phenomenon.

[94] Lutz 1970a, 326-7. For the uncertainty about the location of this

assess the time between manufacture and disposal directly. At the moment, this is a hypothetical possibility only, since none of the independently dated bowls has yet been found in a properly recorded archaeological context, but there is an indirect assessment that can be made in the case of the Cerialis IV and Cibisus bowls.

Cerialis IV is a Rh Ib potter, and has been found with a *dupondius* of Antoninus, 151-2, a *sestertius* of Severus, a *denarius* of Severus, 194-5, and a *denarius* of Severus, 197. The last coin is from A 90, St Magnus House, London, which also has a dendrochronological date for the waterfront timbers of 209-14, and coins to Elagabalus (AD 219 or later) from associated layers.[95] The deposit has an adjusted date of period VIIIb, i.e. *c.* 210-220. The general range of adjusted dates for Cerialis I-V in well-dated/stratified deposits is periods VIIa-Xb, i.e. *c.* 160-280, with a peak in period VIIIb (Appendix 8; Fig. 5.14).[96] If the bowl of Cerialis IV with the impressed coin is typical of his production, and not markedly earlier or later, then the average life-expectancy seems to be in the order of 20-140 years, with peak disposal occurring 70-80 years after earliest possible manufacture; in all, a remarkably long time in circulation, and with significant implications for dating of decorated samian ware in general. However, the coin impressed on the bowl only provides a *terminus post quem* and is subject to the same circulation factors as coins found in stratified deposits. It may have been in circulation for some time before use by the mould-maker, and if this was the case, would consequently reduce the life-expectancy given above. As an example, if the coin had been in circulation for 10 years or more, which would accord with the hoard data analysed in chapter 3, then the life-expectancy range and peak given above can be reduced by at least 10 years.

The adjusted coin dates for Cibisus, all from A 202, Zugmantel, centre on periods VIIIb-IXa, i.e. *c.* 210-240.[97] Similarly to the Cerialis example above, if the Cibisus bowl in question is in the full period of production for this potter, then average life-expectancy is 40-70 years, again a remarkably long time. The coin on the Cibisus bowl is relatively unworn, and may have been fairly close to its minting date when used by the mould-maker, which gives an apparently more accurate date for this bowl than for the Cerialis IV example.

potter, see Lutz 1968, 55-9; 1986d, 218; Kern 1986b, 230; Kern *et al.* 2009, 95; Delage & Mees 2009, 99. It seems probable that Cibisus made moulds at Ittenwiller, but they were also utilised at Mittelbronn, probably by another potter; Goubet & Meyer 2006, 549.

[95] The deposits are, respectively, A 206ay, Enns-Lorch; A 206av, Enns-Lorch; A 206s, Enns-Lorch and A 90, St Magnus House, London. The Enns-Lorch stratigraphic recording is less reliable than that for St Magnus House. See the entries in the Gazetteer for further discussion.

[96] The earliest coins are from the reign of Antoninus, but from less well-stratifed deposits. The coin range as a whole perfectly reflects the earlier bronze and later silver pattern, as discussed in relation to coin circulation in chapter 3.

[97] The contexts are all cellars in the *vicus*; A 202h, 6 coins to J Maesa *denarius*, A 202n, 7 coins to J Mamaea *denarius,* A 202aj, bronze of Hadrian. See Appendix 3, and the discussion of Zugmantel in chapter 3.

In one important respect, it seems inherently unlikely that such long life-expectancies can be regarded as typical, for if it was the case, it would push virtually all later samian production back to the late second century or earlier, including many of the late Rheinzabern, Trier and Westerndorf potters (and would also have significant implications for all earlier samian production back into the first century AD). Other coin-dated deposits, from the kiln-centres themselves, would contradict this conclusion, as they definitely show production at these three centres in the early to mid third century. It would also imply firstly, that samian ware production need not have been at a high volume, since replacements would rarely have been needed, and secondly that samian vessels were carefully conserved during use, and regarded as specialities worthy of preservation.[98] This second inference possibly may have been the case if samian ware was a status symbol (see chapter 6), but on the whole it may be expected that those samian vessels that were actually used regularly would have had a lower life-expectancy. Decorated bowls used for their designed purpose of wine mixing and drinking should, by virtue of being handled and moved a good deal during use, in fact have had a shorter life-expectancy than, for instance, a storage jar, which should have had a more static existence less prone to accidents. This type of life-expectancy pattern is known from the ethnographic record,[99] and available data from this source tend to suggest a relatively short life for most pottery, in the order of 1-3 years, extending up to 10-30 years for durable vessels and in certain societies.[100] Of course, distant modern societies do not give us figures that are glibly transferable to the Roman period, but the model they uphold is a valid one, and unless it can be clearly established that fine pottery such as samian was carefully preserved, it would seem reasonable to follow the hypothesis that most samian ware had a life expectancy in the order of 5-10 years or so rather than the much longer periods suggested by the Cerialis and Cibisus bowls.

To balance this, however, account has to be taken of what is clearly a measurable percentage of survival vessels possibly up to a century old in many archaeological deposits, as the dated deposits in this volume demonstrate.[101] Another factor to bring in at this point is the possibility that samian vessels, particularly the decorated bowls, were not sold immediately after manufacture, but may have spent a significant period in a warehouse or other storage before reaching their consumer destination. This is the line of argument put forward by Joanna Bird, to account for the heterogeneous nature of the samian ware in A 90, St Magnus House, London.[102] Many of the larger deposits of samian ware in this period are either from the kiln-centres

[98] This is discussed by Wallace (2006, 264), drawing on work by Willis (1997) and J. Evans.

[99] E.g. DeBoer & Lathrap 1979; David 1972.

[100] Arnold 1985, 152ff. Peña (2007, chapter 11, esp. Fig 11.3) models the primary use-life of Roman table ware at 3 years.

[101] See also Wallace 2006. Willis (2005, section 5.8.1) discusses the long 'tail' of samian ware in use, especially in the later phases of production and use.

[102] Bird 1986, 139.

themselves or from 'warehouse' or 'shop' deposits, such as A 131, Wroxeter, or D 80, Langenhain, which suggests that a significant amount of the pottery remained at places of manufacture or commercial storage, rather than being disposed of after 'normal' usage by a consumer.[103] In addition, the demonstrable reuse of moulds at Trier, Blickweiler and elsewhere, combined with the plausible suggestion by Delage that moulds could be stored after a production run, then taken off the shelf to be used for another run, possibly many years, even decades after original manufacture,[104] also serve to make the long life-expectancies indicated by the Cerialis and Cibisus bowls less anomalous than the use-life in the ethnographic record would imply. If these factors are a significant element in the life-expectancy of a samian ware decorated bowl, there are implications concerning the relative inefficiency of the distribution system, and the effect this may have had on the decline of production.[105]

A final set of factors to consider in the life expectancy of decorated samian ware is the evaluation of wear, and the incidence of repair to broken vessels. Interior wear as an indicator of usage is not commonly or consistently recorded, but studies by Ward (née Bulmer) at Chester and Piercebridge show an apparent increase through time in the number of worn plain and decorated bowls and plates. Thus, SG and earlier CG examples tend to have little evidence of wear, but later CG and EG examples do, implying conservation of vessels in use for longer periods in the late second and third centuries. The inference from this is that users were aware of the supply problems at this time, and adjusted their usage behaviour towards samian ware accordingly.[106] This is a moot point, as the converse could also be the case, i.e. that usage behaviour was changing in the late second to early third century, for other (unknown) reasons, and that this reduced demand because the replacement rate for samian ware was lower, with consequent economic effects on the viability of the supply chain.[107]

The analysis of repairs to samian bowls is mainly concerned with how much of an assemblage had evidence of lead staples. Results are mixed, in that Piercebridge indicates a higher percentage of repairs in the later period, backing up the wear analysis given above, whilst London samian ware gives a higher percentage of repairs on SG products than on those from CG or EG, implying a greater attention to maintenance of samian ware in the first century, as compared with the second and third centuries. However, it should be noted that lead repairs at both sites only account for c. 1.1-1.3% of the total assemblages.[108] A spectacular example of a lead-repaired CG 37 from Stonea also yields an apparently long life before disposal, since the context is dated to AD 200 or later, and the bowl itself is assigned a manufacture date of the 120s/130s.[109]

To bring this discussion of samian life-expectancy to a close, it is worth noting that, in archaeological terms, any period less than ten years is effectively unmeasurable (except under special conditions such as dated burial sequences). Therefore it may be easiest to assume that manufacture is, to all intents and purposes, analogous to the main period of disposal, or just prior to it, by perhaps 20 years or so, with storage, reuse of moulds, survival and a lower intensity of manufacture accounting for the gradual fall-off in many of the disposal chronologies. This conclusion also assumes that reuse of moulds, and storage in warehouses and shops, while being undoubtedly factors in the chronology, were not, in overall terms, major influences on the lengthening of average life-expectancy of the majority of the decorated samian bowls recorded in the Gazetteer.

## Chronology of Kiln-centres, c. 150-280, based on coin-dated deposit evidence

The chronologies that have been compiled in this chapter are composed of three basic elements: the likely period of discard of products of the kiln-centre sub-groups and their main constituent patterns, the pattern of association of potters with one another in assemblages, and the internal stylistic associations and sequences of the potters. The first is derived from the estimated dates-of-loss of the associated coins, and this gives the basic framework. The last, which of course has not been considered afresh for this thesis and relies upon existing work, provides an important link between the better-dated potters and those with little or no chronological evidence. The same applies to the second element, since it links the better-dated prolific potters with their less productive colleagues, and also serves as a check on the stylistic framework.

The three elements have been combined to form Fig. 5.23, a summary of kiln-centre chronologies, Fig. 5.24, a tentative estimate of the comparative volume of production for the major kiln-centres, and Table 5.XIV, which attributes individual potters to chronological groups. It has not been easy to reconcile some of the contradictions encountered when trying to combine different chronological elements in this way. Janu II of Rh, a potter already mentioned more than once, started out by being stylistically early, but was revised by Bernhard and became a later potter.[110] The coin-associations support this revision but the association with other potters does not. On the whole, it has been felt best to let the revision stand and leave this potter in Rh IIIa.

[103] For discussion of pottery lost before reaching the consumer, and a gazetteer, see Rhodes 1989; also Simon & Köhler 1992 for Langenhain. A recent shop deposit of the mid 3rd century has been excavated at Nantes; Delage *et al.* 2011.

[104] Huld-Zetsche 1993, 52-6; 1998; Petit 2001; Delage 2003, 186-8. For the trade in Lezoux moulds, see Picon 1989.

[105] Discussed further in chapter 7.

[106] Chester: Bulmer 1980, 89; Piercebridge: Ward 1993, 19-20. See the discussions in Peña (2007, 59-60) and Symonds (1992, 64, n61).

[107] Discussed further in chapter 7.

[108] Piercebridge: Ward 1993, 20-1; London: Marsh 1981, 228, fig. 11.18. See the discussion in Peña 2007, 244-8, Table 8.1.

[109] Johns 1996, 409, 412, fig. 137, 413 no. 13; Peña 2007, 237, 244.

[110] Bernhard 1981a. See fn. 1 for the debate about this potter.

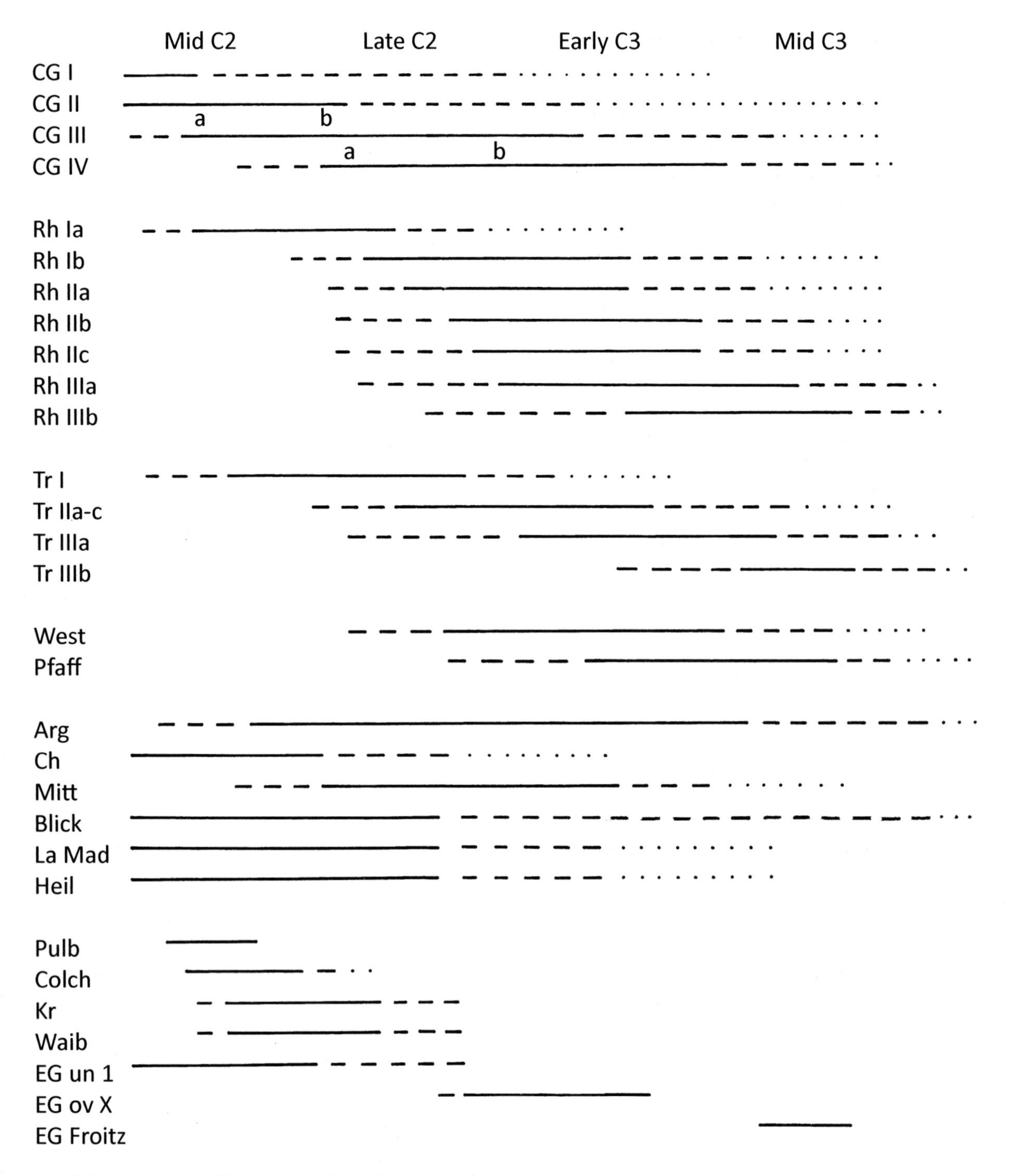


*Fig. 5.23 Diagram of kiln-centre chronologies.*

Banvus of CG also seems to be early in CG IV when coin associations are considered, especially his presence in the Wroxeter 'gutter' find, but associations with other potters point to links with later CG IV potters.[111] In this case, the Wroxeter evidence has been taken as the guiding indicator of a relatively early CG IV date.

Table 5.XIV proposes divisions within CG III and CG IV, which take account of apparent chronological distinctions within these two large groups.[112] CG III products were

[111] See fn. 27; also Delage 1999b; Delage & Séguier 2009.

[112] In general terms, this scheme conforms well to Delage's proposals (2003, 187, Fig. 2), and is even somewhat conservative chronologically in comparison with his datings. He suggests the following:

Paternus group I 140-60, IIa 160-70, IIb 170-210, IIc 180-210, the last 2 groups having continued use of moulds up to c. 240.

Cinnamus group A 140-60, B 150-80, C 170-90, the last 2 groups having continued use of moulds up to c. 220.

Iullinus group I 160-70, IIa 170-90, IIb 190-210, the last 2 groups having continued use of moulds up to c. 220 and 240 respectively.

Doeccus 170-90, with continued use of moulds up to c. 240.

Mercator II 170-210, with continued use of moulds up to c. 250.

Caletus 190-230, with continued use of moulds up to c. 250.

P-33 190-230, with continued use of moulds up to c. 250.

Marcus group Ia, Ib, Ic 210-40, with continued use of moulds up to c. 270.

Fgientinus (Cintinus) 230(?)-260, with continued use of moulds up to c. 270.

See also Delage 1999b for discussion of Q I Balbinus, Iullinus group,

being distributed during the main period for CG, when there must have been a flood of CG pottery on the market, which eventually became incorporated into archaeological deposits in a fairly mixed fashion. Nevertheless, it does seem that Criciro, Cettus, Cinnamus-Cerialis and Cinnamus early styles form a CG IIIa group, while potters such as Laxtucissa, Albucius, Divixtus and Cinnamus main styles form CG IIIb. Not all CG III potters can be allocated to sub-divisions in this way due to paucity of evidence for them, and have been left in the general CG III grouping. CG IIIb overlaps strongly with the early part of CG IV, and in some ways the distinction between them is a fairly artificial one, being based on the absence of the latter from the Antonine Wall. If deposits of this overlap period are examined, especially the shop deposit from the Wroxeter 'gutter', it can be seen that CG IIIb and CG IVa products were on sale and in use at the same time. Nevertheless, the absence of CG IV from the Antonine Wall is a real enough phenomenon, and serves a purpose in providing a useful division to a large mass of potters. CG IVa includes Paternus II, Casurius, Advocisus, Iullinus and others, while CG IVb is mainly Doeccus I and Iustus. As with CG III there are a number of unplaceable minor CG IV potters. It is noticeable that the volume of production falls away in CG IVb, and potters generally acknowledged to be the latest in CG IVb, e.g. Marcus, Caletus and Lucinus, were probably making vessels on a small scale, mainly for a regional rather than long-distance market, and virtually on their own, at least as far as decorated bowls are concerned.[113]

For the other kiln-centres, changes to existing divisions are few and need less comment. Rheinzabern has a clear early period, but Rh II and III have considerable overlap chronologically, both within each group and between the two groups, in all probability due to the intensive sharing of figure-types and styles between potters. There is debate about the viability of the Bernhard (and Bittner) groups used here, and in many ways, these groups, together with the alternative proposed by Mees, may not be the best way of organizing Rheinzabern chronology, since the groups are effectively stylistic affinity groups.[114]

The Argonne potters seem to fall into the sequence Gesatus, Germanus-Africanus and Tribunus, and Tocca. The first named has relatively early coin-dates and is recorded at the Saalburg Erdkastell,[115] a site dated before the mid second century.[116] Tribunus appears to be late second century and possibly a little later, as do Germanus-Africanus and

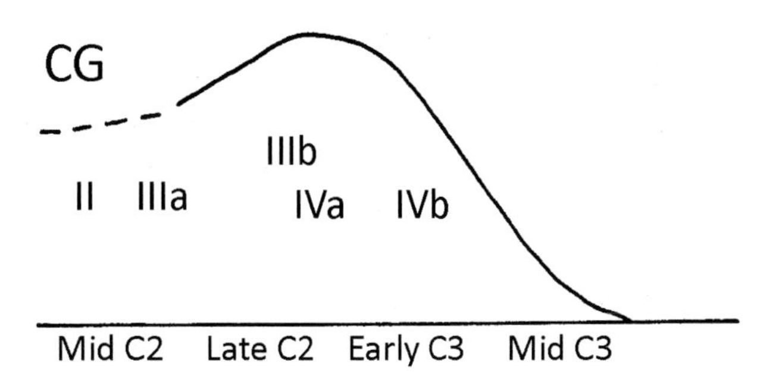


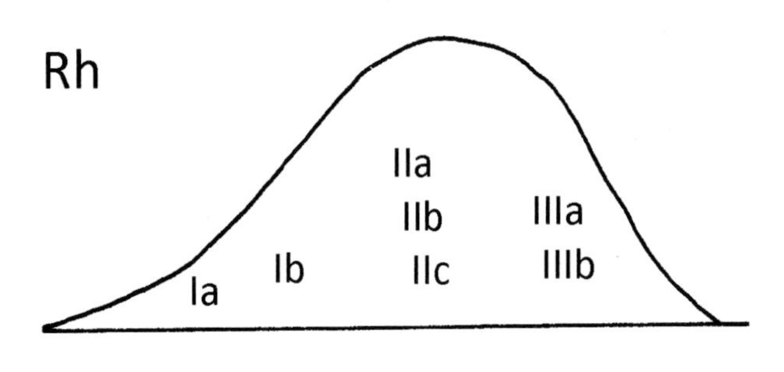


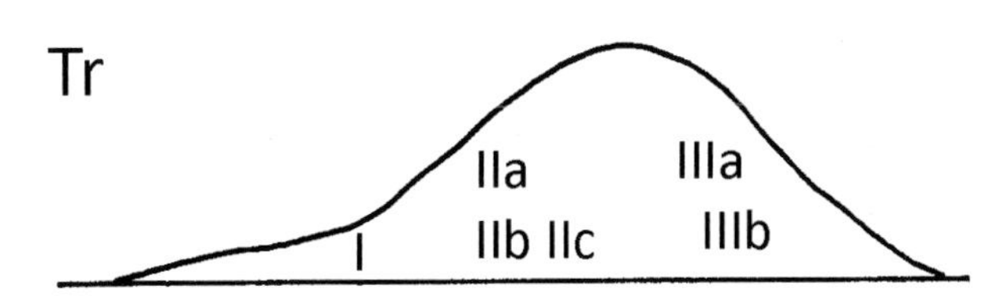


*Fig. 5.24 Tentative estimate of the relative volume of production of the major kiln-centres, based on Table 5.XII.*

Africanus. Tocca is the latest in the sequence, being found at A 90, London and A 146, Titelberg, of early-mid third century date.

Blickweiler and Eschweiler-Hof have been pushed considerably later, on the basis of the excavations at Bliesbruck (D 51) and the work of Petit.[117] He makes a case for continued and periodic reuse of moulds of L.A.L, Avitus and L.AT.AT, up to the 240/50s, and points out the deterioration in the quality of production. He also suggests that these potters should be dated 135/40 to 240/50, because of the reuse of the moulds. Blickweiler is divided by Petit and Heiligmann into four production groups, into the last of which the potters just mentioned are allocated.[118] Other Blickweiler potters are earlier, and seem not to be found much beyond the end of the second century. Eschweiler-Hof is very close to Blickweiler and seems to

Servus group, Paternus group and Banvus group. Q I Balbinus, Servus and Banvus are linked by Delage with late production running into the 3rd century, similar to the other groups above. For further discussion of late CG potters; Delage 2000a (P-33); 2012 (Servus VI); Delage & Séguier 2009 (Banvus & Cracina); Martin 2009b (Cantomallus).

113 See Delage 1998 for distribution maps of the late potters in his phases 7 and 8.

114 See Appendix 5 for further discussion and bibliography concerning the Rheinzabern groups.

115 Ricken 1934, 178.

116 Schönberger & Hartley 1970; but there is no pressing reason why the date could not be advanced later since many of the samian stamps have parallels on the Antonine Wall.

117 Petit 1989; 2001. See also Schaub 1987.

118 Petit 2001, 69; Heiligmann 1990, 157-61, Tab. 13.

*Table 5.XIV Kiln-centre phasing and dating, incorporating changes in chronology proposed in chapter 5.*

* indicates the better-represented potters. The lists of potters do not necessarily include all those known for the kiln-centre.

**CG I** Found as survival pieces in late 2nd century contexts. Potters not listed here, cf Tables 1.I and Appendices 7 and 9.

**CG II** Early potters, especially Quintilianus*, Sacer-Attianus*, X-6* and Drusus II* found as survival pieces in late 2nd/early 3rd century contexts. Later potters (as in Table 1.I) in production/distribution in mid 2nd century, also found in late 2nd century with survivals in early 3rd - the list includes Ianuaris II-Paternus I*, Sissus II, Tetturo, Tittius and perhaps also Attianus of Sacer-Attianus.

**CG III** Can be divided into **CG IIIa**, Criciro*, Cettus*, Cinnamus-Cerialis and Cinnamus early styles, which are produced on a small scale in the mid 2nd century, with main production mid/late 2nd century and survival into the early 3rd; and **CG IIIb**, Cinnamus main styles* (ovolo 3 mainly earlier, ovolo 1 mainly later), Albucius*, Divixtus*. Laxtucissa*, Secundus, Paullus, Pugnus, Q I Balbinus, Servus I, Carantinus I, Martialis, P-23. CG IIIb has main production in late 2nd century, some production/distribution up to end 2nd/early 3rd, with survivals to mid 3rd century. Unplaceable within CG III are Illixo, Moxius, Lastuca, Cantomallus, P-18, P-19, P-22.

**CG IV** Can also be divided. **CG IVa** consists of Paternus II*, Casurius*, Advocisus*. Iullinus*, Censorinus, Servus II-III, Banvus (possibly also CG IVb), Mercator II, Doeccus II (possibly CG III). These potters overlapped with CC IIIb, but their production probably continued to early 3rd century, and many of their products still found up to mid 3rd century. **CG IVb** is Doeccus I*, Iustus, Caletus, Fgientinus (Cintinus), Severus, Marcus, Lucinus (last 2 are late in CG IVb). There is some production in late 2nd century, but mainly end 2nd/early 3rd, with many pieces found in contexts of early/mid 3rd century. Unplaceable within CG IV are Antistii, Caratillus, Atilianus, Priscus, Belsa, Catussa, Ollognatus, ov B184.

**Rh Ia** Main production mid 2nd century, continuing to late 2nd, with survivals to early 3rd century. Janu I*, Reginus I*, Cobnertus I-III*, Firmus I

**Rh Ib** Some production overlapping with Rh Ia, but mainly in late 2nd/early 3rd century, with survivals to mid 3rd century. Cerialis I-V*, Comitialis I-III*, Cerialis group wares A & B, Arvernicus-Lutaevus, Belsus I, Lucanus.

**Rh IIa** Production starts in the late 2nd century, but is mainly early 3rd with survivals to mid 3rd century. Comitialis IV-VI*, B F Attoni*, ov E25/26*, Belsus II-III, Cerialis VI, Respectus, Florentinus, Mammilianus, Firmus II, Pupus-Iuvenis II, Pupus, Atto, Attillus, Reginus II, Iustinus, Iuvenis I, Augustinus I, Castus.

**Rh IIb** Dated as Rh IIa. Julius I*, Julius I-Lupus*, Lupus, Augustinus II-III, Victorinus I, ov E8.

**Rh IIc** Dated as Rh IIa, but production may start later. Helenius*, Primitivus I-IV*, Verecundus I-II, Marcellus I-II, Augustalis, wares A & B with 0382/3.

**Rh IIIa** Production entirely within early 3rd century, but probably some production/distribution to mid 3rd century. Julius II-Julianus I*, Victorinus II-III, Janu II, Respectinus I-II, Marcellinus, ov E48/49.

**Rh IIIb** Dated as Rh IIIa, but with emphasis on later period of early/mid 3rd century. Victor II-Januco*, Victor I, Victor III, Julianus II, Statutus I-II, Perpetuus, Pervincus, Severianus, Severianus-Gemellus, ov E30, ov E34, ov E31, ov E35.

**Tr I** Dates are similar to Rh Ia, but main production may have started slightly later. Werkstatt I is earlier than Werkstatt II*.

**Tr IIa** Dated as Rh IIa. Comitialis*, Dexter*, Censor*, Maiiaavus*, Censor group.

**Tr IIb** Dated basically as Tr IIa, but production may start later. Amator*, Tordilo*, Criciro, Dexter/Censor successors, Marcellinus, Victor.

**Tr IIc** Dated as Tr IIb, but production may start later. Afer*, Afer-Marinus, Atillus-Pussosus.

**Tr IIIa** Dated as Rh IIIa. Dubitatus-Dubitus, Paternianus, Dignus-Primanus, Perpetuus, Gard 1937, Taf 27 nos 1-21.

**Tr IIIb** Dated as Rh IIIb but production/distribution certain for mid 3rd century. Succio, Equitatus, TPCFR, 'late ware'.

**West** Production starts in late 2nd century, main period early 3rd, probably continuous to mid 3rd. Helenius*, Comitialis*, Onniorix, Iassus, Decminus, Erotus, Venerius.

**Pfaff** Production starts in early 3rd century, perhaps after decline of **West**, continues to mid 3rd. Helenius, Dicanus, ov 19, ov 27.

**Arg** Some production in mid 2nd century, main period late 2nd and beginning of 3rd century, some production up to mid 3rd century, with probable continuity to roller-stamped wares. Gesatus and Gesatus-Tribunus* (early), Tribunus*, Germanus-Africanus, Africanus, Tocca (late), ov E, ov F, ov C&G R2/T3 (Les Allieux).

**La Mad** Some production early 2nd century, main period mid 2nd, some production/distribution in late 2nd, with survival pieces to early 3rd. Albillus* (early), Sacer, Virtus, Janu (later), ov A', ov B, ov C (later), ov F, ov K1, ov L.

**Heil** Dated as La Mad. Janu* (= Rh Ia), Reginus (= Rh Ia), Ciriuna, Verecundus, F-master, ov J.

**Blick** Dated as La Mad, but with production from reused moulds up to mid 3rd century. Avitus, LAL, master potter, vase ovolo potter, large figure potter, leaping animal potter, ov 30, ov 31, ov 32, ov 34 (last 4 possibly later).

**Chém** Dated as La Mad, but little in late 2nd century or later contexts. Saturninus-Satto*.

**Mitt** Some production mid 2nd century, main period late 2nd/beginning 3rd, with many survival pieces in early 3rd or later. Saturninus-Satto (early), Cibisus (later).

**Itten** Probably as Heil. Verecundus.

**Kräh** Dated as Rh Ia. Reginus (= Rh Ia).

**Waib** Dated as Rh Ia. Reginus (= Rh Ia), Marinus, ov B.

**Esch** Probably as Blick. LAA, L.AT.AT.

**EG** Ricken 1934 unlocated group 1, dated probably as La Mad. Ov X, dated probably early 3rd century. Clamosus dated early/mid 3rd century. Others in Appendix 9 effectively undated, but probably early-mid 3rd century.

**Brit** **Colch** A, **Colch** B in production mid/late 2nd century (= CG III). Pieces found to end 2nd century, perhaps later. **Pulb** in production mid 2nd century (= CG III, probably IIIa).

For other kiln-centres see notes and bibliography in Appendix 10.

have been a later semi-independent kiln-centre. The other potter associated with this group, Clamosus, has not been allocated to a kiln-centre, and borrowed stylistically from both Rheinzabern and Trier. On the basis of the Bliesbruck finds, he is late, dated 240/60.[119]

Heiligenberg is the other small kiln-site worthy of mention. The current view of dating is late first century – *c.* 150 with potters coming in the sequence Ciriuna, Janu, F-master, Reginus.[120] This end-date seems too early, according to the evidence in the gazetteer, since potters such as Janu are associated with CG and Rheinzabern potters of later date, and there is not such a clear sequence (cf Table 5.V). One reason for the date of *c.* 150 was that Reginus was thought to have gone from Heiligenberg to Kräherwald and Waiblingen, then to Rheinzabern, where he must have been by *c.* 160 at the latest.[121] This inevitably raises the question of what form these migrations actually took – was it movement of personnel, which would imply a sequence, or was it movement of equipment, which could imply contemporaneity? Such questions are unfortunately not answerable using the data in this chapter since chemical analysis of moulds, etc., is required to establish provenances, but there is further discussion of the issue in chapter 6. La Madeleine is involved in these problems too, since Janu, apparently a later La Madeleine potter, is thought to have moved from there to Heiligenberg then to Rheinzabern. The only dating indications for La Madeleine from coin-associations are that Albillus is earlier and ovolo C is later within the dating scheme proposed in Fig. 5.23.

[119] Schaub 1987; Petit 2001.

[120] Garbsch 1982, 57. Janu = Januarius; cf. Simon & Köhler 1992, 18; Heiligmann 1990, 159-60. Heiligmann (1990, 157-61, Tabelle 13) proposes division of Heiligenberg into two groups, and Blickweiler into four, in similar fashion to his sub-divisions of CG and Rheinzabern. Symonds (1992, 42) gives a helpful summary table of the chronology of the minor EG kilns, based on the work by Lutz.

[121] Riedl 2011, 225-7.

The chronology presented here is tentative and obviously liable to future modification. A deliberate feature of it is the imprecision of the absolute dates compared with most previous chronologies, which often attempt datings to the nearest year or five-year interval. All the dating indicators used, coin-associations, historical datings, dendrochronolog-ical dates, etc., can only be imprecisely and flexibly applied to samian ware chronology, due to the inherent complications of the dating methodology, as outlined in chapter 2. Very accurate dates applied to samian ware are spurious, even if accurate dates in general are earnestly desired by archaeologists seeking to marry archaeological remains with specific events in Roman history.[122] The sort of precision, or rather imprecision, presented here, which is accurate only to the reigns of emperors, or their equivalent coin-periods, and uses phrases such as early, mid or late century, are the most compatible with the evident complexity of attempting to date samian ware, for 'In general, complexity and precision bear an inverse relation to one another in the sense that, as the complexity of a problem increases, the possibility of analysing it in precise terms diminishes'.[123]

Finally, has the hypothesis put forward in chapter 1 been maintained or disproved? In part, it has been disproved since the main period of production of Central Gaulish pottery does not go on as late as that of Rheinzabern or Trier. However, it is equally the case that Central Gaulish production did not come to an end as early as usually stated, and that the historical explanation for the end of production can no longer be sustained. Therefore an economic or social explanation for the decline of samian manufacture is still an active hypothesis, and will be pursued further in chapters 6 and 7.

[122] Maxfield 1982, 75, 80.

[123] Zadeh 1973, quoted by Jain 1980 in connection with 'fuzzy' set theory.

# Chapter 6

# The Decline of Samian Ware Manufacture

## Part I: A Review of Production and Distribution

Previous chapters have been concerned largely with matters of methods, chronology and typology. As such they have formed an important part of laying a factual foundation against which ideas and hypotheses can be tested. Various hypotheses will be put forward in this and the following chapter, both on the economics of the pottery industry itself and on wider implications for the archaeology and history of the period. The intent of this chapter is to review existing evidence for the production and distribution of samian ware, taking into account current thinking on the subject. All periods of samian ware production will be considered, as it is difficult to examine the decline of manufacture without assessing the state of the industry in its fully developed form.

### Social Status of the Potters

At the fairly general level of the status of the samian potter in Roman society, Grenier's discussion provides a suitable starting point, as it succinctly puts forward all the main issues.[1] He suggests that the men actually making the pottery in the Gaulish workshops were generally not slaves, on the basis of well-furnished cemeteries near the kilns, which he takes to be those of potters, together with the finding of figure-punches in reasonably well-appointed houses. In Arezzo, however, the potters were slaves, as was clear from the stamps. Grenier was influenced in these suggestions by a desire to derive much of the provincial samian tradition from pre-Roman and Gallo-Belgic potting traditions. There is an underlying assumption that Gauls were free men, and thus their pottery organisation was voluntarily constituted. He concluded by placing the potters in a primary position in the industry, going so far as to suggest that the *negotiatores artis cretariae* were their salesmen and agents.[2] Unfortunately, his evidence and ideological assumptions would not now survive detailed critical analysis: the cemeteries do not certainly contain the remains of potters, and the figure-punches in the houses may not be in primary deposits. However, the questions he attempted to answer are still valid - a) did all samian potters work in the same conditions? b) was the organisation of Gaulish samian production based primarily on imported techniques of red-gloss pottery production, or was the organisation rooted more strongly in local pottery traditions? c) what position did those craftsmen actually making the vessels have in the social structure of the pottery trade?

In order to seek answers to these questions it is necessary to turn first to the Arretine potteries and their conditions of production. The epigraphic evidence in the form of potters' stamps is abundant and sufficiently full to give a reasonable picture of workshop organisation, as Prachner, Fülle and others have shown.[3] They distinguish between proprietors (some of whom were of senatorial status and clearly not engaged in actual production), freedmen and slaves by means of the case-endings and the sequence of names on the stamps in moulds and bowls. A good example is Cn Ateius: there are apparently twenty-two subordinates connected with his name, of which four are slaves, fourteen are freedmen and four are slaves freed during attachment to his workshop. These figures are complicated by the fact that many of the freedmen have Ateius' *nomen*, and it seems possible to assume that most were originally his slaves. Perhaps the skilled potters, especially those working on decorated bowls, were freed by their proprietors, while the slaves were those working on less difficult tasks, possibly following an ancient form of apprenticeship which resulted in their freedom after being trained and working as a potter for some years. Some of the slaves are connected on the stamps with the freedmen rather than Ateius himself, implying that they were working for them rather than the proprietor. The names of the slaves and freedmen are also revealing, in that twelve are Greek, of which ten produced decorated ware, seven are Latin of which only two produced decorated ware, and only three of the names are barbarian in origin (Germullus – Celtic; Mahes – near eastern or Illyrian; Otonius – possibly German). This, together with the find of a workshop graffito written in Greek,[4] would appear to back the idea that the skilled men were coming from the East, although this issue is clouded by the common use of Greek words when naming slaves. The presence of non-Latin and non-Greek names in an appreciable minority throughout the Arretine workshops implies on the other hand that men of various ethnic origins were being trained to do the job.

Ateius was chosen as an example because he seems fairly typical of the other Arretine potters. As Prachner has shown, his is by no means the largest workshop; the Annii, Cornelius, Rasinius and Titius all having at least fifty subordinates, and there is quite a variation in the proportion of freedmen to slaves (from zero out of sixty in the case of Rasinius, but two freedoms granted, to two out of two in the case of M Pescennius).[5] It is not easy to account for such large differences. Generally, however,

[1] Grenier 1938.

[2] 'courtiers et ... commissionaires', Grenier 1938, 89.

[3] Prachner 1980; Fülle 1997; 2000c; Mees 2002. For proprietors of senatorial status, see Wiseman 1963.

[4] Johnston 1985.

[5] Prachner 1980, 220.

the image of the Arretine industry being entirely slave-run is not strictly true, for many were freedmen or eventually made free. In fact, the freedmen as a class were probably the most important element in the industry, as several went on to become workshop proprietors in their own right.[6]

To return to Ateius, it would appear that his workshop was one of the more adventurous of the Italian potteries, for production started at Lyon not long after it had first started at Arezzo and, as is now known, Pisa, and slightly later, at La Graufesenque.[7] The potters at Lyon numbered up to four slaves (i.e. all the slaves known for Ateius) and nine freedmen. The slaves were all except one the property of the freedmen. The styles of pottery they produced were virtually identical to those made in the original workshop, achieved by shipping moulds to Lyon.[8] However, the exact relationship between main workshop and Lyon branch is not really known and presents problems, partly of a typological and chronological nature.[9] Could Lyon have been a semi-independent venture set up by his freedmen, rather than a branch workshop? The evidence of the close stylistic links probably goes against a third possibility; competitive trading by Ateius' subordinates. It is also doubtful that the freedmen could or would want to put themselves in such a position, given their legal (patron-client) obligations to their former master. Other proprietors' names are also known from Lyon, stamped on locally-produced vessels (e.g. Rasinius), so the Ateius transfer was not an isolated case, and there does seem to have been a movement of materials, techniques and organisation to Gaul, giving the best evidence so far available of the way in which samian techniques came to the province. The evidence suggests that both the workshop organisation and relationships as well as the technical skills were introduced, everything in fact except perhaps the proprietors themselves, whom in all probability remained in Italy. A peripheral matter in this last respect is the observation that few if any of the Arretine proprietors appear to have had their commercial interest continued into the second generation. Such lack of continuity may have some bearing on the decline of the Arretine industry, and may perhaps be explained by the potters having some sort of temporary contract with the proprietors (see below).[10]

Arretine ware provides us with fairly good evidence of the social structure of the workshops. However, Gaulish samian potteries are less precise in the information they furnish and it is less easy to talk in terms of juridical status relationships. La Graufesenque is perhaps the most revealing because of the existence of a large number of graffiti scratched on plates before firing in the kilns.[11] Most are lists, probably related to communal firings, which will be discussed below, but one appears to refer to the status of the potters in that it contains the word *puerorum*.[12] This is a rather inexact term for a slave or servant, and it cannot be established whether the people in question were owned by the proprietor, Atelia, or paid by her.[13] The word probably means that freedmen are not being referred to, and it is likely that someone of the status of a freedman is, in fact, inscribing the graffito, perhaps in the capacity of a *magister*.[14] The proprietor does not seem to have been involved in any of the activities mentioned on this particular graffito, or in making the graffito itself. The other graffiti in the form of lists were probably also the work of *magistri* supervising subordinates.

The evidence from the stamps is much harder to interpret, for they are simpler in form than those from Arezzo, referring usually only to one person, except in the earliest period of South Gaul when slave names do seem to occur, e.g. Scottius Damoni A.[15] The single name stamps are often either in the genitive with *officina* or *manu*, or in the nominative with *fecit*. Names with *tria nomina* are rare, and many of them may refer to Imperial freedmen, e.g. T Flavius Secundus.[16] Most of the names are single words, e.g. Acutus, Laetus, Hilarus, of the sort often associated with slaves, or Gaulish names such as Matugenus or Mommo of the sort usually taken to be of peregrine status.[17] For South Gaul, therefore, the evidence seems to suggest a low level of involvement by Roman citizens, most of those using name stamps being peregrines and possibly slaves of peregrines.[18] This conclusion applies *a fortiori* to the more northerly kiln-centres of the second and third centuries, where the stamps have few if any individuals with *tria nomina*, and also few servile-type names. Single provincial names, usually of Celtic ancestry, account for by far the greatest percentage of the stamps.[19]

A source of confusion in the study of name stamps arises when the matter of whom the stamps are referring to is considered. This is especially the case there more than one stamp is present, and Johns and others have drawn attention to the widespread practice of having three names on decorated vessels; cursive mould signatures, large advertisement stamps in the decoration and small stamps

[6] Cf. Garnsey 1981, esp. 368-71; the slave-run model for Arretine production is seen, for instance, in the pages of Pucci 1973; 1981; 1983, 115.

[7] Pisa: Jefferson, Dannell & Williams 1981; La Graufesenque: Hoffmann 1995; Genin, Hoffmann & Vernhet 2002.

[8] Picon 1976, 94.

[9] Wells 1977; Ettlinger 1983, 103-5.

[10] Fülle 1997, 121ff. The type of contract was probably *locatio/conduction* (cf. Wieling 2000), but for a pre-firing graffito on a C21 from Argonne potteries, with the looser *mandatum*, see Raepsaet 2008. Ettlinger (1987) discusses the Arretine market, and links with Lyon.

[11] Marichal 1988; cf also Dannell 2002; Fülle 2000a; Polak 1998; Favory 1974, 96; Marichal 1971.

[12] Marichal 1974; 1988, 226, no. 169; King 1980.

[13] The first line of the graffito begins ]. *ateliae puerorum* which appears to refer to a woman proprietor, Atelia.

[14] Cf. *CIL* XIII 8729 for use of this word in a pottery context.

[15] I.e. Arretine (ware) by Scottius for Damonus; Hartley 2002, 135; Vernhet & Balsan 1975.

[16] Vernhet 1975, 4.

[17] Balsan 1970.

[18] The graffiti demonstrate that La Graufesenque potters were effectively bilingual in Gaulish and Latin, with additionally, Greek-derived words in their vocabulary; Mullen 2013.

[19] The only apparent public building excavated at La Graufesenque is a Romano-Celtic temple, near which a unique samian ware portrait head was found, with the name Calus; he may have been one of the senior potters at the site, perhaps a potter-priest or a guild master; Mees 2012. Cf. Lutz 1977a, 45-6 for the example of the Moselle potters.

under the rim indicating the man or workshop that actually produced the vessel.[20] In these cases the stamps may refer to master-potter, proprietor and vessel-maker respectively, or some other organisational relationship about which there is further discussion below.[21]

To conclude the matter of social status of the potters, reference can be made back to Grenier's suggestion that the potters themselves were in the primary position in the industry, the *negotiatores* being their agents. This appears to be entirely wrong: all the evidence of nomenclature and the material culture of the workshop sites (for which see below) would seem to indicate persons of low status, including the certain use of slaves at Arezzo and their probable use in South Gaul. Workshop *magistri* (and possibly proprietors) seem to have been the only people at the workshops themselves to have been of higher status and in a position to make contracts for selling the products.[22] These men and the *negotiatores* were the wealthy ones in the industry, in all probability bearing the cost of the finished vessels and the risk of distributing them – and of course making any profit to be had. It is particularly the *negotiatores* that are commemorated on inscriptions and tombstones.[23] One *mag(ister) fig(linae)* is known,[24] and one potter, of somewhat uncertain status, but rich enough to be commemorated on a tombstone.[25] *Negotiatores* were probably the key men in the industry, the name itself denoting a person of relatively high status in the mercantile hierarchy,[26] and can be equated very roughly with the middlemen in Peacock's descriptions of ethnological practices in this field.[27]

One area that is completely uncertain is the status of the rather shadowy workshop proprietors. They may not have been connected with the processes of production and distribution of the pottery, perhaps being the land-owners who leased the production sites to the *magistri*,[28] or who used bailiffs as an extension of other estate activities. Of relevance in this context are Egyptian papyri recording contracts for leases, for instance, of a pottery and its works to a skilled illiterate potter for a specified contract in which the land-owner supplied the raw materials.[29] Such a system may have operated for some of the smaller samian kiln-centres, but it seems unlikely that the larger centres had such direct relationships between land-owners and potters. Instead, there are likely to have been business managers (*institores*), who took on the risks of samian ware production and distribution.[30]

## Workshop Organisation

The hints gleaned by considering social status that there were differences between the major samian potteries seem to be confirmed when the details of the organisation of production are examined. Returning to Arezzo, the evidence seems to suggest that the proprietors owned (or perhaps leased) tracts of land in and around the town on which they set up production. M Perennius had a kiln and levigation tanks in the town, and Ateius' workshop has also been located.[31] These and other sparse indications favour more or less integrated production for each workshop. However, the pattern is different at La Graufesenque (and to a lesser extent the other Gaulish kilns) where there is evidence for some activities being organised on a communal basis. Here, the stamps indicate division of labour, such that the potters need not be using moulds of their own manufacture, but often those made by others. The relationship between the mould-makers and the bowl-makers is not entirely clear, some scholars such as Chenet and Gaudron arguing that the mould-maker was subordinate to the potters producing the finished vessels, others, notably Terrisse, Favory, Delplace and Haalebos preferring to see the mould-maker as the master potter who leaves the less creative task of making the bowls to subordinates.[32] A third possibility exists, that the mould-makers operated independently of the vessel-makers, making their moulds available to whoever wished to purchase them. This possibility is supported by the finding of moulds of one kiln-centre being used for making vessels at another centre, e.g. Mougon-Nouâtre moulds in use at Mazières-en-Mauge, or Berne-Enge moulds at Martigny.[33] This would also account for the existence of bowls with identical moulding being stamped with the names of different vessel-makers,[34] equally as well as the possibility that the mould-maker was the master potter.

Another relationship between potters that is of interest is that between mould-makers and punch-makers. The punches are clearly the material remains of the primary stage of manufacture of the moulds, but present a number of problems in their interpretation. Firstly, remarkably few of them have been found. Hofmann was able to say that there were two

[20] Johns 1963; cf. Raistrick 1931 for a Rheinzabern example.

[21] There is extensive discussion of stamps and their meaning, and the subject is only touched upon in this chapter. Cf. Aubert 1994, 287-302; Dannell 2002; Delage 1999b; 2004; Demarolle 2000; Fülle 1997, 114-21; 2000b; Hartley 2002; Hartley & Dickinson 2008a, introduction; Malfitana 2006; Mees 2002; Polak 2000, 39-42; Weber 2012.

[22] The villa of Q Iulius Pri(...) at Aspiran (Hérault), with adjacent kilns for amphorae and samian ware, is a good example of a proprietor or *magister* living next to the workshop (Mauné 2010).

[23] E.g. *CIL* XIII 1906, 2033, Lyon; XIII 8224, 8350, Cologne; XIII 8793, Domburg; cf. Delplace 1978, 56.

[24] *CIL* XIII 8729, Holtedoorn; an alternative reading is *magister figulorum* in the sense of a master of a guild of potters (Pucci 1983, 117). A *collegium figulorum* is mentioned by Pliny (*NH* 35.159).

[25] *fictiliarius*, *CIL* XIII 11361, Metz.

[26] Kneissl 1983; D'Arms 1981, 160. Cf. also Schmidts 2011, 95ff.

[27] Peacock 1982.

[28] As has been suggested for brick production; Helen 1975; Aubert 1994, 217ff.

[29] Cockle 1981; Fülle 1997, 121-2. Mees 2002 has a gazetteer and translation (into German) of relevant papyri and other literary sources.

[30] Aubert 1994, esp. Ch. 4; Fülle 1997, 128-9. Strobel (1987; 1992) argues for a strong and direct role for land and pottery owners at La Graufesenque, but more recent discussion by Fülle 1997, Mees 2002 and Dannell 2002 favour more complex and variable relationships. See also King 1990, 125-31.

[31] Peacock 1982, 121, citing Pasqui 1896; Bartoli *et al*. 1984. Ateius' workshop; Maetzke 1959.

[32] Chenet & Gaudron 1955, 65-8, 151-2; Terrisse 1968, 38; Favory 1974, 95; Delplace 1978, 73; Haalebos 1979, 128.

[33] Delage 2010; Haldimann 1999.

[34] E.g. Medetus and Donnaucus at Les Martres-de-Veyre; Favory 1974, 95.

from La Graufesenque, about twenty from Lezoux and two from Rheinzabern.[35] This is to be compared with hundreds of moulds or bowls, compounding the problem further. Were the punches not used in the kiln and workshop areas? Plicque recorded the find of a group of them in a Roman house at Lezoux, which may back up this suggestion.[36] Another possibility is that they were guarded carefully when in use, and disposed of when worn and useless in such a way that other potters (and subsequent archaeologists) were not able to find and make use of them. An alternative is that a perishable material such as wood was widely used, but there appears to be no sign of this in finished moulds and bowls. The names on the punches, however, are easier to interpret. Several are otherwise unknown, which may be because they were specialist modellers of punches. Others are those who produced the moulds, much as would be expected.

Communal organisation may have existed for firing the pots in the South Gaulish kilns, as the graffiti appear to demonstrate. The Celtic word τυθός or the Latin *furnus* at the head of the more complete lists in graffito probably means kiln or firing.[37] The word is followed by a number between one and ten signifying either the number of the kiln or the number in a sequence of firings. Under this heading is a list of potters' names, each accompanied by a total of vessels of different types, usually in descending size order (the way in which they might have been stacked in the kiln). The grand totals are in the region of 30,000 but occasionally are much higher, above 100,000. This number of vessels was well within the capacity of the large kilns found at samian production centres. One excavated at La Graufesenque was 9 x 7 m with an internal space estimated at 100 $m^3$.[38] The graffiti were apparently incised before firing and the plate with the list then put in the kiln so that a check could be made on unloading the kiln. This seems to indicate that the kilns were used by groups of potters, an observation confirmed for some of the kiln-centres that do not have surviving graffiti by the finding of fused wasters or 'moutons' with different potters represented in the piles of bowls.[39] Unfortunately, it is not easy to discern how these groups were constituted. Three possibilities are a), that each workshop of potters controlled its own kilns, and therefore that the graffiti lists were internal checks on production, or b) that the master-potters controlled the kilns, meaning that the lists were tallies of the work of their subordinates, or c) that the kilns were independently organised as a separate skilled part of the process, so that the lists acted in effect as charge sheets for the space each potter was taking up in the kiln.[40]

The problem of communal organisation in the kiln-centres draws in the matter of the name stamps again. Mees has demonstrated that larger workshops, e.g. Calvus i at La Graufesenque, used many different dies for their name-stamps, and therefore seem to have employed a large workforce. This applies most strongly at La Graufesenque, where overall pottery production volumes were highest; less so at Lezoux, Rheinzabern or Trier.[41]

Many of the vessel-makers stamps were small, often illegible, sometimes illiterate and occasionally not personal names at all.[42] The best explanation of this is that these are identification marks used by vessel-makers to trace their own products through the process, and were not for the sake of the customer.[43] It may also have been necessary for master-potters, proprietors or those running the kilns to have the work of individual potters distinguished.

Another approach to workshop organisation is to examine the links between designs on the decorated bowls. Generally speaking, a similar picture seems to emerge. The major analysis of this by Mees has focused upon Rheinzabern, building on earlier work by Bernhard and Bittner.[44] Evidence is advanced that there are seven main overlapping groups, each acting more-or-less communally but independently. The groups are not chronologically distinct, except perhaps for the earliest potters, and therefore they represent affiliated teams of potters, with shared or inherited decorative punches and moulds. This appears to be similar to Knorr's observations of overlapping styles in South Gaulish products, but contrasts with Stanfield and Simpson's characterisation of early second century Central Gaulish potters as organised more on the lines of self-contained workshops.[45]

[35] Hofmann 1971, n. 17.

[36] Vertet 1976a, 101.

[37] Duval & Marichal 1966; Bémont 1996; Polak 1998, 116-7; Fülle 2000a.

[38] Vernhet 1981; Picon & Vernhet 2008; Schaad 2007, 190-206; Genin 2007. The 'fosse de Cirratus' at La Graufesenque contained 28,448 plain-ware vessels, and the 'fosse de Gallicanus' 40,132; both apparently filled in a short space of time (Genin 2007, 55-70, 83-107), possibly a result of the throwing out of a kiln load. Cf. also *Gallia* 41, 1983, 478-9.

[39] Johns, Tite & Maniatis 1977; Rogers 1977.

[40] Polak (1998, 120-1) argues for the last option, and suggests that many potters at La Graufesenque contracted out the firing of their products. They appear to have used more than one kiln operator, possibly because the kilns themselves were specialised in certain vessel forms. Organisation of the potters, therefore, could easily have been fluid, with temporary rather than permanent co-operation. Fülle (2000a) takes the same general line of interpretation.

[41] Mees 2013. Calvus can be equated with Calus, and thus may have been the 'potter-priest' discussed by Mees 2012.

[42] E.g. Ave Vale from La Graufesenque; Vernhet & Balsan 1975, 27. Polak (2000, 42) makes the interesting suggestion that internal stamps at La Graufesenque were simply a tradition from Italian potteries, and eventually ceased to serve any specific purpose. He bases this on the large percentage of unstamped vessels, and on the prevalence of broken and illiterate stamps.

[43] However, there are clear exceptions to this. The existence of a form of brand name 'ARRETINUM' implies that some stamps were for customer identification of the product, even if the stamp sometimes actually appeared on non-Arretine as well the genuine vessels (Malfitana 2006; Fülle 1997, 116). The large, intra-decoration name stamps, e.g. of Cinnamus, also imply development of a brand image (Delage 2004).

[44] Mees 2002; 1993; 1994a; 2000; Kortüm & Mees 1998. This analysis uses the Jaccard similarity coefficient to create dendrograms from the presence/absence of co-occurring decorative types between potters, i.e. it is a clustering method that groups associated potters. Mees prefers the Jaccard coefficient, on statistical grounds, over that of Yule used by Bittner 1986 and Bernhard 1981a for their matrices and groupings of potters. See also Gimber 1999 for comments on Bittner 1986 and 1996. For a critical comparison of the different types of similarity coefficient, see Jackson *et al.* 1989. Rheinzabern potters' groups are discussed further in Appendix 5.

[45] Knorr 1919; 1952; Mees 1995; Dannell *et al.* 2003. Cf. also Delplace 1978, 69; Stanfield & Simpson 1958, xxiii-xxv.

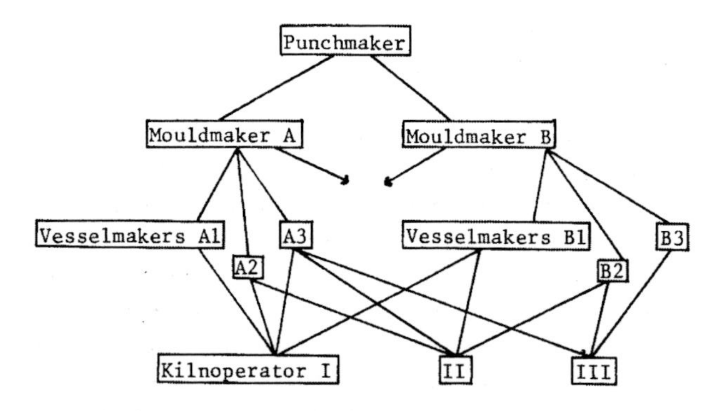


*Fig. 6.1 A model for workshop inter-relationships, based on Rheinzabern (after Bernhard 1981a).*

There seem to have been three major divisions within the Rheinzabern workshop organisation. The largest group was that of vessel-makers (Fig. 6.1), responsible for finished plain and decorated wares, perhaps with the assistance of subordinates preparing clay, slip and so on, but more probably in some sort of communal arrangement. Supplying them with specialised equipment to produce decorated ware were the mould-makers, who were artistically the master-craftsmen, and may also have been in charge of the vessel-makers. Alternatively, there may have been workshops incorporating both mould- and vessel-makers under a *magister* or proprietor, as suggested earlier. The third division is that of the kiln-operators, who may have been operating a specialised service for several small workshops, perhaps under the aegis of one of the larger workshops.[46]

A matter of some relevance in the context of workshop organisation is the question of how far samian production can be regarded as mass-production in the modern sense, a connection that has been made in the archaeological literature.[47] Two relevant criteria seem to be fulfilled: there were apparent stages in the production process, with specialisation at the different stages, and there was high-volume output. However, there is no evidence for a third important criterion, continuous production. Indeed, the rare mention of dates on the South Gaulish and other graffiti concentrate in the period May to September.[48] Production was probably seasonal, even at the large workshops, with the winter for gathering wood, digging clay and allowing it to weather, and the summer for throwing, drying and firing the pottery. In addition, the stages in the manufacturing process may be deceptive, in that they are a reminder of modern production-line assembly systems. A characteristic of the decorated bowls goes a long way to dispelling this notion, in that given the enormous quantity of decorated vessels known, multiple copies and duplicates appear to be rare. It seems likely, in fact, that the moulds were not used for making a great quantity of bowls from each, and may also have been conserved for re-use at a later date or traded to other kiln-centres.[49] A more valid view is to regard the use of samian moulds in the same light as those used in bronze-casting or the production of terracotta figurines. The moulds were an aid in the manufacture of a highly-crafted product, in which the stages of production added to cost and time, not reduced them. The moulds appear to have had significant value, and were used to produce a 'run' of vessels, then put into storage, or alternatively broken up (to enhance the value of the vessels?), which may account for the mould fragments found both at the kiln sites and elsewhere. In certain cases, especially towards the later phases of production at a kiln-centre, moulds might be retrieved from storage and re-used, decades after their original manufacture.

## POSITIONING OF KILN-CENTRES

A matter that has always been of major concern to samian specialists is the positioning of the kiln-centres.[50] The received opinion is that they gradually moved nearer their main markets, presumably as a result of a desire to make economies in transport and other costs. However, a closer look at the development of the industry shows that this simple analysis is not quite the case, and that the issues are somewhat complicated by the relationships between kiln-centres and with the local socio-economic structure.

Mees has suggested that the productive economic zone of Tarraconensis, Narbonensis and Aquitania in the late Republic and early Empire, may have been the stimulus to the establishment of South Gaulish kiln-centres.[51] The zone had a significant development of wine and other high-value agricultural products, for which samian ware would naturally be associated as part of the equipment for consumption of those goods. This plausibly provides a general framework for expansion of the Italian *sigillata* industry into southern Gaul.

The setting up of the Arretine workshops at Lyon does at first sight seem to conform to these ideas. Pottery from the Roman fortress of Haltern shows that the majority comes from Lyon, while the Italian workshops were less well-represented and tended to concentrate on the Mediterranean market.[52] However, if the single largest contributor to the assemblage, the Ateius workshop, is examined, a different picture emerges. 60% comes from

[46] Bernhard 1981a. Cf. Jacob & Leredde 1982 for discussion of kiln-operators elsewhere.

[47] E.g. Hingley 1982; Dark 2001. The economic historiography of the basis of manufacture at Arezzo is discussed by Fülle (1997, 112-4). See also Strobel 1992 and Dannell 2002 for La Graufesenque, and Delage 2001a for Lezoux. For an overview of the Primitive/Modern debate on the ancient economy, see Strobel's introduction to the volume on Roman ceramic industries (Strobel 2000, 1 ff.).

[48] E.g. Marichal 1974, no. 25b.

[49] Reuse is demonstrated at Trier (Huld-Zetsche 1998), Blickweiler (Petit 1989) and also Central Gaul (Delage 2003). Less clear is the situation at Rheinzabern: cf. Reutti 1983, 54-6; Bittner 1986, 254-5; 1996; Gimber 1999; Mees 1993; 2002; Bird 1993, 2; 2002, 33-4 for the debate on this. It does seem, however, that reuse of moulds at Rheinzabern has been detected, but the extent of the practice there is uncertain. For the trade in moulds in the CG area, see Picon 1989.

[50] See, most recently, Goodman 2013 for discussion of samian kiln-centres and the settlement pattern.

[51] Mees 2011, 237ff. The same hypothesis is discussed by Lewit 2013.

[52] von Schnurbein 1982, 167, 170.

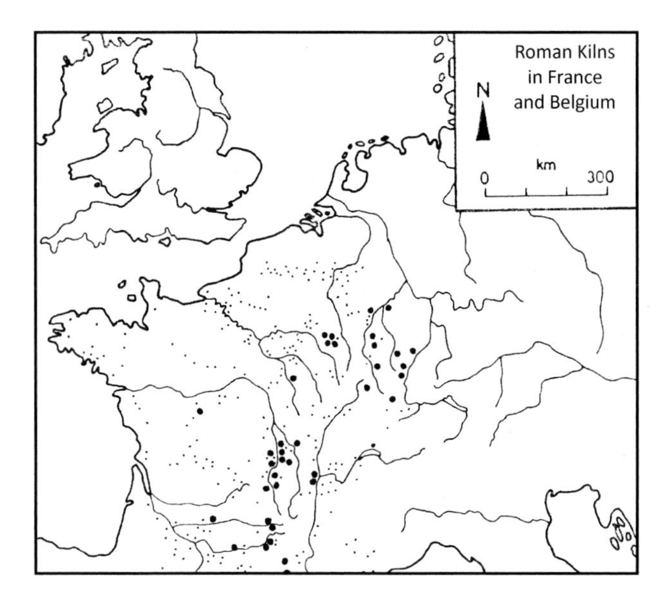


*Fig. 6.2 Map of kilns in France and Belgium, showing kilns producing luxury ware (large dots) and other kilns (small dots). Source: Duhamel 1975.*

Pisa, 30% from Lyon and 10% from Arezzo.[53] In addition, the majority of Ateius sherds from southern and central Gaul are from Pisa. It seems that Lyon acted more as an entrepôt for Pisa products than as the main supplier to the north in its own right. Production at Lyon itself was probably on a small scale as far as Ateius was concerned (unless a greater proportion of Ateius products was made there after Haltern was abandoned in AD 9). It seems that Pisa was the major kiln-centre overall for Ateius, and Arezzo itself was seemingly less significant. Perhaps the latter supplied Italy on a 'nearer' land-based distribution network,[54] while Pisa was established to take advantage of shipping facilities to more distant areas on a 'further' distribution network, using Lyon as a branch.[55]

Another case where recent work tends to present a different view from the usually accepted one is that all the main Gaulish kilns are now known to have been set up early. La Graufesenque emerged before the reign of Tiberius, and Montans and Lezoux probably at the same time or not long afterwards. Both La Graufesenque and Lezoux probably had La Tène III antecedents (but evidence is sparse for the former), and both were in areas that appear to have been difficult for transport compared with Lyon. Why, then, did Lyon fail as a samian ware producer, while being much more favourably positioned, as Marsh has pertinently pointed out?[56] In addition, why did La Graufesenque go from strength to strength, while Lezoux, at first producing very similar vessels, was in quite serious decline during the mid-first century?[57] On the face of it, Lezoux was better placed to capture the expanding northern market, while La Graufesenque was in a good position for the Mediterranean.

An approach to seeking answers to these questions is to attempt to establish the requirements for the production of samian ware. At the level of material requirements this is very simple – clay with calcareous content, water, wood for fuel and a peptising agent (e.g. bark extract) for preparation of the slip.[58] On this basis, production could have been set up virtually anywhere in the Empire, but it was not, and clearly even within the area of most consistent distribution of the product, was quite restricted geographically (Fig. 6.2). Other factors were clearly of importance in the positioning of the kilns, as Nicklin has demonstrated for modern pre-industrial pottery manufacture.[59]

A major factor may have been land: its ownership, cost and requirements for other purposes. Lyon provides a case in point. At the time of the establishment of the colony and its early development open areas for potting may have been easily available. At first there was the site of Loyasse within the colony itself on the hill of Fourvière, later production being away from the centre on the banks of the rivers, e.g. La Muette on the Saône.[60] After this stage, Lyon ceased to be a major kiln-centre, perhaps as a result of increasing land-values at the time of the major developments in the city in the Tibero-Claudian period. The large areas required for potting, especially in the relatively large-scale production of a multi-stage product, as in the case of samian, are not compatible with an urban environment or high land-prices. The relatively low unit-value of Roman pottery (see below) probably could not offset the cost of the land-area necessary for making the pottery. Even the grouping of potters together, perhaps to ease land-costs, as Delplace suggests, appears not to have been a major influence in this respect.[61] Elsewhere, urban kilns were rare, but suburban production was quite common, e.g. Trier or Colchester.[62] In the cases of Lezoux, Rheinzabern, and La Graufesenque, these were probably towns as a result of their pottery production.[63] A further consideration as far as land is concerned is its use for agriculture. It is often stated that potting and agriculture are compatible and complementary activities, for instance in terms of Peacock's estate production model.[64] But large-scale potting and intensive agriculture could easily cause

[53] von Schnurbein 1982; Wells 1977, 3.

[54] There is a majority of Arezzo vessels of Ateius at Bolsena (Picon 1975, 92).

[55] See now the extensive discussion of Arezzo, Pisa, Lyon and La Graufesenque in Mees 2011.

[56] Marsh 1981, 207.

[57] Vertet 1967.

[58] Winter 1978; Picon (2002a, 155; 2002b) stresses the high wood-fuel requirement for the production of true glossy samian ware (his mode C firing). Cf. also Tite *et al.* 1982 for analysis concluding that the gloss and the body of samian sherds came from the same clay source, which eases the logistical implications of clay sourcing and extraction. Mirti *et al.* (1999) discuss the success of Gaulish and Arretine potters in selecting and firing glossy slips.

[59] Nicklin 1979.

[60] Lasfargues 1973; Lasfarges *et al.* 1976.

[61] Delplace 1978, 74.

[62] Goodman (2013, 129-34) discusses suburban and settlement-periphery workshops. For Westerndorf as a kiln-centre on the periphery of *Pons Aeni*, see Radbauer 2013, 153-5.

[63] *contra* Finlay 1973, 21-2; cf. Pucci 1983, 113. Arezzo appears to have become a potting town after its days of greatness were over, and perhaps when land-values were declining there. Cf. also Goodman 2013, 134-6.

[64] Peacock 1982, 129. An example of this is Aspiran; Mauné 2010.

a conflict of interest. This may account for the apparent lack of samian kilns in the intensively farmed areas of Picardy, for instance, despite its physical suitability. There is a tendency for large kiln-centres to be positioned on marginal land, Lezoux and La Graufesenque being good early examples, and the Argonne being a later example.[65] An associated matter is that many of the kiln-centres are in areas suitable for pastoral more than arable agriculture. Perhaps the processes of pottery production, e.g. clay-digging, were more compatible with the pastoral than the arable farming cycle. The positioning of kilns on marginal land may, therefore, have been influenced by land-use and land-values, and leads to the further suggestion that the cost of land may have had a marked effect on the price of the vessels.

Related to this issue are those of land-ownership and the status of the territory in which kilns were located. It is notable that many kiln-sites were peripheral to centres of population and were often located on lands between *civitates* or near their boundaries, e.g. Lezoux between the Arverni and Segusiaves, La Graufesenque between the Ruteni and Volci Arecomici, the Argonne potteries between the Remi and Mediomatrices.[66] These areas may have been *subsecivae* and of low value, or unallocated *ager publicus*.[67] The siting of the larger kiln-centres away from population centres may possibly have a negative correlation with the siting of villas, and could be explained in terms of land-values being higher around the central places of the *civitates*, due to their desirability for villa-type property ownership.[68] An alternative hypothesis is that there was some sort of commercial advantage in having kiln-sites in boundary areas. Indeed, it is notable that La Graufesenque was situated close to the Aquitania/Narbonensis provincial boundary, and Lezoux close to the Aquitania/Lugdunensis boundary. Perhaps some advantages could be taken of inter-provincial *portoria* by being positioned in this way.[69]

Another requirement for production of samian ware is the availability of skilled personnel, which may also have had a bearing on the positioning of the kilns. Fig. 6.2 is notable in having large areas in which little if any fine pottery was produced in Gaul, not for want of raw materials – the distribution of kilns in general demonstrates the contrary – nor for lack of demand, since these areas appear to have imported samian ware in some quantity, but probably because potters versed in samian techniques did not choose to set up establishments in those regions.[70] Such a hypothesis applies even more strongly to Britain. Why this should be so is difficult to ascertain, mainly because little detailed work has been done on distributions of individual potter's products. Perhaps samian potters considered their main market to be in the Mediterranean at first, then in eastern parts of Gaul and Germany, as has traditionally been maintained, and that western Gaul and Britain were too thinly spread as primary markets. A relevant consideration in this respect is that samian potters were clearly prepared to move about, in some cases quite widely. On the general level, potters from Lyon seem to have moved to sites like Lezoux to help establish production there, and, later, potters moved from, for instance, Lezoux to Chémery.[71] On the level of individuals, Hartley has demonstrated a number of moves, e.g. Capitus from Lezoux to East Gaul in the late first century, or Lipuca from La Madeleine to Sinzig to Colchester in the mid second century.[72] Cintugnatus, in particular, is known to have worked at a number of smaller East Gaulish kiln-sites before ending up at Rheinzabern.[73] What is interesting is that these moves do not result in the spread of production throughout the area of distribution, large areas of Gaul and Britain never having any local production but continuing to be major consumers.

The mention of consumers brings to attention another important requirement for production: the existence of a demand for the product. For samian ware this is perhaps self-evident as far as the north-west provinces were concerned, since virtually from the initial conquest of the area this vogue pottery of Italy had become fashionable amongst the Romanised elements of the new provinces, via the catalyst of the example set by Roman officials and the army. Marsh shows clearly in his survey how the popularity of samian increased through the first century and then declined gradually during the second and early third centuries.[74] To this generalised picture Greene has added the important observation that even when supply of samian ware faltered such as at the end of the first century, imitations and analogous types of pottery rose in popularity to plug the gap.[75] The point at issue for the positioning of kiln-centres is whether a realisation that the pottery would be in such demand was a major determinant in the location of potteries. This does not appear to have been the case, for some of the kiln-centres were in what appear to be strange positions relative to their markets, e.g. Banassac in south-west Gaul supplying the Danube area, or Les Martres-de-Veyre supplying Britain and northern Gaul, but not seemingly its own local hinterland.[76] Even Lezoux in its hey-day was right on the southern margin of its distribution area. This seems to imply that demand was there, but that the kiln-centres did not satisfy that demand according to any conception of positioning for the market that would be seen as logical today. It is possible to

[65] As discussed for La Graufesenque by Polak (2000, 34).

[66] These examples could be multiplied. In Britain the Oxford kilns were probably between the Dobunni and the Catuvellauni, and the New Forest kilns between the Belgae and the Durotriges. Even Arezzo was in a peripheral area to a certain extent at the time of samian ware production there.

[67] Duncan-Jones 1976, 7.

[68] Hodder & Millet 1980; Hingley 1982, 33; Gregson 1982, 143ff.

[69] Cf. De Laet 1949, 125ff. Demarolle (1996, 31) discusses the potential advantages gained by Westerndorf and Pfaffenhofen due to their position just within the Illyrican *portorium*.

[70] Picon 2002 explores the skills needed to produce true samian ware.

[71] Vertet 1971; Bémont *et al.* 1983.

[72] Hartley 1977.

[73] Huld-Zetsche *et al.* 2012.

[74] Marsh 1981; it should be noted that this picture is essentially that for London and Britannia, and may be different in other provinces.

[75] Greene 1982.

[76] Hofmann 1977; Groh 1998; Marsh 1981, 201.

suggest as a consequence that the positioning of kilns was decided upon by the potters without explicit reference to the whereabouts of their markets. Since it may have been the case that supply networks were operated largely for other goods than samian ware, the relationship between the potter and his market could have been almost entirely out of his hands and dependent upon the *negotiatores*.

Finally for the subject of kiln positioning, it must be considered in relation to communications, a similar matter to their relations with the market. On this subject, it has nearly always been said that rivers were the main arteries of transportation in the ancient world, and that this particularly applied to Gaul, as was noted by writers such as Strabo.[77] However, this does not seem to have been an undue influence on kiln-positioning, as virtually all the kilns required land transport initially, although many were within 5 km of a river. The major example is La Graufesenque, which was on the River Tarn, but does not appear to have sent products downstream, but sent them by land over hilly country 115-130 km to Béziers or Narbonne.[78] This is especially significant, as the kiln-centre of Montans, 70 km further down the same river, did in fact use the river for distribution. If ease of transport had been a prime consideration, kiln-centres such as La Graufesenque would surely have used their nearest riverine and marine distribution networks. Another relevant matter is that distributions often cut across river-heads, and unless a very slow and circuitous route was used, several transhipments would have been necessary. Banassac to the Danube has already been mentioned, likewise Lezoux to the Danube (see below). All routes that did not use open sea were forced to tranship up to six times, each time adding to cost and probably causing breakages, despite the packing of the pottery in crates.[79] Although this matter is more in the realm of the economics of distribution, to be examined below, if it had been of great importance to the potters, it should have influenced their choice of kiln position. The evidence seems to indicate that it is not at all certain that they were.

The position of samian ware kilns, therefore, is rather a vexed issue. The seven factors outlined above must all have contributed to a greater or lesser extent to the decision as to where to set up a samian pottery centre.

## The Economics of Distribution

The last major aspect to be examined in this chapter is the way in which the pottery reached the consumer. Various relevant points have already been covered, of which one of the most significant is that *negotiatores* appear to have controlled supply, probably from the nearest large town, as nearly all inscriptions to these people come from such towns.[80] It is very likely that pottery was initially shipped to the warehousing facilities used by the *negotiator*, from

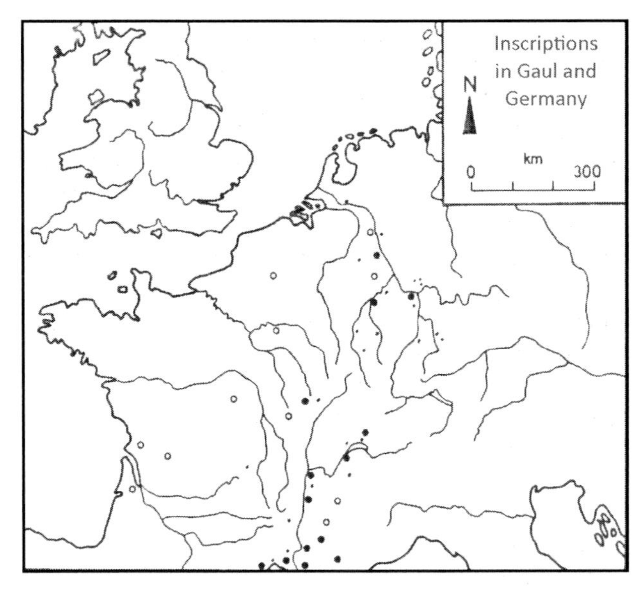


*Fig. 6.3 Map showing main findspots of inscriptions in Gaul and Germany. The large filled circles represent a number of inscriptions, of which some are associated with traders or negotiatores. The small filled circles represent single findspots of inscriptions to traders or negotiatores. The open circles represent other sites with a number of inscriptions. Source: Middleton 1979; Goudineau 1980, 387; Raepsaet 1987, pl. 1; Schmidts 2011*

where it was redistributed. Therefore, Narbonne or Beziers served in this regard for La Graufesenque;[81] Lyon or one of the Loire valley towns for Lezoux. Pliny's famous reference to *samia vasa* is relevant here, as the passage refers to a number of towns held to be well-known for their samian ware.[82] These were in all probability the initial handling points rather than the kiln-centres themselves.

The nature of the supply network and the methods of costing and payment are the subjects of most interest in the discussion of distribution economics. Middleton has discussed the former for the area of Gaul, and the gist of his argument is that the major trade-routes, e.g. along the rivers Rhône-Saône-Rhine, were organised as official supply lines for the army, in such goods as basic foodstuffs and metals. Entrepreneurial trade in samian ware was parasitical: 'long-distance trade in a commodity depended upon the ability of the traders to exploit an official supply route.'[83] For South Gaulish ware this may have been the supply of metal ingots from the Causses area near La Graufesenque.[84] Part of his evidence is the incidence of inscriptions relating to boatmen and *negotiatores*, which he regards as reflecting the trade-pattern (Fig. 6.3). In addition, he fits *negotiatores* into a military context. This view appears to be very deterministic, not allowing for the

77 4.1.2; 4.1.14.

78 Fiches *et al.* 1978; Middleton 1980.

79 Atkinson 1914; Dzwiza 2004.

80 Schmidts 2011, 95-105, Abb. 47. Cf. Raepsaet 1987; 1988; Rhodes 1989, 44-6; Chastagnol 1981.

81 Fiches *et al.* 1978. For Arretine marketing, and the use of Lyon as a redistribution centre, see Ettlinger 1987.

82 *NH* 35.160. Cf. King 1980.

83 Middleton 1979, 90. Cf. also Whittaker 2003, 301. For a critique, see Lewit 2013, 114-6. Weber (2013, 208-9) favours the existence of supply contracts or directed trade in relation to CG supply to the Upper Danube region. Cf. also Mees 2007, 152-3.

84 Middleton 1980; cf. also *idem* 1983.

existence of supply networks outside the military sphere. As far as the inscriptions he uses are concerned, it can be seen from the general distribution of inscriptions in Gaul (Fig. 6.3), that they follow the general distribution. Inscriptions are probably more common in those areas where stone was readily available and where there was an epigraphic tradition. The distribution does not necessarily reflect the wealthy areas or the important trade routes. However, it must be said that army supply was an active consideration for traders in samian ware, as most of the successful kiln-centres had elements of the army within their market areas. An alternative basis for the supply network is one based on the pre-Roman pattern, when, for instance, links between Britain, Gaul and the Mediterranean ran from the Rhône-Saône valley to the Seine valley.[85] Transport costs would also favour this route for the samian trade. A problem in the discussion of this matter is the risk of over-simplifying the way in which archaeological distributions came into being. For samian in particular, it has to be acknowledged that it was probably shipped in small quantities and consequently may have made up only a small part of the supplies being shipped in anyone load. Such is the case for the campanian ware, an analogous type of pottery, from the wreck of the Grand Congloué and for other wrecks carrying pottery as part of the cargo.[86] Because of this, frequent transhipments may have been necessary to convey samian vessels to the consumer, especially if the main cargoes were not being shipped to the same destination.[87] It may be that there was an extensive network of *negotiatores* at ports and towns throughout Gaul, Germany and Britain, who bought and sold consignments of samian ware from and to each other. This would be a suitable system for long-distance overland trade within the Empire, but is a matter that needs further research for clarification of the issue involved. An example of this may be the *negotiatores* at Domburg buying goods from Rhine river shippers, which they then forwarded across the Channel for sale to merchants on the British side.[88] Such a system would have been more flexible than direct long-distance links between the potters and the consumers via a single *negotiator*, but at the same time, would have made the links between the potters and their markets more tenuous, which has implications for the extent to which consumers could influence the choice of product made and the changing fashions of samian ware.

As far as costs are concerned, there is only one inscription that gives the actual cost of a decorated samian vessel. A Dr. 37 of late-2nd century date from Flavia Solva, Austria, has the graffito PANNA VIIRIICUNDAIIS EMPTA VIGIIS, which is probably to be read, 'The bowl of Verecundus, bought for 20 (Asses)'.[89] This price conveys little on its own; however, it is a little under a day's pay for a legionary of the time of Severus,[90] and also some attempt at relative costing is possible, on the basis of prices for other types of pottery. Diocletian's Price Edict gives a maximal price of 1 *denarius* per *sextarius* of volume for a pot.[91] This compares with 4 *denarii* per *sextarius* for black olives, 30 *denarii* per *sextarius* for good wine and 50 *denarii* per day as pay for a wall-builder. Therefore, in the early 4th century, pottery, in this case probably common pottery of the eastern Empire, was very cheap. The work of potting also paid badly; the same document gives a tile preparer as earning 2 *denarii* per 8 tiles (potters not being mentioned). Papyri from Oxyrhyncus (of the early 3rd century) and other Egyptian sites confirm this general range of prices, as does a graffito from Pompeii mentioning a common ware *pultarium* or *patella* as costing 1 *as*.[92] In the case of samian ware, onto the basic cost of a pot has to be added the cost of punches and moulds, together with the labour of their associated personnel, the cost of slip preparation and application, the cost of high wastage rates,[93] and possibly most important of all, transport costs, which can be broken down into costs for storage, transhipment and distance moved. These factors probably made a decorated samian vessel some 10-20 times more expensive than common ware.

On the matter of transport, if it is assumed that transport was usually by water, which to judge from the evidence of Diocletian's Price Edict and of barges found on very minor rivers, such as at Pommeroeul, Hainault,[94] was very probably the case, it is plausible to argue that samian ware was transported by barge down rivers wherever possible, and thence transhipped to larger vessels as part of a mixed cargo (see above). It is also plausible to argue that the cost of moving samian ware would vary as a proportion of the costs of the general rate of flow of goods along particular routes. Thus, a large volume of trade would have reduced the unit-cost of transporting samian ware along those routes. In other words, when the volume of trade changed for any reason, the unit cost of samian shipment would have had a tendency to alter in consequence, if the *negotiatores* were to cover their fixed costs and continue to make the same profit as before.

---

[85] Haselgrove 1984.

[86] Benoit 1961. Pucci (1983, 111) points out the exceptional case of the Riou I wreck, where pottery may have been the main cargo. However, it is not clear in this particular case whether there was a perishable cargo or not (Lequémont & Liou 1975, 79). The same consideration applies to the Cap Creus wreck, which only yielded samian and other pottery (Nieto I Prieto & Haumey 1985).

[87] It is notable that some archaeologically detectable commodities, carried in Dressel 30 amphoras of 2nd-century date, originated in roughly the same area as Lezoux samian ware and also in the lower Rhône valley, but are distributed to the Rhineland, whereas Lezoux samian was not, and in fact cuts across the Lezoux samian distribution network to the Middle Danube area (Peacock 1978).

[88] Hassall 1978; Chastagnol 1981.

[89] Noll 1972; Garbsch 1982, 15. There is also a plain-ware Ludowici Ta' with a graffito indicating a cost of 12 *asses* (Kovacsovics 1987). Cf. Darling 1998; Willis 2005, 1.3; Biddulph 2012, 295.

[90] Biddulph 2012, 295.

[91] Giacchero 1974, 15, 100. Cf. also Peña 2007, 27-8.

[92] Cockle 1981; *CIL* IV, 5380.

[93] The major kiln-centres have many millions of broken vessels on site, all of which must be termed wasters because, even if perfect, they never left the potteries. Another aspect of the wastage rate is reflected in the La Graufesenque pit containing *c.* 40,000 vessels (i.e. 200 days production given a rate of 200 vessels per day), large numbers being by the relatively little-known potter Gallicanus (Labrousse 1980, 467; Genin 2007, 83-107). The more prolific and therefore better-known potters must have had much larger numbers of wasters.

[94] Duncan-Jones 1974, 366; De Boe 1978; cf also Eckoldt 1984; Rhodes 1989, 46.

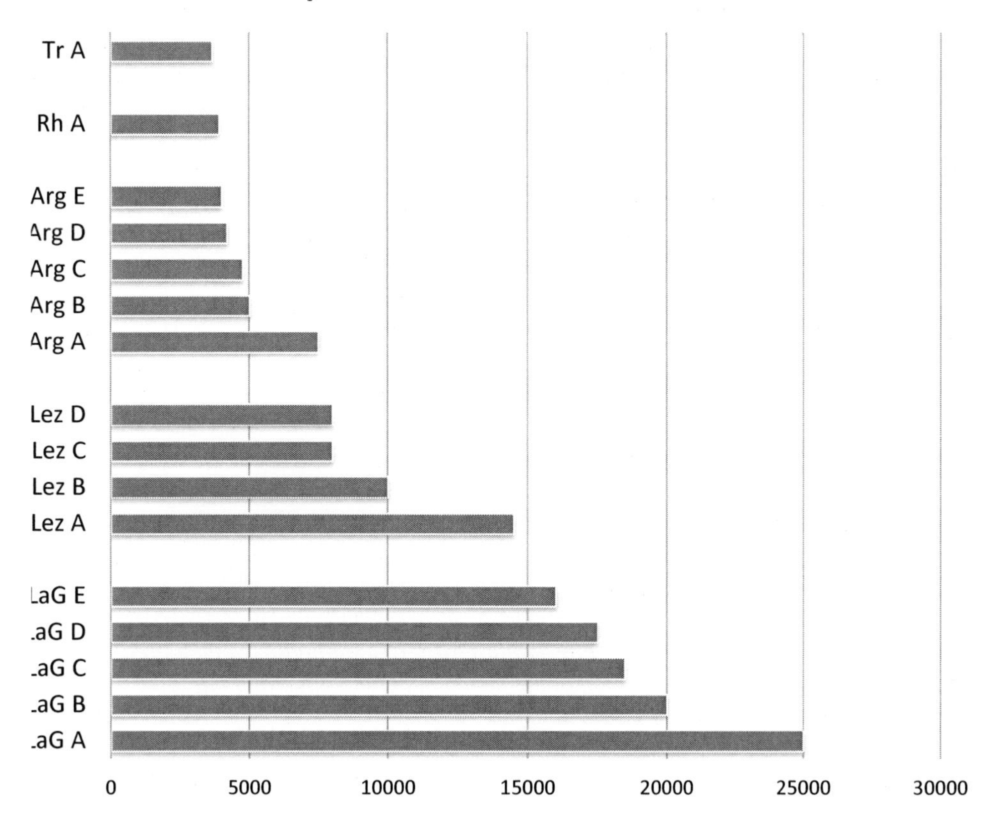


*Fig. 6.4 Relative costs for transporting samian ware to Southern Britain. See text, Table 6.I, and note 95 for explanation of the method of calculation and the scale of units.*

A kiln-centre for which transport costs were probably an important consideration is Lezoux, which was on the southern margin of its distribution area and with natural communications that ran most easily to the north-west. The relative costs of transporting samian ware from this kiln-centre to one of its major markets, Britain (Fig. 6.4), shows that the cheapest route to Britain was via the Middle Loire and the Seine.[95] This would logically have been the best route, but it is not known whether other supplies along some of the alternative routes could have depressed the unit-cost of transporting the pottery enough to make them competitive. The Loire/Atlantic route in particular could have been a major supply route if there was a large quantity of trade along the western seaways and up the Channel.[96]

An interesting aspect of the Lezoux transport costs is that other second- and third-century kiln-centres were clearly in an advantageous position to undercut the transport element of the cost by about half. However, this did not happen in actual fact, as Lezoux held a virtual monopoly of the British samian trade from the early second century onwards, although it did have a cost advantage over La Graufesenque, as Fig. 6.4 demonstrates.

To explain this, either transport costs were not very important in the economy of the potteries and could be overshadowed by other factors (e.g. land-values), or the unit-costs of transport varied a great deal on different routes, so that in this case, Lezoux shipments to Britain were still competitive despite the longer distances over which the pottery was transported. A further consideration in this respect is the shipment of Lezoux samian ware during the mid to late second century to the Danube (Fig. 6.5), another distant and difficult market that was in due course supplied more cheaply from Rheinzabern (or, later, Westerndorf). This also points either to cheap non-transport costs at Lezoux, or an important trade route from Central Gaul to the Danube that held transport costs down.[97]

[95] The costs are computed by using a modified form of the relative land-sea-river costs given in Diocletian's Price Edict (Duncan-Jones 1974, 366-9; Peacock 1978). Peacock used the ratios calculated by Duncan-Jones without alteration in his example, but it is felt that the east Mediterranean flavour of the Edict presents a false picture of costs in the NW provinces, and adjustments have been made to account for the dangers of the Atlantic, the flow of rivers and the hilliness of land routes. Therefore 1 Mediterranean Sea km = 1 unit; 1 Atlantic Ocean/English Channel km = 2 units; 1 downstream river km = 4 units; 1 upstream river km = 8 units; 1 land km = 30-40 units depending on the difficulty of the terrain. No extra value is added for transhipments, although these may have been an additional cost. For details of the routes in Fig 6.4, see Table 6.I. See also King 1981, 69-70; Raepsaet 1987, 21-3; Webster 2001, 297. Polfer (1991, 287-90) discusses land transport costs, and gives the ratio of 1:5.5-6.5:29-40 for land:river:sea costs, very similar to that used here. Cf. also Dannell & Mees 2013; Mees 2011, 259-62, for computer modeling of transport costs.

[96] The Loire route for shipments from Lezoux is discussed in Pinel (1977), drawing on evidence of a barge at Vichy (Corrocher 1971; 1980) and of samian ware dredged from the Loire mouth (Plicque 1887b).

[97] See discussion in Weber 2013, 208-9; Delage 1998.

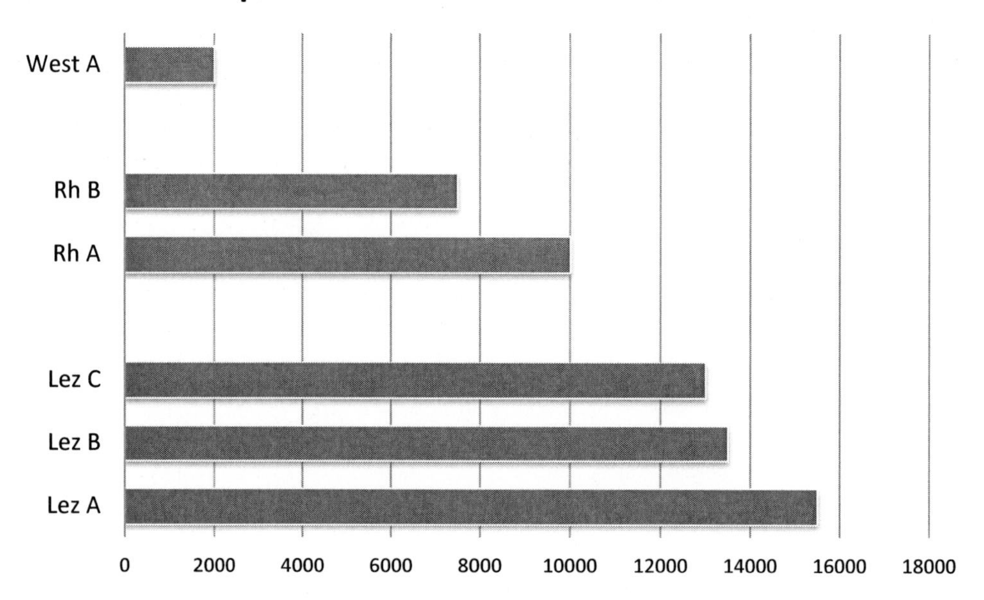


*Fig. 6.5 Relative costs for transporting samian ware to the Middle Danube area. See text, Table 6.I, and note 95 for explanation of the method of calculation and the scale of units.*

Whatever the relative contribution of different elements to the final cost; the result was in all probability, a luxury, not a common product, especially in those provinces where few were wealthy enough to make regular use of metal tableware. Demand also appears to have been heavy, which in conventional economic terms would raise the price of a vessel further. Therefore, when samian ware reached the provincial market place, it was probably quite an expensive item.[98] The question consequently arises as to who was likely to buy the pottery, and how it was paid for. The last question is necessary in view of discussion of the extent of monetisation in the early Empire, especially in a newly-conquered and peripheral province such as Britain.[99] The coins in circulation may not have been of suitably low denominations for the purchase of most goods, and money may have been confined to the market for luxuries, including, probably, samian ware. If this was the case, samian ware, particularly decorated vessels, would be the pottery of the rich – for Britain the army, members of the administration and the tribal aristocracies.

*Table 6.I*

The routes used on Fig. 6.4, from top to bottom:-

| | |
|---|---|
| Tr A | Trier – Moselle/Rhine – Channel – Dover |
| Rh A | Rheinzabern – Rhine – Channel – Dover |
| Arg E | Argonne – Aisne/Seine – Channel – Dover |
| Arg D | Argonne – Verdun – Meuse – Channel – Dover[100] |
| Arg C | Argonne – Aisne – Soissons – Amiens – Somme – Channel – Dover |
| Arg B | Argonne – Verdun – Moselle/Rhine – Channel – Dover |
| Arg A | Argonne – Metz – Moselle/Rhine – Channel – Dover |
| Lez D | Lezoux – Allier/Loire – Orléans – Paris – Seine – Channel – Dover |
| Lez C | Lezoux – Allier/Loire – Atlantic/Channel – Dover |
| Lez B | Lezoux – Allier/Loire – Orléans – Paris – Seine/Oise – Amiens – Somme – Channel – Dover[101] |
| Lez A | Lezoux – Allier/Arroux – Autun – Chalon – Saône – Port-sur-Saône – Nancy – Moselle/Rhine – Channel – Dover |
| LaG E | La Graufesenque – Béziers – Toulouse – Garonne – Atlantic/Channel – Dover |
| LaG D | La Graufesenque – Béziers – Rhône/Saône – Chalon – Châtillon – Seine – Channel – Dover |
| LaG C | La Graufesenque – Béziers – Rhône/Saône – Port-sur-Saône – Nancy – Moselle/Rhine – Channel – Dover |
| LaG B | La Graufesenque – Béziers – Rhône/Saône – Port-sur-Saône – Commercy (Meuse) - Moselle/Rhine – Channel – Dover |
| LaG A | La Graufesenque – Béziers – Mediterranean – Straits of Gibraltar – Atlantic/Channel - Dover |

The routes used in Fig. 6.5:-

| | |
|---|---|
| West A | Westerndorf – Inn/Danube – Carnuntum |
| Rh B | Rheinzabern – Rhine – Bregenz – Kempten – Iller/Danube – Carnuntum |
| Rh A | Rheinzabern – Günzburg – Danube – Carnuntum |

[98] There is a graffito on a form 31 from Ospringe which reads LUCIUS LUCIANUS ULI DIANTUS VICTOR VICTORICUS VICTORINA VAS COMMUNIS (Whiting, Hawley & May 1931, 68, pl LIV, no 498a). This may imply that single ownership of a vessel was beyond the means of these individuals.

[99] Crawford 1970; Hodder 1979a; Reece 1979; Hingley 1982. Picon (2002b) stresses the investment necessary for producing true (mode C) samian ware, and the consequent need for it to be a well-organised, relatively large-scale industry. These factors are also significant in the perception of samian ware as an expensive product.

[100] For discussion of the Meuse as a transport route; Raepsaet 1987, 11-19.

[101] An alternative for the Lezoux-Seine route is via the Loing (provided it was navigable), with a portage between Gien and Montargis (Vauthey & Vauthey 1967b). This reduces the unit total to 4700, which approaches more closely the transport costs of the other kilns. Another alternative, but much more costly Lezoux-Seine route runs via Digoin, Montceau-les-Mines, Chalons, and Avallon (Schmitt 1975).

| | |
|---|---|
| Lez C | Lezoux – Allier/Loire – Feurs – Lyon – Rhône – Lausanne – Yverdon – Aare/Rhine – Bregenz – Kempten – Iller/Danube – Carnuntum |
| Lez B | Lezoux – Lyon – Rhône – Lausanne – Yverdon – Aare/Rhine – Bregenz – Kempten – Iller/Danube – Carnuntum[102] |
| Lez A | Lezoux – Allier/Loire/Arroux – Autun – Chalon – Saône – Port-sur-Saône – Basel – Rhine – Bregenz – Kempten – Iller/Danube – Carnuntum |

[102] This is a close alternative to Lezoux route C, but is overland direct from Lezoux to Lyon, which increases the unit total to approx. 13500.

The last group just mentioned is also the most interesting potential class of purchaser of the pottery, for explanation is needed of why the pottery became popular among non-Roman groups in the newly-conquered provinces. The best explanation is probably that the pottery was regarded as a status symbol, one that had in part been in existence in pre-Roman times, and in part being the ceramic equivalent of the *templa, fora, domos* which the newly-Romanised population of Britain took to with such apparent alacrity.[103]

[103] Cunliffe 1978, 159; Tacitus, *Agr.* 21.

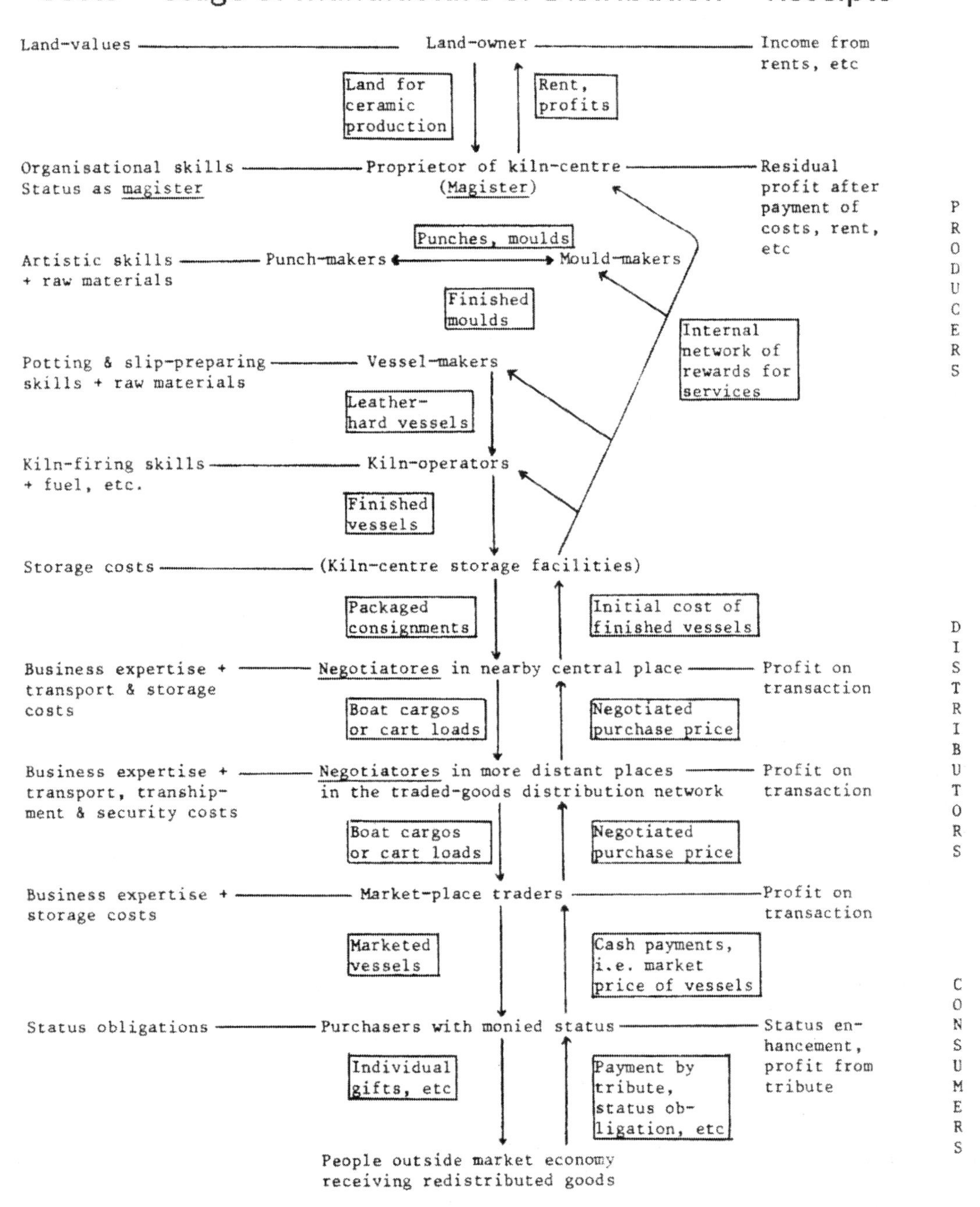


*Fig. 6.6 A model for the relationships in samian ware manufacture and distribution. The costs represent the input at each stage, and the receipts the income from it. The product at each stage is given in a box with an arrow pointing down the page, and the corresponding receipt with an upward arrow.*

If this was the case, the desirability of the pottery may in its own right have put a premium on the cost of a vessel and made it into more of a luxury.[104] Samian ware would fit in very well with the concept of a prestige-goods economy, being a luxury brought-in by the social elite, which was the only group in tribal society in a position to carry out trade easily in a largely moneyless economy.[105] The pottery may have been redistributed as gifts or payments to those further down the social scale. If this was the case, samian would only remain in demand by the social elite if it retained its symbolic status. If obtainable too widely throughout the social spectrum, it may have been in danger of being supplanted by another symbol of wealth, for instance metal vessels. This may have been a contributory factor in the decline of samian ware production, which will be discussed at greater length in chapter 7. For the purposes of the present discussion, it is sufficient to observe that demand for samian ware was a key factor in the success of the industry, and that major changes in consumer preferences may have exerted pressure on the costs and output of the kiln-centres.

[104] Cf. Pucci 1983, 110.
[105] Frankenstein & Rowlands 1978; Hingley 1982, 19.

## Conclusion: an economic model for samian ware

Many aspects of production and distribution have been examined in this chapter, resulting in a somewhat diffuse picture of the economics of samian ware manufacture. By way of conclusion, a model has been drawn up (Fig. 6.6) in order to integrate these aspects as far as possible in a single framework. It shows relationships between producers, distributors and consumers in terms of the product and the reciprocal payment for it. No attempt has been made to show relative values, as these are not known sufficiently well, if at all, for some key relationships, e.g. the amount of profit generated at each stage of the distribution network, or the relative importance of land-values in the economics of production. However, the framework that the model presents is able to serve as a basis for discussion of the decline of manufacture, the subject of the next chapter.

# Chapter 7

# The Decline of Samian Ware Manufacture

## Part II: Factors of Decline

### A brief history of samian ware manufacture c. AD 150-280

In order to set the scene for a discussion of the factors that affected the last century or so of samian ware manufacture, it will be useful to set out here the chronological framework as it is presently understood, incorporating the revisions in dating proposed in earlier chapters and the data on all the known kilns of the period (Fig. 7.1) as given in Appendix 10.

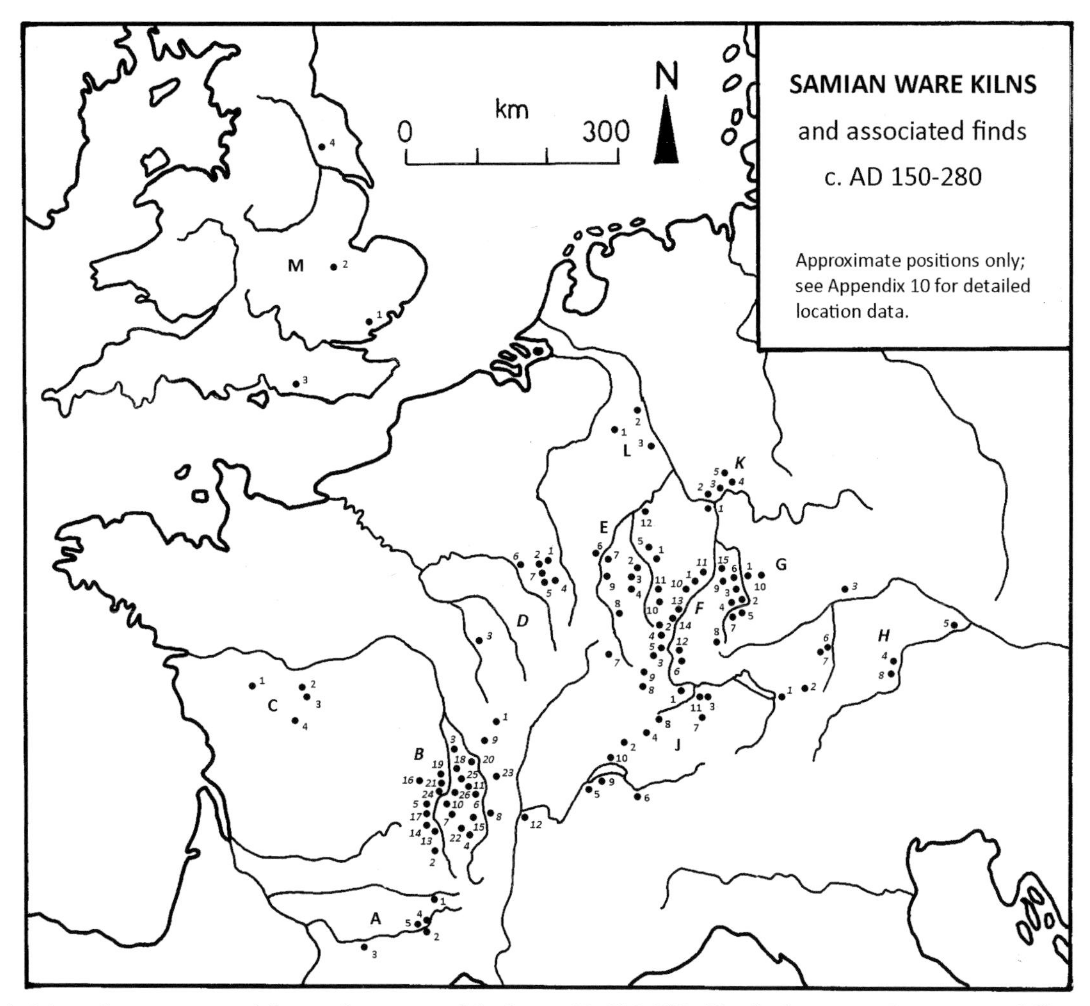


*Fig. 7.1 Map of samian ware kilns and associated finds, c. AD 150-280. The findspots on the map are differentiated by use of Italic and ordinary typeface for the respective numbering of adjacent groups.*

Key to Fig 7.1; see Appendix 10 for location details.

**South Gaulish Area** A1 Banassac, A2 La Graufesenque, A3 Montans, A4 Le Rajol, A5 Le Roc

**Central Gaulish Area** B1 Autun, B2 Brioude, B3 Chantenay-St-Imbert, B4 Chézieu, B5 Clermont-Ferrand, B6 Cordelle, B7 Courpière, B8 Feurs, B9 Gueugnon, B10 Lezoux, B11 Lubié (Lubillé), B12 Lyon, B13 Manglieu, B14 Les Martres-de-Veyre, B15 Montverdun, B16 Neris-les-Bains, B17 Les Queyriaux, B18 St Bonnet, B19 St Didier-la-Forêt, B20 St Pourçain-sur-Besbre, B21 St Remy-en-Rollat, B22 St Romain-le-Puy, B23 Tancon, B24 Terre-Franche, B25 Toulon-sur-Allier, B26 Vichy

**Centre-West Group** C1 Mazières-en-Mauge, C2 Mougon, C3 Nouâtre, C4 Poitiers

**Argonne Group** D1 Avocourt (including Les Allieux and Forêt-de-Hesse), D2 La Chalade (Lachalade), D3 Jaulges/Villiers-Vineux, D4 Lavoye, D5 Pont-des-Rèmes, D6 Reims, D7 Vaux-Régnier

**Moselle and Sarre Region** E1 Blickweiler, E2 Boucheporn, E3 Chémery-Faulquemont, E4 Eincheville-le-Tenig, E5 Eschweiler-Hof, E6 Haute-Yutz (and Daspich-Ebange), E7 Hombourg-Budange, E8 La Madeleine, E9 Metz, E10 Mittelbronn, E11 Sarre-Union, E12 Trier

**Middle Rhine Region** F1 Altenstadt, F2 Heiligenberg-Dinsheim, F3 Horbourg-Wihr, F4 Ittenwiller (or Ittenweiler), F5 Jebsheim, F6 Lehen, F7 Luxeuil-les-Bains, F8 Mathay, F9 Offemont, F10 Reichshoffen, F11 Rheinzabern, F12 Riegel, F13 Schiltigheim, F14 Strasbourg, F15 Stettfeld

**Neckar Region** G1 Bad Cannstatt, G2 Köngen, G3 Kräherwald, G4 Neuhausen-auf-den-Fildern, G5 Nürtingen, G6 Pforzheim, G7 Pfrondorf, G8 Rottweil, G9 Rutesheim, G10 Waiblingen-Beinstein

**Bavaria** H1 Bregenz, H2 Kempten-in-Allgau, H3 Nassenfels, H4 Pfaffenhofen, H5 Pocking, H6 Schwabegg, H7 Schwabmünchen, H8 Westerndorf

**Switzerland** J1 Augst, J2 Avenches, J3 Baden, J4 Bern-Engehalbinsel, J5 Geneva, J6 Martigny, J7 Ottenhusen, J8 Solothurn, J9 Thonon, J10 Vidy-Lausanne, J11 Windisch

**Wetterau** K1 Mainz, K2 Massenheim, K3 Nied, K4 Praunheim (Heddernheim), K5 Saalburg

**Lower Rhine Region** L1 Aachen-Schönforst, L2 Neuss, L3 Sinzig

**Britain** M1 Colchester, M2 Peterborough, M3 Pulborough, M4 York

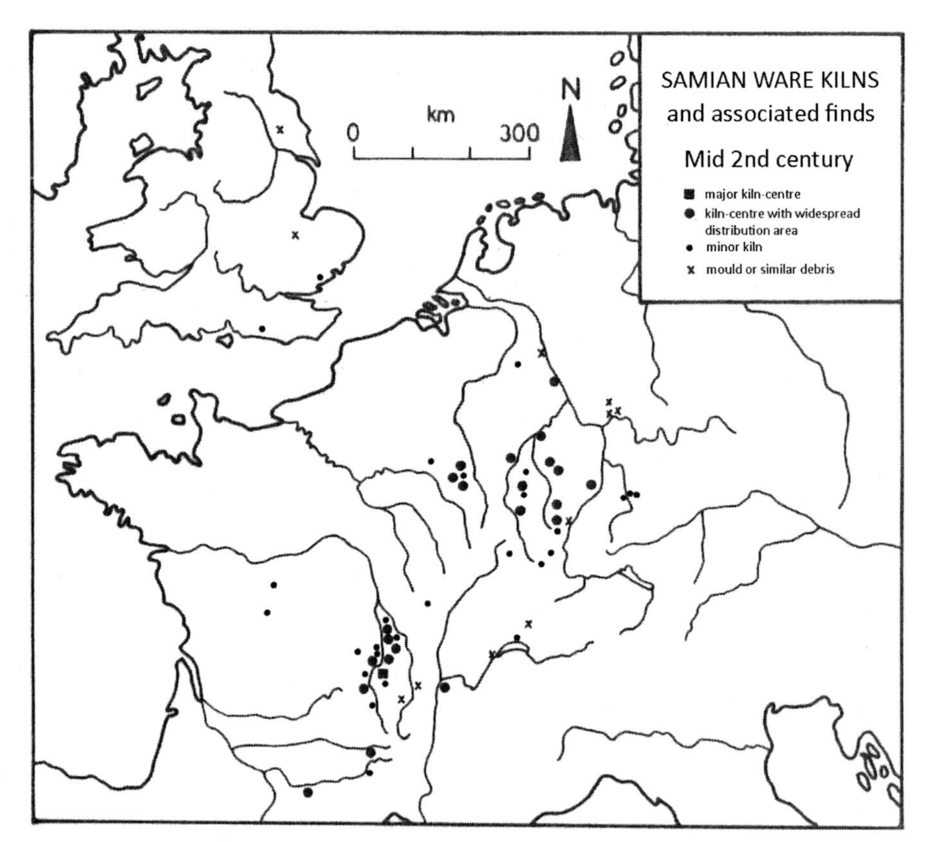


*Fig. 7.2a Map of samian ware kilns and associated finds of the mid-2nd century. Squares indicate major kiln-centres; large circles, kiln-centres with a widespread distribution area; small circles, minor kilns; crosses, finds of moulds or similar debris.*

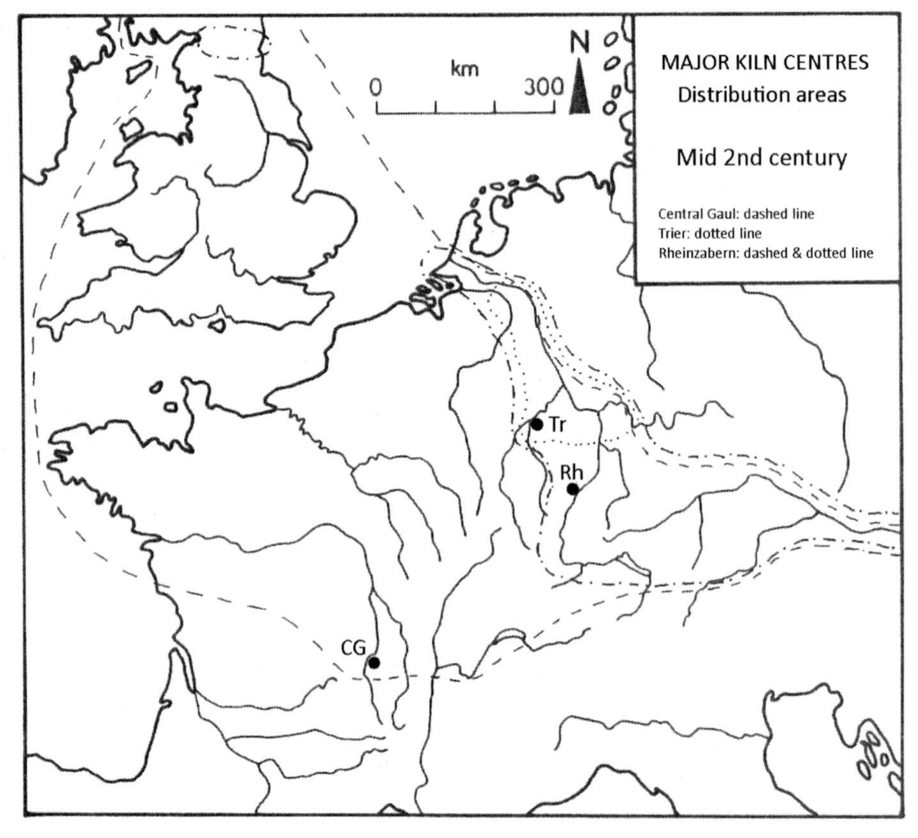


*Fig. 7.2b Generalised distribution map of the products of the major kiln-centres in the mid-2nd century. The dashed line indicates Central Gaul, the dotted line Trier, and the dashed-and-dotted line Rheinzabern.*

Mid Second Century (Fig. 7.2)
The mid second century is, par excellence, the period of Central Gaul. Lezoux is the main kiln-centre, having taken over that role from Les Martres-de-Veyre a bit earlier, and it reaches a peak of production in the mid/late second century. There are also many smaller kilns operating in the region, particularly Terre-Franche, Vichy, Lubié, Toulon, Yzeure and Lyon, all of which had widely distributed products, not only of samian ware, but other ceramics as well such as lamps, figurines and miscellaneous fine wares. The general distribution area for Central Gaulish samian ware (much of which is difficult to attribute to individual kiln-centres due to a high level of internal interaction) covers the northern half of Gaul, Britain, the upper/middle Danube and, to a lesser extent, the Rhineland.

In East Gaul, the period around the middle of the second century is one of much change. A number of small kiln-centres (e.g. Boucheporn, Chémery) which had been operating from the late first or early second centuries, come to an end and are supplanted by others, notably the Argonne kilns, Trier, Rheinzabern and Mittelbronn. The main area where kilns are in operation is in and around the Moselle and Sarre valleys, where La Madeleine, Blickweiler, Eschweiler, Mittelbronn and Trier are producing samian in the mid and late second centuries. None outlasts the second century, except Trier which expands greatly, and Mittelbronn, which appears to continue. Rheinzabern and Heiligenberg are the main kilns in the middle Rhine valley, both in fairly small-scale production, but Rheinzabern is clearly stronger and of course goes on to dominate East Gaul by the end of the century. Heiligenberg appears to have a distinctive distant market in the Danube area. Slightly further east there is local production in the Neckar Valley and to the west of the whole region the Argonne kilns (chiefly Lavoye) have started producing samian ware by the middle of the century and are exporting mainly to the north.

The South Gaulish kilns are well past their prime, although Montans and Banassac are still producing pottery that is widely distributed (to Britain and the Danube respectively). La Graufesenque had been in large scale production up to the time of Trajan, but by the middle of the century was distributing in the local region only.[1]

Two features are worthy of comment when considering the mid-century period as a whole. Firstly, this is perhaps when more samian kilns are in operation than at any other time in the history of manufacture. The great majority of them are engaged in small-scale production, only Lezoux really standing out as a major production centre. A distinction can also be drawn between those kilns that achieved a fairly widespread distribution and those that remained as local suppliers only (e.g. the British kilns). Why this was so is difficult to ascertain, since the design quality of the latter was not always inferior, and it may be that other factors were relevant, such as difficulty of access to the *negotiatores'* traditional distribution system. There are clearly a large number of what may be termed 'peripheral' samian kilns at this time, many of which do not last long unless they have secure markets. Most of the medium-size, exporting kilns are also of relatively limited duration, especially those in rural areas that were positioned specifically for distant markets. Only a few of them survive to expand and dominate the market for later samian ware.

The second notable feature of Fig. 7.2 (and 7.3) is the number of find-spots of samian moulds for decorated ware. This is particularly the case in the Wetterau and Neckar regions. Some of these probably indicate places of manufacture that are as yet unexplored, or use of samian moulds for 'imitation' samian in other fabrics (e.g. Praunheim), but many are certainly the result of the removal of moulds from kiln sites to other places. The clearest case of this is at Kempten (Fig. 7.3) where the mould fragments were all found in a house in the town, well away from the known kilns. Czysz interprets the moulds as being from a shop, since much other pottery was also found, and they were either pieces used for packing samian ware for transport or they were perhaps some form of advertisement.[2] The mould of Drusus I of Les Martres-de-Veyre at York can be also interpreted along these lines, but its provenance is unfortunately rather uncertain.

Late Second/Early Third Century (Fig. 7.3)
By the end of the second century, the picture is different. The number of kiln-centres is less, particularly in East Gaul. There has been consolidation at a few major centres, and the general areas of production are seen to be in a wide band skirting the southern part of the NW provinces, virtually all the somewhat erratic and small-scale production to the north and west of the area having gone.

Lezoux, now with fewer neighbours, dominates Central Gaulish production, but the distribution area has shrunk, mainly due to the loss of the Danube market and the growth of a clear-cut market area for the main East Gaulish products. Although there is consolidation in Central Gaul, it is clear that samian ware is still in demand from this area, since the pottery remains popular in the Gaulish and British distribution areas. Indeed, some local production starts up at this time, at Gueugnon, Jaulges-Villiers-Vineux (to the north) and at two sites near La Graufesenque to the south. South Gaul and Aquitaine are of some interest, since they are essentially outside the NW provinces distribution area and instead orientated towards the Mediterranean. Other forms of samian ware, in different styles, are predominant there, notably locally produced 'terre sigillée claire' (from the lower Rhône Valley) and imported African Red Slip ware.

In East Gaul, the number of kilns has declined markedly, but overall production is higher; the two major kilns,

[1] Lutz (1989, 272) suggests an end to South Gaulish imports to eastern Gaul and the Rhineland in the Hadrianic/Antonine period, and in northern Germany by AD 115/20.

[2] Czysz 1982.

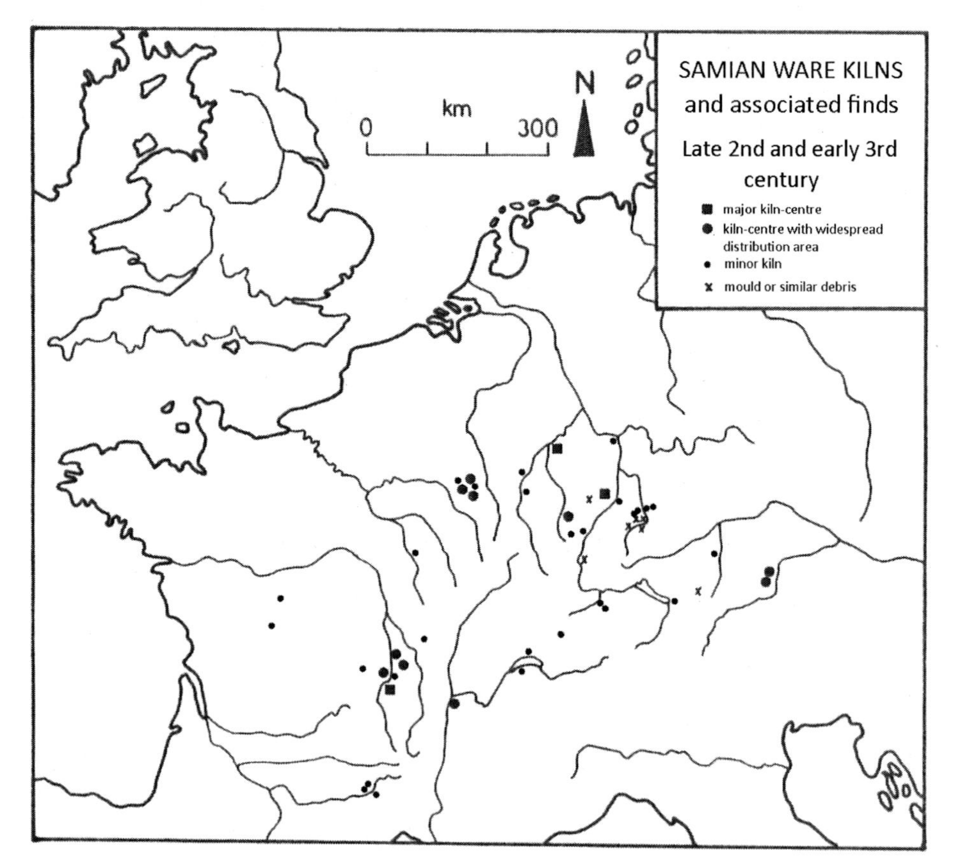


*Fig. 7.3a Map of samian ware kilns and associated finds of the late 2nd/early 3rd century. Key as Fig 7.2a.*

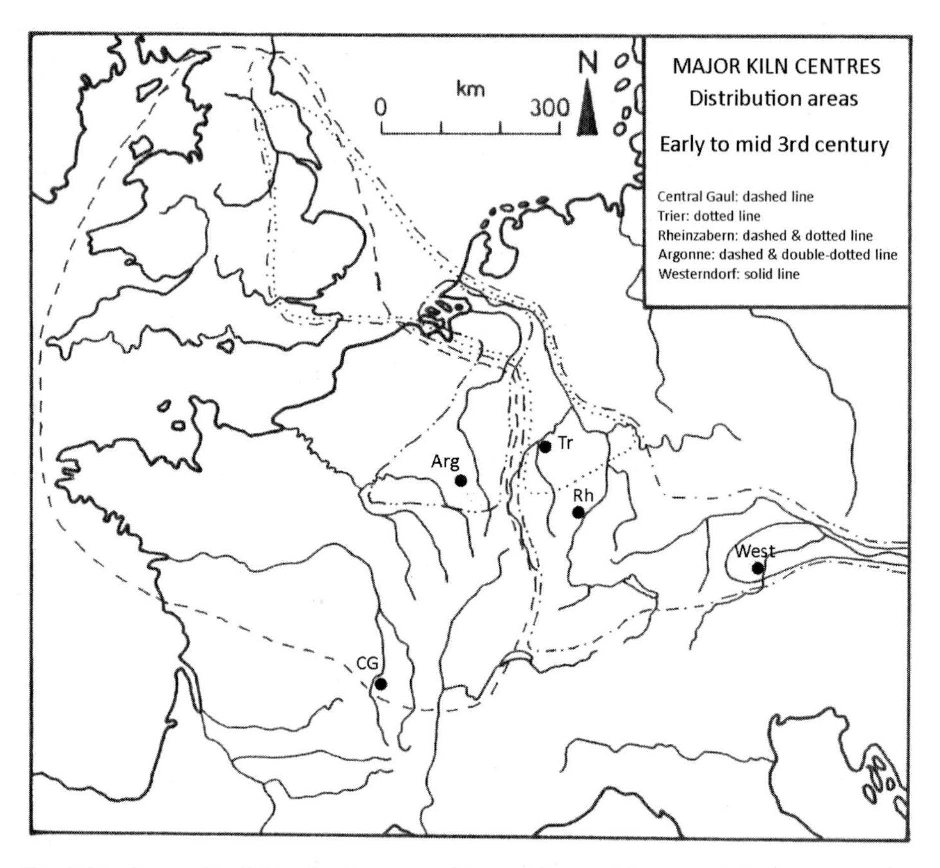


*Fig. 7.3b Generalised distribution map of the products of the major kiln-centres in the late 2nd/early 3rd century. Key as Fig 7.2b, plus continuous line for Westerndorf, and dashed-and-double-dotted line for Argonne.*

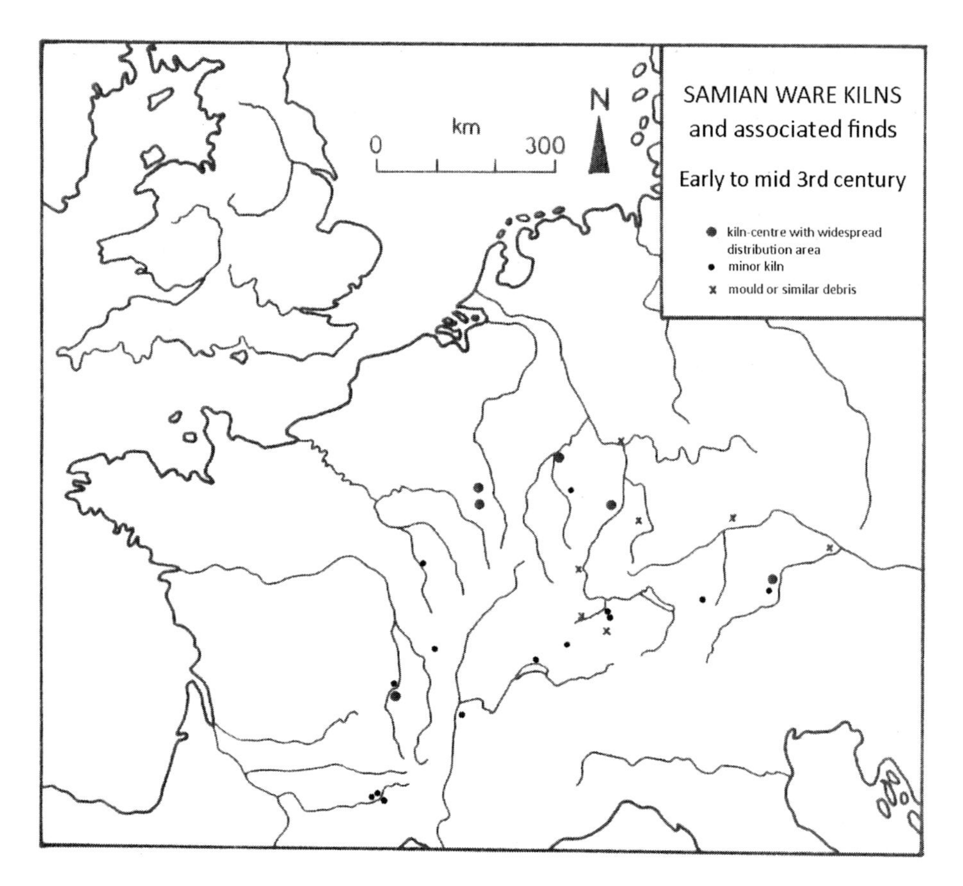


*Fig. 7.4 Map of samian ware kilns and associated finds of the early/mid 3rd century. Key as Fig 7.2a.*

Rheinzabern and Trier, certainly exceeding contemporary Lezoux production, but distributing their pottery over a smaller area. Rheinzabern is the more important kiln-centre, with close-knit groups of potters producing ware that was common throughout the Rhine and Danube areas during the main period of production, the late second to early third centuries. Trier, the only important urban, or rather suburban, late samian ware kiln-centre, had a more northerly and smaller market than Rheinzabern, but production peaks at round about the same time. Of the other kilns, those in the Argonne are still in production, although past their late second century peak. Their products overlap with Lezoux distribution in northern France, but with Rheinzabern/Trier distribution in the Low Countries. Further east, Westerndorf and a bit later Pfaffenhofen are in production from the end of the second century, carving out a distribution area in a zone that was largely supplied by Rheinzabern, but which had lost its Central Gaulish sources not too long before. Local kilns also come into existence in southern Germany and Switzerland, heavily influenced by the styles of the major producers.

The main trend to be seen during this period is the consolidation of both kiln-centres and markets. Distribution areas are dominated by one or two large-scale manufacturers, and there is an important separation to be made between Britain and Gaul, largely the preserve of the Central Gaulish kilns, and the Rhine and Danube areas where Rheinzabern and Trier are dominant. There is little interpenetration of markets, the main exception being in the Low Countries south of the Rhine and in eastern Britain, where products from all three major kiln-centres mingled to a certain extent. The Argonne distribution network also appears to have existed in both market areas.

### Early/Mid Third Century (Fig. 7.4)

By about the 230s AD the number of kilns in operation is further reduced, and the remainder appears to be producing pottery in less quantity. Lezoux is almost certainly still in existence, but production is in its final stages and most of the main workshops have ceased. Some late products are widely distributed, however, reaching Britain and other parts of the traditional Central Gaulish market area. After this time, Lezoux, like all the others in this region, is producing for local distribution only. Fourth century production of a samian 'derivé' is known at the kiln-site, and continuity through the late third century has been established.[3]

Rheinzabern and Trier continue to hold dominant positions in the East Gaulish market, and in this area the situation seems slightly more stable than in Central Gaul. This may be due to the later peak of production that these two kiln-centres had enjoyed, and perhaps also a wider product range (as was made clear in the section on plain wares in chapter 4). Certainly both continue to the mid third

[3] Bet & Gangloff 1987; see bibliography in Appendix 10 entry.

century, although it is noticeable from the 230s/240s that distribution is more localised, and distant transport no longer easy to organise. Neither kiln-centre appears to continue to the late third century or later, and in the case of Rheinzabern part of the site at least was burnt in the 260s. Trier late products are found on local sites of the 270s but not apparently in later deposits.

The Argonne area continues to produce traditional samian ware on a relatively small scale but quite widely distributed probably up to the mid-third century, although certainty about this is not assured in the absence of clear evidence. Some decorated ware is, however, known from sites in the region dating to the 270s, and there appears to be an overlap in some deposits with the production of roller-stamped Argonne ware. It would not be surprising if here, too, there was continuity up to the main period of roller-stamped ware production in the early fourth century.[4]

The other main kiln-centre still in operation is Pfaffenhofen, which is thought to have continued later than Westerndorf, up to the middle of the century. Products were marketed down the Danube to Noricum and Pannonia, where there was also a strong early third century local production, and where the economy was relatively resilient.[5] The latest products are associated with coins of the 270s-80s from local civilian refuges, where late Argonne-style fabrics are also known.

The general impression of samian production from the 230s to the 270s is that there is a reasonable level of activity at first, which falls away towards the middle of the century but continues at a low level in one or two places. Some of these centres revive in the late third century, and although in no case can continuity be clearly demonstrated, the time gap is short enough to suspect that the kilns were not abandoned for any great length of time, if at all.

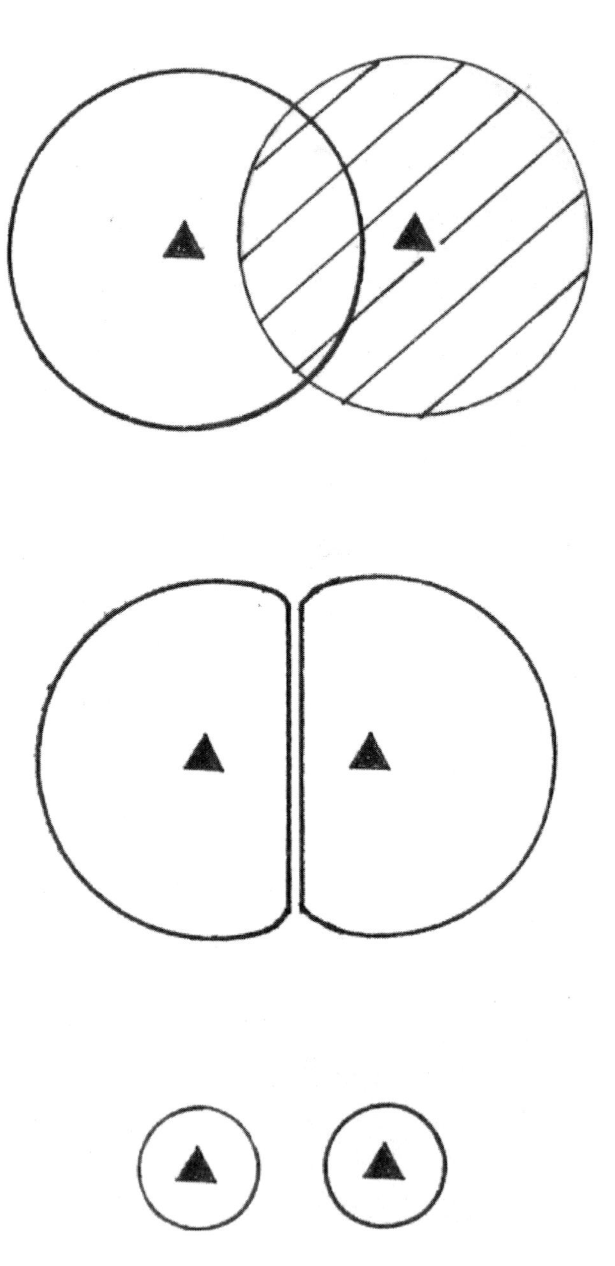

*Fig. 7.5 A model for the development of market areas by the major samian ware kiln-centres.* ***Top:*** *Established kiln and market, with an emergent kiln with developing market shown as a hatched circle,* ***Middle:*** *Both kilns with quasi-monopolistic markets,* ***Bottom:*** *Retreat of markets to local areas of kilns.*

### A descriptive model

Out of the foregoing description of the last century or so of samian ware production, certain general trends are apparent that appear to be common to many of the kiln-centres. If we start with a production and distribution system that is largely the preserve of one kiln-centre (and its smaller neighbours), the way in which another kiln-centre rises to dominance is by becoming established in a small area of the existing market, preferably an area where the dominant kiln-centre has not completely swamped all avenues of distribution and sated the market. Having created a niche, perhaps in company with other neighbouring small kilns, the potential major kiln starts to distribute widely but not in bulk within the existing market area, and is tolerated perhaps because the middlemen handling the pottery of the dominant kiln-centre perceive no threat from the newcomer (Fig. 7.5, Top). After this production expands at the new kiln probably at the expense of some of the neighbouring small kilns, which merge with it or gradually disappear. With expanding production and distribution comes a new situation, where the previously dominant kiln-centre loses or cedes part of its distribution area to the newcomer and is forced to contract. Eventually, distribution areas are established which are mutually exclusive (Fig. 7.5, Middle), with virtually no overlap except in some of the peripheral markets where active competition between middlemen may be taking place.[6] The distributions are quasi-monopolistic, since most consumers would have had no choice as to which kiln-

[4] See Bird 1993, 12 for discussion of 3rd-century Argonne ware in Britain, and the question of continuity.

[5] Fitz 1982, 26-8.

[6] Cf. Bradley 1971.

centre's products they could buy (provided, of course, that they cared about having a choice in the first place). This has certain important implications for the decline of samian manufacture, as will be explored below. The final stage in the model occurs when no new major kiln centre emerges to alter the distribution pattern yet again. In this case production and distribution eventually decline for one reason or another, and the market contracts within the quasi-monopolistic areas (Fig. 7.5, Bottom). Large parts of the distribution network are abandoned as the market is localised around the kilns, and eventually production comes to an end.[7]

This model does not offer explanations for the sequence – that is a matter to be discussed in later sections of this chapter – but it does encompass quite well the expansion of Trier and Rheinzabern at the expense of Central Gaul, also to a lesser extent the rise of the Argonne kilns and Westerndorf, although neither of these manage to establish quasi-monopolies for themselves, but achieve the intermediate position between Figs 7.5, Top and Middle, of a substantial market share within the distribution areas of the major kilns. The model may also be used in earlier periods, since the first two stages are relevant to the rise of South Gaul at the expense of 'Arretine' distribution in the NW provinces, similarly the rise of the early Central Gaulish kilns at the expense of the northern part of South Gaul's distribution. In both these cases, though, the older kiln-centre rapidly declined and did not establish a mutually exclusive distribution. For all kiln-centres, at all times, however, the overall aim in distributional terms seems to have been to gain as much of a monopolistic hold over as many well-defined market areas as possible. This seems to reflect an element of competition between kiln-centres, in other words some sort of competition in economic terms between middlemen for new and existing market areas.

## The economics of decline

The model described above implies, by the use of words like competition and market, that samian ware trading was carried out in a moneyed free market economy. But as Polanyi has forcefully pointed out, we cannot assume that ancient economic systems operated on a self-regulatory exchange basis or independently of other social institutions.[8] To do so would perpetuate the mistaken impression of some economists, anthropologists and others that the system that came to relative maturity in nineteenth-century Europe, the price-fixing market based on relatively independent economic institutions, is the paradigm to which the economic systems of other societies conform to a greater or lesser extent, depending on their individual circumstances.

Polanyi proposed that there were two other major systems used in ancient (and modern, so-called primitive) societies, namely reciprocity and redistribution. Both were defined from an examination of the mechanics of ancient trade and marketing (the 'substantive' approach) rather than from the theoretical basis of the supply-demand price-fixing mechanism of classical economics (the 'formal' approach). As reciprocity is of little consequence in the *milieu* of samian ware manufacture and trading (as opposed to what might happen to the pottery after it was sold), it is to the relative merits of redistribution and classical economic exchange systems that we shall turn.

Redistribution, in Polanyi's wider definition, can be taken to apply to all markets operating under conditions of price-fixing that are not self-regulatory. However, this is not a useful tool for further analysis, as virtually all markets can be said to conform to this definition in some form or another, even modern 'free' market systems.[9] It would be particularly applicable, for instance, to markets under the control of Diocletian's Price Edict, which attempted to institutionalise market prices. If edicts such as this were typical of practices in the Roman world, we should be able to say that trading was, generally speaking, redistributive and artificially priced. There is evidence of town and provincial taxes on various goods and services,[10] but little else is available in the period we are concerned with to indicate the extent of intervention in the market. The extent of government control, therefore, must be left as an open question, for neither the proposition of little state control up to the time of Diocletian, nor of attempts at control throughout the second and third centuries can be defended with any confidence. As far as samian ware is concerned, therefore, we do not really know whether the pottery was sold under the dictates of a fixed-price or under more or less free market conditions.[11]

Returning to the market system in which samian ware was traded, in view of the lack of definitive evidence to the contrary, we may assume that trading in the pottery tended to conform to self-regulatory pricing conditions wherever constraints against these conditions were not in operation. The widespread avoidance of regulations and the desire of traders to strike bargains is brought out in the prolegomena to Diocletian's Price Edict and in Lactantius' observation that the edict was driving goods off the market because the prices were too low.[12] Thus, there was a tendency towards a trading system that operated relatively free of control. If trade in samian ware was carried out under such an ethos, we may make the suggestion that the pottery was regularly being bargained for, and that opportunities were available for under-cutting by cost reduction. The reflection of this

[7] The final stages of CG production conform well to this model; Delage 1998; 2001a. Cf. Picon's cogent comments on 'la fin de l'atelier de Lezoux' in the printed discussion session of the SFECAG conference at Lezoux (*SFECAG Lezoux, 1989,* 106).

[8] Polanyi 1957; 1977. Cf. Hodder 1979a and Reece 1979 for discussion of Polanyi's ideas in relation to coinage and the economy of pre-Roman and Roman Britain.

[9] Plattner 1983.

[10] E.g. *CIL* VIII, 4508, Zarai; cf. De Laet 1949 on *portoria.*

[11] But cf. Finlay 1973; Whittaker 1983 who favour restricted market freedom.

[12] *de mort. pers.* 7.6; Duncan-Jones 1974, 367; Reece 1984, 144.

in the archaeological record may be seen in various cost-cutting tendencies in samian manufacture to be discussed below.

This appears to contradict Polanyi's contention that Roman economies were strongly redistributive, and it is possible to maintain that although the consumers' market may have been quite deeply embedded in social institutions[13] – and thus that the sale of samian ware was not free of non-market constraints – it would appear that the suppliers' market was competitive, particularly between *negotiatores* trading the products of different workshops. Therefore, it seems best to model the sale and distribution of the pottery in terms of a hybrid economic scheme, being partly traded within the *negotiatores* network on a competitive basis, at least as far as the social system of the *negotiatores* would allow (i.e. within their own internal hierarchy, and within the confines of their *collegium* system), and being partly traded in a more redistributive mode at the point of sale, where social constraints may have been more evident.[14]

If this scheme is granted, we may accept that price fluctuations and competition existed in the samian trading system. The quasi-monopolistic distribution areas described above are a response to competition in that they serve to reduce it and thus allow prices to rise higher than they would otherwise have done if competition was evenly distributed and more intense (as may have been the case in the mid second century before the quasi-monopolistic areas emerged).[15] Thus, prices would have had a tendency to drift upwards, either to the price ceiling (if one similar to the Price Edict existed at this time) or to the market tolerance level. Production would be geared to these optimum conditions, and we have a situation in which a drop in price levels, for whatever reason, is almost bound to lead to cost-cutting or contraction of production, as happened from the end of the second century or a bit later.

Possible forms of contraction are:-

1) consolidation of potters into larger workshops to ensure the continuance of volume production and product variety;
2) reduction of the number of smaller centres to the advantage and growth of those better established, so that transport and trading costs are optimised;
3) the movement of potteries nearer to their principal markets, for similar reasons to 2;
4) the reduction of product range and quality, to ensure continued production of particular lines;
5) the consolidation of marketing into smaller quasi-monopolistic regions, and withdrawal from markets involving extensive distribution networks;
6) diversification of production, and experimentation with new lines on the local market;
7) the establishment of dependent branches to large workshops in a main market area, for similar reasons to 2.

It is obvious that these responses to commercial pressure are varied, and in certain cases, mutually contradictory (e.g. 4 and 6). Different kiln-centres made different responses, and it seems from the available data that factor 5 is the most widely documented form of contraction, affecting all major kiln-centres. Lezoux also seems to have reduced product range and quality (4), as did the others to a lesser extent. Rheinzabern and Trier diversified (6) into products previously made in other fabrics in an attempt to preserve production and win new markets within the existing market area. The reduction in the number of kiln-centres (2) occurred early on, from the mid second century, but a comparable phenomenon, the reduction of workshops within the major kiln-centres seems likely to have happened at a later stage, to judge from the small number of potter's names we can definitely associate with the final phases of manufacture. The movement of potters and kilns nearer their markets (3) is not necessarily a characteristic of final contraction of the industry, since this happened in the late first/early second century when contraction was occurring in South Gaul, and new kilns were being set up in East Gaul partly in response to this. In the late period, the clearest example is the establishment of Westerndorf nearer the Danubian market than Rheinzabern. There seems to be little evidence for factor 7, unless Westerndorf was in fact organisationally dependent on Rheinzabern, or for factor 1, unless the small number of known late potters denotes this factor at work as well as a simple reduction in the actual number of workshops.

The forms that contraction of manufacture took were introduced above without prior consideration of why the contraction and the drop from optimum price levels might have come about. The reasons for this are of course the nub of discussion of the decline of samian manufacture, and they can be broadly categorised as follows:- 1) breakdown or curtailment of the distribution network; 2) political intervention and random disruptive events; 3) reduction of consumer purchasing power or removal of one or more principal consumer groups; 4) change in consumer preferences. There is a fifth possibility, a contraction of the resource base (i.e. suitable clay, timber, etc) but this has no available evidence to support it and is not discussed further. The four processes listed will be examined in turn for the extent of each one's contribution to the decline of manufacture, and also to see how far these processes might inter-relate.

### Disruption of the distribution network

It has already been suggested (in Chapter 6) that kiln-centres were positioned without explicit reference to their markets, and depended entirely on the distribution network to bring the pottery to the market. That network had been in

[13] Hodder 1979a; cf Polanyi 1957, 256.

[14] Cf. Plattner 1983 for discussion of traditional economic customs as factors affecting the operation of the 'free' market in pre-industrial societies. See also the discussion in chapter 6 of the economics of distribution.

[15] Cf. Bradley 1971.

existence for some time by the end of the second century, and its origins, whether in military supply or pre-Roman trade were probably no longer relevant except in historic terms. Specialist dealers in pottery (*negotiatores artis cretariae*) are attested on inscriptions of the late second and early third century,[16] presumably able to sustain a trade exclusively in that commodity, but not necessarily filling ships and barges with it. It still seems likely that samian ware was transported as part of mixed cargoes, with the two consequent implications discussed in chapter 6, that consignments were probably transhipped several times before they reached long-distance destinations, and that the cost of moving samian ware would vary as a proportion of the costs of the general rate of flow of goods on particular routes. A large volume of general trade probably accounted in part for the success of Central Gaul (via Lyon to the north and east and via Vichy, the Loire and the Seine to the north and west), Rheinzabern (via Mainz, Strasbourg and the Rhine), Trier (via Trier, the Moselle and Rhine) and the Argonne (via the Meuse, or via Metz and the Moselle). The nature of the other products being traded along these routes is not certain, but included wine, stone, iron and cloth.[17]

Because of this, an obvious suggestion to account for problems in distribution is that there was a decline in the quantity of goods moved in the early/mid third century. This will be discussed in general terms in a later section, but the mechanics of a declining volume of trade are relevant here. Unit costs would rise as difficulties of distribution increased (and also, if it occurred, as demand decreased). Thus, *negotiatores* and *navicularii* would probably be forced to increase their rates as a percentage of the total unit cost, if they were to maintain their standard of service. However, this is counterbalanced by the increased sharpness of inter-*negotiator* competition brought about by a declining market, which would force traders to reduce costs in order to retain their contracts. In the system that prevailed, whereby a *negotiator* bought goods from manufacturers, negotiated shipping costs or percentages with transport owners, and ultimately sold the goods either to another *negotiator* at a different point in the trading network, or direct to the market, there would inevitably come a time when the conflicting interests of maintaining profits or assets, and the need to undercut competitors, would lead to a loss making venture and possible bankruptcy. In this way, it can be seen that a decline in the market and the erosion of trading profitability lead to circumstances where the possibility of making a loss is very much enhanced.

The consequences of this are that outlying areas of the distribution would tend to be given up, and that unpopular or new products would tend not to be traded because of the risk involved (or restricted to a smaller distribution area). Under the Roman system, it would be easy for a trader to cut his losses by no longer carrying certain goods, or not distributing them to all his former market areas, as the manufacturing and trading arms of ancient industry were not closely linked. When *negotiatores* decided that it was no longer in their interests to continue shipping samian ware, or distribute it over such long distances, both trade and manufacture would cease altogether or decline sharply, unless other dealers could step into the abandoned market, or unless local trade was able to sustain a reasonable level of potting activity.

Those kiln-centres with long distribution lines would be particularly vulnerable to this process. Lezoux and the other Central Gaulish kilns are the prime example, as it has already been demonstrated that transport costs must have been higher for their products than for those of Rheinzabern and Trier (Figs 6.4-6.5). The period of decline in Central Gaul has been shown to be a couple of decades earlier than in East Gaul, a difference that may possibly be due to distribution difficulties as outlined above.

Disruption of the trading and distribution system seems to give a satisfactory explanation of how samian ware manufacture declined at the weakest part of the industry as a whole.[18] However, this does not explain why the disruption came about, which will be discussed in the next two sections.

### Political intervention and random disruptive episodes

The suggestion that political events could bring about the decline or end of samian manufacture is the traditional form of explanation, as exemplified by the Birley and Simpson hypothesis for the end of Lezoux. This particular hypothesis has been examined in detail in chapter 1, and there must be considerable doubt that the events during or just after Severus' victory over Albinus at Lyon in AD 197 were in fact a primary cause of the demise of the kilns. The main reason for this is chronological, as the evidence presented in chapter 4 would favour both a later and a less traumatic end for Central Gaulish production. There is also no published evidence for a sudden end at the kiln-site itself.[19]

A lack of evidence for this particular event being a cause of decline does not, of course, preclude the general idea that political manifestations of this sort were detrimental to manufacture and trading. Events like the visit of Caracalla to South Gaul in *c.* 212 and the consequent panic amongst Gaulish office-holders, may have been a case in point.[20] At all times when there was a heightened risk of loss of goods or capital, prices may have risen to account for it, as an ancient form of insurance. This may have driven long-distance traded goods off the market in the manner described in the preceding section, to the advantage of their

[16] Delplace 1978, 56; Hassall 1978; Kuhoff 1984.

[17] Wine from the Mediterranean via Lyon, and within the Moselle/Rhine area; Kneissl 1981. Stone from the Argonne/Metz area; Wightman 1985, 135. Iron from Central Gaul; Buckley 1981, 300. Cloth in East Gaul and around Trier; Drinkwater 1981.

[18] This line of interpretation is also taken by Polak (2000, 36-7) in relation to the decline of South Gaulish production in the early 2nd century.

[19] See chapter 1, and discussion in King 1990, 172-3.

[20] *Hist. Aug.*, Caracalla 5.1-2.

cheaper, local, low-risk rivals (e.g. regionally distributed colour-coated wares).

The other and perhaps more significant threat to trading in the early to mid third century was disruption as a result of what are termed here random episodes, i.e. barbarian raids. The offensive of the Alemanni in 233-5 that ultimately resulted in the death of Severus Alexander at the hand of his own troops near Mainz,[21] can hardly have left the mercantile world unruffled, particularly near the area of the incursions in the middle Rhineland. However, events such as these probably only had a short-term direct effect; the middle Rhineland and *agri decumates* appeared to be functioning relatively normally again in the 250s.[22] Further to the north it may be that the increase of piracy from the 170s reflected later in the building of forts such as Brancaster and Reculver in the early decades of the third century, led to difficulties in cross-Channel shipping.[23] Changes in the garrisoning of the fleet at this time, which brought about the disappearance of the *classis britannica*,[24] and the general success of incursions elsewhere from the 230s onwards, probably marks the period after which the odds were heavily against the normal continuance of seaborne trade in the North.

Actual destruction of a kiln-site may be attested by the burning layer dated to Postumus or later at Rheinzabern, which would fit into the historical context of the presumed incursions into the area from 257 onwards, and Postumus' counter-measures.[25] However, this apparent death-blow to the workshops was inflicted on a virtually lifeless body, if the coin-dated chronology of chapter 5 is correct.

A further disruptive element may have been an internal one. Social unrest is documented in Gaul on the occasion of the revolt of Maternus AD 185-7, serious enough to require legionary help in its suppression.[26] Again, in *c.* AD 207 a revolt was put down, and troops were required in Central Gaul. Brigandage increased and policing work by *beneficarii* was necessary on main roads.[27]

Common to all the political and disruptive events recorded here is their individually transient nature, but their cumulative effect of creating uncertainty, and by that means disrupting long-distance trade. Such trade required security to be carried out economically, and the cost of the threat from piracy, brigandage and the occasional but unpredictable barbarian incursion may ultimately have been prices that were too high for the market to bear. It seems clear that the Roman trading network was vulnerable to continual unsettled conditions even if single events could be weathered. Nevertheless, there was a surprising resilience in trade in the early third century, particularly in the Rhineland, where, paradoxically, the barbarian threat and political upheavals were most immediate. Inscriptions and funerary monuments were set up until the 230s or perhaps later, and Drinkwater has maintained that prosperity in East Gaul and the Rhineland laid the foundations for the Gallic Empire, only to be swept away after its collapse in the 270s.[28] This leads on to the point that there may have been regional differences in the economy of the NW provinces during the early third century, which perhaps had a stronger effect on the decline of samian ware manufacture than the historical events outlined above.

### Consumer purchasing power

We have seen that insecurity in the NW provinces may have caused prices of long-distance items to rise, which in itself could have been an important economic factor affecting the samian ware market. There are also two other monetary matters which are relevant in this context, the strong inflationary tendency and the shortage of coins, both in evidence during the first half of the third century.

Ancient historians seem to be agreed that it was after the reign of Caracalla, and probably due to his pay rise to the troops and subsequent extensive and continued debasements of the coinage, that inflation became a problem in the Empire.[29] Quite what economic effect this had is unclear, except that continued pay rises were necessary to the troops to keep pace with inflation, pay rises that were financed not only by taxes but by forced requisitions from the civilian population,[30] and which must have brought about a large-scale transfer of wealth from those whose assets were relatively fixed, to the army. Civilian purchasing power was therefore undermined, and this presumably affected the market for non-essential items such as samian ware.

Hopkins suggests that inflation at this time led to dislocation of the money supply, which hitherto had been relatively homogeneous throughout the Empire, but from the Severan period became increasingly divergent and regionalised.[31] Although, as Hopkins' Fig. 4 shows, the actual numbers of coins in circulation went up, there may well have been a shortage of coin in some areas. The hoard evidence in chapter 3 (Table 3.VI, Figs 3.1-3.8) indicates that silver coins entered circulation and were hoarded at a faster and faster rate during the third century, and that the rate was faster in Britain than the Rhine or Danube areas in the early part of the century. This may be due to

[21] Herodian 6.8-9; Ensslin 1939, 71.

[22] Drinkwater 1983, 88-9. However, Wightman (1970, 199-200) attributes the end of Trier decorated samian manufacture to the deleterious effects of the frontier problems a couple of decades later in the 270s (cf. also Symonds 1992, 63).

[23] Schönberger 1969, 172; Hassall 1977; Edwards & Green 1977; Philp 1970.

[24] Cleere 1977.

[25] Rau 1977a; Alföldi 1939, 155, 158.

[26] Herodian 1.10.2.

[27] Drinkwater 1983, 84-5.

[28] Drinkwater 1983, 224-6.

[29] Crawford 1975; Beck 1977; Walker 1978, 140-3; Hopkins 1980, 115.

[30] E.g. under Maximinus Thrax; Herodian 7.3.1.

[31] Hopkins 1980, 123, Fig 4. Howgego (1996) lays out the hoard evidence for increasingly local circulation patterns in the 3rd century, from the period of Gordian III onward. Cf. Rathbone (1996) for the situation in 3rd-century Egypt.

the erratic nature of coin supply as well as to the rapid use of coins consequent on inflation. Certainly, coin supplies were disrupted enough to bring about an upsurge in counterfeiting.[32] In addition, the evidence of site finds shows that silver coins were relatively rarer in Britain than the Rhine or Danube (Tables 4.I, 4.IV), which may be a further reflection of regional differences. The areas with greater relative percentages of silver coins, the Danube and to a lesser extent the Rhineland, probably had more stable money supplies and economies than Britain (and perhaps than Gaul also, although the evidence for the latter is not sufficient to be conclusive). The resilience of the Rhenish and Danubian areas economically has already been noted in this chapter, and it is probably not simply a coincidence that these areas were active in the military sphere at the same time, while Britain was quiescent. In other words, the army probably had a considerable effect on regional economies in the early/mid third century, which inevitably must have had consequences for samian manufacture.

Britain is important in this context, since it is likely that after the reign of Caracalla, there was little military activity in the province, and consequently there may have been troop reductions as men were redeployed elsewhere to more urgent theatres.[33] Britain, too, was the main military market for late Central Gaulish ware after its exclusion from Rhenish and Danubian areas, and if, as suggested above, civilian purchasing power was being undermined at this time, the military market would have had relatively greater importance. Therefore, a reduction in the British garrison may have been significant for the decline of Central Gaulish production and perhaps contributed to its earlier demise than that of the East Gaulish kilns. It is relevant to note that Table 5.XII and Appendix 9 have slightly higher percentages of late Central Gaulish samian (CG IV, especially CG IVb) in the southern, civilian parts of Britain than in the north, which may support the suggestion that the military area was acquiring less samian ware at this time, and causing a contraction of supply.

There is, however, a complicating issue in this explanation. It is exemplified by the evidence put forward by Sheldon that the north of Britain suffered less in terms of contraction or abandonment of sites in the early third century than the south, and also by the expansion of the northern military *vici* at this time.[34] This appears to be a contradiction of what has been suggested above, until it is noted that the north in the early third century after Severus had worse problems with lack of coin supply than the rest of Britain.[35] Presumably, a certain measure of resilience in the northern economy accompanied by an apparent diminution of coin use points to a corresponding increase in the non-monetary economy. For the civilians this would mean bartering, and for the army, requisitions and the *annona*. It would seem that the decline of samian ware use in the military areas was not only due to a reduction of the army garrison but also to the diminution of monetisation in the military area.

On the matter of bartering, Humphrey, in an important article, has shown that long-distance trade, and trade in valuables, are made more difficult by bartering, not simply because the goods are not being bought and sold for cash, but because their value is effectively unknown against the normal goods used in barter exchanges.[36] Thus, a samian vessel could be bartered by someone who has previously bought it with money at another point in the trading system, but what that person received in kind for the samian vessel may vary greatly and not be 'worth' the cash originally paid. Also, coins, as Humphrey observed, tend to be bartered in a demonetised economy, which causes their value to vary and therefore would upset the value relationship between coins and samian ware in the bartering area. This seems to point to the conclusion that although the acquisition of long-distance traded items like samian ware was not precluded by a predominantly bartering economy, traditional supply systems may not have been able to cope with the variability of the bartering market and consequently would have confined themselves more to the monetised sector.

The other aspect of the non-monetary economy in north Britain, troop requisitioning and the *annona*, is perhaps more straightforward, if equally hypothetical in nature. The replacement of pay in cash by pay in kind for the troops was suggested by van Berchem to have occurred first in the reign of Severus.[37] There is little clear evidence in support of this at this particular time, especially in view of the number of coins of Severus from the frontier regions. However, after the Severan period, the lack of coinage on northern British sites lends support to the establishment of an *annona* system. This would presumably have stimulated the local bartering economy as troops disposed of surplus requisitioned goods (rather than saving money, as previously), which may account for the apparently flourishing military *vici* of the period. However, this would be a self-contained system, without the circulation of cash for purchase of items like samian ware. Of course, this is not a complete explanation, since if troops were keen to get hold of samian vessels, they could have bartered for them with their requisitioned goods, as they could for anything else they particularly wanted. This raises the issue of whether samian ware was in fact still in demand, to be discussed further in the next section.

The *annona* was not only in apparent operation in Britain at this period, for Nuber cites evidence of troops being present on the German limes after the end of coin supply.[38] However, there are many coins in Germany of the period from the late Severans to Philip (IXa-IXb) which would imply that pay in cash and a monetised economy continued longer than in Britain. This coincides with the continuance

[32] Boon 1974, 110ff.; King (C) 1996, 243.
[33] Jones (R) 1981; James 1984.
[34] Sheldon 1981; Jones (R) 1981, 409; Jones (G) 1984.
[35] Jones (R) 1981, 394-5.
[36] Humphrey 1985.
[37] van Berchem 1936.
[38] Nuber 1969, 141, n39.

of East Gaulish samian supply longer than Central Gaulish by about the same length of time, and therefore leads to the conclusion that samian distribution was closely integrated into the monetary economy. When this started to fail, samian supply also faltered, and thus the decline of samian ware manufacture can be linked to a certain extent to the vicissitudes of the official (i.e. predominantly military) money supply.

The economic evidence presented here emphasises the fact that the terms of trade throughout the NW provinces may have been changing, to the disadvantage of samian ware manufacture, in the early/mid third century. In macro-economic terms, the hypothesis generally put forward is that the system in existence in the early Empire – that of high consumption of imported produce (and also high internal production) in Italy and other Mediterranean lands, bought or levied from the outlying provinces (with the army and official taxes as the principal agents of acquisition) – came under increasing pressure through the second century as a result of the gradual development of the outer provinces, and of the ending of an expansionist policy. Eventually, starting in the mid third century or later, a new system came into being that relied much more on internal self-sufficiency, or trading within a local group of provinces.[39] At its height, in the early fourth century, this system allowed for the movement of goods between provinces on a roughly reciprocal basis. For example, pottery produced in southern Britain was exported to northern Gaul in small quantities, and there was a slightly larger flow in the other direction. Most of the pottery, however, was internally produced and consumed.[40]

The key period, as far as the decline of samian ware is concerned, is precisely when the early system was in the process of collapse, and when the seeds of the new system were being sown. Of course, it is a commonplace among ancient historians and archaeologists that the third century, when this change and associated disruption was at its peak, is a time when both historical and archaeological evidence is minimal and resistant to clear interpretation. However, a few significant facts are known to us that give an indication of the direction that economic events were taking, and when. For instance, a general diminution of spending power can be seen from the time of Marcus Aurelius onwards in the number of Italian and western (except N African) inscriptions recording the erection of new buildings.[41] Trading ports such as Ostia or London have clear evidence of abandonment of living and commercial areas in the late second and early third centuries; and elsewhere, settlements were neither increasing nor expanding.[42] Shipwrecks, often used as an index of trading intensity, are fewer in number after AD 200.[43] Coin circulation becomes erratic and increasingly disparate in different regions, as we have seen above. The cumulative effect is one of increasing dislocation of the economy, accompanied principally by a diminishing trade in all but essentials or high value luxuries, a declining money market and increasing isolationist or provincialist tendencies. The position of samian ware trading in this picture is clear; it would have been most difficult to sustain a healthy long-distance trade in these circumstances, and a decline of samian ware distribution and trading was thus almost inevitable.

### Change in consumer preferences

So far the discussion has centred on questions of supply and has basically charted the economic decline of samian manufacture. However, matters cannot be left there, for this would be to ignore the important issue of demand - that is, whether consumer preferences were swinging away from using samian ware. Gard long ago suggested that Trier samian was incompatible with northern taste due to its ultimately Hellenistic origins, and that a change took place in the mid third century to other styles.[44] The simple fact is that samian ware in its glossy-red, moulded figurative form never came back into production once a more stable economic climate had been restored at the end of the third century. Hitherto, samian kiln-centres had declined singly, to be replaced by others without any real break in supply; and the two fairly major hiccoughs, at the end of Arretine production and the end of South Gaulish production, had both been overcome without the collapse of manufacture as a whole. In the early/mid third century, though, all the samian kiln-centres declined together, within a space of approximately thirty-forty years, and production of moulded decorated wares never recovered.

The main distinctive features of samian ware, its red gloss and its decoration, were also not taken up to any great extent by other ceramic production after samian's decline. The gloss tended to be replaced by a slip with a matt finish on wares that succeeded samian, the so-called 'derivés de sigillée', although it must be noted that most later samian products had poor glosses and anticipated their successors in this respect.[45] The gloss tradition lasted longer on black-gloss wares in forms such as beakers.[46] More fundamental

[39] Reece 1981b.
[40] Fulford 1977.
[41] Duncan-Jones 1974, 352.
[42] Carandini & Panella 1981; Sheldon 1981.
[43] Hopkins 1980, Fig 1.

[44] Gard 1937, 134. Note that this point-of-view reflected prevailing Nazi ideology about the cultural superiority of northern (Germanic) Europe. However, there is no suggestion that Gard himself was actively promulgating this ideology; see his biography by Merten (2012). Wightman (1970, 199-200) also discusses a change of taste in similar terms: 'the debased classical art of the decorated terra sigillata was being rejected in vafour of traditions more pleasing to indigenous taste'.
[45] As described by Delage & Guillier (1997, 258) for phases 7 and 8 of Lezoux production, late 2nd-mid 3rd century (the phases are also given in Bet *et al.* 1989, 38). See also Picon 2002b, and Genin (2007, 163-5) for late production at La Graufesenque in 'mode C' technique; Rigoir & Rigoir 1985. Roth-Rubi 1990 surveys the development of 'spätantike Glanztonkeramik' in the western provinces. A good example of a derivative of samian production that is very similar to late samian products, including incised versions of Dr 37, can be seen at Augst, Auf der Wacht site, dated to early/mid 3rd century; Schmid & Vogel Müller 2012. For the links between Oxfordshire products and samian ware; Bird & Young 1981.
[46] Symonds 1992; Gose 1975; Bird 1993; Roth-Rubi 1990, 936-7.

was the ending of moulded decoration, together with its subject-matter, figurative scenes depicting myths, hunts, animals, and peopled scrolls. It is possible to account for the end of moulding for technical reasons, given that it was more complicated to produce than its common alternatives, stamping or slip-trailing, but the demise of the subject-matter is best explained by a change in consumer preferences.

A brief survey of pottery being made in the third century after samian manufacture had ceased shows that slip-trailing was the main decorative type at all reminiscent of moulded samian decoration. The subject-matter tended to be vegetative, derived from vine scrolls, etc., and less commonly, hunting scenes of dogs, horses and deer.[47] Slip-trailed decoration in fact had its own stylistic traditions going back to the more complicated and often more realistically-modelled designs of the mid/late second century. Human and mythological scenes had little, if anything, to do with this tradition. The other form of decoration that could have continued samian-derived figurative design, stamping, also appears not to have done. Only occasionally do samian-derived features such as ovolos feature as stamps.[48]

The post-samian fine wares are in many ways remarkable for their homogeneity - all have a repertoire of forms that includes several derived from samian ware,[49] but which is mainly rooted in other fine ware types, such as beakers. Slips are sometimes as lustrous as samian glosses but are usually matt.[50] Slip-trailing, where it was a different colour from the body of the vessel, tended to be white or yellow, following the practice of late second century slip-trailed wares. (East Gaulish late samian ware types with white slip highlights were themselves imitative of these wares, as East Gaulish potters attempted to diversify their production away from traditional samian types; see above.) The similarity between some of these fine wares has led to a search for connections, as superficially there appear to be links in forms and types between the Rhineland and British centres such as the Nene Valley, New Forest and Oxfordshire, and also links between these areas and the Argonne. The exact nature and extent of these links is a matter for debate,[51] but in the current context it is enough to note that the new styles of the mid/late third century and later do not cater in any way for consumers wanting traditional decorated samian ware, and it must be presumed that tastes had changed. The change was not for lack of exposure to samian ware, since the evidence in chapter 5 points clearly to decorated vessels remaining in use in small numbers to the late third century, and much greater quantities surviving in rubbish deposits which would have been quite noticeable when disturbed. It is also equally clear that there was a general continuity with earlier potting styles, since certain aspects, such as some samian forms, and the use of semi-literate or illiterate name stamps of samian type did continue, demonstrating the overlap between the use of late samian ware and the manufacture of early post-samian wares.[52] If consumer preferences had moved away from samian styles of decoration, as the indications seem to demonstrate, it must be asked why this happened, and whether the change contributed to the decline of samian manufacture or was a consequence of it. Concrete answers to these questions are not easy to find, but some explanations are attempted in the paragraphs that follow.

### The status of samian ware

A preliminary observation is that there is no evidence for a continuation of figurative decoration of samian type on vessels of other similar materials, e.g. glass.[53] Metal vessels, however, may possibly continue second century styles into the third century,[54] but it must be noted that there are difficulties in assessing the life of luxuries such as these before disposal. The possibility that styles in metal continued while those on samian ware did not, despite the fact that the latter were derived in large part from the former, is perhaps a pointer to the nature of the changes that were occurring. It may be that the patrons of luxury arts such as metalwork, sculpture, mosaic, etc., were more conservative in their taste at this time than the users of such comparatively humble items as samian ware. There certainly appears to be a greater stylistic continuity in these materials through the third century, as Henig has pointed out in connection with jewellery.[55]

An indicator of the extent to which decorated samian ware users may have retained a desire to conserve their bowls and therefore, the styles associated with them, are the twin factors of wear and repair, together with the life-expectancy of decorated vessels. As discussed at the end of chapter 5, there are signs that this may have been a factor in the early third century in northern Britain, perhaps a reflection of the already-declining Central Gaulish supply to that region, and a still-continuing consumer preference at that time for the figurative scenes and glossy finish on samian wares.

At this juncture it is useful to remind ourselves of the original nature of samian ware usage, as outlined in chapter 6. It seems to have started out in the NW provinces in a high-status context, being used by the pre-Roman tribal aristocracy and the Roman army. In other words, it was associated with the elite, and during the rapid Romanisation of the first century AD became a widely-established product that must have been a status symbol

[47] Bird 1993; cf. New Forest, Fulford 1975; Oxford, Young 1977; Nene Valley, Hartley 1960c; Rhineland, Gose 1975; Symonds 1992; North Britain, Gillam 1968.

[48] Principally in the Argonne; Chenet 1941. Also occasionally found on Oxfordshire wares; Young 1977.

[49] E.g. forms 37 (without decoration). 35, 45, 79, 31, 38.

[50] Cf. Rigoir *et al.* 1973 for Lezoux matt slips that succeeded samian production.

[51] Bird & Young 1981; Swan 1984, 109; Roth-Rubi 1990.

[52] Young 1977, 178-80; Dannell 1973a.

[53] inf. J. Shepherd (1985).

[54] Henig 1983, ch. 6.

[55] Henig 1981.

used by those who wished to display their emulation of Roman ways.[56] It was a symbol of *Romanitas*, and had the attributes of its Romanity (classical art-forms and mythology) prominently arrayed upon it.[57] Samian ware was also associated with wine-drinking (see below) and Roman table customs, both also highly visible aspects of Romanisation. Samian ware during the second and third centuries, however, seems to have been subject to the well-documented process that many status symbols undergo – the decline from status as more and more people acquire the symbols in their fulfillment of emulation.[58] Meanwhile, those wishing to maintain social differentiation create new status symbols, which in the Roman NW provinces probably included luxury items like jewellery and metalware. Samian, therefore, probably occupied a special position in early provincial society, being one of the few ceramic products available that had some prestige status (other such ceramics being glazed and fine ware cups, and perhaps also lamps). That status was probably declining during the second and early third centuries, and eventually the symbolic value of the pottery was lost, which meant that samian manufacture would have had to change to become like other more commonplace pottery products (as East Gaul attempted to do) or go out of fashion.

A pertinent problem inherent in samian manufacture, however, was the separation of producer and consumer. This meant that changes in consumer preferences were not directly communicable to the potters, except within the local market area. The consequence of this appears to have been that the long-distance consumers probably had little influence over decorative designs and accepted what was supplied.[59] This would lead to an innate conservatism in the designs on the part of the potters if there was little stimulus to change coming from the market. This may also account in part for the re-use of moulds at several kiln-centres and potters' workshops, up to a century after their original creation. In this context, the Central Gaulish kilns are worthy of note, since they are both distant from the main areas of their distribution, established in a self-contained rural potting region with a small local market (the towns of Vichy and Clermont-Ferrand), and also conservative in their samian traditions. On the model outlined here, this state of affairs would be a recipe for a more rapid decline than kilns which had larger local markets and therefore were more responsive (i.e. in East Gaul), and it is in fact the case that decline came somewhat earlier in Central Gaul.

Nevertheless, conservatism of design can also be seen in late East Gaulish products, albeit with attempts to cater for change. Late moulded designs have fewer figures, more open space and geometric motifs, and a smaller zone of decoration in proportion to the bowl as a whole. In fact, on some bowls the decorative area was so much confined to the lower curved part of the vessel as to be barely visible, and seems to us hardly worth producing at all. Perhaps the social structure within the kiln-centres was such that the high-status potters of moulded wares (see chapter 6) continued to produce decorated bowls as a means of maintaining their positions, even though the market was changing and there was a trend to creating new styles.[60] Such a model of conservatism within the industry may account for the continuance of decorated samian ware until the period of decline, at which point the dominance of the market by samian ware distributors started to slip, for reasons outlined earlier. Once that dominance was broken and supplies became more erratic, the previous acceptance by consumers of samian styles may quite rapidly have changed to preference for other styles instead. Only certain facets of samian ware, e.g. some forms and derivatives of the gloss, were retained in the new style, while features such as moulded figurative decoration soon became part of a bygone age, to be found mainly in sherds lying on rubbish dumps.

The issue that has been sidestepped in discussion so far is why consumer preferences should have changed at this particular period. Some relevant information can be gained by turning briefly to two institutions that to a certain extent were related, wine-drinking and the army. Although there is no direct proof, decorated samian bowls are probably to be connected with wine-drinking: they are the lineal descendents of Arretine drinking and wine mixing vessels (form 11 etc.), some of them are decorated with vintage scenes (e.g. bowls by Saturninus-Satto), and occasionally with exhortatory inscriptions (on Banassac bowls). In broad terms the manufacture of samian ware was in the same area as the growing of vines, and there is even the possibility that the establishment of samian production and viticulture in East Gaul occurred at about the same time in the late first century.[61] Wine-drinking, like samian ware itself (and clearly the two are related), started out by being a prestige institution in pre-Roman times, due to the expense of obtaining the wine and the essential drinking paraphernalia. However, again like samian ware, wine consumption spread rapidly during early Romanisation, to judge from the number of amphorae found, and thereby became a more commonplace and less high-status activity. The matter of relevance to the decline of samian ware is that it is possible wine-drinking habits were changing towards the end of the second and in the third century. New types of drinking beaker were coming into use in the Rhineland, with vinous allusions similar to those on samian ware in their decoration; stylised bunches of grapes, exhortations to drink, etc.[62] With the rise of local viticulture, the drinking institutions themselves appear to have been changing, and

[56] Fulford 1986 discusses the status differences between pottery and metal vessels in Roman society. Cf. Miller 1982.

[57] Webster & Webster 2012 discuss this in relation to selection of motifs at Les Martres-de-Veyre. Cf. also Webster & Webster 2013; Pitts 2012; Monteil 2004, 3; Vertet 1998; Henig 1998; Demarolle 1989; 1993; Bémont 1981; Picard 1981.

[58] Flügel 1940; Thompson 1979. For discussion of this in relation to pottery in Roman Britain; Henig 1998, 64-6.

[59] Cf. Weber 2012, 66 ff. for further discussion.

[60] Cf. Zucker 1977; also Lowe & Lowe 1982.

[61] Cüppers 1970; but date disputed in Kneissel 1981.

[62] Cüppers 1970, 144.

losing their Mediterranean flavour, of which samian bowls were so clear a symbol.

The relevance of the army to a possible change in consumer preferences is different, but in the end also connected with wine-drinking. It is well established that the pattern of recruitment to the army was changing during the early Empire from one dominated by Italians to one where men from the frontier lands formed the great majority of new recruits.[63] Initially the army would have been ethnically 'Mediterranean' in the newly conquered provinces, clearly different from the native population. Their diet and their drinking habits, as represented by samian ware and other artefacts, were subject to emulation by the Romanising population, since the army was part of the new elite and was making use of these easily copied symbols of *Romanitas*.[64] This observation is, of course, simply to repeat what has been stated already above, but the change in the pattern of recruitment (itself a facet of Romanisation) brought with it the consequence that the army population and the civilian population in the late second century were essentially of the same composition, with little new input of 'foreigners' into the army in any particular province, except for those coming from similar provinces. This, combined with the separation of military and civilian into different areas (in Britain more than the Rhine and Danube) and the apparent success of Romanisation in terms of the penetration of such artefacts as samian ware, led to a situation where the pottery had lost its original status, and where the army was no longer in an elite position capable of providing new status symbols for others to emulate. In fact, the army was experiencing some difficulties in recruiting from the local population in the third century,[65] perhaps because of increasing friction between military and civilian (see above), and therefore decided to take on an increasing percentage of 'barbarians', usually from within the Empire, e.g. Thrace. Some of these were organised as ethnic groups in a system of units that seems to have originated in the second century, e.g. *numeri Maurorum*, and the prowess of these units has led Speidel to see in them the nucleus of the new elite, predominantly cavalry, field armies that evolved in the course of the third century.[66]

The significance of this for samian ware usage is that the old associations of the army in terms of their drinking institutions, etc. were no longer relevant as the army's internal structure changed in favour of the new elite, who had no need of such symbols of *Romanitas* and indeed appear to have been proud of their ethnic origins. It seems likely, therefore, that the army, one of the major consumer groups for samian ware, was changing its preferences away from this type of pottery at about the time that manufacture was in decline. This may, in itself, have been a contributory factor in the demise of the industry, and certainly would have been an element in the failure of samian to come back into use in the late third century, by which time the army had undergone a considerable change.

Finally, we should turn to the population as a whole, since the army, albeit important, was not the only consumer group in the NW provinces, and it should have been possible for samian ware manufacture to continue to supply to the civilian population if demand still existed after the economic problems of the third century had been overcome. However, this was clearly not the case, and the best explanation for this is that tastes in pottery styles (and presumably other decorative commodities) were changing throughout the area.

In a preliminary paper on the subject of this volume, the suggestion was put forward that periods of cultural change are sometimes set in motion by widespread socio-psychological insecurity, which had been documented for some modern societies.[67] That such insecurity existed in the Roman Empire is documented for the mid-third century by the increased deposition of hoards, even in provinces not directly affected by barbarian incursions (e.g. Britain), by the building of town-walls in the NW provinces, and by the general tenor of some of the literary references of the time.[68] It was Dodds's 'Age of Anxiety', which in his view was an important contributory factor to religious change.[69]

The link between general changes of this sort and consumer preferences for samian ware was put in the interim report in terms of changes in levels of anxiety or, for instance, achievement motivation, affecting the subconscious structures and overt content of artistic and literary works, which had been demonstrated in a modern cross-cultural and diachronic context.[70] By this was meant that structural attributes of a society (e.g. degree of boundedness, vertical hierarchy, group identity, etc.) are reflected in cultural styles – the concept of the 'art style as a cultural cognitive map',[71] and therefore that changes in these attributes should be reflected in concomitant changes in art styles. This should affect the content of styles rather than technical (i.e. motor) skill and performance, which is only recorded as changing in conditions of long-term stress or trauma.[72]

This model is, however, complicated by the debate between those who argue for universal underlying structures of culture and personality through time and cross-culturally, such as McClelland's and Fischer's research implied,[73]

[63] Mann 1983; Forni 1974.

[64] Cf. King 1984b for discussion of military diet.

[65] Mann 1983, 66-7.

[66] Speidel 1975.

[67] King 1981, 73; Wallace 1970, chap. 5; cf. also Hodder 1979b.

[68] Alföldy 1974. An increase in volcanic activity is documented for the 3rd century, with eruptions in c. 220, 240, 260 (the strongest), 280 and 300; Rossignol & Durost 2007. This was associated with climatic perturbation in 262-8. In contrast, the second century saw an eruption in the 150/60s, followed by climatic perturbation in 164-6. The less favourable climate and the eruptive episodes in the third century may have contributed to the sense of insecurity.

[69] Dodds 1965.

[70] McClelland *et al.* 1953; Aronson 1958; cf. Klein 1982, chap. 10 for a more recent discussion.

[71] Fischer 1961.

[72] Hill 1977, 99-105.

[73] Cf. also Barry 1957; Kaplan & Levine 1981 amongst many other studies.

and those who argue for a more 'situationist' view.[74] The latter put much more emphasis on the social environment and its effect on personality, with the implication that underlying structures, if they are significant at all, vary from culture to culture. Each culture creates its own set of social behaviours with systems of symbolisation that are rooted in its own historical traditions, and which are liable to change at receptive periods (such as internal crisis or external pressure).[75] This is a more satisfactory model in archaeological terms, since it relies more on the internal characteristics of a culture, rather than universal attributes which are difficult to test for in past societies.

This theoretical digression now allows us to return to samian ware and its place as a status symbol. If we accept that the pottery was not simply a commonplace artefact but displayed visible symbols of *Romanitas* that would have been widely significant to people in the NW provinces,[76] then widespread changes in the nature of Roman society's world-view, from one that can be characterised in the second century as expansionist, optimistic and peacefully benevolent,[77] to one in the third century that was defensive, alarmist and insecurely repressive,[78] would lead, according to the model of cultural change outlined above, to the discarding of the old symbols and the establishment of new ones. In this way, figurative traditional samian ware did not survive the 'crisis' of the mid third century, and can be seen to have fallen victim to a major change in cultural preferences.

## Conclusion

The disparate threads of explanation for the decline of samian ware manufacture given in this chapter are difficult to draw together. In general, there is a distinction to be drawn between the mechanism of decline and its underlying dynamic, in that the former can be explained largely in terms of economics, i.e. breakdown of distribution networks, shortage of coin supply, etc., while the latter has to be couched more in a social framework, i.e. the nature of consumer preferences, samian as a status symbol, etc. Explanations of change in classical ceramics have moved from using historical paradigms to economic ones,[79] and have tended to concentrate on production and distribution. However, there is also much scope for a mode of explanation that sees pottery as an integral part of the social fabric of ancient society, towards which this chapter makes a contribution.

In broader terms chronologically, are the factors discussed in this chapter unique to the third century and its problems, or is there wider applicability, for instance to the decline of South Gaulish production in the early/mid second century, or the decline of Arretine production in the first century AD? In many respects, the answer to this is no, as each episode of manufacturing decline has its own set of contributory factors. What is emphasized in this chapter (and volume as a whole) has been the lengthening usage of samian ware, the worsening coin circulation patterns and the insecurity that affected the distribution system and ultimately consumer taste for the product. Earlier declines in samian production had different factors, linked in many respects to both competition from, and production efficiencies in, emerging centres of production, rather than social changes in consumer preferences.

The methodologies outlined in this volume, however, do have wider applicability. Earlier phases of samian ware production, e.g. South Gaulish, could be examined by means of the methods for assessing coin-dated contexts set out here, as indeed, could other classes of pottery and artefact. The method for dating of coin-loss extrapolated from hoard data could also be used for exploring coin-loss in other periods and regions, both within the Roman world, and even, possibly, beyond.

[74] Mischel 1968, 282; Cole & Scribner 1974.
[75] Cf. Deetz 1974.
[76] On the information exchange model of Wobst 1977; cf. Hill 1985 for discussion; also Pollock 1983; Wells 1985.
[77] As reflected in, for instance, Aelius Aristides.
[78] As reflected in Cyprian and the other 3rd-century writers in Alföldy 1974.
[79] Peacock 1982, 3.

# APPENDIX 1

## Percentages of silver coins per period in hoards of the mid second to mid third centuries

For each hoard, for each period, the percentage of coins of that period in the hoard is given.

Key: *Denomination:* D = denarius, R = radiate/antoninianus. *Reference:* R[number] = hoard reference number in Robertson 2000

**a) S Britain** and Wales

| *Site* | *Denom.* | *Latest* | *VI* | *VIIa* | *VIIb* | *VIIIa* | *VIIIb* | *IXa* | *IXb* | *IXc* | *Total* | *Reference* |
|---|---|---|---|---|---|---|---|---|---|---|---|---|
| Itteringham | D | 141+ | 3 | | | | | | | | 62 | Leins 2002 |
| Bryn Gwydion | D | 140-3 | 9 | | | | | | | | 45 | Williams 1875; R171 |
| Chalfont St Giles | D | 146 | 13 | | | | | | | | 40 | Mattingly 1934 |
| Llanymynech | D | 148-9 | 12 | | | | | | | | 33 | Boon 1966 |
| Snettisham | D | 155 | 4 | | | | | | | | 83 | Burnett 1997; R202 |
| Lawrence Weston | D | 157 | 17 | | | | | | | | 677 | Carradice 1988; R215 |
| East Stoke | D | 158-9 | 16 | | | | | | | | 43 | Bland & Williams 1997 |
| Pyrford | D | 159-60 | 12 | | | | | | | | 82 | Carson 1960b |
| London | D | Ant | 18 | | | | | | | | 68 | Chaffers 1847; R172 |
| Allerton Bywater | D | 162 | 21 | 2 | | | | | | | 295 | Mattingly 1925 |
| Long Whatton | D | 164 | 14 | 4 | | | | | | | 84 | Abdy 2002b |
| Fotheringhay | D | 165-6 | 20 | 9 | | | | | | | 45 | Carradice & Burnett 1992a; R234A |
| Hamstead Marshall | D | 169 | 25 | 5 | | | | | | | 84 | Williams & Read 2002 |
| Melbourn | D | 169-70 | 31 | 7 | | | | | | | 29 | Buttrey 1997 |
| Knapwell | D | 170 | 21 | 11 | | | | | | | 72 | Robertson 1939 |
| Braughing | D | 170-1 | 10 | 8 | | | | | | | 60 | Carson 1957b |
| Brundish | D | 170-1 | 25 | 12 | | | | | | | 65 | Bland 1997a |
| Marlingford | D | 171-2 | 23 | 9 | | | | | | | 173 | Bland et al 1997 |
| Potters Bar | D | 175-6 | 21 | 18 | | | | | | | 95 | Meadows et al 1997 |
| Aldworth | D | 176-7 | 33 | 12 | | | | | | | 75 | Carradice 1986; R284 |
| Poughill | D | 176-7 | 25 | 11 | | | | | | | 28 | Sutherland 1939a |
| Caerleon | D | 177 | 29 | 17 | | | | | | | 295 | Mattingly 1932; R316 |
| Caistor by Norwich | D | 177 | 20 | 15 | | | | | | | 20 | Haverfield 1902 |
| Castle Bromwich | D | 177 | 24 | 13 | | | | | | | 199 | Brooke 1910 |
| Wreningham | D | 180 | 31 | 10 | | | | | | | 186 | Davies & Orna-Ornstein 1997 |
| Mere | D | Aur | 16 | 7 | | | | | | | 232 | Baker 1894; R278 |
| Barway | D | 181 | 29 | 12 | 0.5 | | | | | | 463 | Bland & Buttrey 1997; R228A/317 |
| Brixworth | D | 180-3 | 25 | 25 | 4 | | | | | | 24 | Mattingly 1945c |
| Bletchley | D | 186 | 24 | 9 | 1 | | | | | | 913 | Tuckett 1992; R320/319 |
| Lowestoft | D | 186-9 | 24 | 13 | 5 | | | | | | 38 | Carradice 1986b; R339 |
| Postwick | D | 192 | 33 | 23 | 7 | | | | | | 282 | Davies et al 2002; R330 |
| Weston Underwood | D | Comm | 23 | 13 | 1 | | | | | | 166 | Lowndes 1863, 127; R336 |
| Lydney | D | Comm | 23 | 17 | 0.5 | | | | | | 155 | Bagnall-Oakeley 1882 |
| Silchester | D | 194-5 | 21 | 13 | 5 | 1 | | | | | 258 | Boon 1960b, 241-5; R362 |
| Handley | D | 194-5 | 24 | 17 | 8 | 0.5 | | | | | 570 | Robertson 1950; R380 |
| Great Melton | D | 195-7 | 24 | 18 | 5 | 0.5 | | | | | 274 | Davies 2002; R359 |
| Abergele | D | 201-6 | 21 | 7 | 2 | 2 | | | | | 350 | Robertson 1937; R383 |
| Kenilworth | D | 207 | 25 | 8 | 0 | 2 | | | | | 52 | Ireland et al 2002 |
| Bristol | D | 208 | 17 | 9 | 4 | 32 | | | | | 1478 | Mattingly & Pearce 1938 |
| Muswell Hill | D | 209 | 9 | 9 | 4 | 52 | | | | | 654 | Mattingly 1929 |
| Much Hadham | D | 210-11 | 6 | 0 | 2 | 70 | | | | | 128 | Burnett 1992b; R385A |
| Chadwell St Mary | D | 213-7 | 10 | 1 | 5 | 61 | 1 | | | | 99 | Carson 1957a |
| Prestwood | D/R | 220 | 14 | 3 | 5 | 58 | 5 | | | | 111 | Abdy 2002c |
| Akenham | D | 220-2 | 14 | 2 | 8 | 46 | 17 | | | | 59 | Carradice 1984a; R403 |
| Colchester | D/R | 223 | 12 | 12 | 6 | 24 | 36 | 6 | | | 33 | Evans 1891; R405 |
| Shapwick | D | 224 | 6 | 2 | 4 | 62 | 12 | 1 | | | 9196 | Abdy & Minnitt 2002 |
| Llanarmon | D/R | 226 | 5 | 2 | 5 | 62 | 15 | 2 | | | 505 | Mattingly 1923 |
| St Mary Cray | D | 226 | 1 | 1 | 4 | 54 | 22 | 10 | | | 376 | Robertson 1935a |
| Nuneaton | D | 228/31 | | | | 66 | 7 | 24 | | | 29 | Mattingly 1921 |
| E of England | D/R | 231 | 9 | 7 | 8 | 40 | 22 | 4 | | | 3164 | Evans 1898 |
| Hartlebury | D | 240 | | | | 36 | 30 | 29 | 5 | | 56 | Bland 1992; R437A |
| Great Chesterford | D/R | 246-7 | 0.5 | 0.5 | 2 | 36 | 12 | 5 | 43 | | 326 | Pearce 1953; VCH Ex III, 85-6; R448 |
| Elveden | D/R | 248 | 0.5 | 0.5 | 1 | 11 | 32 | 40 | 16 | | 1146 | Carson 1954; R449 |
| Cambridge | D/R | 248 | | | | 9 | 27 | 37 | 27 | | 207 | Boyd 1897; R447 |
| Brickendonbury | D/R | 250 | | | 0.5 | 17 | 28 | 45 | 8 | 1 | 433 | Evans 1896 |
| London | D/R | 249-51 | | | 0.5 | 16 | 18 | 19 | 47 | 0.5 | 587 | Evans 1882; 1883; R460 |
| Rayleigh | D/R | 249-51 | 1 | 0 | 2 | 22 | 26 | 34 | 13 | 3 | 117 | Smith 1850; R464 |
| Poole | R | 254 | | | | | | | 82 | 18 | 34 | Allan 1938 |
| Dorchester | D/R | 257-8 | | | | | 1 | 0.5 | 77 | 22 | 20680 | Mattingly 1939a |
| Caistor by Yarmouth | D/R | 260 | 4 | 2 | 3 | 47 | 17 | 3 | 18 | 3 | 839 | Jenkins 1947 |
| Mattishall | D/R | 260 | 0.5 | 0 | 0.5 | 11 | 27 | 32 | 23 | 6 | 1079 | Carson 1969b; R489 |
| Woodcote | D/R | 260 | | | | | 1 | 0 | 26 | 50 | 78 | Boon 1954, 40-1; R491 |
| Fineshade | D/R | 260-1 | | | | 3 | 10 | 21 | 17 | 43 | 262 | Curteis 1997 |

| | | | | | | | | | | | | |
|---|---|---|---|---|---|---|---|---|---|---|---|---|
| Stevenage | D/R | 263 | | | | 1 | 6 | 9 | 15 | 47 | 2506 | Bland 1988; R485 |
| Exeter | D/R | 263-4 | | | | 3 | 4 | 3 | 15 | 24 | 310 | Shiel 1979; R483 |
| Caerwent | D/R | 260-4 | | | | 1 | 3 | 8 | 46 | 41 | 116 | Boon 1976, 237-8; R477 |
| Alcester | R | 265 | | | | | | | 12 | 40 | 95 | Carson 1969a |
| Crowmarsh | D/R | 266 | | | | 0.5 | 3 | 4 | 19 | 53 | 337 | King 1997b |
| Beachy Head | D/R | 266 | | | | 0.5 | 0.5 | 0.5 | 17 | 30 | 3163 | Carson 1968; R492 |
| Gosbecks I | D/R | 269 | | | | 0.5 | 0.5 | 0.5 | 7 | 33 | 1544 | Bland & Carradice 1986; R696 |
| Gare | D/R | 267-70 | | | | | 9 | 6 | 0 | 15 | 47 | Carson 1971a |
| Welwyn | D/R | 267-70 | | | | 2 | 0 | 1 | 9 | 6 | 149 | Carson 1969c |
| Bassaleg | D/R | 268-70 | | | | | | 0.5 | 9 | 37 | 896 | Besly 1992; R536A |
| Luton | D/R | 268-70 | | | | | 1 | 1 | 5 | 24 | 506 | Evans 1863; R537 |
| Choseley | R | 270 | | | | | | | 3 | 20 | 465 | Carson1952; R548 |
| Selsey | D/R | 270 | | | | | 0.5 | 0.5 | 6 | 26 | 975 | Heron-Allen 1933; R550 |
| Emneth | D/R | 270-1 | | | | 0.5 | 0 | 0.5 | 2 | 6 | 664 | Mattingly 1945 |
| Linwood | R | 270-4 | | | | | 0.5 | 0 | 1 | 2 | 806 | Robertson 1935b |
| Wareham | D/R | 271 | | 0.5 | 0 | 1 | 3 | 5 | 6 | 20 | 1548 | Cheesman & Bland 1997 |
| Purbrook Heath | R | 272 | | | | | | | | 8 | 206 | Burnett 1984b; R565 |
| Gosbecks II | D/R | 273 | | | | 0.5 | 0 | 0.5 | 0 | 3 | 4020 | Bland & Carradice 1986; R696 |
| Gosbecks III | R | 274 | | | | | | | | 2 | 485 | Bland & Carradice 1986; R696 |
| Botley | R | 274 | | | | | | | | 2 | 1365 | Cheesman 1997 |
| Shoreham area | D/R | 274 | | | | | 0.5 | 0.5 | 0.5 | 1 | 4091 | Abdy 1999a |
| Lostwithiel | R | 271-4 | | | | | | | 1 | 1 | 93 | Burnett 1986; R559 |
| Mildenhall, Wilts | D/R | c. 274 | | | 0.5 | 0.5 | 0.5 | 0.5 | 0.5 | 21 | 52777 | Besly & Bland 1983 |
| East Mersea | R | 270-5 | | | | | | | | 1 | 592 | Burnett 1984b; R562 |
| Springhead | R | 270-5 | | | | | | | 2 | 9 | 120 | Smith 1887; R571 |
| Meare Heath | R | 270-5 | | | | | | | | 1 | 385 | Davies 1986; R584 |
| Emneth | R | 270-5 | | | | | | | 0.5 | 2 | 1612 | Robertson 1945 |
| Mildenhall, Suff | D/R | 270-5 | | | | | 0.5 | 0 | 0 | 1 | 1280 | Robertson 1954 |
| Tinwell | D/R | 275 | | | | | | | | 1 | 1811 | Abdy 1999b |
| Lutterfield | R | Tet | | | | | | | | 4 | 254 | Abbot 1956, 25; R573 |
| Deeping St James | R | Tet | | | | | | | | 1 | 515 | Carson 1973; R574 |
| Addington | R | Tet | | | | | | | | 5 | 168 | Besly 1981; R585 |
| Combe Hill | R | Tet | | | | | | | 1 | 1 | 137 | Rudling 1984; R587 |
| Bowcombe | R | 277 | | | | | | | 0.5 | 3 | 448 | Bland et al 1997 |
| Deeping St James | D/R | Aurel | | | | | 0.5 | 0.5 | 1 | 11 | 2815 | Carradice 1984b; R699 |
| Baconsthorpe | D/R | Aurel | | | | | 0.5 | 0 | 1 | 14 | 3679 | Hogg 1884; R700 |
| Wickham Market | R | Aurel | | | | | | | | 6 | 1563 | Burnett et al 1986; R703 |
| Eastbourne | R | Aurel | | | | | | | | 0.5 | 5499 | Bland 1979; R705 |
| Aldbourne | R | Aurel | | | | | | | | 2 | 4808 | Moorhead 1992; R706 |
| Poole | R | Aurel | | | | | | | 0.5 | 5 | 964 | Mattingly 1933; R715 |
| Amlwch | D/R | Aurel | | | | 0.5 | 0 | 0.5 | 0.5 | 0.5 | 399 | Mattingly & Pearce 1939; R732 |
| Chalfont St Peter | D/R | 281 | | | | 0.5 | 0.5 | 0.5 | 4 | 9 | 6116 | Cheesman 1992; R740A |
| Appleshaw | R | 282 | | | | | | | | 0.5 | 2947 | Bland & Burnett 1988a; R744 |
| Hollingbourne | D/R | Prob | | | | | 0.5 | 0.5 | 2 | 6 | 4984 | Carson 1961a; R746 |
| Much Wenlock | R | 282-5 | | | | | | | 0.5 | 0.5 | 2445 | Ivens & Burnett 1981; R822 |

**b) N Britain**

| *Site* | *Denom.* | *Latest* | *VI* | *VIIa* | *VIIb* | *VIIIa* | *VIIIb* | *IXa* | *IXb* | *IXc* | *Total* | *Reference* |
|---|---|---|---|---|---|---|---|---|---|---|---|---|
| Norton | D | 143-4 | 8 | | | | | | | | 39 | Carson 1963 |
| Londonthorpe | D | 153-4 | 8 | | | | | | | | 420 | Carson & Burnett 1979; R214 |
| Sheffield | D | 154-5 | 29 | | | | | | | | 35 | *Antiquary* 42, 1906, 406; R 211 |
| Chester | D | 161-2 | 28 | 14 | | | | | | | 43 | Davies & Longbottom 1923, 47-51; R237 |
| Osgodby | D | 163 | 16 | 2 | | | | | | | 44 | Abdy et al 2002 |
| Kirkby in Ashfield | D | 165-6 | 14 | 7 | | | | | | | 29 | Burnett 1992a; R235A |
| Dewsbury | D | 166 | 11 | 11 | | | | | | | 27 | Mattingly 1939b |
| Rudchester | D | 168 | 10 | 3 | | | | | | | 470 | Craster 1912, 220 |
| Doncaster | D | 169 | 24 | 14 | | | | | | | 63 | Bales 1943; R308 |
| Grinton | D | 170 | 35 | 6 | | | | | | | 52 | Casey & Wenham 1990; R245 |
| Newbiggin | D | 176 | 31 | 9 | | | | | | | 68 | Mattingly 1929 |
| Doncaster | D | 177 | 29 | 12 | | | | | | | 52 | Bales 1943; R309 |
| Hickleton | D | 180 | 20 | 9 | | | | | | | 349 | Leins 2001 |
| Kirkintilloch | D | Aur | 0 | 2 | | | | | | | 47 | Robertson 1961a, 151; R282 |
| Edwinstowe | D | 180 | 15 | 10 | 0.5 | | | | | | 399 | Carradice & Burnett 1992b; R314 |
| Rumbling Bridge | D | 186-7 | 29 | 24 | 5 | | | | | | 180 | Robertson 1957; R335 |
| South Shields | D | 191-2 | 20 | 11 | 7 | | | | | | 120 | Casey 1979, 72-5, 90; R323 |
| Kirkby Thore | D | Comm | 27 | 16 | 0.5 | | | | | | 167 | Shotter 1978, 17-19; R333 |
| Littleborough | D | 193 | 18 | 24 | 10 | 1 | | | | | 72 | Williams & Meadows 1997 |
| Portmoak | D | 196-7 | 29 | 19 | 7 | 2 | | | | | 104 | Macdonald 1918, 264-5; R369 |
| Bottesford | D | 207 | 17 | 9 | 8 | 28 | | | | | 164 | Williams & Rigby 2002 |
| Morton Lodge | D | 210 | 13 | 10 | 1 | 28 | | | | | 138 | Williams 1997; R384 |
| Carrawburgh | D | 211 | 4 | 0 | 7 | 72 | 1 | | | | 67 | Askew 1937 |
| Darfield | D | 213 | 18 | 14 | 2 | 10 | 8 | | | | 495 | Corder 1948 |
| Edston | D | 218-22 | 17 | 5 | 5 | 13 | 9 | | | | 288 | Holmes & Hunter 1997 |
| Wigan | D | 228+ | 6 | 2 | 3 | 50 | 23 | 11 | | | 133 | Cheetham 1926; R422 |
| Falkirk | D | 230 | 16 | 13 | 3 | 5 | 5 | 4 | | | 1924 | MacDonald 1934 |
| Cadeby | D | 235-6 | 4 | 11 | 4 | 26 | 31 | 22 | | | 27 | Smedley 1946a |
| Darfield | D/R | 236-8 | 8 | 4 | 5 | 46 | 16 | 7 | | | 479 | Walker 1946 |

| | | | | | | | | | | | | |
|---|---|---|---|---|---|---|---|---|---|---|---|---|
| Kirkham | D | 238 | 17 | 6 | 6 | 17 | 9 | 14 | | | 35 | Sutherland 1936; R433 |
| Chesterfield | D | 241 | | | | 11 | 16 | 63 | 11 | | 19 | Wade 1939 |
| Ashover | D/R | 238-44 | | | | 12 | 21 | 57 | 10 | | 42 | Peck 1922; R437 |
| Standish | D/R | 240-4 | 1 | 4 | 5 | 20 | 40 | 27 | 1 | | 98 | Leigh 1700, 81, 92-110; R442 |
| Edlington Wood | D/R | 248 | 1 | 0 | 1 | 33 | 40 | 23 | 1 | | 81 | Robertson 1935c |
| Edlington Wood | D/R | 258-9 | | | | 5 | 27 | 36 | 21 | 11 | 528 | Robertson 1935c |
| Barton on Humber | D/R | 253-60 | | | | 8 | 29 | 35 | 9 | 19 | 77 | Burnett & Williams 1986; R471 |
| Austerfield | D/R | 262 | | | | | 8 | 18 | 41 | 24 | 34 | Carson 1964 |
| Piercebridge | D/R | Gall/Post | | | | | | 1 | 1 | 59 | 128 | Casey & Coult 1977; R484 |
| Wortley | D/R | 269-70 | | | | 3 | 8 | 4 | 10 | 57 | 77 | Bland 1997b |
| Folds Farm | R | 270-3 | | | | | | | 0.5 | 4 | 1203 | Smedley 1946b |
| Mytholmroyd | R | 270-4 | | | | | | | 0.5 | 3 | 543 | Carson 1953b |
| Boothstown | R | 270-5 | | | | | | | | 4 | 542 | Carson 1947 |
| Drax | D/R | 275-6 | | | | 0.5 | 0.5 | 1 | 0 | 3 | 326 | Barclay 1997 |
| Throckley | R | Aurel | | | | | | | 0.5 | 2 | 4507 | Clayton 1880; R702 |
| Agden | R | 281-2 | | | | | | | 0.5 | 1 | 2319 | Thompson 1962; R741 |
| Maltby | R | 282 | | | | | | | 0.5 | 1 | 3488 | Carradice 1981; R763 |
| Kirmington | R | Prob | | | | | | | 0.5 | 0.5 | 8414 | Robertson 2000, no 751 |
| Normanby | R/D | 286-93 | | | | | | | | 0.5 | 45650 | Bland & Burnett 1988b; R854 |

**c) France**

| *Site* | *Denom.* | *Latest* | *VI* | *VIIa* | *VIIb* | *VIIIa* | *VIIIb* | *IXa* | *IXb* | *IXc* | *Total* | *Reference* |
|---|---|---|---|---|---|---|---|---|---|---|---|---|
| Amiens | D | 148-9 | 28 | | | | | | | | 43 | Foucray 1990 |
| Kervian-en-Camaret | D | 218-22 | 21 | 20 | 7 | 3 | 1 | | | | 279 | Aubin & Galliou 1979 |
| Bavay | R | 251-3 | | | | | 1 | 0 | 89 | 10 | 1290 | Delmaire 1992 |
| Nanterre | D/R | 255 | | | | 3 | 3 | 5 | 66 | 22 | 1859 | Le Gentilhomme 1946 |
| Sanssac L'Eglise | R | 256-8 | | | | | | | 58 | 42 | 38 | Christol 1976 |
| Raveau | D/R | 258-60 | 0.5 | 0 | 0.5 | 2 | 3 | 2 | 33 | 60 | 181 | Fabre & Mainjoinet 1958b |
| Clamerey | D/R | 259-60 | | | | | 2 | 0.5 | 38 | 60 | 1544 | Giard 1980 |
| Esbarres | D/R | 260 | 0.5 | 0 | 0 | 1 | 1 | 1 | 50 | 47 | 230 | Huvelin et al 1993 |
| Morthonniers | R | 260 | | | | | 2 | 0 | 50 | 49 | 121 | Cothenet 1974 |
| Sancey le Grand | D/R | 260 | 0.5 | 1 | 0 | 11 | 10 | 10 | 48 | 20 | 423 | Dayet 1960 |
| Ecluse de Creil I | R | 260 | | | | | 0.5 | 0 | 60 | 39 | 985 | Amandry *et al.* 1985 |
| Chalandry | R | 261-2 | | | | | | | 25 | 32 | 200 | Matton 1870 |
| Vannes | D/R | 262 | | | | 8 | 3 | 2 | 23 | 47 | 112 | Brenot 1963 |
| Châtenay sur Seine | R | 263 | | | | | 0.5 | 0 | 22 | 42 | 700 | Giard 1963 |
| Lassigny | D/R | 263 | | | | | 1 | 1 | 26 | 25 | 110 | Jouve 1994 |
| Noyers sur Serein | D/R | 263 | | | | | 1 | 0.5 | 56 | 17 | 436 | Fabre & Mainjoinet 1953a |
| Noyon | D/R | 263 | | | | 2 | 2 | 1 | 49 | 39 | 1146 | Amandry 1992 |
| Rouvroy les Merles | D/R | 263 | | | | 5 | 4 | 2 | 33 | 26 | 636 | Fabre & Mainjoinet 1954 |
| Guiry-en-Vexin | R | 263 | | | | | | | 10 | 45 | 606 | Foucray & Hollard 1990 |
| Saint-Boil | D/R | 263 | | | | 0.5 | 1 | 1 | 33 | 29 | 521 | Hollard & Aviseau-Broustet 1998 |
| Lassigny | D/R | 263 | | | | | 1 | 1 | 26 | 25 | 110 | Jouve 1994 |
| Noyon | D/R | 263 | | | | 2 | 2 | 1 | 49 | 39 | 1146 | Amandry 1992 |
| Rocquencourt | D/R | 266 | | | | | 0.5 | 0.5 | 23 | 31 | 4906 | Hollard & Gendre 1986 |
| Lewarde | R | 266 | | | | | | | 1 | 30 | 108 | Delmaire 1986 |
| Allonnes | D/R | 266 | | | | | 0.5 | 0 | 47 | 24 | 1015 | Giard 1962 |
| Souzy-la-Briche | D/R | 267 | | | | 1 | 1 | 2 | 69 | 24 | 5439 | Foucray 1995a |
| Cravent | D/R | 268 | 0.5 | 0.5 | 0.5 | 1 | 1 | 2 | 10 | 28 | 4404 | Hollard & Foucray 1995 |
| Mons-Boubert | D/R | 268 | | 0.5 | 0 | 1 | 1 | 2 | 21 | 22 | 571 | Amandry et al 1987 |
| Etaples | D/R | 268 | | | | 0.5 | 0.5 | 0 | 16 | 20 | 3834 | Delmaire & Coupppé 1988 |
| Autun | D/R | Post | | | | | 15 | 3 | 44 | 31 | 39 | Armand-Calliat & Viallefond 1958 |
| Courcité | R | 270 | | | | | | | 2 | 18 | 3134 | Aubin 1989 |
| Limours | R | 270 | | | | | | | 1 | 19 | 510 | Hollard 1995a |
| Auvilliers | R | 270 | | | | | | | | 0.5 | 907 | Fabre & Mainjoinet 1956 |
| Bonneuil sur Marne | R | 270 | | | | | | | 0.5 | 9 | 1759 | Giard 1966 |
| Chilleurs au Bois | R | 270 | | | | | | | 1 | 14 | 129 | Cothenet & Huvelin 1972 |
| Malicorne | R | 270 | | | | | | | 4 | 13 | 1041 | Giard 1966 |
| Tôtes | D/R | 270 | | | | | | 0.5 | 9 | 17 | 1392 | Fabre 1950 |
| Treffieux | R | 270 | | | | | | | | 8 | 815 | Fabre & Mainjoinet 1953b |
| Ecluse de Creil II | R | 273 | | | | | | | | 2 | 1437 | Amandry *et al.* 1985 |
| Coupvray | R | 272-4 | | | | 1 | 0 | 0 | 1 | 11 | 217 | Foucray 1995b |
| Allonnes | R | 274 | | | | | | | 0.5 | 2 | 3813 | Estiot et al 1986 |
| Montargis | R | 274 | | | | | 0.5 | 0 | 6 | 15 | 376 | Estiot 1992 |
| Morgat-en-Crozon | R | 274 | | | | | 0.5 | 0 | 5 | 8 | 1545 | Eveillard 1980 |
| Bourg Blanc | D/R | 274 | | | | 0.5 | 0 | 0 | 0 | 12 | 154 | Nuolet 1966 |
| Chézy sur Marne | R | 274 | | | | | | | 0.5 | 0.5 | 604 | Fabre & Mainjoinet 1958a |
| Forge les Bains | R | 274 | | | | | 0.5 | 0 | 0 | 0.5 | 878 | Dumas 1967 |
| Auxerre-Vaulabelle | R | 275 | | | | | | | 0.5 | 0.5 | 2151 | Hollard & Amandry 1997 |
| Mane Vechen | D/R | 280-2 | 0.5 | 0.5 | 0.5 | 0.5 | 1 | 0.5 | 22 | 12 | 21459 | André 2003 |
| Brains-sur-les-Marches | R | 282 | | | | | | | 0.5 | 2 | 4357 | Hollard & Lechat 2000 |
| Bavay | R | 289 | | | | | | | 0.5 | 0.5 | 6659 | Gricourt *et al* 1958 |

**d) Low Countries**

| *Site* | *Denom.* | *Latest* | *VI* | *VIIa* | *VIIb* | *VIIIa* | *VIIIb* | *IXa* | *IXb* | *IXc* | *Total* | *Reference* |
|---|---|---|---|---|---|---|---|---|---|---|---|---|
| Balloo | D | 180 | 55 | 35 | 1 | | | | | | 77 | Zadoks-Josephus Jitta 1956 |
| Bargercompascuum | D | 180 | 33 | 13 | 4 | | | | | | 309 | Zadoks-Josephus Jitta 1954 |

| Renkum | D | 197 | 42 | 41 | 9 | 0.5 | | | | | 245 | Zadoks-Josephus Jitta 1960a |
|---|---|---|---|---|---|---|---|---|---|---|---|---|
| Eghezée | D | 227 | 1 | 0 | 3 | 70 | 12 | 7 | | | 67 | Thirion 1967, 75 |
| Paal | D | 238 | 3 | 0 | 3 | 52 | 14 | 26 | | | 145 | Thirion 1967, 236 |
| Vilvoorde | D | 241 | | | | 25 | 25 | 44 | 6 | | 16 | Thirion 1967, 313A |
| Ellignies | D | 241-3 | | 1 | 0.5 | 38 | 31 | 29 | 0.5 | | 275 | Thirion 1967, 79A |
| Thuin | D/R | 246 | | | | 8 | 27 | 39 | 25 | | 102 | Thirion 1967, 293 |
| Eck en Wiel | D/R | 244-7 | | | | | 15 | 26 | 59 | | 34 | Zadoks-Josephus Jitta 1960b |
| Strijp | D/R | 249-51 | | | | 8 | 24 | 16 | 48 | 4 | 25 | Boersma 1963, 49 |
| Sterrebeck | D/R | 253 | | | | | 3 | 0.5 | 87 | 10 | 357 | Thirion 1967, 282 |
| Glavier | D/R | 254 | | | 0.5 | 12 | 23 | 29 | 31 | 4 | 1674 | Thirion 1967, 47B |
| Dailly | D/R | 253-7 | | | | 3 | 18 | 23 | 36 | 20 | 87 | Thirion 1967, 55 |
| St Oedenrode | D/R | 256-9 | | | | 4 | 23 | 35 | 33 | 5 | 168 | Boersma 1963, 56-7 |
| Harchies | D/R | 259-60 | 1 | 0 | 0 | 7 | 10 | 7 | 38 | 38 | 101 | Thirion 1967, 114 |
| Oombergen | D/R | 259-60 | | | | | 2 | 0.5 | 37 | 56 | 161 | Lallemand 1971 |
| Petit Rechain | R | 259-60 | | | | | | | 20 | 80 | 54 | Thirion 1967, 244 |
| Malonne | R | 260 | | | | | | | 20 | 80 | 115 | Thirion 1967, 180 |
| Maisières | R | 260 | | | | | 1 | 0 | 40 | 49 | 240 | Thirion 1967, 178 |
| Dailly | D/R | 261 | | | 0.5 | 2 | 2 | 5 | 30 | 56 | 214 | Thirion 1967, 54 |
| Basècles | R | 263 | | | | | | | 11 | 33 | 489 | Thirion 1967, 19 |
| Belsele | D/R | 263 | | | | 0.5 | 1 | 0.5 | 57 | 36 | 1527 | Thirion 1967, 23 |
| Denderleeuw | D/R | 263 | | | | 10 | 5 | 5 | 35 | 30 | 20 | Thirion 1967, 59 |
| Howardries II | R | 263 | | | | | | | 16 | 51 | 43 | Thirion 1967, 140 |
| Howardries III | R | 263 | | | | | 0.5 | 0 | 6 | 19 | 242 | Thirion 1967, 141 |
| Zottegem Velzeke II | D/R | 263 | 0.5 | 0.5 | 1 | 22 | 15 | 10 | 33 | 10 | 1059 | Thirion 1974a |
| Helmond | D/R | 262-5 | 12 | 4 | 4 | 4 | 0 | 0 | 4 | 0 | 25 | Boersma 1963, 45 |
| Grotenberge | R | 266-7 | | | | | | | 1 | 17 | 2381 | Thirion 1967, 114 |
| Thulin | D/R | 268 | | | | | 0.5 | 0 | 5 | 17 | 698 | Thirion 1967, 295 |
| Lompret | R | 268-9 | | | | | 0.5 | 0 | 74 | 23 | 370 | Thirion 1967, 173 |
| Andenne | R | 269-70 | | | | | | | 0.5 | 13 | 158 | Thirion 1967, 6 |

**e) Rhineland**

| *Site* | *Denom.* | *Latest* | *VI* | *VIIa* | *VIIb* | *VIIIa* | *VIIIb* | *IXa* | *IXb* | *IXc* | *Total* | *Reference* |
|---|---|---|---|---|---|---|---|---|---|---|---|---|
| Stockstadt | D | 167-8 | 32 | 6 | | | | | | | 1353 | Kellner *et al* 1975, 6020 |
| Fröndenburg | D | 175-6 | 5 | 1 | | | | | | | 257 | Korzus 1972, 5084 |
| Lashorst | D | 197 | 32 | 30 | 8 | 2 | | | | | 185 | Korzus 1973, 6089 |
| Flonheim | D | 198-200 | 31 | 25 | 33 | 2 | | | | | 301 | Franke 1960, 1023 |
| Waldkirch | D | 200-1 | 44 | 6 | 0 | 6 | | | | | 18 | Christ 1964a, 2062 |
| Vardingholt | D | 215 | 38 | 19 | 13 | 0 | 6 | | | | 16 | Korzus 1971, 4023 |
| Mainz | D | 217-8 | 2 | 18 | 10 | 49 | 8 | | | | 51 | Franke 1960, 1152 |
| Baden-Baden | D/R | 218-22 | 6 | 6 | 6 | 44 | 22 | | | | 18 | Christ 1964a, 2197 |
| Mainz | D | 222-8 | 13 | 13 | 4 | 42 | 12 | 0.5 | | | 186 | Franke 1960, 1153 |
| Saalburg | D | 226 | | | 4 | 26 | 39 | 30 | | | 23 | Jacobi 1897 |
| Unterdigisheim | D/R | 228-31 | 3 | 0 | 3 | 31 | 22 | 34 | | | 32 | Christ & Franke 1964, 3027 |
| Baden-Baden | D/R | 222-35 | 10 | 9 | 4 | 44 | 17 | 0.5 | | | 562 | Christ 1964a, 2196 |
| Einsiedel | D/R | 222-35 | 4 | 2 | 5 | 56 | 27 | 4 | | | 844 | Christ & Franke 1964, 3300 |
| Welzheim | D/R | 222-35 | 10 | 1 | 4 | 66 | 5 | 0.5 | | | 648 | Christ 1964b, 4596 |
| Köln | D/R | 235 | 9 | 9 | 1 | 32 | 30 | 4 | | | 254 | Hagen 1949 |
| Fridingen | D | 236 | | 6 | 0 | 38 | 25 | 31 | | | 16 | Christ & Franke 1964, 3280 |
| Mainz | D/R | 247 | | | | 3 | 19 | 26 | 52 | | 159 | Franke 1960, 1155 |
| Köngen | D/R | 246-8 | 0.5 | 0 | 1 | 16 | 23 | 32 | 27 | | 613 | Stribrny 1993, 71-122 |
| Mainz Kastel | D/R | 248-9 | | | | 13 | 21 | 46 | 21 | | 63 | Franke 1960, 1185 |
| Ladenburg | D/R | 249-51 | 2 | 0 | 0 | 19 | 19 | 33 | 20 | 2 | 64 | Christ 1963, 1144 |
| Ladenburg | D/R | 249-51 | 6 | 0 | 0 | 9 | 15 | 34 | 24 | 1 | 68 | Christ 1963, 1145 |
| Wiesbach | D/R | 251-3 | 0.5 | 0.5 | 1 | 16 | 17 | 30 | 34 | 1 | 402 | Kienast 1962, 1082 |
| Oberhersdorf | D/R | 251-3 | | | | | 12 | 12 | 56 | 20 | 25 | Binsfeld *et al* 1967 |
| Dalheim | D/R | 257 | | | | 10 | 32 | 30 | 22 | 3 | 50 | Weiller 1972, 78 |
| Neuhofen | R | 257 | | | | | 1 | 0 | 76 | 21 | 349 | Chantraine 1965, 2219 |
| Grosbous | D/R | 253-60 | | | | 2 | 18 | 11 | 33 | 37 | 57 | Weiller 1972, 154 |
| Leimersheim | D/R | 260 | | | | | 1 | 2 | 10 | 18 | 359 | Chantraine 1965, 2069 |
| Spesbach | D/R | 260 | | | | | 2 | 2 | 26 | 29 | 42 | Chantraine 1965, 2102 |
| Mainz | D/R | 261 | 0.5 | 0.5 | 0.5 | 5 | 11 | 13 | 51 | 18 | 1815 | Franke 1960, 1164 |
| Schwarzenacker | D/R | 261 | | | | | 1 | 0.5 | 64 | 28 | 4806 | Kienast 1962, 1023 |
| Ettelbruck | R | 262 | | | | | | | 13 | 28 | 598 | Weiller 1972, 123 |
| Bingen | D/R | 263 | 4 | 0 | 0 | 9 | 17 | 21 | 33 | 4 | 76 | Franke 1960, 1059 |
| Trier | R | 266 | | | | | | | | 13 | 211 | Binsfeld 1972 |
| Alzey | D/R | 268 | | | | 0.5 | 2 | 0.5 | 12 | 12 | 381 | Franke 1960, 1005 |
| Heidelberg | D/R | 260-8 | 3 | 0 | 2 | 25 | 25 | 16 | 12 | 1 | 130 | Christ 1963, 1064 |
| Contern | R | 260-9 | | | | | | | 48 | 26 | 109 | Weiller 1972, 72 |
| Orscholz | R | 270 | | | | | | | | 0.5 | 2773 | Keinast 1962, 1044 |
| Bischoffsheim | R | 275 | | | | | | | 0.5 | 1 | 8057 | Longuet & Banderet 1955 |
| Niederingelheim | R | 274-80 | | | | | | | | 0.5 | 1173 | Franke 1960, 1092 |
| Schwenningen | R | 283-5 | | | | | | | 0.5 | 3 | 168 | Christ & Franke 1964, 3220 |

**f) Danube region**

| *Site* | *Denom.* | *Latest* | *VI* | *VIIa* | *VIIb* | *VIIIa* | *VIIIb* | *IXa* | *IXb* | *IXc* | *Total* | *Reference* |
|---|---|---|---|---|---|---|---|---|---|---|---|---|
| Unterammergau | D | 184 | 9 | 3 | 1 | | | | | | 104 | Kellner 1960a, 1102 |
| Kösching | D | 196-211 | 13 | 6 | 6 | 25 | | | | | 16 | Kellner 1960a, 1114 |

| | | | | | | | | | | | | |
|---|---|---|---|---|---|---|---|---|---|---|---|---|
| Kempten | D/R | 226 | 17 | 18 | 8 | 12 | 13 | 3 | | | 640 | Alföldi *et al* 1962, 7186 |
| Sigmaringen | D | 228 | 2 | 2 | 2 | 43 | 30 | 11 | | | 44 | Nau 1971 |
| Rembrechts | D/R | 230 | 1 | 1 | 5 | 27 | 32 | 28 | | | 82 | Christ & Franke 1964, 3343 |
| Kirchmatting | D/R | 231 | 3 | 1 | 5 | 49 | 28 | 14 | | | 1169 | Kellner 1970, 2116 |
| Marnbach | D/R | 231 | 0.5 | 0 | 1 | 32 | 35 | 30 | | | 167 | Kellner 1960a, 1325 |
| Eining | D | 228-31 | 11 | 0 | 9 | 36 | 28 | 13 | | | 47 | Kellner 1970, 2034 |
| Kempten | D | 228-31 | 19 | 5 | 5 | 14 | 29 | 29 | | | 21 | Alföldi *et al* 1962, 7188 |
| Pfünz | D | 232 | 1 | 0 | 0 | 24 | 35 | 39 | | | 94 | Kellner 1963a, 5042 |
| Wiggensbach | D/R | 231-5 | 2 | 0.5 | 1 | 34 | 32 | 30 | | | 401 | Alföldi *et al* 1962, 7199 |
| Eining | D | 236 | | | | 20 | 35 | 40 | | | 20 | Kellner 1970, 2035 |
| Langengeisling | D | 236 | 3 | 0 | 2 | 32 | 31 | 30 | | | 96 | Kellner 1960a, 1054 |
| Neideraschau | D | 235-6 | 1 | 0.5 | 1 | 32 | 33 | 31 | | | 765 | Kellner 1960a, 1229 |
| Kösching | D/R | 241 | | | 1 | 17 | 36 | 45 | 0.5 | | 240 | Kellner 1960a, 1115 |
| Günzenhausen | D/R | 241-3 | | | 1 | 15 | 34 | 49 | 1 | | 309 | Kellner 1963a, 5057 |
| Burgau | D/R | 251-3 | | | | | 3 | 0 | 78 | 20 | 40 | Alföldi *et al* 1962, 7123 |
| Weissenburg | R | 251-3 | | | | | | | 63 | 37 | 30 | Kellner 1963a, 5100 |
| Mettenbach | R | 255-6 | | | | | | | 64 | 36 | 28 | Kellner 1970, 2075 |
| Klugham | D/R | 257-8 | | | | | 3 | 3 | 21 | 72 | 33 | Kellner 1960a, 1178 |
| Olgishofen | D/R | 258-9 | | | | | 2 | 0 | 63 | 34 | 41 | Alföldi *et al* 1962, 7160 |
| Pfakofen | D/R | 259-60 | 3 | 0 | 3 | 23 | 40 | 23 | 0 | 9 | 35 | Kellner & Overbeck 1978, 3040 |
| Regensburg | D/R | 260-8 | 1 | 0 | 0 | 0 | 1 | 0 | 2 | 19 | 118 | Kellner & Overbeck 1978, 3081 |
| Kisslegg | D/R | 268 | 4 | 0.5 | 1 | 28 | 18 | 21 | 19 | 6 | 274 | Christ & Franke 1964, 3338 |
| Regensburg | D/R | 283-4 | | | | 2 | 0 | 0 | 5 | 27 | 56 | Kellner & Overbeck 1978, 3082 |

# APPENDIX 2

## Percentages of bronze coins per period in hoards of the mid second to mid third centuries

For each hoard, for each period, the percentage of coins of that period in the hoard is given. Hoards indicated as mixed metal (e.g. Ae/D), only have the bronze percentages calculated.

Key: *Denomination:* Ae = bronze, D = denarius, R = radiate/antoninianus. *Reference:* R[number] = hoard reference number in Robertson 2000

**a) S Britain and Wales**

| *Site* | *Denom.* | *Latest* | *VI* | *VIIa* | *VIIb* | *VIIIa* | *VIIIb* | *IXa* | *IXb* | *IXc* | *Total* | *Reference* |
|---|---|---|---|---|---|---|---|---|---|---|---|---|
| Langford | Ae | 154-5 | 4 | | | | | | | | 25 | Burnett 1978; R167 |
| Croydon | Ae | 154-5 | 35 | | | | | | | | 267 | Walters 1907; R216 |
| Snettisham | Ae | 155 | 7 | | | | | | | | 27 | Burnett 1977; R202 |
| Warminster | Ae | 155 | 3 | | | | | | | | 37 | Williams & Leins 2002 |
| Bridport | Ae | 155-6 | 6 | | | | | | | | 47 | King 1997a |
| Croydon | Ae | 167-8 | 22 | 13 | | | | | | | 266 | Walters 1907 |
| Alrewas & Fradley | Ae | 169 | 14 | 3 | | | | | | | 36 | Abdy 2006 |
| Whitchurch | Ae | Aur | 24 | 12 | | | | | | | 17 | Sutherland 1939b |
| Upchurch | Ae | 180 | 16 | 16 | 3 | | | | | | 37 | Gray 1954 |
| Maidstone | Ae | 184 | 23 | 23 | 9 | | | | | | 57 | Cook 1936 |
| South Wonston | Ae | 192 | 26 | 20 | 9 | | | | | | 46 | Abdy & Chaitow 2002 |
| Great Chesterford | Ae | Comm | 25 | 2 | 0.5 | | | | | | 195 | Robertson 2000, no. 324 |
| Newchurch | Ae | 197 | 25 | 43 | 4 | 7 | | | | | 28 | Lyne & Abdy 2007 |
| Whiddon Down | Ae/D | 198 | 34 | 11 | 2 | 1 | | | | | 115 | Ghey & Moorhead 2009 |
| Curridge | Ae | 209 | 25 | 17 | 6 | 2 | | | | | 397 | Abdy *et al.* 2002 |
| Much Hadham | Ae/D | 210-1 | 17 | 17 | 8 | 0 | | | | | 36 | Burnett 1992b; R385A |
| Knapwell | Ae | Sev | 25 | 15 | 0 | 5 | | | | | 20 | Lewis 1877 |
| Leysdown | Ae | 260 | 21 | 28 | 9 | 1 | 0 | 1 | 0.5 | 0 | 495 | Carson 1971b |
| Ramsgate | Ae | 260 | 22 | 26 | 33 | 0 | 0 | 4 | 0 | 0 | 27 | Merrifield 1971 |
| Alcester | Ae | 265 | 29 | 31 | 14 | 0 | 2 | 0 | 0 | 0 | 49 | Carson 1969a |
| Ham Hill | Ae | Post | 26 | 27 | 6 | 1 | 0.5 | 2 | 0.5 | 0 | 749 | Seaby 1949; R506 |
| Gare | Ae | 267-70 | 25 | 33 | 11 | 2 | 0.5 | 2 | 0.5 | 0 | 1036 | Carson 1971a |
| Bourne End | Ae | 268-70 | 19 | 33 | 10 | 5 | 5 | 0 | 5 | 0 | 21 | Burnett 1977b |
| Albury | Ae | 270-5 | 19 | 31 | 10 | 0 | 2 | 3 | 7 | 0 | 58 | Evans 1870; R568 |

**b) N Britain**

| *Site* | *Denom.* | *Latest* | *VI* | *VIIa* | *VIIb* | *VIIIa* | *VIIIb* | *IXa* | *Ixb* | *Ixc* | *Total* | *Reference* |
|---|---|---|---|---|---|---|---|---|---|---|---|---|
| Manchester | Ae | Ant | 24 | | | | | | | | 42 | Conway *et al.* 1909, 18-28; R178 |
| Nottingham | Ae | 156-7 | 25 | | | | | | | | 44 | Robertson 2000, no. 204 |
| Longhorsley | Ae | 175 | 34 | 2 | | | | | | | 44 | Abdy 2003 |
| Hickleton | Ae/D | 180 | 9 | 0 | | | | | | | 35 | Leins 2001 |
| Owston Ferry | Ae | 196 | 23 | 13 | 4 | 0 | | | | | 113 | Carson 1953a |
| Letwell | Ae/R | 269 | 41 | 26 | 22 | 4 | 0 | 0 | 0 | 0 | 27 | Abdy 2006 |
| Adderstone | Ae | 270-5 | 8 | 38 | 15 | 8 | 8 | 0 | 0 | 0 | 13 | Archbold 1858 |

**c) France**

| *Site* | *Denom.* | *Latest* | *VI* | *VIIa* | *VIIb* | *VIIIa* | *VIIIb* | *IXa* | *IXb* | *IXc* | *Total* | *Reference* |
|---|---|---|---|---|---|---|---|---|---|---|---|---|
| Montigny sur Crécy | Ae | 174 | 40 | 8 | | | | | | | 461 | De Roquefeuil 1970 |
| Pécy | Ae | 188-9 | 24 | 20 | 4 | | | | | | 1127 | Amandry 1995 |
| Senlis | Ae | 190 | 17 | 19 | 6 | | | | | | 152 | Foucray 1993 |
| Woignarue | Ae | Comm | 23 | 25 | 9 | | | | | | 716 | Bompaire *et al.* 1987 |
| Paris | Ae | 230 | 29 | 29 | 18 | 0 | 0 | 6 | | | 17 | Brenot 1968 |
| Charny | Ae | 235 | 31 | 21 | 9 | 0 | 0 | 1 | | | 78 | Hollard 1989 |
| Germainville | Ae | 236-8 | 29 | 31 | 15 | 2 | 0 | 3 | | | 177 | Berdeaux-le Brazidec 2001 |
| Arnouville-lès-Gonesse | Ae | 238-9 | 25 | 22 | 10 | 2 | 0.5 | 1 | 0.5 | | 2375 | Turckheim-Pey 1981 |
| Epiais-Rhus | Ae | 241-3 | 26 | 23 | 8 | 1 | 0 | 2 | 1 | | 416 | Mitard 1985 |
| Villaines-la-Carelle | Ae | Gord III | 24 | 19 | 11 | 2 | 0 | 0.5 | 8 | | 254 | Hollard 2006 |
| Château Renaud | Ae | 248 | 24 | 24 | 8 | 4 | 1 | 6 | 2 | | 139 | Armand-Calliat 1956 |
| Couzeix | Ae | 244-9 | 21 | 22 | 10 | 2 | 0.5 | 3 | 1 | | 778 | Desnier 1985 |
| Celle-Conde | Ae | Phil | 22 | 17 | 11 | 0 | 0 | 0 | 0 | | 559 | Cothenet 1973 |
| Rouen | Ae/R | 253-4 | 24 | 23 | 12 | 3 | 0 | 1 | 0.5 | 0 | 701 | Hollard & Pilon 2006 |
| Paris | Ae | 255 | 21 | 29 | 21 | 7 | 0 | 0 | 0 | 0 | 70 | Blanchet 1927 |
| Thimert-Gâtelles | Ae | 260-1 | 20 | 41 | 11 | 5 | 1 | 3 | 0 | 0 | 132 | Hollard 1995b |
| Bourg-Blanc | Ae/R | 261 | 28 | 29 | 10 | 2 | 0.5 | 1 | 0.5 | 0 | 1198 | Amandry & Hollard 2006 |
| Landévennec | Ae | 261 | 26 | 13 | 3 | 0 | 0 | 0 | 6 | 0 | 31 | Hollard 1992a |
| Muirancourt | Ae | 261 | 20 | 28 | 4 | 2 | 0 | 0 | 2 | 0 | 46 | Bastien 1965 |
| Vannes | Ae | 262 | 19 | 30 | 11 | 2 | 0.5 | 3 | 1 | 0 | 458 | Brenot 1963 |
| Méricourt-l'Abbé | Ae | 266-7 | 10 | 12 | 3 | 0.5 | 0 | 0.5 | 0 | 0 | 477 | Gricourt & Hollard 1992 |
| Angicourt | Ae | Post | 16 | 23 | 6 | 2 | 2 | 13 | 2 | 0 | 131 | Blanchet 1900 |
| Dardez | Ae | Post | 35 | 28 | 15 | 3 | 0 | 2 | 2 | 0 | 123 | De Barthélémy 1874 |
| Tavers | Ae | 269 | 23 | 19 | 14 | 1 | 0 | 1 | 1 | 0 | 73 | Bastien & Cothenet 1975 |

**d) Low Countries**

| *Site* | *Denom.* | *Latest* | *VI* | *VIIa* | *VIIb* | *VIIIa* | *VIIIb* | *IXa* | *IXb* | *IXc* | *Total* | *Reference* |
|---|---|---|---|---|---|---|---|---|---|---|---|---|
| Humbeck | Ae | 186-7 | 20 | 30 | 5 | | | | | | 20 | Thirion 1974b |
| Meux | Ae | 186-7 | 14 | 12 | 2 | | | | | | 439 | Thirion 1967, 200 |
| Givenich | Ae | 195 | 23 | 19 | 15 | 4 | | | | | 26 | Weiller 1990, 188-9 |
| Flobecq | Ae | 195 | 24 | 29 | 6 | 2 | | | | | 95 | Thirion 1967, 91 |
| Destelbergen | Ae | 195-6 | 21 | 17 | 21 | 3 | | | | | 112 | Thirion 1967, 62 |
| Mélin | Ae | 213-7 | 24 | 23 | 12 | 0 | 1 | | | | 245 | Thirion 1967, 192 |
| Bornem | Ae | 215 | 10 | 23 | 44 | 21 | 3 | | | | 39 | Thirion 1967, 31 |
| Solre St Géry | Ae | 223 | 25 | 21 | 13 | 0 | 0 | 0 | | | 24 | Thirion 1967, 274 |
| Hautrage | Ae | 225 | 25 | 12 | 14 | 0 | 0 | 2 | | | 51 | Thirion 1967, 122 |
| Manage | Ae | 230 | 22 | 28 | 8 | 0 | 1 | 2 | | | 252 | Thirion 1967, 181 |
| Hautrage II | Ae | 222-35 | 22 | 22 | 11 | 2 | 0 | 2 | | | 123 | Thirion 1970 |
| Roksem | Ae | 238 | 26 | 29 | 16 | 0 | 0 | 0 | | | 38 | Thirion 1971 |
| Beveren Leie | Ae | 235-8 | 22 | 26 | 10 | 0.5 | 0 | 0.5 | | | 421 | Thirion 1967, 27 |
| Merelbeke III | Ae | 235-8 | 7 | 36 | 7 | 21 | 0 | 29 | | | 14 | Thirion 1967, 195 |
| Morialmé | Ae | 241-3 | 29 | 30 | 8 | 2 | 0 | 0 | 0 | | 126 | Thirion 1967, 210 |
| Mompach | Ae/R | 244-9 | 20 | 20 | 13 | 0 | 0 | 0 | 0 | | 15 | Weiller 1990, 291-3 |
| Strijp | Ae | 249-51 | 50 | 25 | 13 | 0 | 0 | 0 | 0 | 0 | 16 | Boersma 1963, 49 |
| Malonne | Ae | 260 | 19 | 32 | 21 | 4 | 0 | 0 | 0 | 0 | 57 | Thirion 1967, 180 |
| Froidmont | Ae | 260 | 22 | 12 | 9 | 0 | 1 | 0 | 0 | 0 | 135 | Thirion 1967, 102; Buttrey 1972, 46-7 |
| Petigny | Ae | 260 | 17 | 14 | 10 | 2 | 0 | 2 | 0 | 0 | 88 | Thirion 1967, 242 |
| Elverdinge | Ae | 262 | 18 | 16 | 7 | 2 | 0.5 | 0.5 | 0 | 0 | 589 | Thirion 1967, 80 |
| Werken | Ae | 266 | 10 | 20 | 25 | 0 | 0 | 0 | 0 | 0 | 20 | Thirion 1967, 331 |
| Nismes | Ae | 267-8 | 20 | 20 | 13 | 0 | 0 | 0 | 0 | 0 | 30 | Thirion 1967, 219 |
| Aardenburg | Ae | 273 | 13 | 38 | 0 | 0 | 0 | 13 | 0 | 0 | 8 | Boersma 1967 |

**e) Rhineland**

| *Site* | *Denom.* | *Latest* | *VI* | *VIIa* | *VIIb* | *VIIIa* | *VIIIb* | *IXa* | *IXb* | *IXc* | *Total* | *Reference* |
|---|---|---|---|---|---|---|---|---|---|---|---|---|
| Walheim | Ae | 156-7 | 49 | | | | | | | | 51 | Stribrny 1993, 176-80; Klein 2002, 578-81 |
| Zugmantel | Ae | 161-76 | 79 | 7 | | | | | | | 14 | Franke 1956 |
| Geilenkirchen | Ae | 186 | 29 | 24 | 10 | | | | | | 21 | Hagen 1956 |
| Faha | Ae | 196-211 | 27 | 22 | 5 | 0.5 | | | | | 681 | Kienast 1962, 1029 |
| Mainz Zahlbach | Ae | 196-211 | 20 | 22 | 11 | 2 | | | | | 114 | Franke 1960, 1203 |
| Scheidgen | Ae | 211-7 | 18 | 16 | 2 | 5 | 2 | | | | 44 | Weiller 1972, 308 |
| Heidelberg | Ae | 228 | 16 | 24 | 0 | 3 | 0 | 0 | | | 37 | Christ 1963, 1065 |

**f) Danube region**

| *Site* | *Denom.* | *Latest* | *VI* | *VIIa* | *VIIb* | *VIIIa* | *VIIIb* | *IXa* | *IXb* | *IXc* | *Total* | *Reference* |
|---|---|---|---|---|---|---|---|---|---|---|---|---|
| Bernbeuren | Ae | 185 | 26 | 38 | 10 | | | | | | 53 | Kellner 1960a, 1250 |
| Eining | Ae | 228-31 | 0 | 32 | 18 | 9 | 5 | 5 | | | 22 | Kellner 1970, 2034 |

**g) S and SW France**

| *Site* | *Denom.* | *Latest* | *VI* | *VIIa* | *VIIb* | *VIIIa* | *VIIIb* | *IXa* | *IXb* | *IXc* | *Total* | *Reference* |
|---|---|---|---|---|---|---|---|---|---|---|---|---|
| Naujac | Ae | 141-5 | 6 | | | | | | | | 140 | Nony 1961 |
| Seyssel | Ae | 177 | 41 | 44 | | | | | | | 188 | Audron 1997 |
| St Marcel d'Ardèche | Ae | 189 | 24 | 35 | 27 | | | | | | 85 | Vian & Bastien 1960 |
| Bordeaux | Ae | 197 | 31 | 34 | 5 | 1 | | | | | 86 | Buttrey 1972 |
| Lombez | Ae | 222/31 | 26 | 11 | 1 | 0 | 0.5 | 1 | | | 263 | Depeyrot *et al.* 1985 |
| Cestas | Ae | Alex | 25 | 27 | 10 | 0 | 0 | 2 | | | 93 | Jouannet 1840, Nony 1961 |
| Plaisians | Ae | 249/51 | 20 | 18 | 10 | 4 | 2 | 16 | 12 | 4 | 49 | Amandry & Hollard 1997 |

**h) Italy**

| *Site* | *Denom.* | *Latest* | *VI* | *VIIa* | *VIIb* | *VIIIa* | *VIIIb* | *IXa* | *IXb* | *IXc* | *Total* | *Reference* |
|---|---|---|---|---|---|---|---|---|---|---|---|---|
| Bassana | Ae | 193 | 31 | 29 | 14 | 5 | | | | | 109 | Horvat 1936 |
| Pozzuoli | Ae | 241-3 | 10 | 17 | 10 | 3 | 10 | 7 | 3 | | 30 | Stazio 1954 |
| S Martino del Pizzolano | Ae | 251-3 | 11 | 18 | 13 | 4 | 0.5 | 25 | 16 | 1 | 639 | Ambrosoli 1897 |
| Villaurbana, Sardinia | Ae | 251-3 | 5 | 5 | 2 | 2 | 1 | 36 | 44 | 2 | 293 | Taramelli 1915 |
| Roma | Ae | 260-1 | 1 | 4 | 1 | 0.5 | 0.5 | 15 | 35 | 41 | 610 | Cesano 1919 |

**i) N Africa**

| *Site* | *Denom.* | *Latest* | *VI* | *VIIa* | *VIIb* | *VIIIa* | *VIIIb* | *IXa* | *IXb* | *IXc* | *Total* | *Reference* |
|---|---|---|---|---|---|---|---|---|---|---|---|---|
| Algiers | Ae | Phil | 7 | 21 | 24 | 8 | 0 | 11 | 16 | | 119 | Mattingly 1945b |
| Cape Matafu | Ae | Dec | 9 | 18 | 11 | 6 | 2 | 19 | 21 | 2 | 130 | Boyce 1947 |
| Guelma | Ae | 255-7 | 7 | 9 | 4 | 1 | 1 | 29 | 33 | 11 | 7460 | Turcan 1963 |

# APPENDIX 3

## Zugmantel coin site-finds: further considerations

Given that the latest coins in the smaller coin groups may well not be reflecting the true period of deposition of these groups at Zugmantel, it remains to ask whether the *terminus ad quem* may in most cases actually be later than the latest coin. At Zugmantel we are fortunate in having a possible episode which may account for the deposition of the contexts in Table B, or at least a majority of them. The latest coins as a whole came from period IXb, when it is thought that sections of the German *limes* may have been abandoned. It is possible that the *vicus* at Zugmantel was abandoned at this time, therefore implying that the *terminus ad quem* for many of the deposits is in fact period IXb.

Table A shows the Zugmantel coins in relation to period IXb. The bottom row gives the period of the latest coin in each deposit (equivalent to totalling the rows in Chapter 3, Table 3.III), and shows what would be expected in the light of Table 3.III, that the majority of deposits, whatever their size, are earlier than IXb according to the latest coin, but most are within 3 periods. These could easily have been deposited in period IXb. It is also, of course, the case that some of the groups, particularly those with latest coins a lot earlier than IXb, may in fact have been deposited somewhat before the hypothetical IXb abandonment episode. The Table also shows the total coins in relation to period IXb. This reflects the overall pattern of Chapter 3, Table 3.II (silver later, bronze earlier), but in a more marked form. If the majority of these coins have a *terminus ad quem* of period IXb, we have in Table A a reflection of the circulation pattern prevalent at the time, a supposition which can be checked by reference to the data available from hoards, as considered in the main body of the chapter.

*Table A Zugmantel: coins in associated groups in relation to period IXb*

| | *Period and number of periods earlier than IXb* | | | | | | | | | | | | | |
|---|---|---|---|---|---|---|---|---|---|---|---|---|---|---|
| | *IXb* | *IXa* | *VIIIb* | *VIIIa* | *VIIb* | *VIIa* | *VI* | *V* | *IV* | *III* | *IIb* | *IIa* | *Ib* | *Ia* |
| | *0* | *1* | *2* | *3* | *4* | *5* | *6* | *7* | *8* | *9* | *10* | *11* | *12* | *13* |
| Silver | 10 | 30 | 26 | 47 | 7 | 11 | 10 | 6 | 12 | 18 | 1 | - | - | 3 |
| Bronze | - | - | 1 | - | 24 | 91 | 68 | 72 | 35 | 36 | 2 | 1 | 2 | 4 |
| Latest coin | 7 | 19 | 10 | 16 | 8 | 12 | 3 | 2 | - | - | - | - | - | - |

*Table B Zugmantel: associated groups of coins (Ar = silver, Ae = bronze)*

| *Context* | *Denom.* | *Period* | | | | | | | | | | | | | |
|---|---|---|---|---|---|---|---|---|---|---|---|---|---|---|---|
| | | *Ia* | *Ib* | *IIa* | *IIb* | *III* | *IV* | *V* | *VI* | *VIIa* | *VIIb* | *VIIIa* | *VIIIb* | *IXa* | *IXb* |
| 83 | Ar | - | - | - | - | - | - | - | - | - | 1 | 5 | 3 | 2 | - |
| 111 | Ar | - | - | - | - | - | - | - | - | - | - | - | - | 1 | - |
| | Ae | - | 1 | - | - | 2 | 2 | - | - | - | 1 | - | - | - | - |
| 120 | Ar | - | - | - | - | 1 | - | - | - | - | - | - | - | 1 | - |
| | Ae | - | - | - | - | - | - | 1 | 1 | - | - | - | - | - | - |
| 168 | Ar | - | - | - | - | - | 2 | - | 1 | 1 | 2 | - | - | - | - |
| | Ae | 1 | - | - | - | 3 | 8 | 8 | 6 | 10 | 3 | - | - | - | - |
| 171 | Ar | - | - | - | - | - | - | - | - | - | - | - | 2 | - | 1 |
| | Ae | - | - | - | - | 2 | 1 | 1 | 2 | 1 | - | - | - | - | - |
| 202 | Ar | - | - | - | - | 1 | - | - | - | - | - | - | - | - | - |
| | Ae | - | - | - | - | - | - | - | 1 | - | 1 | - | - | - | - |
| 208 | Ar | - | - | - | - | 3 | 1 | 1 | 1 | - | - | - | - | - | - |
| | Ae | - | - | - | - | - | - | - | - | 1 | - | - | - | - | - |
| 233 | Ar | - | - | - | - | - | - | - | - | - | - | 1 | - | - | - |
| | Ae | - | - | - | - | - | - | 1 | - | - | - | - | - | - | - |
| 234 | Ar | - | - | - | - | - | - | - | - | - | - | 2 | - | - | - |
| | Ae | - | - | - | - | - | - | - | - | 1 | - | - | - | - | - |
| 234a | Ae | - | - | - | - | - | - | 1 | 1 | 1 | 1 | - | - | - | - |
| 235 | Ar | - | - | - | - | - | - | 1 | - | - | - | 1 | 1 | - | - |
| | Ae | - | - | - | - | - | - | 1 | - | 2 | - | - | - | - | - |
| 236 | Ar | - | - | - | - | - | 2 | - | - | - | - | 2 | - | 1 | - |
| | Ae | - | - | - | - | - | - | - | - | 2 | - | - | - | - | - |
| 242 | Ar | - | - | - | 2 | - | - | - | - | 1 | - | - | - | 1 | - |
| | Ae | - | - | - | - | - | - | 1 | 1 | - | - | - | - | - | - |
| 245 | Ae | - | - | - | - | - | - | - | - | 2 | - | - | - | - | - |
| 255 | Ae | - | - | - | - | - | - | - | - | 2 | - | - | - | - | - |
| 261 | Ar | 1 | - | - | - | 5 | 1 | - | - | - | - | - | - | - | - |
| | Ae | - | - | - | - | - | - | 1 | - | 2 | 1 | - | - | - | - |

| *Context* | *Denom.* | *Period* | | | | | | | | | | | | | |
|---|---|---|---|---|---|---|---|---|---|---|---|---|---|---|---|
| 264 | Ar | - | - | - | - | 1 | - | - | - | - | - | 1 | - | 1 | - |
| 265 | Ae | - | - | - | - | - | - | 1 | 1 | - | 1 | - | - | - | - |
| 271 | Ae | - | - | - | - | - | 1 | - | 2 | 3 | - | - | - | - | - |
| 274 | Ar | - | - | - | - | - | - | 1 | - | - | - | 1 | - | - | - |
| | Ae | - | - | - | - | - | 1 | 1 | - | - | - | - | - | - | - |
| 277 | Ar | - | - | - | - | - | - | 1 | - | - | - | - | - | - | - |
| | Ae | - | - | - | - | 1 | - | 2 | - | - | - | - | - | - | - |
| 278 | Ar | - | - | - | - | - | - | - | - | - | - | 1 | - | - | - |
| | Ae | - | - | - | - | - | - | 1 | 2 | 1 | 1 | - | - | - | - |
| 284 | Ar | - | - | - | - | - | - | - | - | - | - | 1 | - | - | - |
| | Ae | - | - | - | - | - | - | 4 | - | - | - | - | - | - | - |
| 287 | Ar | - | - | - | - | - | - | - | 1 | 2 | - | 1 | - | - | - |
| | Ae | - | - | - | - | - | - | 3 | 1 | 4 | - | - | - | - | - |
| 296 | Ar | - | - | - | - | - | - | - | - | - | - | 1 | 1 | - | - |
| | Ae | - | - | - | - | - | - | 1 | 1 | 1 | - | - | - | - | - |
| 297 | Ar | - | - | - | - | - | - | - | 1 | - | - | - | - | - | - |
| | Ae | - | - | - | - | 1 | 1 | - | - | 1 | - | - | - | - | - |
| 300 | Ae | - | - | - | - | - | - | - | 3 | 1 | - | - | - | - | - |
| 301 | Ar | - | - | - | - | - | - | - | - | 1 | - | 1 | - | - | - |
| | Ae | - | - | - | - | 2 | - | - | - | - | - | - | - | - | - |
| 302c | Ar | - | - | - | - | - | - | - | - | - | - | 1 | 1 | 2 | - |
| | Ae | - | - | - | - | - | - | 1 | - | 2 | - | - | - | - | - |
| 304 | Ar | - | - | - | - | - | - | - | 1 | - | - | 2 | - | 1 | - |
| | Ae | - | - | - | - | 3 | - | - | - | - | - | - | - | - | - |
| 312a | Ar | - | - | - | - | 1 | - | - | - | - | 1 | - | 1 | - | - |
| | Ae | - | - | - | - | - | 1 | 1 | - | - | 2 | - | - | - | - |
| 312b | Ae | - | - | - | - | 1 | - | - | - | 2 | - | - | - | - | - |
| 313a | Ar | 1 | - | - | - | - | - | - | - | - | - | - | 1 | - | - |
| | Ae | - | - | - | - | 1 | 1 | 4 | 2 | 1 | - | - | - | - | - |
| 314 | Ar | - | - | - | - | - | - | - | - | - | - | 2 | - | - | - |
| | Ae | - | - | - | - | 1 | - | - | - | - | 1 | - | - | - | - |
| 315 | Ar | - | - | - | - | - | 1 | - | - | - | - | 1 | - | 2 | - |
| | Ae | - | - | - | - | 1 | 1 | 2 | 3 | 2 | - | - | - | - | - |
| 316 | Ar | - | - | - | - | - | - | - | - | - | - | - | 1 | 1 | - |
| | Ae | - | - | - | - | - | - | - | 2 | 1 | - | - | - | - | - |
| 317 | Ar | - | - | - | - | - | - | - | - | 1 | - | 1 | - | 1 | - |
| | Ae | - | - | - | - | - | - | - | 2 | 1 | - | - | - | - | - |
| 322 | Ar | - | - | - | - | 1 | - | - | - | - | - | - | - | - | 1 |
| | Ae | - | - | - | - | - | - | - | 2 | 1 | - | - | - | - | - |
| 323 | Ar | - | - | - | - | - | - | - | - | - | - | 1 | - | 2 | - |
| | Ae | - | - | - | - | 1 | - | - | - | 3 | - | - | - | - | - |
| 324 | Ar | - | - | - | - | - | 2 | 1 | - | - | - | - | - | - | 1 |
| | Ae | - | - | - | - | 1 | - | 1 | 1 | - | - | - | - | - | - |
| 331 | Ar | - | - | - | - | 1 | - | - | - | - | - | 1 | - | - | - |
| | Ae | - | - | - | 1 | - | 1 | 2 | 1 | 1 | - | - | - | - | - |
| 332 | Ar | - | - | - | - | - | 1 | 1 | - | - | - | 4 | 2 | - | 2 |
| | Ae | - | - | - | - | 3 | - | 3 | 2 | 2 | - | - | - | - | - |
| 333 | Ae | - | - | - | - | - | 1 | 1 | 1 | - | - | - | - | - | - |
| 334 | Ar | - | - | - | - | 1 | - | - | 1 | 1 | 1 | 1 | 2 | 2 | 3 |
| | Ae | - | - | - | - | - | 1 | 3 | 2 | 2 | 3 | - | - | - | - |
| 338 | Ar | - | - | - | - | - | - | - | - | - | - | 1 | 1 | - | - |
| | Ae | - | - | - | - | - | - | 2 | 1 | 1 | 1 | - | - | - | - |
| 339 | Ae | - | - | - | - | - | - | 1 | 1 | - | 1 | - | - | - | - |
| 340 | Ar | - | - | - | - | - | 1 | - | - | - | - | - | - | 1 | - |
| | Ae | - | - | - | - | - | 1 | - | 1 | 2 | 1 | - | - | - | - |
| 341 | Ae | - | - | - | - | - | - | - | 1 | 1 | - | - | - | - | - |
| 348 | Ar | - | - | - | - | - | - | - | - | 2 | - | - | - | - | 1 |
| | Ae | - | - | - | - | - | - | - | 1 | 2 | 1 | - | - | - | - |
| 351 | Ar | - | - | - | - | - | - | - | - | - | - | 1 | - | - | - |
| | Ae | - | - | - | - | 1 | - | - | - | - | - | - | - | - | - |
| 353 | Ar | - | - | - | - | - | - | - | - | - | - | 1 | - | - | - |
| | Ae | - | - | - | 1 | 1 | 2 | 2 | 2 | 2 | - | - | - | - | - |
| 356 | Ae | 2 | - | - | - | - | - | - | - | 2 | - | - | - | - | - |
| 359 | Ar | - | - | - | - | 1 | - | - | - | - | - | 1 | - | - | - |

| *Context* | *Denom.* | *Period* | | | | | | | | | | | | | |
|---|---|---|---|---|---|---|---|---|---|---|---|---|---|---|---|
| | Ae | - | - | - | - | - | - | 1 | - | - | - | - | - | - | - |
| 361 | Ar | - | - | - | - | - | - | - | - | - | - | - | 2 | - | - |
| | Ae | - | - | - | - | 1 | - | - | - | - | - | - | - | - | - |
| 364 | Ae | - | - | 1 | - | - | 1 | 1 | - | 1 | - | - | - | - | - |
| 366 | Ar | - | - | - | - | - | 1 | - | 1 | | - | 1 | 1 | 1 | 1 |
| | Ae | - | - | - | - | 1 | - | - | - | - | - | - | - | - | - |
| 367 | Ar | - | - | - | - | 1 | - | - | - | | - | 1 | - | - | - |
| | Ae | - | - | - | - | - | - | 2 | 1 | 2 | 1 | - | - | - | - |
| 367a | Ar | - | - | - | - | - | - | - | 1 | 1 | - | 3 | 2 | 3 | - |
| | Ae | - | - | - | - | - | 2 | 1 | 4 | 6 | 1 | - | - | - | - |
| 368 | Ar | - | - | - | - | - | - | - | - | - | - | - | 1 | - | - |
| | Ae | - | - | - | - | - | - | 1 | - | - | - | - | - | - | - |
| 369 | Ae | - | - | - | - | 1 | - | - | 1 | - | - | - | - | - | - |
| 370 | Ae | - | - | - | - | - | - | 5 | 2 | 2 | 1 | - | - | - | - |
| 373 | Ar | - | - | - | - | - | - | - | - | - | 2 | 1 | - | - | - |
| | Ae | - | - | - | - | - | - | - | - | 4 | - | - | - | - | - |
| 374 | Ar | - | - | - | - | - | - | - | - | - | - | - | 2 | - | - |
| | Ae | - | - | - | - | - | - | - | 1 | 1 | - | - | - | - | - |
| 375 | Ae | - | - | - | - | - | 1 | - | 1 | 4 | 1 | - | - | - | - |
| 376 | Ar | - | - | - | - | - | - | - | - | - | - | 1 | 1 | 1 | - |
| | Ae | 1 | 1 | - | - | 3 | 4 | 2 | 1 | 1 | 1 | - | - | - | - |
| 379 | Ar | - | - | - | - | - | - | - | - | - | - | - | - | 1 | - |
| | Ae | - | - | - | - | - | - | - | 1 | - | - | - | - | - | - |
| 385 | Ae | - | - | - | - | - | 1 | 1 | 2 | - | - | - | - | - | - |
| 386 | Ar | - | - | - | - | - | - | - | - | - | 1 | - | - | - | - |
| | Ae | - | - | - | - | - | 3 | 1 | 2 | - | 1 | - | 1 | - | - |
| 390 | Ae | - | - | - | - | - | - | - | - | 2 | - | - | - | - | - |
| 393 | Ar | - | - | - | - | - | - | - | - | - | - | - | - | 2 | - |
| | Ae | - | - | - | - | - | - | - | 1 | - | - | - | - | - | - |
| 394 | Ar | - | - | - | - | 1 | - | - | 2 | - | - | - | - | 2 | - |
| | Ae | - | - | - | - | 3 | 1 | 1 | 1 | 1 | - | - | - | - | - |
| 396 | Ar | - | - | - | - | - | - | - | - | - | - | 1 | - | 1 | - |
| | Ae | - | - | - | - | 1 | - | - | 1 | - | - | - | - | - | - |
| 401 | Ar | - | - | - | - | - | - | - | - | - | - | 1 | - | - | - |
| | Ae | - | - | - | - | - | - | - | 1 | 1 | - | - | - | - | - |
| 409 | Ar | 1 | - | - | - | 1 | - | - | - | - | - | - | - | - | - |
| | Ae | - | - | - | - | - | - | - | - | 1 | - | - | - | - | - |
| 427 | Ar | - | - | - | - | - | - | - | - | - | - | 1 | - | - | - |
| | Ae | - | - | - | - | - | - | 1 | - | 1 | - | - | - | - | - |
| 429 | Ar | - | - | - | - | - | - | - | - | - | - | 1 | 1 | - | - |
| | Ae | - | - | - | - | - | - | - | 1 | 1 | - | - | - | - | - |
| 437 | Ae | - | - | - | - | 1 | - | 5 | - | - | - | - | - | - | - |
| 439/40 | Ar | - | - | - | - | - | - | - | - | 1 | - | - | - | - | - |
| | Ae | - | - | - | - | 1 | - | 1 | - | - | - | - | - | - | - |

# APPENDIX 4

## Concordance Table of Argonne potters and ovolos

| *Ovolo* | | | | *Potter* |
|---|---|---|---|---|
| Fölzer 1913 | Ricken 1934 | Oswald 1945 | Chenet & Gaudron 1955 | |
| 454 | - | - | 02 | - |
| 455 | D | - | R7 | Tribunus |
| 457 | - | XLVII | U3 | Tocca |
| 461 | A | I | - | Gesatus |
| 462 | - | L | S6-7 | Tocca |
| 464 | B | II | T4 | Gesatus, Tribunus |
| 465 | G | XI | R5 | Germanus |
| 466 | - | - | X1 | Tribunus? |
| - | E | XXVIII? | V3-4? | Tribunus?, Tocca? |
| VII, no. 54 | F | - | - | - |
| - | C | XXV | T1 | Tribunus, Tocca |
| - | - | XXIV | V1? | Tribunus |
| - | - | XII | V5-6 | Germanus |

# APPENDIX 5

## RHEINZABERN: COMPARISON OF STYLISTIC GROUPS AND CHRONOLOGY

Ricken[1] gave a sequence of potters in his volume of plates illustrating decorative styles of Rheinzabern potters (Table A), which has been utilised widely in a chronological sense, running from early to late. Ricken himself did not date the potters, and the work was essentially a stylistic sequence. It was supplemented by a text volume, analyzing the figure-types, now the standard reference, and a new edition of the plates.[2]

*Table A Sequence of potters in Ricken & Thomas 2005*

Janu I, Reginus I, Janu II, Cobnertus I-III, Firmus I, B F Attoni, Cerialis I-VI, Cerialis group wares A & B, Arvernicus-Lutaevus, Comitialis I-VI, Belsus I-II, Castus, Respectus, Florentinus, E25/26, Mammilianus, Firmus II, Belsus III, Iustinus, Iuvenis I, Pupus-Iuvenis II, Pupus, Atto, Reginus II, Reginus II-Virilis, Augustinus I-III, Julius I, Lupus, Lucanus I-II (=E8), Victorinus I, Verecundus I-II, Peregrinus, Helenius, Attillus, Marcellus I-II, Augustalis, Primitivus I-IV, Julius II-Julianus I, Victorinus II-III, E 48/49, Respectinus I-II, wares A & B with 0 382/383, Victor I, Victor II-Januco, Victor III, Perpetuus, Pervincus I-II (= E31), Regulinus, E30/34, Julianus II, Statutus I-II, Marcellinus, Severianus, Severianus-Gemellus

Bernhard[3] reviewed the earlier work by Ricken, and the work on absolute chronology and groupings derived from it, as given by Karnitsch, Walke, Simon, Pferdehirt and others.[4] He went on to present a correlation table of links between potters (Table B), on the basis of sharing of figure-types, and presented 3 main groups and subdivisions. His groups have been widely used (as indeed in this volume for the analysis in chapter 5), and were reviewed in relation to other production centres by Heiligmann.[5]

*Table B Grouping of potters in Bernhard 1981a, as used in the present volume for the analysis in chapters 4 & 5*

Ia c AD 140-70
Janu I, Reginus I, Cobnertus I-III, Firmus I
Ib c AD 170-early 3rd century
Cerialis I-V, Arvernicus-Lutaevus, Comitialis I-III, Belsus I, Lucanus, Reginus II-Virilis, Cerialis group wares A & B
IIa dated as Ib, probably starting later
Comitialis IV-VI, B F Attoni, Belsus II-III, Cerialis VI, Castus, Respectus, Florentinus, Mammilianus, Firmus II, Iustinus, Iuvenis I, Pupus-Iuvenis II, Pupus, Atto, Reginus II, Attillus, Augustinus I, E25/26
IIb dated as IIa, probably starting later
Augustinus II-III, Julius I, Lupus, Victorinus I, E8
IIc probably early third century
Verecundus I-II, Regulinus, Peregrinus, Helenius, Marcellus I-II, Augustalis, Primitivus I-IV, wares A & B with 0 382/383
IIIa c AD 230-260
Julius II-Julianus I, Victorinus II-III, Janu II, Respectinus I-II, Marcellinus, E 48/49
IIIb c AD 230 or later - 275
Victor I, Victor II-Januco, Victor III, Perpetuus, Julianus II, Statutus I-II, Severianus, Severianus-Gemellus, Pervincus, E30/34, E31, E35

Bittner[6] took Bernhard's correlation analysis further (Table C), drawing extensively on stratified deposits at Rheinzabern (see Gazetteer **B 149**). His proposal to move Janu II earlier was criticised by Gimber,[7] who also had reservations on the overall methodology. Gimber's own work on Janus provided a full conspectus of one of the most significant potter's workshops at Rheinzabern.[8]

[1] Ricken 1942 [1st ed.]; 1948 [2nd ed.].
[2] Ricken & Fischer 1963; Ricken & Thomas 2005.
[3] Bernhard 1981a, 79-81.
[4] Karnitsch 1955; 1959; Walke 1964; Simon 1968; Pferdehirt 1976.
[5] Heiligmann 1990, 159-63.
[6] Bittner 1986; 1996.
[7] Gimber 1999. See also discussion in Zanier 1994, esp. 66-7.
[8] Gimber 1993.

*Table C Grouping of potters in Bittner 1986, Tabelle 10*

Ia 148-53
Janu I
Ia to 160
Cobnertus I-III, Reginus I, Janu II
Ib 160-90
Cerialis I-VI, Cerialis group wares A & B, Arvernicus-Lutaevus, Lucanus, Comitialis I-VI, B F Attoni, Atto, Attillus, Firmus I-II, Belsus I-III, Castus, Respectus, Mammilianus, Florentinus, Iustinus, Iuvenis I, Pupus-Iuvenis II, Pupus, E25/26, Reginus II, Reginus II-Virilis
II 190/210-235/45
Verecundus I-II, Peregrinus, Helenius, Perpetuus, Marcellus I-II, Augustalis, Primitivus I-IV, Pervincus I-II (= E31), Regulinus, E8, Victorinus I-II, Lupus, Julius I-Lupus, Julius I, Julius II-Julianus I, Julianus II, Augustinus I-III, Respectinus I-II, Marcellinus, E30/34, Statutus I-II, wares A & B with O 382/383, Victor I, Victor II-Januco
II after 235/45-260/75
Severianus, Severianus-Gemellus, E35, Victor III (?), Victorinus III (?)

A new direction in analysis was taken by Mees,[9] who discarded the previous correlation analysis on statistical grounds, and instead of the Yule coefficient, used the Jaccard coefficient to establish a series of 7 groups (Table D).[10] Mees stressed that this was a stylistic analysis of the use and sharing of figure-types amongst potters, and had no chronological significance. However, Mees equated his groups 1 and 3 with the Bernhard/Bittner group I, his groups 4-7 with Bernhard/Bittner group II, and his group 2 with the late Bernhard/Bittner group III. Further work proposed a chronological framework for the Jaccard groups,[11] based on a correlation matrix between the potters and various dated sites. This resulted in a modification, so that there was an early group (1 and 3), a middle group (4-6) and a late group 7 and 2), with absolute dates for circulation of wares of the major potters (Table E).

*Table D Grouping of potters, and sequence of groups in Mees 1993, Abb. 3 and 1994a, fig. 3*

| | |
|---|---|
| 1 | Ianu[arius] I, Cerialis I-VI, Cerialis group A & B, Arvernicus-Lutaevus, Comitialis I-III, Belsus I, Lucanus, Cobnertus I |
| 3 | Cobnertus II-III, Firmus I, B F Attoni = Atto I |
| 4 | Comitialis IV, Comitialis VI, Pupus, Pupus-Iuvenis II, Castus, Belsus II-III, E 25, Florentinus, Respectus, Atto II, Helenius, Primitivus I-IV, Marcellus II, Attillus, Augustalis |
| 6 | Verecundus I-II, Peregrinus |
| 5 | Firmus II, Iustinus, Reginus II, Iulius I, Lupus, E 8 = Lucanus II, Pervincus I, Iuvenis I, Victorinus I, Regulinus |
| 7 | Ware B with O 382/383, Victor I, Victor II-Ianuco, Victor III, Statutus I |
| 2 | Ianu[arius] II, Iulius II-Iulianus I, Victorinus II, Respectinus I-II, E 49, Severianus, Marcellinus |
| None | Mamillianus, Ware A with O 382/383, Iulianus II, Perpetuus, Reginus I, E 34/30, Comitialis V, Marcellus I, Victorinus III, Statutus II, Pervincus II, Reginus II-Virilis, Augustinus I-III |

*Table E Dating for the Hauptumlaufzeiten (main circulation periods) of the major Rheinzabern potters, from Kortüm & Mees 1998, 162*

| | |
|---|---|
| Ianu I, Reginus I, Cobnertus I-III | 150/60-190/200 |
| Cerialis I-V | 160/70-220/30 |
| Comitialis I-VI | 170/80-230/40 |
| Primitivus I-VI, Iulius I | 190/200-250/60 |
| Julius II, Victor | 220/30-260/70 |

For further bibliography on Rheinzabern, see Appendix 10, sv Rheinzabern, F11.

[9] Mees 1993; 1994a; 2000; 2002.
[10] Cf. Jackson *et al.* 1989 for a critique of the different types of similiarity coefficient.
[11] Kortüm & Mees 1998, Abb. 1 & 4.

# APPENDIX 6

## THE EXTENT OF RESIDUALITY, AND THE ESTIMATED DATE-RANGE OF THE DEPOSITS GIVEN IN THE GAZETTEER, SECTIONS A-C.

Key: Residual element, * little or none, ** some residual pieces, *** badly affected;
Rate of accumulation, * slow, ** average, *** fast;
Overall reliability, ** average, *** good; U, unkown, -, inapplicable
For Deposit type see Chapter 4.

| Gazetteer number | Site name | Deposit type | Residual element | Rate of accumulation | Quality of excavation | Overall reliability | Coin date | Estimated date of loss |
|---|---|---|---|---|---|---|---|---|
| A1 | Alchester | E | ** | U | C | * | Xa | Xb |
| A2 | Bainbridge | E | * | *** | A | *** | VI | VIIa-Xa |
| A3 | Benwell | E | * | *** | B | ** | VIIb | VIIIa-IXb |
| A4 | Benwell | B | * | ** | A | *** | VIIIa | VIIIa-IXc |
| A5 | Bermondsey | E | * | * | A | ** | VIIb | VIIIa-Xa |
| A6 | Birdoswald | F | * | - | B | * | VIIIb | VIIIb-IXa |
| A7 | Birrens | E | * | *** | A | *** | VI | VIIa-VIIb |
| A8 | Bitterne | E | ** | U | A | * | Xa | Xa |
| A9 | Bitterne | B | ** | ** | A | * | Xb | Xb |
| A10 | Bitterne | B | * | ** | A | ** | Xb | Xb |
| A11 | Boxmoor | E | * | *** | A | *** | VIIIb | VIIIb-IXc |
| A12 | Bradford Down | C | ** | U | A | ** | XI | XI |
| A13 | Braintree | C | * | ** | A | ** | Xa | Xa |
| A14 | Brampton | C | ** | *** | A | *** | VI | VIIa-Xa |
| A15 | Brentford | C | * | ** | A | *** | Xb | Xb |
| A16 | Brentford | E | ** | U | A | ** | V | VI-IXc |
| A17 | Brentford | D | ** | ** | A | ** | Xb | Xb |
| A18 | Brentford | D | * | U | A | ** | VIIIb | VIIIb-IXa |
| A19 | Brockworth | D | ** | * | A | * | Xb | Xb |
| A20 | Caerleon | F | U | - | B | * | VI | VIIa-Xa |
| A21 | Caerleon | B | * | ** | A | *** | VIIa | VIIb-IXc |
| A22 | Caerleon | E | *** | * | A | * | VIIIa | VIIIa-VIIIb |
| A23 | Caerleon | B | ** | ** | A | ** | - | VIIIb+ |
| A24 | Caerleon | B | * | U | A | ** | VI | VIIIa-Xa |
| A25 | Caerleon | E | ** | ** | B | ** | IXa | IXa |
| A26 | Caerleon | F | * | - | A | ** | - | VIIIb+ |
| A27 | Caerleon | E | *** | *** | A | * | Xb | Xb |
| A28 | Caerleon | E | * | *** | A | *** | VIIIa | VIIIa-IXb |
| A29 | Caernarvon | D | * | *** | A | *** | VI | VI-VIIIb |
| A30 | Caerwent | E | ** | *** | A | ** | VIIIb | VIIIb |
| A31 | Canterbury | C | * | ** | A | ** | Xb | Xb |
| A32 | Canterbury | C | ** | *** | A | ** | VI | VIIa-Xa |
| A33 | Canterbury | E | *** | U | A | * | VIIa | VIIa-VIIIa |
| A34 | Canterbury | E | ** | U | A | ** | Xb | Xb |
| A35 | Canterbury | C | ** | *** | A | ** | Xa | Xa |
| A36 | Canterbury | B | * | ** | A | ** | VIIa | VIIb-VIIIb |
| A37 | Canterbury | B | * | * | A | ** | Xb | Xb |
| A38 | Carmarthen | C | ** | U | A | * | XII | XII |
| A39 | Carpow | F | * | *** | A | *** | VIIIb | VIIIb |
| A40 | Carrawburgh | E | * | ** | A | ** | VIIIa | VIIIa-IXb |
| A41 | Chester | C | * | ** | A | ** | Xb | Xb |
| A42 | Chester | C | * | *** | A | *** | VIIIb | IXa-IXc |
| A43 | Chester | C | * | *** | A | *** | IXa | IXa-IXb |
| A44 | Chester | F | * | U | B | * | VIIa | VIIb-IXa |
| A45 | Chester | E | * | * | B | * | Xb+ | Xb+ |
| A46 | Chichester | C | ** | U | A | * | III | III-VIIIa |
| A47 | Chichester | D | ** | ** | A | * | Xb | Xb |

| | | | | | | | | |
|---|---|---|---|---|---|---|---|---|
| A48 | Colchester | E | * | *** | C | ** | VIIa | VIIIa-IXb |
| A49 | Colchester | G | ** | * | A | * | Xb | Xb |
| A50 | Colchester | B | * | ** | A | *** | VIIIb | VIIIb |
| A51 | Colchester | E | * | ** | A | *** | Xa | Xa |
| A52 | Colchester | C | * | * | A | * | XII | XII |
| A53 | Combe Hay | E | *** | ** | A | * | XII | XII |
| A54 | Corbridge | E | * | *** | A | *** | VI | VIIa-VIIIa |
| A55 | Corbridge | E | * | *** | A | ** | VIIa | VIIa-VIIIb |
| A56 | Cox Green | F | * | - | A | ** | IV-VIIIb | VIIIa-Xa |
| A57 | Dorchester | B | * | ** | A | * | VI | VIIa-Xa |
| A58 | Dorchester | B | * | *** | A | *** | VIIb | VIIIb-Xa |
| A59 | Dorchester | E | * | U | A | ** | Xb | Xb |
| A60 | Dover | E | ** | * | A | * | VIIa | VIIb-IXc |
| A61 | Dover | C | * | U | A | ** | VI | VIIa-IXc |
| A62 | Dover | B | * | ** | A | *** | VIIIa | VIIIa-IXa |
| A63 | Dover | B | * | ** | A | *** | V | V-VIIIa |
| A64 | Dover | E | * | ** | A | ** | VI | VIIa-Xa |
| A65 | Dover | B | * | ** | A | *** | VIIa | VIIa-VIIIb |
| A66 | Dover | E | ** | ** | A | ** | IXb | IXb |
| A67 | Dover | E | ** | *** | A | * | Xb | Xb |
| A68 | Ebchester | E | ** | * | A | * | Xb | Xb |
| A69 | Enfield | C | * | ** | A | ** | VIIb | VIIIa-IXc |
| A70 | Enfield | C | ** | ** | A | * | Xb | Xb |
| A71 | Fordcroft | C | ** | * | A | * | XI | XI |
| A72 | Gloucester | B | *** | * | A | * | VIIIa | VIIIa-IXc |
| A73 | Gloucester | E | *** | * | A | * | XII | XII |
| A74 | Holcombe | B | * | ** | A | ** | Xb | Xb |
| A75 | Housesteads | G | * | * | A | ** | VI | VI-VIIb |
| A76 | Ilchester | C | * | U | A | ** | VIIb | VIIIa-Xa |
| A77 | Joyden's Wood | D | * | *** | A | ** | VI | VIIa-Xa |
| A78 | Latimer | B | * | U | A | ** | IV | V-VIIb |
| A79 | Leicester | E | ** | ** | A | ** | VIIa | VIIb-IXc |
| A80 | Leicester | E | ** | ** | A | ** | VIIa | VIIa |
| A81 | Leicester | E | ** | ** | A | ** | VI | VIIa-IXb |
| A82 | Leicester | E | * | ** | A | ** | VIIIa | VIIIa-IXc |
| A83 | Lincoln | E | ** | *** | A | * | VIIb | VIIIa-Xa |
| A84 | Lincoln | E | ** | ** | A | ** | VIIb | VIIIa-Xa |
| A85 | Lincoln | E | ** | *** | A | ** | III | V-VIIIa |
| A86 | Little Chester | C | ** | U | C | * | IXa | IXa-IXc |
| A87 | London | C | * | U | A | ** | IV | VI-Xa |
| A88 | London | G | * | * | A | ** | VI | VIIa-IXa |
| A89 | London | G | * | ** | A | *** | VI | VIIa-Xa |
| A90 | London | E | * | *** | A | *** | VIIIb | VIIIb |
| A91 | *Margidunum* | E | * | U | C | ** | VI | VIIa-Xa |
| A92 | *Margidunum* | E | ** | U | A | ** | VI | VIIa-Xa |
| A93 | Maryport | E | ** | * | A | * | VIIa | VIIIb-Xa |
| A94 | Mumrills | E | * | *** | A | *** | VI | VI-VIIIb |
| A95 | Nettleton | E | * | U | A | * | VI | VIIa-Xa |
| A96 | Nettleton | B | * | U | A | ** | VI | VIIa-Xa |
| A97 | Newhaven | D | * | ** | A | ** | VI | VIIb-IXc |
| A98 | Old Ford | B | * | * | A | ** | Xb | Xb |
| A99 | Portchester | F | * | - | A | ** | XI | XI+ |
| A100 | Rapsley | F | ** | - | A | ** | VIIa | VIIb-IXc |
| A101 | Richborough | D | ** | *** | C | * | Xb | Xb |
| A102 | Rochester | E | ** | *** | A | ** | VIIa | VIIa-VIIIb |
| A103 | Scole | B | ** | ** | A | ** | Xa | Xa |
| A104 | Scole | B | * | ** | A | ** | Xb | Xb |
| A105 | Silchester | D | ** | ** | A | ** | VIIa | VIIIa-IXc |
| A106 | Silchester | E | * | *** | A | ** | VIIIa | VIIIa-IXc |
| A107 | Silchester | E | ** | ** | A | * | Xb | Xb |
| A108 | South Shields | E | * | U | A | ** | VIIIa | VIIIb-IXc |
| A109 | South Shields | E | * | U | A | ** | IV | VI-IXc |
| A110 | South Shields | E | * | U | A | ** | VIIIb | VIIIb-IXb |
| A111 | Springhead | B | ** | ** | A | ** | IXa | IXa-IXb |
| A112 | Springhead | B | ** | ** | A | ** | VI | VIIa-IXb |

| | | | | | | | | |
|---|---|---|---|---|---|---|---|---|
| A113 | Springhead | B | ** | ** | A | ** | VI | VI-VIIIb |
| A114 | Springhead | F | * | - | A | ** | VI | VIIa-Xa |
| A115 | Springhead | B | * | ** | A | ** | VI | VIIa-Xa |
| A116 | Springhead | E | * | ** | A | ** | VI | VIIa-IXb |
| A117 | Springhead | C | ** | * | C | * | XI | XI |
| A118 | Staines | C | ** | * | A | * | VIIIb | VIIIb-IXc |
| A119 | Stonham Aspal | D | * | ** | A | *** | IXa | IXa-IXc |
| A120 | Thorplands | C | * | *** | A | *** | VIIIb | VIIIb-IXc |
| A121 | Towcester | C | * | ** | A | ** | VI | VIIb-Xa |
| A122 | *Verulamium* | E | * | *** | A | *** | VIIa | VIIa-VIIb |
| A123 | *Verulamium* | E | * | ** | A | *** | VI | VI-VIIIa |
| A124 | *Verulamium* | E | * | ** | A | ** | VIIIa | VIIIa-IXb |
| A125 | Watercrook | E | ** | U | A | ** | Xb | Xb |
| A126 | Whitchurch | E | * | ** | A | ** | Xb | Xb |
| A127 | Wiggonholt | C | ** | * | A | * | Xa | Xa |
| A128 | Winchester | E | ** | *** | A | * | VIIb | VIIIa-Xa |
| A129 | Winchester | B | * | * | A | ** | Xb | Xb |
| A130 | Wroxeter | E | * | U | A | ** | VIIIb | VIIIb-IXc |
| A131 | Wroxeter | E | * | *** | A | *** | VI | VI |
| A132 | Wroxeter | E | * | *** | B | *** | VIIa | VIIb-IXc |
| A133 | York | D | * | ** | A | ** | VIIb | VIIIa-Xa |
| A134 | York | B | * | ** | A | ** | VIIIa | VIIIa-IXc |
| A135 | York | E | * | ** | A | ** | VIIIa | VIIIa-IXc |
| A136 | York | E | * | *** | A | *** | VI | VIIa-VIIIb |
| A137 | Cosne | E | * | ** | A | ** | V | VIIa-Xa |
| A138 | Keradennec | B | * | ** | A | ** | VIIb | VIIb-IXc |
| A139 | La Roche-Maurice | E | * | *** | A | ** | V | VIIb-IXc |
| A140 | Lewarde | B | * | ** | A | ** | VIIa | VIIa |
| A141 | Limoges | C | ** | *** | A | ** | Xb | Xb |
| A142 | Malain | E | * | *** | A | *** | IXb | IXb-IXc |
| A143 | Merlines | B | * | U | C | ** | VIIa | VIIb-IXa |
| A144 | St Martial | A | * | *** | C | *** | VIIb | VIIIa-Xa |
| A145 | St Thiboult | E | ** | *** | C | * | XII | XII+ |
| A146 | Titelberg | E | * | *** | A | *** | Xb | Xb |
| A147 | Braives | C | * | U | A | ** | VIIa | VIIb-Xa |
| A148 | Gerpinnes | A | * | *** | B | ** | VIIa | VIIb-IXc |
| A149 | Haccourt | E | ** | *** | B | ** | Xa | Xa |
| A150 | Jette | E | * | *** | A | *** | IXc | IXc |
| A151 | Pommeroeul | E | ** | ** | A | ** | IXc | IXc |
| A152 | Tongeren | D | * | U | B | ** | VIIIb | VIIIb-IXc |
| A153 | Tongeren | E | * | ** | B | ** | IXb | IXb-IXc |
| A154 | Tournai | B | * | U | A | ** | Xb | Xb |
| A155 | Druten | B | * | *** | A | *** | VIIb | VIIb-Xa |
| A156 | Rockanje | F | * | - | C | ** | VIIb | VIIIb-Xa |
| A157 | Utrecht | C | * | U | B | ** | VIIb | VIIIa-Xa |
| A158 | Zwammerdam | F | ** | - | A | *** | VIIIa | VIIIa-IXa |
| A159 | Beiderweis | C | * | ** | B | ** | VIIa | VIIb-Xa |
| A160 | Cannstatt | A | * | *** | B | *** | V | VIIb-Xa |
| A161 | Cannstatt | A | * | *** | B | *** | VIIa | VIIb-IXc |
| A162 | Cannstatt | A | * | *** | B | *** | VI | VI-VIIb |
| A163 | Degerfeld | F | ** | - | B | ** | V | V-VI |
| A164 | Froitzheim | D | * | *** | A | *** | Xb | Xb |
| A165 | Gauting | E | *** | * | C | * | IXa | IXa-IXb |
| A166 | Heddernheim | B | * | ** | A | ** | VIIIa | VIIIa-IXc |
| A167 | Heddernheim | C | * | U | A | ** | VIIb | VIIb-IXb |
| A168 | Heddernheim | E | * | *** | B | *** | IXc | IXc-Xa |
| A169 | Heddernheim | C | * | *** | A | *** | IXb | IXb-IXc |
| A170 | Heddernheim | E | * | *** | A | *** | IXa | IXa |
| A171 | Holzhausen | B | ** | * | B | ** | IXa | IXa-IXc |
| A172 | Holzhausen | B | * | * | B | ** | VIIIb | VIIIb-IXc |
| A173 | Holzhausen | E | * | *** | B | *** | IXa | IXa-IXb |
| A174 | Holzhausen | E | * | ** | B | ** | IXa | IXa-IXb |
| A175 | Holzhausen | E | * | U | B | ** | IXa | IXa-IXc |
| A176 | Holzhausen | C | * | U | B | ** | IXa | IXa-IXb |
| A177 | Künzing | C | * | * | B | ** | VI | VIIa-Xa |

| | | | | | | | | |
|---|---|---|---|---|---|---|---|---|
| A178 | Künzing | C | * | U | A | ** | VIIIb | VIIIb-IXc |
| A179 | Künzing | C | ** | U | B | ** | VIIIb | VIIIb-IXc |
| A180 | Künzing | C | * | U | B | ** | Ia | VIIa-IXb |
| A181 | Leonardspfunzen | A | * | *** | B | *** | V | VIIIa-Xa |
| A182 | Mainz | E | * | ** | A | ** | VIIIa | VIIIa-IXc |
| A183 | Mainz-Kastel | C | * | U | B | ** | VIIIb | VIIIb-IXb |
| A184 | Marzoll | E | * | ** | A | ** | VI | VIIa-Xa |
| A185 | Murrhardt | E | * | *** | A | *** | VIIa | VIIb-Xa |
| A186 | Neuburg | A | * | *** | A | *** | V | VI-Xa |
| A187 | Niederbieber | F | * | - | C | ** | IXc | IXc |
| A188 | Pfaffenhofen | E | * | *** | A | *** | IXa | IXa |
| A189 | Pfaffenhofen | E | * | ** | A | ** | Xb | Xb |
| A190 | Pfaffenhofen | E | * | *** | A | *** | Xb | Xb |
| A191 | Pfaffenhofen | E | * | ** | A | ** | VIIb | VIIb-IXa |
| A192 | Pocking | E | * | *** | A | *** | IXb | IXb-IXc |
| A193 | Regensburg | A | * | *** | C | ** | VIIb | VIIb-Xa |
| A194 | Regensburg | A | * | *** | A | *** | VIIIb | VIIIb-Xa |
| A195 | Reichenhall | A | * | *** | B | ** | VI | VIIa-Xa |
| A196 | Speyer | E | * | ** | A | ** | Xb | Xb |
| A197 | Straubing | E | ** | U | B | ** | IV | V-IXc |
| A198 | Trier | E | * | ** | A | ** | VIIa | VIIb-Xa |
| A199 | Walldürn | F | * | - | A | ** | VIIIa | VIIIa-IXa |
| A200 | Walldürn | F | * | - | A | ** | VIIIa | VIIIb-IXb |
| A201 | Xanten | E | * | ** | A | ** | VIIIa | VIIIa-IXc |
| A202 | Zugmantel | E | * | - | C | ** | - | - |
| A203 | *Carnuntum* | E | * | ** | B | ** | IXb | IXb-Xa |
| A204 | *Carnuntum* | E | * | ** | C | ** | Xa | Xa |
| A205 | Enns-Lorch | A | * | *** | A | *** | VIIIa | VIIIa-IXa |
| A206 | Enns-Lorch | G | * | - | C | ** | - | - |
| A207 | Salzburg | A | * | *** | C | ** | VI | VIIa-Xa |
| A208 | Zalalövö | G | * | U | B | ** | VIIa | VIIb-Xa |
| | | | | | | | | |
| B1 | Alchester | B | * | U | C | ** | | |
| B2 | Aldborough | E | ** | ** | A | ** | | |
| B3 | Bar Hill | F | * | - | C | ** | | |
| B4 | Bath | B | * | U | A | ** | | |
| B5 | Benwell | D | * | *** | A | *** | | |
| B6 | Bishopstone | C | * | U | A | ** | | |
| B7 | Bitterne | D | * | U | A | ** | | |
| B8 | Bothwellhaugh | F | * | - | A | *** | | |
| B9 | Brancaster | F | * | - | A | ** | | |
| B10 | Brecon | C | * | U | B | ** | | |
| B11 | Brentford | C | * | ** | A | ** | | |
| B12 | Brentford | E | * | ** | A | ** | | |
| B13 | Brentford | D | * | U | A | ** | | |
| B14 | Brentford | C | * | U | A | ** | | |
| B15 | Caerleon | E | *** | U | A | * | | |
| B16 | Caerleon | G | * | * | A | ** | | |
| B17 | Caistor | B | * | U | C | ** | | |
| B18 | Canterbury | C | * | ** | A | ** | | |
| B19 | Canterbury | B | * | U | A | ** | | |
| B20 | Canterbury | B | * | U | A | ** | | |
| B21 | Carzield | F | * | - | B | ** | | |
| B22 | Catterick | B | * | U | A | ** | | |
| B23 | Chester | C | * | * | A | ** | | |
| B24 | Chester-le-Street | F | * | - | A | ** | | |
| B25 | Chichester | E | * | U | A | ** | | |
| B26 | Chichester | C | ** | * | A | * | | |
| B27 | Colchester | C | * | ** | A | ** | | |
| B28 | Corbridge | E | * | *** | A | *** | | |
| B29 | Ditchley | D | * | * | A | ** | | |
| B30 | Dorchester | E | * | U | A | ** | | |
| B31 | Dorchester | E | * | *** | A | ** | | |
| B32 | Dover | D | * | ** | A | ** | | |
| B33 | Dover | D | * | ** | A | ** | | |

| B34 | Dover | D | * | ** | A | ** |
|---|---|---|---|---|---|---|
| B35 | Dover | B | * | ** | A | ** |
| B36 | Dover | E | * | *** | A | ** |
| B37 | Enfield | C | ** | U | A | ** |
| B38 | Enfield | C | * | U | A | ** |
| B39 | Ewell | D | ** | U | A | ** |
| B40 | Exeter | B | * | ** | A | ** |
| B41 | Fishbourne | F | *** | - | A | * |
| B42 | Gloucester | E | * | U | A | ** |
| B43 | Gloucester | B | * | ** | A | ** |
| B44 | Gloucester | E | ** | *** | A | ** |
| B45 | Heronbridge | E | * | ** | A | ** |
| B46 | Heronbridge | E | * | ** | A | ** |
| B47 | High Cross | D | ** | U | A | ** |
| B48 | High Cross | C | * | U | A | ** |
| B49 | Hob's Ditch | D | * | U | A | ** |
| B50 | Housesteads | E | * | ** | A | ** |
| B51 | Ilkley | F | * | - | A | *** |
| B52 | Leicester | E | ** | ** | A | ** |
| B53 | Lincoln | E | ** | *** | A | ** |
| B54 | Little Chester | E | * | *** | A | *** |
| B55 | Little Chester | B | * | U | A | ** |
| B56 | London | E | ** | *** | A | ** |
| B57 | London | E | ** | ** | A | * |
| B58 | London | E | * | *** | A | *** |
| B59 | Lyne | E | * | ** | A | *** |
| B60 | Mansfield | D | * | U | A | ** |
| B61 | Nettleton | E | ** | U | A | ** |
| B62 | Nettleton | C | ** | U | A | ** |
| B63 | Newstead | D | * | ** | A | ** |
| B64 | Newstead | D | * | ** | A | ** |
| B65 | Newstead | D | * | ** | A | ** |
| B66 | Newstead | C | ** | ** | A | ** |
| B67 | Ravenglass | E | * | *** | A | *** |
| B68 | Ravenglass | C | * | U | A | ** |
| B69 | Rochester | B | * | ** | A | ** |
| B70 | Rochester | E | * | *** | A | ** |
| B71 | Rough Castle | F | * | - | A | ** |
| B72 | South Shields | B | * | U | A | ** |
| B73 | Southwark | C | * | ** | A | ** |
| B74 | Southwark | C | * | ** | A | ** |
| B75 | Southwark | C | * | ** | A | ** |
| B76 | Springhead | E | * | *** | A | *** |
| B77 | *Verulamium* | D | * | ** | A | ** |
| B78 | Wiggonholt | C | * | ** | A | ** |
| B79 | Winterton | E | * | U | A | ** |
| B80 | Wroxeter | B | * | U | A | ** |
| B81 | York | B | * | U | A | ** |
| B82 | Amiens | E | * | *** | A | *** |
| B83 | Amiens | E | * | U | A | ** |
| B84 | Amiens | D | * | U | A | ** |
| B85 | Amiens | D | * | U | A | ** |
| B86 | Eyrein | C | * | ** | B | ** |
| B87 | Guiry-Gadancourt | C | * | U | A | ** |
| B88 | Guiry-Gadancourt | C | * | U | A | ** |
| B89 | Koenigshoffen | C | * | ** | B | ** |
| B90 | Lyon | G | * | * | A | ** |
| B91 | Strasbourg | E | * | *** | B | *** |
| B92 | Strasbourg | B | * | U | B | ** |
| B93 | Pommeroeul | G | * | U | C | ** |
| B94 | Robelmont | E | * | ** | A | ** |
| B9S | Robelmont | E | * | ** | A | ** |
| B96 | Robelmont | E | * | ** | A | ** |
| B97 | Rosmeer | F | ** | - | B | ** |
| B98 | Rijswijk | F | * | - | A | ** |

| | | | | | | |
|---|---|---|---|---|---|---|
| B99 | Altenstadt | C | * | U | A | ** |
| B100 | Altenstadt | D | * | U | A | ** |
| B101 | Altenstadt | D | * | U | A | ** |
| B102 | Altenstadt | C | * | U | A | ** |
| B103 | Altenstadt | C | * | ** | A | ** |
| B104 | Altenstadt | C | * | ** | A | ** |
| B105 | Altenstadt | C | * | U | A | ** |
| B106 | Böhming | E | * | *** | B | ** |
| B107 | Butzbach | F | * | - | B | ** |
| B108 | Degerfeld | D | ** | U | B | ** |
| B109 | Degerfeld | C | * | U | B | ** |
| B110 | Degerfeld | C | * | U | B | ** |
| B111 | Degerfeld | C | * | U | B | ** |
| B112 | Degerfeld | C | * | U | B | ** |
| B113 | Epfach | A | * | *** | B | *** |
| B114 | Epfach | A | * | *** | B | *** |
| B115 | Epfach | A | * | *** | B | *** |
| B116 | Epfach | A | * | *** | B | *** |
| B117 | Epfach | A | * | *** | B | *** |
| B118 | Faimingen | F | ** | - | A | ** |
| B119 | Gross-Gerau | E | * | ** | B | ** |
| B120 | Günzburg | E | ** | *** | A | ** |
| B121 | Hackenbroich | C | * | ** | A | ** |
| B122 | Holzhausen | C | * | U | B | ** |
| B123 | Holzhausen | C | * | U | B | ** |
| B124 | Holzhausen | C | * | U | B | ** |
| B125 | Holzhausen | C | * | U | B | ** |
| B126 | Kriftel | C | * | U | B | ** |
| B127 | Kriftel | C | * | U | B | ** |
| B128 | Kriftel | C | * | U | B | ** |
| B129 | Künzing | C | * | U | B | ** |
| B130 | Künzing | A | * | *** | A | *** |
| B131 | Künzing | C | * | ** | A | ** |
| B132 | Künzing | C | * | U | A | ** |
| B133 | Künzing | C | * | U | A | ** |
| B134 | Künzing | C | * | ** | A | ** |
| B135 | Leonhardspfunzen | A | * | *** | B | *** |
| B136 | Miltenberg | F | * | - | B | ** |
| B137 | Munningen | C | * | ** | B | ** |
| B138 | Murrhardt | C | * | ** | A | ** |
| B139 | Ohringen-West | D | * | U | B | ** |
| B140 | Ohringen-West | C | * | U | B | ** |
| B141 | Ohringen-West | C | * | U | B | ** |
| B142 | Pfaffenhofen | E | * | ** | A | ** |
| B143 | Pfaffenhofen | E | * | * | A | ** |
| B144 | Pocking | E | ** | U | A | ** |
| B145 | Pocking | C | * | U | B | ** |
| B146 | Regensburg | F | * | - | C | ** |
| B147 | Regensburg | A | * | *** | A | *** |
| B148 | Regensburg | F | ** | - | C | *** |
| B149 | Rheinzabern | C | * | *** | A | *** |
| B150 | Rheinzabern | C | * | U | A | ** |
| B151 | Rosendahlsberg | A | * | *** | B | *** |
| B152 | Rosendahlsberg | A | * | *** | B | *** |
| B153 | Straubing | C | * | U | B | ** |
| B154 | Straubing | C | * | U | B | ** |
| B155 | Trier | C | * | ** | C | ** |
| B156 | Trier | E | * | ** | A | ** |
| B157 | Trier | E | * | U | A | ** |
| B158 | Xanten | E | ** | U | A | ** |
| B159 | Wiesendangen | F | * | - | B | ** |
| B160 | Schaan | F | * | - | A | ** |
| B161 | *Carnuntum* | E | * | ** | A | ** |
| B162 | *Aquincum* | E | * | *** | C | *** |
| B163 | Zalalövö | E | * | ** | A | ** |
| B164 | Zalalövö | E | * | U | A | ** |

| | | | | | | | | |
|---|---|---|---|---|---|---|---|---|
| C1 | Atworth | F | * | - | A | ** | Xa-XII | XII |
| C2 | Bozeat | D | * | U | A | ** | VIIa | VIIa-VIIIa |
| C3 | Brancaster | D | * | ** | A | ** | VIIIb | VIIIb-IXc |
| C4 | Brean Down | F | * | - | A | ** | XII | XII |
| C5 | Brigstock | F | * | - | A | ** | Xa-XII | XII |
| C6 | Caerleon | B | * | ** | B | ** | VIIIa | VIIIb-Xa |
| C7 | Caernarvon | F | * | - | A | ** | VI | VI-VIIIb |
| C8 | Caistor | C | * | U | A | ** | Xb | Xb |
| C9 | Canterbury | E | ** | *** | A | ** | VI | VIIa-Xa |
| C10 | Canterbury | B | ** | U | A | * | VI | VIIa-Xa |
| C11 | Canterbury | C | * | ** | A | ** | Xa-XII | XII |
| C12 | Canterbury | B | * | U | A | ** | Xa | Xa |
| C13 | Carrawburgh | B | * | *** | A | ** | - | - |
| C14 | Chew Park | C | * | * | A | ** | XI | XI |
| C15 | Chichester | A | * | *** | A | *** | VI | VIIa-Xa |
| C16 | Chilgrove | D | * | *** | A | ** | IXa | IXa-IXc |
| C17 | Clear Cupboard | F | * | - | C | ** | XII | XII |
| C18 | Darenth | D | * | * | A | ** | Xa | Xa |
| C19 | Dorchester | C | * | ** | A | ** | Xb | Xb |
| C20 | Dover | E | * | U | A | ** | VIIIb | VIIIb-IXc |
| C21 | Dover | B | * | ** | A | ** | VIIa | VIIb-Xa |
| C22 | Downton | B | * | U | A | ** | Xa | Xa |
| C23 | Droitwich | C | * | ** | A | ** | Xb | Xb |
| C24 | Dunstable | C | * | *** | A | *** | Xb | Xb |
| C25 | Durrington Walls | C | * | *** | A | ** | - | - |
| C26 | Exning | C | * | *** | A | *** | IXa | IXa-IXc |
| C27 | Faversham | E | ** | *** | A | ** | XII | XII |
| C28 | Fulham | F | * | - | A | ** | XII | XII |
| C29 | Gloucester | F | * | - | A | ** | XI | XI |
| C30 | Harlow | B | * | U | B | ** | VI | VIIIa-Xa |
| C31 | Lincoln | E | * | *** | A | ** | Xa | Xa |
| C32 | Little Waltham | C | ** | U | A | ** | Xb | Xb |
| C33 | Lullingstone | E | * | ** | A | ** | IXa | IXa-IXc |
| C34 | Lympne | B | ** | ** | A | ** | XII | XII |
| C35 | Lynch Farm | F | ** | - | A | ** | XII | XII |
| C36 | *Margidunum* | C | * | ** | A | ** | XI | XI |
| C37 | Nettleton | E | * | U | A | ** | VIIIb | VIIIb-IXc |
| C38 | Norwood | D | ** | U | C | * | XII | XII |
| C39 | Reculver | B | * | U | A | ** | VIIIb | VIIIb-IXc |
| C40 | Richborough | C | ** | U | C | * | Xb | Xb |
| C41 | Scole | B | * | ** | A | ** | Xb | Xb |
| C42 | Shakenoak | B | * | ** | A | ** | V | VIIb-Xa |
| C43 | Shakenoak | B | ** | ** | A | ** | VIIIb | VIIIb-IXb |
| C44 | Silchester | E | ** | *** | A | ** | VI | VIIa-Xa |
| C45 | Slonk Hill | D | ** | ** | A | * | VIIb | VIIIa-Xa |
| C46 | Slonk Hill | C | * | ** | A | ** | VI | VIIa-IXb |
| C47 | Sompting | A | * | *** | A | *** | VIIIa | VIIIa-IXa |
| C48 | Towcester | B | * | U | A | ** | IXa | IXa-IXc |
| C49 | Towcester | B | * | U | A | ** | VIIIa | VIIIa-IXc |
| C50 | Towcester | B | * | U | A | ** | VIIa | VIIb-IXc |
| C51 | *Verulamium* | C | * | *** | A | ** | VI | VIIa-Xa |
| C52 | *Verulamium* | E | * | *** | A | *** | Xb | Xb |
| C53 | Walton | B | * | U | A | ** | Xa-XI | XI |
| C54 | Winchester | B | * | * | A | ** | IXc | IXc-Xa |
| C55 | Etalon | E | * | U | B | ** | Xb | Xb |
| C56 | Malain | E | * | ** | B | ** | IXa | IXa-IXc |
| C57 | Nivelles | E | * | ** | A | ** | Xa | Xa |
| C58 | Roche Ste-Anne | F | * | - | A | *** | Xb | Xb |

# APPENDIX 7

## Dated samian ware sherds in deposits of *c.* 150-280+, from Gazetteer section A, based on dates of minting of associated coins

Each entry is given as a pair of figures: on the left the number of sherds, on the right the number of deposits.
Key: *, large quantity; ov, ovolo; K1955, Karnitsch 1955; K1959, Karnitsch 1959; R1934, Ricken 1934; C&G, Chenet & Gaudron 1955

| Kiln ph. | Potter | I-III | IV | V | VI | VIIa | VIIb | VIIIa | VIIIb | IXa | IXb | IXc | Xa-b | XI+ |
|---|---|---|---|---|---|---|---|---|---|---|---|---|---|---|
| **Central Gaul** | | | | | | | | | | | | | | |
| I | X-2 | | | | | | | | | | | | 1-1 | |
| | Drusus I | | | | 3-3 | 1-1 | 1-1 | | 1-1 | | | | 2-1 | |
| | Igocatus | | | | 2-2 | 1-1 | | | | | | | 2-2 | |
| | X-8/10 | | | | | 2-2 | | | | | | | | |
| | X-11/12 | | 1-1 | | 3-2 | | 1-1 | | | | | | | |
| | Sacirius | | | 1-1 | | 3-3 | | 1-1 | | 1-1 | | | | |
| | Libertus | | | | 1-1 | | | | | | | | 1-1 | |
| II | Quintilianus | | | | 2-1 | 1-1 | 3-3 | 3-2 | | 5-1 | | | | 1-1 |
| | Geminus | | | | | | | 2-1 | | | | | | |
| | X-5 | | | | | | | | 1-1 | | | | | |
| | X-6 | | 1-1 | 1-1 | 4-2 | | 1-1 | | | 7-1 | | | | 1-1 |
| | Large S | | | | | 1-1 | | | | | | | | |
| | Sacer-Attianus | | | | 4-4 | 9-5 | 1-1 | 2-2 | 1-1 | 5-2 | | | 2-2 | 1-1 |
| | Drusus II | | | 1-1 | | 4-2 | 1-1 | | | 1-1 | | | 1-1 | |
| | Secundinus I | | | 1-1 | | 1-1 | | | | | | | | |
| | Butrio | | | | 1-1 | | 3-1 | | 1-1 | | | | | |
| | Austrus | | | | 2-2 | 1-1 | | | | 1-1 | | | | |
| | Docilis | | | | 2-2 | 2-1 | | | | | | | 2-2 | |
| | Tittius | | | | 1-1 | | | | | | | | | |
| | Arcanus | | | | 1-1 | | | | | 1-1 | | | | |
| | Acurio | | | | | | | | | 1-1 | | | | |
| | Sissus | | | 1-1 | | | | | | | | | | |
| | Me ... | | | | | | 1-1 | | | | | | | |
| | Tetturo | | | 1-1 | | | 1-1 | | | | | | | |
| | Ianuaris II-Paternus I | | 1-1 | | 1-1 | 1-1 | | | | | | | | |
| III | P-18 | | | | 1-1 | | | | | | | | | |
| | P-19 | | | 1-1 | | | | | | | | | | |
| | P-23 | | | | 1-1 | | 1-1 | | | | | | | |
| | Criciro | | | | 9-6 | 4-3 | 4-2 | 3-1 | 1-1 | 2-1 | | | | |
| | Cettus | | | 1-1 | 3-3 | 1-1 | 1-1 | 2-1 | | 2-2 | | | 1-1 | 2-2 |
| | Cinnamus-Cerialis; early Cinnamus | | | | 1-1 | 5-2 | | 1-1 | | | | | | |
| | Cinnamus | 5-2 | 1-1 | 5-3 | 45-18 | 25-6 | 8-6 | 44-6 | 9-4 | 90-3 | 2-2 | | 11-7 | 5-4 |
| | Secundus | | | 2-2 | 3-3 | 2-2 | | | 1-1 | | | | 2-1 | |
| | Pugnus | | | 1-1 | 1-1 | | | 3-2 | 1-1 | 2-1 | | | | |
| | Paullus | | | | 7-3 | 1-1 | | | 1-1 | | | | 1-1 | |
| | Laxtucissa | 1-1 | | | 4-3 | 4-4 | 1-1 | 2-2 | 1-1 | | | | 2-2 | |
| | Albucius | 1-1 | | | 9-5 | 5-4 | 1-1 | 2-2 | 1-1 | 4-3 | | | | 3-3 |
| | Q I Balbinus | | | | | | | | 2-2 | | | | | |
| | Servus I | | | | 1-1 | | | | | | | | | |
| | Carantinus II | | | | 1-1 | | | | | 1-1 | | | | |
| | Illixo | | | | 1-1 | | | | | | | | | |
| | Divixtus | | | 1-1 | 3-2 | 3-3 | | 2-2 | 2-2 | 2-2 | | | 1-1 | 1-1 |
| | Lastuca | | | | 1-1 | | | 1-1 | | 2-1 | | | | |
| | Martialis | | | | 1-1 | | | | | | | | | |
| IV | Casurius | | | | 7-2 | 3-2 | | 4-2 | 2-2 | 1-1 | 1-1 | | 2-2 | 2-2 |
| | Paternus II | | | 2-2 | 28-7 | 5-4 | 3-2 | 8-2 | 10-3 | 10-4 | 2-1 | | 1-1 | 1-1 |

| | | | | | | | | | | | | | | |
|---|---|---|---|---|---|---|---|---|---|---|---|---|---|---|
| | Censorinus | | | | 3-1 | | | 2-2 | 2-1 | 1-1 | 1-1 | | 1-1 | |
| | Mercator II | | | | | | 1-1 | 1-1 | 1-1 | | | | | |
| | Advocisus | | | | 8-4 | 3-2 | 1-1 | 2-1 | 2-1 | | | | 1-1 | |
| | Iustus | | | | 1-1 | 1-1 | 1-1 | 2-1 | 1-1 | 1-1 | | | 1-1 | |
| | Iullinus | | | | 1-1 | 1-1 | | 1-1 | 1-1 | 1-1 | | | 3-3 | 2-1 |
| | Doeccus I | | | | 6-6 | 4-4 | 1-1 | 4-3 | 7-3 | 3-2 | | | 5-5 | 7-3 |
| | Banvus | | | | 1-1 | 1-1 | | 2-2 | 1-1 | 1-1 | | | 2-2 | |
| | Servus II | | | | | | 2-2 | 1-1 | 2-1 | | | | | |
| | Severus | | | | | | | | 2-1 | 1-1 | | | | 1-1 |
| | Caletus | | | 1-1 | 1-1 | | 1-1 | | 2-2 | | | | | 1-1 |
| | Priscus | | | | | 1-1 | | | | | | | | |
| | Caratillus | | | | | 1-1 | | | 1-1 | | | | | |
| | 'Cintusmus' | | | | | | | | 1-1 | | | | | |
| | Marcus | | | | | | | | | | | | | 1-1 |
| **Rheinzabern** | | | | | | | | | | | | | | |
| **Ia** | Janu I | | | | 1-1 | 1-1 | | 4-2 | 3-3 | 2-1 | | | | |
| | Reginus I | 1-1 | | 2-2 | 1-1 | 3-3 | 2-1 | 2-1 | | 9-2 | 1-1 | | 2-2 | |
| | **Cobnertus I** | | | 1-1 | | 1-1 | | | | | | | | |
| | Cobnertus III | | | 3-2 | | 1-1 | | 2-1 | | 1-1 | | | | |
| | Firmus I | | | 1-1 | | 1-1 | 1-1 | | 1-1 | | | 1-1 | 1-1 | |
| | Firmus | | | 1-1 | | | | 2-2 | 1-1 | | | | | |
| **Ib** | Cerialis I | | | | 1-1 | | 1-1 | 1-1 | 2-2 | 1-1 | | | | |
| | Cerialis II | | 1-1 | | | | | | | | | | 1-1 | |
| | Cerialis III | | | | 1-1 | 1-1 | 1-1 | | 2-2 | | 1-1 | | | |
| | Cerialis IV | | | | 1-1 | | | 2-2 | 1-1 | | | | | |
| | Cerialis V | | | 1-1 | 1-1 | | | 1-1 | 1-1 | 1-1 | | 1-1 | 1-1 | |
| | Cerialis | | | | 1-1 | | 1-1 | 1-1 | | | | | 1-1 | |
| | Cerialis group B | | | | | | | 1-1 | 1-1 | | | | | |
| | Arvernicus-Lutaevus | | | | | | | 1-1 | | 1-1 | | | | |
| | Comitialis II | | | | | | | 6-6 | 2-2 | 1-1 | 2-2 | | | |
| | Comitialis III | | | | | | | 2-2 | 3-3 | 1-1 | | | 1-1 | |
| | Belsus I | 1-1 | | | | 1-1 | 1-1 | 1-1 | 1-1 | | | | | |
| | Lucanus | | | | | | | | 2-2 | | | | | |
| IIa | Comitialis IV | | | | | 1-1 | 1-1 | 2-2 | 2-2 | 5-5 | 1-1 | | 1-1 | |
| | Comitialis V | | | 2-2 | 1-1 | 2-2 | 1-1 | 4-3 | 5-4 | | 1-1 | | 1-1 | |
| | Comitialis VI | | | | 1-1 | 2-2 | | 3-3 | 1-1 | 1-1 | 1-1 | 2-1 | 1-1 | |
| | Comitialis | | | | | 3-3 | | 2-2 | 3-3 | 4-4 | 2-2 | | | |
| | B F Attoni | | | | 4-4 | | | | | | | | | |
| | Belsus III | | | | | | | | | | | | | |
| | Cerialis VI | | | | | | | | | | | | | 1-1 |
| | Respectus | | | | 1-1 | 2-2 | | 3-3 | 1-1 | 1-1 | | | | |
| | Florentinus | | | | | | | | 1-1 | 1-1 | | | | |
| | E 25/26 | | | | 2-2 | | | 2-2 | 2-2 | 1-1 | 1-1 | | | |
| | Mammil ianus | | | 1-1 | | 1-1 | | | | | 1-1 | | | |
| | Firmus II | | | | | | | | | 2-2 | | | | |
| | Pupus-Iuvenis II | | | 8-1 | | | | 1-1 | 1-1 | | 1-1 | | | |
| | Pupus | | | | | | | | | | | 1-1 | | |
| | Atto | | | | | | 2-2 | 1-1 | 2-2 | | | | | |
| | Reginus II | | | | | | 1-1 | 1-1 | 1-1 | | | | | |
| | Attillus | | 1-1 | | 1-1 | | | 1-1 | 1-1 | | | | | |
| **IIb-c** | Augustinus II | | | | | | | | | | 1-1 | | 1-1 | |
| | Julius I | | | | | | | 4-2 | 2-2 | | | | 1-1 | |
| | Julius I-Lupus | | | | | | 1-1 | 1-1 | 3-1 | | | | 1-1 | |
| | Lupus | | | | | 1-1 | | 1-1 | | 1-1 | | 1-1 | | |
| | E8 | | | | | | | 1-1 | 1-1 | | | | | |
| | Victorinus I | | | | | | | 1-1 | | 1-1 | 1-1 | | | |
| | Verecundus I-II | | | | | | | | | 2-2 | | | | |
| | Helenius | | 1-1 | | | | 1-1 | 1-1 | 2-2 | | 1-1 | | 1-1 | |
| | Marcellus II | | | | | | | | 1-1 | 2-2 | | | | |
| | Primitivus I | | 1-1 | | | 2-2 | | 1-1 | 4-4 | 4-3 | | 1-1 | 2-2 | |
| | Primitivus II | | | | | | | 1-1 | | | | | | |
| | Primitivus III | | | | | | | 2-2 | | 2-2 | 1-1 | | | |

| | | | | | | | | | | | | | | |
|---|---|---|---|---|---|---|---|---|---|---|---|---|---|---|
| | Primitivus IV | | | | | | | 2-2 | 1-1 | 2-2 | | | 1-1 | |
| | Primitivus | | | | | | | 2-2 | 1-1 | 1-1 | | | | |
| | O 382/3 | | | | | | | | | 1-1 | | | | |
| III | Julius II-Julianus I | | | 1-1 | 1-1 | 2-2 | 1-1 | 2-2 | 7-5 | 15-8 | 6-4 | | 8-6 | |
| | Victorinus II-III | | | | | | | | | 1-1 | | 1-1 | | |
| | Janu II | | | | | 1-1 | 1-1 | 4-3 | | 3-1 | | | | |
| | Respectinus I | | | | | | | | | | | | 1-1 | |
| | Victor I | | | | 1-1 | | | | 1-1 | | | | | |
| | Victor II-Januco | | | | | | | | | 2-2 | | | | 2-2 |
| | Julianus II | | | | | | | | | 1-1 | | | 1-1 | |
| | Statutus I-II | 1-1 | | | | | | | 1-1 | | 1-1 | | | |
| | E 31 | | | | | | | | 1-1 | | | | | |
| | Pervincus | | | | 1-1 | | | | | | | 1-1 | | |
| | | | | | | | | | | | | | | |
| **Trier** | | | | | | | | | | | | | | |
| | Werkstatt I | | | | | | | 3-1 | 1-1 | | | 2-1 | | |
| | Werkstatt II | | | | 2-1 | 2-2 | 1-1 | 30-2 | | 1-1 | | 19-1 | | 1-1 |
| | Comitialis | | | | | | | 6-1 | 1-1 | | | | | |
| | Dexter | | | 1-1 | | 4-3 | | 5-2 | 3-1 | 3-3 | | 8-1 | 1-1 | |
| | Censor | | | | | 1-1 | 1-1 | 2-1 | 1-1 | 1-1 | | 10-1 | 1-1 | |
| | Censor group | | | | | | | | | | | 7-1 | | |
| | Censor/Dexter successors | | | | | | | 15-1 | | | | 8-1 | | |
| | Maiiaavus | | | 1-1 | 1-1 | | | 7-1 | | | | | | |
| | Criciro | | | | | | | | 1-1 | | | 2-1 | | |
| | Amator | | | | | 1-1 | | 5-1 | 1-1 | | | 6-1 | | |
| | Tordilo | | | | | | | 4-1 | | 1-1 | | 7-1 | | |
| | Atillus-Pussosus | | | | | | | 5-1 | | | | 1-1 | | |
| | Afer | | | | | | | 13-1 | 2-2 | 1-1 | | | | |
| | Afer-Marinus | | | | | | | | 2-1 | | | 1-1 | | |
| | Dubitatus-Dubitus | | | | | | | | 2-2 | | | 1-1 | | |
| | Paternianus | | | | | | | | 1-1 | | | | | |
| | Primanus | | | | | | | | | | | 4-1 | | |
| | Late ware | | | | | | | | | | | | 2-1 | |
| | F 939 | | | | | 1-1 | | | | | | | | |
| | F 943 | | | | | | | | | 1-1 | | | | |
| | F 954 | | | | | | | | | | | | 2-2 | |
| | F 955/6 | | | 1-1 | | | | | | | | | | |
| | | | | | | | | | | | | | | |
| **Westerndorf** | | | | | | | | | | | | | | |
| | Helenius | | | | 1-1 | 2-2 | 7-3 | 1-1 | 1-1 | 21-4 | 9-2 | | 8-3 | 3-1 |
| | Comitialis | | | | 1-1 | | 5-1 | 1-1 | | 69-2 | 2-1 | | 16-5 | |
| | Iassus | | | | | | | | | 1-1 | | | | |
| | Onniorix | | | | | | | | | 2-1 | 1-1 | | 3-1 | |
| | Decminus | | | | | | | | | 1-1 | | | | |
| | | | | | | | | | | | | | | |
| **Pfaffenhofen** | | | | | | | | | | | | | | |
| | Helenius | | | | | | 25-2 | | | 1-1 | | | 13-2 | |
| | Dicanus | | | | | | 2-1 | | | 1-1 | | | 4-3 | |
| | ov 27 | | | 1-1 | | | | | | | | | | |
| | K1959/101E | | | | 1-1 | | | | | | | | | 1-1 |
| | | | | | | | | | | | | | | |
| **Argonne** | | | | | | | | | | | | | | |
| | Tribunus | | | 1-1 | 1-1 | | | 2-2 | 1-1 | | | | | 1-1 |
| | Tocca | | | | | | | | 1-1 | | | | 1-1 | |
| | Africanus | | | | 1-1 | | | | | | | | | |
| | Gesatus-Tribunus | | | 3-3 | | 1-1 | 3-2 | 3-1 | | | 1-1 | | 2-2 | |
| | Germanus-Africanus | | | | | | | 1-1 | | | | | 1-1 | |
| | ov E | | | | | | | 2-1 | | | | | | |

| | | | | | | | | | | | | | | |
|---|---|---|---|---|---|---|---|---|---|---|---|---|---|---|
| | ov F | | | | | | | | | | | | 1-1 | |
| | C&G R2/T3 | | | | | | | 1-1 | | | | | | |
| | unattrib. | | | 1-1 | | 3-1 | 1-1 | | | | | | 4-2 | |
| | | | | | | | | | | | | | | |
| **La Madeleine** | | | | | | | | | | | | | | |
| | Albillus-ov A-ov H | | | | 2-2 | | | 5-3 | | | | | | |
| | Sacer | | | | | | | 2-1 | | | | | | |
| | Janu | | | | | | | 1-1 | | | | | | |
| | ov A' | | | | | 3-1 | | | | | | | | |
| | ov B | | | | 2-2 | | | | 1-1 | 1-1 | | | 1-1 | |
| | ov C | | | | 2-1 | 2-2 | | | | | | | 1-1 | |
| | ov K1 | | | 1-1 | | | | | | | | | | |
| | ov L | | | | | 1-1 | | | | | | | | |
| | unattrib. | | | | | | | 5-2 | 1-1 | | | | | |
| | | | | | | | | | | | | | | |
| **Chémery/Mittelbronn** | | | | | | | | | | | | | | |
| | Saturninus-Satto | | | | | 1-1 | 1-1 | 5-2 | | | | | | |
| | Cibisus | | | 1-1 | | | | | 1-1 | 1-1 | | | | |
| | | | | | | | | | | | | | | |
| **Sinzig** | | | | | | | | | | | | | | |
| | Group 1, workshop 2 | | | | | 11-1 | | | | | | | | |
| | | | | | | | | | | | | | | |
| **Heiligenberg** | | | | | | | | | | | | | | |
| | Janu | | | | 6-2 | | | | | | | | | |
| | Reginus | | | | | | | | | | | | | 1-1 |
| | Ciriuna | 1-1 | | | | 1-1 | 1-1 | | | 2-1 | | | | |
| | F-master | | | | 1-1 | | | | | 1-1 | | | | |
| | R 1934/10J | | | | | | | | | | | | 1-1 | |
| | unattrib. | | | | | | | | | 1-1 | | | | |
| | | | | | | | | | | | | | | |
| **Blickweiler** | | | | | | | | | | | | | | |
| | Avitus | | | | | 1-1 | | 1-1 | | | 1-1 | | | |
| | LAL | | | | | | | 2-2 | | | | | | |
| | master potter | | | 1-1 | | | | 2-1 | | | | | | |
| | ov 30 | | | | 2-1 | | | 1-1 | | | | | | |
| | ov 31 | | | | | 1-1 | | | | | | | | |
| | ov 32 | | | | 1-1 | 1-1 | | 3-1 | | | | | | |
| | ov 34 | | | | | 1-1 | | | | | | | | |
| | unattrib. | | | | 1-1 | | | | | | | | | |
| | | | | | | | | | | | | | | |
| **Ittenviller** | | | | | | | | | | | | | | |
| | Verecundus | | | | | | | | | | 1-1 | | | |
| | | | | | | | | | | | | | | |
| **Kräherwald** | | | | | | | | | | | | | | |
| | Reginus | | | 1-1 | 2-1 | | | | | | | | | |
| | | | | | | | | | | | | | | |
| **Waiblingen** | | | | | | | | | | | | | | |
| | Reginus | | | | | 1-1 | | | | | | | | |
| | ov B | | | | | 1-1 | | | | | | | | |
| | | | | | | | | | | | | | | |
| **East Gaulish - Unlocated Wares** | | | | | | | | | | | | | | |
| | R1934 group 1 | | | 1-1 | | | | | | | | | | |
| | ov X | | | | | | | | | 1-1 | | | | |
| | K1955/92/2-3 | | | | | | | | | | | | 1-1 | |
| | Froitzheim | | | | | | | | | | | | 1-1 | |
| | | | | | | | | | | | | | | |
| **Britain** | | | | | | | | | | | | | | |
| | Colchester A&B | | | | | *-1 | | | | | | | | |
| | Colchester B | | | | | | | | | | | | | 1-1 |
| | Pulborough | | | | | | | | | | | | 1-1 | |

# APPENDIX 8

## Dated samian ware sherds in deposits of *c.* 150-280+, from Gazetteer section A, based on estimated dates of loss of associated coins.

Key:
**a** number of sherds per coin-period;
**b** as **a** but well-dated deposits only;
**c** number of deposit equivalents per coin-period (see text);
**d** as **c** but well-dated deposits only;
**e** Pfaffenhofen kiln deposits, sherd numbers per coin-period.

| | | V | VI | VIIa | VIIb | VIIIa | VIIIb | IXa | IXb | IXc | Xa | Xb | XI |
|---|---|---|---|---|---|---|---|---|---|---|---|---|---|
| CG I | a | - | 4.5 | 2.3 | 2.3 | 2.2 | 3.4 | 2.1 | 1.8 | 1.4 | 1.1 | 5.0 | 1.0 |
| | b | - | 4.3 | 1.6 | 1.6 | 0.6 | 1.6 | 0.3 | - | - | - | 5.0 | 1.0 |
| | c | - | 6 | 9 | 9 | 12 | 14 | 12 | 11 | 9 | 7 | 5 | 2 |
| | d | - | 4 | 4 | 4 | 2 | 3 | 1 | - | - | - | 5 | 2 |
| CG II | a | 2.2 | 6.7 | 12.3 | 11.5 | 7.9 | 7.5 | 7.0 | 6.8 | 5.9 | 4.3 | 6.0 | 3.0 |
| | b | 2.0 | 6.1 | 10.5 | 9.5 | 2.2 | 2.0 | 1.7 | 1.7 | 1.2 | 2.0 | 6.0 | 3.0 |
| | c | 7 | 17 | 29 | 29 | 33 | 32 | 30 | 29 | 26 | 13 | 7 | 4 |
| | d | 6 | 13 | 18 | 17 | 6 | 6 | 5 | 5 | 4 | 2 | 7 | 4 |
| CG III | a | 1.1 | 20.1 | 18.2 | 16.3 | 10.8 | 14.5 | 16.5 | 10.2 | 6.9 | 2.7 | 7.0 | 7.0 |
| | b | 0.9 | 19.8 | 16.4 | 13.7 | 4.3 | 8.2 | 10.2 | 3.9 | 1.8 | 1.0 | 7.0 | 7.0 |
| | c | 4 | 22 | 41 | 43 | 43 | 48 | 46 | 40 | 29 | 10 | 7 | 7 |
| | d | 3 | 20 | 30 | 28 | 13 | 19 | 17 | 11 | 6 | 1 | 7 | 7 |
| CG III + Cinn | a | 3.1 | 34.1 | 31.7 | 30.8 | 27 .0 | 33.9 | 52.7 | 26.7 | 15.7 | 6.1 | 17.0 | 16.0 |
| | b | 2.2 | 32.8 | 25.4 | 22.7 | 10.9 | 18.4 | 37.4 | 11.6 | 3.6 | 2.0 | 17.0 | 16.0 |
| | c | 7 | 30 | 66 | 72 | 78 | 86 | 83 | 77 | 55 | 24 | 13 | 12 |
| | d | 4 | 24 | 36 | 34 | 18 | 27 | 25 | 20 | 9 | 2 | 13 | 12 |
| CG IV | a | 0.3 | 38.5 | 10.2 | 5.4 | 11.1 | 38.1 | 25.8 | 16.7 | 9.6 | 4.1 | 12.5 | 17.5 |
| | b | 0.3 | 38.5 | 8.6 | 2.9 | 4.5 | 31.5 | 19.2 | 10.1 | 3.8 | 2.0 | 12.5 | 17.5 |
| | c | 1 | 10 | 25 | 25 | 45 | 66 | 61 | 55 | 38 | 16 | 17 | 17 |
| | d | 1 | 10 | 13 | 9 | 12 | 33 | 28 | 22 | 9 | 2 | 17 | 17 |
| Sacer-Attianus | a | 0.3 | 0.9 | 3.5 | 3.7 | 2.4 | 2.1 | 2.1 | 1.9 | 1.4 | 1.3 | 2.0 | 1.0 |
| | b | 0.3 | 0.9 | 3.2 | 3.2 | 1.1 | 0.8 | 0.8 | 0.8 | 0.3 | 1.0 | 2.0 | 1.0 |
| | c | 1 | 3 | 7 | 8 | 10 | 9 | 9 | 8 | 7 | 3 | 2 | 1 |
| | d | 1 | 3 | 5 | 5 | 3 | 2 | 2 | 2 | 1 | 1 | 2 | 1 |
| Criciro | a | 0.3 | 3.3 | 2.5 | 2.8 | 2.3 | 2.3 | 2.3 | 2.0 | 1.8 | 0.5 | - | - |
| | b | 0.3 | 3.3 | 2.3 | 2.6 | 0.6 | 0.6 | 0.6 | 0.3 | 0.3 | - | - | - |
| | c | 1 | 4 | 5 | 6 | 7 | 7 | 7 | 6 | 5 | 2 | - | - |
| | d | 1 | 4 | 4 | 5 | 2 | 2 | 2 | 1 | 1 | - | - | - |
| Laxtucissa | a | 0.5 | 2.5 | 2.0 | 1.2 | 1.5 | 2.3 | 2.0 | 1.0 | 0.8 | 0.4 | 1.5 | 0.5 |
| | b | 0.3 | 2.3 | 1.6 | 0.6 | 0.3 | 1.3 | 1.0 | - | - | - | 1.5 | 0.5 |
| | c | 2 | 3 | 5 | 5 | 7 | 7 | 6 | 5 | 4 | 2 | 2 | 1 |
| | d | 1 | 2 | 3 | 2 | 1 | 2 | 1 | - | - | - | 2 | 1 |
| Albucius | a | 0.3 | 4.3 | 4.2 | 3.2 | 1.9 | 1.9 | 2.6 | 1.6 | 0.6 | 0.3 | 1.0 | 3.0 |
| | b | 0.3 | 4.3 | 3.9 | 2.9 | 1.4 | 1.4 | 2.1 | 1.1 | 0.3 | - | 1.0 | 3.0 |
| | c | 1 | 3 | 9 | 9 | 7 | 7 | 7 | 6 | 3 | 2 | 1 | 2 |
| | d | 1 | 3 | 7 | 6 | 4 | 4 | 4 | 3 | 1 | - | 1 | 2 |
| Divixtus | a | - | 1.7 | 2.3 | 1.5 | 1.0 | 1.7 | 1.4 | 0.4 | 0.4 | - | 1.0 | 1.0 |
| | b | - | 1.7 | 2.3 | 1.3 | 0.6 | 1.3 | 1.0 | - | - | - | 1.0 | 1.0 |
| | c | - | 2 | 4 | 4 | 4 | 4 | 3 | 2 | 2 | - | 1 | 1 |

| | | V | VI | VIIa | VIIb | VIIIa | VIIIb | IXa | IXb | IXc | Xa | Xb | XI |
|---|---|---|---|---|---|---|---|---|---|---|---|---|---|
| | d | - | 2 | 4 | 3 | 2 | 2 | 1 | - | - | - | 1 | 1 |
| Cinnamus | a | 2.0 | 14.0 | 13.5 | 14.5 | 16.2 | 19.4 | 36.2 | 16.5 | 8.8 | 3.4 | 10.0 | 9.0 |
| | b | 1.3 | 13.0 | 9.0 | 9.0 | 6.6 | 10.2 | 27.2 | 7.7 | 1.8 | 1.0 | 10.0 | 9.0 |
| | c | 3 | 8 | 25 | 29 | 35 | 38 | 37 | 37 | 26 | 14 | 6 | 5 |
| | d | 1 | 4 | 6 | 6 | 5 | 8 | 8 | 9 | 3 | 1 | 6 | 5 |
| Casurius | a | - | 6.0 | 2.1 | 0.3 | 1.3 | 2.3 | 1.3 | 2.3 | 0.5 | 1.1 | 1.5 | 1.5 |
| | b | - | 6.0 | 2.0 | - | 0.8 | 1.8 | 0.8 | 1.8 | - | 1.0 | 1.5 | 1.5 |
| | c | - | 1 | 2 | 2 | 4 | 5 | 4 | 5 | 3 | 2 | 2 | 2 |
| | d | - | 1 | 1 | - | 1 | 2 | 1 | 2 | - | 1 | 2 | 2 |
| Paternus II | a | 0.3 | 22.6 | 1.4 | 2.1 | 3.0 | 10.2 | 10.9 | 4.9 | 3.7 | 0.7 | 0.5 | 1.5 |
| | b | 0.3 | 22.6 | 0.9 | 0.9 | 0.6 | 7.8 | 8.5 | 2.5 | 1.5 | - | 0.5 | 1.5 |
| | c | 1 | 2 | 7 | 10 | 14 | 16 | 17 | 17 | 12 | 5 | 1 | 2 |
| | d | 1 | 2 | 3 | 3 | 2 | 5 | 6 | 6 | 2 | - | 1 | 2 |
| Advocisus | a | - | 5.3 | 2.0 | 1.0 | 1.2 | 3.2 | 0.7 | 0.7 | 0.2 | 0.2 | 0.5 | 0.5 |
| | b | - | 5.3 | 1.8 | 0.8 | 1.0 | 3.0 | 0.5 | 0.5 | - | - | 0.5 | 0.5 |
| | c | - | 2 | 5 | 4 | 4 | 5 | 3 | 3 | 2 | 2 | 1 | 1 |
| | d | - | 2 | 3 | 2 | 2 | 3 | 1 | 1 | - | -- | 1 | 1 |
| Iullinus | a | - | 0.3 | 0.3 | 0.3 | 0.6 | 1.6 | 1.1 | 0.8 | - | - | 3.0 | 2.0 |
| | b | - | 0.3 | 0.3 | 0.3 | 0.6 | 1.6 | 1.1 | 0.8 | - | - | 3.0 | 2.0 |
| | c | - | 1 | 1 | 1 | 2 | 3 | 3 | 2 | -- | - | 3 | 1 |
| | d | - | 1 | 1 | 1 | 2 | 3 | 3 | 2 | - | - | 3 | 1 |
| Doeccus | a | - | 0.3 | 3.2 | 1.5 | 2.0 | 8.3 | 3.3 | 2.0 | 1.6 | 1.4 | 3.5 | 6.5 |
| | b | - | 0.3 | 2.6 | 0.9 | 0.6 | 6.9 | 1.9 | 0.6 | 0.6 | 1.0 | 3.5 | 6.5 |
| | c | - | 1 | 8 | 7 | 9 | 12 | 11 | 9 | 7 | 4 | 4 | 3 |
| | d | - | 1 | 4 | 3 | 2 | 5 | 4 | 2 | 2 | 1 | 4 | 3 |
| Iustus | a | - | - | 1.2 | 0.2 | 0.4 | 1.0 | 2.0 | 1.0 | 0.5 | - | 0.5 | 0.5 |
| | b | - | - | 1.0 | - | - | 0.6 | 1.6 | 0.6 | 0.3 | - | 0.5 | 0.5 |
| | c | - | - | 2 | 1 | 2 | 4 | 5 | 4 | 2 | - | 1 | 1 |
| | d | - | - | 1 | - | - | 2 | 3 | 2 | 1 | - | 1 | 1 |
| Rh Ia | a | 4.9 | 6.5 | 5.7 | 5.4 | 5.7 | 6.8 | 7.2 | 5.4 | 3.4 | 1.9 | 2.0 | - |
| | b | 4.8 | 6.1 | 5.2 | 4.5 | 2.7 | 3.8 | 4.2 | 2.4 | 0.6 | 1.0 | 2.0 | - |
| | c | 5 | 10 | 11 | 13 | 20 | 23 | 22 | 19 | 15 | 6 | 2 | - |
| | d | 4 | 6 | 6 | 6 | 6 | 9 | 8 | 5 | 2 | 1 | 2 | - |
| Rh Ib | a | 0.1 | 0.1 | 1.1 | 1.3 | 5.3 | 14.4 | 11.4 | 9.9 | 5.6 | 2.5 | 3.0 | - |
| | b | - | - | 0.3 | 0.3 | 2.7 | 11.1 | 8.1 | 6.6 | 2.5 | 1.0 | 3.0 | - |
| | c | 1 | 1 | 8 | 10 | 26 | 44 | 42 | 38 | 27 | 12 | 3 | - |
| | d | - | - | 1 | 1 | 9 | 23 | 21 | 17 | 7 | 1 | 3 | - |
| Rh IIa | a | 0.1 | 0.5 | 3.8 | 5.8 | 14.1 | 24.0 | 27.9 | 23.0 | 12.5 | 4.7 | 2.0 | - |
| | b | - | 0.3 | 2.3 | 3.2 | 9.5 | 18.0 | 21.9 | 17.0 | 6.7 | 1.3 | 2.0 | - |
| | c | 1 | 3 | 14 | 23 | 47 | 73 | 85 | 76 | 53 | 23 | 2 | - |
| | d | - | 1 | 2 | 5 | 19 | 38 | 50 | 41 | 19 | 2 | 2 | - |
| Rh IIb-c | a | - | 0.3 | 0.4 | 0.8 | 6.0 | 14.1 | 18.0 | 16.8 | 6.6 | 3.3 | 5.0 | - |
| | b | - | - | - | - | 4.0 | 11. 7 | 15.6 | 14.4 | 4.4 | 2.3 | 5.0 | - |
| | c | - | 3 | 4 | 7 | 25 | 37 | 48 | 46 | 25 | 10 | 5 | - |
| | d | - | - | - | - | 12 | 22 | 33 | 31 | 11 | 2 | 5 | - |
| Rh III | a | 0.1 | 0.1 | 0.3 | 1.1 | 3.2 | 8.2 | 19.9 | 11.5 | 6.6 | 5.2 | 4.0 | 1.0 |
| | b | - | - | - | 0.3 | 2.0 | 6.8 | 18.5 | 10.1 | 5.2 | 4.5 | 4.0 | 1.0 |
| | c | 1 | 1 | 3 | 7 | 14 | 22 | 33 | 27 | 19 | 10 | 4 | 1 |
| | d | - | - | - | 1 | 6 | 13 | 24 | 18 | 10 | 5 | 4 | 1 |

| | | V | VI | VIIa | VIIb | VIIIa | VIIIb | IXa | IXb | IXc | Xa | Xb | XI |
|---|---|---|---|---|---|---|---|---|---|---|---|---|---|
| Janu I | a | 1.0 | 2.0 | 1.3 | 1.3 | 1.4 | 2.2 | 1.9 | 1.4 | 1.1 | - | - | - |
| | b | 1.0 | 2.0 | 1.3 | 1.3 | 0.6 | 1.4 | 1.1 | 0.6 | 0.3 | - | - | - |
| | c | 1 | 2 | 2 | 2 | 4 | 6 | 5 | 4 | 3 | - | - | - |
| | d | 1 | 2 | 2 | 2 | 2 | 4 | 3 | 2 | 1 | - | - | - |
| Reginus I | a | 2.9 | 3.0 | 2.6 | 3.0 | 1.5 | 1.5 | 1.5 | 1.5 | 0.8 | 1.5 | 1.0 | - |
| | b | 2.8 | 2.8 | 2.3 | 2.3 | 0.5 | 0.5 | 0.5 | 0.5 | - | 1.0 | 1.0 | - |
| | c | 3 | 4 | 4 | 6 | 7 | 7 | 7 | 7 | 5 | 3 | 1 | - |
| | d | 2 | 2 | 1 | 1 | 1 | 1 | 1 | 1 | - | 1 | 1 | - |
| Cerialis I-V | a | 0.1 | 0.1 | 0.9 | 1.0 | 2.4 | 7.2 | 5.4 | 4.3 | 3.2 | 2.3 | 2.0 | - |
| | b | - | - | 0.3 | 0.3 | 0.9 | 5.1 | 3.3 | 2.2 | 1.1 | 1.0 | 2.0 | - |
| | c | 1 | 1 | 7 | 8 | 14 | 24 | 22 | 20 | 17 | 10 | 2 | - |
| | d | - | - | 1 | 1 | 3 | 10 | 8 | 6 | 3 | 1 | 2 | - |
| Comitialis II-III | a | - | - | - | - | 1.8 | 4.8 | 4.3 | 3.9 | 1.8 | 0.1 | 1.0 | - |
| | b | - | - | - | - | 1.2 | 4.1 | 3.6 | 3.2 | 1.1 | - | 1.0 | - |
| | c | - | - | - | - | 7 | 13 | 13 | 11 | 7 | 1 | 1 | - |
| | d | - | - | - | - | 4 | 9 | 9 | 7 | 3 | - | 1 | - |
| Comitialis IV-VI | a | - | 0.4 | 0.6 | 1.2 | 4.0 | 8.0 | 9.3 | 8.2 | 5.0 | 2.5 | 2.0 | - |
| | b | - | 0.3 | 0.3 | 0.3 | 2.5 | 5.7 | 7.0 | 5.9 | 2.7 | 1.3 | 2.0 | - |
| | c | - | 2 | 4 | 7 | 15 | 24 | 30 | 28 | 20 | 9 | 2 | - |
| | d | - | 1 | 1 | 1 | 6 | 11 | 17 | 15 | 7 | 2 | 2 | - |
| Comitialis (all) | a | - | 0.4 | 0.8 | 1.9 | 8.5 | 14.6 | 20.1 | 16.1 | 7.0 | 2.6 | 3.0 | - |
| | b | - | 0.3 | 0.3 | 0.6 | 6.0 | 11.2 | 16.7 | 12.7 | 3.8 | 1.3 | 3.0 | - |
| | c | - | 2 | 5 | 10 | 27 | 43 | 53 | 47 | 28 | 10 | 3 | - |
| | d | - | 1 | 1 | 2 | 13 | 24 | 34 | 28 | 10 | 2 | 3 | - |
| B F Attoni | a | - | - | 0.4 | 1.0 | 2.2 | 2.5 | 4.0 | 1.5 | 0.7 | 0.4 | - | - |
| | b | - | - | - | 0.6 | 1.8 | 2.1 | 3.6 | 1.1 | 0.3 | - | - | - |
| | c | - | - | 4 | 6 | 10 | 11 | 13 | 7 | 5 | 4 | - | - |
| | d | - | - | - | 2 | 6 | 7 | 9 | 3 | 1 | - | - | - |
| E25/26 | a | - | - | 0.3 | 0.3 | 0.5 | 2.1 | 1.4 | 1.9 | 1.6 | 0.3 | - | - |
| | b | - | - | - | - | - | 1.6 | 0.9 | 1.4 | 1.1 | - | - | - |
| | c | - | - | 1 | 1 | 2 | 5 | 5 | 6 | 5 | 1 | - | - |
| | d | - | - | - | - | - | 3 | 3 | 4 | 3 | - | - | - |
| Julius I, Lupus | a | - | 0.1 | 0.2 | 0.4 | 2.0 | 6.4 | 3.9 | 3.4 | 0.4 | 0.2 | 2.0 | - |
| | b | - | - | - | - | 1.6 | 5.8 | 3.3 | 2.8 | - | - | 2.0 | - |
| | c | - | 1 | 2 | 3 | 7 | 11 | 11 | 9 | 3 | 1 | 2 | - |
| | d | - | - | - | - | 4 | 7 | 7 | 5 | - | - | 2 | - |
| Helenius | a | - | 0.1 | 0.1 | 0.1 | 0.8 | 1.1 | 1.1 | 1.4 | 0.8 | 0.6 | 1.0 | - |
| | b | - | - | - | - | 0.3 | 0.6 | 0.6 | 0.9 | 0.3 | 0.3 | 1.0 | - |
| | c | - | 1 | 1 | 1 | 4 | 5 | 5 | 6 | 4 | 3 | 1 | - |
| | d | - | - | - | - | 1 | 2 | 2 | 3 | 1 | 1 | 1 | - |
| Primitivus I-IV | a | - | 0.1 | 0.1 | 0.3 | 2.3 | 5.4 | 8.7 | 7.2 | 4.0 | 2.5 | 1.0 | - |
| | b | - | - | - | - | 1.2 | 4.1 | 7.4 | 5.9 | 2.7 | 2.0 | 1.0 | - |
| | c | - | 1 | 1 | 3 | 11 | 17 | 23 | 22 | 14 | 6 | 1 | - |
| | d | - | - | - | - | 4 | 9 | 15 | 14 | 6 | 2 | 1 | - |
| Julius II- | a | - | - | - | 0.6 | 1.2 | 5.6 | 14.3 | 7.2 | 5.1 | 3.8 | 2.0 | - |
| Julianus I | b | - | - | - | 0.3 | 0.9 | 5.1 | 13.8 | 6.7 | 4.6 | 3.5 | 2.0 | - |
| | c | - | - | - | 3 | 5 | 11 | 18 | 14 | 11 | 6 | 2 | - |
| | d | - | - | - | 1 | 3 | 8 | 15 | 11 | 8 | 4 | 2 | - |
| Janu II | a | - | - | - | 0.2 | 1.4 | 1.4 | 1.4 | 1.1 | 0.6 | 0.2 | - | - |
| | b | - | - | - | - | 0.8 | 0.8 | 0.8 | 0.5 | - | - | - | - |

| | | V | VI | VIIa | VIIb | VIIIa | VIIIb | IXa | IXb | IXc | Xa | Xb | XI |
|---|---|---|---|---|---|---|---|---|---|---|---|---|---|
| | c | - | - | - | 1 | 5 | 5 | 5 | 4 | 3 | 1 | - | - |
| | d | - | - | - | - | 2 | 2 | 2 | 1 | - | - | - | - |
| Trier | a | 0.5 | 1.2 | 1.2 | 3.4 | 33.0 | 47.2 | 38.1 | 5.2 | 2.5 | 0.3 | 5.0 | - |
| | b | 0.5 | 1.1 | 0.9 | 2.2 | 31.1 | 45.1 | 36.0 | 3.1 | 0.6 | - | 5.0 | - |
| | c | 1 | 4 | 5 | 11 | 24 | 36 | 30 | 17 | 11 | 2 | 4 | - |
| | d | 1 | 3 | 3 | 5 | 15 | 26 | 21 | 7 | 2 | - | 4 | - |
| Dexter, Censor | a | - | 0.1 | 0.4 | 2.2 | 3.4 | 7.4 | 5.8 | 1.8 | 0.8 | - | 2.0 | - |
| | b | - | - | 0.3 | 1.6 | 2.6 | 6.6 | 5.0 | 1.0 | - | - | 2.0 | - |
| | c | - | 1 | 2 | 6 | 8 | 10 | 10 | 6 | 4 | - | 2 | - |
| | d | - | - | 1 | 3 | 4 | 6 | 6 | 2 | - | - | 2 | - |
| West | a | - | - | 0.2 | 1.3 | 1.7 | 2.3 | 4.1 | 8.9 | 7.1 | 6.8 | 4.0 | - |
| | b | - | - | - | 1.0 | 1.0 | 1.6 | 3.4 | 8.2 | 6.4 | 6.3 | 4.0 | - |
| | c | - | - | 2 | 4 | 6 | 8 | 11 | 14 | 11 | 8 | 4 | - |
| | d | - | - | - | 1 | 1 | 3 | 6 | 9 | 6 | 4 | 4 | - |
| | e | - | - | - | 2.0 | 2.0 | 2.0 | 91.0 | 0.2 | 0.2 | - | 20.0 | - |
| Pfaff | a | - | - | 0.1 | 0.1 | 0.3 | 0.3 | 0.3 | 0.3 | 0.3 | 1.3 | 1.0 | - |
| | b | - | - | - | - | - | - | - | - | - | 1.0 | 1.0 | - |
| | c | - | - | 1 | 1 | 2 | 2 | 2 | 2 | 2 | 3 | 1 | - |
| | d | - | - | - | - | - | - | - | - | - | 1 | 1 | - |
| | e | - | - | - | 6.8 | 6.8 | 6.8 | 8.8 | - | - | - | 15.0 | - |
| Helenius | a | - | - | 0.1 | 1.2 | 1.4 | 2.0 | 2.8 | 6.1 | 5.3 | 3.7 | 2.0 | - |
| | b | - | - | - | 1.0 | 1.0 | 1.6 | 2.4 | 5.7 | 4.9 | 3.3 | 2.0 | - |
| | c | - | - | 1 | 3 | 4 | 6 | 8 | 9 | 7 | 5 | 2 | - |
| | d | - | - | - | 1 | 1 | 3 | 5 | 6 | 4 | 2 | 2 | - |
| | e | - | - | - | 7.0 | 7.0 | 7.0 | 26.0 | 0.2 | 0.2 | - | 19.0 | - |
| Arg | a | 0.5 | 0.5 | 2.2 | 0.5 | 3.5 | 5.2 | 4.2 | 3.4 | 2.4 | 9.2 | 3.0 | - |
| | b | 0.5 | 0.5 | 2.0 | - | 2.3 | 3.8 | 2.8 | 2.0 | 1.0 | 8.0 | 3.0 | - |
| | c | 1 | 1 | 3 | 4 | 10 | 13 | 12 | 10 | 9 | 11 | 3 | - |
| | d | 1 | 1 | 1 | - | 4 | 6 | 5 | 3 | 2 | 5 | 3 | - |
| La Mad | a | - | 1.3 | 2.3 | 3.0 | 6.4 | 6.1 | 4.8 | 2.0 | 1.7 | 2.0 | - | - |
| | b | - | 1.3 | 2.1 | 2.1 | 4.5 | 4.2 | 2.9 | 0.3 | - | 2.0 | - | - |
| | c | - | 3 | 6 | 8 | 15 | 13 | 11 | 5 | 4 | 2 | - | - |
| | d | - | 3 | 5 | 5 | 10 | 8 | 6 | 1 | - | 2 | - | - |
| Chém/Mitt | a | - | 0.4 | 0.5 | 0.5 | 2.3 | 2.5 | 3.5 | 0.7 | 0.4 | 0.1 | - | - |
| | b | - | 0.3 | 0.3 | 0.3 | 1.9 | 2.1 | 3.1 | 0.3 | - | - | - | - |
| | c | - | 2 | 3 | 3 | 6 | 6 | 7 | 4 | 3 | 1 | - | - |
| | d | - | 1 | 1 | 1 | 3 | 3 | 4 | 1 | - | - | - | - |
| Heil | a | - | - | 1.2 | 1.3 | 1.5 | 1.5 | 1.5 | 2.5 | 1.1 | 0.3 | 1.0 | - |
| | b | - | - | - | - | - | - | - | 1.0 | - | - | 1.0 | - |
| | c | - | - | 4 | 5 | 6 | 6 | 6 | 7 | 4 | 2 | 1 | - |
| | d | - | - | - | - | - | - | - | 1 | - | - | 1 | - |
| Blick | a | - | 1.1 | 1.6 | 1.8 | 4.7 | 3.6 | 3.3 | 1.7 | 0.2 | 0.2 | - | - |
| | b | - | 1.1 | 1.4 | 1.4 | 4.3 | 3.2 | 2.9 | 1.3 | - | - | - | - |
| | c | - | 3 | 5 | 7 | 13 | 10 | 9 | 5 | 2 | 2 | - | - |
| | d | - | 3 | 4 | 4 | 10 | 7 | 6 | 2 | - | - | - | - |

# APPENDIX 9

## Regional distribution and complete listing of identified samian ware in deposits *c.* 150-280+, in Gazetteer sections A and B

All deposits except for kiln products from kiln-centre deposits (i.e. A 48, A 188-191, B 27, B 142-3, B 149-50, B 155-6). Key as Appendix 7 and Table 5.II

| Kiln-centre | Potter | S Brit | Wales & W Brit | N Brit | France | Low Countries | Rhineland | Danube | Total |
|---|---|---|---|---|---|---|---|---|---|
| CG I | X-2 | 2 | - | 1 | - | - | - | - | 3 |
| | Drusus I | 7 | 4 | - | - | - | - | - | 11 |
| | Igocatus | 4 | 1 | 2 | - | - | - | - | 7 |
| | X-8/10 | 1 | - | 5 | - | - | - | - | 6 |
| | X-11/12 | 7 | 2 | 3 | - | - | - | - | 12 |
| | Sacirius | 5 | - | 4 | - | 1 | - | 2 | 12 |
| | Libertus A-C | 3 | 1 | - | - | - | - | - | 4 |
| | rosette | 1 | - | - | - | - | - | - | 1 |
| CG II | Avitus-Vegetus | 2 | - | 1 | - | - | - | - | 3 |
| | Quintilianus | 7 | 2 | 13 | - | - | - | 7 | 29 |
| | Geminus | 1 | - | 8 | 1 | - | - | - | 10 |
| | X-5 | - | - | 4 | - | 1 | - | - | 5 |
| | X-6 | 6 | - | 9 | - | - | 2 | 7 | 24 |
| | large S | 1 | - | - | - | - | - | - | 1 |
| | Secundinus I | 3 | - | 1 | - | - | - | - | 4 |
| | Butrio | 3 | 2 | 6 | - | - | - | - | 11 |
| | Acaunissa | - | 1 | 1 | - | - | 1 | - | 3 |
| | Austrus | 7 | 2 | 2 | - | - | - | - | 11 |
| | Docilis | 5 | - | 4 | - | - | - | 1 | 10 |
| | Arcanus | 2 | - | - | - | - | - | 1 | 3 |
| | Acurio | 1 | - | - | - | - | - | 1 | 2 |
| | Drusus II | 11 | 1 | 1 | - | - | - | 1 | 14 |
| | Sacer-Attianus | 20 | 7 | 10 | - | - | - | 5 | 42 |
| | Birrantus II | - | - | 1 | - | - | - | 1 | 2 |
| | Me... | 1 | - | 1 | - | - | - | - | 2 |
| | Tittius | 1 | - | - | - | - | - | - | 1 |
| | Sissus I-II | - | - | 2 | - | - | - | - | 2 |
| | Tetturo | 1 | - | 2 | - | - | - | - | 3 |
| | Ianuaris II-Paternus I | 2 | 1 | 3 | 1 | - | - | - | 7 |
| | ov B212 | - | - | - | - | - | - | 1 | 1 |
| | I/II style | 8 | 4 | 3 | - | - | - | 1 | 16 |
| CG III | Criciro | 6 | 5 | 16 | - | 2 | - | 4 | 33 |
| | Cettus | 6 | 1 | 14 | 1 | - | - | 1 | 23 |
| | Cinnamus-Cerialis and early styles | 5 | - | 10 | - | - | - | - | 15 |
| | Cinnamus main style | 89 | 46 | 99 | 3 | 4 | - | 95 | 336 |
| | Secundus | 4 | 2 | 7 | - | - | - | - | 13 |
| | Pugnus | 6 | 4 | 3 | 1 | 1 | 1 | 1 | 17 |
| | Paullus | 6 | 2 | 7 | - | - | - | - | 15 |
| | Laxtucissa | 9 | 5 | 6 | - | - | - | 1 | 21 |
| | Albucius | 14 | 8 | 15 | 3 | - | - | 6 | 46 |
| | Q I Balbinus | - | 1 | - | - | - | - | - | 1 |
| | Servus I | 1 | 1 | - | - | - | - | - | 2 |
| | Carantinus II | 2 | - | - | - | - | - | - | 2 |
| | Illixo | - | - | 1 | - | - | - | - | 1 |
| | Divixtus | 7 | 6 | 9 | 1 | - | - | 2 | 25 |

| Kiln-centre | Potter | S Brit | Wales & W Brit | N Brit | France | Low Countries | Rhineland | Danube | Total |
|---|---|---|---|---|---|---|---|---|---|
| | Lastuca | 1 | 1 | - | - | - | - | - | 2 |
| | Martialis | - | 1 | - | - | - | - | - | 1 |
| | Moxius | - | 1 | - | - | - | - | - | 1 |
| | P-18 | 1 | - | - | - | - | - | - | 1 |
| | P-19 | - | - | 1 | 1 | - | - | - | 2 |
| | P-22 | - | - | - | - | - | - | 1 | 1 |
| | P-23 | - | 1 | 1 | - | - | - | - | 2 |
| CG IV | Casurius | 11 | 11 | 10 | 1 | - | - | 2 | 35 |
| | Paternus II | 27 | 38 | 17 | 12 | 2 | - | 13 | 109 |
| | Censorinus | 3 | 5 | 3 | 1 | 1 | - | 1 | 14 |
| | Mercator II | 1 | 3 | 3 | 2 | - | - | - | 9 |
| | Advocisus | 10 | 9 | 13 | 1 | - | - | - | 33 |
| | Iustus | 3 | 2 | 4 | 4 | - | - | - | 13 |
| | Iullinus | 11 | 3 | 9 | 2 | - | - | - | 25 |
| | Doeccus I | 32 | 7 | 19 | 6 | - | - | - | 64 |
| | Doeccus II | - | - | 1 | - | - | - | - | 1 |
| | Banvus | 7 | 4 | 1 | 2 | - | - | - | 14 |
| | Servus II | 3 | - | 5 | 2 | - | - | - | 10 |
| | Servus III | - | - | 1 | - | - | - | - | 1 |
| | Severus | 1 | 2 | 2 | 2 | - | - | - | 7 |
| | Caletus | 2 | 1 | 2 | 1 | - | - | - | 6 |
| | Priscus | 2 | - | 1 | - | - | - | - | 3 |
| | Antistii | - | - | - | 1 | - | - | - | 1 |
| | Caratillus | 1 | - | 1 | - | - | - | - | 2 |
| | Fgientinus | 1 | - | - | - | - | - | - | 1 |
| | Atilianus | - | - | - | 1 | - | - | - | 1 |
| | Marcus | 1 | - | - | 1 | - | - | - | 2 |
| | Lucinus | 1 | - | - | - | - | - | - | 1 |
| | 'Cintusmus' - late | - | - | 1 | - | - | - | - | 1 |
| | ov B184 | - | - | - | 1 | - | - | - | 1 |
| | III/IV style | 35 | 14 | 30 | 17 | 3 | 1 | 17 | 117 |
| | | | | | | | | | |
| Rh Ia | Janu I | 2 | 2 | 8 | - | - | 1 | 9 | 22 |
| | Reginus I | 3 | 1 | 6 | - | 1 | 6 | 26 | 43 |
| | Cobnertus I | - | - | 2 | - | - | 1 | 1 | 4 |
| | Cobnertus II | - | 1 | - | - | - | - | - | 1 |
| | Cobnertus III | - | - | 3 | 1 | - | 6 | 5 | 15 |
| | Firmus I | - | - | 1 | - | - | 1 | 5 | 7 |
| | Firmus | - | - | - | - | - | 5 | - | 5 |
| Rh Ib | Cerialis I | 1 | - | - | - | 2 | 1 | 3 | 7 |
| | Cerialis II | - | - | - | - | - | 2 | 1 | 3 |
| | Cerialis III | 3 | - | 1 | - | 1 | 2 | 4 | 11 |
| | Cerialis IV | 1 | - | - | - | - | - | 4 | 5 |
| | Cerialis V | - | - | - | - | - | 2 | 6 | 8 |
| | Cerialis group A | - | - | - | - | - | - | 2 | 2 |
| | Cerialis group B | - | - | - | - | - | 4 | 4 | 8 |
| | Cerialis | - | - | - | - | - | 2 | 3 | 5 |
| | Avernicus-Lutaevus | - | - | 1 | - | - | - | 3 | 4 |
| | Comitialis I. | 1 | - | - | - | - | 1 | 2 | 4 |
| | Comitialis II | - | - | - | - | 1 | 3 | 10 | 14 |
| | Comitialis III | 2 | - | 1 | - | 1 | 4 | 3 | 11 |
| | Belsus I | - | - | - | - | 1 | - | 6 | 7 |
| | Lucanus | 1 | - | - | - | - | - | 3 | 4 |
| | I style | 3 | - | - | - | - | 2 | 1 | 6 |
| Rh IIa | Comitialis IV | 1 | 1 | - | - | - | 6 | 11 | 19 |

| Kiln-centre | Potter | S Brit | Wales & W Brit | N Brit | France | Low Countries | Rhineland | Danube | Total |
|---|---|---|---|---|---|---|---|---|---|
| | Comitialis V | 3 | - | - | 1 | 1 | 15 | 14 | 34 |
| | Comitialis VI | - | - | - | - | - | 6 | 14 | 20 |
| | Comitialis | - | - | - | - | - | 15 | - | 15 |
| | B F Attoni | - | - | 1 | - | 1 | 6 | 13 | 21 |
| | Belsus II | - | - | 1 | - | - | - | 2 | 3 |
| | Belsus III | 1 | - | - | - | - | - | 1 | 2 |
| | Cerialis VI | 1 | - | - | - | - | - | 1 | 2 |
| | Respectus | - | - | - | - | 1 | 1 | 8 | 10 |
| | Florentinus | - | - | - | - | - | 1 | 3 | 4 |
| | ov E25/26 | 1 | - | - | - | 1 | 3 | 11 | 16 |
| | Mammilianus | - | - | - | - | - | 3 | 2 | 5 |
| | Firmus II | 1 | - | - | - | - | 1 | 5 | 7 |
| | Pupus-Iuvenis II | - | - | - | - | - | - | 11 | 11 |
| | Pupus | - | - | - | - | - | 4 | 2 | 6 |
| | Atto | 1 | - | - | - | 1 | 2 | 4 | 8 |
| | Reginus II | 1 | 1 | 1 | - | - | 2 | - | 5 |
| | Attillus | 1 | - | - | - | - | 5 | 3 | 9 |
| Rh IIb | Augustinus II | 1 | - | - | - | - | 1 | 2 | 4 |
| | Julius I | - | 1 | - | - | 2 | 34 | 5 | 42 |
| | Julius I-Lupus | 4 | - | 2 | - | 4 | 1 | 1 | 12 |
| | Lupus | - | - | - | - | - | 6 | - | 6 |
| | ov E8 | - | 1 | - | - | - | 1 | 1 | 3 |
| | Victorinus I | - | - | - | - | - | 3 | 1 | 4 |
| Rh IIc | Verecundus I-II | - | - | - | - | - | 1 | 2 | 3 |
| | Helenius | 2 | - | - | - | - | 7 | 4 | 13 |
| | Marcellus II | - | - | - | - | - | 2 | 1 | 3 |
| | Primitivus I | 4 | - | 1 | - | 1 | 6 | 22 | 34 |
| | Primitivus II | - | - | - | - | - | - | 2 | 2 |
| | Primitivus III | - | - | - | - | - | 1 | 3 | 4 |
| | Primitivus IV | 1 | - | - | - | - | 3 | 4 | 8 |
| | Primitivus | 1 | - | - | - | - | 5 | - | 6 |
| | ware O382/3 | - | - | - | - | - | 2 | 1 | 3 |
| | Augustalis | - | - | - | - | - | - | 2 | 2 |
| | II style | 2 | - | 4 | - | - | 18 | 4 | 28 |
| Rh IIIa | Julius II-Julianus I | 6 | - | 1 | - | 3 | 29 | 18 | 57 |
| | Victorinus II-III | - | - | - | - | - | 2 | - | 2 |
| | Janu II | - | - | - | - | 1 | - | 10 | 11 |
| | Respectinus I | - | - | - | - | - | - | 1 | 1 |
| | Respectinus II | - | - | - | - | - | 1 | - | 1 |
| | Marcellinus | - | - | - | - | - | 2 | - | 2 |
| Rh IIIb | Victor I | - | 1 | - | - | - | 1 | 2 | 4 |
| | Victor II-Januco | - | - | - | - | - | 3 | 5 | 8 |
| | Julianus II | - | - | - | - | - | 2 | - | 2 |
| | Statutus I-II | - | - | - | - | - | 3 | - | 3 |
| | Pervincus | 1 | - | - | - | - | 3 | - | 4 |
| | ov E31 | - | 1 | - | - | - | - | - | 1 |
| | III style | - | - | - | 1 | - | 3 | - | 4 |
| | | | | | | | | | |
| Tr I | Werkstatt I | 1 | - | - | - | 3 | 4 | - | 8 |
| | Werkstatt II | 2 | - | 1 | - | 30 | 33 | - | 66 |
| Tr IIa | Comitialis | 2 | - | - | - | 10 | - | - | 12 |
| | Dexter | 4 | - | - | - | 4 | 22 | - | 30 |
| | Censor | 1 | - | - | - | 3 | 19 | - | 22 |
| | Censor group | - | - | - | - | - | 7 | - | 7 |
| | Maiiaavus | - | - | - | - | 7 | 16 | - | 23 |

| Kiln-centre | Potter | S Brit | Wales & W Brit | N Brit | France | Low Countries | Rhineland | Danube | Total |
|---|---|---|---|---|---|---|---|---|---|
| Tr IIb | Censor/Dexter successors | 1 | - | - | - | 16 | 9 | - | 26 |
| | Criciro | 1 | - | - | - | - | 2 | - | 3 |
| | Amator | 1 | - | - | - | 5 | 9 | - | 16 |
| | Tordilo | - | - | - | - | 4 | 9 | - | 13 |
| Tr IIc | Atillus-Pussosus | - | - | - | - | 5 | 3 | - | 8 |
| | Afer | 1 | - | - | - | 14 | 4 | - | 19 |
| | Afer-Marinus | 2 | - | - | - | - | 2 | - | 4 |
| Tr IIIa | Dubitatus-Dubitus | 1 | - | - | - | - | 4 | - | 5 |
| | Paternianus | 1 | - | - | - | - | - | - | 1 |
| | Dignus-Primanus | 1 | - | - | - | 1 | 4 | - | 6 |
| Tr IIIb | late ware | - | - | - | - | - | 2 | - | 2 |
| Tr | ov F939 | - | - | - | - | - | 1 | - | 1 |
| | ov F941 | - | - | - | - | 1 | 1 | - | 2 |
| | ov F943 | - | - | - | - | - | 1 | - | 1 |
| | ov F954 | - | - | - | - | 1 | 1 | - | 2 |
| | ov F955/6 | - | - | - | - | - | 2 | - | 2 |
| | ov F960 | - | - | - | - | - | 1 | - | 1 |
| | unattrib. | 7 | - | 1 | - | 7 | 15 | - | 31 |
| | | | | | | | | | |
| West | Helenius | 2 | - | 1 | - | 1 | - | 23 | 27 |
| | Comitialis | - | - | - | - | - | - | 15 | 15 |
| | Onniorix | - | - | - | - | - | - | 1 | 1 |
| | ov as R&F E57 | - | - | - | - | - | - | 1 | 1 |
| | unattrib. | - | - | - | - | 1 | - | 1 | 2 |
| Pfaff [1] | Dicanus | - | - | - | - | - | - | 3 | 3 |
| | ov 19 | - | - | - | - | - | - | 1 | 1 |
| | ov 27 | - | - | - | - | - | - | 1 | 1 |
| | K 1959/101E | - | - | - | - | - | - | 1 | 1 |
| | unattrib. | - | - | - | - | - | - | 15 | 15 |
| Arg | Gesatus-Tribunus | - | - | 5 | 2 | 9 | 6 | - | 22 |
| | Tribunus | 2 | - | 3 | - | 5 | 2 | - | 12 |
| | Germanus-Africanus | - | - | - | - | 2 | - | - | 2 |
| | Africanus | 2 | - | - | - | - | - | - | 2 |
| | Tocca | 1 | - | - | - | - | 1 | - | 2 |
| | ov E | - | - | - | - | 2 | - | - | 2 |
| | ov F | - | - | - | - | 1 | - | - | 1 |
| | ov C&G R2/T3 | - | - | - | - | 2 | - | - | 2 |
| | unattrib. | 3 | - | - | 5 | 9 | 1 | - | 18 |
| La Mad | Albillus | 1 | - | 2 | - | 4 | 2 | - | 9 |
| | Sacer | - | - | - | - | 2 | - | - | 2 |
| | Virtus | - | - | - | - | - | 1 | - | 1 |
| | Janu | - | - | - | - | 1 | - | - | 1 |
| | ov A | - | - | - | - | - | 3 | - | 3 |
| | ov B | - | - | 1 | - | 2 | 1 | - | 4 |
| | ov C | 1 | - | - | - | 1 | 2 | - | 4 |
| | ov F | - | - | - | - | - | 1 | - | 1 |
| | ov K1 | - | - | - | - | - | 2 | - | 2 |
| | ov L | - | - | - | - | - | 1 | - | 1 |
| | unattrib. | 2 | - | 6 | - | 1 | - | - | 9 |
| Heil | Janu | 1 | 1 | - | - | 1 | - | 7 | 10 |
| | Reginus | 1 | - | - | - | - | - | - | 1 |
| | Ciriuna | - | - | 1 | - | - | 1 | 4 | 6 |
| | Verecundus | - | - | - | - | - | - | 1 | 1 |
| | F-master | - | - | - | - | - | - | 2 | 2 |

| Kiln-centre | Potter | S Brit | Wales & W Brit | N Brit | France | Low Countries | Rhineland | Danube | Total |
|---|---|---|---|---|---|---|---|---|---|
| | ov L | - | - | - | - | - | 1 | - | 1 |
| | unattrib. | 2 | - | 6 | - | 1 | - | - | 9 |
| Heil | Janu | 1 | 1 | - | - | 1 | - | 7 | 10 |
| | Reginus | 1 | - | - | - | - | - | - | 1 |
| | Ciriuna | - | - | 1 | - | - | 1 | 4 | 6 |
| | Verecundus | - | - | - | - | - | - | 1 | 1 |
| | F-master | - | - | - | - | - | - | 2 | 2 |
| | R 1934/10/J | - | - | - | - | - | - | 1 | 1 |
| | unattrib. | - | - | - | - | - | - | 2 | 2 |
| Blick | Avitus | - | - | - | - | - | 6 | - | 6 |
| | LAL | - | - | - | - | 1 | 1 | - | 2 |
| | master | - | - | - | - | 2 | 1 | - | 3 |
| | vase ovolo | - | - | - | - | 1 | 1 | - | 2 |
| | large figure | - | - | - | - | - | 2 | - | 2 |
| | leaping animal | - | - | - | - | - | 1 | - | 1 |
| | ov 30 | - | - | - | - | 1 | 2 | - | 3 |
| | ov 31 | - | - | - | - | - | 1 | - | 1 |
| | ov 32 | 1 | - | - | - | 3 | 2 | - | 6 |
| | ov 34 | - | - | - | - | - | 1 | - | 1 |
| | unattrib. | 1 | - | 1 | - | - | - | - | 2 |
| Chém | Saturninus-Satto | 1 | - | 2 | - | - | 1 | - | 4 |
| | unattrib. | - | - | - | - | - | - | 1 | 1 |
| Mitt | Saturninus-Satto | - | - | - | - | 4 | 4 | 1 | 9 |
| | Cibisus | - | - | - | - | - | 4 | 1 | 5 |
| Itten | Verecundus | - | - | - | - | - | - | 1 | 1 |
| Kräh | Reginus | - | - | - | - | - | 3 | - | 3 |
| Waib | Reginus | - | - | - | - | - | 1 | - | 1 |
| | Marinus | - | - | - | - | - | 1 | - | 1 |
| | ov B | - | - | - | - | - | 1 | - | 1 |
| Esch | LAA | - | - | - | - | - | 3 | - | 3 |
| EG | R 1934 group 1 | - | - | 1 | - | - | 2 | - | 3 |
| | ov X | - | - | - | - | - | 1 | - | 1 |
| | K 1955/92/2-3 | - | - | - | - | - | - | 1 | 1 |
| | Froitzheim | - | - | - | - | - | 1 | - | 1 |
| | Holzhausen | - | - | - | - | - | 1 | - | 1 |
| | Ohringen | - | - | - | - | - | 1 | - | 1 |
| | unattrib. | 3 | 1 | 1 | 1 | - | 1 | - | 7 |
| Brit | Colch B | 1 | - | - | - | - | - | - | 1 |
| | Pulb | 2 | - | - | - | - | - | - | 2 |

1. Helenius of Pfaffenhofen is attested at the kiln-site but not in other deposits.

# APPENDIX 10

## LIST AND BIBLIOGRAPHY OF SAMIAN WARE KILN-SITES AND RELATED DISCOVERIES DATING TO C. 150-250

Each entry in the following list represents either a kiln-site thought to have been producing samian ware, or a find-spot that is suggestive, perhaps because of the discovery of samian kiln debris or of moulds. Spain, the Mediterranean and the Balkan provinces are not covered in this list. The format of the entries is as follows:-

Name of site, region (map reference on Fig 7.1)

1. Latitude & longitude [NB accuracy in " is approximate]
2. Nature of site (e.g. large centre, individual kiln, mould fragment)
3. Dating
4. Distribution
5. Bibliography relative to site, excavations, pottery production and the samian products from the site. Explanatory subheadings are given to elucidate the bibliography. More important contributions have an asterisk. Journal abbreviations are the same as those used in the main Bibliography.

Some of the general works on South Gaul have been included under La Graufesenque, on Central Gaul under Lezoux, on the Argonne under Lavoye, on Satto/Saturninus and the Moselle under Chémery-Faulquemont.

SOUTH GAULISH AREA

A1 **Banassac**, Lozère

1 44° 26′ 03″ N, 3° 12′ 05″ E
2 Kiln-centre
3 50/60 - 150/180, main period very late 1st-mid 2nd century
4 The late products have been recorded in the Upper Danube area (cf e.g. Gauting, A 165 in gazetteer), and also in SW France. Earlier distribution in late 1st and early 2nd century much wider, to Britain, E France, Alpine regions, N Italy, Upper and Middle Danube, Dacia.
5 Most of the bibliography is relevant only to the 1st and early 2nd century production, and is not given here.
*Excavations*: Hofmann 1970a; Mitard & Hofmann 1963
*Products and typology*: Hofmann 1966a*; 1981*; 1986; Mees 1994b*; 1995; Morel 1957; Morel & Peyre 1973; 1975*; Picon & Hofmann 1974. Polak 2000, 27-30; Rogers 1970*
*Distribution*: Groh 1998; Hofmann 1977; Mees 1994b

A2 **La Graufesenque**, Millau, Aveyron

1 44° 05′ 46″ N, 3° 05′ 33″ E
2 Major kiln-centre
3 5 BC/5 AD - 250-260, main period 10/20 - 110/120, revival in 4th/early 5th century
4 Products of the early 2nd century are uncommon but still widely distributed, i.e. Britain, France, Low Countries, Rhine and Danube, but those made after Trajanic times are local only. The 4th/5th century products are found in S and SW France.
5 There is a large bibliography for this site: only those with a bearing on later periods of production are given here.
*General surveys*: Dannell *et al.* 2003*; Déchelette 1904*; Eschbaumer & Faber 1988; Haalebos *et al.* 1991; Hermet 1934*; Mees 1995*; 2007*; 2011; Pferdehirt 1978; 1986; Polak 1998; 2000, 22-5; Riccioni 1977; Vernhet 1975*; 1986; Vernhet & Balsan 1975
*Excavations*: Balsan 1950; 1954; Causse 1965; Reutti & Schulz 2010; Schaad 2007*; 2010; Vernhet 1981*; *Gallia* 11, 1953, 346; 12, 1954, 193-5; 13, 1955, 182-3; 24, 1966, 412-5; 26, 1968, 517-21; 28, 1970, 398-402; 30, 1972, 472-6; 32, 1974, 456-61; 34, 1976, 463-7; 36, 1978, 391-3; 38, 1980, 464-7; 41, 1983, 476-9.
*Late products*: Bémont 1971; Bémont *et al* 1982; Bourgeois 1979; Bousquet 1963; Fromols 1937; 1938; Genin 2007, 163-5*; Knorr 1919; 1952; Labrousse 1981; Lafon 1978; Martin 1986a; Mees 2007*; Renard 1955; Vernhet 1977*; Vernhet & Vertet 1976

A3 **Montans**, Tarn

1 43° 51′ 54″ N, 1° 53′ 03″ E
2 Kiln-centre
3 10 - 130/40, late production to 160+
4 Late products are known from N Britain and SW France.
5 Most of the bibliography is relevant only to the 1st century production, and is not given here.
*General surveys*: Labrousse 1975*; Martin 1986b; Polak 2000, 18-20
*Excavation*: Martin 1974*; 1977a*; 1977c; Reutti & Schulz 2010; *Gallia* 26, 1968, 554-6; 28, 1970, 435; 30, 1972, 507-8; 32, 1974, 491-3; 34, 1976, 495-6; 36, 1978, 424; 38, 1980, 500; 41, 1983, 499.
*Products and typology*: Durand-Lefebvre 1946; 1954; Martin 1977b; 1979; 1986; 2009; Mees 1995; Simpson 1976*; 1987; Tilhard 1972; 1977; Wild 2012

A4 **Le Rajol**, Millau, Aveyron
1 44° 05′ 59″ N, 3° 04′ 56″ E
2 Kiln-site
3 Late $2^{nd}$/mid $3^{rd}$ century
4 Local region
5 Vernhet 1977

A5 **Le Roc**, Millau, Aveyron
1 44° 05′ 40″ N, 3° 04′ 09″ E
2 Kiln-site
3 Late $2^{nd}$/mid $3^{rd}$ century
4 Local only
5 Vernhet 1977; *Gallia* 24, 1966, 412-3

Central Gaulish Area

B1 **Autun**, Saône-et-Loire
1 46° 57′ 03″ N, 4° 18′ 04″ E
2 Mould fragments found, probably of Lezoux origin, in a pottery and figurine workshop
3 Mid/late $2^{nd}$ century
4 Not known
5 Majurel 1969; Vertet 1980, 20; *Gallia* 30, 1972, 457

B2 **Brioude**, Haute-Loire
1 45° 17′ 40″ N, 3° 23′ 02″ E
2 Mould fragments found, probably from a kiln site
3 Not known
4 Not known
5 Vertet 1980, 23

B3 **Chantenay-St-Imbert**, Nièvre
1 46° 43′ 59″ N, 3° 11′ 00″ E
2 Samian production debris
3 Not known
4 Not known
5 Vertet 1979, 146; 1980, 23

B4 **Chézieu**, Loire
1 45° 34′ 29″ N, 4° 06′ 16″ E
2 Mould fragment found, in style of X-2
3 Early $2^{nd}$ century
4 Not known
5 Dumoulin 1997, 501

B5 **Clermont-Ferrand**, Puy-de-Dôme
1 45° 46′ 37″ N, 3° 05′ 13″ E
2 Moulds and other production debris found, but most of the discoveries are $19^{th}$ century and somewhat doubtful.
3 $2^{nd}$ century; $1^{st}$ – $2^{nd}$ century non-samian pottery production definitely attested.
4 Not known
5 Fournier 1970, 240-2; Vertet 1980, 24

B6 **Cordelle**, Loire
1 45° 56′ 13″ N, 4° 02′ 34″ E
2 Mould fragments found, at Les Garioux site, one attributable to Libertus B
3 Early/mid $2^{nd}$ century
4 Not known
5 Dumoulin 1997, 501

B7 **Courpière**, Puy-de-Dôme
1 45° 45′ 15″ N, 3° 32′ 19″ E
2 Kiln-site
3 Late $1^{st}$ – $2^{nd}$ century, probably equivalent to nearby Lezoux: moulds of early $2^{nd}$ century amongst finds.
4 Not known
5 Bet, Valaude & Vertet 1986; Pinel 1970, 22; Vertet 1979, 146; 1980, 25-6

B8 **Feurs**, Loire
1 45° 44′ 38″ N, 4° 13′ 28″ E
2 Probable kiln site. Moulds found, possibly from the Roman town, of Lezoux type and probably imported from there; chemical analysis also indicates local mould production, of late potters such as Iullinus.
3 Mid/late $2^{nd}$ century and later. The majority of potters represented are CG IV, including $3^{rd}$ century Iullinus and Ollognatus.
5 Dumoulin 1997*; Vertet 1980, 26-7

B9 **Gueugnon**, Saône-et-Loire
1 46° 36′ 04″ N, 4° 03′ 51″ E
2 Kiln-centre
3 Late $2^{nd}$ - mid $3^{rd}$ century
4 Brittany; lower Loire; Sarthe region
5 Gaillard & Parriat 1975*; Groupe Archéologique de Gueugnon-Montceau 1974; Hofmann 1967c; Mitard 1982; Notet 1977; 1981; 1982; 1986; 1996*; Notet & Mitard 1987; Vauthey & Vauthey 1968; Vertet 1980, 28; *Gallia* 24, 1966, 409; 26, 1968, 496-500; 28, 1970, 389-90; 30, 1972, 457; 34, 1976, 456; 37, 1979, 456-7; 39, 1981, 432; 41, 1983, 407-8

B10 **Lezoux**, Puy-de-Dôme
1 45° 49′ 42″ N, 3° 22′ 46″ E extending as far north as 45° 50′ 47″ N, 3° 23′ 39″ E (Serve-d'Ervier site), and south to 45° 18′ 16″ N, 3° 22′ 23″ E (Ocher site)
2 Major kiln-centre, spreading over several $km^2$, with 5 main centres (see map Bet & Delage 2009, 478, fig. 61)
3 10 - 40/50 for early products; possible continuity of production up to main period 100/110 - 220/30; some late $3^{rd}$ – $4^{th}$ century moulded figurative bowl production in fabric similar to terre sigillée claire B.
4 Britain, France (except the S), Upper Danube (until late $2^{nd}$ century). Only early/mid $2^{nd}$ century products reach the Rhineland and N part of the Low Countries. Early and late products generally local only, but $3^{rd}$ century products also found in western Gaul. $4^{th}$-century distribution very local.
5 The bibliography for the $1^{st}$ century kiln-centre is not given here.
***General surveys***: Bet & Vertet 1986; Déchelette 1904*; Delage 1999a*; Lewit 2013; Pinel 1975; Plicque 1887a; Stanfield & Simpson 1958*; 1990*; Vertet 1975a*; 1978; 1980, 29; 1989
***Excavations***: Bet 1988*; Bet & Delage 2009*; 2010; Bet & Gangloff 1987*; Caillaud 1914; Chalut 1970; 1971; Delage 2001a*; Frere & Hartley 1966; Picon 1973*; Pinel 1970a; Reutti & Schulz 2010; Vertet 1967b; 1970; 1974; 1975b; 1979*; Vertet & Bet 1978; 1980a*; 1980b; Vertet & Hartley 1968; *Gallia* 2, 1944, 279; 4, 1946, 344; 5, 1947, 223; 6, 1948, 281; 7, 1949,

298; 8,1959, 232; 10, 1952, 124; 11, 1953, 345; 12, 1954, 553; 14, 1956, 137; 15, 1957, 322; 16, 1958, 486; 17, 1959, 503; 21, 1963, 498; 23, 1965, 408-10; 25, 1967, 314-22; 27, 1969, 332-7; 29, 1971, 327-32; 31, 1973, 445-8; 33, 1975, 431-5; 35, 1977, 426-7; 37, 1979, 476; 39, 1981, 453.

***Distribution***: Berke 1988; Corrocher 1977; Delage 1998*; Ferdière 1974; Gabler 1964; Gabler & Vaday 1986; King 1981; Marsh 1981; Pinel 1977; Plicque 1887b; Raepsaet 1987; Smith 1907; 1909; Vauthey & Vauthey 1967b

***Products and typology*** (apart from the standard references, for which see site gazetteer abbreviations): Argyropoulos 1995; Bémont 1972; 1973; 1975a; 1975b; 1977a*; 1980; Bémont *et al* 1982; 1983; Bémont & Rogers 1977; 1978*; 1979*; 1980*; Bet *et* al 1989*; Blanc 1964; 1965; Boon 1970; Comité Archéologique de Lezoux 1957a; 1957b; 1957c; 1958a; 1958b; De Groot 1967; Delage 1999b*; 2000a; 2009; 2012; Delage & Seguier 2009; Detsicas 1960b; 1962; 1963b; 1964a; 1964b; 1966; 1967; Dickinson 2005; Ferdière 1972; Gendron 1971; Grezillier 1962; Hartley 1972a*; Hofmann 1966b; 1966c; 1967b; 1967d; 1969b; Johns 1971; Knorr 1939; Marandet 1960; Morel & Peyre 1973; Morlet 1957, 1958; Oswald 1929; 1930; 1931; 1948; Pinel 1970b; Pitts 2012; Rogers 1970; Rogers & Laing 1966; Romeuf 1970; Romeuf-Vialatte 1970; Sanquer 1967; Sauvaget 1970; Sauvaget & Vauthey 1970; Sauvaget & Vertet 1967; Simpson 1957a, 1971; 1973; 1977; Simpson & Rogers 1969*; Société Archéologique de Neuville 1978; Stanfield 1929; 1935; 1937; Vauthey & Vauthey 1970a; 1977b; Vertet 1961a; 1961b; 1971; 1972a; 1972b; 1973a; 1976a*; 1976b; 1976c; Vertet & Pic 1961; Vialette 1968; Vialatte & Vertet 1967; Wild 2005; Zumstein 1964

***Late production***: Bet 1985; Bet & Gangloff 1987; Bet & Wittmann 1995; Delage 2001a; Delage & Guillier 1997; Rigoir *et al* 1973; Vertet, Picon & Vichy 1970; Vertet, Rigoir & Raignoux 1970*; *Gallia* 27, 1969, 337

B11 **Lubié** (Lubillé), Lapalisse, Allier
1 46° 15′ 38″ N, 3° 37′ 28″ E
2 Kiln-centre
3 Mid/late 2nd - mid 3rd century
4 Not known, but probably as Lezoux, since the site is a satellite. Banvus, Casurius, Marcus and other wares were produced at this site.
5 Bet & Delage 2000*; Vertet 1975, 49; 1979, 146; 1980, 31; 1986b; Vertet & Pic 1961, 36

B12 **Lyon**, Rhône
1 45° 45′ 49″ N, 4° 50′ 07″ E
2 Probable production centre for appliqué ware
3 Early 2nd - 4th century, main period late 2nd - early 3rd century
4 S France, Rhineland
5 Desbat 1981*.with earlier references therein; Vertet 1969*

B13 **Manglieu**, Puy-de-Dôme
1 45° 36′ 45″ N, 3° 21′ 01″ E
2 Kiln-site
3 2nd century and perhaps later.
4 Not known, but probably as Lezoux, since the site is a satellite. Paternus, Laxtucissa and contemporary wares were produced at this site.
5 Bet, Delage & Murat 2000

B14 **Les Martres-de-Veyre**, Puy-de-Dôme
1 45° 41′ 09″ N, 3° 11′ 29″ E
2 Major kiln centre
3 90/100 - 150/160, main period up to 120/30
4 France, Britain, some products found in Rhineland and Upper Danube
5 ***General surveys and excavations***: Romeuf 1986; Romeuf & Romeuf 1977a, 1977b; 2001*; Terrisse 1954; 1958a; 1958b; 1960b; 1968*; Vertet 1979, 146; 1980, 30; *Gallia* 12, 1954, 200; 13, 1955, 188; 27, 1969, 338; 33, 1975, 435-6; 35, 1977, 427-8; 37, 1979, 476-8; 39, 1981, 453-5; 41, 1983, 425-7
***Products and typology***: Bemman 1981; Blanc 1965; Detsicas 1963a*; Hatt 1958; Hofmann 1969b; Johns et al 1977; Lutz 1963b; Rogers 1972; 1977; Romeuf & Romeuf 1978; Terrisse 1960a; 1963a; 1963b; Webster & Webster 2012

B15 **Montverdun**, Loire
1 45° 42′ 56″ N, 4° 04′ 03″ E
2 Mould fragments found, probably made at Lezoux
3 Not known
4 Not known
5 Dumoulin 1997, 501

B16 **Neris-les-Bains**, Allier
1 46° 17′ 17″ N, 2° 39′ 35″ E
2 Kiln-site
3 Early 1st century production definitely attested; late 2nd century kilns known, but not certainly producing samian
4 Not known
5 Vertet 1979, 146; 1980, 31-2; *Gallia* 29, 1971, 323-4; 31, 1973, 449; 33, 1975, 423-7; 37, 1979, 469-71

B17 **Les Queyriaux**, Cournon-d'Auvergne, Puy-de-Dôme
1 45° 43′ 43″ N, 3° 12′ 23″ E
2 Kiln site
3 120/30-160/70 for moulds of Cinnamus and associates (group 1); later group of vessels includes Banvus, Marcus and Advocisus, suggesting probable continued production into early 3rd century.
4 Not known, but probably as Lezoux, in view of the potters represented.
5 Bet *et al* 1998; Delage 2001b

B18 **St Bonnet**, Yzeure, Allier
1 46° 34′ 21″ N, 3° 20′ 59″ E
2 Samian production debris, from kiln-centre
3 Probably mid 2nd century for samian production, when figurine production declined. The Flavian kilns did not produce samian, and most of the 2nd century products were figurines.

4 Uncertain, but the figurines were widely distributed to Central and N Gaul, and Britain.
5 Abauzit & Vertet 1976; Déchelette 1904, I, 207-8; Vertet 1979, 146, 148; 1980, 41; *Gallia* 27, 1969, 317; 35, 1977, 421-3

B19 **St Didier-la-Forêt**, Allier
1 46° 13′ 34″ N, 3° 20′ 41″ E
2 Samian production debris
3 Not known
4 Not known
5 Vertet 1979, 146; 1980, 32-3

B20 **St Pourçain-sur-Besbre**, Allier
1 46° 28′ 32″ N, 3° 38′ 24″ E
2 Samian production debris, from kiln-centre
3 Probably mid 2nd century and later for samian ware. Main production was figurines and coarse ware.
4 Not known
5 Vertet 1980, 35

B21 **St Remy-en-Rollat**, Allier
1 46° 11′ 05″ N, 3° 23′ 29″ E
2 Kiln-centre
3 Moulded glazed and coarse ware produced in early 1st century, samian production possible in 2nd century but uncertain
4 Not known
5 Vertet 1961; 1979, 146; 1980, 35-6

B22 **St Romain-le-Puy**, Loire
1 45° 33′ 17″ N, 4° 07′ 27″ E
2 Figure punch found
3 Probably mid/late 2nd century
5 *Gallia* 29, 1971, 415-6

B23 **Tancon**, Sâone-et-Loire
1 46° 12′ 04″ N, 4° 15′ 47″ E
2 Mould fragment found, of Cinnamus or Paullus style
3 Mid 2nd century or later
4 Not known
5 Dumoulin 1997, 501

B24 **Terre-Franche**, Bellerive-sur-Allier, Vichy, Allier
1 46° 06′ 19″ N, 3° 24′ 40″ E
2 Kiln-centre
3 120-230; main period for samian ware mid/late 2nd century
4 Not known, but products of Cinnamus, Servus II and contemporaries were made here, which were probably distributed as widely as their Lezoux products.
5 ***General surveys and excavations***: Corrocher 1981; Groupe de Fouilles de Terre-Franche 1970* (and earlier references therein); Hofmann 1973; Lantier 1954, 553; Vauthey & Vauthey 1957; 1963b; 1967a; 1986; Vertet 1980, 21-2; *Gallia* 17, 1959, 363; 19, 1961, 355; 21, 1963, 485; 25, 1967, 296.
***Products and typology***: Blanc 1965; Corrocher 1981; 1983; Corrocher & Randoin 1974; 1977; Ferdière 1972; Hofmann 1969a; Mitard 1965; Morlet 1957; 1958; Picon & Vauthey 1975; Vauthey & Vauthey 1958; 1959; 1963a; 1966; 1967a; 1970a; 1970b; 1973; 1974; 1975; 1976; 1977; Vauthey *et al* 1967; Vertet 1973b

B25 **Toulon-sur-Allier**, Allier
1 46° 31′ 04″ N, 3° 21′ 36″ E
2 Kiln-centre, 2 sites known 1km apart on either side of a small stream
3 Early-late 2nd century samian production known, with figurines probably being produced during approximately the same period.
4 Uncertain, but since the site was a satellite of Lezoux, distribution may have been widespread.
5 Bet & Vertet 1980; Féraudy & Vertet 1986; Vertet 1959a*; 1959b; 1977; 1979, 146, 154-5; 1980, 37-9; *Gallia* 17, 1959, 364-5; 19, 1961, 357; 37, 1979, 471-2; 39, 1981, 447-9

B26 **Vichy**, Allier
1 46° 07′ 55″ N, 3° 25′ 31″ E
2 Kiln-centre, of about 14 kilns under the site of the station; other sites on the periphery of the ancient town also known.
3 Uncertain, but probably mid 2nd century
4 Not known, but possibly widespread, as the site was a satellite of Lezoux.
5 Corrocher 1981, 142ff; Vertet 1975, 49 (reference to early finds); 1979, 146; 1980, 40; 1986a; *Gallia* 37, 1979, 472

Centre-West Group

C1 **Mazières-en-Mauge**, Maine-et-Loire
1 47° 02′ 46″ N, 0° 48′ 58″ W
2 Kiln-site using moulds made at Mougon and Nouâtre
3 As Mougon and Nouâtre
4 Probably as Mougon and Nouâtre
5 Delage 2000b; 2010

C2 **Mougon**, Crouzilles, Indre-et-Loire
1 47° 06′ 59″ N, 0° 28′ 22″ E
2 Kiln-site
3 Mid-late 2nd century, with earlier period back to mid/late 1st century, and later period to mid 3rd century
4 Brittany; lower Loire; Sarthe region
5 Delage 1997; 2006; 2010; Ferdière 1975, 92-4; 1988; 1989; Ferdière & Gendron 1986a; 1986b; Gendron 1977; Guitton 2004 ; Tilhard 2004; *Gallia* 32, 1974, 315; 34, 1976, 320; 38, 1980, 330

C3 **Nouâtre**, Indre-et-Loire
1 47° 03′ 04″ N, 0° 32′ 58″ E
2 Kiln-site
3 Mid-late 2nd century, with earlier period back to mid/late 1st century, and later period to mid 3rd century
4 Brittany; lower Loire; Sarthe region
5 Delage 1997; Ferdière 1975, 92-4; 1988; 1989; Ferdière & Gendron 1986c; Gendron 1977

C4 **Poitiers**, Vienne
1 46° 34′ 48″ N, 0° 20′ 25″ E
2 Kiln-site (probable) and mould fragments
3 Probably as Mougon and Nouâtre
4 Local region only?

5 Ferdière 1988; 1989; Ferdière & Gendron 1986d; Gendron 1977, 279; Tilhard 2004*

ARGONNE GROUP

D1 **Avocourt**, Meuse
1 49° 13′ 07″ N, 5° 08′ 33″ E (Avocourt); 49° 11′ 25″ N, 5° 05′ 26″ E (Les Allieux)
2 Kiln-centre, of at least 2 sites (including **Les Allieux** and **Forêt-de-Hesse**) spread over *c* 1 km$^2$
3 Mid 2nd – 4th century, producing moulded ware in the mid 2nd - early 3rd century, and stamped ware later. 1st century production is known, but not of samian ware.
4 Low Countries, NE France, the Rhineland, some to Britain.
5 Brulet *et al.* 2000; Chenet 1941*; Chenet & Gaudron 1955* (and earlier references therein); Feller 1989; Gazenbeek & Van der Leeuw 2003*; Mitard 1979; Mitard, Hofmann & Lutz 1986, 204-7; Vanderhoeven 1969; *Gallia* 26, 1968, 380; 36, 1978, 334; 38, 1980, 416

D2 **La Chalade** (Lachalade), Meuse
1 49° 10′ 01″ N, 4° 57′ 34″ E
2 Mould fragments in the style of Tribunus, probably from a destroyed kiln-site
3 Probably late 2nd - early 3rd century
4 Not known
5 Chenet & Gaudron 1955; Gazenbeek & Van der Leeuw 2003, 303

D3 **Jaulges/Villiers-Vineux**, Yonne
1 47° 56′ 31″ N, 3° 47′ 21″ E (not on Fig 7.9 – the site is to the SW of the map)
2 Kiln-centre
3 Late 2nd – 4th century, producing Argonne style wares in the late period. Pottery produced at this site in 1st century, but not samian ware.
4 Local region
5 Bémont *et al* 1980; Jacob & Leredde 1974*; 1975; 1979; 1985*; 1986; *Gallia* 30, 1972, 465-7; 37, 1979, 468; 39, 1981, 439; 41, 1983, 413

D4 **Lavoye**, Meuse
1 49° 02′ 35″ N, 5° 07′ 49″ E
2 Kiln-centre, spreading over c 1 km into neighbouring village of Autrecourt
3 Mid-2nd – 4th century, as Avocourt (q.v.). Evidence of 1st century non-samian production.
4 As for Avocourt
5 Bémont 1974; Chenet 1941*; Chenet & Gaudron 1955*; de Maeyer 1933; Deschieter *et al.* 2012; Fölzer 1913*; Gazenbeek & Van der Leeuw 2003*; Hanut & Henrotay 2006, fig. 23; Hofmann 1961; 1968*; 1970b; 1979*; Mitard, Hofmann & Lutz 1986, 196-201; Oswald 1945; Ricken 1934*

D5 **Pont-des-Rèmes**, Florent-en-Argonne, Marne
1 49° 06′ 30″ N, 4° 59′ 43″ E
2 Kiln-site
3 Mid/late 2nd century
4 Not known, but probably as for Avocourt and Lavoye
5 Chenet & Gaudron 1955; Gazenbeek & Van der Leeuw 2003; Mitard, Hofmann & Lutz 1986, 201-3

D6 **Reims**, Marne
1 49° 14′ 34″ N, 4° 02′ 28″ E
2 Kiln centre at parc-Saint-Rémi to S of the Roman city, producing gallo-belgic ware, including moulded grey-ware beakers in Argonne-derived styles
3 Probably mid/late 2nd century for the moulded pieces, but production generally goes back to early 1st century
4 Probably local region
5 *Gallia* 31, 1973, 410-3

D7 **Vaux-Régnier**, Florent-en-Argonne, Marne
1 49° 08′ 28″ N, 4° 58′ 07″ E
2 Kiln-site
3 Late 2nd - early 3rd century
4 Not known, but probably as for Avocourt and Lavoye
5 Chenet & Gaudron 1955; Gazenbeek & Van der Leeuw 2003

MOSELLE AND SARRE REGION

E1 **Blickweiler**, Saarland
1 49° 12′ 51″ N, 7° 15′ 18″ E
2 Kiln-centre
3 105 - 150/60 and later. Products from reused moulds up to early/mid 3rd century
4 Local region, Rhineland, Low Countries, some to Britain
5 Bohn 1923; Heiligmann 1990; Klumbach 1933; Knorr & Sprater 1927*; Lutz 1970b; Oldenstein-Pferdehirt 1986; Petit 1989; 2001*; Pferdehirt 1987; Ricken 1934; Roller 1966; Schumacher 1988

E2 **Boucheporn**, Moselle
1 49° 08′ 20″ N, 6° 36′ 33″ E
2 Kiln-centre
3 20/40 - 160, main period early 2nd century
4 Late products in local region only
5 Hatt 1964b; 1979; Hoerner 2000; Lutz 1962; 1964b; 1977a*; 1977c; 1986a; *Gallia* 18, 1960, 224; 22, 1964, 344-7; 24, 1966, 294-5; 26, 1968, 382-5

E3 **Chémery-Faulquemont**, Moselle
1 49° 00′ 57″ N, 6° 34′ 49″ E
2 Kiln centre
3 90 - 150/60, main period early 2nd century
4 Local region, Rhineland, Low Countries
5 ***Excavations and products***: Bémont *et al* 1983; Delort 1953*; Hatt 1958; Hoerner 2000; Lutz 1963a; 1963b; 1966; 1986b; Welter 1936; Zumstein 1964; *Gallia* 40, 1982, 327
***Saturninus-Satto***: Delort 1935; 1948; Demarolle 1987; 1989; Fischer 1987; Fölzer 1913; Lutz 1964a; 1965a; 1969; 1970°; 1970b; 1971; 1977b; 1977c; 1977d

E4 **Eincheville-le-Tenig**, Moselle
1 48° 59′ 46″ N, 6° 35′ 26″ E

2 Probable kiln-site, satellite of Chémery-Faulquemont
3 Early/mid 2nd century, coarse ware of 1st century
4 As for Chémery-Faulquemont
5 Coispine 1987; Lutz 1984; 1986c; Lutz & Weiler 1981; *Gallia* 38, 1980, 414; 40, 1982, 327

E5 **Eschweiler-Hof**, Saarland
1 49° 18′ 25″ N, 7° 11′ 38″ E
2 Kiln-site
3 135-60 or later
4 Local region and Rhineland
5 Fölzer 1913; Knorr & Sprater 1927*; Lutz 1972; Petit 1989; 2001*; Roller 1966; Reutti & Schulz 2010

E6 **Haute-Yutz** (and **Daspich-Ebange**), Thionville, Moselle
1 49° 20′ 47″ N, 6° 11′ 37″ E
2 Kiln-site
3 130/40 - 210
4 Local region, Rhineland, some to Low Countries
5 Fölzer 1913; Huld 1969; Stiller 1986; Stiller *et al* 1960*; *Gallia* 20, 1962, 483-92; 22, 1964, 340

E7 **Hombourg-Budange**, Thionville, Moselle
1 49° 17′ 45″ N, 6° 20′ 38″ E
2 Kiln-site
3 Late 2nd century
4 Not known, but probably local region and Rhineland. Stylistic links to Metz and Haute-Yutz
5 Gérard 1999

E8 **La Madeleine**, Laneuveville-devant-Nancy, Meurthe-et-Moselle
1 48° 38′ 37″ N, 6° 16′ 00″ E
2 Kiln-centre
3 105 - 70/80 or later
4 Local region, Rhineland, Low Countries, some to Britain
5 Bemman 1985; Fölzer 1913; France-Lanord 1979; France-Lanord & Beck 1986; Goury 1939; Oelmann 1911; Oldenstein-Pferdehirt 1986; Ricken 1934*; *Gallia* 26, 1968, 376-7

E9 **Metz**, Moselle
1 49° 06′ 42″ N, 6° 10′ 06″ E
2 Samian production debris (equivalent in style to Trier Werkstatt 1 and Sinzig phase 1) found at the Caserne de Lattre, to S of the Roman town
3 Late 2nd - early 3rd century (production more likely in the earlier part of this time-frame, i.e. late 2nd century)
4 Local region and Middle Rhine
5 Biehler & François 1977; Demarolle 1995; Lutz 1986e; Weiss-König 2011*; *Gallia* 30, 1972, 364-7

E10 **Mittelbronn**, Moselle
1 48° 46′ 17″ N, 7° 13′ 35″ E
2 Kiln-centre
3 Production starts mid 2nd century, main period late 2nd century and later. Satto and Cibisus products from reused moulds from late 2nd century. Non-samian production to mid/late 3rd century.
4 Mainly local region and Rhineland; some to Danube
5 Gabler 1987; Goubet & Meyer 2006*; Helmer & Deiber 1985; Lutz 1959; 1960; 1964c; 1965b; 1968; 1986d; 1970a*; Lutz & Morand-Hartmann 1955; *Gallia* 11, 1953, 147; 12, 1954, 478-9; 14, 1956, 289-93; 16, 1958, 322-3; 18, 1960, 233-4; 38, 1980, 452

E11 **Sarre-Union**, Bas-Rhin
1 48° 56′ 29″ N, 7° 5′ 30″ E
2 Samian production debris found at rue de Bitche, parcel 32, and nearby sites
3 Probably mid/late 2nd century. Stylistically attributed to the Saturninus-Satto group.
4 Not known
5 Gervreau *et al* 2009*; Hatt 1966

E12 **Trier**, Rheinland-Pfalz
1 49° 44′ 36″ N, 6° 37′ 46″ E
2 Major kiln-centre, located in southern outskirts of the Roman town
3 1st period 125-50, 2nd (main) period 145 - 250/75, possible production of plain ware up to 300. Other pottery made 1st – 4th century.
4 Rhineland, especially lower Rhine, Low Countries, some to Britain
5 Binsfeld 1977; Fölzer 1913*; Frey 1993; 2000; Gard 1937*; Haalebos 1973; Hanut & Henrotay 2006, fig. 23; Huld 1969; Huld-Zetsche 1971a; 1971b; 1971c; 1972*; 1978; 1986; 1993*; 1998; Kalee 1973; Loeschcke 1921; Lutz 1969; Merten 1993; 2011; Reutti & Schulz 2010; Weidner 2010

### Middle Rhine Region

F1 **Altenstadt**, Wissembourg, Bas-Rhin
1 49° 01′ 46″ N, 7° 58′ 01″ E
2 Mould fragment of Cerialis, Belsus or Mammilianus of Rheinzabern
3 Late 2nd - early 3rd century
5 Forrer 1911, 193; Lafon 1986b; Simon 1977a, 472

F2 **Heiligenberg-Dinsheim** (or Dinsheim-Heiligenberg), Bas-Rhin
1 48° 32′ 25″ N, 7° 24′ 10″ E
2 Kiln-site
3 105 - early 3rd century, main period mid 2nd century
4 Mainly to Upper Danube, Switzerland and the local region
5 Biegert 2003; Delage & Mees 2009; Forrer 1911*;Gabler 1987; Hatt 1964a; Hatt *et al* 1973, 132; Imlau 1969; Kern 1986a; Kern *et al.* 2009*; Knorr 1906; Pastor 2013; Reutti & Schulz 2010; Simon 1977b; *Gallia* 20, 1962, 510-1

F3 **Horbourg-Wihr**, Haut-Rhin
1 48° 04′ 42″ N, 7° 23′ 44″ E
2 Kiln site with mould fragments found of Luxeuil ware
3 Early/mid 2nd century
4 Probably local region
5 Hatt *et al* 1973, opposite p. 129; Jehl & Bonnet 1969; Lafon 1986b; *Gallia* 26, 1968, 433-4

F4 **Ittenwiller** (or Ittenweiler), Saint Pierre, Bas-Rhin
1 48° 23′ 00″ N, 7° 27′ 20″ E
2 Kiln-centre
3 120 - 150/75 or later
4 Local region, Rhineland and Upper Danube
5 Biegert 2003; Forrer 1911*;Gabler 1987; Hatt *et al* 1973, 132; Kern 1986b; Kern & Helmer 1982; Lutz 1968

F5 **Jebsheim**, Haut-Rhin
1 48° 07′ 29″ N, 7° 28′ 39″ E
2 Mould fragment found, of Julius II-Julianus I of Rheinzabern
3 Probably early/mid 3rd century
5 Forrer 1911, 194; Hatt *et al* 1973, 132; Lafon 1986b; Simon 1977a

F6 **Lehen**, Freiburg-in-Breisgau, Baden-Württemberg
1 48° 01′ 02″ N, 7° 48′ 04″ E
2 Kiln site
3 Early/mid 2nd century; stylistically related to Luxeuil
4 Local region
5 Nuber 1989

F7 **Luxeuil-les-Bains**, Haute-Saône
1 47° 49′ 22″ N, 6° 22′ 56″ E
2 Kiln centre to N of *vicus* and thermal baths
3 90 - 130 and later; non-samian production late 1st – end 2nd century
4 Local region, some to Rhineland
5 Card 2008*; Fölzer 1913; Jeannin 1967; Kahn 1986; Lerat 1961; 1982; Lerat & Jeannin 1960*; Reutti & Schulz 2010; *Gallia* 18, 1960, 252-3; 34, 1976, 419; 40, 1982, 383; 42, 1984, 337-8

F8 **Mathay,** Mandeure, Doubs
1 47° 27′ 0″ N, 6° 47′ 17″ E
2 Kiln-site. Moulds for form 30 in simple decorative styles, producing 'Mode C' products. Other types of pottery also manufactured.
3 Mid 2nd century onwards; abandonment at end of 2nd century
4 Local region
5 Lame & Mazimann 1993*

F9 **Offemont**, Belfort
1 47° 39′ 47″ N, 6° 52′ 44″ E
2 Kiln-site
3 130 - 50, associated with Luxeuil production
4 Probably local region
5 Forrer 1911, 222; Rilliot 1969; 1976; 1986; *Gallia* 22, 1964, 375-6; 24, 1966, 345; 26, 1968, 435-6; 28, 1970, 345; 30, 1972, 421-2; 32, 1974, 425-6; 34, 1976, 436-7; 36, 1978, 387; 40, 1982, 387; 42, 1984, 338

F10 **Reichshoffen**, Bas-Rhin
1 48° 56′ 00″ N, 7° 40′ 03″ E
2 Mould fragment found (no details) at possible kiln site
3 Not known
5 Forrer 1911, 193; Lafon 1986b

F11 **Rheinzabern**, Rheinland-Pfalz
1 49° 06′ 56″ N, 8° 16′ 36″ E
2 Major kiln centre
3 140/50 - 235/60, with non-samian production from late 1st century
4 Rhineland, Danube, Alpine region, some to E Gaul, Low Countries and Britain, especially S and E Britain. Many exports beyond the *limes,* as far as Poland and Slovakia
5 ***General surveys***: Garbsch 1982, 60-74; Ludowici 1904; 1905; 1908; 1912; 1927; Roller 1965
***Excavations***: Bernhard 1981b; 1990*; Rau 1976; 1977a*; 1977b; Reutti 1983*; 1984; Reutti & Schulz 2010*; Schulz 1999*; Sprater 1930
***Products and typology***: Bernhard 1981a*; Bittner 1986*; 1996*; 2011*; Delmaire 1971; De Maeyer 1933; Fischer 1968; Garbsch 1966; Gimber 1986; 1993*; 1999; Gschwind 2006; Hofmann 1970b; Kortüm & Mees 1998*; Lutz 1970b; Mees 1993*; 1994a; 2002*; Nuber 1969; Oldenstein-Pferdehirt 1986; Pferdehirt 1971; Reubel 1912; Ricken 1948*; Ricken & Fischer 1963*; Ricken & Thomas 2005*; Ruprechtsburger 1974; Schönberger 1963; Stanfield 1929; Trimpe-Burger 1961
***Distribution***: Berke 1988; Gabler 1964; Gabler & Vaday 1986; Gschwind 2006; Laser 1998; Mees 2002*; Raepsaet 1987

F12 **Riegel**, Emmendingen, Baden-Württemberg
1 48° 09′ 05″ N, 7° 44′ 57″ E
2 Mould fragments found, in the style of Giamillus of Lehen, and Rheinzabern styles
3 Not known
4 Not known
5 Simon 1977a

F13 **Schiltigheim**, Strasbourg, Bas-Rhin
1 48° 36′ 18″ N, 7° 44′ 54″ E
2 Mould found, of Victorinus II of Rheinzabern, and other possible production debris. A possible kiln site.
3 Late 2nd - early 3rd century
5 Forrer 1911, 189-90; Lafon 1986b; Simon 1977a

F14 **Strasbourg**, Bas-Rhin
1 48° 34′ 54″ N, 7° 44′ 44″ E
2 Mould fragment found in rue Ste Barbe to W of the Roman fortress and town, in style of Janus of Heiligenberg; no other production debris associated.
3 Mid 2nd century
5 Forrer 1927, 464-5

F15 **Stettfeld**, Ubstadt-Weiher, Karlsruhe, Baden-Württemberg
1 49° 10′ 54″ N, 8° 38′ 37″ E
2 Kiln site, mainly for coarse ware, but some moulded samian produced, derived from Reginus I of Rheinzabern
3 Late 2nd century
4 Local region
5 Schallmayer 1982; 1984

## Neckar Region

G1 **Bad Cannstatt**, Baden-Württemberg
1 48° 48′ 18″ N, 9° 12′ 56″ E
2 Kiln site, with possible samian ware production debris, and pieces in style of Reginus and Janu (of Rheinzabern?).
3 Late 2nd century
4 Local region
5 Paret 1921; 1932, 133-5; Riedl 2011, 29-32*

G2 **Köngen**, Baden-Württemberg
1 48° 40′ 46″ N, 9° 21′ 59″ E
2 Mould fragment found, of Comitialis V of Rheinzabern
3 Late 2nd - early 3rd century
5 Simon 1977a

G3 **Kräherwald**, Stuttgart-Feuerbach, Baden-Württemberg
1 48° 47′ 00″ N, 9° 08′ 59″ E
2 Kiln site
3 160 - 200
4 Local region, some to Upper Danube
5 Knorr 1905, 41; 1906, 89; Paret 1932, 135; Riedl 2011, 20-3*; Simon 1984; *FS* 18, part 2, 1967, 119

G4 **Neuhausen-auf-den-Fildern**, Baden-Württemberg
1 48° 40′ 58″ N, 9° 16′ 41″ E
2 Mould fragments found, possibly for copying Rheinzabern styles (e.g. of Verecundus II) in local wares. Probably linked to nearby Nürtingen
3 Late 2nd - early 3rd century
5 Simon 1977a

G5 **Nürtingen**, Baden-Württemberg
1 48° 37′ 27″ N, 9° 21′ 03″ E
2 Kiln site, using locally-produced moulds in the style of Comitialis, Primitius and Verecundus of Rheinzabern
3 Late 2nd - early 3rd century
4 Local region, some to Upper Danube
5 Luik 2005a*; 2005b; 2012*; Paret 1932, 352; Riedl 2011, 32-7*; Simon 1977a

G6 **Pforzheim**, Baden-Württemberg
1 48° 53′ 27″ N, 8° 42′ 48″ E
2 Mould fragments found, in Rheinzabern styles: Julius II –Julianus I and Julianus II
3 Late 2nd-early 3rd century
5 Kortüm 1995, 213-5

G7 **Pfrondorf**, Tübingen, Baden-Württemberg
1 48° 32′ 52″ N, 9° 06′ 38″ E
2 Mould fragment from kiln site (which does not seem to have produced samian ware)
3 Not known, but probably late 2nd - early 3rd century
5 Paret 1932, 142; Simon 1977a

G8 **Rottweil**, Baden-Württemberg
1 48° 09′ 25″ N, 8° 38′ 43″ E
2 Mould found (no details); much evidence for potting but no direct evidence of samian production
3 Unknown; imitation plain samian made in 1st century
5 Rüsch 1981, 80

G9 **Rutesheim**, Baden-Württemberg
1 48° 48′ 29″ N, 8° 56′ 42″ E
2 Mould fragments found, of Julius II-Julianus I and Ware B with O 382/3 of Rheinzabern
3 Early/mid 3rd century
5 Knorr 1905; Simon 1977a

G10 **Waiblingen-Beinstein**, Baden-Württemberg
1 48° 49′ 20″ N, 9° 20′ 56″ E
2 Kiln centre, with evidence of moulds and figure punches. Mainly production of Reginus, with links to Heiligenberg
3 160 - early 3rd century
4 Local region, some to Upper Danube
5 Kaiser 2006; Paret 1932, 135; 1938; Pferdehirt 1974; Ricken 1938*; Riedl 2011, 23-9*; Simon 1984*; *FB-W* 10, 1985, 581-2

## Bavaria and Austria

H1 **Bregenz**, Vorarlberg
1 47° 30′ 02″ N, 9° 44′ 32″ E
2 Mould fragments found, in style of Reginus II of Rheinzabern and the Neckar area and Cerialis II of Rheinzabern
3 Late 2nd - early 3rd century
5 Forrer 1911, 169; Kellner 1962; 125-6; Knorr 1905, 33; Simon 1977a

H2 **Kempten-in-Allgau**, Schwaben
1 47° 43′ 35″ N, 10° 19′ 28″ E
2 Mould fragments found in pottery shop in the Roman town, of Helenius of Westerndorf (also local production suspected in Westerndorf-derived style)
3 *c* 200 and later
5 Czysz 1982; Kellner 1962, 119-25

H3 **Nassenfels**, Eichstatt, Mittel-Franken
1 48° 47′ 50″ N, 11° 13′ 42″ E
2 Mould fragment found, in Trier-derived style
3 Probably early/mid 3rd century
5 Böhme 1961; Kellner 1962, 119

H4 **Pfaffenhofen**, Schechen, Oberbayern
1 47° 53′ 26″ N, 12° 07′ 27″ E
2 Kiln centre
3 190 - 260
4 Local region and Middle Danube
5 Christlein & Kellner 1969*; Christlein *et al* 1976*; Gabler 1978; Garbsch 1982, 86-8 ; Kellner 1964; 1968; 1971b; 1973; Picon 1974

H5 **Pocking**, Niederbayern
1 48° 24′ 05″ N, 13° 18′ 39″ E
2 Mould fragment found, in local style probably connected with Westerndorf
3 Early/mid 3rd century
5 Kellner 1962, 116-9

H6 **Schwabegg**, Augsburg, Schwaben
1 48° 11′ 00″ N, 10° 41′ 20″ E

2 Kiln site
3 170/80 – 230. Set up as a branch establishment of Schwabmünchen, and also with links to Rheinzabern
4 Local region, some to Middle Danube
5 Czysz 1981; 2000; Czysz & Sommer 1983, 27; Gabler 1996; Sölch 1999*

H7 **Schwabmünchen**, Augsburg, Schwaben
1 48° 11′ 27″ N, 10° 45′ 23″ E
2 Kiln site
3 170/80 – 230. Other pottery production from late 1st century
4 Local region, some to Middle Danube
5 Czysz 1980; 2000; Czysz & Sommer 1983*; Gabler 1996; Garbsch 1982, 75-6; Sölch 1999*; Sorge 2001*

H8 **Westerndorf**, Oberbayern
1 47° 49′ 18″ N, 12° 04′ 41″ E
2 Kiln centre
3 170 - 235 and later
4 Local region and Middle Danube, some to Rhineland, Britain and N Italy
5 ***General surveys and excavations***: Garbsch 1982, 77-85; Kellner 1961*; 1963b; 1968; 1971b; 1973; 1980; Prammer 1975; Radbauer 2013*; Von Hefner 1863*; Von Wiebeking 1824
***Products and typology***: Kellner 1981*; Kiss 1948*; Knorr 1906; Picon 1974; Streitberg 1971; 1973.
***Distribution***: Gabler 1966; 1983; Kellner 1962; Rutkowski 1967

## Switzerland and Savoy

J1 **Augst**, Basel-Landschaft
1. 47° 32′ 13″ N, 7° 43′ 15″ E
2. Derivative of sigillata production at Auf der Wacht site, including incised-decorated Dr 37. Mould fragment also found, of Reginus I of Rheinzabern
3. Early/mid 3rd century for the Auf der Wacht products. Mid/late 2nd century for the mould fragment
4 Local region
5 Schmid & Vogel Müller 2012; Vogel Müller 1990

J2 **Avenches**, Vaud
1 46° 52′ 50″ N, 7° 02′ 40″ E
2 Mould fragment found; probable local production centre
3 Mould of Iustus (of Lezoux), late 2nd century. Other local products of uncertain date due to plainness of decoration, possibly early/mid 2nd century
4 Local region
5 Castella & Meylan Krause 1999; Ettlinger 1966; Roth-Rubi 1986

J3 **Baden**, Aargau
1 47° 28′ 25″ N, 8° 18′ 23″ E
2 Kiln centre, using moulds in a Westerndorf-derived style; also mould of Cobnertus of Rheinzabern found.
3 Late 2nd - mid 3rd century, main period early/mid 3rd century
4 Local region
5 Ettlinger 1966; Ettlinger & Roth-Rubi 1979*; Forrer 1911, 173; Hedinger 1999; Roth-Rubi 1986; Simon 1977a; Vogt 1941

J4 **Bern-Engehalbinsel**, Bern
1 46° 58′ 23″ N, 7° 26′ 58″ E
2 Kiln centre
3 Early/mid 3rd century
4 Local region
5 Ettlinger 1966; Ettlinger & Roth-Rubi 1979*; Müller-Beck & Ettlinger 1963; Roth-Rubi 1984; 1986; Vogt 1941

J6 **Geneva**, Genève
1 46° 12′ 06″ N, 6° 08′ 51″ E
2 Mould fragment found, in Lezoux style
3 Probably mid/late 2nd century
5 Deonna 1925, 206; Ettlinger 1966

J7 **Martigny**, Valais
1 46° 05′ 41″ N, 7° 04′ 13″ E
2 Local production using moulds of potter E6 of Berne-Enge
3 Late 2nd-early 3rd century
4 Not known, probably local region
5 Haldimann 1999

J8 **Ottenhusen**, Hohenrain, Luzern
1 47° 09′ 50″ N, 8° 19′ 41″ E
2 Mould fragment found, from villa site, in local Baden/Berne/Windisch style
3 Early/mid 3rd century
5 Ettlinger & Roth-Rubi 1979, 38; Meyer-Freuler 1984

J9 **Solothurn**, Solothurn
1 47° 12′ 31″ N, 7° 32′ 16″ E
2 Mould fragment found, of Regulinus of Rheinzabern
3 Early/mid 3rd century
5 Ettlinger 1966, 237; Simon 1977a; Vogt 1941, 98

J10 **Thonon**, Haute-Savoie
1 46° 22′ 20″ N, 6° 28′ 54″ E
2 Mould fragment found at kiln site
3 Late 2nd - early 3rd century
4 Not known, probably local region
5 Paunier 1975, 132 & fig 14; *Gallia* 31, 1973, 546-7

J11 **Vidy-Lausanne**, Vaud
1 46° 31′ 07″ N, 6° 35′ 55″ E
2 Kiln centre
3 Main period mid 1st century, making plain ware and using imported SG moulds. Production to early 3rd century, and a punch and moulds are known in late SG/Banassac style, Lyon appliqué style and a local style (probably late 2nd - mid 3rd century).
4 Local region
5 Ettlinger 1966; Ettlinger & Roth-Rubi 1979; Laufer 1980; Paunier & Kaenel 1981*; Roth-Rubi 1986

J12 **Windisch**, Aargau
1 47° 28′ 40″ N, 8° 13′ 00″ E

2 Mould fragments found, in local Westerndorf-derived style and in style of Cobnertus of Rheinzabern. Probable kiln site.
3 Late 2nd - mid 3rd century
5 Ettlinger & Roth-Rubi 1979; Hedinger 1999; Kellner 1962; Simon 1977a; Vogt 1941, 98

Wetterau

K1 **Mainz**, Rheinland-Pfalz
1 50° 00′ 16″ N, 8° 16′ 44″ E
2 Moulds and waster found, possibly from kiln site but provenances mostly uncertain, in styles of Verecundus (from the Rhine), Comitialis and B F Attoni of Rheinzabern. Possible production of ware with ovolo X.
3 Late 2nd - early 3rd century (also Aco and 'Arretine' moulds of early 1st century)
4 Local region
5 Behrens 1915; Fremersdorf 1950; Klumbach 1972; Schleiermacher 1958; Simon 1977a

K2 **Massenheim**, Wiesbaden, Hessen
1 50° 02′ 28″ N, 8° 23′ 11″ E
2 Mould fragment found, but provenance uncertain, in style of Victor I of Rheinzabern
3 Early/mid 3rd century
5 Simon 1977a

K3 **Nied**, Höchst, Hessen
1 50° 05′ 53″ N, 8° 34′ 01″ E
2 Mould fragment found, of Sacer of La Madeleine, in kiln centre, but no other evidence of samian production
3 Mid 2nd century
5 Simon 1977a, 471

K4 **Praunheim** (Heddernheim), Hessen
1 50° 08′ 41″ N, 8° 36′ 25″ E
2 Mould fragment found, of Janu of Rheinzabern; it was used for making colour-coated ware 'imitation' samian. From kiln site producing non-samian ware, in *vicus*.
3 Mid/late 2nd century
5 Biegert 1999, 45-6; Fischer 1980; Huld-Zetsche 1982, 287; Simon 1977a; *FH* 5/6, 1966, 165-6

K5 **Saalburg**, Hessen
1 50° 16′ 22″ N, 8° 33′ 53″ E
2 Two mould fragments found, of Janu I of Rheinzabern, one from *vicus* to SE of fort
3 Mid/late 2nd century
5 Jacobi 1924, 73; Simon 1977a

Lower Rhine Region

L1 **Aachen-Schönforst**, Nordrhein-Westfalen
1 50° 45′ 46″ N, 6° 08′ 02″ E
2 Kiln-site
3 Early/mid 2nd century
4 Local region
5 Mayer 1934

L2 **Neuss**, Nordrhein-Westfalen
1 51° 11′ 54″ N, 6° 41′ 42″ E
2 Mould fragment found, in style of Alpinius of Haute-Yutz/Werkstatt II of Trier, from the *vicus* of the auxiliary fort
3 Mid/late 2nd century
5 Müller 1971, 368-9

L3 **Sinzig**, Rheinland-Pfalz
1 50° 32′ 33″ N, 7° 14′ 48″ E
2 Kiln centre; also imported mould fragment found of Satto of East Gaul
3 140/5 - 155 and later
4 Local region, and Colchester (where a workshop was established)
5 Daszkiewicz *et al.* 2003; Fischer 1969*; Funk 1910 (for now disproved samian kiln site at nearby Remagen); Symonds 1987

Britain

M1 **Colchester**, Essex
1 51° 53′ 25″ N, 0° 53′ 27″ E
2 Kiln site
3 Mid/late 2nd century ware with stylistic links to Sinzig, Germany
4 Local region
5 Hart *et al.* 1987; Hull 1934; 1963*; Rodwell 1982b; Simpson 1982a; Symonds 1987*

M2 **Peterborough**, Cambridgeshire
1 52° 32′ 27″ N, 0° 19′ 12″ W
2 Mould fragment found, probably for local samian derivative
3 Mid/late 2nd century
5 Hull 1963, 47.1; Watson 1983

M3 **Pulborough**, West Sussex
1 50° 57′ 25″ N, 0° 29′ 51″ W
2 Samian production debris, from probable kiln site
3 Mid 2nd century
4 Local region
5 Bennet 1978; Marsh 1979; Praetorius 1910; Simpson 1952; Webster 1974; 1975*

M4 **York,** Yorkshire
1 53° 57′ 19 N, 1° 05′ 13″ W
2 Mould fragment found, but provenance uncertain (possibly not from York), of Drusus I of Martres-de-Veyre
3 Early 2nd century
5 Bulmer 1979, 23; Hull 1963, 47.2

# Gazetteer of Deposits

The gazetteer has four major divisions:-
A, groups with decorated samian and coins;
B, groups with decorated samian but not having coins associated;
C, groups with plain ware and coins;
D, as A, but a summary of selected more recent publications, not used for the analysis in chapters 4 and 5.

Within each of these divisions an alphabetical arrangement of sites is followed, subdivided by country or region (e.g. Danube region for Austria, Hungary, etc.). Each entry is given a reference number, which has been used where necessary in the main text when individual deposits have been referred to.

## Key to arrangement of gazetteer entries

There are 8 sections in each entry, but they are not necessarily all completed in each case. They are as follows:-

1 Name of site, region of site; site type; brief deposit description and excavator's stratigraphic reference

2 Deposit type. Key:- A, burial; B, occupation layer, 'build-up', or road-surface; C, pit or well; D, ditch; E, destruction debris, burnt levels, or dumps; F, general association only, usually between several deposits in one phase; G, other type of deposit, specified in the entry.

3 Standard of recovery and documentation. Key:-
A, full stratigraphic details;
B, excavation by workmen semi-stratigraphically, or by 'planum' method, but with full details given;
C, either A or B with only partial details published (e.g. phasing information only).

4 Listing of samian ware pieces present. Decorated ware is given first, the entry for each piece being:-
Form number in the Dragendorff 1895/Déchelette 1904/Knorr 1907/Walters 1908 series - otherwise as referenced in the list of abbreviations (number of joining pieces if known given in brackets after the form number);
kiln centre;
potter or potters;
details of the decorative elements and style;
figure number or other reference in original report.
Stamped plain wares are given similarly:-
form number;
kiln centre;
potter and die number of stamp in Hartley & Dickinson 2008a-2012;
reference number.
Plain wares are given by their form and kiln centre, with the number of pieces or vessels in brackets after each entry. Larger groups of plain ware have been tabulated.

5 Presence of other fine pottery noted.

6 Coins present, given as a list, each entry being:-
Emperor or reign (number of coins if more than one identical specimen found);
denomination;
reference number in RIC, BMC or C - see abbreviations;
date;
state of wear;
reference number in original report.

7 Comments on the deposit.

8 Sources of information.

## Abbreviations used in gazetteer entries

N.B. Expansions of the names of Roman emperors, coin names, and county/regional names are not given here, as these are widely available in textbooks of Roman history, Roman numismatics, and European atlases respectively.

| | |
|---|---|
| Ae | bronze coin |
| Alzei | Unverzagt 1916 |
| Arg | Argonne |
| Barb Rad | Barbarous Radiate |
| BB | Black-burnished |
| Blick | Blickweiler |
| BMC | Mattingly & Carson 1923-62 |
| Brit | British samian |
| Bushe-Fox | Bushe-Fox 1926 (form type) |
| C | (in coins section) Cohen 1880-92 |
| C | (in samian section) Curle 1911 (form type) |
| CCW | Colour-coated ware |
| CG | Central Gaulish |
| C&G | Chenet & Gaudron 1955 (figure type) |
| Chenet | Chenet 1941 |
| CIL | Corpus Inscriptionum Latinarum |
| Colch | Colchester |
| D | Déchelette 1904 (figure type) |
| Déch | *ibid.* II, 192-234 (appliqué type) |
| dec | decoration |
| EG | East Gaulish |
| F | Fölzer 1913 (figure type) |
| H | Hofmann 1968 (figure type) |
| Heil | Heiligenberg-Dinsheim |
| Itten | Ittenwiller |
| K&S | Knorr & Sprater 1927 (figure type) |
| La Mad | La Madeleine |
| Lez | Lezoux |
| Lud | Ludowici 1927, 277ff (Kat. V) (form type) |
| MdV | Les Martres-de-Veyre |
| Mitt | Mittelbronn |
| mort | mortarium |
| NF | New Forest |
| Nied | Oelmann 1914 (form type) |
| NV | Nene Valley |
| O | Oswald 1936-7 (figure type) |
| O&P | Oswald & Pryce 1920 |
| Oxf | Oxfordshire |
| Pfaff | Pfaffenhofen |
| R | Rogers 1974 (decoration type) |
| R&F | Ricken & Fischer 1963 (figure type) |
| Rheinz | Rheinzabern |
| Rhen | Rhenish |
| RIB | Collingwood & Wright 1965 |
| RIC | Mattingly, Sydenham *et al* 1923-81 |
| Ritt | Ritterling 1913 (form type) |
| SG | South Gaulish |
| S&S | Stanfield & Simpson 1958 |
| Syd | Sydenham 1952 |
| U | uncertain or unassignable |
| W | Walters 1908 (form type) |
| West | Westerndorf |

# Section A: Deposits Associated with Coins

## BRITAIN

**A 1**

1 Alchester, Oxfordshire; *vicus*; rubbish tip east of Rough Rooms II and III

2 E

3 C

4 37 (2 pieces); SG; Biragillus; details not given here; fig 5 nos 1-2

30; CG; Avitus; ovolo R B114, man with diaulos O 614, ornamental stand R Q42, rosette R C172, trifid terminal R C93, cf S&S pl. 62, 7; pl. XXIX no. 2

30; CG; Avitus; ovolo R B114, rosette R C172, trifid R C96, Venus O 293A, Bacchus as O 581; pl. XXIX no. 3

37; CG; X-11 (Ioenalis I); leaf R J128, lioness O 1518, scroll in lower part, festoons above; fig. 5 no. 3

37; CG; X-13 (Donnaucus); cross of wreaths as S&S pl. 43 no. 499, lion O 1404, sea-horse to left S&S pl. 39 no. 460; fig. 5 no. 4

37; CG; X-11 (Ioenalis I); this piece illustrated in S&S pl. 36 no. 421; fig. 5 no. 5 and fig. 4 no. 18

37; CG; Secundinus I; tripod R Q8 (in which publication this piece is referred to); fig. 5 no. 6

37; CG; Secundinus I; rosette R C292 in place of ovolo; fig. 5 no. 7

37 (2 pieces); CG; Arcanus; ornamental stand R Q40, Venus O 286, Apollo O 83, Vulcan O 66, very similar dec to S&S pl. 78 nos 4-5; fig. 5 nos 8 and 12

37 (2 pieces); CG; Drusus I (X-3); these pieces are illustrated in Detsicas 1963a, pl. III no. 41 and pl. VI no. 64, the design is identical to *ibid* pl. XIII no. 157 from MdV; fig. 5 nos 9 and 10

37; CG; Drusus II; vine scroll R M2, maenad O 368; fig. 5 no. 11

37; CG; Attianus (stamped in mould); this piece illustrated in S&S pl. 85, 1 and pl. 50, 591; fig. 5 no. 13

37; CG; possibly Cinnamus; large leaf, winding scroll and small birds as S&S pl. 162, 57-8, but the ovolo is not clearly of Cinnamus; fig. 5 no. 14

37; CG; Austrus; ovolo S&S fig. 25 no. 2, Mars as O 145, figure to right O 929, Bacchus O 562, all between vertical bead-rows crossed by astragali R R18, part of same bowl as in deposit B1, cf S&S pl. 95 no. 21 for similar design; fig. 5 no. 15 37 (2 pieces); CG; Cinnamus; ovolo 3, S&S fig. 47 no. 3, boar O 1666, over small gladiator in festoon, metope style; fig. 5 nos 16 and 17

37; CG; Tittius (stamped in mould); unique piece illustrated in S&S pl. 146 no. 1; fig. 5 no. 18

37; CG; potter not certain; lion as O 1497K, probably early/mid-2nd century date; fig. 5 no. 19

6 Claud II (2); Rad; 268-70; from rubbish tip beside Rough Rooms

7 The coin is not definitely associated with the pottery, as the report is not clear on this point. However, if it is associated, the samian assemblage must be redeposited as it is a relatively homogeneous group of mid-2nd century.

8 Hawkes 1927

**A 2**

1 Bainbridge, West Yorkshire; fort; Antonine II destruction level in AB

2 E

3 A

4 37; CG; Paternus II (stamped); no details available

38; CG; stamped by Muxtullus

There are decorated pieces by Doeccus, Casurius, and Paternus II in levels underlying.

6 Ant; As; damaged and burnt

7 The excavator suggests that some of the samian, including the Paternus piece, is residual. He dates the destruction to the events of AD 196-7.

8 Hartley 1960a

**A 3**

1 Benwell, Tyne & Wear; fort; *sacellum* cellar fill

2 E

3 B

4 37; CG; Criciro, early Cinnamus or Paullus; lion and boar O 1491, ornament as O·2155 but unclear (Criciro, Attianus and others), metope and medallion style; fig. 2

31 (2); 27 (1)

6 Ant; HS; worn

Comm; HS; worn

As; illeg

7 The material all appears to come from the bottom part of the fill.

8 Spain 1930

**A 4**

1 Benwell, Tyne & Wear; *vicus* of fort; occupation debris, over ditch filling, in building A

2 B

3 A

4 37; CG; possibly Donnaucus style; ovolo as S&S fig. 11 (3 positioned upside-down), other details not identifiable, metope style; fig. 3 no. 44

37; CG; probably Geminus; trifid S&S fig. 15 no. 3; metope style; fig. 3 no. 45

37; CG; Geminus; trifid S&S fig. 15 no. 3, vine-scroll *ibid* fig. 15 no. 5, metope style; fig. 3 no. 46

37; CG; probably Quintilianus group; ovolo possibly S&S fig. 17 no. 4, hare O 2116; fig. 3 no. 48

37; CG; Quintilianus group; ovolo S&S fig. 17 no. 1, rosette *ibid* fig. 17 no. 7, circle as *ibid* fig. 17 no. 26; fig. 3 no. 49

37 (2 pieces); CG; Cinnamus; ovolo S&S fig. 47 no. 1, sea bull O 42, metope style; fig. 3 no. 53

37; CG; Criciro; trifid R G67, bud as R G138, style as S&S pl. 102 no. 15 (Censorinus); fig .3 no. 54

37; CG; Cinnamus; male figure O 581, metope style; fig. 3 no. 55

37; CG; Cinnamus; dolphin and basket R Q58, metope and medallion style; fig. 3 no. 57

37; CG; Paternus II; leaf R H75, deer O 1784, free style; fig. 3 no. 59

37; CG; ovolo as R B23 (Secundinus III); fig. 3 no.61

37; CG; Criciro; ornament S&S fig. 33 no. 5, bear O 1588, deer O 1743, free style; fig. 3 no. 63

37; CG; Cettus; charioteer O 98, lioness O 1518, bear O 1595, free style; fig. 3 no. 64
30; CG; Cinnamus; ovolo S&S fig. 47 no. 3, dancer O 322, metope and medallion style; fig. 4 no. 66
30; CG; Cinnamus; ovolo S&S fig. 47 no. 3; fig. 4 no. 67
30; CG; Cinnamus; ovolo S&S fig. 47 no. 3, male figure O 234, metope style; fig. 4 no. 68
30; CG: Cinnamus; male figure O 644, metope and medallion style; fig. 4 no. 69
30; CG; Cinnamus; ovolo S&S fig. 47 no. 1, metope style; fig. 4 no. 70
37; CG; Cinnamus; male figure O 204 in medallion; fig. 4 no. 75
37; CG; Cinnamus; ovolo S&S fig. 47 no. 1, male figure O 234, metope and medallion style; fig. 4 no. 74
37; CG; Criciro; ovolo as S&S fig. 33 no. 2, Hercules O 783, caryatid O 1206, hare O 2061, bird as O 2252, metope style; fig. 4 no. 73
37; CG; Cinnamus; horseman O 245 in medallion, metope and medallion style; fig. 4 no. 76
37; CG; Cinnamus or associate; cupid O 450 in medallion, metope and medallion style; fig. 4 no. 77
37; CG; Cinnamus; horseman O 245, deer as O 1743. winding scroll style; fig. 4 no. 78
37; CG; Cinnamus; ovolo S&S fig. 47 no. 3, bird O 2239B; fig. 4 no. 80
37; CG; Laxtucissa, Paternus II or associate; ovolo R B105; fig. 4 no. 81
37; CG; Paternus II; ovolo R B105, leaf as R H21, bird O 2365, winding scroll style; fig. 4 no. 82
37; CG; Pugnus; ovolo as S&S fig. 45 no. 1, bird O 2315 in medallion, metope and medallion style; fig. 4 no. 85
37; CG; Cinnamus (early style), Cettus, or associate; Jupiter O 13, winding scroll style; fig. 4 no. 86
37; CG; Cinnamus, Casurius or successor; Pan mask O 1214, metope style; fig. 5 no. 88
37; CG; possibly Cettus, rosette as R C65; fig. 5 no. 90
37; Rheinz; Janu I; ovolo R&F E19a, free style; fig. 5 no. 93
37 (2 pieces); Rheinz, Janu I; ovolo R&F E19a, circle *ibid* K48, cupid *ibid* M121, cupid *ibid* M112, metope and medallion style; fig. 5 nos 94-5
30; Rheinz; Cobnertus III (stamped in mould); leaf as R&F P91, trifid *ibid* P120, metope, medallion and St Andrew's cross style, as Ricken 1948 Taf. 32 nos 3-4, probably from same mould; fig. 5 no. 97
30; Rheinz; Cobnertus III; Mercury R&F M77, tree *ibid* P1, identical to Ricken 1948 Taf. 30 no. 12; fig. 5 no. 98
37; La Mad; leaf F 66; fig. 5 no. 99
37; La Mad; spiral as ovolo Ricken 1934 Taf. IX no. 1; fig 5 no. 101
37; La Mad; spiral as previous, trifid F 89; fig. 5 no. 102
37; La Mad; spiral as basal wreath Ricken 1934 Taf. VII no. 34, trifid not in *ibid* or F, metope style; fig. 5 no. 109
37; La Mad; ware with ovolo Ricken 1934 Taf VIIA; ovolo *ibid*; fig. 5 no. 106
37; La Mad; possibly ware with ovolo A; circle and rosette Ricken 1934 Taf. IX no. 10; fig. 5 no. 103
37; Trier; Werkstatt II; basal wreath F 905-6, seated figure F 470, standing figure F 536, free style; fig. 5 no. 104
37; Trier; probably Werkstatt II; bust F 578; fig. 5 no. 108
37; EG - probably Trier; ovolo as F 946; fig. 5 no. 105
37; Arg; ware with ovolo C; trifid as basal wreath Ricken 1934 Taf. XII no. 17, medallion style; fig. 5 no. 110
Also from this deposit but not illustrated:
37; CG; Divixtus (stamped in mould)
37; Rheinz; Janu I (stamped in mould)

6 Faust II; Den; on road surface stratigraphically earlier
Sev; Den; in building A
7 Building A was constructed over the filled in vallum (deposit B5) and was in turn replaced by later buildings (which contain Aur Den (2); Elag Den; late 3rd century Rad).
8 Birley 1947a; Birley, Brewis & Charlton 1934; Swinbank 1955

**A 5**

1 Bermondsey, Greater London; river channel; layer V
2 E
3 A
4 72; probably CG; incised dec
72; CG; appliqué dec; the vessel is fully described in Detsicas 1960a, with reference to Déchelette's catalogue of appliqué types (1904, II, 192-234); relevant moulded figure type equivalents are bird O 2316 and hare O 2116, both used by a number of late potters; this type of vessel was dated by Déchelette to the closing years of Lezoux production.
33; CG; 38
5 Rhenish CCW beaker
6 Comm; As; RIC 663; 180-1
8 Detsicas 1960a; Marsden 1967

**A 6**

1 Birdoswald, Cumbria; fort, 1928-9 excavation period 11
2 F
3 B
4 37; CG; 'Cintusmus' (bowl-finisher working for unknown potter); ovolo not in R, large trifid not in R but as S&S pl. 135 no. 36 (Casurius), small trifid as R G226, bird O 2315 (late Cinnamus), figure as O 205 (Iustus), no borders, free style, published in S&S fig. 49; fig. 8
37; CG; possibly Caratillus but attribution in S&S uncertain; no ovolo, column as R P50 but without capital in one case, stand R Q48 (lower part only), trifid as R G154 but doubled so that 5 leaves are visible, bird O 2315, metope style, published in S&S pl. 96 no. 4; fig. 9
5 NV CCW beaker
6 Traj; HS; illeg
Geta; Den; RIC 17-18; 200-2
J Domna; Den; illeg
Car; As; RIC 415d; 202
Elag; Den; RIC 77; 218-22
7 The 2 pieces of samian both come from room 'a' of period II, but the coins are general finds. There is also an inscription of 205-8 (RIB 1909) that the excavators use to date the start of the period.
8 Richmond & Birley 1930

**A 7**

1 Birrens, Dumfries & Galloway; fort; 1962-7 excavations, upper burned layer
2 E
3 A
4 37; CG; possibly Tittius, Pugnus, X-6 or contemporary; ovolo as R B233, bird O 2286A; fig. 52 no. 7
30 (11 pieces); CG; Criciro; festoon R F16, sea horse O 48A, hare as O 2128, erotic group O B in medallion R E26, metope and medallion style; fig. 52 no. 8
37 (2 pieces); CG; Criciro; ovolo S&S fig. 33 no. 1, trifid R G67, lion O 1450, caryatid O 1207A, metope style; fig. 52 no. 9
37 (14 pieces); CG; Cinnamus; ovolo S&S fig. 47 no. 2, cupid O 450, Pan mask O 1214, panther O 1570, panther O

1518, metope and medallion style, rivetted; fig. 52 no. 10
37 (7 pieces); CG; Cinnamus; ovolo S&S fig. 47 no. 5, dancer O 322, warrior O 234, man O 688, metope and medallion style; fig. 53 no. 11
37; CG; Cinnamus; ovolo S&S fig. 47 no. 3; fig. 53 no. 12
37; CG; Paullus or Cinnamus; ovolo S&S fig. 47 no. 3; fig. 53 no. 13
37; CG; possibly Secundus; horseman as S&S pl. 155 no. 21 (not in O); fig. 53 no. 16
37; CG – possibly Vichy; probably Docilis or early Cinnamus; ovolo S&S fig. 24 no. 1; fig. 53 no. 17
37 (2 pieces); CG; Albucius; ovolo and border S&S fig. 35 no. 1, reclining woman O 554, bird O 2317, bird O 2326, figure O 633, circle R E48, metope and medallion style; fig. 53 no. 22
37 (6 pieces); La Mad; ovolo Ricken 1934 Taf. VII B
Plain ware: 33(6); 18/31 or 31(15); 31 type (2); 18/31R or 31R (7); 31R; C15; 43 or C21; 38(3); U
CG and EG were differentiated in the general total, but not in the detailed listing for the burned layer.
6 M Ant; Den (5); all very worn
Dom; Den; RIC 176; 93-4; slightly worn
Traj; HS; RIC 492; 103-11; fairly worn
Faust I; Ae; RIC (Ant) 1102a; 141+; slightly worn
7 The burned layer marks an episode which brought the Antonine I period of the fort to a close. Rebuilding in Antonine II is conventionally associated with an inscription of 158 from the well of the *principia* (RIB 2110).
8 Robertson 1975; Wild 1975

**A 8**

1 Bitterne, Hampshire; *vicus*; period IXA construction of stone building IIA
2 E
3 A
4 30 (6 pieces); CG; Casurius - early style; ovolo S&S pl. 132 no. 1 (ovolo no. 5), wavy line borders, man O 599, metope style; fig. 14 nos 12A-E
30 (3 pieces); CG; Doeccus (probably); ovolo as S&S fig. 44 no. 2, column R P63 (Iustus), hare O 2116, medallion style; fig. 14 nos 13A-B
37; CG; unknown potter but identified as 'close to the style of Attianus or his group' (Simpson); ovolo as S&S fig. 23 no. 2, five-leafed palmette as R G17 or 20; fig. 15 no. 12
37 CG (11 small sherds); 30 SG (2 small sherds); 18/31SG; 18/31CG; 18/31; 27; 42SG; 42CG; U (29 small sherds)
5 Rhenish CCW beaker; NF indented CCW beaker
6 HS; 2nd century type; very worn; coin 5
From period VIII underlying this level came:
Claud II (consecratio); Rad; RIC 261; 270; coin 15
7 The excavator assigns this phase to the late 4th century (see re-assessment of phasing and dating to 3rd century in King 1991b). There is clearly some earlier samian mixed with a predominantly late group. See **A 9** for overlying material.
8 Cotton & Gathercole 1958, 115-6; Pearce 1958; Simpson 1958

**A 9**

1 Bitterne, Hampshire; *vicus*; period IXB occupation of stone building IIA
2 B
3 A
4 37; CG; Cinnamus or Doeccus; no details given
37; CG; Casurius; hen attributable to Casurius (Simpson), no details given
Plain ware: 37 SG (2); 37 CG (3); 37 CG/EG; 18 SG; 18/31 SG (4); 18/31 CG (6); 18/31 EG; 27 SG; 27 CG (2); 33 CG (2); 33; 35/36; 45 EG; U SG (6); U CG (20)
5 NF indented CCW beakers; Rhenish CCW beaker
6 Gall; Rad; as RIC 159; 253-68; coin 8
Salonina; Rad; RIC (Gall sole reign) 76; 260-8; coin 13
Tet I; Rad; illeg; 270-3; coin 29
7 The excavator assigns this level to the late 4th century (see re-assessment in King 1991b). There is clearly some earlier samian mixed with a predominantly late group. See **A 8** for underlying material.
8 Cotton & Gathercole 1958, 116-7; Pearce 1958; Simpson 1958

**A 10**

1 Bitterne, Hampshire; *vicus*; period XB occupation of stone building IIB
2 B
3 A
4 37; CG; Doeccus (or possibly Quintilianus group); trifid as R G259, rosette as R C170; fig. 15 no. 2
Plain ware: 18/31 CG (2); 18/31 EG; 18/31 (2); 27 SG (2); 33 CG; 35/36
5 NF CCW beakers; Rhenish CCW beakers
6 Tet I; Rad (barbarous); illeg; coin 29
Tet I; Rad (barbarous); as RIC 146 or 148; coin 30
Barb Rad: coin 37
7 This phase is assigned to the late 4th century (see re-assessment in King 1991b).
8 Cotton & Gathercole 1958, 118-9; Pearce 1958; Simpson 1958

**A 11**

1 Boxmoor, Hertfordshire; villa; period 3 destruction and overlying occupation of period 4
2 E
3 A
4 From period 3 destruction:
33 CG; 31R CG; 33 EG
From period 4 occupation:
37; CG; Pugnus (stamped in mould); rosette as S&S pl. 155 no. 20, eagle O 2167 in medallion, as S&S *loc cit*; fig. 55 no. 16
31R EG
6 From immediately under period 3 destruction:
Plautilla; Den; 211-7
7 The upper limit of the period 4 occupation may be the 250s, since it contained no coins, but the overlying period 5 rebuilding contained coins of Gall to Const.
8 Curnow 1976; Dannell 1976; Neal 1976, 65-7

**A 12**

1 Bradford Down, Dorset; rural settlement; depression A1
2 C
3 A
4 37 (3 pieces); CG; Marcus or an associate; ovolo R B184 - only attested at one other place, York, Venus O 322, squared beaded border, metope style; fig. 16 nos 9-10
6 Claud II (consecratio); Rad; RIC 265; 270
Allect; Rad; RIC 55; 293-6
7 The coins come from the topsoil over the depression, but may have been associated prior to modern disturbance. An imperfect association for an important attestation of a known late CG potter.

8 Field 1982; Simpson 1982c

**A 13**

1 Braintree, Essex; settlement; pit F8
2 C
3 A
4 30; Rheinz; Primitivus I (stamped in mould); ovolo R&F E11, ornament *ibid* O113, bird *ibid* T222, archer *ibid* M174a, metope and medallion style; fig. 19 no. 2
33; Colch; stamped by Senilis iv die la
45 CG; 31 CG; 38 CG; 79 CG; 31 EG; 45 EG; 31 Colch (presences only)
6 From the upper layer in pit F8 at 30cm depth:
Valerian; Ant; RIC 98; 253-9
Post; Rad; RIC 64; 259-68
7 It is not clear from the report whether the coins and the samian were found in the same layer, or whether the coins were immediately over the samian.
8 Drury 1976; Reece 1976; Rodwell 1976

**A 14**

1 Brampton, Norfolk; *vicus*; pit B layers 30-34
2 C
3 A
4 29 (2 pieces); Lez; 1st century type of Flavian date; details not given here
37; CG; Casurius; ovolo S&S pl. 133 no. 17, leaf, beads and astragalus *ibid* pl. 133 no. 19, metope style; fig. 25 no. 36
37; CG; Paternus II or Iustus; ovolo S&S pl. 104 no. 5, bead row of Iustus type; fig. 25 no. 40
Plain ware:
33 CG (5 – one stamped by Catullus ii die 4b); 33 CG/EG (2); 79 CG (5); 36 CG; 18/31 CG (2); 18/31 Colch (stamped by Miccia vii die 1a); 18/31 or 31 CG; 31 CG (10); C15 CG; U SG; U 1st c. Lezoux ware; U CG (5); U CG/EG (2); U EG
5 NV CCW beaker; Colch CCW with barbotine *phalli*
6 Ant; As; RIC 934; 152-3; little wear; coin 1 from layer 32
7 Layers 30-34 are the middle fill of pit B and are interpreted by the excavator as a rapid fill, particularly as sherds joined across the layers.
8 Bird 1977a; Green 1977

**A 15**

1 Brentford, Greater London; *vicus*; Northumberland Wharf site C, F10
2 C
3 A
4 37; CG; Cinnamus style; ovolo 3 S&S fig. 47 no. 3, beaded border, scroll with bird O 2228, cf S&S pl. 162, 57; no. 3
37; CG; Cinnamus style; identical scheme to previous but seems to be from a different vessel; no. 4
8 sherds of plain ware - not described
5 2 CCW beakers, 1 with 'hunt-cup' type barbotine; 2 Oxf mortaria; Oxf red CCW mortarium; BB type bowls
6 Sev; Den cast in AE; as RIC 266; 202-10; no12
Gall; Rad; as RIC 207; 260-68; no13
Barb Rad; Tet II type
Barb Rad; Pax type
Barb Rad; illeg
7 It is possible that the two sherds are in fact from different sides of the same vessel, for the decoration is identical and Marsh suggests they are different on the basis of their thickness.
8 Laws 1976; Marsh 1976; Merrifield 1976

**A 16**

1 Brentford, Greater London; *vicus*; site 9, feature 28
2 E
3 A
4 29; SG; Flavian date; no details given here
67; SG; late Flavian date; no details given here
37; CG; X-13; deer O 1768; fig. 82 no. 5
37; CC; Cinnamus; ovolo S&S fig. 47 no. 3; fig. 82 no. 6
37; CG; Drusus II; ovolo S&S pl. 88 no. 1; fig. 82 no. 7
37; CG; Secundus; ovolo as Hartley 1972c no. D117, seahorse O 42, joins with a piece from deposit **A 17**; fig. 82 no. 9
37 CG; 30 CG
6 Nero; Dup; RIC 341-3; very worn
Had; HS; RIC 969; 134-8; slightly worn
7 Some redeposited material ·from Flavian levels on the site is present.
8 Bird 1978a; Canham 1978; Hammerson 1978

**A 17**

1 Brentford, Greater London; *vicus*; site 9, feature 211
2 D
3 A
4 37; SG; Flavian; no details given here; fig. 86 no. 14
37; CG; Drusus I; ornament as ovolo S&S fig. 4 no. 1, rosette *ibid* fig. 4 no. 3; fig. 86 no. 6
37; CG; Drusus I; ovolo S&S fig. 4 no. 1, bifid *ibid* fig. 4 no. 9; fig. 86 no. 7
37; CG; Secundus; ovolo as Hartley 1972c, no. D117, sea horse O 42, joins with piece from deposit **A 16**; fig. 82 no. 9
37; CG; Secundus; ovolo as Hartley 1972c, no. D117; fig. 86 no. 13
37; CG; Censorinus; eagle as O 2183, metope and St Andrew's cross style; fig. 86 no. 11
37; CG; probably Cinnamus; winding scroll style; no. 15
37; CG; Cinnamus, Criciro or Pugnus; trifid R G67; fig. 86 no. 12
37; Rheinz; no. 16
37; CG (2)
Stamps on plain ware:
18/31; CG; Martialis 11 die 1c
33; CG; Quintus V die 5a
38; Heil; Nivalis die la
31; Heil or Rheinz; Suadullius die 3a
5 NV CCW beakers with barbotine dec
6 Traj; HS; RIC 503/592; 106-17; slightly worn
Claud II (Barb); Rad; very worn
7 The excavator considers the ditch to have been filled in the 2nd century, but with a certain amount of filling in the late 3rd.
8 Bird 1978a; Canham 1978; Hammerson 1978

**A 18**

1 Brentford, Greater London; *vicus*; site 9, feature 212
2 D
3 A
4 37; Rheinz; Janu I; ovolo R&F E19a, rosette *ibid* O42, rosette *ibid* O43, leaf *ibid* O31, medallion *ibid* K48, metope and medallion style, possibly from same mould as Ricken 1948 Taf. 4 no. 14; fig. 80 no. 1
37; CG; Antonine date
6 Car; Den; RIC 83; 206; good condition
8 Bird 1978a; Canham 1978; Hammerson 1978

**A 19**

1 Brockworth, Gloucestershire; rural settlement; ditch 6 and ditch 2
2 D
3 A
4 37; CG; Docilis; trifid S&S fig. 24 no. 5 in triple circle or festoon; no S6
flat dish; Rheinz; stamped by Victorinus ii die 7j ; no S36
45 (2); 79 (2) ; 18/31 (2) ; 38 EG
5 BB1; Oxf base with nonsense stamp
6 Barb Rad; illeg; coin 4
7 Sherds in ditch 6 join with some in ditch 2, and the fills are apparently the same. It is possible that the ditches were silting over a period.
8 Burge 1981; Rawes 1981

**A 20**

1 Caerleon, Gwent; fortress; Golledge's Field barracks VIII and IX
2 F
3 B
4 37; CG; Drusus I; no details given; from timber layer barrack IX
Stamp of Paullus CG from timber layer barrack VIII
79 from timber layer between barracks VIII and IX
6 Ant; HS; no details given; from make-up of stone paving barrack VIII
7 These finds are given as part of Boon's evidence for an Antonine not Trajanic stone reconstruction of the fortress. Only a general association is possible.
8 Boon 1972, 119-20

**A 21**

1 Caerleon, Gwent; fortress; Museum St, occupation soil north of wall 3
2 B
3 A
4 37; CG; Paternus II; 'twist' S&S fig. 30 no. 18, free style
37CG (2 fragments); 33 CG (4); 31 CG; 35/6 CG; 18/31 CG
6 Had; Den; very worn
From a contemporary hearth south of wall 3:
Aur; HS; as RIC 1140; 174-5; worn
8 Boon 1965a; Murray-Threipland 1965; Simpson 1965

**A 22**

1 Caerleon, Gwent; fortress; Museum St, period III remetalling of road
2 E
3 A
4 37; CG; Quintilianus group; ovolo S&S fig. 17 no. 2, other details not given
6 Sev; Den; BMC 238; 197; slightly worn
7 The sherd is very worn, probably by water. It could derive from a culvert in the road, and thus be a good example of redeposition.
8 Boon 1965a; Murray-Threipland 1965; Simpson 1965

**A 23**

1 Caerleon, Gwent; fortress; North corner, hearth 3 of barrack VIII (period 4)
2 B
3 A
4 37; Rheinz; Janu I or Cerialis II; ovolo as R&F E39, Amazon *ibid* M155
Lud Ob Rheinz
General finds from period 4:
37; CG; Divixtus; ovolo as S&S fig. 33 no. 1
29 SG; 37 SG; 37 CG (2); 18/31 SG; 27 SG; 27 CG
6 Barrack VIII hearth 5 and elsewhere in the barrack has tile stamps of Leg II Aug Antoniana, dated by Boon (1984, 14) to 213-22.
7 The general finds from period 4 are mixed and are probably redeposited.
8 Boon & Simpson 1967; Murray-Threipland 1967

**A 24**

1 Caerleon, Gwent; fortress; Priory Gardens, occupation levels, period III
2 B
3 A
4 From trench A:
37; CG; Laxtucissa or Paternus II; ovolo S&S fig. 30 no. 1; fig. 4 no. 12
31 EG; 45
From trench B:
37; CG; Drusus I (X-3); basal wreath S&S fig. 4 no. 8, bifid *ibid* fig. 4 no. 9, acanthus *ibid* fig. 4 no. 13, astragalus *ibid* fig. 4 no. 15, tripod *ibid* fig. 4 no. 20, metope and medallion style; fig. 4 no. 11
37; CG; Criciro; ovolo S&S fig. 33 no. 2, man O 684A; fig. 4 no. 10
6 Ant; As; worn; from trench A
8 Boon 1964

**A 25**

1 Caerleon, Gwent; fortress; Prysg Field, barracks 3, 6 and 7, floors of stone phase
2 E
3 B
4 From barrack 3 (summary of identifiable pieces only as full details are not available):
37; CG; Paternus II, Censorinus, Iustus, Doeccus or Servus II; sea bull O 52A, dolphin O 2393; no. 86
37; CG; probably Paternus II (stamped on bowl by Doeccus II); dolphin O 2393, metope style; fig. 48 no. 88
37; CG; Cinnamus; leaf S&S fig. 47 no. 5, female figure O 809, bird O 2239, horseman O 245, bear O 1609, metope and medallion style; fig. 48 no. 91
37; CG; probably Pugnus; caryatid O 1206, stag O 1781, metope and medallion style; no. 92
From barrack 6:
37; SG; Flavian style; no. 105
37; CG-MdV; Trajanic style; no. 141
37; CG; Cinnamus or Advocisus; male figure O 234, bird O 2315, Vulcan O 66, boar O 1642, Minerva O 126, metope style; no. 111
37; CG; Cinnamus; female figure O 331, leaf R J58, winding scroll style; fig. 49 no. 115
37; CG; Banvus or Advocisus; cupid O 383, metope style; no. 120
37; CG; Cinnamus; leaf as R H21, winding scroll style; fig. 49 no. 121
37; CG; Censorinus, Iustus, Cinnamus or associate; male figure O 905, metope and medallion style; no. 122
37; CG; Cinnamus; leaf R J15, cupid O 401, Pan O 711, Pan mask O 1214, female figure O 331, dolphin and basket R Q58, metope and medallion style: fig. 49 nos 123a-b (see no. 150 from barrack 7 which may be the same vessel)
37; CG; Cinnamus; sea panther O 46, dog O 1980, winding scroll and medallion style; nos 124 and 137

37; CG; Cinnamus; lion O 1421, acanthus R K12, winding scroll style; no. 126
37; CG; Cinnamus or Doeccus; leaf R J1, winding scroll style; no. 128
37; CG; Pugnus; caryatid O 1206, Diana O 106, metope style; no. 130
37; CG; Cinnamus; stand as R Q48, boar O 1641, Amazon O 241, metope style; nos 134 and 136
37; CG; probably Cinnamus; acanthus R K12, lozenge as S&S fig. 47 no. 15, lioness as O 1537, metope and medallion style; no. 139
37; CG; Censorinus or Banvus; male figure O 606, metope style; no. 143
30; CG; Cinnamus (stamped in mould with large stamp); dolphin and basket R Q58, male figure as reverse of O 1191, metope and medallion style; fig. 65 no. 20
From barrack 7:
29; SG; Flavian style; fig. 47 no. 156
30; SG; Flavian style; no. 144
37; SG; Flavian style; no. 146
37; CG; Albucius; female figure O 554, metope style; no. 148
37; CG; Paternus II (stamped in mould); ovolo S&S fig. 30 no. 1, leaf *ibid* fig. 30 no. 22, rosette *ibid* fig. 30 no. 3, bird O 2365, winding scroll style; fig. 65 no. 55
37; CG; Cinnamus (stamped in mould with large stamp); ovolo S&S fig. 47 no. 1, leaf *ibid* fig. 47 no. 31, female figure O 331, male figure O 234, Pan mask O 1214, Pan O 711, dolphin and basket R Q58, bird O 2315, metope and medallion style, identical to S&S pl. 160 no. 35 (BM) and probably from same mould; fig. 50 no. 150 (see no. 123 from barrack 6 which may be the same vessel)
37; CG; Lastuca; bear O 1589, deer O 1732, dog O 1940, goat O 1849, free style; fig. 49 no. 151
37; CG; Lastuca or Paternus II; leaf R H35; no. 152
37; CG; Cinnamus; horseman O 245, male figure O 688, lozenge as R U1, lioness as O 1569, metope and medallion style; fig. 50 no. 160
37; CG; Cinnamus; trifid R G66, female figure O 322, winding scroll and medallion style; no. 163
37; CG; Paternus II; sea-horse O 33, Pan O 709, mask as O 1289, metope style; fig. 50 no. 165
37; CG; Iustus; ovolo S&S fig. 31 no. 1, sea bull O 52A, metope style; fig. 51 no. 166
37; CG; Sacer-Attianus, Criciro or Cinnamus; lion O 1421, metope and medallion style; no. 167
37; CG; Cinnamus; trifid R G66, female figure O 322, metope and medallion style; no. 173
37; CG; Cinnamus; bear O 1609, gladiator O 1059, metope style; no. 174
37; CG; Doeccus; dolphin O 2382, dolphin O 2393, sea-horse O 33, fish O 2417, sea-creature O 54, dolphin O 2401, metope style; fig. 51 no. 175
37; CG; Laxtucissa, Paternus II, Iustus, Doeccus or contemporary; triton O 19, metope style; no. 176
37; CG; probably Paternus II; dog O 1834, metope style; fig. 51 no. 178
37; CG; Cinnamus; leaf as R H21, winding scroll style; fig. 51 no. 185
37; CG; Cinnamus or Pugnus; acanthus R K12, male figure O 644, lozenge R U1, cornucopia R U245, metope and medallion style; fig. 52 no. 187
37; CG; probably Cinnamus; male figure O 581, female figure O 126, bird O 2239, winding scroll style; no. 190
37; CG, Cinnamus; female figure O 322, mask as O 1337, female figure O 111, bear as O 1627, deer O 1720, metope and medallion style; no. 193
37; CG; Cinnamus; leaf R H72, acanthus R K12, lioness as O 1537, metope and medallion style; fig. 51 no. 194
37; CG; Cinnamus or associate; stand R Q42, dolphin and basket R Q58, metope style; no. 196
37; CG; Divixtus; ovolo as S&S fig. 33 no. 2, erotic group O H, caryatid O 1207A, metope and medallion style; fig. 52 no. 204
37; CG; Sacer-Attianus, Criciro, Cinnamus or associate; bear O 1588, free style; no. 205
37; CG; Doeccus; triton O 19, lozenge R U34, metope style; fig. 52 no. 210
37; CG; Banvus, Caletus, Iustus or Mercator II; trifid R G57 in medallion; fig. 52 no. 211
37; CG; Cinnamus or Doeccus; female figure O 809, dolphin O 2401, metope and medallion style; no. 212
37; CG; Albucius; bear O 1608, gladiator O 1059, metope and medallion style; no. 213
37; CG; probably Paternus II; female figure O 926, mask O 1215; no. 215
37; CG; Cinnamus (stamped in mould with large stamp); ovolo S&S fig. 47 no. 1, metope style; fig. 65 no. 22
37; CG; Paternus II; leaf R J119, metope and medallion style; fig. 50 no. 169
37; EG-uncertain location; fig. 51 no. 201

6 From barrack 3:
Faust II; AE
Traj; HS
Alex; AE; 222-3; worn
Hoard from barrack 3, room 18:
Vesp Ae; Traj Den (2); Had HS; Had Den; Comm HS; Sev Den
From barrack 6:
Comm; Ae
From barrack 7:
Traj; HS
Faust I; AE
Had; Ae.
Ant; Ae
Hoard from barrack 7, room 37 latest floor:
Rep Den (5); Nero Den (2); Otho Den; Vitellius Den (2); Vesp Den .(23); Titus Den (6); Dom Den (12); Nerva Den (5); Traj Den (51); Traj HS; Had Den (52); Ant Den (53); Faust I Den (12); Aur Den (37); Aur HS; Faust II Den (20); L Verus Den (6); Lucilla Den (4); Comm Den (4)

7 The associations are only generalised, since more than one occupation stratum is involved in certain areas of the barracks. There are only 2 other 3rd century coins from the barracks - Car Ae; Alex Den. The deposits are not closed but appear to be relatively homogeneous.

8 Mattingly 1932; Nash-Williams 1931-2; Simpson 1962, 105-7

**A 26**

1 Caerleon, Gwent; fortress; The Hall period 4a
2 F
3 A
4 37; CG; Casurius; leaf S&S fig. 40 no. 12, eagle O 2167, bull O 1886
6 A tile stamp of Leg II Aug Antoniniana dated 213-22 (Boon 1984, 14) is assigned to this period.
7 General association only
8 Boon 1969a; Murray-Threipland 1969

**A27**

1 Caerleon, Gwent; fortress; The Hall period 5 levelling of courtyard
2 E
3 A
4 37; SG; Flavian type; no details given here
37; SG; Flavian type; no details given here
37; CG; Paternus II; ovolo S&S fig. 30 no. 8, goat O 1849A
27 SG; 29 SG; 38 CG; 32 CG (2); C11 SG; 27 SG; 27 CG; 33 CG
6 Victorin; Rad; RIC 42; slight wear
Aurelian; Rad; RIC 41; worn
7 A mixed deposit with a majority of pieces of 1st century date.
8 Boon 1969a; Bowes 1969; Murray-Threipland 1969

**A 28**

1 Caerleon, Gwent; quayside; metalling of the quays
2 E
3 A
4 From first quay:
45 EG
From hard standing behind the quays:
37; Rheinz; Reginus II; ovolo R&F E57, circles as Ricken 1942 Taf. 136 no. 2; fig. 11 no. 16
37; Rheinz; ware with ovolo E8; ovolo R&F E8, cupid as *ibid* M110; fig. 11 no. 17
5 NV CCW with barbotine dec; Oxf mortarium
6 From first quay:
Sev; Den; RIC 82; 205; worn
From second quay:
Sev; Den; RIC 46; 195; very worn
Sev; Den; RIC 116a; 210; slightly worn
From rubble of second quay:
Dom; HS; very worn
7 Boon dates the coarse ware up to the late 3rd century on the basis of a similar group from Caerleon parade ground of 260-95. However, there are no post-260 coins from the quays.
8 Boon 1978a

**A 29**

1 Caernarvon, Gwynedd; fort; inner ditch primary silt
2 D
3 A
4 37; CG; Drusus I (X-3); ovolo S&S fig. 4 no. 1, rosette *ibid* fig. 4 no. 6, dolphin ornament *ibid* fig. 4 no. 19, gladiator as O 1027, metope style; fig. 5 no. 7
37; CG; Paternus II; warrior O 188, mask O 1214, metope style; fig. 5 no. 4
31 CG; 18/31 CG; 18 or 18/31 SG; 35/6 SG
6 Ant; HS; RIC 616a; 140-3; no. 8
7 The deposit comes from a ditch that is dated mid to late 4th century by the excavator. Overlying silts in the ditch certainly contain later material, but the primary silt does not. Either it is redeposited with no admixture of 4th century material, or the ditch is in fact earlier, perhaps associated with the Severan stone defences, but kept clear of debris, except for the primary silt, until the 4th century.
8 Casey 1974; Greene 1974

**A 30**

1 Caerwent, Gwent; town; building XXVIIs, charcoal layer on floor of room 7
2 E
3 A
4 37; CG; Drusus I (X-3); no details given here since it is clearly redeposited - sherds of this vessel occur also under the floor levels elsewhere in the building; published in S&S pl. 15 no. 112; fig. 3 no. S16
37; probably EG; rouletted dec in two horizontal zones replacing moulded ornament; fig. 3 no. S27
18 SG; 18/31 CG
6 Car; Den; 202; good condition
8 Nash-Williams 1930

**A 31**

1 Canterbury, Kent; town; Burgate Street, CXIV N I 4
2 C
3 A
4 37; CG; Cettus; ovolo possibly R B263, rosette probably R C145=C37, leaf probably R H31 (Criciro), leaf probably R H18 (Doeccus), small circles in field, in scroll decoration; fig. 137 no. 4
5 Rhenish and coarse wares dated by excavator to 3rd century (fig. 117, 639-45)
6 Rad; illeg
7 The samian sherd is very large and could easily be a survival. From the layer above this in the same pit were more mid-3rd century coins: Tet I; Rad; illeg; Barb Rad; illeg.
8 Frere & Stow 1983, 117-20, 160-3, 319

**A 32**

1 Canterbury, Kent; town; Burgate Street, trench C pit 1
2 C
3 A
4 29; SG; Primus style (probably); no details given here; broken in several pieces with clean breaks; pl. IV no. 4
37; CG; Doeccus; dancer O 344
27; SG; Firmo; stamped; fig. 8,1
6 Faust I; HS; 141+
7 The SG pieces are almost certainly redeposited, the breaks in the form 29 probably occurring when the pit was filled with 'heavy grey soil and large nodules of flint' (Williams 1947, 71). The excavator suggests that, 'The pit must have been cut and filled in quite soon after layer 8 had been deposited in the middle-late 2nd century' (*ibid*).
8 Williams 1947, 68-87

**A 33**

1 Canterbury, Kent; town; 47 Burgate Street, section 1 layer 3 and section 2 layer 3
2 E
3 A
4 Section 1 layer 3:
30; SG; Mercator; head of Minerva O 1208, goose O 2244, goose O 2286; fig. 6 no. 8
37; Rheinz; Reginus I; orange gloss, very poor execution, boxer R&F M193b=O 1185 (blurred), stag as R&F T105=O 1732/1740; fig. 6 no. 19
Section 2 layer 3:
30; CG; Donnaucus; man O 659, dancer O 353, circle R E2, leaf R J65, rosette R C244; fig. 6 no. 14
33; CG; stamped R]EBURRI OF; stamp no. 12
6 Vesp; As; RIC 494; 71; coin no. 5, section 1 layer 3
Aur; Den; 140-7; coin no. 8, section 2 layer 3
Aur; HS; 162-3; coin no. 9, section 2 layer 3
7 These two layers are equivalent according to the excavator, and also equate with section 4 layer 4 which contains Salonina; Ant; *c* 260; coin no. 14. Such a late date may go with the EG sherd, but it is clear that material has been redeposited.
8 Jenkins 1950

**A 34**

1 Canterbury, Kent; town; 47 Burgate Street, section 5 layer 3
2 E
3 A
4 37 (2 pieces); CG; probably Doeccus; deer D 852, lioness, small deer, dog; fig. 6 nos 12 and 13
6 Tet I; Rad; RIC 132-3; 270-3; coin no. 18
7 Possibly redeposited
8 Jenkins 1950

**A 35**

1 Canterbury, Kent; town; St George's Street, pit R6
2 C
3 A
4 37; Rheinz; no details
6 Gall; Rad; 260-8
7 From a pit fill of 'soft, black soil' whose 'homogeneous nature ... indicated that each pit was quickly filled' (Williams 1946, 66). This refers not only to pit R6 but also to pits R4 and R7 where an 18/31 fragment with a coin of Tet I and a 45 fragment with a coin of Const I were found respectively. There was also a gully with a 31 fragment and a coin of Tet I. However, as Williams points out, 'Some of the sherds were abraded and had obviously been lying about for some time before reaching the midden' (*ibid*). Unfortunately the abraded sherds are not specified.
8 Williams 1946

**A 36**

1 Canterbury, Kent; town; theatre site, CXVII D III layer 33
2 B
3 A
4 37; CG; Advocisus, Doeccus or Cinnamus; Victory O 809 in double medallion; fig. 6 no. 13
37; CG; not known; double medallion and small circle of CG III-IV type; fig. 6 no. 6
5 NV rouletted CCW
6 Aur; As; RIC 1321; 154/5; fair
7 This layer is considered part of the occupation of a house apparently contemporary with the rebuilt theatre of AD 210 onwards. The layer itself is dated 235-50.
8 Frere 1970, 107; Simpson 1970

**A 37**

1 Canterbury, Kent; town; theatre site, CXVII DIII 39
2 B
3 A
4 37; CG; Banvus or Doeccus; large border, plain double medallion; fig 6 no. 5
37; West; Helenius; ovolo cf Karnitsch 1959, Taf. 182 nos 6-8 and Taf. 183 no. 1, Kellner 1961, Abb. 12 and Abb. 13 no. 1, Kellner 1962, Taf. 6 no. 5
37; CG; Albucius or Paternus; ovolo
5 NV CCW with white-slipped tendrils; red CCW copying form 46; Rhenish beakers; Oxf red CCW bowl
6 From layer DIII 39 and its equivalent in D IV (Frere 1970, 107):
Sev; Den (plated)
Gall; Rad (2)
Tet I; Rad (6 +1 copy)
Tet II; Rad
Claud II
Barb Rad (4)
Const I; Ae
7 The excavator states that the stratum was not sealed until medieval times, thus giving an explanation for the Const coin as a stray. 'It is clear that the main deposit took place *c* AD 275-300' (Frere 1970, 108), and the coins, apart from Const, are consonant with a group not later than 290-300. The layer is mixed dark soil overlying a house near the theatre, which may have built up over a period, but equally well could contain pottery that was roughly contemporary in use.
8 Frere 1970, 107-8; Simpson 1970

**A 38**

1 Carmarthen, Dyfed; town; Church Street well phase VI
2 C
3 A
4 37; SG; Biragillus; no details given here; no. 37
37; SG; Biragillus; no details given here; no. 38
30 (several pieces); CG; Doeccus (stamped in mould with die 5a); ovolo S&S fig. 44 no. 2, leaf *ibid* fig. 44 no. 32, leaf *ibid* fig. 44 no. 27, rosette R C274, 'twist' S&S fig. 47 no. 4, hare O 2116, hare O 2061, metope and medallion style; no. 47
30 (several pieces); CG; Doeccus; ovolo S&S fig. 44 no. 2, leaf *ibid* fig. 44 no. 27, shield R U210, rosette R C50, leaf S&S fig. 44 no. 38, rosette *ibid* fig. 44 no. 5, ring *ibid* fig. 44 no. 12, man O 687, metope and medallion style, rivetted; no. 48
37; CG; Divixtus; erotic group O B in medallion; no. 75
37; CG; Albucius; dancer D 217, metope style; no. 76
37; CG; probably Albucius; ovolo R B107; no. 77
37; CG; Iullinus; ovolo S&S fig. 36 no. 2, acorn *ibid* fig. 36 no. 2, leaf *ibid* fig. 36 no. 8, stag O 1732, metope style; no. 78
37; CG; Iullinus; pedestal R U214, Pan O 710; no. 79
37; CG; Casurius; ovolo as R B176; no. 80
37; CG; Doeccus; ovolo S&S fig. 44 no. 1, panther as O 1542; no. 82
37; CG; Doeccus; stand R Q63, metope style; no. 83
37 (several pieces); CG; Severus; ovolo S&S fig. 37 no. 2, 'twist' as *ibid* pl. 128, acanthus *ibid* fig. 40 no. 11 (= R J11), deer (3x) O 1732A, bear O 1626, hunter O 1086C, panther O 1510, boar (2x) as O 1674, lion and boar (5x) as O 1491, deer as O 1815, horse (2x) O 1904, panther O 1518, deer as O 1704A, lion as O 1403A, lion O 1427, deer not in O, free style; no. 88
6 Barb Rad; Tet I type (2)
Caraus; Rad; RIC 478; slightly worn
Const I; Follis; RIC 429; 323-4; slightly worn
7 The samian, apart from the two SG pieces, forms a coherent late group, but is probably redeposited in view of the coin evidence.
8 Boon 1978b; James 1978

**A 39**

1 Carpow, Tayside; fortress; general finds
2 F
3 A
4 37; CG; Casurius, Pugnus or Cettus: warrior O 188, eagle O 2167 in double medallion; rosettes not in R; metope style with rope-like borders; fig. 6
Plain ware: 33 (2), 31 (5), 38 (2), 45 (7), beaker with barbotine decoration
6 From 1961-2 excavations, associated with the samian:
Had; HS; RIC 743; 134-8; worn; coin 1
Faust II; HS; RIC (Aur) 1715; 176-80; very worn; coin 2
Car; Den; RIC 65; 2021 mint; coin 3
Plautilla; Den; RIC (Car) 361; 202-3; mint; coin 4
From the later excavations and early casual finds:

Tit; Den; 79-81
Faust I or II
Vesp; Den; 69-79
Faust I; Den; 141+
Lucilla; Den; 164-9
Sev; Den; 193-211
Car; Den; 198-209
Car; Den; 198-209
2 unidentified Den, probably early 3rd century
7 This site is usually dated on historical grounds to 208-11 (Leach & Wilkes 1977, 59) when the fort was established for Severus' campaigns in Scotland. The coins seem to confirm this, and the samian was undoubtedly in use on the site.
8 Birley, A R 1963; Birley, E & Dodds 1963; Birley, R 1963; Leach & Wilkes 1977

**A 40**

1 Carrawburgh, Northumberland; *vicus* of fort; stone debris at east end of site
2 E
3 A
4 37; CG; Advocisus (stamped in mould); Diana O 106, caryatid O 1207, metope style; fig. 5 no. 4
37; CG; Advocisus; trifid as R G73, tree R N4, mask O 1218, bear O 1578, horizontal zone and festoon style; fig. 5 no. 7
37; CG; Banvus (stamped in mould); column R P3, other details not attributable, metope style; fig. 5 no. 5
37; CG; Cinnamus; ovolo S&S fig. 47 no. 2; fig. 5 no. 6
37 (12 pieces); CG; Cinnamus; ovolo S&S fig. 47 no. 1, Hercules O 774, athlete O 652, 'twist' S&S fig. 47 no. 4, leaf *ibid* fig. 47 no. 5, circle *ibid* fig. 47 no. 11, Diana O 106, dolphin O 2401, metope and medallion style; fig. 5 no. 10
37; CG; Cinnamus; ovolo S&S fig. 47 no. 3, dancer O 322, ornament S&S fig. 47 no. 19, figure O 905, metope and medallion style; fig. 5 no. 11
37 (2 pieces); CG; Cinnamus; ovolo S&S fig. 47 no. 1, Perseus O 234, deer O 1704, metope and medallion style; fig. 5 no. 12
37; CG; Cinnamus; ovolo S&S fig. 47 no. 5, bird O 2297 in festoon, metope style; fig. 5 no. 13
37; CG; Cinnamus; figure O 204 in medallion; no. 15
37; CG; Casurius; male figure O 638, mask Stanfield 1935 no. 46, sea horse O 33, caryatid as O 1206, leaf S&S fig. 40 no. 9, leaf *ibid* fig. 40 no. 12, metope style; fig. 5 no. 16
37; CG; Casurius; eagle O 2167, leaf S&S fig. 40 no. 12, metope style; fig. 5 no. 14
37; CG; Casurius; no details given
37 (2 pieces); Chémery; Satto-Saturninus; festoon and hanging bud F 249, rosette as F 282, horizontal zone and festoon style; fig. 5 no. 8
37 (13 pieces); Rheinz; Reginus I; deer R&F T94, leaf ibid P47a, circle as ibid O 137 or O 140, free style; fig. 5 no. 18
37 (2 pieces); Rheinz; Janu I; ovolo R&F E19a, mask ibid M19 in medallion; fig. 5 no. 15
37 (2 pieces); Rheinz; probably Reginus I; ovolo as R&F E55; fig. 5 no. 17
Plain ware:
37 CG (5 fragments); 37 EG (2 fragments); 80 CG; 38 EG; 36 CG; 31 and 31R CG (7 - 1 stamped by Cambus); 18/31R CG; 79 CG; 33 CG (3)
6 Nero; As
Sev; Den; 201
8 Charlesworth 1967; Hartley 1967

**A 41**

1 Chester, Cheshire; fortress; Castle Street, well II layers 1-2
2 C
3 A
4 53 (19 pieces); EG; barbotine dec; fig. 33 no. 219 (pieces of the same vessel also found in well I)
5 Rhen CCW indented beaker; NV CCW
6 J Mamaea; Den; RIC (Alex) 360; little wear; no. 223
Severan type plated Den; no. 224
Post; Rad; little wear; no. 226
Tet I; Rad; RIC 135-6; 270-3; worn; no. 227
Tet I; Rad; RIC 127; 270-3; little wear; no. 228
Tet I; Rad; no. 230
Tet I; Rad (Barb); no. 229
Barb Rad (4); nos 231, 233, 235-6
Rad of mid to late 3rd century (2); nos 232, 234
7 See comments to **A 42-3**.
8 Bulmer 1980; Mason 1980; Robinson 1980

**A 42**

1 Chester, Cheshire; fortress; Castle Street, well II layer 3
2 C
3 A
4 37 (13 pieces); Rheinz; ware with ovolo E31; ovolo R&F E31, stand *ibid* O161a, hare *ibid* T1636, acanthus *ibid* P114, metope style using stands as dividers; fig. 29 no. 154
Plain ware:
C15 CG; 18/31 CG; 18/31R CG; 31 CG; 31 EG; 31R CG; 31R EG; 32 CG; 33 CG; 45 CG (2)
5 Oxf CCW rouletted beaker; Oxf imitation 18/31 with illiterate stamp; Rhen CCW
6 Elag; Den; RIC 146; 218-22; no. 181
Female head of early 3rd century; Den; no. 182
7 The excavators date the coarse pottery to late-3rd/mid-4th century. They suggest that the samian ware is 'a compact group of vessels which, in view of the wear some of them received before breakage, could have continued in use well into the third century, if not later' (Mason 1980, 52). Underlies **A 41** and overlies **A 43**.
8 Bulmer 1980; Mason 1980; Robinson 1980

**A 43**

1 Chester, Cheshire; fortress; Castle Street, well II layers 4-7
2 C
3 A
4 37; Rheinz; Comitialis IV or associate; ovolo R&F E25, lion *ibid* T17, deer as O 1721 or 1726, panther R&F T46, free style; fig. 25 no. 74
37; CG; Iullinus; figure group O 238, Hercules O 748, acanthus R K7, 'twist' S&S pl. 127 no. 24, metope style; fig. 25 no. 75
37; CG; Cinnamus; ovolo S&S fig. 47 no. 1, no other details given
37; CG; Paternus II; no details given
37; CG; possibly Cettus; no details given
Plain ware:
18R SG; C11 CG; 18/31 CG (2); 18/31R CG (5-6); 18/31R or 31R CG (4); 31 CG (4); 31 EG; 31R CG (4); C23 CG; 27 CG; 32 CG; 33 CG (7-8); 35 CG; 36 CG (3-4); 37 CG (7); 37 EG; 38 CG; 43 EG; 45 CG (2); 80 CG; U CG (11) (the Dr 37 count includes dec pieces listed above)
5 Oxf type imitation 38 CCW bowl; Rhen CCW beaker; CG CCW; NV CCW

6 Geta; Den; RIC 45; 203-8; slightly worn; no. 138
Alex; Den; RIC 32; 2231 slightly worn; no. 139
Ae with diademed head; mid-4th century?; no. 140
7 Most of the pottery and the last coin come from the lowest of this group of layers (7). There is no indication of any exclusively 4th century pottery - and the coin appears to be a stray (but difficult to explain in such a deep context). The link between material in wells I and II **A 41-3** suggests that finds on the surface, of largely early-mid 3rd century date, were placed in the wells, perhaps at a much later date, mid 4th century. It is also possible that they were 'heirlooms', as Ward (1996, 77) suggests.
8 Bulmer 1980; Mason 1980; Robinson 1980

**A 44**

1 Chester, Cheshire; fortress; Deanery Field, 'Antonine' levels in barracks
2 F
3 B
4 From over rooms 16 and 17:
37; CG; Criciro (cursive signature in mould); leaf R H31 or possibly H33, leaf R H41, bird O 2252, bird O 2298, winding scroll style, also published as S&S pl. 118 no. 14 (with slight variations in the drawing); pl. XLI no. 5
Another sherd with Criciro's cursive signature is recorded from the same level
6 From over rooms 7 and 7a:
Aur; Ae; Greek provincial issue; BM Cat Gk Coins, Nicaea 35; 161-80
Faust II; Den
7 A general association only, for despite the levels being equivalent the coins and samian were *c.* 15m apart.
8 Droop & Newstead 1931, 114, 116

**A 45**

1 Chester, Cheshire; fortress; Deanery Field, upper Roman stratum over barracks
2 E
3 B
4 37; CG; Sacer-Attianus; ornament probably S&S fig. 22 no. 6, deer O 1772, cupid O 396, metope style; pl. XII no. 12
37; CG; Cinnamus; horseman as O 245, deer O 1720, deer O 1704, free style; pl. XII no. 13
37 (3 pieces); CG; Quintilianus group; ovolo as S&S fig. 17 no. 1, trifid R C32, lion as O 1428, Apollo O 83, free style; pl. XII no. 14
37; CG; Cinnamus; vase S&S fig. 47 no. 6 in medallion, acanthus *ibid* fig. 47 no. 21, metope and medallion style; pl. XII no. 15
37; CG; Sacer; deer O 1781 in medallion R E2, metope and medallion style; pl. XII no. 16
37; CG; Mercator II; bird O 2316 in medallion as R E14, draped figure O 923, metope and medallion style; pl. XII no. 18
37; CG; Cinnamus or associate; hare O 2116 in medallion, metope and medallion style; pl. XII no. 20
37; CG; dolphin O 2393-4 (Paternus II or contemporary); pl. XII no. 19
37; CG; Doeccus or possibly Catussa I; ovolo as R B165, but poorly illustrated, rosette S&S fig. 44 no. 4, festoon R F34, Apollo O 93, fish not in O, metope style; pl. XII no. 21
37; CG; Pugnus; fish as O 2416, hare O 2116, gadroon R U153, metope and medallion style; pl. XII no. 22
37; CG; Casurius; sea horse O 33, figure O 638, leaf S&S fig. 40 no. 12, metope style; pl. XIII no. 23
37; CG; Iustus; draped figure O 905, sea bull O 42 in festoon as R F7 or F9, metope style; pl. XIII no. 24
37; CG; probably Censorinus; cockerel O 2361, bear O 1627, metope style; pl. XIII no. 25
37; CG; Banvus, ovolo S&S fig. 41 no. 1, vase R T3, lozenge as R U33-4, metope and medallion style; pl. XIII no. 26
30; CG; Laxtucissa; ovolo S&S fig. 27 no. 1, trifid *ibid* fig. 27 no. 2, leaf *ibid* fig. 27 no. 1; pl. XIII no. 27
37; CG; Cinnamus; boar O 1638, draped figure O 905, metope style; pl. XIII no. 28
30; CG; Advocisus; ovolo as S&S pl. 113 no. 22, lion O 1387, branch R L22, free style; pl. XIII no. 29
30; CG; probably Austrus; ovolo as S&S pl. 95 no. 15, Apollo O 92, metope style; pl. XIII no. 30
37; CG; probably Cinnamus; stand R Q43, metope and medallion style; pl. XIII no. 31
37; CG; Cinnamus; leaf R J1, winding scroll style; pl. XIII no. 32
37; CG; Cinnamus; leaf R H24, winding scroll style; pl. XIII no. 33
37; CG; Cinnamus; leaf R J1, bird O 2298, metope style; pl. XIII no. 34
6 From occupation of rooms 7 and 7a underlying (see deposit **A 44**):
Aur; Greek Ae; BM Cat Gk Coins Nicaea 35; 161-80
Faust II; Den
From the upper Roman stratum:
Comm; Den
Gall; Rad
Tet I; Rad
Constans; Ae
7 The layer is an unsealed black earth deposit incorporating a fairly homogeneous group of samian, but later coins. The coins underlying give a terminus post quem which is probably close to the date of the pottery. There may have been more coins from the upper stratum than are listed above.
8 Droop & Newstead 1931; Newstead & Droop 1936

**A 46**

1 Chichester, West Sussex; town; Chapel Street, X10
2 C
3 A
4 37; CG; Laxtucissa (stamped in mould); ovolo S&S fig. 27 no. 1, leaf *ibid* no. 3, bead-row R A10, horizontal dentils S&S pl. 98 no. 13, man O 913, lion O 1511, eagle O 2183, erotic group as in S&S pl. 102 no. 11 (Censorinus), metope style; fig. 112 no. 54
6 Dom; As/Dup; illeg
7 From part of a timber-lined latrine phased period 5 phase 2, i.e. early/mid-4th century. However the dating evidence is not strong and the latest pottery was CCW dated 270+. The coin and samian may be redepositions.
8 Dannell 1981; Down 1981; Lintott 1981

**A 47**

1 Chichester, West Sussex; town; Tower Street, ditch area 2, layers 2, 3 and 5
2 D
3 A
4 Layer 2:
37; CG; Butrio: dancer O 360, Bacchus O 578C; Fig. 3 nos 1-2
30; CG; Divixtus; lion O 1404, cf S&S pl. 117 no. 7; Fig. 3 no. 5
29; SG; possibly Albus; head O 1322; Fig. 3 no. 4
Flanged bowl; Lez - 1st century kilns; cf O&P pl. 71 no. 16

Layer 3:
18; SG; 'Flavian'
37; SG; 'late 1st century'
Layer 5:
31; CG
6 Barb Rad; late 3rd century; coin no. 5 from layer 5
7 Layer 5 is the lowest layer in the ditch, and forms the ditch silt. The coin and the samian from that layer could possibly be contemporary. However, the two overlying layers contain a variety of mixed material and are good examples of redeposited dumps into the feature.
8 Dannell 1966; Down 1966

**A 48**

1 Colchester, Essex; kiln site; 1933 excavations, dump over kilns 19-22
2 E
3 C
4 Large quantity of moulds, kiln debris, wasters, and vessels of Colch potters A and B, not described here, but given in Hull 1963, 43ff.
Non-local samian:
30; CG; Cinnamus; ovolo S&S fig. 47 no. 3, goat O 1836, metope style; fig. 43 no. 1
37 (2 pieces); CG; Cinnamus or Casurius; mask O 1214, dolphin O 2382, metope style; fig. 43 nos 2 and 2a
30 (2 pieces); CG; Banvus; ovolo S&S fig. 41 no. 1, female figure O 1142, male figure not in O, bear as O 1617, free style; fig. 43 no. 3
37 (6 pieces); CG; Paternus II; ovolo R B178, 'twist' S&S fig. 30 no. 21, bear O 1589, bear O 1578, free style; fig. 43 no. 4
37 (2 pieces); CG; Cinnamus; hare O 2116, sphinx O 854, sphinx O 857, dancer O 348, cockerel as O 2350, metope and medallion style; fig. 43 no. 5
37; CG; Cinnamus; ovolo S&S fig. 47 no. 1, cockerel O 2348, metope style; fig. 43 no. 6
37 (3 pieces); CG; Cinnamus; ovolo S&S fig. 47 no. 1, Minerva O 126B, metope and medallion style; fig. 43 no. 7
37 (2 pieces); CG; Cinnamus; ovolo S&S fig. 47 no. 4, dancer O 322, faun O 711, metope and medallion style; fig. 43 no. 8
37 (12 pieces); CG; Sacer-Attianus or P-23; ovolo as R B93, rosette R C23, circle R E2, dolphin not in O, metope and medallion style; fig. 43 no. 10
37 (2 pieces); CG; Iullinus; ovolo S&S fig. 36 no. 1, vase *ibid* fig. 36 no. 4, column *ibid* fig. 36 no. 5, trifid *ibid* fig. 36 no. 9, rosette as R C53, metope and arcade style; fig. 43 no. 11 and fig. 44 no. 18
37; CG; probably Cinnamus; deer O 1743, free style; fig. 43 no. 12
37; CG; Cinnamus; ovolo S&S fig. 47 no. 2, free style; fig. 43 no. 13
37; CG; group III or IV potter; warrior as O 195A, warrior as O 212, metope and medallion style; fig. 43 no. 14
37; CG; Cinnamus; horseman O 245, figure O 688 in medallion; fig. 43 no. 15
37 (3 pieces); CG; Paullus; horseman O 258, bear as O 1606, deer O 1784, deer O 1815, free style; fig. 44 nos 17a-b
37 (2 pieces); CG; Sacer-Attianus; ovolo R B14, figure as S&S pl. 82 no. 1 (= O 1073), free style; fig. 44 nos 23a-b
37; CG; possibly Caratillus; overlapping ovolo apparently as S&S fig. 26 no. 1 but with single border as *ibid* pl. 96 no. 2, free style; fig. 44 no. 25
30; CG; Albucius; ovolo S&S fig. 35 no. 1, astragalus border, sphinx stand as S&S pl. 69 no. 12, bird O 2324, metope style; fig. 44 no. 28
37; CG; Cinnamus or associate; fragment in metope and medallion style; fig. 43 no. 9
37 (2 pieces); EG - probably La Mad; ovolo similar to Ricken 1934 Taf. VIIIC, leaf as *ibid* Taf. X no. 21, spiral *ibid* Taf. VII no. 33, ornament R U123, metope style; fig. 44 no. 19
37; CG - but possibly EG; lion as O 1373-4, figure O 592-3, spiral not in R, F, H or R&F, free style; fig. 44 no. 22
37 (10 or more pieces); Sinzig; group 1 workshop 2; identical to Fischer 1969 Taf. 33 no. 203 (and fully described in that publication); fig. 42 no. 1
37 (2 pieces); Sinzig; as previous; identical to *ibid* Taf. 28 no. 167; fig. 36 no. 8 and fig. 42 no. 2
37 (2 pieces); Sinzig; as previous; identical to *ibid* Taf. 30 no. 181; fig. 42 nos 3-4
37; Sinzig; as previous; identical to *ibid* Taf. 32 no. 199; fig. 42 no. 5
37; Sinzig; as previous; identical to *ibid* Taf. 23 no. 131; fig. 42 no. 6
37; Sinzig; as previous; identical to *ibid* Taf. 32 no. 200; fig. 42 no. 7
37 (2 pieces); Sinzig; as previous; identical to *ibid* Taf. 22 no. 127; fig. 42 nos 9-10
37; Sinzig; as previous; identical to *ibid* Taf. 27 no. 156; fig. 42 no. 12
37; possibly Sinzig; cupid *ibid* M13, erotic group *ibid* M32-3, spiral *ibid* O13, border *ibid* O37, free style; fig. 42 no. 8
37; possibly Sinzig; cupid *ibid* M13, Diana *ibid* M6, metope style; fig. 42 no. 11
37; possibly Sinzig; seated figure *ibid* M4-4a; fig. 42 no. 13
5 Large quantity of Colch CCW with barbotine dec
6 Dom; As; very worn; no. 2
Had; As; RIC 577; slightly worn; no. 3
Aur; HS; RIC 960/696; 164+; very worn; no. 4
Aur?; As; illeg; very worn; no. 5
7 The stratigraphy of the dump is unclear, and it is certain that it was moved and redeposited when the later kilns (20 etc) were in use. No sections were recorded to document the exact sequence of the dumps. The main conclusion, however, is that the dump contains wasters of the Colch samian potters, together with pieces by their Sinzig predecessors and contemporary CG potters - all brought together in the rubbish dump after the kiln went out of use. The Sinzig ware was described by Hull as his potter C, but has been recognized for its true origin since.
8 Hull 1963; Fischer 1969, 196; Simpson 1982a

**A 49**

1 Colchester, Essex; town; Insula 15 'Mithraeum' lower fill of drain running from room D
2 G, drain fill
3 A
4 37 (3 pieces); CG; Laxtucissa; rosette and frond S&S fig. 27 no. 9, circle *ibid* fig. 27 no. 7, rosette *ibid* fig. 27 no. 11, horizontal 'column' *ibid* fig. 27 no. 13, caryatid O 1199, male figure O 779, metope style; fig. 51B no. 2
30; CG; Cinnamus; ovolo S&S fig. 47 no. 3, lion O 1421; fig. 51B no. 9
37; CG; Docilis (cursive signature in mould); ovolo S&S fig. 24 no.1, no border, stand as R Q8, mask not in O, lozenge R U28, Victory with rudder not in O, bud R G145, lion O 1403A, Hercules club R Q5, palm frond as S&S fig. 24 no. 15, Venus O 280, bifid R U30, two small birds

not exact in O, bud R Q259, acanthus R K3, column R P3, rosette R C35, Hercules O 774, cupid O 408, caryatid not in O, circle S&S fig. 24 no. 7, Mars O 151, metope style, published in S&S pl. 91 no. 1; fig. 51a
37; CG; Attianus II (stamped in mould); ornament S&S fig. 23 no. 3, horseman O 251, bear O 1595, lioness O 1566, free style, published in S&S pl. 85 no. 3; fig. 51B no. 1
31; Rheinz; stamped by Iassus
79; CG; stamped by Namil-Croesi
5 Oxf imitation samian 37 with incised dec from half-way up fill
6 Had; HS; illeg; fair condition
Gall?; Rad
From upper fill of drain:
Claud II; Rad
Claud II; Rad
7 There is the possibility of long-term or episodic deposition in the drain fill.
8 Harden & Green 1978, 171-2; Hull 1958, 107-45

**A 50**

1 Colchester, Essex; town; Insula 15 'Mithraeum' lowest layer in room D
2 B
3 A
4 37; CG; Doeccus (stamped in mould); ovolo as S&S fig. 44 no. 2, leaf *ibid* fig. 44 no. 37 in medallion, astragalus *ibid* fig. 44 no. 3, rosette *ibid* fig. 44 no. 4, cupid O 442A, shell S&S fig. 44 no. 6, figure not in O but as O 389 without wings, metope and medallion style; fig. 50 no. 11
37; Rheinz; Comitialis III; ovolo as R&F E10, athlete *ibid* M195, deer *ibid* T96, circle *ibid* K48, stand *ibid* O11, medallion style, as Ricken 1942 Taf. 83; fig. 50 no. 12
6 Traj; HS; fair condition
Had; HS; illeg, worn
Had; HS; illeg; good
Had; HS; illeg; fair
Had; Den (plated); mutilated
Ant; HS; illeg
Ant; HS; illeg
Faust II; As; RIC (Aur) 1647; good
J Domna; Den; RIC (Car) 559; 196-211; very good
Car; Den (plated); illeg; good
Constans; Ae; very good
From rubble above lowest layer:
Victorin - Tet II; 12 Rad
7 C Green has revised the original date given by Hull for this deposit from the mid-4th century to the early or mid-3rd (Harden & Green 1978, 171-2). The coin of Constans seems to be intrusive or mis-recorded. The two samian pieces fit well with the revised dating.
8 Harden & Green 1978, 171-2; Hull 1958, 107-45

**A 51**

1 Colchester, Essex; town; Lewis's Gardens, destruction levels of house III
2 E
3 A
4 37; Rheinz; Cerialis II-III or Primitivus I; Venus as R&F M48, no other details given
37; CG; Paullus; bird D 1037
31R CG; 45
5 Mortarium stamped by Cunopectus who also made samian at Colchester
6 Gall; Rad; unrecorded type; 259
8 Carson 1961; Hartley 1961a; Richardson 1961

**A 52**

1 Colchester, Essex; religious building in town suburb; 22 Crouch Street, pit A in apse
2 C
3 A
4 37; Colch; ovolo of potter B, Hull 1963 fig. 41 no. 115, bifid as *ibid* fig. 42 nos 1, 3-5, 9 used by potter C, small medallions in horizontal zones; fig. 111 no. 4
5 Rhenish beaker; large globular vase in polished red ware with rouletting and white painted dec
6 Nerv; Dup; very worn
Traj; HS; very worn
Aur; HS; RIC 948
Aur; HS; RIC 948
Aur; HS; RIC 886 or 1397; worn
Sev; HS: RIC 657; 193; worn
Post-Tet II; 13 Rad
Allect; Rad
129 4th to early 5th century coins
7 The earlier coins are from the lower levels of the pit, but unfortunately the relative position of the pottery is not given. Therefore the dating is very vague. However, the context appears to be votive, built up over a period, possibly starting in the late 2nd or 3rd century since all the 1st and 2nd century coins are worn or very worn and could have been in circulation at that time. The published pottery is more likely to date to the 3rd century rather than the 4th.
8 Dannell 1971a; Dunnett 1971, 78-84; Hull 1958, 245-8

**A 53**

1 Combe Hay, Somerset; rural settlement; VIII layer 4
2 E
3 A
4 37; CG; Sacer; ovolo S&S fig. 22 no. 4; microfiche fig. 25SA2
37; CG; Quintilianus and Arcanus; vine scroll
37; CG; X-6; ovolo S&S pl. 76 nos 28-30, hare O 2136 in festoon as S&S pl. 75 no. 20, leaf-tip *ibid* pl. 75 no. 15; microfiche fig. 25SA5/30
37; CG; Casurius; microfiche fig. 25SA6
37; Trier or, less possibly, Sinzig; leaf F 1916, sea horse as O 36 but smaller; microfiche fig. 25SA20
37; Trier; griffin O 877
37 CG fragment; 33 CG (2); 18 CG; 18/31 CG; 31 CG (3); 31 EG; 38 EG
6 Gall; Rad; RIC 480-1; 260-8; very good condition
Barb Rad (2)
5 coins of House of Const
5 coins of House of Valent
7 This seems a clear case of redeposition. The rubbish deposit derives from the dismantling of putative iron-smelting kilns.
8 Price & Watts 1980; Reece 1980a; Wild 1980

**A 54**

1 Corbridge, Northumberland; town; burnt level in site XX
2 E
3 A
4 37; CG; Divixtus; ovolo S&S fig. 33 no. 1, Bacchus O 571, metope and medallion style; fig. 7 no. S1
37 (2 pieces); CG; Albucius; column R P3; dancer O 360, Jupiter O 3, female figure O 926, Hercules O 779, male figure O 663, metope and medallion style; fig. 7 no. S2
6 From under the burnt layer:
Traj; HS

Ant; Den; RIC 222; 152-3
Faust II; As; illeg
7 Part of the so-called 'AD 197' destruction deposit
8 Corbitt 1955; Richmond & Gillam 1955, 238-42

**A 55**

1 Corbridge, Northumberland; town; destruction deposit of Antonine II in and near site XI
2 E
3 A
4 More than 800 samian sherds were found according to Richmond & Gillam 1950, 181-2, but only a tiny proportion of the decorated ware has been published:
37; CG; X-9; leaf R U161, rosette S&S fig. 9 no. 7; fig. 15 no. 24
37; CG; Sacer-Attianus; ovolo S&S fig. 22 no. 1, bear O 1588, deer O 1743, free style; fig. 15 no. 25
37; CG; Cinnamus; ovolo S&S fig. 47 no. 4, goat O 1836, metope style; fig. 15 no. 26
37; CG; Cinnamus-Cerialis; ovolo as R B144, prisoner on trolley O 1139, goat O 1852, rosette S&S fig. 47 no. 26, leaf R H24, winding scroll style; fig. 15 no. 27a-b
There were 2-300 pieces in the style of Cinnamus from the deposit - only the two above were published because they had unusual designs.
37; CG; 'Aventinus II' (bowl finisher for Cinnamus); rosettes S&S fig. 46 no. 9 arranged around a medallion, metope and medallion style; fig. 16 no. 28
37; CG; Advocisus (stamped in mould); ovolo S&S fig. 33 no. 2, ornament *ibid* fig. 33 no. 1, cupid O 442, cupid O 503, mask O 1330, metope style; fig. 16 no. 29
37; CG; Ianuaris II-Paternus I; ovolo S&S fig. 34 no. 1, lion O 1430, bear O 1617, deer O 1732, free style; fig. 16 no. 30
37; CG; Paternus II; ovolo S&S fig. 30 no. 1, branch R L22, bear O 1617, free style; fig. 16 no. 31
37; CG; Albucius; ovolo S&S fig. 35 no. 1, fish O 2417, dolphin O 2384, dolphin O 2393, sea horse O 33, sea bull O 52A, free style, published as S&S pl. 121 no. 8; fig. 16 no. 32
37; CG; Albucius; ovolo S&S fig. 35 no. 1, leaf *ibid* fig. 35 no. 2, stand R Q6, cupid O 444, cupid O 420, cupid O 440, metope style; fig. 16 no. 33
37; CG; Secundus; ovolo S&S fig. 45 no. 4, Perseus O 234, Pan mask O 1214, deer O 1777, female figure O 801, panther O 1508, dolphin O 2401, metope and medallion style, published as S&S pl. 155 no. 22; fig. 17 no. 34
37; Rheinz; Cobnertus I (stamped in mould die c); ovolo R&F E44a, leaf *ibid* P59, leaf *ibid* P78, free style, virtually identical to Ricken 1948 Taf. 21 no. 6; fig. 17 no. 36
37; La Mad; probably ware with ovolo C; ovolo as Ricken 1934 Taf. VII C; fig. 17 no. 38
Probably from the same deposit, from excavations of 1957-8:
37; CG; Cinnamus; ovolo S&S fig. 47 no. 1, boar O 1666, metope and medallion style; Birley 1959, fig. 2 no. 3
37; CG; Cinnamus (early style); ovolo S&S fig. 47 no. 3, figure with pan-pipes O 617A, circle S&S fig. 47 no. 11, leaf R H24, winding scroll style; Birley 1959, fig. 2 no. 4
37; CG; Laxtucissa; ovolo S&S fig. 27 no. 1; Birley 1959, fig. 2 no. 5
37; CG; Divixtus (stamped in mould); ovolo S&S fig. 33 no. 2, bird O 2252, mask O 1262, mask O 1328, caryatid O 1199, lioness O 1570, lioness O 1518, metope and medallion style; Birley 1959, fig. 2 no. 6
37; CG; Advocisus; (stamped in mould); ovolo S&S fig. 33 no. 2, ornament *ibid* fig. 33 no. 1, dancer O 353, man on rock O 842, caryatid as O 1206; Birley 1959, fig. 2 no. 7
Also thought to be from the same deposit, because of their burnt appearance (Hartley 1972a, 46):
Quintilianus group; Attianus; Tetturo; EG-La Mad; Cinnamus-Cerialis
6 At least 4 coins were found in the destruction deposit, including:
Rep; Den; M Antony type
Faust II; Den
Sev; Den; 198+
7 The stratigraphy of this deposit is very difficult. There appear to be two burning levels that post-date the construction of site XI (Forster & Knowles 1912, 162), the first of which may have brought about the abandonment of the building programme (Gillam & Tait 1971, period VB-C). It is now impossible to establish from which level the coins and pottery came, although the Severan coin was definitely from the lower level (Craster 1911). Elsewhere in Corbridge it seems that the lower destruction was fairly widespread, and is recorded in deposit A54, and also in Forster & Knowles (1912, 174) where bowls of Cinnamus and Divixtus are mentioned in association with Vesp; HS, Had; HS, Had; As, Had; Den, Aur; Dup (2) dated 155 (in good condition). In all probability most, if not all, the samian from site XI comes from the lower level since it appears to be similar to these other deposits. Some may have been disturbed and redeposited, as Hartley suggests (1972a, 46), probably including the Severan coin, which could be intrusive. The samian listed here is a selection only and is difficult to use in a quantified way. Plain ware was very common; 31 and 18/31, 33, 27 and 38 being most frequent, in that order (Richmond & Gillam 1950, 182).
8 Birley 1959; Craster 1911; Dore 1988, 220-1; Forster & Knowles 1912; Gillam nd; Gillam & Tait 1971; Hartley 1972a, 45-8; Richmond & Gillam 1950, 177-83; Simpson 1953

**A 56**

1 Cox Green, Berkshire; villa; period I
2 F
3 A
4 37; CG; X-13 (Donnaucus); leaf R H161, rosette R C280, female figure not in O, beaded border in two sizes, metope and St Andrew's cross style; fig. 6 no. 1
6 HS; 2nd century type; illeg
7 A general association only. From above this level came several pieces of late plain ware: 31 CG; 38 CG (2); 33 CG; 44 var EG; 45.
8 Bennett 1962; Hartley 1962; Kent 1962

**A 57**

1 Dorchester, Dorset; town; Library site, cobbles west of pit N near road 1
2 B
3 A
4 37 (2 pieces); CG; Albucius; ovolo R B105, border R A9, female figure D 334, metope style as S&S pl. 122 no. 24; fig. 16 no. 17
6 Faust I; HS; possibly RIC (Ant) 1099; 141+
7 The cobbles from which the sherd comes are part of the initial road make-up. The coin was found on edge in the worn surface of the road. An imperfect association as a result.
8 Aitken & Aitken 1982; Pengelly 1982

**A 58**

1 Dorchester, Dorset; town; Library site, surface of road 26
2 B
3 A
4 37; CG; Cinnamus; figure O 644, lion O 1450, dog O 1980, free style; fig. 16 no. 19
6 Comm; HS; RIC 326; 181-2; very worn
7 Sherd and coin come from the road flints. From brown clay at the edge of the road, possibly to be associated with the town rampart, comes Faust II; HS; RIC (Aur) 1693; *c* 175-80.
8 Aitken & Aitken 1982; Pengelly 1982

**A 59**

1 Dorchester, Dors; town; Wadham House site, trench 5 layer 6
2 E
3 A
4 37; CG; Iullinus; as S&S pl. 126 - no other details given
5 NF indented CCW beakers; BB1 dishes and jars
6 Barb Rad; as Tet I RIC 86; good copy but much worn, estimated as lost *c* 280-320
7 All the pottery apart from the samian appears to be contemporary with the coin.
8 Draper & Chaplin 1982

**A 60**

1 Dover, Kent; fort; Battle of Britain Homes, DV 2684 and 2545-7, fill of latrine sewer B89
2 E
3 A
4 37; SG; parallels in Grimes 1930, nos 16, 29, 44 (dated 90-110); fig. 52 no. 358
37; CG; Doeccus or Casurius; beads as S&S pl. 149, 27 and pl. 136, 46
Plain ware: 33 EG; 36 SG; 31 CG (2); C 21 prob EG
6 Vesp; Dup; illeg; 69-79; coin 5
Had; Dup; illeg; 117-28; coin 31
Aur; Dup/As; RIC (Ant) 1354a; 159-60; coin 50
8 Bird & Marsh 1981; Philp 1981

**A 61**

1 Dover, Kent; fort; Burial Ground, DV28 pit fill in guard room of B13
2 C
3 A
4 37; CG; Cinnamus/Cerialis style; ovolo S&S fig. 47 no. 3b
33 CG; U·CG (2)
6 Traj; HS; RIC 503; 103-11; coin 19
Ant P; HS; RIC 643; 140-4; coin 41
8 Bird & Marsh 1981; Philp 1981

**A 62**

1 Dover, Kent; fort; Car Park, DV 536/683 period III occupation in B20
2 B
3 A
4 37; CG; Iullinus; square beads S&S pl. 126, 11, small circle *ibid*·pl. 127, 29, 32, Victory as O 812 and S&S pl. 126, 13; fig. 49 no. 307
Plain ware: 31 CG/EG; 45 EG
6 Had; Den; RIC 42a; 118; coin 20
Comm; Den; RIC 241; 192; coin 56
Sev; Den; type of 202-10; coin 63
Adjacent contemporary road surface has:
Sev; Den; RIC 125a; 198-200; coin 60
8 Bird & Marsh 1981; Philp 1981

**A 63**

1 Dover, Kent; fort; Car park, DV 556/643 period II occupation in B20
2 B
3 A
4 37 (3 pieces); CG; caryatid as O 1198A; fig. 48 nos 302-4
37; CG; Tetturo; gladiator O 1059, warrior as O 177, many similar features on S&S pl. 131, 1; fig. 48 no. 305
Plain ware: 18/31 CG; 27 CG; 33 CG (2); 46 EG
6 Nerva; HS; RIC 93; 97; coin 14
Had; Den; RIC 355; 134-8; coin 21
8 Bird & Marsh 1981; Philp 1981

**A 64**

1 Dover, Kent; fort; Cause-is-Altered, DV 2051/2096/2136 dump in B19 forming period II floors
2 E
3 A
4 37; CG; Cinnamus; ovolo 3 S&S fig. 47, 3, goat smaller than O 1836; fig. 48 no. 297
37; CG; Cinnamus; ovolo 1 S&S fig. 47, 1
Plain ware: 30 CG; 31 CG; 33 CG
6 Ant; As; RIC 934; 154-5; coin 44
8 Bird & Marsh 1981; Philp 1981

**A 65**

1 Dover, Kent; fort; Cause-is-Altered, DV 2130 B19 period III occupation
2 B
3 A
4 37; CG; Albucius - stamp of Albucius ii die 6h in mould; dolphin O 2382; fig. 48 no. 298
6 Aur; Den; RIC 207; 168-9; coin 51
Adjacent contemporary deposits have:
Ant; Den; RIC 136; 145-61; coin 38
Sev; Den; RIC 125a; 200; coin 62
8 Bird & Marsh 1981; Philp 1981

**A 66**

1 Dover, Kent; fort; School Yard, DV 720/788 soil above B25
2 E
3 A
4 37; CG; Censorinus, Laxtucissa or Paternus II; ovolo R B138, bear not in O; fig. 49 no. 317
37; CG; Casurius; saltire S&S pl. 135, 36, foliage as *ibid*
30; CG; Cinnamus; warrior as S&S pl. 160, 41, bird as *ibid* pl. 161, 47
37; CG; fragment of animal and scroll
37; CG; broken ovolo
37; Arg; Tribunus; ovolo Oswald 1945 fig. 8 no. 27, hare O 2140A/B; fig. 49 no. 318
37; Heil; Reginus; ovolo not paralleled but see Forrer 1911 Taf. 27 no. 2 for the egg, vertical lattice *ibid*, large rosette *ibid* Taf. 27 no. 6, bud in place of ovolo tongue *ibid*; fig. 49 no. 319
33; Lez; Iustus II die 2a
33; Lez; Pottacus die 2b
Plain ware: 32 EG; 38 CG (2); 31 CG (2); 31 EG (2); 33 CG (3); 45 CG (2); 45 EG (2)
6 Titus; Den; RIC 9; 79-81; coin 7
J Domna; Den; RIC (Sev) 572; 196-211; coin 66
J Domna; Den; RIC (Sev) 577; 196-211; coin 67
Car; Den; Sol type of Sev; 203-10; coin 68
J Maesa; Den; as RIC (Elag) 263; 218-22; coin 73
Alex; Den; RIC 133; 222-35; coin 75

Alex; As; RIC 577; 222-31; coin 78
Phil; Ant; RIC 276; 244-9; coin 80
Allect; Rad; as RIC 28/86; 293-6; coin 84
7 This part of the fort has later coins and samian than elsewhere. The excavator suggests that this area was a dump for the adjacent headquarters or commandant's building which may have continued in some sort of occupation mid/late 3rd century (Philp 1981, 56). However the coin of Allectus may be intrusive.
8 Bird & Marsh 1981; Philp 1981

**A 67**

1 Dover, Kent; *vicus* of fort; Market Square, level 4a destruction
2 E
3 A
4 37; CG; Albucius; dolphin O 2392, bust O 650
18/31; Lez; Briccus stamp
6 Two hoards probably associated with the deposit, conflated in the report:
Phil II; Ant; RIC 219
Gall (7); rad
Claud II; rad
Claud II; rad; *consecratio* issue (3)
Post; rad (2)
Vict; rad
Tet I; rad (5); 270-3
Tet II; rad (5); 270-3
Barb rad (31)
Illeg (15)
7 The hoards were deposited in the top of the destruction over the wall foundations. It is not clear from the excavator's account if the samian, which was in rather than from the top of the destruction, was stratigraphically earlier or contemporary.
8 Birley & Simpson 1957; Murray-Threipland 1957; O'Neil 1957

**A 68**

1 Ebchester, County Durham; fort; dark soil between period VII buildings
2 E
3 A
3 37 (2 pieces); CG - MdV; X-2 or Drusus I; ovolo and bead row, no details given; no. 76
37; CG; Cinnamus; ovolo S&S fig. 47 no. 1; no. 77
27 SG; 18/31R CG-MdV; 31 CG; 31R CG (2); 43 or 45 CG
5 BB1 and BB2 of late 2nd to 3rd century date
6 Nerva; HS; illeg
Barb Rad
7 The deposit possibly built up over a period, and is associated with buildings of mid to late 3rd century.
8 Casey 1975; Hartley, Dickinson & Pengelly 1975; Maxfield & Reed 1975

**A 69**

1 Enfield, Greater London; *vicus;* F1 lower part, pit fill
2 C
3 A
4 37; CG; Quintilianus group; ovolo S&S fig. 29 no. 3, horse O 1902 (3 times), horse O 1892 (2 times), dolphin not in O, free style; fig. 17 no. 1
30; CG; unknown potter; spiral R S68 (assigned to Igocatus (X-4) and Me...; this piece is not by Igocatus), eagle larger than O 2167, metope style; fig. 17 no. 2
37; CG; Cinnamus; astragalus as S&S fig. 47 no. 41, sea monster O 46, no. 32
6 Faust II; HS; RIC (Aur) 1635; 161-75; fairly worn; coin 23
Comm; HS; RIC (Aur) 1599; 179; fairly worn; coin 25
2 coins of the period 268-73
4 coins of the period 270-80
4 house of Const
1 house of Valent
2 house of Theod
7 The pit has been disturbed and recut in the 4th century, but it is thought that the samian and the two 2nd century coins are part of the original fill. The differentiation is not made clear in the report.
8 Gentry, Ivens & McClean 1977; Hammerson & Coxshall 1977; Webster 1977

**A 70**

1 Enfield, Greater London; *vicus*; F64 pit fill
2 C
3 A
4 37; Rheinz; Reginus I; ovolo R&F E56, Minerva *ibid* M29A, rosette *ibid* O42, metope style; fig. 18 no. 33
6 Lucilla; HS; RIC (Aur) 1730-2; 161-9; very worn; coin 24
Claud II (*consecratio*); Rad; RIC 290; 270; slightly worn; coin 45
7 The other pottery suggests contemporaneity with the general run of 2nd century pits on the site. However, the two coins and the samian might be contemporary depositions.
8 Gentry, Ivens & McClean 1977; Hammerson & Coxshall 1977; Webster 1977

**A71**

1 Fordcroft, Orpington, Kent; villa; pit 2
2 C
3 A
4 30 (14 pieces); CG; Doeccus; ovolo S&S fig. 44 no. 2,astragalus *ibid* fig. 44 no. 9, rhomboid *ibid* fig. 44 no. 17, shield R U210, base of stand not in R or S&S, Mercury O 532, sea horse O 42, fish O 2412, fish O 2419, metope style, rivetted; fig. 7 nos 5-10
30; CG; Doeccus; Bacchus O 584, standing on mask as O 1237, leaf not in R, metope style; fig. 7 no. 12
37 (4 pieces); CG; Cinnamus; circle S&S fig. 47 no. 11, leaf R H21, winding-scroll style; fig. 7 no. 13
37 (2 pieces); CG; Albucius; leaf-tips as S&S pl. 121 no. 13, pygmy O 699, male figure as O 660, astragalus borders, metope style, smeared on removal from mould; fig. 7 no. 14
37; CG; Drusus I; ovolo Detsicas 1963a fig. 3 no. 1; fig. 7 no. 15
37; CG; Cettus; ovolo S&S fig. 42 no. 2, leaf-stalk *ibid* fig. 42 no. 4, Venus O 281; fig. 7 no. 16
37 (3 pieces); CG; Acurio; leafy branch R N14, leaf-tips S&S pl. 165 nos 1-2, lion O 1459, panther O 1503, deer as O 1720, dog O 1980, horse as O 1904, panther O 1512, deer as O 1732, free style, similar to S&S pl. 165; fig. 8 nos 17-l8
30 (2 pieces); CG; rouletted dec
Plain ware: 15/17 SG (3); 18 SG; 18 CG; 27 CG; 33 CG (8 - 1 stamped by Catullus); 33 EG (2); 38 CG (2); 36 CG (5); C11 SG; C11 CG; C15 CG; 79 CG; 46/80 CG; 18/31 CG (4 - 1 stamped by Bononus); 18/31R CG; 31 CG (5); 31R CG
6 Coin nos 119-35 in the report
Aur; HS; RIC 1009; 170-1
Aur; HS; RIC 992
Aur?; As; worn

Gall ; Rad; illeg
Vict; Rad; RIC 41; 265-70
Vict/Tet I; Rad (3)
Tet I; Rad (2 +1 uncertain)
Claud II; Rad; consecratio issue
Allectus; Ae; RIC 55; 293-6 (2)
Barb Rad (2) + 1 illeg

7 The coin evidence points apparently to a very late dated group, but the composition of the samian is against this. However, the number of joining sherds may suggest that the group is not redeposited. The explanation may be that the stratigraphy in the pit was more complicated than given by the excavator. He points out (Tester 1969, 55) that some pottery at the bottom of the pit was 1st century (possibly including the SG plain ware), but that the considerable quantity above was 2nd and 3rd century in character. The Aurelius coins are most consonant with the decorated samian and the majority of the plain pieces. Perhaps the late 3rd century coins are part of a later levelling of a slump in the pit.

8 Detsicas 1969; Tester 1969

**A 72**

1 Gloucester, Gloucestershire; town; New Market Hall, occupation of 1st masonry building north of street

2 B

3 A

4 29; SG; mid-Flavian style, details not given here; fig. 8 no. 28
29; SG; similar to previous; fig. 8 no. 30
37; SG; St Andrew's cross and leaf tendril, late Flavian style; fig. 8 no. 29
37; CG; Laxtucissa; ovolo S&S fig. 27 no. 1 with wavy line below; fig. 8 no. 31
Plain ware: 31 CG stamped by Satono; 33 CG stamped by November; 31, 36 and 44 CG and EG; 18, 18/31, 27, 31, 33, 36, 44 and 45 SG, CG, EG (unspecified in report)

6 J Domna; Den; RIC (Sev) 572; 196-211; coin 10

7 There is a large proportion of 1st century material here, probably residual. However, the piece by Laxtucissa, the stamped plain ware and some of the other plain wares may be contemporary with the coin. The excavators date the occupation to 150-250.

8 Bird 1974a; Hartley 1974; Hassall & Rhodes 1974

**A 73**

1 Gloucester, Gloucestershire; tile kiln: St Oswald's Priory, abandonment levels, phase RA

2 E

3 A

4 37; CG; Iustus; ovolo S&S fig. 31 no. 2, lozenge *ibid* fig. 31 no. 10, wavy line border, deer O 1720, metope and medallion style; fig. 7 no. 4
37; CG; Doeccus; leaf S&S fig. 44 no. 39, rosette *ibid* fig. 44 no. 5 in medallion; fig. 7 no. 5
37; Rheinz; Cerialis VI; ovolo R&F E40, trace of winding scroll; fig. 7 no. 6

5 Coarse ware includes material from the 1st century to the mid-4th

6 Faust II; Ae; as RIC (Ant) 1154-1200; coin 105
Victorin; Rad; RIC 114; coin 82
1 house of Const, 1 Honorius

7 The deposit is certainly mixed, but the samian element is unusual in having no plain ware and being of roughly contemporary pieces.

8 Heighway & Parker 1982; Watkins 1982; Wild 1982

**A 74**

1 Holcombe, Devon; villa; phase IV midden debris in room 9

2 B

3 A

4 37; CG; Iullinus; dancer O 322, see S&S pl. 127 nos 24 and 35 for style, metope style; fig. 12 no. 8

6 Ant; HS; RIC 618
Gall; Rad; RIC 270
Claud II; Rad; RIC 103; 268-70

7 This phase is dated to the late 3rd century. Therefore Pollard considers the samian to be residual. However, it is noteworthy that the other decorated samian includes pieces, one with the ovolo of Avitus and Ianuaris II and one in Cinnamus style, that Simpson considers to be late, possibly copies, of late 2nd to 3rd century date. There is also some incised samian.

8 Carson & Bosanko 1974; Pollard 1974; Simpson 1974b

**A 75**

1 Housesteads, Northumberland; fort; commandant's house latrine drain, rooms 8-9

2 G - silt in drain

3 A

4 37; CG; Iullinus; Venus O 278, dolphin and basket R Q59, ornament S&S fig. 36 no. 7, metope style; no. 15
37; CG; Advocisus; Pan O 709, metope style; no. 16
37; CG; Doeccus (stamped on rim with small stamp); rim only; no. 1
37; Rheinz; Firmus or BF Attoni; eagle and hare R&F T204; no. 8
Lud VMe type; Rheinz, barbotine dec of dolphins and scrolls; no. 12
jar (2 vessels); CG; appliqué dec, black CG; nos 13-14
37 (2)
Plain ware: 31 (2); 31R (2); 35; 36; C15 or 23 (2); 38 (2); 33 (3 - 1 stamped by Mammius CG); Lud Tx; 45 (2); 18/31; 18/31R or 31R (2); U (5)

5 CCW indented beakers

6 Dom; As; RIC 340
Ant; Dup; illeg
Ant; Dup; illeg
Faust I; Den; RIC (Ant) 361; 141+
Faust I; Dup; illeg

7 The drain was altered and the overlying fill had a coin of Alex; Den; RIC 7

8 Charlesworth 1975; Curnow 1975; Pengelly 1975

**A 76**

1 Ilchester, Somerset; town; site R10, layer 94 pit fill

2 C

3 A

4 37; CC; Ioenalis/Ranto group; winding scroll and horizontal wreath; fig. 65 no. D58

6 Comm; As; worn

8 Isaac 1982; Leach 1982; Rodwell 1982a

**A77**

1 Joyden's Wood, Bexley, Kent; enclosure; ditch AB

2 D

3 A

4 37; CC; Doeccus; ovolo probably S&S fig. 44 no. 2, bird O 2197 in festoon, sphinx O 858, warrior O 204 in double circle R E8; fig. 2
Plain ware: 18/31; 31 CG; 33 CG stamped by Quintus; 33 CG; Ritt 8; 46 CG

6 Ant; Ae

The conjoining ditch AC had: Comm; HS
7 The ditch sections cleared were long - AB was 147 feet. Thus associations are tentative. However, the excavators state that 'from the upright position of many of the sherds and the absence of lines of natural bedding it may be concluded that the main contents were the result of deliberate in-filling rather than slow accumulation' (Tester & Caiger 1954, 169).
8 Tester & Caiger 1954

**A 78**

1 Latimer, Buckinghamshire; villa; room 19 layer 8
2 B
3 A
4 37; CG; Ianuaris II; ovolo S&S fig. 34 no. 1, leaf *ibid* fig. 34 no. 1, rosette *ibid* fig. 34 no. 5, free style; fig. 34 no. 397
6 Vesp; As; illeg; worn
Traj; HS; 97-117
8 Branigan 1971; Detsicas 1971; Robinson 1971

**A 79**

1 Leicester, Leicestershire; town; Jewry Wall period V, courtyard surface
2 E
3 A
4 37; CG; Cinnamus or associate; tree R N2, cupid O 419, dog O 1980, metope style; fig. 8 no. 6
37; CG; Cinnamus; Diana O 111, panther O 1518, metope style; fig. 8 no. 7
37 (3 pieces); CG; Casurius; ovolo S&S fig. 40 no. 1, leaf *ibid* fig. 40 no. 10, ornament *ibid* fig. 40 no. 3, ornament R U295, figure 0 638, arcade style; fig. 8 no. 8
37; CG; Cinnamus; ovolo only (no details)
67 CG with incised dec
6 Ant; Dup; from period IV underlying
Vesp; Dup
Ant; As
Faust II; As; RIC (Aur) 1395
7 There is a certain amount of residual material in the level, not reflected in the samian ware listed here.
8 Kenyon 1948; Oswald 1948b

**A 80**

1 Leicester, Leicestershire; town; Jewry Wall period VI, courtyard surface
2 E
3 A
4 37; CG; Albucius; ovolo S&S fig. 35 no. 1, cupid O 450, metope and medallion style; fig. 9 no. 1
37; CG; Advocisus; ovolo S&S fig. 33 no. 1, boar O 1642, panther O 1542, free style; fig. 9 no. 4
37; CG; probably Iustus; ovolo as R B177, vine scroll R M50, metope style; fig. 9 no. 5
37; CG; Laxtucissa; ovolo S&S fig. 27 no. 1, horse or deer O 1974A; fig. 9 no. 6
37; CG; probably Austrus; ovolo as S&S fig. 25 no. 2 (blurred), goat O 1851, free style; fig. 9 no. 10
37; CG; Doeccus; ovolo S&S fig. 44 no. 2, bifid *ibid* fig. 44 no. 15; fig. 9 no. 11
37; CG; Divixtus; ovolo S&S fig. 33 no. 3, astragalus *ibid* fig. 33 no. 1, caryatid O 1199, erotic group O B, metope and medallion style, from the same mould as a piece from Carlisle in S&S pl. 116 no. 8; fig. 9 no. 13
37; CG; Casurius; ovolo S&S fig. 40 no. 1, cupid O 382; fig. 9 no. 14
37; CG; Casurius; leaf S&S fig. 40 no. 10; fig. 9 no. 15
72 CG with incised dec
6 Vesp; As
Vesp; Dup
Traj; As
Traj; HS
Had; HS
Had; Den
Ant; Dup; RIC 908; 152-3
Ant; As; RIC 934; 155-6
(Faust II As from underlying level, see previous entry)
7 Residual early material was present, but was not listed.
8 Kenyon 1948; Oswald 1948b

**A 81**

1 Leicester, Leicestershire; town; Jewry Wall period VII, courtyard surface
2 E
3 A
4 37 (2 pieces); CG; Laxtucissa; ovolo S&S fig. 27 no. 1, leaf *ibid* fig. 27 no. 12, panther O 1509, bear O 1617, dog O 1985A, free style; fig. 9 no. 16
37; CG; Pugnus, Paullus or Cettus; Mercury O 532; fig. 9 no. 18
37; CG; Advocisus, Cinnamus or Casurius; stand R Q42; fig. 9 no. 20
37; CG; Cinnamus; ovolo S&S fig. 47 no. 1, lozenge *ibid* fig. 47 no. 15, circle *ibid* fig. 47 no. 11, leaf and flower *ibid* fig. 47 no. 39, dolphin and basket *ibid* fig. 47 no. 18, leaf *ibid* fig. 47 no. 31, ornament R U247, leaf as R J99, cock O 2348, male figure O 204, Vulcan O 66, Venus O 331, metope and medallion style; fig. 9 no. 21
37; Trier; Werkstatt II; ovolo F 955, pipe player F 541, vine scroll F 727, free style; fig. 9 no. 22
6 Traj; Dup
Had; HS
Ant; Dup; RIC 1154; 141-5
(Ant As of 155-6 from underlying level, and Faust II As from level under that, see deposits **A 79-80**).
7 Residual early material was present, but was not listed.
8 Kenyon 1948; Oswald 1948b

**A 82**

1 Leicester, Leicestershire; town; Jewry Wall period IX, courtyard surface
2 E
3 A
4 37; CG; Albucius; ovolo S&S fig. 35 no. 1; fig. 10 no. 1
37; CG; Cinnamus; dancer O 322, metope and medallion style; fig. 10 no. 3
37; Trier; Werkstatt II; ovolo F 954, leaf F 772, free style; fig. 10 no. 4
Plain ware:
31 (2); 32; 33 (2); 38 (9); 45 (3) ; 79 CG (2)
5 Oxf type CCW in form 45
6 Traj; HS
Const I; Ae; 313-5 ; possibly intrusive
(Traj Dup; Comm Den; Sev Den 202-10 from underlying level VIII)
7 There is little or no residual material from this level.
8 Kenyon 1948; Oswald 1948h

**A 83**

1 Lincoln, Lincolnshire; town; Bishop's Palace, *colonia* rampart
2 E
3 A

4 37; CG; Drusus I (X-3); ovolo S&S fig. 4 no. 1, arcade style; fig. 4 no. 10
37; CG; Sacer-Attianus; rosette R C280, hare O 2116, metope and medallion style; fig. 4 no. 11
Plain wares (presence only):
15 CG-MdV; 36 CG; 18/31 CG-MdV (3); 27 SG (2); 18 SG; 27 SG-MdV; 33 CG
6 Comm; HS; BMC 474; 181-2; fairly worn
7 The pottery could all be redeposited material of early to mid-2nd century. However, the overall phasing of the rampart has been modified by Jones (1980, 51-3) and two phases may have been conflated in Petch's report. This makes the association of coin and samian somewhat uncertain.
8 Carson 1960c; Hartley 1960b; Petch 1960

**A 84**

1 Lincoln, Lincolnshire; town; Flaxengate site, make-up for floors of building B
2 E
3 A
4 37 (2 pieces); SG; late Flavian date, no details given here; fig. 9 no. 16
37; SG; no details given here; fig. 10 no. 21
37; CG; dolphin O 2382 in medallion, used by many group III-IV potters; fig. 9 no. 17
37; CG; Cinnamus; ovolo S&S fig. 47 no. 3; fig. 9 no. 18
37 (4 pieces); CG; Cinnamus; ovolo S&S fig. 47 no. 3, draped figure O 905, Diana O 111, boar O 1666, dolphin not in O, dolphin O 2384, dolphin O 2401, dolphin O 2402, fish O 2419, astragalus S&S fig. 47 no. 40, stand R Q42, scroll R M31, metope and small medallion style; fig. 9 no. 19
37; Rheinz; Comitialis IV; ovolo R&F E25, Apollo *ibid* M72, soldier as *ibid* M269, medallion style; fig. 10 no. 20
37; Rheinz; probably Atto; flautist R&F M167, stand *ibid* O215, bifid *ibid* P145, arcade style; fig. 10 no. 23
37; Rheinz; Helenius; bust R&F M12, head *ibid* M15, Venus *ibid* M42, boxer as *ibid* M191, free style; fig. 10 no. 25
37; Trier; wreath F 904, leaf as F 737, dog as F 376; fig. 10 no. 24
37; CG fragment
45 EG with barbotine dec and lion's head spout
Plain ware listed in report as presences only, not given here.
U (4 fragments made into *tesserae*)
5 Rhenish CCW beaker with motto; U CCW beakers with barbotine dec, and boxes
6 Comm; As; RIC 427; 183-4; worn; no. 7
7 The construction of building B is dated to the mid-3rd century or later by the excavator, but no supporting evidence apart from the coarse ware date ranges is available.
8 Bird 1973; Coppack 1973; Wilson & Kent 1973

**A 85**

1 Lincoln, Lincolnshire; town; rampart of *colonia*
2 E
3 A
4 37; SG; style of Germanus, no details given here; fig. 4 no. 8
37; CG; Albucius or Paternus II; ovolo S&S fig. 30 no. 1; fig. 4 no. 11
37; CG; Cinnamus or Pugnus; leaf R H109; fig. 4 no. 12
37; CG; Cinnamus; ovolo S&S fig. 47 no. 3; fig. 4 no. 13
37 (2 pieces); CG; Cinnamus; ovolo S&S fig. 47 no. 3, figure O 905, bird O 2297 in festoon, metope style; fig. 4 no. 15
37 (4 pieces); CG; Cinnamus (stamped in mould); ovolo probably S&S fig. 47 no. 3, Diana O 111 in medallion, lozenge S&S fig. 47 no. 15, 'twist' as *ibid* fig. 47 no. 4, lozenge R U36, vine scroll R M3, metope and medallion style; fig. 5 no. 16
37; probably EG; ovolo blurred, not in R or R&F, figure not in O or R&F; fig. 4 no. 14
35/36 SG; 29 SG (2); 18/31 CG; 31 CG
6 Dom; As; 86; fairly worn
7 There is clearly Flavian and late 2nd century material mixed together. The date of the rampart may be *c* 200 according to finds elsewhere (deposit **A 83**).
8 Birley 1956; Thompson 1956

**A 86**

1 Little Chester, Derbyshire; fort; well
2 C
3 C
4 37; CG; Austrus; ovolo R B18, festoon R F16; fig. 1 no. 5
37; SG; late Flavian date, no details given here; fig. 1 no. 6
5 CCW indented or rouletted beakers; CCW boxes
6 Had; HS; very worn
Alex; Den (plated); RIC 160; 222-8; good condition
7 There appears to be some 4th century material from the top of the well, which has not been differentiated in the finds report.
8 Brassington 1969

**A 87**

1 London, City of London; town; Aldgate, pit 7
2 C
3 A
4 37; MdV; Ioenalis; bird O 2298, metope style as Wheeler 1926, S77 and S&S pl. 41 no. 478; fig. 7 no. 9
37; Rheinz; Helenius; ovolo R&F E7; fig. 7 no. 11
37; Rheinz; Primitivus I or III; dog R&F T138, leaf *ibid* P30, free style; fig. 7 no. 12
5 NV CCW beaker (fig. 17 no. 255); BB2 bowls; 2 CG mother-goddess figurines
6 Nerva; Dup: RIC 61 or 84; 96-7; very worn; coin no. 7
7 The coin is clearly older than the samian ware, but appears to have been in circulation a long time.
8 Chapman 1973; Dannell 1973b; Merrifield 1973

**A 88**

1 London, City of London; town; Angel Court, layer 20 stream bed silt
2 C - stream bed silt
3 A
4 37; CG; Docilis or Sacer; ovolo S&S fig. 24 no. 1, Venus O 305, metope style as S&S pl. 84 no. 1; fig. 14 no. 389
37; CG; Doeccus; no details given
37; La Mad; Albillus; ovolo F 123 with a faint tongue, bead row below, long astragalus F 100, figure F 48, figure F 49, bear F 57, deer F 54, small animal as F 58, free style; fig. 14 no. 390
46; Arg; stamped by Premo die 2a
Plain ware:
18/31 CG (2); 31 Montans; 31 CG (3); 31R CG; 31R EG (2); 32 EG; 33 CG (4); 33 EG; 36 CG; 38 EG; 43 CG: 45 CG; 72 CG; 72 EG; 81 CG; 30 CG; 37 CG
5 BB1; BB2; Much Hadham; Portchester 'D'; NV CCW; Colch CCW; Arg CCW
6 Claud?; Dup (copy); illeg; very worn; coin 411
Vesp?; Dup; illeg; very worn; coin 412
Had; Dup; illeg; 117-22; very worn; coin 413

Ant; As; illeg; worn; coin 414
Faust I; As; RIC (Ant) 1161; 141+; worn coin 415
7 This deposit is later than the coins, to judge from the samian and more especially, the other pottery. It could have built up over a period.
8 Blurton 1977; Dannell 1977; Merrifield 1977

**A 89**

1 London, City of London; waterfront of town; Custom House III-42, deposit in front of timber quay
2 G - sand and gravel riverine deposit
3 A
4 37; CG; Sacer-Attianus; metope style; fig. 27 no. 15
30; CG; Cinnamus; figure O 204, metope and medallion style, possibly from the same mould as Hartley 1972c no. D115 from Verulamium; fig. 27 no. 17
37; Arg-Lavoye; ovolo as Oswald 1945 fig 6 nos xxvii and xlix; fig. 27 no. 16
5 NV CCW ‚hunt-cup'; BB2; Speicher ware
6 Ant; As; illeg; coin 505
7 A dendrochronological date of AD 137-42 has been established for the quay in front of which this deposit built up (Fletcher 1982), with dates in the following decade for timbers in front of it.
8 Bird 1974b; Fletcher 1982; Merrifield 1974; Tatton-Brown 1974

**A 90**

1 London; waterfront of town; St Magnus House (New Fresh Wharf), layers associated with Roman wharf
2 E
3 A
4 37 (2 pieces); CG; Carantinus; ovolo R B114, dog and festoon as K 1959 Taf. 75 no. 2, metope and medallion style; no. 2.13
37; CG; Divixtus or associate; bead row and rosette terminal as S&S pl. 116 no. 8, dolphin O 2383, dolphin O 2394A, leaf not in R, metope style; no. 2.14
30; CG; Cinnamus ii (stamped in mould); cushion as S&S pl. 161 no. 50 (not in R), rosette *ibid* pl. 161 no. 55, naked figure in medallion as *ibid* pl. 164 no. 7, stand as R Q43; unused; no. 2.16
37; CG; Cinnamus; leopard O 1521, stand R Q27, 'twist' S&S fig. 47 no. 4, crane O 2199, metope style; unused; no. 2.18
37; CG; Cinnamus; ovolo S&S fig. 47 no. 1, astragalus *ibid* fig. 47 no. 40, leaf R H21, dancer O 322 in medallion, leaf R J15. lozenge S&S fig. 47 no. 1, bird as O 2316-8, winding scroll and medallion style as S&S pl. 162 no. 60; no. 2.19
37; CG; Censorinus; ovolo S&S fig. 29 no. 2, St Andrew's cross *ibid* fig. 29 no. 12, Venus O 334, metope style; no. 2.26
30; CG; Advocisus (stamped in mould); Venus O 293A, rosette and border S&S pl. 114 no. 33, Venus O 305, Apollo as O 92, dolphin not in O but pair of S&S pl. 114 no. 28, metope style; no. 2.24
37 (4 pieces); CG; Advocisus; ovolo S&S fig. 33 no. 1, ornament *ibid* fig. 33 no. 5, astragalus *ibid* fig. 33 no. 1, Diana O 106, Victory O 809, caryatid as O 1206, leaves as S&S pl. 113 no. 16, trifid R G73, metope style; no. 2.25
37 (2 pieces); CG; Paternus II, Advocisus or Laxtucissa; ovolo as R B105, ovoid bead row, dolphin O 2392, cupid O 443B, vase R 75; no. 2.23
30; CG; Laxtucissa; ovolo R B105, trifid S&S fig. 27 no. 2, bead and reel border R A10, rosette S&S fig. 27 no. 10, leaf cluster as R L1-7, metope style; no. 2.22
30; CG; probably Censorinus; ovolo S&S fig. 29 no. 3, bead and reel border, circle *ibid* fig. 29 no. 6, bud R G208, eagle O 2183 in double medallion, woman O 931, man O 648, metope style; unused; no. 2.27
37 (2 pieces); CG; Laxtucissa or Paternus II; rosette R C227, column R P3 split into two sections, panther O 1509-10, Apollo O 83, satyr as O 571; unused; no. 2.28
37; CG; Paternus II; ovolo R B135, bird (not in O) and winding scroll as S&S pl. 107 no. 26; no. 2.29
30 (4 pieces); CG; Paternus II; ovolo R B114: leaf R J85, beaded and corded borders, panther O 1509, trifid R G55, 'twist' S&S fig. 30 no. 18, deer O 1732, cupid O 444, cupid O 440, metope style; no. 2.30
37; CG; Paternus II; ovolo as S&S pl. 104 no. 10, cupid O 440 or 444, circle R E57, Apollo O 94, Vulcan O 68; no. 2.32
37; CG; Paternus II; ovolo S&S fig. 30 no. 1, corded border, leaf R J14, deer as O 1784; no. 2.33
37 (2 pieces); CG; Paternus II; ovolo R B178, leaf S&S fig. 30 no. 8, astragalus border, 'twist' *ibid* fig. 30 no. 18, metope and medallion style; no. 2.34
37; CG; Paternus II; ovolo S&S fig. 30 no. 3, panther O 1509, hare O 2127, twig R L22, free style; no. 2.35
37 (2 pieces); CG; Iullinus; ovolo S&S fig. 36 no. 2, corded border, column *ibid* fig. 36 no. 5 in arcade, warrior O 186, circle and general design as S&S fig. 127 no. 22, metope and arcade style; no. 2.42
37 (4 pieces); CG; Severus; bear O 1630, panther O 1509, man as O 673 with bead row spear in right hand as S&S pl. 128 no. 2, 'twist' and overall design as on *ibid*, free style; unused; no. 2.43
37; CG; Caletus; cupid O 443B, stand R T29, rosette R C39; no. 2.44
37; CG; Servus II (iv) (signed in mould); dolphin basket R Q58, deer as O 1704A, Pan as O 707; no. 2. 40
37; CG; Servus II (iv) (signed in mould); tripod as R Q16, stand R Q1, sea bull as O 52A; no. 2.41
37; CG; Banvus; ovolo and border S&S fig. 41 no. 1, leaf *ibid* fig. 41 no. 12, leaf *ibid* fig. 41 no. 8, winding scroll style as *ibid* pl. 139 no. 3; no. 2.45
30 (5 pieces); CG; Doeccus i (stamped in mould); ovolo S&S fig. 44 no. 2, rosette *ibid* fig. 44 no. 1, astragalus *ibid* fig. 44 no. 3, trifid as R G1S9, leaf S&S fig. 44 no. 31, deer O 1752A, deer O 1704A, bird O 2250A, cupid O 432A; no. 2.48
30; CG; Doeccus i (stamped in mould); corded motif as S&S pl. 148 no. 23, rosette *ibid* fig. 44 no. 5, dolphin basket *ibid* fig. 44 no. 28, vase *ibid* pl. 147 no. 6 (not in R), metope style; no. 2.49
37; CG; Doeccus; leaf S&S fig. 44 no. 27, lozenge *ibid* fig. 44 no. 17, sea horse O 33, bird O 2250A, cupid O 445; no. 2.50
30; CG; Doeccus; ovolo S&S fig. 44 no. 1, rosette *ibid* fig. 44 no. 4, sea horse O 33 in festoon, mounted Amazon O 246, metope style; no. 2.51
37; CG; Doeccus; ovolo S&S fig. 44 no. 1, saltire of square beads and medallion as *ibid* pl. 149 no. 33, leaf R H37 (apparently not R H17); no. 2.52
37 (2 pieces); CG; Casurius, Doeccus or associate; beads R A15, Apollo O 73A, Minerva O 126, rosette S&S fig. 44 no. 5, metope and St Andrew's cross style - not used by Casurius or Doeccus; no. 2.53

37; La Mad; ieaf, rosette and bead row as in Ricken 1934 Taf. 8 no. 13, lion *ibid* Taf. 7 no. 107, leaf in wreath not paralleled; no. 2.56

37; Arg-Lavoye; Tocca; lion Oswald 1945 fig. 9 no. 42, twig *ibid* fig. 9 no. 44 and C&G fig. 57G, chevron column *ibid* fig 58F; no. 2.59

37: Trier; Werkstatt I; arcade, column, beads as Huld-Zetsche 1972 Taf. 3 no. A18; no. 2.60

37; Trier; Comitialis; ovolo and bead row Haalebos 1977 Taf. 50 no. 354, leaf Holwerda 1923 afb. 84 no. 10, grapes *ibid* afb. 84 no. 11, medallion Kalee 1973 afb. 8 no. 26; no. 2.64

37; Trier; Dexter; ovolo, floral swags from columns, astragalus wreath F Taf. 15 no. 14, grapes F Taf. 15 no. 10; no. 2.66

37 (4 pieces); Trier; Dexter; ovolo, rope festoon F Taf. 15 no. 39, astragalus wreath F Taf. 15 no. 14, crane F 669; no. 2.67

37; Trier; Dexter; ovolo, astragalus row F Taf. 15 no. 33, basket F 733; no. 2.68

37; Trier; Amator; ovolo F 952 (= Gard 1937 R17), leaf and ornament F Taf. 19 no. 26, medallion F Taf. 19 no. 20, rosette F Taf. 19 no. 19; no. 2.70

37; Trier; Criciro; ovolo Oelmann 1914 Taf. 6 no. 21, cock *ibid*, panther and rosette F Taf. 17 no. 15, deer F Taf. 17 no. 27; no. 2.71

37; Trier; Afer; ovolo Gard 1937 R20, cogged medallion *ibid* Taf. 14 no. 19; no. 2.74

37 (2 pieces); Trier; Afer-Marinus; circle Oelmann 1914 Taf. 8 no. 8, cogged medallion Gard 1937 Taf. 14 no. 7, hare *ibid* Taf. 14 no. 20, cupid O 451B-C (not in F); unused; no. 2.75

37 (3 pieces); Trier; Afer-Marinus; ovolo F 942 (= Gard 1937 R8), leaf Oelmann 1914 Taf. 8 no. 8, very similar overall design in *ibid* Taf. 8 no. 7; no. 2.76

37; Trier; Paternianus iii (stamped in mould); leaf F 752, figure F 520, gladiator probably O 1053, two large figures not in F; no. 2.83

37 (2 pieces); Trier; probably Dubitatus; ovolo and arcade Oelmann 1914 Taf. 6 no. 8, deer Gard 1937 Taf. 14 no. 16, blobs *ibid* Taf. 23 no. 5, fish F 702, lobster F 694, style as Gard 1937 Taf. 19 no.19; unused; no. 2.84

37; Trier; Dubitus-Dubitatus; ovolo Gard 1937 Taf. 23 no. 6, cock *ibid*, corded border in similar arrangement *ibid* Taf. 23 no. 8; no. 2.85

37 (2 pieces); Trier; Dignus and Primanus (stamped in mould); ovolo and rosette Gard 1937 Taf. 25-6, bear *ibid* Taf. 26 nos 6-7, hound *ibid* Taf. 26 no. 2, dog Oelmann 1914 Taf. 8 no. 26, cow new to these potters (no details given); unused; no. 2.87

37; Trier; Dignus, Primanus, Perpetuus group; ovolo, column, arcade Gard 1937 Taf. 26 no. 31, crane *ibid* Taf. 25 no. 13; no. 2.88

37; Rheinz; Cerialis I; ovolo R&F E1, rosette *ibid* O52 in a circle *ibid* O82a, wreath *ibid* R34, leaf *ibid* P145, lion *ibid* T2, horse *ibid* T114, bear *ibid* T53, figure *ibid* M203, free style similar to Ricken 1948 Taf. 46 no. 7 and Taf. 50 no. 1; no. 2.90

37 (3 pieces); Rheinz; Cerialis III; ovolo R&F E44, cupid *ibid* M116, cupid *ibid* M117, figure *ibid* M268, men with prisoner *ibid* M269, dog *ibid* T141, figure *ibid* M249, leopard *ibid* T35a, cornucopia *ibid* O160a; unused; no. 2.91

37; Rheinz; Cerialis IV; ovolo R&F E38, leaf *ibid* P59a, medallion *ibid* K32, bird *ibid* T259; no. 2.92

37 (2 pieces); Rheinz; Comitialis III (stamped in mould); ovolo R&F E10, panther *ibid* T44, deer *ibid* T96, hare *ibid* T163, tripod *ibid* O11, rosette *ibid* O50, medallion *ibid* K48, festoon *ibid* KB89, identical to a mould from Rheinz (Ricken 1948 Taf. 83 no. 10); no. 2.94

37; Rheinz; Comitialis V; ovolo R&F E17, column *ibid* O287, bead row *ibid* O262, panther *ibid* T35, leaf *ibid* P38, circle ibid K19a, festoon *ibid* KB76, metope and medallion style, as Ricken 1948 Taf. 100, 101, 103; no. 2.95

37 (2 pieces); Rheinz; Comitialis V-VI; ovolo R&F E23, Abundantia *ibid* M36, leaf *ibid* P75, panther *ibid* T35, bead row *ibid* O262, festoon part only of *ibid* K20a, metope and medallion style as Ricken 1948 Taf. 103; no. 2.97

37 (3 pieces); Rheinz; 'ware with E25/26'; ovolo R&F E26, festoon *ibid* KB138, bead row *ibid* O261, trifid *ibid* P116, leaf *ibid* P145, geometric style as Ricken 1948 Taf. 114 nos 13-17; unused; no. 2.99

37 (4 pieces); Rheinz; Belsus III (stamped in mould); ovolo R&F E25, beads *ibid* O263, leaf *ibid* P145, hare *ibid* T154, dog *ibid* T138a, medallion *ibid* K20, trophy *ibid* O214, rosette *ibid* O48, metope and medallion style from same mould as Ricken 1948 Taf. 126 no. 16; no. 2.101

37 (2 pieces); Rheinz; Reginus II (stamped in mould by Reginus vi); ovolo R&F E18, wrestler *ibid* M196, medallion *ibid* K53, medallion as *ibid* K21, medallion style as Ricken 1948 Taf. 136 no. 6; no. 2.102

37; Rheinz; Julius I-Lupus; ovolo R&F E46, border *ibid* O273, leaf *ibid* P145, cornucopia *ibid* O16a, medallion *ibid* K6, metope and medallion style as Ricken 1948 Taf. 155 no. 6 and Taf. 157 no. 1; unused; no. 2.104

37 (2 pieces); Rheinz; Julius I-Lupus; ovolo R&F E46, medallion *ibid* K6, border *ibid* O273, leaf *ibid* P145, crane *ibid* T2l4, bird *ibid* T254, bird *ibid* T244, metope and medallion style; no. 2.105

37 (3 pieces); Rheinz; Julius I-Lupus; ovolo as R&F E46, eagle *ibid* T205a, leaf *ibid* P145, cornucopia *ibid* O160a, medallion *ibid* K11, border as *ibid* O273, bird *ibid* T244; no. 2.106

37 (3 pieces); Rheinz; Lucanus; ovolo R&F E53, leaf *ibid* P99, rosette *ibid* O37, bird *ibid* T258, lion *ibid* T2, dog *ibid* T133, hare *ibid* T168b, deer *ibid* T84, free style; unused; no. 2.108

30; Rheinz; Primitivus I; ovolo R&F E40, Venus *ibid* M60B, crown *ibid* O113, arcade *ibid* KB108, border *ibid* O242, astragalus *ibid* O196, leaf *ibid* P142a, dog *ibid* T144, leaf *ibid* P81a, dancer *ibid* M97a, metope and medallion style; no. 2.110

37; Rheinz; Julius II-Julianus I; ovolo R&F E17, pedestal *ibid* O151, circle *ibid* K11 with cross *ibid* O53 within, geometric style; no. 2. 113

37; Rheinz; Julius II-Julianus I; ovolo R&F E23, trifid *ibid* O169, bud *ibid* O170, pedestal *ibid* O179, acanthus *ibid* P111, arcade *ibid* KB73, arcade style from the mould illustrated in Ricken 1948 Taf. 205 no. 4; unused; no. 2.114

37 (2 pieces); Rheinz; Julius II-Julianus I (stamped in mould by Julius viii); ovolo R&F E23, bead row *ibid* O256, geometric style as Ricken 1948 Taf. 212 nos 13, 15, 19, 23; no. 2.116

37; EG - probably Rheinz; ovolo as R&F E40-3 but impressed with broken punch; no. 2.121

6 Sev; Den; 197; from layer 309 under the timbers; details of type not known. Timbers from the waterfront have given a dendrochronological date of 209-14. Other coins from as-

sociated layers Vesp-Had Ae (15), Ant-Comm Ae (15), Elag Den (plated 219+).
7 This is one of the major stratified deposits of the early 3rd century. The stratigraphy of the dumps and fills between the wharf timbers appears to be one of roughly contemporary filling as there are many joins between layers. More detailed consideration of the stratigraphy and the subdivision of the pieces listed above within the layers is given in the main part of chapter 5. All the pieces are dated by the coin or the date given to the timbers except nos 2.18 and 2.29 which come from the layer immediately below the coin. These two, however, have been included because of the similarity of the fill irom which they came to the rest of the stratigraphy.
8 Bird 1986; Museum of London, Department of Urban Archaeology archive report compiled by J. Bird; Hillam & Morgan 1981; Merrifield 1983, 149-51; Richardson & Tyers 1984; cf. also Bird 1987; 1993

**A 91**

1 *Margidunum*, Nottinghamshire; *vicus*; dump of Antonine pottery on floor of 'schola'
2 E
3 C
4 37; CG; Advocisus (stamped in mould); ovolo S&S fig. 33 no. 1, boar O 1642, panther O 1536, bear O 1627, lion O 1404,scroll R M50, metope style; fig. 14 no. 1
31; Rheinz; stamped by Probus
5 CCW with indented and scale dec
6 Ant; Dup; BMC 1966; 154-5
7 The association seems fairly secure from the description, but should be treated cautiously in view of Todd's assessment (1969) of Oswald's excavations.
8 Oswald 1941, 41, 54-6

**A 92**

1 *Margidunum*, Nottinghamshire; *vicus*; workshop deposit in cutting 3
2 E
3 A
4 37; CG-MdV; Igocatus; manacled man O 1146, sea bull O 42, bifid S&S fig. 6 no. 4, metope style; fig. 20a no. 5
37; CG; Criciro; ovolo S&S fig. 33 no. 1, deer O 1743, ornament S&S fig. 33 no. 5, free style; fig. 20a no. 6
5 Mica-dusted ware
6 From below associated clay floor:
Vesp; As; 72-79; worn; no. 4
Traj; HS; RIC 584; 103-11; very worn; no. 11
Ant; HS; RIC 546/646; 139-40; worn; no. 13
Ant; HS; RIC 642; 140-4; worn; no. 14
7 The coins appear to provide a *terminus post quem* for the clay floor, which is adjacent to the workshop deposit and may be part of the floor of the workshop.
8 Cotterill & Todd 1969; Todd 1969, 62, 65

**A 93**

1 Maryport, Cumbria; fort; clay below period II east barrack block
2 E
3 A
4 37; CG; Donnaucus group; ovolo as S&S fig. 11, 'twist' *ibid* fig. 11 no. 25 or 26, rosette *ibid* fig. 11 no. 1, Vulcan O-66, cupid not in O; no. 14
18/31 SG
6 Lucilla: HS; illeg: very worn: no. 6
7 A very mixed association which is complicated by the possibility that the coin was trodden into the clay after the barrack was built.
8 Casey 1976; Greene 1976; Jarrett 1976

**A 94**

1 Mumrills, Central Region; fort; destruction deposit in outer west ditch
2 E
3 A
4 From 1950s excavations:
37; CG; Quintilianus group (probably Ianuaris I); rosette R C290, figure O 581, dog as D 930-4, metope style; fig. 5 no. 1
37; CG; Quintilianus group; ovolo S&S fig. 14 no. 1 (= R B228), bifid as wreath below ovolo R G361, metope style; fig. 5 no. 2
37 (3 pieces); CG; Docilis; ovolo as R B176, stand R Q42, male figure not in O (but as O 360 without scarf), figure O 656, cupid O 508, warrior O 193, metope style; fig. 5 no. 3, cf Hartley 1972c no. D116
37 (37 pieces); CG; Secundus; ovolo R B143, Perseus O 234, Diana O 111, Pan O 709, hare O 2115, bear O 1609, panther O 1507, dolphin as O 2401, metope and medallion style; fig. 5 no. 4
37; CG; Paullus; ovolo R B144, metope and medallion style; fig. 5 no. 5
37 (6 pieces); CG; Paullus; ovolo R B144, Minerva O 126, Vulcan O 66, Perseus O 234, bear O 1627, male figure O 581, dolphin and basket R Q58, column as R P4, metope and medallion style; fig. 5 no. 6
37 (2 pieces); CG; Paullus; ovolo as R B144, medallion R E21, medallion and winding scroll style; fig. 5 no. 7
37 (4 pieces); CG; Paullus; ovolo as R B144, lion O 1450, deer O 1772, free style; fig. 5 no. 8
37 (3 pieces); CG; Cinnamus or Paullus; ovolo as R B143/4, lion O 1450, metope style; fig. 6 no. 9
37 (2 pieces); CG; Cinnamus or Paullus; leopard as O 1510, leopard O 1521, sphinx O 857, medallion not in R, metope and medallion style; fig. 6 no. 10
30; CG; Cinnamus; ovolo S&S fig. 47 no. 3, metope style, joins with piece found in 1920s, see below; fig. 6 no. 11
37; CG; Cinnamus (stamped in mould on joining piece found in 1920s); ovolo S&S fig. 47 no. 1, leaf *ibid* fig. 47 no. 5, horseman O 245, bear O 1588, free style; fig. 6 no. 12
37; CG; Cinnamus; ovolo S&S fig. 47 no. 1, lozenge *ibid* fig. 47 no. 15, vase *ibid* fig. 47 no. 6, metope and medallion style; fig. 6 no. 13
37 (3 pieces); CG; Illixo or Carantinus II; ovolo R B145, bear as O 1588; fig. 6 no. 14
37 (2 pieces); CG; Criciro; ovolo R B52, ornament O 2155, lion O 1450, bear O 1588, free style; fig. 6 no. 15
37; CG; probably Criciro; ovolo not found in R; fig. 6 no. 16
30 (2 pieces); CG; Divixtus; satyr O 627, metope style; fig. 6 no. 17
37; CG; Divixtus, Advocisus or associate; cupid O 383, caryatid O 1207A, metope style; fig. 6 no. 18
37; CG; Cettus or Ianuaris II; bifid R G326, horse as O 1897; fig. 6 no. 19
37; CG; Albucius; ovolo S&S fig. 35 no. 2, joins with piece found in 1920s, see below; fig. 6 no. 20
37 (3 pieces); CG; Albucius; ovolo S&S fig. 35 no. 1; fig. 6 no. 21
30; CG; Sacer-Attianus or associate; leaf R H72, winding scroll style; fig. 6 no. 22

37 CG (9 fragments)
From 1920s excavations:
37; CG; Cinnamus (stamped in mould with large stamp); ovolo S&S fig. 47 no. 1, leaf *ibid* fig. 47 no. 5, horseman O 245, bear O 1588, lion O 1450, lioness O 1562, lioness O 1537, lion O 1421, horse O 1976, free style, joins with piece found in 1950s, see above; fig. 77 no. 8
30; CG; Cinnamus; ovolo S&S fig. 47 no. 3, figure O 905, Venus O 331, figure O 204, metope and medallion style, joins with piece found in 1950s, see above; fig. 79 no. 32
37; CG; Albucius; ovolo S&S fig. 35 no. 2, leaf *ibid* fig. 35 no. 2, dolphin O 2382, metope style, joins with piece found in 1950s, see above; fig. 79 no. 37
37; CG; unknown potter, rosette R C278, Diana in *biga* not in O but similar format to O 117, metope and medallion style; fig. 79 no. 35

6 Rep; Den; M Antonius 'legionary' issue; very worn
Nero; Den; RIC 45; 64-8; worn
Nero; As; RIC 361; 54-68; slightly worn
Dom; As; minted under Vesp or Titus
Ant; As; RIC 934; 154-5; slightly worn

7 A key deposit for assessing the final period of occupation of the Antonine Wall.

8 Hartley 1961b; MacDonald & Curle 1929; Robertson 1961; Steer 1961

**A 95**

1 Nettleton, Wiltshire; temple; circular shrine phase I construction and use
2 E
3 A
4 37; CG; Cinnamus; ovolo S&S fig. 47 no. 5; fig. 71 no. 127
37; CG; X-6; bifid R G367; fig. 71 no. 128
37; CG; X-6; triton as O 25, warrior O 216, leaf R H113, free style; fig. 71 no. 130ii
37 CG (5); 35 CG; 18/31 or 31 CG
6 Faust I; Ae; 145+
7 Details of findspots have not been given, so the association is a general one only. Further, roughly contemporary sherds (nos 131-50, 152) may come from roughly equivalent stratigraphy.
8 Simpson 1982b; Wedlake 1982

**A 96**

1 Nettleton, Wiltshire; *vicus*; occupation of building XI
2 B
3 A
4 37; CG; Cinnamus; lion O 1450, free style; fig. 70 no. 104
37; CG; Cinnamus; stand R G42, metope and medallion style; fig. 70 no. 105
37; Arg; possibly Africanus; circle as H 469, ovolo similar to F 124 (La Mad), free style; fig. 70 no. 102
37; EG; ovolo attributed to R&F E33 (Pervincus) by Simpson, but the drawing is inaccurate; fig. 70 no. 103
6 Faust I; Ae; no details given
8 Simpson 1982b; Wedlake 1982

**A 97**

1 Newhaven, East Sussex; villa; site 6, ditch, layer 1
2 D
3 A
4 37 (2 pieces); CG; Laxtucissa; ovolo S&S fig. 27 no. 1, trifid *ibid* fig. 27 no. 5, astragalus *ibid* fig. 27 no. 3, circle *ibid* fig. 27 no. 7, sea horse O 33 in double circle, Apollo O 92; fig. 38 nos 7-8
31; CG; stamped by Advocisus
From site 1, ditch, layer 1 (continuation of same feature):
31; CG; stamped by Ritogenus; very worn
6 Ae; illeg; very worn
From site 5, ditch, layer 1 (probably the same feature and contemporary):
Ant; As (probably)
7 The upper layer of the ditch contains destruction debris including plaster and tiles. Although the identified coin was found some way from the bulk of the pottery and the samian, the associated dates are consistent.
8 Bell 1976; Detsicas 1976

**A 98**

1 Old Ford, Greater London; *vicus*; Appian Road, trench 2 layer 5
2 B
3 A
4 37; CG; Doeccus style; ovolo S&S pl. 149, 28, square bead row
Plain wares: 31 CG (2); 31 CG/EG; 31 EG; 45 CG; 38 EG; 33 CG; 33 EG; Lud Tg EG; U CG (2); U EG (3)
5 Oxf flanged bowl (from B-3)
6 Faust II; HS; RIC (Aur) 1663; fairly heavy wear; no. 1
HS of 1st-2nd century; very heavy wear; no. 2
Claud II; Rad; 270-2; average wear; no. 9
Tet I; Rad; 270-3; average wear; no. 15
7 The gravelly layer from which these pieces came could have accumulated over a period, but the underlying sand (Sheldon 1972, 111) has a coin of Julia Maesa that provides a *terminus post quem* (J Maesa; Den; RIC (Elag) 271; 218-22; light wear; no. 3).
8 Hammerson 1972; Morris 1972; Sheldon 1972

**A 99**

1 Portchester, Hampshire; fort; general finds from site
2 F
3 A
4 37; CG; Cinnamus; ovolo S&S fig. 47 no. 1, style as *ibid* pl. 162 no. 60
Plain ware: 18 SG (very worn); 18/31 CG (2); 18/31 CG/EG; 18/31 EG; 18/31 or 31 CG/EG; 18/31 or 31 EG; 31 CG (3); 31 CG/EG; 31 EG (4); 31R CG/EG (2); 33 CG (3 - 1 stamped by Priscus of Lez); 33 EG; 43 or 45 CG/EG; 43 or 45 EG; 45 CG; 45 EG; 36 CG; 36 CG/EG; 37 EG; 38 EG (3); C15 EG (2); C21 EG
6 There are many coins from the site but their details are not relevant here.
7 Cunliffe (1975, 421) gives a construction date for the fort of 286-90, there being no evidence of earlier occupation apart from coins of Salonina (1) and Gallienus (2) in layers immediately predating the construction. The samian accounted for 0.3% of the total assemblage by weight (1200g), more than 4th century Argonne ware, for instance, and came from all levels and a variety of features. It is possible that the samian came to the site with redeposited soil, but this seems unlikely in view of the fact that no other early finds were made, apart from some Conquest period coarse ware, with which the worn SG might be associated. As Morris concludes (1975, 277-8), the best explanation is probably that the samian was brought to the site by the first occupants of the fort.
8 Cunliffe 1975; Morris 1975

**A 100**

1 Rapsley, Ewhurst, Surrey; villa; period III

2 F
3 A
4 37; EG; Cerialis style; tree D 1129; fig. 26 no. 15
37; CG; Quintilianus group; ovolo S&S fig. 17 no. 1, *ibid* fig. 15 no. 2; fig. 26 no. 14
37 (4 pieces); CG; Priscus; ovolo R B174, standing figure O 599, Mercury O 533 with bead row as staff in right hand, metope style; fig. 26 no. 10
37 (8 pieces from 4 different deposits); SG; Biragillus; details of dec not given here; fig. 26 nos 11-13
37 (5 pieces from 2 different deposits); CG; Sacer-Attianus; ovolo as R B231, rosette S&S fig. 23 no. 1, bifid *ibid* fig. 23 no. 12, stand as R G10 but smaller, metope style with St Andrew's crosses; fig. 26 nos 7-8
37; EG; no details given
29; SG; no details given
Plain ware: 31 CG (3 – 1 stamped Bovillus, 2 stamped Ritogenus); 31 EG (stamped Augustinus); 33 CG (stamped Atticus); 33 Blick (stamped Placidus); 72 CG; 79/80 CG; C11 SG; 31R CG; 43/45 CG; 38 CG (2)
6 Traj; Den; BMC 203; 103-11; very worn; coin 2
Traj; As; illeg; very worn; coin 3
As; late 2nd century type; illeg; very worn; coin 5
7 The dating of this period (200-20) is later than that suggested by the samian and coins. The succeeding period IV is dated 220-80 on the basis of the presence of Oxf ware mortaria, and has 37 EG (2) and Aur; HS; BMC 1376; 169-70. These early pieces are explained by the excavator as survival, 'On a civil site in this rural area one would not expect the owners to have a very quick turn-over of their material goods, and fine tableware might be in use for 40 to 50 years before ending up in the midden ' (Hanworth 1968, 9). The Biragillus 37 SG is interesting in being accompanied by late 2nd century samian in two different contexts.
8 Detsicas 1968a; Hanworth 1968

**A 101**

1 Richborough, Kent; fort; filling of inner ditch of 3rd century earth fort
2 D
3 C
4 37; Trier; Dexter; ovolo with urn in egg F pl. XV, 2, 14; pl. XXIX no. 4
Plain ware from same part of filling; 31 and 33
From elsewhere in the filling; 30, 37, 31 (2), Lud Ka
5 CCW beaker with white barbotine; Colch CCW
6 From elsewhere in the ditches of the earth fort:
Claud II (2); Rad (and earlier coins)
7 There is clearly redeposited material in the ditches, the filling of which was probably in the period 270-285, but much of the samian is late in character and could have been in use when the earth fort was constructed not long before (in Bushe-Fox's opinion, 1932, 24).
8 Bushe-Fox 1932, 24-5; Pryce 1932

**A 102**

1 Rochester, Kent; town; The Common, layer 18
2 E
3 A
4 37; CG; Cettus; ovolo S&S fig. 42 no. 2, leaf-stalk *ibid* fig. 42 no. 4; fig. 4 no. 6
37; CG; Drusus I, X-2 or Quintilianus group; ovolo Detsicas 1963a fig. 3 no. 1; fig. 4 no. 8
37; CG; Secundinus I; vine-scroll R M2, ovolo Rogers & Laing 1966 fig. V no. 5; fig. 4 no. 13
37; SG; Biragillus; details not given here; fig. 5 no. 22
Plain ware: 27 SG; 27 CG (3); 33 CG; 33 EG (2); 18 SG; 18R SG; 18/31 CG; 31 EG; 31R CG; 38 CG (2); 36 CG (3)
6 Aur; Den; 161-5
7 Since the deposit is a dump there is a chance of redeposited material. See deposits **B 69-70** for further material associated with the town rampart.
8 Detsicas 1970a; Harrison 1970

**A 103**

1 Scole, Norfolk; *vicus*; layers 30, 179, 218 and 362
2 B
3 A
4 30; Rheinz; Primitivus IV (stamped die 15c); cupid R&F M111a in medallion; fig. 72 no. D34
Plain ware: 18/31 SG (3); 18/31 CG (3); 18/31R CG; 31 CG (6 - 1 stamped by Mercator iv die 5a of Lez); 31R CG (3 - 1 stamped by Gippus die 2a, 1 rivetted); 30 or 37 SG; 30 or 37 CG; 30 or 37 EG/Colch; 33 CG (3); 36 CG; 35/36 SG; 38 or 44 CG; 79 CG; 80 CG; C23 CG; mort EG; dish CG
6 Aur; Den; RIC 285b; 172-3; worn; coin 7
Crispina; Den; RIC (Aur) 286a; 177-83; unworn; coin 8
Alex; Den; RIC 172; 222-8; unworn; coin 9
possibly Gall; Rad; 253-68; unworn; coin 10
7 Layers 179, 218 and 362 are sub-units of surface 30. The coin possibly of Gallienus did not have a complete inscription surviving.
8 Gregory 1977; Hartley & Dickinson 1977; Rogerson 1977

**A 104**

1 Scole, Norfolk; *vicus*; layers 79 and 206
2 B
3 A
4 From layer 79:
37 (2 pieces); CG; Libertus; Mercury as D 288, dolphin and trident D 1060, Apollo D 45, figure D 547, free style; fig. 69 nos D12a-b (one piece is derived from an earlier layer)
37; CG; Cinnamus, Pugnus or an associate; ovolo not in R or S&S but as R B233, tree R N8, bird O 2214A in festoon, mask O 1214, eagle O 2167 in medallion, metope and medallion style; fig. 71 no. D22
37; CG; Cinnamus or associate; ovolo S&S fig. 47 no. 5, as border; fig. 71 no. D23
37; CG; Cinnamus; vase R T3, mask O 1214, caryatid O 1199, metope and medallion style; fig. 71 no. D25
37; CG; Cinnamus; ovolo S&S fig. 47 no. 3, basket *ibid* fig. 47 no. 18; fig. 71 no. D30
37; CG; Banvus; mask O 1214, vase as R T26 in medallion; fig. 71 no. D31
37; La Mad; rosette Ricken 1934 Taf. VIII no. 2, cupid *ibid* no. 85, lion *ibid* no. 107, see *ibid* Taf. IX no. 6 for similar metope arrangement, metope and medallion style; fig. 70 no. D16
From layer 206:
37; CG-MdV; Igocatus (X-4); ovolo S&S fig. 6 no. 1, vase *ibid* fig. 6 no. 3, stand *ibid* fig. 6 no. 2, wavy-line borders, lioness in festoon as *ibid* pl. 17 no. 211, philosopher O 905, woman O 949, metope and arcade style with circles as vertical spacers, see S&S pl. 18 for parallels, rivetted; fig. 70 no. D17
Stamped plain ware from layer 79:
18/31; MdV; Balbinus die 2a
33; CG; Pugnus ii
33; CG; Habilis die Sb
31; CG; Muxtullus die la
31; CG; Satono die la

33; Colch; Senilis iv die la
6 Barb Rad from underlying surface of layer 125
7 Layers 206 and 79 both overlie 125
8 Gregory 1977; Rartley & Dickinson 1977; Rogerson 1977

**A 105**

1 Silchester, Hampshire; town; inner earthwork ditch fill, trench B layer VI
2 D
3 A
4 30; SG; Germanus; no details given here; fig. 9 no. 11
37; CG; Sacer-Attianus; tree as R N7, free style; fig. 9 no. 17
37; CG; Criciro; trifid R G67, metope style; fig. 9 no. 18
37; CG; Potter of the large S; stand R Q5, spiral R S71, metope style; fig. 9 no. 19
37; CG; Criciro; ovolo S&S fig. 33 no. 4, metope and medallion style; fig. 9 no. 20
37; CG; Laxtucissa; ovolo S&S fig. 27 no. 1, astragalus *ibid* fig. 27 no. 3, metope style; fig. 9 no. 21
Other decorated pieces were found but have not been listed by Boon.
6 Had; HS; RIC 969; 128-38; worn
Faust I; Dup; 141+; very worn
Aur; Dup; RIC 1035; 171-2; very worn
7 The lower layers of ditch fill had rather earlier samian and coins, which probably accounts for the 30 SG. Trench A layer V was similar in composition and yielded Aur; HS; 177; worn.
8 Boon 1969b, 8, 46, 55-6

**A 106**

1 Silchester, Hampshire; town; town wall construction trench
2 E
3 A
4 From Hartley 1983b:
37; CG; Servus; no details given, dated by Hartley 160-200
31 CG (3); 33 CG (5); 18 SG; SC scrap
From Pryce 1947:
37; CG; Doeccus; ovolo R B161, stand R Q40 in arcade, circle as E70 metope and arcade style; pl. XXXVII no. 9
37; CG; rosette as R C170-1, metope and medallion style; pl. XXXVII no. 10
37; CG; hare in free style decoration; pl. XXXVII no. 13
37 CG (2 fragments); 45; 31 (11); 32; 33 (2); 38; 18 (CG dated late 2nd century by Pryce); 43; flanged bowl (2)
5 Rouletted black CCW beaker; Rhenish beaker with barbotine slip; Rhenish/Colch CCW; NV CCW 'hunt-cup'; Trier style white painted CCW motto beaker.
6 No coins came from these 2 groups, but in 1909 a coin of Severus (probably a Den) was found 6 feet from the top of the mound of the bank, probably in the wall construction trench.
7 The associations here are not strong since the 3 sections involved were all in different sectors of the defences. However, if the wall construction was a roughly contemporaneous event, the coin and the samian may be grouped together. Collis dates most of the coarse ware to the early/mid 3rd century, and says that there was little residual material.
8 Collis 1983, phase C; Cotton 1947; Hartley 1983b; Hope & Stephenson 1910, 325; Pryce 1947

**A 107**

1 Silchester, Hampshire; town; fill overlying town wall construction trench (phase D)
2 E
3 A
4 37; CG; Drusus II, no details given
Plain ware: 18 SG; 18/31 or 31 CG; 31 CG (2); 33 CG (4); 33 EG; 79 EG; 38 or 44 CG (2 - 1 stamped by Catianus of Lez); 31R CG; U CG
6 Barb Rad (2)
7 A good example of a relatively mixed, probably redeposited, group. It is underlain by deposit **A 106** which may be associated with a coin of Severus.
8 Collis 1983; Hartley 1983b; Reece 1983

**A 108**

1 South Shields, Tyne & Wear; fort; 1977 layers 14, 16 and 25
2 E
3 A
4 37; Arg; Tribunus; leaf H 372, arcade style; fig. 25 no. 116
37 (3 pieces); CG; Iustus; ovolo S&S fig. 31 no. 2, lozenge *ibid* fig. 31 no. 11, dolphin O 2382, dolphin O 2392, metope and medallion style; fig. 25 no. 120
6 Sev; Den; RIC 125; 198-200; worn; no. 18
7 The coin comes from layer 7 underlying and provides a *terminus post quem*.
8 Casey 1983; Dore 1983; Miket 1983

**A 109**

1 South Shields, Tyne & Wear; fort; 1978 layer 56 over Hadrianic drain
2 E
3 A
4 37; CG; X-6; ovolo R B35, trifid arrangement as S&S pl. 74 no. 8; fig. 25 no. 275
18/31 CG (2); 18/31R CG; 31 CG (3); 31 EG; 31R CG; 33 CG; 37 CG (3 fragments); U (6)
6 Traj; As; extremely worn; no. 12
8 Casey 1983; Dore 1983; Miket 1983

**A 110**

1 South Shields, Tyne & Wear; fort; 1979, layer 126, F66 and layers 102, 111 and 130
2 E
3 A
4 From layer 126:
37 CG (2 fragments); 18/31 La Mad
From F 66:
37; CG; Cinnamus; ovolo R B144
18/31 La Mad; 31 EG; 31 CG; 31R CG; 33 CG (2); 33 EG; 33 (2); 44 EG
From layers 102, 111 and 130:
37; CG; Paternus II; tripod S&S fig. 30 no. 9, trifid *ibid* fig. 30 no. 4, metope style; fig. 26 no. 347
37; CG; Paternus II; ovolo R B106, 'twist' S&S fig. 30 no. 18, horseman O 246, free style; fig. 26 no. 382
37; CG; Iustus; ovolo R B234, bird O 2295A, corded border, metope style; fig. 26 no. 387
31R; CG; stamped by Cadgatis die la
43 EG - other plain ware not given here
6 From layer 126:
Elag; Den; RIC 162; 218-22; slightly worn; no. 23
From F 66:
Sev; Den; corroded; no. 20
7 Layer 126 underlies both the other deposits, and therefore the Elag coin provides a date for all three groups.
8 Casey 1983; Dore 1983; Miket 1983

**A 111**

1 Springhead, Kent; *vicus*; site A key deposit IV
2 B

3 A
4 37; CG; Carantinus II; leaf R H20, leaf R J2, ovolo indecipherable on drawing, bird as O 2252, bird as O 2298, winding scroll style, trace of cursive mould signature visible; fig. 9 no. 1
37; CG; Paternus II; 'twist' S&S fig. 30 no. 18, bear O 1616, dog O 1917, dog O 1984, free style; fig. 9 no. 2
37; CG; Albucius; cupid O 440, bird as O 2316, astragalus border, metope and medallion style, probably from same bowl as in the layer below (**A 112**); fig. 9 no. 3
33 SG? stamped by Corius?
18/31 SG
6 Had; Dup; RIC 360
Aur Caes; As; RIC (Ant) 1322
Aur Caes; As; RIC (Ant) 1322
Faust II; As; RIC (Ant) 1405a
Alex; Den; RIC 7; 222
7 This is the abandonment level of the site, and there is some redeposition from levels underneath.
8 Penn 1957

**A 112**

1 Springhead, Kent; *vicus*; site A key deposit VI
2 B
3 A
4 37; CG; Lastuca; ovolo as S&S pl. 100 no. 2, gladiator O 1057, mask O 1215, 'twist' as S&S pl. 100 no. 3, metope and medallion style; fig. 9 no. 4
37; CG; Albucius; bird O 2316, bird O 2324, bifid as S&S fig. 35 no. 7, probably from same bowl as in deposit **A 111**; fig. 9 no. 5
37; CG; Cinnamus; leaf R J58, leaf as R H72, circle S&S fig. 47 no. 11, winding scroll style; fig. 9 no. 6
37; CG; Doeccus; ovolo probably S&S fig. 44 no. 2, cupid O 440 in festoon with beaded border S&S pl. 148 no. 14, metope and medallion style; fig. 9 no. 8
37; CG; possibly P-18; palm branch as R J118, bird as O 2298 in medallion, metope and medallion style; fig. 9 no. 9
37; CG; Cinnamus; stand as R Q2, sphinx O 853 in festoon, metope style; fig. 9 no. 10
37; CG; unattributed from drawing; fig. 9 no. 7
Plain ware: (CG/EG was not differentiated in the report) 15/17 SG (2); 18 SG; 27 SG (3); 18/31 SG (3); 18/31 CG/EG (7); 33 CG/EG (5 - 1 stamped Avitus Rheinz, 1 stamped Miccio Rheinz, 1 stamped Elvillus CG); 31 CG/EG (11); 38 CG/EG (2); 79 CG/EG (3 - 1 stamped Atilianus CG); 81 CG/EG; C23 CG/EG
6 Traj; Den; RIC 353
Had; Den; RIC 297
Had; Dup; RIC 360
Ant; Dup; RIC 932; 154-5
8 Penn 1957

**A 113**

1 Springhead, Kent; *vicus*; site A key deposit VII
2 B
3 A
4 29; SG; details not given here, dated Claud/early Flav; fig. 9 no. 11
37; CG; identification to potter not possible from drawing, but standing figure as O 538 of Butrio, other details not of this potter but of the same period or slightly later; fig. 9 no. 12
37; CG; possibly Cinnamus; bear as O 1609, metope style; fig. 9 no. 13
Plain ware: (CG/EG was not differentiated in the report) 15/17 SG; 18 SG (2); 18/31 SG; 18/31 CG/EG (2); 31 CG/EG; 33 CG/EG (3 - 1 stamped Osbimanus CG); 79 CG/EG
6 Faust I; Den; RIC (Ant) 339a; 139-40
8 Penn 1957

**A 114**

1 Springhead, Kent; temple in *vicus*; temple 1 phase C
2 F
3 A
4 37; CG; probably Paternus II; leaf as S&S fig. 30 no. 2, deer O 1732, metope style; fig. 7 no. 3
Plain ware: 31 CG stamped Aestivus; 36 CG/EG; C15 CG/EG
6 Ant; As; RIC 533; 139
7 The pottery forms a reasonably homogeneous late group, somewhat later than the coin.
8 Penn 1959

**A 115**

1 Springhead, Kent; temple in *vicus*; temple III stratum E
2 B
3 A
4 37 (2 pieces); CG; Attianus; leaf R H72, leaf R J4, winding scroll style; fig. 7 nos 2-3
Plain ware: 33 CG stamped Sacrillus; 33 CG stamped Sedatus; Lud Sa EG stamped Malliacus; 31 CG/EG
6 Ant; HS; RIC 638; 140-4; coin 8
7 The layer below also has samian of this general group.
8 Penn 1960

**A 116**

1 Springhead, Kent; temple in *vicus*; temple III stratum F
2 E
3 A
4 37; CG; Iustus (stamped in field with large stamp); ovolo S&S fig. 31 no. 1, cupid O 440 in medallion, leaf R H129, leaf R J51, leaf as S&S pl. 109 no. 9 (small leaf), small 'twist' not in S&S or R, bird O 2365, bird as O 2239B, winding scroll and medallion style as S&S pl. 110 no. 10; fig. 7 no. 10
37; CG; Paternus II (stamped in field with large stamp); ovolo S&S fig. 30 no. 1, cupid O 440 in medallion, astragalus S&S fig. 30 no. 12, stand *ibid* fig. 30 no. 9, 'column' *ibid* fig. 30 no. 25, dolphin O 2382, in festoon R F15, dolphin O 2392, metope and medallion style; fig. 7 no. 5
37; CG; unknown potter associated with Cinnamus group; tree R N4, 'column' R P3, leaf R H24 in medallion, Venus O 331 on small trifid, metope and medallion style; fig. 8 no. 3
37; CG; Paternus II, Doeccus or an associated potter; cupid O 440 in medallion; fig. 7 no. 4
37; CG; unknown potter contemporary with the others in this group; bird O 2356 in medallion, trifid not in R, medallion style; fig. 7 no. 9
37 (6 pieces); Heil; Janus; vertical rope-like border with bifids on it and smaller bifids attached by tendrils identical to a piece from Rottenburg in Knorr 1910 Taf. XI no. 4, Venus O 322, metope style; fig. 8 no. 1
37; Rheinz; Reginus, Janu I, Cobnertus, Cerialis group; warrior O 176; fig. 7 no. 7
Plain ware: 18 SG (5); 18/31 (8); 24/25; 31 (3); 33 (8); 38 (3); 42; 46; Ritt 1; C11; C15; C21 (3); Lud Ob (2); Lud Oc; Lud Sa stamped Calenus Rheinz; Lud Sa stamped Maternus Rheinz; 33 stamped Rufinus EG; 33 stamped Tintirus EG

5 Several CCW 'hunt-cups'; glass dated late 2nd to early 3rd century
6 Vesp; Den; RIC 10; 69-71; coin 1
Faust I; As; RIC (Ant) 1163; 141+; coin 3
The layer below has:
Ant; HS; RIC 638; 140-4; coin 8
7 An unusual group of decorated samian, with several pieces in styles not easy to attribute to a particular potter.
8 Penn 1960

**A 117**

1 Springhead, Kent; *vicus*; well F19
2 C
3 C
4 29 (2 pieces); SG; hare O 2048, winding scroll style in upper zone, dated Flav; fig. 4 no. 3
37; CG; Paternus II (stamped in field with large stamp); ovolo S&S fig. 30 no. 1, leaf *ibid* fig. 30 no. 16 in medallion, Apollo O 94A, metope and medallion style; fig. 4 no. 1
37 (5 pieces); CG; Cettus; leaf R H155, deer O 1704, horseman O 245, boar O 1641, free style; fig. 4 no. 2
37; CG; Cinnamus; basket S&S fig. 47 no. 18, 'twist' *ibid* fig. 47 no. 4, bird *ibid* fig. 47 no. 8, caryatid O 1199, metope style; fig. 4 no. 4
37; CG; Cinnamus; man O 644
30; CG; Caletus; man O 689
37; EG; fragment of ovolo only
Plain ware: 18 SG (2); 35/36 SG; 35/36 CG; 3l/3lR CG; 33 EG; 79 CG (2); C11 CG; 45 CG/EG
6 From 4 feet down: Gall; Rad; RIC 280
From 8 feet down: Allect; Rad; RIC 79F
From 12 feet down: Ant; HS; RIC 792
7 No details of the stratigraphy of the fill are given, but it is suggestive from the coin evidence that it may be a question of more than one episode of filling.
8 Detsicas 1970b; Harker 1970

**A 118**

1 Staines, Surrey; small town; Friends Burial Group, layer 59
2 C
3 A
4 37; CG; Sacer style; ovolo S&S fig. 22 no. 4, twist S&S pl. 183 nos 11 and 12, leaf as R G147; no. 66
6 Had; As; RIC 617; 121-2; slightly worn; no. 11
Car; Den (Ar plated Ae copy); illeg; early 3rd century?; no. 18
7 The earlier coin is contemporary with the samian, and this seems a case of redeposition. Other samian from the same phase includes 2 Flavian SG 37, CG 37 of X-6 style, and a CG 37 of Aventinus II. Only the last seems contemporary with the coin date. There is also an Ant As from the same phase.
8 Crouch & Shanks 1984; Hammerson 1984; Marsh 1984

**A 119**

1 Stonham Aspal, Suffolk; villa; ditch A
2 D
3 A
4 37; EG - probably Trier; charioteer as F 503, hare as F 667, dog not in F, free style; fig. 39a
30 (2 pieces); Rheinz; Primitivus I; figure R&F M196a/b, see Ricken 1948 Taf. 188, 5 and 6, Taf. 189, 12 and Taf. 191, 12, medallion style; fig. 39e and f
45; EG
From the rubble layer in the top of ditch A:
37; Trier; dog F 642, wreath F 904, ovolo probably F 958, see F Taf. XXIII no. 5, free style; fig. 39b
30; CG; Doeccus; ovolo S&S fig. 44 no. 2, leaf *ibid* fig. 44 no. 32 in medallion, rosette *ibid* fig. 44 no. 5, Venus O 331, see S&S pl. 148 no. 15 for similar arrangement, metope and medallion style; fig. 39c
5 BB1; CCW hunt-cup
6 J Domna; Den; RIC (Sev) 560; 193-211
Alex; As; RIC 543; 222-35
7 The coins and the first 3 pieces of samian come from the lower fill of the ditch. The last 2 pieces of samian are from the rubble perhaps from a rebuilding or the destruction of the bath-house. The building appears to date from the early 3rd century.
8 Hartley 1966a; Smedley & Owles 1966

**A 120**

1 Thorplands, Northamptonshire; rural settlement; pit 26
2 C
3 A
4 37; CG; Paullus (but possible mould signature of Mercator i below decoration); ovolo R B206, dancer O 348 in medallion, bear O 1627, sea horse O 42, deer O 1815, Mars O 143, metope and medallion style; fig. 7 no. 10
Plain ware: (many of the pieces were abraded) 31R CG (9); 31 CG (10 - 1 stamped by Paullus of Lez, 1 stamped by Ianuaris ii of Lez); 31 EG; 33 CG (14 - 1 stamped by Geminus vi of Lez); 18/31 CG (3); 18/31R CG (2); 36 CG; 36 EG; 38 CG (3); 23 CG; 45 CG; 45 EG; 79 CG; U CG 'a number'; U EG
5 NV CCW beaker with barbotine dec; 'Castor boxes'; Oxf mortaria; BB1
6 Elag; Den; RIC 131; 218-22
7 The filling of this large pit, with *c* 1000 vessels present, was probably made in a short space of time, to judge from the stratigraphy (Hunter & Mynard 1977, 104, 130). However, the pottery includes samian of the late 2nd century and mortaria of the late 3rd if the conventional datings are followed. The excavator suggests that the samian is residual and that the period of filling was 250-300, but there is nothing to suggest that the pottery and the coins are not roughly contemporary.
8 Burnett 1977a; Hunter & Mynard 1977; Pengelly 1977a

**A 121**

1 Towcester, Northamptonshire; town; Park Street site, F94 and F176
2 C
3 A
4 37 (3 pieces - 2 redeposited in other features); CG; associate of Docilis/Casurius/Doeccus; ovolo R B24, leaf R H167, bear D 808, panther D 804, hare D 950A, dog not in O or D, leaf R H101, free style; fig. 19 no. 14
37; CG; Cinnamus (stamped by Cinnamus ii die Sb in mould); ovolo R B143, leaves *ibid* H5l, H99, H101, rosette not in R, bird D 1038, see S&S. pl. 162 no. 61 for similar style; no. W5
74 var; CG-Lez; almost complete vessel in many fragments, appliqué figures, deer O 1777 but with antlers as O 1822N, deer as O 1784, dog as O 1983, dog smaller copy of D 934 (= O 1979), these figure-types have connections with Illixo and Paternus II, the same appliqué deer are on a black-slip vessel from a deposit in the Verulamium theatre (Simpson 1957a, 41 no. 31 and fig. 2 no. 31) dated to the end of the 2nd century and the form is paralleled at Exeter (Simpson 1973, 47 no. 29 and fig. 1 no. 29), bronze-brown matt slip, erratically fired; fig. 18 no. 12, ref. W29
Stamped plain ware:

31; MdV; Aelianus die 21
33; MdV; Buccula die 2a
33; MdV; Buccula die 2a
27; CG; Canaus ii die 2a
31; CG; Coccillus die 2a
31; CG; Cracuna i die 2a
33; Rheinz; Dagodubnus ii die la
18/31; CG; Ericus die Ib
27; CG; Gongius die 2a
33; CG; Illiomaris ii die la
18/31R; CG; Muxtullus die Ib; rivetted
31; CG; Muxtullus die Ib
18/31R; CG; Secundus v die Ib
31; MdV; Suobnus die 2a
Other plain ware: 42 CG; C15 CG; 18/31 CG; 31 CG; 18/31R CG; 37 CG rim; 79 CG

5 Roughcast beakers; imitation BB1; rouletted CCW beaker; large glass assemblage

6 Ant?; As; illeg

7 This feature is a pit cut into the top of a well, which contains a few pieces of samian including a piece by Attianus II. The coin and the first piece of samian are from F94, the top of the pit. The rest of the pottery is a homogeneous group in F176. Several of the foot rings are worn.

8 Esmonde-Cleary 1980; Lambrick 1980; Pengelly 1980; Simpson 1980

**A 122**

1 *Verulamium*, St Albans, Hertfordshire; town; Insula XIV, period IID fire deposits

2 E

3 A

4 37; CG-MdV; ovolo and bead row as Terrisse 1968 pl. 43 no. 260; no. D114
30; CG; Cinnamus; ovolo S&S fig. 47 no. 2, athlete O 204, Pan mask O 1214, dolphin and basket S&S fig. 47 no.18, medallion R E21, metope and medallion style; no. D115
37; CG; Docilis; ovolo not in R or S&S, stand S&S fig. 24 no. 13, small figure O 210A, bird O 2251, metope style; no. D116
37; CG; Secundus; ovolo as R B227 (Ollognatus), column R P16, bird O 2252, hare O 2115, athlete O 204, panther O 1518, metope and medallion style; no. D117
37; CG; Cinnamus, Cerialis, Paullus or associate; ovolo R B144; no. D118
37; CG; Cinnamus-Cerialis; sphinx O 853, panther O 1521, metope and medallion style; no. D119
37; CG; Sacer-Attianus; ovolo S&S fig. 23 no. 1, circle *ibid* fig. 23 no. 9, trifid *ibid* fig. 22 no. 4, leaf as R H37 (larger), deer O 1772, bird O 2252, bird O 2298, bird O 2316, bird O 2324, winding scroll style; no. D120
37; CG: Sacer-Attianus; ovolo as R B185, Hercules O 783, caryatid O 1206, metope style; no. D121
37; CG; Cinnamus (stamped by Cintusmus as bowl finisher); ovolo S&S fig. 47 no. 2, stand R Q43, Vulcan O 66, deer O 1720, metope and medallion style; no. D122
37; CG; X-10 (Silvio); winding scroll style, dated by Hartley to Hadrianic period; no. D123
37; CG; Sacer-Attianus; ovolo as R B185; no. D124
37; CG; Drusus II; vine scroll as R M22, winding scroll style; no. D125
37; CG; Drusus II; ovolo not in R, Vulcan O 66; no. D127
37; CG; unknown potter of group II; ovolo as R B189, leaf R H73, spiral R S16, Pan O 723 (Aventinus I), dolphins and gladiator not in R; no. D128
37; CG; Cinnamus (early); leaf R H24, winding scroll style; no. D129
37; CG; probably Sacer-Attianus; Amazon O 241, acanthus as R K22; no. D130
37; CG; Docilis; stand S&S fig. 24 no. 13, stand R Q42, metope style; no. D133
37; CG; Criciro or Sacer-Attianus; ornament S&S fig. 33 no. 5, lion O 1450, deer O 1772, free style; no. D135
37; CG; Cinnamus; ovolo S&S fig. 47 no. 3, cupid O 401, hare O 2116, bird O 2315, circle as R E17, metope and medallion style; no. D136
37; CG; Sacer-Attianus; trifid as fig. 22 no. 4, deer O 1772, metope style; no. D137
37; CG; Igocatus; figure O 905, lioness O 1537, Perseus O 234, metope style; no. D138
37; CG; Docilis; lozenge R U28, bifid R G350, Hercules O 751, metope style; no. D139
37; CG; possibly Drusus II; circles in place of ovolo, style as S&S pl. 89 no. 12, metope style; no. D140
37; CG; Austrus or Secundinus I; bear O 1620, free style; no. D141
37; CG; Cinnamus; ovolo S&S fig. 47 no. 3, leaf R H21, leaf as R H99, winding scroll style; no. D142
37; Blick; ovolo K&S Taf. 82 no. 32, triton *ibid* Taf. 71 no. 14, triton *ibid* Taf. 71 no. 15, bird *ibid* Taf. 80 no. 7, bird *ibid* Taf. 80 no. 8, ship *ibid* Taf. 57 no. 7, vine as *ibid* Taf. 81 no. 22, bifid *ibid* Taf. 81 no. 51, free style, as *ibid* Taf. 33 no. 2 (with Austrus ovolo); no. D126
37; Chémery; Satto-Saturninus; ovolo as F 276, bifid F 240, bifid F 239, horizontal zone style; no. D132
(9 of the above pieces are from disturbed burning deposits)
Plain ware and undescribed decorated pieces (excluding those from disturbed deposits):
30 SG; 37 SG (6); 18/31 SG; CII SG; 18 SG (14); 29 SG (5); 18R SG; cup SG; 27 SG (8); 33 SG; 42 CG; C15 CG (4); 46 CG (5); inkwell CG; 37 CG (18 - 2 Cinnamus, 1 Sacer-Attianus, 1 Acaunissa, 1 Bassus); 30 CG (2); 33 CG (64); 31 CG (54); 31R CG (11); 18/31 CG (21); 18/31R CG (2); jar CG (2 - incised dec); CII CG (7); 44 CG (3); 38 CG (7); 27 CG (21); 35 CG (4); 36 CG (9); 32 CG; C23 CG; C21 CG

6 From undisturbed deposits:
Rep; Den; M Antony type.
Dom; Den; RIC 144
Nerva; HS; RIC 93 or 104
Traj; HS; RIC 663
Traj; Dup
Had; As; RIC 669
Ant; ?; 139
Faust II; As
Faust II; ?; 145-6
From disturbed deposits:
Barb Rad
Gall; Rad; RIC 164
Tet I; Rad; RIC 90
Tet II; Barb Rad
Victorin; Rad; RIC 118
Claud II; Rad; RIC 168
Constans; Ae (2)
House of Const; Barb Ae

7 The fire deposit is an amalgam of layers associated with a burning episode. It is dated 150-60 by Hartley on the basis of the samian ware.

8 Frere 1972; Hartley 1972c

**A 123**

1 *Verulamium*, St Albans, Hertfordshire; town; insula XXVIII building 1, make-up layers

2 E

3 A
4 37; CG; Cinnamus or associate; deer O 1720, dog O 1980, free style; no. D78
37; CG; Criciro; ovolo not in R, bird O 2250A, bird R G138, festoon R F60, hare, O 2057, trifid as R G76, metope style; no. D79
37; CG; Criciro or Sacer; ovolo not in R, leopard O 1518, bear O 1588, horseman O 249, free style; no. D80
37; CG; Attianus; leaf R R58, bird as O 2298, winding scroll style; no. D81
37; CG; X-6; ovolo R B233, lion O 1497K, ornament R U92, dog O 1980, deer D 885, free style; no. D82
37; CG; Cinnamus; leaf R N15, leopard O 1521, deer O 1720, dog O 1980, free style; no. D83
37; CG; Carantinus, Cinnamus or Illixo; ovolo R B145, leaf R J154, leaf R J160, lion O·1425, panther O 1546, leopard O 1518, deer O 1743, deer O 1777, horseman O 258, free style; no. D84
37; CG; X-6; ovolo R B32, trifid R G97, panther O 1542, wavy line borders, metope style; no. D85
37; CG; Cinnamus; deer O 1781; no. D86
37; CG; Cinnamus; 'twist' as S&S fig. 47 no. 35, trifid R G66, Osiris O 711, metope and medallion style; no. D87
Stamps on plain ware:
33; CG; Aventinus i die la; no. S64
27; CG; Martius iii die 3b; no. S65
31; CG; Aventinus i die la; no. S66
Plain ware (including stamped pieces):
37 CG (12 fragments); 37 EG; 31 CG (16); 31R CG (3); 80 CG (2); 38 CG (2); 79 CG (3); 33 CG (8); 36 CG (2); 27 CG; 81 CG (4); 72 CG; 45 EG
5 Oxf mort
6 Faust I; Den; RIC (Ant) 360a
Ant; RS (copy); as RIC 600
7 It is possible that some earlier material (i.e. SG samian) has been omitted (Frere 1983, 252).
8 Dickinson 1984; Frere 1983

### A 124

1 *Verulamium*, St Albans, Hertfordshire; town; make-up for road, period III, surrounding theatre
2 E
3 A
4 37; CG; Cinnamus; ovolo as S&S fig. 47 no. 3, festoon R F13, bird O 2214A, pygmy O 696A, bear O 1609, metope style; fig. 9 no. 3
Presence of forms: 37; 31; 33; 18/31; 38; 35; 27
7 Faust I; probably Ae; RIC (Ant) 1154ff; good condition
Sev; Den
8 Kenyon 1934, 230, 254

### A 125

1 Watercrook, Cumbria; fort; NE gate, E chamber layer 1
2 E
3 A
4 37 (5 pieces); Rheinz; Julius I or Lupus; ovolo as R&F E18, grapes *ibid* P164, leaf *ibid* P37, rosette *ibid* O48, metope and medallion style; fig. 114 no. 12
33; CG; stamped by Martius IV die Ib; no. S19
6 Barb Rad (4 - Claud II, 2 Victorin, Tet I)
7 There are two pieces of the 37 Rheinz from the associated layer underneath, plus scraps of CG and EG vessels.
8 Potter 1979; Shotter 1979; Wild 1979b

### A 126

1 Whitchurch, Shropshire; *vicus*; E1 layer 8 and associated layers in stone building III
2 E
3 A
4 37; CG; Doeccus or Casurius; large beads, no other details given; no. 30
Plain ware: 33 CG; 31R CG (2); 18/31 or 31 CG; fragment of 1st century Lezoux ware
5 BB jars; NV CCW
6 Victorin; Barb Rad; 268-70; very worn; coin 5
Tet II; Rad; 270-4; very worn: coin 7
7 The material is somewhat disturbed in the medieval period, but the pottery from the building rubble would appear to be fairly homogeneous in character.
8 Jones & Webster 1968; Wild 1968

### A 127

1 Wiggonholt, West Sussex; rural settlement; site A pit 11
2 C
3 A
4 37; Brit; Aldgate/Pulborough potter; horseman O 249, circle Webster 1975 e, circle Webster 1975 f, free style; Webster 1975 no. 12, but see section 7 below.
37; CG; possibly Cinnamus; lion as O 1378, small tendril tips used as field decoration as S&S pl. 163 no. 66, free style, burnt; Webster 1974 fig. 18 no. 13
18/31; CG; stamped by Tittius die XIa
6 Nero; As; BMC 387; coin 3
Had; Ae; BMC 1163; coin 12
Had; As; worn; coin 11
Evans (1974, 108) also records a coin of Postumus from this pit. It may be coin 13 in Archibald's report:
Post; Rad; RIC 90
7 There is a problem with this association, for the Aldgate/Pulborough piece is recorded in Webster 1975 as coming from A20c10, a context which is not found in Evans' excavation report. However, Webster states (1975, 169n) that this piece was residual in a later pit, and can probably be related to the piece that comes from pit 11 referred to in Webster 1974, 144. The pit itself had a fill of burnt material, perhaps from a nearby wooden building: the pottery and coins came from above the burnt layer.
8 Archibald 1974; Evans 1974; Hartley & Dickinson 1974; Webster 1974; 1975

### A 128

1 Winchester, Hampshire; town; County Council offices, enlargement of defensive bank
2 E
3 A
4 29; SG; mid-Flavian style
37; SG; late Flavian style
37; CG; Drusus II; stand R Q40, Venus O 286, metope decoration
37; CG; Quintilianus group; lion and small double circle as S&S pl. 74 no. 34
37 CG (fragment); 18/31 CG (2 - 1 rivetted); 27 CG (late type); 31 CG
From Colebrook Street, infill against back of wall face:
37; CG; Cinnamus; ovolo S&S fig. 47 no. 4, see *ibid* pl. 162 no. 61 for the style
18 CG; 18/31R CG; 27 CG (2); 15/17 SG
6 Comm; probably Ae; 180-92; no details given

7 Redeposited material is clearly present here. The two deposits of samian ware are from different sectors of the walls, but the excavator associates them with the same building episode (Cunliffe 1962, 80).
8 Cunliffe 1962; Dannell 1962

**A 129**

1 Winchester, Hampshire; town; Kingdon's Workshop, level V, occupation of first masonry building
2 B
3 A
4 37; CG; Igocatus (X-4); ovolo S&S fig. 6 no. 1
18/31 CG; 27 CG; 31 CG; 33 CG
6 Dom; As
Barb Rad
7 Basically an early to mid-2nd century group not sealed until the second masonry building was constructed *c* 270.
8 Cunliffe 1964; Dannell 1964

**A 130**

1 Wroxeter, Shropshire; town; baths, third layer above hall (period I) of baths
2 E (probably)
3 A
4 37; CG; Butrio; rosette S&S fig. 13 no. 10, stand *ibid* fig. 13 no. 7, caryatid O 577, metope style; fig. 5 no. 33
37; CG; Paternus II, Banvus, Carantinus or Lastuca; dancer O 360 in medallion; fig. 5 no. 34
37; CG; Criciro; caryatid O 1207A, Hercules O 783, metope and medallion style; fig. 5 no. 35
37; CG; possibly Caletus; ovolo as R B90, wavy line border (unusual for Caletus); fig. 5 no. 36
37; CG; Q I Balbinus; column as S&S fig. 35 no. 10 (Albucius), stand *ibid* fig. 35 no. 1 (Balbinus), cupid O 450, Victory O 826, dolphin O 2382, panther O 1570, astragalus border, rosette as R C167, metope and medallion style; fig. 5 no. 39
37; CG; Secundus; ovoloR B143, guide line under ovolo, metope and medallion style; fig. 5 no. 40
37; CG; Cinnamus; ovolo R B143, ornament R U245, astragalus S&S fig. 47 no. 40, metope and medallion style; fig. 5 no. 41
37; CG; Cinnamus; ovolo S&S fig. 47 no. 3, lozenge *ibid* fig. 47 no. 15, acanthus *ibid* fig. 47 no. 21, leaf R J89, male figure O 905, bird O 2298, metope and medallion style; fig. 5 no. 43
37; CG; Cinnamus (stamped in mould with large stamp); ovolo S&S fig. 47 no. 1, edge of leaf as *ibid* fig. 47 no. 36, metope and medallion style; fig. 5 no. 44
37 (2 pieces); CG; Paternus II; ovolo S&S fig. 30 no. 1, cupid O 440, cupid O 444; fig. 6 nos 46-7
37; CG; Caletus or Severus; basket R T29, Pan O 710, metope style; fig. 6 no. 49
37; CG; Doeccus; figure O 204 in medallion; fig. 6 no. 51
37; CG; Mercator II; ovolo S&S fig. 43 no. 2, rosette *ibid* fig. 43 no. 1, circle *ibid* fig. 43 no. 6, column R P3, Apollo O 83, seated figure not in O (as O 622 and 571), metope style; fig. 6 no. 54
37; CG; Paternus II (stamped in mould with large stamp); ovolo S&S fig. 30 no. 1, astragalus *ibid* fig. 30 no. 12, stand *ibid* fig. 30 no. 9, rosette *ibid* fig. 30 no. 1, ornament *ibid* fig. 30 no. 24, triton O 19, sea bull O 52A, mask O 1215, mask O 1330, astragalus borders, metope and medallion style, early Paternus style with many details in common with Ianuaris II-Paternus I; fig. 6 no. 56
37; CG; Albucius; ovolo S&S fig. 35 no. 1, metope style; fig. 6 no. 57
37 CG (2) with winding scroll designs of group III-IV; fig. 5 no. 42, fig. 6 no. 53
6 Car; Den; RIC 89; 207
8 Kenyon 1940; Stanfield 1940

**A 131**

1 Wroxeter, Shropshire; town; destruction deposit in the forum and the east portico gutter
2 E
3 A
4 From the 'stalls' in the east portico gutter:
37; CG; Advocisus (stamped in mould); ovolo S&S fig. 33 no. 1, stand R Q49, Victory O 809, Venus O 281, caryatid O 1207, Diana O 106, metope and medallion style; pl. 33 no. G1
37; CG; Albucius (stamped in mould); ovolo S&S fig. 35 no. 1, trifid *ibid* fig. 35 no. 9, circle *ibid* fig. 35 no. 5, lozenge as R U32, column R P3, column R P37, astragalus R R8, vase R T17, trifid as R G161, ornament as R U260, bifid as R G282, male figure O 607 with trifid as R G185 in place of right hand, dolphin (upside-down) O 2382, Pan mask O 1214, cupid O 450, Victory O 826, metope, medallion and arcade style, published in S&S pl. 120 no. 1; pl. 33 no. G2
37; CG; Paternus II (stamped in mould with large stamp); ovolo S&S fig. 30 no. 1, dolphin O 2382, dolphin O 2384, dolphin O 2392, dolphin O 2393, triton O 19, female figure O 926, metope and medallion style; pl. 34 no. G3
37; CG; Paternus II (stamped in mould with large stamp); ovolo S&S fig. 30 no. 1, column *ibid* fig. 30 no. 25, astragalus *ibid* fig. 30 no. 12, sea bull O 52A, centaur O 744, sea horse O 33, metope style; pl. 34 no. G4
37; CG; Paternus II (stamped in mould with large stamp); ovolo S&S fig. 30 no. 3, circle *ibid* fig. 30 no. 17, leaf *ibid* fig. 30 no. 22, rosette *ibid* fig. 30 no. 3, circle *ibid* fig. 30 no. 15, column R P70, seated figure O 913, bird O 2365, winding scroll and medallion style; pl. 34 no. G5
37; CG; Paullus (stamped in mould); ovolo R B144, vine scroll R M31, draped figure O 905, deer O 1781, bear O 1627, boar O 1666, Minerva O 126, hare O 2116, sphinx O 735A, warrior O 177, metope and small medallion style; pl. 32A and pl. 35 no. G6
37; CG; Paternus II; ovolo S&S fig. 30 no. 1, trifid *ibid* fig. 30 no. 4, stand *ibid* fig. 30 no. 9, astragalus *ibid* fig. 30 no. 12, rosette *ibid* fig. 30 no. 1, cupid O 444, mask O 1215, mask O 1330, cupid O 440; pl. 33 no. G7
30; CG; Mercator II; ovolo S&S fig. 43 no. 1, leaf R H117, dog O 1917, goat O 1840, lioness O 1537, deer O 1770, lioness O 1534, deer O 1732, free style; pl. 32B and pl. 35 no. G8
37; CG; Casurius; ovolo S&S fig. 40 no. 1, leaf *ibid* fig. 40 no. 12, leaf R H47, acanthus R K3, mask O 1293, cupid O 382, Minerva O 126, metope style; pl. 36 no. G9
37; CG; Paternus II; ovolo S&S fig. 30 no. 1, 'twist' *ibid* fig. 30 no. 21, lion O 1540, bear O 1589, dog O 1917, horseman O 246, boar O 1674, dog O 1985, dog O 1980, free style; pl. 36 no. G10
37; CG; Censorinus; ovolo and bead row S&S fig. 29 no. 2, leaf R J153, column as R P3, caryatid O 1207, satyr O 627, deer O 1784, lioness O 1501, Apollo O 92, free style with medallions; pl. 35 no. G11

37; CG; Paternus II; ovolo S&S fig. 30 no. 1, stand *ibid* fig. 30 no. 9, female figure O 926, metope and medallion style; pl. 33 no. G12

37 (8 pieces); CG; Laxtucissa; leaf S&S fig. 27 no. 1, leaf *ibid* fig. 27 no. 12, leaf R H117, lion O 1455, lion O 1509, boar O 1589, bear O 1590, bear O 1578, boar O 1674, deer O 1720, deer O 1752A, horse O 1904, dog O 1917, free style; pl. 37 no. G13a-g

From the destruction level in the forum:

37; CG; Advocisus (stamped in mould); female figure O 923; pl. 37 no. H1

37; CG; Advocisus (stamped in mould); ovolo S&S fig. 33 no. 1, Bacchus O 571, dolphin O 2392, Pan O 709, seated figures O 970, metope style; pl. 33 no. H2

37; CG; Advocisus (stamped in mould); ovolo S&S fig. 33 no. 1, trifid R G70, Pan O 709, cupid O 508, mask O 1330, dolphin O 2382, cupid O 504, mask O 1215, dolphin O 2392, metope and small medallion style; pl. 33 no. H3

30; CG; Divixtus (stamped in mould); metope style; no. H4

37; CG; Martialis (signed in mould); ornament S&S fig. 33 no. 5 (Criciro), lion O 1450, deer as O 1781, free style; pl. 37 no. H7

37; CG; Paternus II (stamped in mould with large stamp); ovolo S&S fig. 30 no. 1, 'twist' *ibid* fig. 30 no. 21, horseman O 246, boar O 1674, horse O 1910, free style; pl. 34 no. H8

37; CG; Paternus II (stamped in mould with large stamp); 'twist' S&S fig. 30 no. 18, ornament as *ibid* fig. 30 no. 24, bear O 1616, horse O 1910, deer O 1732, free style: pl. 37 no. H9

37 (2 pieces); CG; Paternus II; ovolo S&S fig. 30 no. 1, branch or club R U281, triton O 19, dolphin O 2382, dolphin O 2384, dolphin O 2393, metope style; pl. 34 no. H12

37; CG; Paternus II; ovolo S&S fig. 30 no. 1, leaf R H125, acanthus not in R, sea bull O 52A, metope style; pl. 34 no. H13

37; CG; Paternus II: ovolo S&S fig. 30 no. 1, triton O 19, metope and medallion style; pl. 37 no. H14

37; CG; Paternus II; ovolo S&S fig. 30 no. 1, column *ibid* fig. 30 no. 25, metope and medallion style; pl. 39 no. H15

37; CG; Paternus II; ovolo S&S fig. 30 no. 1, 'twist' ibid fig. 30 no. 18, horseman O 246, lion as O 1403, free style; pl. 39 no. H16

37; CG; Paternus II; ovolo S&S fig. 30 no. 1, lioness O 1534, boar O 1674, free style; pl. 39 no. H17

37; CG; Paternus II or associate; ovolo S&S fig. 30 no. 1, long 'twist' not in *ibid* fig. 30, deer O 1732, horse O 1904, gladiator O 202, dog O 1983, lioness O 1534, free style; pl. 40 no. H18

37 (3 pieces); CG; Paternus II, ovolo S&S fig. 30 no. 1, 'twist' *ibid* fig. 30 no. 18, dog O 1940, lion O 1540, dog O 1980, deer O 1777, panther O 1509, free style; pl. 39 nos H19-20

37; CG; Albucius; ovolo S&S fig. 35 no. 1, leaf *ibid* fig. 35 no. 2, leaf tips in field as *ibid* pl. 123 no. 33, deer O 1732, dog O 1917, panther O 1509, free style; pl. 39 no. H21

37; CG; Paternus II or associate; ovolo S&S fig. 30 no. 1, goat O 1849, free style; pl. 39 no. H22

37; CG; Paternus II or associate; ovolo S&S fig. 30 no. 1; pl. 39 no. H23

37; CG; Paullus; ovolo not in R but as R B175 (poorly impressed); shield R U210, sphinx O 857, sphinx O 853, sphinx O 735A, sea bull O 42, lioness/dog not in O, male figure not in O, metope and small medallion style; pl. 40 no. H24

37; CG; Cinnamus; ovolo S&S fig. 47 no. 1, Diana O 106, male figure O 648, Pan mask O 1214, deer O 1704, cupid O 408, circle R E16, festoon R F11, metope and medallion style; pl. 40 no. H25

37; CG; Casurius; ovolo S&S fig. 40 no. 1, leaf *ibid* fig. 40 no. 6, leaf *ibid* fig. 40 no. 10, ornament *ibid* fig. 40 no. 3, acanthus R K16, male figure O 638, Minerva O 126, Pan mask O 1214, mask O 1293, metope style; pl. 40 no. H26

37; CG; Cinnamus; ovolo R B85, 'twist' S&S fig. 47 no. 4, ornament R U247, seated figure O 111, bird O 2197, bust not in O, metope style; pl. 40 no. H27

37; CG; P-23; ovolo R B93, rosette R C21, vine scroll as R M10, lion O 1421, caryatid O 1206, metope style; pl. 40 no. H28

37; CG; Casurius or Iustus; ovolo S&S fig. 40 no. 3, leaf R H14, leaf R J146, dolphin O 2393, lioness O 1534, draped figure O 926, metope and medallion style (ovolo and style of Casurius, details of Iustus); pl. 35 no. H29

37 (4 pieces); CG; probably Censorinus; ovolo as S&S fig. 29 no. 3, rosette as R C181 (Namilianus-Croesus), leaf as R J127, Venus O 331, erotic group O B, cupid O 497, metope and medallion style; pl. 41 no. H30

37; CG; probably Censorinus; dancer O 355, eagle O 2813, metope and medallion style; pl. 39 no. H31

37; CG; Casurius; ovolo S&S fig. 40 no. 1, cruciform ornament as *ibid* pl. 135 no. 36, sea horse O 33, metope style; pl. 39 no. H32

37; CG; Casurius; ovolo S&S fig. 40 no. 1, festoon R F47, bird O 2239, caryatid O 1207, metope and medallion style; pl. 39 no. H33

37; CG; Casurius; ornament R U295, metope style; pl. 39 no. H34

30 (2 pieces); CG; Paternus II or Lastuca; ovolo S&S fig. 30 no. 2, trifid *ibid* fig. 30 no. 6, centaur O 744, gladiator O 1060, gladiator O 1061A, Hercules O 750, dog O 1940, bird O 2278, bird O 2324, metope and medallion style; pl. 40 no. H36

30; CG; Banvus; ovolo R B5, rosette S&S fig. 41 no. 4, column R P3, dolphin O 2382, metope style; pl. 42 no. H37

37; CG; Laxtucissa; ovolo S&S fig. 27 no. 1, column *ibid* fig. 27 no. 13, circle *ibid* fig. 27 no. 7, Pan O 709, dancer O 360, metope style; pl. 40 no. H38

37; CG; Secundus; ovolo S&S fig. 45 no. 3, trifid R G29, female figure O 819A, fore part of lioness O 1537, dog O 1980, hare O 2115, metope and medallion style; pl. 41 no. H39

37; CG; Paternus II or associate; ovolo S&S fig. 30 no. 3 (poorly·impressed), Apollo O 84, seated figure O 913, metope style; pl. 41 no. H40

37 (5 pieces); CG; Cinnamus; ovolo S&S fig. 47 no. 1, acanthus R K26, caryatid O 1207, metope and medallion style; pl. 42 no. H41

37; CG; Criciro; vine scroll R M50, erotic group O B, Hercules O 783, metope style; pl. 42 no. H42

37; CG; Cinnamus; ovolo S&S fig. 47 no. 1, stand R Q42, acanthus R K12, lioness O 1518, lioness O 1573D, metope style; pl. 42 no. H43

37 (2 pieces); CG; Cinnamus; ornament R U245, Pan O 717, caryatid O 1199, metope and medallion style; pl. 42 no. H45

37; CG; possibly Servus I; leaf R J8, beaded border, metope and medallion style; pl. 42 no. H46

37; CG; Paternus II or associate; sea bull O 52A in medallion; pl. 42 no. H47

37; CG; Casurius; ovolo S&S fig. 40 no. 1, leaf *ibid* fig. 40 no. 10, Minerva O 126, male figure O 638, Pan mask O 1214, metope and arcade style; pl. 41 no. H48
37; CG; Cinnamus; ovolo as S&S fig. 47 no. 2, leaf *ibid* fig. 47 no. 38, bird O 2317, bird O 2252, winding scroll style; pl. 40 no. H49
37; CG; Cinnamus; ovolo S&S fig. 47 no. 3, bird O 2239B, winding scroll and medallion style; pl. 42 no. H50
37; CG; Pugnus, ovolo S&S fig. 45 no. 1, leaf R H22, dancer O 360 without scarf, winding scroll style; pl. 43 no. H51
37; CG; Cinnamus; trifid R G66, acanthus R K12, deer O 1704, winding scroll and medallion style; pl. 43 no. H52
37; CG; Cinnamus; ovolo S&S fig. 47 no. 3, astragalus border, tree R N2, individual leaves from the tree in field, deer O 1720, lion O 1450, horse O 1976, lioness O 1537, dog O 1917, free style; pl. 40 no. H54
37; CG; Criciro; ovolo S&S fig. 33 no. 2, ornament *ibid* fig. 33 no. 5, Amazon O 241, lion O 1570, warrior as O 780 with spear in right hand made from bead row, deer O 1772, panther O 1518, horseman O 251, free style; pl. 41 no. H55
37 (2 pieces); CG; Advocisus; ovolo R B103, tendril in field R M50 (part only), lion and boar O 1491, lion O 1369, horse O 1911, free style; pl. 41 no. H56
37; CG; Paternus II; leaf as R H129, 'twist' S&S fig. 30 no. 21, panther O 1509, dog O 1917, free style; pl. 43 no. H57
37; CG; Paternus II; dog O 1983, 'twist' S&S fig. 30 no. 21, free style; pl. 43 no. H58
37; CG; Albucius; leaf S&S fig. 35 no. 2, gladiator O 177, dog as O 1917, free style; pl. 43 no. H59
37 (several pieces); CG; Libertus B; ovolo R B214, Hercules O 759, caryatid O 1206/7, caryatid O 599, Diana O 107, Diana O 115, figure Bémont & Rogers 1979 Pe194, mask O 1310, metope style; pl. 36 no. H62
37; CG; X-11/12; notched circle in place of ovolo as S&S pl. 35 no. 413, vine scroll as *ibid* pl. 37 no. 431, horizontal zone style; pl. 42 no. H63
37; CG; X-11/12; similar overall composition to previous piece; pl. 42 no. H64
37; CG; Igocatus (X-4); stand S&S fig. 6 no. 2, male figure O 905, Venus O 331, metope and arcade style; pl. 42 no. H65
30; CG; Austrus; festoon R F56, Silenus O 647, bird O 2316, hare O 2061, metope style; pl. 43 no. H66
37; CG; probably Ianuaris II-Paternus I; ovolo as S&S fig. 30 no. 8, horseman O 249, free style; no. G67
37; CG; Casurius, Cinnamus, Pugnus or associate; ovolo R B223, cursive inscription below bead row reading TOCAC/VOGAS, probably part of a Celtic inscription, see Déchelette 1904, I, 218 for identical inscription from same mould from Lezoux, cf also Detsicas 1966; pl. 37 no. H11
37; Rheinz; Janu I (stamped in mould); ovolo R&F E396, warrior *ibid* M210, warrior *ibid* M207, Vulcan *ibid* M80, dancer *ibid* M60, bifid *ibid* P142, metope style, from same mould as Ricken 1948 Taf. 3 no. 18; pl. 38 no. H5
37 CG (3) not attributed - nos H35, H44, H53
37 CG (4) not analysed here since they are identified by the excavator as early pieces (Sacer, Drusus II, etc) certainly from a disturbed pre-destruction deposit in east reom 3 - nos H6, H10, H60-1

6 Vesp; As; BMC 846-7; no. 27; east room 3
Vesp; HS; illeg; no. 34; east room B
Dom; Den; BMC 246; no. 45; entrance
Nerva; As; illeg; no. 48; east room B
Traj; Dup; BMC 719; no. 49, east portico
Traj; HS; illeg; no. 63; east room 1
Traj; Den; BMC 103; no. 50; east room A
Traj; Den; BMC 123; no. 51; east room A
Traj; HS; BMC 1042; no. 61; east room A
Traj; Den; BMC 204; no. 53; east room B
Traj; HS; illeg; no. 63; east room B
Traj; HS; BMC 782; no. 55; west room 1
Traj; HS; BMC 812; no. 58; west room 1
Had; HS; BMC 1130-1; no. 64; east portico
Had; Dup; illeg; no. 68; east portico
Had; As; illeg; no. 73; east room 1 west
Had; HS; BMC 1211-2; no. 67; east room 4
Had; As; BMC 1175 ; no. 66; east room B
Ant; As; RIC 934; 155; no. 77; east room 3
Ant; Dup; RIC 668; 140-3; no. 74; east room B
Faust I; Ae; RIC (Ant) 1154f; no. 79; east portico
Faust I; Ae; illeg; no. 82; east portico
Faust I; Den; RIC (Ant) 350a; no. 80; east room 1
Faust I; Ae; illeg; no. 82; east room 3
Const I; Ae; 309-13; no. 179; east portico; regarded as intrusive by the excavator

7 The gutter deposit is accepted to be a shop or stall deposit destroyed in the forum fire. There is also the possibility that there was a store of pottery in East Rooms 1 and 2 in the forum and its vicinity, since a large quantity of fairly homogeneous pieces was found there (nos 1, 4, 7-8, 11, 15-18, 21-3, 27-8, 31-4, 36-7, 40, 43, 45-7, 49-50, 55, 57-8). The coins and pottery from the destruction level in fact were positioned·under the fallen roof debris of the destruction and above the floors.

8 Atkinson 1942; Hartley 1972a, 27; Weber 2012, 62-3; 2013, 190-2

**A 132**

1 Wroxeter, Shropshire; town; water cistern construction deposit
2 E
3 B
4 Summary only given in report:
37; CG; Cinnamus (stamped)
37; CG; Paternus II
37; CG; Paternus II
37; CG; Sacer-Attianus or Criciro
37 (3 pieces); CG; Sacer-Attianus or Drusus II
6 Dom; HS; RIC 347
Aur; HS; RIC 1302a; 150-2; worn
8 Houghton 1965

**A 133**

1 York, Yorkshire; suburb of town; Blossom Street, ditch under road B
2 D
3 A
4 37; CG; Paternus II; ovolo probably S&S fig. 30 no. 1, rosette *ibid* fig. 30 no. 8, sea horse O 33 in medallion, Apollo O 94A, fish O 2418, metope and medallion style; fig. 7 no. 1
37; CG; Caletus; basket R T29, Pan O 710, caryatid O 1199, metope style; fig. 7 no. 2
37; CG; Criciro or Attianus; ovolo as S&S fig. 33 no. 1, but closer to R B93 (Attianus, P-23), sea horse O 48A in festoon R F16, bird O 2252, rosette R C125, metope and medallion style; fig. 7 no. 3
37; CG; Laxtucissa (stamped in mould); astragalus as S&S fig. 27 no. 3, metope and medallion style; fig. 7 no. 4

37; CG; P-23 or Cinnamus; ovolo as R B12 or B28, stand R Q42, Jupiter as O 3, metope style; fig. 7 no. 5
30; CG; Doeccus; ovolo S&S fig. 44 no. 2, leaf *ibid* fig. 44 no. 30, medallion, rosette *ibid* fig. 44 no. 1, leaf *ibid* fig. 44 no. 22, leaf *ibid* fig. 44 no. 27, stand *ibid* fig. 44 no. 7, flower R G259, metope and medallion style; fig. 7 no. 6
37; CG; Cinnamus (stamped in mould with large stamp); leaf R R72, leaf R J86, winding scroll style; fig. 7 no. 7
37; CG; X-6; giant O 624, dwarf O 699, ornament S&S fig. 18 no. 17, lozenge R U33, free style; fig. 7 no. 8
37; CG; Cettus; ovolo S&S fig. 42 no. 2, spiral *ibid* fig. 42 no. 1, leaf *ibid* fig. 42 no. 4, metope style; fig. 7 no. 9
37; CG; Albucius (stamped in mould); fig. 7 no. 10
37; CG; Butrio (stamped in mould); ovolo S&S fig. 13 no. 2, leaf *ibid* fig. 13 no. 8, deer O 1822A, dog O 2024, free style; fig. 7 no. 11
37; CG; Butrio; ornament S&S fig. 13 no. 7, erotic group O H, mask O 1330, Pan O 709, metope style; fig. 7 no. 12
37 (3 pieces); CG; Criciro (signed in mould); rosette R C125, cupid O 426, trifid R G67, metope style; fig. 7 no. 13
37; CG; Quintilianus group; ovolo S&S fig. 17 no. 1, dwarf O 698, dwarf O 693, goat as O 1842, dog O 2001, panther O 1555, ornament S&S fig. 17 no. 20, basal wreath *ibid* fig. 17 no. 4, free style; fig. 7 no. 14
37; CG; Butrio; ovolo S&S fig. 13 no. 2, Bellerophon and Pegasus O 835, Venus O 305, Mercury O 538, mask O 1330, mask O 1215, metope style, very similar to S&S pl. 58 no. 659 (London); fig. 8 no. 15
37 (3 pieces); CG; Criciro; ovolo S&S fig. 33 no. 1, ornament O 2155, bear O 1588, lion O 1450, panther O 1581, free style; fig. 8 nos 16-17
37; CG; Servus II; seated figure O 641, Venus O 290, Venus O 305, metope and medallion style; fig. 8 no. 18
37; CG; Tetturo; Bacchus O 571, gladiator O 1059, metope style; fig. 8 no. 19
37; CG; Servus II; ovolo as S&S pl. 131 no. 6, hare O 2057A in festoon, metope style; fig. 8 no. 20
37; Heil; Ciriuna; lion R&F J10, stand *ibid* O160; fig. 9 no. 30
37; Rheinz; Reginus II, Iulius I, Lupus or associate; ovolo R&F E42, rosette *ibid* O37, rosette and divided bead row *ibid* O271, metope and arcade style, very similar to Ricken 1948 Taf. 161 no. 2; fig. 9 no. 31
37 (2 pieces); Rheinz; Reginus I (stamped in mould); gladiator R&F M266, altar *ibid* O224, medallion style; fig. 9 nos 26-7
37; Rheinz; Reginus I; circles in place of ovolo R&F R14, acanthus *ibid* O139, stand *ibid* O224, free style; fig. 9 no. 28
37; Rheinz; Reginus II or B F Attoni; gladiator R&F M204a, leaf *ibid* P78; fig. 9 no. 29
37; Rheinz; Mammilianus, Firmus II, Reginus II or Victorinus I; ovolo R&F E18, winding scroll style; fig. 9 no. 33
37; Rheinz; Attillus, Augustalis or Primitivus I; ovolo R&F E40, panther *ibid* T47b, mask *ibid* M9, medallion style; fig. 9 no. 34
37; West; Helenius; ovolo von Hefner 1863 Taf III no. 121, bird *ibid* Taf III no. 77 (= R&F T2l8), trifid not in von Hefner 1863 or Kellner 1963, free style with festoons; fig. 9 no. 32
37; Arg; ware with ovolo A; ovolo Ricken 1934 Taf. XIII, A, Mars *ibid* Taf. XIII no. 43, leaf *ibid* Taf. XIII no. 45, free style; fig. 9 no. 35
37; Arg; ware with ovolo A; ovolo Ricken 1934 Taf. XIII, A, festoon *ibid* Taf. XIII no. 20, rosette as *ibid* Taf. XIII nos l-2, festoon style; fig. 9 no. 36
37; Arg; ware with ovolo B; ovolo Ricken 1934 Taf. XIII, B, acanthus *ibid* Taf. XIII no. 12, bird *ibid* Taf. XIII no. 13, medallion style; fig. 9 no. 37
37; Trier; tree F 760, basal wreath F 727, metope style; fig. 9 no. 38

6 Comm; HS; no details given; 181-92; no13
7 The coin comes from under the surface of road B, not from the ditch, and is therefore in an analogous stratigraphic position to the samian ware, but not closely associated.
8 Bowes 1965; Wenham 1965

**A 134**

1 York, Yorkshire; town; Bishophill, period 1 features sealed by terrace
2 B and D
3 A
4 37; CG; Attianus or Criciro; athlete O 684, ornament O 2155, free style; no. 260
37; CG; Cinnamus; ovolo S&S fig. 47 no. 1; no. 261
37; CG; Mercator II; ovolo S&S fig. 43 no. 1, bird O 2317; no. 259
38; CG; stamped by Privatus iii die la; no. 238
Plain wares (presences only): 18/31 CG; 31 CG; 31R CG; 33 CG; 38 CG; inkwell CG; jar with incised dec CG; 31 EG; 32 EG; 33 EG
5 York CCW with barbotine dec; other CCW; African RSW; CG CCW
6 Sev; Den (plated); as RIC 61; 195+
7 The associations are loose, since only the 38 CG is from the same ditch layer as the coin. However, the other features are considered to be roughly contemporary.
8 Carver *et al* 1978, 30; Casey 1978, 41; Hartley & Dickinson 1981; Perrin 1981, 50-1

**A 135**

1 York, Yorkshire; town; Bishophill, period 2 terrace build-up
2 E
3 A
4 37; CG; Sacer; ovolo S&S fig. 22 no. 1; no. 262
37; CG; Cinnamus; ovolo S&S fig. 47 no. 1; no. 263
37; CG; Censorinus; ovolo R B105, trifid R G102, metope style; no. 264
37; CG; Doeccus; ovolo S&S fig. 44 no. 1, cupid O 455 in medallion; no. 265
37; CG; Casurius; festoon R F38; no. 266
37; CG; Doeccus; ovolo S&S fig. 44 no. 2, dolphin (2x) O 2394, warrior O 177A, metope and medallion style; no. 267
37; Heil or Rheinz; Janu I; ovolo R&F E19, rosette *ibid* O42, dog *ibid* T130, metope style; no. 268
Stamps:
31; Heil; stamped by Patruitus die 2a; no. 239
33; CG; stamped by Tintirio die la; no. 240
33; CG; stamped by Albinus ii die 6b; no. 241
33; CG; stamped by Vagiro/us die 7a; no. 242
Plain ware (presences only): 18/31 CG; 27 CG; 31 CG; 31R CG; 33 CG; 38 CG; 79/80 CG
5 NV CCW beakers with scale and rouletted dec
6 Sev; Den (plated); as RIC 61; 195+
7 The coin comes from underlying deposits and is also referred to in the previous entry. There is an inscription of *c.* 200 which may come from this context (RIB 658). The coarse pottery is dated by Perrin (1981, 51-5) to *c.* 200, on comparison with groups from Corbridge and Carpow.
8 Carver *et al* 1978, 30-2; Casey 1978; Hartley & Dickinson 1981; Perrin 1981, 51-5

**A 136**

1 York, Yorkshire; town; Skeldergate, burnt layer between roads III and IV
2 E
3 A
4 37; Blick; no details given; no. 248
37; CG; Doeccus; no details given; no. 249
Plain ware (presences only): 31 CG; 33 CG; 37 CG; 37 EG
5 NV CCW
6 Ant; Den; RIC 175; 158-9; worn; no. 294
7 A date of mid to late 3rd century is suggested by Perrin (1981, 75)
8 Carver *et al* 1978, 7; Casey 1978; Hartley & Dickinson 1981; Perrin 1981, 47

## FRANCE

**A 137**

1 Cosne-sur-Loire, Nièvre; settlement; cellar layer I
2 E
3 A
4 37; CG; Paternus II; ovolo as S&S fig. 30 no. 5; pl. III
37; CG; possibly Caletus; pl. IV nos 1-2
79/80; CG; stamped by Severianus
45 CG; 72 CG
From layer II:
37; probably Arg; pl. IV no. 6
6 Had; HS; 119-22; very worn
7 Layers I and II are associated, but are covered with rubble (layer III) and then layer IV which contained 45 EG, Arg CCW and 2 Barb Rad. Layer IV is thought by the excavator to be a deliberate later fill.
8 Bouthier 1972; 1977

**A 138**

1 Keradennec, Finistère; villa; lower occupation layers in rooms I-A, I-E and E facade
2 B
3 A
4 37; CG; Paternus II (stamped); fig. 16 from I-A
30; CG; Mercator II; fig. 26 no. 4 from I-E
37; CG; Servus II; from E facade
37; CG; probably Paternus II; fig. 23f from E facade
37; CG; Paternus II or Advocisus type ovolo; from I-A
37; CG; probably Iustus; from I-A
37; CG; sea bull O 52A used by several late potters such as Paternus, Iustus or Doeccus; from I-A
5 Lez CCW with incised dec
6 Aur (Caes); HS; 146; worn
Comm; HS; 184
7 The associations are fairly loose because the layers are equivalent to each other, according to the excavators, but not directly linked stratigraphically. There is, surprisingly, a C14 date for these layers of 190ad±100 (Gif 1304). Overlying floor levels contained a coin of Claud II. Two of the pieces listed above are composed of erotic group designs, which is unusual.
8 Sanquer & Galliou 1970

**A 139**

1 La Roche-Maurice, Finistère; villa; burnt layer
2 E
3 A
4 30; CG; Divixtus (stamped); fig. 17 no. 714C4
37; CG; Cinnamus; ovolo S&S fig. 47 no. 1; fig. 17 no. 714C5
37; CG; Paternus II; ovolo S&S fig. 30 no. 1; fig. 17 no. 714C6
37; CG; probably Casurius; fig. 17 no. 714C7
37; CG; Cinnamus or Pugnus
37; CG; P-19; stand R Q43, vase R T22
37; CG; probably Cettus
37 CG (2) not attributable to a potter
Stamps:
79R; CG; Clemens die IIId
79; CG; Venerandus
80; CG; Matarianus die Ia
Plain ware: 35 CG; 33; 18/31 CG; 36 (2); 79 (8); 80; C21 (5); 45 type CG
6 Lucius Verus; HS; 161; little wear
Had; HS; very worn
As of 1st to 2nd century; very worn
7 The coins come from floor levels immediately under the burnt layer, and therefore provide a *terminus post quem* but are not directly associated. Some of the stratigraphic details are rather vague.
8 Sanquer & Galliou 1972

**A 140**

1 Lewarde, Nord; settlement; sondage 2 level 2
2 B
3 A
4 30; CG; Doeccus or Banvus; fig. 3 no. 19
37; CG; fig. 4 no. 21
37; CG; fig. 4 no. 24
37; Arg; bird O 2259A; fig. 4 no. 20
37; Arg; fig. 4 no. 23
37; Rheinz; possibly Cobnertus III or Comitialis V; fig. 4 no. 22
18/31; CG; stamped by Attius
18/31; CG; stamped by Maternus
18/31 (2); 27 (2); 33 (2); 35/6
6 2 Gaulish coins
Dom; Ae; (3)
Traj; Ae
Had; Ae
Faust II; Ae; (2)
Aur; Den; 164
7 The level is a floor surface and associated occupation level.
8 Demolon *et al* 1979

**A 141**

1 Limoges, Haute-Vienne; town; rue Soeurs-de-la-Rivière, well
2 C
3 A
4 From layer 1:
37; CG: Iullinus
From below layer 1:
37; CG; rouletted decoration
72; CG; incised trifid and floral decoration
38 variant with high flange and very small foot ring; CG
6 From layer 1:
Claud II; Rad
Tet I; Rad (2)
From below layer 1:
Gall; Rad
Claud II; Rad (2)
Aurelian; Rad (2)
Tet I; Rad (5)
Tet II; Rad

Barb Rad + 1 illeg
7 Layer 1 is the mouth of the well, which may be a filling subsequent to the layers below, and contain redeposited material. The other layers are fairly homogeneous.
8 Berland & Lintz 1975; Roche 1975

**A 142**

1 Mâlain, Côte-d'Or; town; town house burnt layer
2 E
3 A
4 37; CG; Severus
6 Faust I (no details given)
L Verus
From associated cellar fills:
Ant (2)
Crispina (2)
Aur
Had
Max Thrax
7 The cellar fills, although not burnt, are associated by the excavator with the burnt layer and therefore provide the latest coin association.
8 Roussel 1971

**A 143**

1 Merlines, Corrèze; villa; occupation level
2 B
3 C
4 37; CG; Doeccus; ovolo S&S fig. 44 no. 2; fig. 5
6 Traj; Den; 101-2
Aur; HS; 171
8 Desbordes 1979, 480-1

**A 144**

1 St Martial-de-Gimel, Corrèze; burial
2 A
3 C
4 37; CG (5) - the drawings are too poor to allow allocation to a potter, but the general style is of CG groups III or IV
5 CCW with rouletted borders and barbotine dec
6 Comm; Ae; worn
7 The coin was found in a cinerary chest, and the samian came from around the chest.
8 Fournier 1961, 358-9

**A 145**

1 St Thiboult, Cher; villa; destruction debris over 2nd floor
2 E
3 C
4 37; EG - Rheinz or a late-derivative workshop; bird as O 2222 = R&F T255 - poorly formed, rosette as *ibid* O45, concentric circles and rosette borders, no parallel for style; fig. 16 (published upside-down)
Other sherds of samian were found but no details are available.
6 Coins of late 3rd to 4th century date
7 The association is not secure because the context was destruction debris, and the sherd may have been redeposited.
8 Picard 1966, 247-9

## LOW COUNTRIES

**A 146**

1 Titelberg, Grand-Duché de Luxembourg; *vicus*; cellar 4
2 E
3 A
4 37; Trier; bifid as ovolo F 908 (late ware); Taf. VII no. 1
37; Trier; ovolo as basal wreath F 943, ovolo not in F (probable late ware); Taf. VII no. 4
37; Arg; Tocca or successor; Taf. VII no. 3
37; Arg; ovolo as F 464; Taf. VII no. 2
40 EG; 35 EG; 38 EG (4); 45 EG (10) with devolved lion's head spouts; Nied 14 EG (2); 23 EG; O&P pl. 65 no. 5 EG; O&P pl. 61 no. 5 EG
5 Rhenish CCW beakers with barbotine dec and mottos; Rhenish CCW beakers with incised dec; CCW indented and rouletted beakers; Speicher type inturned rim bowls
6 44 coins in all, only summary given here:
Celtic (2); Aug (1); Had (2HS, 1 Dup); Ant (2 HS); Aur (2 HS, 1 Dup); Valerian (1 Ant); Claud II (1 Rad); Post (1 Rad); Victorin (6 Rad); Tet I-II (17 Rad); Barb Rad of Gallic Emperors (7); latest regular coin 271-3
7 A coin of Comm (HS) was found in the earth fill beside the cellar, and may provide a *terminus post quem* for its construction. The fill of the cellar consisted of burnt building debris and objects.
8 Thill, Metzler & Weiller 1971; Huld-Zetsche 1971a, 245

**A 147**

1 Braives, Liège; *vicus*; sector C pit 15
2 C
3 A
4 37; Arg; ovolo C&G fig. 54B no. 05, bird *ibid* fig. 56E; no. 76
45 EG with lion-head spout
6 Aur; HS; 172-7
8 Brulet 1981

**A 148**

1 Gerpinnes, Hainault; burial
2 A
3 B
4 37; Arg; ovolo Ricken 1934 Taf. XIIIB; fig. 2F
6 Had; As; 134-8
Ant; Dup ; 157-8
Faust II; Ae; 161-75
7 A casual discovery, subsequently checked by controlled excavation.
8 Brulet 1968

**A 149**

1 Haccourt, Liège; villa; destruction levels
2 E
3 B
4 From main part of villa:
37; La Mad; ovolo Ricken 1934 Taf. VIIB; fig. 11 no. 6
37; La Mad; ovolo Ricken 1934 Taf. VIIC; fig. 11 no. 7
37 (3 pieces); Arg; probably ovolo C potter; rosette in place of ovolo Ricken 1934 Taf. XII no. 12; fig. 11 no. 8
37 (2 pieces); Arg; spiral in place of ovolo F taf. VII no. 56; fig. 11 no. 9
37; possibly CG; ovolo as R B102 (Advocisus, P-19, Prisus/Clemens); fig. 11 no. 10
Late Arg ware form Chenet 320 with roller-stamp dec
Plain ware (presences only - not quantified): 37 EG; 18/31 EG; 33 EG; 32 EG; 40 EG; 45 EG; 37 CG: 18/31 CG; 27 CG; 31 CG; 33 CG; 38 CG; 40 CG; 45 CG; 27 SG; 18/31 SG; 35 SG; 35/36 SG
From the bath-house:
29; SG; fig. 12 no. 1
37; CG; Cinnamus-type winding scroll fragment; fig. 12 no. 3

37; Arg; ovolo C potter; fig. 12 no. 5
Plain ware (presences only - not quantified): 27 EG - probably Blick - stamped by Tocca (2); 18/31 EG; 27 EG; 33 EG; 40 EG (2); 45 EG; 18/31 CG; 27 CG; 31 CG; 33 CG; 18 SG; 18/31 SG; 27 SG; 33 SG
6 From the main part of the villa:
Aug; As (2)
Nero; Semis
Dom; HS
Traj; Dup (copy)
Car/J Domna; Den (copy)
3rd century empress; Den
From the bath-house:
Claud; As
Vesp; As
Had; As
Post; Rad; 263
7 The excavator states that the finds are nearly all from the destruction debris, but the finds reports do not have provenances. All the samian and coins have been given, since much is late, but there is clearly an admixture of earlier material. The roller-stamped Arg piece is of some interest in its context.
8 De Boe 1975; 1976

**A150**

1 Jette, Bruxelles; villa; burnt layer in cellar
2 E
3 A
4 30; Rheinz; Primitivus I; fig. 6 no. 2
33 CG; 52 Rheinz
5 Trier CCW motto beaker
6 Had; As; very worn
Valerian; Ant; RIC 92; 254; good condition
8 Matthys 1973

**A 151**

1 Pommeroeul, Hainault; *vicus*; debris over building, layer b
2 E
3 A
4 30 (2 pieces); EG; rouletted dec, slightly flaring profile; fig. 6
6 Alex; HS; 228
Under this layer was an occupation level with a coin hoard of Sev-Valerian (258)
7 Possibly redeposited during the 3rd century.
8 Demory & Huysecom 1984

**A 152**

1 Tongeren, Limburg; suburb of town; extra-mural building, ditch south of building A
2 D
3 B
4 37; CG; Cinnamus; pl. III no. 2
37; CG; Cinnamus; pl. III no. 3
37; CG; Pugnus; pl. III no. 4
37; CG; X-5; Hercules O 760; pl. IV no. 7
37; Arg; ovolo Ricken 1934 Taf. XII C; pl. IV no. 2
18/31; CG; stamped by Reditus
C21 EG
6 Level associated with the ditch has:
Elag; Ant; RIC 138; 218-22
7 The association is fairly loose.
8 Mertens & Vanvinckenroye 1975

**A 153**

1 Tongeren, Limburg; suburb of town; extra-mural building, quarry cutting
2 E
3 B
4 37; Arg; ware with ovolo Ricken 1934 Taf. XIII B-C; pl. IV no. 1
6 Had; Ae; worn
Had; HS; worn
Gord III/Phil II; Ant (hybrid copy)
7 The quarry is not closed stratigraphically and may date to a later period, but all the Roman material could be contemporary.
8 Mertens & Vanvinckenroye 1975

**A 154**

1 Tournai, Hainault; town; La Loucherie, layer above 2nd floor
2 B
3 A
4 37; Trier; ovolo F 954
37; probably EG; little surviving decoration; fig. 11 no. 14
Lud SMb; Rheinz; with barbotine dec
6 From burning layer overlying were coins of Phil I, Gall, Claud II, and Tet I (copy),
7 Not a true association as such. The building appears to have been erected in the mid-2nd century, and the samian listed above comes from the level immediately below the coin-dated destruction.
8 Mertens & Remy 1974

**A 155**

1 Druten, Utrecht; river-barge; layer within the barge
2 B
3 A
4 37; Rheinz; Julius II-Julianus I; fig. 8 no. 2
5 Rhenish CCW beaker
6 HS; very worn; dated to 2nd or early 3rd century by the Kon. Penningkabinet
7 The finds appear to be part of the barge's inventory.
8 Hulst & Lehmann 1976

**A 156**

1 Rockanje, Zuid-Holland; settlement; general finds
2 F
3 C
4 37; Trier; Censor, Criciro, Tordilo, or Amator; afb. 3.1
37; Trier; Werkstatt II; afb. 3.2
37; Rheinz; possibly Atto (R&F T138a or b, P142a); afb. 3.3
37; Rheinz; probably Julius I or Lupus; afb. 3.4
37; Rheinz; Cerialis I, Comitalis I-II or contemporary; ovolo R&F E2; afb. 3.6b
37; Arg; ornament as F 448; afb. 3.5
37 EG (5 fragments); Lud Sb (2); 45; 33 EG; 40 (2); Lud SMb/c EG;
2 pieces of Trier fabric
6 Ant; Dup; 148-9; very worn
Comm; HS; 190; very worn
2nd or 3rd century Quadrans; very worn
7 The group is fairly homogeneous, but it is from casual discoveries on a building site. Probably only one pit or level is involved.
8 Bogaers 1952

**A 157**

1 Utrecht; fort; well; finds groups 61, 68, 72, 78, 80, 83
2 C

3 B
4 Few detaiis are given in the report:
37 EG (2); 37 Trier as F Taf. XX; 37 Rheinz (2); 45 EG (2); 43/ Lud RSM EG; 33 EG; 18/31 Trier stamped by Minutius with graffito 'ex ge[r inf]'; U Arg
6 HS very worn
7 The well is part of the stone period of the fort, usually dated from the late 2nd to mid-3rd centuries. Van Giffen (1948, 52-3) gives the date as 190+ on the basis of tile stamps and stratigraphy.
8 Van Giffen *et al* 1934; Van Giffen 1948

**A 158**

1 Zwammerdam, Zuid-Holland; fort; Period III general finds
2 F
3 A
4 Summary only:
29; SG; pre-Flavian (3)
37; SG; late Flavian (3)
37; CG; Donnaucus (1)
37; Blick; LAL (1)
37; Blick; 'master-potter' (2)
37; Blick; ware with ovolo K&S Taf. 82 no. 30 (1)
37; Blick; ware with ovolo *ibid* no. 32 (3)
37; probably Mittel; Saturninus/Satto (4)
37; La Mad; ware with ovolo Ricken 1934 Taf. VII A (2)
37; La Mad; ware with ovolo *ibid* B (1)
37; La Mad; ware with ovolo *ibid* H (1)
37; La Mad; ware with ovolo *ibid* K3 (1)
37; La Mad; Sacer (2)
37; La Mad (1)
37; Arg; Gesatus-Tribunus (3)
37; Arg; ware with ovolo E (2)
37; Arg; Germanus-Africanus or Verus (1)
37; Arg; ovolo C&G fig. 54bis, R2 (1)
37; Trier; Werkstatt I (3)
37; Trier; Werkstatt II (28)
37; Trier; Maiiaaus group (7)
37; Trier; Comitialis (6)
37; Trier; Dexter (4)
37; Trier; Censor (2 - 1 stamped)
37; Trier; Censor and Dexter's successors (15)
37; Trier; Amator (5)
37; Trier; Tordilo group (4)
37; Trier; Atillus-Pussosus (5)
37; Trier; Afer (13)
37; Trier (4)
37; Rheinz; Janu II (1)
37; Rheinz; B F Attoni (1)
37; Rheinz; Belsus I (1)
37; Rheinz; Cerialis I (1)
37; Rheinz; Respectus (1)
37; Rheinz; Comitialis II (1)
37; Rheinz; Comitialis III (1)
37; Rheinz; Comitialis V (1)
37; Rheinz; Julius I-Lupus (1)
37; Rheinz; Julius I (2)
37; Rheinz; Julius II-Julianus I (1)
37; Rheinz; ovolo R&F E17 (1)
37; Rheinz; ovolo *ibid* E44 (1)
From underlying period II:
SG (34); CG (8); Blick (3); Saturninus-Satto (8); La Mad (19); Arg (11); Sinzig (1); Trier (15, of which; Trier II, 5; Comitialis, 6; Censor group, 2; Amator, 1); Rheinz (1 - Janu II)
6 Sev; Den; RIC 479; 194-7
Vesp; Dup
Traj; HS; BMC 772
Traj; Dup; very worn
Aur; Dup; BMC 1190; 164+
7 Period III is placed by the excavator after AD 178 on the basis of tile stamps of Didius Julianus (governor in that year) associated with the stone walling. There is a little late Trier ware from surface finds (Dubitatus, 6; Primanus, 8; late wares, 2).
8 Haalebos 1977

## GERMANY

**A 159**

1 Beiderweis, Niederbayern; fort; trench 2, pit A
2 C
3 B
4 37; Rheinz; Primitivus I
6 Aur; Dup; RIC 1591; 178
7 The sherd came from higher in the pit than the coin, but the stratigraphy appears to be homogeneous.
8 Schönberger 1956

**A 160**

1 Cannstatt, Baden-Württemburg; cemetery; grave 7
2 A
3 B
4 37; probably Kräherwald; Reginus; Taf. 2 no. A2
6 Had; As; RIC 678; 125-8; very worn
8 Nierhaus 1959

**A 161**

1 Cannstatt, Baden-Württemburg; cemetery; grave 16
2 A
3 B
4 37; Rheinz; Reginus I; Taf. 2 no. H7
37 (4 pieces); Rheinz; Comitialis V; Taf. 2 nos H5-6
37 (14 pieces); Rheinz; Comitialis VI; Taf. 2 nos H3-4
37 (2 pieces); Waiblingen; Reginus; Taf. 2 nos H1-2
37 (5 pieces); Waiblingen; ovolo B group; Taf. 2 nos H8-10
32 EG (4-5); 33 EG
6 Had; As; very worn
Lucilla; As; RIC (Aur) 1752; 164-9; slightly worn
8 Nierhaus 1959

**A 162**

1 Cannstatt, Baden-Württemburg; cemetery; grave 82
2 A
3 B
4 37; Kräherwald; Reginus; Taf. 10 no. H3
37; Kräherwald; Reginus; Taf. 10 no.H4
6 Ant; As; RIC 818; 145-61; slightly worn
8 Nierhaus 1959

**A 163**

1 Degerfeld in Butzbach, Hessen; fort; general finds from prestone levels
2 F
3 B
4 From sealed deposits:
37; CG; X-6; Fundn. 8106
37; Rheinz; Cobnertus III; Fundn. 8106
37; Arg; ware with ovolo B; Fundn. 8049
37; Trier; Maiiaaus; Fundn. 8049
37; Rheinz; Reginus I; Fundn. 8049
37; Rheinz; Cobnertus III; Fundn. 8049

From other deposits;
37; SG; Mascuus
37; EG; Saturninus-Satto (2)
37; La Mad; ware with ovolo K1
37; Arg; ware with ovolo A
37; Arg; ware with ovolo A/B
37; Arg; ware with ovolo D
37; Blick; 'master potter'
37; Trier; ovolo F 955/6
37; EG - unlocated; Ricken 1934 group 1
6 Had; As; 134-8; very good condition
7 The 2 sealed deposits from which the first 6 pieces came are less mixed than the unsealed material and may immediately precede the building of the stone fort. Simon (1968, 16) puts the end of the earth fort at 150-60, partly on the basis of the Trier sherds in the earlier levels.
8 Simon 1968

**A 164**

1 Froitzheim, Nordrhein-Westfalen; defended enclosure; fill of inner and outer ditches
2 D
3 A
4 From inner ditch:
37; Trier; ovolo F 594, shell F 708; fig. 24 no. 1
37; Trier; ovolo, blurred
37 (4 pieces); Arg; large square ovolo
37; Rheinz; fragment only
From outer ditch, lowest level:
37; Trier; Censor or Amator; ornament F 794 in place of ovolo; fig. 24 no. 2
From outer ditch, middle level:
37; Trier; ornaments as F 842 and 853; fig. 24 no. 3
From outer ditch, upper level:
37; EG - unknown kiln site; column as F 879, bifid F 902, rosette as F 842, other decoration not in F or R&F; fig. 24 no. 4
Alzey 1; Arg; roller stamp decoration, type 97
From elsewhere on the site:
37; Rheinz; Julianus II
37; Rheinz; Augustinus II
37 EG (2)
Plain ware from the site as a whole, given as vessel, not fragment, counts:
45 EG (30); 43 EG (5); 44 EG (15); Lud SMa and SMc (3); 32 EG (8-10); 36 EG (5); 31 EG (5-7); Lud Ti (3); 33 EG (3); 38 EG (3); cups EG (7); Lud VSb EG; 72 EG with incised dec; Lud VMk EG with barbotine dec; vases EG (3); U EG (11)
6 From inner ditch (summary only):
Gall (4); Claud II (2); Aurel (1); Post (1); Victorin (1); Tet I (17); Const II (1); Valens (1); 1st-2nd century As very worn
From outer ditch, middle level:
Tet I (2)
From outer ditch, upper level:
Tet I (5)
7 The construction, use, and filling of the ditches is placed by the excavator in the period shortly before and after AD 274. Most of the material is contemporary with this, and includes some very late Trier samian types (cf Huld-Zetsche 1971a, 244). There is a late 2nd to early 3rd century villa nearby, but contamination seems slight. Some 4th century material is present, particularly in the upper filling of the ditches.
8 Barfield 1968; Hagen 1968; Johns 1968

**A 165**

1 Gauting, Oberbayern; *vicus*; ‚Scherbenlager'
2 E
3 C
4 Summary only:
29; SG (4)
37; SG; mainly late Flavian - early Trajanic (56); may include some Banassac pieces
37; Banassac (32)
37; CG; Donnaucus style (1)
37; CG; Quintilianus group (5)
37; CG; Arcanus (1)
37; CG; X-6 (7)
37; CG; Sacer-Attianus (4)
37; CG; Divixtus (1)
37; CG; Criciro (2)
37; CG; Cettus (1)
37; CG; Casurius (1)
37; CG; Albucius (1)
37; CG; Drusus II (1)
37; CG; Acurio (1)
37; CG; Cinnamus (67, of which 3 stamped in mould with large stamp; 16 ovolo 1; 5 ovolo 2; 11 ovolo 3; 1 ovolo 4; 1 with ovolo as S&S pl. 157 no. 13)
37; CG; Paternus II (1 - ovolo 3)
37; CG (7)
37; Heil; F-master (1)
37; Heil; Ciriuna (2)
37; Heil (1)
37; Rheinz; Janu I (2)
37; Rheinz; Reginus I (8)
37; Rheinz; B F Attoni or Firmus (1)
37; Rheinz; Cobnertus III (1)
37; Rheinz; Janu II (3)
37; Rheinz; Respectus (1)
37; Rheinz; Verecundus (1)
37; Rheinz (5)
37; West; Helenius (1)
6 Tib; As
Had; Dup
Had; As
Max; Den; 235-8
7 The deposit is a burnt layer *c* 1 m thick, consisting mainly of samian ware: one sixth decorated out of 4000 rims/walls and 900 bases. There was another deposit 50 m to the north, mainly non-samian pottery and glass. Several of the buildings in the *vicus* had been burnt, possibly in the late Trajanic period. This may account for part of the deposit, which was possibly clearance from the burnt buildings, but there is a great deal of later pottery. Possibly there was a second fire, or the deposit may have been built up over a period, or its stratigraphy has not been properly recognized during the long period of salvage recording in the wake of building operations.
8 Kellner 1960a (FMRD I, i, 1266); Walke & Walke 1966; Weber 2013, 198-9

**A 166**

1 Heddernheim, Hessen; town; Parz. 106, occupation level
2 B
3 A
4 37; Rheinz; Helenius; Taf. 1 no. 1a-b
37; Rheinz; Attillus (stamped in mould); Taf. 1 no. 2a-b
6 Plautilla; Den; RIC (Car) 361; 202-4
8 Nuber 1969

**A 167**

1 Heddernheim, Hessen; town; Parz. 106, well
2 C
3 A
4 37; Rheinz; Lupus (stamped in mould); Taf. 1 no. 3
32 (2 pieces); Rheinz; stamped by Belatullus
6 Dom; Quadrans; RIC 427; 84-96
Faust I; HS; RIC (Ant) 1146a; 141+
L Verus; HS; RIC (Aur) 1284; 161
HS very worn, late 1st/early 2nd century
8 Nuber 1969

**A 168**

1 Heddernheim, Hessen; town; Parz. 302/21, cellar
2 E
3 B
4 37; Rheinz; Julius II-Julianus I (stamped); Abb. 3 no. 1
37; Rheinz; Julius II-Julianus I, Comitialis V, Victorinus II or Severianus; Abb. 3 no. 2
37; Rheinz; Julius II-Julianus I, Janu II, Victorinus II or contemporary; Abb. 3 no. 3
37; Rheinz; Comitialis I; made from reused mould (Spätausformung); Fasold 1994, Abb. 2, no. 4
33 EG; 31 EG; 43 or 45 EG; beaker Oelmann 1914 type 24b with incised dec; all indicated as presences only
6 Faust II; Dup
Max Thrax; HS; 235-6
Treb Gall; Ant; RIC 37; 251-2
Gall; Ant; 258; good condition
7 A division in the stratigraphy is alluded to by the excavators - the 3 earlier coins coming from the lower level, and the coin of Gall from higher up. The exact context of the sherds is not indicated in the excavation report, but Nuber (1969, 147) indicates that the samian was found in the same level as the coin of Treb Gall, whilst Fasold (1994, 72) states that the mass of the pottery came from a level associated with the coins of Faust and Max Thrax. The pottery was re-examined by Fasold, who also identified a bowl by Comitialis I, made in a reused mould, probably in the late period of Rheinzabern production.
8 Fasold 1994; Fischer & Schleiermacher 1962; Nuber 1969, 147

**A 169**

1 Heddernheim, Hessen; town; Parz. 359/78, well, burnt debris level
2 C
3 A
4 37; Rheinz; Julius II-Julianus I; Taf. 3 no. 4
37; Rheinz; Julius II-Julianus I (stamped in mould); Taf. 3 no. 5
Plain ware, probably all Rheinz: Lud SMc (2); Lud SR var; Nied 15; 43 (2); 33
6 Aur; HS; RIC 1029; 171-2
Alex; Den; RIC 235; 231-5
Otacilia; Ant; RIC (Phil I) 127/8; 246-8
8 Nuber 1969

**A 170**

1 Heddernheim, Hessen; town; Parz. 515/108, cellar
2 E
3 A
4 From the interior of the cellar:
37; Rheinz; Marcellus II; Taf. 2 no. 1
37; Rheinz; Primitivus IV; Taf. 2 no. 7
37; Rheinz; Julius II-Julianus I; Taf. 2 no. 3
37; Rheinz; Julius II-Julianus I; Taf. 2 no. 5
37; Rheinz; Julius II-Julianus I; Taf. 2 no. 6
37; Rheinz; Julius II-Julianus I; Taf. 2 no. 4
37; Rheinz; Julius II-Julianus I (stamped in mould); Taf. 2 no. 10
37; Rheinz; Victorinus III; Taf. 2 no. 8
37; Rheinz; Julianus II; Taf. 2 no. 9
37; Trier; ovolo as F 943, dog F 649, lobster F 694, shell F 707, bird Gard 1937, T128, metope style; Taf. 2 no. 11
Lud SSa Rheinz; Lud SMc (3 pieces) with barbotine dec
From the entrance to the cellar:
43 Rheinz with barbotine dec; 32 Rheinz stamped by Comitialis
6 From the entrance to the cellar:
Had; Dup; RIC 974i; 134-8
Ant; HS; RIC 946; 155-6
Ant; HS; RIC 776; 145-61
Sev; Den; RIC 351A; 193
Sev; HS; RIC 667; 194
Sev; Den; RIC 84; 196-7
Geta; Den; RIC 18; 200-2
Elag; Den; RIC 100; 218-22
Elag; Den; RIC 131; 218-22
Alex; Den; RIC 29; 223
Alex; Den; RIC 70; 227
7 The group of coins is possibly a scattered hoard. The entrance and interior of the cellar are apparently the same stratigraphically.
8 Nuber 1969

**A 171**

1 Holzhausen, Hessen; fort; black layer east of building A
2 B
3 B
4 37 (2 pieces); Rheinz; Comitialis IV (stamped in mould); A11
37; Rheinz; Comitialis IV; joins with pieces in deposits **A 175-6**; A12
37; Rheinz; ware with ornament R&F O382/3; A63
Nied 19 EG; 43 EG; 45 EG (3); Nied 56 EG
6 Car; Den; as RIC 134; 201-6; very worn; no. 13
Alex; Den; RIC 14; 222; no. 18
7 The association is slightly uncertain, as the layer probably accumulated over the abandoned fort and contained mixed material.
8 Nass 1934; Pferdehirt 1976

**A 172**

1 Holzhausen, Hessen; fort; black layer over pit 22
2 B
3 B
4 37; Rheinz; Julius II-Julianus I; joins with piece from deposit **A 173**; A43
37; Rheinz; Statutus I; A74
37; Trier; Afer group; A150
37; Trier; Dubitatus-Dubitus; A162
37 EG (3); 44 EG; 45 EG (2)
6 J Soemias; Den; no. 15
7 The association is slightly uncertain because the material comes from an abandonment accumulation.
8 Nass 1934; Pferdehirt 1976

**A 173**

1 Holzhausen, Hessen; fort; cellar K1
2 E
3 B
4 37; Rheinz; Comitialis III; A8

37; Rheinz; Lupus; A18
37; Rheinz; Verecundus II; A22
37; Rheinz; Primitivus I; A32
37; Rheinz; Primitivus I; A33
37; Rheinz; Primitivus III; A37
37; Rheinz; Primitivus IV; A38
37 (4 pieces); Rheinz; Julius II-Julianus I (joins with a piece from deposit **A 172**); A43
37; Rheinz; Julius II-Julianus I; A50
37; Rheinz; Julius II-Julianus I; A56
37; Rheinz; Victor II-Januco; A67
37; Rheinz; Lucanus, ware with ovolo E8 or Victorinus I; A77
37; Rheinz; Janu I, Marcellus II or Primitivus I; A92
37; Rheinz; Cerialis VI; Attillus, Marcellus II, Primitivus I or III; A98
37; Trier; Werkstatt II; A11
37; Trier; Censor; A128
37; Trier; Comitialis, Afer, Dubitatus or Paternianus; A180
37; Trier; Dexter, Dubitatus-Dubitus or ware Gard 1937 Taf. 21 nos 1-8; A181
37 EG (10); 44 EG; 45 EG (10); 32 EG (3); 33 EG; 40 EG; Niederbieber 19 EG; ibid I2b EG (3); ibid 27 EG; cup EG
6 Lucilla; HS; RIC (Aur) 1730; no. 9
J Maesa; Den; RIC (Elag) 268; no. 16
Alex; Den; RIC 73; 228; no. 24
7 The finds come from various parts of the cellar.
8 Nass 1934; Pferdehirt 1976

**A 174**

1 Holzhausen, Hessen; fort; drain channel in cellar K1
2 E - or silt in drain
3 B
4 37; Rheinz; Julius II-Julianus I; A47
37; Rheinz; Julius II-Julianus I; A52
37; Rheinz; ovolo R&F E25 (used by number of group 11 potters); A100
37 EG; Nied 12b EG (2)
6 Comm; HS; RIC (Aur) 1530; 175; no. 10
7 The general fill of the cellar is associated with this context, and has a coin of Alex (deposit **A 173**).
8 Nass 1934; Pferdehirt 1976

**A 175**

1 Holzhausen, Hessen; fort; on Roman 'surface' between well 1 and fort rampart
2 E
3 B
4 37; EG - unlocated; ware with ovolo X (Schleiermacher 1958, 74); A4
37; Rheinz; Comitialis IV (joins with pieces in deposits **A 171** and **A 176**); A12
37; Rheinz; Marcellus II; A28
37; Rheinz; Firmus II or Belsus III; A76
37 (3); 45 (2) - both probably EG
6 Alex; Den; RIC 27; 223; no. 19
7 The association is not absolutely secure.
8 Nass 1934; Pferdehirt 1976

**A 176**

1 Holzhausen, Hessen; fort; pit 19
2 C
3 B
4 37; Rheinz; Comitialis IV; joins with pieces in deposits **A 171** and **A 175**; A12
37; Rheinz; probably Firmus II; A16
37; Rheinz; Primitivus I; A31
37; Rheinz; Julius II-Julianus I; A46
37; Rheinz; Victor II-Januco; A64
37; Trier; Afer; A148
37 EG (2); Nied 19 EG; Nied 21b EG; 45 EG (8); 32 EG (3); Nied 5b EG; Nied 27 EG; 33 EG (4); U Rheinz (stamped by Vitalis)
6 Ant; Den; corroded; no. 3
Alex; Den; RIC 74; 228; slightly worn; no. 22
8 Nass 1934; Pferdehirt 1976

**A 177**

1 Künzing, Niederbay; fort; hollow 170
2 C
3 B
4 37; CG; Cinnamus; ovolo S&S fig. 47 no. 1; no. 36
37; probably Chémery; no. 37
37; Rheinz; Reginus I (stamped in mould); no. 43
37; Rheinz; Cerialis III; no. 44
37; Rheinz; Cerialis V; no. 45
37; Rheinz; Comitialis V; no. 51
37; Rheinz; Comitialis VI; no. 52
37; Rheinz; ware with ovolo E25/26; no. 58
37; Rheinz; Victor I; no. 75
37; Rheinz; B F Attoni or Belsus II; no. 78
37; Rheinz; ware with ovolo E25/26 or Attillus; no. 79
37 Rheinz
6 Ant; As; as RIC 569; 139-56; very corroded
7 The deposit may apparently have built up over a period.
8 Schönberger 1975

**A 178**

1 Künzing, Niederbayern; fort; trench 2 pit 83
2 C
3 A
4 37; Rheinz; Cerialis VI; no. 20
37; Rheinz; Primitivus IV; no. 28
32; Rheinz; stamped by Peppo; no. 43
6 Car; Den; RIC 251; 211-7
7 The features were dug separately from the upper levels, which were dug by the planum method.
8 Kellner 1959; Schönberger 1959

**A 179**

1 Künzing, Niederbayern; fort; well 134
2 C
3 B
4 37; SG; late ware; no. 22
37; Banassac; late ware; no. 17
37; Rheinz; Cerialis V or Comitialis II; no. 46
37; Rheinz; Comitialis IV; no. 48
37; Rheinz; Respectus or Belsus II; no. 55
37; Rheinz; Florentinus (stamped in mould); no. 56
37; Rheinz; ware with ovolo E 25/26; no. 57
37; Rheinz; Marcellus II; no. 64
37; Rheinz; Primitivus I; no. 65
37; Rheinz; Julius II-Julianus I (stamped in mould by Julius); no. 69
37 Rheinz
6 Elag; Den; RIC 88; 218-22
8 Schönberger 1975

**A 180**

1 Künzing, Niederbayern; fort; well 487
2 C
3 B
4 37; CG; Cinnamus; ovolo S&S fig. 47 no. 3; no. 31

37; CG; Cinnamus; ovolo S&S fig. 47 no. 2; no. 32
37; Heil; Ciriuna; no. 38
37; Rheinz; Belsus I (stamped in mould); no. 53
6 Republic; Den; GkE-Syd. 1215ff; 32-1BC; very worn
8 Schönberger 1975

**A 181**

1 Leonardspfunzen, Oberbay; cemetery; grave 75
2 A
3 B
4 37 (25+ pieces); Rheinz; Cobnertus I; Abb. 24 no. 2
37 (5 pieces); Rheinz; Firmus I; Abb. 25 nos 1-2
37 (11 pieces); Rheinz; Mammilianus; Abb. 25 nos 4-5
37; Rheinz; Janu I, Cerialis I, Comitialis I-II, Belsus I, Reginus II or Augustinus III; Abb. 25 no. 3
30 (8 pieces); Pfaffenhofen; ovolo type 27; Abb. 23 no. 1 and Abb. 24 no. 1
32; EG; stamped by Sodalis
32; Rheinz; stamped by Firmus
33; Rheinz; stamped by Firmus
31; Rheinz; stamped by Belatullus
32 EG (3); O&P pl. 55 no. 22 EG; 33 West; cup EG
6 Had; As; 125-38; very worn
7 The brooch from this grave was very similar to another from grave 73, which was associated with 4 Ant Ae coins (but no pottery recorded).
8 Kellner 1968

**A 182**

1 Mainz, Rheinland-Pfalz; town; construction level for town wall, Interfactorbank layer 7
2 E
3 A
4 37; Rheinz; Comitialis III or B F Attoni; Abb. 3 no. 3
43; EG; with barbotine dec
6 Sev; Den; RIC 152; 201
7 The layer is not under the wall, but is associated by the excavator with its foundation trench. The material from the layer is fairly homogeneous, with apparently little redeposited.
8 Stümpel 1978

**A 183**

1 Mainz-Kastel, Hessen; fort; pit
2 C
3 B
4 37; Rheinz; Attillus; Abb. 4 no. 3
53 Rheinz with barbotine dec; 43 Rheinz with barbotine dec
33 Rheinz (3)
6 Sev; Den
Car; Den
A number of clay coin-moulds with coin types up to Elag; Den; 221
8 Behrens 1921

**A 184**

1 Marzoll, Oberbayern; villa; period 5, dump deposits
2 E
3 A
4 From between earlier and later floors in room 5:
37 (5 pieces); West; Comitialis (stamped by Ripanus on bowl); Abb. 9 nos 1-5
37; CG; Cinnamus; ovolo S&S Fig. 47 no. 3; Abb. 9 no. 9
33 West; 32 West; 31 West
From rubbish deposit later than the building construction phase of period 5:
37; Pfaffenhofen; ovolo Karnitsch 1955 Taf. 101E
37 EG; 18/31 Rheinz; 33 West; plate as O&P pl. 53 no. 21 West
6 From the rubbish deposit:
Ant; HS; RIC 766; 145-61
7 The first group is probably earlier than the second.
8 Christlein 1963

**A 185**

1 Murrhardt, Baden-Württemburg; fort; burning level over period I
2 E
3 A
4 37; Rheinz; Cerialis III; no. 18
37; Blick; later group; ovolo K&S Taf. 82 no. 31; no. 19
37; Blick; later group; ovolo K&S Taf. 82 no. 34; no. 20
37 Rheinz (2 pieces)
6 Aur; Dup; RIC 900; 164-5; no. 6
7 This group of pottery and coins provides the dating evidence for the end of period I of the fort. The samian comes from the burning level itself, and the coin from a dump cut into the burning level which is, however, earlier than period II construction levels. The period commenced with the building of the outer *limes* in the 150s, and a well associated with period I construction had a dendrochronological date of AD 159.
8 Krause 1984, 325-6

**A 186**

1 Neuburg-an-der-Donau, Niederbayern; cemetery; grave 10
2 A
3 A
4 37; Rheinz; Reginus I (stamped in mould); Abb. 3 no. 39 and Abb. 12
6 Had; As; RIC 669; 125-8
8 Hübener 1957

**A 187**

1 Niederbieber, Rheinland-Pfalz; fort; general finds
2 F
3 C
4 Attributions based on drawings in Oelmann 1914, Taf. VI-VIII:
37; Trier; Werkstatt I (2 - possibly from reused moulds)
37; Trier; Werkstatt II (19 - 17 possibly from reused moulds)
37; Trier; Censor (10 - 2 stamped in mould)
37; Trier; Dexter (8)
37; Trier; Censor group (7)
37; Trier; Censor/Dexter successors (8)
37; Trier; Criciro (2 - stamped in mould)
37; Trier; Censor or Criciro or Dexter (1)
37; Trier; Comitialis (4 - 1 stamped in mould)
37; Trier; Amator (6)
37; Trier; Amator or Atillus-Pussosus (1)
37; Trier; Tordilo (7)
37; Trier; Maiiaaus (13 - 1 stamped in mould)
37; Trier; Afer-Marinus (1)
37; Trier; Primanus (3 +1 possible)
37; Trier; Dubitus-Dubitatus (1 - stamped in mould)
37; Rheinz; probably Firmus I (1)
37; Rheinz; Cerialis V (1)
37; Rheinz; Comitialis VI (2 stamped in mould)
37; Rheinz; Victorinus II (1 stamped in mould)
37; Rheinz; Pupus (1 stamped in mould)
37; Rheinz; Lupus (1 stamped in mould)
37; Rheinz; Pervincus (1)

Plain ware (all EG):
31 (30); Lud Tc etc (2); Nied 3; 36 (8); 32 (160); Lud Ti[1] and Tf (7); 46 (2); Lud Bb and Bc (3); 33 (30-40); 40 (70); Lud Schd (10); 41 (15); Lud Nb (7); Nied 14; Nied 15 (4); Lud Se etc (15); 37 (400); 44 (25-30); Lud SMa etc (15); 38 (4); 43 (25); 45 (150-200); Nied 23; 54 (10); Lud Vd-g (3); Lud VSb etc (4); Lud MVg etc (5); Nied 24d (2); Lud VMa; 53 (5); Lud Kc (6); Lud KMa (3)
6 Tile stamps from the bath building in the fort provide an apparent *terminus post quem* of 185-92.
Coins from excavations of 1897-8 and 1900:
Traj HS; Had Den; Had HS; Aur Ae; Lucilla Ae; Sev Den (5); J Domna Den; Car Den (3); Alex Den (3); Alex HS; J Mamaea Den; Gord III Ant (5); Phil I Ant (3); Decius Ant; Etruscilla Ant (2); Gall Ant or Rad
Coin hoard I (all Ant):
Car; Elag; Balbinus; Gord III (77); Phil I (72); Otacilia Severa (11); Phil II (8); Decius (7); Etruscilla (4); Etruscus (2); Treb Gall (4); Volusian (2); Valerian (2); Gall - dubious - otherwise latest coin dates to 254
Coin hoard II:
Denarii - Clod Alb (3); Sev (17); J Domna; Car (5); Geta; Elag (11); J Paula; J Maesa (3); Alex (32); J Mamaea (7); Max (2); Maximus; Gord III (4)
Antoniniani - Macrinus; Elag; Gord III (85); Phil I (39); Otacilia Severa (7); Phil II (13); Decius (17); Etruscilla (10); Etruscus (5); Treb Gall (20); Volusian (20); Aemilian (2); Valerian I (29); Gall (34); Salonina (10); Valerian II (6); Saloninus (2)
7 There is certainly more decorated samian than listed here, since passing references to other pieces have been made in publications since Oelmann 1914. In all possibility, the published pieces have been selected, in view of the high incidence of stamps in the Rheinz section.
8 Huld-Zetsche 1972, 70, 91, Taf 66; Oelmann 1914; Ritterling 1901; 1911; 1936

**A 188**

1 Pfaffenhofen, Oberbayern; samian kiln centre; trench B/1969, layer V, destruction debris
2 E
3 A
4 37; Rheinz; Reginus I
37; Rheinz; B F Attoni; Abb. 20 no. 6
37; Rheinz; Julius II-Julianus I; Abb. 20 no. 7
37; West; Comitialis (67 pieces, 1 mould); see Abb. 18-21
37; West; Helenius (17 pieces); see Abb. 18-21
30; West; Helenius; Abb. 19 nos 3 and 7
37; West; Iassus; Abb. 18 no. 11
37; West; Onniorix (2 pieces)
37; West; Decminus (stamped in mould); Taf. 3 no. 2
37; Pfaffenhofen; Dicanus; Abb. 19 no. 5
mould for 37; Pfaffenhofen; Helenius; Taf. 1 no. 2
moulds for 37; Pfaffenhofen (3 pieces); Taf. 1 no. 3-5
6 Had; Den; RIC 164c; 125-8; no. 4
Ant; Den; RIC 395c; 141+; no. 8
Aur; Den; RIC 516; 163-4; no. 16
Clod Alb; Den; RIC la; 193; no. 19
Sev; Den; RIC 330; 196-7; no. 20
Sev; Den; RIC 386; 203-8; no. 21
Alex; Den; RIC 64; 227; no. 24
Alex; Den; RIC l65a; 222-8; no. 27
Alex; Den; RIC 190a; 228-31; no. 29
Alex; Den; RIC 202; 228-31; no. 30
7 The excavator considers the coins to be a scattered hoard associated with the incursion of the Alemanni in AD 233 - they all come from burning debris in the top part of the layer.
8 Christlein *et al.* 1976; Kellner 1976

**A 189**

1 Pfaffenhofen, Oberbayern; samian kiln centre; trench B/1969, layer XI, stone and gravel layer
2 E
3 A
4 37; Heil ; ovolo Ricken 1934 Taf. 10J
37; West; Comitialis (10 pieces)
30; West; Comitialis; Abb. 22 no. 10
37; West; Helenius (5 pieces); Abb. 22
30; West; Helenius; Abb. 22 no. 2
37; West; Onniorix (3 pieces); Abb. 22 no. 11
37; Pfaffenhofen; Helenius (3 pieces); Abb. 22 nos 3-4, 9
37; Pfaffenhofen (15 pieces); Abb. 22 no. 5
6 Aurel; Rad (3); RIC 261K; 270-5; nos 66-8
Probus; Rad; 276-82; illeg; no. 77
7 Pfaffenhofen style mould fragments and other pieces by potters including Dicanus come from the overlying but associated layer XII. Deposit **A188** underlies this one.
8 Christlein *et al.* 1976; Kellner 1976

**A 190**

1 Pfaffenhofen, Oberbayern; samian kiln centre; trench C/1967 building 2 burning level
2 E
3 A
4 37; CG; X-13; rosette R C80; Abb. 12 no. 14
37; Rheinz; Cerialis group; Abb. 12 no. 4
37; West; uncertain potter; Abb. 16 no. 4
37; Pfaffenhofen; Helenius (10 vessels); Abb. 19 nos 3 and 7, Abb. 20 nos 5 and 7, Abb. 21 nos 2-4, 8, 12-13
37; Pfaffenhofen; Dicanus (2 vessels); Abb. 22 no. 7, Abb. 25 no. 1
beaker West/Pfaff with incised dec
6 Tet; Rad; illeg; no. 8
8 Christlein & Kellner 1969

**A 191**

1 Pfaffenhofen, Oberbayern; samian kiln centre; trench D/1967 layer III
2 E
3 A
4 37; West; Comitialis (5 vessels); Abb. 13 nos 2-3, 5, 7, 12
37; West; Helenius (4 vessels); Abb. 14 nos 2-3, 7-8
37; Pfaffenhofen; Helenius (2 vessels); Abb. 19 no. 1, Abb. 20 no. 6
6 Comm; Den; RIC 144; 186-7; no. 3
8 Christlein & Kellner 1969

**A 192**

1 Pocking, Niederbayern; *vicus*; cellar 5, upper burnt fill
2 E
3 A
4 37; CG; Paternus II; ovolo S&S fig. 30 no. 1; Abb. 9 no. 5
37 (2 pieces); CG; Paternus II; ovolo S&S fig. 30 no. 3; Abb. 9 nos 1 and 2
37; CG; Cinnamus; ovolo S&S fig. 47 no. 2; Abb. 9 no. 4
37; CG; Paternus II, Albucius or Laxtucissa; ovolo R B105; Abb. 9 no. 3
37; Ittenweiler; Verecundus; Abb. 9 no. 6
37; Rheinz; Comitialis VI; Abb. 9 no. 7
37; Rheinz; Juvenis II; Abb. 9 no. 13
37; Rheinz; Augustinus; Abb. 9 no. 15

37 (2 pieces); Rheinz; Julius II-Julianus I; Abb. 9 nos 10-11
37; Rheinz; Cerialis III or V; Abb. 9 no. 12
37; Rheinz; ornament R&F O160 (Firmus I, B F Attoni, Comitialis IV-VI and contemporaries); Abb. 9 no. 14
37; Rheinz; ovolo R&F E26 (B F Attoni or contemporary, ware B with O 382/3); Abb. 9 no. 8
37; West; Comitialis; Abb. 10 no. 13
37; West; Comitialis; Abb. 10 no. 12
37; West; Helenius; Abb. 10 no. 4
37 (2 pieces); West; Helenius; Abb. 10 nos 8-9
37; West; Helenius; Abb. 10 no. 3
37; West; Helenius; Abb. 10 no. 1
37; West; Helenius; Abb. 10 no. 6
37; West; Helenius; Abb. 10 no. 7
37; West; Helenius; Abb. 10 no. 2
37; West; Helenius; Abb. 10 no. 5
37 (2 pieces); West; Onniorix; Abb. 10 nos 10-11
Plain ware: 41 Rheinz with incised dec; 30 EG with rouletted dec; 33 Rheinz; 33 West (2); 31 West; 32 EG (4); C1S CG or EG; bowl as O&P pl. 45 nos 6-7 EG
From the same fill, but not in the cellar:
37; West; Comitialis; Taf. IIB no. 3
37 (2 pieces); West; Helenius; Taf. IIB nos 4-5
37; West; Helenius; Taf IIB no. 6
6 Max Thrax; HS; RIC 85; 236-8
Max Thrax; HS; RIC 93; 236-8
Gord III; Ant; RIC 83; 241-3
7 The burnt layer fills the upper part of the cellar and covers the surrounding area as well.
8 Kellner 1960b

**A 193**

1 Regensburg, Niederbayern; cemetery of fortress; finds group 633
2 A
3 C
4 37; Rheinz; Belsus I (stamped in mould); Taf. 78 no. 5
6 Aur; Ae; RIC 1714; 176-80; no. 502
7 These finds come from an early excavation, apparently without an associated grave. The association is not absolutely certain.
8 von Schnurbein 1977, 233

**A 194**

1 Regensburg, Niederbayern; cemetery of fortress; grave 847
2 A
3 A
4 37; Rheinz; figure R&F M246 (Cobnertus III, Comitialis V, Attillus or Julius II-Julianus I); Taf. 114 no. 3
23; Rheinz; stamped by Silvinus
6 Car; As; 198-211; no. 528
7 The 37 Rheinz is not certainly an original part of the grave.
8 von Schnurbein 1977, 199

**A 195**

1 Reichenhall, Oberbayern; cemetery; grave 202
2 A
3 B
4 37; CG; Advocisus or Mercator II
6 Ant; Ae; no details given
8 von Chlingensperg auf Berg 1896

**A 196**

1 Speyer, Rheinland-Pfalz; town; Stiftungskrankenhaus cellar 11
2 E
3 A
4 37; Rheinz; Comitialis III; Abb. 5 no. 8
37; Rheinz; Julius II-Julianus I, Marcellus II or Primitivus I; Abb. 5 no. 9
37; Rheinz; Julius I; Abb. 5 no. 10
37; Rheinz; Primitivus I-III; Abb. 5 no. 11
37; Rheinz; Julius II-Julianus I or Janu II; Abb. 5 no. 7
41 EG with incised dec
6 Claud II; Rad; *consecratio* type; 270
7 The finds come from a layer under the burnt rubble fill in the upper part of the cellar.
8 Bernhard 1979, 110

**A 197**

1 Straubing, Niederbayern; military *vicus*; cellar K26
2 E
3 B
4 37; CG; Cinnamus
37; Rheinz; Cerialis II-III; Taf. 28 no.14
37; Rheinz; Attillus (stamped in mould); Taf. 32 no. 5
6 Traj; As; 104-11
8 Walke 1965

**A 198**

1 Trier, Rheinland-Pfalz; town; Porta Nigra, deposit 8
2 E
3 A
4 37; Trier; probably Werkstatt II
33 EG
6 Wall adjoining contains in its mortar:
Aur; As; RIC 1133; 174-5
7 The deposit lies up against the wall and presumably postdates it.
8 Cüppers 1973

**A 199**

1 Walldürn, Baden-Württemburg; bath-house of fort; earlier bath, general finds
2 F
3 A
4 37; Rheinz; B F Attoni; no. 2
plate; Rheinz; stamped by Patruinus
6 Faust I; Den; RIC (Ant) 363; 141+; slightly worn
Aur; Ae; RIC 798-802 or 828-32; 161-2; slightly worn
Aur; Dup; RIC 966; 168-9; fairly worn
Sev; Den; RIC 125; 199-200; good condition
7 The earlier bath was probably founded when the outer *limes* was set up in the 150s according to the tile stamps. It was burnt and the later bath built in 232, according to inscription CIL XIII, 6592.
8 Baatz 1978

**A 200**

1 Walldürn, Baden-Württemburg; bath-house of fort; later bath, general finds
2 F
3 A
4 37; Rheinz; ware with ovolo E25/26 or Firmus II; no. 5
37 (2 pieces); Rheinz; Julius I; no. 8
37; Rheinz; Julius I or style of Augustinus III; no. 9
37; Rheinz; Julius II-Julianus I or Respectinus II; no. 14
6 Had; HS; 134-8; very worn; no. 2
Traj or Had; HS; 103-38; very worn; no. 3
Comm; As; 180-7; fairly worn; no. 7
Comm; HS; RIC 582; 190; slightly worn; no. 8
Ant; Aur or Comm; As; very worn; no. 9
Sev; Den; RIC 556; 196-211; slightly worn; no. 11

7 An inscription recording the rebuilding of the bath in 232 (CIL XIII, 6592) is suggested by Baatz to date the later bath. He puts the end of the bath between 248 and 260 on the basis that the latest (unstratified) coin from the site dated to 248 (Phil I; Ant).
8 Baatz 1978

**A 201**

1 Xanten; Nordrhein-Westfalen; pottery kiln outside town; kiln 2
2 E
3 A
4 37; Trier; Dexter; ovolo F 948
37; EG; ovolo fragment unidentified
37 EG; 31 EG; 27 or 32 EG stamped by Lutevus; 31 EG stamped by Melissus; 33 EG
5 The kiln produced CCW
6 Clod Alb; Den; RIC 7b; 194-5
8 Heimberg & Rüger 1972

**A 202**

1 Zugmantel, Hessen; military *vicus*; various locations
2 mainly E
3 C
4/6 The usual format is not followed here because only stamped sherds have been recorded:
a) cellar 441: Rheinz, Victorinus
Coins: Traj Den; Traj HS; Traj Ae; Had HS; Had Ae; Ant Den; Faust I Ae; Alex Den
b) well 434: Rheinz, Janu I; Trier, Dexter
Coin: Faust II Den
c) channel 120: Rheinz, B F Attoni; Rheinz, Comitialis; Trier, Dexter
Coins: Dom Den; Had HS; Ant HS; Alex Den (229)
d) cellar 180: Blick, Avitus; Rheinz, Lupus; Rheinz, Primitivus; Rheinz, Victorinus; Trier (3 vessels)
Coins: Nero Ae; Car Den (203)
e) cellar 185: Trier, Dexter
Coins: Faust I Den; L Verus Ae
f) near building 202: Rheinz, Cerialis; EG, Satto
Coins: Dom Den; Faust I Ae; Comm HS (182)
g) cellar 234: Rheinz, Primitivus
Coins: Faust II Ae; Sev Den (194); Sev Den (198/201)
h) cellar 235: Mitt, Cibisus
Coins: 1st century Ae; Had Ae; Aur Ae; L Verus Ae; J Domna Den; J Maesa Den
i) cellar 236: Rheinz, Firmus
Coins: Nerva Den; Traj Den; Aur Ae; Lucilla HS; Sev Den; J Domna Den; J Mamaea Den
j) cellar 243: Rheinz, Firmus
Coin: Sev Den (195)
k) cellar 245: Rheinz, Mammilianus
Coins: Faust II HS; Aur Ae
l) well 237: Trier, Dexter
Coin hoard: 29 Ar coins - nearly all Severan - latest Max (236)
m) well 111: Rheinz, Julius II
Coins: Calig HS; Vesp HS; Dom Ae; Traj Ae; Traj HS; Comm Ae; Max Den (236)
n) cellar 302: Mitt, Cibisus; Rheinz, Comitialis; Rheinz, Julius II-Julianus I (Jacobi 1911, Abb 23)
Coins: Had HS; Faust II HS; Lucilla Ae; Sev Den; Elag Den; J Mamaea Den; J Mamaea Den
o) cellar 287: Rheinz, Comitialis; Rheinz, Firmus
Coins: Had Ae; Faust I HS; Ant Den; Aur Den; Aur Ae; Faust II HS; Faust II Ae; Faust II Den; Geta Caes Den
p) cellar 301: Rheinz, Comitialis
Coins: Dom Ae; Dom Ae; Faust II Den; Clod Alb Den; underlying deposit has J Maesa Den
q) well 296: Rheinz, Atto
Coins: Had HS; Ant HS; Aur Ae; Sev Den; Elag Den
r) well 300: Rheinz, Reginus
Coins: Faust I Ae; Ant HS; Ant Ae; Faust II HS
s) cellar 282: Trier, Dexter
Coin: Had Ae (cos III)
t) cellar 267: Rheinz, Reginus; Rheinz, Statutus
Coins: Dom Ae; 1st century Ae
u) cellar 271: Rheinz, Comitialis
Coins: Traj HS; Ant Ae; Faust I HS; Aur HS; Aur HS (178); Lucilla HS
v) cellar 261: Trier, Censor
Coins: Republican Den; Vesp Den (4x); Titus Den; Traj Den; Had HS; Faust II HS; Aur HS; Comm HS (190)
w) cellar 278: Blick, LAL; Rheinz, Cerialis
Coins: Had Ae; Ant HS; Ant Ae; Aur Ae; Comm Ae; Sev Den (194)
x) cellar 264: Rheinz, Comitialis IV; Rheinz, Comitialis; Trier, Tordilo
Coins: Vesp Den; Sev Den; Max Den
y) cellar 277: Rheinz, Comitialis V
Coins: Dom Ae; Had Den; Had Ae; Had Ae
z) well 251: Rheinz; Comitialis
Coins: Traj Ae; Elag Den (221)
aa) well 274: Rheinz, Comitialis V
Coins: Traj HS; Had HS; Had Den; Aur Ae; Sev Den (193)
ab) well 275: Rheinz, Attillus
Coin: Faust I Ae (141+)
ac) cellar 331: Rheinz, Comitialis
Coins: Nero Ae; Dom Den; Traj HS; Had HS; Had Ae; Ant Ae; L Verus HS; Car Den (197)
ad) cellar 322: Rheinz, Comitialis II
Coins: Titus Au; Faust I Ae; Faust I Ae; Lucilla Ae; Phil II Ant (248)
ae) cellar 324: Blick, Avitus; Rheinz, Comitialis II; Rheinz, Mammilianus
Coins: Dom Ae; Traj Den; Traj Den; Had Den; Aelius Ae; Ant Ae; Phil I Ant
af) cellar 364: Blick, Avitus; Rheinz, Comitialis
Coins: Claud Ae; Traj Ae; Had Ae; Faust II Ae
ag) cellar 367: Rheinz, Firmus; Rheinz, Primitivus; Trier, Censor
Coins: Vesp Den; Had Ae; Had HS; Ant HS; Ant Ae; Lucilla Ae; Comm HS; Car Den (202); possibly coin of Alex
ah) cellar 368: Rheinz, Belsus; Rheinz, Comitialis; Rheinz, Comitialis V; Rheinz, Helenius
Coins: Had Ae; Diadumenius Den
ai) cellar 373: Rheinz, Comitialis V (2)
Coins: Aur Ae; Aur Ae; Faust II Ae; Faust II Ae; Comm Den; Comm Den; Sev Den
aj) cellar 382: Mitt, Cibisus; Rheinz, Cobnertus; Rheinz, Firmus; Rheinz, Julius; Rheinz, Comitialis V
Coin: Had Ae
ak) cellar 390: Rheinz, Comitialis V; 13 complete vessels, mainly in Trier, Dexter and Rheinz, Julius styles
Coins: Aur HS; Aur HS
al) cellar 340: Rheinz, Primitivus
Coins: Traj Den; Traj Ae; Faust I Ae; Aur Ae; Aur Ae; Comm Ae; Alex Den
am) cellar 348: Rheinz, Julius
Coins: Ant HS; Ant Den; Aur HS; Faust II HS; Crispina HS; Aur Den; Gord Ant
an) cellar 369: Rheinz, Julius

Coins: Dom Ae; Ant HS
ao) cellar 315: Rheinz, Comitialis (2); Trier; Dexter
Coins: Tit Ae; Traj Den; Traj HS; Had HS; Had Ae; Ant Ae; Ant Ae; Faust I HS; Aur Ae; Faust II HS; Sev Den; Alex Den; Alex Den (225); possibly Max Den (235) from underlying deposit
ap) cellar 317: Rheinz, Comitialis; Rheinz, Julius I-Julianus I
Coins: Ant HS; Faust I Ae; Aur HS; Faust II Den; J Domna Den; J Mamaea Den
aq) feature 332: Rheinz, Victorinus (2); Rheinz, Comitialis; Rheinz, Reginus; Rheinz, Statutus
Coins: Vesp Ae; Dom Ae; Dom Ae; Traj Den; Had Den; Had Ae; Ant Ae; Ant Ae; Ant Ae; Faust I Ae; Aur Ae; Aur HS; Sev Den; Sev Den; Sev Den; Car Den; J Domna Den; Elag Den; Gord Ant; Phil Den

8 Jacobi 1909; 1910; 1911; 1912; 1924; 1930

## MIDDLE DANUBE REGION

**A 203**

1 *Carnuntum*, civil settlement, Niederösterreich; extra-mural building in town; trench III room 2, debris under latest floor
2 E
3 B
4 37; West; Helenius; Taf. 11 no. 3
From under the floor of room 3:
37; Rheinz; Helenius; Taf. 11 no. 2
6 Phil I; HS; C268 (not in RIC)
7 The floors in rooms 2 and 3, with their preceding levelling layers, are contemporary.
8 Reinfuss 1957

**A 204**

1 *Carnuntum*, civil settlement, Niederösterreich; town; Spaziergarten house, corridor 2, finds under latest floor
2 E (probably)
3 C
4 37; Rheinz; Victor II-Ianuco; Taf. III no. 9
37; West; Helenius; Taf. III no. 11
37; West; Helenius; Taf. III no. 12
37; West; Helenius; Taf. III no. 13
37; Pfaffenhofen; ovolo and ware Karnitsch 1955 type E, Taf. 91, 92, 101; Taf. III no. 15
5 Green glazed jar with scale dec
6 Gall; Rad; RIC 163
4th century Ae; Gloria Exercitus with 2 standards
7 The finds are not allocated to layers in the finds report, but the description of the stratigraphy refers to most of the finds coming from a burnt layer and levelling under the latest floor. The samian and the coin of Gall are a probable association - however, the 4th century coin is uncertain and may come from overlying destruction debris.
8 Swoboda-Milenović 1956

**A 205**

1 Enns-Lorch, Oberösterreich; cemetery of fortress; Georgenberg grave 1
2 A
3 A
4 37; Rheinz; B F Attoni; Taf. 2 no. 13
6 Sev; Den; RIC 121 or 233; 210; slightly worn
8 Sydow 1982

**A 206**

1 Enns-Lorch, Oberösterreich; fortress; finds from planum levels
2 G - no stratigraphy given other than levels and positions
3 C
4/6 This section is arranged differently from other entries, since the associations in many cases are fairly general and Karnitsch's arrangement precludes the analysis of individual deposits. The samian is listed first, followed by the associated coins.
a) 37; Rheinz; Janu I
37; Rheinz; B F Attoni
37; Rheinz; Cerialis I
37; Rheinz; Comitialis II
37; Rheinz; Comitialis III
37; Rheinz; Primitivus I
Coin: J Maesa; Den; RIC (Elag) 268
b) 37; Rheinz; Janu II
37; Rheinz; Julius I-Julianus I
37; West; Helenius
Coin: Aur; HS; RIC 931; 166
c) 37; Rheinz; Firmus I
Coin: Comm; Den; RIC 117; 185
d) 37; Rheinz; Cerialis V
37; Rheinz; Comitialis II
37; Rheinz; Comitialis VI
Coins: Ant; As; RIC 996; 157-8
Sev; Den; RIC 434; 195
Sev; As; RIC 732; 196
Alex; Den; RIC 294
Barbia Orbiana; Den; RIC (Alex) 319
J Mamaea; Den; RIC (Alex) 341
e) 37; Rheinz; Cerialis group Ware B
37; Rheinz; Comitialis II
Coins: Sev; Den; RIC 61; 195
Sev; Den; RIC 389; 194-5
Car; Den
Elag; Den; RIC 161; 218-22
f) 37; Rheinz; Comitialis IV
Coins: Faust I; Ae; RIC (Ant) 1187; very worn
J Mamaea; Den; RIC (Alex) 335
g) 37; Rheinz; Comitialis IV
37; Rheinz; Comitialis VI
37; Rheinz; Respectus
Coin: Aur; HS; RIC 1160; 175-6; very worn
h) 37; Rheinz; Comitialis VI
Coin: Sev; HS
i) 37; Rheinz; Respectus
Coin: Lucilla; HS; RIC (Aur) 1756
j) 37; Rheinz; Iuvenis II-Pupus
Coin: Car; Den; RIC 83; 206
k) 37; Rheinz; Julius II-Julianus I
Coin: Lucilla; HS; RIC (Aur) 1756
l) 37; West; Comitialis
Coin: Sev; Den; RIC 430a; 194-5
m) 37; Rheinz; Janu II (2)
Coins: Had; Den; RIC 200; 125-8
Sev; Den
n) 37; Rheinz; Comitialis II
37; Rheinz; Primitivus III
37; Rheinz; Primitivus IV
37; Rheinz; Iuvenis II-Pupus
37; Rheinz; Atto
Coin: Sev; Den; RIC 111a; 197-8
o) not used - n) and o) have been combined
p) 37; Rheinz; Janu II

Coin: Comm; HS
q) 37; Rheinz; Comitialis IV
Coin: Gall; Rad
r) 37; Rheinz; Janu II
Coin: Sev; Den; RIC as 280; 202-10
s) 37; Rheinz; Cerialis IV
37; Rheinz; Cerialis group, ware B
Coin: Sev; Den; RIC 411; 194-5
t) 37; Rheinz; Firmus I
Coins: Comm; Dup: RIC (Aur) 1614; 179
Claud II; Rad; RIC 257; 268-70
u) 37; Rheinz; B F Attoni
Coin: Ant; HS; RIC 904; 152-3
v) 37; Rheinz; Comitialis VI
Coins: Gall; Rad; RIC 163
Claud II; Rad
w) 37; Rheinz; ware with ovolo E25/26
Coin: Alex; Den; RIC 168; 227-8
x) 37; Rheinz; Firmus I
Coins: Car; Den; RIC 54a; 201
J Maesa; Den; RIC (Elag) 268
y) 37; Rheinz; B F Attoni
Coin: Comm; Den; RIC 219; 190-1
z) 37; Rheinz; Arvernicus
Coins: Aur; HS; RIC 1096; 174
Alex; Den; RIC 32; 223
aa) 37; Rheinz; Comitialis V
Coin: Max; HS; RIC 109; 235-8
ab) 37; Rheinz; Comitialis V
37; Rheinz; Julius II-Julianus I
Coin: Elag; Den; 218-22
ac) 37; Rheinz; Comitialis V
Coin: Elag; Den; RIC 136; 218-22
ad) 37; Rheinz; Julius I
Coins: Aur; HS; RIC 1001; 170-1
Sev; Den; RIC 88; 196-7
J Domna; Den; RIC (Sev) 580
J Domna; Ae; RIC (Car) 597
Car; Den
ae) 37; Rheinz; Primitivus III
37; Rheinz; Julius II-Julianus I (2)
Coins: Sev; Den; RIC 113; 197-8
Elag; Den; RIC 52; 222
Balb; HS; RIC 22; 238
af) 37; Rheinz; Julius II-Julianus I
37; West; Comitialis (2)
Coins: Gall; Rad; RIC 160
Gall; Rad; RIC 481
Gall; Rad; as RIC 192a
ag) 37; Rheinz; Julius I-Julianus I
Coin: Gall; Rad
ah) 37; Rheinz; B F Attoni
Coin: Ant; HS; RIC 636; 140-2
ai) 37; Rheinz; Respectus
37; West; Helenius
Coins: Comm; HS; RIC 513; 187-8
Sev; HS; RIC 701; 195-6
aj) 37; Rheinz; B F Attoni
Coin: Ant; Dup; RIC 1018; 158-9
ak) 37; Rheinz; B F Attoni
37; Rheinz; Comitialis II
37; Rheinz; Comitialis IV
37; Rheinz; Primitivus I
Coins: Aur; HS; RIC (Ant) 1338; 156-7
Sev; As; RIC 813
Sev; Den; RIC 189b; 203

ah) 37; Rheinz; Cerialis I
37; Rheinz; Primitivus IV
37; West; Comitialis (2)
37; West; Helenius
Coins: Ant; Den
Comm; Den; RIC 254a; 192
Sev; HS
Sev; HS
Alex; Den; 222-35
am) 37; Rheinz; Comitialis IV
37: Rheinz; Comitialis VI
37; Rheinz; Julius I
37; Rheinz; Atto
37; Rheinz; Lucanus
37; Rheinz; ware with ovolo E8
37; Rheinz; Helenius
37; Rheinz; Primitivus I
37; Rheinz; Julius II-Julianus I
37; Rheinz; Victor I
Coins: Comm; Dup; RIC 420; 183-4; worn
Car; As; RIC 506; 210-l3
J Domna; Den; RIC (Sev) 560
an) 37; Rheinz; Cerialis I
37; Rheinz; Respectus
Coin: Aur; HS; RIC (Ant) 1328; 155-6
ao) 37; Rheinz; Cerialis V
37; Rheinz; Comitialis II
37; Rheinz; Comitialis VI
37; Rheinz; Respectus
37; Rheinz; Primitivus IV
Coin: J Domna; As; burnt
ap) 37; Rheinz; Florentinus (stamped)
Coin: Alex; Den; burnt
aq) 37; Rheinz; ware with ovolo E25/26
Coins: Alex; As; RIC 175
J Maesa; Den; RIC (Elag) 272
Gord III; HS; RIC 337; 238-44
ar) 37; Rheinz; Cerialis III (stamped)
Coin: Comm; HS
as) 37; Rheinz; Primitivus III (stamped)
Coin: Sev; Den; RIC 176; 201
at) 37; Rheinz; Cerialis III
37; West; Helenius
Coins: Had; Dup
Sev; Den; RIC 69; 195-6
Car; Den
au) 37; Pfaffenhofen; Dicanus
Coins: Aur; Dup; RIC 1100; 173-4
Sev; Den; RIC 411; 194-5
J Domna; Den; RIC (Sev) 536; 193-6
Claud II, Rad; RIC 104; 268-70
Valentinian I; RIC 15a; 364-75
av) 37; Rheinz; Cerialis IV
Coin: Sev; HS; burnt
aw) 37; Rheinz; Cerialis V
37; Rheinz; Comitialis V
37; Rheinz; Helenius
Coins: Sev; Den; RIC 40 or 345; 194-5
Claud II, Rad; RIC 14; 268-70
ax) 37; Rheinz; Respectinus I
Coins: Claud II; Rad; RIC 109; 268-70
Claud II; Rad; RIC 197; 268-70
ay) 37; Rheinz; Cerialis IV
Coin: Ant; Dup; RIC 894; 151-2
az) 37; West; Helenius
Coin: Aur; HS; RIC 923; 165-6

ba) 37 (2 pieces); EG - unlocated; Karnitsch Taf. 92 nos 2-3
Coins: Claud II; Rad; RIC 66; 268-70
Aurel; Rad; RIC 259; 270-5
bb) 37; Rheinz; Cerialis V
37; Rheinz; Iuvenis II-Pupus (8 – 6 stamped)
Coins: Had; Den; RIC 86; very worn
M Antonius; Republican Den; very worn
bc) 37; Rheinz; Arvernicus
37; Rheinz; Comitialis IV
37; Rheinz; Comitialis VI (stamped)
37; Rheinz; ware with ovolo E25/26
37; Rheinz; Primitivus II
Coins: Car; Den; RIC (Sev) 65; 202
Claud II; Rad; RIC 267a; 268-70; from 30cm above the other finds
bd) 37; Rheinz; Comitialis II; from between floors 4 and 5
Coins: Sev; Den; RIC 68; 195-6; from between floors 4 and 5
Sev; Den; RIC 118; 197-8; from nearby, but not from the floors
be) 37; Rheinz; Comitialis II
Coin: Sev; Den; RIC 176; 201
bf) 37; Rheinz; Primitivus I
Coin: L Verus; As; RIC (Aur) 1288; 161
bg) 37; Rheinz; Julius II-Julianus I
Coins: Gord III; Ant; RIC 86; 241-3
Gall; Rad; RIC 108
bh) 37; West; Helenius
Coin: Alex; Den; RIC 92; 229
bi) 37; Rheinz; Julius I-Julianus I
Coins: Gall; Rad; RIC 159
Gall; Rad; RIC 160
Claud II; Rad; RIC 209; 268-70
bj) 37; West; Comitialis
Coin: Claud II; Rad; RIC 33; 268-70
bk) 37; West; Comitialis
37; West; Helenius
Coins: Gall; Rad
Claud II; Rad; RIC 66; 268-70
bl) 37; West; Comitialis
Coins: Geta; As; RIC (Sev) 148; 209
Gall; Rad; RIC 160
Gall; Rad; RIC 159

7 These :associations appear to be by proximity only, i.e. samian and coins at roughly the same depth and in the same area (although a wide latitude has been allowed in determining 'proximity'). No stratigraphic details are given, except on rare occasions (e.g. deposit bd). All the finds come from levels associated with the legionary fortress, founded in the reign of M. Aurelius.
8 Karnitsch 1955; 1960

**A 207**

1 Salzburg-Eichhof, Salzburg; cemetery; grave in Zaunergasse
2 A
3 C
4 37; West; Helenius
37; CG; Cinnamus
6 Faust I; As; 141+
8 Kellner 1961, 178, n52 (brief details only)

**A 208**

1 Zalalövö, Hungary; town; trench K/2, level 85-115cm
2 G - probable planum level
3 B
4 37; Heil; Ciriuna
6 Aur; HS; BMC 1088; 163-4
7 The association is not absolutely secure.
8 Rédö, Lányi & Gabler 1978

# SECTION B: Deposits of decorated samian ware not associated with coins

## BRITAIN

**B 1**

1 Alchester, Oxfordshire; *vicus*; B(ii) level between Long Room I and Rough Room I
2 B
3 C
4 37; CG; Cinnamus style; hare O 2116 in double medallion, with bead row and rosette, metope and medallion style; fig. 4 no. 21
37; CG; Austrus; ovolo S&S fig. 25 no. 2, Pan O 718, Bacchus O 562, between vertical bead rows crossed by astragali R R18, metope style, part of same bowl as in deposit **A 1**, cf S&S pl. 95, 21 for similar design; fig. 4 no. 23
37; CG; Cinnamus style; leaf R H21, leaf R H72, circle S&S fig. 4 no. 11, in winding scroll dec; fig. 4 no. 24
7 A small group of associated sherds, also connected to deposit **A 1** which has a coin of Claud II
8 Hawkes 1927

**B 2**

1 Aldborough, West Yorkshire; town; rampart of town wall
2 E
3 A
4 From Section I, 1938:
37; SG; Flavian date; fig. 22 no. 9
37; CG; attributed by Oswald to Birrantus; Hercules not in O; fig. 22 no. 5
37; CG; X-12 (Ioenalis); Pan O 717 in arcade; fig. 22 no. 6
37; CG; Sacer; leaf S&S fig. 22 no. 6, trifid *ibid* fig. 22 no. 4, linked festoon style, virtually identical to *ibid* pl. 82 no. 7 (Corbridge); fig. 22 no. 7
37; CG; Albucius (stamped in mould); ovolo S&S fig. 35 no. 1, cupid O 450, cupid O 440, rosette S&S fig. 35 no. 5, metope style; fig. 22 no. 8
37; Rheinz; Ianu I; ovolo R&F E396, medallion *ibid* K50, bifid *ibid* P140, rosette *ibid* O42, large rosette *ibid* O37a, metope and medallion style; fig. 23
From Section III, 1934-5:
37; CG; Cinnamus or Doeccus; dancer O 322 in medallion; fig. 8 no. 7
37; CG; X-5; ovolo S&S fig. 16, ornament with wavy line *ibid* fig. 16 no. 1; fig. 8 no. 6
7 The rampart consists of dumps which may well contain earlier material.
8 Myres *et al.* 1959; Oswald 1959

**B 3**

1 Bar Hill, Strathclyde; fort; general finds
2 F
3 C
4 30; CG; Medetus-Ranto or Donnaucus (X-13); acanthus R K10 in St Andrew's cross motif; fig. 45 no. 2
30; CG; Cettus; ovolo S&S fig. 42 no. 4; fig. 45 no. 3
30; CG; Cinnamus; ovolo as S&S fig. 47 no. 1; fig. 45 no. 4
37 (3 pieces); CG; Divixtus; ovolo S&S pl. 116 no. 8, which is virtually identical in overall design; erotic group O B, metope and medallion style; fig. 45 no. 7
37 (10 pieces); CG; Cinnamus (stamped in mould); ovolo S&S fig. 47 no. 1; Perseus O 147A, sea creature O 46, Vulcan O 66, metope and medallion style; fig. 45 no. 10a
37 (3 pieces); CG; Cinnamus; ovolo S&S fig. 47 no. 1, Perseus O 147A, sea creature O 46, it is not clear whether this is the same bowl as the last or an identical one, metope and medallion style; fig. 45 no. 10b
37; CG; Cinnamus or Paullus; dancer O 348 in medallion, metope and medallion style; fig. 45 no. 11
37; CG; Cinnamus, Paullus, Iustus or Attianus II; sea horse O 42 in festoon; fig. 45 no. 12
37 (3 pieces); CG; Cinnamus; as S&S fig. 47 no. 5; fig. 45 no. 13
30; CG; Cinnamus (stamped in mould with small stamp); ovolo S&S fig. 47 no. 3, sea creature O 52 in medallion; fig. 45 no. 14
37 (4 pieces); CG; possibly Laxtucissa; trifid as S&S pl. 99 no. 19 in small medallion as *ibid*, rivetted, very worn; fig. 45 no. 16
37 (2 pieces); CG; Casurius or Cinnamus; ovolo as S&S fig. 47 no. 1, medallion as R E26; fig. 46 no. 17
37 (3 pieces); CG; possibly Cinnamus; medallion and trace of figures as S&S pl. 160 no. 35; fig. 46 no. 18
37 (2 pieces); CG; Cinnamus, Cerialis, Paullus or associate; Venus O 286, metope style; fig. 46 no. 19
37 (2 pieces); CG; Butrio; ovolo as S&S fig. 13 no. 2; leaf as *ibid* fig. 13 no. 13, Victory O 809, dolphin as O 2391, metope and medallion style; fig. 46 nos. 20a-b
37 (3 pieces); CG; possibly X-5; ovolo as S&S pl. 67 no. 1, rivetted; fig. 46 no. 21
37; CG; X-10 (Ranto-Silvio); ovolo as S&S pl. 33 no. 391, dancer O 819A; fig. 46 no. 22
37; CG; Albucius, Servus or Q I Balbinus; stand as R Q77; fig. 46 no. 24
37 (6 pieces); CG; Cinnamus; ovolo S&S fig. 47 no. 1, figure as O 147A or O 169; metope style; fig. 46 no. 25
37 (2 pieces); CG; Cinnamus; ovolo S&S fig. 47 no. 3, erotic group O B in medallion, bird O 2239B, winding scroll and medallion style; fig. 46 no. 27
37 (2 pieces); CG; Albucius, Doeccus, Advocisus or associate; leaf as R H27, female figure O 353, winding scroll style; fig. 46 no. 28
37 (2 pieces); CG; Cinnamus; ovolo S&S fig. 47 no. 3, lead *ibid* fig. 47 no. 38, winding scroll style; fig. 46 no. 29
37 (5 pieces); CG; Cinnamus; leaf as R H24, winding scroll style; fig. 46 no. 30
37; CG; Cinnamus; ovolo S&S fig. 47 no. 1, part of winding scroll; fig. 46 no. 31
37 (3 pieces); CG; Cinnamus; ovolo S&S fig. 47 no. 1, dolphin motif as *ibid* fig. 47 no. 18, leaf as R H21, winding scroll style; fig. 46 no. 32
37 (2 pieces); CG; Cinnamus; ovolo S&S fig. 47 no. 3, bear O 1627, lioness O 1518, lion O 1497J, free style; fig. 47 no. 33
37 (3 pieces); CG; Cinnamus; ovolo S&S fig. 47 no. 3, lion O 1497J, lioness O 1537, lioness O 1542, bear as O 1630, free style; fig. 47 no. 34

37 (11 pieces); CG; Cinnamus (stamped in mould); ovolo S&S fig. 47 no. 1, lion as O 1497J, lioness O 1537, lion O 1421, bear O 1633L, deer O 1728, leaf S&S fig. 47 no. 5, free style; fig. 47 no. 35
37; CG; X-8 or X-9; column with trifid above - not in R, wavy line above; fig. 47 no. 36
37; CG; Cettus or Casurius; leaf as S&S fig. 40 no. 6; fig. 47 no. 37
37; CG; Quintilianus group; basal circle and small scroll alternating as S&S pl. 71 nos 29 and 30; fig. 47 no. 38
37 (3 pieces); CG; Cinnamus or Albucius; ovolo as S&S fig. 47 no. 2, stand R Q42, dancer O 343, female figure O 644, bird O 2239, free style; fig. 47 no. 39
37 (2 pieces); CG; Divixtus; ovolo as S&S pl. 115 no. 1; fig. 47 no. 40
37 ( 3 pieces); CG; Cinnamus; ovolo S&S fig. 47 no. 3; fig. 47 no. 44
37; CG; Cinnamus; as previous; fig. 47 no. 46a
37; CG; Cinnamus; as previous; fig. 47 no. 46a
37 (5 pieces); CG; Cettus; ovolo S&S fig. 42 no. 4; fig. 47 no. 46b
37; CG; Cettus; as previous; fig. 47 no. 48a
37; CG; Cinnamus; ovolo S&S fig. 45 no. 3; fig. 47 no. 48b
30 CG (4); 30 or 37 CG; 37 CG (59 pieces from at least 22 bowls - 2 rivetted)
Plain ware: 27 CG (14 pieces from *c* 10 vessels); 33 CG (61 pieces from *c* 42 vessels); 18/31 and 31 CG and EG? (94 pieces from 55-60 vessels); 31 CG and EG (42 pieces from 25-30 vessels); 31R CG and EG (15 pieces from 7 vessels); 46 EG; 51 EG (6 pieces from 3 vessels); Lud Tb EG; 51 or Lud Tb; Lud TZ ? EG; C11 with barbotine dec; C11 (4 pieces from 2 vessels); 38 CG or EG (8 pieces from 3 vessels); C 21?; bowls (5 pieces); beakers (7 pieces); U (15 pieces)

8 Docherty & Wild 1975; Robertson *et al.*1975

**B 4**

1 Bath, Avon; town; Abbey Green, trench 1 layer 7
2 B
3 A
4 37; CG; Casurius; ovolo S&S fig. 40 no. 1
37; CG; Criciro; Venus on pedestal S&S pl. 117 no. 11, horse *ibid* pl. 117 no. 17
37; CG; Ioenalis; Perseus S&S pl. 40 no. 468
37 (2); 31 CG (3); 31 EG; 33 (3)
5 CG CCW beaker
8 Green 1979

**B 5**

1 Benwell, Tyne & Wear; *vicus* of fort; Vallum ditch filling
2 D
3 A
4 37; SG; Flavian type, no details given here; fig. 2 no. 19
37; SG; as above; fig. 2 no. 39
37; CG; Avitus-Vegetus; leaf S&S fig. 14 no. 16, basal wreath *ibid* fig. 14 no. 2, figure O 676, metope and medallion style, published in S&S pl. 64 no. 23; fig. 2 no. 24
37; CG; Geminus; ovolo S&S fig. 15 no. 1; fig. 1 no. 1
37; CG; Geminus; ovolo S&S fig. 15 no. 1, rosette *ibid* fig. 15 no. 6, ornament *ibid* fig. 15 no. 10, astragalus *ibid* fig. 15 no. 8, circle not in R or S&S, metope and small medallion style; fig. 1 no. 2
37; CG; probably Geminus; circle as in previous piece; fig. 1 no. 3
37; CG; Geminus; ovolo S&S fig. 15 no. 1, Minerva O 126A; fig. 1 no. 5
37; CG; Quintilianus group; ovolo S&S fig. 17 no. 3, leaf *ibid* fig. 17 no. 11; fig. 1 no. 7
37; CG; Quintilianus group (stamped in mould by Paterclus); basal wreath S&S fig. 17 no. 1, rosette *ibid* fig. 17 no. 6, metope style; fig. 1 no. 8
37 (several pieces); CG; Quintilianus group; ovolo S&S fig. 17 no. 1, basal wreath *ibid* fig. 17 no. 1, astragalus *ibid* fig. 17 no. 13, rosette *ibid* fig. 17 no. 7, circle *ibid* fig. 17 no. 14, vine scroll R M5, stand R Q7, figure O 173A, dwarf O 698, Pan O 707, man with trophy not in O, metope style, published in S&S pl. 69 no 4; fig. 1 no. 9
37; CG; X-6; ovolo as S&S fig. 18 no. 4, rosette *ibid* fig. 18 no. 11, Diana as O 103A-D, metope style; fig. 1 no. 10
37; CG; X-6; ovolo S&S fig. 18 no. 1; fig. 1 no. 11
37; CG; X-6; as above; fig. 1 no. 12
37; CG; possibly X-6; ovolo as S&S fig. 18 no. 3; fig. 1 no. 13
37; CG; possibly X-5 or X-7; ovolo as S&S fig. 19; fig. 1 no. 14
37; CG; Quintilianus group; ovolo S&S fig. 17 no. 1; fig. 1 no. 15
37; CG; X-6; ovolo not attributable, spiral S&S fig. 18 no. 8, trifid *ibid* fig. 18 no. 2, gladiator O 1001, metope style; fig. 2 no. 21
37; CG; unknown potter, possibly Me... ; stand R Q15, cornucopia as R U245, metope style; fig. 2 no. 25
37; CG; Criciro; ovolo S&S fig. 33 no. 1, lioness O 1518, free style; fig. 2 no. 26
37; CG; Austrus or Criciro; circle R E2, scarf dancer not in O but possibly O 361, metope and medallion style, see S&S pl. 50 no. 595; fig. 2 no. 28
37; CG; probably Sacer-Attianus; ovolo as S&S fig. 23 no. 2; fig. 2 no. 34
37; CG; Advocisus or Censorinus; trifid as R G70-1 in St Andrew's cross design; fig. 2 no. 35
37; CG; Cinnamus or Casurius; Pan mask O 1214, bird O 2239 in festoon, metope and medallion style; fig. 2 no. 36
37; CG; Attianus (stamped in mould); fig. 2 no. 37
37; CG; probably Laxtucissa; deer O 1752A, winding scroll style; fig. 2 no. 40
37; CG; probably Laxtucissa; bud R G208, bird O 2365; fig. 2 no. 41
37; CG; Sacer-Attianus or Cinnamus; leaf R H22, winding scroll style; fig. 2 no. 42
37; Rheinz, Janu I; trifid R&F P127, metope style; fig. 2 no. 33
7 Several pieces were not possible to attribute easily and have been omitted. The Vallum ditch filling was probably a single episode, and this deposit is sealed by **A 4**.
8 Birley 1947a; Birley, Brewis & Charlton 1934; Swinbank 1955

**B 6**

1 Bishopstone, East Sussex; rural settlement; feature 1, pottery group iv
2 C
3 A
4 37; CG; Paternus II; no details given
31; Rheinz; Iucundus V; stamped with die 5a
31 CG; bowl; EG
5 Mortarium and BB1 bowl attributed to 3rd century
8 Bell 1977; Bird 1977b

**B 7**

1 Bitterne, Hampshire; *vicus*: site C2 ditch silt level 4
2 D
3 A

4 37 (2 pieces); CG; Libertus C; ovolo largely cut away in finishing process, no border, sea horse O 48, charioteer O 102A, mask O 1330, apparently free style; fig. 14 nos 19-20
37 (2 pieces); CG; unattributed but later than Libertus; Apollo as O 96 but not exact, a figure-type only recorded for Libertus A and B, but this instance is clearly later in an unknown style, stand, acanthus and ovolo not in R, metope style; fig. 15 nos 18-19
37; CG; too small for attribution but mid-2nd century or later; fig. 15 no. 8
66/68; CG; Libertus/Butrio: black gloss, Mars O 148, stand not in R but Butrio type, this piece also published in Simpson 1973 no. 33; fig. 15 no. 31
Plain ware: 18/31 SG (5 - 1 stamped Vitalis); 18/31 CG (14); 18/31 EG; 27 SG (2); 27 CG; 33 SG (3): Lud Tb EG; C11 var EG; unicum SG (cf Simpson 1958 fig. 18 no. 8); U CG (26); U EG
7 An unusual and highly specific group of decorated ware, including a piece of black gloss samian, which has a marked concentration of distribution in southern Britain. The plain ware has a wider chronological spread.
8 Cotton & Gathercole 1958; Simpson 1958

**B 8**

1 Bothwellhaugh, Strathclyde; fort; general finds from bath-house
2 F
3 A
4 37; CG; ovolo - very abraded, deer in free style, assigned to Had-early Ant by Webster; no. 4
37; CG; Cettus; astragalus as R R62, leaf R J144, metope style; fig. 24 no. 5
37 (6 pieces); CG; probably Cinnamus; lion as O 1456, lioness O 1537, free style; no. 6
37 (2 pieces); CG; Cinnamus; ovolo S&S fig. 47 no. 3 (= ovolo 3a), rivetted; no. 7
37; CG; Acaunissa; ovolo S&S fig. 21; no. 8
37; CG; Cinnamus; cushion S&S pl. 161 no. 50 (not in R), metope and medallion style; fig. 24 no. 9
37; CG; Cinnamus; ovolo S&S fig. 47 no. 3 (= ovolo 3a), metope and medallion style; fig. 24 no. 10
37; CG; Cinnamus; lozenge R D33, metope and medallion style; fig. 24 no. 11
37; CG; Cinnamus; ovolo S&S fig. 47 no. 1, metope and medallion style; no. 12
37; CG; Cinnamus; ovolo S&S fig. 47 no. 3; no. 13
37; CG; Cinnamus or associate; Minerva as O 126B, goat O 1836, metope and medallion style; no. 14
37; CG; Cinnamus; leaf R H13, winding scroll style; fig. 24 no. 15
37; CG; Cinnamus-Cerialis group; ovolo R B144, metope and medallion style; fig. 24 no. 16
37; CG; Laxtucissa; dolphin as O 2384, astragalus as S&S fig. 30 no. 28, corded and beaded borders, assigned by Webster and Dickinson to a late date in the work of this potter, since it has similarities to the work of Paternus II, metope and medallion style; fig. 24 no. 17
37; CG; Cinnamus; ovolo S&S fig. 47 no. 3 (= ovolo 3a); no. 21
Plain ware and total of form 37 minimum vessels:
18/31 CG (17); 18/31R or 31R CG (2); 18/31 or 31 CG (3); 27 CG (2); 33 CG (9); 38 CG (4); C11 SG - interpreted as an antique by Webster; CG jars (2); 37 CG (31)
Stamped plain ware:
31; CG; Sextus v die 5b
18/31; CG; Beliniccus i die 11a
33; CG; Minatio die la
31; CG; Sinturo/Sinturus die 3a
5 NV CCW hunt cup; BB1
7 The pottery comes from the bath-house, principally its debris levels, and is composed largely of late pieces for the Antonine occupation of Scotland. There is an As of 159-60 from the site.
8 Dickinson 1981; Keppie 1981; Webster 1981, 80-4

**B 9**

1 Brancaster, Norfolk; *vicus* of fort; general finds
2 F
3 A
4 From site 13:
37; Trier; Cocus iv-Comitialis group; ovolo; no. 773312
37; Rheinz; Cerialis I-V or Comitialis I; deer R&F T106, dog *ibid* T130, free style; no. 773331
37; Rheinz; probably B F Attoni, Comitialis VI, Belsus III or contemporary; dog R&F T138a, bear possibly *ibid* T61a, free style; no. 773826
37; Rheinz; Julius I or Lupus; ovolo R&F E46; no. 773731
37 (8 pieces); CG; Doeccus; ovolo R B160, leaf R H59 in medallion, female figure O 926, leaf R J63, dancer O 368, circle R E54, metope and medallion style; nos 773661, 774172, 773733, 773774-6, 774217, 774175
37; CG; Cerialis-Cinnamus group; lion D 737, cupid O 401, mask O 1341, metope style; no. 773330
37; CG; Advocisus or Priscus; ovolo R B103, metope style; no. 773398
37; CG; Doeccus; leaf R H15, metope style; no. 773389
37 (3 pieces); CG; Doeccus; stand R Q6, leaf R H16 in medallion, deer O 1732 in medallion, metope and medallion style; nos 773441, 773570, 773595
37; CG; probably Paternus II; warrior O 188 in medallion; no. 773656
37 (4 pieces); CG; Doeccus; ovolo R B160, shell R U76, cup R T14, dolphin O 2401, metope style; nos 773735, 773783, 774174, 773635
37; CG; Paternus II; cupid O 444 in medallion; no. 773734
37; Arg; festoon F 451, ornament C&G fig. 621, 59B, crane *ibid* fig. 63, 6; no. 773646
37; Arg; Tribunus or Africanus; cock F 385, acanthus as F 386, free style; no. 773934
37 (3 pieces); Arg; ovolo C&G fig. 54bis; leaf *ibid* fig. 63, 11; nos 773844, 774033, 774094
37 (2 pieces); CG - probably Terre-Franche or Lubié rather than Lezoux; Banvus (stamped in mould with die 2a); Apollo O 92, metope style; nos 773846, 774007
37; CG; ovolo,-festoon and metope assigned to Had-Ant period by Dickinson; no. 773845
37; CG; Advocisus; no details available; no. 774077
37 (2 pieces); CG; Priscus; ovolo R B103, lozenge R U30; nos 774032, 774057
30; CG; Iullinus or Mercator II; ovolo R B156; no. 774040
37 (2 pieces); CG; Iullinus; ovolo R B153, Victory O 812 in medallion; nos 774075, 774130
37; CG; rouletted rather than moulded, as O&P pl. LXXV
72 (3 pieces); CG; barbotine scrolls, appliqué male figure Déch 20, similar figure not in Déch; nos 773589, 773628-9
From excavations by C Green:
37; CG; Banvus; bird O 2296A in medallion, cupid as O 433, column R P76, rosette S&S fig. 41 no. 3, metope and medallion style, worn internal bowl; no. 774407

37; CG; Iullinus; ovolo S&S fig. 36 no. 1, Venus O 339; no. 774403
37; CG; Casurius; ovolo R B223; no. 774405
37; Rheinz; JuliusII-Julianus I; ovolo R&F E17, Venus *ibid* M47, figure *ibid* M246, column *ibid* O210; no. 774408
Stamps from both sites:
33; CG; Martinus iii die 2a; no. 773311
31R; CG; Maximinus i die 2a; no. 773487
31; CG; Albusa die la
33; CG; Martius iv die 1b
31R; CG; Potitianus ii die 2a
31; Rheinz; Crassiacus die la
79 type; CG; Carus ii die la
31; CG; Maximinus i die 2a
33; CG; Martinus iii die 7a
31; CG; Celsus ii die 2a
31; CG; Albillus i die 1b
31; CG; Albusa die la
31R; Rheinz; Severianus ii die 4b
31R; Arg; Caupius die 4a
Plain ware from both sites:
18/31R CG; 18/31R or 31R CG; 31 CG (77); 31 CG/EG (8); 31 EG (44); 31 Rheinz (3); 31R CG (59 - 2 rivetted); 31R EG (32); 31R Rheinz; 31R Trier; 31R Arg; 33 CG (20); 33 EG (23); 35 EG; 35/36 CG; 36 CG (8); 36 EG (11); 46 CG; C15 CG (3); 79 CG (10); 79 EG (2); 79/80 CG; C15/23 CG (12); C23 CG (11); C23 EG riveted; 32 EG (9); 38 CG (4); 38 EG (8); 38/44 CG (3); Lud SM6 EG (2); C21 EG (3); 43 EG (3); 43/45 EG (5); 45 CG (33 - 2 rivetted); 45 CG/EG (2); 45 EG (15); 45 Trier; 45 Arg; mort CG (20); mort CG/EG; mort EG (3); Bushe-Fox 84 CG; Ritt 13 CG (3); 54 EG (6 - barbotine dec); 72 CG (4 - 1 barbotine, 1 appliqué; 72 EG; 30 CG; 30/37 CG (13); 30/37 EG (2); 37 CG (43); 37 EG (5); 37 Rheinz (5); 37 Trier; 37 Arg (5); jar CG with incised dec; U CG (70 - 1 rivetted); U CG/EG (20); U EG (60)

6 Faust I; 141-6
Faust II; 161-75
J Domna; 193-211
Sev; 193-211
Elag; 218-22
Traj Dec; 249-51
Claud II; 268-9

7 The sites are dated from late 2nd to early 4th centuries according to the phasing. On the face of it, the lack of coins of 270+ would run contrary to the later date given.

8 Department of the Environment, Central Excavation Unit archive reports by B Dickinson and J Bird (for the samian ware and coins listings given in sections 4 and 6); Curnow 1985; Dickinson & Bird 1985; Hinchliffe & Sparey Green 1985; Sparey Green 1985

**B 10**

1 Brecon, Powys; fort; well in *principia*
2 C
3 B
4 37; CG; Casurius; gadroon R V151, metope style; Simpson 1963 fig. 9(c) no. 2
37; Rheinz; Cobnertus II; ovolo as R&F R44b, Mercury *ibid* M77, caryatid *ibid* M56, warrior *ibid* M261, vertical border *ibid* P14, metope and medallion style, as Ricken 1948 Taf. 23 no. 1; fig. 75 no. 599
31 (2); 31 CG (2); Lud Tf EG
8 Pryce & Oswald 1926; Simpson 1963a, 16-37; Wheeler 1926

**B 11**

1 Brentford, Greater London; *vicus*; site 9, feature Z6B
2 C
3 A
4 37; CG; Paternus II; cupid O 444A, medallion and winding scroll style; fig. 81 no. 15
37; CG; Albucius or Servus I; ovolo S&S fig. 35 no. 1, metope and medallion style; fig. 81 no. 16
37; CG; Paternus II or associate; ovolo S&S fig. 31 no. 1; fig. 81 no. 17
7 There are several SG pieces from the same feature, but the excavator has distinguished two fills in the stratigraphy.
8 Bird 1978a; Canham 1978

**B 12**

1 Brentford, Greater London: *vicus*; site 9, feature Z9A dark soil
2 E
3 A
4 37; CG; Pugnus; ovolo S&S pl. 155 no. 20; fig. 83 no. 1
37; CG; Doeccus; large square beads; fig. 83 no. 2
8 Bird 1978a; Canham 1978

**B 13**

1 Brentford; Greater London; *vicus*: site 9, feature Z15
2 D
3 A
4 37; CG; Igocatus; ovolo S&S fig. 6 no. 1; fig. 87 no. 1
37; CG; Drusus II; ovolo S&S pl. 89 no. 12, Hercules O 783, metope style; fig. 87 no. 2
37; CG; Cinnamus; ovolo S&S fig. 47 no. 1, winding scroll style; fig. 87 no. 3
8 Bird 1978a; Canham 1978

**B 14**

1 Brentford, Greater London; *vicus*; site 9, feature Z35
2 C
3 A
4 37; Rheinz; Julius II-Julianus I; ovolo R&F E23, hare *ibid* T160a, plant *ibid* P111, stand *ibid* O179, arcade style, cut to make a disc; fig. 89 no. 1
5 Oxf CCW; NV CCW; Verulamium CCW indented beaker with rouletted bands; Oxf mortarium
7 The interest of this group is the other fine pottery which constitutes 12.4% of the assemblage. Their general dating is late 2nd to early 4th century. Oxf ware is supposed to be widely distributed from *c* 250.
8 Bird 1978a; Canham 1978

**B 15**

1 Caerleon, Gwent; fortress; Goldcroft Common, debris levels 1 and 1a in furnace house
2 E
3 A
4 From level 1:
37 SG (2); 18/31 SG or CG
From level 1a:
37; SG; erotic group O J
37; CG; vine leaf from winding scroll on probable late vessel
18 SG; 15/17 SG; SG or CG fragments (2)
6 Vesp; Dup: RIC 740; 72-3; little wear
7 A clear case of redeposition, as Simpson points out (1959, 130), in this case to build up the clay bank of the rampart over the furnace house. Only the 37 CG is probably contemporary.

8 Murray-Threipland 1959; Rigold 1959; Simpson 1959 and pers. comm.

**B 16**

1 Caerleon, Gwent; quayside; mud and peat behind the breakwater
2 G - silt accumulation
3 A
4 37; Rheinz; Reginus I; ovolo R&F E55, rosettes *ibid* O45, free style; fig. 11 no. 18
37 (2 pieces); Rheinz; Julius I; ovolo R&F E42, metope and medallion style as Ricken 1948 Taf. 153 nos 1-5; fig. 11 no. 19
37; Rheinz; Victor I; gladiator R&F M217, border *ibid* O275, metope and medallion style; fig. 11 no. 20
7 These pieces may be contemporary with the quays themselves (deposit **A 28**), but the rate of accumulation of the mud and peat is difficult to establish, as is the stratigraphy relative to the quays.
8 Boon 1978a

**B 17**

1 Caistor-by-Norwich, Norfolk; town; south of south wall room 14 in forum
2 B
3 C
4 37; CG; Paternus II style; ovolo 3 (S&S fig. 30 no. 3, R B206), beaded border below, rosette prob R C126 but appears more like R C130, small double circle as S&S pl. 108, 37
37; CG; Divixtus style; hare O 2061 at base of panelled dec, vertical bead-row on each side, and feet of stands for caryatids as S&S pl. 115 no. 7
37; CG; base with part of large scroll
7 Stratigraphic details are unclear, but the sherds appear to be an associated group.
8 Frere 1971, 24

**B 18**

1 Canterbury, Kent; town; Burgate Street, CXIV M I 26
2 C
3 A
4 37; Rheinz; probably Primitivus I-IV; ovolo as R&F E11, trifid as *ibid* P116-7; fig. 137 no. 3
36; 'late Antonine'
31R: 'late Antonine'
5 CCW and coarse wares dated by excavator to mid-3rd century (fig. 116, 603-6)
7 A late, apparently contemporary, group. The layers above (22 and 19), which slump into and seal the pit, contain coins of late 3rd to 4th century.
8 Frere & Stow 1983, 113-8, 160-2, 319

**B 19**

1 Canterbury, Kent; town; St George's Street apsed building, layers CXV SII 22 and 25
2 B
3 A
4 37; CG; Docilis; ovolo probably S&S fig. 24 no. 1, triangular panel design formed by beaded borders linked by astragali as S&S pl. 91 no. 2, bird as O 2214a; fig. 137 no. 5
37; CG; Cinnamus; leaf R H24, bird O 2315 but smaller; fig. 137 no. 6
7 Found, according to the excavator, in layers of a building constructed AD 190-220 and demolished before 250. The dates come from coarse wares. The Cinnamus sherd comes from a primary floor (layer 25) and the Docilis sherd from a secondary floor (layer 22). A sherd of Austrus (fig. 137 no. 2) came from soil overlying the building, but this may be redeposited.
8 Frere & Stow 1983, 41-9, 319

**B 20**

1 Canterbury, Kent; town; Watling Street, grey layer in cutting AA[1]
2 B
3 A
4 37; CG; Cinnamus; ovolo S&S fig. 47 no. 1, part of hare in festoon; pl. VI no. 6
30; CG; Paternus II; stag O 1770, small circle; pl. VI no. 7
18/31; Lez; stamped G]IPPI·M
Plain wares: 2 x 31, 38, 45
8 Williams 1947, 87-100

**B 21**

1 Carzield, Dumfries and Galloway; fort; general finds
2 F
3 B
4 37; CG; X-6; ovolo S&S fig. 18 no. 4 (= R B2), trifid S&S fig. 18 no. 13, figure O 571, Diana O·106, metope style, this piece published as S&S pl. 76 no. 28; fig. 1 no. 1
37; CG; Quintilianus group; rosette R C29, dancer O 347, metope style; fig. 1 no. 2
37; CG; Pugnus; ovolo S&S fig. 45 no. 2, leaf as *ibid* fig. 45 no. 9, deer O 1781, free style, this piece published as S&S pl. 153 no. 11; fig. 1 no. 3
37; CG; Albucius (stamped in mould); ovolo and border S&S fig. 35 no. 1, Jupiter O 3, metope style; fig. 1 no. 5
37 (2 pieces); Arg; possibly ware with ovolo A/B; rosette Ricken 1934 Taf. 13 no. 48 and C&G fig. 57J, dog not in H, medallion style; fig. 1 no. 6
7 Birley interprets the pottery as a whole as being of the period 140-60, but the group presented here seems fairly mixed.
8 Birley 1947b, 70-2

**B 22**

1 Catterick, North Yorkshire; town; building II, lower occupation
2 B
3 A
4 37 (4 pieces); CG; Paternus II; ovolo S&S fig. 30 no. 4; fig. 7 no. 5
37; CG; probably Severus; ovolo as S&S fig. 37 no. 2; fig. 7 no. 6
37 CG fragment; presence of 31 CG and 33 CG
From sandy layer above lower occupation and below floor:
37; CG; Iullinus; mask O 1214, leaf S&S fig. 36 no. 8, metope style; fig. 7 no. 2
37; CG; Advocisus; leaf S&S fig. 33 no. 4, draped woman as O 923, metope style; fig. 7 no. 3
5 Rhenish CCW beaker; NV CCW cup
7 The sandy layer may be make-up for the upper floor rather than part of the lower occupation.
8 Hildyard 1957; Simpson 1957b

**B 23**

1 Chester, Cheshire; fortress; Castle Street, well II layer 8
2 C
3 A
4 37; CG; Butrio or Attianus; Mercury O 538, border R A2, metope style; fig. 21 no. 25

37 (4 pieces); CG; Cinnamus; ovolo R B143, Pan mask O 1214, dolphin and basket R Q58, Vulcan O 66, metope and medallion style; fig. 21 no. 27
37 (22 pieces); CG; Advocisus (stamped in mould with die 8a); ovolo R B103, rosette R C122, Victory O 809, ornament R U104, caryatid O 1205, astragalus R R81, panther O 1536, bear O 1630, metope and medallion style; fig. 21 no. 28
37 (18 pieces); CG; Casurius; ovolo S&S fig. 40 no. 1, sea horse O 33, male figure O 638, astragalus R R2, leaf R H68, base as R U295, metope style; fig. 21 no. 29
37; CG; probably Paternus II; erotic group as O Y, 'twist' S&S fig. 30 no. 21; fig. 21 no. 30
37; CG; Cinnamus; ovolo S&S fig. 47 no. 2; no other details given
37; CG; Albucius; no details given
37; CG; Banvus or Iullinus; no details given
37; Heil; Janu; ovolo R&F E69, bifid *ibid* P140, cupid *ibid* M126, metope style; fig. 21 no. 26
Stamps on plain ware:
18/31; CG; Malledo die 4b
33; CG; Gratius ii die 7a
33; CG; Peculiaris i die 5a
33; CG; Caratillus die 6a
33; CG; Osbimanus die 7b
33; CG; Sanciro die la
33; CG; Elvillus die la
33; CG; Martius iv die 1h
38; CG; Draucus ii die la
Plain ware (including those listed above): C15 CG; 18/31 CG (9-10); 18/31 EG; 18/31R CG (4); 31 CG; 31R CG; 33 CG (8); 38 CG; 30 CG (1-2); 37 CG (23-24); 37 EG; U CG (4)

5 Oxf CCW bowl imitation 38

7 This is the lowest silt in the well, and the material (including a skeleton) probably accumulated during the use of the well.

8 Bulmer 1980; Mason 1980

**B 24**

1 Chester-le-Street, County Durham; fort; general finds

2 F

3 A

4 From 1970s excavations:
37; CG; Paternus II; rosette R C281; no. 34
37; CG; Cinnamus or Paullus; sea-bull O 42, bird O 2239, metope style; no. 81
37; CG; probably Cinnamus; deer O 1720; no. 35
37; Trier; Werkstatt II Style E; strigil F 895, circle as F Taf. 22 no. 3, free style; no. 77
72 CG (2) with incised dec; 45 CG with incised dec
From earlier excavations:
37; CG; X-13 or Sacer; ovolo as R B14
37; CG; X-5; column R P62, border R A23, metope style
37; CG; Cinnamus; ovolo S&S fig. 47 no. 1, bird O 2250A, metope style
37 (2 pieces); CG; Cinnamus or Casurius; ovolo S&S fig. 47 no. 1
37; CG; Cinnamus; ovolo S&S fig. 47 no. 1
37; CG; Casurius; bird as O 2239 (closer to Stanfield 1935 pl. IX no. 27), acanthus R K16, metope style
37; CG; Casurius; ovolo R B223, sea horse O 33, metope style
37; CG; Casurius, ovolo R B223, trifid Stanfield 1935 pl. IX no. 16A, metope style
37; CG; Cinnamus, Pugnus, Iullinus, Severus or contemporary; caryatid as O 1199, metope style
37; CG; Iullinus; ovolo S&S fig. 36 no. 2
37; CG; probably Iullinus; column as R P37, astragalus as R R61
37; CG; Priscus, Caletus or associate; ovolo as R B77, leaf R J78, rosette as R C103, metope style
30; CG; festoon as R F2 (Mercator II, Caletus, Fgientinus), winding scroll style
30; CG; possibly Caletus; rosette as R C39, metope style
37; CG; Doeccus; lioness O 1533, metope style
37; CG; Paternus II; 'twist' S&S fig. 30 no. 18, horse O 1911, bear as O 1616, dog as O 1917, dog as O 1940, free style
37; CG; Paternus II or Albucius; ovolo R B106
37; CG; Paternus II, Albucius or Sissus II; ovolo R B107
37; CG; Sissus I; ovolo as R B98
30; CG; Advocisus; Venus O 305, female figure as O 923, metope style
37; Arg; Tribunus; ovolo C&G T6
37; Rheinz; Janu I; ovolo R&F E19
30; Rheinz; Cobnertus III; cupid R&F M111, eagle *ibid* T166, metope and medallion style
37; Rheinz; Comitialis III; ovolo R&F E10, circle *ibid* K48, tripod *ibid* O11, medallion style
30; Rheinz; Primitivus I (stamped in mould); metope style
37; Rheinz; Cobnertus III, Primitivus I-IV or contemporary; ovolo R&F E11
30; Rheinz; Cobnertus III or Primitivus III; rosette R&F O78, metope style
37; Rheinz; B F Attoni or Cerialis IV; ovolo R&F E3
37; Rheinz; Julius I, Lupus or associate; ovolo as R&F E46
37; Rheinz; probably Julius II-Julianus I or contemporary; ovolo R&F E23
37; Rheinz; Julius II-Julianus I; rosette R&F O66, circle *ibid* K9, festoon *ibid* KB100, stand *ibid* O161
72 CG with barbotine dec

8 King 1991a

**B 25**

1 Chichester, West Sussex; town; Central Girls' School, trench G layer 29

2 E

3 A

4 37: Rheinz; Julius II-Julianus I; ovolo R&F E23, cross *ibid* O53 in circle *ibid* K11 or circle *ibid* K14, medallion style, cf Karnitsch 1955, Taf. 98; fig. 10.11, no. 40

5 NV CCW; Oxf and NF CCW - early types

7 This layer is dated late 3rd century on the basis of the fine wares (Down 1978, 266). The samian could be contemporary, or certainly in use up to the mid-3rd century. An overlying layer has a late 3rd century radiate coin.

8 Dannell 1978a; Down 1978

**B 26**

1 Chichester, West Sussex; town; Gospel Hall, trench P layer 37

2 C

3 A

4 37 (2 pieces); Rheinz; Firmus II (stamped in mould); ovolo as R&F E26, rosette *ibid* O48, column *ibid* O220, medallion style; fig 10.11 no. 38
Plain ware: pre-Flavian (1), Flavian (3), early 2nd (5), Antonine i.e. CG (6), late 2nd/early 3rd i.e. EG (2)

5 NF CCW dated to end 3rdcentury (pp. 262-5); Colch and Lez CCW; absence of Oxf CCW

7 This pit is placed in phase 5, 3rd to early 4th century, by the excavator. The NF pottery is placed at the end of the 3rd

century but there is no reason why it should not be earlier. The amount of early samian suggests a measure of redeposition. A contemporary pit (trench O layer 40) has similar contents (samian - 1st century (1), Hadrianic (2), Antonine i.e. CG (7), late 2nd/early 3rd i.e. EG (2)).

8 Dannell 1978a; Down 1978

**B 27**

1 Colchester, Essex; kiln site; pit C17
2 C
3 A
4 30; CG; Cinnamus (stamped in mould with large stamp); cupid O 401, metope and medallion style; fig. 44 no. 21
Fragments of Colch samian over-fired and discarded as wasters.
5 Colch CCW rough-cast beakers over-fired and discarded as wasters.
7 Important for its relationship to the Colch samian kiln.
8 Hull 1963, 90

**B 28**

1 Corbridge, Northumberland; town; destruction level of Antonine II (period V) in area of 'temples' I-III
2 E
3 A
4 37 (many pieces); CG; Cettus; ovolo as S&S fig. 42 no. 1, trifid *ibid* fig. 42 no. 6, trifid *ibid* fig. 42 no. 9, rosette *ibid* fig. 42 no. 7, spiral *ibid* fig. 42 no. 1, leaf R H62, leaf reverse of R J57, lion O 1457, lion O 1404, metope style; fig. 2 no. 16
37 (2 pieces); CG; Tetturo; Jupiter O 3, trifid as R G65, rosette as R C277, metope and medallion style; fig. 3 no. 17
37; CG; Cinnamus; ovolo S&S fig. 47 no. 3 (= R B144), panther O 1533, free style; fig. 3 no. 18
37; CG; Cinnamus; ovolo S&S fig. 47 no. 3, leaf *ibid* fig. 47 no. 38, bird O 2239B, winding scroll and medallion style; fig. 3 no. 19
37; CG; probably Cinnamus; winding scroll and medallion style; fig. 3 no. 20
37; Rheinz; B F Attoni; ovolo R&F E3, leaf *ibid* P58, acanthus *ibid* P145, winding scroll style very similar to Ricken 1948 Taf. 40 no. 2; fig. 3 no. 21
7 Apparently part of the so-called 'AD 197' destruction deposit.
8 Simpson1922

**B 29**

1 Ditchley, Oxfordshire; villa; ditch to west of entrance to courtyard
2 D
3 A
4 37 (several pieces); CG; Cinnamus (early style); ovolo S&S fig. 47 no. 3, warrior O 177, dancer O 819A, pygmy O 696A, hare O 2116, metope style; pl. XI nos 4 and 13
37; CG; Libertus; cupid O 498, metope style; pl. XI no. 5
37 (2 pieces); CG; Butrio; ovolo S&S fig. 13 no. 9, leaf *ibid* fig. 13 no. 5, female figure O 943, metope style; pl. XI nos 6-7
37; CG; Austrus; ovolo not in R but as B10, festoon R F16, trifid as R G71, stand R Q53, lion O 1570, metope style; pl. XI no. 8
37; CG; Drusus I; ovolo R B28, rosette R C280, metope style; pl. XI no. 9
37; CG; X-13; ovolo R B6, warrior O 197, rosette R C280, metope style; pl. XI no. 10
37; CG; Sacer-Attianus; lioness O 1518, bear O 1595, free style; pl. XI no. 12
37; CG; possibly Quintilianus group; metope style; pl. XI no. 11
7 The deposit was a thick dark layer 'of thatch fallen from the roof of the southern building' (Radford 1936, 50).
8 Pryce 1936; Radford 1936

**B 30**

1 Dorchester, Dorset; town; library site, beneath chalk floor of building 1
2 E
3 A
4 37; CG; Divixtus; Venus O 365, metope and medallion style; fig. 16 no. 8
37; CG; Casurius; stand R Q42, female figure O 339, metope style; fig. 16 no. 10
37; CG; Iullinus or associate; column as R P21, Venus O 278, possibly arcade style; fig. 16 no. 11
80; CG; stamped by Maximus ii die 9a
7 The overlying floor formed part of a building dated late 2nd to early 3rd century for its construction.
8 Aitken & Aitken 1982; Pengelly 1982

**B 31**

1 Dorchester, Dorset; town; Trinity Street, layers 6 and 7, burnt deposit
2 E
3 A
4 37; Trier; Censor; ovolo as F 937, stand F 795, Venus as O 315 but smaller, arcade and metope style; p. 51 no. 111a
Plain ware: 33 CG stamped by Mammus; 37 CG stamped by Uxopillus; 43; 32; C21; 33; 18/31
5 NF wares from the same layers. Kirk gives the number of sherds per thousand of the total of sherds in each layer as follows:
Layer 9: samian 79
Layer 7: samian 46; NF 1
Layer 6: samian 53; NF 1
Layer 5: samian 37; 'imitation samian' 1; NF 10
Layer 4: samian 11; 'imitation samian' 14; NF 53
7 Layer 5 is probably a mid to late 3rd century construction deposit incorporating earlier material. Layers 6 and 7, from which the samian listed above came, may date up to that period but also incorporate some earlier material.
8 Kirk 1940

**B 32**

1 Dover, Kent; fort; Burial Ground, DV 39/97/100/102/147-8 upper fill of 2nd fort ditch
2 D
3 A
4 37; Rheinz; B F Attoni; Cerialis V or Primitivus III; ladder made of bead-rows cf Ricken 1948 Taf. 38 no. 16, Taf. 64 no. 20, Taf. 198 no. 8; fig. 48 no. 290
37; CG; probably Criciro; blurred ovolo as S&S pl. 117 no. 1, lioness possibly *ibid* pl. 117 no. 3
37; CG; narrow candelabrum and fine wavy lines, rivetted
37; CG; Paternus II, Iullinus or Catussa I; Victory as O 812 in double medallion
Plain ware: 31 CG (6); 31R CG/EG; 31R EG; 31/31R CG/EG; 31/31R EG; 33 CG (2); 79 CG/EG; 36 CG; 37 CG (2); 38 CG; U CG (2); U EG
8 Bird & Marsh 1981; Philp 1981

**B 33**

1 Dover, Kent; fort; Durham Hill North, DV 1992 central fill of 2nd fort ditch
2 D
3 A
4 37; CG; Servus II; ovolo R B147, leaf (2) R H133, wavy line border S&S pl. 131 no. 1, acanthus leaf S&S pl. 131 no. 2, Venus O 290, Venus O 331, metope style; fig. 48 no. 287
37; CG; Paternus II; ovolo S&S pl. 105 no. 12, large rosette *ibid* pl. 107 no. 27, braided small circle *ibid* pl. 107 no. 30, large bead *ibid*, circle *ibid* pl. 108 no. 37, beaded double medallion *ibid* pl. 107 no. 31, cupid O 444, medallion and scroll style; fig. 48 no. 288
37; CG; Iullinus or Mercator II; vase as R T16; fig. 48 no. 289
33; Lez; Pottacus die 2a
31; Lez; Cintusmus i die 2b
31R; Lez; Sextus v die 4c
Plain ware: 33 CG (2); 31 CG (2); 31R CG
8 Bird & Marsh 1981; Philp 1981

**B 34**

1 Dover, Kent; fort; Durham Hill North, DV 1993 lower fill of 2nd fort ditch
2 D
3 A
4 37; CG; Sacer-Attianus; circles and bead-row S&S pl. 84 no. 15, leaf-tips *ibid* pl. 83 no. 9, warrior O 177, metope style; fig. 48 no. 285
30; CG; Cinnamus; ovolo S&S fig. 47 no. 3, hare O 2116, in festoon S&S pl. 157 no. 7, bead-and-reel border *ibid* pl. 160 no. 35, warrior O 204, metope style; fig. 48 no. 286
37; CG; fragment with sea-beast in medallion; fig. 48 no. 284
Plain ware: 33 CG (2)
8 Bird & Marsh 1981; Philp 1981

**B 35**

1 Dover, Kent; fort; Durham Hill South, DV 1902-3 loam over floor in B 30
2 B
3 A
4 37; SG; Meddillus-Quintus style; details not given here, very worn bowl; fig. 51 no. 353
37; CG; probably Cinnamus; lozenge S&S fig. 47 no. 15, in arrangement as *ibid* pl. 159 no. 24; fig. 51 no. 348
37; CG; Albucius; wreath border S&S pl. 120 no. 6, bead-row terminal *ibid*, leaf *ibid* pl. 122 no. 27, metope style; fig. 51 no. 349
37; La Mad; ovolo Ricken 1934 Taf. VIIC, mask *ibid* Taf. VII no. 70, vase *ibid* Taf. VII no. 77, robed figure *ibid* Taf. IX no. 15, basal wreath possibly *ibid* Taf. XI no. 8; fig. 51 no. 350
37; CG; Doeccus or Pugnus; figure as O 243; fig. 51 no. 351
37; CG; Cinnamus; ovolo S&S fig. 47 no. 3, bead-row *ibid* pl. 157 no. 1, small leaf, festoon, rosette and small circle all *ibid* pl. 157 no. 12, charioteer O 1159, metope style; fig. 51 no. 352
37; CG; fragmentary ovolo
33; Lez; Mattius ii die4a
18/31R; Lez; Banvillus die 2a
Plain ware: 18 SG; 18/31 CG; 18/31R CG (rivetted); 37 SG; 37 CG; 38 CG; 31 CG (3); 33 CG (7)
7 The excavator suggests that the SG vessels may be derived from another deposit (Philp 1981, 61) but the very worn condition of the 37 SG may be due to use over a long period, and hence survival.
8 Bird & Marsh 1981; Philp 1981

**B 36**

1 Dover, Kent; *vicus* of fort; Market Square, level 3b of destruction
2 E
3 A
4 37 (6 pieces); Rheinz; Reginus I; ovolo Ricken 1948 Taf. 12 no. 9, tripod *ibid* Taf. 13 no. 25a, cupid R&F M91; fig. 13
37; CG; Ioenalis or Donnaucus; Diana as the moon in a biga O 117A, dolphin not in O or D
37 (3 pieces); CG; Cinnamus; 'small bowl ovolo' = S&S fig. 47 no. 3, large 10-petalled rosette, winding scroll style
18/31; Lez; Saciro stamp
18/31; Lez; Sextus stamp
18/31; Lez; Aestivus stamp
31; Lez; Uxopillus stamp
31; Lez; Ritogenus ii stamp
31; Lez; Albus stamp
8 Birley & Simpson 1957; Murray-Threipland 1957

**B 37**

1 Enfield, Greater London; *vicus*; F42 pit fill
2 C
3 A
4 29; SG; mid-Flavian style, no details given here; fig. 18 no. 25
37; CG; Doeccus; ovolo S&S fig. 44 no. 3; no. 20
37; CG; Cinnamus; ovolo S&S fig. 47 no. 1; no. 21
37 (2 pieces); CG; Cinnamus; ovolo S&S fig. 47 no. 2; no. 22
37 (3 pieces); EG - possibly La Mad; lion O 1497K, warrior O 201, Pan as O 717, bird as O 2361, spiral ornament, metope style; no. 23
6 Coin of 268-73
Coin of 355-60
7 The pit was initially filled in the 2nd century, but was later consolidated in the 4th. This accounts for the later coins which have not been differentiated stratigraphically in the report.
8 Gentry, Ivens & McClean 1977; Hammerson & Coxshall 1977; Webster 1977

**B 38**

1 Enfield, Greater London; *vicus*; F48 layer 2, pit fill
2 C
3 A
4 37; CG; Paternus II; ovolo as R B234; no. 28
37; CG; Fgientinus; ovolo as R B50, leaf as R H23; no. 29
7 From the disturbed layer above this comes Had; Quad; RIC 623; 119-21, Sev; Den (plated); *c* 200, and a coin of the house of Const. The earlier two may be associated with the fill of the pit, disturbed in the 4th century.
8 Gentry, Ivens & McClean 1977; Hammerson & Coxshall 1977; Webster 1977

**B 39**

1 Ewell, Surrey; *vicus*; ditch in cuttings I and IA
2 D
3 A
4 From cutting I:
37; CG; Paternus II; ovolo probably S&S fig. 30 no. 1, mask O 1330 in double circle, trifid S&S fig. 30 no. 11 in festoon, metope style with rope-like borders; pl. V no. 1

30; CG; Pugnus; ovolo S&S fig. 45 no. 2, panther O 1518 in festoon, small circle S&S fig. 45 no. 7, trifid terminal to vertical wavy line borders S&S fig. 45 no. 1 and pl. 153 no. 6, warrior O 177, identical to S&S pl. 153 no. 1 from Corbridge and probably from the same mould; pl. V no. 3 and fig. 9 no. 3
37; CG; small ovolo with rosette, probably early 2nd century; rivetted; pl. V no. 2
27; CG; stamped by Pateratus
Plain ware: 37 prob SG; 37 CG; 38 CG; 30 CG; 31
From cutting IA:
37; CG; Cinnamus; ovolo S&S fig. 47 no. 1, part of festoon; pl. V no. 13
37; CG; Doeccus; sea bull O 52A, triton O 21, hare O 2057A in double circle, 4-leaved rosette S&S fig. 44 no. 2, bifid *ibid* fig. 44 no. 13, shell *ibid* fig. 44 no. 6 in small double circle, large double circle R E8, metope style; pl. V no. 14
Plain ware: 18/31 CG; 31; 33 CG; 36 EG?; 37 prob SG; 37; 38 CG; 80 EG? stamped with rosette

7 These two deposits are linked by virtue of the form 38 from each cutting probably coming from the same vessel. A fairly homogenous group, but mixed with some fragments of earlier material, e.g. 37 SG. There is also plain samian from cutting V, including 18/31 CG, 31 CG (4), 36 CG (2), which are probably trom the same ditch.

8 Frere 1943

**B 40**

1 Exeter, Devon; town; South Gate, occupation sealed by tail of rampart

2 B

3 A

4 37 (17 pieces); CG; Paullus; warrior D 103, lioness D 789, lioness D 798, bear D 817, stag D 874, shield R U210, leaf as on signed bowl by Paullus (Hartley 1961c, fig. 7 no. 21), free style with sparse vertical divisions; fig. 6 no. 1
37; CG; Albucius (stamped in mould); ovolo S&S fig. 35 no. 2, lion and bear as D 778, warrior D 140 with slight difference in right arm, figure D 382, bear as O 1626, bestiarius D 631, free style; fig. 6 no. 2
37; CG; Cinnamus; ovolo S&S fig. 47 no. 4, dancer O 322, bird as O 2297 in double medallion; dolphin D 1050, Pan mask D 675, hare D 950a in festoon, athlete D 394, Pan D 413, metope, festoon and medallion style; fig. 6 no. 3
37; CG; Paullus or associate; ovolo only
Plain ware includes 31; 33; 38

8 Fox 1968; Hartley 1968

**B 41**

1 Fishbourne, West Sussex; villa; period 3 destruction levels

2 F

3 A

4 Details of the following pieces are not given here, see Dannell 1971b, 295-6. His dates have been used.
37; SG; dated 70-85
37; SG; dated 75-90
37; SG; Biragillus; dated 80-100
37; SG; Martialis and Marinus; dated 65-80
37; GG; Attianus; dated 125-50
37; CG; dated 150+
37; CG; Doeccus; dated 160-90

6 The coins have been grouped in a different manner from the samian. However, from period 3 occupation levels (i.e. underlying) come:
Rep; Den (plated)
Claud; Ae; illeg (3)
Nero; Ae; illeg
Vesp; Den
Vesp; Ae (3)
Nerva; Ae
Had; HS (2)
Post; Rad
Claud II; Rad (3)
Tet I; Rad
Tet II; Rad
Barb Rad

7 This is a good example of mixed redeposition, since the samian closely reflects the pattern from the occupation levels of the 'palace'. The coins too are probably largely redeposited. It is just possible that the later samian (e.g. by Doeccus) could have been in use in period 3 occupation - there are several late CG bowls in the robbing trenches. There are problems in making clear associations because of the way in which the samian and the coins have been generalised into phases, without specific contexts being given.

8 Cunliffe 1971; Dannell 1971b; Reece 1971

**B 42**

1 Gloucester, Gloucestershire; town; Bon Marché site, layer 90 and associated layers

2 E

3 A

4 37; CG; Paternus II; ovolo S&S fig. 30 no. 1, leaf R H2, rosette R C242, virtually identical to S&S pl. 107 no. 27, winding scroll style; fig. 7 no. 6
37; CG; Pugnus; ovolo R B32, St Andrew's cross as S&S pl. 153 no. 7 with same details; fig. 7 no. 7
37; CG; rim only

8 Hunter 1963; Simpson 1963b

**B 43**

1 Gloucester, Gloucestershire; town; Bon Marché site, 4th street surfaces

2 B

3 A

4 37; CG; Divixtus; ovolo as S&S pl. 116 no. 10, metope with circles; fig. 7 no. 14
37; CG; Doeccus; bifid S&S fig. 44 no. 15, metope and medallion style; fig. 7 no. 15
37; CG; Iullinus; vase R T16, 'bowl' R U64; fig. 7 no. 16
37; CG; Paternus II (stamped in mould); fragment of animal and medallion; fig. 7 no. 17

8 Hunter 1963; Simpson 1963b

**B 44**

1 Gloucester, Gloucestershire; town; King's Square, layer 2 of bank of town wall upper levels

2 E

3 A

4 37; CG; Cinnamus; ovoloS&S fig. 47 no. 3
37; CG; Advocisus; ovolo S&S fig. 33 no. 2, bird O 2314 in festoon, Amazon O 244, metope style; fig. 3 no. 1
37; CG; Cinnamus; ovolo S&S fig. 47 no. 2, bird as *ibid* pl. 161 no. 47 in festoon, metope and medallion style; fig. 3 no. 3
37; CG; Casurius; ovolo as S&S pl. 134 no. 26, female figure not in O, metope style; fig. 3 no. 2
37; CG; Pugnus; leaf S&S fig. 45 no. 6; fig. 3 no. 6

Plain ware: 37 CG (2 fragments); 18/31 (4); 31 (10); 33 CG (2); 27 (late type)
From lower levels of layer 2:
37; CG; Pugnus; caryatid O 1199, bird O 2197, sphinx O 735A in festoon, metope style; fig. 3 no. 7
Plain ware: 24/25 SG; 81/31 CG; 42 CG
5 CCW 'hunt-cup'
7 Both upper and lower parts of layer 2 can probably be taken together. The upper level is more homogeneous and has no admixture of SG pieces.
8 O'Neil 1958

**B 45**

1 Heronbridge, Cheshire; *vicus*; group E from between buildings II and III
2 E
3 A
4 37; CG; Attianus; ornament O 2155, leaves S&S fig. 22 no. 6, lion O 1450, horseman O 251, boar O 1668, free style; fig. 7 no. 16
37; CG; Drusus II (signed in mould); ovolo S&S pl. 89 nos 12-13, deer O 1697, trifid as R G89, vine scroll R M10, metope style, also published in S&S pl. 89 no. 12; fig. 7 no. 17
37; CG; Cinnamus or associate; acanthus as R K12; fig. 7 no. 18
37; CG; Divixtus; hare as O 2131, metope style; fig. 7 no. 20
37; CG; Cinnamus or Sacer; ovolo as S&S fig. 47 no. 3, bird O 2315, winding scroll style; fig. 7 no. 19
Plain ware: 27; 36; 31; 33 (all probably CG)
5 NV CCW beaker with barbotine dec
7 The gap between the two buildings is narrow, and the deposit is probably deliberate rubbish fill.
8 Hartley 1952

**B 46**

1 Heronbridge, Cheshire; *vicus*; group F from under second road surface
2 E
3 A
4 30; CG; Sacer; ovolo as S&S fig. 22 no. 1, trifid *ibid* fig. 22 no. 4, shrine roof R U269, bird O 2324, hare O 2061, Apollo as O 91, bird as O 2266, caryatid O 1199, erotic group O K, metope style; fig. 8 no. 23
37; CG; Attianus; ovolo probably S&S fig. 23 no. 4, leaf R J1, leaf R H72, bird as O 2270, winding scroll style, possibly from same mould as S&S pl. 87 no. 21 (Chester); fig. 8 no. 25
37; CG; Advocisus (stamped in mould); gladiators as O 1003-4, spiral as R S18, metope and medallion style; fig. 8 no. 26
37; CG; Sacer; ovolo S&S fig. 22 no. 1, Jupiter O 3, metope style; fig. 8 no. 27
37; CG; Acaunissa; rosette S&S fig. 21 no. 5, trifid *ibid* fig. 21 no. 2, metope style; fig. 8 no. 28
30 (2 pieces); CG; Divixtus (stamped in mould); Diana O 106, metope style; fig. 8 nos 29 and 31
37; CG; possibly P-1; bifid as R G304, metope style; fig. 8 no. 30
37; CG; Advocisus; ovolo as R B102, metope style; fig. 8 no. 32
Plain ware: 37 CG fragment; 27 CG stamped by Paulus; 33 CG stamped by Acapa; 79 probably CG; 31 Rheinz or Heil stamped by Virilis
5 NV CCW beaker
6 There was an Ae coin of Traj of 104-11 from the underlying road surface.
7 The group may be redeposited rubbish from the building used to level the roadway.
8 Hartley 1952

**B 47**

1 High Cross, Leicestershire; *vicus*; ditch F34
2 D
3 A
4 37; SG; late Flavian date, no details given here; fig. 4 no. 7
37; Blick or CG; ovolo as S&S fig. 22 no. 1 (Sacer), but attributed by Hartley to Blick; fig. 5 no. 14
37; CG; probably Drusus II; ovolo as R B38, ornament O 2155, free style; fig. 5 no. 17
37; CG; Drusus II; ovolo as R B38, rosette R C280, vine scroll R M10, metope style; fig. 5 no. 21
37; CG; Mercator II; ovolo S&S fig. 43 no. 2, leaf R H18, medallion style; fig. 5 no. 32
8 Greenfield & Webster 1965; Hartley 1965

**B 48**

1 High Cross, Leicestershire; *vicus*;pit F45
2 C
3 A
4 37; CG-MdV; possibly X-2; figure similar to O 571A; fig. 5 no. 13
37; CG-MdV; Drusus I; lion O 1424, lioness O 1520, metope style; fig. 5 no. 15
37; CG; Quintilianus group; ovolo S&S fig. 17 no. 1, straight line below top bead row as *ibid* pl. 70 no. 19; fig. 5 no. 20
37; CG; Paternus II; cupid O 444A, winding scroll and medallion style; fig. 5 no. 29
37; Rheinz; Janu I; ovolo R&F E39, tripod *ibid* O11, trifid *ibid* P127, metope style; fig. 5 no. 24
37; CG; free style, unattributed to potter; fig. 5 no. 31
33; CG; stamped by Osbimanus
7 The samian comes from the top part of the pit (layer 5).
8 Greenfield & Webster 1965; Hartley 1965

**B 49**

1 Hob's Ditch Causeway, Warwickshire; linear earthwork; layer 16/18
2 D
3 A
4 37; CG; Cinnamus; ovolo S&S fig. 47 no. 2; no. S12
37; CG; Cinnamus or associate; stand R Q32; no. S13
37; CG; Casurius; ovolo S&S fig. 40 no. 3; no. S14
Plain ware: 37 CG (2 fragments - 1 rivetted); 31 CG; 31R CG; 33 CG; 35 CG; U CG (2); U CG or EG (5)
8 Hutty 1975

**B 50**

1 Housesteads, Northumberland; *vicus* of fort; rubbish on floor of phase II
2 E
3 A
4 37; CG; Criciro; ovolo probably S&S fig. 33 no. 2, ornament *ibid* fig. 33 no. 5, lion O 1450, bear O 1627, free style; fig. 5 no. 2
37; CG; Geminus; ovolo S&S fig. 15 no. 1, wavy line border; fig. 5 no. 5
37; CG; Sacer-Attianus; ovolo S&S fig. 23 no. 1; fig. 5 no. 7
37 (3 pieces);CG; Docilis-Doccalus; ovolo as S&S pl. 91 no. 5, bud *ibid* fig. 24 no. 18, frond *ibid* fig. 24 no. 4, figure

as O 593, dwarf O 698A, lion O 1403A, lion not in O, deer as O 1770, bird as O 2313, metope style; fig. 5 no. 9

37 (2 pieces); CG; Divixtus; ovolo as S&S fig. 33 no. 3, caryatid O 1207A, metope and medallion style; fig. 5 no. 10

37; CG; X-11; bifid R G371, bud R G151, lioness O 1518, metope style; fig. 5 no. 11

37; CG; probably by a contemporary of Geminus; fig. 5 no. 4

37; EG - unlocated but stylistically dependent on Trier Wk I and Sinzig; Ricken 1934 '1st unlocated group'; similar to a sherd from Saalburg (Huld 1966, 104); fig. 5 no. 12

7 The deposit is overlain by a circular building of late 2nd or early 3rd century date, thought to be a temple to Mars Thincsus.

8 Birley, A 1962; Birley, E 1962

**B 51**

1 Ilkley, West Yorkshire; fort; general finds

2 F

3 A

4 From Woodward 1925 (only pieces attributable to potter given):

37; SG; Flavian; pl. XIX no. 13

37; SG; late Flavian, no details given here; pl. XVII no. 1

37; SG; Flavian or early Trajanic; pl. XVII no. 2

37; CG; X-8 to X-ll; Moxius; leaf as R J128; pl. XVII no. 3

30 (2 pieces); CG; Doeccus (stamped in mould); deer O 1752A, metope style; pl. XVII no. 4

30; CG; Doeccus; ovolo S&S fig. 44 no. 2, leaf *ibid* fig. 44 no. 24, metope style; pl. XVII no. 5

30; CG; Doeccus; mask as O 1352; pl. XVII no. 6

37; CG; Advocisus; ovolo as S&S fig. 33 no. 1, Pan O 709, metope style; pl. XVII no. 7

37; CG; Doeccus; ovolo as R B160, dancer O 362, leaf S&S fig. 44 no. 21, metope style; pl. XVII no. 8·

37; CG; Doeccus; shell S&S fig. 44 no. 29, rosette *ibid* fig. 44 no. 1, mask O 1214 in medallion, woman O 331, metope and medallion style; pl. XVII no. 9

37; CG; Iullinus; ovolo possibly as S&S pl. 125 no. 10, Venus O 278, metope style; pl. XVII no. 10

37; CG; Iullinus, Advocisus or contemporary; caryatid O 1207, metope style; pl. XVII no. 11

37 (2 pieces); CG; Cinnamus; erotic group O B in medallion, Vulcan O 66, metope and medallion style; pl. XVII no. 12

37; CG; Criciro; trifid R G67, metope and medallion style; pl. XVII no. 14

37; CG; Advocisus; dancer O 353, metope and medallion style; pl. XVII no. 15

37; CG; Cinnamus, Banvus, Iustus or Servus III; ornament probably R U247; pl. XVII no. 16

37; CG; Doeccus; leaf S&S fig. 44 no. 27, metope style; pl. XVII no. 17

37; CG; Paternus II; column S&S fig. 30 no. 25, 'twist' *ibid* fig. 30 no. 21, metope and medallion style; pl. XVII no. 18

37; CG; Doeccus; leaf probably S&S fig. 44 no. 27, metope style; pl. XVII no. 19

37; CG; Paternus II, Doeccus, Iustus or contemporary; dolphin O 2392; pl. XVII no. 20

37; CG; Doeccus; ovolo S&S fig. 44 no. 1, rosette *ibid* fig. 44 no. 12; pl. XVII no. 21

37; CG; Doeccus; ovolo S&S fig. 44 no. 1, leaf *ibid* fig. 44 no. 34, leaf *ibid* fig. 44 no. 26, dolphin basket *ibid* fig. 44 no. 28, rosette *ibid* fig. 44 no. 4, seated figure O 151, metope and medallion style; pl. XVII no. 22

37 (2 pieces); CG; possibly P-19; leaf as R H140, acanthus R K14 or K10, winding scroll and medallion style; pl. XVII no. 23

37; CG; Doeccus; leaf S&S fig. 44 no. 30 in medallion; pl. XVII no. 24

37; CG; Cinnamus, Paternus II or contemporary; leaf as R H21, winding scroll style; pl. XVII no. 25

37; CG; Criciro or Paternus II; leaf R H28, winding scroll style; pl. XVII no. 26

37; CG; leaf not in R but closest to R J15-16 (Cinnamus, Doeccus); pl. XVII no. 27

37 (9 pieces); CG; Severus (stamped in mould); ovolo S&S fig. 37 no. 2, 'twist' *ibid* fig. 37 no. 2, man O 673 (without rosette), man O 688, lioness O 1509, lion O 1497B, bear O 1630, hare O 2116, free style, also published (slightly differently) in S&S pl. 128 no. 2; pl. XVIII no. 1

37 (4 pieces); CG; Secundus or Pugnus; ovolo S&S fig. 45 no. 3 (beaded), Pan O 717, draped man O 905, Bacchus O 571, leaf S&S fig. 47 no. 5, rosette R C98, trifid R G67, gadroon R U153, caryatid O 1199, metope, medallion and arcade style; pl. XVIII no. 2 and Hartley 1966b, fig. 8 no. 108

37; Advocisus; ovolo probably S&S fig. 33 no. 1; pl. XIX no. 1

37; CG; Servus II; ovolo S&S pl. 131 no. 1, lion O 1564; pl. XIX no. 8

37 (3 pieces); CG; probably Servus II; tripod R Q16, stand R Q1, deer as O 1786, divided free style; pl. XIX nos 9-10

37 (3 pieces); CG; probably Iustus; lion O 1540, leaf tips as S&S pl. 110, but see also *ibid* pl. 81 no. 22 (Acaunissa), free style; pl. XIX no. 11

37; CG: Igocatus (X-4); ovolo S&S fig. 6 no. 1; pl. XIX no. 14

37 (several pieces); CG; X-12 (Ioenalis); rosette R C292 no ovolo and basal wreath, vine R M18 forming winding scroll; pl. XIX nos 15 and 18, Hartley 1966b, fig. 7 no. 90

37; CG; Censorinus; ovolo S&S fig. 29 no. 1; pl. XIX no. 17

37; CG; Servus III; ovolo S&S pl. 138 no. 1; pl. XIX no. 21

37 (2 pieces); CG; Censorinus or Paternus II; ovolo and astragalus border, no details given; nos 54-5

37 (2 pieces); CG; Iullinus; ovolo probably S&S fig. 36 no. 1; nos 59-60

37; CG; Doeccus; no details given; no. 61

37; CG; Paternus II; ovolo S&S fig. 30 no. 4; no. 62

37; CG; Paternus II (stamped in mould); ovolo S&S fig. 30 no. 1; no. 63

37; CG; Cinnamus; ovolo S&S fig. 47 no. 1; no. 64

37; CG; probably Sacer; very large ovolo, no details given; no. 65

37; CG; Paullus; ovolo Hartley 1961b, p. 103 nos 5-8; no. 66

37; CG; Iullinus; no details given; no. 67

37; CG; Criciro; ovolo, no details given; no. 68

37; CG; Servus II; ovolo S&S pl. 131 no. 1; no. 69

37; CG; Casurius (stamped by Apolauster on rim of bowl); no. 70

37; Arg; ware with ovolo A and B; rosette Ricken 1934 Taf. XIII no. 1, festoon *ibid* Taf. XIII no. 20, metope and arcade style; pl. XVII no. 13

37 (3 pieces); Arg; ware with ovolo C; ovolo as F463, leaf scroll Ricken 1934 Taf. XII no. 57, leaf *ibid* Taf. XII no. 14, bird *ibid* Taf. XII no. 53, spiral as F 423, winding scroll and free style; pl. XIX no. 42

37; Chémery; Satto or associate; ovolo F 275, bear F 204, leaf and scroll as F 270, winding scroll and panel style; pl. XIX no. 7

From Hartley 1966b (excavations of 1962, only pieces attributable to potter given):

SG decorated (19 pieces)

37; CG-MdV; Igocatus (X-4); captive D 643; no. 90
37; CG; possibly X-13 or Sacer; ovolo as R B14, lioness O 1502; no. 92
37; CG; Cinnamus; ovolo S&S fig. 47 no. 1, athlete O 651 in medallion; no. 93
37; CG; Cinnamus; ovolo S&S fig. 47 no. 1, trace of medallion; no. 94
37; CG; Cinnamus or associate; Neptune O 66, metope-and medallion style; no. 95
37; CG; Doeccus; ovolo S&S fig. 44 no. 1, rosette *ibid* fig. 44 no. 12, metope and medallion style; no. 96
37; CG; Doeccus; ovolo R B160, metope style; no. 97
37; CG; Casurius; ovolo S&S fig. 40 no. 2, Venus O 339, metope style; no. 98
37; CG; probably Iullinus, cupid O 450; no. 99
37 (several pieces); CG; Ianuaris II-Paternus I; ovolo S&S fig. 34 no. 2, 'twist' *ibid* fig. 30 no. 21, boar O 1674, deer O 1732, horse O 1910, dog O 1917, dog O 1940, lion as O 1459, free style; no. 100
37; CG; Albucius or Q I Balbinus; ovolo S&S fig. 35 no. 2; no. 101
37; CG; Iullinus; legs of animal as deer O 1732, small ring as S&S pl. 127 no. 29; no. 102
37; CG; Albucius or Q I Balbinus; ovolo S&S fig. 35 no. 2; no. 103
37; CG; Paternus II or associate; ovolo S&S fig. 30 no. 1, dog O 1940; no. 104
37; CG; Advocisus; ovolo S&S fig. 33 no. 2; no. 105
37; CG; Pugnus or Secundus; trifid, probably from same mould as Atkinson 1942, pl. 41 no. H39 (Wroxeter forum destruction); no. 107
37; Rheinz; Reginus I; ovolo R&F E66, festoon *ibid* KB121, medallion *ibid* O137, metope and festoon style; no. 112
From Raistrick 1931 (not certainly from fort - possibly from *vicus*):
37; Rheinz; Arvernicus - Lutaevus (stamped by the former and signed by the latter in the mould - also stamped by Lucius on the rim of the bowl); ovolo R&F E1, figure *ibid* M31, goat *ibid* T124, eagle *ibid* T205, flower *ibid* P99, basal wreath *ibid* R33, metope style, also published in Ricken 1942 Taf. 74 no. 3
Hartley (1966b, 50) gives totals for both groups as follows (with some differences from the list given above):
SG 21; Igocatus 2; MdV 1; Doeccus 13; Paternus, Censorinus and associates 7; Iullinus 5 (1 uncertain); Cinnamus 5 (1 uncertain); Advocisus 4; Criciro 3; Albucius and associates 2; Pugnus-Secundus 2; Servus II 2; Servus III 1; Casurius 2; Sacer 1 (uncertain); Severus 1; Banvus 1; Paullus 1; CG unattributed 19; EG 7.
There is a small associated group from the 1962 excavations: nos 98, 100, 102, 103 and 104 were found in debris over the Antonine building behind the west rampart.

7 The fort is known to have had a break in occupation in the mid-2nd century, which accounts for the division of the samian into two chronological groups - SG, Igocatus and MdV from the early fort and the rest from later levels. Reoccupation is considered by Hartley to be by AD 169 at the latest, on the basis of a building inscription (RIB 636).

8 Hartley 1966b; Raistrick 1931; Woodward 1925

**B 52**

1 Leicester, Leicestershire; town; Jewry Wall, period III courtyard surface

2 E

3 A

4 37; CG; X-11/13; ovolo as S&S fig. 10 no. 1, ornament R U64; fig. 7 no. 11
37; CG; Arcanus (signed in mould); fig. 7 no. 12
37; CG; Austrus; figure O 604; fig. 7 no. 14
37; CG; Cettus; spiral S&S fig. 42 no. 1, leaf as *ibid* fig. 42 no. 4, panther O 1518, bear O 1620, metope style; fig. 7 no. 16
37; CG; Cinnamus; ovolo S&S fig. 47 no. 3, leaves R L11, Perseus O 234, metope style; fig. 7 no. 17
37; CG; Cinnamus; ovolo S&S fig. 47 no. 3, bird O 2239B; fig. 7 no. 18
37; CG; Cinnamus; lozenge S&S fig. 47 no. 15, man O 688, free style; fig. 7 no. 19
37; CG; Cinnamus (stamped in mould with large stamp); ovolo as S&S fig. 47 no. 1, metope and medallion style; fig. 7 no. 20
37; CG; Cinnamus; ovolo S&S fig. 47 no. 1, lozenge *ibid* fig. 47 no. 15, acanthus *ibid* fig. 47 no. 21, winding scroll style; fig. 7 no. 21

7 Period II which precedes this was associated with coins - Nero As; Vesp As; Ant As (155-6); Faust II; Den; RIC (Ant) 517; 145-61. Some residual material was present, but was not listed.

8 Kenyon 1948; Oswald 1948b

**B 53**

1 Lincoln, Lincolnshire; town, rampart of *colonia*

2 E

3 A

4 37; SG; late Flavian, no details given here; fig. 10 no. 10
37; CG; Advocisus; ovolo S&S fig. 33 no. 2; fig. 10 no. 8
37; CG; Albucius; dog O 1940, horse O 1904, free style; fig. 10 no. 9
37; CG: triton as O 20 (Libertus, Carantinus, Silvio); fig. 10 no. 11
72; CG; incised dec
37 CG fragment; 27 CG (2); 33 CG; 38 CG; 67 CG with barbotine dec

7 Redeposited material is clearly present. The deposit may be dated *c* 200 by reference to finds from elsewhere (deposit **A 83**).

8 Webster 1949

**B 54**

1 Little Chester, Derbyshire; fort; burnt daub above upper clay floor

2 E

3 A

4 37; CG; Cinnamus; Victory O 809, dolphin O 2401 in medallion; fig. 8 no. 34
37 (3 pieces); CG; Mercator II; ovolo S&S fig. 43 no. 3, cornucopia *ibid* fig. 43 no. 4, small circle *ibid* pl. 145 no. 6, deer O 1784, metope style; fig. 8 no. 40
37; CG; probably Doeccus (stamped by Moxima as bowl-finisher); fig. 8 no. 42
37 (2 pieces); Rheinz; probably Belsus II; ovolo R&F E25, bifid *ibid* P145, metope and medallion style, as Ricken 1948 Taf. 110 no. 14; fig. 9 no. 47

8 Hartley 1961c; Webster 1961

**B 55**

1 Little Chester, Derbyshire; fort; layer XIII in trenches A, B and C

2 B

3 A

4 37; CG; Paternus II; ovolo S&S fig. 30 no. 1, dolphin O 2382 in festoon R F15, column S&S fig. 30 no. 25, tripod *ibid* fig. 30 no. 9, circle *ibid* fig. 30 no. 15, Apollo O 94, Bacchus as O 562, metope style; fig. 4 no. 1
37; CG; Paternus II; leaf as R H21, winding scroll style; fig. 4 no. 4
37; CG; Doeccus or Casurius; figure O 638; fig. 4 no. 5
37; CG; probably Butrio; ovolo as R B109, triton O 19, sea horse O 33, free style; fig. 4 no. 6
37; CG; X-11, X-13, Quintilianus or Cinnamus; vine scroll R M27; fig. 4 no. 2
37; CG; free style fragment; fig. 4 no. 3
38 CG
5 NV CCW with rouletted dec
8 Brassington 1967; Hartley & Dickinson 1967

**B 56**

1 London, City of London; town extra-mural area; Goodman's Yard, dump layers
2 E
3 A
4 37; CG; part of double medallion and beaded border; layer 180
37; EG; layer 180
37; CG; layer 175
37; SG; rosette-tongued ovolo with bands of wreaths and gadroons below; layer 253
37; CG; Divixtus style; caryatid O 1199 and double-bordered medallion, identical to S&S pl. 116 no. 8; layer 251
37; Arg; treble-bordered ovolo with plain tongue; layer 217
37; EG; double-bordered ovolo with plain tongue; layer 217
37; CG; layer 250
37; CG; layer 223
37; CG; double-bordered 'hammerhead' ovolo with fragment of panel decoration (2 sherds); layer 215
U; EG; cut-glass decoration; layer 179
Plain wares: 31 CG (2); 31 EG (2); 45 CG (12); 45 CG/EG; 45 CG?; 18 SG (3); 35 MdV; 38 CG (5); 38 CG/EG (2); 38 CG?; 38 EG (10); 38 Arg; 18/31 MdV; C11 CG; 33 CG (2); 33 EG (2); 27 SG; C21 CG; W79 CG; 44 CG; U CG (9); U MdV; U CG/EG? (3); U EG (5); U Arg
5 2 BB1 jars; 2 BB1 bowls and BB2 bowl; grey ware jar with roller-stamped decoration (fig. 7 no. 3), equivalent to sherds in the Colchester Mithraeum and kiln 28, now redated to mid-3rd century by Harden & Green 1978; Nene Valley CCW beaker with barbotine dec; 2 Nene Valley CCW sherds and similar flagon; Oxf mortarium (Young 1977, M18); Colch form 306, also redated by Harden & Green 1978 as above; Much Hadham face flagon; Rhenish CCW motto beaker; Rhenish CCW indented beaker.
6 Nero; As; RIC 329; 66-8; layer 182
7 The layers are considered by the excavator to be 'apparently deposited over a short period of time (Whytehead 1980, 36) and to be a series of dumps within a quarrying area. The coin clearly does not date the sequence, particularly as it came from a dark earth deposit overlying the other layers. However, the pottery group is fairly homogeneous apart from some residual or survival SG samian, and probably all of late 2nd - early/mid 3rd century date. McIsaac dates the other pottery to late 3rd/early 4th century and points out that this differs from the samian dating. However, this group can be brought earlier, to mid-3rd century, on the basis of the Colchester Mithraeum group and the presence of Oxf and Much Hadham wares. The BB and CCW could be early-mid 3rd century. This allows the samian and the other pottery to be roughly contemporary.
8 McIsaac 1980; Marsh 1980; Whytehead 1980

**B 57**

1 London, City of London; town; Tower of London, White Tower 1956-7, room IV fill
2 E
3 A
4 Fill of room IV
37; CG; Cinnamus style; vine-scroll
Plain wares: 31 CG (2); 18/31 MdV (2); 33; U SG
Top of fill of room IV:
37; Rheinz; Attillus; ovolo R&F E11, trifid as Ricken 1948 Taf. 180 no. 7, double medallion
37; CG; Servus II; stag O 1732, general style as S&S pl. 131
37; EG; wall sherd
Plain wares: 45 CG; U CG; plate CG
5 Cameron's discussion places the other pottery in the period late 2nd to early 3rd century. The upper fill (III 4) certainly contains vessels paralleled in late 3rd to early 4th century contexts.
6 The upper fill contains: Sev; Den (plated); types of Sev of 200-1 and Car of 200
7 The construction of room IV is dated to the same period as the building of the city wall and its bank (which is immediately adjacent). The wall in its turn is dated elsewhere in the city to AD 190-225 on coin evidence: thus the material here may be contemporary, but the reasons for its accumulation in the room, and its origin, are not known. The coin and the samian from the upper fill of room IV are probably part of this early 3rd century group, disturbed and redeposited about a century later.
8 Butcher 1982; Cameron 1982; Curnow 1982; Dickinson & Hartley 1982; Parnell 1982

**B 58**

1 London, City of London; waterfront of town; St Magnus House (New Fresh Wharf), layer 37
2 E
3 A
4 37; CG; Doeccus; dolphin basket S&S fig. 44 no. 28, small wreath as *ibid* pl. 149 no. 28
37; CG; Doeccus; stand S&S fig. 44 no. 7, beaded festoon as *ibid* pl. 151 no. 61
37; CG; Ollognatus-Doeccus group; ovolo B 227
37; Trier; Dexter-Censor; basal row of astrgali as F Taf. 15 no. 2 and Taf. 16 no. 11
37; Rheinz; ovolo R&F E17, medallion *ibid* K19
37; Rheinz; Janu I, Cerialis, Belsus or Pupus-Iuvenis II; figure R&F M126
7 This group is associated with the much larger deposit **A 90**.
8 Bird 1986; Museum of London, Department of Urban Archaeology archive report compiled by J Bird.

**B 59**

1 Lyne, Borders Region; fort; on intervallum road under tail of rampart
2 E
3 A
4 37; CG; Cettus; ovolo S&S fig. 42 no. 2
37 (4 pieces); CG; Cettus; parallels for motifs in S&S pl. 141-4, no details given
37; CG; Cinnamus; ovolo S&S fig. 47 no. 1
37; CG; probably Cinnamus; free style, no details given
31 CG

7 The samian is probably to be associated with the occupation of the fort, which is put by the excavators into the Antonine II period.
8 Steer & Feachem 1962

**B 60**

1 Mansfield Woodhouse, Nottinghamshire; villa; ditch, lower filling
2 D
3 A
4 37; CG; Iullinus; ovolo S&S fig. 36 no. 1, column *ibid* fig. 36 no. 5, Venus O 278, man as O 591, mask O 1214, metope and arcade style; pl. 1 no. 5
37; CG; Banvus (stamped in mould); ovolo as S&S fig. 41 no. 1, leaf *ibid* fig. 41 no. 15, leaf *ibid* fig. 41 no. 8, leaf as R J14 but smaller, winding scroll and medallion style; pl. 1 no. 6
8 Oswald, A, 1949

**B 61**

1 Nettleton, Wiltshire; *vicus*; lower filling of cellar in building XIII
2 E
3 A
4 37 (2 pieces); CG; Geminus; ovolo S&S fig. 15 no. 1, rosette *ibid* fig. 15 no. 6, metope style; fig. 70 nos 112-3
37; CG; Drusus II or Martialis; caryatid O 1207, trifid R G113, bifid R G345, metope style; fig. 70 no. 114
7 There are Constantinian coins from the cellar, but the destruction episode associated with the coins is probably unconnected with the samian.
8 Simpson 1982b; Wedlake 1982

**B 62**

1 Nettleton, Wiltshire; *vicus*; pit below building XIX
2 C
3
4 37; SG; late Flavian date, no details given here; fig. 69 no. 79
30; SG; no details given here; fig. 70 no. 83
37; CG; Advocisus or Divixtus; ovolo R B103, metope style; fig. 69 no. 78
37; CG; possibly Paternus II; dolphin O 2392, metope and medallion style; fig. 70 no. 80
31; CG; stamped by Cintusmus
33 CG; 31 CG
8 Simpson 1982b; Wedlake 1982

**B 63**

1 Newstead, Borders Region; fort; inner ditches in west annexe
2 D
3 A
4 From inner ditch:
37; CG; Cinnamus; dancer O 322, stand R Q42, metope style; no. 67
37; CG; Cinnamus; sea bull O 42, erotic group O B in medallion, metope and medallion style; no. 68
37; CG; Cinnamus (stamped in mould with large stamp); bear O 1588, pygmy as O 696a, metope style; no. 69
37; CG; possibly Pugnus; festoon as R F16, trifid as R G175, wavy line borders, lion O 1566, bear not in O, metope and medallion style; no. 70
From outer ditch:
37; CG; Albucius or Paternus II; ovolo S&S fig. 30 no. 1, cupid O 440 in medallion; no. 71
37; CG; Divixtus (stamped in mould); caryatid O 1199, mask O 1328, metope and medallion style; no. 73
37; CG; ovolo not attributable from drawing, bird O 2252 in small medallion and festoon (Cinnamus or contemporary); no. 72
8 Curle 1911, 219

**B 64**

1 Newstead, Borders Region; fort; inner ditch of later fort on west side
2 D
3 A
4 37; CG; Cinnamus; ovolo S&S fig. 47 no. 1, acanthus R K20, festoon as R F40, bird O 2252, metope style; no. 64
37; CG; Cinnamus; ovolo S&S fig. 47 no. 3, Perseus O 234, metope style; no. 65
37; Rheinz; Reginus I; circles in place of ovolo R&F R15, ornament *ibid* O166, trifid *ibid* P128, circle *ibid* O122, festoon *ibid* KB137, festoon style as Ricken 1948 Taf. 18 no. 126; no. 66
8 Curle 1911, 218-9

**B 65**

1 Newstead, Borders Region; fort; inner ditch in east annexe
2 D
3 A
4 37; CG; Sacer-Attianus; ovolo as S&S fig. 23 no. 2, leaf-tips S&S pl. 85 no. 1, horseman O 249, bear O 1575, lioness O 1537, free style; no. 74
37 (3 pieces); CG; Cettus; ovolo S&S fig. 42 no. 1, leaf *ibid* fig. 42 no. 5, large trifid *ibid* fig. 42 no. 9, vertical divider *ibid* fig. 42 no. 5, small man below decoration *ibid* fig. 42 no. 3, trifid *ibid* fig. 42 no. 6, leaf as R H21, border R A30, metope style; no. 75
37; CG; Cinnamus; ovolo probably S&S fig. 47 no. 3, lozenge *ibid* fig. 47 no. 1, acanthus *ibid* fig. 47 no. 21, deer O 1704, bear O 1627, male figure O 234, mask O 1328, mask O 1214, philosopher O 905, astragalus borders, metope and medallion style; no. 77
37; La Mad; possibly Avitus; ovolo and pelta, cf. *Ann. Inst Arch. Luxembourg* 110/111, 1979/80, no. 18, Fig. 6.2, from Arlon, cf. also S&S 19, fig. 6, metope and St Andrew's cross style; no. 76
8 Curle 1911, 219-20

**B 66**

1 Newstead, Borders Region; fort; pit LIX
2 C
3 A
4 29; SG; 3 vessels represented, no details given here; nos 36-8
67; SG or CG
From a higher level in the pit than the pieces given above:
37; CG; Paullus; ovolo S&S fig. 47 no. 3, vine scroll R M10, bird O 2315, winding scroll style; no. 83
37; CG; Criciro; bird O 2252 in festoon, bear O 1616, ornament O 2155 (part only), metope style; no. 84
37; CG; Cinnamus; ovolo S&S fig. 47 no. 4, leaf R J89, winding scroll style; no. 85
37; Rheinz; Cerialis III; Venus R&F M44, flute player *ibid* M165, palm branch *ibid* P15, vase as *ibid* O13, metope style; no. 86

7 The filling appears to be divided between an Antonine fill from which the four CG pieces came, and the bottom black filling below 20 feet, of Flavian date.
8 Curle 1911, 130, 222

**B 67**

1 Ravenglass, Cumbria; fort; destruction of barrack blocks, phase 2/3
2 E
3 A
4 37 (11 pieces); CG; Secundinus I, II or III; ovolo R B23, festoon R F41, acanthus R K5, column not in R, dancer O 348, metope style; fig. 48 no. 8
37 (7 pieces); CG; Sissus; triton as O 25 in place of ovolo, Bacchus O 566, Diana O 109, Hercules O 782, Apollo O 78, leaf R J22, acanthus R K6, arcade style; fig. 49 no. 9
37 (12 pieces); CG; Cinnamus (stamped in mould with large stamp die 5b); ovolo S&S fig. 47 no. 1, leaf *ibid* fig. 47 no. 5, horseman O 245, deer O 1743, figure O 644, boar O 1641, free style; fig. 49 no. 11
37; CG; Secundus; ovolo as S&S fig. 47 no. 1, caryatid O 1201, metope and medallion style; fig. 49 no. 12
37; CG; Cinnamus or associate; Apollo O 84, metope style; fig. 49 no. 10
7 There is a worn Hadrian As from the preceding phase.
8 Potter 1979; Wild 1979a

**B 68**

1 Ravenglass, Cumbria; fort; pit FF, phase 2/3
2 C
3 A
4 37; CG; X-6; basal wreath S&S fig. 18 no. 3, Amazon O 241, free style; fig. 49 no. 13
37; CG; Cinnamus or Paullus; deer O 1781, bear O 1627, metope style; fig. 49 no. 14
37; CG; Cinnamus; ovolo S&S fig. 47 no. 2, winding scroll style; fig. 49 no. 15
37 (2 pieces); CG; Divixtus (stamped in mould with die 9d); warrior O 213, erotic group O H, metope and medallion style; fig. 50 no. 16
37; CG; Advocisus, ovolo S&S fig. 33 no. 1, Minerva O 126, metope style; fig. 50 no. 17
37; CG; Censorinus or Mammius; bifid R G359, border R A10, metope style; fig. 50 no. 18
37 (3 pieces); CG; Paternus II; ovolo S&S fig. 30 no. 1, leaf *ibid* fig. 30 no. 7, winding scroll style; fig. 50 no. 19
7 This deposit may be slightly later than that in the previous entry.
8 Potter 1979; Wild 1979a

**B 69**

1 Rochester, Kent; town, The Common, layer 20
2 B
3 A
4 37 (7 pieces); CG; Quintilianus group; ovolo S&S fig. 17 no. 4, large rosette *ibid* fig. 17 no. 5, astragalus *ibid* fig. 17 no. 5, acanthus *ibid* fig. 17 no. 17, female figure O 339, metope and arcade style; fig. 4 nos 4-5
37 (3 pieces); CG; Paullus; ovolo S&S fig. 47 no. 3, bear O 1627, deer O 1772, free style, very similar to a piece from Mumrills (**A94**) Hartley 1961b, fig. 6 no. 8; fig. 4 no. 7
37; CG; Cinnamus; ovolo S&S fig. 47 no. 3, leaf *ibid* fig. 47 no. 38, leaf R H152, winding scroll style; fig. 4 no. 9
37; CG; Austrus; ovolo S&S fig. 25 no. 2; fig. 4 no. 12
37 (8 pieces); CG; Cettus; ovolo S&S fig. 42 no. 3, lion O 1450, boar O 1641, male figure O 660, lion O 1404, lion O 1457, male figure O 637, free style with vertical dividers; fig. 5 nos 17-19
37; CG; ovolo with worn rosette; fig. 5 no. 14
Plain ware: 27 CG (3); 33 CG; 33 EG (3); 18 SG; 18/31 CG (stamped by Pateratus); 31 EG; 31R CG
7 See deposit **A 102** for overlying layer associated with a coin of Aurelius.
8 Detsicas 1970a; Harrison 1970

**B 70**

1 Rochester, Kent; town; Northgate, cutting B, layer 12, rampart
2 E
3 A
4 37; West; Helenius; spiral Kiss 1948 pl. VI no. 64, pl. XV nos 1 and 3, half medallion *ibid* pl. VI no. 80, cupid O 459A (= R&F M142); fig. 15 no. 1
37; CG; Advocisus; ovolo S&S fig. 33 no. 1, bird O 2317, basket on tripod R Q32; fig. 15 no. 2
37; CG; Cinnamus; ovolo S&S fig. 47 no. 5, overlapped ovolo; fig. 15 no. 3
37; CG; Ianuaris II; ovolo S&S fig. 34 no. 1; fig. 15 no. 4
From rampart in cutting A, layer 7:
37; CG; Cinnamus; ovolo S&S fig. 47 no. 3, bear O 1619; fig. 15 no. 5
7 The last sherd is stratigraphically contemporary with the main group but from a different part of the defences.
8 Detsicas 1968; Harrison & Flight 1968

**B 71**

1 Rough Castle, Central Region; fort; general finds
2 F
3 A
4 From excavations of 1957-61:
37; CG; Albucius; leaf S&S fig. 35 no. 2, free style; no. 21
37; CG; Cettus; cupid as O 458A, figure O 660; no. 24
37; CG; Cinnamus, Pugnus or Caletus; Perseus O 234; no. 33
37; CG; Cinnamus, Paullus or associate; lioness O 1518, metope style; no. 36
37; CG; Criciro, Divixtus or Secundus; ovolo R B52, sphinx O 857; no. 40
37; CG; Cinnamus; ovolo R B143, bird O 2239B, winding scroll style, rivetted; no. 46
37 (2 pieces); CG; Quintilianus group; ovolo R B28, trifid R G164, lion O 1425, warrior O 219A, goat D 885; no. 49
37; CG; Cinnamus; ovolo R B145, leaf R H13, leaf R J89, trifid R G66, bird O 2298, erotic group O B, winding scroll and medallion style; no. 50
37; CG; Cinnamus; ovolo R B223, bird O 2315, winding scroll style; no. 51
37; CG; Cinnamus; leaf R H21; no. 51
From earlier excavations, now in National Museum of Antiquities of Scotland:
37 (2 pieces); CG; Cerialis-Cinnamus; ovolo R B144, eagle O 2167, Apollo O 83, medallion with rosettes as S&S pl. 156 nos 3 and 7, metope style; no. 55
37; CG; Criciro; ovolo R B52 with wavy line below; no. 56
37; CG; Cinnamus; ovolo R B223; no. 57
37; CG; Criciro; ovolo R B12, caryatid O 1257A, erotic group O B, bird O 2295A, metope style; no. 58
37; SG-Montans; Felicio; fan-shaped plant, chevrons, festoons; no. 59
37; CG; Cinnamus; leaf R J1, leaf R J153, bird - reverse of O 2315, winding scroll style; no. 60

37; CG; Cerialis-Cinnamus; ovolo R B144, leaf R H21, bird O 2252, winding scroll style; no. 61
37; CG; Paternus I; deer O 1204A in double medallion, ornament R U103, tree as R N2; no. 62
37; CG; Cerialis-Cinnamus; vine scroll R M31, lozenge R U36, mask O 1293, athlete O 688, dolphins and basket R Q58, metope style; no. 63
37; CG; Cettus; ovolo R B263, Apollo O 83, medallions and astragali as S&S pl. 143 no. 44, metope style; no. 64
37; CG; Cerialis-Cinnamus; ovolo R B144, leaf R H22, bird O 2252, winding scroll style; no. 65 - the same as no. 61?
37; CG; Cerialis-Cinnamus; ovolo R B144, bird O 2252, winding scroll style; no. 66
37; CG; Butrio; ovolo R B114, cupid O 450, Venus O 334, female figure O 943, warrior O 1060, bird O 2234, Apollo O 100, Hercules O 792, philosopher O 905, figure as O 159, Hercules D 456, leaf as R G137-47, free style; no. 67
37; CG; unknown potter connected with Drusus II; festoon R F37; no. 68
37; CG; possibly Laxtucissa; leaf R H7, bird O 2315, ring-tongued ovolo, type not specified, winding scroll style; no. 69
37; CG; Secundus; straight line beneath ovolo; no. 70
37; CG; Quintilianus; rosettes R C21 as basal wreath, hare O 2116, metope style; no. 71
37; CG; Docilis; ovolo R B208, stand R Q42; no. 72
Stamps in the National Museum:
37; CG; Cinnamus ii die 5B
18/31; CG; Doeccus i die 11a
18/31; CG; Peculiaris i die 2A
18/31; CG; Suobrus die 2a
33; CG; Tasgillus ii die 9b surmoulage copy
Plain ware from excavations of 1957-61:
18/31R CG; 31R CG; 33 CG (5); 31 CG (22); 18/31-31 MdV; 27 La Mad; 30 or 37 (4); C11 CG; C21 CG; U CG (2)
8 Hartley & Dickinson 1980; MacIvor *et al* 1980

**B 72**

1 South Shields, Tyne & Wear; fort; 1979 layer 100 above 2nd intervallum road
2 B
3 A
4 37; Rheinz; Cobnertus I; figure R&F M243, palm frond border *ibid* P14, arcade style as Ricken 1948 Taf. 22 no. 10; fig. 25 no. 338
37; La Mad; spirals Ricken 1934 Taf. 7 no. 33, rosette *ibid* Taf. 7 no. 37, trifid *ibid* Taf. 7 no. 11, metope and medallion style; fig. 26 no. 339
37 (2 pieces); La Mad; festoon Ricken 1934 Taf. 9 no. 5, acanthus as *ibid* Taf. 7 no. 25, metope style; fig. 26 no. 340
33 (3 pieces); CG; stamped by Suobnillus die 4a
18/31R EG; 31 CG (3); U (7)
8 Dore 1983; Miket 1983

**B 73**

1 Southwark, Greater London; suburb of town; Saxon St/ Great Dover St, ditch B 11-2, layer 2-3
2 C
3 A
4 37; Trier; scrolls as Huld-Zetsche 1972 O33-6, guide-line on each side; fig. 214 no. 206
37; Rheinz; Augustinus II; ovolo R&F E59
37; EG; no details given
There is a high proportion of EG plain ware from the ditch as a whole (26.2%).
5 NV CCW; Loire 'à l'éponge' ware
7 The excavator puts the ditch fill in the second half of the 3rd century from the coarse pottery. It is covered by a black-earth deposit containing a Constantinian coin.
8 Bird & Marsh 1978a; Graham 1978

**B 74**

1 Southwark, Greater London; suburb of town; 1-7 St Thomas Street, large pit bottom fill, layer 190
2 C
3 A
4 37; CG; leaf R H152 (Advocisus, Doeccus or contemporary. Lucinus); fig. 142 no. 128
37; CG; Paternus II, or P-17; ovolo R B135, leaf as R J180 but reversed, astragalus border, Amazon O 241, bear O 1578, free style; fig. 142 no. 130
37; Arg; possibly Africanus; ovolo Ricken 1934 Taf. XII C, boar *ibid* Taf. XII no. 44, bird *ibid* Taf. XII no. 53, leaf *ibid* Taf. XII no. 10, bifid H 405, stand Ricken 1934 Taf. XIV no. 1, free style, very similar to ibid Taf. XII no. 68; fig. 142 no. 129
Stamps:
33; CG; stamped by Albucianus die 6b
27; SG; stamped by Patricius i die 5b
31; CG; stamped by Saturninus ii die Ic
Plain ware: 31 CG (2); 33 CG; 35 CG
8 Bird & Marsh 1978b; Dennis 1978

**B 75**

1 Southwark, Greater London; suburb of town; 8 Union Street, well
2 C
3 A
4 37; Rheinz; Comitialis I· ovolo R&F E1, pygmy *ibid* M151, female figure *ibid* M56; fig. 98 no. 82
37; Rheinz; Comitialis V; dog R&F T139, deer *ibid* T98, bird *ibid* T245A, leaf *ibid* P38, medallion *ibid* KB140, rivetted; fig. 98 no. 83
Plain ware: 15/17 SG; 31 CG; 31 CG/EG; 31 EG; 33 CG (4); 33 CG/EG; 33 EG (2); 31R EG; 38 CG; 38 EG; 45 CG; 43 or 45 CG/EG; 46 EG
5 Coarse ware of early to mid-3rd century type as recognised by Green (Harden & Green 1978).
8 Marsh 1978

**B 76**

1 Springhead, Kent; *vicus*; building B18
2 E
3 A
4 29 (3 pieces); SG; bird O 2220, bird O 2257, bird O 2247, winding scroll in upper part, festoon in lower part; fig. 1 nos 20-1
30 (4 pieces); SG; Masclus; panther O 1573, metope and St Andrew's cross style; fig. 2 nos 22-3
37 (2 pieces); SG; cupid O 435, metope style with wreaths above and below, an early form of 37; fig. 1 no. 19
37 (2 pieces); SG-probably Banassac; hare O 2098A, dog as O 1925, lion O 1444, hare O 2073 or 2074, winding scroll style, poorly impressed; fig. 1 nos 16-17
30 (5 pieces); CG; Laxtucissa; ovolo S&S fig. 27 no. 1, astragalus *ibid* fig. 27 no. 3, circle *ibid* fig. 27 no. 7, rosette *ibid* fig. 27 no. 11, Mercury O 547 in double circle, erotic group O K, trifid S&S fig. 27 no. 2, mask O 1218, metope and medallion style; fig. 1 no. 18

37 (10 pieces); CG; X-2;ovolo S&S fig. 3, bud *ibid* fig. 3 no. 10, tendril junction *ibid* fig. 3 no. 4, pygmy O 696A, warrior O 218, wreath S&S fig. 3 no. 2, winding scroll style, from the same mould as a piece from London S&S pl. 4 no. 41; fig. 2 no. 24
37 (18 pieces); CG; Drusus I (X-3); wreath as ovolo Detsicas 1963a fig. 2 no. 3, cup *ibid* fig. 2 no. 16, rosette *ibid* fig. 2 no. 5, acanthus *ibid* fig. 2 no. 26, leaf-tips *ibid* fig. 2 no. 7, leaf *ibid* fig. 2 no. 20, tendril junction *ibid* fig. 2 no. 18, winding scroll style; fig. 2 nos 25-26
37 (6 pieces); CG; 'potter of the rosette'; rosette S&S fig. 7 no. 20, Bacchus O 588, leaf S&S fig. 7 no. 37, panther O 1499, St Andrew's cross made up of S&S fig. 7 nos 17, 24, 26, 31, leaf-tip *ibid* fig. 7 no. 36, circle *ibid* fig. 7 no. 10, astragalus *ibid* fig. 7 no. 17, wreath *ibid* fig. 7 no. 4, dog O 1984, metope style, rivetted; fig. 2 nos 27-8
37 (17 pieces); CG; Cinnamus (stamped in mould); ovolo S&S fig. 47 no. 1, lion O 1421, pygmy O 696A, dog O 1980, deer O 1720, panther O 1518, horse Karnitsch 1959 Taf. 54 no. 7, deer O 1781, lion and boar O 1491, leaf S&S fig. 47 no. 5, free style; fig. 3 no. 29
37 (3 pieces); CG; Austrus; ovolo S&S fig. 25 no. 2, vase *ibid* fig. 25 no. 30, panther O 1573D, metope style; fig. 3 nos 30-1
Plain ware: 15/17 SG (5 pieces); 18 SG; 18R SG stamped by Primus; 18/31 EG stamped by Tarra; 18/31 CG stamped by Paterclus; 18/31 CG; 31 EG stamped by Aprilis; 31R CG stamped by Pateratus; 31R CG stamped by Patricius; 31R EG stamped by Pridianus; 32 EG; 36 SG; 42 probably SG; C11 SG (2); C15 CG; 27 CG; 33 CG (2); 33 EG (2); 33 CG stamped by Soellus; 33 CG stamped by Cracuna; 33 EG stamped by Lupus; 38 CG stamped by Mettius; 38 CG stamped by Cintusmus; 38/44 CG stamped by Sinturus; 79 EG stamped by Festus

7 This is a problematic deposit. The outer limits of dating are 45-200 on stylistic grounds (Detsicas 1968, 227). However the pottery all comes from a homogeneous burnt deposit on the floor of buidling 18. Many of the sherds are burnt and seem to have reached the deposit as a result of a single episode. Penn suggested that the site was a samian ware shop but Detsicas was unconvinced (1968, 227), 'For not only is it very improbable that such a shop would have held stocks of samian over such a long period of time, but also the pottery itself was burnt after breakage as the evidence of many conjoining sherds amply demonstrates.' Detsicas suggested that the building was burnt down, and then that samian ware was deposited there in partly burnt refuse. This is equally unconvincing. The fact that the sherds were burnt after breakage could be explained by the collapse of the building in which the pots were stored, their breakage and then a fire in amongst the debris. Subsequent levelling also appears to have taken place leading to further breakage. A possible explanation for the unusual collection of samian in a comparatively humble building is perhaps that it was a store-room. It may even have been for sale of old pieces or a repair shop.

8 Detsicas 1968b

**B 77**

1 *Verulamium*, St Albans, Hertfordshire; town-house; site G period II ditch silt

2 D

3 A

4 37; CG; Cinnamus, Paullus or Casurius; hare as O 2116 in medallion; fig. 5 no. 3
37; Rheinz; Janu I or Cerialis I-V - probably Cerialis III; tree R&F P6, lion *ibid* T21, free style, see Ricken 1948 Taf. 57 for general type; fig. 5 no. 6
38; 31 (several)

7 Period III construction is dated, on pottery evidence alone, to AD 170-90.

8 Cotton & Wheeler 1949, 36, 59-60

**B 78**

1 Wiggonholt, West Sussex; rural settlement; site D pit DA4

2 C

3 A

4 37; Brit; Aldgate/Pulborough potter; dog S&S pl. 88 no. 1, sphinx O 854, stand S&S pl. 89 no. 13, column Webster 1975k, acanthus *ibid* n, rosette *ibid* i, circle and rosette *ibid* h, beaded circle *ibid* g, free style; Webster 1975 no. 10
37; CG; X-6; ovolo S&S fig. 18 no. 4, winding scroll style; Webster 1974 fig. 18 no. 15
37; CG; Cinnamus; ovolo Simpson & Rogers 1969 fig. 1 no. 3a, stag O 1704a, astragalus S&S fig. 47 no. 40, metope and festoon style; Webster 1974 fig. 18 no. 16
37; EG - La Mad, Heil or Rheinz; gladiator R&F M215; Webster 1974 fig. 18 no. 17
Plain ware: 31 CG stamped by Geminus v die Xlc?; 36/C11 Brit; 18/31 Brit

8 Evans 1974; Hartley & Dickinson 1974; Webster 1974; 1975

**B 79**

1 Winterton, North Lincolnshire; villa; building G, context eg under room 1

2 E

3 A

4 37; CG; bird as O 2252, metope and medallion style; the sherd is described as 'A very small, thick bowl in pinkish micaceous fabric with blotchy red-brown coat, closer to a colour-coat than the normal samian glaze .... This kind of bowl is relatively rare in Britain, but is common at Lezoux in groups of the end of the 2nd century or the early 3rd century, being made by such potters as Lucinus. The styles of decoration are crude and poorly executed, involving reduced copies of figure-types used by earlier potters. As often with these bowls, the technique of finishing is very poor, and here the clumsy foot ring has not been properly luted to the bowl. '; fig. 52 no. 47
Plain ware: 18/31 CG; 18/31R CG: 31 CG (2); 79 CG; 31R CG

8 Hartley & Pengelly 1976; Stead 1976

**B 80**

1 Wroxeter, Shropshire; town; street section layer 5

2 B

3 A

4 37; CG; Divixtus; erotic group as O H; fig. 4 no. 9
37; CG; Sacer, Attianus or Drusus II; trifid R G76; fig. 4 no. 10
37; CG; Moxius; spiral R S20, as S&S pl. 152 no. 4, metope style; fig. 6 no. 11

7 The layer is sealed by ditch fill associated with one of the road levels.

8 Hartley 1970; Webster & Daniels 1970

**B 81**

1 York, Yorkshire; fortress; Low Petergate, trench 2 layer 15

2 B

3 A

4 37; CG; Iustus; ovolo present, no details given; no. 10

37; CG; Casurius; ovolo probably S&S fig. 40 no. 1, hare O 2120A; no. 11
Plain ware present: 17 (?); 31; 33
5 NV CCW; tile stamp of LEG VI VIC PF
7 The layer is dated by coarse ware to 2nd/4th century, but none is illustrated. All the fine ware could be late 2nd or early 3rd century.
8 Hartley 1972b; Wenham 1972

## FRANCE

**B 82**

1 Amiens, Somme; town; Chambre de Commerce site, cellar 32
2 E
3 A
4 37; CG; Cinnamus (stamped with small signature as S&S pl. 157 no. 4); pl. 4 no. 1
37; CG; Albucius; ovolo S&S fig. 35 no. 1; pl. 4 no. 2
37; CG; Paternus II; pl. 4 no. 3
37; CG; Cinnamus, Pugnus or Secundinus I; ovolo R B143; pl. 4 no. 4
37; CG; Advocisus, Priscus or Clemens; ovolo R B102; pl. 4 no. 5
37; CG; possibly Geminus or late Butrio; pl. 4 no. 6
79/80 CG; 27 CG; 33 CG
8 Bayard 1980, 156

**B 83**

1 Amiens, Somme; town; 'Courrier Picard' site, layer between 1st and 2nd fire deposits
2 E
3 A
4 37; CG; Pugnus; pl. 9 no. 1
37; CG; probably Servus II; pl. 9 no. 2
37 (2 pieces); CG; Paternus II; pl. 9 nos 3-4
37; CG; Paternus II or Laxtucissa; pl. 9 no. 5
Lud Tk' or Tn' Rheinz
8 Bayard 1980, 162

**B 84**

1 Amiens, Somme; town; rue Vanmarcke group IVb
2 D
3 A
4 37; CG; Iullinus; pl. 13 no. 13
37; CG; probably Mercator II; pl. 13 no. 14
37; CG; metope style - late 2nd century type; pl. 13 no. 16
37; Arg; ovolo probably Ricken 1934 Taf. XIIIB; pl. 13 no. 15
37; Arg; ovolo as Ricken 1934 Taf. XIIIA; pl. 13 no. 19
37; Trier; circle as F 838; pl. 13 no. 18
18/31 CG stamped by Pugnus
33 CG stamped by Maccalus
33 CG stamped by Martius
40 probably EG
8 Bayard 1980, 168-70

**B 85**

1 Amiens, Somme; town; rue Vanmarcke group IVc
2 D
3 A
4 37; CG; Paternus II; pl. 16 no. 68
37; probably CG; broken column not R, F or R&F; pl. 16 no. 72
37; CG; probably Doeccus; pl. 16 no. 74
37 (3 pieces); CG; not identifiable from pl. 16 nos 69-71
37; Arg; leaves F 519, style as C&G fig. 58A no. M23; pl. 16 no. 75
10/54; CG or Arg; incised dec
18/31; CG; stamped by Materninus
37 CG fragment; 18/31 CG; 33 CG; 35/6 CG; 38 CG
7 Ensemble IX which may be contemporary has 45 CG; 40 CG (2) associated with coins of the 260s (Bayard 1980, 184).
8 Bayard 1980, 172

**B 86**

1 Eyrein, Corrèze; villa; 'Chambon' ditch
2 C
3 B
4 37; CG; Casurius
37; CG; Paternus II
37; CG; unknown potter in late style; ornament R Q80 (Marcus), tree R N8 (Cinnamus, Catussa II, Talussa), rosette as R C25 (Cettus, Attianus), leaf not in R, ovolo and border as S&S pl. 153 no. 7 (Pugnus), cupid O 431, arcade style; pl. 2
Lagena in unique form; CG or local samian product; figure types not in O or R; pl. 1
72; CG; incised dec
72; CG; incised dec
3 plates in unique form with wide flat rims, 2 of which carry incised dec.
plate in unique form with narrower rim and deeper bowl, the rim has rouletted dec.
45; CG; reduced size lion's head spout
35/36 CG (2); 40 CG with white barbotine dec; 79/80 CG (2) both possibly stamped by Pistillus; 43 CG (2); 39 CG variant with sloping handle (4); 40 CG; 18/31 CG with steep rim; C15 CG - fragments only
5 CCW flagon with barbotine and incised dec - probably CG; CG CCW cups of form 34 with barbotine dec; marbled slip imitation of form 38
7 Found during agricultural operations, which had scattered some of the material from the pit.
8 Antignac 1977

**B 87**

1 Guiry-Gadancourt, Val-d'Oise; villa; pit 38
2 C
3 A
4 37; CG; Cinnamus; no. 16
37; CG; Iustus; no. 17
37; CG; Doeccus; no. 19
37; CG; Paternus II; no. 20
37; CG; Ianuaris II-Paternus I; no. 21
37 (4 pieces); CG; Censorinus; nos 22-22a
37; CG; Antistii; no. 23
37; CG; Banvus; no. 24
37; CG; Paternus II; no. 25
37 (2 pieces); CG; Severus; no. 26
37; CG; possibly Atilianus or Talussa; rosette as R C235 densely scattered as only element of decoration; no. 27
37; CG; Doeccus; no. 29
37; CG; tree R N4 used by many potters including Advocisus, Cinnamus, Criciro, Geminus; no. 31
32; CG; Iustus; no. 32
37; CG; ovolo R B177 (Iustus, Marcus), leaf R M29 (Maccius, Maccirra), another piece from this bowl in pit 79 (deposit **B 88**); no. 35
37; EG - probably Rheinz; dec not possible to identify precisely; no. 28

37; Rheinz; Cobnertus III, Firmus I or Comitialis V - most likely the last; no. 30
8 Hofmann 1967a

**B 88**

1 Guiry-Gadancourt, Val-d'Oise; villa; pit 79
2 C
3 A
4 37; CG; free style dec with leaf not in R, other figure types by Censorinus, Paternus II, Doeccus and Casurius; no. 33
37 (2 pieces); CG; Iustus; no. 34
37; CG; ovolo R B177 (Iustus, Marcus), leaf R M29 (Maccius, Maccirra), another piece from this bowl in pit 38 (**B 87**); no. 35
37; CG; Paternus II; no. 36
37; CG; Albucius; no. 37
37; CG; probably Paternus II; no. 38
37; CG; Albucius; no. 39
37; possibly Arg or EG; dancer O 332; no. 39B
37; CG; bear O 1588, figure as O 779, probably late CG potter; no. 39A
8 Hofmann 1967a

**B 89**

1 Koenigshoffen, Bas-Rhin; cemetery area of town; Route des Romains, pit
2 C
3 B
4 37; Rheinz; Florentinus (stamped in mould); fig. 25A
37; Rheinz; Pupus (stamped in mould); fig. 25B
43 Rheinz with barbotine dec; 39 Rheinz (2) with barbotine dec - 1 stamped by Verinus; Lud VSb EG with incised dec; all on fig. 25
7 No other pieces were found in the deposit, thus its composition is unusual, possibly funerary in character.
8 Petry 1972, 397-8

**B 90**

1 Lyon, Rhône; town; Tolozan site, drain B1
2 G - possibly a silt deposit
3 A
4 37; CG; Doeccus; ovolo S&S fig. 44 no. 1
37; CG; Doeccus; ovolo *ibid* no. 2
37; CG; Banvus; ovolo *ibid* fig. 41 no. 2
37; CG; ovolo as R B184 (unknown potter)
37 CG (2); 30 CG; jars CG with incised dec
large quantity of terre sigillée claire
7 Apparently one of the latest deposits of samian ware from Lyon.
8 Notes and rubbings made at Lyon Museum

**B 91**

1 Strasbourg, Bas-Rhin; town; Rue du Sanglier, burning level
2 E
3 B
4 37; Rheinz; Pervincus; fig. 10 no. 10
37; Rheinz; Pervincus; fig. 10 no. 15
37; Rheinz; Atto; fig. 10 no. 16
5 Niederbieber style coarse wares
7 Assigned by the excavator to AD 235 on historical grounds: the deposit overlies the occupation level given in the following entry.
8 Hatt 1949, 182

**B92**

1 Strasbourg, Bas-Rhin; town; Rue du Sanglier, occupation level
2 B
3 B
4 37; Rheinz; Julius II-Julianus I (stamped by Julius in mould); fig. 10 nos 5 and 8
37; Rheinz; Comitialis V; fig. 10 no. 2
37; Rheinz; probably ware with ovolo E8; fig. 10 no. 3
37; Rheinz; Julius II-Julianus I; fig. 10 no. 6
37; Rheinz; Julius II-Julianus I; fig. 10 no. 19
37; Rheinz; Primitivus I; from same mould as Ricken 1948 Taf. 190 no. 10; fig. 10 no. 1
8 Hatt 1949, 177

## LOW COUNTRIES

**B 93**

1 Pommeroeul, Hainault; *vicus*; assemblage PO 355
2 G - not known
3 C
4 30; CG; Cinnamus (stamped in mould with large stamp); ovolo S&S fig. 47 no. 2; fig. 5 no. 6
30; CG; Censorinus; fig. 5 no. 7
37; CG; Paternus II; ovolo S&S fig. 30 no. 1; fig. 6 no. 8
37; CG; Paternus II; ovolo S&S fig. 30 no. 1; fig. 6 no. 9
7 No stratigraphic details are available.
8 Vanderhoeven 1981

**B 94**

1 Robelmont, Luxembourg (Belgium); villa; trench A2 layer V
2 E
3 A
4 37; EG - possibly Chémery; master of the shields and helmets (X-I); no. 26
37; Arg; Gesatus; no. 27
37 (3 pieces); Trier; Censor; nos 29, 32, 123
8 Raepsaet 1974

**B 95**

1 Robelmont, Luxembourg (Belgium); villa; trench A3 layer IV
2 E
3 A
4 37; Arg; ovolo C&G 73; no. 48
37; CG; free style of Cinnamus, Paternus II or contemporary; no. 62
37; CG; possibly Cinnamus; no. 64
8 Raepsaet 1974

**B 96**

1 Robelmont, Luxembourg (Belgium); villa; trench A3 layer V
2 E
3 A
4 37; Arg; Tribunus; no. 66
37; CG; Criciro; no. 67
37; CG; Criciro; no. 152
37; Blick; 'potter with the vase-ovolo'; no. 70
37; EG; possibly Saturninus-Satto style; network of beaded borders; no. 69
37; La Mad; Albillus; no. 154
7 Lies below deposit **B 95**.
8 Raepsaet 1974

**B 97**

1 Rosmeer, Limburg (Belgium); villa; general finds
2 F

3 B
4 37; Rheinz; Reginus I; pl. VI no. 8
37; Arg, ware with ovolo A and B; pl. VI no. 9
37; Arg; ovolo F 465; pl. VI no. 10
37; probably Arg; pl. VI no. 11
37; Arg; pl. VI no. 12
37; Arg; ovolo De Schaetzen & Vanderhoeven 1954 pl. 44 no. 7; pl. VI no. 13
37; West; pl. VI no. 14
Lud VMc; Rheinz; barbotine dec
37 EG (3 fragments)
Plain ware: 18 SG; 18/31 SG (4); 18/31 CG (2); 18/31 EG (2); 15/17 CG; 32 CG; 32 EG (7); 33 CG (2); 33 EG (8); 38 EG; 40 EG (13); 44 EG; 45 EG (14 - 3 with lion's head spouts); beaker EG
6 Aug; As
Nerva; HS
Treb Gall; Ant; 251-3
Gall; Ant; 257-8
7 The samian and the coins are not allocated to context in the report, but it appears that the majority of finds came from a cellar (De Boe & Van Impe 1979, 30).
8 De Boe & Van Impe 1979

**B 98**

1 Rijswijk, Zuid-Holland; rural settlement; phase III
2 F
3 A
4 37; SG; M Crestio; no. 587/5636
37; EG; Janus-group; see Ricken 1934, 176; no. 333
37; Arg; fragment of ovolo; no. 579/5620
37; Arg; column Ricken 1934 Taf. XIII no. 19 (ovolo A and B); no. 689/5850
37; probably Arg; fragment of ovolo; no. 758/5806
37; probably Arg; no. 806/5887
37; Arg; Tribunus group; man H 280, man H 218; no. 808/5888
37; Arg; possibly ovolo A, festoon as Ricken 1934 Taf. XII no. 23; no. 832/5922
37 (3 pieces); Trier; Comitialis; nos 198, 599/5528, 599/5710
37; Trier; Werkstatt II Style B; no. 331/5420
37; Trier; Comitialis; no. 565/5380
37; Trier; ovolo F 941; no. 579/5543
37 (2 pieces); Trier; Primanus group; nos 581/5523, 706/5734
37; probably Trier; no. 587/5636
37 (2 pieces); Trier; Comitialis; nos 620/5043 and 832/5922
37; Trier; Afer; no. 808/5888
37; Trier; Dexter/Censor group; no. 832/5922
37; Trier; Comitialis; no. 832/5922
37; Rheinz; Lupus, Julius I or Perpetuus; ovolo R&F E42; no. 16
37; Rheinz; Cerialis III; no. 31
37; Rheinz; Julius I, Lupus, Reginus 11 type ware; ovolo R&F E40; no. 334/5408
37; Rheinz; ovolo R&F E25/6; no. 579/5525
37; Rheinz; Julius II-Julianus I; no. 691/5805
18/31; West; Pergamus (Helenius group potte); no. 937
7 The association is a general one only, in phase III, which is dated by the excavator AD 200-250/70. There is an unstratified coin of Tet I, but no later material from the site. Five of the sherds listed above (from 832/5922) form a small associated group.
8 Bloemers 1978, 240-53, 302, Beilage 7

## GERMANY

**B 99**

1 Altenstadt, Hessen; fort; trench 7, pit 27
2 C
3 A
4 37; Trier; Tordilo; Taf. 16 no. 155
37; Rheinz; Cerialis I; Taf. 17 no. 181
37; Rheinz; Firmus I, Comitialis V, Attillus, Julius II-Julianus I or Severianus; Taf. 19 no. 272
8 Schönberger & Simon 1983

**B 100**

1 Altenstadt, Hessen; fort; trench 10, ditch period 2/3
2 D
3 A
4 37; CG; X-6; Taf. 12 no. 10
37; CG; Acaunissa; Taf. 12 no. 12
37; CG; X-14 or Pugnus; Taf. 12 no. 16
37; CG; Venus O 286 (Albucius, Arcanus, Drusus II, Cinnamus, Cinnamus-Cerialis, Paullus); Taf. 12 no. 17
37; Chémery; Saturninus/Satto ware; Taf. 13 no. 25
37; Blick; master of the large figures; Taf. 13 no. 36
37; Blick; potter of the vase ovolo; ovolo K&S Taf. 82 no. 27; Taf. 13 no. 40
37; La Mad; ware with ovolo A; no. 64
37; Trier; Werkstatt I, group B; Taf. 16 no. 108
8 Schönberger & Simon 1983

**B101**

1 Altenstadt, Hessen; fort; trench 10, ditch period 6
2 D
3 A
4 37; Trier; Afer; Taf. 16 no. 162
37; Trier; Dubitatus-Dubitus; Taf. 17 no. 163
37; Rheinz; Julius II-Julianus I; no. 253
37; Rheinz; ovolo R&F E17; no. 283
8 Schönberger & Simon 1983

**B 102**

1 Altenstadt, Hessen; fort; trench 10, pit 24/25
2 C
3 A
4 37; Trier; Censor; no. 130
37; Rheinz; Comitialis V (stamped in mould); Taf. 18 no. 203
37; EG; rouletted dec
8 Schönberger & Simon 1983

**B 103**

1 Altenstadt, Hessen; fort; trench 11, pits 59 and 60
2 C
3 A
4 From pit 59:
37; EG - unlocated kiln-centre; ovolo Ricken 1934 Taf. 10 no. 16; Taf. 15 no. 105
37; Rheinz; Reginus I; Taf. 17 no. 174
From pit 60:
Another piece of the 37 EG from pit 59; no. 105
37; Blick; Avitus; Taf. 13 no. 46
37; Rheinz; Cerialis group, ware B; no. 194
37; Rheinz; ovolo R&F E44; no. 305
7 These two adjacent pits were probably filled from the same source.
8 Schönberger & Simon 1983

**B 104**

1 Altenstadt, Hessen; fort; trench 11, pits 63 and 64
2 C
3 A
4 From pit 63:
37; EG - perhaps Mitt; Saturninus/Satto ware; ovolo Lutz 1970a 02; Taf. 13 no. 24
37; Blick; master of the large figures; Taf. 13 no. 32
37; Trier; Comitialis; Taf. 16 no. 153
37; Rheinz; CerialisV; Taf. 17 no. 189
37; Rheinz; Pupus; Taf. 18 no. 226
37; Rheinz; ovolo R&F E66 (Comitialis IV, Mammilianus or Pupus); no. 312
From pit 64:
37; Trier; Dexter; Taf. 16 no. 150
37; Rheinz; Cobnertus III; Taf. 17 no. 176
37; Rheinz; Pupus; Taf. 18 no. 226 - joins with a piece from pit 63
37; Rheinz; ovolo R&F E17; no. 284
7 These pits are adjacent and may have been filled from the same source.
8 Schönberger & Simon 1983

**B 105**

1 Altenstadt, Hessen; fort; trench 11, pit 73/74
2 C
3 A
4 37; Trier; Werkstatt II, group E; Taf. 16 no. 117
37; Trier; Censor; no. 130
37; Trier; Dexter; Taf. 16 no. 149
37; Trier; Dexter; Taf. 16 no. 150
37; Trier; Amator; Taf. 16 no. 156
37; Trier; Dubitatus-Dubitus; Taf. 17 no. 165
37; Rheinz; B F Attoni; no. 179
37; Rheinz; Comitialis I-II; no. 183
37; Rheinz; Comitialis IV; Taf. 18 no. 202
37; Rheinz; Julius I; Taf. 18 no. 228
37; Rheinz; Firmus II, Reginus II or Victorinus I; no. 232
37; Rheinz; Helenius; no. 234
37; Rheinz; Julius II-Julianus I; Taf. 18 no. 250
37; Rheinz; Marcellinus; Taf. 19 no. 270
37; Rheinz; Marcellinus; Taf. 19 no. 271
37; Rheinz; ovolo R&F E40 (Cerialis VI, Comitialis III, Attillus, Marcellus II, Primitivus I-III); no. 302
8 Schönberger & Simon 1983

**B 106**

1 Böhming, Schwaben; fort; burning level of timber fort
2 E
3 B
4 Certainly from the burnt level:
37; Rheinz; Belsus I; Abb. 1 no. 1
37; Rheinz; Comitialis V; Abb. 1 no. 5
33; 31
Probably from the burnt level:
37; CG; Cinnamus; ovolo S&S fig. 47 no. 4; Abb. 1 no. 2
37; CG; Cinnamus; Abb. 1 no. 3
37; CG; Cinnamus or Paternus II; leaf as R H21; Abb. 1 no. 4
7 Kellner puts the building of the subsequent stone fort to AD 181 on the basis of an inscription which he associates with that fort (Vollmer 1915, 291). He dates the burning level to the Marcomannic War on historical grounds.
8 Kellner 1965, 162-5

**B 107**

1 Butzbach, Hessen; fort; level VII
2 F
3 B
4 37; La Mad; ware with ovolo A; Taf. 2 no. 1
37; La Mad; ware with ovolo C; Taf. 2 no. 2
37; La Mad; ware with ovolo B; Taf. 2 no. 3
37; La Mad; ware with ovolo C; Taf. 2 no. 4
37; Blick; late potter; ovolo K&S Taf. 82 no. 32
37; Blick; ware with small ovolo as K&S Taf. 82 no. 30
37; Blick; ware with small ovolo as K&S Taf. 82 no. 30
37; Trier; Werkstatt II; ovolo F 944; Taf. 2 no. 6
37; Trier; Werkstatt II; ovolo F 944 as basal wreath; Taf. 2 no. 5
37; Trier; Maiiaaus ovolo F 941; Taf. 2 no. 7
6 From level VI:
Vesp; As; 72-9; illeg
Traj; HS; 103-17; illeg
Faust I; Den; BMC (Ant) 40; 138-9
7 The coins provide a *terminus post quem* for the level with the samian. Coins from the overlying topsoil (level VIII) run to Phil I; Ant; 247-9 (plus some from the late 4th century).
8 Müller 1962

**B 108**

1 Degerfeld in Butzbach, Hessen; fort; ditch of stone fort
2 D
3 B
4 From 1930s excavations:
37; La Mad; ware with ovolo A'
37; Rheinz; Comitialis
37; Rheinz; Comitialis
37 ; Trier; Dexter
37; Trier; Censor
37; Trier; ovolo as F 939
37 Trier (2)
From 1960s excavations:
37; La Mad; ware with ovolo A'
37; La Mad; probably ware with ovolo A'; cross in place of ovolo Ricken 1934 Taf. VII no. 20
37; La Mad; ware with ovolo L
37; Trier; Dexter
37; Trier; Amator or Atilli-Pusso
37; Rheinz; ovolo R&F E44, bear *ibid* T61-2 (Cerialis II-III, Pupus-Iuvenis II, ware B with O382-3)
37; Rheinz; grapes R&F P164a (B F Attoni, Cerialis V-VI, Comitialis VI, Belsus II, Respectus, ware with ovolo E 25/26, Pupus-Iuvenis II)
37 Trier
6 General coins from the stone fort are Ant; As; 140-4 and Aur; HS; 164
7 The deposit seems fairly mixed as the ditch of the preceding earthen fort contains many similar pieces.
8 Schleiermacher 1936; Simon 1968

**B 109**

1 Degerfeld in Butzbach, Hessen; fort; pit in trench 5
2 C
3 B
4 37; Trier; Dexter
37; Rheinz; Attillus (stamped in mould)
8 Simon 1968

**B 110**

1 Degerfeld in Butzbach, Hessen; fort; pit 14
2 C
3 B
4 37; La Mad; ware with ovolo K, group 3

37; Rheinz; Belsus III or Firmus II
8 Simon 1968

**B 111**

1 Degerfeld in Butzbach, Hessen; fort; pit 33
2 C
3 B
4 37; Arg; ware with ovolo A/B
37; Blick; 'potter of the leaprng animals', K&S Taf. 25 no. 2
7 The deposit comes from a pit associated with the earthen fort preceding the stone phase.
8 Simon 1968

**B 112**

1 Degerfeld in Butzbach, Hessen; fort; pit 41
2 C
3 B
4 37; La Mad; Virtus
37; Trier; Dexter
37; Rheinz; Comitialis III (stamped in mould)
8 Simon 1968

**B 113**

1 Epfach, Oberbayern; cemetery; grave 1d
2 A
3 B
4 37; CG; Cinnamus, Paternus II or associate; Hercules O 757 in medallion; no. 1
37 (2 pieces); Rheinz; Primitivus I; no. 2
37 (6 pieces); West; Comitialis; no. 3
7 The provenance of the CG piece is slightly uncertain.
8 Walke 1964; Werner *et al* 1964

**B 114**

1 Epfach, Oberbayern; cemetery; grave 5
2 A
3 B
4 37 (4 pieces); Rheinz; Janu I style; no. 1
37 (4 pieces); Rheinz; B F Attoni, Belsus or Victor I; no. 2
37 (2 pieces); Rheinz; Primitivus I; no. 3
37 (5 pieces); Rheinz; Primitivus I; no. 4
37 (6 pieces); Rheinz; Primitivus I (stamped); no. 5
37 (4 pieces); Rheinz; Atto; no. 7
37; Rheinz; Lucanus; no. 8
37 (9 pieces); CG; Casurius; no. 6
8 Walke 1964; Werner *et al* 1964

**B 115**

1 Epfach, Oberbayern; cemetery; grave 7
2 A
3 B
4 37; CG; Albucius (stamped); no. 1
37 (2 pieces); Rheinz; Comitialis II (stamped by Ioventus as bowl finisher); no. 2
8 Walke 1964: Werner *et al* 1964

**B 116**

1 Epfach, Oberbayern; cemetery; grave 12
2 A
3 B
4 37; Itten or Mitt; Cibisus (stamped); no. 1
37; CG; Paternus II; no. 2
37; Rheinz; Cerialis group, ware B; no. 3
8 Walke 1964; Werner *et al* 1964

**B 117**

1 Epfach, Oberbayern; cemetery; grave 47
2 A
3 B
4 37 (6 pieces); Banassac; Natalis; no. 1
37 (2 pieces); Rheinz; Cobnertus III; no. 2
8 Walke 1964; Werner *et al* 1964

**B 118**

1 Faimingen, Schwaben; temple; phase I general finds
2 F
3 A
4 37; SG; Mercato-Mascuus; no. 7
37; Banassac; Natalis; no. 21
37 SG (8 small pieces)
37; CG; Cinnamus; no. 39
37; CG; Cinnamus or Pugnus; no. 42
37 CG (1 fragment)
37; Heil; Januarius; no. 44
37; Heil; Januarius; no. 47
37 (2 pieces); Heil; Januarius; no. 47a and b
37; Heil; F-master; no. 48
37; Heil; Januarius; no. 52
37; Heil; Januarius; no. 53
37 Heil (4 small pieces)
37; Rheinz; Cerialis II-IV; no. 57
37 Rheinz (2 small pieces)
6 Had; HS; RIC 748c; 134-8; very worn
Ant; Ae; RIC 1238; 140-4· fairly worn
7 Destruction levels around the temple have coins of the Severan dynasty. This, coupled with the lack of late Rheinz samian, has led the excavator to date phase I to the 2nd half of the 2nd century. Some upper levels have been removed, since the proportion of Rheinz samian is much higher in the disturbed levels.
8 Weber 1981

**B 119**

1 Gross-Gerau, Hessen; *vicus*; trench 19, cellar
2 E
3 B
4 37; Rheinz; Julius I-Lupus
37 (6 pieces); Rheinz; Respectinus II (stamped in mould); Abb. 4 no. 1
37 Rheinz
8 Simon 1965

**B 120**

1 Günzburg, Schwaben; *vicus*; trench 2, upper cellar fill
2 E
3 A
4 37; SG; Sabinus; late Flavian - early Trajan; no. 16
37; Heil; Januarius; no. 21
37; EG - Heil or La Mad; no. 23
37; Rheinz; ware B with O 382/3; no. 24
37 SG (5); 37 Heil; 45 EG; 27; 31 EG; 37 EG
7 Clearly there is early redeposited material amongst a small 2nd century group.
8 Walke 1959

**B 121**

1 Hackenbroich, Nordrhein-Westfalen; cemetery; pit by grave 1
2 C
3 A
4 37; Rheinz; Respectus; Bild 10 no. 1

37; Trier; ovolo F 941; Bild 10 no. 2
8 Müller 1971

**B 122**

1 Holzhausen, Hessen; fort; pit 16
2 C
3 B
4 37; Trier; Maiiaaus; A 146
37; Trier; Dexter, Maiiaaus or Tordilo; A 171
37 EG (3); 45 EG (2); U EG stamped by Severus
8 Nass 1934; Pferdehirt 1976

**B 123**

1 Holzhausen, Hessen; fort; pit 21
2 C
3 B
4 37; Rheinz; Julius II-Julianus I; A 51
37; Trier; Tordilo, Afer or Dubitatus-Dubitus; A 172
37 EG; 44 EG (2); 45 EG (5); 32 EG (3); 33 EG (3); Nied 21b EG; Nied 5b EG (5); Nied 11b EG; Nied 27 EG; U EG
8 Nass 1934; Pferdehirt 1976

**B 124**

1 Holzhausen, Hessen; fort; pit 24
2 C
3 B
4 37; Rheinz; Cerialis group ware B; A 5
37; Rheinz; Comitialis I; A 6
37; Trier; Censor-Dexter; A 134
37; Trier; Marinus; A 152
37; Trier; Atillus group; A 157
37; EG - unlocated
37 EG (5); 45 EG (5); 32 EG; Nied 5b EG; 33 EG; Nied 12 EG; U EG (stamped by Ursulus)
8 Nass 1934; Pferdehirt 1976

**B 125**

1 Holzhausen, Hessen; fort; post-hole 30
2 C
3 B
4 37; Trier; Amator; A 147
37; Trier; Atillus; A 158
37; Trier; Dexter, Maiiaaus or Tordilo; A 170
37; Trier; Afer or Dubitatus; A 173
Nied 19 EG; Nied 21b EG; 45 EG (6)
8 Nass 1934; Pferdehirt 1976

**B 126**

1 Kriftel, Hessen; *vicus*; pit 1
2 C
3 B
4 37; Arg; ware with ovolo C; Abb. 7 no. 15
37; Rheinz; Cobnertus I; Abb. 7 no. 6
37; Trier; crosses in place of ovolo F 960; Abb. 7 no. 23
37 Rheinz
8 Schoppa 1964

**B 127**

1 Kriftel, Hessen; *vicus*; pit 5
2 C
3 B
4 37; Rheinz; Primitivus I or III; Abb. 7 no. 5
37; Rheinz; B F Attoni, Cerialis VI, Respectus, Primitivus I or III, or ware with ovolo E 25/26; Abb. 7 no. 7
37; Rheinz; Comitialis V; Abb. 7 no. 16
37; Rheinz; Cobnertus III, Comitialis V; Marcellus II, Primitivus I or II; Abb. 7 no. 18
37; Rheinz; Cerialis III; Abb. 7 no. 19
37; Rheinz; Lupus; Abb. 7 no. 21
8 Schoppa 1964

**B 128**

1 Kriftel, Hessen; *vicus*; pit 7
2 C
3 B
4 37; Rheinz; B F Attoni; Abb. 7 no. 1
37; Rheinz; Cobnertus II or Comitialis V; Abb. 7 no. 13
37; Rheinz; Comitialis V; Abb. 7 no. 14
8 Schoppa 1964

**B 129**

1 Künzing, Niederbayern; fort; pit 113
2 C
3 B
4 37; Rheinz; Comitialis IV; no. 49
37; Rheinz; Primitivus II; no. 66
37; Rheinz; Julius II-Julianus I; no. 71
37; Rheinz; Victor II-Januco; no. 76
37; Rheinz; Victor II-Januco; no. 77
8 Schönberger 1975

**B 130**

1 Künzing, Niederbayern; *vicus*; trench 0/1, grave 45
2 A
3 A
4 37; West; Helenius; no. 237
37; Rheinz; Julius I, Lupus or Perpetuus; ovolo R&F E42; no. 238
37; Rheinz; Pupus; no. 239
37; Rheinz; Comitialis VI (stamped in mould); no. 240
7 Possibly a burning area rather than an actual grave.
8 Rieckhoff-Pauli 1979, 115-6

**B 131**

1 Künzing, Niederbayern; *vicus*; trench W/12, pit 2
2 C
3 A
4 From layer 6:
37; Rheinz; leaf R&F P61 (used by several potters of groups IIa-b, also Cerialis V and Belsus I); no. 117
37; Rheinz; Cerialis I-III; no. 118
33 EG; 18/31 EG (6); 27 EG
From layer 8:
37; CG; Cinnamus; no. 131
37; Rheinz (or Heil?); Reginus I; no. 132
18/31
From layer 9:
33 EG; beaker EG
7 The layers appear to be contemporary.
8 Rieckhoff-Pauli 1979, 102-4

**B 132**

1 Künzing, Niederbayern; *vicus*; trench W/12, pit 3
2 C
3 A
4 37; Rheinz; Victor II-Januco; no. 149
37; Rheinz; Ware with ovolo R&F E 25/26; no. 150
37 Rheinz (2); 33 EG (2); 18/31 EG
8 Rieckhoff-Pauli 1979, 104-6

**B 133**

1 Künzing, Niederbayern; *vicus*; trench W/12, pit 4
2 C
3 A
4 37; Rheinz; Comitialis VI, Belsus II-III, Respectus or ware with E 25/26; no. 170
37; Rheinz; Attillus; no. 171
31 EG (2)
8 Rieckhoff-Pauli 1979, 106-8

**B 134**

1 Künzing, Niederbayern; *vicus*; trench W/12, pit 6
2 C
3 A
4 From layer 4:
37; Rheinz; B F Attoni; no. 179
32 EG
From layer 5:
37; CG; Cinnamus; no. 185
7 The layers appear to be contemporary.
8 Rieckhoff-Pauli 1979, 108-10

**B 135**

1 Leonhardspfunzen, Oberbayern; cemetery; grave 12
2 A
3 B
4 37; Pfaffenhofen; ovolo type 19, stamped by Victorinus on the rim; Abb. 21 nos 1a-b
37; CG; Quintilianus group; Abb. 22 no. 1
37 (4 pieces); Rheinz; Reginus I; Abb. 22 nos 2-5
31; CG; stamped by Gippus
32 (4); 33
8 Kellner 1968

**B 136**

1 Miltenberg-Altstadt, Baden-Württemberg; fort; general finds
2 F
3 B
4 37; Trier; Dexter; Abb. 27 no. 8
37; Blick; Avitus (stamped in mould); Abb. 27 no. 1
37; Blick; Avitus/Cambo; Abb. 26 no. 3
37 (2 pieces); Arg; Gesatus; Abb. 27 no. 2
37; Rheinz; Julius II-Julianus I; Abb. 27 no. 5
37; Rheinz; probably Julius I; Abb. 26 no. 4
37; Rheinz; Helenius; Abb. 26 no. 2
37; Rheinz; Julius II-Julianus I; Abb. 27 no. 4
37 (2 pieces); Rheinz; Comitialis VI or Belsus III; Abb. 27 no. 3
37 (3 pieces); Rheinz; Helenius; Abb. 26 nos 6-8
37; Rheinz; Cerialis I or V, Comitialis I; Abb. 26 no. 5
37; Rheinz; Julius II-Julianus I or Respectinus II; Abb. 27 no. 6
37; Rheinz; Comitialis V (stamped in mould); Abb. 27 no. 7
37 (3 pieces); Rheinz; Cobnertus III; Abb. 26 no. 1
Chenet 320 EG with roller stamp dec
32 EG; Lud Tl EG; 43 EG; 33 Rheinz (2 stamped); 37 CG (stamped in bowl by Cracuna); 37 Rheinz; 31 Arg (stamped); 31 Blick (stamped)
6 Stray coin finds from the excavations:
Flavian (2 Ae); Nerva (1 Ae); Traj (5 Ae); Had (1 Ae, 1 Den); Ant (1 Ae, 2 Den); Aur (1 Ae); Comm (1 Den); Sev (2 Den); Alex (1 Den); Max (1 Den); Gord III (1 Ant); Phil I (1 Ant)
7 These finds are of interest since they are from a fort apparently founded in the 150s.
8 Beckmann 1977, 94ff

**B 137**

1 Munningen, Baden-Württemberg; fort; hollow, upper level
2 C
3 B
4 37; CG; Cinnamus; ovolo S&S fig. 47 no. 2; Abb. 22 no. 51
37; Mitt; Saturninus-Satto: ovolo Lutz 1970a 02; no. 61
37; Heil; Januarius; Abb. 22 no. 70
7 Some burnt items from high in this level are associated by the excavator with a burning episode of *c* AD 170.
8 Baatz 1976; Simon 1976

**B 138**

1 Murrhardt, Baden-Württemberg; fort; pit 79/88, period I
2 C
3 A
4 37; Rheinz; Janu I or Cerialis II; no. 16
37; Rheinz; Janu I or Cerialis II; no. 17
37 (4 pieces); Waiblingen; Marinus; ovolo Simon 1984 no. 12; no. 21
7 Period I probably falls between the late 150s and the late 160s-170s (see deposit **A 185**).
8 Krause 1984, 325

**B 139**

1 Ohringen-West, Baden-Württemberg; fort; ditch 37
2 D
3 B
4 37; Heil; Ciriuna; Abb. 3 no. 1
37; Eschweiler; LAA potter; Abb. 3 no. 8
37; Eschweiler; LAA potter; Abb. 3 no. 9
37; Eschweiler; LAA potter (or late Blick ware); Abb. 3 no. 10
37; Rheinz; ware with ovolo E 25/26; Abb. 4 no. 23
37; Rheinz; Mammilianus; Abb. 4 no. 25
37; Rheinz; Reginus II; no. 26
37; EG - unlocated, possibly from a south German kiln; Abb. 4 no. 43
7 The fort is part of the outer *limes*, occupied probably from the 140s. The following coins come from the fort as a whole (Christ 1964b= FMRD II, 4, 4408): Calig HS; Traj HS, Dup, Ae; Had As, Ae; Aur HS, Ae, As, Dup, Den; Comm HS, Dup As; Clod Alb Den; Car Den; Alex Den; Phil I Ant.
8 Schönberger 1972

**B 140**

1 Ohringen-West, Baden-Württemberg; fort; pit 22
2 C
3 B
4 37; Rheinz; probably B F Attoni; Abb. 4 no. 15
37; Rheinz; Cerialis group ware B; no. 20
37; Rheinz; ware with ovolo E 25/26; no. 24
7 See comments for **B 139**.
8 Schönberger 1972

**B 141**

1 Ohringen-West, Baden-Württemberg; fort; pit 36
2 C
3 B
4 37; Blick; late ware; ovolo K&S Taf 82 no. 32; Abb. 3 no. 6
37; Rheinz; Cerialis group ware B; Abb. 4 no. 19
37; Rheinz; Reginus II; no. 27
37; Rheinz; Helenius; Abb. 4 no. 29
37; Rheinz; Attillus; Abb. 4 no. 30
37; Rheinz; Primitivus IV; Abb. 4 no. 31
37; Rheinz; ware with ornament O 382/383; Abb. 4 no. 36
37; Rheinz; Victor II-Januco; Abb. 4 no. 37
37 Rheinz

7 See comments for **B 139**.
8 Schönberger 1972

**B 142**

1 Pfaffenhofen, Oberbayern; samian kiln centre; trench B/1967 layer VI
2 E
3 A
4 37; Rheinz; Pupus; Abb. 12 no. 6
37; West; Comitialis; Abb. 13 no. 6
8 Christlein & Kellner 1969

**B 143**

1 Pfaffenhofen, Oberbayern; samian kiln centre; trench D/1967 layer IV
2 E
3 A
4 37; Rheinz; Julius II-Julianus I; Abb. 12 no. 5
37; Rheinz; B F Attoni; Abb. 12 no. 12
37; West or Pfaffenhofen; Helenius (2 vessels); Abb. 16 nos 5-6
37; Pfaffenhofen; Helenius (13 vessels); Abb. 18 no. 2, Abb. 19 nos 2, 6, Abb. 20 nos 2-4, 8-9, Abb. 21 nos 5, 7, 9, 10, 14
41 Pfaff with incised dec; 41 Pfaff with incised inscription and dec; 33 Pfaff; 31 Pfaff; O&P pl. 59 no. 10 Pfaff; 32 Pfaff (4); Nied 6a Pfaff
moulds for 37; Pfaffenhofen; Helenius (23 moulds); Abb. 17 nos 1-12, 14-24
moulds for 37; Pfaffenhofen; Dicanus (2 moulds); Abb. 22 nos 1-2
7 The deposit is underlain by deposit **A 191**, which contained a Denarius of Commodus. However, there is no overlying layer, and there is the possibility that it accumulated slowly in the late Roman period. The kiln debris is probably contemporary.
8 Christlein & Kellner 1969

**B 144**

1 Pocking, Niederbayern; *vicus*; cellar 5, lower fill
2 E
3 A
4 37; CG; Paternus II, Albucius or Laxtucissa; ovolo R B105
37; CG; Divixtus; ovolo S&S fig. 33 no. 1
37; West; ovolo as R&F E57
37; West; Comitialis
Plain ware: cup SG; 27 SG; 33 CG; cup CG; 18/31 CG; 54 Rheinz (2); O&P pl. 79 nos 9-13 Rheinz
7 Kellner suggests that this is an occupation deposit in the cellar.
8 Kellner 1960b

**B 145**

1 Pocking, Niederbayern; *vicus*; pit 2
2 C
3 B
4 37; CG; Docilis; ovolo S&S fig. 24 no. 1; Abb. 2 no. 1
37; CG; Cinnamus; ovolo S&S fig. 47 no. 1; Abb. 2 no. 4
37; Rheinz; Arvernicus-Lutaevus; ovolo R&F E2; Abb. 2 no. 2
37; Rheinz; Primitivus I; Abb. 2 no. 3
37; Rheinz; Firmus II; Abb. 3
37; Rheinz; Comitialis V; Abb. 2 no. 5
37; West; Comitialis; Abb. 2 no. 6
Plain ware: 37 West (fragment); 33 CG; 33 CG or EG; 31 EG; 18/31 CG or EG; 31 Rheinz; 32 Rheinz (2)
8 Kellner 1960b

**B 146**

1 Regensburg, Niederbayern; cemetery of fortress; general finds
2 F
3 C
4 Summary only; all 37 Rheinz:
Janu I (1); Reginus I (2); Janu II (2); Cobnertus III (1); Firmus I (1); B F Attoni (1); Cerialis IV (1); Cerialis A ware (2); Cerialis B ware (1); Comitialis I (2); Comitialis II (1); Comitialis III (2); Comitialis IV (3); Comitialis V (5); Comitialis VI (4); Belsus I (3); Belsus II (1); Respectus (1); Ware with ovolo E 25/26 (3); Mammilianus (1); Firmus II (4); Atto (1); Julius I (3); Lucanus (1); Victorinus I (1); Verecundus I (1); Attillus (1); Augustalis (2); Primitivus I (12); Julius II-Julianus I (3); Perpetuus (1)
7 The cemetery is associated with the legionary fortress, which was founded by AD 179 and apparently suffered destruction in the 230s and the 260s. There is some 4th century occupation.
8 von Schnurbein 1977, 267

**B 147**

1 Regensburg, Niederbayern; cemetery of fortress; grave 1012
2 A
3 A
4 37; Rheinz; Victorinus I; Taf. 138 no. 1
37;Rheinz; Augustalis; Taf. 137 no. 4
37; Rheinz; ovolo R&F E17 (Firmus I, B F Attoni, Julius II-Julianus I, Perpetuus and others); Taf. 137 no. 3
8 von Schnurbein 1977, 212

**B 148**

1 Regensburg-Kumpfmühl, Niederbayern; fort and *vicus*; general finds and a burnt layer
2 F and E
3 C
4 From the Kariopp collection:
29 SG (3); 30 SG (1); 37 SG (15); 37 Banassac (17); 30 Heil (1) (summary figures - no details given here)
37; CG; Quintilianus group; Abb. 15 no. 80
37; CG; Attianus; Abb. 15 no. 81
37; CG; Birrantus; Abb. 15 no. 82
37; CG; Criciro; Abb. 15 no. 83
37; CG; Cinnamus; ovolo R B182; Abb. 15 no. 84
37; CG; Cinnamus; ovolo R B145; Abb. 15 no. 85
37; CG; Cinnamus; ovolo R B223; Abb. 15 no. 86
37; CG; Cinnamus; Abb. 15 no. 87
37; CG; Cinnamus; Abb. 15 no. 88
37; CG; ovolo R B208 (Docilis, Laxtucissa or Quintilianus group); Abb. 16 no. 89
37; CG; Abb. 16 no. 90
37; Rheinz; Janu I style; Abb. 16 no. 91
From a burnt deposit in the apsidal building in the *vicus*:
37; CG; Albucius; ovolo R B107; Abb. 16 no. 92
37; CG; Paternus II; ovolo R B105; Abb. 16 no. 93
37; CG; Laxtucissa; ovolo R B102; Abb. 17 no. 94
37; CG; ovolo R B212 (unknown potter); Abb. 17 no. 95
37; Rheinz; Janu I style; Abb. 17 no. 96
37; Rheinz; Janu I (stamped by Avitus on the rim); Abb. 17 no. 97
37; Rheinz; Janu I; Abb. 17 no. 98
37; Rheinz; Reginus I; Abb. 18 no. 99
37; Rheinz; Reginus I; Abb. 18 no. 100
37 (2 pieces); Rheinz; Reginus I; Abb. 18 no. 101
37; Rheinz; Reginus I; Abb. 19 no. 102

37; Rheinz; Reginus I; Abb. 19 no. 103
37; Rheinz; Reginus I; Abb. 19 no. 104
37; Rheinz; Reginus I; Abb. 19 no. 105
37 (2 pieces); Rheinz; Reginus I; Abb. 19 no. 106
37; Rheinz; Reginus I; Abb. 19 no. 107

7 The latest coin from the site is Aur; Dup; 171-2, and both fort and *vicus* appear to have been burnt down and abandoned probably in the 170s. Fischer (1981, 66) suggests that the founding of the Regensburg legionary fortress in AD 179 provides a *terminus ante quem* for the burning and abandonment of the Kumpfmühl fort.

8 Fischer 1981

**B 149**

1 Rheinzabern, Rheinland-Pfalz; samian kiln centre; pit 17c (79/657) associated with overfired kiln load
2 C
3 A
4 Summary only; all 37 Rheinz or moulds:
Ware with ovolo E31 = Pervincus II (108); Julius II-Julianus I (92); Regulinus (91); Primitivus I (77); Victorinus I (50); Julianus II (45); Pervincus (25); Julius I (25); Ware with ovolo E49 (25); Julius I-Lupus (12); Primitivus III (12); Ware B with O382/3 (8); Respectinus II (8); Primitivus IV (7); Comitialis V (6); Marcellus II (5); Comitialis VI (4); Helenius (4); Comitialis II (3); Victorinus II (3) Marcellinus (3); Belsus II (2); Primitivus II (2); Ware with ovolo E34/30 (2); Janu II (1); Firmus I (1); Cerialis I (1); Comitialis III (1); Lucanus (1); Comitialis IV (1); Statutus (1); unknown (22)
7 The excavator considers the potters represented by 45 or more pieces to be working at the nearby kiln. Regulinus was the most common potter in terms of moulds. There is evidence for the reuse of moulds in the case of Janu II, Firmus I, Comitialis II-IV and Lucanus I. Bittner dates the assemblage to 235-45.
8 Reutti 1983, 55-6; Bittner 1986, 249-58; 1996; 2011

**B 150**

1 Rheinzabern, Rheinland-Pfalz; samian kiln centre; well 16g
2 C
3 A
4 Summary of presences only; all 37 Rheinz or moulds:
Majority of the sherds: Julius I; Reginus II/Julius I/ Lupus style; Abbo (stamped on mould in style of Reginus II/Julius I/Lupus)
Other pieces by: Comitialis VI; Julius II-Julianus I; Victor I; Lupus; B F Attoni
7 This is probably material from a kiln workshop, but the nearest known kiln is 50m distant.
8 Reutti 1983, 60

**B 151**

1 Rosendahlsberg, Nordrhein-Westfalen; cemetery in free Germany; grave 256
2 A
3 B
4 37 (2 pieces); Rheinz; Cobnertus III or Firmus I; Abb. 23 nos 3-4
37; Rheinz; Helenius; Abb. 23 no. 5
37; Rheinz; Victorinus or Julius II-Julianus I; Abb. 23 no. 7
37; Trier; Werkstatt II; Abb. 23 no. 9
37 (2 pieces); Trier; Werkstatt I; Abb. 23 no. 10
37; Trier; figure F 499; Abb. 23 no. 8
37; Trier; Censor; Abb. 23 no. 14
8 von Petrikovits & von Uslar 1950

**B 152**

1 Rosendahlsberg, Nordrhein-Westfalen; cemetery in free Germany; grave 268
2 A
3 B
4 37; Rheinz; Helenius; Abb. 23 no. 6
37; Trier; Werkstatt II; Abb. 23 no. 11
37; Trier; Werkstatt I
8 von Petrikovits & von Uslar 1950

**B 153**

1 Straubing, Niederbayern; military *vicus*; well B20
2 C
3 B
4 37; Rheinz; Reginus I (stamped in mould)
37; Rheinz; Reginus I
37; Heil; Verecundus; Taf. 17 no. 6
8 Walke 1965

**B 154**

1 Straubing, Niederbayern; military *vicus*; well B14
2 C
3 B
4 37; Rheinz; Belsus II (stamped in mould); Taf. 30 no. 11
37; Rheinz; ware with ovolo E25/26; Taf. 31 no. 4
37; Rheinz; Helenius; Taf. 32 no. 3
8 Walke 1965

**B 155**

1 Trier, Rheinland-Pfalz; samian kiln centre; Louis Lintzstr., pit
2 C
3 C
4 37; Trier; Dignus/Primanus (stamped in mould)
37; Trier; Dignus/Primanus (stamped in mould)
mould fragments for 37 Trier
many late types of plain ware present
5 Rhenish/Trier CCW beakers with barbotine hunt scenes and drinking mottos; Speicher 'à l'éponge' ware
7 The pit is dated by the excavator to AD 259/60, on historical grounds. There is no internal dating evidence.
8 Loeschcke 1921

**B 156**

1 Trier, Rheinland-Pfalz; samian kiln centre; 'Massenfund'
2 E
3 A
4 A large quantity of bowls was found, together with *c* 350 moulds.
Estimates of relative quantities have been made by counting the illustrated pieces in Gard 1937:
Werkstatt I (1); Werkstatt II (8); Maiiaaus group (3); Comitialis (3); Censor (3); Dexter - early (3); Dexter - late (50); Catu... (1); Dexter successors (7); Amator (1); Victor (1); Afer/Marinus (23); Atillus/Pussosus (27); Siser (1); Paternianus (7); Dubitatus-Dubitus (*c* 120); Perpetuus/Dignus/Primanus (2); ware Gard Taf. 27 no. 1ff (22); ...]ianus (1); ware with Rheinz figure types (1)
The plain ware includes stamps of TPCFR.
7 The deposit is a dump within the pottery kilns, which is interpreted as a single event. There is no dating evidence, but it has been associated with disturbances of the mid-3rd century. Huld-Zetsche makes a case from this and other deposits for reuse of earlier moulds by later potters.
8 Gard 1937; Huld-Zetsche 1971b; 1972; 1978

**B 157**

1 Trier, Rheinland-Pfalz; town; Simeonstift, dump against town wall
2 E
3 A
4 37; Trier; probably Werkstatt I; Abb. 24 no. 5
37; Trier; Werkstatt II; Abb. 24 no. 1
37; Trier; Werkstatt II; Abb. 24 no. 2
37; Trier; Werkstatt II; Abb. 24 no. 6
37; Trier; probably Werkstatt II; Abb. 24 no. 3
7 The wall is dated to the period after *c* AD 180 according to coin finds from elsewhere in the circuit.
8 Cüppers 1973

**B 158**

1 Xanten, Nordrhein-Westfalen; town; Siegfriedstr 7a
2 E
3 A
4 37; La Mad; ovolo as F Taf. 1 no. 36, Mercury F 31
37; Trier; ovolo F 956
37; Trier; Dexter; ovolo F 947
18/31 SG stamped by Flavus and Germanus; 38 EG; 33 EG; 45 EG (3)
5 Rhenish CCW with barbotine dec
7 The pottery is related to the 'frühe Niederbieber-Horizont'.
8 Bruckner & Hinz 1962

## ALPINE REGION

**B 159**

1 Wiesendangen, Zürich; villa; general finds
2 F
3 B
4 37; Mittelbronn; Cibisus (stamped in mould); Abb. 5 no. 6
37 (2 pieces); Rheinz; Comitialis V; Abb. 5 no. 7
37; Rheinz; Comitialis VI; Abb. 5 no. 8
37; Rheinz; Comitialis VI; Abb. 5 no. 9
31; Rheinz; stamped by Victorinus
32; Mittelbronn; stamped by Cibisus
32; Rheinz; stamped by Iulius
32; Swiss workshop; stamped by Iustus
31 EG (4); Nied 19 EG with barbotine dec
6 Summary only:
Ant HS; Faust II HS; Gall (5); Post (2); Tet I; Tet II; Claud II (4); Quint; Aurel; Prob (2); Dio; Max Herc (2)
7 90% of the total assemblage comes from a black layer in room 5. Unfortunately, the particular pieces from the layer are not specified and so the association is general only. The coins are general finds from the villa.
8 Drack, Wiedemer & Ettlinger 1961

**B 160**

1 Schaan, Leichtenstein; fort; general finds
2 F
3 A
4 37; Rheinz; Victor II
plate EG
spindle-whorl made from EG ware
7 The fort does not appear to have earlier occupation than the end of the 3rd century. The pieces are probably survivals (see Portchester).
8 Ettlinger 1959

## MIDDLE DANUBE REGION

**B 161**

1 *Carnuntum*, Niederösterreich; fortress; trench V, 1970, cistern
2 E
3 A
4 37; Rheinz; Augustinus II; Taf. 5 no. 10·
37; West; Helenius; Taf. 6 no. 8
8 Grünewald 1979

**B 162**

1 *Aquincum*, Budapest, Hungary; town; pottery shop burnt deposit
2 E
3 C
4 30; Rheinz; Cobnertus III (stamped in mould); animal R&F T40, eagle *ibid* T199, metope style very similar to Ricken 1948 Taf. 25 no. 4F; táb. II no. 9
30; Rheinz; Cobnertus III; trifid R&F P120, leaf *ibid* P91, 'twist' *ibid* O236, all in St Andrew's cross design as Ricken 1948 Taf. 32 nos 3-4; táb. II no. 10
37; CG; Albucius (stamped in mould); ovolo S&S fig. 35 no. 1, bead and reel border, leaf and astragalus *ibid* fig. 35 no. 1, Neptune O 13, metope style; táb. I no. 1
37 (2 pieces); CG; Paternus II; ovolo S&S fig. 30 no. 1, tripod R Q16, Mercury O 529, metope style; táb. I nos 2-3
37 (3 pieces); CG; Paternus II; ovolo S&S fig. 30 no. 1, tripod as R Q16 = S&S fig. 30 no. 9, rosette on top of vertical bead row as *ibid* pl. 107 no. 29, rosette *ibid* fig. 30 no. 1, 'twist' *ibid* fig. 30 no. 21, cupid O 440 inside two concentric double medallions, cupid O 444 in similar, female figure O 926, metope and medallion style; táb I nos 4-6
37 (3 pieces); CG; Paternus II; ovolo S&S fig. 30 no. 1, cupid O 440, cupid O 444, 'column' R P3, 'twist' S&S fig. 30 no. 21, deer O 1732 in festoon, metope style; táb. I nos 7-9
37 (7 pieces); CG; Cinnamus; ovolo S&S fig. 47 no. 1, leaf R H21, leaf R H22, leaf R H13, leaf R J93, bird O 2239, winding scroll style; táb. I nos 10-14 and táb. II nos 1-2
37 (6 pieces); CG; Cinnamus (stamped by Cintusmus on rim); ovolo S&S fig. 47 no. 1, sea horse O 52 in festoon, dancer O 322 in medallion repeated at least 4 times, small figure as O 939, philosopher O 905, horse O 1976 (wrongly drawn as a dog in O), lozenge S&S fig. 47 no. 15, astragalus *ibid* fig. 47 no. 40, circle *ibid* fig. 47 no. 11, metope and medallion style; táb. II nos 3-8
37 (2 pieces); CG; Cinnamus; lion O 1421, lioness O 1512 in medallion, Pan mask O 1214, caryatid O 1199, cupid O 401, metope and medallion style; táb. II nos 11-12
37 (6 pieces); CG; Criciro (signed in mould below dec); ovolo as S&S pl. 117 no. 8, cupid O 426 (4 times), goat O 1842, dog not in O but as O 1948-9, sea horse O 48A, leaf R J58, trifid R G67, metope and St Andrew's cross style; táb. II nos 13-17 and táb. III no. 1
37 (3 pieces); CG; Paternus II (stamped in mould); ovolo S&S fig. 30 no. 3, leaf R H35, rosette as S&S fig. 30 no. 3, seated figure O 913 in medallion (2 times), winding scroll and medallion style; táb. III nos 2-4
37 (2 pieces); CG; Censorinus; ovolo R B206, bud R G208, Venus O 305, male figure with staff not in O, bead and reel vertical border, free style with some vertical divisions; táb. III nos 5-6
37 (2 pieces); CG; Paternus II or Censorinus; ovolo R B206, bud R G208, figure with sword O 628 in medallion,

rosette S&S fig. 30 no. 5, winding scroll and medallion style; táb. III nos 7-8
37 (4 pieces); CG; Paternus II; ovolo R B206, leaf S&S fig. 30 no. 14, deer O 1805, dog O 1940 without tip of tail, dog O 1985, deer O 1752A, boar O 1674, bear as O 1617, free style; táb. III nos 9-12
37; CG; possibly Paternus; warrior O 191, warrior as O 189, bead and reel border, metope style; táb. IV no. 1
37 (2 pieces); CG; Albucius; ovolo as R B107, cupid as O 399A, Venus O 338, bird O 2324, metope style; táb. IV nos 2-3
37; CG; Cinnamus or Paullus; ovolo S&S fig. 47 no. 3, dancer O 348 in medallion, bear O 1627, caryatid O 1207, metope and medallion style; táb. IV no. 4
37 (2 pieces); CG; Cinnamus; Vulcan O 66 without tongs, female figure O 819A in medallion, astragalus S&S fig. 47 no. 40, circle *ibid* fig. 47 no. 11, tree R N4, metope and medallion style; táb. IV nos 5-6
37 (3 pieces); CG; Paternus II; ovolo R B105, warrior O 188 in medallion, cupid O 450 in medallion, rosette S&S fig. 30 no. 26, astragalus *ibid* fig. 30 no. 12, 'twist' *ibid* fig. 30 no. 21, metope and medallion style; táb. IV nos 7-8
37 (2 pieces); CG; Cinnamus; ovolo as S&S fig. 47 no. 3, vine scroll R M3, lozenge S&S fig. 47 no. 15, metope style; táb. IV nos 9-10
37; CG; Criciro or Divixtus; caryatid O 1207A, rosette and border as S&S pl. 117 no. 11, metope and medallion style; táb. IV no. 11
37; CG; Cinnamus; ovolo S&S fig. 47 no. 3, trace of bird in festoon, metope and medallion style; táb. IV no. 12
37; CG; Cinnamus; bird O 2252 in festoon; táb. IV no. 13
37; CG; Albucius; ovolo R B105, gladiator as O 1060; táb. IV no. 14
30; CG; unknown potter; ovolo as R B78 of P-22, trace of acanthus; táb. IV no. 15
37; CG; probably Paternus II; sphinx O 857 in festoon; táb. IV no. 16
37; CG; trace of probable basal wreath similar to S&S pl. 76 no. 23 of X-6; táb. IV no. 17
U; CG; wall sherd with incised leaf dec; táb. IV no. 18
7 The deposit is a group of samian apparently from a burnt shop in a portico, subsequently rebuilt with the burnt deposit used as levelling.
8 Juhász 1936

**B 163**

1 Zalalövö, Hungary; town; 1979 A/IV-A/III-B/IV grey fill in channel
2 E
3 A
4 37; CG; Pugnus; no. 63
37; CG; Cinnamus; ovolo S&S fig. 47 no. 4; no. 68
37; CG; Cinnamus; ovolo R B144; no. 69
37; Rheinz; Comitialis V; no. 77
8 Gabler 1981; Rédö 1981

**B 164**

1 Zalalövö, Hungary; town; 1980-1, construction of building b
2 E
3 A
4 37; Rheinz; Comitialis V; no. 92
37; Rheinz; Belsus III; no. 93
37; Rheinz; Florentinus; no. 94
37; West; Comitialis-Decminus/Venerius/Luppo; ovolo Kellner 1961 E2; no. 96
37; Pfaffenhofen; Dicanus; no. 97
37 Rheinz
7 The association appears to be a fairly general one.
8 Gabler 1982; Rédö 1982

# SECTION C: Deposits of plain samian ware associated with coins

## BRITAIN

**C 1**

1 Atworth, Wiltshire; villa; general finds
2 F
3 A
4 38 (2); 33 (2); 79 (2); 18/31 CG; 38 CG; 31; 36; 32; mortarium
6 Coins from Gall - Theod, but mainly late 3rd century and Const
7 The excavators discuss the starting date of the villa and note the absence of early coins, but take account of the lack of coins in Britain of the early 3rd century. Therefore they suggest that period I starts *c* AD 200 with the samian 'not inconsistent with an initial date of AD 200, but whether they support the later margin of AD 250 is debatable' (Mellor & Goodchild 1940, 89).
8 Mellor & Goodchild 1940; Mattingly 1940; Oswald 1940

**C 2**

1 Bozeat, Northamptonshire; rural settlement; ditch 1
2 D
3 A
4 45; probably CG
6 Aur; Den; RIC 59; 163; good condition
8 Hall & Nickerson 1970

**C 3**

1 Brancaster, Norfolk; *vicus* of fort; site 13 ditch 72 layer 54
2 D
3 A
4 30 or 37 CG; 31R CG; 33 CG; 31R EG - possibly Trier
6 Elag; Den; 218-22
7 The ditch has been phased to the late 3rd century, but clearly there is a group of material of early 3rd century date.
8 Department of the Environment, Central Excavation Unit archive report by B Dickinson

**C 4**

1 Brean Down, Somerset; temple; general finds
2 F
3 A
4 79 CG (2); 31 CG (2); 31 EG (4)
7 The temple is dated mid- to late 4th century, and no earlier occupation is apparent. Boon comments, 'Samian in this sort of quantity is a well-known feature of late Roman sites and does not, of itself, suggest an occupation earlier than the foundation of the temple. The fact that all the scraps of samian are derived from dishes suggests that they represent the ritual service in the temple'.
8 ApSimon 1965; Boon 1965b

**C 5**

1 Brigstock, Northamptonshire; temple; general finds
2 F
3 A
4 33 CG (2); 31R CG stamped by Cintusmus; 33 CG (6); 31 CG (3); 31R CG (3)
7 The excavator considers the site to have been occupied from *c* AD 260 to the end of the 4th century. There are a few coins earlier than this, of mainly late 2nd century date. The samian and the coins could be survivals.
8 Greenfield 1963; Hartley 1963a

**C 6**

1 Caerleon, Gwent; amphitheatre of fortress; occupation layer over period III ramp in entrance C and adjoining road
2 B
3 B
4 72 CG (2) with incised dec; fig. 17 no. 4
45; 43; C21; 33
6 Underlying layers:
Had; Den
Aur; 2 AE; RIC (Ant) 1321; 155
Contemporary layers:
Sev; As; RIC 666; 194; worn
Subsequent layers have 19 coins Gall to Allect
7 This group can be associated with the 3rd century rebuilding work dated by tile stamps of AD 213-22 (Boon 1984, 14) and the subsequent occupation.
8 Wheeler & Wheeler 1928

**C 7**

1 Caernarvon, Gwynedd; *mithraeum*; phase I
2 F
3 A
4 33 CG; almost complete
30 CG
5 CCW beaker in orange fabric
6 Faust I; Den; RIC (Ant) 328b; 138-9
7 The coin comes from the make-up for phase I and therefore provides a *terminus post quem*. Boon considers this phase to be early 3rd century (1960a, 144). Later phases may run up to the 290s, but since there are no post-260 coins except in the destruction debris, it is possible that the *mithraeum* dates entirely to the early and mid-3rd century.
8 Boon 1960a

**C 8**

1 Caistor-by-Norwich, Norfolk; town; pit 36
2 C
3 A
4 31; 33; 38; 45 (numbers and kiln not known)
5 Rhenish and NV CCW; CCW with stamped rosettes
6 Gall; Claud II; Post; Tet I (5); Tet II (2); 260-90 unidentified (17); Barb Rad (6)
7 The samian was mainly small fragments, considered by the excavator to be residual. However, they are all late types.
8 Atkinson 1937, 206-7

**C 9**

1 Canterbury, Kent; town defences; Burgate Lane, CXXVI CW 28
2 E

3 A
4 38; CG-Lez; Doccius ii, die 4c; 53
U; CG-Lez; Marcus v, die 4a; 52
33; 'Antonine'; 37; 'Antonine'
5 Coarse ware probably dated 3rd century, according to excavator
6 Ant; Dup; RIC 658; 140-44; coin no. 10
7 An overlying deposit (22), has a coin of Tet I (Rad; coin no. 21). This layer is argued by the excavator to be part of the same dump in the rampart as that from which the sherds came, thus confirming evidence from elsewhere that the defences were constructed in the later 3rd century. The dump considered here is probably redeposited, perhaps from strata analogous to the layers excavated from under the rampart dump. From these underlying layers came:
37; CG; Tetturo or Servus; bird, reduced version of O 2250a; D2 (fig. 64, 2) CXXVI CW 35
37; CG; Paternus II; cupid O 450; D1 (fig. 64, 1) CXXI CW III 5
33; CG-Lez; Reburrus ii die 41; CXIII CW 46
These sherds could easily be contemporary with those from the overlying dump.
8 Frere, Stow & Bennett 1982, 34-6, 126, 141-3

**C 10**

1 Canterbury, Kent; town; Burgate Street, trench C layer 8
2 B
3 A
4 27; SG; Verecundus; stamped
38; CG; Albucius; possibly stamped (text unclear), high gloss; fig. 4, 13
6 Ant; HS; RIC 772; 145-61; good condition
7 Unclear circumstances of deposition.
8 Williams 1947, 68-87

**C 11**

1 Canterbury, Kent; town; 47 Burgate Street, well
2 C
3 A
4 45; very worn fragment of lion's head spout; fig. 15 no. 82
5 Arg with roller stamp, very worn fragments
7 These sherds were found together 12'6" (3.8m) down the well (Jenkins 1950, 89 and fig 4 section 7). Several coins of Claud II-Gratian were found 5' (1.52m) above them. The filling seems generally late, but the lower part with the sherds may be late 3rd to early 4th century. The pottery may represent worn survivals.
8 Jenkins 1950

**C 12**

1 Canterbury, Kent; town; 5 Watling Street, key deposit 3
2 B
3 A
4 45; Lez ware quartz gritted, cf O&P pl. 74, 1
6 Traj; Den; BMC 281-7; 101-11
Salonina; Ant; 253-68
7 Overlain by black earth containing mainly late 4th century artefacts.
8 Jenkins 1952

**C 13**

1 Carrawburgh, Northumberland; *mithraeum*; period IIc early group
2 B
3 A
4 45 CG (2) with lion's head spouts - both nearly complete and little worn
5 NV CCW beakers
7 There is no independent dating evidence, but the other pottery is generally 3rd century. The group is unusual and is thought to be vessels in use in the temple. Earlier phases are also thought to be 3rd century.
8 Richmond & Gillam 1951

**C 14**

1 Chew Park, Avon; villa; well
2 C
3 A
4 6 pieces of 2nd century samian recorded according to depth in the well:
37 (20' = 6.1m); 18/31 (20' = 6.1m); 31 CG (20' = 6.1m); 37 (23' = 7m); 31 (29' = 8.8m); 31 EG = Lud Sb with illiterate herringbone stamp (30' = 9.1m - the bottom)
6 Coins are also recorded according to depth in the well:
Caraus; Rad; RIC 89; 25-6' = 7.6-7.9m
Tet II; Rad; RIC 254; 26-7' = 7.9-8.2m
Claud II; Rad; RIC 48/9; 26-7' = 7.9-8.2m
Caraus; Rad; 27-8' = 8.2-8.5m
Tet II; Rad; 27-30' = 8.2-9.1m
Unstratified from higher in the well:
Tet I Rad; Tet II Rad (2); 4th century (3)
7 The well is associated with a villa probably constructed in the late 3rd century, continuing into the 4th. The lower part of the fill appears to be the period of use of the well and consists of a gradual accumulation (Rahtz & Greenfield 1977, 270-1). The unstratified coins are also probably from the upper part of this slow filling. The sherds of samian appear to be the earliest pottery in the assemblage and could easily represent survivals.
8 Boon 1977; Boon & Hartley 1977; Rahtz & Greenfield 1977

**C 15**

1 Chichester, West Sussex; cemetery; St Pancras, burial 251
2 A
3 A
4 36; prob CG; 'Hadrianic'
27; CG; stamped Regini·M; 'Antonine'
6 Faust I; As; RIC (Ant) 1162a; 141+; coin no. 3
8 Down & Rule 1971, 117

**C 16**

1 Chilgrove, West Sussex; villa; villa 2 ditch 1
2 D
3 A
4 'Antonine' plain ware - 3 pieces
5 CG CCW (11); Rhenish CCW (13); NV CCW (3); NF CCW of early type (16); Oxf CCW (4) - includes type C26 (Young 1977) from top of fill - dated 270-400
6 J Maesa; Den (plated Ae); as RIC (Alex) 55
7 The lower fill of the ditch was a gradual silt, followed by dumps from which most of the pottery came. On this was building rubble in which the Oxf ware was found. The excavator suggests these layers were roughly contemporary and homogeneous (Down 1979, 97, 189). Another ditch, no. 2, was similar and probably contemporary. It contained: samian plain ware 'Antonine' (7); CG CCW (11); Rhenish CCW (3); NF CCW of early type (10). The samian (4 dec pieces) from the site in general is late, but includes a sherd of Libertus from the upper fill of ditch 2 - probably redeposited.
8 Dannell 1979; Down 1979; Lintott 1979

**C 17**

1 Clear Cupboard, Farmington, Gloucestershire; villa; general finds
2 F
3 C
4 31 (4 fragments of one vessel) of 2nd century date
6 coins run from Const-Magnentius
7 The excavator states that the villa was occupied from the 1st quarter to the middle of the 2nd half of the 4th century, 'The site produced no evidence of occupation before or after this period'(Gascoigne 1969, 34). The samian piece could just possibly have been a survival.
8 Gascoigne 1969

**C 18**

1 Darenth, Kent; villa; F14 water channel
2 D
3 A
4 31 CG; U CG (3); U EG
6 Victorin; Rad; 265-70
7 The deposit is sealed by a black layer with 4th century coins.
8 Bird 1984, 95; Philp 1984

**C 19**

1 Dorchester, Dorset; town; Library site, pit K
2 C
3 A
4 31R CG with well worn footring, dated by Pengelly mid to late Antonine
5 NF CCW
6 Gall; Rad; 253-68; little worn
Victorin; Rad; RIC 71; 269-70; little worn
Claud II; Rad; RIC 259; 270; little worn
Tet I; Rad; RIC 70/71; 270-3; little worn
Tet I; Rad; RIC 270/71; 270-3
7 The sherd came from the bottom of the pit, but the whole filling (except the top metre which was a 4th century infill) seems contemporary with the 3rd century coins.
8 Aitken & Aitken 1982; Pengelly 1982

**C 20**

1 Dover, Kent; fort; Durham Hill South, DV 1946/1951 over B16
2 E
3 A
4 37; CG; base only
72; CG; incised dec; fig. 48 no. 292
Plain ware: 18/31 CG; 45 Arg; 33 Rheinz; 31 EG; 37? EG
6 Comm; Den; RIC 241; 192; coin 57
Car?; Den: illeg; early 3rd century; coin 70
8 Bird & Marsh 1981; Philp 1981

**C 21**

1 Dover, Kent; fort; School Yard, DV 728 occupation period IIIA in B25
2 B
3 A
4 37; CG or EG
Plain ware: 45 Arg; 31 EG; 18/31 CG
6 Aur; HS; RIC 844; 162-3; coin 52
Underlying occupation has Faust II; As; RIC (Ant) 1395; 145-76
8 Bird & Marsh 1981; Philp 1981

**C 22**

1 Downton, Wiltshire; villa; hypocaust in room V
2 B
3 A
4 31 CG (5 weathered fragments, but fairly unworn footing)
6 Claud II; Rad; RIC 145; 268-70; coin 2
7 The villa appears to date from the later 3rd century with no evidence of earlier activity except for a very worn Ant HS found outside the villa and 2 other pieces of 31 CG.
8 Boon 1963; Hartley 1963; Rahtz 1963

**C 23**

1 Droitwich, Worcestershire; *vicus*; pits 6 and 7
2 C
3 A
4 From pit 6: 31 CG
From pit 7: 45 CG; C15 CG
6 From pit 6: Gall Rad; Tet I Rad; Barb Rad (11)
From pit 7:
Claud II; Rad; RIC 71; 268-70
Rad illeg
7 The two roughly contemporary pits were near a villa-like building within the defences.
8 Curnow 1957; Gelling 1957

**C 24**

1 Dunstable, Bedfordshire; *vicus*; well
2 C
3 A
4 79; probably CG
32; Rheinz; stamped by Domitius
A total of 15 vessels was found; details not given
5 Imitation samian, probably Oxf; NV CCW hunt cups; CCW indented beakers with rouletted bands
6 Tet I; Rad; 270-3
7 Similar types of pottery were found throughout the filling, which appears to have taken place over a fairly short period.
8 Matthews & Hutchings 1972

**C 25**

1 Durrington Walls, Wiltshire; rural settlement; feature 19
2 C
3 A
4 18/31 or 18/31R CG; burnt; dated Had-Ant
7 The sherds of this vessel were freshly broken, and joining pieces occurred in the corn-drying oven and feature 64/65, suggesting that this vessel was broken and entered the fill of these features more or less at the same time. Nearly all the other material from the site is late 3rd to 4th century in date.
8 Swan 1971; Wainwright 1971

**C 26**

1 Exning, Suffolk; rural settlement; well
2 C
3 A
4 31; CG; stamped; date given as 160-90
Lud Vi or similar EG; 79 CG
5 NV CCW indented beakers
6 Had; As; illeg
Alex; Den; RIC 23; 223
J Mamaea; Den; RIC (Alex) 343; 222
7 Hartley states that the filling of the well below 29' (8.8m) was more homogeneous and of 3rd century character than that from above 29' (which was more mixed 2nd to early

4th century, including coins of Constantine, from above 12' = 3.7m). This conflicts with the observation of Johnston that the fill below 12' was the result of a single operation. The finds listed above all come from below 29' and appear to be a reasonable association.
8 Hartley 1959; Johnston 1959

**C 27**

1 Faversham, Kent; villa; cellar filling
2 E
3 A
4 18/31; Rheinz; stamped MA[ ... ]LLIO, perhaps Marcellus
5 Coarse ware includes many types dated by the excavator late 2nd to early 3rd century.
6 Barb Rad
Const II; Ae; 320-4
7 The coins are indicated to be from the cellar area only, and therefore may not be closely associated. The excavator suggests a date of AD 200-25 for the filling of the cellar.
8 Philp 1968

**C 28**

1 Fulham, Greater London; enclosure; Palace Moat, general finds
2 F
3 A
4 Plain wares: 31 CG (3); 38 CG (2); 45 EG; 33 CG; U CG; U EG
6 2nd century HS (Aur, very worn); Gallic Emp - late 3rd cent (26); later (31)
7 The site does not appear to have been occupied until the mid 3rd century at the earliest, and there is no evidence of any substantial residual element in the coarse ware (i.e. securely dated pre-250). The samian comes from all phases, and is associated with much churned material of late 3rd to late 4th century date.
8 Arthur & Whitehouse 1978; Johns 1978

**C 29**

1 Gloucester, Gloucestershire; town; Westgate Street, period 2B, general finds
2 F
3 A
4 31R; CG; stamped by Carussa die 3C'
31R CG (3); 31/31R CG; 36 CG - almost complete
5 Oxf mortarium - imitation samian 45
6 HS; illeg; 2nd century; coin 116
Sev; Den; RIC 150; 200; coin 155
Sev; Den; RIC 433; 195; coin 72
Gall; Rad; RIC 230 or 574; 259-68; coin 70
Barb Rad and illeg Rad (8); 260-90
Illeg 3rd to 4th century Ae (4)
7 The coins appear to run to *c* AD 290, but possibly up to c 330.
8 Heighway & Garrod 1980; Reece 1980b; Vince & Goudge 1980

**C 30**

1 Harlow, Essex; temple; Roman filling of the fore-building
2 B
3 B
4 33 sherd
5 Coarse ware of 3rd to 4th century date
6 Faust I; Ae; 141+; worn almost smooth
8 Wheeler 1928

**C 31**

1 Lincoln, Lincolnshire; town; burnt tile level in the east gate
2 E
3 A
4 31; CG; stamped by Satto
6 Gall; Rad; illeg
7 The coin comes from a sandy level stratigraphically below the burnt tile level.
8 Hartley 1973; Thompson & Whitwell 1973

**C 32**

1 Little Waltham, Essex; rural settlement; feature 339 well
2 C
3 A
4 38 CG (late type); 18 SG fragment; 2 chips - possibly 1st century
5 Indented beaker; Oxf red CCW; 1st century Colch ware
6 Gall; Rad; RIC 189
Barb Rad (2)
7 Clearly much of the material is residual, but the 38 CG may be a survival contemporary with the coins.
8 Drury 1978; Reece 1978a; Rodwell 1978

**C 33**

1 Lullingstone, Kent; villa; grey rubbish deposit in room 10
2 E
3 A
4 67; prob Rheinz; as O&P pl. 77 no. 6
Lud VSb; Rheinz
Beaker; incised dec; possibly the piece illustrated in Oswald 1952a fig. 6 no. S1
6 Alex; Den; prob RIC 141c; 222-8; fair
7 The excavator suggests that there was an abandonment of the villa in the early to mid 3rd century, but this appears to be a fairly homogeneous deposit of exactly that date. In general the evidence of the coins and samian would suggest an active early 3rd century phase - the majority of the published samian is late CG and EG, and early 3rd century coins are surprisingly abundant for a villa.
8 Meates 1979, 50-1; Oswald 1952a; Pearce 1952

**C 34**

1 Lympne, Kent; fort; occupation layers listed in Cunliffe 1980, 275
2 B
3 A
4 7 CG sherds, very abraded
5 2 Arg, 4 German CCW sherds, very abraded
7 The occupation layers are 4th century, with coins up to Gratian. All the sherds from them are CG, but from disturbed layers there are 12 CG, 1 SG, and 7 EG pieces. There is only one coin earlier than AD 259 from the site (found in 1850; Cunliffe 1980, 261). It is difficult to assess whether the samian is redeposited or not, although the abraded condition and wide chronological range is suggestive that it might be, perhaps brought in with make-up material. See Portchester (**A 99**) for possible use of samian when that fort was established in the late 3rd century.
8 Cunliffe 1980; Young 1980

**C 35**

1 Lynch Farm, Cambridgeshire; cemetery; general finds
2 F
3 A
4 31 CG (4); 31 EG (3); 33 CG; 33 EG; U EG (5)
6 Coins of 350-402

7 These pieces are almost certainly late in date, but are probably residual on the site. There are some 3rd century type CCW indented beakers with scale dec.
8 Jones 1975

**C 36**

1 *Margidunum*, Nottinghamshire; *vicus*; well R
2 C
3 A
4 36 EG; Lud Sa EG; Lud Sb. EG
5 CCW beaker with scale dec; CCW of 3rd to 4th century date
6 Tet I Rad; Car Rad
7 The coins are below the Lud Sa and Lud Sb pieces, but apparently in a different layer from the form 36 which was below the coins. The 36 may be from an earlier filling episode in the well.
8 Oswald 1926; 1952b

**C 37**

1 Nettleton, Wiltshire; temple; circular shrine phase II, octagonal podium
2 E
3 A
4 33; CG; stamped by Minulus; no. 151
6 Plautilla; Den; RIC (Car) 367
7 The position of the coin suggests that it provides a *terminus post quem* for the octagonal shrine.
8 Reece 1982; Simpson 1982b; Wedlake 1982

**C 38**

1 Norwood, Cambridgeshire; enclosure; 1961 enclosure ditch
2 D
3 C
4 18/31 CG (6); 38 CG; 45 CG; 79 CG
5 2 indented beakers, 1 with scale dec; 'Castor box'; NV CCW with barbotine dec; Oxf CCW; large quantity of NV cooking ware some with CC
6 Barb Rad fragment
Const I; Ae; RIC Arles 194; 319
7 Much of the non-samian pottery could date to the late 3rd to early 4th centuries as suggested by the coins, but some could equally well be of late 2nd to mid 3rd century date. Some redeposition is probable.
8 Johns 1981; Potter 1981, 104-16; Shotter 1981

**C 39**

1 Reculver, Kent; fort; key deposit VII
2 B
3 A
4 45; no details given
5 Rhenish CCW beaker
6 Elag; Den; RIC 88; 218-22
8 Philp 1959

**C 40**

1 Richborough, Kent; town; site III pit 26
2 C
3 C
4 'Twenty to thirty fragments of the late first century onwards'
5 CCW beakers with barbotine dec, one with hunt scene
6 Faust II; Ae (2); *c* 160
Gall; Rad (7); 254-68
Claud II; Rad (4); 268-70
Tet I-II; Rad (11+4 Barb); 270-3
Also 2nd century (2), Radiates (25), Barb Rad or unidentifiable (80)
7 This pit is well known for providing the *terminus post quem* for the building of the Saxon Shore fort, since it underlies the fort wall. However, in this context, it is of interest for the apparent association of samian with mid/late 3rd century coins, but since no details are available of the samian, it cannot be clearly established whether much of it was residual or came to the pit as survivals.
8 Bushe-Fox 1928, 33-4

**C 41**

1 Scole, Norfolk; *vicus*; layer 27
2 B
3 A
4 31 CG; 31R CG; 33 CG; 38 EG (2); 79 CG; 3 fragments
6 Aur; Den; RIC (Ant) 431; 145-7; moderate wear; coin 11
Tet I; Rad; RIC 77; 270-3; moderate wear; coin 12
Honorius; Ae4; 394-5; worn; coin 13
7 The last coin is considered by the excavator to be intrusive from the layer above (Rogerson 1977, 120).
8 Gregory 1977; Hartley & Dickinson 1977; Rogerson 1977

**C 42**

1 Shakenoak, Oxfordshire; villa; period B3a floor of room BXII
2 B
3 A
4 72 type (6 pieces); CG; barbotine dec and appliqué leaf (Déch 157); no. 117
35/36 SG
6 Had; HS; RIC 759; 'at least 50 years' wear'; no. 183
8 Brodribb, Hands & Walker 1971; Hartley 1971

**C 43**

1 Shakenoak, Oxf; villa; surface of diagonal path north of fishpond 11
2 B
3 A
4 33 CG stamped by Severus iii die 6e
37 CG/EG (2); 37 EG; 18 SG; 27 SG; 27 CG; 31 CG; 31 CG/EG; 31 EG (2); 31R EG; 33 CG/EG; 33 EG (2); 36 CG/EG; 36 EG; U SG (2); U CG (5); U CG/EG (2); U EG (4)
6 Traj; As; very worn
Car; Den; RIC 13a; worn
Geta; Den; RIC 9a; worn
Elag; Den; RIC 101 (brockage); 218-22
7 The deposit is associated with building K, which is believed by the excavators to date AD 200-250. There are a number of samian deposits also associated with the building, all generally of late CG and EG pieces.
8 Bird 1978b; Brodribb, Hands & Walker 1978

**C 44**

1 Silchester, Hampshire; town; town defensive bank
2 E
3 A
4 29 SG (2); 37 CG (5 - fragments, or not possible to identify to individual potters - generally dated to the Antonine period)
18 SG stamped by Sabinus; 18/31 (4); 31 CG (3); 67 CG; 33 CG
6 Had; As; RIC 678; 118-22; coin 5
Ant; As; RIC 934; 154-5; coin 6
8 Allen 1947; Cotton 1947; Pryce 1947

**C 45**

1 Slonk Hill, West Sussex; rural settlement; boundary ditch layer 1
2 D
3 A
4 37; SG; dated Flavian/Trajanic; no details given
18/31 SG; 18/31 CG; 31 CG; 45 CG; 79 CG
6 Crispina; Ae
7 This layer is the top of the ditch and therefore not a closed deposit. It is dated by Fulford to the 4th century, but could be 3rd century with some material redeposited of somewhat earlier date. Underlying levels in the ditch have 37 MdV; 30 CG; 37 CG; 37 CG. This is a more homogeneous group than layer 1 and perhaps supports the possibility of redeposition in the latter case.
8 Fulford 1978; Hartridge 1978; Rudling 1978

**C 46**

1 Slonk Hill, West Sussex; rural settlement; pit 8
2 C
3 A
4 18/31R CG (2); C15 CG
6 Had; As; RIC 678
Faust II; Ae; RIC (Ant) 1395
Faust II; Ae; RIC (Ant) 1395
7 The associated coarse ware is placed later than the dates suggested in this relatively well-dated group.
8 Fulford 1978; Hartridge 1978; Rudling 1978

**C 47**

1 Sompting, West Sussex; burial
2 A
3 A
4 33; CG; Maximinus die IIa
33; CG; Maximinus die IIa
31; CG; Victor die Ia
39; Rheinz; Favvo die Ia
39; Rheinz; Iuvenis die XVd
79 CG (2)
6 Geta; Den; 198-209; little worn
8 Ainsworth & Ratcliffe-Densham 1974

**C 48**

1 Towcester, Northamptonshire; town; Alchester Road suburb, building 2/5, layer 184
2 B
3 A
4 31 CG; 31R CG (11 fragments from 1 vessel); 31R CG; Lud Tg CG (2); 36 type CG; 4 CG fragments
6 Elag; Den; 219; coin CW 28
Alex; Den (plated); RIC 61; 227; coin CW 30
7 The general phase dating for this context is AD 175-270.
8 Bird & Pengelly 1983; Brown & Woodfield 1983; Woodfield 1983

**C 49**

1 Towcester, Northamptonshire; town; Alchester Road suburb, building 2/6, layer 199
2 B
3 A
4 31 CG; 31R CG; CG fragment
6 Car; Den; RIC 11; 196-8; coin CW 34
7 The general phase dating for this context is AD 175-270.
8 Bird & Pengelly 1983; Brown & Woodfield 1983; Woodfield 1983

**C 50**

1 Towcester, Northamptonshire; town; Alchester Road suburb, stone floor of building 2/1, layer 181
2 B
3 A
4 37 EG (rim only); 45 EG; 36 CG (2); CG fragment
6 Ant; HS; illeg; coin AB 767
Ant; HS; illeg; coin AB 769
Faust II; HS; Fortuna type; 146-75; coin AB 768
7 The phase from which the material comes is dated AD 175-270 by the excavator.
8 Bird & Pengelly 1983; Brown & Woodfield 1983; Woodfield 1983

**C 51**

1 *Verulamium*, St Albans, Hertfordshire; town; insula XVII, building 1, pit 3 and gully
2 C
3 A
4 From pit 3: 45 and 33
From the gully: 33 CG stamped by Divicatus; 31
5 NV CCW jug
6 From the gully:
Had; HS; RIC 752; 117-38; very worn
Ant; As; RIC 934; 154-5; very worn
7 The two features have identical fills and are deemed to be contemporary by the excavator.
8 Richardson 1944, 88-9

**C 52**

1 *Verulamium*, St Albans, Hertfordshire; town; site G destruction level
2 E
3 A
4 45 CG or EG (2); 37 (3 fragments)
5 NV CCW rouletted beaker
6 Alex Den; Valerian Ant; Gall Rad; Tet I Rad (3); Claud II Rad; Barb Rad (2)
8 Cotton & Wheeler 1953

**C 53**

1 Walton, Bucks; rural settlement; layer group II
2 B
3 A
4 38 EG; 33 (2); 31R (3); 18/31; 18/31R; 31; 36
5 Oxf CCW
6 mid- to late 3rd century Rad (2)
7 A fairly loose association, since four or five layers have been grouped together.
8 Mynard & Woodfield 1977; Pengelly 1977b; Woodfield 1977

**C 54**

1 Winchester, Hampshire; town suburb; Radley House, layer 7, dark soil over burials
2 B
3 A
4 45 CG
5 NF CCW indented beaker; Oxf red CCW imitation samian
6 Valerian; Ant; RIC 126; 253-9
7 This and overlying layers succeed the use of the site as an inhumation area. These layers could have accumulated over a period, and continue into the 4th century.
8 Collis 1978; Dannell 1978b; Reece 1978b

## FRANCE AND BELGIUM
(selection only)

**C 55**

1 Etalon, Somme; settlement; cellar B4
2 E
3 B
4 45 EG with very devolved lion-head spout
6 Post Rad; Tet II Rad; Barb Rad
7 Few details of stratigraphy given.
8 Vasselle 1974

**C 56**

1 Malain, Côte-d'Or; town; town-house room XIII cellar fill
2 E
3 B
4 45; Gueugnon
6 (no details given) Had; Ant; Max Thrax
7 Courtyard XVII nearby also has 46 Gueugnon, 45 Gueugnon and barbotine/incised samian cups in loose association with coins of Traj, Ant and Tet.
8 Roussel 1975

**C 57**

1 Nivelles, Namur; *vicus*; cellar II
2 E
3 A
4 18/31 CG; 18/31; 32 EG (2); 32 (2); 45 EG (2)
5 CCW hunt cup
6 Gord III Ant; Gall Rad; Crispus Ae (thought by excavator to be intrusive)
8 Dewert & Severs 1982

**C 58**

1 Roche Ste-Anne, Nismes, Namur; defended refuge; general finds
2 F
3 A
4 45 EG (approx 10); 45 Arg; 27 CG
6 Had; As; very worn
Aur; Dup; very worn
Comm; HS; very worn
Sev; Den
Many coins of Gall, Post-Tet II and Barb Rad
7 The site is placed by the excavators in the context of the events of the Gallic Empire, and is dated AD 256/9-272/4+. The stratigraphy indicates a very short occupation.
8 Doyen & Warmenbol 1979; Warmenbol 1979

# SECTION D: Deposits of decorated samian ware, mainly associated with coins – selective summary of recent publications, not utilised for the analysis in chapters 4 & 5

## BRITAIN

### D 1

1 Alcester, Warwickshire; *vicus*; pit D II 29, layer 29A
2 C
3 A
4 Largely complete vessels:
37; CG; Sacer ii (st); from very worn mould; fig. 49 no. 271
37; CG; Maccius (st); fig. 49 no. 272
37; CG; Tittius-Cassius I (st); possibly from worn mould; fig. 49 no.273
37; CG; Pugnus ii (st); probably from worn mould; fig. 50 no. 274
37; CG; Tetturo style; fig. 50 no. 275
37; CG; Laxtucissa (st); fig. 50 no. 276
37; CG; Laxtucissa (st); fig. 50 no. 277
37; CG; Criciro v (cursive signature); fig. 50 no. 278
37; CG; Criciro v (cursive signature); fig. 51 no. 279
37; CG; Cinnamus ii style; ovolo 2; fig. 51 no. 280
37; CG; Cinnamus ii style; ovolo 2; fig. 51 no. 281
37; CG; Cinnamus ii (st); ovolo 3; fig. 51 no. 282
37; CG; Cinnamus ii (st); ovolo 3; fig. 51 no. 283
37; CG; Cinnamus ii style; ovolo 3; fig. 52 no. 284
37; CG; Cinnamus ii (st); ovolo 3; fig. 52 no. 285
37; CG; Cinnamus ii style; ovolo 3; fig. 52 no. 286
37; CG; Cinnamus ii style; ovolo 3; fig. 52 no. 287
37; CG; Cinnamus ii style; ovolo 3; fig. 52 no. 288
37; CG; Cinnamus ii (st); ovolo 3; fig. 52 no. 289
37; CG; Cinnamus ii (st); ovolo 1; fig. 53 no. 290
37; CG; Cinnamus ii (st); ovolo 1; fig. 53 no. 291
More fragmentary pieces from the deposit:
29; SG; Flavian; not illus.
37; CG; Arcanus style; fig. 53 no. 292
37; MdV; Cettus style; fig. 53 no. 293
37; CG; Albucius ii style; fig. 53 no. 294
37; CG; ovolo of Quintilianus group; not illus., no. 295
37; CG; Cinnamus ii style; ovolo 2; not illus., no. 296
37; CG; Cinnamus ii style; ovolo 1; not illus., no. 297
37; CG; Cinnamus ii style; fig. 53 no. 298
37; CG; Antonine; fig. 53 no. 299
7 There are no associated coins, but this represents a large, mainly unused group of fairly complete vessels, dumped in a pit. It is dated AD 150-60 by Hartley. The excavator places the pit in phase II, dated later 2nd to early 3rd century (?). He notes 'there was also a large and clearly *in situ* group of mid-2nd-century samian and other material' (Langley 1994, 63), together with glass vessels and BB1, in the pit, but the latest material therein dates to the late 3rd to 4th century.
8 Hartley *et al.* 1994, 106-10, figs 49-53; Langley 1994, 60-3, figs 56-8; Rhodes 1989, 55

### D 2

1 Caister-on-Sea, Norfolk; fort, dump deposits
2 E
3 A
4 From Upper Refuse:
37; CG; probably Caletus; no. 1
37; CG; Mercator iv style; fig. 134 no. 2
68; CG; probably Paternus v or associate; black gloss; no. 3
37; CG; Servus II style; no. 4
37; CG; Cantomallus (st); fig. 134 no. 5
37; Trier; Maiiaaus or Tordilo style; fig. 134 no. 6
37; CG; probably Priscus iii or Clemens ii style; fig. 134 no. 7
37; CG; Paternus v style; moulded from much-used mould; Rheinz fabric (from visual inspection); fig. 134 no. 8
37; CG; Banvus style; no. 9
29; SG; mid 1st c.; no. 26
From Lower Refuse:
37; Trier; Dubitatus/Dubitus style; fig. 135 no. 10
37 (similar to this form); Arg; rouletted; no. 25
37; Rheinz; Iulius viii die 5c (st); fig. 135 no. 27
From Upper or Lower Refuse:
37; Trier; Werkstatt II style; fig. 135 no. 21
From Rampart Spill:
37; CG; Banvus style; no. 11
37; CG; ovolo probably of Iustus ii; no. 12
From Spill:
37; Trier; ovolo of Amator, Attillus or Pussosus; no. 13
37: CG; probably Doeccus i style; no. 14
37; CG; Servus II (iv) style; almost certainly in Rheinz fabric (from visual inspection), presumably from a mould acquired from Lezoux; fig. 135 nos 15 & 16
Flagon; Trier; p. 160, no. 2
Other dec pieces:
37; CG; Priscus iii style; fig. 135 no. 19
30; CG; Doeccus i style; no. 20
37; CG; Caletus style; almost certainly in Rheinz fabric (from visual inspection); fig. 135 no. 22
37; Rheinz; Severianus style; fig. 135 no. 23
37; Rheinz; BF Attoni or Cerialis VI style; re-use of old mould; no. 24
37; Rheinz; not attributed to a potter; no. 17
37; Trier; ovolo F 953; no. 18
Flagon; Trier; fig. 136, no. 206
6 From Lower Refuse:
Coin hoard 6; 15 coins to c. 340/45
Coin hoard 7; 14 coins to c. 340/45
7 The deposits were carefully recorded, but due to the long lapse of time between the excavation and its report, the associations are fairly general. The site is interpreted by the report writers as being established as a fort on unoccupied ground in the early 3rd century. The coin hoards from the Lower Refuse are mid 4th century, and imply that the dumping in the fort may have been a long-lasting episode.
8 Darling & Gurney 1993, 6-15; Dickinson & Bird 1993; Reece 1993

### D 3

1 Castleford, West Yorkshire; *vicus* of fort, 'pottery shop' burnt deposit, phase 3, site 1, level 3
2 E
3 A
4 Summary of dec pieces:
CG; X-9 (2)
CG; X-12 (1)
CG; Acaunissa (6)

CG; Avitus-Vegetus (2 + 1?)
CG; Austrus (3)
CG; Bassus iv (1)
CG; Butrio (2)
CG; Catul- and X-6 (12)
CG; Cerialis-Cinnamus (129)
CG; Criciro (1)
CG; Drusus ii (5)
CG; Geminus iv (3)
CG; Paternus iv (3)
CG; Pugnus ii or associates (6)
CG; Pugnus ii/X-6/Cassius (15)
CG; Quintilianus group (6)
CG; Sacer group (20)
CG; Secundinus ii (1)
CG; A-10 (1)
CG; P-14 = Pugnus ii (9)
CG; X-9 (2)
CG; X-12 (1)
CG; large S potter (2)

6 Nero; Den; plated copy, poor condition; no. 161
Titus; Den; slightly worn; no. 208
Dom; Den; fairly good; no. 212
Had; Quadrans; fair condition; 119-38; no. 261
Had; As; worn; 117-38; no. 268
Illeg.; As; no. 280
Const II as Caesar; Ae; no. 298
Valentinian; Ae; c. 370s; no. 304

7 The pottery listed here is all burnt, and represents a store or shop deposit, apparently stock that was in circulation and/or for sale during the period 140-50, according to Dickinson and Hartley. Much of it seems unworn and probably unused, though some of the decorated ware was made from worn moulds, and may have been either seconds, or possibly made from moulds in use for some time. There is some old stock, e.g. by X-9 and X-12, whose moulds originated at MdV, otherwise all of the assemblage comes from Lezoux. Weber (2012, 64) estimates the date at the middle of the century, to judge from the wear on the associated coins up to Hadrian. However, there has been some disturbance of the burnt material, as the 4th-century coins testify.

8 Abramson & Fossick 1999, 132-5; Dickinson & Hartley 2000, 33-56; Mattingly & Pirie 1998; Weber 2012, 64-6; 2013, 192-4

**D 4**

1 Corbridge, Northumberland; town, burnt deposit, 1980, Trench 2, context 167
2 E
3 A
4 37; CG; Doeccus, Banvus, Attianus or Acaunissa style; sphinx D 496; fig. 111 no. 62
37; CG; Advocisus style; fig. 111 no. 63
37; CG; Albucius style; fig. 111 no. 69
37; CG; Cinnamus style; ovolo R B143; fig. 111 no. 70
37; CG; Cinnamus style; ovolo 2 (R B231); fig. 111 no. 80
7 This is the equivalent of the 'destruction deposit' (A 55), and the comments made for A 55 are releavnt to this deposit also.
8 Dore 1988, 109, 220-1, 237-43

**D 5**

1 Cramond, Edinburgh; fort, east ditch extension, site VI, highest fill layer, 16
2 D
3 A
4 From context 16:
37; CG – MdV; Cettus style; fig. 46 no. 4
Other dec pieces:
37; Montans; Felicio iii style; fig. 46 no. 1
37; Montans; Hadrianic-Antonine; fig. 46 no. 2
37; Montans; Hadrianic-Antonine; fig. 46 no. 10
37; CG; Bassus iv style; fig. 46 no. 3
37; CG; probably Had-Ant potter; lion D 753, fig. 46 no. 5
37; CG; possibly Albucius ii style; fig. 46 no. 6
37; CG; Criciro v style; fig. 46 no. 7
37; CG; Doeccus i style; fig. 46 no. 8
37; CG; Banvus style; fig. 46 no.9
37; CG; Attianus ii style; fig. 46 no. 11
37; CG; X-6 style; fig. 46 no. 12
37; CG – MdV; Cettus style; fig. 46 no. 13
37; CG; Cinnamus ii style; ovolo 2 (R B231); fig. 46 no. 15
37; CG; Iullinus ii style; fig. 46 no. 16
37; CG; Cinnamus ii or Pugnus ii style; ovolo 2 (R B231); fig. 46 no. 18
37; CG; X-5 style; fig. 46 no. 19
37; CG; Cinnamus ii style; ovolo R B143; fig. 46 no. 20
37; CG; Albucius ii (st) die 6b; fig. 47 no. 22
37; CG; Arcanus style; rivetted; fig. 47 nos 23-4
37; CG; Cinnamus ii style; fig. 47 nos 25-6
37; CG; X-6 style; fig. 47 nos 28-31
37; CG; ovolo R B102; bowl probably a *surmoulage* of Advocisus, late 2nd or early 3rd c.; fig. 48 nos 32-3
37; CG; Cinnamus ii style; fig. 48 no. 34
37; CG; X-6 style; fig. 48 no. 35
37; CG; Docilis I style; fig. 48 no. 36
37; CG; Cerialis ii/Cinnamus ii group; fig. 48 no. 37
37; CG; X-6 style; fig. 48 no. 42
37; CG; Maccirra style; fig. 48 no. 43
37 CG Had-Ant style (7)
6 From context 16:
Comm; Den; moderately worn; no. 12
Car (Plautilla); Den; slight wear; 202-5; no. 21
Car (Plautilla); Den; slight wear; 202-5; no. 22
7 The coin finds as a whole (Holmes 2003, 94-9) suggest an Antonine phase that may continue to the period of M Aurelius, and a Severan phase, of the first decade of the 3rd century. The samian listed above for the ditch fill (16) certainly relates to the Antonine phase, even if it was deposited in the early 3rd century. It is a small sherd, and could have been redeposited. The rest of the decorated samian assemblage is exclusively CG, which could have come to the site in the Antonine phase. Only fig. 48, nos 32-3 could be linked to the Severan phase. However, many of the vessels could still have been in use in the Severan phase. There is a very limited quantity of EG plain ware in a predominantly CG plain ware assemblage.
8 Dickinson 2003; Holmes 2003

**D 6**

1 Dover, Kent; *vicus* of fort, period V, dump deposits
2 F
3 A
4 37; CG; Sacer style; fig. 27 no. 58
6 Had; HS; 118; no. 1
7 The association is a general one within the phase, in the dumps underlying the 'Painted House'. The excavator dates the period up to AD 180.
8 Kent 1989; Bird 1989; Philp 1989, 27-9

**D 7**

1 Dover, Kent; *vicus* of fort, period V, robber-trench deposits
2 F

3 A
4 29 SG Flav (1)
37 SG Flav (3)
37 SG Flav-Traj (2)
37; SG; Germanus i style; fig. 27 no. 66
37; CG; Donnaucus style; fig. 27 no. 60
37; CG; X-6 style; burnt; fig. 27 no. 62
6 Had; Ae; 117-36; no. 2
7 See comments to D 6, above.
8 Kent 1989; Bird 1989; Philp 1989, 27-9

**D 8**

1 Dover, Kent; *vicus* of fort, period VI, 'Painted House' construction levels
2 F
3 A
4 37; CG; Donnaucus style; fig. 28 no. 68
37; CG; Cinnamus style; ovolo 3a or 3b
6 Comm; Den; 176-7; no. 4
Illeg; Ae; no. 3
7 The association is a general one within the phase. The excavator dates the construction to c. AD 200.
8 Kent 1989; Bird 1989; Philp 1989, 44

**D 9**

1 Dover, Kent; *vicus* of fort, period VI, 'Painted House', drain fill
2 G/F
3 A
4 37; CG; Paternus II, Albucius or Q I Balbinus; fig. 28 no. 68
37; CG – MdV; Cettus/Satus style; fig. 28 no. 69
6 Sev; Ae; 193-211; no. 6
Illeg; Ae
7 The drain fills are from the usage phase of the 'Painted House'.
8 Kent 1989; Bird 1989; Philp 1989, 44

**D 10**

1 Dover, Kent; *vicus* of fort, period VII, clay-walled building
2 F
3 A
4 37; SG; Germanus style; fig. 28 no. 70
Plain ware includes Antonine CG and late 2nd/early 3rd cent. EG.
6 Sev Alex; Den; 222-35; no. 7
7 The coin was found inside the clay wall of phase 2 of the building. The pottery in general and the building are dated by the excavator to AD 210-50, with the latest modifications dated 250-70. The decorated piece is clearly residual.
8 Kent 1989; Bird 1989; Philp 1989, 48-9

**D 11**

1 Dover, Kent; *vicus* of fort, period VIII, demolition prior to Saxon Shore fort
2 F/E
3 A
4 37 CG Antonine (2)
37 EG late 2nd/early 3rd cent., burnt (1)
37 Rheinz
37; Trier; Censor style; fig. 28 no. 71
6 Had; HS; no. 11
Ant; As; no. 12
J Mamaea (Sev Alex); Den; 222-35; no. 13
Illeg; Ae; no. 14
7 General association, but note that the illegible bronze coin was found in the hypocaust channels of the 'Painted House', together with the Trier bowl. The excavator dates the demolition to after AD 240, probably 250-70.
8 Kent 1989; Bird 1989; Philp 1989, 50-1

**D 12**

1 Dover, Kent; *vicus* of fort, period VIII, dump of material over demolition debris, to form base of Saxon Shore fort rampart bank
2 E
3 A
4 37; CG; Antonine; fig. 28 no. 72
37; Arg – Lavoye; Germanus style; fig. 28 no. 73
37 CG/EG
Plain ware includes 53/VMe Rheinz with barbotine dec, and a majority of EG ware.
6 Sev Alex; Den; no. 16
Sev Alex; Den; no. 17
Pupienus; Den; 238; no. 15
Gord III; Ant; 238-44; no. 18
7 The coin association is tentative, since they came from a collapse of a stratigraphic section. The excavator places them stratigraphically at the interface between the demolition rubble (D 11) and the dumped material above. They were probably a small group/hoard, perhaps in a purse. The dumping for the fort rampart dates to after c. 270.
8 Kent 1989; Bird 1989; Philp 1989, 50-1

**D 13**

1 Kelvedon, Essex; *vicus*, area B3, dump F321, in back-filled quarry pit F317
2 E
3 A
4 37; Rheinz; Helenius style; fig. 74 no. 52
6 Barb Rad; illeg; 270-90; no. 14
8 Reece 1988; Rodwell (K) 1988, 7-9; Rodwell (W) 1988, 97-8

**D 14**

1 Piercebridge, County Durham; fort; secondary ditch, Housing Scheme, context 280
2 D
3 A
4 37; Trier; Werkstatt I style; no. 968
6 Claud II; Rad; slight wear; no. 497
Barb Rad; late 3rd cent.; no. 1348
7 The fort defences are thought to have been constructed in the mid 3rd century, following an early 3rd century period of legionary activity at the site. The ditches and associated features in **D 14-22** indicate occupation and dumping from the mid 3rd century onwards, but with material from the early 3rd century incorporated. For the samian ware, see Ward 2008, chapter 9 Digital, 19-31. It is uncertain how much of the earlier material had been conserved in use into the mid/late 3rd-early 4th century, or was redeposited rubbish.
8 Cool & Mason 2008, 68-77; context, coin and samian ware databases; Ward 2008, 9D.28-9, no. 28

**D 15**

1 Piercebridge, County Durham; fort; main ditch, Housing Scheme context 465
2 D
3 A
4 37; CG; Cinnamus ii, early group; no. 43
37; CG – MdV?
6 Dom; As; very worn; no. 15
Had; As; very worn; no. 42

Aelius; As; worn; no. 48
Ant; As; worn; no. 60
Aur (Faust II); 161-75; worn; no. 75
7 Some uncertainty about the stratigraphy of this context, according to the digital context database entry. See comment to **D 14**.
8 Cool & Mason 2008, 68-77; context, coin and samian ware databases; Ward 2008, 9D.23, no. 41.

**D 16**

1 Piercebridge, County Durham; fort; secondary ditch, upper ash layer, Housing Scheme context 538
2 D
3 A
4 37; Rheinz; Belsus ii style; no. 1071
37; Heil; Janus ii style; no. 1073
37; CG; Attianus ii or P-23 style; riveted; no. 1087
37; CG; later 2nd century; prob. riveted; no. 1088
6 63 coins (poss. hoard) to Const I; 320-1; unworn; no. 1569
7 Dated by the excavator to the early 4th century. There is a Severan denarius amongst the coins, which may not be part of the putative hoard, and which could easily be contemporary with the samian ware. See comment to **D 14**.
8 Cool & Mason 2008, 72-3; context, coin and samian ware databases; Ward 2008, 9D.29-30, nos 34-6

**D 17**

1 Piercebridge, County Durham; fort; secondary ditch, smithing slag and ash dump, Housing Scheme context 539
2 D
3 A
4 37; CG; Albucius ii style; no. 1101
6 11 coins to Const I; 318-9; unworn; no. 1564
7 Probably later than the previous entry. See comment to **D 14**.
8 Cool & Mason 2008, 68-77; context, coin and samian ware databases

**D 18**

1 Piercebridge, County Durham; fort; secondary ditch, Housing Scheme context 550
2 D
3 A
4 37; Trier; Criciro style; reuse of old mould; no. 1132
6 8 coins; Gallien to Caraus; 280-93; slight wear; no. 1511
7 Noted by the excavator as being contaminated by recent (i.e. modern) material, but significant for the presence of the late Trier product. See comment to **D 14**.
8 Cool & Mason 2008, 68-77; context, coin and samian ware databases; Ward 2008, 9D.30-1, no. 37

**D 19**

1 Piercebridge, County Durham; fort; main ditch, stone spread, Housing Scheme context 907
2 D
3 A
4 37; Trier; poss. Catu... style; no. 27
37; CG; Doeccus i style; no. 28
6 Claud II; Rad; 268-70; no. 432
Victorin; Rad; 268-70; slight wear; no. 633
7 See comment to **D 14**.
8 Cool & Mason 2008, 68-77; context, coin and samian ware databases; Ward 2008, 9D.22, nos 25-6

**D 20**

1 Piercebridge, County Durham; fort and *vicus*; E-W road, Housing Scheme context 1006
2 B
3 A
4 37; Rheinz; Ware A/B with O 382/383; poss. Riveted; no. 2076
6 Tet II (Caes); Rad; 270-3; no. 1072
7 Recorded as being contaminated by a modern intrusion. See comment to **D 14**.
8 Cool & Mason 2008, 64-7; context, coin and samian ware databases; Ward 2008, 9D.38, no. 5

**D 21**

1 Piercebridge, County Durham; fort; secondary ditch, Housing Scheme context 1054
2 D
3 A
4 37; CG; Iullinus ii (st); no. 45
6 5 coins Gallic Emp to Barb Rad; late 3rd cent.; no. 1362
7 See comment to **D 14**.
8 Cool & Mason 2008, 68-77; context, coin and samian ware databases; Ward 2008, 9D.24-5, no. 51

**D 22**

1 Piercebridge, County Durham; fort; NW corner, metalled surface, Housing Scheme context 1070
2 B
3 A
4 37; CG; Secundus v style; no. 1696 (11 pieces in total)
6 Tet I copy; Rad; late 3rd cent.; worn; no. 972
7 See comment to **D 14**.
8 Cool & Mason 2008, 29-33; context, coin and samian ware databases; Ward 2008, 9D.4, no. 4

**D 23**

1 Piercebridge, County Durham; fort and *vicus*; E-W road foundations, clay layer associated with kiln, Housing Scheme context 1357
2 E
3 A
4 37; CG; Criciro v style; no. 2189
6 Traj; no details; no. 33
7 Dated by the excavators to the late 2nd century. See comment to **D 14**.
8 Cool & Mason 2008, 63-4; context, coin and samian ware databases; Ward 2008, 9D.39, no. 12

**D 24**

1 Piercebridge, County Durham; fort; NW corner/E-W road, cobble layer, Housing Scheme context 1747
2 B
3 A
4 37; CG; Doeccus i style; no. 2217
6 4 coins Gallic Emp to Tet II; 270-3; very worn; no. 1105
7 See comment to **D 14**.
8 Cool & Mason 2008, 63-7; context, coin and samian ware databases

**D 25**

1 Piercebridge, County Durham; *vicus*; NE corner, fill of rooms/sleeper trenches, Housing Scheme context 1869
2 B
3 A
4 37; SG; late Flavian to early 2nd century; no. 1632
37; SG; late Flavian to early 2nd century; no. 1659

37; CG – MdV; X-12 style; no. 1658
37; CG; mid-late 2nd century
6 Dom; As; 81-96; very worn; no. 13
7 An early context, associated with civilian activity prior to the later military occupation.
8 Cool & Mason 2008, 104-5; context, coin and samian ware databases; Ward 2008, 9D.35, nos 3-6

**D 26**

1 Piercebridge, County Durham; *vicus*; surface of track, Tofts Field 1974 context 3209
2 B
3 A
4 37; CG; X-5 style; no. 3263
6 Ant (Faust I div); Den; 141-60; no. 62
7 The context is associated with Phase 3 Kiln 1. The samian report lists this as a Phase 4 context.
8 Cool & Mason 2008, 96-101; context, coin and samian ware databases; Ward 2008, 9D.67, no. 93

**D 27**

1 Piercebridge, County Durham; *vicus*; Phase 4 road surface, Tofts Field 1974, context 3230
2 B
3 A
4 37; CG; Doeccus i style; no. 3444
37; CG; Casurius ii style; no. 3445
37; CG; Censorinus style; no. 3446
6 Constans; no details; 347-8; slight wear; no. 1681
7 This is the latest phase of the road, dated to the 4th century.
8 Cool & Mason 2008, 96-101; context, coin and samian ware databases; Ward 2008, 9D.70-1, nos 129-31

**D 28**

1 Piercebridge, County Durham; *vicus*; Phase 2 occupation layer within southern building, Tofts Field 1974, context 3252
2 B
3 A
4 37; CG; Avitus-Vegetus ii or X-6 style; no. 3562
37; CG; Cinnamus ii, early group; no. 3563
37; CG; Cinnamus ii style; poss. riveted; no. 3564
37; CG; Cinnamus ii style; no. 3566
6 Vesp; As; 69-79; no. 4
7 The samian report lists this as a Phase 3 context.
8 Cool & Mason 2008, 99; context, coin and samian ware databases; Ward 2008, 9D.63-4, nos 61-4

**D 29**

1 Piercebridge, County Durham; *vicus*; Tofts Field 1974, Phase 2 context 3256
2 unknown
3 A/C
4 37; CG; X-6 or Tittius style; no. 3589
6 Traj; Dup; 98-102; slight wear; no. 25
8 Cool & Mason 2008, 96-101; context, coin and samian ware databases; Ward 2008, 9D.59, no. 24

**D 30**

1 Piercebridge, County Durham; *vicus*; Tofts Field 1974, context 3295 associated with Phase 2 North building
2 unknown
3 A/C
4 37; CG; Cinnamus or Secundus style; no. 3718
6 Traj; HS; worn; no. 31
Ant (Faust I div); Den; 141-61; slight wear; no. 64
7 The samian report lists this as a Phase 3 context.
8 Cool & Mason 2008, 96-101; context, coin and samian ware databases; Ward 2008, 9D.65-6, no. 84

**D 31**

1 Piercebridge, County Durham; *vicus*; Tofts Field 1974, Phase 3 context 3296
2 unknown
3 A/C
4 37; SG; Flavian; no. 3725
6 Vesp/Titus; Den; no. 9
Sev; Den; 202-10; unworn; no. 98
7 Very likely to have been a largely redeposited context.
8 Cool & Mason 2008, 96-101; context, coin and samian ware databases; Ward 2008, 9D.66, no. 87

**D 32**

1 Piercebridge, County Durham; *vicus*; debris of the Phase 3 Kilns, Tofts Field 1974, context 3306
2 E
3 A
4 30; CG; Paternus v style; no. 3769
37; CG; Casurius ii style; no. 3771
37; CG; Sacer i style; no. 3775
6 Vesp; As; no. 8
Dom; Dup; 81-96; no. 14
7 The samian ware report lists this as a Phase 2 context.
8 Cool & Mason 2008, 96-101; context, coin and samian ware databases; Ward 2008, 9D.62, nos 49-51

**D 33**

1 Piercebridge, County Durham; *vicus*; possible temple, Room 1/Stairway, Tofts Field 1975, context 3404
2 B or E
3 A
4 37; Rheinz; Belsus ii style; no. 3795
6 Caraus; Aurel; 287-93; unworn; no. 1487
7 The samian ware from this building dates mainly to the 3rd century, and may be associated with the construction and use of a possible shrine to Jupiter Dolichenus in the early 3rd century. The stratigraphy, however, including this deposit, contains much 4th-century coarse pottery, and appears to represent dumping into a building that had been abandoned after brief usage of c. 50 years.
8 Cool & Mason 2008, 101-4; context, coin and samian ware databases; Ward 2008, 9D.79, no. 2

**D 34**

1 Piercebridge, County Durham; *vicus*; retaining wall, Kilngarth Field 1974, context 3608
2 B
3 A
4 30; Rheinz; Cobnertus iv (st); no. 3966 (6 pieces)
6 Sev?; Den; unworn; no. 83
Tet II; Rad; 270-3; slight wear/worn; no. 1102
7 The finds in this deposit were recovered from the structure of the wall. The samian ware comes from context 3609 (5 pieces) and 3608 (1 piece).
8 Cool & Mason 2008, 113-4; context, coin and samian ware databases; Ward 2008, 9D.85-6, no. 9

**D 35**

1 Piercebridge, County Durham; *vicus*; Kilngarth Field 1974, context 3628
2 unknown
3 A/C

4 37; Rheinz; later 2$^{nd}$ or 3$^{rd}$ c. potter; no. 4032
6 Tet I; Rad; 270-3; slight wear; no. 845
8 Cool & Mason 2008, 113-6; context, coin and samian ware databases; Ward 2008, 9D.86, no. 14

**D 36**

1 Piercebridge, County Durham; *vicus*; Northern Nursery area A, context 3702
2 unknown
3 A/C
4 37; CG; poss. Banvus style; no. 4087
6 9 coins Gallien to Barb Rad; late 3$^{rd}$ cent.; slight wear; no. 1292
8 Cool & Mason 2008, 116-7; context, coin and samian ware databases

**D 37**

1 Piercebridge, County Durham; *vicus*; Northern Nursery area A, context 3704
2 unknown
3 A/C
4 37; CG; Servus iv style; no. 4110
6 Ant; HS; 140-4; slight wear/worn; no. 57
8 Cool & Mason 2008, 116-7; context, coin and samian ware databases; Ward 2008, 9D.87, no. 1

**D 38**

1 Piercebridge, County Durham; *vicus*; Northern Nursery area A, context 3706
2 unknown
3 A
4 37; Rheinz; Comitialis IV style; no. 4114
6 Victorin; Rad; 268-70; slight wear; no. 670
8 Cool & Mason 2008, 116-7; context, coin and samian ware databases; Ward 2008, 9D.87, no. 3

**D 39**

1 Piercebridge, County Durham; *vicus*; Northern Nursery area A, context 3711
2 unknown
3 A/C
4 37; CG; Servus iv style; no. 4147
6 Salonina; Rad; 252-8; worn; no. 301
8 Cool & Mason 2008, 116-7; context, coin and samian ware databases; Ward 2008, 9D.87-8, no. 7

**D 40**

1 Piercebridge, County Durham; *vicus*; road cobbles, Northern Nursery area A, context 3717
2 B
3 A
4 37; Rheinz; later 2$^{nd}$ or 3$^{rd}$ century potter; no. 4164
6 Barb Rad; late 3$^{rd}$ cent.; slight wear; no. 1276
8 Cool & Mason 2008, 116; context, coin and samian ware databases; Ward 2008, 9D.88, no. 9

**D 41**

1 Piercebridge, North Yorkshire; *vicus* S of R Tees; Holme House 71-2, Section A between limestone revetting, context 4133
2 unknown
3 A/C
4 37; Trier; Dexter style; poss reuse of old mould; no. 4897
6 Aur (Faust II); As; 161-75; very worn; no. 74
8 Cool & Mason 2008, 123-6; context, coin and samian ware databases; Ward 2008, 9D.102, no. 70

**D 42**

1 Piercebridge, North Yorkshire; *vicus* S of R Tees; Holme House 71-2, context 4138
2 unknown
3 A/C
4 37; Rheinz; Comitialis group; no. 4996
37; CG; Iullinus ii style; no. 5008
37; CG; Paternus v style; no. 5009
6 Tet I; Rad; 270-3; slight wear; no. 842
8 Cool & Mason 2008, 123-6; context, coin and samian ware databases; Ward 2008, 9D.104-5, nos 82, 86

**D 43**

1 Piercebridge, County Durham; fort; Bath-house, Glen View 76-77, context 4664
2 unknown
3 A/C
4 37; CG; Banvus style; no. 5163
6 Tet I; Rad; 270-3; worn; no. 843
8 Cool & Mason 2008, 40-5; context, coin and samian ware databases; Ward 2008, 9D.12, no. 6

**D 44**

1 Piercebridge, County Durham; fort; Bath-house, floor, phase 3, Tees View 78-79, context 4888
2 B
3 A
4 37; CG; Advocisus style; no. 5209
6 Had (Sabina); HS; very worn; no. 46
Ant; Dup; very worn; no. 55
Aur; HS; worn; no. 70
Aur; HS; very worn; no. 71
Sev; Den; worn; no. 90
Sev; Den; 202-10; slight wear; no. 99
7 The coins may constitute a small scattered hoard.
8 Cool & Mason 2008, 47-51; context, coin and samian ware databases; Ward 2008, 9D.13, no. 14

**D 45**

1 Piercebridge, County Durham; fort; Courtyard Building, courtyard, PB73-74, context 5206
2 B
3 A
4 37; Rheinz; late 2$^{nd}$ or early 3$^{rd}$ century; no. 5401
6 Elag; Den; c. 220; no. 133
8 Cool & Mason 2008, 33-7; context, coin and samian ware databases; Ward 2008, 9D.7, no. 3

**D 46**

1 Ribchester, Lancashire; fort; phase 5.1, degradation of the site
2 F
3 A
4 37; SG; Flav-Traj; fig. 45 no. 12
37; SG; Flav; fig. 45 no. 13
37; MdV; Drusus I (X-3) style; fig. 45 no. 16
37; MdV; Drusus I (X-3) style; fig. 46 no. 27
37; CG; Geminus iv style; fig. 46 no. 22
37; CG; Geminus iv style; fig. 46 no. 27
37; CG; Sacer i (st); fig. 46 no. 24
30; CG; Cinnamus ii style; fig. 46 no. 25
37; CG; Cinnamus ii style; fig. 47 no. 30
37; CG; Cinnamus ii style; ovolo 3; fig. 47 no. 31
37; CG; Cinnamus ii style; ovolo 4; fig. 49 no. 51
37; CG; X-6 style; fig. 47 no. 29
37; CG; Docilis i style; fig. 48 no. 43

37; CG; Docilis i style; rivetted; fig. 48 no. 43
37; CG; Advocisus style; fig. 49 no. 54
37; CG; Casurius ii style; fig. 50 no. 55
37; CG; Paternus v (st); fig. 50 no. 57
37; CG; fig. 48 no. 47
37; La Mad; fig. 48 no. 40

6 Geta; Den; 200
Plautilla; Den; 204

7 This is a general association only. The excavators suggest that the phase could date late 2nd-early 3rd century. Destruction, phase 5.2, took place 3rd-mid 4th century.

8 Buxton & Howard-Davis 2000, 133; Dickinson 2000; Shotter 2000

**D 47**

1 Shadwell, Greater London; settlement and bath-house, phase 6, boundary ditch Structure 4

2 D

3 A

4 29; SG – La Graufesenque; Flavian; fig. 17 no. SAM2; context 360
29; SG – La Graufesenque; Flavian; fig. 17 no. SAM1; context 645, joining to piece from 710 (phase 2)
37; SG – La Graufesenque; fig. 17 no. SAM5; contexts 361, joining to pieces from 80, 233, 700, 721, 751
30; CG – Lezoux; Antonine, CG IV; fig. 17 no. SAM13, context 278
37; Arg – Lavoye; probably Gesatus; fig. 18 no. SAM22; context 327
37; Rheinz; Attillus; fig. 20 no. SAM50; context 370, joining to pieces from 1438 and F29
37; Rheinz; Julius II-Julianus I style; fig. 21 no. SAM62; contexts 651 and 657
37; Rheinz; Lupus style; fig. 19 no. SAM43; context 360, joining with piece from 144
37; Rheinz; Perpetuus style; fig. 21, no. SAM65; context 357
37; Rheinz; Primitivus I style; fig. 20, no. SAM52, context 357
37; Rheinz; Primitivus II style; fig. 20 no. SAM57; context 261
37; Rheinz; Primitivus IV style; fig. 20 no. SAM56; context 327
37; Rheinz; Primitivus IV style; fig. 20 no. SAM55; context 361, joining to piece from 659
37; Rheinz; Verecundus II style; fig. 19 no. SAM47; context 261, joining to pieces from 19, 648, 649, 657
Stamps: 33; CG – Lezoux; Severianus I die 7a; context 656
31R; Rheinz; Maianus iii die 2d; context 358
Plain ware and other dec pieces with no details:
18 SG; 18/31 SG; 18/31 CG; 30 CG; 30/37 CG (2); 30/37 EG; 31 CG (3); 31 EG (5); 31R CG (5); 31R EG (6); 31/37 hybrid rouletted externally EG; 32 EG (9); 33 CG (9); 33 EG (3); 36 EG; 37 CG (6); 37 EG (9); 38? CG; 38 EG (7); C15 CG; mort EG (5); fr SG (2); fr CG (3); fr EG (14)

5 Portchester 'D' ware; Nene Valley CCW; Oxf CCW; Lakin 2002, Tables 7 & 8

6 Lower fills, western sector:
Coin of 270-85 (context 288)
Upper fills, western sector:
Coin of 270-90 (context 253)
Eastern sector:
Coins of 324-8 (context 357) and 332-4 (context 146)

7 This ditch is associated with a tower, possibly a mausoleum or signal tower (cf. Douglas *et al.* 2011, 152, 165ff; Bird (D) 2008 for discussion of the interpretation of the tower), and seems to have a relatively homogeneous fill, albeit with some earlier material (including the SG pieces listed). The assemblage from Shadwell as a whole is unusual in having virtually no CG samian; it is dominated by Rheinzabern and Trier, mainly the late phases of these kiln-centres. The significance of this group is discussed by Bird (2011; also 2002; 1993; 1987).
There are some coin-dated contexts with decorated samian from the excavations of 2002 (e.g. A1028, B250, B435, B721; Douglas *et al.* 2011, 173-91), but the layout of the report does not permit classification of the context type, or evaluation of the significance of the contexts and their phasing.

8 Bird 2002; Dickinson 2002; Hammerson 2002; Lakin 2002. See also Bird 1987; 1993; 2011.

**D 48**

1 Silchester, Hampshire; town; forum/basilica, well F127, upper fills 254 and 346

2 C

3 A

4 37; CG; Cinnamus group (prob); st on rim by Apolauster 4a; fig. 105 no. 28 (context 346)
37; CG; late potter, poss Doeccus but not certain; R Q6; not illus (context 254)
EG plain ware fragments (2)

5 NF and Oxf CCW; BB1

6 Comm; HS; 180-182; very worn; context 254, no. 82

7 The well was constructed in mid 2nd century, and deliberately infilled by the end of the 3rd century, including the clay layer 346. The silty layer 254 above is material in a subsequent slump in the well infill.

8 Bird & Dickinson 2000; Boon 2000; Fulford & Timby 2000, 69-71

**D 49**

1 Stonea Grange, Cambridgeshire; Romano-Celtic temple; pit P10

2 C

3 A

4 37; CG; Advocisus (st) die 8a; fig. 137 no. 13

7 No coins, but apparently a single dump of many pieces of moderately or little worn plain ware of similar date. The excavators link the pit to the temple and date it to the late 2nd/early 3rd century.

8 Jackson & Potter 1996, 219-20; Johns 1996

## FRANCE

**D 50**

1 Allonnes, Sarthe; religious sanctuary; Horizon 6b, destruction by fire, portico and east courtyard, contexts 1501 and 1515

2 E

3 A/C

4 Presence of 37 CG by Caletus, Libertus II, Marcus, Casurius, Paternus II (style b)
Plain ware includes 45 CG, 72 CG, C21 CG

6 No coins directly associated with the contexts.
From Horizon 6b in the south gallery of the sanctuary, Crispus; Ae; 321-3 (Brouquier-Reddé & Gruel 2004, 351).

7 The destruction levels contain a relatively homogeneous group of samian ware of very late CG. The whole pottery assemblage totals 2743 pieces, and is dated by Bazin and Delage to the late 3rd century. The excavators date the de-

struction to the early 4th century, on the basis of the coin, and the coin assemblage from the overlying Horizon 7.
8 Bazin & Delage 2005; Brouquier-Reddé & Gruel 2004

**D 51**

1 Bliesbruck, Moselle; *vicus*; destruction deposits in buildings 1-14
2 E
3 A
4/6 As for A 202 and A 206, the format here is to have the samian ware first, followed by the coins, in each building.
1) 37; EG; Clamosus
37; Esch; L.AT.AT (3)
37; Blick; Cambo style
37; Trier; Werkstatt II 'Spätausformung'
Coins: Had HS; Aur Den; Sev Den (2) (200)
3) 37; EG; Clamosus
Coins: Ant As; Aur HS (163/4)
4) 37 ; EG ; Clamosus (st)
37 ; Blick ; L.A.L (2)
37 ; Blick ; Avitus (2)
Coins: Traj Dup; Ant As; Alex Den (2); Gord III Ant (242/4)
5) 37; EG; Clamosus
37; Blick; L.A.L (2)
37; Esch/Blick; L.AT.AT or L.A.L
Coins: Traj As; Had Dup; Ant Den; Comm HS; Sev Den (2); Elag Den (2); Alex Den (222)
6) 37; EG; Clamosus
37; Blick; L.A.L
37; Esch; L.AT.AT (2)
37; Rheinz
Coins: Traj As; Had Den; Ant Den; Aur HS (2); Sev Den (2); Car Den; Elag Ant; Gord III Ant (238/9)
7) 37; EG; Clamosus (st) (6)
37; Blick; L.A.L
37; Esch; L.AT.AT (2)
Coins: Nero As; Traj HS; Ant Dup; Aur HS (2); Comm HS (2); Sev Den; Elag Den; Alex Den (222/35)
8) 37; EG; Clamosus
37; Blick; Avitus
Coins: Nero As; Vesp Den; Traj HS; Had As; Had HS (2); Ant HS (2); Aur HS; Aur Dup; Aur As; Sev Den (202/10)
9) 37; EG; Clamosus (2)
37; Blick; Avitus (st)
37; Rheinz?
Coins: Had As (119/21)
11) 37; Blick; L.A.L
37; Blick; Avitus (st)
Coins: Had HS; Sev Den (202/10)
7 The burnt destruction deposits are interpreted as a single episode, dated by Petit (1989) to the 250s, on the basis of a posthumous coin of Valerian of AD 257/8, from building 14. Building 7 is the most prolific assemblage, and was studied separately by Schaub, particularly for Clamosus, a then-unknown potter from an unspecified EG workshop. Petit (1989; 2001) makes a case for continued and periodic reuse of moulds of L.A.L, Avitus and L.AT.AT, up to the 240/50s, and points out the deterioration in the quality of production. He also suggests that these potters should be dated 135/40 to 240/50, because of the reuse of the moulds. Clamosus seems to be late, dated 240/60.
8 Petit 1989; 2001; Schaub 1987

**D 52**

1 Boulogne, Pas-de-Calais; fortress; Palais de Justice site, drain
2 G
3 A/C
4 29; SG; Flavian
37; SG; Flavian (7)
37; SG; late Flavian – Trajanic (2)
37; CG; mid 2nd cent.
37; Arg; late 2nd cent.
6 Galba; As
Had; Ae
Had; As
Faust II; As/Dup
Comm; HS
Valerian?; Rad
Post; Rad
Tet I; Barb Rad
7 The deposit also contained a gold ring of late 3rd/early 4th cent., and a lead seal with a Christian symbol of early 4th cent. The context is a good example of a long period of accumulation, and seems very mixed.
8 Dhaeze & Seillier 2005

**D 53**

1 Châlons-sur-Marne (Châlons-en-Champagne), Marne; town; rue Saint-Dominique, deposit on floor of building
2 B?
3 A/C
4 37; Arg-Lavoye (2)
Presence of 45 Arg; Chenet 302, 303, 325, 326 Arg
6 coins of Post; 260-269
8 Lenoble 1985

**D 54**

1 Châteaubleau, Seine-et-Marne; *vicus*; Grands Jardins site, well F23/Z01
2 C
3 A/C
4 37; CG; Doeccus; complete, worn
6 Fragment of mould for coin imitations – Barb Rad – of late 3rd cent.
7 The samian was apparently in use and conserved as a prestige piece, according to the excavators. Doeccus dated 170/200 by Rogers 1999, and distributed up to 240, according to Delage 2003.
8 Bertin & Pilon 2006, 366-7, 373

**D 55**

1 Corseul, Côtes-d-Armor; town; Horizon IV, bâtiment 5
2 F
3 C
4 Presence of 37 CG, Paternus II, Iustus, Laxtucissa, Iullinus, Albucius, Casurius, Butrio, Cinnamus, Quintilianus
45 CG; 79/80 CG; 72 CG
6 Aug; Dup, As, Semis
Traj; HS, Dup, As
Had; 2 HS
Faust II; 2 HS
Tet I; Rad
7 General association only
8 Kerébel 2001

**D 56**

1 Corseul, Côtes-d-Armor; town; Horizon V
2 F
3 C
4 37; CG; 3rd century style; fig 149, 1-5
Chenet 320; Arg
6 Coin hoards up to Aurelian

7 Destruction levels, dated to late 3rd century or possibly early 4th century.
8 Kerébel 2001

**D 57**

1 Lezoux, Puy-de-Dôme; kiln-centre; ZAC de l'Enclos, kiln F55, fill of firing chamber
2 E
3 A/C
4 Presence of Caletus (most numerous of the list given here), Banvus, Priscus, Marcus, Advocisus, Doeccus, Iullinus, Gemelinus, Servus, Paternus II, Catussa, Censorinus, Attianus, Severus, Pugnus, Casurius, Cinnamus
Moulds form about a third of the decorated assemblage, which totals 135 kg (decorated vessels and moulds).
6 No coins found
7 The fill is a dump within a very large samian ware kiln, and is considered by the excavators to date to the mid-3rd century. It is very similar to an assemblage from building F83 on the same site, which has a similar date attribution (see below).
8 Bet & Gangloff 1987, 148-51

**D 58**

1 Lezoux, Puy-de-Dôme; kiln-centre; ZAC de l'Enclos, building F83, demolition debris
2 E
3 A/C
4 Presence of Caletus (most numerous), other potters not named
Poinçons found in the assemblage
Plain ware 45 CG, incised vessels
6 Coins of Gord III, Phil, Traj Decius
7 The excavators date the underlying tiled floor of the building to the end of the 2nd century or early 3rd century. The function of the building is linked to the nearby samian kilns, but its exact use is unclear.
8 Bet & Gangloff 1987, 154-7

**D 59**

1 Lezoux, Puy-de-Dôme; kiln-centre; ZAC de Parc intercommunal entre Dore et Allier, Serve-d'Ervier samian ware kiln F111/112
2 E
3 A/C
4 37; CG; Cinnamus; ovolo R B231; O 2252, R A2; tendril scroll style; fig. 22 no. F111-10
68; CG mould; Paternus; Bémont 1977, GR56 types 1, 6, 7, 14, 30, 39; fig. 22 no. F111-12 & 13
37; CG; Paternus (st); ovolo R B106; R A12; fig. 22 no. F111-56
37; CG; Cinnamus; O 717, O 1201a, R A2, R M27, R Q27; metope style; fig. 22 no. F112-136
37; CG; Paternus; O 1533, O 1578, O 1720(?), O 1915a, O 1917, R U281, free style; fig. 22 no. F112-137
37; CG; Paternus (st); O 19, R A40; fig. 22 no. F112-138
37; CG; Paternus; O 538, O 907, R A12, R P68; fig. 22 no. F112-139
37; CG; Iullinus; O 33, O 2384, R A34, R as C167, R G73; metope style; fig. 22 no. F112-140
37; CG; Cinnamus (st); R A2, R M3; fig. 22 no. F112-141
37; CG; Paternus/Iustus; ovolo R B234; O 1061, O 1510, O 1842, R A23, R H129; tendril scroll and medallion style; fig. 22 no. F112-142
Plain ware includes 33, 36, 43, 44, 45, 79, all probably made at the kiln.
6 No coins recorded
7 The assemblage is considered to be material dumped at the kiln, and in all probability made there. A date of the 3rd quarter of the 2nd century is assigned by the excavators.
8 Bet & Delage 2009, 453-64; 2010

**D 60**

1 Lezoux, Puy-de-Dôme; kiln-centre; ZAC de Parc intercommunal entre Dore et Allier, Serve-d'Ervier samian ware waster dump F090/091
2 E
3 A/C
4 37; CG mould; Sanvillus (cursive signature in base of mould); ovolo R B138; O 84, O 1214, O 1215, O 2393, O K, R A10, R A24, R H117, R R7; metope style; Sanvillus is previously unknown, and the style is close to Censorinus and Paternus; fig. 30, fig. 31 no. F90-16
37; CG mould; not known; ovolo R B180(?); R A2, R G89, fig. 31 no. F90-05
37; CG; Butrio; O 907, O 2382, O 2392, R A23, R C213(?), R K35; metope style; fig. 31 no. F90-22
37; CG; Albucius; ovolo R B105; R A9, R E58; fig. 31 no. F90-21
37; CG; Albucius; ovolo R B105; O 207, O 826, R A9, R E58, R P3; metope and medallion style; fig. 31 no. F90-23
37; CG; Paternus; O 440, R E18, R H2, R R71; fig. 31 no. F90-20
37; CG; Cinnamus group; O 2315, R H24; not illus
68; CG; Doeccus; O 2250a, O 2417; fig. 34 no. F91-56
6 No coins recorded
7 The deposit is slightly mixed, and also contains 1st-century material. However, the kiln furniture, potters' tools, moulds and the CG decorated vessels all appear to date from the mid 2nd century or later. The general composition is earlier than the kiln at this site (see above). Another broadly contemporary waster heap, F 106 (Bet & Delage 2009, 470-1), has vessels by Cinnamus, Pugnus, Paternus, a mould by Quintilianus and a residual mould fragment in the 1st-century style of Titos.
8 Bet & Delage 2009, 464-70

**D 61**

1 Lyon, Rhône; town (lower city); place des Célestins, levelling dump
2 E
3 A/C
4 Presence of Maccirra, Docilis, Sacer/Attianus, Pugnus, Pugnus/Cinnamus, Paternus II, Doeccus, Iullinus II, Mercator II, P-33
5 Terre Sigillée Claire B
6 None
7 The decorated samian is dated by Delage to the early 3rd cent. The context is dated by the excavators to the late 2nd or early 3rd cent.; most probably early 3rd cent. The deposit contains 30,000 pieces of pottery in total, of which 22,000 are amphorae.
8 Bonnet *et al.* 2003

**D 62**

1 Le Mans, Sarthe; town; Ilot 7, ave P Mendès-France, well F1
2 C
3 A
4 Presence of:
37; CG; Iustus, Mercator II, Banvus

37; CG; Marcus; ovolo R B89; O 2225, O 2324, O 2382, O 2392, R C130, R F40, R P76; fig. 7 no. 6
37; CG; Marcus; O 450, R J36, R T13; fig. 7 no 8
37; CG; Banvus (later style); ovolo R B106; O 212, O 246, O 644, O 856, O 1115a; fig. 7 no. 7
6 Ant; Ae
Car; Ae; 214
Alex; Den; 222-34
8 Delage & Guillier 1997, 262-7

**D 63**

1 Le Mans, Sarthe; town; Les Halles; context 2006, unspecified single context (not closed)
2 G
3 A/C
4 37; CG; Marcus; ovolo R B89; R J53; fig. 12 no. 9
37; CG; Marcus; R H72, R M5, R P76, R R86; fig. 12 no. 12
37; CG; Banvus; O 1115a, O 2382, O 4038; fig. 12 no. 11
37; CG-Lubié; fig. 12 no. 13
Presence of 37 CG, Casurius, Cantomallus, Pugnus, Paternus I/Ianuarius II, Censorinus, Iustus, Iullinus, Advocisus, Carantinus II, Paternus II, Laxtucissa, Fgientinus
6 Traj; As
Had; As
Ant; 2 HS
Comm; HS
J Domna; HS
Elag; Rad
Claud II; Rad; 268-70
Tet; 2 barb rad
Tet; 2 Rad; 272-3
8 Delage & Guillier 1997, 268-71

**D 64**

1 Le Mans, Sarthe; town; Les Halles; context 1007, unspecified single context
2 G
3 A/C
4 37; CG; unknown; unpublished ovolo; O 171a, O 204, O 562, R C251; fig. 15 no. 3
37; CG; Caletus (reutilised mould); ovolo R B90; R C39, R E68, R T2, R T7, R U35; fig. 15, no. 4
37; CG; Paternus II (reutilised mould); O 33, O 450, O 1510, O 1533, R E56, R Q16; fig. 16 no. 1
37; CG; Mercator II/Caletus (reutilised mould); ovolo R B258; O 92, O 450, O K, R E3, R R89; fig. 16 no. 2
37; CG; Iullinus (reutilised mould); ovolo R B164; O 111, O 966, R T40, R U87; fig. 16 no. 3
37; CG; Fgientinus; ovolo R B234; R G53, R G152, R R13; fig. 17 no.1
37; CG; Fgientinus; ovolo R U288; O 46, R F40, R G21, R H2, R J2, R J154, R N4; fig. 17 no. 2, joins to a piece in context 2006 (see above)
37;CG; Fgientinus; ovolo R B50; R C251, R F2, R H89, R H152, R J20, R U288; fig. 17 no. 3
37; CG; Fgientinus; ovolo R B151; O 2183, O 2365, O 2418, R C251; fig. 17 no. 4
37; CG; Fgientinus; ovolo R B151; O 2134, R H117, R H130, R R2; fig. 17 no. 5
37; CG; Iullinus; ovolo R B164; O 1732, R T40; not illus
Presence of 37 CG, Marcus
72 CG, incised and barbotine (many pieces)
6 Traj; Dup
Had; 2 HS
Ant; Dup
Comm; Dup
Post; Rad
Tet; 4 barb rad (c 270-3)
8 Delage & Guillier 1997, 271-6

**D 65**

1 La Mézière, Ille-et-Vilaine; rural settlement; general finds
2 F
3 A
4 37; CG; Anunus II style; fig. 4 no. 77
37; CG; Cinnamus style; fig. 4 nos 126 and 152 (2)
37; CG; Attianus II, Criciro or Sacer II group; fig. 4 no. 124
37; CG; Sissus II (st); fig. 4 no. 443
37; CG; Albucius style; fig. 4 no. 143
37; CG; Maccirra style (prob.); fig. 4 no. 153
68; CG; Paternus II/Laxtucissa group; black-gloss; fig. 5 no. 226
6 No coins mentioned.
7 A general association only, apparently with no coins, but interesting as a later 2nd-century group from a rural establishment in western Gaul.
8 Simon 2002

**D 66**

1 La Plaine d'Hermesnil, Seine-Maritime; rural settlement; pit-group
2 C
3 A/C
4 37; CG; Servus II
37; CG; Priscus/Clemens
37; CG; Paternus II/Iustus (2)
37; CG; late style
37: EG (2)
6 5 coins (As/Dup) to Comm
7 From a group of pits filled contemporaneously over a short period.
8 Coffineau & Dubant 2002

**D 67**

1 Poitiers, Vienne; town; couvent des Cordeliers, pottery shop deposit, P222, destruction debris of fire
2 E
3 A/C
4 37; CG; Fgientinus/Cintinus; ovolo R B206; O 857, O 1512, R A13, R E69, R H89, R H117, R P61, R R13; metope style; identical to a mould in MAN, Rogers 1999, 103-5, pl. 37, no. 34; fig. 11 no. 31
37; CG; Caletus; ovolo R B258; O 21, O 450, O 970, O 1836, O 2234, erotic scene unpub, R A13, R as C171; R E7, R J78, R R89; metope style; from the same mould as one from the ZAC de l'Enclos, Lezoux, dated to 3rd quarter of the 3rd cent (Delage 1999a, V, pl. 9, 4230); fig. 11 no. 32
Plain ware catalogued but not given here.
5 Non-samian catalogued but not given here.
6 None recorded.
7 The fire at the pottery shop is dated by the excavators to the 2nd half of the 3rd century, but the basis for this dating (apart from the pottery itself) is not given.
8 Wittmann & Jouquand 2009

**D 68**

1 St Germain-la-Gâtine, Eure-et-Loir; *vicus*; building 8, cellar F14-03, fire and destruction deposit
2 E
3 A/C

4 37; CG; Censorinus; ovolo R B128?; O 84, O 93, O 443b, O 497, O 638, O 688, O 854, O 857, O 1214, O 1374, O 1834, R A2, R C123, R G162, R R7
37; CG; Cinnamus (early); ovolo R B144; O 1491, O 1627, O 1666, O 1781, R A9, R C53, R H51, R J178, R K12, R Q2, R R8; fig. 8 no. 9
37; CG; Cinnamus (st); ovolo R B143; O 711, R A9, R H21, R H101, R K12, R Q27, R R70, R U33, R U36, R U266; fig. 8 no. 10
37: CG; Paternus II (style a); ovolo R B114 var. 2; O 440, O 444, O 907, O 1215, O 1230, O 2316, O 2324, R A12, R A40, R R60
37; CG; Paternus II (style a); ovolo R B114 var. 2; O 1578, O 1696i, O 1842, O 1915a, O 1984, O 1985a, R A12
37; CG; Paternus II (style b) (st); ovolo R B106; O 450, O 929, O2382, O 2392, R A12, R A36, R R60; fig. 8 no. 11
Plain ware catalogued but not given here.
5 Non-samian catalogued but not given here.
6 Ant; Dup; 139
7 The excavators interpret the deposit as having been the material in the cellar at the time of the fire, which they date to 160/180. The pottery is later than the coin, and is estimated to be prior to 190, due to the absence of form 45, and potters such as Doeccus, Iullinus, Mercator II, etc.
8 Delage, Morin & Sellès 2007

**D 69**

1 St Romain-en-Gal, Rhône; town; Small North Baths, phase 6 fills
2 E/F
3 A/C
4 Presence of 37 SG, 37 CG (late 2nd century styles), 37 CG Censorinus
6 Nerva; As
Had; As
Ant; As
Comm; As; 185-92
7 Appears to be a largely contemporaneous group, built up over a period.
8 Leblanc 2003

**D 70**

1 St Romain-en-Gal, Rhône; town; Thermes des Lutteurs, abandonment levels
2 E/F
3 A/C
4 Presence of much SG (La Graufesenque and Banassac), MdV, CG-Lezoux (late 2nd century styles)
6 Gall; Rad
Valerian; Rad
Claud II; Rad
Tet; Rad; 270-3
7 This group contains much redeposited material, unlike the previous group.
8 Leblanc 2003

**D 71**

1 Senlis, Oise; town; 4 Impasse du Courtillet, zone 2, layers 2 and 3
2 E
3 A
4 37; CG; Iustus (st)
37 CG (4)
6 Coin hoard dated to 190
7 Few stratigraphic details, but enough to indicate a coin-dated association.
8 Pissot 1993

**D 72**

1 Tavers, Loiret; villa; rubbish pit
2 C
3 C
4 37; CG; Marcus
37; CG; Banvus (st)
37; CG; Iullicus (prob)
37 CG (22 other vessels, including one in style of Donnaucus MdV)
Plain ware includes 45 CG, 79 CG/EG, 72 CG, C21 CG, Lez 96 CG; much of this probably comes from Terre-Franche kiln site.
6 Aur; no details
7 The pit contained 2243 pieces of pottery in total, and is dated by the excavator to the early 3rd century.
8 Moireau 1992

**D 73**

1 Le Thovey, Haute-Savoie; *vicus* or *mansio*; phase 3/4 abandonment levels
2 E/F
3 A/C
4 Presence of Paternus II, Banvus, Albucius, Casurius, Cinnamus, Caletus
6 14 2nd cent.
6 early 3rd cent.
Gallien; Rad; 267-8
7 The samian is all post 170/90 according to Delage.
8 Landry 2003

**D 74**

1 Vieux, Calvados; town; building A, cellar, context 1173
2 E
3 A
4 Presence of 37 CG Marcus, 45 CG, Lezoux type 96 CG, 72 CG (late style)
5 3rd century coarse ware
6 1st century As
Ant for Faust I div; As
8 Jardel 2002, 144-8

**D 75**

1 Vieux, Calvados; town; abandonment level, context 1111/1079/1080
2 E
3 A
4 Presence of CG of late production (Delage phases 7 and 8), 37 CG Libertus II (Rogers 1999, dated to 150-70), 72 CG, 45 CG, C21/Lezoux type 97 CG
5 3rd century coarse ware, including BB1 of types found associated with Oxf and NF
6 Gall; Victorin; Tet II; 4 Rad in total
8 Jardel 2002, 148-55

## GERMANY

**D 76**

1 Echzell, Hessen; *vicus;* 'Geschirrfund'
2 E
3 A/C
4 Dec pieces:
Trier; Werkstatt I (1)
Trier; Werkstatt II (36)

Trier; Mai.iaaus (1)
Trier; Amator (4)
Trier; Dexter (95)
Trier; miscellaneous (20)
Rheinz; Comitialis V (6)
6 11 coins to Comm, 183/4
7 Dated by Huld-Zetsche to 190/200.
8 Huld-Zetsche 1993, 57-8; Huld-Zetsche & Steidl 1994

**D 77**

1 Günzenhausen, Bayern; cemetery; graves 1, 2 and 8
2 A
3 A
4 Grave 1: 37; SG; Mascuus
Grave 2: 37 SG (2)
Grave 8: 37; SG; Germanus
6 Grave 1: Dom; As
Traj; As; 103-17
Grave 2: Traj; As
Aur; As; 161-2
Grave 8: Dom; Dup
Traj; HS
Had; As; 119-22
7 A good example in the case of Grave 2, of apparent conservation of a samian vessel for a long period after manufacture.
8 Fasold 1988

**D 78**

1 Köngen, Baden-Württemberg; *vicus*, Abfallgrube Flurstück 3640, findspot 182
2 C
3 A
4 37; SG; Mercato-Mascuus (2)
37; CG; Ioenalis
37; EG; Satto-Saturninus (2)
37; Blick; Haupttöpfer style
37; Heil; Janu
37; Rheinz; Janu I (3)
37; Rheinz; Janu I style
18/31; Heil; Sacco
18/31; Rheinz/Blick; Bitunus
6 Ant; As (2)
8 Luik 1996, 83

**D 79**

1 Köngen, Baden-Württemberg; *vicus;* Adolf-Ehmann Str 35, findspot 300, wooden well
2 C
3 A
4 In fill of well:
37; SG; prob Bannassac
37; prob CG
37; EG; Satto-Saturninus (2)
37; Blick; Haupttöpfer style (several pieces)
37 (poss); Heil; F-master
37; EG; Janu style (2)
6 Dendrochronological (felling) date of 131-151 for the wood construction of the well.
8 Luik 1996, 106

**D 80**

1 Langenhain, Hessen; *vicus;* 'Geschirrfund' in cellar 1
2 E
3 A
4 Dec pieces:
Trier; Werkstatt II (2)
Trier; Comitialis (1)
Trier; Mai.iaaus group (1)
Trier; Censor (2)
Trier; Censor-Dexter group (5)
Trier; Censor-Dexter & followers (7)
Trier; Dexter (23)
Trier; Afer-Marinus (1)
Trier; Afer-Marinus (poss) (10)
Trier; Atillus (7)
Trier; Atillus (poss) (4)
Trier; Atillus group (1)
Trier; Dubitatus (5)
Trier; Dubitus (63)
Trier; misc and poss (74)
Rheinz; Comitialis III (1)
Rheinz; Comitialis V (1)
Rheinz; Comitialis VI (1)
Rheinz; Julius I (2)
Rheinz; Julius I or Lupus (16)
Rheinz; Lupus (15)
Rheinz; Attillus (1)
Rheinz; Marcellus II (1)
Rheinz; Julius II-Julianus I (3)
Rheinz; Ware B with O 382/383 (2)
Rheinz; Victor I (1)
Rheinz; Marcellinus (10)
Rheinz; misc (13)
Arg-Lavoye; Gesatus (1)
CG; Pugnus (1)
Heil; Ianuarius (1)
EG unlocated (1)
6 Aug/Tib; As, very worn
Dom; Dup
Dom; As
Traj; As
Had; Dup
Comm; Dup
Sev; Den
Car; Den
Car; As
Geta; As
Elag; Den (12)
Alex; Den (3), latest 222-35
7 Dated to 233 on historical grounds, and associated with a burning episode.
8 Huld-Zetsche 1993, 58-9; Huld-Zetsche & Steidl 1994; Simon & Köhler 1992

**D 81**

1 Regensburg-Kumpfmühl, Niederbayern; *vicus* of fort, cellar fill of 'Erdkeller 1979'
2 E
3 A
4 29; SG; Vitalis style; Abb. 8 no. 80
37; SG – Bannassac; late Flavian/Trajanic; Abb. 11 no. 81
37; Heil; Janu style; Abb. 11 no. 82
37; Rheinz; Reginus I style; Abb. 12 no. 83
37; Rheinz; Reginus I style; Abb. 12 no. 84
37; Rheinz; Janu I style; Abb. 13 no. 85
37; Rheinz; Janu I style; Abb. 13 no. 86
31 CG (st) Lallus; Abb 14 no. 99
7 No coins were found in the cellar, but the fort and *vicus* are considered to have been destroyed in the Marcomannic War in 170/175, prior to the construction of the Regens-

burg legionary fortress. Much of the material in the cellar fill had been burnt.

8 Fischer (T) 1984

**D 82**

1 Regensburg-Kumpfmühl, Niederbayern; *vicus* of fort, finds location Vicus 3/2

2 F

3 C

4 37; SG; Mercato style; Abb. 46 no. 18
37; SG; no. 19
37; CG; Paternus II style; no. 20
37; Esch or Blick; late 2nd century; no. 21
37; Heil; Janu style; Abb. 46 no. 22
37; Heil; Ciriuna style; Abb. 46 no. 23
37; Heil; Ciriuna style; Abb. 46 no. 24
37; Rheinz; Reginus I style; Abb. 46 no. 25
37; Rheinz; Reginus I style; no. 26
37; Rheinz; Cerialis I style; no. 27
37; Rheinz; Cerialis I style; Abb. 46 no. 28
37; Rheinz; Cerialis I or II; no. 29
30; Rheinz; Comitialis V style; no. 30
37; Rheinz; Pupus/Iuvenis II style, no. 31
37; Rheinz; Victor I style; Abb. 47 no. 32
37; Rheinz; Bernhard group Ia-IIa potter; no. 33
37; West; Helenius style; Abb. 47 no. 34

6 Vesp; As; no. 12
Dom; As; no. 39
Had; Den; 119/22; no. 80

7 General association only, from early 20th-century excavations using planum method. The assemblage is significant for the probable destruction date of 170/175 for the fort and *vicus* as a whole (see previous entry). This deposit is dated by Faber to the mid/late 2nd century occupation of the *vicus*, without being able to be more precise.

8 Faber 1994, 349-55

**D 83**

1 Regensburg-Kumpfmühl, Niederbayern; *vicus* of fort, finds location Vicus 10

2 F

3 C

4 30; SG – La G; Medillus style; no. 30
30; SG – La G; Calus style; no. 31
30; SG – La G; Mercato group; Abb. 56 no. 32
37; SG – La G; Germanus style; nos 33-34 (2)
37; SG – La G; Frontinus style; Abb. 56 no. 35
37; SG – La G; M Crestio style; Abb. 56 no. 36
37; SG – La G; Flavian; Abb. 56 no. 37
37; SG – La G; Flavian; no. 38
37; SG – La G; Coelus or Bassus style; Abb. 56 no. 39
37; SG – La G; Mercato group; no. 40
37; SG – La G; L Cosius style; no. 41
37; SG – La G; Mercato group; nos 42-44 (3)
37; SG – La G; L Cosius Virilis style; no. 45
37; SG – La G; Mercato group; nos 46-47 (2)
78; SG – La G; Germanus (st); Abb. 56. No. 48
78; SG – La G; Mercato group; no. 49
37; SG – Banassac; Biragil style; no. 50
37; SG – Banassac; Germani F Ser style; Abb. 56 no. 51
37; SG – Banassac; Natalis group; Abb. 56 nos 52-54 (3)
37; SG – Banassac; Germani F Ser style (prob.); Abb. 56 no. 55
37; SG; early 2nd cent.; no. 56
37; SG – Banassac; early 2nd cent.; no. 57
37; MdV; X-11/X-12 style; Abb. 56 no. 58
37; MdV; Ranto style (prob.); no. 59
37; CG; Docilis/Docalus style; Abb. 57 no. 60
37; CG; Sissus II style (prob.); no. 61
37; CG; Attianus style; Abb. 57 no. 62
37; CG; Cinnamus style; nos 63-68 (6)
37; CG; Criciro style; no. 69
37; CG; Laxtucissa style; no. 70
37; CG; Albucius style; Abb. 57 no. 71
37; Heil or Rheinz; Reginus I style; no. 72
37; Rheinz; Janus I style; no. 73
37; Rheinz; Bernhard group Ib; Abb. 57 no. 74

6 Tib; As; no. 6
Vesp; Den; worn; no. 9
Traj; As (2); slight wear; nos 59-60
Traj; As/Dup; very worn
Had; HS; 119; fairly worn; no. 84
Quadrans; late 1st-mid 2nd cent.; good condition; no. 41

7 See previous entry for comments on the nature of the deposit. A mixed group, interesting for the CG and Rheinzabern products, apparently in use at the time of the destruction of the fort and *vicus*. Faber (1994, 374) notes that the last-listed piece, of Bernhard group Ib, may be later than the destruction date.

8 Faber 1994, 364-74

**D 84**

1 Regensburg-Kumpfmühl, Niederbayern; *vicus* of fort, finds location Vicus 10/21, trough

2 C

3 C

4 From 10/21-3:
37; SG; Germanus style; no. 3
37; SG; Mercato group (2); nos 5-6
37; Banassac; Germani F Ser style (2); Abb. 83, nos 7-8
37; CG; Cinnamus (3); nos 9-11
37; CG; Attianus or Criciro; Abb. 83, no. 12
37; Heil; F master style; Abb. 83, no. 13
37; Rheinz; Cobnertus II style; no. 14

6 From 10/21-3:
Dom; HS; no. 37
Nerva; As; very worn; no. 49
From 10/21-2 (underlying planum):
Ant; HS; 154-5; good condition; no. 98

7 The trough underlies the SW corner of the Period 2 house (Vicus 10/29-10/40). There were some medieval and modern finds from 10/21-3, so the context has some disturbance or contamination.

8 Faber 1994, 400-5

**D 85**

1 Regensburg-Kumpfmühl, Niederbayern; *vicus* of fort, finds location Vicus 10/53-3, planum level within a strip-house

2 F

3 C

4 29; SG; mid 1st-century style; Abb. 91, no. 7
37; SG; Germanus style (2); nos 8-9
37; Banassac; Germani F Ser style; no. 10
37; CG; Cinnamus early style; Abb. 91, no. 11
37; Heil; Janus style; Abb. 91, no. 12

6 Dom; HS; no. 32
Nerva; As; no. 47
Traj; As; no. 70
Had (Sabina); HS; 128-30; no. 93

8 Faber 1994, 41-5

**D 86**

1 Regensburg-Kumpfmühl, Niederbayern; *vicus* of fort, finds location Vicus 10/75, pit
2 C
3 C
4 37; Banassac; early 2nd-century style (2); Abb. 114-5, nos 13, 17
37; Banassac; Natalis group (3); Abb. 115, nos 14-16
37; CG; Cinnamus early style; Abb. 115, no. 18
37; CG; Cinnamus main style (3); nos 19-21
37; Rheinz; Janus I style; Abb. 115, no. 22
6 Traj; HS; no. 73
Had; Den; 119-22; no. 79
7 A pit filled with burnt material, possibly associated with the Marcomannic destruction.
8 Faber 1994, 437-52

**D 87**

1 Rottweil, Baden-Württemberg; north *vicus*; building K, cellar fill
2 E
3 A
4 37; Rheinz; Bernhard group IIa (4 vessels); Taf. 71, nos 10-13
6 Sev; Den; 194-5, no. 23
8 Klee 1986, 36, 92, 145

**D 88**

1 Saalburg, Hessen; *vicus* of fort; Find no. 10, cellar fill
2 E
3 C
4 37; Trier; Dexter style; Taf. 2, no. 11
37; Trier; Dubitatus style; Taf. 3, no. 2
37; Rheinz; Marcellinus style; Taf. 3, no. 1
37; Rheinz; Lupus style; Taf. 3, no. 3
6 Worn bronze coins (date not recorded)
Vesp; Den
7 Deposits **D 88-94** represent the recovery of stratigraphic and contextual data from late 19th- and early 20th-century excavations. The finds themselves do not survive in every case. In general, the Saalburg *vicus* is considered to have come to an end in the early/mid 3rd century, and many of the cellar fills and other deposits are associated with the abandonment of the site.
8 Moneta 2010, vol. 1, 230-1; vol. 2, 8-9

**D 89**

1 Saalburg, Hessen; *vicus* of fort; Find no. 11, cellar fill
2 E
3 C
4 37; Rheinz; Marcellinus style; Taf. 4, no. 1
6 Sev (Car); Den; 196; no. 4
7 The finds come from the bottom of the fill.
8 Moneta 2010, vol. 1, 232; vol. 2, 9-10

**D 90**

1 Saalburg, Hessen; *vicus* of fort; Find no. 67, well
2 E
3 C
4 37; Rheinz; Comitialis V (st); Taf. 8, no. 8
6 Sev (Geta); Den; 198-200; no. 2
7 Both the samian and the coin come from c. 3.5 m depth in the well.
8 Moneta 2010, vol. 1, 236; vol. 2, 32-3

**D 91**

1 Saalburg, Hessen; *vicus* of fort; Find no. 92, well
2 C
3 C
4 37; Trier; Dexter; Taf. 12, no. 1
6 No coins
7 The well contains an inscription to Jupiter Dolichenus (CIL XIII.11950), with the name of Geta erased, implying a date of 205 or later for the inscription, and after 212 for the *damnatio memoriae*, and subsequent deposition.
8 Hörig & Schwertheim 1987, 318; Moneta 2010, vol. 1, 240; vol. 2, 43-4

**D 92**

1 Saalburg, Hessen; *vicus* of fort; Find no. 1070, cellar fill
2 E
3 C
4 37; Rheinz; Lupus style; no. 1
39; Rheinz; Verinus ii (st); Taf. 19, no. 11
6 Ant; Dup; no. 5
Comm (Crispina); HS; 180-3; no. 4
7 Only a loose association is indicated for this deposit.
8 Moneta 2010, vol. 1, 247; vol. 2, 97-8

**D 93**

1 Saalburg, Hessen; *vicus* of fort; Find no. 1153, post-hole
2 C
3 C
4 From near the post-hole:
37; Trier; Dexter style; Taf. 22, no. 11
6 In the post-hole:
Ant; HS; no. 1
From near the post-hole:
Aur; HS; 171-2; no. 2
7 See comment to **D 92**.
8 Moneta 2010, vol. 1, 250; vol. 2, 111

**D 94**

1 Saalburg, Hessen; *vicus* of fort; Find no. 5040, interior layer in building
2 B/E
3 C
4 37; Rheinz; Ware with ovolo E34; Taf 49, no. 15
6 Aur; HS; no. 1
Comm; HS; no. 2
Sev; HS; 194; no. 3
7 The samian and the coins are recorded in the archove notes as having been found together.
8 Moneta 2010, vol. 1, 277; vol. 2, 347

**D 95**

1 Sulz, Baden-Württemberg; *vicus;* cellar, Fundn. 7
2 E
3 A
4 Dec pieces:
Itten/Mitt; Cibisus (15)
Itten/Mitt; Cibisus? (1)
Itten/Mitt; Verecundus (8)
Itten/Mitt; Cibisus/Verecundus (4)
Heil; F-master (3)
Heil; Ciriuna (4)
Heil; Ciriuna/Janus I (1)
Heil; Ianus I (4)
Heil; Reginus I (1)
EG unlocated; Cibisus/Ianus II (1)
EG unlocated; Cibisus/Reginus I (1)
EG unlocated, perhaps Rheinz or Heil; Reginus I (1)
. Rheinz; Ianus I (1)

Rheinz; Reginus I (6)
Rheinz; Reginus I? (1)
Rheinz; Cobnertus III (1)
Rheinz; Cerialis I (1)
Rheinz; Cerialis III/IV (1)
Rheinz; Cerialis IV (1)
Rheinz; Augustinus I? (1)
Rheinz; Ianus II (8)
Rheinz; uncertain (5)
6 10 coins, up to:
Comm (Crispina); HS; 180/83
7 The coin is only slightly worn, and probably provides a realistic date for the assemblage. The composition of the samian group is significant for early Rheinzabern and links with other EG kiln centres.
8 Gimber 1999, 383-4; Nuber 1992; Schaub 1994, 442; 1996

**D 96**

1 Walheim, Baden-Württemberg; *vicus* of fort; cellar 604
2 E
3 A
4 37; Heil; F-master style; Taf. 47, no. 9
37; Blick; master potter style; Taf. 47, no. 10
37; Rheinz; Pupus-Iuvenis II style; Taf. 47, no. 11
37; Blick; Avitus, Cambo or L.A.L.; Taf. 47, no. 12
6 Ant (Faust I div); HS; 141-61; worn; no. 259
7 The forts and *vicus* of Walheim are on the Neckar *limes.* There is a burning episode, c. AD 155/60, with rebuilding thereafter and occupation up the period of Severus Alexander, c. 233, according to the material evidence, then apparently abandonment. Most of the deposits in **D 96-113** can be linked to the late 2[nd]-early 3[rd] century phase, and include important groups of early Rheinzabern wares. The finds from the fort ditches, not included here, also have Satto/Saturninus pieces from Chémery and Mittelbronn.
8 Klein 2004; Kortüm & Lauber 2004, vol. II, 57-8

**D 97**

1 Walheim, Baden-Württemberg; *vicus* of fort; fill 745
2 E
3 A
4 37; Rheinz; Mammilianus style; Taf. 48, no. 11
37; Rheinz or Heil; Janus I, Cobnertus I or Cerialis II; Taf. 48, no. 15
37; Rheinz; Janus I style; Taf. 48, no. 16
37; Rheinz; Janus I or II; Taf. 48, no. 17
37; Rheinz; Julius I-Lupus style; Taf. 48, no. 18
37; Heil; F-master style; Taf. 48, no. 19
6 Comm; HS; 184-5; no. 329
8 Klein 2004; Kortüm & Lauber 2004, vol. II, 61-3

**D 98**

1 Walheim, Baden-Württemberg; *vicus* of fort; stokehole 945
2 E
3 A
4 37; Blick; Avitus style; Taf. 60, no. 9
37; Blick; Avitus style; Taf. 60, no. 21
37; Rheinz; Reginus I style; Taf. 60, no. 11
37; Rheinz; Janus I style; Taf. 60, no. 12
37; Rheinz; Cobnertus III style; Taf. 60, no. 13
37; Rheinz; Janus I or Mammilianus; Taf. 60, no. 14
37; Rheinz; Mamilianus or Reginus II; Taf. 60, no. 15
37; Rheinz; Reginus I style; Taf. 60, no. 16
37; Rheinz; Cobnertus I style; Taf. 60, no. 17
37; Rheinz; Cobnertus III (st); Taf. 60, no. 18
37 Rheinz
37 SG
6 Titus; As; worn; no. 38
Had; Dup; 134-8; worn; no. 181
8 Klein 2004; Kortüm & Lauber 2004, vol. II, 75-9

**D 99**

1 Walheim, Baden-Württemberg; *vicus* of fort; rubble layer 1078, over building 10
2 E
3 A/C
4 37; Rheinz; Lucanus (st); no. 28 (not illus.)
37; Rheinz; Helenius style; no. 29
37; Rheinz; Primitivus II style; no. 30
37; Rheinz; Comitialis V style (3); nos 31, 42, 45
37; Rheinz; Mammilianus style; no. 32
37; Rheinz; Julius II-Julianus I style; no. 33
37; Blick; Avitus style (2); nos 38-9
37; Rheinz; Janus I style (3); nos 40-1, 46
37; Rheinz; Mammilianus or Reginus II; no. 44
37; Rheinz; Pupus style; no. 47
37; Rheinz; Cerialis IV or B F Attoni̅; no. 48
37; Rheinz; Comitialis VI, E 25/26, Atto or Attillus; no. 49
6 Had; As; worn; no. 186
Comm; HS; 180-3; worn; no. 336
7 A loose association only, because of the nature of the stratigraphy.
8 Klein 2004; Kortüm & Lauber 2004, vol. II, 89-95

**D 100**

1 Walheim, Baden-Württemberg; *vicus* of fort; cellar fill 1309
2 E
3 A
4 37; Rheinz; Janus I style; Taf. 85, no. 38
37; Rheinz; Janus I or Reginus I; Taf. 85, no. 40
37; Rheinz; Reginus II, Julius I or Lupus; Taf. 85, no. 41
37; Rheinz; Reginus I style; Taf. 85, no. 42
37; Rheinz; Helenius style; Taf. 85, no. 45
37; Rheinz; Julius I-Lupus style (2); Taf. 85, nos 46-7
37; Rheinz; Janus II style; Taf. 85, no. 50
6 Had; HS; worn; no. 194
Aur; Dup; worn; no. 278
L Verus; Dup; very worn; no. 318
Comm; As; 180-3; worn; no. 337
8 Klein 2004; Kortüm & Lauber 2004, vol. II, 109-13

**D 101**

1 Walheim, Baden-Württemberg; *vicus* of fort; latrine 1376
2 E
3 A
4 37; Heil; Janus style; Taf. 96, no. 6
37; Blick; potter of the leaping animals style; Taf. 95, no. 7
37; Rheinz or Heil; Reginus style; Taf. 95, no. 8
37; Rheinz; Reginus style; Taf. 95, no. 11
37; Rheinz or Heil; Janus style; Taf. 95, no. 12
6 Had; HS; 119-22; worn; no. 150
8 Klein 2004; Kortüm & Lauber 2004, vol. II, 120-3

**D 102**

1 Walheim, Baden-Württemberg; *vicus* of fort; cellar fill 1461
2 E
3 A
4 37; Rheinz; Helenius style; Taf. 106, no. 19
37; Rheinz; Ware A with O 382/383; Taf. 106, no. 22
37; Rheinz; Respectus style; Taf. 106, no. 23
6 Aur; HS; no. 276
Elag (J Soaemias); Den; 218-22; slight wear; no. 363

7 The coin of Elagabalus comes from an upper level in the fill, and the samian ware from a little lower down.
8 Klein 2004; Kortüm & Lauber 2004, vol. II, 131-3

**D 103**

1 Walheim, Baden-Württemberg; *vicus* of fort; cellar fill 1686
2 E
3 A
4 37; Blick; L.AT.AT style; Taf. 119, no. 18
37; Rheinz; Cerialis Ware B; Taf. 119, no. 19
37; Rheinz; Cerialis VI style; Taf. 120, no. 20
37; Rheinz; Primitivus I or III; Taf. 120, no. 21
37; Rheinz; Comitialis VI style (2); Taf. 120, nos 22, 24
37; Rheinz; B F Attoni style; Taf. 120, no. 23
37; Rheinz; Comitialis IV, Belsus II, Castus or Respectus; Taf. 119, no. 25
37; Rheinz; Comitialis IV or VI, Florentinus, E 25/26 or Attillus; Taf. 119, no. 26
37; Rheinz; Mammilianus, Reginus II or Julius I-Lupus; Taf. 119, no. 27
37; Rheinz; Verecundus I style; Taf. 119, no. 28
37; Rheinz; Cerialis IV style; Taf. 119, no. 30
37; Rheinz; E 25/26 style; Taf. 120, no. 36
37; Rheinz; Comitialis VI, Respectus, Florentinus or E 25/26; Taf. 120, no. 37
37; Rheinz; B F Attoni atyle; Taf. 120, no. 38
37; Rheinz; Cerialis III style; Taf. 120, no. 43
37; Rheinz; Cerialis group Ware B; Taf. 120, no. 44
37; Rheinz; Mammilianus, Firmus II or Reginus II; Taf. 120, no. 46
6 Aur (Comm); As; 177-8; worn; no. 312
8 Klein 2004; Kortüm & Lauber 2004, vol. II, 148-55

**D 104**

1 Walheim, Baden-Württemberg; *vicus* of fort; pit 1747
2 C
3 A
4 37; Blick; Avitus style; Taf. 132, no. 28
37; Rheinz; Reginus I style (2); no. 27 (not illus) and Taf. 133, no. 29
37; Rheinz; Mammilianus style; Taf. 133, no. 30
37; Rheinz; Cerialis group; Taf. 133, no. 31
6 Titus (Dom); Den; 80; worn; no. 37
8 Klein 2004; Kortüm & Lauber 2004, vol. II, 159-63

**D 105**

1 Walheim, Baden-Württemberg; *vicus* of fort; cellar fill 1888
2 E
3 A
4 37; Rheinz; Cerialis VI (st); Taf. 147, no. 27
37; Rheinz; O 382/383 style; Taf. 147, no. 28
37; Rheinz; Augustinus I or II; Taf. 147, no. 29
37; Rheinz; Comitialis IV style; Taf. 147, no. 31
37; Rheinz; Cobnertus III style; Taf. 147, no. 32
6 Traj; HS; worn (2); nos 89, 93
L Verus (Lucilla); HS; very worn; no. 323
Sev; Den; 193-211; little wear; no. 347
7 The coins came from higher in the fill than the samian ware. A stone statuette of Jupiter was also found in this cellar.
8 Klein 2004; Kortüm & Lauber 2004, vol. II, 173-7

**D 106**

1 Walheim, Baden-Württemberg; *vicus* of fort; latrine 2635
2 E
3 A
4 37; Heil; Janus style (3); Taf. 176, nos 9, 11, 12
37; Heil; F-master style; Taf. 176, no. 13
6 Vesp; As; 69-79; very worn; no. 26
8 Klein 2004; Kortüm & Lauber 2004, vol. II, 215-7

**D 107**

1 Walheim, Baden-Württemberg; *vicus* of fort; pit 2975
2 C
3 A
4 37; Rheinz; Janus I style; Taf. 198, no. 6
37; Rheinz; Janus I or similar potter; Taf. 198, no. 7
37; Rheinz; Cerialis VI, Belsus I or Respectus; Taf. 197, no. 8
6 Had; HS; 134-8; worn/very worn; no. 179
8 Klein 2004; Kortüm & Lauber 2004, vol. II, 250-1

**D 108**

1 Walheim, Baden-Württemberg; *vicus* of fort; latrine 3160
2 E
3 A
4 37; SG; Masculus style; Taf. 203, no. 6
Plain ware includes SG; Banassac; Chém; SG/Blick?
6 Traj; As; 103-11; worn/very worn; no. 99
8 Klein 2004; Kortüm & Lauber 2004, vol. II, 262-3

**D 109**

1 Walheim, Baden-Württemberg; *vicus* of fort; cellar 3177
2 E
3 A
4 37; Rheinz; B F Attoni style; Taf. 204, no. 4
6 Aur; Dup; 163-4; worn; no. 279
8 Klein 2004; Kortüm & Lauber 2004, vol. II, 265-6

**D 110**

1 Walheim, Baden-Württemberg; *vicus* of fort; cistern or latrine 3200
2 E
3 A
4 37; Rheinz; E 25/26 style; Taf. 205, no. 4
37; Rheinz; Attillus style; Taf. 205, no. 5
6 Ant; HS; 143-4; no. 214
8 Klein 2004; Kortüm & Lauber 2004, vol. II, 266-8

**D 111**

1 Walheim, Baden-Württemberg; *vicus* of fort; large pit 3399
2 C
3 A
4 37; Rheinz; Primitivus II style; Taf. 213, no. 35
37; Rheinz; Firmus I style (2); Taf. 213, nos 36, 46
37; Rheinz; Verecundus I style; Taf. 213, no. 37
37; Rheinz; Julius I-Lupus or similar potter; Taf. 213, no. 38
37; Rheinz; Belsus II (st); Taf. 213, no. 40
37; Rheinz; E 25/26 style (2); Taf. 213, nos 41, 50
37; Rheinz; Cerialis II style; Taf. 213, no. 44
37; Rheinz; Cerialis IV style; Taf. 213, no. 45
37; Rheinz; Reginus II-Virilis style; Taf. 213, no. 49
37; Rheinz; Cerialis group Ware B; Taf. 214, no. 52
6 Flavian; As; 69-81; very corroded; no. 43
8 Klein 2004; Kortüm & Lauber 2004, vol. II, 274-80

**D 112**

1 Walheim, Baden-Württemberg; *vicus* of fort; cistern or latrine 3446
2 E
3 A
4 37; Rheinz; Janus II style; Taf. 221, no. 14
37; Rheinz; Pupus-Iuvenis II style; Taf. 221, no. 18

6 Traj; Aureus; 114-7; little wear; no. 110
8 Klein 2004; Kortüm & Lauber 2004, vol. II, 282-5

**D 113**

1 Walheim, Baden-Württemberg; *vicus* of fort; cellar fill 4058
2 E
3 A
4 37; Blick; Avitus or Cambo; Taf. 233, no. 16
37; Blick; master potter style; Taf. 233, no. 20
37; Heil; Ciriuna style; Taf. 233, no. 17
37; Heil; Janus style (2); Taf. 233, nos 18, 21
37; Heil; Reginus I style; Taf. 233, no. 19
37; Rheinz or Heil; Reginus style; Taf. 233, no. 23
37; Rheinz or Schwäbische kiln; Reginus I style; Taf. 233, no. 22
6 Dom; HS; very worn; no. 57
Ant; Dup; 157-8; slightly worn; no. 234
8 Klein 2004; Kortüm & Lauber 2004, vol. II, 299-304

**D 114**

1 Zugmantel, Hessen; *vicus* of fort; cellar 256
2 E
3 C
4 37; Rheinz; Julius II-Julianus I or Victorinus II or Respectinus II; fig. 1 no. 1
37; Rheinz; Julius II-Julianus I or Perpetuus; fig. 1 no. 2
37; Rheinz; Pervincus style; fig. 1 no. 3
37; Rheinz; Julius II-Julianus I style; fig. 1 no. 4
6 None, but see general coin finds from the cellars at the site, **A 202**.
7 This is a group of decorated and plain samian ware, possibly associated with the immediately adjacent Jupiter Dolichenus shrine. The cellar was infilled at the same time as the others in the *vicus* (see **A 202** and chapter 3).
8 Schücker & Thomas 2004

## SWITZERLAND

**D 115**

1 Augst, Basel-Landschaft; town; site between Women's Baths and the Theatre, Bauphase Cc, SchARE2A01.Cc.1001-Kern
2 F
3 A
4 37 Banassac (prob.)
37 EG (2)
37 Helvetic sigillata; ovolo Ettlinger & Roth-Rubi 1979, 70, E2
6 Sev (Geta); Den
Car; Den
Alex; Den (2)
Alex (J Mamaea); Den
Phil I; HS; 244/9; good condition, little wear
7 A general association only, but apparently well dated by the coins.
8 Engeler-Ohnemus 2006, 290-305

**D 116**

1 Augst, Basel-Landschaft; town; near East Gate, FK 2006.058.F01284
2 F
3 A
4 37; CG; Butrio, Libertus or Advocisus; prob. early 2nd cent.
37; CG; Quintilianus, Bassus, Ianuarius or Paterclus; mid 2nd cent. (2)
37; CG; X-9 or X-11
37; CG; Curmillus (st)
37; Heil; F-master
37 CG
37 Heil
6 Aug; As; halved
Aug; As; imitation
Claud; As; imitation
Titus; As
Dom; HS; 88/9
7 A general association, with the samian approximately 50 years later than the Flavian coins in the phase.
8 Schaub 2007, 164-9

**D 117**

1 Kaiseraugst, Aargau; fort and *vicus*; DH Implenia site (2008.003), phase 3-4, dark soil fill of quarry
2 E
3 A/C
4 Late Rheinz incised dec plate; fig. 4 no. 3
Chenet 320; Arg; roulette-decorated
6 Small Ae; 323-4
7 Dated to late 3rd and early 4th centuries on the basis of the range of ceramic material. The late Rheinzabern plate is probably from the earlier end of this date range.
8 Ammann *et al.* 2009

# Index of sites in the Gazetteer
## Arranged according to the regions used in Table 4.I and elsewhere

France

Allonnes D50
Amiens B82-5
Bliesbruck D51
Boulogne D52
Châlons-sur-Marne D53
Châteaubleau D54
Corseul D55-6
Cosne-sur-Loire A137
Etalon C55
Eyrein B86
Guiry-Gadancourt B87-8
Keradennec A138
La Mezière D65
La Plaine d'Hermesnil D66
La Roche-Maurice A139
Le Mans D62-4
Le Thovey D73
Lewarde A140
Lezoux D57-60
Limoges A141
Lyon B90, D61
Malain A142, C56
Merlines A143
Poitiers D67
St Germain-la-Gâtine D68
St Martial-de-Gimel A144
St Romain-en-Gal D69-70
St Thiboult A145
Senlis D71
Tavers D72
Vieux D74-5

Low Countries

Braives A147
Druten A155
Gerpinnes A148
Haccourt A149
Jette A150
Nivelles C57
Pommeroeul A151, B93
Rijswijk B98
Robelmont B94-6
Roche-Ste Anne C58
Rockanje A156
Rosmeer B97
Tongeren A152-3
Tournai A154
Utrecht A157·
Zwammerdam A158

Rhineland

Altenstadt B99-105
Butzbach B107
Cannstatt A160-2
Degerfeld-in-Butzbach A163, B108-12
Echzell D76
Froitzheim A164
Gross-Gerau B119
Hackenbroich B121
Heddernheim A166-70
Holzhausen A171-6, B122-5
Koenigshoffen B89
Köngen D78-9
Kriftel B126-8
Langenhain D80
Mainz A182
Mainz-Kastel A183
Miltenburg-Altstadt B136
Murrhardt A185, B138
Niederbieber A187
Ohringen-West B139-41
Rheinzabern B149-50
Rosendahlsberg B151-2
Rottweil D87
Saalburg D88-94
Speyer A196
Strasbourg B91-2
Sulz D95
Titelberg A146
Trier A198, B155-7
Walheim D96-113
Walldürn A199-200
Wiesendangen B159
Xanten A201, B158
Zugmantel A202, D114

Danube and Alpine regions

*Aquincum* B162
Augst D115-6
Beiderweis A159
Böhming B106
*Carnuntum* A203-4, B161
Enns-Lorch A205-6
Epfach B113-7
Faimingen B118
Gauting A165
Günzburg B120
Günzenhausen D77
Kaiseraugst D117
Künzing A177-80, B129-134
Leonardspfunzen A181, B135
Marzoll A184
Munningen B137
Neuburg-an-der-Donau A186
Pfaffenhofen A188-91, B142-3
Pocking A192, B144-5
Regensburg A193-4, B146-7
Regensburg-Kumpfmühl B148, D81-6
Reichenhall A195
Salzburg-Eichhof A207
Schaan B160
Straubing A197, B153-4
Zalalövö A208, B163-4

# BIBLIOGRAPHY

## Abbreviations and List of Journals

Journal abbreviations loosely follow those in *Année Philologique* and *American Journal of Archaeology*, but with many variations. Journals not in the above lists have been given appropriate abbreviations in the same general format.

| ***Abbreviation*** | ***Title*** | ***Publisher*** |
|---|---|---|
| *AAB-W* | *Archäologische Ausgrabungen Baden-Württemberg* | Stuttgart: Konrad Theiss Verlag |
| *AAel* | *Archaeologia Aeliana* | Newcastle: Society of Antiquaries of Newcastle |
| *AAHung* | *Acta Archaeologica Academiae Scientiarum Hungaricae* | Budapest: Akadémiai Kiadó |
| *AARBordeaux* | *Actes de l'Académie Royale des Sciences, Belles-Lettres et Arts de Bordeaux* | Bordeaux: Académie Royale des Sciences, Belles-Lettres et Arts de Bordeaux |
| *AB* | *Annales de Bretagne et des Pays de l'Ouest* | Rennes: Presses Universitaires de Rennes |
| *ABelg* | *Archaeologia Belgica* | Brussels: Institut Royal du Patrimoine Artistique, Service des Fouilles |
| *ACamb* | *Archaeologia Cambrensis* | Cardiff: Cambrian Archaeological Association |
| *ACant* | *Archaeologia Cantiana* | Maidstone: Kent Archaeological Society |
| *AÉrt* | *Archaeologiai Értesítő* | Budapest: Akadémiai Kiadó |
| *AIIN* | *Annali dell'Istituto Italiano di Numismatica* | Rome: Istituto Italiano di Numismatica |
| *AJ* | *Archaeological Journal* | London: Royal Archaeological Institute |
| *AJA* | *American Journal of Archaeology* | Boston, MA: Archaeological Institute of America |
| *AJB* | *Das Archäologische Jahr in Bayern* | Stuttgart: Konrad Theiss Verlag |
| *AK* | *Archäologisches Korrespondenzblatt* | Mainz: von Zabern |
| *ALUB* | *Annales Littéraires de l'Université de Besançon* | Besançon: Université de Besançon |
| *AmAnt* | *American Antiquity* | Washington DC: Society for American Archaeology |
| *AmAnthro* | *American Anthropologist* | Washington DC: American Anthropological Association |
| *AMIIN* | *Atti e Memorie dell'Istituto Italiano di Numismatica* | Rome: Istituto Italiano di Numismatica |
| *AmNat* | *The American Naturalist* | Chicago: University of Chicago |
| *AN* | *Antiquités Nationales* | Saint-Germain-en-Laye: Musée des Antiquités Nationales |
| *ANB* | *Archäologische Nachrichten aus Baden* | Freiburg i Br.: Förderkreis für die Ur- und Frühgeschichtliche Forschung in Baden |
| *ANSMN* | *American Numismatic Society Museum Notes* | New York: American Numismatic Society |
| *AntCl* | *L'Antiquité Classique* | Brussels: L'Antiquité Classique |
| *AntJ* | *Antiquaries Journal* | London: Society of Antiquaries of London |
| *ANRW* | H. Temporini & W. Haase (ed) *Aufstieg und Niedergang der Römischen Welt* | Berlin: Walter de Gruyter |
| *APA* | *Acta Praehistorica et Archaeologica* | Berlin : Bruno Hessling Verlag |
| *Apulum* | *Apulum. Acta Musei Apulensis* | Alba Iulia: Muzeul de Istorie Alba Iulia |
| *Arch* | *Archaeologia* | London: Society of Antiquaries of London |
| *Archaeometry* | *Archaeometry* | Oxford: Wiley-Blackwell |
| *Archaeonautica* | *Archaeonautica* | Paris: CNRS |
| *Archaeo-Physika* | *Archaeo-Physika* | Bonn: Rheinisches Landesmuseum |

| *Abbreviation* | *Title* | *Publisher* |
|---|---|---|
| *Archéologia* | *Archéologia. Trésors des âges* | Dijon: Archéologia |
| *Archéologie* | *Archéologie* | Brussels: Centre National de Recherches Archéologiques en Belgique |
| *ArchPol* | *Archeologia Polski* | Warsaw: Instytut Historii Kultury Materialnej (Polska Akademia Nauk) |
| *AR-P* | *Archäologie in Rheinland-Pfalz* | Mainz: Verlag Philipp von Zabern |
| *Aquitania* | *Aquitania* | Bordeaux: Presses Universitaires de Bordeaux |
| *AS* | *Archäologie der Schweiz* | Basel: Schweizerische Gesellschaft fur Ur- und Fruhgeschichte |
| *ASA* | *Anzeiger für Schweizerische Altertumskunde* | Zürich: Schweizerischen Landesmuseum |
| *ASAHFNivelles* | *Annales de la Société d'Archéologie, d'Histoire et de Folklore de Nivelles et du Brabant Wallon* | Brussels: Musée de Nivelles |
| *ASFNA* | *Annuaire de la Société Française de Numismatique et d'Archéologie* | Paris: Société Française de Numismatique et d'Archéologie |
| *ASHAL* | *Annuaire de la Société d'Histoire et Archéologie de la Lorraine* | Metz: Société d'Histoire et Archéologie de la Lorraine |
| *ASR* | *American Sociological Review* | Washington DC: American Sociological Association |
| *Athenaeum* | *Athenaeum. Studi periodici di letteratura e storia dell'antichità* | Pavia: Università di Pavia |
| *AVNassau* | *Annalen. Verein für Nassauische Altertumskunde* | Wiesbaden: Verein für Nassauische Altertumskunde und Geschichtsforschung |
| *AYork* | *The Archaeology of York* | York: York Archaeological Trust |
| *BACTH* | *Bulletin Archéologique du Comité des Travaux Historiques et Scientifiques* | Paris: Editions du Comité des Travaux Historiques et Scientifiques |
| *BAL* | *Bulletin des Antiquités Luxembourgeoises.* | Luxembourg: Société des Antiquités Nationales |
| BAR | *British Archaeological Reports* | Oxford: Archaeopress |
| *BAVexin* | *Bulletin Archéologique du Vexin Français* | Guirey-en-Vexin : Centre de Recherches Archéologiques du Vexin Français |
| *BBB* | *Bericht der Bayerischen Bodendenkmalpfege* | Munich: Selbstverlag des Bayerischen Landesamts für Denkmalpflege |
| *BBCS* | *Bulletin of the Board of Celtic Studies* | Cardiff: University of Wales Press |
| *BCAAmphora* | *Bulletin du Club Archéologique Amphora* | Braine-l'Alleud: Club Archéologique Amphora |
| *BCALezoux* | *Bulletin du Comité Archéologique de Lezoux* | Lezoux: Comité Archéologique de Lezoux |
| *BCEN* | *Bulletin Trimestriel du Cercle d'Études Numismatiques* | Brussels: Cercle d'Études Numismatiques |
| *BedsAJ* | *Bedfordshire Archaeological Journal* | Luton: Bedfordshire Archaeological Council |
| *BerksAJ* | *Berkshire Archaeological Journal* | Reading: Berkshire Archaeological Society |
| *BIAL* | *Institute of Archaeology, University of London. Bulletin* | London: Institute of Archaeology |
| *BIALiege* | *Bulletin de l'Institut Archéologique Liégeois* | Liège: Institut Archéologique Liégeois |
| *BIO* | *Das Bayerische Inn-Oberland* | Rosenheim: Verlag des Historischen Vereins Rosenheim und Umgebung |
| *BJ* | *Bonner Jahrbucher* | Cologne: Rheinland Verlag |
| *BNJ* | *British Numismatic Journal* | London: British Numismatic Society |
| *BRGK* | *Bericht der Römisch-Germanischen Kommission* | Frankfurt: Römisch-Germanische Kommission des Deutschen Archäologischen Instituts |
| *Brit* | *Britannia* | London: Society for the Promotion of Roman Studies |

| *Abbreviation* | *Title* | *Publisher* |
|---|---|---|
| *BROB* | *Berichten van de Rijksdienst voor het Oudheidkundig Bodemonderzoek* | Amersfoort: Rijksdienst voor het Oudheidkundig Bodemonderzoek (Rijksdienst voor het Cultureel Erfgoed since 2009) |
| *BSAC* | *Bulletin de la Société Archéologique Champenoise* | Reims: Société Archéologique Champenoise |
| *BSAO* | *Bulletin de la Société des Antiquaires de l'Ouest.* | Poitiers: Société des Antiquaires de l'Ouest |
| *BSAP* | *Bulletin Trimestriel de la Société des Antiquaires de Picardie* | Amiens: Société des Antiquaires de Picardie. |
| *BSDSaarland* | *Bericht der Staatlichen Denkmalpflege im Saarland* | Saarbrücken: Staatliches Konservatoramt |
| *BSFN* | *Bulletin de la Société Française de Numismatique* | Paris: Société Française de Numismatique |
| *BSHAVichy* | *Bulletin de la Société d'Histoire et d'Archéologie de Vichy et des Environs* | Vichy: Société d'Histoire et d'Archéologie de Vichy et des Environs |
| *BV* | *Bayerische Vorgeschichtsblätter* | Munich: C. H. Beck and Kommission für Bayerische Landesgeschichte |
| *BW* | *Bodenaltertümer Westfalens* | Münster: Aschendorff/Mainz: von Zabern |
| *CAAAH* | *Cahiers Alsaciens d'Archéologie, d'Art et d'Histoire* | Strasbourg: Société pour la Conservation des Monuments Historiques d'Alsace |
| *Caesarodunum* | *Caesarodunum* | Limoges: Presses Universitaires de Limoges |
| *CAP* | *Cahiers Archéologiques de Picardie* | Amiens: Société des Antiquaires de Picardie |
| *CCALezoux* | *Cahiers du Centre Archéologique de Lezoux* | Lezoux: Centre Archéologique de Lezoux |
| *CurrArch* | *Current Archaeology* | London: Current Publishing Ltd |
| *CCM* | *Cahiers de Civilisation Médiévale* | Poitiers: Université de Poitiers, Centre d'Études Supérieures de Civilisation Médiévale |
| *Celticum* | *Celticum* | Rennes: Ogam-Celticum, Amis de la Tradition Celtique |
| *CH* | *Coin Hoards* | London: Royal Numismatic Society |
| *CHRB* | *Coin Hoards from Roman Britain* | London: Royal Numismatic Society and British Museum |
| *CIL* | *Corpus Inscriptionum Latinarum,* | Berlin: G. Reimer Verlag |
| *CJ* | *Carnuntum Jahrbuch* | Vienna: Verlag der Österreichischen Akademie der Wissenschaften |
| *CL* | *Les Cahiers Lorrains* | Metz: Société d'Histoire et d'Archéologie de la Lorraine |
| *CLPA* | *Cahiers Ligures de Préhistoire et d'Archéologie* | Bordighera: Institut International d'Études Ligures |
| *CNSS* | *Actes du [number] Congrès Nationale des Sociétés Savantes* | Paris: Editions du Comité des Travaux Historiques et Scientifiques |
| *CollLatomus* | *Collection Latomus* | Brussels: Société d'Études Latines de Bruxelles - Latomus |
| *CRAI* | *Comptes Rendus des Séances de l'Académie des Inscriptions et Belles-Lettres* | Paris: Académie des Inscriptions et Belles-Lettres |
| DAF | *Documents d'Archéologie Française* | Paris: Editions de la Maison des Sciences de l'Homme |
| *DCRAA* | *Les Dossiers du Centre Régional Archéologique d'Alet* | Saint-Malo: Centre Régional Archéologique d'Alet |
| *DerbAJ* | *Derbyshire Archaeological Journal* | Derby: Derbyshire Archaeological Society |
| *Der Limes* | *Der Limes* | Bad Homburg: Deutsche Limeskommission |
| *DHA* | *Dialogues d'Histoire Ancienne* | Paris: Les Belles Lettres/CNRS |

| ***Abbreviation*** | ***Title*** | ***Publisher*** |
|---|---|---|
| *DialArch* | *Dialoghi di Archeologia* | Milan: Il Saggiatore di Alberto Mondadori Editore |
| *Digressus* | *Digressus* (online journal www.digressus.org ) | Birmingham & Nottingham: Departments of Classics, Universities of Birmingham and Nottingham |
| *DossArch* | *Les Dossiers de l'Archéologie* | Dijon: Archéologia |
| *DurhamAJ* | *Durham Archaeological Journal* | Durham: Architectural and Archaeological Society of Durham and Northumberland |
| *EAAR* | *East Anglian Archaeology Report* | Oxford: Oxbow Books and East Anglian Archaeology Editorial Board |
| *EAH* | *Essex Archaeology and History* | Chelmsford: Essex Archaeological Society |
| *FABT* | *Funde und Ausgrabungen im Bezirk Trier* | Trier: Rheinisches Landesmuseum |
| *FB-W* | *Fundberichte aus Baden-Württemberg* | Stuttgart: Konrad Theiss Verlag |
| *FH* | *Fundberichte aus Hessen* | Bonn: Rudolf Habelt |
| *Figlina* | *Figlina. Documents du Laboratoire de Céramologie de Lyon* | Lyon: Société Française d'Étude de la Céramique Antique en Gaule |
| *FMRD* | *Die Fundmünzen der Römischen Zeit in Deutschland* | Berlin: Verlag Gebrüder Mann |
| *FÖ* | *Fundberichte aus Österreich* | Horn: Verlag Berger |
| *Forum* | *Forum* | Paris: Touring Club de France |
| *FS* | *Fundberichte aus Schwaben* | Stuttgart: Konrad Theiss Verlag |
| *Gallia* | *Gallia. Fouilles et monuments archéologiques en France métropolitaine* | Paris: CNRS |
| *Gallia Supp* | *Gallia Supplément* | Paris: CNRS |
| *Germ* | *Germania. Anzeiger der Römisch-Germanischen Kommission des Deutschen Archäologischen Instituts* | Berlin: Deutsches Archäologisches Institut |
| *GlasgowAJ* | *Glasgow Archaeological Journal* | Glasgow: Glasgow Archaeological Society |
| *GRBS* | *Greek, Roman and Byzantine Studies* | Durham, NC: Duke University |
| *Gymnasium* | *Gymnasium. Zeitschrift für Kultur der Antike und Humanistische Bildung* | Heidelberg: Universitätsverlag Winter |
| *Helinium* | *Helinium* | Wetteren: Universa |
| *HelvArch* | *Helvetia Archaeologica* | Basel: Schweizerische Gesellschaft für Ur- und Frühgeschichte |
| *Hémecht* | *Hémecht. Zeitschrift für Luxemburger Geschichte = Revue d'Histoire Luxembourgeoise* | Luxemburg: Sankt Paulus-Druckerei |
| *HertsArch* | *Hertfordshire Archaeology* | St Albans: Hertfordshire Archaeology Editorial Committee |
| *IEEE Trans SMC* | *Institute of Electrical and Electronics Engineers Transactions on Systems, Man and Cybernetics* | New York: Institute of Electrical and Electronics Engineers |
| *IJNAUE* | *International Journal of Nautical Archaeology and Underwater Exploration* | Oxford: Blackwell and Nautical Archaeology Society |
| *IntArch* | *Internet Archaeology* (online journal http:// intarch.ac.uk ) | York: Council for British Archaeology |
| *JAA* | *Journal of Anthropological Archaeology* | Amsterdam: Elsevier |
| *JAK* | *Jahresberichte aus Augst und Kaiseraugst* | Liestal: Amt für Museen und Archäologie des Kantons Basel-Landschaft |
| *JAN* | *Journal of Archaeological Numismatics* | Brussels: European Centre for Numismatic Studies |
| *JAS* | *Journal of Archaeological Science* | London: Academic Press/Elsevier |

| ***Abbreviation*** | ***Title*** | ***Publisher*** |
|---|---|---|
| *JASP* | *Journal of Abnormal and Social Psychology* | Washington DC: American Psychological Association |
| *JBAA* | *Journal of the British Archaeological Association* | London: British Archaeological Association |
| *JBB* | *Jahresbericht der Bayerischen Bodendenkmalpflege* | Munich: Landesamt für Denkmalpflege |
| *JCAS* | *Journal of the Chester Archaeological Society* | Chester: Chester Archaeological Society |
| *JHVL* | *Jahrbuch des Historischen Vereins für das Fürstentum Liechtenstein* | Vaduz: Historischer Verein für das Fürstentum Liechtenstein |
| *JMP* | *Jaarboek voor Munt- en Penningkunde* | Amsterdam: Koninklijk Nederlands Genootschap voor Munt- en Penningkunde |
| *JOM* | *Jahrbuch des Oberösterreichischen Musealvereines* | Linz: Oberösterreichischer Musealverein |
| *JRA* | *Journal of Roman Archaeology* | Portsmouth, RI: Journal of Roman Archaeology |
| *JRGZM* | *Jahrbuch des Römisch-Germanischen Zentralmuseums Mainz* | Mainz: Römisch-Germanische Zentralmuseum |
| *JRPS* | *Journal of Roman Pottery Studies* | Oxford: Oxbow Books and Study Group for Romano-British Pottery |
| *JRS* | *Journal of Roman Studies* | London: Society for the Promotion of Roman Studies |
| *JSGU* | *Jahrbuch der Schweizerischen Gesellschaft für Urgeschichte* | Basel: Schweizerische Gesellschaft für Urgeschichte |
| *JSGUF* | *Jahrbuch der Schweizerischen Gesellschaft für Ur- und Frühgeschichte* | Basel: Schweizerische Gesellschaft für Ur- und Frühgeschichte (Archäologie Schweiz since 2006) |
| *JVT* | *Jaarverslag van de Vereeniging voor Terpenonderzoek* | Groningen: J. B. Wolters |
| *Klio* | *Klio. Beiträge zur Alten Geschichte* | Berlin: Akademie Verlag |
| *Ktèma* | *Ktèma. Civilisations de l'Orient, de la Grèce et de Rome Antiques* | Strasbourg: Université de Strasbourg, Centre de Recherche sur le Proche-Orient et la Grèce Antiques |
| *LAAA* | *Liverpool Annals of Archaeology and Anthropology* | Liverpool: University of Liverpool |
| *Latomus* | *Latomus. Revue d'Études Latines* | Brussels: Société d'Études Latines de Bruxelles - Latomus |
| *Laverna* | *Laverna. Beiträge zur Wirtschafts- und Sozialgeschichte der Alten Welt* | St. Katharinen: Scripta Mercaturae Verlag |
| *LF* | *Limesforschungen. Studien zur Organisation der römischen Reichsgrenze an Rhein und Donau* | Darmstadt: von Zabern |
| *LHA* | *Lincolnshire History and Archaeology* | Lincoln: Society for Lincolnshire History and Archaeology |
| *LondArch* | *London Archaeologist* | Tonbridge: London Archaeologist Association |
| *Man* | *Man. Journal of the Royal Anthropological Institute* | London: Royal Anthropological Institute |
| *MANMetz* | *Mémoires de l'Académie Nationale de Metz* | Metz: Académie Nationale de Metz |
| *MAW* | *Mitteilungen der Altertumskommission für Westfalen* | Münster: Altertumskommission für Westfalen |
| *MBAH* | *Münstersche Beiträge zur Antiken Handelsgeschichte.* | St. Katharinen: Scripta Mercaturae Verlag |
| MF | microfiche | |
| *MHJ* | *The Medieval History Journal* | New Delhi: Sage Publications |

| ***Abbreviation*** | ***Title*** | ***Publisher*** |
|---|---|---|
| *MHVP* | *Mitteilungen des Historisches Vereins der Pfalz* | Speyer: Verlag des Historischen Vereins der Pfalz |
| *Mnemosyne* | *Mnemosyne. Bibliotheca Classica Batava* | Leiden: Brill |
| *MSNAF* | *Mémoires de la Société Nationale des Antiquaires de France* | Paris: Société Nationale des Antiquaires de France |
| *MZ* | *Mainzer Zeitschrift* | Mainz: von Zabern |
| *NA* | *Nassauische Annalen* | Wiesbaden: Verlag des Vereins für Nassauische Altertumskunde und Geschichtsforschung |
| *NC* | *Numismatic Chronicle* | London: Royal Numismatic Society |
| *NhantsArch* | *Northamptonshire Archaeology* | Northampton: Northamptonshire Archaeological Society |
| *NKG* | *Neues Kunst- und Gewerbblatt* | Munich: Polytechnischer Verein für das Königreich Bayern |
| *NLB-W* | *Nachrichtenblatt der Landesdenkmalpflege Baden-Württemberg* | Esslingen: Landesamt für Denkmalpflege im Regierungspräsidium Stuttgart. |
| *NorfArch* | *Norfolk Archaeology* | Norwich: Norfolk and Norwich Archaeological Society |
| *Numismatika* | *Numismatika. Vjesnik Numismatičkog društva u Zagrebu* | Zagreb: Tisak Zaklade tiskare narodnih novina |
| *OAVG* | *Oberbayerisches Archiv für Vaterländische Geschichte* | Munich: Historischer Verein von Oberbayern |
| *Ogam* | *Ogam* | Rennes: Ogam-Celticum, Amis de la Tradition Celtique |
| *OJA* | *Oxford Journal of Archaeology* | Oxford: Blackwell |
| *OM* | *Oudheidkundige Mededeelingen van het Rijksmuseum van Oudheden te Leiden* | Leiden: Rijksmuseum van Oudheden |
| *Oxo* | *Oxoniensia* | Oxford: Oxfordshire Architectural and Historical Society |
| *Pallas* | *Pallas. Revue d'Études Antiques.* | Toulouse: Presses Universitaires du Mirail |
| *PATAR* | *Portable Antiquities & Treasure Annual Report* | London: Dept for Culture, Media and Sport |
| *PCAS* | *Proceedings of the Cambridge Antiquarian Society* | Cambridge: Cambridge Antiquarian Society |
| *PDAS* | *Proceedings of the Devon Archaeological Society* | Exeter: Devon Archaeological Society |
| *PDNHAS* | *Proceedings of the Dorset Natural History and Archaeology Society* | Dorchester: Dorset Natural History and Archaeology Society |
| *PHFCAS* | *Proceedings of the Hampshire Field Club and Archaeological Society* | Winchester: Hampshire Field Club and Archaeological Society |
| *Phys* | *La Physiophile* | Montceau-les-Mines: La Physiophile |
| *PLPLS* | *Proceedings of the Leeds Philosophical and Literary Society* | Leeds: Leeds Philosophical and Literary Society |
| *PPS* | *Proceedings of the Prehistoric Society* | London: The Prehistoric Society |
| *PSAL* | *Proceedings of the Society of Antiquaries of London* | London: Society of Antiquaries of London |
| *PSAS* | *Proceedings of the Society of Antiquaries of Scotland* | Edinburgh: Society of Antiquaries of Scotland |
| *PSIA* | *Proceedings of the Suffolk Institute of Archaeology* | Bury St. Edmunds: Suffolk Institute of Archaeology and Natural History |
| *PUBSS* | *Proceedings of the University of Bristol Spelaeological Society* | Bristol: University of Bristol Spelaeological Society |
| *RA* | *Revue Archéologique* | Paris: Presses Universitaires de France |

| *Abbreviation* | *Title* | *Publisher* |
|---|---|---|
| *RAC* | *Revue Archéologique du Centre de la France* | Vichy: Revue Archéologique du Centre de la France |
| *RAECE* | *Revue Archéologique de l'Est et du Centre-Est* | Dijon: CNRS |
| *RAL* | *Revue Archéologique du Loiret* | Neuville-aux-Bois: Fédération archéologique du Loiret |
| *RAM* | *Rapportage Archeologische Monumentenzorg* | Amersfoort: Rijksdienst voor het Cultureel Erfgoed |
| *RAN* | *Revue Archéologique de Narbonnaise* | Montpellier: Service des Publications de l'Université Paul Valéry |
| *RAP* | *Revue Archéologique de Picardie* | Amiens: Société des Antiquités Historiques de Picardie |
| *RCRFA* | *Rei Cretariae Romanae Fautorum Acta* | Frankfurt [and other locations]: Rei Cretariae Romanae Fautores |
| *REA* | *Revue des Études Anciennes* | Pessac: Université Michel de Montaigne, Maison de l'Archéologie. |
| *RecBucks* | *Records of Buckinghamshire* | Aylesbury: Buckinghamshire Archaeological Society |
| *Relicta* | *Relicta. Archeologie, Monumenten- en Landschapsonderzoek in Vlaanderen* | Brussels: Vlaams Instituut voor het Onroerend Erfgoed |
| *RGévaudan* | *Revue du Gévaudan, des Causses et des Cévennes* | Mende: Société Des Lettres, Sciences et Arts de la Lozère |
| *RhAusgr* | *Rheinische Ausgrabungen* | Cologne: Rheinland Verlag |
| *Rhodania* | *Rhodania* | Vienne: Rhodania: Association des Préhistoriens, des Archéologues Classiques et des Numismates du Bassin du Rhône |
| *RIN* | *Rivista Italiana di Numismatica e Scienze affini* | Milan: Società Numismatica Italiana. |
| *RK* | *Römisch-germanisches Korrespondenzblatt* | Trier: J. Lintz |
| *RNord* | *Revue du Nord* | Villeneuve-d'Ascq: Université Charles-de-Gaulle – Lille III |
| *RNum* | *Revue Numismatique* | Paris: Société Française de Numismatique |
| *RRouergue* | *Revue du Rouergue* | Rodez: P. Carrière |
| *RSP* | *Rivista di Studi Pomeiani* | Rome: « L'Erma » di Bretschneider |
| *SA* | *Les Saisons d'Alsace* | Strasbourg: La Nuée bleue |
| *SANH* | *Somerset Archaeology and Natural History* | Taunton: Somerset Archaeological and Natural History Society |
| *SFECAG* | *Société Française d'Étude de la Céramique Antique en Gaule, Actes du Congrès de [place]* | Marseille: Société Française d'Étude de la Céramique Antique en Gaule |
| SFMA | *Studien zu Fundmünzen der Antike* | Mainz: von Zabern and Akademie der Wissenschaften und der Literatur |
| *SGRPNews* | *Study Group for Roman Pottery Newsletter* | Wisbech: Study Group for Roman Pottery |
| *SHR* | *Scottish Historical Review* | Edinburgh: Edinburgh University Press |
| *Sites* | *Revue Archéologique Sites* | Avignon: La Revue Archéologique Sites |
| *SJ* | *Saalburg Jahrbuch* | Mainz: von Zabern |
| *SM* | *Schweizer Münzblätter* | Lausanne: Schweizerische Numismatische Gesellschaft |
| *SNUQ* | *Specimina nova dissertationum ex Instituto Historico Universitatis Quinqueecclesiensis de Iano Pannonio nominatae* | Pécs: Janus Pannonius Tudományegyetem, Történettudományi Tanszékének Évkönyve |
| *SyAC* | *Surrey Archaeological Collections* | Guildford: Surrey Archaeological Society |
| *SxAC* | *Sussex Archaeological Collections* | Lewes: Sussex Archaeological Society |
| *TAR* | *Treasure Annual Revue* | London: Dept for Culture, Media and Sport |
| *TBGAS* | *Transactions of the Bristol and Gloucestershire Archaeological Society* | Gloucester/Bristol: Bristol and Gloucestershire Archaeological Society |
| *TBWAS* | *Transactions of the Birmingham and Warwickshire Archaeological Society* | Birmingham: Birmingham and Warwickshire Archaeological Society. |

| *Abbreviation* | *Title* | *Publisher* |
|---|---|---|
| *TCWAAS* | *Transactions of the Cumberland and Westmorland Antiquarian and Archaeological Society* | Kendal/Carlisle: Cumberland and Westmorland Antiquarian and Archaeological Society |
| *TDGNHAS* | *Transactions of the Dumfriesshire and Galloway Natural History and Antiquarian Society* | Dumfries: Dumfriesshire and Galloway Natural History and Antiquarian Society Council |
| *TEAS* | *Transactions of the Essex Archaeological Society* | Chelmsford: Essex Archaeological Society |
| *TLAHS* | *Transactions of the Leicestershire Archaeological and Historical Society* | Leicester: Leicestershire Archaeological and Historical Society |
| *TLAS* | *Transactions of the Leicestershire Archaeological Society* | Leicester: Leicestershire Archaeological Society |
| *TLCAS* | *Transactions of the Lancashire and Cheshire Antiquarian Society* | Manchester: Lancashire and Cheshire Antiquarian Society |
| *TLMAS* | *Transactions of the London and Middlesex Archaeology Society* | London: London and Middlesex Archaeology Society |
| *TM* | *Trésors Monétaires* | Paris: Bibliothèque Nationale de France |
| *TSAS* | *Transactions of the Shropshire Archaeological Society* | Shrewsbury: Shropshire Archaeological Society |
| *TStAHAAS* | *Transactions of the St Albans and Hertfordshire Architectural and Archaeological Society* | St Albans: St Albans and Hertfordshire Architectural and Archaeological Society |
| *TTS* | *Transactions of the Thoroton Society of Nottinghamshire* | Nottingham: Thoroton Society of Nottinghamshire |
| *TZ* | *Trierer Zeitschrift für Geschichte und Kunst des Trierer Landes und seiner Nachbargebiete.* | Trier: Rheinisches Landesmuseum |
| *US* | *Ur-Schweiz* | Basel: Schweizerische Gesellschaft für Urgeschichte |
| *WA* | *World Archaeology* | London: Routledge |
| *WANHM* | *Wiltshire Archaeological and Natural History Magazine* | Devizes: Wiltshire Archaeological and Natural History Society |
| *WAM* | *Wiltshire Archaeological Magazine* | Devizes: Wiltshire Archaeological and Natural History Society |
| *YAJ* | *Yorkshire Archaeological Journal* | Leeds: Yorkshire Archaeological Society |
| *ZPE* | *Zeitschrift für Papyrologie und Epigraphik* | Bonn: Habelt |
| *ZSAK* | *Zeitschrift für Schweizerische Archäologie und Kunstgeschichte* | Zürich: Schwegler |

# Bibliography


Abauzit, P. & Vertet, H. 1976: Africanus et les potiers de St Bonnet, Yzeure (Allier): un mythe? *RAC* 15, 113-22

Abbott, R. 1956: Roman discoveries at Goadby Marwood. *TLAHS* 32, 17-35

Abdy, R. A. 1999a: Shoreham area, West Sussex. *TAR* 2, 118

----- 1999b: Tinwell, Rutland. *TAR* 2, 118-9

----- 2002a: *Romano-British Coin Hoards*, Princes Risborough

----- 2002b: Long Whatton, Leicestershire. *CHRB* 11, 97-101

----- 2002c: Prestwood A, Buckinghamshire. *CHRB* 11, 163-8

----- 2003: Worn *sestertii* in Roman Britain and the Longhorsley hoard. *NC* 163, 137-46

----- 2004: Letwell, South Yorkshire: twenty-nine Roman copper-alloy *sestertii* and three base-silver *radiates*. *TAR* 7, 178

----- 2006: Alrewas and Fradley, Staffordshire: 38 Roman copper-alloy sestertii and associated pottery. *TAR* 8, 190-1

-----, Brunning, R. A. & Webster, C. J. 2001: The discovery of a Roman villa at Shapwick and its Severan coin hoard of 9238 silver *denarii*. *JRA* 14, 358-72

----- & Chaitow, E. 2002: South Wonston, Hampshire. *CHRB* 11, 129-31

-----, Johns, C. & Hill, J. D. 2002: Osgodby, Lincolnshire. *CHRB* 11, 93-6

----- & Minnitt, S. 2002: Shapwick villa, Somerset. *CHRB* 11, 169-233

-----, Read, C. & Rigby, V. 2002: Curridge, Berkshire. *CHRB* 11, 147-58

Abramson, P. & Fossick, M. R. 1999: The major trenches: excavations of the *vicus*, 1974 and 1980-82. In P. Abramson *et al.*, *Roman Castleford. Excavations 1974-85. Volume II, the structural and environmental evidence,* Leeds, 126-51

Ainsworth, C. & Ratcliffe-Densham, H. 1974: Spectroscopy and a Roman cremation from Sompting, Sussex. *Brit* 5, 310-6

Aitken, G. & Aitken, N. 1982: Excavations on the Library site, Colliton Park, Dorchester, 1961-3. *PDNHAS* 104, 93-126

Alföldi, A. 1939: The invasions of peoples from the Rhine to the Black Sea. In S. Cook *et al.* (ed), *Cambridge Ancient History XII*, Cambridge, chap. 5

Alföldi, M. R. *et al.* 1962: *FMRD I, vii, Schwaben*, Berlin

Alföldy, G. 1974: The crisis of the third century as seen by contemporaries. *GRBS* 15, 89-111

Allan, J. 1938: Roman coins from Poole harbour. *NC* ser 5, 18, 300

Allen, D. F. 1947: Coins. In Cotton 1947, 147-9

Amandry, M. 1992: Le dépôt monétaire de la propriété Florencia à Noyon (Oise). *RAP* 1992, 1/2, 93-107

----- 1995: Le dépôt monétaire de Pécy (Seine-et-Marne): 1133 sesterces et sous-multiples de la fin du règne de Commode. *TM* 15, 23-33

-----, Delestrée, L.-P., Hollard, D., Metzger, C. 1987: Le trésor de Mons-Boubert (Somme). *TM* 9, 31-45

----- & Hollard, D. 1997: Le trésor be bronzes romains de Plaisians (Drôme). *TM* 16, 21-3

----- & ----- 2006: Le trésor de Bourg-Blanc 1989 (Finistère). *TM* 22, 119-32

-----, Rigault, P. & Trombetta, P. J. 1985: Le trésor monétaire de l'Ecluse de Creil (commune de Saint-Maximin, Oise). *RAP* 1985, 1/2, 65-111

Ambrosoli, S. 1897: Il ripostiglio di San Martino del Pizzolano. *RIN* 10, 507-11

Ammann, S., Fünfschilling, S., Waddington, S., Peter, M. 2009: Ensembles céramiques de l'antiquité tardive de la fouille *DH Implenia* à Kaiseraugst – rapport préliminaire. *SFECAG Colmar, 2009,* 215-30

Anderson, A. C. & Anderson, A. S. 1981: *Roman Pottery Research in Britain and North-West Europe,* Oxford

André, P. 2003: Le trésor monétaire du Mane Vechen en Plouhinec (Morbihan), 22,000 monnaies du IIIème siècle. *DCRAA* 31, 11-22

Anon 1854: Roman antiquities, Fifeshire. *PSAS* 1, 60-6

Antignac, J.-L. 1977: La fosse-dépotoir du 'Chambon' à Eyrein (Corrèze). *RAC* 16, 147-64, 339-56

ApSimon, A. M. 1965: The Roman temple on Brean Down, Somerset. *PUBSS* 10, 195-258

Archbold, J. 1858: Roman remains found at Adderstone, nr. Bamburgh, Northumberland. *AAel* ser 2, 2, 14-6

Archibald, M. 1974: The coins. In Evans 1974, 121-4

Argyropoulos, V. 1995: A characterization of the compositional variations of Roman samian pottery manufactured at the Lezoux production centre. *Archaeometry* 37/2, 271-85

Armand-Calliat, L. 1956: Un trésor monetaire romaine découvert à Château-Renaud (Sa-et-L). *RAECE* 7, 179-85

----- & Viallefond, G. 1958: Amphores et monnaies romaines trouvées en 1956 à Autun. *RAECE* 9, 275-8

Arnold, D. 1985: *Ceramic Theory and Cultural Process*, Cambridge

Aronson, E. 1958: The need for achievement as measured by graphic expression. In J. Atkinson (ed), *Motives in Fantasy, Action and Society*, Princeton

Arthur, P. A. & Whitehouse, K. 1978: Report on excavations at Fulham Palace Moat, 1972-1973. *TLMAS* 29, 45-72

Askew, G. 1937: Notes on two hoards of Roman coins from Carrawburgh, North. *NC* ser 5, 17, 144-7

Atkinson, D. 1914: A hoard of samian ware from Pompeii. *JRS* 4, 27-64

----- 1937: Roman pottery from Caistor-next-Norwich. *NorfArch* 26, 197-230

----- 1942: *Report on Excavations at Wroxeter in the County of Salop 1923-7*, Oxford
Aubert, J.-J. 1994: *Business Managers in Ancient Rome. A social and economic study of Institores, 200 B.C.-A.D. 250,* Leiden
Aubin, G. 1989: Le trésor de Courcité (Mayenne): antoniniani et imitations de Gordien III à Victorien. *TM* 11, 55-77
----- & Galliou, P. 1979: L'enfouissement de deniers de Kervian-en-Camaret. *TM* 1, 17-43
Audron, A. 1997: Le dépôt monétaire de Seyssel (Haute-Savoie): 188 sesterces et sous-multiples de la fin du règne de Marc Aurèle. *TM* 16, 15-20
Baatz, D. 1976: Das Kastell Munningen im Nördlinger Ries. *SJ* 33, 11-62
----- 1978: Das Badegebäude des Limeskastells Walldürn (Odenwaldkreis). *SJ* 35, 61-107
Bagnall-Oakeley, M. E. 1882: Roman coins found in the Forest of Dean, Gloucs. *NC* ser 3, 2, 52-6
Baker, T. H. 1894: Find of Roman coins at Mere cemetery in 1856. *WANHM* 27, 176-7
Bales, P. G. 1943: Doncaster, two Roman hoards. *YAJ* 35, 84-95
Balsan, L. 1950: Reprise des fouilles à La Graufesenque (Condatomagos), campagne 1950. *Gallia* 8, 1-13
----- 1954: Les fouilles de La Graufesenque. Campagnes 1953, 1954. *RRouergue* 8, 44-51, 399-404
----- 1970: Observations sur quelques estampilles de potiers de La Graufesenque. *RAC* 9, 99-109
Barclay, C. 1997: Drax, North Yorkshire. *CHRB* 10, 258-63
Barfield, L. H. 1968: Ein Burgus bei Froitzheim, Kr. Düren. *RhAusgr* 3, 9-120
Barker, P. 1977: *Techniques of Archaeological Excavation*, London
Barry, H. 1957: Relationships between child training and the pictorial arts. *JASP* 54, 380-3
Bartoli, D., Bruschetti, P., Porten-Palange, P., Scarpellini-Testi, M., Zamarchi-Grassi, P. 1984: *M. Perennius Bargathes*, Rome
Bastien, P. 1965: Trouvaille de Muirancourt (Oise). *SM* 60, 137-42
----- 1967: *Le Monnayage de Bronze de Postume*, Wetteren
----- & Cothenet, A. 1975: La trouvaille de monnaies romaines de Tavers (Loiret). *BCEN* 12, 21-6
Bayard, D. 1980: La commercialisation de la céramique commune à Amiens du milieu du IIe à la fin du IIIe siècle après J.C. *CAP* 7, 147-209
Bazin, B. & Delage, R. 2005: Un lot de céramiques de la fin du Haut-Empire à Allonnes (Sarthe). *SFECAG Blois, 2005,* 649-53
Beck, J.-J. 1977: Problèmes économiques del'empire romain au 3[e] siècle, de l'époque des Sévères à Dioclétian. *BAL* 8, 159-76
Beckmann, B. 1973: Review of Huld-Zetsche 1972. *RCRFA* 14/15, 136-45
----- 1977: Neuere Ausgrabungen im römischen Limeskastell Miltenburg-Altstadt und im mittelalterlichen Walehausen. *JBB* 17/18, 62-131
Behrens, G. 1915: Beiträge zur römischen Keramik. *MZ* 10, 90-103
----- 1921: Eine römische Falschmünzerwerkstätte in Mainz-Kastell. *MZ* 15/16, 25-31
Bell, M. 1976: The excavation of an early Romano-British site and Pleistocene landforms at Newhaven, Sussex. *SxAC* 114, 218-305
----- 1977: Excavations at Bishopstone. *SxAC* 115, *passim*
Bemmann, H. 1981: Ein Model-Graffito des mittelgallischen Sigillata-Töpfers Sacirius aus Bonn. *BJ* 181, 393-4
----- 1985: Eine neue Ware des Virtus von La Madeleine. *SJ* 40/41, 5-27
Bémont, C. 1971: Notes sur C. CINO SENOVIRI. *Gallia* 29, 200-17
----- 1972: Signatures sur moules sigillées de la collection Plicque. *AN* 4, 63-82
----- 1973: A propos de Catussa. *Gallia* 31, 81-122
----- 1974: Un gobelet à décor moulé en sigillée claire B. *Gallia* 32, 83-105
----- 1975a: Décors sur sigillée dans le style de Paternus II: moules et gobelets Déch 68. *Gallia* 33, 171-202
----- 1975b: Cruche à décor sigillé du centre de la Gaule. *AN* 7, 64-7
----- 1977: Moules de gobelets ornés de la Gaule centrale au Musée des Antiquités Nationales. *Gallia Supp* 33
----- 1980: Styles et moules: essai de méthodologie. *RCRFA* 19/20, 5-24
----- 1981: Quelques aspects de l'imagerie mythologique sur la céramique gallo-romaine décorée de reliefs. In L. Kahil & C. Augé (ed.), *Mythologie gréco-romaine, Mythologies périphériques: études d'iconographie,* Paris, 37-40
----- 1996: Les comptes de potiers de La Graufesenque. *DossArch* 215, 122-7
-----, Blanc, N., Jacob, J.-P., Leredde, H. 1980: Décors sur céramique sigillée et classification automatique. *DossArch* 42, 80-2
-----, Duval, A., Gautier, J., Lahanier, C. 1982: Lezoux, La Graufesenque et le potier à la rosette. *Gallia* 40, 239-55
----- & Jacob, J.-P. 1986: (ed) *La Terre Sigillée Gallo-Romaine. Lieux de production du Haut-Empire: implantations, produits, relations,* Paris [DAF 6]
-----, Lutz, M., Duval, A., Gautier, J., Lahanier, C., Malfoy, J.-M. 1983: Lezoux, Chémery et le potier à la rosette. *RAECE* 34, 135-51
----- & Rogers, G. B. 1977: Quelques poinçons-matrices signés du nom de Libertus et leurs relations avec les décors de l'atelier. *AN* 9, 66-70
----- & ----- 1978: *Libertus* (ou *Liberti?*) I. Les premiers styles à estampilles. *Gallia* 36, 89-142
----- & ----- 1979: *Libertus* (ou *Liberti?*) II. Le style aux graffites. *Gallia* 37, 141-200
----- & ----- 1980: Un potier inconnu: P-1. Remarques sur la détermination des officines anonymes. *Gallia* 38, 169-96
Bennet, J. 1978: A further vessel by the Aldgate-Pulborough potter. *Brit* 9, 393-4

Bennett, C. M. 1962: Cox Green Roman villa. *BerksAJ* 60, 62-91

Benoit, F. 1961: L'épave du Grand Congloué à Marseille. *Gallia Supp* 14

Berdeaux-le Brazidec, M.-L. 2001: Le trésor de bronzes romaines de Germainville (Eure-et-Loir). *AN* 33, 171-88

Berke, S. 1988: Zum Export mittelgallischer und früher Rheinzaberner Terra Sigillata in das Barbaricum nördlich der mittleren Donau. *MBAH* 7.1, 46-61

Berland, L. & Lintz, G. 1975: Un puits gallo-romain comblé au IIIe siècle à Limoges. *RAC* 14, 15-30

Bernhard, H. 1979: Neue Grabungen im römischen und mittelalterlichen Speyer. *AK* 9, 101-13

----- 1981a: Zur Diskussion um die Chronologie Rheinzaberner Relieftöpfer. *Germ* 59, 79-93

----- 1981b: Untersuchungen im frührömischen Rheinzabern. *AK* 11, 127-37

----- 1985: Studien zur spätrömischen Terra Nigra zwischen Rhein, Main und Neckar. *SJ* 40/41, 34-120

----- 1990: Rheinzabern. In H. Cüppers (ed.), *Die R*ömer in Rheinland-Pfalz, Stuttgart, 532-9

Bertin, P. & Pilon, F. 2006: Reconnaissance et charactérisation des assemblages céramiques de la seconde moitié du IIIe siècle du quartier nord dit des *Grands Jardins* à Châteaubleau (Seine-et-Marne). *SFECAG Pézenas, 2006,* 365-79

Besly, E. M. 1981: Addington, near Croydon, hoard of antoniniani. *CHRB* 2, 3-6

----- 1984: The Aldbourne, Wilts., hoard. *CHRB* 4, 63-104

----- 1992: Bassaleg and Caerleon, Gwent. *CHRB* 9, 87-104

----- & Bland, R. 1983: *The Cunetio Treasure: Roman coinage of the third century AD*, London

Bet, P. 1985: Les sigillées moulées et à reliefs d'appliqué du Ive siècle à Lezoux. *SFECAG Reims, 1985*, 47-8

----- 1988: Groupes d'ateliers et potiers de Lezoux (Puy-de-Dôme) durant la période gallo-romaine. *SFECAG Orange, 1988,* 221-41

-----, Boudriot, G., Chappet, C. & Vallat, P. 1998: Un nouveau centre de production de céramique sigillée en Gaule, le site des Queyriaux Cournon d'Auvergne (Puy-de-Dôme). *SFECAG Istres, 1998*, 263-9

----- & Delage, R. 2000: Du nouveau sur le centre de production de céramique sigillée de Lubié (Allier): étude préliminaire du mobilier issu d'un sondage récent. *SFECAG Libourne, 2000*, 441-59

----- & ----- 2009: L'atelier de la Serve d'Ervier à Lezoux (Puy-de-Dôme). *SFECAG Colmar, 2009*, 453-79

----- & ----- 2010: *Instants furtifs du Haut-Empire romain à Lezoux: les sites du Parc d'activité intercommunal*, Bron [Inrap pamphlet]

-----, ----- & Murat, R. 2000: En Gaule centrale, le centre de production sigillée de Manglieu (Puy-de-Dôme). *SFECAG Libourne, 2000,* 511-14

----- & Delor, A. 2000: La typologie de la sigillée lisse de Lezoux et de la Gaule centrale. Révision décennale. *SFECAG Libourne, 2000,* 461-84

-----, Fenet, A. & Montineri, D. 1989: La typologie de la sigillée lisse de Lezoux, Ier-IIIe s. Considérations générales et formes inédites. *SFECAG Lezoux, 1989,* 37-54

----- & Gangloff, R. 1987: Les installations de potiers gallo-romains sur le site de la Z.A.C. de l'Enclos à Lezoux (Puy-de-Dôme). *SFECAG Caen, 1987,* 145-58

----- & Montineri, D. 1990: La sigillée lisse de Lezoux, typologie des formes du Haut-Empire. *Sites* 43, 5-13

----- & Vertet, H. 1980: Fouilles de sauvetage d'un habitat de la zone des ateliers du second siècle à Toulon-sur-Allier, au lieudit 'La Forêt' (Allier). In Vertet, Bet & Corrocher 1980, 73-87

----- & ----- 1986: Centre de production de Lezoux. In Bémont & Jacob 1986, 138-44

-----, Valaude, P. & Vertet, H. 1986: Courpière. In Bémont & Jacob 1986, 144-5

----- & Wittmann, A. 1995: La production de la céramique sigillée à Lezoux (Auvergne, France) durant le Bas-Empire. *RCRFA* 34, 205-20

Biddulph, E. 2012: Costing the (figured) earth: using samian to estimate funerary expenditure. In Bird (D) 2012, 295-304

----- 2013: The blind potter: the evolution of samian ware and its imitations. In Fulford & Durham 2013, 368-80

Biegert, S. 1999: *Römische Töpfereien in der Wetterau,* Frankfurt am Main

----- 2003: Chemische Analysen zu glatten Sigillata aus Heiligenberg und Ittenweiler. In Liesen & Brandl 2003, 7-28

Biehler, E. & François, M.-F. 1977: Une officine de céramique romaine découverte à Metz dans l'enceinte de la caserne De-Lattre-de-Tassigny. *CL* 4, 99-103

Binsfeld, W. 1972: Ein Münzschatz in Trier aus der Zeit des Postumus. *TZ* 35, 127-33

----- 1977: Töpferviertel. In *Führer zu vor- und frühgeschichtlichen Denkmälern 32, Trier I*, Mainz, 223-5

-----, Cüppers, H., Gollub, S. 1967: Jahresbericht 1962-5. *TZ* 30, 225-91

Bird, D. 2008: 'The rest to some faint meaning make pretence, but Shadwell never deviates into sense' (further speculation about the Shadwell 'tower'). In J. Clark *et al.* (ed), *Londinium and Beyond. Essays on Roman London and its hinterland for Harvey Sheldon,* York, 96-101

----- 2012: (ed) *Dating and Interpreting the Past in the Western Roman Empire. Essays in honour of Brenda Dickinson*, Oxford

Bird, J. 1973: Samian ware. In Coppack 1973, 78-81

----- 1974a: Decorated samian ware. In Hassall & Rhodes 1974, 34-7

----- 1974b: The samian ware. In Tatton-Brown 1974, 151-5

----- 1977a: The samian ware. In Green 1977, 58-63

----- 1977b: The samian pottery. In Bell 1977, 179-80

----- 1978a: Samian pottery. In Canham 1978, 78-81

----- 1978b: The samian. In Brodribb, Hands & Walker 1978, 40-8

----- 1984: The samian ware. In Philp 1984, 95-7
----- 1986: Samian wares. In Miller, Schofield & Rhodes 1986, 139-85
----- 1987: Two groups of late samian in Britain. *RCRFA* 25/6, 325-30
----- 1989: The samian ware. In Philp 1989, 67-74
----- 1993: 3rd-century samian ware in Britain. *JRPS* 6, 1-14
----- 1998: (ed) *Form and Fabric. Studies in Rome's material past in honour of B. R. Hartley,* Oxford
----- 2002: Samian wares. In Lakin 2002, 31-48
----- 2003: Samian studies, 1985-96: a review. *JRPS* 10, 117-24
----- 2011: The samian. In Douglas *et al.* 2011, 71-4, 173-83
----- 2012: Arena scenes with bulls on South Gaulish samian. In Bird (D) 2012, 135-48
----- 2013: Samian in religious and funerary contexts: a question of choice. In Fulford & Durham 2013, 326-39
----- & Dickinson, B. 2000: The sigillata. In Fulford & Timby 2000, 183-96
----- & Marsh, C. 1978a: Decorated samian. In Graham 1978, 482
----- & ----- 1978b: Decorated samian. In Dennis 1978, 333-7
----- & ----- 1981: The samian ware. In Philp 1981, 178-202
----- & Pengelly, H. 1983: The samian ware. In Brown & Woodfield 1983, 68-71
----- & Young, C. 1981: Migrant potters – the Oxford connection. In Anderson & Anderson 1981, 295-312
Birley, Angela 1962: The pottery. In Birley, E. 1962, 129-33
Birley, A. R. 1963: The coins. In Birley, R. 1963, 201
Birley, E. 1947a: Figured samian from Benwell, 1938. *AAel* ser 4, 25, 52-67
----- 1947b: The samian ware. pp. 70-72 in E. Birley & J. Gillam: The pottery from the Roman fort at Carzield. *TDGNHAS* ser 3, 24, 68-78
----- 1956: The samian ware. In Thompson 1956, 28
----- 1959: Excavations at Corstopitum, 1906-1958. *AAel* ser 4, 37, 1-31
----- 1962: Housesteads *vicus*, 1961. *AAel* ser 4, 40, 117-33
-----, Brewis, P. & Charlton, J. 1934: Report for 1933 of the North of England Excavation Committee. *AAel* ser 4, 11, 176-84
----- & Dodds, W. 1963: Other finds. In Birley, R. 1963, 201-7
----- & Simpson, G. 1957: Samian. In Murray-Threipland 1957, 33-5
Birley, R. E. 1963: Excavation of the Roman fortress at Carpow, Perthshire, 1961-2. *PSAS* 96, 184-207
Bishop, M. C. & Dore, J. N. 1988: *Corbridge. Excavations of the Roman fort and town, 1947-80,* London
Bittner, F.-K. 1986: Zur Fortsetzung der Diskussion um die Chronologie der Rheinzaberner Reliefköpfer. *BV* 51, 233-59
----- 1996: Zur Fortsetzung der Diskussion um die Chronologie der Rheinzaberner Relieftöpfer. *BV* 61, 143-74
----- 2011: Erweiterte Bildstempellisten der Rheinzaberner Relieftöpfer. *BV* 76, 177-218
Blagg, T. F. C. & King, A. C. 1984: (ed) *Military and Civilian in Roman Britain. Cultural relationships in a frontier province*, Oxford
Blanc, A. 1964: Etudes techniques sur la poterie gallo-romaine de Lezoux. *RAC* 3, 39-48
----- 1965: La terre sigillée gallo-romaine. Quelques observations faites au laboratoire de Valence. *RAC* 4, 21-30
Blanchet, A. 1900: Trouvailles de monnaies. *RNum* ser 4, 4, 104-6
----- 1927: Trouvailles. *RNum* ser 4, 30, 237
Bland, R. F. 1979: The 1973 Beachy Head treasure trove of third-century antoniniani. *NC* 139, 61-107
----- 1988: Stevenage, Hertfordshire. *CHRB* 8, 43-73
----- 1992: Hartlebury, Hereford and Worcester. *CHRB* 9, 81-5
----- 1996: The development of gold and silver denominations, AD 193-253. In King & Wigg 1996, 63-100
----- 1997a: Brundish, Suffolk. *CHRB* 10, 104-7
----- 1997b: Wortley, South Yorkshire. *CHRB* 10, 206-11
----- & Abdy, R. 2002: Hoards of the Severan period from Britain. *CHRB* 11, 19-45
----- & Burnett, A. 1988a: Appleshaw, Hampshire. *CHRB* 8, 91-107
----- & ----- 1988b: Normanby, Lincolnshire. *CHRB* 8, 114-215
----- & Buttrey, T. V. 1997: Barway, Cambridgeshire (addenda). *CHRB* 10, 127-30
----- & Carradice, I. A. 1986: Three hoards from Oliver's Orchard, Colchester. *CHRB* 6, 65-118
-----, Cepas, A. & Tosdevin, M. 1997: Bowcombe, Isle of Wight. *CHRB* 10, 264-78
-----, Davies, J. & Sheffield, C. 1997: Marlingford, Norfolk. *CHRB* 10, 108-14
----- & Williams, J. 1997: East Stoke, Dorset. *CHRB* 10, 88-90
Bloemers, J. H. F. 1978: *Rijswijk (Z.H.), 'De Bult'. Eine Siedlung der Cananefaten*, Amersfoort
Blurton, T. R. 1977: Excavations at Angel Court, Walbrook, 1974. *TLMAS* 28, 14-100
Böhme, O. 1961: Zur Topographie des römischen Nassenfels. *BV* 26, 143-7
Boersma, J. S. 1963: De Romeinse muntvondsten in de provincie Noord-Brabant. *JMP* 50, *passim*
----- 1967: The Roman coins from the province of Zeeland. *BROB* 17, 65-97
Bogaers, J. 1952: Bewoning uit de Romeinse tijd: 2e helft van de 2e en 1e helft van de 3e eeuw na Christus; Rockanje. *BROB* 3, 4-8
Bohn, O. 1923: Eine ‚Töpferrechnung' aus Blickweiler in der Westpfalz. *Germ* 7, 64-8
Bolin, S. 1958: *State and Currency in the Roman Empire to 300 AD*, Stockholm

Bompaire, M., Delestrée, L. P., Delestrée, B. & Piton, D. 1987: Le trésor monétaire de Woignarue (Somme). *RAP* 1987, 3/4, 65-81

Bonnet, C., Batigne Vallet, C., Delage, R., Desbat, A., Lemaître, S., Marquié, S., Silvino, T. 2003: Mobilier céramique du IIIe siècle à Lyon. Les cas de trois sites de la Ville Basse: place des Célestins, rue de la République/rue Bellecordière et place Tolozan. *SFECAG St Romain-en-Gal, 2003,* 145-81

Boon, G. C. 1954: Hoards of Roman coins in the Reading Museum and Art Gallery. *Oxo* 19, 38-44

----- 1960a: A temple of Mithras at Caernarvon - Segontium. *ACamb* 109, 136-72

----- 1960b: Hoards of Roman coins found at Silchester. *NC* ser 6, 20, 241-52

----- 1963: The coins. In Rahtz 1963, 336

----- 1964: Three small excavations at Caerleon. *ACamb* 113, 16-40

----- 1965a: Coins. In Murray-Threipland 1965, 140-1

----- 1965b: The samian ware. In ApSimon 1965, 249

----- 1966: The Llanymynech Roman Imperial treasure trove. *NC* ser 7, 6, 155-6

----- 1969a: Coins, glass, antefixes and tile stamps. In Murray-Threipland 1969, 101-9

----- 1969b: Belgic and Roman Silchester: the excavations of 1954-8 with an excursus on the early history of Calleva. *Arch* 102, 1-82

----- 1970: Un nouveau décor du potier Anunus 'II'. *RAC* 9, 32-5

----- 1972: *Isca. The Roman Legionary Fortress at Caerleon, Mon.,* Cardiff

----- 1974: Counterfeit coins in Roman Britain. In Casey & Reece 1974, 95-172

----- 1976: A list of Roman hoards in Wales – first supplement 1973. *BBCS* 26, 237-40

----- 1977: Roman and later coins. In Rahtz & Greenfield 1977, 295-302

----- 1978a: Excavations on the site of a Roman quay at Caerleon and its significance. In G. C. Boon (ed), *Monographs and Collections I, Roman Sites*, Cardiff, 1-24

----- 1978b: Sigillata. In James 1978, 85-97

----- 1984: *Lateranum Iscanum: the Antefixes, Brick and Tile Stamps of the Second Augustan Legion*, Cardiff

----- 2000: The coins. In Fulford & Timby 2000, 127-79

----- & Hartley, B. R. 1977: The samian ware. In Rahtz & Greenfield 1977, 206-16

----- & Simpson, C. 1967: Samian. In Murray-Threipland 1967, 51-3

Bourgeois, A. 1979: La diffusion de la céramique paléochrétienne grise et orangée dans les Grands Causses. *RAN* 12, 201-51

Bourne, R. J. 2001: *Aspects of the Relationship between the Central and Gallic Empires in the Mid to Late Third Century AD with Special reference to Coinage Studies* (BAR Int. Ser. 963), Oxford

Bousquet, J. 1963: Circonscription de Rennes – Blain, Loire-Atlantique. *Gallia* 21, 427

Bouthier, A. 1972: Un sous-sol/cave du IIe siècle à Cosne-sur-Loire (Nièvre). *RAECE* 23, 385-433

----- 1977: L'exploitation et l'utilisation de la houille en Gaule romaine. *Actes du 98e CNSS, St Etienne 1973*, 143-56

Bowes, H. K. 1965: Samian ware. In Wenham 1965, 548-51

----- 1969: Samian. In Murray-Threipland 1969, 111-3

Boyce, A. A. 1947: A hoard of sestertii from Cape Matafu (Algeria). *ANSMN* 2, 35-51

Boyd, W. C. 1897: A find of Roman denarii near Cambridge. *NC* ser 31 17, 119-26

Braat, W. C. 1930: Een nieuwe collectie vormschotels uit Lezoux. *OM* 11, 20-8

Bradley, R. 1971: Trade competition and artefact distribution. *WA* 2, 347-52

Branigan, K. 1971: *Latimer*, Bristol

Brassington, M. 1967: Roman material recovered from Little Chester, Derby, 1965. *DerbAJ* 87, 39-69

----- 1969: Roman wells at Little Chester. *DerbAJ* 89, 115-9

----- 1975: A reappraisal of the western enclave and environs, Corstopitum. *Brit* 6, 62-75

Breeze, D. J. & Dobson, B. 1976: *Hadrian's Wall*, London

Brenot, C. 1963: Le trésor de Vannes (Morbihan). *RNum* ser 6, 5, 159-63

----- 1968: Un dépôt de monnaies romaines du Haut Empire découvert sur le parvis de Notre-Dame de Paris. *BSFN* 23, 267

Brodribb, A. C., Hands, A. R., Walker, D. R. 1971: *Excavations at Shakenoak Farm ... II*, Oxford

-----, ----- & ----- 1978: *Excavations at Shakenoak Farm ... V*, Oxford

Brooke, G. C. 1910: A find of Roman denarii at Castle Bromwich. *NC* ser 4, 10, 13-40

----- 1912: The Edwinstowe find of Roman coins. *NC* ser 4, 12, 149-78

Brouquier-Reddé, V. & Gruel, K. 2004: (ed) Le sanctuaire de Mars Mullo chez les Aulerques Cénomans (Allonnes, Sarthe), Ve s. av. J.-C. – IVe s. ap. J.-C. Etat des recherches actuelles. *Gallia* 61, 291-396

Brown, A. E. & Woodfield, C. 1983: Excavations at Towcester, Northamptonshire: the Alchester Road suburb. *NhantsArch* 18, 43-140

Bruce, J. C. 1978: *Handbook to the Roman Wall* (13th ed. by C. M. Daniels), Newcastle

Bruckner, A. & Hinz, H. 1962: Xanten. pp. 572-4 in H. von Petrikovits, Bericht über die Tatigkeit des Rheinisches Landesmuseums Bonn im Jahre 1960. *BJ* 162, 507-94

Brulet, H. 1968: Gerpinnes: sepulture gallo-romaine. *Helinium* 8, 269-76

Brulet, R. 1981: *Braives Gallo-Romain I, La zone centrale*, Louvain-la-Neuve

-----, Misonne, B. & Feller, M. 2000: La terre sigillée tardive et ses derivées dans le nord de la Gaule. In Strobel 2000, 219-33

Bruun, P. 1978: Site finds and hoarding behaviour. In R. Carson & C. Kraay (ed), *Scripta Nummaria Romana*, London, 114-23

Buckley, B. 1981: The Aeduan area in the third century. In King & Henig 1981, 287-315

Bulmer, M. 1979: An introduction to Roman samian ware, with special reference to collections in Chester and the North West. *JCAS* 62, 5-72

----- 1980: Samian. In Mason 1980

Bursche, A. 2011: Roman coins from the bog sacrifice at Illerup Ådal, Jutland (DK). In G. Pardini (ed), *Preatti del I Workshop Internazionale di Numismatica,* Rome, 229-32

Burge, D. 1981: The coins. In Rawes 1981, 69

Burnett, A. M. 1977a: The coins.In Hunter & Mynard 1977, 109

----- 1977b: Bourne End find, 1976. *CH* 3, 77-8

----- 1978: The Langford find (1977). *CH* 4, 45

----- 1984a: The Purbrook Heath, Hants., hoard. *CHRB* 4, 33-7

----- 1984b: The E. Mersea, Essex, hoard (1980-81). *CHRB* 4, 39-44

----- 1986: Lostwithiel, Cornwall, hoard. *CHRB* 6, 157-60

----- 1992a: Kirkby in Ashfield, Nottinghamshire. *CHRB* 9, 41-2

----- 1992b: Much Hadham, Hertfordshire. *CHRB* 9, 73-80

----- 1997: The coins. In C. Johns, *The Snettisham Roman Jeweller's Hoard*, London, 76-84

-----, Bland, R. F. & Plouviez, J. 1986: The Wickham Market, Suffolk, hoard. *CHRB* 6, 119-42

----- & Williams, D. 1986: The Burwell Farm, Barton upon Humber, treasure trove. *CHRB* 6, 59-63

Bushe-Fox, J. P. 1926: *First Report of the Excavation of the Roman Fort at Richborough, Kent*, London

----- 1928: *Second Report ... Richborough, Kent*, Oxford

----- 1932: *Third Report ... Richborough, Kent*, Oxford

Butcher, S. A. 1982: Excavation of a Roman building on the east side of the White Tower, 1956-7. In Parnell 1982, 101-5

Buttrey, T. V. 1972: A hoard of sestertii from Bordeaux and the problem of bronze circulation in the third century AD. *ANSMN* 18, 33-58

----- 1997: Melbourn, Cambridgeshire. *CHRB* 10, 101-3

Buxton, K. & Howard-Davis, C. 2000: *Bremetenacum. Excavations at Roman Ribchester 1980, 1989-90,* Lancaster

Caillaud, G. 1914: Un four de potier gallo-romain de Lezoux. *BACTH* 1914, 447-60

Callu, J-P. 1969: *La Politique Monétaire des Empereurs Romains de 238 à 311*, Paris

Cameron, F. 1982: The other Roman pottery. In Parnell 1982, 107-15

Canham, R. 1978: *2000 Years of Brentford*, London

Carandini, A. & Panella, C. 1981: Trading connections of Rome and Central Italy in the late second and third centuries: the evidence of the Terme del Nuotatore excavations, Ostia. In King & Henig 1981, 487-503

Card, C. 2008 Nouvelles données sur les productions des ateliers de potiers gallo-romains de Luxeuil-les-Bains (Haute-Saône): la vaiselle en céramique non sigillée. *RAECE* 57, 205-26

Carradice, I. A. 1981: Maltby, South Yorkshire, treasure trove (1978). *CHRB* 2, 27-48

----- 1984a: The Akenham, Suffolk, hoard. *CHRB* 4, 30-2

----- 1984b: The Market Deeping, Lincs., hoard. *CHRB* 4, 45-62

----- 1986a: The Aldworth, Berkshire, hoard. *CHRB* 6, 39-44

----- 1986b: The Lowestoft hoard. *CHRB* 6, 45-6

----- 1988: Lawrence Weston, Avon. *CHRB* 8, 23-31

----- & Burnett, A. M. 1992a: Fotheringhay, Northamptonshire. *CHRB* 9, 43-5

----- & ----- 1992b: Ollerton ('Edwinstowe'), Nottinghamshire. *CHRB* 9, 46-9

Carson, R. A. 1947: A find of antoniniani at Boothstown, Lancs. *NC* ser 6, 7, 74-9

----- 1952 The Roman coin finds at Choseley. *NorfArch* 30, 353-7

----- 1953a: Owston Ferry hoard of Roman Imperial coins. *NC* ser 6, 13, 138-40

----- 1953b: A third-century Roman hoard from Mytholmroyd, Yorks. *NC* ser 6, 13, 140-1

----- 1954: The Elveden (Suffolk) treasure trove. *NC* ser 6, 14, 204-7

----- 1957a: The Chadwell St Mary find of Roman denarii. *NC* ser 6, 17, 238

----- 1957b: The Braughing treasure trove of Roman denarii. *NC* ser 6, 17, 239

----- 1960a: The Barway, Cambs, treasure trove of Roman coins. *NC* ser 6, 20, 237-9

----- 1960b: Pyrford Roman treasure trove. *NC* ser 6, 20, 235

----- 1960c: Coins. In Petch 1960, 54

----- 1961a: Hollingbourne treasure trove. *NC* ser 7, 1, 211-23

----- 1961b: Coins. In Richardson 1961, 28-30

----- 1963: Norton (Malton) Roman Imperial treasure trove. *NC* ser 7, 3, 67

----- 1964: Austerfield (1963) Roman Imperial treasure trove. *NC* ser 7, 4, 139

----- 1968: Beachy Head treasure trove of Roman imperial silver coins. *NC* ser 7, 8, 67-79

----- 1969a: Alcester (Warwickshire) find of Roman antoniniani and sestertii. *NC* ser 7, 9, 123-8

----- 1969b: Mattishall (Norfolk) treasure trove of Roman Imperial silver coins. *NC* ser 7, 9, 129-42

----- 1969c: Welwyn treasure trove of Roman Imperial denarii. *NC* ser 7, 9, 143-4

----- 1971a: Gare (Cornwall) find of Roman silver and bronze coins. *NC* ser 7, 11, 181-8

----- 1971b: Leysdown (Kent) hoard of early Roman Imperial bronzes. *NC* ser 7, 11, 189-97

----- 1973: A hoard of third-century Roman coins from Deeping St James, Lincs. *NC* ser 7, 13, 69-74

----- 1983: Coin hoards and Roman coinage of the third century AD. In C. Brooke *et al.* (ed.), *Studies in Numismatic Method presented to Philip Grierson,* Cambridge, 65-74

----- & Bland, R. 1976: Meare Heath, Somerset, find of Roman coins. *CH* 2, 46-51

----- & Bosanko, J. 1974: Coins. In Pollard 1974, 109-10

----- & Burnett, A. M. 1979: The Londonthorpe treasure trove (1976). *CHRB* 1, 9-24

Carver, M. O. H., Donaghey, S. & Sumpter, A. B. 1978: Riverside structures and a well in Skeldergate and buildings in Bishophill. *AYork* 4, 1-54

Casey, P. J. 1974: Excavations outside the north-east gate of Segontium, 1971. *ACamb* 123, 54-77

----- 1975: Coins. In Maxfield & Reed 1975, 67-8

----- 1976: Coins. In Jarrett 1976, 46-8

----- 1978: Coins. pp. 41-7 in A. MacGregor, Roman finds from Skeldergate and Bishophill. *AYork* 17, 31-66

----- 1983: The coins. In Miket 1983, 48-52

----- & Coult, R. 1977: The Piercebridge (Co. Durham) hoard of mid-third century 'antoniniani' and a note on Elmer 593 (Postumus). *CH* 3, 72-6

----- & Reece, R. 1974: (ed) *Coins and the Archaeologist*, Oxford

----- & Wenham, P. 1990: A second-century *denarius* hoard from Grinton, North Yorkshire. *YAJ* 62, 9-11

Castella, D. & Meylan Krause, M.-F. 1999: Témoins de l'activité des potiers à *Aventicum* (Avenches, Suisse), capitale des Helvètes, des Ier au IIIe siècle après J.-C. *SFECAG Fribourg, 1999,* 71-88

Causse, C. 1965: A La Graufesenque, une grande 'industrie' gallo-romaine. *Archéologia* 7, 23-7

Cesano, L. 1919: Sulla circolazione delle monete di bronzo nei primi tre secoli dell'impero romano. Ripostiglio del Testaccio. *AMIIN* 3, 35-69

Chaffers, W. 1847: [Well Street, London, hoard]. *JBAA* 2, 272-4

Chalut, J.-L. 1970: L'implantation gallo-romaine. *BCALezoux* 3, 14-16

----- 1971: Lezoux gallo-romain: essai de restitution topographique. *RAC* 10, 54-8

Chantraine, H. 1965: *FMRD IV, ii, Pfalz*, Berlin

Chapman, H. 1973: Excavations at Aldgate, 1972. *TLMAS* 24, 1-56

Charlesworth, D. 1967: Excavations on the Carrawburgh car park site, 1967. *AAel* ser 4, 45, 1-16

----- 1975: The commandant's house, Housesteads. *AAel* ser5, 3, 17-42

Chastagnol, A. 1981: Une firme de commerce maritime entre l'île de Bretagne et le contient gaulois à l'époque des Sevères. *ZPE* 43, 63-6

Cheesman, C. 1992: Chalfont St Peter, Buckinghamshire. *CHRB* 9, 154-205

----- 1997: Botley, Hampshire. *CHRB* 10, 241-57

----- & Bland, R. 1997: Wareham, Dorset. *CHRB* 10, 212-40

Cheetham, F. H. 1926: Roman coins found near Wigan. *AntJ* 6, 318-9

Chenet, G. 1941: *La Céramique gallo-romaine d'Argonne du IVe siècle et la terre sigillée decorée à la molette*, Macon

----- & Gaudron, G. 1955: La céramique sigillée d'Argonne des IIe et IIIe siècles. *Gallia Supp* 6

Christ, K. 1963: *FMRD II, i, Nordbaden*, Berlin

----- 1964a: *FMRD II, ii, Sudbaden*, Berlin

----- 1964b: *FMRD II, iv, Nordwürttemburg*, Berlin

----- & Franke, P. R. 1964: *FMRD II, iii, Sudwürttemburg-Hohenzollern*, Berlin

Christlein, R. 1963: Ein römisches Gebaude in Marzoll, Ldkr. Berchtesgaden. *BV* 28, 30-57

----- & Kellner, H.-J. 1969: Die Ausgrabungen 1967 in Pons Aeni. *BV* 34. 76-161

-----, Czysz, W., Garbsch, J., Kellner, H.-J., Schroter, P. 1976: Die Ausgrabungen 1969-74 in Pons Aeni. *BV* 41, 1-106

Christol, M. 1976: Le trésor de Sanssac-l'Eglise (arrond. du Puy, Haute-Loire). *BSFN* 31, 50-4

Clarke, D. L. 1968: *Analytical Archaeology*, London

Clayton, J. 1880: Discovery of a hoard of Roman coins on the Wall of Hadrian, in Northumberland. *AAel* ser 2, 8, 256-80

Cleere, H. 1977: The *Classis Britannica*. In D. Johnston (ed), *The Saxon Shore*, London, 16-19

Cockle, H. 1981: Pottery manufacture in Roman Egypt: a new papyrus. *JRS* 71, 87-97

Coffineau, E. & Dubant, D. 2002: La céramique commune du site de La Plaine d'Hermesnil (Seine-Maritime) de la seconde moitié du IIe siècle de notre ère. *SFECAG Bayeux, 2002,* 131-9

Cohen, H. 1880-92: *Description Historique des Monnaies Frappées sous l'Empire Romain*, Paris

Coispine, J.-M. 1987: La sigillée unie d'Eincheville-Le Tenig (Moselle). *RAECE* 38, 23-34

Cole, M. & Scribner, S. 1974: *Culture and Thought. A psychological introduction*, New York

Collingwood, R. G. & Wright, R. P. 1965: *The Roman Inscriptions of Britain I*, Oxford

Collis, J. 1974: Data for dating. In Casey & Reece 1974, 173-83

----- 1978: Radley House, St Cross Road. In *Winchester Excavations II: 1949-1960*, Winchester, 12-23

----- 1983: Excavations at Silchester, Hants, 1968. *PHFCAS* 39, 57-68, MF

Comité Archéologique de Lezoux 1957a: Les découvertes de Lezoux. Vase à relief d'applique représentant Mithra sacrifiant le taureau et moule à relief d'applique figurant la déesse gallo-romaine Epona. *Ogam* 9, 147-50

----- 1957b: Les découvertes de Lezoux. Poinçon-matrice de Mithra, moules à relief d'appliques et vases moulés au Dioscure au fouet. *Ogam* 9, 255-60

----- 1957c: Les découvertes de Lezoux. Vases de la forme 30 de l'officine de Cinnamus. *Ogam* 9, 374-6

----- 1958a: Les découvertes de Lezoux. Vases hémisphériques (forme 37). *Ogam* 10, 179-87

----- 1958b: Les découvertes de Lezoux. Vases hors séries. *Ogam* 10, 259-64

Conway, R., MacInnes, J. & Brooke, G. C. 1909: The Roman coins of Manchester. In F. A. Bruton (ed.), *The Roman Fort at Manchester*, Manchester, 18-28

Cook, N. 1936: A hoard of Roman coins from Maidstone. *ACant* 48, 249-51

Cool, H. E. M. & Leary, R. S. 2012: Aspects of the use of samian pottery in Romano-British funerary practices. In Bird (D) 2012, 305-18

----- & Mason, D. J. P. 2008 (ed.) *Roman Piercebridge. Excavations by D. W. Harding and Peter Scott 1969-1981,* Durham; data archive: http://archaeologydataservice.ac.uk/archives/view/piercebridge_eh_2008/

Coppack, G. 1973: The excavation of a Roman and Medieval site at Flaxengate, Lincoln. *LHA* 8, 73-114

Corbitt, J. H. 1955: Coins from site XX. In Richmond & Gillam 1955, 251-2

Corder, P. 1948: A second hoard of Roman denarii from Darfield. *NC* ser 6, 8, 78-81

Corrocher, J. 1977: Chargement de sigillée ledosienne coulé dans l'Allier à Vichy. *BCALezoux* 10, 9-12

----- 1980: Un bateau gallo-romain coulé dans l'Allier. *Archéologia* 138, 62-4

----- 1981: *Vichy Antique*, Clermont-Ferrand

----- 1983: La céramique à glaçure plombifère de Vichy (Allier). *RAC* 22, 14-40

----- & Randoin, B. 1974: Un document céramique original livré par l'officine gallo-romaine de Terre-Franche (Allier). *RAC* 13, 113-22

----- & ----- 1977: Mortiers en sigillée de l'officine de Terre-Franche (Bellerive-sur-Allier). *RAC* 16, 363-8

Cothenet, A. 1973: Le trésor de la Celle-Conde (arr. St Amand-Montrond, canton de Lignières, Cher). *BSFN* 28, 405-6

----- 1974: Le trésor de Morthonniers (Cher). *BSFN* 29, 525

----- & Huvelin, H. 1972: Trouvaille d'antoniniani à Chilleurs-au-Bois (Loiret). *RNum* ser 6, 14, 169-83

Cotterill, A. & Todd, M. 1969: The coins. In Todd 1969, 82-5

Cotton, M. A. 1947: Excavations at Silchester 1938-9. *Arch* 92, 121-68

----- & Gathercole, P. W. 1958: *Excavations at Clausentum, Southampton, 1951-1954*, London

----- & Wheeler, R. E. M. 1953: Verulamium, 1949. *TStAHAAS* 1953, 13-97

Cracknell, S. 1996: *Roman Alcester: defences and defended area,* York

Craster, H. H. 1911: Comment on the coins. p. 165 in R. H. Forster & W. H. Knowles, Corstopitum: report on the excavations in 1910. *AAel* ser 3, 7, 143-267

----- 1912: The coins. In Forster & Knowles 1912, 210-63

Crawford, M. H. 1969: Bletchley treasure trove of Roman Imperial denarii. *NC* ser 7, 9, 113-22

----- 1970: Money and exchange in the Roman world. *JRS* 60, 40-48

----- 1975: Finance, coinage and money from the Severans to Constantine. In H. Temporini (ed), *ANRW II, 2,* Berlin, 560-93

Crouch, K. R. & Shanks, S. A. 1984: *Excavations at Staines. 1975-6, The Friends' Burial Ground Site*, Dorking

Crummy, P. & Terry, R. 1979: Seriation problems in urban archaeology. In M. Millett (ed), *Pottery and the Archaeologist*, London, 49-60

Cüppers, H. 1970: Wein und Weinbau zur Römerzeit in Rheinland. *Gymnasium* Beiheft 7, 138-45

----- 1973: Die Stadtmauer des römischen Trier und das Graberfeld an der Porta Nigra. *TZ* 36, 133-222

Cunliffe, B. W. 1962: The Winchester city wall. *PHFCAS* 22, 51-81

----- 1964: *Winchester Excavations, 1949-60, I,* Winchester

----- 1971: *Excavations at Fishbourne, 1961-1969,* London

----- 1975: *Excavations at Portchester Castle, I, Roman,* London

----- 1978: *Iron Age Communities in Britain* (2nd ed.), London

----- 1980: Excavations at the Roman fort at Lympne, Kent, 1976-8. *Brit* 11, 227-88

Curle, J. 1911: *A Roman Frontier Post and its People. The Fort of Newstead in the parish of Melrose*, Glasgow

Curnow, P. 1957: Handlist of coins. In Gelling 1957, 20-1

----- 1975: Coins. In Charlesworth 1975, 42

----- 1976: The coins. In Neal 1976, 99-101

----- 1982: The coins. In Parnell 1982, 106

----- 1985: The coins from the 1977 excavations. In Hinchliffe & Sparey Green 1985, 41

Curteis, M. 1997: Fineshade, Northamptonshire. *CHRB* 10, 180-90

Czysz, W. 1980: Eine neue raetische Sigillata-Manufaktur bei Schwabmünchen, Ldkr. Augsburg. *JBB* 21, 155-74

----- 1981: Eine Töpferei von Sigillata-Gefässen bei Schwabegg, Ldkr. Augsburg. *AJB 1980*, 138-9

----- 1982: Der Sigillata-Geschirrfund von Cambodunum-Kempten. *BRGK* 63, 281-348

----- 2000: Handwerksstrukturen im römischen Töpferdorf von Schwabmünchen und in der Sigillata-Manufaktur bei Schwabegg. In Strobel 2000, 55-88

----- & Sommer, S. 1983: *Römische Keramik aus der Töpfersiedlung von Schwabmünchen im Landkreis Augsburg*, Kallmünz

Dannell, G. B. 1962: Samian ware. In Cunliffe 1962, 72-4

----- 1964: Samian ware. In Cunliffe 1964, 76-82

----- 1966: The samian ware. In Down 1966, 50-2

----- 1971a: Samian. In Dunnett 1971, 83

----- 1971b: The samian pottery. In Cunliffe 1971, vol II, 260-316

----- 1973a: The potter Indixivixus. In A. P. Detsicas (ed), *Current Research in Romano-British Coarse Pottery*, London, 139-42

----- 1973b: The samian ware. In Chapman 1973, 14-17

----- 1976: The samian. In Neal 1976, 102-5

----- 1977: Samian. Iin Blurton 1977, 53-5

----- 1978a: The samian pottery. In Down 1978, 225-33

----- 1978b: The samian. In Collis 1978, 20

----- 1979: The samian ware. In Down 1979, 200

----- 1981: The samian ware. In Down 1981, 263-9

----- 2002: Law and practice: further thoughts on the organization of the potteries at la Graufesenque. In Genin & Vernhet 2002, 211-42

-----, Dickinson, B. M., Hartley, B. R., Mees, A. W., Polak, M., Vernhet, A., Webster, P. V. 2003: *Gestempelte Südgallische Reliefsigillata (Drag. 29) aus den Werkstätten von La Graufesenque,* Mainz

----- & Mees, A. W. 2013: New approaches to samian distribution. In Fulford & Durham 2013, 165-87

Dapoto, P. 1987: Circolazione monetale a Pompei. Cenni su problemi di economia. *RSP* 1, 107-10

Dark, K. 2001: Proto-industrialization and the economy of the Roman Empire. In M. Polfer (ed), *L'Artisanat Roman. Evolutions, continuités et ruptures (Italie et provinces occidentales),* Montagnac, 19-29

Darling, M. J. 1998 Samian from the city of Lincoln: a question of status? In Bird 1998, 169-77

----- & Gurney, D. 1993: *Caister-on-Sea: excavations by Charles Green, 1951-55,* Gressenhall

D'Arms, J. H. 1981: *Commerce and Social Standing in Ancient Rome*, Cambridge, Mass.

Daszkiewicz, M., Liesen, B. & Schneider, G. 2003: Chemische und technische Analysen an Terra Sigillata aus Sinzig. In Liesen & Brandl 2003, 29-38

David, N. 1972: On the life span of pottery, type frequencies, and archaeological inference. *AmAnt* 37, 141-2

Davies, J. A. 1986: The Meare Heath, Somerset, hoard and the coinage of barbarous radiates. *NC* 146, 107-18

----- 2002: Great Melton, Norfolk (addenda 1996). *CHRB* 11, 133-4

----- 2009: *The Land of Boudicca. Prehistoric and Roman Norfolk,* Oxford

-----, Beverly, J. & Leins, I. 2002: Postwick, Norfolk (addenda 1997-2001). *CHRB* 11, 125-8

----- & Orna-Ornstein, J. 1997: Wreningham, Norfolk. *CHRB* 10, 121-7

Dayet, J. 1960: Trésor du IIIe siècle trouvé à Sancey-le-Grand. *BSFN* 15, 437-40

De Barthélémy, A. 1874: Trésor de Dardez. *ASFNA* 4, 343-4

De Boe, G. 1975: Haccourt II. Le corps de logis de la grande villa. *ABelg* 174

----- 1976: Haccourt III. Les bains de la grande villa. *ABelg* 182

----- 1978: Roman boats from a small river harbour at Pommeroeul, Belgium. In J. du Plat Taylor & H. Cleere (ed), *Roman Shipping and Trade: Britain and the Rhine Provinces*, London, 22-30

----- & Van Impe, L. 1979: Nederzetting uit de Ijzertijd en Romeinse villa te Rosmeer. *ABelg* 216

DeBoer, W. R. & Lathrap, D. W. 1979: The making and breaking of Shipibo-Conibo ceramics. In C. Kramer (ed), *Ethno-archaeology. Implications of Ethnography for Archaeology*, New York, 102-38

Déchelette, J. 1904: *Les Vases Céramiques Ornés de la Gaule Romaine (Narbonnaise, Aquitaine et Lyonnaise),* Paris

Deetz, J. 1974: A cognitive historical model for American material culture: 1620-1835. In C. B. Moore (ed), *Reconstructing Complex Societies*, Massachusetts, 21-7

De Groot, J. 1967: Un poinçon inconnu de Libertus. *RA* 1967, 287-90

De Laet, S. J. 1949: *Portorium. Etude sur l'organisation douanière chez les Romains, surtout à l'époque du Haut-Empire*, Brugge

Delage, R. 1997: Premier aperçu de la diffusion de la céramique du Groupe Centre-Ouest dans l'ouest de la Gaule (régions Pays-de-Loire et Bretagne). *SFECAG Le Mans, 1997*, 279-92

----- 1998: Première approche de la diffusion des céramiques sigillées du Centre de la Gaule en Occident romain. *SFECAG Istres, 1998,* 271-314

----- 1999a: *Contribution à l'Etude des Sites de Production du Centre de la Gaule et de leurs Céramiques sigillées moulées,* thèse de doctorat, Université de Paris I – Panthéon Sorbonne

----- 1999b: Réflexions sur la classification des décors sur sigillées du Centre de la Gaule des IIe et IIIe siècles: le rôle des marques épigraphiques et des différents critères d'analyse. *SFECAG Fribourg, 1999*, 311-37

----- 2000a: P-33: un nouvel ensemble stylistique sur sigillée moulée de Lezoux (Puy-de-Dôme). *RAC* 39, 113-36

----- 2000b; Les productions de céramique sigillée du choletais et la question du groupe du Centre-Ouest de la Gaule. In G. Berthaud (ed), *Mazières-en-Mauge (Maine-et-Loire): un quartier artisanal et domestique,* Angers, 64-73

----- 2001a: Les structures de production des ateliers de potiers à Lezoux du Ier au IVe s., reflets de l'évolution des stratégies commerciales et de l'organisation du travail. In M. Polfer (ed), *L'Artisanat Roman. Evolutions, continuités et ruptures (Italie et provinces occidentales),* Montagnac, 117-36

----- 2001b: Essai de caractérisation de la période d'activité du centre de production des Queyriaux (Puy-de-Dôme) à partir de la sigillée moulée. *RAC* 40, 115-32

----- 2003: Les sigillées du Centre de la Gaule peuvent-elles contribuer à la datation des niveaux du IIIe s.? *SFECAG Saint-Romain-en-Gal, 2003*, 183-90

----- 2004: L'écrit en 'représentation': les marques de grand format au sein des décors sur sigillée du Centre de la Gaule. *Gallia* 61, 145-52

----- 2006: Sigillée du groupe Centre-Ouest à Thésée-Pouillé (Loir-et-Cher). *SFECAG Pézenas, 2006,* 569-78

----- 2009: Nouvel examen du cas RENTIO. *CCALezoux* 3, 161-9

----- 2010: La céramique sigillée du Centre-Ouest de Mazières-en-Mauge revisitée. *SFECAG Chelles, 2010*, 621-6

----- 2012: 'Servus VI' potier(s) décorateur(s) de Lezoux. In Bird (D) 2012, 74-91

----- & Guillier, G. 1997: La céramique confrontée au problème de la datation des niveaux du IIIe siècle: quatre exemples manceaux (Sarthe). *SFECAG Le Mans, 1997*, 255-78

----- & Mees, A. W. 2009: Le commerce de la céramique sigillée de Dinsheim-Heiligenberg et de la Gaule de l'est. In Kern *et al.* 2009, 99-104

-----, Monteil, G., Rouzeau, N. & Pascal, J. 2011: A third-century samian shop group from Nantes (Loire-Atlantique, France). *SGRPNews* 52, 20-5

-----, Morin, J.-M. & Sellès, H. 2007: Le vaisselier d'une maison gallo-romaine incendiée au cours des années 160/180 à Saint-Germain-la-Gâtine (Eure-et-Loir). *SFECAG Langres, 2007,* 585-94

----- & Séguier, J.-M. 2009: CRACINA, potier et décorateur lézovien méconnu. A propos de la découverte d'un vase moulé à Saint-Sauveur-lès-Bray (Seine-et-Marne). *RAC* 48, 143-54

Delmaire, R. 1971: Un nouveau fragment de Dr. 37 signé de Cerealis. *RNord* 53, 619-20

----- 1986: Le trésor de Lewarde, Nord (Gordien III-Postume). *TM* 8, 47-50

----- 1992: Trésor d'antoniniens découvert à Bavay en 1990. *RNord* 74, 143-61

----- & Couppé, J. 1988: Un lot du trésor trouvé à Etaples en 1964. *TM* 10, 55-7

Delor, A. & Devevey, F. 2004: Gueugnon (Saône-et-Loire), 'La Plaine du Fresne'. Premier bilan des découvertes d'avril 2003. *SFECAG Vallauris, 2004,* 443-52

Delort, E. 1935: La céramique de Satto et de Saturninus. *ASHAL* 44, 355-406

----- 1948: L'atelier de Satto. Vases unies - 3000 marques. *MANMetz* ser 2, 17, 96-127

----- 1953: *Vases ornés de la Moselle*, Nancy

Delplace, C. 1978: Les potiers dans la société et l'économie de l'Italie et de la Gaule au Ier siècle av. et au Ier siècle ap. J-C. *Ktèma* 3, 55-76

De Maeyer, R. 1933: Uit het Museumbezit der Gentsche Universiteit. 1. Terra Nigra Sigillata uit Lavoye. 2. Primitius van Rheinzabern. *AntCl* 2, 37-41

Demarolle, J.-M. 1987: Trois décors de Saturninus-Satto: un type de discours iconographique. *RAECE* 38, 35-42

----- 1989: Recherches sur l'organisation de l'espace décoratif dans la sigillée (décors de Saturninus-Satto). *Latomus* 48, 135-49

----- 1993: Imaginaires: le bestiaire de la sigillée ornée au Haut-Empire. *DHA* 19.2, 187-212

----- 1995: La sigillée ornée de l'atelier de Metz. Approche méthodologique des décors à arcades et à festons. *RCRFA* 34, 187–194

----- 1996: Commercialisation de la sigillée au Haut-Empire. *DossArch* 215, 24-31

----- 2000: Estampilles à deux noms sur sigillée lisse: la question des 'associations' de potiers. In Strobel 2000, 43-54

Demolon, P., Tuffreau-Libre, M., Vadet, A. 1979: Le site gallo-romain des 'Terres Noires' à Lewarde (Nord). *RNord* 61, 873-922

Demory, A. & Huysecom, E. 1984: Pommeroeul V: ensemble monétaire (196-258) dispersé sur le sol d'une pièce d'habitation. *Helinium* 24, 53-67

Dennis, G. 1978: 1-7 St Thomas St. In J. Bird *et al.* (ed), *Southwark Excavations 1972-4*, London, 291-422

Deonna, W. 1925-6: Vases gallo-romains à glaçure rouge et à décor moulé, trouvés à Genève. *ASA* ser 2, 27, 205-14; *ibid* ser 2, 28, 14-26, 87-97, 154-69, 254-9

Depeyrot, G., Cairou, R. & Lassure, J.-M. 1985: Le trésor de sesterces de Lombez (Gers) (vers 230-240). *Aquitania* 3, 141-7

De Roquefeuil S. 1970: Un trésor de monnaies romaines du Haut Empire trouvés à Montigny-sur-Crécy (Aisne). *RNord* 52, 463-7

Desbat, A. 1981: Vases à medaillons d'applique des fouilles récentes de Lyon. *Figlina 5/6, passim*

Desbordes, J.-M. 1979: Circonscription du Limousin. *Gallia* 37, 479-94

De Schaetzen, P. & Vanderhoeven, M. 1954: La terre sigillée de Tongres I. La sigillée ornée. *BIALiège* 70, 1-284

Deschieter, J., De Clercq, W. & Vilvorder, F. 2012: Balancing between tradition and innovation: the potter EBΛRΛS and the mould-decorated beakers from the Argonne. In Bird (D) 2012, 92-106

Desnier, J.-L. 1985: Le trésor du Puy-Dieu. *TM* 7, 33-104

Detsicas, A. P. 1960a: Some samian ware of form 72. *AntJ* 40, 195-9

----- 1960b: The Central Gaulish potter LAXTUCISSA. *AntJ* 40, 227-8

----- 1962: Some samian mould fragments. *AntJ* 42, 30-7

----- 1963a: The anonymous Central Gaulish potter known as X-3 and his connections. *CollLatomus* 64

----- 1963b: Central Gaulish samian mould fragments. *AntJ* 43, 214-7

----- 1964a: A samian bowl by the potter Belsa and an Arretine vessel, from Canterbury. *AntJ* 44, 152-8

----- 1964b: Central Gaulish samian mould fragments. *AntJ* 44, 159-64

----- 1964c: Central Gaulish mould fragments. *RAC* 3, 55-61

----- 1966: A samian bowl from Eccles, Kent. In M. G. Jarrett & B. Dobson (ed), *Britain and Rome*, Kendal, 105-8

----- 1967: Central Gaulish samian mould fragments. *AntJ* 47, 60-9

----- 1968a: Samian ware. In Hanworth 1968, 56-62

----- 1968b: A deposit of samian ware from Springhead. *ACant* 83, 217-27

----- 1968c: Romano-British pottery. In Harrison & Flight 1968, 81-93

----- 1969: The samian ware. In Tester 1969, 56-64

----- 1970a: Roman pottery. In Harrison 1970, 101-8

----- 1970b: The samian ware. In Harker 1970, 146-8

----- 1971: Samian ware. In Branigan 1971, 132-4

----- 1976: The samian ware. In Bell 1976, 287-8

Dewert, J.-P. & Severs, L. 1982: Vestiges d'établissement rural d'époque romaine à Nivelles. *ASAHFNivelles* 24, 37-98

Dhaeze, W. & Seillier, C. 2005: La céramique de l'égout collecteur du camp de la *classis britannica* à Boulogne-sur-Mer (Pas-de-Calais). *SFECAG Blois, 2005,* 609-38

Dickinson, B. M. 1981: Samian potters' stamps. In Keppie 1981, 85

----- 1984: The samian ware. In S. S. Frere, *Verulamium Excavations III*, Oxford, 174-99

----- 1990: The samian ware. In M. R. McCarthy, *A Roman, Anglian and Medieval Site at Blackfriairs Street, Carlisle*, Kendal, 213-36

----- 2000: Samian. In Buxton & Howard-Davis 2000, 202-26

----- 2002: Samian potters' stamps. In Lakin 2002, 48-9

----- 2003: Samian ware. In Holmes 2003, 41-7

----- 2005: P-14 unmasked, and what happened next. *JRPS* 12, 97-105

----- & Bird, J. 1985: The samian ware. In Hinchliffe & Sparey Green 1985, 74-82

----- & ----- 1993: Decorated samian. In Darling & Gurney 1993, 157-60

----- & Hartley, B. R. 1982: The samian. In Parnell 1982, 106-7

----- & ----- 2000: The samian. In P. Rush *et al.*, *Roman Castleford. Excavations 1974-85. Volume III, the pottery,* Leeds, 5-88

Docherty, K. & Wild, F. 1975: Samian ware. In Robertson *et al.* 1975, 127-37

Dodds, E. R. 1965: *Pagan and Christian in an Age of Anxiety*, Cambridge

Dore, J. N. 1983: The samian. In Miket 1983, 53-60

----- 1988: The pottery. In Bishop & Dore 1988, 219-86, MF M4: C1-D6

Douglas, A., Gerrard, J. & Sudds, B. 2011: *A Roman Settlement and Bath House at Shadwell. Excavations at Tobacco Dock and Babe Ruth Restaurant, The Highway, London,* London

Down, A. 1966: Excavations in Tower Street, Chichester, 1965. *SxAC* 104, 46-55

----- 1978: *Chichester Excavations III*, Chichester

----- 1979: *Chichester Excavations IV*, Chichester

----- 1981: *Chichester Excavations V*, Chichester

----- & Rule, M. 1971: *Chichester Excavations I*, Chichester

Doyen, J.-M. 2011: Cliométrie et numismatique contextuelle: compter et quantifier le passé? Petite histoire de la méthode. *JAN* 1, 9-46

----- & Warmenbol, E. 1979: Nismes: un éperon barré de l'époque de Postume. *Archéologie* 1979, 1, 19-20

Drack, W., Wiedemer, H. R., Ettlinger, E. 1961: Spuren eines römischen Gutshofes bei Weisendangen. *JSGU* 48, 84-94

Dragendorff, H. 1895: Terra Sigillata. Ein Beitrag zur Geschichte der griechischen und römischen Keramik. *BJ* 96/7, 18-155

Draper, J. & Chaplin, C. 1982: *Dorchester Excavations I*, Dorchester

Drinkwater, J. F. 1981: Money-rents and food-renders in Gallic funerary reliefs. In King & Henig 1981, 215-33

----- 1983: *Roman Gaul*, Beckenham

Droop, J. P. & Newstead, R. 1931: Excavations in the Deanery Field, Chester. *LAAA* 18, 6-18, 113-47

Drury, P. J. 1976: Braintree: excavations and research, 1971-76. *EAH* 8, 1-143

----- 1978: *Excavations at Little Waltham, 1970-71*, London

Duhamel, P. 1975: Les ateliers céramiques de la Gaule romaine. *DossArch* 9, 12-20

Dumas, F. 1967: Trouvaille de Forge-les-Bains (IIIe siècle). *RNum* ser 6, 9, 140-65

Dumoulin, F. 1997: Les moules à sigillée découverts à Feurs (Loire). *SFECAG Le Mans, 1997*, 495-502

Duncan-Jones, R. P. 1974: *The Economy of the Roman Empire. Quantitative Studies*, Cambridge

----- 1976: Some configurations of land-holding in the Roman Empire. In M. I. Finlay (ed.), *Studies in Roman Property*, Cambridge, 7-33

----- 1994: *Money and Government in the Roman Empire*, Cambridge

----- 1996: Empire-wide patterns in Roman coin hoards. In King & Wigg 1996, 139-52

----- 2001: The denarii of Septimius Severus and the mobility of Roman coin. *NC* 161, 75-89; and discussion, *NC* 162, 2002, 339-45

Dunnett, B. R. 1971: Excavations in Colchester, 1964-68. *TEAS* ser 3, 3, *passim*

Durand-Lefebvre, M. 1946: Etude sur les vases de Montans du Musée Saint-Raymond de Toulouse. *Gallia* 4, 137-94

----- 1954: Etude sur la décoration des vases de Montans. *Gallia* 12, 73-88

Duval, P.-M. & Marichal, R. 1966: Un 'compte d'enfournement' inédit de La Graufesenque. In R. Chevallier (ed), *Mélanges d'Archéologie offerts à André Piganiol*, Paris, 1341-52

Dzwiza, K. 2004: Ein Depotfund reliefverzierter südgallischer Terra Sigillata-Schüsseln aus Pompeji. *JRGZM* 51, 381-587

Eckoldt, M. 1984: Navigation on small rivers in Central Europe in Roman and Medieval times. *IJNAUE* 13, 3-10

Edwards, D. & Green, C. 1977: The Saxon Shore fort and settlement at Brancaster, Norfolk. In D. Johnston (ed), *The Saxon Shore*, London, 21-9

Engeler-Ohnemus, V. 2006: Abfälliges aus Augusta Raurica. Deponien und Zerfallserscheinungen zwischen den Frauenthermen und dem Theater. *JAK* 27, 209-322

Ensslin, W. 1939: The Senate and the army. In S. Cook *et al.* (ed), *Cambridge Ancient History XII*, Cambridge, chap. 2

Eschbaumer, P. & Faber, A. 1988: Die südgallischer Reliefsigillata – kritische Bemerkungen zur Chronologie und zu Untersuchungsmethoden. Eine Stellungnahme zu dem Aufsatz von B. Pferdehirt im Jahrbuch RGZM 33, 1986. *FB-W* 13, 223-47

Esmonde-Cleary, A. S. 1980: The Roman coins. In Lambrick 1980, 60

Estiot, S. 1992: Le trésor de Montargis-Les Closiers (Loiret): un trésor d'antoniniens à double terminus, Victorin et Aurélien. *TM* 13, 107-34

-----, Amandry, M., Bompaire, M., Aubin, G. 1986: Le trésor d'antoniniani d'Allonnes II. *TM* 8, 51-110

Ettlinger, E. 1959: Die Kleinfunde aus dem spätrömischen Kastell Schaan. *JHVL* 59, 229-99 (= Ettlinger, *Kleine Schriften,* Augst 1977, 94 ff.)

----- 1966: Neues zur Terra-sigillata-fabrikation in der Schweiz. In R. Degen *et al.* (ed), *Helvetia Antiqua*, Zürich, 233-40

----- 1983: *Novaesium IX. Die italische Sigillata von Novaesium*, Berlin

----- 1987: How was Arretine ware sold? *RCRFA* 25/26, 5-19

----- & Roth-Rubi, K. 1979: *Helvetische Reliefsigillata und die Rolle der Werkstatt Bern-Enge*, Bern

Evans, J. 1863: Account of a hoard of Roman coins found near Luton, Bedfordshire. *NC* ser 2, 3, 112-8

----- 1870: Note on a hoard of coins found on Pitstone Common, near Tring, 1870. *NC* ser 2, 10, 125-32

----- 1882: Roman coins discovered in Lime Street, London. *NC* ser 3, 2, 57-60

----- 1883: Further notice of some Roman coins discovered in Lime Street, London. *NC* ser 3, 3, 278-81

----- 1891: Find of Roman coins at Colchester. *NC* ser 3, 11, 413-7

----- 1896: Roman coins found at Brickendonbury, Hertford. *NC* ser 3, 16, 191-208

----- 1898: A hoard of Roman coins. *NC* ser 3, 18, 126-84

Evans, J. 1996: Samian: a note. In Cracknell 1996, 77

Evans, K. J. 1974: Excavations on a Romano-British site, Wiggonholt, 1964. *SxAC* 112, 97-151

Eveillard, J.-Y. 1980: La trouvaille d'*antoniniani* de Morgat-en-Crozon (Finistère). *TM* 2, 31-58

Faber, A. 1994: *Das Römische Auxiliarkastell und der Vicus von Regensburg-Kumpfmühl,* Munich

Fabre, G. 1950: La trouvaille de Tôtes. *RNum* ser 5, 12, 13-52

----- & Mainjoinet, M. 1953a: Trésor de Noyers-sur Serein (Yonne). *RNum* ser 5, 15, 131-4

----- & ----- 1953b: Trésor de Treffieux (Loire-Inf.). *RNum* ser 5, 15, 135-9

----- & ----- 1954: Trésor de Rouvroy-les-Merles (Oise). *RNum* ser 5, 16, 183-7

----- & ----- 1956: Trésor d'Auvilliers (Loiret). *RNum* ser 5, 18, 233-40

----- & ----- 1958a: Trésor de Roches, commune de Chézy-sur-Marne (Aisne). *RNum* ser 6, 1, 190-2

----- & ----- 1958b: Trésor de la Forêt de la Bertrange, commune de Raveau (Nièvre). *RNum* ser 6, 1, 193-6

Fasold, P. 1988: Eine römische Grabgruppe auf dem Fuchsberg bei Günzenhausen, Gem. Eching, Lkr. Freising. *BBB* 28/29, 181-215

----- 1994: Die Keramik aus dem Dendrophorenkeller von Nida-Heddernheim. *SJ* 47, 71-8

Favory, F. 1974: Le monde des potiers gallo-romaines. *DossArch* 6, 90-102

Feller, M. 1989: Céramique gallo-romaine d'Argonne. Les méthodes de prospection terrestre appliquées à la reconnaissance des ateliers du groupe du massif de Hesse et de la vallée de la Buante. *SFECAG Lezoux, 1989,* 223-31

Féraudy, L. de &Vertet, H. 1986: Toulon-sur-Allier – Le Lary. In Bémont & Jacob 1986, 153-5

Ferdière, A. 1972: Notes de céramologie de la région Centre. *RAC* 11, 132-7

----- 1974: Notes de céramologie de la région du Centre, Ve série. *RAC* 13, 59-86

----- 1975: Notes de céramologie de la région Centre VII - Les ateliers de potiers gallo-romains de la région Centre. *RAC* 14, 85-111

----- 1988: Elaboration du répertoire des poinçons décoratifs des sigillées du groupe Centre-Ouest. *SFECAG Orange, 1988,* 215-20

----- 1989: Catalogue des poinçons décoratifs sur sigillée du 'Groupe Centre-Ouest'. *RAC* 28, 180-215

----- 2011: *La Gaule Lyonnaise*, Paris

----- & Gendron, C. 1986a: Groupe du Centre-Ouest. In Bémont & Jacob 1986, 130-1

----- & ----- 1986b: Mougon. In Bémont & Jacob 1986, 131-2

----- & ----- 1986c: Nouâtre. In Bémont & Jacob 1986, 133-5

----- & ----- 1986d: Poitiers. In Bémont & Jacob 1986, 136

Fiches, J.-L., Guy, M., Poncin, L. 1978: Un lot de vases sigillées des premières années du règne de Néron dans l'un des ports de Narbonne. *Archaeonautica* 2, 185-219

Field, N. H. 1982: The Iron Age and Romano-British settlement on Bradford Down, Pamphill, Dorset. *PDNHAS* 104, 71-92

Finlay, M. I. 1973: *The Ancient Economy*, London

Fischer, C. 1968: Zum Beginn der Terra-Sigillata-Manufaktur von Rheinzabern. *Germ* 46, 321-3

----- 1969: *Die Terra-Sigillata-Manufaktur von Sinzig am Rhein*, Dusseldorf

----- 1980: Verscheidene Firniswaren aus Nida-Heddernheim und Praunheim. *FH* 19/20, 725-43

----- 1987: Une coupe Drag. 29 de Saturninus-Satto du vicus de Nida-Heddernheim. *RAECE* 38, 43-5

Fischer, J. L. 1961: Art styles as cultural cognitive maps. *AmAnthro* 63, 79-93

Fischer, T. 1981: Zur Chronologie der römischen Fundstellen um Regensburg. *BV* 46, 63-104

----- 1984: Ein Keller mit Brandschutt aus der Zeit der Markomannenkriege (170/175 n. Chr.) aus dem Lagerdorf des Kastells Regensburg-Kumpfmühl. *BBB* 24/25, 24-64

----- 1994: Archäologische Zeugnisse der Markomannenkriege (166-180 n. Chr.) in Raetien und Obergermanien. In Friesinger *et al.* 1994, 341-54

----- 2009: Zerstörungshorizonte. Germanische Übergriffe und ihr archäologischer Niederschlag. In *2000 Jahre Varusschlacht. Konflikt,* Stuttgart, 109-13

Fischer, U. & Schleiermacher, W. 1962: Eine Dendrophoreninschrift aus Heddernheim. *Germ* 40, 73-84

Fitz, J. 1982: *The Great Age of Pannonia (AD 193-284),* Budapest

Fletcher, J. 1982: The waterfront of *Londinium*: the date of the quays at the Custom House site reassessed. *TLMAS* 33, 79-84

Flügel, J. C. 1940: *The Psychology of Clothes*, London

Fölzer, E. 1913: *Die Bilderschüsseln der ostgallischen Sigillata-Manufakturen*, Bonn

Forni, G. 1974: Estrazione etnica e sociale dei soldati delle legioni. In H. Temporini (ed), *ANRW II, 1*, Berlin, 339-91

Forrer, R. 1911: *Die Römischen Terrasigillata-Töpfereien von Heiligenberg-Dinsheim und Ittenweiler im Elsass*, Stuttgart

----- 1927: *Das Römische Strassburg-Argentorate*, Strasbourg

Forster, R. H. & Knowles, W. H. 1912: Corstopitum: report on the excavations in 1911. *AAel* ser 3, 8, 137-263

Foucray, B. 1990: Amiens XIII. Un trésor de deniers Rue des Jacobins. *TM* 12, 11-17

----- 1993: Un trésor monétaire au 4 Impasse du Courtillet à Senlis (Oise). *RAP* 1993, 3/4, 135-47

----- 1995a: Le trésor de deniers et d'antoniniens de *La Grosse Haie* à Souzy-la-Briche (Essonne). *TM* 15, 35-70

----- 1995b: Le trésor d'antoniniens de Coupvray (Seine-et-Marne). Un nouveau cas de *terminus* mixte Victorien/Aurélien. *TM* 15, 137-50

----- & Hollard, D. 1990: Le trésor d'antoniniens de Guiry-en-Vexin (Val-d'Oise). *TM* 12, 19-30

Fournier, P.-F. 1961: Circonscription de Clermont-Ferrand. *Gallia* 19, 355-67

----- 1970: La poterie sigillée de Clermont-Ferrand. *RAC* 9, 225-42

Fox, A. 1968: Excavations at the South Gate, Exeter, 1964-5. *PDAS* 26, 1-20

France-Lanord, A. 1979: *L'Atelier de Céramique gallo-romain de La Madeleine à Laneuveville-devant-Nancy*, Nancy

----- & Beck, F. 1986: La Madeleine. In Bémont & Jacob 1986, 244-7

Franke, P. R. 1956: Die römische Fundmünzen aus dem Saalburg-Kastell. *SJ* 15, 5-28

----- 1960: *FMRD IV, i, Rheinhessen*, Berlin

Frankenstein, S. & Rowlands, M. J. 1978: The internal structure and regional context of Early Iron Age society in south-western Germany. *BIAL* 15, 73-112

Fremersdorf, F. 1950: Die Herstellung von Relief-Sigillata im römischen Mainz. *MZ* 44/5, 34-7

Frere, S. S. 1943: A Roman ditch at Ewell County School. *SyAC* 48, 45-60

----- 1967/1978: *Britannia*, London

----- 1970: The Roman theatre at Canterbury. *Brit* 1, 83-113

----- 1971: The forum and baths at Caistor by Norwich. *Brit* 2, 1-26

----- 1972: *Verulamium Excavations I*, London

----- 1973: *Verulamium Excavations II*, London

----- 1984: British urban defences in earthwork. *Brit* 15, 63-74

----- & Hartley, B. R. 1966: Fouilles de Lezoux (Puy-de-Dôme) en 1963. *CCM* 9, 557-63

----- & Stow, S. 1983: *Excavations in the St George's Street and Burgate Street Areas, Canterbury*, Maidstone

-----, Stow, S. & Bennett, P. 1982: *Excavations on the Roman and Medieval Defences of Canterbury*, Maidstone

Frey, M. 1993: Die römischen Terra-sigillata-Stempel aus Trier. *TZ* Beiheft 15

----- 2000: Die letzten Reliefsigillaten aus Trier und ihre Zeitstellung. In Strobel 2000, 209-18

Friedrich, S. 2012: Die Grabungen der Reichs-Limeskommission im Kastell Niederbieber. *Der Limes* 6/2, 24-7

Friesinger, H., Tejral, J. & Stuppner, A. 1994: (ed.) *Markomannenkriege. Ursachen und Wirkungen*, Brno

Fromols, J. 1937-8: Le vase orné à légendes de Crucuro. *BSAC* 31, 14-17; 32, 31-3

Fulford, M. G. 1975: *New Forest Roman Pottery*, Oxford

----- 1977: Pottery and Britain's trade in the later Roman period. In D. P. S. Peacock (ed), *Pottery and Early Commerce*, London, 35-84

----- 1978: The Romano-British pottery. In Hartridge 1978, 119-31

----- 1984: *Silchester Defences 1974-80*, London

----- 1986: Pottery and precious metals in the Roman world. In M. Vickers (ed.), *Pots and Pans. A colloquium on precious metals and ceramics*, Oxford, 153-60

----- 2013: Gallo-Roman sigillata: fresh approaches, fresh challenges, fresh questions. In Fulford & Durham 2013, 1-17

----- & Durham, E. 2013: (ed) *Seeing Red. New social and economic perspectives on* terra sigillata, London

----- & Timby, J. 2000: *Late Iron Age and Roman Silchester. Excavations on the site of the Forum-Basilica 1977, 1980-86*, London

Fülle, G. 1997: The internal organization of the Arretine *terra sigillata* industry: problems of evidence and interpretation. *JRS* 87, 111-55

----- 2000a: Die Organisation der Terra sigillata-Herstellung in La Graufenseque. Die Töpfergraffiti. *MBAH* 19.2, 62-99

----- 2000b: Die Organisation der Terra sigillata-Herstellung in La Graufenseque. Die Herstellersignaturen. *Laverna* 11, 44-70

----- 2000c: Scherben und Strukturen. Zu methodischen Grundproblemen der Sigillataforschung. In Strobel 2000, 23-41

Funk, E. 1910: Römische Töpfereien in Remagen. *BJ* 119, 322-34

Gabler, D. 1960: Az importált terra sigillaták forgalma Pannóniában. *AÉrt* 91, 94-110

----- 1966: Westerndorfer und späterrömische Sigillata in Nordpannonien. *BV* 31, 123-33

----- 1978: Die Sigillata von Pfaffenhofen in Pannonien. *AAHung* 30, 77-147

----- 1981: Terra Sigillata (1979). In Redö 1981, 309-28

----- 1982: Terra Sigillata. In Redö 1982, 345-61

----- 1983: Die Westerndorfer Sigillata in Pannonien. Einige Besonderheiten ihrer Verbreitung. *JRGZM* 30, 349-58

----- 1987: La céramique sigillée de la Gaule de l'Est en Pannonnie. *RAECE* 38, 47-56

----- 1994: Über die Aussagekraft der Terra Sigillata-Funde bezüglich der Zerstörungen in den Provinzen. In Friesinger *et al.* 1994, 355-69

----- 1996: Die Ware der Sigillatamanufaktur Schwabmünchen II in den mittleren Donauprovinzen. *RCRFA* 33, 135-9
----- & Vaday, A. H. 1986: *Terra Sigillata im Barbaricum zwischen Pannonien und Dazien,* Budapest
Gaillard, H. & Parriat, H. 1975: L'officine gallo-romaine de Gueugnon (Saône-et-Loire). *RAECE* 26, 307-412
Garbsch, J. 1966: Die Rheinzaberner Sigillata-Formschüsseln der Prähistorischen Staatssammlung München. *BV* 31, 108-22
----- 1982: *Terra Sigillata. Ein Weltreich im Spiegel seines Tafelgeschirrs*, München
Gard, L. 1937: *Beitrage zur Kenntnis der Reliefsigillata des III und IV Jahrhunderts aus Trier*, unpub thesis, Tübingen
Garnsey, P. 1981: Independent freedmen and the economy of Roman Italy under the Principate. *Klio* 63, 359-71
Gascoigne, P. E. 1969: Clear Cupboard villa, Farmington, Gloucestershire. *TBGAS* 88, 34-67
Gazenbeek, M. & Van der Leeuw, S. 2003: L'Argonne dans l'Antiquité: étude d'une région productrice de céramique et de verre. *Gallia* 60, 269-317
Gechter, M. 1979: Die Anfänge des Niedergermanischen Limes. *BJ* 179, 1-138
Gelling, P. S. 1957: Report on excavations in Bays Meadow, Droitwich, Worcestershire, 1954-5. *TBWAS* 75, 1-23
Gendron, C. 1971: Une forme mythique de sigillée: la forme 73 de Déchelette. *RAC* 10, 303-6
----- 1977: La production de sigillée ornée du Centre-Ouest (Groupe Mougon-Nouâtre, Indre-et-Loire). *BSAO* ser 4, 14, 277-96
Genin, M. 2007: *La Graufesenque (Millau, Aveyron) II, Sigillées lisses et autres productions*, Pessac
-----, Hoffmann, B. & Vernhet. A. 2002: Les productions anciennes de la Graufesenque. In Genin & Vernhet 2002, 45-104
----- & Vernhet, A. 2002: (ed) *Céramiques de la Graufesenque et autres productions d'époque romaine. Nouvelles recherches. Hommages à Bettina Hoffmann,* Montagnac
Gentry, A., Ivens, J., McClean, H. 1977: Excavations at Lincoln Road, London Borough of Enfield, November 1974-March 1976. *TLMAS* 28, 101-89
Gérard, F. 1999: Une nouvelle officine de céramique sigillée en Moselle. *SFECAG Fribourg, 1999,* 349-60
Gervreau, J.-B., Goubet, F., Meyer, N., Nüsslein, P., Orditz, C., Vauthier, S. 2009: Les ateliers céramiques gallo-romains de Sarre-Union (Bas-Rhin). Des centres de production méconnus. *SFECAG Colmar, 2009,* 13-32
Ghey, E. 2013: The Beau Street hoard, Bath. *CurrArch* 278, 26-32
----- & Moorhead, S. 2009: Whiddon Down, Devon, February 2008-March 2009. *NC* 169, 338-9
Giacchero, M. 1974: *Edictum Diocletiani et Collegarum de Pretiis Rerum Venalium*, Genoa
Giard, J.-B. 1962: Le trésor d'Allonnes (Sarthe). *RNum* ser 6, 4, 217-25
----- 1963: Le trésor de Châtenay-sur-Seine. *RNum* ser 6, 5, 153-8
----- 1965: Le trésor d'Etaples. *RNum* ser 6, 7, 206-24
----- 1966: Malicorne et Bonneuil-sur-Marne: deux trésors monétaires du temps de Victorin. *RNum* ser 6, 8, 144-80
----- 1980: Le trésor de Clamerey. *TM* 2, 9-29
Gillam, J. P. 1968: *Types of Roman Coarse Pottery Vessels in Northern Britain*, Newcastle
----- nd: *The Corbridge Destruction Deposit*, typescript of the mid 1970s, in response to Hartley 1972a
----- & Tait, J. 1971: The investigation of the commander's house area, on site XI, Corbridge, 1958 to 1970; the structures. *AAel* ser 4, 49, 1-28
Gimber, M. 1985: Ein Beleg für eine bisher unbekannte Formschüssel des Rheinzaberner Ianus-Ateliers. *FB-W* 10, 143-6
----- 1993: *Das Atelier des Ianus in Rheinzabern,* Karlsruhe
----- 1999: Anmerkungen zur Fortsetzung der Diskussion um die Chronologie der Rheinzaberner Relieftöpfer. *BV* 64, 381-92
Going, C. 1992: Economic 'long waves' in the Roman period? A reconnaissance of the Romano-British ceramic evidence. *OJA* 11, 93-117
Goodman, P. J. 2013: The prodcution centres: settlement hierarchies and spatial distribution. In Fulford & Durham 2013, 121-36
Gose, E. 1975: *Gefässtypen der Römischen Keramik im Rheinland*, Bonn
Goubet, F. & Meyer, N. 2006: Atelier de l'Oxenzoung, Mittelbronn (Moselle). Nouvelles données et actualisation du catalogue des marques sur sigillée lisse et support de cuisson. *SFECAG Pézenas, 2006,* 541-50
Goudineau, C. 1980: Les villes de la paix romaine. In G. Duby (ed.), *Histoire de la France urbaine, Tome 1, La ville antique des origines au IXe siècle,* Paris, 233-391
Goury, G. 1939: L'atelier de céramique gallo-romaine de La Madeleine. *REA* 41, 329-38
Graham, A. 1978: Swan Street/Great Dover Street. In J. Bird *et al.* (ed), *Southwark Excavations 1972-4,* London, 473-97
Gray, P. H. 1954: A hoard of sestertii (Domitian-Commodus) from Slayhills Marsh, Upchurch, Kent. *NC* ser 6, 14, 201-3
Green, C. 1977: Excavations in the Roman kiln field at Brampton, 1973-4. *EAA* 5, 31-95
Green, J. A. 1965: *Sets and Groups*, London
Greene, J. P. 1979: Abbey Green 1971. In B. W. Cunliffe (ed), *Excavations in Bath, 1950-1975,* Bristol, 72-7
Greene, K. T. 1974: The samian pottery. In Casey 1974, 62-7
----- 1976: Pottery. In Jarrett 1976, 54-65
----- 1982: Terra Sigillata: imitations and alternatives. *RCRFA* 21/22, 71-8
Greenfield, E. 1963: The Romano-British shrines at Brigstock, Northants. *AntJ* 43, 228-63
----- & Webster, G. 1965: Excavations at High Cross 1955. *TLAS* 40, 3-41

Gregory, T. 1977: The coins. In Rogerson 1977, 127-9

Gregson, M. 1982: The villa as private property in Roman Britain. In K. Ray (ed), *Young Archaeologist*, Cambridge, 143-91

Grenier, A. 1938: Sur la 'coutume ouvrière' des potiers gallo-romaines. In *Festschrift für August Oxé*, Darmstadt, 84-9

Grézillier, A. 1962: Une collection de moules de Lezoux au musée de Rochechouart (Hte-Vienne). *Ogam* 14, 249-72

Gricourt, D. & Hollard, D. 1992: Le trésor de bronzes romains de Méricourt-l'Abbé. Recherches sur les monnayages d'imitation tardifs de Postume. *TM* 13, 15-43

Gricourt, J. *et al.* 1958: Trésors monétaires et plaques-boucles de la Gaule romaine: Bavai, Montbouy, Chécy. *Gallia Supp* 12

Grimes, W. F. 1930: *Holt, Denbighshire: the works-depot of the twentieth legion at Castle Lyons,* London

Groh, S. 1998: Importations tardives du Sud de la Gaule dans le Norique. La circulation des produits de Banassac dans les Alpes orientales. *SFECAG Istres, 1998,* 315-19

Groot, T. de, Kort, J. de, Aarts, J & Os, B. van 2012: Onderzoek naar de context van een laat-Romeinse muntschat in Sint Anthonis (Noord-Brabant). *RAM* 203

Groupe Archéologique de Gueugnon-Montceau 1974: L'officine céramique gallo-romaine de Gueugnon. Les fouilles de 1971 à 1974. *Phys* 81, 24-61

Groupe de Fouilles de Terre-Franche, de Vichy et Environs 1970: L'officine de céramique gallo-romaine de Terre-Franche. *BSHAVichy* 77, *passim*

Grueber, H. A. 1910: A find of Roman coins at Nottingham. *NC* ser 4, 10, 205-6

Grünewald, M. 1979: Die Gefässkeramik des Legionslagers von Carnuntum (Grabungen 1968-74). *Der Römische Limes In Österreich* 29

Gschwind, M 2006: Späte Rheinzaberner Sigillata in Raetien. *BV* 71, 63-86

Guidobaldi, F., Pavolini, C. & Pergola, P. 1998: *I Materiali Residui nello Scavo Archeologico,* Rome

Guitton, D. 2004: Contribution à l'étude de la diffusion des céramiques sigillées du groupe Centre-Ouest: l'estuaire de la Loire. *SFECAG Vallauris, 2004,* 289-314

Haalebos, J. K. 1973: Zu den Trierer Bilderschüsseln von Zwammerdam. *RCRFA* 14/15, 55-60

----- 1977: *Zwammerdam-Nigrum Pullum*, Amsterdam

----- 1979: Primus, Celadus und Senicio. *RCRFA* 19/20, 121-35

-----, Mees, A. W., & Polak, M. 1991: Töpfer und Fabriken. Verzierte Terra-Sigillata des ersten Jahrhunderts. *AK* 21, 79-91

Hagen, W. 1949: Nachtrag zum Kölner Münzschatzfund vom Jahre 1909. *BJ* 149, 287-309

----- 1956: Jahresbericht 1951-3 C. Münzfunde. *BJ* 155/6, 544-601

----- 1968: Die Münzen. In Barfield 1968, 56-60

Hahn, W. 1976: *Die Fundmünzen der Römischen Zeit in Österreich III, I, Carnuntum*, Vienna

Haldimann, M.-A. 1999: A la recherche des productions de céramique gallo-romaine en Valais. *SFECAG Fribourg, 1999,* 131-8

Hall, D. N. & Nickerson, N. 1970: Circular Roman building at Bozeat, Northamptonshire, 1964. *BedsAJ* 5, 57-65

Hammerson, M. J. 1972: Coins from the excavations. In Sheldon 1972, 129-36

----- 1978: Coins. In Canham 1978, 135-8

----- 1984: The coins. In Crouch & Shanks 1984, 88-9

----- 2002: Roman coins. In Lakin 2002, 53-7

----- & Coxshall, R. 1977: The coins. In Gentry *et al.* 1977, 161-8

Hanut, F. & Henrotay, D. 2006: Le mobilier céramique des IIe et IIIe siècles du site 'NEU' à Arlon/*Orolaunum* (province de Luxembourg, Belgique). *SFECAG Pézenas, 2006,* 287-339

Hanworth, R. 1968: The Roman villa at Rapsley, Ewhurst. *SyAC* 65, 1-70

Harden, D. & Green, C. 1978: A late Roman grave-group from the Minories, Aldgate. In J. Bird *et al.* (ed), *Collectanea Londiniensis*, London, 163-75

Harker, S. R. 1970: Springhead – the well, F. 19. *ACant* 85, 139-48

Harrison, A. C. 1970: Excavations in Rochester. *ACant* 85, 95-112

----- & Flight, C. 1968: The Roman and Medieval defences of Rochester in the light of recent excavations. *ACant* 83, 55-104

Hart, F. A., Storey, J. M. V., Adams, S. J., Symonds, R. P., Walsh, J. N. 1987: An analytical study, using inductively coupled plasma (ICP) spectrometry, of samian and colour-coated wares from the Roman town at Colchester together with related continental samian wares. *JAS* 14, 577-98

Hartley, B. R. 1952: Excavations at Heronbridge 1947-8. *JCAS* 39, 1-20

----- 1959: Pottery from the Exning well. In Johnston 1959, 16-20

----- 1960a: The Roman fort at Bainbridge. Excavations of 1957-9. *PLPLS* 9, 107-31.

----- 1960b: The samian ware. In Petch 1960, 55-6

----- 1960c: *Notes on the Roman Pottery Industry in the Nene Valley*, Peterborough

----- 1961a: Samian pottery. In Richardson 1961, 18-19

----- 1961b: The samian ware. In Steer 1961, 100-110

----- 1961c: Samian pottery. In Webster 1961, 95-104

----- 1962: The samian ware. In Bennett 1962, 78-80

----- 1963a: Samian. In Greenfield 1963, 254-5

----- 1963b: Samian pottery. In Rahtz 1963, 334

----- 1965: Samian. In Greenfield & Webster 1965, 14-20

----- 1966a: The samian. In Smedley & Owles 1966, 241-3

----- 1966b: The Roman fort at Ilkley. Excavations of 1962. *PLPLS* 12, 23-72

----- 1967: Samian. In Charlesworth 1967, 6-16

----- 1968: Samian pottery. In Fox 1968, 14-17

----- 1969: Samian ware or Terra Sigillata. In R. G. Collingwood & I. A. Richmond, *The Archaeology of Roman Britain*, London, chap. 13
----- 1970: Samian. In Webster & Daniels 1970, 19-21
----- 1971: The samian ware. In Brodribb, Hands & Walker 1971, 59-70
----- 1972a: The Roman occupation of Scotland: the evidence of samian ware. *Brit* 3, 1-55
----- 1972b: Samian ware. In Wenham 1972, 104-6
----- 1972c: The samian ware. In Frere 1972, 216-62
----- 1973: Samian ware. In Thompson & Whitwell 1973, 172-3
----- 1974: Samian potters' stamps. In Hassall & Rhodes 1974, 37-9
----- 1977: Some wandering potters. In J. Dore & K. Greene (ed), *Roman Pottery Studies in Britain and Beyond*, Oxford, 251-61
----- 1983a: The enclosure of Romano-British towns in the second century AD. In B. Hartley & J. Wacher (ed.), *Rome and her Northern Provinces*, Gloucester, 84-95
----- 1983b: The samian. In Collis 1983, 64-5, MF M18-21
----- 2002: Associations of potters on stamps from la Graufesenque. In Genin & Vernhet 2002, 133-8
----- & Dickinson, B. M. 1967: Little Chester samian 1965. In Brassington 1967, 47-51
----- & ----- 1974: Index of potters' stamps. In Evans 1974, 149
----- & ----- 1977: The samian ware. In Rogerson 1977, 155-72
----- & ----- 1980: Samian ware. In MacIvor *et al.* 1980, 243-7
----- & ----- 1981: Samian ware. In Perrin 1981, 70-73
----- & ----- 2008a: *Names on* Terra Sigillata. *An index of makers' stamps and signatures on Gallo-Roman* terra sigillata *(samian ware), volume 1 (A to Axo)*, London
----- & ----- 2008b: *Names on* Terra Sigillata. *An index of makers' stamps and signatures on Gallo-Roman* terra sigillata *(samian ware), volume 2 (B to Cerotcus)*, London
----- & ----- 2008c: *Names on* Terra Sigillata. *An index of makers' stamps and signatures on Gallo-Roman* terra sigillata *(samian ware), volume 3 (Certianus to Exsobano)*, London
----- & ----- 2009a: *Names on* Terra Sigillata. *An index of makers' stamps and signatures on Gallo-Roman* terra sigillata *(samian ware), volume 4 (F to Klumi)*, London
----- & ----- 2009b: *Names on* Terra Sigillata. *An index of makers' stamps and signatures on Gallo-Roman* terra sigillata *(samian ware), volume 5 (L to Masclus I)*, London
----- & ----- 2010: *Names on* Terra Sigillata. *An index of makers' stamps and signatures on Gallo-Roman* terra sigillata *(samian ware), volume 6 (Masclus I-Balbus to Oxittus)*, London
----- & ----- 2011a: *Names on* Terra Sigillata. *An index of makers' stamps and signatures on Gallo-Roman* terra sigillata *(samian ware), volume 7 (P to Rxead)*, London
----- & ----- 2011b: *Names on* Terra Sigillata. *An index of makers' stamps and signatures on Gallo-Roman* terra sigillata *(samian ware), volume 8 (S to Symphorus)*, London
----- & ----- 2012: *Names on* Terra Sigillata. *An index of makers' stamps and signatures on Gallo-Roman* terra sigillata *(samian ware), volume 9 (T to Ximus)*, London
-----, ----- & Pengelly, H. 1975: Samian ware. In Maxfield & Reed 1975, 80-8
----- & Pengelly, H. 1976: Samian ware. In Stead 1976, 102-16
-----, ----- & Dickinson, B. 1994: Samian ware. In S. Cracknell & C. Mahany (ed.), *Roman Alcester: southern extra-mural area, 1964-1966 excavations, Part 2: finds and discussion,* York, 93-119
Hartridge, R. 1978: Excavations at the prehistoric and Romano-British site on Slonk Hill, Shoreham, Sussex. *SxAC*116, 69-141
Haselgrove, C. 1984: 'Romanisation' before the Conquest: Gaulish precedents and British consequences. In Blagg & King 1984, 5-63
Hassall, M. 1977: The historical background and military units of the Saxon Shore. In D. Johnston (ed), *The Saxon Shore*, London, 7-10
----- 1978: Britain and the Rhine provinces: epigraphic evidence for Roman trade. In J. du Plat Taylor & H. Cleere (ed), *Roman Shipping and Trade: Britain and the Rhine Provines*, London, 41-8
----- & Rhodes, J. 1974: Excavations at the new Market Hall, Gloucester, 1966-7. *TBGAS* 93, 15-100
Hatt, J.-J. 1949: Le passé romain de Strasbourg. *Gallia* 7, 161-94
----- 1958: Les céramiques des Martres-de-Veyre (Allier) et de Chémery (Moselle) au Musée Archéologique de Strasbourg. *Gallia* 16, 251-61
----- 1964a: L'atelier du maitre F de Heiligenberg. *RAECE* 15, 313-27
----- 1964b: Les fouilles de Boucheporn. *RAECE* 15, 353-8
----- 1966: Fouilles de Sarre-Union. *CAAAH* 10, 59-68
----- 1979: La chronologie de l'officine de terre sigillée de Boucheporn d'après les fouilles de 1963 à 1967. *RCRFA* 19/20, 72-6
-----, Pétry, F., Thévenin, A, Will, R. 1973: L'archéologie en Alsace. *SA* 46, *passim*
Haverfield, F. 1902: Find of Roman coins near Caistor, Norfolk. *NC* ser 4, 2, 186-8
Hawkes, C. F. 1927: Excavations at Alchester, 1926. *AntJ* 7, 147-84
Hedinger, B. 1999: La production de céramique entre *Vindonissa* et Eschenz. Etat de la question. *SFECAG Fribourg, 1999,* 19-24
Heesch, J. van 2010: Les monnaies: un dépôt mais deux lots monétaires. In Paridaens *et al.* 2010, 227-45
Heighway, C & Garrod, P. 1980: Excavations at Nos 1 and 30 Westgate Street, Gloucester: the Roman levels. *Brit* 11, 73-114
----- & Parker, A.J. 1982: The Roman tilery at St Oswald's Priory, Gloucester. *Brit* 13, 25-77
Heiligmann, J. 1990: *Der „Alb-Limes". Ein Beitrag zur römischen Besetzungsgeschichte Südwestdeutschlands,* Stuttgart

Heimberg, U. & Ruger, C. B. 1972: Eine Töpferei im Vicus vor der Colonie Ulpia Traiana. *RhAusgr* 12, 84-118

Helen, T. 1975: *Organisation of Roman brick production in the first and second centuries AD. An interpretation of Roman brick stamps*, Helsinki

Helmer, L. & Deiber, C. 1985: Du nouveau sur le répertoire de Cibisus. Fouilles d'Ehl (Bas-Rhin). *RAECE* 36, 305-10

Henig, M. 1981: Continuity and change in the design of Roman jewellery. In King & Henig 1981, 127-43

----- 1983: (ed) *A Handbook of Roman Art*, Oxford

----- 1998: Romano-British art and Gallo-Roman samian. In Bird 1998, 59-67

Hermet, F. 1934: *La Graufesenque, Condatomagos, vases sigillées, graffites*, Paris

Heron-Allen, E. 1933: A hoard of Roman coins from a villa-site at Selsey. *SxAC* 74, 140-63

Hildyard, E.J. 1957: Cataractonium, fort and town. *YAJ* 39, 224-65

Hill, J. N. 1977: Individual variability in ceramics and prehistoric social organisation. In J. N. Hill & J. Gunn (ed), *The Individual in Prehistory*, New York, 55-108

----- 1985: Style: a conceptual evolutionary framework. In B. A. Nelson (ed), *Decoding Prehistoric Ceramics*, Carbondale, 362-85

Hillam, J. & Morgan, R. 1981: Dendro dates from Sheffield. *CurrArch* 7, 286-7

Hinchliffe, J. & Sparey Green, C. 1985: *Excavations at Brancaster 1974 and 1977,* Gressenhall

Hingley, R. 1982: Roman Britain: the structure of Roman Imperialism and the consequences of Imperialism on the development of a peripheral province. In D. Miles (ed), *The Romano-British Countryside*, Oxford, 17-52

Hobley, A. S. 1998 *A Examination of Roman Bronze Coin Distribution in the Western Empire AD 81-192* (BAR Int. Ser. 688), Oxford

Hodder, I. 1979a: Pre-Roman and Romano-British tribal economies. In B. Burnham & H. Johnson (ed), *Invasion and Response. The Case of Roman Britain*, Oxford, 189-96

----- 1979b: Economic and social stress and material culture patterning. *AmAnt* 44, 446-54

----- & Millett, M. 1980: Romano-British villas and towns: a systematic analysis. *WA* 12, 69-76

----- & Reece, R. 1980: An analysis of the distribution of coins in the western Roman Empire. *Archaeo-Physika* 7, 179-92

Hoerner, B. 2000: Zu den Anfängen der ostgallischen Terra Sigillata-Industrie im 1. Jahrhundert n. Chr.: Chémery-Faulquemont und Boucheporn (Lothringen). In Strobel 2000, 103-50

Hörig, M. & Schwertheim, E. 1987: *Corpus Cultus Iovis Dolicheni (CCID),* Leiden

Hofmann, B. 1961: La céramique argonnaise orné au moule. *RCRFA* 3, 23-33

----- 1966a: Oves et marques de potiers de Banassac (fouilles 1961-1964). *RCRFA* 8, 23-44

----- 1966b: Etude d'un vase inedit en terre sigillée de Gaule centrale. *Ogam* 18, 71-9

----- 1966c: Notes de céramologie antique I. *Ogam* 18, 477-86

----- 1967a: Etude de la céramique sigillée moulée de la villa gallo-romaine des Terres-Noires de Guiry-Gadancourt. *BAVexin* 3, 97- 108

----- 1967b: Notes de céramologie antique II. *Ogam* 19, 129-36

----- 1967c: Notes de céramologie antique III. *Ogam* 19, 215-23

----- 1967d: Notes de céramologie antique IV. *Ogam* 19, 457-74

----- 1968: Catalogue des poinçons pour moules à vases sigillés des décorateurs argonnais. *Ogam* 20, 273-343

----- 1969a: Quelques marques sur vases unis de l'atelier de Terre-Franche (Allier). *RAC* 8, 293-300

----- 1969b: Notes de céramologie antique VI. *Ogam* 21, 179-210

----- 1970a: Aperçu général sur nos fouilles à Banassac (Lozère). *Forum* 1, 3-15

----- 1970b: Verbindungen zwischen den Reliefschüsseln der Argonnen-töpfereien und Rheinzabern. *RCRFA* 11/12, 30-3

----- 1971: Les relations entre potiers fabricants de moules et artistes producteurs de poinçons. *RCRFA* 13, 5-20

----- 1973: Contribution à l'étude de l'atelier de Terre Franche à Bellerive-sur-Allier (Allier). *Forum* 3, 12-20

----- 1977: Les exportations de céramiques sigillées de Banassac vers les provinces danubiennes de l'Empire romain. *Caesarodunum* 12, 410-7

----- 1979: L'Argonne, témoin de l'évolution des techniques céramiques au cours du IIIe siècle. *RCRFA* 19/20, 214-35

----- 1981: *L'Atelier de Banassac*, Gonfaron

----- 1986: Banassac. In Bémont & Jacob 1986, 103-10

Hoffmann, B. 1995: A propos des relations entre les sigillées de la Graufesenque et les sigillées d'Italie. Ateius e le sue fabbriche. In *La Produzione di Sigillata ad Arezzo, a Pisa e nella Gallia Meridionale*, Pisa, 389-402

Hogg, A. H. A. & Stevens, C. E. 1937: The defences of Roman Dorchester. *Oxo* 2, 41-73

Hogg, M. A. 1884: Notice of Roman coins found at Baconsthorpe. *NorfArch* 9, 25-32

Hollard, D. 1989: Le trésor de Charny (Seine-et-Marne). *TM* 11, 25-33

----- 1992a: Le trésor de bronzes romains de Landévennec (Finistère). *TM* 13, 11-14

----- 1992b: La thésaurisation du monnayage de bronze de Postume, structure et chronologie des dépôts monétaires. *TM* 13, 73-105

----- 1995a: Le trésor d'antoniniens des environs de Limours (Essonne). *TM* 15, 115-35

----- 1995b: Le trésor de Thimert-Gâtelles (Eure-et-Loir): bronzes romains de Domitien à Postume. *TM* 15, 253-6

----- 1996: La circulation monétaire en Gaule au IIIe siècle après J.-C. In King & Wigg 1996, 203-17

----- 2006: Le trésor de bronzes de Villaines-la-Carelle (Sarthe). *TM* 22, 37-55

----- & Amandry, M. 1997: Le trésor d'antoniniens d'Auxerre-Vaulabelle (Yonne), 1992. *TM* 17, 31-54

-----, ----- & Foucray, B. 2000: Le trésor d'antoniniens de Reignac (Charente). *TM* 19, 1-32

----- & Avisseau-Broustet, M. 1998: Le trésor de Saint-Boil (Saône-et-Loire): bijoux et monnaies de Septime Sévère à Postume. *TM* 17, 11-30

----- & Foucray, B. 1995: Le trésor multiple de deniers et d'antoniniens de Cravent (Yvelines). *TM* 15, 71-114

----- & Gendre, P. 1986: Le trésor de Rocquencourt et la transformation du monnayage d'imitation sous le règne de Postume. *TM* 8, 9-45

----- & Lechat, S. 2000: Le trésor de Brains-sur-les-Marches (Mayenne). *TM* 19, 57-116

----- & Pilon, F. 2006: Le trésor et les monnaies de site de l' 'Espace du palais' à Rouen (Seine-Maritime). *TM* 22, 57-118

Holmes, N. 2003: *Excavation of Roman Sites at Cramond, Edinburgh,* Edinburgh

----- 2006: Two denarius hoards from Birnie, Moray. *BNJ* 76, 1-44

----- & Hunter, F. 1997: Edston, Peebles-shire. *CHRB* 10, 149-68

Holwerda, J. H. 1923: *Arentsburg, een Romeinsch militair vlootstation bij Voorburg*, Leiden

----- 1925: Terra sigillata van Lezoux. *OM* ser 2, 6, 12-30

----- 1926a: Nieuwe fragmenten uit Lezoux. *OM* ser 2, 7, 6-9

----- 1926b: Een zeldzame vaas van terra sigillata. *OM* ser 2, 7, 77-8

Hope, W. H. & Stevenson, M. 1910: Excavations about the site of the Roman city at Silchester, Hants, in 1909. *Arch* 62, 317-32

Hopkins, K. 1980: Taxes and trade in the Roman Empire (200 BC-AD 400). *JRS* 70, 101-25

Hopkins, R. 2012: New Central Gaulish poinçons. In Bird (D) 2012, 184-94

Horvat, B. 1936: Nalaz rimskih sestercija kod Bassana (Italija). *Numismatika* 2/4, 70-93

Houghton, A. 1965: A water cistern at Viroconium (Wroxeter). *TSAS* 58, 19-26

Howgego, C. 1996: The circulation of silver coins, models of the Roman economy, and crisis in the third century AD: some numismatic evidence. In King & Wigg 1996, 219-36

Hubener, W. 1957: Ein römisches Graberfeld in Neuburg-an-der-Donau. *BV* 22, 71-96

Huld, I. 1966: Zur relativen Chronologie des 'ersten gallischen Töpfers'. *SJ* 23, 104-5

----- 1969: Reliefsigillata des ALPINIUS aus Haute-Yutz (dép Moselle) und die sog. ALPINIUS-Ware aus Trier. *TZ* 32, 221-31

Huld-Zetsche, I. 1971a: Zum Forschungsstand über Trierer Reliefsigillaten. *TZ* 34, 233-45

----- 1971b: Glatte Sigillata des 'Massenfundes' aus Trier. *RCRFA* 13, 21-39

----- 1971c: Eierstäbe auf Trierer Reliefsigillaten. *Vortrag, Tagung Rei Cretariae Romanae Fautores, Nijmegen*, Nijmegen

----- 1972: *Trierer Reliefsigillata Werkstatt I*, Bonn

----- 1978: Spät ausgeformte römische Bilderschüsseln. *BJ* 178, 315-34

----- 1979: 150 Jahre Forschung in Nida-Heddernheim. *NA* 90, 5-38

----- 1982: Frankfurt am Main – Heddernheim – Praunheim. In D. Baatz, F.-R. Herrmann (ed), *Die Römer in Hessen*, Stuttgart, 275-93

----- 1986: Premiers fabricants trévires de sigillée ornée et leurs relations avec d'autres ateliers. In Bémont & Jacob 1986, 251-6

----- 1993: *Trierer Reliefsigillata Werkstatt II*, Bonn

----- 1998: Zur Verwertbarkeit von Reliefsigillaten des 2. und 3. Jahrhunderts. In Bird 1998, 147-9

-----, Eschbaumer, P. & Thomas, M. 2012: Der Wandertöpfer CINTVGNATVS. In Bird (D) 2012, 107-11

----- & Steidl, B. 1994: Die beiden neuen Geschirrdepots von Echzell und Langenhain. *MBAH* 13.2, 47-59

Hull, M. R. 1934: Eine Terra-Sigillata-Töpferei in Colchester (Camulodunum). *Germ* 18, 27-36

----- 1958: *Roman Colchester*, Oxford

----- 1963: *The Roman Potters' Kilns of Colchester*, Oxford

Hulst, R. S. & Lehmann, L. T. 1974: The Roman barge of Druten. *BROB* 24, 7-24

Humphrey, C. 1985: Barter and economic disintegration. *Man* ser 2, 20, 48-72

Hunter, A. G. 1963: Excavations at the Bon Marché site, Gloucester, 1958-59. *TBGAS* 82, 25-65

Hunter, R. & Mynard, D. 1977: Excavations at Thorplands near Northampton, 1970 and 1974. *NhantsArch* 12, 97-154

Hutty, B. D. 1975: Hob's Ditch Causeway, first excavation report (1965-1969). *TBWAS* 87, 89-110

Huvelin, H., Meissonnier, J. & Gaillard de Sémainville, H. 1993: Le trésor d'Esbarres 1979 (Côte-d'Or): 236 monnaies et 3 bijoux *ca.* 260. *TM* 14, 9-16

Imlau, T. 1969: Ein Scherben des Heiligenberger 'F-Meisters' aus Straubing. *BV* 34, 200-1

Ireland, S., Wise, P. J. & Williams, J. 2002: Kenilworth, Warwickshire (addenda 1997). *CHRB* 11, 89-90

Isaac, P. J. 1982: The coins. In Leach 1982, 235-40

Isserlin, R. M. J. 2012: Calibrating ceramic chronology: four case studies of timber building sequences, and their implications. In Bird (D) 2012, 28-40

Ivens, S. & Burnett, A. M. 1981: Much Wenlock treasure trove (1977). *CHRB* 2, 49-61

Jackson, D. A., Somers, K. M., Harvey, H. H. 1989: Similarity coefficients: measures of co-occurrence and association or simply measures of occurrence? *AmNat* 133, 436-53

Jackson, R. & Potter, T. W. 1996: *Excavations at Stonea, Cambridgeshire, 1980-87,* London

Jacob, J. P. & Leredde, H. 1974: L'officine céramique gallo-romaine de Jaulges-Villiers-Vineux (Yonne). *RAECE* 25, 365-86

----- & ----- 1975: Jaulges-Villiers-Vineux. *DossArch* 9, 71-8

----- & ----- 1979: A propos des jattes de forme 'Chenet 323'. *RCRFA* 19/20, 77-84

----- & ----- 1982: Un aspect de l'organisation de production céramique: le mythe du 'cartel'. *RCRFA* 21/2, 89-94

----- & ----- 1985: Les potiers de Jaulges/Villiers-Vineux (Yonne): étude d'un centre de production gallo-romain. *Gallia* 43, 167-92

----- & ----- 1986: Jaulges-Villiers-Vineux. In Bémont & Jacob 1986, 238-40

Jacobi, H. 1909: Das Kastell Zugmantel. In E. Fabricius *et al.* (ed), *Der Obergermanisch-Raetische Limes des Römerreiches B, II, no. 8,* Berlin & Leipzig

----- 1910: Die Ausgrabungen. *SJ* 1, 28-60

----- 1911: Die Ausgrabungen. *SJ* 2, 10-58

----- 1912: Die Ausgrabungen. *SJ* 3, 6-71

----- 1924: Die Ausgrabungen, II, Kastell Zugmantel. *SJ* 5, 1-105

----- 1930: Die Ausgrabungen der Jahre 1925-8. *SJ* 7, 8-91

Jacobi, L. 1897: *Das Römerkastell Saalburg*, Homburg-vor-der-Höhe

Jain, R. 1980: Fuzzyism and real world problems. In Wang & Chang 1980, 129-32

James, H. 1978: Excavations at Church Street, Carmarthen, 1976. In G. C. Boon (ed), *Monographs and Collections I, Roman Sites*, Cardiff, 63-106

James, S. 1984: Britain and the late Roman army. In Blagg & King 1984, 161-86

Jardel, K. 2002: Le mobilier céramique du IIIe siècle issu du site 'Les Préaux' à Vieux (Calvados). *SFECAG Bayeux, 2002,* 141-58

Jarrett, M. G. 1976: *Maryport, Cumbria: a Roman fort and its garrison*, Kendal

Jeannin, Y. 1967: Céramique sigillée de Luxeuil: nouveaux fragments. *RAECE* 18, 149-55

Jefferson, T. O., Dannell, G. B., Williams, D. F. 1981: The production and distribution of terra sigillata in the area of Pisa, Italy. In Anderson & Anderson 1981, 161-71

Jehl, M. & Bonnet, C. 1969: Horbourg, un centre artisanal aux IIe et IIIe siècles. *CAAAH* 13, 59-72

Jenkins, F. 1950: Excavations in Burgate St, 1946-8. *ACant* 63, 82-118

----- 1952: Canterbury excavations, June-December 1947. *ACant* 65, 114-36

Jenkins, G. K. 1947: The Caister-by-Yarmouth hoard. *NC* ser 6, 7, 175-9

Jilek, S. 1994: Ein Zerstörungshorizont aus der 2. Hälfte des 2. Jhs. n. Ch. im Auxiliarkastell von Carnuntum. In Friesinger *et al.* 1994, 387-405

Johns, C. M. 1963: Gaulish potters' stamps. *AntJ* 43, 288-9

----- 1968: Terra sigillata. In Barfield 1968, 61-9

----- 1971: A black samian vessel from Redbridge, Hampshire. *RCRFA* 13, 40-6

----- 1978: The samian ware. In Arthur & Whitehouse 1978, 63

----- 1981: The samian. In Potter 1981, 116

----- 1996: The samian. In Jackson & Potter 1996, 409-21

-----, Tite, M., Maniatis, Y. 1977: A group of samian wasters from Les Martres-de-Veyre. In J. Dore & K. Greene (ed), *Roman Pottery Studies in Britain and Beyond*, Oxford, 235-43

Johnston, A. W. 1985: A Greek graffito from Arezzo. *OJA* 4, 119-24

Johnston, D. E. 1959: A Roman well at Exning, Suffolk. *PCAS* 52, 11-20

Jones, G. D. B. 1984: "Becoming different without knowing it." The role and development of the *vici.* In Blagg & King 1984, 75-91

----- & Webster, P. V. 1968: Mediolanum: excavations at Whitchurch 1965-6. *AJ* 125, 193-254

Jones, M. J. 1980: *The Defences of the Upper Roman Enclosure*, London

Jones, R. F. J. 1975: The Romano-British farmstead and its cemetery at Lynch Farm, near Peterborough. *NhantsArch* 10, 94-137

----- 1981: Change on the frontier: northern Britain in the third century. In King & Henig 1981, 393-414

Jost, C. A. 2002: Neue Ausgrabungen im römischen Kastell Niederbieber, Stadt Neuwied. *AR-P* 2002, 103-6

----- 2009: Kastell Niederbieber bei Neuwied. *Der Limes* 3/1, 8-11

Jouannet, F. 1840: Notice sur quelques antiquités récemment découvertes à Bordeaux et aux environs. *AARBordeaux* 2, 295-317

Jouve, M. 1994: Le trésor monétaire gallo-romain de Lassigny (Oise). *RAP* 1994, 3/4. 39-50

Juhász, G. 1936: A Lezouxi terrasigillata gyárak Aquincumi lerakata. *AÉrt* 49, 33-48

Kaiser, H. 2006: Zum Beispiel Waiblingen. Römische Töpfereien in Baden-Württemberg. In S. Schmidt & M. Kempa, *Imperium Romanum. Roms Provinzen an Neckar, Rhein und Donau*, Stuttgart, 403-8

Kahn, P. 1986: Luxeuil: atelier du Chatigny. In Bémont & Jacob 1986, 241-4

Kalee, C. A. 1973: Trierer Bilderschüsseln in Museum Kam, Nijmegen. *RCRFA* 14/15, 61-105

Kaplan, F. S. & Levine, D. M. 1981: Cognitive mapping of a folk taxonomy of Mexican pottery: a multivariate approach. *AmAnthro* 83, 868-84

Karnitsch, P. 1955: Die verzierte Sigillata von Lauriacum. *Forschungen in Lauriacum* 3, *passim*

----- 1959: *Die Reliefsigillata von Ovilava*, Linz

----- 1960: Münzdatierte Rheinzabern- und Westerndorf-Sigillata von den Grabungen 1951-6 in Enns-Lorch. *Forschungen in Lauriacum* 6/7, 119-30

Kehne, P. 2009: Rom in Not. Zur Geschichte der Markomannenkriege. In *2000 Jahre Varusschlacht. Konflikt,* Stuttgart, 98-108

Kellner, H.-J. 1959: Die Fundmünzen. In Schönberger 1959, 145-6

----- 1960a: *FMRD I, i, Oberbayern*, Berlin

----- 1960b: Die römische Ansiedlung bei Pocking. *BV* 25, 132-64

----- 1961: Zur Sigillata-Töpferei von Westerndorf *BV* 26, 165-203

----- 1962: Die raetischen Sigillata-Töpfereien und ihr Verhältnis zu Westerndorf. *BV* 27, 115-29

----- 1963a: *FMRD I, v, Mittelfranken*, Berlin

----- 1963b: Die keramischen Funde aus den Grabungen den 'Römersektion' in und bei Westerndorf. *BIO* 33, 5-50

----- 1964: Die Sigillata-Töpferei in Pfaffenhofen am Inn und ihr Formenschatz. *Germ* 42, 80-91

----- 1965: Raetien und die Markomannenkriege. *BV* 30, 154-75

----- 1968: Beitrage zum Typenschatz und zur Datierung der Sigillata von Westerndorf und Pfaffenhofen. *BIO* 35, 5-72

----- 1970: (ed) *FMRD I, ii, Niederbayern*, Berlin

----- 1971a: *Die Römer in Bayern*, Mjinchen

----- 1971b: Sigillatatöpferei Westerndorf und Strassenstation Pons Aeni (Pfaffenhofen). In *Führer zu vor- und frühgeschichtlichen Denkmalern 19, Rosenheim*, Mainz, 13-16

----- 1973: *Die Sigillatatöpfereien von Westerndorf und Pfaffenhofen*, Stuttgart

----- 1980: Beobachtungen in Westerndorf-St Peter 1976. *JBB* 21, 175-81

----- 1981: Die Bilderstempel von Westerndorf. Comitialis und lassus. *BV* 46, 121-89

-----, Overbeck, B., Overbeck, M. 1975: *FMRD I, vi, Unterfranken,* Berlin

----- & Overbeck, M. 1978: *FMRD I, iii/iv, Oberpfalz und Oberfranken*, Berlin

Kent, J. P. C. 1962: The coins. In Bennett 1962, 71-6

----- 1989: The Roman coins. In Philp 1989, 56-7

Kenyon, K. M. 1934: The Roman theatre at Verulamium, St Albans. *Arch* 84, 213-61

----- 1940: Excavations at Viroconium, 1936-7. *Arch* 88, 175-228

----- 1948: *Excavations at the Jewry Wall site, Leicester*, Oxford

Keppie, L. J. F. 1981: Excavation of a Roman bath-house at Bothwellhaugh. *GlasgowAJ* 8, 46-94

Kerébel, H. 2001 *Corseul (Côtes-d'Armor), un quartier de la ville antique*, Paris [DAF 88]

Kern, E. 1986a: Dinsheim-Heiligenberg. In Bémont & Jacob 1986, 226-9

----- 1986b: Ittenwiller. In Bémont & Jacob 1986, 230-1

----- & Helmer, L. 1982: Nouveaux décors et poinçons du potier Cibisus. *RAECE* 33, 202-3

-----, Oswald, G., Pastor, L. 2009: (ed) *De Terra Sigillata. Histoire de la céramique sigillée et des potiers gallo-romains de Dinsheim-Heiligenberg,* Molsheim

Kerrick, J. E. & Clarke, D. L. 1967: Notes on the possible misuse and errors of cumulative percentage frequency graphs for the comparison of prehistoric artefact assemblages. *PPS* 33, 57-69

Kienast, D. 1962: *FMRD, III, Saarland*, Berlin

King, A. C. 1980: A graffito from La Graufesenque and *'samia vasa'*. *Brit* 11, 139-43, plus corrigendum, *Brit* 12, 1981, 311

----- 1981: The decline of samian ware manufacture in the North West provinces: problems of chronology and interpretation. In King & Henig 1981, 55-78

----- 1983: The Roman church at Silchester reconsidered. *OJA* 2, 225-37

----- 1984a: The decline of Central Gaulish sigillata manufacture in the early third century. *RCRFA* 23/4, 51-9

----- 1984b: Animal bones and the dietary identity of military and civilian groups in Roman Britain, Germany and Gaul. In Blagg & King 1984, 187-217

----- 1985: *The Decline of Samian Ware Manufacture in the North West Provinces of the Roman Empire*, unpub PhD thesis, University of London

----- 1990: *Roman Gaul and Germany,* London

----- 1991a: Discussion of the decorated samian ware, and, The samian ware. In J. Evans, R. F. J. Jones & P. Turnbull, Excavations at Chester-le-Street, Co. Durham, 1978-1979. *Durham Archaeol J* 7, 42-5, fig. 28, MF 68-82

----- 1991b: The date of the stone defences of Roman Bitterne. In V. Maxfield and M. Dobson (ed.), *Roman Frontier Studies 1989*, Exeter, 108-10

----- & Henig, M. 1981: (ed) *The Roman West in the Third Century*, Oxford

----- & Millett, M. 1993: Samian. In P. J. Casey & J. L. Davies, *Excavations at Segontium (Caernarfon) Roman Fort, 1975-1979,* London, 234-49

King, C. E. 1996: Roman copies. In King & Wigg 1996, 237-63

----- 1997a: Race Down Farm, Bridport, Dorset. *CHRB* 10, 74-87

----- 1997b: Crowmarsh, Oxfordshire. *CHRB* 10, 191-205

----- & Wigg, D. G. 1996: (ed.) *Coin Finds and Coin Use in the Roman World* (SFMA 10), Berlin

Kirk, G. E. 1940: A Roman site in Trinity Street, Dorchester. *PDNHAS* 61, 48-59

Kiss, K. 1948: A Westerndorfi Terra-szigillata gyár. *AÉrt* 7/9, 216-74

Klee, M. 1986: *Arae Flaviae III. Der Nordvicus von Arae Flaviae,* Stuttgart

Klein, S. B. 1982: *Motivation. Biosocial Approaches*, New York

Klein, U. 2004: Die Fundmünzen aus dem Grabungen der Jahre 1980 bis 1989 im Nordvicus von Walheim. In Kortüm & Lauber 2004, vol. 1, 551-613

Klejn, L. S. 1982: *Archaeological Typology*, Oxford

Klumbach, H. 1933: Der Sigillata-Töpfer L.A.L. *MZ* 28, 60-8

Kneissl, P. 1981: Die Utriclarii. Ihr Rolle im gallo-römischen Transportwesen und Weinhandel. *BJ* 181, 169-204

----- 1983: Mercator-Negotiator. Römische Geschäftsleute und die Terminologie ihrer Berufe. *MBAH* 2, 1, 73-90

Knorr, R. 1905: *Die verzierten Terra-Sigillata-Gefässe von Cannstatt und Köngen-Grinario*, Stuttgart

----- 1906: Die Westerndorf-Sigillaten des Museums Stuttgart. *FS* 14, 73-90

----- 1907: *Die verzierten Terra-Sigillata-Gefässe von Rottweil*, Stuttgart

----- 1910: *Die verzierten Terra-Sigillata-Gefässe von Rottenburg-Sumelocenna*, Stuttgart

----- 1919: *Töpfer und Fabriken verzierter Terra-Sigillata des ersten Jahrhunderts*, Stuttgart

----- 1939: Frühe und späte Sigillata des Arcanus. *Germ* 23, 163-8
----- 1952: *Terra-Sigillata-Gefässe des ersten Jahrhunderts mit Töpfernamen*, Stuttgart
----- & Sprater, F. 1927: *Die westpfalzischen Sigillata-Töpfereien von Blickweiler und Eschweiler Hof*, Speyer
Kortüm, K. 1995: *PORTUS – Pforzheim. Untersuchungen zur Archäologie und Geschichte in römischer Zeit*, Pforzheim
----- 1998: Zur Datierung der römischen Militäranlagen im Obergermanisch-Rätischen Limesgebiet. Chronologische Untersuchungen anhand der Münzfunde. *SJ* 49, 5-65
----- & Lauber, J. 2004: *Walheim I. Das Kastell II und die nachfolgende Besiedlung*, Stuttgart, 2 vols
----- & Mees, A. 1998: Die Datierung der Rheinzaberner Reliefsigillata. In Bird 1998, 157-68
Korzus, B. 1971: *FMRD VI, iv, Munster*, Berlin
----- 1972: *FMRD VI, v, Arnsberg*, Berlin
----- 1973: *FMRD VI, vi, Detmold*, Berlin
Kovacsovics, W. K. 1987: As XII – Eine Preisangabe auf einem Sigillatateller aus Salzburg. *Germ* 65, 222-5
Krause, R. 1984: Neue Untersuchungen am römischen Kohortenkastell in Murrhardt, Rems-Murr-Kreis. *FB-W* 9, 289-358
Kuhoff, W. 1984: Der Handel im römischen Suddeutschland. *MBAH* 3, 1, 77-107
Kuzmová, K. 1994: Die Markomannenkriege und der Terra Sigillata-Import im Vorfeld des nordpannonischen Limes. In Friesinger *et al.* 1994, 245-50
Labrousse, M. 1975: Céramiques et potiers de Montans. *DossArch* 9, 59-70
----- 1980: Circonscription de Midi-Pyrenées. *Gallia* 38, 463-505
----- 1981: Les potiers de La Graufesenque et la gloire de Trajan. *Apulum* 19, 57-63
Lafon, X. 1978: Un moule à médaillon d'applique de La Graufesenque (Aveyron). *Gallia* 36, 243-60
----- 1986a: Les ateliers de l'Est de la France. La fin des ateliers. In Bémont & Jacob 1986, 183-93
----- 1986b: Ateliers alsaciens secondaires. In Bémont & Jacob 1986, 233-5
Lakin, D. 2002: *The Roman Tower at Shadwell, London: a reappraisal*, London
Lallemand, J. 1971: Trésor de monnaies romaines à Oombergen: antoniniens de Caracalle à Valérien-Gallien (Salonin). *Helinium* 11, 48-60
Lame, M. & Mazimann, J.-P. 1993: L'atelier de potiers du Champ-des-Isles à Mathay (Doubs) et sa production. *RAECE* 44, 429-69
Lambrick, G. 1980: Excavations in Park Street, Towcester. *NhantsArch* 15, 35-118
Landry, C. 2003: Les céramiques du IIIe siècle sur le site du Thovey (Haute-Savoie). *SFECAG St Romain-en-Gal, 2003*, 115-22
Langley, R. S. 1994: Site D. In C. Mahany (ed.), *Roman Alcester: southern extra-mural area, 1964-1966 excavations, Part 1: stratigraphy and structures*, York, 60-84
Lantier, R. 1935: Neue Töpfereien im römischen Gallien. *Germ* 19, 317-23
----- 1954: Recherches publiées en 1952 – periode historique. *Gallia* 12, 527-63
Laser, R. 1998: *Terra Sigillata-Funde aus den östlichen Bundesländern*, Bonn
Lasfargues, J. 1973: Les ateliers de potiers lyonnais, étude topographique. *RAECE* 24, 525-35
-----, Lasfargues, A., Vertet, H. 1976: L'atelier de potiers augustéen de la Muette à Lyon. In M. Leglay & A. Audin (ed), *Notes d'Epigraphie et d'Archéologie Lyonnaises*, Lyon, 61-80
Latchmore, F. 1889: On a find of Roman coins near Cambridge. *NC* ser 3, 9, 332-4
Lathrap, D. W. 1983: Recent Shipibo-Conibo ceramics and their implications for archaeological interpretation. In D. K. Washburn (ed.), *Structure and Cognition in Art*, Cambridge, 25-39
Laufer, A. 1980: *La Péniche. Un atelier de céramique à Lousonna*, Lausanne
Laws, A. 1976: Excavations at Northumberland Wharf, Brentford. *TLMAS* 27, 179-205
Leach, J. D. & Wilkes, J. J. 1977: The Roman military base at Carpow, Perthshire, Scotland: summary of recent investigations (1964-70, 1975). In J. Fitz (ed), *Limes*, Budapest, 47-62
Leach, P. 1982: *Ilchester I, excavations 1974-5*, Bristol
Leblanc, O. 2003: Contextes des IIe et IIIe siècles sur le site de Saint-Romain-en-Gal (Rhône). *SFECAG St Romain-en-Gal, 2003*, 21-51
Le Gentilhomme, P. 1946: La trouvaille de Nanterre. *RNum* ser 5, 9, 15-114
Leins, I. 2001: Hickleton, South Yorkshire: 350 Roman silver coins and 36 copper-alloy coins. *TAR* 4, 94-5
----- 2002: Itteringham, Norfolk. *CHRB* 11, 77-83
Lenoble, M. 1985: Céramique sigillée provenant d'un entrepôt rue Saint-Dominique à Châlons-sur-Marne. *SFECAG Reims, 1985*, 73-7
Lequément, R. & Liou, B. 1975: Les épaves de la côte de Transalpine. *CLPA* 24, 76-82
Lerat, L. 1961: Un fragment de céramique sigillée de Luxeuil au Musée de Lons-le-Saunier. *RAECE* 12, 207-9
----- 1982: Un bol Dr. 37 'luxovien' à Strasbourg. *RAECE* 33, 27-9
----- & Jeannin, Y. 1960: La céramique sigillée de Luxeuil. *ALUB* 31, *passim*
Lewis, S. S. 1877: Roman coins found at Knapwell, near Cambridge. *NC* ser 2, 17, 167-8
Lewit, T. 2013: The mysterious case of La Graufesenque? Stimuli to lsrge-scale fine pottery production and trade in the Roman Empire. In Fulford & Durham 2013, 111-20
Liesen, B. 2011: (ed) *Terra-Sigillata in den germanischen Provinzen*, Mainz
----- & Brandl, U. 2003: (ed) *Römische Keramik. Herstellung und Handel*, Mainz
Light, A. 1983: A Romano-British waster heap at Allen's Farm, Rockbourne. *PHFCAS* 39, 69-75, MF

Lintott, R. 1979: The Roman coins from the sites. In Down 1979, 132-44
----- 1981: The Roman coins from the North-West Quadrant. In Down 1981, 180-3
Lockyear, K. 2012: Dating coins, dating with coins. *OJA* 31, 191-211
Loeschcke, S. 1909: Keramische Funde in Haltern: ein Beitrag zur Geschichte der augusteische Kultur in Deutschland. *MAW* 5, 101-322
----- 1921: Töpfereiabfall den Jahre 259/60 in Trier aus einer römischen Grube in der Louis-Linzstrasse. *Jahresber 1921 Provinzialmuseums Trier* Beilage II, 103-7
Longuet, H. & Banderet, A. 1955: La trouvaille de Bischoffsheim, près Strasbourg. *RNum* ser 5, 17, 153-226
Lowe, J. W. & Lowe, E. D. 1982: Cultural pattern and process: a study of stylistic change in women's dress. *AmAnthro* 84, 521-44
Lowndes, C. 1863: On the Manor and Chase of Whaddon, with its 'finds'. *RecBucks* 2, 118-27
Ludowici, W. 1904: *Stempel-Namen Römischer Töpfer von meinen Ausgrabungen in Rheinzabern, Tabernae Rhenanae, 1902-4*, München
----- 1905: *Stempel-Bilder Römischer Töpfer aus meinen Ausgrabungen in Rheinzabern nebst dem II Teil der Stempel-Namen 1901-5*, München
----- 1908: *Urnengraber Römischer Töpfer in Rheinzabern und III Folge dort gefundener Stempel-Namen und Stempel-Bilder bei meinen Ausgrabungen 1905-8*, München
----- 1912: *Römische Ziegelgräber, Katalog IV meiner Ausgrabungen in Rheinzabern 1908-12, Stempel-Namen, Stempel-Bilder, Urnengraber*, München
----- 1927: *Stempel-Namen und Bilder Römischer Töpfer, Legionsziegelstempel, Formen von Sigillata- und anderen Gefässe aus meinen Ausgrabungen in Rheinzabern 1901-14*, München
Luik, M. 1996: *Köngen-Grinario I. Topographie, Funstellenverzeichnis, ausgewählte Fundgruppen*, Stuttgart
----- 2005a: Eine neue TS Manufaktur von Nürtingen (Kreis Esslingen, Baden-Württemberg). *RCRFA* 39, 19-24
----- 2005b: „Schwäbischer Fleiß" in der Antike. Die neu entdeckte Sigillata-Manufaktur von Nürtingen (Kreis Esslingen). *NLB-W* 34, 129-33
----- 2012: Die Terra-Sigillata-Töpferei von Nürtingen, Lkr. Esslingen. *FB-W* 32/2, 201-332
Lutz, M. 1959: L'officine de céramique gallo-romaine de Mittelbronn (Moselle). *Gallia* 17, 101-60
----- 1960: La céramique de Cibisus à Mittelbronn. *Gallia* 18, 111-61
----- 1962: Une nouvelle officine de céramique gallo-romaine en Moselle: Boucheporn. Considérations sur quelques tessons recueillis en surface. *ASHAL* 61, 30-43
----- 1963a: Relations entre les officines de céramique gallo-romaines de Moselle et de Sarre. *ASHAL* 63, 29-35
----- 1963b: Le 'Maitre aux Boucliers et aux Casques', potier de la Gaule de l'Est de filiation arverne? *RAC* 2, 5-13
----- 1964a: Saturninus et Satto et le groupe des potiers. *RAECE* 15, 329-335
----- 1964b: Premier aperçu sur les maitres potiers de Boucheporn qui ont fabriqué de la céramique sigillée à relief. *RAECE* 15, 347-52
----- 1964c: Mittelbronn. L'une des officines de Saturninus et de Satto. *Archéologia* 1, 76-9
----- 1965a: La céramique de la Gaule de l'Est en général et de Saturninus-Satto en particulier. *Celticum* 12, 357-8
----- 1965b: Un type d'ove inconnu chez Cibisus. *US* 29, 46-50
----- 1966: Etat actuel de nos connaissances sur la céramique sigillée de la Gaule de l'Est. *RAC* 5, 130-57
----- 1968: Catalogue des poinçons employés par le potier Cibisus. *Gallia* 26, 55-117
----- 1969: Saturninus et Satto et la sigillée de Trèves. *TZ* 32, 215-20
----- 1970a: L'atelier de Saturninus et de Satto à Mittelbronn (Moselle). *Gallia Supp* 22
----- 1970b: Relations entre Saturninus/Satto et les ateliers de Blickweiler et Rheinzabern. *RCRFA* 11/12, 59-65
----- 1971: Les vases de la forme Drag. 29 et 29/37 de Saturninus et Satto. *RCRFA* 13, 56-81
----- 1972: Neue Grabung im Bereich der Sigillata-Manufaktur Eschweilerhof. *BSDSaarland 19, Abt. Bodendenkmalpflege*, 65-72
----- 1977a: La sigillée de Boucheporn (Moselle). *Gallia Supp* 32
----- 1977b: Importation et exportation de vases sigillés chez les Mediomatriques. *Caesarodunum* 12, 430-5
----- 1977c: Cheminement d'un style de la Gaule du Sud à la Gaule de l'Est. *RAC* 16, 107-16
----- 1977d: La céramique en Gaule de l'Est. Importations et exportations. *BAL* 8, 56-9
----- 1984: L'officine de céramique gallo-romaine d'Eincheville-Le Tenig. *RCRFA* 23/4, 37-49
----- 1986a: Boucheporn. In Bémont & Jacob 1986, 210-14
----- 1986b: Chémery. In Bémont & Jacob 1986, 214-16
----- 1986c: Eincheville-Le-Tenig. In Bémont & Jacob 1986, 217
----- 1986d: Mittelbronn. In Bémont & Jacob 1986, 218-21
----- 1986e: Metz. In Bémont & Jacob 1986, 224
----- 1989: Remous autour de la chronologie sigillaire: mise au point concernant deux publications allemands. *RAECE* 40, 269-75
----- & Morand-Hartmann, R. P. 1955: La céramique de Mittelbronn. *ASHAL* 54, 75-96
----- & Weiler, P. 1981: Eincheville-Le Tenig, nouvel atelier de potiers? *CL* 1981, 33-50
Lyne, M. & Abdy, M. 2007: Newchurch, Isle of Wight: 57 copper-alloy *sestertii* and *sestertius* fractions. *PATAR* 1, 178

McClelland, D. C., Atkinson, J. W., Clark, R. A., Lowell, E. L. 1953: *The Achievement Motive*, New York

Macdonald, G. H. 1918: Roman coins found in Scotland. *PSAS* 52, 203-76

----- 1934: A hoard of Roman denarii from Scotland. *NC* ser 5, 14, 1-30

----- 1935: The dating value of samian ware. A rejoinder. *JRS* 25, 187-200

----- & Curle, A. O. 1929: The Roman fort at Mumrills, near Falkirk. *PSAS* 63, 396-575

MacIvor, I., Thomas, M. C., Breeze, D. J. 1980: Excavations on the Antonine Wall fort of Rough Castle, Stirlingshire, 1957-61. *PSAS* 110, 230-85

McIsaac, W. 1980: The other Roman pottery. In Whytehead 1980, 38-41

Maetzke, G. 1959: Notizie sulla esplorazione dello scarico della fornace di Cn ATEIUS in Arezzo. *RCRFA* 2, 25-7

Majurel, R. 1969: Un fragment de moule de céramique sigillée en provenance d'Autun. *Ogam* 21, 227-32

Malfitana, D. 2006: Appropriazione di '*copyright*', falsificazione o ingannevole messagio pubblicitario nel marchio *ARRETINUM*? Nota sui rapporti fra archeologia e storia del diritto romano. *MBAH* 25.2, 149-68

Mann, J. C. 1983: *Legionary Recruitment and Veteran Settlement during the Principate*, London

Marabini Moevs, M. T. 1980: New evidence for an absolute chronology of decorated Late Italian Sigillata. *AJA* 84, 319-27

Marandet, C. 1960: Deux tessons en terre sigillée de Lezoux, décorés de dessins au trait. *Gallia* 18, 197-9

Marichal, R. 1971: Quelques graffites inédits de La Graufesenque (Aveyron). *CRAI* 1971, 188-212

----- 1974: Nouvelles graffites de La Graufesenque IV. *REA* 76, 266-92

Marsden, P. R. 1967: A boat of the Roman period discovered on the site of New Guy's House, Bermondsey, 1958. *TLMAS* 21, 118-31

Marsh, G. 1976: The samian ware. In Laws 1976, 200

----- 1978: 8, Union Street. In J.Bird *et al.* (ed), *Southwark Excavations 1972-4*, London, 220-32

----- 1979: Three vessels by the Aldgate-Pulborough potter from London. *TLMAS* 30, 185-7

----- 1980: Samian. In Whytehead 1980, 37-8

----- 1981: London's samian supply and its relationship to the development of the Gallic samian industry. In Anderson & Anderson 1981, 173-238

----- 1984: Samian wares. In Crouch & Shanks 1984, 34-44

Martin, T. 1974: Deux années de recherches archéologiques à Montans (Tarn). *RAC* 13, 123-43

----- 1977a: Fouilles de Montans. Note préliminaire sur les résultats de la campagne 1975. *Figlina* 2, 51-78

----- 1977b: Vases sigillées de Montans imitant des formes en verre? *Gallia* 35, 249-57

----- 1977c: Des fours de potiers mis au jour à Montans. *Archéologia* 111, 74-5

----- 1979: Données nouvelles sur la chronologie des ateliers de Montans. *RCRFA* 19/20, 170-81

----- 1986a: Les ateliers du Sud de la Gaule. Le déclin. In Bémont & Jacob 1986, 43-5

----- 1986b: Montans. In Bémont & Jacob 1986, 58-71

----- 2009a: Contribution à l'étude des styles décoratifs du potier *Attillus* I de Montans. *SFECAG Colmar, 2009*, 707-21

----- 2009b: Réflexions sur un vase orné de CANTOMALLUS découvert sur la *villa* de Montcaret (Dordogne). *CCALezoux* 3, 5-10

Mason, D. J. P. 1980: *Excavations at Chester, 11-15 Castle Street and neighbouring sites, 1974-8*, Chester

Massy, J.-L. 1972: La commercialisation sur le marché ambien de la céramique sigillée gallo-romaine. *BSAP* 54, 258-75

Mathonnière-Plicque, A. & Grenier, A. 1961: Nouvelles fouilles à Lezoux (Puy-de-Dôme). *Gallia* 19, 55-69

Matthews, C. L. & Hutchings, J. B. 1972: A Roman well at Dunstable. *BedsAJ* 7, 21-34

Matthys, A. 1973: La villa gallo-romaine de Jette. *ABelg* 152

Mattingly, H. 1921: Find of Roman denarii near Nuneaton. *NC* ser 5, 1, 145-9

----- 1923: Find of Roman denarii in Denbighshire. *NC* ser 5, 3, 152-5

----- 1925: Allerton Bywater. *NC* ser 5, 5, 400-1

----- 1929: Hoards of Roman coins. *NC* ser 5, 9, 314-9

----- 1932: Coins. In Nash-Williams 1931-2, part 2, 100-4

----- 1933: Poole hoard of Roman coins. *NC* ser 5, 13, 229-32

----- 1934: The Chalfont St Giles hoard. *NC* ser 5, 14, 219-20

----- 1939a: The great Dorchester hoard of 1936. *NC* ser 5, 19, 21-61

----- 1939b: The Dewsbury hoard, 1938. *NC* ser 5, 19, 104

----- 1940: The coins. In Mellor & Goodchild 1940, 76-87

----- 1945a: The Emneth hoard. *NorfArch* 28, 107-10

----- 1945b: A hoard of Roman sestertii from Algeria. *NC* ser 6, 5, 163

----- 1945c: The Brixworth hoard. *NC* ser 6, 5, 164-5

----- & Carson, R. A. 1923-62: *Coins of the Roman Empire in the British Museum*, London

----- & Pearce, B. W. 1938: The Bristol hoard of denarii, 1937. *NC* ser 5, 18, 85-98

----- & ----- 1939: The Amlwch hoard. *BBCS* 9, 168-87

----- & Pirie, E. J. E. 1998: Catalogue of the coins from the *vicus* (Site 1 (74) and T10). In H. E. M. Cool & C. Philo (ed.), *Roman Castleford. Excavations 1974-85. Volume I, the small finds,* Leeds, 18-22

-----, Sydenham, E. A., *et al.* 1923-81: *Roman Imperial Coinage*, London

Matton, M. 1870: Trouvailles de monnaies faites en France: Aisne, Chalandry. *ASFNA* 3, 370-1

Mauné, S. 2010: La villa de Quintus Iulius Pri(...) à Aspiran (Hérault). Uncentre domanial de Gaule Narbonnaise (Ier –Ve s. apr. J.-C.). *Pallas* 84, 111-43

Maxfield, V. 1982: Mural controversies. In B. Orme (ed), *Problems and Case Studies in Archaeological Dating*, Exeter, 57-81

----- & Reed, A. 1975: Excavations at Ebchester Roman fort 1972-3. *AAel* ser 5, 3, 43-104
Mayer, O. E. 1934: Eine neue Sigillata-Töpferei in Aachen-Schönforst. *Germ* 18, 102-9
Meadows, A., Orna-Ornstein, J. & Williams, J. 1997: Potters Bar, Hertfordshire. *CHRB* 10, 116-20
Meates, G. W. 1979: *The Roman Villa at Lullingstone, Kent, I: the site*, Maidstone
-----, Greenfield, E. & Birchenough, E. 1952: The Lullingstone Roman villa, second interim report. *ACant* 65, 26-78
Mees, A. W. 1993: Zur Gruppenbildung Rheinzaberner Modelhersteller und Ausformer. *JAK* 14, 227-55
----- 1994a: Potiers et moulistes. Observations sur la chronologie, les structures et la commercialisation des ateliers de terre sigillée décorée. *SFECAG Millau, 1994,* 19-40
----- 1994b: Datierung und Vertrieb von reliefverzierten Sigillaten aus Banassac. *MBAH* 13.2, 31-46
----- 1995: *Modelsignierte Dekorationen auf Südgallischer Terra Sigillata,* Stuttgart
----- 2000: Terra Sigillata multivariata. Vergleichende Untersuchungen zur Produktionsstruktur römischer Großtöpfereien in Rheinzabern, Arezzo und Cincelli. In Strobel 2000, 163-9
----- 2002: *Organisationsformen römischen Töpfer-Manufakturen am Beispiel von Arezzo und Rheinzabern,* Mainz
----- 2007: Diffusion et datation des sigillées signées et décorées de La Graufesenque en Europe. L'influence de l'armée sur l'évolution du pouvoir d'achat et du commerce dans les provinces romaines. *SFECAG Langres, 2007*, 145-208
----- 2011: *Die Verbreitung von Terra Sigillata aus den Manufakturen von Arezzo, Pisa, Lyon und La Graufesenque. Die Transformation der italischen Sigillata-Herstellung in Gallien*, Mainz
----- 2012: The portrait of the potter Calus: a potter priest at La Graufesenque? In Bird (D) 2012, 41-57
----- 2013: The internal organisation of *terra sigillata* (samian) workshops. In Fulford & Durham 2013, 66-96
----- & Polak, M. 2013: Scattered pots. Exploring spatial and chronological aspects of samian ware. In Fulford & Durham 2013, 36-48
Mellor, A. S. & Goodchild, R. 1940: The Roman villa at Atworth, Wilts. *WAM* 49, 46-95
Merrifield, R. 1971: A Roman coin-hoard from Ramsgate, 1969. *NC* ser 7, 11, 199-201
----- 1973: The coins. In Chapman 1973, 45-6
----- 1974: The coins. In Tatton-Brown 1974, 204
----- 1976: The coins. In Laws 1976, 202-3
----- 1977: Coins. In Blurton 1977, 57-8
----- 1983: *London. City of the Romans*, London
Merten, J. 1993: Elvira Fölzer und die Erforschung der römischen Keramik in Trier. *FABT* 25, 44-56
----- 2011: *Reliefsigillata und Heimatgeschichte.* Der Trierer Archäologe und Journalist Leo Gard (1911-1976). *FABT* 43, 71-85
Mertens, J. & Remy, H. 1974: Tournai: fouilles à la Loucherie. *ABelg* 165
----- & Vanvinckenroye, W. 1975: Een Romeins gebouwencomplex extra-muros te Tongeren. *ABelg* 180
Meyer-Freuler, C. 1984: Ein römisches Formschüsselfragment aus Ottenhusen. *HelvArch* 57/60, 185-94
Middleton, P. 1979: Army supply in Roman Gaul: an hypothesis for Roman Britain. In B. Burnham & H. Johnson (ed), *Invasion and Response. The Case of Roman Britain*, Oxford, 81-97
----- 1980: La Graufesenque: a question of marketing. *Athenaeum* 58, 186-91
----- 1983: The Roman army and long distance trade. In P. Garnsey and C. Whittaker (ed), *Trade and Famine in Classical Antiquity*, Cambridge, 75-83
Miket, R. 1983: *The Roman Fort at South Shields; excavation of the defences 1977-1981*, Gateshead
Miller, D. 1982: Structures and strategies: an aspect of the relationship between social hierarchy and cultural change. In I. Hodder (ed), *Symbolic and Structural Archaeology*, Cambridge, 89-98
Miller, L., Schofield, J. & Rhodes, M. 1986: *The Roman Quay at St Magnus House, London. Excavations at New Fresh Wharf, Lower Thames Street, London 1974-78*, London
Miller, S. N. 1921: Samian ware and the chronology of the Roman occupation. *SHR* 18, 199-205
Millett, M. J. 1979: An approach to the functional interpretation of pottery. In M. Millett (ed), *Pottery and the Archaeologist*, London, 35-48
----- 1980: Aspects of Romano-British pottery in West Sussex. *SxAC* 118, 57-68
----- 1983: *A Comparative Study of some Contemporaneous Pottery Assemblages from Roman Britain*, unpub DPhil thesis, Oxford University
----- 1987a: A question of time? Aspects of the future of pottery studies. *BIAL* 24, 99-108
----- 1987b: Boudicca, the first Colchester potters' shop and the dating of Neronian samian. *Brit* 18, 93-124
Mirti, P., Appolonia, L., Casoli, A. 1999: Technological features of Roman *terra sigillata* from Gallic and Italian centres of production. *JAS* 26, 1427-35
Mischel, W. 1968: *Personality and Assessment*, New York
Mitard, P.-H. 1965: Les têtes de lion-déversoirs sur terrines Drag. 45 de l'officine de céramique de Terre Franche (Vichy, rive gauche). *RAC* 4, 141-52
----- 1979: Mortiers Drag. 45 de la Gaule de l'Est: l'atelier argonnais du Champ-des-Bierres à Avocourt (Meuse). *RCRFA* 19/20, 85-95
----- 1982: Les mortiers Drag. 45 de l'atelier de Gueugnon. *Phys* 96, 77-80
----- 1985: Le trésor d'Epiais-Rhus (Val-d'Oise). *TM* 7, 9-32
----- 2005: Les mortiers Drag. 45: leur place dans l'étude des céramiques d'époque romaine. *JRPS* 12, 145-8
----- & Alegoët, C. 1975: Les terrines à déversoir drag. 45 dans l'est de la Saône-et-Loire. *RAECE* 26, 217-26

----- & Hofmann, B. 1963: Fouilles de Banassac. *RGévaudan* ser 2, 9, 61-80

------, ----- & Lutz, M. 1986: Les ateliers de l'Est de la France. Goupe d'Argonne. In Bémont & Jacob 1986, 196-207

Moireau, F. 1992: Le dépotoir des 'Murgets', à Tavers (Loiret): étude de la céramique. *RAC* 31, 177-88

Moneta, C. 2010: *Der Vicus des römischen Kastells Saalburg,* 3 vols, Mainz

Monteil, G. 1999: *New Fresh Wharf and St Magnus. An assessment of part of the publication and archive of an important waterfront site in London and suggestions for a review of the evidence,* unpub MA dissertation, Leicester University

----- 2004: Samian and consumer choice in Roman London. In B. Croxford *et al.* (ed), *TRAC 2003. Proceedings of the Thirteenth Annual Theoretical Roman Archaeology Conference, Leicester 2003,* Oxford, 1-15

Moorhead, T. S. 1992: Aldbourne, Wiltshire (addenda). *CHRB* 9, 105-15

Morel, C. 1957: Quelques aspects des céramiques gallo-romaines de Banassac (Lozère). *Rhodania* 31, 54-62

----- & Peyre, P. 1973: *Banassac et Lezoux*, La Canourgue

----- & ----- 1975: *La Céramique gallo-romaine de Banassac (Lozère). L'atelier de Germanus*, La Canourgue

Morelli del Franco, V. C. & Vitale, R. 1989: L'*insula* 8 della *Regio* I: un campione d'indagine socio-economica. *RSP* 3, 185-221

Morlet, A. 1957: Libertus, Cinnamus – et d'autres potiers de Lezoux – ont-ils travaillés à Vichy? *Ogam* 9, 264-6

----- 1958: Vichy et Lezoux. L'art religieux de Cinnamus. *Ogam* 10, 311-20

Morris, J. 1972: Samian and North-African redware. In Sheldon 1972, 145

----- 1975: The samian. In Cunliffe 1975, 276-8

Mullen, A. 2013: The language of the potteries: communication in the production and trade of Gallo-Roman *terra sigillata.* In Fulford & Durham 2013, 97-110.

Müller, G. 1962: Kastell Butzbach. *LF* 2, 5-66

----- 1968: Das Lagerdorf des Kastells Butzbach; die reliefverzierte Terra sigillata. *LF* 5

----- 1971: Römische Brandgraber mit Truhenresten aus Hackenbroich, Kreis Grevenbroich. *RhAusgr* 10, 200-18

Müller-Beck, H. & Ettlinger, E. 1963: Die Besiedlung der Engehalbinsel in Bern. *BRGK* 43/4, 107-53

Murray-Threipland, L. 1957: Excavations in Dover. *ACant* 71, 14-37

----- 1959: Excavations at Caerleon 1956. *ACamb* 108, 126-33

----- 1965: Caerleon: Museum Street site, 1965. *ACamb* 114, 130-45

----- 1967: Excavations at Caerleon, 1966. *ACamb* 116, 23-56

----- 1969: The Hall, Caerleon, 1964: excavations on the site of the legionary hospital. *ACamb* 118, 86-123

Mynard, D. C. & Woodfield, C. 1977: A Roman site at Walton, Milton Keynes. *RecBucks* 20, 351-83

Myres, J. N., Steer, K. A., Chitty, A. M. 1959: The defences of *Isurium Brigantium* (Aldborough). *YAJ* 40, 1-77

Nash-Williams, V. E. 1930: Further excavations at Caerwent, Monmouth-shire, 1923-5. *Arch* 80, 229-88

----- 1931-2: The Roman legionary fortress at Caerleon in Monmouthshire. Report on the excavations carried out in the Prysg Field, 1927-9. *ACamb* 86, 99-157; 87, 48-104; 87, 265-349

Nass, K. 1934: Kastell Holzhausen. Grabungen 15. Juli bis 30. November 1932. *NA* 54, 233-69

Nau, E. 1971: Münzen aus Raum D. Pp. 188-96 in P. Filtzinger, Römische Strassenstation bei Sigmaringen. *FS* ser 2, 19, 175-206

Neal, D. S. 1976: Three Roman buildings in the Bulbourne Valley. *HertsArch* 4, 1-135

Newstead, R. & Droop, J. P. 1936: Excavations in the Deanery Field and Abbey Green, 1935. *LAAA* 23, 3-50

Nicklin, K. 1979: The location of pottery manufacture. *Man* 14, 436-58

Nierhaus, R. 1959: *Das Römische Brand- und Körpergräberfeld 'Auf der Steig' in Stuttgart-Bad Cannstatt*, Stuttgart

Nieto-i-Prieto, F. X. & Haumey, C. 1985: Un navire romain et sa cargaison. *Archéologia* 198, 18-21

Noll, R. 1972: Eine Sigillataschussel mit Eigentumsvermerk und Preisangabe aus Flavia Solva. *Germ* 50, 148-52

Nony, D. 1961: Le trésor d'Escoussans et les trésors de monnaies romaines en Gironde. *RNum* ser 6, 3, 91-107

Notet, J.-C. 1977: Fouilles de 1975 et 1976. *Phys* 86, 56-76

----- 1981: L'officine céramique gallo-romaine de Gueugnon. *Phys* 94, 33-43

----- 1982: La sigillée de l'officine de Gueugnon. *Phys* 96, 59-76

----- 1986: Gueugnon. In Bémont & Jacob 1986, 166-71

----- 1996: Gueugnon. 25 ans de fouilles extensives. *DossArch* 215, 118-21

----- & Mitard, P. H. 1987: Une découverte exceptionelle de moules sur le site de l'atelier céramique du Vieux-Fresne à Gueugnon (Saône-et-Loire). *RAECE* 38, 201-9

Nuber, E. 1992: Funde antiker Münzen: Sulz am Neckar. *FB-W* 17/2, 249-66

Nuber, H. U. 1969: Zum Ende der reliefverzierten Terra-Sigillata-Herstellung in Rheinzabern. *MHVP* 67, 136-47

----- 1989: A. Giamilus – ein Sigillatatöpfer aus dem Breisgau. *ANB* 42, 3-9

Nuolet, H. 1966: Trouvaille de Bourg-Blanc (Finistère). *RNum* ser 6, 8, 181-98

Oelmann, F. 1911: Sigillatamanufakturen in La Madeleine bei Nancy. *RK* 1911, 90-3.

----- 1914: *Die Keramik des Kastells Niederbieber*, Frankfurt

Oldenstein-Pferdehirt, B. 1983: Zur Sigillatabelieferung von Obergermanien. *JRGZM* 30, 359-80

----- Recherches sur l'origine des repertoires de poinçons des potiers de Gaule de l'Est et de Germanie Supérieure. In Bémont & Jacob 1986, 257-60

O'Neil, B. H. 1957: Coins. In Murray-Threipland 1957, 23-7

O'Neil, H. E. 1958: 1-5, King's Square, Gloucester, 1958. *TBGAS* 77, 5-22

Orton, C. 1980: *Mathematics in Archaeology*, Cambridge

----- & Orton, J. 1975: It's later than you think: a statistical look at an archaeological problem. *LondArch* 2, 285-7

Oswald, A. 1949: A re-excavation of the Roman villa at Mansfield Woodhouse, Nottinghamshire, 1936-39. *TTS* 53, 1-14

Oswald, F. 1926: The pottery of a third century well at Margidunum. *JRS* 16, 36-44

----- 1929: Bowls by Acaunissa from Birdoswald, Mainz and Cologne. *JRS* 19, 120-4

----- 1930: The decorated work of the potter Butrio. *JRS* 20, 71-7

----- 1931: Bowls of Acaunissa from the North of England. *JRS* 21, 251-5

----- 1936-7: *Index of Figure-Types on Terra Sigillata*, Liverpool

----- 1940: Samian ware (terra sigillata). In Mellor & Goodchild 1940, 71-2

----- 1941: Margidunum. *JRS* 31, 32-62

----- 1945: Decorated ware from Lavoye. *JRS* 35, 49-57

----- 1948a: The work of the Trajanic potter G. lulius Vibinus or Vibius of Lezoux. *LAAA* 28, 55-61

----- 1948b: Samian ware. In Kenyon 1948, 43-72

----- 1952a: Notes on the samian. In Meates *et al.* 1952, 41-9

----- 1952b: *Excavation of a Traverse of Margidunum*, Nottingham

----- 1959: Samian ware. Samian pottery, 1938. In Myres et al. 1959, 37-9, 72-3

----- & Pryce, T. D. 1920: *An Introduction to the Study of Terra Sigillata*, London

Paret, O. 1921: Der Töpferofen. In P. Goessler & R. Knorr, *Cannstatt zur Römerzeit*, Stuttgart, 18-9

----- 1932: *Die Siedlungen des Römischen Württemberg* (Die Römer in Württemberg III), Stuttgart

----- 1938: Die römische Töpferei von Waiblingen-Beinstein. In *Festschrift für August Oxé*, Darmstadt, 57-64

Paridaens, N. *et al.* 2010: Une cachette d'objets de valeur des années 260 apr. J.-C. dans une *villa* de la cité des Nerviens (Merbes-le-Château, Belgique). *Gallia* 67.2, 209-53

Parnell, G. 1982: The excavation of the Roman city wall at the Tower of London, and Tower Hill, 1954-76. *TLMAS* 33, 85-133

Pastor, L. 2013: Classification of decorations of the potter Ianus from the workshop of Dinsheim-Heiligenberg: a preliminary study. In Fulford & Durham 2013, 137-50

Paunier, D. 1975: Etude du matériel de l'établissement gallo-romain de Bernex GE, II, la terre sigillée ornée. *JSGUF* 58, 129-56

----- & Kaenel, G. 1981: Moules pour la fabrication de céramique sigillée à Lousonna (Lausanne-Vidy VD). *AS* 4, 120-6

Pavlinec, M. 1996: Zur Datierung römischzeitlicher Fundstellen in der Schweiz. *JSGUF* 75, 117-32

Peacock, D. P. S. 1978: The Rhine and the problem of Gaulish wine in Britain. In J. du Plat Taylor & H. Cleere (ed), *Roman Shipping and Trade: Britain and the Rhine provinces*, London, 49-51

----- 1982: *Pottery in the Roman World: an ethnoarchaeological approach*, London

Pearce, B. W. 1952: Detailed coin list. In Meates *et al.* 1952, 67-76

----- 1953: The Great Chesterfield hoard of denarii and antoniniani, 1952. *NC* ser 6, 13, 136

----- 1958: Coins. In Cotton & Gathercole 1958, 135-8

Peck, H. 1922: A find of Roman denarii and an early British coin at Ashover, Derbyshire. *BNJ* 16, 369-70

Peña, J. T. 2007: *Roman Pottery in the Archaeological Record,* Cambridge

Pengelly, H. 1975: The samian ware. In Charlesworth 1975, 30-7

----- 1977a: The samian. In Hunter & Mynard 1977, 111-3

----- 1977b: Samian ware. In Mynard & Woodfield 1977, 373

----- 1980: The samian. In Lambrick 1980, 69-76

----- 1982: The samian ware. In Aitken & Aitken 1982, 118-9

Penn, W. S. 1957: The Romano-British settlement at Springhead. Excavation of the Bakery, site A. *ACant* 71, 53-105

----- 1959: The Romano-British settlement at Springhead. Excavation of Temple I, site C1. *ACant* 73, 1-61

----- 1960: Springhead: Temples III and IV. *ACant* 74, 113-40

Perrin, J. R. 1981: Roman pottery from the colonia: Skeldergate and Bishophill. *AYork* 16, 45-111

Petch, D. F. 1960: Excavations at Lincoln, 1955-58. *AJ* 117, 40-70

Peter, M. 1996: Bemerkungen zur Kleingeldversorgung der westlichen Provinzen im 2. Jahrhundert. In King & Wigg 1996, 309-20

Petit, J.-P. 1989: La céramique sigillée dans la bourgade gallo-romain de Bliesbruck (Moselle) au milieu du IIIe siècle après J.-C. Révélation d'une production tardive de vases ornés des potiers Avitus, L.A.L. et L.ÂT.ÂT. de Blickweiler et Eschweiler-Hof. *JRGZM* 36, 473-519

----- 2001: La diffusion de la sigillée moulée à Bliesbruck (Moselle). Contribution à l'étude de Blickweiler et Eschweiler-Hof. In J.-M. Demarolle (ed), *Histoire et Céramologie en Gaule mosellane (Sarlorlux),* Montagnac, 63-180

Petry, F. 1972: Circonscription d'Alsace. *Gallia* 30, 379-419

Pferdehirt, B. 1971: Neue Punzen für Belsus I oder II. *BV* 36, 332

----- 1974: Eine Formschüssel aus Waiblingen-Beinstein. *Germ* 52, 480-2

----- 1976: Die Keramik des Kastells Holzhausen. *LF* 16

----- 1978: *Die Römischen Terra-Sigillata-Töpfereien in Sudgallien*, Stuttgart

----- 1986: Die römische Okkupation Germanikens und Rätiens vonder Zeit des Tiberius bis zum Tode Trajans. Untersuchungen zur Chronologie südgallischer Reliefsigillata. *RRGZM* 33, 221-313

----- 1987: Austrus: un potier de vases décorés à Blickweiler? *RAECE* 38, 57-66

Philp, B. 1959: Reculver. Excavations on the Roman fort in 1957. *ACant* 73, 96-115

----- 1968: *Excavations at Faversham, 1965*, Crawley

----- 1970: *The Roman Fort at Reculver*, Dover

----- 1981: *The Excavations of the Roman Forts of the Classis Britannica at Dover, 1970-1977,* Dover

----- 1984: *Excavations in the Darent Valley, Kent*, Dover

----- 1989: *The Roman House with Bacchic Murals at Dover,* Dover

Picard, G.-C. 1966: Circonscription du Centre. *Gallia* 24, 239-56

----- 1981: La mythologie au service de la Romanisation dans les provinces occidentales de l'Empire romain. In L. Kahil & C. Augé (ed.), *Mythologie gréco-romaine, Mythologies périphériques: études d'iconographie,* Paris, 41-52

Picon, M. 1973: *Introduction à l'Etude technique des Céramiques sigillées de Lezoux*, Dijon

----- 1974: Recherches techniques sur les céramiques de Westerndorf et Pfaffenhofen. *BV* 39, 185-91

----- 1975: Céramique antique et determination des provenances. *DossArch* 9, 85-93

----- 1976: A propos de la vérification du catalogue des marques de l'atelier de la Muette: réflexions sur la valeur des preuves. *Figlina* 1, 89-96

----- 1989: Quelques exemples de la diffusion des moules de Lezoux. *SFECAG Lezoux, 1989,* 79-80

----- 2002a: Les modes de cuisson, les pâtes et les vernis de la Graufesenque: une mise au point. In Genin & Vernhet 2002, 139-63

----- 2002b: À propos des sigillées, présigillées et imitations de sigillées: questions de 'coûts' et de marchés. *SFECAG Bayeux, 2002,* 345-56

----- & Hofmann, B. 1974: La terre sigillée de Banassac (Lozère). Problèmes de composition. *Forum* 4, 17-25

----- & Vauthey, M. 1975: Les céramiques de l'atelier de Terre-Franche. Problèmes de composition et problèmes techniques. *RAC* 14, 284-302

----- & Vernhet, A. 2008: Les très grands fours à sigillées en Gaule, et notamment à La Graufesenque: observations techniques. *SFECAG L'Escala-Empúries, 2008,* 553-66

Pinel, R. 1970a: Travaux de sauvetage. *BCALezoux* 3, 17-22

----- 1970b: Les marques des potiers de Lezoux. *BCALezoux* 3, 26-32

----- 1975: A Lezoux, du nouveau, sur les céramiques gallo-romaines? *Forum* 5, 59-64

----- 1977: La commercialisation de la vaisselle fine gallo-romaine. *BCALezoux* 10, 5-8

Pissot, V. 1993: La céramique gallo-romaine du 4 Impasse du Courtillet à Senlis (Oise). *RAP* 1993, 3/4, 155-72

Pitts, R. A. 2012: The influences on the designs of the potters at Lezoux. In Bird (D) 2012, 178-83

Plattner, S. 1983: Economic custom in a competitive marketplace. *AmAnthro* 85, 848-58

Plicque, A. E. 1887a: *Etude de Céramique arverno-romaine*, Caen

----- 1887b: *Expédition des poteries romaines par l'Allier et la Loire et marques céramiques du Musée de Nantes*, Nantes

Plog, S. 1980: *Stylistic Variation in Prehistoric Ceramics*, Cambridge

Polak, M. 1998: Old wine in new bottles. Reflections on the organization of the production of terra sigillata at La Graufesenque. In Bird 1998, 115-21

----- 2000: *South Gaulish Terra Sigillata with Potters' Stamps from Vechten,* Nijmegen

Polanyi, K. 1957: The economy as instituted process. In K. Polanyi, C. Arensberg, H. Pearson (ed), *Trade and Market in the Early Empires*, Glencoe, Ill., 243-70

----- 1977: *The Livelihood of Man*, New York

Polfer, M. 1991: Der Transport über den Landweg – ein Hemmschuh für die Wirtschaft der römischen Kaiserzeit? *Helinium* 31, 273-95

Pollard, S. 1974: A late Iron Age settlement and a Romano-British villa at Holcombe, near Uplyme, Devon. *PDAS* 32, 59-161

Pollock, S. 1983: Style and information: an analysis of Susiana ceramics. *JAA* 2, 354-90

Potter, T. W. 1979: *Romans in North-West England*, Kendal

----- 1981: The Roman occupation of the central Fenland. *Brit* 12, 79-133

Pownall, A. 1871: Account of a find of Roman coins at Lutterworth. *NC* ser 2, 11, 169-81

Prachner, G. 1980: *Die Sklaven und Freigelassenen im arretinischen Sigillatagewerbe*, Wiesbaden

Praetorius, C. J. 1910: The excavation of a Roman building near Pulborough, Sussex. *PSAL* ser 2, 23, 121-9

Prammer, J. 1975: Ein Sigillata-Brennofen aus Westerndorf-St Peter. *BV* 40, 129-42

Price, R. & Watts, L. 1980: Rescue excavations at Combe Hay, Somerset, 1968-73. *SANH* 124, 1-49, MF

Pryce, T. D. 1932: The decorated samian. In Bushe-Fox 1932, 94-123

----- 1936: Terra sigillata. In Radford 1936, 61-2

----- 1947: Samian pottery. In Cotton 1947, 149-51

----- & Oswald, F. 1926: The terra sigillata or samian ware. In Wheeler 1926, 122-213

Pucci, G. 1973: La produzione della ceramica aretina. Note sull' "industria" nella prima età imperiale romana. *DialArch* 7, 255-93

----- 1981: La ceramica italica (terra sigillata). In A. Giardini & A. Schiavone (ed), *Merci, Mercati e Scambi nel Mediterraneo*, Rome, 99-121, 275-7

----- 1983: Pottery and trade in the Roman period. In P. Garnsey, K. Hopkins, C. Whittaker (ed), *Trade in the Ancient Economy*, London, 105-17

Radbauer, S. 2013: The Roman *terra sigillata*-production of Westerndorf (South Bavaria, Germany): history, location and technology. In Fulford & Durham 2013, 151-64

Radford, C. A. R. 1936: The Roman villa at Ditchley, Oxon. *Oxo* 1, 24-69

Raepsaet, G. 1974: *La Céramique en Terre sigillée de la Villa belgo-romaine de Robelmont (campagnes 1968-71)*, Brussels

----- 1987: Aspects de l'organisation du commerce de la céramique sigillée dans le Nord de la Gaule au IIe siècle de notre ère I: les données matérielles. *MBAH* 6.2, 1-29

----- 2008: Un contrat de mandatum. In Brulet, R. *et al.* (ed), *Liberchies V, vicus gallo-romain,* Louvain-la-Neuve, 267-70

Raepsaet-Charlier, M.-T. & Raepsaet-Charlier, G. 1988: Aspects de l'organisation du commerce de la céramique sigillée dans le Nord de la Gaule au IIe et IIIe siècles notre ère II: négociants et transporteurs. La géographie des activités commerciales. *MBAH* 7.2, 45-69

Rahtz, P. A. 1963: A Roman villa at Downton. *WAM* 58, 303-41

----- & Greenfield, E. 1977: *Excavations at Chew Valley Lake, Somerset*, London

Raistrick, A. 1931: On samian ware from Ilkley, now in the Craven Museum, Skipton. *YAJ* 30, 178-81

Rathbone, D. 1996: Monetisation, not price-inflation, in third-century AD Egypt? In King & Wigg 1996, 321-39

Rau, H. G. 1976: Römische Töpferwerkstatten in Rheinzabern. *AK* 6, 141-7

----- 1977a: Die römische Töpferei ln Rheinzabern. *MHVP* 75, 47-73

----- 1977b: Ausgrabungen in Rheinzabern 1976. *AK* 7, 55-8

Rawes, B. 1981: The Romano-British site at Brockworth, Glos. *Brit* 12, 45-77

Rédö, F. 1981: Römische Forschungen in Zalalövö 1978-1979. *AAHung* 33, 273-346

----- 1982: Römische Forschungen in Zalalövö 1980-1981. *AAHung* 34, 323-62

-----, Lanyi, V., Gabler, D. 1978: Römische Forschungen in Zalalövö 1976. *AAHung* 30, 349-430

Reece, R. M. 1971: The Coins. In Cunliffe 1971, vol. 11, 92-100

----- 1972: A short survey of the Roman coins found on fourteen sites in Britain. *Brit* 3, 269-76

----- 1973: Roman coinage in Britain and the western Empire. *Brit* 4, 227-51

----- 1974: Numerical aspects of Roman coin hoards in Britain. In Casey & Reece 1974, 78-94

----- 1976: The coins. ln Drury 1976, 15-7

----- 1978a: Roman coins. In Drury 1978, 94

----- 1978b: The Roman coins. In Collis 1978, 20

----- 1979: Roman monetary impact. In B. Burnham & H. Johnson (ed), *Invasion and Response. The Case of Roman Britain*, Oxford, 211-7

----- 1980a: Coins. In Price & Watts 1980, MF M148-52, 321-5

----- 1980b: The Roman coins from 1 Westgate Street. In Heighway & Garrod 1980, 99-103

----- 1981a: The 'normal' hoard. In C. Carcassone & T. Hackens (ed), *Statistics and Numismatics*, Strasbourg, 299-308

----- 1981b: The third century: crisis or change? In King & Henig 1981, 27-38

----- 1982: The Roman coins. In Wedlake 1982, 112-8

----- 1983: The coins. In Collis 1983, 65, MF M23

----- 1984: Mints, markets and the military. In Blagg & King 1984, 143-60

----- 1988: The Roman coins. In Rodwell (K) 1988, 79-81

----- 1993: The Roman coin hoards. In Darling & Gurney 1993, 62-5

Reinfuss, G. 1957: Gräberstrasse 1957. *CJ* 3, 81-99

Renard, M. 1955: La légende de Pero et de Micon sur des vases de La Graufesenque. *Latomus* 14, 285-9

Reubel, G. 1912: *Römische Töpfer in Rheinzabern. Ein Beitrag zur verzierten Terra-Sigillata*, Speyer

Reutti, F. 1983: Tonverarbeitende Industrie im römischen Rheinzabern. *Germ* 61, 33-69

----- 1984: *Neue Archäologische Forschungen im römischen Rheinzabern,* Rheinzabern

----- & Schulz, R. 2010: Brennöfen für Terra Sigillata in Rheinzabern. Befunde und Rekonstruktion. *RCRFA* 41, 567-87

Rhodes, M. 1989: Roman pottery lost en route from the kiln site to the user. A gazetteer. *JRPS* 2, 44-58

RIC *Roman Imperial Coinage*

Riccioni, G. 1977: *Problemi di archeologia gallo-romana I. La terra sigillata della Gallia meridionale*, Bologna

Richardson, B. & Tyers, P. A. 1984: North Gaulish pottery in Britain. *Brit* 15, 133-41

Richardson, K. M. 1944: Report on excavations at Verulamium: Insula XVII, 1938. *Arch* 90, 81-126

----- 1961: Excavations in Lewis's Gardens, Colchester, 1955 and 1958. *TEAS* ser 3, 1, 6-32

Richmond, I. A. & Birley, E. 1930: Excavations on Hadrian's Wall, in the Birdoswald-Pike Hill sector. *TCWAAS* ser 2, 30, 169-205

----- & Gillam, J. P. 1950: Excavations on the Roman site at Corbridge 1946-1949. *AAel* ser 4, 28, 152-201

----- & ----- 1951: The temple of Mithras at Carrawburgh. *AAel* ser 4, 29, 1-92

----- & ----- 1955: Some excavations at Corbridge, 1952-1954. *AAel* ser 4, 33, 218-52

Ricken, H. 1934: Die Bilderschüsseln der Kastelle Saalburg und Zugmantel I. *SJ* 8, 130-82

----- 1938: Die Bilderschüsseln der Töpferei von Waiblingen-Beinstein. In *Festschrift für August Oxé*, Darmstadt, 64-83

----- 1942: *Die Bilderschüsseln der römischen Töpfer von Rheinzabern* (Tafelband), 1st ed., Darmstadt

----- 1948: *Die Bilderschüsseln der römischen Töpfer von Rheinzabern* (Tafelband), 2nd ed., Speyer

----- & Fischer, C. 1963: *Die Bilderschüsseln der römischen Töpfer von Rheinzabern* (Textband), Bonn

----- & Thomas, M. 2005: *Die Dekorationsserien der Rheinzaberner Reliefsigillaten. Textband zum Katalog VI der Ausgrabungen von Wilhelm Ludovici in Rheinzabern 1901-1914,* Bonn

Rieckhoff-Pauli, S. 1979: Römische Siedlungs- und Grabfunde aus Künzing, Ldkr. Deggendorf (Niederbayern). *BV* 44, 79-122

Riedl, H. 2011: *Die Schwäbische Reliefsigillata. Untersuchungen zur Bilderschüssel-produktion des 2. und 3. Jahrhunderts im mittleren Neckarraum,* Stuttgart

Rigoir, J. 1968: Les sigillées paléochrétiennes grises et orangées. *Gallia* 26, 177-244

Rigoir, Y. & Rigoir, J. 1985: Les dérivés-des-sigillées dans la moitié sud de la France. *SFECAG Reims, 1985,* 49-56

-----, ----- & Vertet, H. 1973: Essai de classement synthetique des céramiques sigillées. *RAC* 12, 69-76

Rigold, S. E. 1959: Coins. In Murray-Threipland 1959, 132-3

Rilliot, M. 1969: Fouilles archéologiques à Offemont (Territoire de Belfort). *RAECE* 20, 247-70

----- 1976: Offemont. Atelier de potier au lieu dit 'La Cornée'. *RAECE* 27, 171-95

----- 1986: Offemont. In Bémont & Jacob 1986, 231-3

Ritterling, E. 1901: Zwei Münzfunde aus Niederbieber. *BJ* 107, 95-131

----- 1911: Das Kastell Niederbieber. *BJ* 120, 259-78

----- 1913: Das frührömische Lager bei Hofheim im Taunus. *AVNassau* 40, *passim*

----- 1936: Das Kastell Nieder-Bieber. In E. Fabricius *et al.* (ed), *Der Obergermanisch-Raetische Limes des Römerreiches B, I, no. 1a,* Berlin & Leipzig

Robertson, A. S. 1935a: The St Mary Cray hoard. *NC* ser 5, 15, 62-6

----- 1935b: The Linwood (March) hoard. *NC* ser 5, 15, 57-62

----- 1935c: The Edlington Wood find. *NC* ser 5, 15, 202-7

----- 1937: A hoard of Roman silver from Abergele, Denbighshire. *BBCS* 8, 188-201

----- 1939: A hoard of denarii from Knapwell, Cambs. *NC* ser 5, 19, 175-7

----- 1945: A Roman coin hoard from Emneth, Norfolk. *NC* ser 6, 5, 147-53

----- 1950: A hoard of denarii from Handley, Dorset. *NC* ser 6, 10, 311-5

----- 1954: A Roman coin hoard from Mildenhall, Suffolk. *NC* ser 6, 14, 40-52

----- 1957: A hoard of Roman silver coins from Briglands, Rumbling Bridge, Kinross-shire. *PSAS* 90, 241-6

----- 1961a: Roman coins found in Scotland, 1951-60. *PSAS* 94, 133-83

----- 1961b: The coins. In Steer 1961, 99-100

----- 1975: *Birrens (Blatobulgium),* Edinburgh

----- 1978: The circulation of Roman coins in North Britain: the evidence of hoards and site-finds from Scotland. In R. A. Carson & C. M. Kraay (ed), *Scripta Nummaria Romana. Essays presented to Humphrey Sutherland,* London, 186-216

----- 1983: Roman coins found in Scotland, 1971-82. *PSAS* 113, 405-48

-----, Scott, M., Keppie, L. 1975: *Bar Hill: a Roman fort and its finds*, Oxford

Robinson, D. J. 1980: Coins. In Mason 1980

Robinson, P. 1971: Coins. In Branigan 1971, 159-62

Roche, J.-L. 1975: Etude des monnaies. In Berland & Lintz 1975, 28-30

Rodwell, K. 1988: *The Prehistoric and Roman Settlement at Kelvedon, Essex,* London

Rodwell, W. J. 1976: The terra sigillata. In Drury 1976, 38-42

----- 1978: Terra sigillata. In Drury 1978, 93-4

----- 1982a: Group 3: the samian pottery. In Leach 1982, 129-38

----- 1982b: The production and distribution of pottery and tiles in the territory of the Trinovantes. *EAH* 14, 15-76

----- 1988: The samian. In Rodwell (K) 1988, 92-100

Rogers, G. B. 1970: Banassac and Cinnamus. *RCRFA* 11/12, 98-106

----- 1972: Un group de ratés de four de la Gaule centrale. *RAC* 11, 322-6

----- 1974: Poteries sigillées de la Gaule centrale I. Les motifs non figurés. *Gallia Supp* 28

----- 1977: A group of wasters from Central Gaul. In J. Dore & K. Greene (ed), *Roman Pottery Studies in Britain and Beyond*, Oxford, 245-50

----- 1999: *Poteries sigillées de la Gaule centrale II. Les potiers*, Lezoux

----- & Laing, L. R. 1966: *Gallo-Roman pottery from Southampton and the distribution of terra nigra in Great Britain*, Southampton

Rogerson, A. 1977: Excavations at Scole, 1973. *East Anglian Archaeol* 5, 97-224

Roller, O. 1965: *Die Römischen Terra-Sigillata-Töpfereien von Rheinzabern*, Stuttgart

----- 1966: Die römischen Töpfereien von Blickweiler, Kr. St Ingbert, und Eschweilerhof. Gem. Kirkel-Neuhäusel, Kr. Homburg. In *Führer zu vor- und frühgeschichtlichen Denkmalern 5, Saarland*, Mainz, 134-8

Romeuf, A.-M. 1986: Les Martres-de-Veyre. In Bémont & Jacob 1986, 145-52

----- & Romeuf, J. 1977a: Chantier des Martres-de-Veyre (Puy-de-Dôme), *RAC* 16, 271-80

----- & ----- 1977b: Un quartier artisanal aux Martres-de-Veyre, *Archéologia* 108, 76-7

----- & ----- 1978: Chantier des Martres-de-Veyre (Puy-de-Dôme) III – poinçon-matrice figurant un lion (campagne de 1975). *RAC* 17, 235-8

----- & ----- 2001: *Les Martres-de-Veyre (Puy-de-Dôme), le quartier artisanal,* Lezoux

Romeuf, J. 1970: Cinnamus de Lezoux, par Anne-Marie Vialatte. *RAC* 9, 336-7

Romeuf-Vialatte, A.-M. 1970: Cinnamus (inscriptions sur vases et moul es). *BCALezoux* 3, 33-5

Rossignol, B. & Durost, S. 2007: Volcanisme global et variations climatiques de courte durée dans l'histoire romaine (Ie s. av. J.-C. – IVe s. ap. J.-C.). *JRGZM* 54, 395-438

Roth, R. E. 2003: Towards a ceramic approach to social identity in the Roman world: some theoretical considerations. *Digressus* Suppl 1, 35-45 http://www.digressus.org

Roth-Rubi, K. 1984: Nachlese zur Sigillata-Produktion in der Schweiz. *AS* 7, 16-20

----- 1986: La production de terre sigillée en Suisse aux IIe et IIIe s. Problèmes de définition. In Bémont & Jacob 1986, 269-75

----- 1990: Spätantike Glantonkeramik im Westen des römischen Imperiums. *BRGK* 71, 905-71

Roussel, L. 1971: Fouilles de Mâlain lieu dit 'La Boussière' parcel1e 22. *RAECE* 22, 127-59

----- 1975 Mâlain-Mediolanum – Fouilles de 'La Boussière' 1968-72. *RAECE* 26, 7-68

Rudling, D. R. 1978: The Coins. In Hartridge 1978, 100-1

----- 1984: A hoard of Roman coins from Combe Hill, East Sussex. *SxAC* 122, 218-9

Rüsch, A. 1981: *Das Römische Rottweil,* Stuttgart

Ruprechtsberger, E. M. 1974: Zum Typenschatz des Terra-Sigillata-Töpfers Januarius (II) von Rheinzabern. *JOM* 119, 1, 23-8

Rutkowski, B. 1967: The export of the Westerndorf ware. *ArchPol* 18, 55-70

Sanquer, R. 1967: Le style des 'Antistii', potiers de Lezoux. *AB* 74, 167-72

----- & Galliou, P. 1970: Le château gallo-romain de Keradennec en Saint-Frégant (Finistère). *AB* 77, 163-225

----- & ----- 1972: Une maison de campagne gallo-romaine à la Roche-Maurice (Finistère). *AB* 79, 215-51

Sauvaget, R. 1970: Le potier Servus II de Lezoux. *RAC* 9, 127-42

----- & Vauthey, M. 1970: Les deux Servus, un seul et même potier? *RAC* 9, 143-4

----- & Vertet, H. 1967: Remarques sur le potier Servus II. *RAC* 6, 275; *RAECE* 18, 200-1

Schaad, D. 2007: *La Graufesenque (Millau, Aveyron) I,* Condatomagos, *une agglomération de confluent en territoire rutène, II s.a.C. – III s.p.C.,* Pessac

----- 2010: Le grand four de La Graufesenque: histoire d'un four. *SFECAG Chelles, 2010,* 417-32

Schallmayer, E. 1982: Ein römischer Töpferbezirk bei Stettfeld, Gde Ubstadt-Weiher, Landkreis Karlsruhe. *AAB-W* 1982, 106-9

----- 1984: Eine Terra-Sigillata-Imitation aus Stettfeld, Gem. Ubstadt-Weiher, Ldkr. Karlsruhe. *ANB* 33, 23-32

----- 1987: Zur Chronologie in der Römischen Archäologie. *AK* 17, 483-97

----- 1995: (ed) *Der Augsburger Siegesaltar. Zeugnis einer unruhigen Zeit,* Bad Homburg

----- 1996: (ed) *Niederbieber, Postumus und das Limesfall. Bericht des ersten Saalburgkolloquiums,* Bad Homburg

Schaub, A. 1994: Markomannenkriegszeitliche Zerstörungen in Sulz am Neckar – ein tradierter Irrtum. Bemerkungen zu reliefverzierter Terra Sigillata vom Ende des zweiten Jahfhunderts. In Friesinger *et al.* 1994, 439-45

----- 1996: Zur Chronologie des Rheinzaberner Relieftöpfers Ianu II. In Schallmayer 1996, 90-2

Schaub, J. 1987: Le potier Clamosus: sa production revelée par les fouilles de Bliesbruck. *RAECE* 38, 67-76 [*Mélanges offerts à Marcel Lutz*]

Schaub, M. 2007: Archäologie vor Ort vermittelt: die Publikumsgrabung 2006.058 in Augusta Raurica bringt ein Fundensemble um 100 n. Chr. aus Licht. *JAK* 28, 125-95

Scherrer, P. 1994: Der grosse Markomanneneinfall des Jahres 170 und seine Folgen im Lichte der neuen Ausgrabungen in Aelium Cetium/St. Pölten. In Friesinger *et al.* 1994, 447-55

Schleiermacher, W. 1936: Die Einzelfunde der 4. und 5. Strecke. In E. Fabricius *et al.* (ed), *Der Obergermanisch-Raetische Limes des Römerreiches A, II, 2,* Berlin & Leipzig, 181-227

----- 1958: Eine Sigillata-Form-Schüssel mit Eierstab X. *SJ* 17, 74-5

Schmid, D. & Vogel Müller, V. 2012: Eine Terra-Sigillata-ähnliche Keramikproduktion des 3. Jahrhunderts in Augusta Raurica. In Bird (D) 2012, 112-29

Schmidts, T. 2011: *Akteure und Organisation der Handelsschiffahrt in den Nordwestlichen Provinzen des Römischen Reiches,* Mainz

Schmitt, M. P. 1975: Les liaisons de l'Arar vers l'Ocean. *Caesarodunum* 10, 124-8

Schönberger, H. 1956: Das Römerkastell Boiodurum-Beiderweis zu Passau-Innstadt. *SJ* 15, 42-78

----- 1959: Das Römerkastell Quintana-Künzing. *BV* 24, 109-46

----- 1963: Zur 'Sigillata-Formschüssel' aus Alem, Noord-Brabant. *BROB* 12/13, 577-8

----- 1969: The Roman frontier in Germany: an archaeological survey. *JRS* 59, 144-97

----- 1972: Das Römerkastell Öhringen-West (Burgkastell). *BRGK* 53, 233-96

----- 1975: Kastell Künzing-Quintana. *LF* 13

----- & Hartley, B. R. 1970: Die Namenstempel auf glatter Sigillata aus dem Erdkastell der Saalburg. *SJ* 27, 21-30

----- & Simon, H.-G. 1983: Die Kastelle in Altenstadt. *LF* 22

Scholz, M. 2003: Keramik und Geschichte des Kastells Kapersburg – eine Bestandsaufnahme. *SJ* 52/3, 9-281

Schoppa, H. 1964: Eine römische Strassenstation bei Kriftel, Maintaunuskr. *FH* 4, 98-116

Schücker, N. & Thomas, M. 2004: Der Sigillata-Sammelfund aus Keller 256 des Zugmantelvicus – ein Gefässensemble aus dem Heiligtum für *Iuppiter Dolichenus*? *SJ* 54, 161-95

Schulz, R. 1999: Wirtschaftsbedingte Strukturen und Strukturwandel im Töpfervicus Rheinzabern. In N. Hanel & C. Schucany (ed.), *Colonia – municipium – vicus. Struktur und Entwicklung städtischer Siedlungen in Noricum, Rätien und Obergermanien,* Oxford, 65-82

Schumacher, F.-J. 1988: Die Töpferei von Blickweiler. In *Führer zu Archäologischen Denkmälern in Deutschland, 18, Saar-Pfalz-Kreis*, Stuttgart, 151-4

Seaby, W. A. 1949: Coinage from Ham Hill in Taunton Museum. *NC* ser 6, 9, 166-79

Séguier, J.-M. & Delage, R. 2009: Les assemblages céramiques du IIIe siècle après J.-C. dans le secteur Seine-Yonne: datation, faciès et approvisionnements. *SFECAG Colmar, 2009,* 501-62

Sheldon, H. 1972: Excavations at Parnell Road and Appian Road, Old Ford, E3. *TLMAS* 23, 101-47

----- 1981: London and south-east Britain. In King & Henig 1981, 363-82

Shotter, D. C. 1976: Coin evidence and the northern frontier in the second century AD. *PSAS* 107, 81-91

----- 1978: Roman coins from Kirkby Thore. *TCWAAS* 78, 17-22

----- 1979: Coins. In Potter 1979, 291-9

----- 1981: The coins. In Potter 1981, 116

----- 2000: Coins. In Buxton & Howard-Davis 2000, 227-34

Simon, H.-G. 1965: Die römische Funde aus dem Grabungen in Gross-Gerau 1962/63. *SJ* 22, 38-99

----- 1968: Das Kleinkastell Degerfeld in Butzbach, Kr. Friedberg (Hessen); Datierung und Funde. *SJ* 25, 5-64

----- 1976: Terra Sigillata: Bilderschüsseln und Töpferstempel auf glatter Ware. In Baatz 1976, 37-53

----- 1977a: Neufunde von Sigillata-Formschüsseln im Kreis Esslingen. *FB-W* 3, 463-73

----- 1977b: Heiligenberger Töpfereifunde im Saalburgmuseum. *SJ* 34, 88-97

----- 1984: Terra Sigillata aus Waiblingen. Grabung 1967. *FB-W* 9, 471-546

----- & Köhler, H.-J. 1992: *Ein Geschirrdepot des 3. Jahrhunderts. Grabungen im Lagerdorf des Kastells Langenhain,* Bonn

Simon, L. 2002: Mobiliers domestiques en usage au cours du troisième quart du IIe siècle dans une communauté rurale armoricaine: le site du Manoir de la Coudre à La Mézière (Ille-et-Vilaine). *SFECAG Bayeux, 2002,* 185-203

Simpson, G. 1952: The Aldgate potter: a maker of Romano-British samian ware. *JRS* 42, 68-71

----- 1953: The figured samian ware. Pp. 242-53 in I. A. Richmond & J. P. Gillam, Buildings of the first and second centuries north of the granaries at Corbridge. *AAel* ser 4, 31, 205-53

----- 1957a: Metallic black slip vases from Central Gaul with applied and moulded decoration. *AntJ* 37, 29-42

----- 1957b: Samian ware. In Hildyard 1957, 247-51

----- 1958: Pottery: the samian ware. In Cotton & Gathercole 1958, 50-8

----- 1959: The samian ware, and a note on 'samian survival'. In Murray-Threipland 1959, 130-1

----- 1962: Caerleon and the Roman forts in Wales in the second century AD, part 1. *ACamb* 111, 103-66

----- 1963a: Caerleon and the Roman forts in Wales in the second century AD, part 2. *ACamb* 112, 13-76

----- 1963b: The samian ware. In Hunter 1963, 43-6

----- 1965: Samian. In Murray-Threipland 1965, 141-2

----- 1966: The chronological interpretation of Antonine samian pottery. *ACamb* 115, 88-93

----- 1970: The decorated samian ware and potters' stamps. In Frere 1970, 111-2

----- 1971: The close of Period la on Hadrian's Wall, and some Gaulish potters. *AAel* ser 4, 49, 109-18

----- 1972: Samian pottery and a Roman road at Corbridge. *AAel* ser 4, 50, 217-33

----- 1973: More black slip vases from Central Gaul with applied and moulded decoration in Britain. *AntJ* 53, 42-51

----- 1974a: Haltwhistle Burn, Corbridge and the Antonine Wall: a reconsideration. *Brit* 5, 317-39

----- 1974b: The samian pottery. In Pollard 1974, 111-5

----- 1976: Decorated terra sigillata at Montans (Tarn) from the manuscript of Elie Rossignol at Albi. *Brit* 7, 244-73

----- 1977: La marque Sacer.F in tabula ansata et quelques oves de Sacer de Lezoux. *RAC* 16, 85-8

----- 1980: An appliqué metallic slip vase from Central Gaul. In Lambrick 1980, 73-5

----- 1982a: A revised dating for the Colchester samian kiln. *EAH* 14, 149-53

----- 1982b: The samian pottery. In Wedlake 1982, 154-76

----- 1982c: The samian pottery. In Field 1982, 88-9

----- 1987: Production céramique de Montans (Tarn) et masque de théâtre de Wilderspool dans le Cheshire. *RAECE* 38, 251-5

----- 1992: Make your own index. *JRPS* 5, 125-6

----- & Brassington, M. 1980: Concordia and Discipulina on the North British frontier. In W. S. Hanson & L. J. Keppie (ed), *Roman Frontier Studies 1979*, Oxford, 141-50

----- & Rogers, G. 1969: Cinnamus de Lezoux et quelques potiers contemporains. *Gallia* 27, 3-14

Smedley, N. 1946a: The Cadeby (Doncaster) hoard. *NC* ser 6, 6, 151

----- 1946b: The Folds Farm (Doncaster) hoard. *NC* ser 6, 6, 69-72

----- & Owles, E. J. 1966: A Romano-British bath-house at Stonham Aspal. *PSIA* 30, 221-51

Smith, C. R. 1850: Roman denarii found near Rayleigh, Essex. *JBAA* 5, 355-8

----- 1887: Discovery of a hoard of Roman coins at Springhead. *NC* ser 3, 7, 312-5

Smith, R. A. 1907: On the wreck on Pudding Pan Rock, Herne Bay, Kent. *PSAL* ser 2, 21, 268-92

----- 1909: Diving operations on Pudding-pan Rock, Herne Bay, Kent and on the Gallo-Roman red ware recently recovered from the Rock. *PSAL* ser 2, 22, 396-414

Société Archéologique de Neuville 1978: Quatre poinçons inédits du potier IULLINUS sur un vase en terre sigillée découvert à Ingrannes. *RAL* 4, 31-2

Sölch, R. 1999: *Die Terra-Sigillata-Manufaktur von Schwabmünchen-Schwabegg*, Kallmünz

Sommer, C. S. 1988: Kastellvicus und Kastell. Untersuchungen zum Zugmantel im Taunus und zu den Kastellvici in Obergermanien und Rätien. *FB-W* 13, 457-707

Sorge, G. 2001: *Die Keramik der Römischen Töpfersiedlung Schwabmünchen, Landkreis Augsburg,* Kallmünz

Spain, G. R. B. 1930: The treasure vault of the Roman fort at Benwell (Condercum). *AAel* ser 4, 7, 126-30

Sparey Green, C. 1985: The coins from the 1974 excavations. In Hinchliffe & Sparey Green 1985, 41

Speidel, M. P. 1975: The rise of ethnic units in the Roman Imperial army. In H. Temporini & W. Haase (ed), *ANRW II, 3*, Berlin, 202-31

Sprater, F. 1930: Römische Tongewinnung in der Pfalz. pp. in Römisch-Germanischen Zentralmuseum (ed), *Schumacher Festchrift*, Mainz, 265-9

Spurrell, F. C. 1881: Roman coins from the hoard found at Baconsthorpe, Norfolk, in 1878. *AJ* 38, 433-4

Stanfield, J. A. 1929: Unusual forms of terra sigillata. *AJ* 86, 113-51

----- 1935: A samian bowl from Bewcastle, with a note on the potters Casurius and Apolauster. *TCWAAS* 35, 182-205

----- 1937: Unusual forms of terra sigillata, 2nd series. *AJ* 93, 101-16

----- 1940: Samian pottery from Wroxeter. In Kenyon 1940, 194-208

----- & Simpson, G. 1958: *Central Gaulish Potters*, Oxford

----- & ----- 1990: *Les Potiers de la Gaule Centrale*, Gonfaron (2nd ed. of Stanfield & Simpson 1958)

Stazio, A. 1954: Ripostigli monetali del Museo Nazionale di Napoli. *AIIN* 1, 113-26

Stead, I. M. 1976: *Excavations at Winterton Roman Villa*, London

Steer, K. A. 1961: Excavations at Mumrills Roman fort, 1958-60. *PSAS* 94, 86-132

----- & Feachem, R. W. 1962: The excavations at Lyne, Peebleshire, 1959-63. *PSAS* 94, 208-18

Stiller, G. 1986: Haute-Yutz. In Bémont & Jacob 1986, 221-3

-----, Muller, H., Zumstein, H., Hatt, J.-J. 1960: Découverte d'une officine de céramique gallo-romaine à Haute-Yutz (Moselle). *ASHAL* 60, 5-40

Streitberg, G. 1971: Der Kreis des COMITIALIS. Ein Beitrag zur Sigillata-Töpferei von Westerndorf. *BV* 36, 325-31

----- 1973: Namenstempel und Stempelmarken Westerndorfer Sigillatatöpfer. *BV* 38, 132-53

Stribrny, K. 1993: *FMRD II, iv, Nachtrag 1, Nordwürttemberg*, Berlin

Strobel, K. 1987: Einige Bemerkungen zu den historisch-archäologischen Grundlagen einer Neuformulierung der Sigillatenchronologie für Germanien und Rätien und zu wirtschaftsgeschichtlichen Aspekten der römischen Keramikindustrie. *MBAH* 6.2, 75-115

----- 1992: Produktions- und Arbeitsverhältnisse in der südgallischen Sigillatenindustrie: zu Fragen der Massenproduction in der römischen Kaiserzeit. *SNUQ* 8, 27-57

----- 2000: (ed) *Forschungen zur römischen Keramikindustrie. Produktions-, Rechts- und Distributionsstrukturen,* Mainz

Stümpel, B. 1978: Zur Datierung der römischen Stadtmauer in Mainz. *BJ* 178, 291-303

Stuppner, A. 1994: Zu den Auswirkungen der Markomannenkriege im niederösterreichischen Limesvorland. In Friesinger *et al.* 1994, 285-98

Sutherland, C. H. 1936: Three Roman coin hoards. *NC* ser 5, 16, 316-20

----- 1939a: The Poughill (Devonshire) hoard of Roman coins. *NC* ser 5, 19, 170-5

----- 1939b: Coins. In *Victoria County History, Oxford I*, London, 324-30

Swan, V. 1971: The coarse pottery. In Wainwright 1971, 100-16

----- 1984: *The Pottery Kilns of Roman Britain*, London

Swinbank, B. 1955: Pottery from levels of the second and third century, covering the vallum at Benwell. *AAel* ser 4, 33, 142-62

Swoboda-Milenović, R. M. 1956: Ausgrabungen in der Zivilstadt 1952. *CJ* 2, 31-44

Sydenham, E. A. 1952: *Coinage of the Roman Republic*, London

Sydow, W. 1982: Eine römische Nekropole auf dem Georgenberg in Enns. *FÖ* 21, 187-206

Symonds, R. P. 1987: La production de la sigillée à Colchester en Angleterre, et les liens avec les ateliers de la Gaule de l'Est: quelques résultats des analyses chimiques. *RAECE* 38, 77-81

----- 1992: *Rhenish Wares. Fine dark-coloured pottery from Gaul and Germany,* Oxford

----- 2008: *Terminus post quem.* Datation systématique et représentation numérique et graphique de la chronologie des céramiques. *SFECAG L'Escala-Empúries, 2008,* 607-16

Taramelli, A. 1915: Ripostiglio di grandi bronzi imperiali di Villaurbana (Cagliari). *RIN* 28, 73-84

Tatton-Brown, T. W. 1974: Excavations at the Custom House site, City of London, 1973. *TLMAS* 25, 117-219

Terrisse, R. 1954: Eine Sigillata-Töpferei in Martres-de-Veyre (Frankreich). *Germ* 32, 171-5

----- 1958a: L'officine gallo-romaine des Martres-de-Veyre (Puy-de-Dôme). *Ogam* 10, 221-42

----- 1958b: Le dossier des tournettes gallo-romaines peut-être fermé. *Ogam* 10, 417-9

----- 1960a: A propos du potier Drusus. *Ogam* 12, 27-30

----- 1960b: Que de tournettes... *Ogam* 12, 241-2

----- 1963a: Sigillée des Martres-de-Veyre (Puy-de-Dôme): principaux styles. *Gallia* 21, 227-39

----- 1963b: Bref aperçu sur les styles des potiers des Martres-de-Veyre (Puy-de-Dôme). *RAC* 2, 267-92

----- 1968: Les céramiques sigillées gallo-romaines des Martres-de-Veyre (Puy-de-Dôme). *Gallia Supp* 19

Tester, P. J. 1969: Excavations at Fordcroft, Orpington. *ACant* 84, 39-77

----- & Caiger, J. E. 1954: Excavations on the site of a Romano-British settlement in Joyden's Wood, near Bexley. *ACant* 68, 167-83

Thill, G., Metzler, J., Weiller, R. 1971: Neue Grabungsergebnisse vom Titelberg. *Hémecht* 23, 79-91

Thirion, M. 1967: *Les Trésors Monétaires gaulois et romains trouvés en Belgique*, Brussels

----- 1970: Hautrage II. Trésor. *BCEN* 7, 62-3

----- 1971: Trouvailles. Roksem trésor. *BCEN* 8, 18-19

----- 1974a: Le trésor de Zottegem-Veizeke II: argent jusqu'à Postume. *BCEN* 11, 12-15

----- 1974b: Un trésor de sesterces découvert à Humbeek. *BCEN* 11, 77-8

Thompson, F. H. 1956: Roman Lincoln, 1953. *JRS* 46, 22-6

----- 1962: A hoard of antoniniani from Agden, near Altrincham, Cheshire. *NC* ser 7, 2, 143-55

----- & Whitwell, J. B. 1973: The gates of Roman Lincoln. *Arch* 104, 129-208

Thompson, M. 1979: *Rubbish Theory*, Oxford

Tilhard, J.-L. 1972: Deux vases sigillés signés DIO. *RAC* 11, 327-34

----- 1976: *La céramique sigillée du Musée Archéologique de Saintes I. Les estampilles*, Saintes

----- 1977: *La céramique sigillée du Musée Archéologique de Saintes II. Les vases à décor moulé*, Saintes

----- 2004: *Les Céramiques sigillées du Haut-Empire à Poitiers d'après les estampilles et les décors moulés,* Marseille

Tite, M. S., Bimson, M. & Freestone, I. C. 1982: An examination of the high gloss surface finishes on Greek Attic and Roman Samian wares. *Archaeometry* 24, 117-26

Todd, M. 1969: The Roman settlement at Margidunum: the excavations of 1966-8. *TTS* 73, 1-104

Torrence, R. 1978: Chipping away at some misconceptions about sampling lithic assemblages. In J. Cherry, C. Gamble, S. Shennan (ed), *Sampling in Contemporary British Archaeology*, Oxford, 373-98

Trimpe-Berger, J. A. 1961: De Romeinse vormschotel uit Alem. *BROB* 10/11, 555-61

Tuckett, T. 1992: Bletchley, Buckinghamshire. *CHRB* 9, 50-64

Turcan, R. 1963: *Le Trésor de Guelma*, Paris

Turckheim-Pey, S. de 1981: La trouvaille d'Arnouville-lès-Gonesse. *TM* 3, 17-31

Unverzagt, W. 1916: *Die Keramik des Kastells Alzei*, Frankfurt

Van Berchem, D. 1936: L'annone militaire dans l'empire romain au IIIe siècle. *MSNAF* 1936, 117-202

Vanderhoeven, M. 1969: Terre sigillée de Tongres decorée et signée. *CollLatomus* 103, 622-36

----- 1981: Terre sigillée de Matagne-la-Petite, Pommeroeul et Saint-Mard. *ABelg* 243

Van Giffen, A. E. 1948: Inheemse en Romeinse terpen. Opgravingen in de dorpswierde te Ezinge en de Romeinse terpen van Utrecht, Valkenburg ZH en Vechten. *JVT* 29/32, *passim*

-----, Vollgraff, C. W., Van Hoorn, G. 1934: *Opgravingen op het Domplein te Utrecht*, Haarlem

Vanhoutte, S., De Clercq, W., Deschieter, J., Dijkman, W. 2012: The samian ware supply at the Roman fort of Oudenburg (West-Flanders, Belgium). *SGRPNews* 54, 8

-----, Dhaeze, W. & De Clercq, W. 2009a: Pottery consumption c. AD 260-70 at the Roman coastal defence fort in Oudenburg, Northern Gaul. *JRPS* 14, 95-139

----- *et 18 alii* 2009b: De dubblele waterput uit het laat-Romeins *castellum* van Oudenburg (prov. West-Vlaanderen): tafonomie, chronologie en interpretatie. *Relicta* 5, 9-142

Van Oyen, A. 2012: Knowledge systems in the production of *terra sigillata*. Moving beyond the local/global paradox. In M. Duggan *et al.* (ed), *TRAC 2011. Proceedings of the 21st Theoretical Roman Archaeology Conference, Newcastle 2011*, Oxford, 48-59

Vasselle, F. 1974: Structures gallo-romaines à Etalon. *CAP* 1, 103-14

Vauthey, M. & Vauthey, P. 1957: Terre Franche. Officine de la céramique rouge de Vichy I. Historique du site et premières découvertes. *Ogam* 9, 368-73

----- & ----- 1958: Terre Franche, officine de la céramique rouge de Vichy II – marques et signatures des potiers de Vichy-rive gauche. *Ogam* 10, 87-94

----- & ----- 1959: Terre Franche, officine de la céramique rouge de Vichy (Allier). *Ogam* 11, 455-68

----- & ----- 1963a: Officine de Terre-Franche. Deux moules de vases 30 signés Cinnamus. *RAC* 2, 48-56

----- & ----- 1963b: L'officine céramique de Terre-Franche (Allier). Le site, les elements de fours, les accessoires de fabrication, la poterie rouge non décorée. *RAC* 2, 319-34

----- & ----- 1966: A propos de deux estampilles 'Minusu' et de quelques autres livrées par l'officine de Terre-Franche (Allier). *RCRFA* 8, 51-5

----- & ----- 1967a: Introduction a l'étude du potier arverne Servus II. La fouille 561 de Vichy-Terre-Franche. *RAC* 6, 145-56

----- & ----- 1967b: Les grandes officines de céramique sigillée de la Gaule centrale II: les voies fluviales et maritimes d'exportation de la sigillée arverne vers la Grande-Bretagne. *BSHAVichy* 71, 266-81; also in *Actes du 91e CNSS, Rennes 1966*, 177-200

----- & ----- 1968: L'officine céramique de Gueugnon (S-et-L). *RAC* 7, 265-8

----- & ----- 1970a: Un moule de vase Drag. 37 avec graffito d' «Anunus». *RAC* 9, 36-41

----- & ----- 1970b: Deux vases Drag. 30 de Servus II découverts à Argentomagus (Indre). *RAC* 9, 145-52

----- & ----- 1973: Deux moules de potiers arvernes d'une époque précoce (Trajan-Hadrien). *RAC* 12, 315-21

----- & ----- 1974: Un potier arverne anonyme, officine de Terre-Franche-sur-Allier. *RAC* 13, 319-33

----- & ----- 1975: Inventaires de Terre-Franche. Marques et estampilles sur céramique sigillée I, 1957-1969. *RAC* 14, 130-41

----- & ----- 1976: Inventaires de Terre-Franche. Le potier 'Z', facteur de moules original. *RAC* 15, 325-41

----- & ----- 1977a: Inventaires de Terre-Franche. Le potier 'Z' (suite), le poinçon de la cornucopie. *RAC* 16, 369-75

----- & ----- 1977b: A propos de certains vases à reliefs d'applique et barbotine. *Actes du 98e CNSS, St Etienne 1973*, 431-46
----- & ----- 1986: Terre-Franche. In Bémont & Jacob 1986, 155-61
-----, -----, Martinet, Y. 1967: Répertoire des poinçons, style et art decoratif du potier arverne Servus II. *RAC* 6, 230-56
Vernhet, A. 1975: *Notes sur la terra sigillata de La Graufesenque*, Millau
----- 1977: Les dernières productions de La Graufesenque et la question des sigillées claires B. *Figlina* 2, 33-49
----- 1981: Un four de La Graufesenque (Aveyron): la cuisson des vases sigillés. *Gallia* 39, 25-43
----- 1986: Centre de production de Millau, atelier de La Graufesenque. In Bémont & Jacob 1986, 96-103
----- & Balsan, L. 1975: La Graufesenque. *DossArch* 9, 21-34
----- & Vertet, H. 1976: T. Flavius Secundus de La Graufesenque. *Figlina* 1, 29-38
Vertet, H. 1959a: L'officine de Toulon-sur-Allier. *RCRFA* 2, 69-73
----- 1959b: Découverte de poterie peinte à Toulon-sur-Allier (Allier). *Gallia* 17, 216-23
----- 1961a: Note sur un moule du potier Cettus et sur la massue de Diane. *RAECE* 12, 199-207
----- 1961b: A mould of the potter CETTUS, and a note on the club as a religious symbol. *AntJ* 41, 233-5
----- 1967a: Céramique sigillée tiberienne à Lezoux. *RA* 1967, 255-86
----- 1967b: Les fouilles de Lezoux. *RAC* 6, 368-70
----- 1969: Observations sur les vases à medaillons d'applique de la vallée du Rhone. *Gallia* 27, 93-133
----- 1970: Les fouilles officielles. *BCALezoux* 3, 8-13
----- 1971: Remarques sur l'influence des ateliers céramiques de Lyon sur ceux du Centre et du Sud de la Gaule. *RCRFA* 13, 92-111
----- 1972a: Manches de patères ornés en céramique de Lezoux. *Gallia* 30, 5-40
----- 1972b: Projet d'un répertoire des vases à décor moulé fabrique à Lezoux. *RAC* 11, 283-98
----- 1973a: Appliques et vases gallo-romaines fabriqués avec des moules brisés. *RAC* 12, 79-85
----- 1973b: Moule de flanc de gourde de Vichy. *RAC* 12, 299-301
----- 1974: Pauvres potiers, pauvre misère. *DossArch* 6, 85-9
----- 1975a: Lezoux et les ateliers du centre de la Gaule. *DossArch* 9, 35-50
----- 1975b: Nécropoles de Lezoux. *BCALezoux* 8, 20-3
----- 1976a: Les poinçons-matrices de sigillée du Musée de Moulins: problèmes techniques, catalogue. *Figlina* 1, 97-142
----- 1976b: Reliefs d'applique tirés de moules de vases sigillés. *RAC* 15, 319-23
----- 1976c: Remarques sur les rapports entre les ateliers céramiques de Lezoux, de la vallée de l'Allier, de La Graufesenque et ceux de Lyon. *Actes du 96e CNSS, Toulouse 1971*, 191-210
----- 1977: Remarques sur une forme de sigillée moulée peu courante dans les ateliers arvernes: fm. 38. *Actes du 98e CNSS, St Etienne 1973*, 309-15
----- 1978: Les influences romaines sur les ateliers de potiers de la Gaule centrale, observations. *Sites* 1, 5-23
----- 1979: Les fours de potiers gallo-romains du Centre de la Gaule. *APA* 9/10, 145-57
----- 1980: Carte des ateliers de potiers de la Gaule centrale. In Vertet, Bet & Corrocher 1980, 13-41
----- 1986a: Vichy-Gare. In Bémont & Jacob 1986, 161-2
----- 1986b: Lubié. In Bémont & Jacob 1986, 162-3
----- 1989: Recherches sur les ateliers de la Gaule central, résultats, problèmes, projets. *SFECAG Lezoux, 1989,* 11-19
----- 1998: Lezoux – La Graufesenque et la Romanisation. In Bird 1998, 127-32
----- & Bet, P. 1978: Fouilles récentes sur le site de Lezoux (Puy-de-Dôme). *Sites* 1, 43-9
----- & ----- 1980a: Fouille du terrain de l'Oeuvre Grancher a Lezoux (63) (1977-9) – Les structures gallo-romaines du second siècle. In Vertet, Bet & Corrocher 1980, 43-72
----- & ----- 1980b: Une tombe d'enfant sous tuiles du second siècle à Lezoux. In Vertet, Bet & Corrocher 1980, 89-104
-----, ----- & Corrocher, J. 1980: *Recherches sur les Ateliers de Potiers gallo-romaines de la Gaule centrale*, Le Blanc Mesnil
----- & Hartley, B. R. 1968: Fouilles de Lezoux 1967. *RAC* 7, 213-23
----- & Pic, G. 1961: Tessons de céramique sigillée signés du potier Doeccus. *RAECE* 12, 34-41
-----, Picon, M. & Vichy, M. 1970: Note sur la composition des céramiques du IVe siècle de Lezoux. *RAC* 9, 243-50
-----, Rigoir, Y. & Raignoux, R. 1970: Céramique du IVe siècle trouvée à Lezoux. *RCRFA* 11/12, 130-42
Vialatte, A.-M. 1968: *Cinnamus, potier de Lezoux*, unpub 3e cycle thesis, Clermont-Ferrand
----- & Vertet, H. 1967: Remarques sur le potier Cinnamus d'après les fouilles des ateliers du Centre de la Gaule. *RAC* 6, 275; *RAECE* 18, 200
Vian, P.-C. & Bastien, P. 1960: Trésor de Saint-Marcel-d'Ardèche. *BSFN* 15, 474-6
Vince, A. G. & Goudge, C. E. 1980: The Roman pottery from 1 Westgate Street. In Heighway & Garrod 1980, 88-99
Vogel Müller, V. 1990: Ein Formschüsselfragment und ein Bruchstück helvetischer Reliefsigillata aus Augst. *JAK* 11, 147-52
Vogt, E. 1941: Terrasigillatafabrikation in der Schweiz. *ZSAK* 3, 95-109
Vollmer, F. 1915: *Inscriptiones Baivariae Romanae*, München
Von Chlingensperg auf Berg, M. 1896: *Die Römischen Brandgräber bei Reichenhall in Oberbayern*, Braunschweig
Von Hefner, J. 1863: Die römische Töpferei in Westerndorf. *OAVG* 22, 1-93

Von Petrikovits, H. & Von Uslar, R. 1950: Die vorgeschichtlichen Funde um den Neuburger Hof (Rheinwupperkreis). *BJ* 150, 167-91

Von Schnurbein, S. 1977: *Das Römische Gräberfeld von Regensburg*, Kallmünz

----- 1981: Untersuchungen zur Geschichte der römischer Militarlager an der Lippe, *BRGK* 62, 5-101

----- 1982: Die unverzierte Terra Sigillata aus Haltern. *BW* 19, *passim*

Von Wiebeking, R. 1824: Ueber die Reste zweier römischer Töpferöfen bei dem Dorfe Westerndorf am Inn, eine halbe Stunde unterhalb Rosenheim in Baiern. *NKG* 10, 321-3

Wade, W. V. 1939: A hoard of Roman coins from Chesterfield, Derbys. *NC* ser 5, 19, 284-9

Wainwright, G. 1971: The excavation of prehistoric and Romano-British settlements near Durrington Walls, Wiltshire, 1970. *WAM* 66, 76-128

Walke, N. 1959: Zum römischen Gunzburg. *BV* 24, 86-109

----- 1964: Verzierte Terra Sigillata von Epfach-Dorf und aus dem Gräberfeld Mühlau. In Werner 1964, 43-69

----- 1965: Das römische Donaukastell Straubing-Sorviodunum. *LF* 3

----- & Walke, I. 1966: Reliefsigillata von Gauting. *BRGK* 46/7, 77-132

Walker, D. R. 1978: *The Metrology of the Roman silver coinage III. From Pertinax to Uranius Antoninus*, Oxford

Walker, J. 1946: The Darfield hoard of Roman denarii. *NC* ser 6, 6, 147-50

Wallace, A. F. 1970: *Culture and Personality*, New York

Wallace, C. 2006: Long-lived samian? *Brit* 37, 259-72

Walters, F. A. 1907: A find of early Roman bronze coins in England. *NC* ser 4, 7, 353-72

Walters, H. D. 1908: *Catalogue of the Roman Pottery in the Department of Antiquities of the British Museum*, London

Wang, P. P. & Chang, S. K. 1980: *Fuzzy Sets. Theory and Applications to Policy Analysis and Information Systems*, New York & London

Ward, M 1993: A summary of the samian ware from excavations at Piercebridge. *JRPS* 6, 15-22

----- 1996: Samian ware. In Cracknell 1996, 74-7, MF

----- 2008: The samian ware. In Cool & Mason 2008, 169-96, CD-Rom, digital chapter in archive: http://archaeologydataservice.ac.uk/catalogue/adsdata/arch-870-1/dissemination/pdf/Ch9DSamian.pdf

----- 2010: Samian ware from northern Britain: models of supply, demand and occupation. In T. Saunders (ed.), *Roman North West England. Hinterland or 'Indian country'?*, Manchester, 74-104

Warmenbol, E. 1979: Roche Sainte-Anne (Nismes). Fouilles 1976-1977 (rapport préliminaire). *BCAAmphora* 1-18 (reprint), 1-3

Waterman, D. M. 1947: Excavations at Clausentum 1937-8. *AntJ* 27, 151-71

Watkin, W. T. 1884: Further notes on the recent find of Roman coins at Ulnes Walton. *TLCAS* 2, 87-91

Watkins, M. J. 1982: The coins. In Heighway & Parker 1982, 38

Watson, G. R. 1969: *The Roman Soldier*, London

Watson, M. 1983: *British Samian Production, Imitations and Copies, AD 43-AD 250*, unpub BA thesis, London

Weber, G. 1981: Neue Ausgrabungen am 'Apollo-Grannus-Heiligtum' in Faimingen. *BRGK* 62, 103-217

Weber, M. 2012: The devil is in the (samian) detail – potters' stamps on samian ware and their implications for the Roman provincial economy. In M. Duggan *et al.* (ed), *TRAC 2011. Proceedings of the 21st Theoretical Roman Archaeology Conference, Newcastle 2011*, Oxford, 60-75

----- 2013: A reassessment of pre-consumption deposits and samian export in the Antonine period. In Fulford & Durham 2013, 188-209

Webster, G. 1949: The legionary fortress at Lincoln. *JRS* 39, 57-78

----- 1961: An excavation on the Roman site at Little Chester, Derby, 1960. *DerbAJ* 81, 85-110

----- & Daniels, C. M. 1970: A street section at Wroxeter in 1962. *TSAS* 59, 15-23

Webster, J. & Webster, P. 2012: 'Is your figure less than Greek?' Some thoughts on the decoration of Gaulish samian ware. In Bird (D) 2012, 195-215

----- & ----- 2013: Classical figures in a provincial landscape. A study in the iconography of samian. In Fulford & Durham 2013, 340-8

Webster, P. V. 1974: The samian ware. In Evans 1974, 144-8

----- 1975: More British samian ware by the Aldgate-Pulborough potter. *Brit* 6, 163-70

----- 1977: The samian pottery. In Gentry *et al.* 1977, 127-34

----- 1981: The Roman pottery. In Keppie 1981, 80-93

----- 2001: Earth, fire and water: the making and marketing of Roman samian ware. In N. J. Higham (ed), *Archaeology of the Roman Empire. A tribute to the life and works of Professor Barri Jones*, Oxford, 289-302

----- 2005: *Roman Samian Pottery in Britain*, York [reprint of 1996 edition]

----- 2013: Samian, soldiers and civilians in Roman Wales. In Fulford & Durham 2013, 210-23

Wedlake, W. J. 1982: *The Excavation of the Shrine of Apollo at Nettleton, Wiltshire, 1956-71*, London

Weidner, M. K. N. 2010: The Roman pottery district in Trier. Remarkable findings from kiln no. 5. *RCRFA* 41, 603-9

Weiller, R. 1972: *Monnaies Antiques découvertes au Grand-Duché de Luxembourg I*, Berlin

----- 1990: *Monnaies Antiques découvertes au Grand-Duché de Luxembourg IV*, Berlin

Weiss-König, S. 2011: Reliefsigillata der ersten Gruppe aus Metz. In Liesen 2011, 97-135

Wells, C. M. 1972: *The German Policy of Augustus*, Oxford

----- 1977: L'implantation des ateliers de céramique sigillée en Gaule. Problématique de la recherche. *Figlina* 2, 1-11

Wells, P. S. 1985: Material symbols and the interpretation of cultural change. *OJA* 4, 9-17

Welter, M. T. 1936: La poterie de Chémery-Faulquemont (Moselle). Les fouilles de 1934. *ASHAL* 45, 137-56

Wenham, L. P. 1965: Blossom Street excavations, York, 1953-1955. *YAJ* 41, 524-53

----- 1972: Excavations in Low Petergate, York, 1957-8. *YAJ* 44, 65-113

Werner, J. 1964: *Studien zu Abodiacum-Epfach*, München

Wheeler, R. E. M. 1926: *The Roman Fort near Brecon*, London

----- 1928: A 'Romano-Celtic' temple near Harlow, Essex; and a note on the type. *AntJ* 8, 300-26

----- & Wheeler, T. V. 1928: The Roman amphitheatre at Caerleon, Monmouthshire. *Arch* 78, 111-218

Whiting, W., Hawley, W. & May, T. 1931: *Excavation of the Roman Cemetery at Ospringe, Kent*, Oxford

Whittaker, C. R. 1983: Late Roman trade and traders. In P. Garnsey, K. Hopkins, C. Whittaker (ed), *Trade in the Ancient Economy*, London, 163-80

----- 2003: Roman proto-industry in southern France: some Indian comparisons. *MHJ* 6, 293-301

Whytehead, R. 1980: Excavations at Goodman's Yard, 1978. *TLMAS* 31, 29-46

Wieling, H. 2000: Vertragsgestaltung der römischen Keramikproduktion. In Strobel 2000, 9-21

Wightman, E. M. 1970: *Roman Trier and the Treveri,* London

----- 1985: *Gallia Belgica*, London

Wild, F. C. 1968: The samian pottery. In Jones & Webster 1968, 215-21

----- 1975: Samian ware. In Robertson 1975, 141-77

----- 1979a: Samian ware. In Potter 1979, 123-33

----- 1979b: Samian ware. In Potter 1979, 269-91

----- 1980: Samian ware. In Price & Watts 1980, MF M138-9, 300-3

----- 1982: Samian ware. In Heighway & Parker 1982, 46-8

----- 2005: Paternus, I or II? *JRPS* 12, 201-3

----- 2012: Montans to Musselburgh: a group of South Gaulish decorated samian ware of the Antonine period. *SGRPNews* 54, 6-7

Williams, A. 1946: Canterbury excavations: September-October 1944. *ACant* 59, 64-81

----- 1947: Canterbury excavations in 1945. *ACant* 60, 68-100

Williams, J. 1997: Morton Lodge, Derbyshire (addenda). *CHRB* 10, 143-8

----- & Leins, I. 2002: Warminster, Wiltshire. *CHRB* 11, 85-7

----- & Meadows, A. 1997: Littleborough, Greater Manchester. *CHRB* 10, 135-9

----- & Read, C. 2002: Hamstead Marshall, Berkshire. *CHRB* 11, 103-7

----- & Rigby, V. 2002: Bottesford, North Lincolnshire. *CHRB* 11, 139-46

Williams, W. W. 1875: Roman coins, Caernarvonshire. *ACamb* ser 4, 6, 128-34

Willis, S. H. 1997: Samian: beyond dating. In K. Meadows *et al.* (ed), *TRAC 96. Proceedings of the Sixth Annual Theoretical Roman Archaeology Conference, Sheffield 1996*, Oxford, 38-54

----- 1998: Samian pottery in Britain: exploring its distribution and archaeological potential. *AJ* 155, 82-133

----- 2005: Samian pottery, a resource for the study of Roman Britain and beyond: the results of the English Heritage funded Samian Project, including an interrogatable database of samian pottery. *IntArch* 17 http://intarch.ac.uk/journal/issue17/willis_index.html

----- 2011: Samian ware and society in Roman Britain and beyond. *Brit* 42, 167-242

----- 2013: Red from the green field: samian ware at villas and other rural sites in Roman Britain. An examination of site evidence and general trends. In Fulford & Durham 2013, 224-41

Wilson, C. & Kent, J. P. C. 1973: Coin report. In Coppack 1973, 84-7

Winter, A. 1978: *Die Antike Glanztonkeramik. Practische Versuche*, Mainz

Wiseman, T. P. 1963: The potteries of Vibienus and Rufrenus at Arretium. *Mnemosyne* ser 4, 16, 275-83

Wittmann, A. & Jouquand, A.-M. 2009: Un lot de sigillées du IIIe siècle découvert à Poitiers (Vienne) dans la boutique d'un marchand de vases. *CCALezoux* 3, 11-33; more-or-less the same also in *SFECAG St Romain-en-Gal, 2003*, 621-41

Wobst, H. M. 1977: Stylistic behaviour and information exchange. In C. E. Cleland (ed), *For the Director: Research Essays in Honor of James B. Griffin*, Michigan, 317-42

Woodfield, C. T. P. 1983: List of coins, Alchester Road suburbs, Towcester. In Brown & Woodfield 1983, MF M18-31

Woodfield, P. 1977: The coins. In Mynard & Woodfield 1977, 375-6

Woodward, A. M. 1925: The Roman fort at Ilkley. *YAJ* 28, 137-321

Wright, R. P. 1965: Roman Britain in 1964, II, Inscriptions. *JRS* 55, 221-8

Young, C. J. 1977: *Oxfordshire Roman Pottery*, Oxford

----- 1980: The pottery. In Cunliffe 1980, 274-83

Zadeh, L. A. 1973: Outline of a new approach to the analysis of complex systems and decision processes. *IEEE Trans SMC*-3, 28-44

----- *et al.* 1975: *Fuzzy Sets and their Applications to Cognitive and Decision Processes*, New York

Zadoks-Josephus Jitta, A. N. 1954: Bargercompascuum (Dr.). *JMP* 41, 109-10

----- 1956: Balbo (Dr.) 1839. *JMP* 43, 98-9

----- 1960a: Renkum (G.) 1811. *JMP* 47, 89-91

----- 1960b: Eck en Weil (G.) 1908. *JMP* 47, 91-2

Zanier, W. 1992: *Das römische Kastell Ellingen,* Mainz

----- 1994: Handelsfragen der Rheinzaberner Sigillata. *MBAH* 13.2, 60-69

Zucker, L. G. 1977: The role of institutionalisation in cultural persistance. *ASR* 42, 726-43

Zumstein, H. 1964: La céramique du 'potier aux boucliers et aux casques' au Musée de Strasbourg. *RAECE* 15, 335-47